THE Southern Living®
GARDEN BOOK

Edited by Steve Bender,
Senior Writer, *Southern Living*

Oxmoor
House®

Hollyhocks and poppies surround a French olive jar

Southern Living® Garden Book
Editor: Steve Bender
Managing Editor: Fiona Gilsenan
Art Director, Design and Production Manager: Alice Rogers
Consulting Art Director: James Boone
Consulting Editors: Bob Doyle, Philip Edinger, Suzanne Normand Eyre
Senior Editor: Pamela Cornelison
Associate Editor: Tom Wilhite
Writers: Hazel White, Ruth Rogers Clausen, Lance Walheim
Researchers: Barbara Brown, Wendy Fowler, Allison Ingram, Tena Payne,
    Susan Ray, Dave Widgington
Editorial Assistant: Tishana Peebles
Production Coordinator: Patricia S. Williams
Chief Copy Editor and Indexer: Carolyn McGovern
Copy Editors: Barbara J. Braasch, Fran Haselsteiner, Marsha Lutch Lloyd
Proofreaders: Desne Border, David Sweet, Lura Dymond,
    Linda M. Bouchard
Computer Production: Elaine Holland, Joan Olson
Botanical Illustrator: Mimi Osborne
Map Design and Cartography: Reineck & Reineck, San Francisco

Southern Living®
Editor: John Alex Floyd, Jr.
Executive Editor: Eleanor Griffin
Garden Editor: Linda C. Askey
Assistant Garden Design Editors: Joann Catherine Kellum,
    Rebecca Bull Reed
Assistant Garden Editor: Charles Thigpen
Photographers: Van Chaplin, Sylvia Martin, Tina Cornett, Jean Allsopp,
    Allen Rokach, Meg McKinney Simle, Mary-Gray Hunter, Beth Maynor,
    Mary Carolyn Pindar

Copyright 1998 by Oxmoor House, Inc.
Book Division of Southern Progress Corporation
P.O. Box 2463, Birmingham, Alabama 35201

Southern Living® is a federally registered trademark of
Southern Living, Inc.

Cover photograph: Pink azalea, Van Chaplin
Title page photograph: European cranberry bush in bloom, Van Chaplin
Copyright page photograph: Van Chaplin

90 QPD/QPD 9 8 7 6 5 4 3 2 1

Library of Congress Catalog Card Number: 97-81295 Hardcover
edition: ISBN 0-8487-2017-2. Softcover edition: 0-8487-2023-7
Printed in the United States of America.

Foreword

Every month, *Southern Living* magazine appears in the homes of more than two million families. In the 30-plus years since its founding, the magazine has become a faithful resource for Southerners who enjoy home, food, travel, and gardening. A hallmark of our philosophy is that good gardening and good design go hand-in-hand. In the many beautiful gardens featured in our pages, we've tried to set the tone for good practices throughout the South.

I am pleased to introduce our first comprehensive gardening book for the people of the American South. The *Southern Living Garden Book* showcases plants that form the backbone of Southern gardens. Spearheaded by Senior Writer Steve Bender, an active gardener and horticulturist, it describes more than 5,000 plants that fit the needs of gardeners across our region. We hope our book, which includes helpful climate maps and outstanding plants selection guides, will become the Bible of Southern gardening.

Whether you live in Lubbock, Texas; Hagerstown, Maryland; Fort Smith, Arkansas; or Tampa, Florida, you'll find this book invaluable. I hope you enjoy reading and using it as much as the *Southern Living* gardening staff enjoyed producing it.

John Alex Floyd, Jr.
Editor, *Southern Living*

CONTENTS

THE SPIRIT OF SOUTHERN GARDENING

  Gardens in the South have their own character. Here, editor Steve Bender reflects on the history, climate, and plants that make our gardens unique. Glorious photos celebrate the best of Southern gardening.

THE 5 CLIMATE ZONES

 Regional maps and descriptions of the five climate zones of the Southern states. To help you choose plants for your garden, all plants listed in the Plant Selection Guide and Encyclopedia are rated for these zones.

A GUIDE TO PLANT SELECTION

 Twenty-six plant lists, organized by theme and illustrated with hundreds of color photographs, to help you create special effects, tackle difficult landscaping situations, or lay out a basic garden framework.

A TO Z PLANT ENCYCLOPEDIA

PRACTICAL GARDENING DICTIONARY

RESOURCE DIRECTORY

INDEXES

Trey and Valerie Vaughan garden
Atlanta, Georgia

The Spirit of Southern Gardening

What Makes a Garden Southern?

It's more than geographical location; it's more than a practiced style. True Southernness grows from a fervent quest for continuity—an instinctive recognition that the seeds we sow and the bulbs we share tell the world who we are and where we've been.

One hundred years ago, the majority of Southerners earned their living from the land. Farmers belonged to a noble, honored profession and were lauded by Thomas Jefferson as "the chosen people of God." Their beliefs, values, and practices shape our gardens still.

"God Almighty first planted a garden. And indeed, it is the purest of human pleasures."

Francis Bacon
"Of Gardens"

Planting corn, Shenandoah Valley, Virginia

7

Homegrown bounty

Coneflowers and Queen Anne's lace

Garden tool art

Farms of a hundred years ago were truly "out there." Neighbors lived far apart, roads were poor, and news and transportation moved slowly. About the only time people got together on a regular basis was on Sunday for church. Families had to rely on themselves.

This isolation and self-reliance produced a conservative outlook, not only in politics and religion, but also in gardening. Thus, today's Southern gardeners aren't trendy—we don't pine for the latest scientific gardening techniques like hydroponics or tissue culture. And we don't trust any ornamental grass that can't be mown.

Instead, Southerners go with what works. We prefer the plants our parents grew, whether these be native or long-established exotics. Oh, from time to time we may flavor the stew with something new, but we never forsake the old family recipe.

Our garden designs are conservative, too. Granted, some of us assault the neighborhood with garish colors and bizarre geometric shapes. But in general, Southerners like gardens that fit in. The most satisfying examples pay homage to local topography, native vegetation, and regional style. Their distinctive looks tell us instantly where we are.

Conservatism doesn't translate into regimentation, however. If it did, how would we explain the glorious anarchy of the classic Southern cottage garden, where flowers and found art conquer all? Every garden needs that spark of innovation, that willingness to bend the rules a little to show that the gardener is alive. In the words of Rufus T. Firefly, author of the epic *White Trash Gardening,* "Garden planning never works. It's just like family planning—if everybody did it, it'd never happen."

Insect-eating pitcher plants and wildflowers at the Minamac Wildflower Bog in Silverhill, Alabama

We often hear that the South is a region that celebrates its eccentrics. If so, it celebrates eccentric plants as well. In addition to azaleas, hollies, roses, crepe myrtles, hydrangeas, and other mainstream plants, Southerners treasure those that are just a bit odd. We prize the flower of the angel's trumpet *(Brugmansia)* as it pinwheels open at night. We tout the pregnant onion *(Ornithogalum caudatum),* which splits open to give birth to babies. We covet the explosive touch-me-not *(Impatiens balsamina),* which showers the unwary gardener with seed. Why? Because having a plant your neighbor doesn't have makes it a conversation piece. And conversation to a Southerner is like oxygen to an astronaut. Without it, life is short.

"Gardeners cheat. If we can grow a plant that's not hardy, we do. And if we can grow a plant out of season, so much the better."

Linda Askey
Birmingham, Alabama

Vicki and Alex Cureton garden
Tallahassee, Florida

The Never-Ending Challenge

As a group, Southerners spend more time gardening than do people in almost any other region. Gardening here isn't a summertime diversion. In much of the South, men and women garden ten, eleven, and even twelve months out of the year.

It isn't always easy. Most of our soils are harder than bronze. A new generation of ravenous insects knocks at the gate every thirty seconds. The merciless weather plagues us with droughts, pelts us with hailstorms, and slicks us with ice. No wonder that halfway through another steamy summer most of us would like to throw in the trowel.

Yet we persevere. For Southern gardeners can no more cast off their heritage than a coon dog can give up the chase. Coaxing plants from the soil is inborn. And although we sometimes fail, we revel in every attempt.

"There are no green thumbs or black thumbs," wrote Henry Mitchell, the late, great columnist for the *Washington Post*. "There are only gardeners and non-gardeners. Gardeners are the ones who ruin after ruin get on with the high defiance of nature herself, creating, in the very face of chaos and tornado, the bower of roses and the pride of irises."

Or, as Mississippi author Felder Rushing likes to put it, "Gardening is an attitude, not a skill."

*Ornamental cabbage
and paper whites*

"Once I touch a plant, I have no concept of time. I can go on gardening forever."

Jim Powell
Jackson, Mississippi

*Alice and Don Williams garden
Atlanta, Georgia*

12

Butterfly Garden, Biltmore Estate
Asheville, North Carolina

A Tradition of Sharing

Gardeners Kay and Sarah Fuston
Birmingham, Alabama

In *White Trash Gardening,* the insightful Mr. Firefly sets down seven golden rules of gardening, one of which states, "Don't buy anything you can borrow." Folks in some parts of the country frown upon such behavior. But here in the South, we not only accept it, we expect it. Shared tools, plants, and knowledge are part of our social contract.

We learn gardening not at the library table, but at our parents' and grandparents' knees. We listen to their colorful names for things, like heart's-a-bustin' *(Euonymus americana),* Moses-in-the-cradle *(Rhoeo spathacea),* Grancy graybeard *(Chionanthus virginicus),* and cry-baby tree *(Erythrina crista-galli).* We feel more comfortable with common, vernacular names than scientific, botanical ones.

As we chat across the garden fence, we also share plants. The hallowed tradition of swapping is rooted in our agrarian past, when farm wives would trade plants at church meetings and socials and also advertise them in market bulletins. Today, many of the South's state departments of agriculture continue to publish market bulletins. These unique periodicals offer all sorts of strange and wonderful plants, bulbs, and seeds, often for little more than a stamped, self-addressed envelope.

French hydrangea

Peeping Tom daffodils

16

Foxgloves and anemones, Stratford Hall, Stratford, Virginia

Still, many of us find our biggest botanical treasures in the gardens of family and generous friends. Indeed, to a gardener, all other gardeners are family and worthy of a leafy inheritance. So we pass along seeds, bulbs, and divisions, always with a piece of gardening advice.

This willingness to share preserves many old Southern heirlooms, such as single jonquils *(Narcissus jonquilla),* Saint Joseph's lily *(Hippeastrum johnsonii),* and butcher's broom *(Ruscus),* which have nearly disappeared from commerce. Each time we view them in our gardens, we immediately recall the persons who gave them. As you read this book, look for the symbol 🏛, which designates certain plants as cherished Southern heirlooms.

"Watering is great therapy. There's something simple, direct, and ancient about standing there on the end of a hosepipe."

Lee May
Atlanta, Georgia

Heart's-a-bustin'

Saint Joseph's lily

Bluebonnets and Indian paintbrush
Independence, Texas

A Chorus of Voices

The American South, as defined by *Southern Living,* stretches from the shorelines of Maryland and Delaware to the deserts of West Texas to the tip of Key West in Florida. It embraces pockets of sympathizers in the boot-heel of Missouri and the southern portions of Illinois and Indiana. No other section of the country boasts a stronger regional identity. Because of this, folks from elsewhere tend to think we speak with a single voice.

Yet our gardens belie this assumption. The intimate, formal courtyards of New Orleans and Savannah hardly seem in the same country as the bucolic borders of Virginia's horse country. And gardens carved from plantations in the Mississippi Delta contrast mightily with the spanking new lawns of Charlotte and Birmingham. Such diversity creates a chorus of voices, enriching our culture, adding to the South's mystique.

No better example exists than Texas, a land of stark contradictions. On the one hand, it's home to great numbers of gardeners determined to grow plants better suited to Tennessee. These folks replace the native soil, install expensive watering systems, and dispense chemicals at the drop of a ten-gallon hat. Yet the Lone Star State boasts the South's strongest native plant and organic gardening movements.

Louisiana iris
Little Elm, Texas

Impatiens and palms
Miami, Florida

Azaleas and live oaks, Afton Villa Gardens, St. Francisville, Louisiana

For all that divides our region, one thing unites us, the most telling factor of all—our climate. While our friends up north shiver in long johns and curse cars that won't crank in the January freeze, we Southerners enjoy short, mild winters with something in bloom almost every month.

Of course, we pay for this privilege with torrid summers and humidity sufficient to grow mold on talcum powder. But given the choice between heat and cold, we inevitably opt for heat. It allows us to grow a wonderfully wide miscellany of plants, both regional natives and exotics from all over the world.

"A weed is a plant dealing with an unhappy person."

J. C. Raulston
Former director of the
North Carolina
State Arboretum
Raleigh, North Carolina

John and Dianne Avlon garden
historic Benjamin Phillips house
Charleston, South Carolina

Florida flame azalea

Monarch butterfly atop Lochinch butterfly bush

Why We Garden

Southerners garden for many reasons. For beauty.
Curiosity. Relaxation. Exercise. Solitude. Fellowship. Knowledge.
Mystery. Conformity. Individuality. Food. Fun.

We garden to establish a link with the past. We garden
to build a road to the future.

But mostly we garden because we are indomitable opti-
mists. We treasure the heritage beneath our feet, knowing that
however many catastrophes beset our efforts, a new day awaits
within every bulb and seed. We are sure that genuine effort
and resolute faith pay off.

In the words of honorary Southerner Rudyard Kipling:

> *Oh, Adam was a gardener, and*
> *God who made him sees*
> *That half a proper gardener's work is*
> *done upon his knees.*

Steve Bender

Sugar maples, Hunt Valley, Maryland

THE FIVE CLIMATE ZONES *of the South*

"Everywhere there are violent winds, startling once-per-five-centuries floods, unprecedented droughts, record-setting freezes, abusive and blasting heats never known before. There is no place, no garden, where these terrible things do not drive gardeners mad."

Henry Mitchell, *The Essential Earthman*

Forgive Henry Mitchell if he seems a bit beleaguered. But if thirty straight days of temperatures in the high 90s had turned your prized hostas into steamed vegetables, you might be somewhat steamed yourself.

The vagaries of Southern weather do indeed make gardening a challenge. Nearly all of the South faces temperatures above the century mark in summer, with sufficient humidity to turn concrete into sponge. And winters, although short, are often frigid. For example, during the freak March blizzard of 1993, Birmingham woke to find itself, at minus 2 degrees, the coldest spot in the nation. Anchorage, Alaska, was balmy by comparison.

Despite the weather, gardening *can* be satisfying in the South, provided you have the necessary resources. And no resource is more critical than a good growing map. Knowing what climate zone you're in can help answer everyday questions: When should I put out my tomato transplants? Why won't my lilac bloom? Can I leave my hibiscus outdoors for the winter? Should my lawn be zoysia or St. Augustine?

FIVE GROWING ZONES

Southern Living divides the South into five broad growing zones—the Upper South, Middle South, Lower South, Coastal South, and Tropical South. Over the years, we've adapted and refined these zones, according to new horticultural and climatological information made available to us. We're aware that more detailed climate maps exist. However, we feel a simple map that's easy to read and understand beats a complicated map that intimidates and confuses.

Most hardiness ratings for plants indicate cold-hardiness alone. But in the South, heat is as much a limiting factor as cold. For example, if we recommend forsythia for the Upper, Middle, and Lower South, we mean that it will survive not only the winters there, but the summers too, and it will perform satisfactorily. We won't recommend forsythia for the Coastal or Tropical South, because while it's obviously winter-hardy there, in the summer it either dies or looks wretched.

To help you pinpoint the climate zone where you garden, we've greatly enlarged the map that regularly appears in *Southern Living*. We've also added many more details, such as major cities, rivers, and interstate highways. After you've identified your climate zone, turn to the plant listings in the encyclopedia to find out what grows well in your area.

SORRY, NO GUARANTEE

Keep in mind, though, that the zones provide guidelines, not guarantees. Many factors other than heat and cold determine a plant's ultimate fate—such as elevation, soil pH, topography, prevailing winds, sun exposure, humidity, and proximity to water. Taken together, these produce a multitude of tiny microclimates, which can create quite different growing conditions even within a small area.

A good example comes from the Tropical South. Tampa and St. Petersburg lie scarcely 15 miles apart on Florida's west coast. Yet because St. Petersburg sits on a peninsula, the surrounding water buffers winter cold snaps by about 5 degrees. This means that tropical plants that can freeze in Tampa escape unscathed in St. Pete.

When you get right down to it, all of the scientific data in the world are no substitute for your own real-life experience and that of your fellow gardeners. If you wonder whether a particular plant will do in your area, first consult our map. Then ask neighbors, friends, garden club members, and local garden centers.

And if by some sinister quirk of fate, a brutal March cold snap makes pudding out of your just-leafed-out hydrangea, pause a moment and consider the observation of Texas writer Scott Ogden, "There is no reasonable way to prepare for these periodic disasters except to remind oneself that, after all, plants, like other living things, are mortal and therefore not meant to live forever."

Then go out and plant something else.

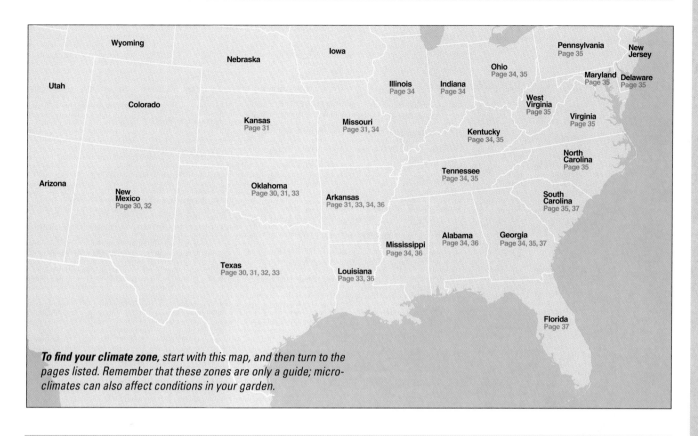

To find your climate zone, start with this map, and then turn to the pages listed. Remember that these zones are only a guide; micro-climates can also affect conditions in your garden.

THE UPPER SOUTH

The Upper South experiences the short-est summers and longest winters in our region. Summers are hot and humid, with the mercury often topping out at 100 degrees or more in July and August. Fortu-nately, such sizzling temperatures seldom persist for more than two to three days. Summer nights usually drop into the 60s, a necessity for the many cool-weather plants that grow here. Winter lows range from 0 to minus 10 degrees, but savage arctic fronts can occasionally push down the tempera-ture to as low as minus 20 degrees in West Virginia, Kentucky, and the Appalachians.

Many conifers, especially those from mountainous habitats, such as spruces and hemlocks, love this climate. Rhododen-drons and lilacs thrive, hostas and other perennials do fabulously, and Japanese yew is a standard foundation plant. Lawns con-sist of bluegrass, fescue, or perennial rye-grass. Cabbage, broccoli, kale, asparagus, raspberries, and rhubarb perform better here than farther south. So do bunch grapes and highbush blueberries.

Cold winters bring constraints, however. Frozen soil means digging dahlias, cannas, gladiolus, and other summer-flowering bulbs in autumn. Crepe myrtles, camellias, and figs may not be cold-hardy in all areas. And flowers are nearly absent from Decem-ber to March.

Sprucing Up the Yard

A majestic Colorado blue spruce *(Picea pungens)* is a common sight in the Upper South, where cold winters provide the growing conditions this mountain-born conifer likes. Gardeners here prize it for its conical shape and beautiful needles, which range in color from bluish green to a glacial silvery blue. Many blue spruces begin as live Christmas trees, which are planted out in the yard after the holidays. Folks enjoy the beauty of the trees and the memories they bring for generations.

THE MIDDLE SOUTH

The Middle South forms the transition zone between warm-weather and cool-weather growing areas. Here you often find plants indigenous to the Northeast, Midwest, and Pacific Northwest growing side by side with those from the Southeast.

Summers, like everywhere else in the South, are hot and humid in this zone. But nights cool off in the mountains. Most perennials and bulbs do quite well, although you have to dig up dahlias and cannas in the autumn for winter storage. Winter lows don't usually drop below zero, but temperatures of minus 15 degrees have been recorded.

Tall fescue is the lawn grass of choice, although Bermuda and zoysia also grow here. Camellias, azaleas, and rhododendrons do well. Vegetable gardeners can grow okra, watermelons, and other long-season, hot-weather crops. Both highbush and rabbiteye blueberries flourish, as do bunch grapes and most muscadines. But the lower Middle South marks the cutoff point for many plants that are well suited to the North. Spruces and hemlocks gradually give way to pines and red cedars, while European beech, white birch, and tulip poplar surrender to sweet gum, red maple, black gum, and red oak.

Coming Up Roses

Roses *(left)* are just some of the lovely plants you can grow in the in-between climate of the Middle South. Plants that need hot summers, such as figs, chaste tree, and watermelons, thrive here. But the region also supplies a needed rest period for plants that require a yearly winter chill, including peony, clematis *(below)*, lilac, apple, tulip, and forsythia.

THE LOWER SOUTH

Spring in the Lower South begins in early February with the blooming of daffodils, star magnolia, and Lenten rose. Flowering dogwood, the South's signature tree, blossoms gloriously by late March. Summer is hot, sticky, often dry, and seemingly endless. Nighttime temperatures during summer usually fall no lower than the mid-70s. The short winter is seldom colder than 10 to 15 degrees. Snow is rare, but ice storms are not.

Spanish moss appears in warmer areas. Backyard orchardists grow muscadines, rabbiteye blueberries, and figs. Lilacs and rhododendrons often flop, but crepe myrtles, camellias, native azaleas, and magnolias triumph. Cannas, dahlias, glads, and elephant's ears usually overwinter in the ground. Warm-weather lawn grasses—Bermuda, buffalo grass, centipede, St. Augustine, and zoysia—predominate. However, tall fescue is a popular alternative for lightly shaded lawns in the upper half of this zone.

The Lower South marks the northern limit for many mild-weather plants, such as Lady Banks's rose, holly fern, Indian hawthorn, and windmill palm. Tulips and hyacinths may need refrigeration in order to bloom well. But pansies, violas, and snapdragons can be planted in autumn.

Queen of the South

Basking in the summer heat, crepe myrtle is one of summer's best-loved trees in the Lower South. It needs weeks of afternoon temperatures above 90 degrees in order to bloom its best.

THE COASTAL SOUTH

Two large bodies of water—the Atlantic Ocean and the Gulf of Mexico—rule the Coastal South. Their close proximity ensures that winters are mild and nearly momentary, while summers are long, warm, and perpetually humid.

Although winter lows can reach 17 to 25 degrees at the northern end of this zone and 25 to 32 degrees at the southern end, many winters are frost-free, turning impatiens, coleus, caladium, and lantana into temporary perennials. Spring commences in January, when oriental magnolias bloom. Fall color is nearly absent, but Chinese tallow trees turn brilliant shades of red, orange, and yellow in early December. Winter is ideal for growing greens and other cool-weather vegetables.

The luxurious growth associated with the Old South is promoted by high rainfall. Massive live oaks enshrouded with Spanish moss form leafy cathedrals above coastal streets. Southern Indica azaleas grow as big as a bus. Let a St. Augustine lawn go a summer week without mowing and you might as well start grazing cattle.

Subtropical plants abound—oleander, Chinese hibiscus, bougainvillea, Indian hawthorn, gingers, palms, Japanese pittosporum, ixora, bottlebrush, loquat, and holly fern. Citrus trees grow in the southern end of the range. Of course, every few years a freeze comes through and annihilates these and other tender plants. But gardens recover so quickly here that the damage is soon forgotten.

Tomorrow's Forecast: Humid

Close proximity to the Atlantic Ocean and the Gulf of Mexico produces hot, humid summers and mild, rainy winters in much of the Coastal South. Copious moisture and a long growing season give live oaks *(Quercus virginiana)*, like these at Orton Plantation in Wilmington, North Carolina, the conditions they need to develop huge canopies and massive, sprawling limbs.

THE TROPICAL SOUTH

Compared to the rest of the South, the Tropical South is almost another world. It rarely feels frost. Because of this, gardens here enjoy an exotic, tropical look. Rainfall averages about 25 inches a year in the extreme south of Texas and more than twice that over the lower Florida peninsula. While most of the South experiences dry summers and wet winters, the Tropical South sees just the opposite.

Palms, palmettos, cycads, birds of paradise, and orchid trees thrive. Bougainvillea, allamanda, and passion vine bloom with abandon. In the lower half of this zone, gardeners succeed with tree fern, coconut palm, jacaranda, royal poinciana, heliconia, as well as with bromeliads and orchids. St. Augustine is the lawn grass of choice, although Bahia and carpetgrass are options for Florida, and Bermuda for South Texas.

The lack of winter chilling comes at a price, however. While you can grow citrus (and in the lower Tropical South, mangoes, bananas, and avocados), apples, peaches, pears, blueberries, grapes, and other popu-

The Heat Is On

Winter ranges from momentary to entirely absent in the Tropical South. This results in a year-round growing season, with something in bloom every month. Exotic tropical plants flourish—so much so that most gardeners here favor them much more than native plants. In fact, cabbage palm *(Sabal palmetto)* is one of the few native palms you'll see.

lar fruits fail. So do many traditional flowering shrubs of the South, including azaleas, camellias, forsythia, spiraea, and quince. On the other hand, since there is no real winter to speak of, flower and vegetable gardening are year-round sports in the Tropical South.

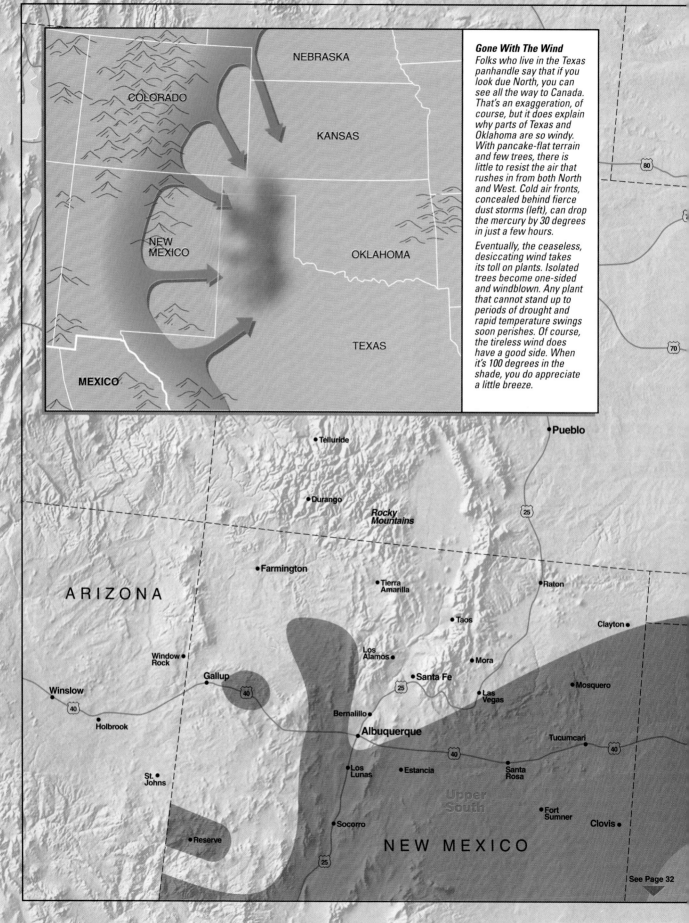

Gone With The Wind

Folks who live in the Texas panhandle say that if you look due North, you can see all the way to Canada. That's an exaggeration, of course, but it does explain why parts of Texas and Oklahoma are so windy. With pancake-flat terrain and few trees, there is little to resist the air that rushes in from both North and West. Cold air fronts, concealed behind fierce dust storms (left), can drop the mercury by 30 degrees in just a few hours.

Eventually, the ceaseless, desiccating wind takes its toll on plants. Isolated trees become one-sided and windblown. Any plant that cannot stand up to periods of drought and rapid temperature swings soon perishes. Of course, the tireless wind does have a good side. When it's 100 degrees in the shade, you do appreciate a little breeze.

NEBRASKA

COLORADO

KANSAS

NEW MEXICO

OKLAHOMA

TEXAS

MEXICO

Telluride

Pueblo

Durango

Rocky
Mountains

25

Farmington

Raton

ARIZONA

Tierra
Amarilla

Taos

Clayton

Window
Rock

Los
Alamos

Mora

Gallup

40

Santa Fe

Mosquero

Winslow

40

25

Las
Vegas

Holbrook

Bernalillo

Albuquerque

Tucumcari

40

40

Los
Lunas

Estancia

Santa
Rosa

St.
Johns

Upper
South

Socorro

Fort
Sumner

Clovis

Reserve

NEW MEXICO

25

See Page 32

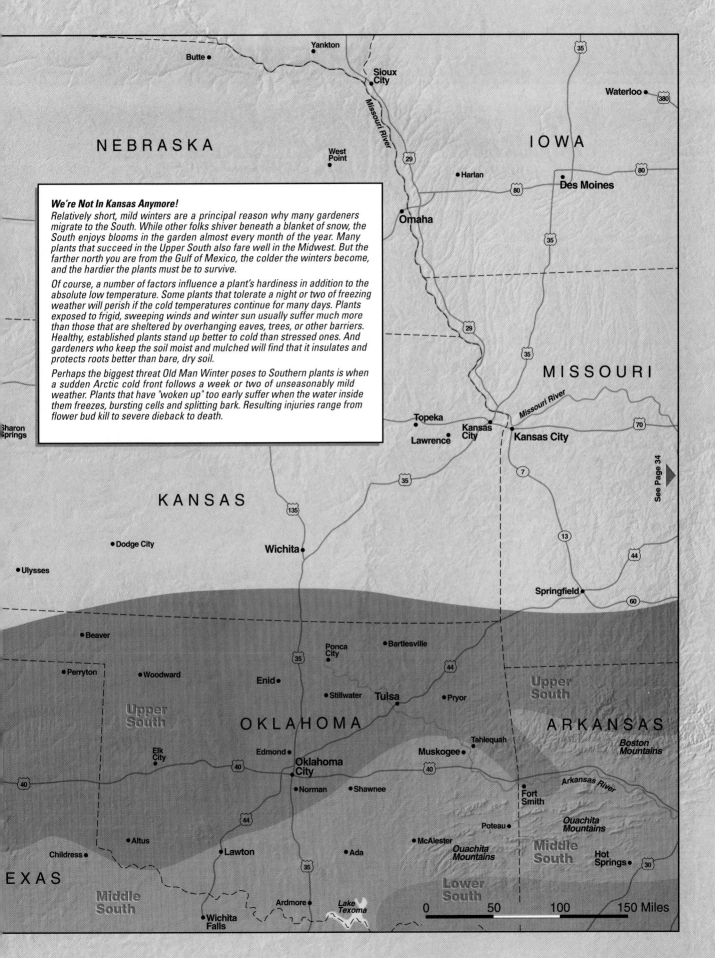

We're Not In Kansas Anymore!

Relatively short, mild winters are a principal reason why many gardeners migrate to the South. While other folks shiver beneath a blanket of snow, the South enjoys blooms in the garden almost every month of the year. Many plants that succeed in the Upper South also fare well in the Midwest. But the farther north you are from the Gulf of Mexico, the colder the winters become, and the hardier the plants must be to survive.

Of course, a number of factors influence a plant's hardiness in addition to the absolute low temperature. Some plants that tolerate a night or two of freezing weather will perish if the cold temperatures continue for many days. Plants exposed to frigid, sweeping winds and winter sun usually suffer much more than those that are sheltered by overhanging eaves, trees, or other barriers. Healthy, established plants stand up better to cold than stressed ones. And gardeners who keep the soil moist and mulched will find that it insulates and protects roots better than bare, dry soil.

Perhaps the biggest threat Old Man Winter poses to Southern plants is when a sudden Arctic cold front follows a week or two of unseasonably mild weather. Plants that have "woken up" too early suffer when the water inside them freezes, bursting cells and splitting bark. Resulting injuries range from flower bud kill to severe dieback to death.

See Page 34

31

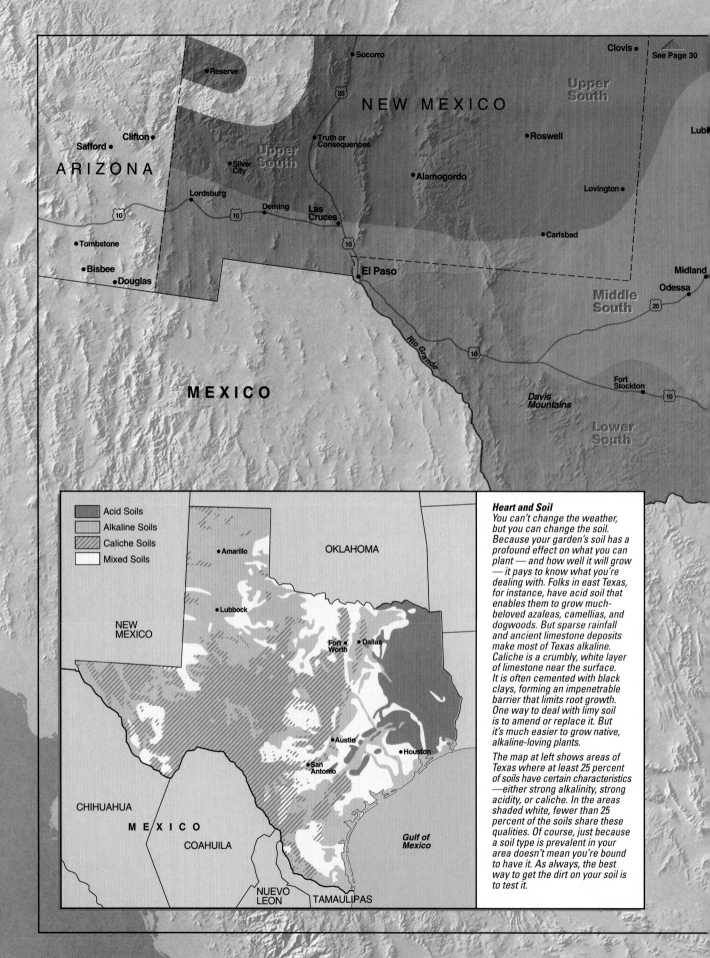

Reserve

Socorro

Clovis

NEW MEXICO

Upper South

Safford • Clifton

Truth or Consequences

• Roswell

A R I Z O N A

Silver City

Upper South

• Alamogordo

Lovington •

Lordsburg

Deming

Las Cruces

• Carlsbad

• Tombstone

El Paso

Midland

Odessa

Middle South

• Bisbee

• Douglas

Rio Grande

M E X I C O

Davis Mountains

Fort Stockton

Lower South

■ Acid Soils	
■ Alkaline Soils	
▨ Caliche Soils	
□ Mixed Soils	

OKLAHOMA

• Amarillo

NEW MEXICO

• Lubbock

Fort Worth • • Dallas

CHIHUAHUA

M E X I C O

• Austin

• San Antonio

• Houston

COAHUILA

Gulf of Mexico

NUEVO LEON **TAMAULIPAS**

Heart and Soil

You can't change the weather, but you can change the soil. Because your garden's soil has a profound effect on what you can plant — and how well it will grow — it pays to know what you're dealing with. Folks in east Texas, for instance, have acid soil that enables them to grow much-beloved azaleas, camellias, and dogwoods. But sparse rainfall and ancient limestone deposits make most of Texas alkaline. Caliche is a crumbly, white layer of limestone near the surface. It is often cemented with black clays, forming an impenetrable barrier that limits root growth. One way to deal with limy soil is to amend or replace it. But it's much easier to grow native, alkaline-loving plants.

The map at left shows areas of Texas where at least 25 percent of soils have certain characteristics — either strong alkalinity, strong acidity, or caliche. In the areas shaded white, fewer than 25 percent of the soils share these qualities. Of course, just because a soil type is prevalent in your area doesn't mean you're bound to have it. As always, the best way to get the dirt on your soil is to test it.

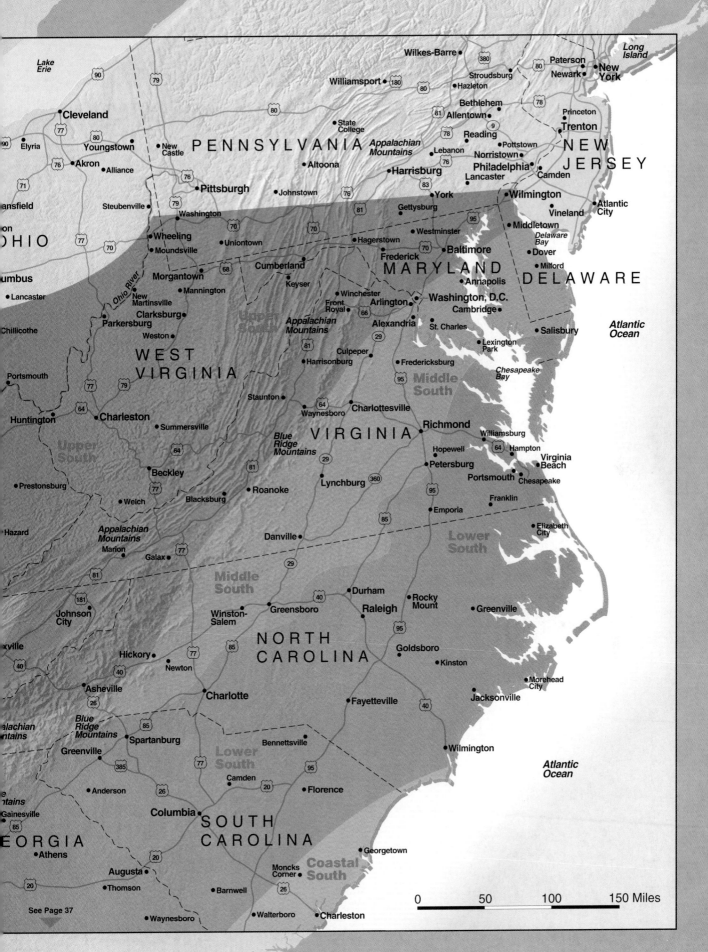

Lake Erie

Cleveland

Elyria

Youngstown

Akron

Alliance

OHIO

mansfield

Lancaster

Steubenville

ansfield

umbus

Chillicothe

Portsmouth

Huntington

Prestonsburg

Hazard

xville

Gainesville

EORGIA

Athens

New Castle

Washington

Wheeling

Moundsville

Morgantown

Mannington

New Martinsville

Clarksburg

Parkersburg

Weston

WEST VIRGINIA

Upper South

Charleston

Summersville

Beckley

Welch

Appalachian Mountains

Marion

Galax

Johnson City

Blue Ridge Mountains

Asheville

Hickory

Newton

Charlotte

Blue Ridge Mountains

Spartanburg

Greenville

Anderson

Columbia

SOUTH CAROLINA

Augusta

Thomson

Barnwell

Waynesboro

Walterboro

Charleston

PENNSYLVANIA

State College

Altoona

Pittsburgh

Johnstown

Appalachian Mountains

Harrisburg

York

Gettysburg

Cumberland

Keyser

Uniontown

Hagerstown

Frederick

Westminster

Baltimore

MARYLAND

Annapolis

Washington, D.C.

Winchester

Front Royal

Arlington

Alexandria

Cambridge

Harrisonburg

Staunton

Culpeper

Fredericksburg

Charlottesville

Waynesboro

VIRGINIA

Richmond

Lynchburg

Roanoke

Blacksburg

Danville

Middle South

Winston-Salem

Greensboro

Durham

Raleigh

Rocky Mount

NORTH CAROLINA

Goldsboro

Kinston

Fayetteville

Jacksonville

Lower South

Bennettsville

Camden

Florence

Georgetown

Moncks Corner

Coastal South

Wilkes-Barre

Williamsport

Hazleton

Stroudsburg

Bethlehem

Allentown

Reading

Lebanon

Norristown

Pottstown

Philadelphia

Lancaster

Camden

Wilmington

Middletown

Dover

Milford

DELAWARE

Delaware Bay

Paterson

Newark

New York

Long Island

Princeton

Trenton

NEW JERSEY

Vineland

Atlantic City

Salisbury

Lexington Park

Chesapeake Bay

Atlantic Ocean

Middle South

Williamsburg

Hopewell

Petersburg

Hampton

Virginia Beach

Portsmouth

Chesapeake

Franklin

Emporia

Lower South

Elizabeth City

Greenville

Morehead City

Wilmington

Atlantic Ocean

St. Charles

Ohio River

Appalachian Mountains

See Page 37

Map Labels

ARKANSAS

Hot Springs •
• Stuttgart
Pine Bluff
Dumas •
El Dorado •
• Crossett
Oak Grove
Minden •
• Bastrop
Monroe
Winnsboro •
Winnfield •
Natchitoches •

MISSISSIPPI

• Batesville Oxford **Tupelo**
Aberdeen •
Birmingham •
Columbus •
• Greenville • Winona
Vicksburg • **Jackson** Meridian •
• Waynesboro
• Hattiesburg

Middle South

Gadsden
• Piedmont
• Anniston
Pell City
• Lafayette
• Clanton Auburn
Tuscaloosa • Columbus
ALABAMA
• Demopolis • Selma **Montgomery**
Lower South
• Troy
Monroeville •
Dothan •
• Brewton
• Atmore
Coastal South
Chattahoo
• Crestview

LOUISIANA

• Leesville
Alexandria •
• Marksville
• De Ridder
Natchez •
Ville Platte
Coastal South
Lafayette •
Lake Charles •
• New Iberia
• Abbeville

Lower South

Baton Rouge Hammond
Lake Maurepas Lake Pontchartrain
Picayune
Gulfport Biloxi • Pascagoula
Mobile • Pensacola Pana City
Lake Borgne
New Orleans • Chalmette
Houma

See Page 33

Arkansas River
Mississippi River
Mississippi River

See Page 33

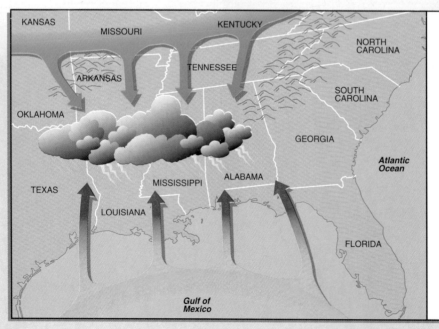

KANSAS MISSOURI KENTUCKY
NORTH CAROLINA
ARKANSAS TENNESSEE
OKLAHOMA
SOUTH CAROLINA
TEXAS
GEORGIA
Atlantic Ocean
MISSISSIPPI ALABAMA
LOUISIANA
FLORIDA
Gulf of Mexico

The South's Weather Machine

Nothing has a more profound effect on our region's climate and weather than the Gulf of Mexico. In winter, the warm waters of the Gulf (between 60 and 70 degrees) heat the air. But when a savage cold front pushes through, tender plants pampered by mild winter temperatures may be killed. In spring, tropical air from the Gulf marches north to battle cold Canadian air headed south, creating a convergence zone; thunderstorms, tornadoes, and flash floods can be the result. By summer (left), water temperatures rise into the mid 80s. Hot, humid air dominates. Afternoon downpours can drop 2 or 3 inches in just a few hours. Houston receives 48 inches of rain per year; Tallahassee gets 62; and New Orleans receives 57. Mobile, the wettest major city in the continental United States, receives 67 inches of rain per year. That's 28 more than "rainy" Seattle.

SOUTH
CAROLINA

•Athens See Page 35

•Georgetown

Augusta•

•Moncks
Corner

•Thomson

•Barnwell

•Charleston

•Waynesboro

•Walterboro

•Hardwick

Lower
South

•Hilton
Head
Island

GEORGIA

•Savannah

•Eastman

•Vidalia

Coastal
South

•Jesup

•Douglas

Atlantic
Ocean

•Brunswick

•Waycross

•Valdosta

Okefenokee
Swamp

•Jacksonville

Tallahassee•

•Lake
City

•St.
Augustine

Live
Oak

•Perry

Coastal
South

•Palatka
Lake
George

Gainesville•

•Daytona
Beach

•Ocala

FLORIDA

•Deltona

•Cape
Canaveral

•Orlando

Spring•
Hill

•Kissimmee

•Melbourne

•Lakeland

Florida's Turnpike

Tampa•

Lake
Wales

St.
Petersburg•

•Fort Pierce

•Sebring

Sarasota•

Port•
Charlotte

Lake
Okeechobee

West
Palm
Beach

Gulf of
Mexico

•Clewiston

•Belle
Glade

Cape•
Coral

Fort
Myers•

Boca
Raton

•Lehigh
Acres

Tropical
South

Fort
Lauderdale

Sanibel
Island

•Hialeah

Naples•

Miami

The
Everglades

•Homestead

Florida
Keys

0   50   100   150 Miles

Key West•

37

A Guide to
PLANT SELECTION

Showy perennials fill a border with color

The thousands of plants described in the A to Z Plant Encyclopedia (beginning on page 113) include an infinitely varied assortment of sizes, shapes, textures, and colors. The pleasure of choosing from this rich assortment is available to anyone with a sense of adventure and a bit of earth. But such abundance can sometimes lead to bewilderment. The lists of plants that follow, used with the plant encyclopedia, will help you to select the right plants—whether you are looking to achieve a special effect with flowers or foliage, tackling a difficult landscape situation, or starting out with the basics.

SUN

☼ Grows best with unobstructed sunlight all day long or almost all day—you can overlook an hour or so of shade at the beginning or end of a summer day

☼ Needs partial shade—that is, shade for half the day or for at least 3 hours during the hottest part of the day

● Prefers little or no direct sunlight—for example, it does best on the north side of a house or beneath a broad, dense tree

WATER

◖ Thrives with less than regular moisture—moderate amounts for some plants, little for those with more drought tolerance

◖ Performs well with regular moisture

◖◖ Takes more than regular moisture—includes plants needing constantly moist soil, bog plants, and aquatic plants

CLIMATE

A plant's climate adaptability is shown after the ✄. The letters refer to the climate zones (see pages 26–37) where the plants will grow best.

LANDSCAPE PLANTS
with Showy Flowers

Crabapple
Malus 'Liset'

You can talk about form and function all you want. But the fact is, when it comes to plants, everyone loves flowers. People want flowers from every plant in the garden, not just from annuals and perennials. Fortunately, many trees, shrubs, ground covers, and vines flaunt striking blooms at different times of the year. To help you plan multiple seasons of bloom, we've arranged this list according to the season in which different plants flower.

Spring garden with white viburnum

Cherry, flowering
Prunus

SPRING
Trees

Black locust
☼ ◑ ❄ ✀ US, MS, LS, CS
Robinia pseudoacacia   p. 359

Bottlebrush
☼ ◑ ❄ ✀ CS, TS
Callistemon   p. 160

Bradford pear
☼ ◑ ❄ ✀ US, MS, LS, CS
Pyrus calleryana 'Bradford'   p. 348

Catalpa
☼ ◑ ◐ ❄ ✀ US, MS, LS, CS
          p. 169

Cherry, peach, plum
☼ ◑ ❄ ✀ ZONES VARY
Prunus (flowering)   p. 342

Crabapple
☼ ◑ ❄ ✀ US, MS, LS
Malus   p. 288

Empress tree
☼ ◑ ◐ ❄ ✀ US, MS, LS
Paulownia tomentosa   p. 314

Flowering dogwood
☼ ◑ ◐ ✀ US, MS, LS, CS
Cornus florida   p. 192

Goldenchain tree
☼ ◑ ◐ ❄ ✀ US
Laburnum   p. 267

Grancy graybeard
☼ ◑ ❄ ✀ US, MS, LS, CS
Chionanthus virginicus   p. 177

Hawthorn
☼ ◑ ❄ ✀ ZONES VARY
Crataegus   p. 195

Jacaranda
☼ ◑ ✀ CS, TS
Jacaranda mimosifolia   p. 260

Kousa dogwood
☼ ◑ ◐ ❄ ✀ US, MS, LS
Cornus kousa   p. 192

Magnolia (most deciduous)
☼ ◑ ◐ ❄ ✀ ZONES VARY
          p. 284

Orchid tree
☼ ◑ ❄ ✀ TS
Bauhinia   p. 145

Red horsechestnut
☼ ◑ ◐ ❄ ✀ US, MS, LS
Aesculus carnea   p. 120

Redbud
☼ ◑ ◐ ❄ ✀ ZONES VARY
Cercis   p. 173

Serviceberry
☼ ◑ ◐ ❄ ✀ US, MS, LS
Amelanchier   p. 126

Silver bell
◑ ◐ ✀ US, MS, LS
Halesia   p. 240

Snowbell
☼ ◑ ◐ ✀ ZONES VARY
Styrax   p. 389

SPRING
Shrubs

Acacia (most)
☼ ◑ ✀ ZONES VARY
          p. 114

Azalea and rhododendron
◑ ◐ ◑ ❄ ✀ ZONES VARY
Rhododendron   p. 353

Banana shrub
☼ ◑ ◐ ✀ LS, CS
Michelia figo   p. 294

Beauty bush
☼ ◑ ◐ ❄ ✀ US, MS, LS
Kolkwitzia amabilis   p. 267

Flowering dogwood
Cornus florida 'Rubra'

Goldenchain tree
Laburnum

Grancy graybeard
Chionanthus virginicus

Jacaranda
Jacaranda mimosifolia

Orchid tree
Bauhinia

Red horsechestnut
Aesculus carnea

Plant listings continue ▶

39

'Bow Bells' Rhododendron

Black jetbead
☼ ◑ ◐ ● ◐ ✂ US, MS, LS
Rhodotypos scandens   p. 357

Mountain laurel
☼ ◑ ◐ ● ◐ ✂ US, MS, LS, CS
Kalmia latifolia   p. 265

Mountain laurel
Kalmia latifolia

Camellia, common
◑ ◐ ● ✂ US, MS, LS, CS
Camellia japonica   p. 161

Myrtle
☼ ◑ ◐ ✂ CS
Myrtus communis   p. 299

Chinese fringe
☼ ◑ ◐ ● ✂ MS, LS, CS
Loropetalum chinense   p. 281

Pearl bush
☼ ◐ ● ✂ US, MS, LS
Exochorda   p. 221

Daphne
◐ ✂ NEEDS, ZONES VARY
                             p. 203

Photinia
☼ ◐ ● ◐ ✂ ZONES VARY
                             p. 326

Pearl bush
Exochorda macrantha

Deutzia
☼ ◑ ◐ ● ◐ ✂ US, MS, LS
                             p. 205

Pieris
◐ ● ◐ ✂ ZONES VARY
                             p. 328

Deutzia, slender
Deutzia gracilis

Dwarf flowering almond
☼ ◐ ● ✂ US, MS, LS
Prunus glandulosa   p. 344

Red buckeye
☼ ◑ ◐ ● ◐ ✂ US, MS, LS, CS
Aesculus pavia   p. 120

Firethorn
☼ ◐ ● ✂ ZONES VARY
Pyracantha   p. 347

Rose
☼ ◑ ◐ ● ✂ ZONES VARY
Rosa   p. 359

Flowering quince
☼ ◐ ● ◐ ✂ US, MS, LS, CS
Chaenomeles   p. 174

Spiraea (some)
☼ ◑ ◐ ● ◐ ✂ ZONES VARY
                             p. 383

Forsythia
☼ ◐ ● ◐ ✂ US, MS, LS
                             p. 226

Sweet mock orange
☼ ◑ ◐ ● ◐ ✂ US, MS, LS, CS
Philadelphus coronarius   p. 323

Fothergilla
☼ ◑ ◐ ● ✂ US, MS, LS
                             p. 227

Texas mountain laurel
☼ ◐ ● ◐ ✂ LS, CS
Sophora secundiflora   p. 381

Hardy orange
☼ ◐ ● ✂ ALL ZONES
Poncirus trifoliata   p. 184

Viburnum (some)
NEEDS VARY
                             p. 407

Rose
Rosa 'Belle Story'

Honeysuckle
☼ ◑ ◐ ● ✂ ZONES VARY
Lonicera   p. 280

Virginia sweetspire
☼ ◑ ◐ ● ◐ ✂ US, MS, LS, CS
Itea virginica   p. 260

Indian hawthorn
☼ ◑ ◐ ● ◐ ✂ LS, CS
Raphiolepis indica   p. 351

Weigela florida
☼ ◑ ◐ ● ✂ US, MS, LS
                             p. 411

Japanese kerria
☼ ◑ ◐ ● ✂ US, MS, LS
Kerria japonica   p. 266

Winter hazel
☼ ◑ ◐ ● ✂ US, MS, LS
Corylopsis   p. 193

Lilac
Syringa

Jasmine
☼ ◑ ◐ ● ✂ ZONES VARY
Jasminum (some)   p. 261

Yellow bells
☼ ◐ ● ✂ CS, TS
Tecoma stans   p. 394

Leucothoe
◑ ● ◐ ● ◐ ✂ ZONES VARY
                             p. 273

Yesterday-today-and-tomorrow
◐ ● ◐ ✂ CS, TS   p. 155
Brunfelsia pauciflora 'Floribunda'

Sweet mock orange
Philadelphus coronarius

Lilac
☼ ◑ ◐ ● ✂ ZONES VARY
Syringa   p. 391

SPRING
Ground Covers

Mahonia
NEEDS, ZONES VARY
                             p. 288

Carpet bugleweed
☼ ◑ ◐ ● ◐ ✂ US, MS, LS
Ajuga reptans   p. 122

Mexican orange
☼ ◑ ◐ ● ✂ LS, CS, TS
Choisya ternata   p. 178

Cheddar pink
☼ ◐ ✂ US, MS, LS
Dianthus gratianopolitanus   p. 206

Mahonia

Yellow bells
Tecoma stans

For growing symbol explanations, please see page 38.

Mazus
Mazus reptans

Bougainvillea

Carolina jessamine
Gelsemium sempervirens

Clematis

Coral tree
Erythrina

Cinquefoil
☼ ◐ ◖ ∤ ZONES VARY
Potentilla (some)   p. 340

Golden globes
☼ ◐ ◖ ∤ MS, LS, CS
Lysimachia congestiflora   p. 283

Mazus
☼ ◐ ◖ ∤ US, MS, LS, CS
Mazus reptans   p. 292

Periwinkle
◐ ● ◖ ∤ ZONES VARY
Vinca   p. 409

Thrift
☼ ◐ ◖ ∤ US, MS, LS, CS
Phlox subulata   p. 325

SPRING
Vines

Allamanda, common
☼ ◖ ◊ ∤ TS
Allamanda cathartica   p. 123

Bougainvillea
☼ ◐ ◖ ◖ ∤ CS, TS
                                        p. 153

Carolina jessamine
☼ ◐ ● ◖ ◊ ∤ MS, LS, CS
Gelsemium sempervirens   p. 231

Cat's claw
☼ ◐ ◖ ∤ LS, CS
Macfadyena unguis-cati   p. 283

Cherokee rose
☼ ◐ ◖ ∤ LS, CS, TS
Rosa laevigata   p. 365

Clematis
☼ ◖ ∤ ZONES VARY
                                        p. 184

Confederate jasmine
☼ ◖ ∤ LS, CS, TS
Trachelospermum jasminoides   p. 400

Crossvine
☼ ◐ ◖ ◊ ∤ ALL ZONES
Bignonia capreolata   p. 150

Lady Banks's rose
☼ ◐ ◖ ∤ LS, CS, TS
Rosa banksiae   p. 364

Trumpet honeysuckle
☼ ◐ ◖ ∤ US, MS, LS, CS
Lonicera sempervirens   p. 281

Wisteria
☼ ◖ ◊ ∤ US, MS, LS, CS
                                        p. 412

SUMMER
Trees

Catalpa
☼ ◐ ◖ ◊ ∤ US, MS, LS, CS
                                        p. 169

Chaste tree
☼ ◖ ◊ ∤ ALL ZONES
Vitex agnus-castus   p. 410

Chitalpa
☼ ◖ ∤ MS, LS, CS
Chitalpa tashkentensis   p. 177

Coral tree
☼ ◖ ◊ ∤ ZONES VARY
Erythrina (some)   p. 216

Crepe myrtle
☼ ◖ ∤ US, MS, LS, CS
Lagerstroemia indica   p. 267

Desert willow
☼ ◖ ∤ MS, LS, CS
Chilopsis linearis   p. 176

Franklin tree
☼ ◐ ◖ ∤ US, MS, LS
Franklinia alatamaha   p. 227

Gold medallion tree
☼ ◖ ◊ ∤ TS
Cassia leptophylla   p. 168

Goldenrain tree
☼ ◖ ◊ ∤ US, MS, LS, CS
Koelreuteria paniculata   p. 267

Harlequin glorybower
◐ ◖ ∤ MS, LS, CS, TS
Clerodendrum trichotomum   p. 186

Japanese pagoda tree
☼ ◐ ◖ ◊ ∤ US, MS, LS
Sophora japonica   p. 381

Jerusalem thorn
☼ ◖ ◊ ∤ CS, TS
Parkinsonia aculeata   p. 312

Loblolly bay
☼ ◐ ◖ ◖ ∤ LS, CS, TS
Gordonia lasianthus   p. 235

Royal poinciana
☼ ◖ ∤ TS
Delonix regia   p. 204

Silver trumpet tree
☼ ◐ ◖ ∤ TS
Tabebuia argentea   p. 392

Southern magnolia
☼ ◐ ◖ ∤ US, MS, LS, CS
Magnolia grandiflora   p. 285

Stewartia
☼ ◐ ◖ ∤ ZONES VARY
                                        p. 385

Sweet bay
☼ ◐ ◖ ◊ ∤ US, MS, LS, CS
Magnolia virginiana   p. 287

SUMMER
Shrubs

Abelia
☼ ◐ ◖ ∤ US, MS, LS
                                        p. 114

Wisteria

Chitalpa
Chitalpa tashkentensis

Harlequin glorybower
Clerodendrum trichotomum

Southern magnolia
Magnolia grandiflora

Royal poinciana
Delonix regia

Plant listings continue ▸

Blue mist
Caryopteris clandonensis

Butterfly bush
Buddleia

Cinquefoil
Potentilla fruticosa

Hydrangea, French
Hydrangea macrophylla

Jasmine, shining
Jasminum nitidum

Bird of paradise bush
☼ ♦ ◑ ♦ ⚡ CS, TS
Caesalpinia gilliesii   p. 158

Blue mist
☼ ♦ ◑ ⚡ US, MS, LS, CS
Caryopteris clandonensis   p. 167

Bottlebrush buckeye
☼ ◑ ♦ ♦ ⚡ US, MS, LS, CS
Aesculus parviflora   p. 120

Brazilian plume
◑ ◐ ♦ ⚡ CS, TS
Justicia carnea   p. 262

Butterfly bush
☼ ◑ ◐ ♦ ⚡ ZONES VARY
Buddleia   p. 156

Cape plumbago
☼ ◐ ♦ ⚡ CS, TS
Plumbago auriculata   p. 335

Cinquefoil
◑ ◐ ⚡ ZONES VARY
Potentilla   p. 340

Coral plant
◑ ◐ ♦ ♦ ⚡ TS
Jatropha multifida   p. 262

Flame of the woods
☼ ♦ ⚡ CS, TS
Ixora coccinea   p. 260

Gardenia, common
☼ ◑ ♦ ♦ ⚡ MS, LS, CS
Gardenia jasminoides   p. 230

Glorybower
◑ ◐ ♦ ⚡ ZONES VARY
Clerodendrum   p. 186

Hibiscus
☼ ♦ ◖ ⚡ ZONES VARY
                              p. 246

Hydrangea
☼ ◑ ◐ ♦ ⚡ ZONES VARY
                              p. 251

Indigo bush
☼ ♦ ◐ ⚡ US, MS, LS, CS
Amorpha fruticosa   p. 126

Jasmine
☼ ◑ ◐ ♦ ⚡ ZONES VARY
Jasminum (some)   p. 261

Oleander, common
☼ ◐ ♦ ⚡ LS, CS, TS
Nerium oleander   p. 302

Pentas
☼ ◑ ◐ ◖ ♦ ⚡ CS, TS
Pentas lanceolata   p. 321

Plumeria
☼ ◑ ◐ ♦ ⚡ TS
                              p. 335

Plumleaf azalea
◑ ♦ ◖ ♦ ⚡ US, MS, LS, CS
Rhododendron prunifolium   p. 357

Pomegranate
☼ ◐ ♦ ⚡ MS, LS, CS, TS
Punica granatum   p. 346

Princess flower
☼ ◑ ♦ ⚡ TS
Tibouchina urvilleana   p. 398

Rose
☼ ◑ ◐ ♦ ⚡ ALL ZONES
Rosa   p. 359

Rose of Sharon
☼ ◐ ♦ ⚡ US, MS, LS, CS
Hibiscus syriacus   p. 247

Sage
☼ ◐ ♦ ⚡ ZONES VARY
Salvia (several)   p. 369

Senna
☼ ◑ ◐ ♦ ⚡ ZONES VARY
Cassia   p. 167

Spiraea (some)
☼ ◑ ◐ ♦ ♦ ⚡ ZONES VARY
                              p. 383

St. Johnswort
☼ ◑ ◐ ♦ ⚡ ZONES VARY
Hypericum   p. 252

Sweet pepperbush
◑ ◐ ♦ ⚡ US, MS, LS, CS
Clethra alnifolia   p. 186

Texas sage
☼ ◐ ♦ ⚡ MS, LS, CS
Leucophyllum frutescens   p. 273

Turk's cap
◑ ◐ ♦ ◐ ♦ ⚡ LS, CS, TS   p. 290
Malvaviscus arboreus drummondii

Yellow bells
☼ ◐ ♦ ⚡ CS, TS
Tecoma stans   p. 394

Yellow shrimp plant
☼ ◑ ◐ ♦ ⚡ CS, TS
Pachystachys lutea   p. 309

Yesterday-today-and-tomorrow
◑ ◐ ♦ ⚡ CS, TS   p. 155
Brunfelsia pauciflora 'Floribunda'

SUMMER
Ground Covers, Vines

Allamanda, common
☼ ◑ ◐ ♦ ⚡ TS
Allamanda cathartica   p. 123

Black-eyed Susan vine
☼ ◑ ◐ ♦ ⚡ CS, TS
Thunbergia alata   p. 397

Bleeding heart vine
◑ ◐ ♦ ⚡ CS, TS
Clerodendrum thomsoniae   p. 186

Bower vine
☼ ◑ ◐ ♦ ⚡ CS, TS
Pandorea jasminoides   p. 311

Rosa
Rosa

St. Johnswort
Hypericum 'Hidcote'

Turk's cap
Malvaviscus arboreus

Yellow shrimp plant
Pachystachys lutea

Allamanda, common
Allamanda

For growing symbol explanations, please see page 38.

Clematis

Confederate jasmine
Trachelospermum jasminoides

Lantana, common
Lantana camara

Mandevilla
Mandevilla splendens 'Red Riding Hood'

Passion vine
Passiflora

Cape plumago
☼ ◐ ◊ ⚡ CS, TS
Plumbago auriculata   p. 335

Ceratostigma
☼ ◐ ◊ ⚡ US, MS, LS, CS   p. 172
Ceratostigma plumbaginoides

Clematis (some)
☼ ◐ ◊ ⚡ ZONES VARY
                              p. 184

Confederate jasmine
☼ ◐ ● ◊ ◊ ⚡ LS, CS, TS   p. 400
Trachelospermum jasminoides

Coral vine
☼ ◊ ◊ ⚡ LS, CS, TS
Antigonon leptopus   p. 129

Creeping liriope
◐ ● ◊ ◊ ⚡ ALL ZONES
Liriope spicata   p. 279

Crossvine
☼ ◐ ◊ ⚡ ALL ZONES
Bignonia capreolata   p. 150

Cypress vine
☼ ◊ ◊ ⚡ ALL ZONES
Ipomoea quamoclit   p. 257

Honeysuckle
☼ ◐ ◊ ⚡ ZONES VARY
Lonicera   p. 280

Hyacinth bean
☼ ◊ ⚡ LS, CS, TS
Dolichos lablab   p. 209

Jasmine
☼ ◐ ◊ ⚡ ZONES VARY
Jasminum (some)   p. 261

Lantana, common
☼ ◊ ◊ ⚡ MS, LS, CS, TS
Lantana camara   p. 270

Mandevilla
☼ ◐ ◊ ⚡ ZONES VARY
                              p. 291

Moonflower
☼ ◊ ◊ ⚡ ALL ZONES
Ipomoea alba   p. 256

Morning glory, common
☼ ◊ ◊ ⚡ ALL ZONES
Ipomea purpurea   p. 257

Passion vine
☼ ◊ ◊ ⚡ ZONES VARY
Passiflora   p. 313

Pink
☼ ◊ ⚡ US, MS, LS
Dianthus   p. 206

Pink trumpet vine
☼ ◐ ◊ ◊ ⚡ CS, TS
Podranea ricasoliana   p. 336

Potato vine
☼ ◐ ◊ ◊ ◊ ⚡ CS, TS
Solanum jasminoides   p. 380

Trumpet creeper
☼ ◐ ◊ ◊ ⚡ ZONES VARY
Campsis   p. 164

Verbena
☼ ◊ ◊ ⚡ ZONES VARY
                              p. 406

Wedelia trilobata
☼ ◐ ◊ ⚡ CS, TS
                              p. 411

AUTUMN
Trees

Autumn flowering cherry
☼ ◊ ◊ ⚡ US, MS, LS   p. 343
Prunus subhirtella 'Autumnalis'

Floss silk tree
☼ ◐ ◊ ◊ ⚡ TS
Chorisia   p. 178

Hong Kong orchid tree
☼ ◐ ◊ ◊ ⚡ TS
Bauhinia blakeana   p. 145

AUTUMN
Shrubs

Abelia
☼ ◐ ◊ ⚡ US, MS, LS
                              p. 114

Angel's trumpet
☼ ◐ ◊ ◊ ◊ ◊ ⚡ CS, TS
Brugmansia   p. 155

Butterfly bush
☼ ◐ ◊ ◊ ⚡ ZONES VARY
Buddleia   p. 156

Caesalpinia
☼ ◊ ◊ ◊ ⚡ ZONES VARY
                              p. 158

Galphimia glauca
☼ ◊ ◊ ⚡ CS, TS
                              p. 230

Hibiscus (some)
☼ ◊ ● ◊ ⚡ ZONES VARY
                              p. 246

Mexican bush sage
☼ ◊ ◊ ⚡ LS, CS, TS
Salvia leucantha   p. 370

Princess flower
☼ ◐ ◊ ◊ ⚡ TS
Tibouchina urvilleana   p. 398

Rose
☼ ◐ ◊ ◊ ⚡ ALL ZONES
Rosa (some)   p. 359

Sasanqua camellia
◐ ● ◊ ◊ ⚡ ALL ZONES
Camellia sasanqua   p. 163

Senna
☼ ◐ ◊ ◊ ⚡ ZONES VARY
Cassia (some)   p. 167

Potato vine
Solanum jasminoides

Angel's trumpet
Brugmansia versicolor 'Charles Grimaldi'

Princess flower
Tibouchina urvilleana

Rose
Rosa 'Charmian'

Plant listings continue ▶

Witch hazel, common
Hamamelis virginiana

Honeysuckle
Lonicera

Mandevilla

Cornelian cherry
Cornus mas

Purple orchid tree
Bauhinia variegata 'Candida'

Shrub bush clover
☼ ◑ ● ℤ US, MS, LS
Lespedeza thunbergii   p. 272

'Tardiva' hydrangea
☼ ◐ ● ℤ US, MS, LS, CS
Hydrangea paniculata   p. 251

Witch hazel, common
☼ ◐ ● ℤ US, MS, LS, CS
Hamamelis virginiana   p. 240

Yellow bells
☼ ● ● ℤ CS, TS
Tecoma stans   p. 394

AUTUMN
Ground Covers, Vines

Allamanda, common
☼ ● ● ℤ TS
Allamanda cathartica   p. 123

Bleeding heart vine
◐ ● ℤ CS, TS
Clerodendrum thomsoniae   p. 186

Cape honeysuckle
☼ ◐ ● ● ℤ CS, TS
Tecomaria capensis   p. 395

Cape plumbago
☼ ● ℤ CS, TS
Plumbago auriculata   p. 335

Flame vine
☼ ◐ ● ℤ CS, TS
Pyrostegia venusta   p. 347

Honeysuckle
☼ ◐ ● ℤ ZONES VARY
Lonicera (some)   p. 280

Mandevilla (some)
☼ ◐ ● ℤ ZONES VARY
                              p. 291

Potato vine
☼ ◐ ● ● ● ℤ CS, TS
Solanum jasminoides   p. 380

Silver lace vine
☼ ● ● ℤ US, MS, LS
Polygonum aubertii   p. 337

WINTER
Trees

Bailey acacia
☼ ● ℤ CS, TS
Acacia baileyana   p. 114

Cornelian cherry
☼ ◐ ● ℤ US, MS, LS
Cornus mas   p. 192

Japanese flowering apricot
☼ ● ● ℤ US, MS, LS, CS
Prunus mume   p. 344

'Okame' flowering cherry
☼ ● ● ℤ US, MS, LS, CS
Prunus 'Okame'   p. 343

Purple orchid tree
☼ ◐ ● ℤ TS
Bauhinia variegata   p. 145

Red maple
☼ ◐ ● ● ℤ US, MS, LS, CS
Acer rubrum   p. 117

Yulan magnolia
☼ ◐ ● US, MS, LS
Magnolia denudata   p. 285

WINTER
Shrubs

Camellia (many)
◐ ● ● ℤ US, MS, LS, CS
                              p. 161

Flowering quince
☼ ● ● ℤ US, MS, LS, CS
Chaenomeles   p. 174

Leatherleaf mahonia
☼ ◐ ● ℤ US, MS, LS, CS
Mahonia bealei   p. 288

Senna
☼ ● ● ℤ ZONES VARY
Cassia (most)   p. 167

Winter daphne
◐ ● ● ● ℤ MS, LS
Daphne odora   p. 203

Winter hazel
☼ ◐ ● ℤ US, MS, LS
Corylopsis   p. 193

Winter honeysuckle
☼ ◐ ● ℤ US, MS, LS, CS
Lonicera fragrantissima   p. 280

Wintersweet
☼ ◐ ● ℤ US, MS, LS, CS
Chimonanthus praecox   p. 176

Witch hazel
☼ ◐ ● ℤ US, MS, LS
Hamamelis (most)   p. 240

WINTER
Ground Covers, Vines

Flame vine
☼ ◐ ● ℤ CS, TS
Pyrostegia venusta   p. 347

Lenten rose
◐ ● ● ● ● ℤ US, MS, LS
Helleborus orientalis   p. 244

Sweet autumn clematis
☼ ● ℤ US, MS, LS, CS
Clematis dioscoreifolia   p. 185

Sweet viburnum
☼ ◐ ● ℤ CS, TS
Viburnum odoratissimum   p. 408

Winter jasmine
☼ ◐ ● ℤ US, MS, LS, CS
Jasminum nudiflorum   p. 261

Camellia

Flowering quince
Chaenomeles

Winter daphne
Daphne odora 'Marginata'

Winter honeysuckle
Lonicera fragrantissima

Lenten rose
Helleborus orientalis

For growing symbol explanations, please see page 38.

ANNUALS
for Seasonal Color

Annuals are the foundation of a good flower border, offering continuous bloom over a long period and an almost boundless variety of colors, shapes, and sizes. Yes, they die after only one season, but that's good—it gives you the chance to try something new. This chart lists both cool-season and warm-season annuals. The former generally bloom in fall and spring but also blossom in winter during mild weather. The latter hate frost, but they love the heat, and beautify our summers. Plants marked with the symbol ☙ are actually tender perennials and may live from year to year in mild-winter areas.

Sweet pea
Lathyrus odoratus

Delphinium

Foxglove
Digitalis

Poppy
Papaver

Pot marigold
Calendula officinalis

COOL-SEASON ANNUALS

Annual lobelia
☀ ● ◐ ◐ ◔ ∕ ALL ZONES
Lobelia erinus — p. 280

Delphinium
☀ ◐ ◔ ∕ ZONES VARY
— p. 204

English daisy
☀ ☼ ◐ ◐ ◐ ∕ ALL ZONES
Bellis perennis — p. 148

English wallflower
☀ ☼ ◐ ◐ ∕ ZONES VARY
Erysimum cheiri — p. 216

Flowering cabbage or kale
☀ ☼ ◐ ∕ ALL ZONES
— p. 158

Forget-me-not
☼ ◐ ◐ ◐ ∕ US, MS, LS
Myosotis sylvatica — p. 298

Foxglove
☼ ◐ ◐ ◔ ∕ US, MS, LS, CS
Digitalis — p. 208

Larkspur
☀ ☼ ◐ ◔ ∕ ALL ZONES
Consolida ambigua — p. 109

Lupine
☀ ☼ ◐ ◔ ∕ ZONES VARY
Lupinus — p. 281

Monkey flower
☀ ☼ ◐ ◔ ∕ ALL ZONES
Mimulus hybridus — p. 294

Pansy, viola, violet
☀ ☼ ◐ ● ◔ ∕ ZONES VARY
Viola — p. 409

Poppy
☀ ☼ ◐ ◔ ∕ ZONES VARY
Papaver (some) — p. 311

Pot marigold
☀ ◐ ∕ ALL ZONES
Calendula officinalis — p. 169

Primrose
☼ ◐ ◐ ◐ ∕ ZONES VARY
Primula (many) — p. 341

Snapdragon
☀ ☼ ◐ ∕ ALL ZONES
Antirrhinum majus — p. 129

Stock
☀ ☼ ◐ ∕ ALL ZONES
Matthiola incana — p. 292

Sweet pea
☀ ☼ ◐ ◐ ∕ ALL ZONES
Lathyrus odoratus — p. 270

Sweet William
☀ ☼ ◐ ∕ ALL ZONES
Dianthus barbatus — p. 206

WARM-SEASON ANNUALS

Ageratum
☀ ☼ ◐ ◔ ∕ ALL ZONES
Ageratum houstonianum — p. 121

Amethyst flower ☙
☼ ◐ ∕ ALL ZONES
Browallia — p. 155

Annual phlox
☀ ☼ ◐ ◔ ∕ ALL ZONES
Phlox drummondii — p. 325

Bachelor's button
☀ ☼ ◐ ∕ ALL ZONES
Centaurea cyanus — p. 171

Begonia ☙
☼ ● ◐ ◐ ∕ ALL ZONES
— p. 147

Black-eyed Susan vine ☙
☀ ☼ ◐ ◔ ∕ ALL ZONES
Thunbergia alata — p. 397

Snapdragon
Antirrhinum majus

Sweet William
Dianthus barbatus

Black-eyed Susan vine
Thunbergia alata

Cockscomb
Celosia

Plant listings continue ▶

Coleus
Coleus hybridus

Cosmos, common
Cosmos bipinnatus

Flowering tobacco
Nicotiana

Madagascar periwinkle
Catharanthus roseus

Marigold
Tagetes tenuifolia 'Lemon Gem'

Melampodium
Melampodium paludosum

Blue daze
:☼: ◐ ◑ ⚡ ALL ZONES
Evolvulus glomeratus   p. 221

Calliopsis
:☼: ◑ ⚡ ALL ZONES
Coreopsis tinctoria   p. 190

Cockscomb
:☼: ◑ ⚡ ALL ZONES
Celosia argentea   p. 171

Coleus
:☼: ◐ ◑◑ ⚡ ALL ZONES
Coleus hybridus   p. 188

Copper leaf
:☼: ◐ ◑ ⚡ ALL ZONES
Acalypha wilkesiana   p. 115

Cosmos, common
:☼: ◑ ⚡ ALL ZONES
Cosmos bipinnatus   p. 194

Creeping zinnia
:☼: ◑ ◑ ⚡ ALL ZONES
Sanvitalia procumbens   p. 372

Dusty miller
:☼: ◑ ◑ ⚡ ALL ZONES
Senecio cineraria   p. 376

Fanflower
:☼: ◑ ◑ ⚡ ALL ZONES
Scaevola aemula   p. 374

Flowering tobacco
:☼: ◐ ◑ ◑ ⚡ ALL ZONES
Nicotiana   p. 302

Garden nasturtium
:☼: ◐ ◑ ⚡ ALL ZONES
Tropaeolum majus   p. 402

Geranium
:☼: ◐ ◑ ◑ ⚡ ALL ZONES
Pelargonium   p. 318

Globe amaranth
:☼: ◐ ◑ ◑ ⚡ ALL ZONES
Gomphrena   p. 235

Impatiens
:☼: ◑ ◐ ◑ ⚡ ALL ZONES
                              p. 255

Indian blanket
:☼: ◑ ⚡ ALL ZONES
Gaillardia pulchella   p. 229

Lantana
:☼: ◑ ◑ ⚡ ALL ZONES
                              p. 219

Lisianthus
:☼: ◐ ◑ ◑ ⚡ ALL ZONES
Eustoma grandiflorum   p. 221

Madagascar periwinkle
:☼: ◐ ◑ ◑ ⚡ ALL ZONES
Catharanthus roseus   p. 169

Marigold
:☼: ◑ ⚡ ALL ZONES
Tagetes   p. 393

Melampodium
:☼: ◑ ⚡ ALL ZONES
Melampodium paludosum   p. 292

Mexican heather
:☼: ◐ ◑ ⚡ ALL ZONES
Cuphea hyssopifolia   p. 198

Mexican sunflower
:☼: ◑ ◑ ⚡ ALL ZONES
Tithonia rotundifolia   p. 398

Morning glory
:☼: ◐ ◑ ⚡ ALL ZONES
Ipomoea   p. 256

Moss rose
:☼: ◐ ◑ ◑◑ ⚡ ALL ZONES
Portulaca grandiflora   p. 339

Pentas
:☼: ◐ ◑ ◑◑ ⚡ ALL ZONES
Pentas lanceolata   p. 321

Pepper, ornamental
:☼: ◐ ◑ ⚡ ALL ZONES
                              p. 321

Perilla
:☼: ◐ ◑ ◑ ⚡ ALL ZONES
Perilla frutescans   p. 321

Petunia
:☼: ◑ ◑ ⚡ ALL ZONES
Petunia hybrida   p. 322

Pink (some)
:☼: ◑ ◑ ⚡ ALL ZONES
Dianthus   p. 206

Scarlet sage
:☼: ◑ ◑ ⚡ ALL ZONES
Salvia splendens   p. 370

Silk flower
:☼: ◑ ◑ ⚡ ALL ZONES
Abelmoschus moschatus   p. 114

Spider flower
:☼: ◑ ◑ ⚡ ALL ZONES
Cleome hasslerana   p. 185

Strawflower
:☼: ◑ ◑ ⚡ ALL ZONES
Helichrysum bracteatum   p. 243

Sunflower, common
:☼: ◑ ◑ ⚡ ALL ZONES
Helianthus annuus   p. 242

Sweet alyssum
:☼: ◐ ◑ ⚡ ALL ZONES
Lobularia maritima   p. 280

Verbena (some)
:☼: ◑ ⚡ ALL ZONES
                              p. 406

Wishbone flower
:☼: ◐ ◑ ⚡ ALL ZONES
Torenia fournieri   p. 400

Zinnia
:☼: ◑ ⚡ ALL ZONES
                              p. 416

Petunia
Petunia hybrida

Spider flower
Cleome hasslerana

Strawflower
Helichrysum bracteatum

Sunflower, common
Helianthus annuus

Verbena

Zinnia
Zinnia elegans

For growing symbol explanations, please see page 38.

BULBS
and Bulblike Plants

Freesia

Daffodil
Narcissus

Iris

Few plants endure for as long as bulbs. Because they're often dormant during the most desolate weather, they can survive with little care. Many become heirlooms, dug and passed along from generation to generation. Some—tulips, hyacinths, and crocuses—need 10 to 12 weeks of winter cold to bloom well. Other bulbs, such as daffodils, snowflakes, and lilies, can thrill us without the chill. Bulbs, corms, tubers, and rhizomes may flower for only a few weeks each year, but when you multiply that by the scores of blossoms they'll produce in a lifetime, they make the garden rich with flowers.

AUTUMN-PLANTED BULBS

Atamasco lily
☼ ◑ ✹ ALL ZONES
Zephyranthes atamasco   p. 415

Blackberry lily
☼ ◐ ◑ ✹ US, MS, LS, CS
Belamcanda   p. 148

Camass
☼ ◑ ◕◑ ✹ US, MS, LS
Camassia   p. 161

Crocus
☼ ◑ ◑ ✹ US, MS, LS
    p. 197

Daffodil
☼ ◐ ◑ ✹ US, MS, LS, CS
Narcissus   p. 299

Dog-tooth violet
◐ ◑ ◕◑ ✹ US, MS, LS
Erythronium dens-canis   p. 217

Foxtail lily
☼ ◑ ✹ US, MS
Eremurus   p. 215

Freesia
☼ ◑ ◑ ✹ CS, TS
    p. 228

Glory-of-the-snow
◐ ◑ ✹ US, MS
Chionodoxa   p. 177

Grape hyacinth
☼ ◐ ◑ ✹ US, MS, LS
Muscari   p. 298

Hyacinth, common
☼ ◐ ◑ ◕ ✹ US, MS, LS, CS
Hyacinthus orientalis   p. 251

Iris
NEEDS, ZONES VARY
    p. 257

Jack-in-the-pulpit
◐ ◑ ◕◑ ✹ US, MS, LS
Arisaema triphyllum   p. 136

Lily
☼ ◑ ◑ ✹ ALL ZONES
Lilium   p. 275

Lily-of-the-Nile
☼ ◐ ◑ ◕◑ ✹ ZONES VARY
Agapanthus   p. 120

Ornamental allium
☼ ◐ ◑ ✹ ZONES VARY
Allium   p. 123

Oxalis
☼ ◐ ◑ ✹ ALL ZONES
Oxalis rubra   p. 308

Oxblood lily
☼ ◑ ◑ ✹ MS, LS, CS
Rhodophiala bifida   p. 357

Persian ranunculus
☼ ◑ ✹ ALL ZONES
Ranunculus asiaticus   p. 350

Rain lily
☼ ◑ ✹ ZONES VARY
Zephyranthes   p. 415

Snowdrop
☼ ◐ ◑ ◕ ✹ US, MS
Galanthus   p. 229

Snowflake
☼ ◐ ◑ ✹ ZONES VARY
Leucojum   p. 273

Spanish bluebell
☼ ◐ ◑ ✹ US, MS, LS, CS
Endymion hispanicus   p. 213

Spring star flower
☼ ◐ ◑ ✹ US, MS, LS, CS
Ipheion uniflorum   p. 256

Squill
☼ ◐ ◑ ◕ ✹ US, MS, LS
Scilla   p. 375

Lily-of-the-Nile
Agapanthus

Spanish bluebell
Endymion hispanicus

Tulip
Tulipa

Lily
Lilium Asiatic hybrid

Hyacinth, common
Hyacinthus orientalis

Plant listings continue ▶

Windflower
Anemone

Canna

Dahlia

Gladiolus

Spider lily
Lycoris

Star of Bethlehem
☼ ♦ ◊ ⚡ US, MS, LS, CS
Ornithogalum umbellatum   p. 307

Sternbergia
☼ ♦ ◊ ⚡ US, MS, LS
Sternbergia lutea   p. 385

Tulip
☼ ♦ ◊ ⚡ US, MS, LS, CS
Tulipa   p. 403

Virginia bluebells
☼ ◐ ♦ ◊ ⚡ US, MS, LS
Mertensia virginica   p. 293

Windflower
☼ ◐ ♦ ◊ ♦ ◊ ⚡ US, MS, LS
Anemone   p. 127

Winter aconite
◐ ◊ ⚡ US, MS
Eranthis hyemalis   p. 214

Yellow star grass
☼ ◐ ♦ ◊ ⚡ US, MS, LS, CS
Hypoxis hirsuta   p. 253

SPRING-PLANTED BULBS

Achimenes
◐ ♦ ⚡ CS, TS
          p. 118

Amaryllis
☼ ◐ ♦ ⚡ LS, CS, TS
Hippeastrum   p. 248

Calla
☼ ◐ ♦ ◊ ⚡ CS, TS
Zantedeschia   p. 414

Canna
☼ ♦ ◊ ◊ ⚡ LS, CS, TS
          p. 164

Chinese ground orchid
◐ ♦ ⚡ MS, LS, CS
Bletilla striata   p. 151

Crinum
☼ ◐ ♦ ◊ ◊ ♦ ◊ ⚡ ZONES VARY
          p. 196

Crocosmia
☼ ◐ ♦ ◊ ⚡ US, MS, LS, CS
          p. 197

Dahlia
☼ ◐ ♦ ◊ ⚡ US, MS, LS
          p. 202

Elephant's ear
◐ ◊ ◊ ♦ ⚡ LS, CS, TS
Colocasia esculenta   p. 189

Fancy-leafed caladium
☼ ◐ ♦ ◊ ◊ ♦ ⚡ TS
Caladium bicolor   p. 158

Giant alocasia
◐ ♦ ◊ ◊ ♦ ⚡ LS, CS, TS
Alocasia macrorrhiza   p. 124

Gladiolus
☼ ♦ ⚡ ZONES VARY
          p. 233

Glory lily
☼ ◐ ♦ ◊ ⚡ TS
Gloriosa rothschildiana   p. 234

Hymenocallis
☼ ◐ ♦ ◊ ⚡ ZONES VARY
          p. 252

Lily
◐ ♦ ⚡ ALL ZONES
Lilium, Asiatic hybrids   p. 276

Magic lily
☼ ◐ ♦ ◊ ⚡ US, MS, LS, CS
Lycoris squamigera   p. 283

Society garlic
☼ ♦ ⚡ LS, CS, TS
Tulbaghia violacea   p. 402

Spider lily
☼ ◐ ♦ ◊ ⚡ ZONES VARY
Lycoris   p. 282

Tuberose
☼ ◐ ♦ ◊ ⚡ ALL ZONES
Polianthes tuberosa   p. 337

Tuberous begonia
◐ ♦ ◊ ⚡ TS
Begonia   p. 148

Walking iris
☼ ◐ ♦ ◊ ⚡ CS, TS
Neomarica gracilis   p. 301

SUMMER-PLANTED BULBS

Amaryllis
☼ ◐ ♦ ◊ ⚡ LS, CS, TS
Hippeastrum   p. 248

Crocus (fall-flowering)
☼ ◐ ♦ ◊ ⚡ US, MS, LS
          p. 197

Cyclamen (except florists' types)
☼ ◐ ♦ ◊ ⚡ ZONES VARY
          p. 199

Meadow saffron
☼ ◐ ♦ ◊ ⚡ US, MS, LS
Colchicum   p. 188

PLANT ANY TIME

Daylily
☼ ◐ ♦ ◊ ⚡ ALL ZONES
Hemerocallis   p. 244

Kaffir lily
☼ ◐ ♦ ◊ ⚡ TS
Clivia miniata   p. 187

Morea iris
☼ ◐ ♦ ◊ ⚡ LS, CS, TS
Dietes   p. 208

Daylily
Hemerocallis

Crocus

Meadow saffron
Colchicum

Kaffir lily
Clivia miniata

Society garlic
Tulbaghia violacea

For growing symbol explanations, please see page 38.

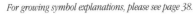

AUTUMN FOLIAGE COLOR

Sugar maple *(Acer saccharum)* in brilliant autumn raiment

F ew things in life have the power to awe as much as a fiery autumn. But whether a plant changes color or not depends on the kind of plant, where it grows, and the particular weather that year. In general, plants develop better fall color in the Upper and Middle South, where autumns are cool and dry. Fall color is hit-or-miss in the Lower South; gardeners in the Coastal and Tropical South see hardly any color. When the right conditions exist, the following plants put on a show. Because leaf color often varies within a species, shop for plants when they're in color. And don't forget about the color that fruits and berries can bring (see page 53).

Crepe myrtle
Lagerstroemia indica

Flowering dogwood
Cornus florida

Grancy graybeard
Chionanthus virginicus

Hawthorn
Crataegus

Honey locust
Gleditsia triacanthos

Black gum
Nyssa sylvatica

Callery pear
Pyrus calleryana

Chinese pistache
Pistacia chinensis

TREES

American beech
☼ ◑ ◐ ✦ US, MS, LS, CS
Fagus grandifolia — p. 222

Ash
☼ ◐ ✦ ✦ ZONES VARY
Fraxinus — p. 227

Bald cypress
☼ ◐ ✦ ✦✦ US, MS, LS, CS
Taxodium distichum — p. 394

Beech
☼ ◑ ◐ ✦ ZONES VARY
Fagus — p. 222

Birch
☼ ◐ ✦✦ ✦ ZONES VARY
Betula — p. 149

Black cherry
☼ ◐ ✦ ✦ US, MS, LS, CS
Prunus serotina — p. 344

Black gum
☼ ☼ ◑ ◐ ✦ ✦ US, MS, LS, CS
Nyssa sylvatica — p. 304

Black locust
☼ ◐ ✦ ✦ US, MS, LS, CS
Robinia pseudoacacia — p. 359

Callery pear
☼ ◐ ✦ ✦ US, MS, LS, CS
Pyrus calleryana — p. 347

Carolina silverbell
☼ ◐ ✦ ✦ US, MS, LS
Halesia carolina — p. 240

Chinese parasol tree
☼ ☼ ◐ ✦ ✦ MS, LS, CS, TS
Firmiana simplex — p. 226

Chinese pistache
☼ ◐ ✦ ✦ US, MS, LS, CS
Pistacia chinensis — p. 329

Chinese quince
☼ ☼ ◐ ✦ ✦ US, MS, LS
Pseudocydonia sinensis — p. 345

Chinese tallow
☼ ◐ ✦ ✦ LS, CS, TS
Sapium sebiferum — p. 372

Crepe myrtle
☼ ◐ ✦ US, MS, LS, CS
Lagerstroemia indica — p. 267

Dawn redwood
☼ ◐ ✦ US, MS, LS — p. 294
Metasequoia glyptostroboides

Edible fig
☼ ◐ ✦ MS, LS, CS, TS
Ficus carica — p. 225

Flowering dogwood
☼ ☼ ◐ ✦ US, MS, LS, CS
Cornus florida — p. 192

Franklin tree
☼ ☼ ◐ ✦ US, MS, LS
Franklinia alatamaha — p. 227

Goldenrain tree
☼ ◐ ✦ ✦ US, MS, LS, CS
Koelreuteria paniculata — p. 267

Grancy graybeard
☼ ◐ ✦ ✦ US, MS, LS, CS
Chionanthus virginicus — p. 177

Hackberry
☼ ☼ ◐ ✦ US, MS, LS
Celtis — p. 171

Hawthorn
☼ ◐ ✦ ZONES VARY
Crataegus (some) — p. 195

Plant listings continue ▸

Larch
Larix

Maidenhair tree
Ginkgo biloba

Maple
Acer

Mountain ash
Sorbus

Oak
Quercus

Honey locust
☼ ◐ ● ⚡ US, MS, LS
Gleditsia triacanthos   p. 234

Ironwood
☼ ☼ ● ● ⚡ US, MS, LS, CS
Carpinus caroliniana   p. 166

Japanese maple
☼ ☼ ● ● ⚡ US, MS, LS, CS
Acer palmatum   p. 116

Japanese zelkova
☼ ● ● ⚡ US, MS, LS
Zelkova serrata   p. 415

Jujube
☼ ● ⚡ US, MS, LS, CS
Ziziphus jujuba   p. 416

Juneberry
☼ ● ● ● ⚡ US, MS, LS
Amelanchier arborea   p. 126

Katsura tree
☼ ☼ ● ● ⚡ US, MS
Cercidiphyllum japonicum   p. 173

Kentucky coffee tree
☼ ● ● ⚡ US, MS, LS
Gymnocladus dioica   p. 236

Larch
☼ ● ⚡ ZONES VARY
Larix   p. 270

Linden
☼ ● ⚡ ZONES VARY
Tilia   p. 398

Maidenhair tree
☼ ● ● ● ⚡ US, MS, LS, CS
Ginkgo biloba   p. 233

Maple
☼ ☼ ● ● ● ⚡ ZONES VARY
Acer (many)   p. 115

Mountain ash
☼ ☼ ● ● ⚡ ZONES VARY
Sorbus   p. 381

Oak
☼ ● ⚡ ZONES VARY
Quercus (deciduous)   p. 348

Ohio buckeye
☼ ☼ ● ● ⚡ US, MS
Aesculus glabra   p. 120

Osage orange
☼ ● ● ⚡ US, MS, LS
Maclura pomifera   p. 284

Pawpaw
☼ ☼ ● ● ⚡ US, MS, LS, CS
Asimina triloba   p. 139

Persimmon
☼ ● ● ⚡ ZONES VARY
Diospyros   p. 322

Quaking aspen
☼ ● ● ⚡ US, MS
Populus tremuloides   p. 339

Redbud
☼ ☼ ● ● ⚡ ZONES VARY
Cercis   p. 173

Sassafras
☼ ● ● ⚡ US, MS, LS, CS
Sassafras albidum   p. 373

Shagbark hickory
☼ ☼ ● ⚡ US, MS, LS, CS
Carya ovata   p. 167

Sourwood
☼ ☼ ● ● ⚡ US, MS, LS
Oxydendrum arboreum   p. 308

Southern wild crab
☼ ● ● ⚡ US, MS, LS
Malus angustifolia   p. 289

Stewartia
☼ ☼ ● ● ⚡ ZONES VARY
          p. 385

Sweet gum
☼ ● ● ⚡ ALL ZONES
Liquidambar styraciflua   p. 277

Tulip poplar
☼ ● ● ⚡ US, MS, LS, CS
Liriodendron tulipifera   p. 278

Yellow wood
☼ ● ⚡ US, MS, LS
Cladrastis lutea   p. 184

Yoshino flowering cherry
☼ ● ● ⚡ US, MS, LS
Prunus yedoensis   p. 343

Yulan magnolia
☼ ☼ ● ● ⚡ US, MS, LS
Magnolia denudata   p. 285

SHRUBS

Azalea
☼ ● ● ◉ ● ⚡ ZONES VARY
Rhododendron (deciduous)   p. 353

Beautyberry
☼ ☼ ● ● ⚡ US, MS, LS, CS
Callicarpa   p. 160

Blueberry
☼ ● ● ⚡ ZONES VARY
Vaccinium   p. 151

Bottlebrush buckeye
☼ ☼ ● ● ⚡ US, MS, LS, CS
Aesculus parviflora   p. 120

Chinese jujube
☼ ● ⚡ US, MS, LS, CS
Ziziphus jujuba   p. 416

Chokeberry
☼ ☼ ● ● ● ● ⚡ US, MS, LS
Aronia   p. 137

Cotoneaster (most deciduous)
☼ ● ⚡ ZONES VARY
          p. 194

Persimmon
Diospyros

Redbud
Cercis

Stewartia

Sweet gum
Liquidambar styraciflua

For growing symbol explanations, please see page 38.

Japanese barberry
Berberis thunbergii 'Rose Glow'

Oakleaf hydrangea
Hydrangea quercifolia

Persian parrotia
Parrotia persica

Sumac
Rhus

Crepe myrtle
☼ ◑ ◔ ✂ US, MS, LS, CS
Lagerstroemia indica   p. 267

Devil's walking stick
☼ ◑ ◔ ◔ ◔ ✂ US, MS, LS, CS
Aralia spinosa   p. 135

Dusty zenobia
◑ ◔ ◔ ✂ US, MS, LS, CS
Zenobia pulverulenta   p. 415

Farkleberry
☼ ◑ ◔ ✂ MS, LS, CS
Vaccinium arboreum   p. 405

Fothergilla
☼ ◑ ◔ ✂ US, MS, LS
                              p. 227

Heart's-a-bustin'
☼ ◑ ◔ ◔ ◔ ✂ US, MS, LS, CS
Euonymus americana   p. 218

Japanese barberry
☼ ◑ ◔ ◔ ◔ ✂ US, MS, LS, CS
Berberis thunbergii   p. 149

Japanese kerria
☼ ◑ ◔ ◔ ✂ US, MS, LS
Kerria japonica   p. 266

'Miss Kim' lilac
☼ ◑ ◔ ◔ ✂ US, MS, LS
Syringa patula 'Miss Kim'   p. 312

Nandina
☼ ◑ ◔ ◔ ◔ ✂ US, MS, LS, CS
Nandina domestica   p. 299

Oakleaf hydrangea
☼ ◑ ◔ ◔ ✂ US, MS, LS, CS
Hydrangea quercifolia   p. 251

Oriental photinia
☼ ◔ ◔ ◔ ✂ US, MS, LS
Photinia villosa   p. 326

Persian parrotia
☼ ◔ ◔ ✂ US, MS, LS
Parrotia persica   p. 312

Pomegranate
☼ ◔ ◔ ◔ ✂ MS, LS, CS, TS
Punica granatum   p. 346

Redvein enkianthus
☼ ◑ ◔ ◔ ✂ US, MS, LS
Enkianthus campanulatus   p. 213

Rose
☼ ◑ ◔ ✂ ALL ZONES
Rosa (some)   p. 359

Shadblow serviceberry
☼ ◑ ◔ ◔ ◔ ✂ US, MS, LS
Amelanchier canadensis   p. 126

Smoke tree
☼ ◔ ◔ ✂ US, MS, LS
Cotinus coggygria   p. 194

Spicebush
☼ ◑ ◔ ● ◔ ✂ US, MS, LS
Lindera benzoin   p. 277

Star magnolia
☼ ◑ ◔ ◔ ✂ US, MS, LS, CS
Magnolia stellata   p. 287

Sumac
☼ ◔ ◔ ✂ ZONES VARY
Rhus   p. 358

Sweet pepperbrush
☼ ◑ ◔ ◔ ✂ US, MS, LS, CS
Clethra alnifolia   p. 186

Sweetshrub, common
☼ ◑ ◔ ◔ ◔ ✂ US, MS, LS
Calycanthus floridus   p. 161

Sweetbells
◑ ◔ ● ◔ ◔ ✂ US, MS, LS, CS
Leucothoe racemosa   p. 274

Titi
☼ ◑ ◔ ◔ ◔ ✂ ALL ZONES
Cyrilla racemiflora   p. 201

Van Houtte spiraea
☼ ◑ ◔ ◔ ◔ ✂ US, MS, LS, CS
Spiraea vanhouttei   p. 383

Viburnum (many)
NEEDS, ZONES VARY
                              p. 407

Virginia sweetspire
☼ ◑ ◔ ● ◔ ✂ US, MS, LS, CS
Itea virginica   p. 260

Winged euonymus
☼ ◑ ◔ ◔ ✂ US, MS, LS
Euonymus alata   p. 218

Winterberry
☼ ◑ ◔ ◔ ✂ US, MS, LS, CS
Ilex verticillata   p. 255

Wintersweet
☼ ◑ ◔ ◔ ✂ US, MS, LS, CS
Chimonanthus praecox   p. 176

Witch hazel, common
☼ ◑ ◔ ◔ ✂ US, MS, LS, CS
Hamamelis virginiana   p. 240

VINES

Bittersweet
☼ ◔ ✂ US, MS, LS
Celastrus   p. 170

Boston ivy
☼ ◑ ◔ ● ◔ ✂ US, MS, LS
Parthenocissus tricuspidata   p. 313

Grape
☼ ◔ ✂ ZONES VARY
                              p. 236

Virginia creeper
☼ ◑ ◔ ◔ ◔ ✂ US, MS, LS, CS
Parthenocissus quinquefolia   p. 313

Wisteria
☼ ◔ ◔ ✂ US, MS, LS, CS
                              p. 412

Viburnum

Winged euonymus
Euonymus alata

Witch hazel, common
Hamamelis

Virginia creeper
Parthenocissus quinquefolia

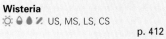

Boston ivy
Parthenocissus tricuspidata

DECIDUOUS PLANTS
for Winter Interest

American beech
Fagus grandifolia

Most Southerners prefer evergreens for their long season of color (see page 103). Still, deciduous plants offer a special beauty, especially in gardens in the Upper South, where winters can be long. Peeling bark, contorted limbs, and sculptural silhouettes cause us to reflect on the subtleties of gardening, those quiet details that make every day outdoors an adventure of learning.

Chinese elm
Ulmus parvifolia

TREES

American beech
☼ ◑ ◐ ✿ US, MS, LS, CS
Fagus grandifolia   p. 222

Birch
☼ ◐ ◑ ✿ ZONES VARY
Betula (most)   p. 149

Black walnut
☼ ◐ ✿ US, MS, LS, CS
Juglans nigra   p. 410

Chinese elm
☼ ◐ ✿ US, MS, LS, CS
Ulmus parvifolia   p. 404

Coral bark maple
☼ ◑ ◐ ◑ ✿ US, MS, LS, CS
Acer palmatum 'Sango Kaku' p. 116

Corkscrew willow
☼ ◐◑ ✿ US, MS, LS
Salix matsudana 'Tortuosa' p. 369

Crepe myrtle
☼ ◐ ✿ US, MS, LS, CS
Lagerstroemia indica   p. 267

Dogwood, flowering
☼ ◑ ◐ ✿ US, MS, LS, CS
Cornus florida   p. 192

Ironwood
☼ ◑ ● ◐ ✿ US, MS, LS, CS
Carpinus caroliniana   p. 166

Japanese flowering cherry
☼ ◐ ◑ ✿ ZONES VARY
Prunus serrulata   p. 343

Kentucky coffee tree
☼ ◐ ◑ ✿ US, MS, LS
Gymnocladus dioica   p. 236

Lacebark pine
☼ ◐ ◑ ✿ US, MS, LS
Pinus bungeana   p. 330

Maidenhair tree
☼ ◐ ◑ ✿ US, MS, LS, CS
Ginkgo biloba   p. 233

Paperbark maple
☼ ◑ ◐ ◑ ✿ US, MS
Acer griseum   p. 116

Saucer magnolia
☼ ◑ ◐ ✿ US, MS, LS, CS
Magnolia soulangiana   p. 286

Shagbark hickory
☼ ◐ ◑ ✿ US, MS, LS, CS
Carya ovata   p. 167

Stewartia
☼ ◑ ◐ ✿ ZONES VARY
                         p. 385

Sycamore
☼ ◐ ◑ ✿ US, MS, LS, CS
Platanus occidentalis   p. 332

White oak
☼ ◐ ◑ ✿ US, MS, LS, CS
Quercus alba   p. 348

SHRUBS

Curly filbert
☼ ◐ ◑ ✿ US, MS, LS
Corylus avellana 'Contorta' p. 193

Heart's-a-bustin'
☼ ◐ ● ◐ ✿ US, MS, LS, CS
Euonymus americana   p. 218

Japanese kerria
☼ ◑ ◐ ✿ US, MS, LS
Kerria japonica   p. 266

Japanese tree lilac
☼ ◑ ◐ ✿ US
Syringa reticulata   p. 392

Oakleaf hydrangea
☼ ◑ ◐ ✿ US, MS, LS, CS
Hydrangea quercifolia   p. 251

Redtwig dogwood
☼ ◑ ◐ ✿ US, MS, LS
Cornus stolonifera   p. 192

Winged euonymus
☼ ◑ ● ◐ ✿ US, MS, LS
Euonymus alata   p. 218

Crepe myrtle
Lagerstroemia indica

Paperbark maple
Acer griseum

Stewartia

Sycamore
Platanus occidentalis

Curly filbert
Corylus avellana 'Contorta'

Redtwig dogwood
Cornus stolonifera

For growing symbol explanations, please see page 38.

COLORFUL FRUITS AND BERRIES

I f you judge a plant solely on the merits of its flowers, you may be doing it a great injustice. Many plants sport showy fruits and berries, principally in fall and winter, when the garden is often devoid of bright color. Not only do these fruits catch your eye, but they often attract hungry birds as well. If you'd like to join them for a snack, look for plants with the 🍐 next to their name. This tells you that people can eat the fruit, too, either fresh or in jams and jellies.

Mandarin orange
Citrus

Viburnum
Viburnum plicatum tomentosum 'Mariesii'

Crabapple
Malus 'Red Jade'

Hawthorn
Crataegus

Mountain ash
Sorbus

TREES

Citrus 🍐
☼ 💧 ⚡ CS, TS
p. 181

Cornelian cherry 🍐
☼ 🌤 💧 ⚡ US, MS, LS
Cornus mas p. 192

Crabapple 🍐
☼ 💧 ⚡ US, MS, LS
Malus p. 288

Dogwood
☼ 🌤 💧 ⚡ ZONES VARY
Cornus kousa & florida p. 192

Eastern red cedar
☼ 🌤 💧 ⚡ US, MS, LS, CS
Juniperus virginiana p. 264

Flamegold
☼ 💧 ⚡ CS, TS
Koelreuteria elegans p. 267

Goldenrain tree
☼ 💧 ⚡ US, MS, LS, CS
Koelreuteria paniculata p. 267

Harlequin glorybower
🌤 💧 ⚡ MS, LS, CS, TS
Clerodendrum trichotomum p. 186

Hawthorn
☼ 💧 ⚡ ZONES VARY
Crataegus p. 195

Holly
☼ 🌤 💧 ⚡ ZONES VARY
Ilex (many) p. 253

Juneberry 🍐
☼ 🌤 💧 ⚡ US, MS, LS
Amelanchier arborea p. 126

Korean evodia
☼ 💧 ⚡ US, MS, LS
Evodia daniellii p. 221

Litchi tree 🍐
☼ 💧 ⚡ CS, TS
Litchi chinensis p. 278

Loquat 🍐
☼ 💧 ⚡ LS, CS, TS
Eriobotrya japonica p. 216

Mountain ash
☼ 🌤 💧 ⚡ ZONES VARY
Sorbus p. 381

Persimmon 🍐
☼ 💧 ⚡ ZONES VARY
Diospyros p. 322

Sea grape 🍐
☼ 💧 ⚡ TS
Coccoloba uvifera p. 187

Southern magnolia
☼ 🌤 💧 ⚡ US, MS, LS, CS
Magnolia grandiflora p. 285

SHRUBS

American elderberry 🍐
☼ 🌤 💧 ⚡ US, MS, LS, CS
Sambucus canadensis p. 369

Beautyberry
☼ 🌤 💧 ⚡ US, MS, LS, CS
Callicarpa p. 160

Bayberry
☼ 🌤 💧 ⚡ US, MS
Myrica pensylvanica p. 298

Black jetbead
☼ 🌤 💧 ⚡ US, MS, LS
Rhodotypos scandens p. 357

Blueberry 🍐
☼ 💧 ⚡ ZONES VARY
Vaccinium p. 151

Chinese photinia
☼ 💧 ⚡ US, MS, LS, CS
Photinia serrulata p. 326

Persimmon
Diospyros

Beautyberry
Callicarpa

Blueberry
Vaccinium

Plant listings continue ▶

Chokeberry
☼ ◑ ◔ ◔ ◔ ⚡ US, MS, LS
Aronia   p. 137

Cotoneaster
☼ ◔ ⚡ ZONES VARY
                                          p. 194

Elaeagnus
☼ ◑ ◔ ◔ ⚡ ZONES VARY
                                          p. 212

Firethorn
☼ ◔ ⚡ ZONES VARY
Pyracantha   p. 347

Golden dewdrop
☼ ◔ ◔ ⚡ TS
Duranta repens   p. 210

Holly
☼ ◑ ◔ ⚡ ZONES VARY
Ilex (many)   p. 253

Honeysuckle
☼ ◑ ◔ ⚡ ZONES VARY   p. 280
Lonicera (most shrubby types)

Japanese aucuba
☼ ◑ ● ◔ ⚡ ALL ZONES
Aucuba japonica   p. 142

Japanese barberry
☼ ◑ ● ◔ ⚡ US, MS, LS, CS
Berberis thunbergii   p. 149

Japanese skimmia
◑ ● ◔ ⚡ US
Skimmia japonica   p. 379

Jerusalem cherry
☼ ◑ ● ◔ ◔ ⚡ CS, TS
Solanum pseudocapsicum   p. 380

Mahonia
NEEDS, ZONES VARY
                                          p. 288

Marlberry
NEEDS, ZONES VARY
Ardesia   p. 136

Nandina
☼ ◑ ● ◔ ◔ ⚡ US, MS, LS, CS
Nandina domestica   p. 299

Natal plum   🍐
☼ ◑ ◔ ⚡ TS
Carissa macrocarpa   p. 166

Oriental photinia
☼ ◔ ◔ ⚡ US, MS, LS
Photinia villosa   p. 326

Pomegranate   🍐
☼ ◔ ◔ ⚡ MS, LS, CS, TS
Punica granatum (some)   p. 346

Prickly pear cactus   🍐
☼ ◑ ◔ ⚡ ZONES VARY
Opuntia   p. 306

Rose   🍐
☼ ◑ ◔ ⚡ ALL ZONES
Rosa (especially rugosas)   p. 359

Sapphireberry
☼ ◔ ⚡ US, MS, LS
Symplocos paniculata   p. 391

Sea buckthorn   🍐
☼ ◔ ◔ ⚡ US
Hippophae rhamnoides   p. 248

Spicebush
☼ ◑ ● ◔ ⚡ US, MS, LS
Lindera benzoin   p. 277

Staghorn sumac
☼ ◔ ◔ ⚡ US, MS, LS
Rhus typhina   p. 358

Turk's cap
◑ ● ◔ ◔ ⚡ LS, CS, TS   p. 290
Malvaviscus arboreus drummondii

Viburnum (many)
NEEDS, ZONES VARY
                                          p. 407

Winged euonymus
☼ ◑ ● ◔ ◔ ⚡ US, MS, LS
Euonymus alata   p. 218

Yew
☼ ◑ ● ◔ ◔ ◔ ⚡ US, MS
Taxus   p. 394

PERENNIALS

Blackberry lily
☼ ◑ ◔ ⚡ US, MS, LS, CS
Belamcanda   p. 148

Gladwin iris
◑ ● ◔ ⚡ US, MS
Iris foetidissima   p. 259

Italian arum
◑ ● ◔ ◔ ⚡ US, MS, LS, CS
Arum italicum   p. 138

Jack-in-the-pulpit
◑ ● ◔ ◔ ⚡ US, MS, LS
Arisaema triphyllum   p. 136

Lily of China
◑ ◔ ◔ ⚡ MS, LS, CS
Rohdea japonica   p. 359

Partridgeberry
● ◔ ◔ ◔ ⚡ US, MS, LS
Mitchella repens   p. 295

VINES

American bittersweet
☼ ◔ ⚡ US, MS, LS
Celastrus scandens   p. 171

Honeysuckle
☼ ◑ ◔ ⚡ ZONES VARY
Lonicera (some)   p. 280

Porcelain berry
☼ ◑ ● ◔ ◔ ⚡ US, MS, LS, CS   p. 126
Ampelopsis brevipedunculata

Chokeberry
Aronia

Cotoneaster

Firethorn
Pyracantha

Holly (Winterberry)
Ilex verticillata

Mahonia, Burmese
Mahonia lomariifolia

Nandina
Nandina domestica

Natal plum
Carissa macrocarpa

Rose
Rosa

Viburnum

American bittersweet
Celastrus scandens

For growing symbol explanations, please see page 38.

SHOWY PERENNIALS
for Beds and Borders

Beard tongue
Penstemon

W e've heard it said that a perennial is any plant that, had it lived, could have come back year after year. Fortunately, many perennials are tougher than this description, offering us decades of dazzling flowers and foliage. Among their ranks you'll find an astonishing array of choices, literally something for everybody. Trying out new and unfamiliar plants each year is one of the things that makes gardening fun.

Perennial border

Alstroemeria

Aster

Astilbe

Balloon flower
Platycodon grandiflorus

Alstroemeria
☼ ◑ ◐ ◊ ☇ MS, LS, CS
p. 125

Aster
☼ ◑ ◐ ☇ US, MS, LS
p. 141

Astilbe
☼ ◑ ◐ ☇ US, MS
p. 141

Baby's breath
☼ ◐ ☇ US, MS
Gypsophila paniculata   p. 239

Balloon flower
☼ ◐ ☇ US, MS, LS, CS
Platycodon grandiflorus   p. 332

Beard tongue
☼ ◑ ◐ ◐ ☇ ZONES VARY
Penstemon (many)   p. 320

Bear's breech
☼ ◑ ◐ ◐ ☇ US, MS, LS, CS
Acanthus mollis   p. 115

Bee balm
☼ ◑ ◐ ◐ ☇ US, MS, LS
Monarda didyma   p. 296

Bellflower
☼ ◑ ◐ ◐ ☇ US, MS, LS
Campanula   p. 164

Bergenia
☼ ◐ ◐ ☇ US, MS, LS
p. 149

Betony
☼ ◐ ☇ US, MS, LS
Stachys officinalis   p. 384

Bird of Paradise
☼ ◑ ◐ ☇ CS, TS
Strelitzia reginae   p. 388

Blanket flower
☼ ◐ ☇ ALL ZONES
Gaillardia grandiflora   p. 229

Blazing star
☼ ◐ ◐ ☇ US, MS, LS, CS
Liatris   p. 274

Bleeding heart, common
◑ ◐ ◐ ☇ US, MS, LS
Dicentra spectabilis   p. 207

Blue star
☼ ◑ ◐ ◐ ☇ US, MS, LS   p. 126
Amsonia tabernaemontana

Butterfly weed
☼ ◐ ◐ ☇ ALL ZONES
Asclepias tuberosa   p. 139

Cardinal flower
◑ ◐ ◐ ◐ ☇ US, MS, LS, CS
Lobelia cardinalis   p. 278

Chrysanthemum
☼ ◐ ☇ ZONES VARY
p. 178

Cinquefoil
◑ ◐ ☇ ZONES VARY
Potentilla   p. 340

Columbine
☼ ◑ ◐ ◐ ☇ ZONES VARY
Aquilegia   p. 134

Coneflower
☼ ◑ ◐ ◐ ☇ ZONES VARY
Rudbeckia   p. 366

Coral bells
☼ ◑ ◐ ☇ US, MS, LS
Heuchera sanguinea   p. 246

Coreopsis
☼ ◐ ☇ US, MS, LS, CS
p. 190

Cranesbill
☼ ◑ ◐ ☇ US, MS, LS
Geranium   p. 231

Crocosmia
☼ ◑ ◐ ☇ US, MS, LS, CS
p. 197

Bellflower
Campanula

Bleeding heart, common
Dicentra spectabilis 'Alba'

Cardinal flower
Lobelia cardinalis

Cranesbill
Geranium

Plant listings continue ▶

Chrysanthemum

Coneflower
Rudbeckia

Daylily
Hemerocallis

Delphinium

Goldenrod
Solidago

Cupid's dart
☼ ◗ ✿ ✿ ⁄ US, MS, LS
Catananche caerulea   p. 169

Daylily
☼ ◗ ◗ ✿ ⁄ ALL ZONES
Hemerocallis   p. 244

Delphinium
☼ ◗ ✿ ⁄ ZONES VARY
          p. 204

Euphorbia
☼ ◗ ● ◗ ✿ ◗ ⁄ ZONES VARY
          p. 219

Euryops
☼ ◗ ✿ ⁄ CS, TS
Euryops pectinatus   p. 220

Evergreen candytuft
☼ ◗ ✿ ⁄ US, MS, LS
Iberis sempervirens   p. 253

False indigo
☼ ◗ ✿ ⁄ US, MS, LS, CS
Baptisia   p. 145

Filipendula
◗ ◗ ◗ ✿ ⁄ US, MS, LS
          p. 225

Fountain grass
☼ ◗ ◗ ◗ ✿ ⁄ ZONES VARY
Pennisetum   p. 320

Four o'clock
☼ ◗ ✿ ◗ ⁄ ALL ZONES
Mirabilis jalapa   p. 295

Gaura
☼ ◗ ◗ ✿ ⁄ US, MS, LS, CS
Gaura lindheimeri   p. 230

Geranium
☼ ◗ ◗ ◗ ✿ ⁄ CS, TS
Pelargonium   p. 318

Gerbera daisy
☼ ◗ ◗ ✿ ⁄ CS, TS
Gerbera jamesonii   p. 232

Geum
☼ ◗ ◗ ✿ ⁄ US, MS, LS
Geum chiloense   p. 232

Ginger lily
☼ ◗ ◗ ◗ ✿ ⁄ ZONES VARY
Hedychium   p. 241

Globe centaurea
☼ ◗ ✿ ⁄ US, MS, LS
Centaurea macrocephala   p. 171

Globeflower
☼ ☼ ◗ ◗ ◗ ✿ ⁄ US, MS
Trollius   p. 402

Globe thistle
☼ ◗ ◗ ✿ ⁄ US, MS, LS
Echinops   p. 211

Goat's beard
◗ ◗ ✿ ⁄ US, MS
Aruncus   p. 138

Golden aster
☼ ◗ ◗ ✿ ⁄ US, MS, LS
Chrysopsis   p. 180

Golden marguerite
☼ ◗ ◗ ✿ ⁄ US, MS, LS
Anthemis tinctoria   p. 128

Golden ray
◗ ◗ ◗ ◗ ✿ ⁄ ZONES VARY
Ligularia   p. 274

Goldenrod
☼ ☼ ◗ ◗ ✿ ⁄ US, MS, LS, CS
Solidago and Solidaster   p. 380

Gooseneck loosestrife
☼ ◗ ◗ ✿ ⁄ US, MS, LS
Lysimachia clethroides   p. 283

Heliconia
☼ ☼ ◗ ◗ ✿ ⁄ TS
          p. 243

Hellebore
☼ ◗ ● ◗ ◗ ◗ ✿ ⁄ ZONES VARY
Helleborus   p. 244

Hosta
☼ ◗ ◗ ◗ ✿ ⁄ US, MS, LS
          p. 249

Iris
NEEDS, ZONES VARY
          p. 257

Jacob's ladder
◗ ◗ ◗ ✿ ⁄ US, MS, LS
Polemonium caerulum   p. 337

Japanese anemone
◗ ◗ ◗ ✿ ⁄ US, MS, LS
Anemone hybrida   p. 127

Jerusalem sage
☼ ◗ ◗ ◗ ✿ ⁄ US, MS, LS
Phlomis fruticosa   p. 324

Joe-Pye weed
☼ ☼ ◗ ◗ ◗ ✿ ⁄ US, MS, LS, CS
Eupatorium purpureum   p. 219

Ladybells
☼ ◗ ◗ ◗ ◗ ✿ ⁄ US, MS
Adenophora   p. 119

Lavender
☼ ◗ ◗ ✿ ⁄ ZONES VARY
Lavandula   p. 271

Lily-of-the-Nile
☼ ☼ ◗ ◗ ◗ ✿ ⁄ ZONES VARY
Agapanthus   p. 120

Live-forever sedum
☼ ◗ ◗ ✿ ⁄ US, MS, LS, CS
Sedum telephium   p. 376

Lungwort
◗ ◗ ◗ ◗ ✿ ⁄ US, MS, LS
Pulmonaria   p. 345

Lupine
☼ ◗ ◗ ✿ ⁄ ZONES VARY
Lupinus   p. 281

Iris

Lavender
Lavandula

Meadow rue
Thalictrum

Mullein
Verbascum

For growing symbol explanations, please see page 38.

Mexican evening primrose
Oenothera speciosa

Nepeta

Obedient plant
Physostegia virginiana

Peony
Paeonia

Pink
Dianthus

Meadow rue
☼ ◑ ◐ ⚡ ZONES VARY
Thalictrum   p. 395

Mexican evening primrose
☼ ◑ ◐ ⚡ MS, LS
Oenothera speciosa   p. 305

Monkshood
☼ ◑ ◐ ◑ ⚡ US
Aconitum   p. 118

Mullein
☼ ◐ ⚡ US, MS, LS
Verbascum   p. 405

Nepeta
☼ ◑ ◐ ⚡ US, MS, LS
                                    p. 301

Obedient plant
☼ ◑ ◐ ⚡ US, MS, LS, CS
Physostegia virginiana   p. 327

Ox-eye
☼ ◑ ◐ ◐ ⚡ US, MS, LS, CS
Heliopsis helianthoides   p. 244

Pampas grass
☼ ◐ ◐ ◐ ⚡ MS, LS, CS, TS
Cortaderia selloana   p. 192

Peony
☼ ◑ ◐ ⚡ ZONES VARY
Paeonia (herbaceous)   p. 309

Perennial blue flax
☼ ◐ ◐ ⚡ US, MS, LS
Linum perenne   p. 277

Perennial hibiscus
☼ ◐ ◐◐ ⚡ ALL ZONES
Hibiscus moscheutos   p. 247

Phlox
☼ ◑ ◐ ⚡ ZONES VARY
                                    p. 325

Pincushion flower
☼ ◑ ◐ ⚡ US
Scabiosa   p. 373

Pink
☼ ◐ ⚡ US, MS, LS
Dianthus   p. 206

Plume poppy
☼ ◑ ◐ ⚡ US, MS, LS
Macleaya cordata   p. 284

Purple coneflower
☼ ◐ ⚡ US, MS, LS, CS
Echinacea purpurea   p. 211

Red-hot poker
☼ ◑ ◐◐ ⚡ US, MS, LS, CS
Kniphofia uvaria   p. 266

Rose campion
☼ ◑ ◐ ⚡ US, MS, LS
Lychnis coronaria   p. 282

Russian sage
☼ ◐ ⚡ US, MS, LS, CS
Perovskia   p. 321

Sea holly
☼ ◐ ⚡ US, MS, LS, CS
Eryngium amethystinum   p. 216

Sea lavender
☼ ◐ ⚡ ZONES VARY
Limonium   p. 276

Sedge
◑ ● ◐◐ ⚡ US, MS, LS, CS
Carex   p. 165

Showy sedum
☼ ◐ ◐ ⚡ US, MS, LS, CS
Sedum spectabile   p. 376

Sneezeweed, common
☼ ◐ ⚡ US, MS, LS
Helenium autumnale   p. 242

Snow-in-summer
☼ ◐ ◐ ⚡ US, MS, LS
Cerastium tomentosum   p. 172

Society garlic
☼ ◐ ⚡ LS, CS, TS
Tulbaghia violacea   p. 402

Speedwell
☼ ◐ ◐ ⚡ ZONES VARY
Veronica   p. 406

Spiderwort
☼ ◑ ● ◐◐ ⚡ US, MS, LS, CS
Tradescantia virginiana   p. 401

Stokesia
☼ ◐ ⚡ ALL ZONES
Stokesia laevis   p. 386

Thrift, common
☼ ◐ ◐ ⚡ US, MS
Armeria maritima   p. 137

Thyme
☼ ◑ ◐ ⚡ ZONES VARY
Thymus   p. 397

Toad lily
◑ ● ◐◐ ⚡ US, MS, LS
Tricyrtis   p. 401

Valerian
☼ ◑ ◐ ⚡ US, MS, LS
Centranthus ruber   p. 172

Wand loosestrife
☼ ◐ ⚡ US, MS, LS
Lythrum virgatum   p. 283

White turtlehead
☼ ◐ ◐ ⚡ US, MS, LS, CS
Chelone glabra   p. 175

Wormwood, common
☼ ◐ ⚡ US, MS, LS
Artemisia absinthium   p. 137

Yarrow
☼ ◐ ⚡ US, MS, LS
Achillea   p. 117

Yucca
☼ ◐ ◐ ⚡ ZONES VARY
                                    p. 413

Russian sage
Perovskia atriplicifolia

Snow-in-summer
Cerastium tomentosum

Thrift, common
Armeria maritima

Yarrow
Achillea

FERNS

for Foliage Interest

Holly fern
Cyrtomium falcatum

Ferns are much more than simply plants for moist shade. In fact, some members of this amazingly diverse group tolerate a surprising amount of sun and drought. In size, they range from forest-floor creepers to majestic tree ferns that seem to belong to the age of dinosaurs. Some ferns are deciduous, while others are evergreen. Some form clumps, others spread by rhizomes, and one fern listed here climbs. But ferns share one especially valuable garden trait—beautiful foliage that's a joy to observe all by itself or in combination with that of other plants.

Southern shield fern
Thelypteris kunthii

Cinnamon fern
Osmunda cinnamomea

Hay-scented fern
Dennstaedtia punctilobula

Royal fern
Osmunda regalis

Ostrich fern
Matteuccia struthiopteris

Sensitive fern
Onoclea sensibilis

Sword fern
Nephrolepis

Wood fern
Dryopteris

American maidenhair fern
☼ ● ◑ ◐ ✂ US, MS
Adiantum pedatum   p. 119

Australian tree fern
☼ ☼ ◑ ✂ TS
Cyathea cooperi   p. 199

Autumn fern
☼ ◑ ◑ ✂ MS, LS, CS
Dryopteris erythrosora   p. 210

Blunt-lobed woodsia
☼ ☼ ◑ ✂ US, MS, LS
Woodsia obtusa   p. 412

Chain fern
☼ ◑ ✂ US, MS, LS, CS
Woodwardia   p. 413

Christmas fern
☼ ● ◑ ✂ US, MS, LS, CS
Polystichum acrostichoides   p. 338

Cinnamon fern
☼ ● ◑ ◑ ✂ US, MS, LS
Osmunda cinnamomea   p. 308

Ebony spleenwort
☼ ● ◑ ◐ ✂ US, MS, LS
Asplenium platyneuron   p. 140

Hay-scented fern
☼ ◑ ◑ ✂ US, MS
Dennstaedtia punctilobula   p. 205

Holly fern
☼ ● ◑ ✂ LS, CS, TS
Cyrtomium falcatum   p. 201

Japanese climbing fern
☼ ◑ ✂ MS, LS, CS, TS
Lygodium japonicum   p. 283

Japanese painted fern
☼ ● ◑ ◑ ✂ US, MS, LS
Athyrium nipponicum 'Pictum'   p. 142

Lady fern
☼ ● ◑ ✂ ZONES US, MS, LS
Athyrium filix-femina   p. 142

New York fern
☼ ☼ ● ◑ ✂ US, MS
Thelypteris noveboracensis   p. 396

Marginal shield fern
☼ ● ◑ ✂ US, MS, LS
Dryopteris marginalis   p. 210

Ostrich fern
☼ ◑ ◑ ✂ US, MS
Matteuccia struthiopteris   p. 292

Royal fern
☼ ☼ ● ◑ ◑ ✂ US, MS, LS, CS
Osmunda regalis   p. 308

Sensitive fern
☼ ◑ ◑ ✂ US, MS, LS
Onoclea sensibilis   p. 305

Southern maidenhair
☼ ● ◑ ◑ ✂ US, MS, LS
Adiantum capillus-veneris   p. 119

Southern shield fern
☼ ● ◑ ◑ ✂ MS, LS, CS
Thelypteris kunthii   p. 396

Sword fern
☼ ● ◑ ✂ TS
Nephrolepis   p. 302

Tasmanian tree fern
☼ ☼ ● ◑ ✂ TS
Dicksonia antarctica   p. 207

Tassel fern
☼ ● ◑ ✂ US, MS, LS
Polystichum polyblepharum   p. 338

Wood fern
☼ ● ◑ ✂ ZONES VARY
Dryopteris   p. 210

For growing symbol explanations, please see page 38.

FRAGRANT PLANTS

Grancy graybeard
Chionanthus virginicus

A garden's fragrance can be as memorable as its appearance; the perfume of a particular blossom can evoke a past experience even years later. Scent is usually most pronounced on warm and humid days; less so when weather is dry and hot. Use fragrant plants where they're most noticeable: in containers on a deck or terrace; beneath a window so the pleasant aroma can drift into the house; or in a part of the garden where you like to sit or walk.

Banana shrub
Michelia figo

Magnolia

Texas mountain laurel
Sophora secundiflora

Angel's trumpet
Brugmansia versicolor 'Charles Grimaldi'

Citrus
'Bearss'

TREES

Black locust
☼ ◐ ♦ ❄ ✔ US, MS, LS, CS
Robinia pseudoacacia   p. 359

Citrus
☼ ♦ ✔ CS, TS
                              p. 181

Crabapple
☼ ◐ ♦ ❄ ✔ US, MS, LS
Malus (some)   p. 288

Fragrant snowbell
☼ ◑ ♦ ✔ US, MS, LS
Styrax obassia   p. 389

Grancy graybeard
☼ ◐ ♦ ❄ ✔ US, MS, LS, CS
Chionanthus virginicus   p. 177

Harlequin glorybower
◑ ♦ ✔ MS, LS, CS, TS
Clerodendrum trichotomum   p. 186

Japanese flowering apricot
☼ ◐ ♦ ❄ ✔ US, MS, LS, CS
Prunus mume   p. 344

Jerusalem thorn
☼ ◐ ♦ ❄ ✔ CS, TS
Parkinsonia aculeata   p. 312

Magnolia (many)
☼ ◑ ♦ ✔ ZONES VARY
                              p. 284

Mimosa
☼ ◑ ♦ ✔ US, MS, LS, CS
Albizia julibrissin   p. 122

Russian olive
☼ ◑ ♦ ◐ ✔ US, MS
Elaeagnus angustifolia   p. 212

Sweet acacia
☼ ♦ ✔ TS
Acacia farnesiana   p. 115

Texas mountain laurel
☼ ◑ ♦ ◐ ✔ LS, CS
Sophora secundiflora   p. 381

Yellow wood
☼ ♦ ✔ US, MS, LS
Cladrastis lutea   p. 184

SHRUBS

Alabama azalea
◐ ♦ ◑ ♦ ✔ MS, LS
Rhododenron alabamense   p. 356

Angel's trumpet
☼ ◐ ♦ ◑ ♦ ✔ LS, CS, TS
Brugmansia   p. 155

Anise tree
◐ ♦ ◐ ♦ ✔ ZONES VARY
Illicium   p. 255

Banana shrub
☼ ◐ ♦ ✔ LS, CS
Michelia figo   p. 294

Bottlebrush buckeye
◐ ♦ ◑ ✔ US, MS, LS, CS
Aesculus parviflora   p. 120

Broom
☼ ◐ ✔ US, MS, LS
Cytisus   p. 201

Butterfly bush
☼ ◑ ♦ ◐ ✔ ZONES VARY
Buddleia   p. 156

Carissa
☼ ◑ ♦ ✔ TS
                              p. 165

Cestrum (some)
◑ ♦ ◐ ✔ ZONES VARY
                              p. 173

Daphne (many)
♦ ✔ NEEDS, ZONES VARY
                              p. 203

Butterfly bush
Buddleia

Daphne
Daphne burkwoodii

Gardenia
Gardenia jasminoides 'Radicans'

Bottleabrush buckeye
Aesculus parviflora

Plant listings continue ▸

Jasmine, pink
Jasminum polyanthum

'Iceberg' rose
Rosa 'Iceberg'

Japanese pittosporum
Pittosporum tobira

Mock orange
Philadelphus

Sweet pepperbush
Clethra alnifolia

Elaeagnus
☼ ◐ ◕ ● ◆ ⚡ ZONES VARY
p. 212

Florida flame azalea
◐ ◕ ● ◑ ◆ ⚡ US, MS, LS, CS
Rhododendron austrinum p. 356

Fothergilla
☼ ◐ ● ◆ ⚡ US, MS, LS
p. 227

Fragrant snowball
☼ ◐ ● ◆ ⚡ US, MS, LS
Viburnum carlcephalum p. 407

Gardenia
☼ ◐ ● ◆ ⚡ MS, LS, CS
p. 230

Hardy orange
☼ ● ◆ ⚡ ALL ZONES
Poncirus trifoliata p. 184

Japanese pittosporum
☼ ◐ ● ◆ ⚡ LS, CS, TS
Pittosporum tobira p. 329

Jasmine
☼ ◐ ● ◆ ⚡ ZONES VARY
Jasminum (some) p. 261

Korean spice viburnum
☼ ◐ ● ◆ ⚡ US, MS, LS
Viburnum carlesii p. 407

Leatherleaf mahonia
☼ ◐ ● ◆ ⚡ US, MS, LS, CS
Mahonia bealei p. 288

Lilac
☼ ◐ ● ◆ ⚡ ZONES VARY
Syringa (many) p. 391

Mexican orange
☼ ◐ ● ◆ ⚡ LS, CS, TS
Choisya ternata p. 178

Mock orange
☼ ● ◕ ● ◆ ⚡ ZONES VARY
Philadelphus (most) p. 323

Orange jessamine
☼ ◐ ● ◆ ⚡ CS, TS
Murraya paniculata p. 297

Osmanthus (most)
☼ ◐ ● ◕ ● ◆ ⚡ ZONES VARY
p. 307

Piedmont azalea
☼ ◐ ● ◕ ● ◑ ◆ ⚡ US, MS, LS, CS
Rhododendron canescens p. 356

Plumeria
☼ ◐ ● ◆ ⚡ TS
p. 335

Raphiolepis 'Majestic Beauty'
☼ ◐ ● ◕ ● ◆ ⚡ LS, CS
p. 351

Rose
☼ ◐ ● ◆ ⚡ ZONES VARY
Rosa p. 359

Spicebush
☼ ◐ ● ◆ ⚡ US, MS, LS
Lindera benzoin p. 277

Star magnolia
☼ ◐ ● ◆ ⚡ US, MS, LS, CS
Magnolia stellata p. 287

Swamp azalea
☼ ◐ ● ◕ ● ◑ ◆ ⚡ US, MS, LS, CS
Rhododendron viscosum p. 357

Sweet azalea
☼ ◐ ● ◕ ● ◑ ◆ ⚡ US, MS, LS
Rhododendron arborescens p. 356

Sweet box
◐ ● ◕ ● ◆ ⚡ LS
Sarcococca p. 372

Sweet pepperbush
☼ ◐ ● ◕ ● ◆ ⚡ US, MS, LS, CS
Clethra alnifolia p. 186

Sweetspire
☼ ◐ ● ◕ ● ◆ ⚡ ZONES VARY
Itea p. 260

Sweetshrub, common
☼ ◐ ● ◕ ● ◑ ◆ ⚡ US, MS, LS
Calycanthus floridus p. 161

Sweet viburnum
☼ ◐ ● ◆ ⚡ CS, TS
Viburnum odoratissimum p. 408

Winter hazel
☼ ◐ ● ◆ ⚡ US, MS, LS
Corylopsis p. 193

Winter honeysuckle
☼ ◐ ● ◆ ⚡ US, MS, LS, CS
Lonicera fragrantissima p. 280

Wintersweet
☼ ◐ ● ◆ ⚡ US, MS, LS, CS
Chimonanthus praecox p. 176

Witch hazel
☼ ◐ ● ◆ ⚡ US, MS, LS
Hamamelis p. 240

VINES

Armand clematis
☼ ● ◆ ⚡ MS, LS, CS
Clematis armandii p. 184

Carolina jessamine
☼ ◐ ● ◕ ● ◆ ⚡ MS, LS, CS
Gelsemium sempervirens p. 231

Chilean jasmine
☼ ◐ ● ◆ ⚡ LS, CS, TS
Mandevilla laxa p. 291

Confederate jasmine
☼ ◐ ● ◕ ● ◆ ⚡ LS, CS, TS p. 400
Trachelospermum jasminoides

Japanese honeysuckle
☼ ◐ ● ◆ ⚡ US, MS, LS, CS
Lonicera japonica p. 280

Sweetshrub, common
Calycanthus floridus

Winter hazel
Corylopsis

Wintersweet
Chimonanthus praecox

Confederate jasmine
Trachelospermum jasminoides

Chocolate cosmos
Cosmos atrosanguineus

For growing symbol explanations, please see page 38.

Purple passion flower
Passiflora alatocaerulea

Crinum, Powell's hybrid
Crinum powellii 'Album'

Flowering tobacco
Nicotiana alata

Garden nasturtium
Tropaeolum majus

Tall bearded iris

Jasmine
☼ ◐ ◖ ⚡ ZONES VARY
Jasminum · p. 261

Madagascar jasmine
◐ ◖ ⚡ TS
Stephanotis floribunda · p. 385

Moonflower
☼ ◐ ◖ ⚡ ALL ZONES
Ipomoea alba · p. 256

Purple passion flower
☼ ◐ ◖ ⚡ TS
Passiflora alatocaerulea · p. 313

Sweet autumn clematis
☼ ◖ ⚡ US, MS, LS, CS
Clematis dioscoreifolia · p. 185

Sweet pea
☼ ◐ ◖ ⚡ ALL ZONES
Lathyrus odoratus · p. 270

Wax flower
◐ ◖ ⚡ TS
Hoya carnosa · p. 250

Wisteria
☼ ◖ ⚡ US, MS, LS, CS
· p. 412

PERENNIALS, ANNUALS, BULBS

Chocolate cosmos
☼ ◖ ⚡ MS, LS, CS
Cosmos atrosanguineus · p. 193

Crinum
☼ ◐ ◖ ◖ ◍ ⚡ ZONES VARY
· p. 196

Crocus
☼ ◐ ◖ ⚡ US, MS, LS
Crocus chrysanthus · p. 197

Daffodil
☼ ◐ ◖ ⚡ US, MS, LS, CS
Narcissus (many) · p. 299

English primrose
◐ ◖ ⚡ US, MS
Primula vulgaris (some) · p. 341

English wallflower
☼ ◐ ◖ ◖ ⚡ US, MS
Erysimum cheiri · p. 216

Flowering tobacco
☼ ◐ ◖ ◍ ⚡ ALL ZONES
Nicotiana alata · p. 303

Four o'clock
☼ ◖ ◍ ⚡ ALL ZONES
Mirabilis jalapa · p. 295

Fragrant plantain lily
◐ ◖ ◖ ⚡ US, MS, LS
Hosta plantaginea · p. 249

Freesia
☼ ◐ ◖ ⚡ CS, TS
· p. 228

Garden nasturtium
☼ ◐ ◖ ⚡ ALL ZONES
Tropaeolum majus · p. 402

Ginger lily
☼ ◐ ◖ ⚡ ZONES VARY
Hedychium · p. 241

Hyacinth
☼ ◐ ◖ ◖ ⚡ US, MS, LS, CS
Hyacinthus · p. 251

Hymenocallis
☼ ◐ ◖ ◖ ⚡ ZONES VARY
· p. 252

Iris, bearded (many)
☼ ◖ ◖ ⚡ US, MS, LS
· p. 258

Lavender
☼ ◖ ⚡ ZONES VARY
Lavandula · p. 271

Lemon daylily
☼ ◐ ◖ ⚡ US, MS, LS, CS
Hemerocallis lilio-asphodelus · p. 245

Lily
☼ ◖ ⚡ ZONES VARY
Lilium (many) · p. 275

Lily-of-the-valley
◐ ◖ ◖ ⚡ US, MS, LS
Convallaria majalis · p. 189

Indian lotus
☼ ◐ ◖ ◖ ⚡ ALL ZONES
Nelumbo nucifera · p. 301

Pansy
☼ ◐ ◖ ◖ ⚡ ALL ZONES
Viola wittrockiana · p. 409

Peony
☼ ◐ ◖ ⚡ ZONES VARY
Paeonia (many) · p. 309

Perennial phlox (esp. light colors)
☼ ◐ ◖ ◖ ⚡ US, MS, LS, CS
Phlox paniculata · p. 325

Petunia
☼ ◖ ◖ ⚡ ALL ZONES
Petunia hybrida · p. 322

Pink
☼ ◖ ⚡ US, MS, LS
Dianthus · p. 206

Stock
☼ ◐ ◖ ⚡ ALL ZONES
Matthiola · p. 292

Sweet sultan
☼ ◖ ⚡ ALL ZONES
Centaurea moschata · p. 172

Sweet violet
☼ ◐ ◖ ⚡ US, MS, LS
Viola odorata · p. 409

Tuberose
☼ ◐ ◖ ⚡ ALL ZONES
Polianthes tuberosa · p. 337

Indian lotus
Nelumbo nucifera

Lily
Lilium 'Stargazer'

Perennial phlox
Phlox paniculata

Pink
Dianthus

61

Yarrow and blanket flower
Achillea and *Gaillardia*

FLOWERS
for Cutting

A garden isn't meant to be enjoyed only outdoors. You can cut many different kinds of flowers and bring them indoors. The ones you see here generally last about a week in water. Many of them, indicated by the symbol 💐, are easy to dry for permanent arrangements. Annuals and biennials must be planted every year; perennials and most bulbs provide flowers year after year.

Larkspur
Consolida ambigua

Bachelor's button
Centaurea cyanus

Cosmos, common
Cosmos bipinnatus

Marigold, signet
Tagetes tenuifolia 'Lemon Gem'

ANNUALS, BIENNIALS

Annual phlox
☼ 🌢 ◗ ✎ ALL ZONES
Phlox drummondii   p. 325

Bachelor's button   💐
☼ ◗ ✎ ALL ZONES
Centaurea cyanus   p. 171

Bells-of-Ireland   💐
☼ ◗ ◆ ✎ US, MS, LS
Moluccella laevis   p. 296

Chinese lantern plant   💐
☼ 🌢 ◗ ✎ ALL ZONES
Physalis alkekengi   p. 327

Cockscomb   💐
☼ ◗ ✎ ALL ZONES
Celosia argentea   p. 171

Cosmos, common   💐
☼ ◗ ✎ ALL ZONES
Cosmos bipinnatus   p. 194

Globe amaranth   💐
☼ 🌢 ◗ ✎ ALL ZONES
Gomphrena globosa   p. 235

Larkspur   💐
☼ ◗ ◆ ✎ ALL ZONES
Consolida ambigua   p. 189

Lisianthus
☼ 🌢 ◗ ◆ ✎ ALL ZONES
Eustoma grandiflorum   p. 221

Love-in-a-mist   💐
☼ 🌢 ◗ ✎ ALL ZONES
Nigella damascena   p. 303

Marigold
☼ ◗ ✎ ALL ZONES
Tagetes (most)   p. 393

Mexican sunflower   💐
☼ ◗ ◆ ✎ ALL ZONES
Tithonia rotundifolia   p. 398

Money plant   💐
☼ 🌢 ◗ ✎ US, MS, LS, CS
Lunaria annua   p. 281

Pincushion flower   💐
☼ 🌢 ◗ ◆ ✎ ALL ZONES
Scabiosa atropurpurea   p. 373

Pot marigold   💐
☼ ◗ ✎ ALL ZONES
Calendula officinalis   p. 159

Sea lavender   💐
☼ ◗ ✎ ALL ZONES
Limonium sinuatum   p. 276

Snapdragon
☼ ◗ ✎ ALL ZONES
Antirrhinum majus   p. 129

Spider flower
☼ ◗ ◆ ✎ ALL ZONES
Cleome hasslerana   p. 185

Stock
☼ 🌢 ◗ ✎ ALL ZONES
Matthiola   p. 292

Strawflower   💐
☼ ◗ ✎ ALL ZONES
Helichrysum bracteatum   p. 243

Sunflower, common   💐
☼ ◗ ✎ ALL ZONES
Helianthus annuus   p. 242

Sweet pea
☼ ◗ ◆ ✎ ALL ZONES
Lathyrus odoratus   p. 270

Zinnia   💐
☼ ◗ ✎ ALL ZONES
          p. 416

PERENNIALS, BULBS

Alstroemeria
☼ 🌢 ◗ ◆ ✎ MS, LS, CS
          p. 125

Mexican sunflower
Tithonia rotundifolia

Pincushion flower
Scabiosa atropurpurea

Sunflower, common
Helianthus annuus

For growing symbol explanations, please see page 38.

Snapdragon
Antirrhinum majus

Sweet pea
Lathyrus odoratus

Balloon flower
Platycodon grandiflorus

Dahlia

Alstroemeria

Angel's trumpet
☼ ◐ ● ♦ ◊ ✂ LS, CS, TS
Brugmansia — p. 155

Aster ⛰
☼ ◐ ◐ ● ✂ US, MS, LS
— p. 141

Baby's breath ⛰
☼ ◐ ● ✂ US, MS
Gypsophila paniculata — p. 239

Balloon flower
☼ ◐ ● ✂ US, MS, LS, CS
Platycodon grandiflorus — p. 332

Black-eyed Susan
☼ ◐ ● ◐ ● ✂ ALL ZONES
Rudbeckia hirta — p. 366

Blanket flower
☼ ◐ ● ✂ ALL ZONES
Gaillardia grandiflora — p. 229

Calla
☼ ◐ ● ✂ CS, TS
Zantedeschia — p. 414

Chrysanthemum (some) ⛰
☼ ◐ ● ✂ ZONES VARY
— p. 178

Columbine meadow rue
◐ ● ✂ US, MS
Thalictrum aquilegifolium — p. 395

Coreopsis (most)
☼ ◐ ● ✂ US, MS, LS, CS
— p. 190

Crinum
☼ ◐ ● ◐ ● ♦ ✂ ZONES VARY
— p. 196

Daffodil
☼ ◐ ● ✂ US, MS, LS, CS
Narcissus — p. 299

Dahlia ⛰
☼ ◐ ● ✂ US, MS, LS
— p. 202

Fernleaf yarrow ⛰
☼ ◐ ● ✂ US, MS, LS
Achillea filipendulina — p. 117

Fountain grass ⛰
☼ ◐ ● ◐ ● ✂ ZONES VARY
Pennisetum — p. 320

Gerbera daisy
☼ ◐ ● ● ✂ ALL ZONES
Gerbera jamesonii — p. 232

Ginger lily, common
☼ ◐ ● ◐ ✂ MS, LS, CS, TS
Hedychium coronarium — p. 242

Gladiolus ⛰
☼ ● ● ✂ ZONES VARY
— p. 233

Globe thistle ⛰
☼ ● ● ✂ US, MS, LS
Echinops — p. 211

Golden aster ⛰
☼ ◐ ● ● ✂ US, MS, LS
Chrysopsis — p. 180

Goldenrod ⛰
☼ ◐ ● ● ✂ US, MS, LS, CS
Solidago and Solidaster — p. 380

Iris
NEEDS, ZONES VARY
— p. 257

Japanese anemone
◐ ● ● ♦ ✂ US, MS, LS
Anemone hybrida — p. 127

Lavender ⛰
☼ ● ● ✂ ZONES VARY
Lavandula — p. 271

Lily
◐ ● ✂ ALL ZONES
Lilium — p. 275

Ox-eye ⛰
☼ ◐ ● ● ● ✂ US, MS, LS, CS
Heliopsis helianthoides — p. 244

Pentas
☼ ◐ ● ● ◐ ✂ ALL ZONES
Pentas lanceolata — p. 321

Perennial phlox
☼ ◐ ● ✂ US, MS, LS, CS
Phlox paniculata — p. 325

Persian ranunculus
☼ ● ✂ ALL ZONES
Ranunculus asiaticus — p. 350

Pincushion flower ⛰
☼ ◐ ● ● ✂ US
Scabiosa (some) — p. 373

Pink
☼ ● ✂ US, MS, LS
Dianthus (many) — p. 206

'Powis Castle' artemisia ⛰
☼ ● ✂ US, MS, LS
Artemisia 'Powis Castle' — p. 138

Purple coneflower ⛰
☼ ● ✂ US, MS, LS, CS
Echinacea purpurea — p. 211

Spike blazing star ⛰
☼ ● ● ✂ US, MS, LS, CS
Liatris spicata — p. 274

Spike speedwell
☼ ● ● ✂ US, MS, LS, CS
Veronica spicata — p. 407

Stokesia ⛰
☼ ● ● ✂ ALL ZONES
Stokesia laevis — p. 386

Sunflower ⛰
☼ ● ● ✂ ZONES VARY
Helianthus — p. 242

Tulip
☼ ● ● ✂ US, MS, LS, CS
Tulipa — p. 403

Gerbera daisy
Gerbera jamesonii

Gladiolus

Lavender
Lavandula

Spike blazing star
Liatris spicata

Purple coneflower
Echinacea purpurea

ORNAMENTAL GRASSES

Bamboo

Denizens of prairie, marsh, seashore, and forest, the ornamental grasses are enormously varied. In contrast to the familiar lawn grasses, these decorative cousins are not for mowing. Their beauty lies in their fountains and shaving-brushes of foliage, in their range of texture, color, and character. Many mount a significant floral display, producing reedlike stems with plumes or pendants of tiny floral structures. And some even offer colorful fall foliage.

Blue fescue
Festuca ovina 'Glauca'

Blue oat grass
Helictotrichon sempervirens

Fountain grass, Oriental
Pennisetum orientale

Japanese blood grass
Imperata cylindrica 'Rubra'

Bamboo ZONES VARY p. 143	**Japanese silver grass** US, MS, LS, CS *Miscanthus sinensis* p. 295	
Blue fescue US, MS *Festuca ovina* 'Glauca' p. 223	**Lindheimer's muhly** US, MS, LS, CS *Muhlenbergia lindheimeri* p. 297	
Blue lyme grass US, MS, LS, CS *Elymus arenarius* 'Glaucus' p. 213	**Maiden grass** US, MS, LS, CS *Miscanthus* p. 295	
Blue oat grass US, MS *Helictotrichon sempervirens* p. 243	**Moor grass** US, MS *Molinia caerulea* p. 295	
Bluestem US, MS, LS *Andropogon* p. 127	**Palm grass** CS, TS *Setaria palmifolia* p. 377	
Broom sedge US, MS, LS, CS *Andropogon virginicus* p. 127	**Pampas grass** MS, LS, CS, TS *Cortaderia selloana* p. 192	
Feather grass US, MS, LS *Stipa* p. 386	**Rattlesnake grass** ALL ZONES *Briza maxima* p. 154	
Feather reed grass US, MS, LS *Calamagrostis acutifolia* 'Stricta' p. 159	**Ravenna grass** US, MS, LS *Erianthus ravennae* p. 215	
Fountain grass NEEDS, ZONES VARY *Pennisetum* p. 320	**Ribbon grass** US, MS, LS, CS *Phalaris arundinacea* p. 323	
Giant reed ALL ZONES *Arundo donax* p. 138	**River oats** US, MS, LS, CS *Chasmanthium latifolium* p. 175	
Hair grass US, MS *Deschampsia* p. 205	**Sedge** US, MS, LS, CS *Carex* p. 165	
Horsetail ALL ZONES *Equisetum hyemale* p. 214	**Switch grass** US, MS, LS *Panicum virgatum* p. 311	
Japanese blood grass US, MS *Imperata cylindrica* 'Rubra' p. 256	**Zebra grass** US, MS, LS, CS *Miscanthus sinensis* 'Zebrinus' p. 295	

Feather grass, giant
Stipa gigantea

Feather reed grass
Calamagrostis acutifolia 'Stricta'

Pampas grass
Cortaderia selloana 'Pumila'

Ribbon grass
Phalaris arundinacea 'Picta'

For growing symbol explanations, please see page 38.

Plants that Attract
BIRDS

Mimosa
Albizia julibrissin

American bittersweet
Celastrus scandens and mockingbird

Birds and blossoms seem to go together. Spying a cardinal, goldfinch, or bluebird sitting in a nearby tree can be just as exciting as spotting a new rose in bloom. Attracting birds to your garden isn't hard—just provide water, shelter, and plenty of food. These plants offer nourishment for birds in the form of fruits, seeds, and nectar.

FRUIT/SEED-EATING BIRDS
Ground Covers, Vines, Perennials

American bittersweet
☼ ◐ ✿ US, MS, LS
Celastrus scandens — p. 171

Black-eyed Susan
☼ ◑ ◐ ✿ ALL ZONES
Rudbeckia hirta — p. 366

Boston ivy
☼ ◑ ◐ ✿ US, MS, LS
Parthenocissus tricuspidata — p. 313

Grape
☼ ◐ ✿ ZONES VARY
— p. 236

Honeysuckle
☼ ◑ ◐ ✿ ZONES VARY
Lonicera — p. 280

Ironweed
☼ ◑ ◐ ◐ ✿ US, MS, LS
Vernonia noveboracensis — p. 406

Porcelain berry
☼ ◑ ◐ ✿ US, MS, LS, CS — p. 126
Ampelopsis brevipedunculata

Virginia creeper
☼ ◑ ◐ ◐ ✿ US, MS, LS, CS
Parthenocissus quinquefolia — p. 313

Wintercreeper euonymus
☼ ◑ ◐ ◐ ✿ US, MS, LS, CS
Euonymus fortunei — p. 218

FRUIT/SEED-EATING BIRDS
Shrubs

American elderberry
☼ ◑ ◐ ✿ US, MS, LS, CS
Sambucus canadensis — p. 369

Barberry
☼ ◑ ◐ ◐ ✿ US, MS, LS, CS
Berberis — p. 149

Bayberry
☼ ◑ ◐ ✿ US, MS
Myrica pensylvanica — p. 298

Beautyberry
☼ ◑ ◐ ◐ ✿ US, MS, LS, CS
Callicarpa — p. 160

Blueberry
☼ ◐ ◐ ✿ ZONES VARY
Vaccinium — p. 151

Carolina buckthorn
☼ ◑ ◐ ✿ US, MS, LS, CS
Rhamnus caroliniana — p. 352

Chokeberry
☼ ◑ ◐ ◐ ◐ ✿ US, MS, LS
Aronia — p. 137

Coralberry
☼ ◐ ✿ US, MS, LS
Symphoricarpos orbiculatus — p. 391

Cotoneaster
☼ ◐ ✿ ZONES VARY
— p. 194

Dogwood
☼ ◑ ◐ ✿ ZONES VARY
Cornus — p. 191

Elaeagnus
☼ ◑ ◐ ◐ ✿ ZONES VARY
— p. 212

Euonymus
NEEDS, ZONES VARY
— p. 218

Firethorn
☼ ◐ ✿ ZONES VARY
Pyracantha — p. 347

Holly
☼ ◑ ◐ ✿ ZONES VARY
Ilex — p. 253

Japanese snowball
☼ ◑ ◐ ✿ US, MS, LS
Viburnum plicatum plicatum — p. 408

Mahonia
NEEDS, ZONES VARY
— p. 288

Photinia
☼ ◐ ◐ ✿ ZONES VARY
— p. 326

Cotoneaster
Cotoneaster apiculatus

Dogwood
Cornus

Firethorn
Pyracantha

Holly (winterberry)
Ilex verticillata 'Afterglow'

Porcelain berry
Ampelopsis brevipedunculata

Wintercreeper euonymus
Euonymus fortunei

Beautyberry, purple
Callicarpa dichotoma

Plant listings continue ▶

Japanese snowball
Viburnum plicatum plicatum

Mahonia

Crabapple
Malus 'Red Jewel'

Hawthorn
Crataegus

Juniper
Juniperus communis

Privet
☼ ◑ ◗ ◆ ✂ ZONES VARY
Ligustrum   p. 274

Rose
☼ ◑ ◆ ✂ ZONES VARY
Rosa (some)   p. 359

Rosemary
☼ ◆ ✂ MS, LS, CS
Rosmarinus officinalis   p. 366

Sargent crabapple
☼ ◆ ◗ ✂ US, MS, LS
Malus sargentii   p. 290

Serviceberry
☼ ◑ ◆ ◗ ✂ US, MS, LS
Amelanchier   p. 126

Spicebush
☼ ◑ ◆ ◗ ✂ US, MS, LS
Lindera benzoin   p. 277

Viburnum (deciduous)
☼ ◑ ◆ ✂ ZONES VARY
                                   p. 407

FRUIT/SEED-EATING BIRDS
Trees

American beech
☼ ◑ ◆ ✂ US, MS, LS, CS
Fagus grandifolia   p. 222

Arborvitae
☼ ◑ ◆ ◗ ✂ ZONES VARY
Thuja   p. 396

Beach plum
☼ ◆ ◗ ✂ US, MS
Prunus maritima   p. 344

Birch
☼ ◆ ◗ ✂ ZONES VARY
Betula   p. 149

Black cherry
☼ ◆ ◗ ✂ US, MS, LS, CS
Prunus serotina   p. 344

Black gum
☼ ◑ ◆ ◗ ✂ US, MS, LS, CS
Nyssa sylvatica   p. 304

Carolina cherry laurel
☼ ◆ ◗ ✂ US, MS, LS, CS
Prunus caroliniana   p. 342

Chickasaw plum
☼ ◑ ◆ ◗ ✂ US, MS, LS, CS
Prunus angustifolia   p. 343

Crabapple
☼ ◆ ◗ ✂ US, MS, LS
Malus   p. 288

Dogwood
☼ ◑ ◆ ◗ ✂ ZONES VARY
Cornus   p. 191

Fir
☼ ◑ ◆ ◗ ✂ ZONES VARY
Abies   p. 114

Glossy privet
☼ ◑ ◆ ◗ ✂ LS, CS, TS
Ligustrum lucidum   p. 275

Hackberry
☼ ◑ ◆ ✂ US, MS, LS
Celtis   p. 171

Hawthorn
☼ ◆ ✂ ZONES VARY
Crataegus   p. 195

Hemlock
☼ ◑ ◆ ◗ ✂ ZONES VARY
Tsuga   p. 402

Holly
☼ ◑ ◆ ◗ ✂ ZONES VARY
Ilex   p. 253

Ironwood
☼ ◑ ◆ ◗ ✂ US, MS, LS, CS
Carpinus caroliniana   p. 166

Juniper
☼ ◑ ◆ ◗ ✂ ZONES VARY
Juniperus   p. 262

Larch
☼ ◆ ✂ ZONES VARY
Larix   p. 270

Magnolia
☼ ◑ ◆ ✂ ZONES VARY
                                   p. 284

Maple
☼ ◑ ◆ ◗ ✂ ZONES VARY
Acer   p. 115

Mountain ash
☼ ◑ ◆ ◗ ✂ ZONES VARY
Sorbus   p. 381

Mulberry, common
☼ ◑ ◆ ✂ ZONES VARY
Morus   p. 296

Oak
☼ ◆ ✂ ZONES VARY
Quercus   p. 348

Pine
☼ ◑ ◆ ✂ ZONES VARY
Pinus   p. 329

Russian olive
☼ ◑ ◆ ◗ ✂ US, MS
Elaeagnus angustifolia   p. 212

Sassafras
☼ ◆ ✂ US, MS, LS, CS
Sassafras albidum   p. 373

Serviceberry
☼ ◑ ◆ ◗ ✂ US, MS, LS
Amelanchier   p. 126

Spruce
☼ ◑ ◆ ◗ ✂ US, MS
Picea   p. 327

Sweet gum
☼ ◆ ◗ ✂ ALL ZONES
Liquidambar stryaciflua   p. 277

Maple
Acer

Mountain ash
Sorbus

Oak
Quercus

Serviceberry
Amelanchier

Spruce
Picea

For growing symbol explanations, please see page 38.

Butterfly weed
Asclepias tuberosa

Cardinal flower
Lobelia cardinalis

Geranium
Pelargonium

Iris

Montbretia
Crocosmia crocosmiiflora

Wax myrtle
☼ ◑ ◐ ● ● ● ⁄ MS, LS, CS, TS
Myrica cerifera   p. 298

HUMMINGBIRDS
Annuals, Perennials, Bulbs

Aloe
☼ ◑ ● ● ● ⁄ TS
                                   p. 124

Alstroemeria
☼ ◑ ● ● ⁄ MS, LS, CS
                                   p. 125

Beard tongue
☼ ◑ ● ⁄ ZONES VARY
Penstemon (many)   p. 320

Bee balm
☼ ◑ ● ● ● ⁄ US, MS, LS
Monarda didyma   p. 296

Bird of paradise
☼ ◑ ● ⁄ CS, TS
Strelitzia reginae   p. 388

Butterfly weed
☼ ● ● ● ⁄ ALL ZONES
Asclepias tuberosa   p. 139

Canna
☼ ● ● ●● ⁄ LS, CS, TS
                                   p. 164

Cape fuchsia
☼ ◑ ● ⁄ US, MS, LS, CS
Phygelius capensis   p. 326

Cardinal flower
◑ ● ● ● ● ● ● ⁄ US, MS, LS, CS
Lobelia cardinalis   p. 278

Columbine
☼ ◑ ● ⁄ ZONES VARY
Aquilegia   p. 134

Coral bells
☼ ◑ ● ⁄ US, MS, LS
Heuchera sanguinea   p. 246

Delphinium
☼ ● ⁄ ZONES VARY
                                   p. 204

Flowering tobacco
☼ ◑ ● ● ● ⁄ ALL ZONES
Nicotiana   p. 303

Four o'clock
☼ ● ● ● ⁄ ALL ZONES
Mirabilis jalapa   p. 295

Foxglove
◑ ● ● ⁄ US, MS, LS, CS
Digitalis   p. 208

Geranium
☼ ◑ ● ● ⁄ CS, TS
Pelargonium   p. 318

Ginger lily
☼ ◑ ●● ⁄ ZONES VARY
Hedychium   p. 241

Gladiolus
☼ ● ⁄ ZONES VARY
                                   p. 233

Hollyhock
☼ ● ⁄ ALL ZONES
Alcea rosea   p. 122

Impatiens
☼ ◑ ● ● ⁄ ALL ZONES
                                   p. 255

Indian paintbrush
☼ ◑ ● ⁄ US, MS, LS
Castilleja coccinia   p. 168

Iris
NEEDS, ZONES VARY
                                   p. 257

Montbretia
☼ ◑ ● ⁄ US, MS, LS, CS
Crocosmia crocosmiiflora   p. 197

Nasturtium, garden
☼ ◑ ● ⁄ ALL ZONES
Tropaeolum majus   p. 402

Pentas
☼ ◑ ● ●● ⁄ ALL ZONES
Pentas lanceolata   p. 321

Phlox
☼ ◑ ● ⁄ ZONES VARY
                                   p. 325

Red-hot poker
☼ ◑ ● ● ⁄ US, MS, LS, CS
Kniphofia uvaria   p. 266

Rose campion
☼ ◑ ● ⁄ US, MS, LS
Lychnis coronaria   p. 282

Sage
☼ ● ⁄ ZONES VARY
Salvia (many)   p. 369

Snapdragon
☼ ● ⁄ ALL ZONES
Antirrhinum majus   p. 129

Speedwell
☼ ● ● ⁄ ZONES VARY
Veronica   p. 406

Spider flower
☼ ● ● ⁄ ALL ZONES
Cleome hasslerana   p. 185

Zinnia
☼ ● ⁄ ALL ZONES
                                   p. 416

HUMMINGBIRDS
Ground Covers, Vines

Bean, scarlet runner
☼ ● ⁄ ALL ZONES
                                   p. 146

Cape honeysuckle
☼ ◑ ● ● ● ⁄ CS, TS
Tecomaria capensis   p. 395

Red-hot poker
Kniphofia uvaria

Rose campion
Lychnis coronaria

Sage
Salvia

Spider flower
Cleome hasslerana

Flame vine
Pyrostegia venusta

Plant listings continue ▸

Trumpet creeper, common
Campsis radicans

Cape honeysuckle
Tecomaria capensis

Honeysuckle
Lonicera

Bird of paradise
Strelitzia reginae

Cypress vine
☼ ◐ ◑ ◗ ✦ ALL ZONES
Ipomoea quamoclit .... p. 257

Flame vine
☼ ◐ ◑ ◗ ✦ CS, TS
Pyrostegia venusta .... p. 347

Honeysuckle
☼ ◐ ◑ ◗ ✦ ZONES VARY
Lonicera .... p. 280

Morning glory, common
☼ ◑ ◗ ✦ ALL ZONES
Ipomoea purpurea .... p. 257

Trailing lantana
☼ ◗ ◗ ✦ MS, LS, CS, TS
Lantana montevidensis .... p. 270

Trumpet creeper
☼ ◐ ◑ ◗ ✦ ZONES VARY
Campsis .... p. 164

HUMMINGBIRDS
Shrubs

Abelia
☼ ◐ ◗ ✦ US, MS, LS
.... p. 114

Acacia
☼ ◗ ✦ ZONES VARY
.... p. 114

American elderberry
☼ ◐ ◑ ◗ ✦ US, MS, LS, CS
Sambucus canadensis .... p. 369

Beauty bush
☼ ◐ ◑ ◗ ✦ US, MS, LS
Kolkwitzia amabilis .... p. 267

Bird of paradise
☼ ◐ ◗ ✦ CS, TS
Strelitzia reginae .... p. 388

Bird of paradise bush
☼ ◗ ◗ ✦ CS, TS
Caesalpinia gilliesii .... p. 158

Butterfly bush
☼ ◐ ◑ ◗ ✦ ZONES VARY
Buddleia .... p. 156

Cape honeysuckle
☼ ◐ ◑ ◗ ✦ CS, TS
Tecomaria capensis .... p. 395

Cestrum
☼ ◗ ◗ ✦ ZONES VARY
.... p. 173

Cotoneaster
☼ ◗ ✦ ZONES VARY
.... p. 194

Flowering quince
☼ ◗ ◗ ✦ US, MS, LS, CS
Chaenomeles .... p. 174

Hibiscus
☼ ◗ ◗ ✦ ZONES VARY
.... p. 246

Honeysuckle
☼ ◐ ◗ ✦ ZONES VARY
Lonicera .... p. 280

Lavender
☼ ◗ ✦ ZONES VARY
Lavandula (many) .... p. 271

Lemon bottlebrush
☼ ◗ ◗ ✦ CS, TS
Callistemon citrinus .... p. 160

Lilac
☼ ◐ ◗ ✦ ZONES VARY
Syringa .... p. 391

Mexican firebush
☼ ◗◗ ✦ CS, TS
Hamelia patens .... p. 241

Pineapple guava
◐ ◗ ✦ LS, CS, TS
Feijoa sellowiana .... p. 223

Rosemary
☼ ◗ ✦ MS, LS, CS
Rosmarinus officinalis .... p. 366

Shrimp plant
☼ ◐ ◗ ◗ ✦ CS, TS
Justicia brandegeana .... p. 262

Yellow shrimp plant
☼ ◐ ◗ ✦ CS, TS
Pachystachys lutea .... p. 309

Texas sage
☼ ◗ ✦ MS, LS, CS
Leucophyllum frutescens .... p. 273

Weigela
☼ ◐ ◗ ✦ US, MS, LS
Weigela florida .... p. 411

HUMMINGBIRDS
Trees

Chinaberry
☼ ◗ ◗ ✦ MS, LS, CS
Melia azedarach .... p. 292

Citrus
☼ ◗ ✦ CS, TS
.... p. 181

Coral tree
☼ ◗ ◗ ◗ ✦ ZONES VARY
Erythrina .... p. 216

Desert willow
☼ ◗ ✦ MS, LS, CS
Chilopsis linearis .... p. 176

Eucalyptus
☼ ◗ ◗ ✦ ZONES VARY
.... p. 217

Horsechestnut
☼ ◐ ◗ ◗ ✦ ZONES VARY
Aesculus .... p. 120

Mimosa
☼ ◐ ◗ ◗ ✦ US, MS, LS, CS
Albizia julibrissin .... p. 122

Flowering qunice
Chaenomeles

Lavender
Lavandula

Weigela
Weigela florida

Coral tree
Erythrina

Mimosa
Albizia julibrissin

For growing symbol explanations, please see page 38.

Plants that Attract
BUTTERFLIES

Butterfly weed
Asclepias tuberosa

Aster
Aster novi-belgii

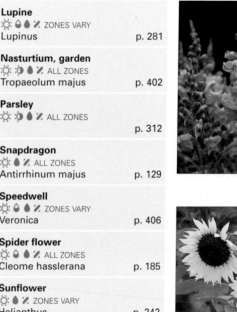

Bleeding heart, common
Dicentra spectabilis

Hollyhock
Alcea rosea

Butterflies are nature's music on the wing. They add movement, color, and moments of subtle wonder to the garden. Choose the right plants and you can encourage them to stay a while and return next year. Butterfly larvae (caterpillars) need food plants; adult butterflies need plants that offer nectar-bearing flowers. Most welcoming are sunny areas such as meadows and borders that are sheltered from the wind and contain butterfly-friendly features such as leaf litter, rock crevices, water, and even a few weeds. Never use pesticides in butterfly gardens, unless you can target the specific pest without harming butterflies or their larvae.

Sunflower
Helianthus

BUTTERFLY LARVAE
Annuals, Biennials, Perennials

Aster
☼ ◐ ◗ ✎ US, MS, LS
p. 141

Beard tongue
☼ ☼ ◐ ◗ ✎ ZONES VARY
Penstemon
p. 320

Bleeding heart
☼ ◗ ◐ ◗ ✎ ZONES VARY
Dicentra
p. 207

Blue-leafed rue
☼ ◐ ◗ ✎ US, MS, LS
Ruta graveolens
p. 367

Butterfly weed
☼ ◐ ◗ ✎ ALL ZONES
Asclepias tuberosa
p. 139

Dill
☼ ◗ ✎ ALL ZONES
Anethum graveolens
p. 128

Fennel, common
☼ ◐ ◗ ✎ ZONES VARY
Foeniculum vulgare
p. 226

Foxglove, common
☼ ◐ ◗ ✎ US, MS, LS, CS
Digitalis purpurea
p. 208

Geum
☼ ☼ ◐ ✎ US, MS, LS
Geum chiloense
p. 232

Hollyhock
☼ ◗ ✎ ALL ZONES
Alcea rosea
p. 122

Joe-Pye weed
☼ ☼ ◐ ◗ ✎ US, MS, LS, CS
Eupatorium purpureum
p. 219

Lupine
☼ ◐ ◗ ✎ ZONES VARY
Lupinus
p. 281

Nasturtium, garden
☼ ☼ ◐ ✎ ALL ZONES
Tropaeolum majus
p. 402

Parsley
☼ ☼ ◗ ✎ ALL ZONES
p. 312

Snapdragon
☼ ◗ ✎ ALL ZONES
Antirrhinum majus
p. 129

Speedwell
☼ ◐ ◗ ✎ ZONES VARY
Veronica
p. 406

Spider flower
☼ ◐ ◗ ✎ ALL ZONES
Cleome hasslerana
p. 185

Sunflower
☼ ◗ ✎ ZONES VARY
Helianthus
p. 242

Swamp milkweed
☼ ◗ ◐◗ ◗ ✎ ALL ZONES
Asclepias incarnata
p. 139

Sweet white violet
☼ ◐ ◗ ✎ US, MS, LS
Viola blanda
p. 409

BUTTERFLY LARVAE
Vines

Dutchman's pipe
☼ ☼ ◗ ◐ ◗◗ ✎ US, MS, LS, CS
Aristolochia durior
p. 137

Passion vine
☼ ◐ ◗ ✎ ZONES VARY
Passiflora
p. 313

Snapdragon
Antirrhinum majus

Sunflower
Helianthus

Purple passion flower
Passiflora alatocaerulea

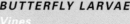

Plant listings continue ▸

Hibiscus

Rose
Rosa 'Leander'

Senna
Cassia

Dogwood, flowering
Cornus florida

Wisteria
☼ ◐ ◑ ⚡ US, MS, LS, CS
p. 412

BUTTERFLY LARVAE
Shrubs

Cape plumbago
☼ ◐ ⚡ CS, TS
Plumbago auriculata   p. 335

Hibiscus
☼ ◐ ◑ ⚡ ZONES VARY
p. 246

Mallow
☼ ◔ ◐ ⚡ US, MS, LS
Malva   p. 290

Rose
☼ ◔ ◐ ⚡ ALL ZONES
Rosa   p. 359

Senna
☼ ◐ ◑ ⚡ ZONES VARY
Cassia   p. 167

Spicebush
☼ ◔ ◐ ◑ ⚡ US, MS, LS
Lindera benzoin   p. 277

Spiraea
☼ ◔ ◐ ◑ ⚡ ZONES VARY
p. 383

Viburnum
☼ ◔ ◐ ⚡ ZONES VARY
p. 407

BUTTERFLY LARVAE
Trees

Birch
☼ ◔ ◐ ◑ ⚡ ZONES VARY
Betula   p. 149

Cherry, peach, plum
☼ ◔ ◐ ⚡ ZONES VARY
Prunus   p. 342

Citrus
☼ ◐ ⚡ CS, TS
p. 181

Crabapple
☼ ◐ ◑ ⚡ US, MS, LS
Malus   p. 288

Dogwood
☼ ◔ ◐ ⚡ ZONES VARY
Cornus   p. 191

Douglas fir
☼ ◔ ◐ ◑ ⚡ US, MS
Pseudotsuga menziesii   p. 345

Hackberry
☼ ◔ ◐ ⚡ US, MS, LS
Celtis   p. 171

Hawthorn
☼ ◐ ⚡ ZONES VARY
Crataegus   p. 195

Honey locust
☼ ◐ ◑ ⚡ US, MS, LS
Gleditsia triacanthos   p. 234

Horsechestnut
☼ ◔ ◐ ◑ ⚡ ZONES VARY
Aesculus   p. 120

Oak
☼ ◐ ⚡ ZONES VARY
Quercus   p. 348

Pawpaw
☼ ◔ ◐ ◑ ⚡ US, MS, LS, CS
Asimina triloba   p. 139

Pine
☼ ◐ ◑ ⚡ ZONES VARY
Pinus   p. 329

Red bay
☼ ◔ ◐ ◑ ⚡ ALL ZONES
Persea borbonia   p. 322

Sassafras
☼ ◔ ◐ ⚡ US, MS, LS, CS
Sassafras albidum   p. 373

Sweet bay
☼ ◔ ◐ ◑ ⚡ US, MS, LS, CS
Magnolia virginiana   p. 287

Sycamore
☼ ◔ ◐ ⚡ ZONES VARY
Platanus   p. 332

Tulip poplar
☼ ◐ ⚡ US, MS, LS, CS
Liriodendron tulipifera   p. 278

Willow
☼ ◐◑ ⚡ US, MS, LS
Salix   p. 368

ADULT BUTTERFLIES
Annuals, Biennials, Perennials

Aster
☼ ◔ ◐ ⚡ US, MS, LS
p. 141

Astilbe
☼ ◔ ◐ ⚡ US, MS
p. 141

Beard tongue
☼ ◔ ◐ ◑ ⚡ ZONES VARY
Penstemon   p. 320

Bee balm
☼ ◔ ◐ ◑ ⚡ US, MS, LS
Monarda   p. 296

Black-eyed Susan
☼ ◔ ◐ ◑ ⚡ ALL ZONES
Rudbeckia hirta   p. 366

Blanket flower
☼ ◐ ⚡ ALL ZONES
Gaillardia grandiflora   p. 229

Blazing star
☼ ◔ ◐ ⚡ US, MS, LS, CS
Liatris   p. 274

Douglas fir
Pseudotsuga menziesii

Oak
Quercus

Sycamore
Platanus

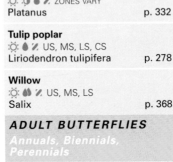

Bee balm
Monarda

Black-eyed Susan
Rudbeckia hirta

For growing symbol explanations, please see page 38.

Cosmos

Dame's rocket
Hesperis matronalis

English wallflower
Erysimum cheiri

Lantana

Sage, pineapple
Salvia elegans

Borage
☼ ◐ ● ◌ ● ⚡ ALL ZONES
Borago officinalis   p. 152

Butterfly weed
☼ ◌ ⚡ ⚡ ALL ZONES
Asclepias tuberosa   p. 139

Candytuft
☼ ◌ ⚡ ZONES VARY
Iberis   p. 253

Cardinal flower
◐ ● ◌ ◔ ⚡ ⚡ US, MS, LS, CS
Lobelia cardinalis   p. 278

Catmint
☼ ◐ ◌ ⚡ US, MS, LS
Nepeta faassenii   p. 301

Ceratostigma
☼ ◐ ◌ ⚡ US, MS, LS, CS   p. 172
Ceratostigma plumbaginoides

Columbine
☼ ◐ ◌ ⚡ ZONES VARY
Aquilegia   p. 134

Coreopsis
☼ ◌ ⚡ US, MS, LS, CS
          p. 190

Cosmos
☼ ◌ ⚡ ALL ZONES
          p. 193

Cupid's dart
☼ ◌ ⚡ US, MS, LS
Catananche caerulea   p. 169

Dame's rocket
☼ ◐ ◌ ⚡ ALL ZONES
Hesperis matronalis   p. 246

English wallflower
☼ ◐ ◌ ⚡ ALL ZONES
Erysimum cheiri   p. 216

Giant hyssop
☼ ◐ ◌ ⚡ ZONES VARY
Agastache   p. 121

Globe amaranth
☼ ◐ ◌ ⚡ ALL ZONES
Gomphrena   p. 235

Globe thistle
☼ ◌ ◌ ⚡ US, MS, LS
Echinops   p. 211

Goldenrod
☼ ◐ ◌ ⚡ US, MS, LS, CS
Solidago and Solidaster   p. 380

Impatiens
☼ ◐ ◌ ◌ ⚡ ALL ZONES
          p. 255

Joe-Pye weed
☼ ◐ ◌ ◔ ⚡ US, MS, LS, CS
Eupatorium purpureum   p. 219

Lantana
☼ ◌ ⚡ ⚡ ALL ZONES
          p. 269

Lavender
☼ ◌ ⚡ ZONES VARY
Lavandula   p. 271

Lily
☼ ◐ ◌ ⚡ ALL ZONES
Lilium   p. 275

Lily-of-the-Nile
☼ ◐ ◌ ◌ ⚡ ZONES VARY
Agapanthus   p. 120

Marigold
☼ ◌ ⚡ ZONES VARY
Tagetes   p. 393

Mexican sunflower
☼ ◌ ◌ ⚡ ALL ZONES
Tithonia rotundifolia   p. 398

Oregano
☼ ◌ ⚡ US, MS, LS
Origanum vulgare   p. 307

Pentas
☼ ◐ ◌ ◔ ⚡ ALL ZONES
Pentas lanceolata   p. 321

Phlox
☼ ◐ ◌ ⚡ ZONES VARY
          p. 325

Pincushion flower
☼ ◐ ◌ ◌ ⚡ ZONES VARY
Scabiosa   p. 373

Pink
☼ ◌ ⚡ US, MS, LS
Dianthus   p. 206

Primrose
☼ ◌ ◌ ◔ ⚡ ZONES VARY
Primula   p. 341

Purple coneflower
☼ ◌ ⚡ US, MS, LS, CS
Echinacea purpurea   p. 211

Ranunculus
NEEDS, ZONES VARY
          p. 350

Sage
☼ ◌ ⚡ ZONES VARY
Salvia   p. 369

Sea holly
☼ ◌ ⚡ US, MS, LS, CS
Eryngium   p. 216

Shasta daisy
☼ ◌ ⚡ US, MS, LS, CS
Chrysanthemum maximum   p. 179

Showy sedum
☼ ◌ ⚡ US, MS, LS, CS
Sedum spectabile   p. 376

Snapdragon
☼ ◌ ⚡ ALL ZONES
Antirrhinum majus   p. 129

Spider flower
☼ ◌ ◌ ⚡ ALL ZONES
Cleome hasslerana   p. 185

Sea holly
Eryngium amethystinum

Sweet alyssum
Lobularia maritima

Thrift, common
Armeria maritima

Yarrow
Achillea

Plant listings continue ▶

Valerian
Centranthus ruber

Abelia

Butterfly bush
Buddleia

Chaste tree
Vitex agnus-castus

Cinquefoil
Potentilla fruticosa

Stonecrop
:☼: ◐ ● ⚡ US, MS, LS
Sedum (tall)   p. 375

Sweet alyssum
:☼: ◐ ● ⚡ ALL ZONES
Lobularia maritima   p. 280

Thrift, common
:☼: ● ● ⚡ ZONES VARY
Armeria   p. 137

Turtlehead
:◐: ● ● ⚡ US, MS, LS, CS
Chelone   p. 175

Valerian
:☼: :◐: ● ⚡ US, MS, LS
Centranthus ruber   p. 172

Verbena
:☼: ● ⚡ ALL ZONES
Verbena bonariensis   p. 406

Wand loosestrife
:☼: ● ⚡ US, MS, LS
Lythrum virgatum   p. 283

Wild ageratum
:☼: :◐: ● ⚡ ALL ZONES
Eupatorium coelestinum   p. 219

Yarrow
:☼: ● ⚡ US, MS, LS
Achillea   p. 117

ADULT BUTTERFLIES
Shrubs

Abelia
:☼: :◐: ● ⚡ US, MS, LS
                                p. 114

American elderberry
:☼: :◐: ● ⚡ US, MS, LS, CS
Sambucus canadensis   p. 369

Azalea
:◐: ● ● ◊ ⚡ ZONES VARY
Rhododendron   p. 353

Bluebeard
:☼: ● ⚡ US, MS, LS, CS
Caryopteris   p. 167

Blueberry
:☼: ● ⚡ ZONES VARY
Vaccinium   p. 151

Buttonbush
:☼: :◐: ● ● ⚡ ALL ZONES
Cephalanthus occidentalis   p. 172

Butterfly bush
:☼: :◐: ● ● ⚡ ZONES VARY
Buddleia   p. 156

Cape plumbago
:☼: ● ⚡ CS, TS
Plumbago auriculata   p. 335

Chinese hibiscus
:☼: ● ● ⚡ CS, TS
Hibiscus rosa-sinensis   p. 247

Cinquefoil
:◐: ● ⚡ ZONES VARY
Potentilla   p. 340

Devil's walking stick
:☼: :◐: ● ● ⚡ ZONES VARY
Aralia spinosa   p. 135

Honeysuckle
:☼: :◐: ● ● ⚡ ZONES VARY
Lonicera   p. 280

Lilac
:☼: :◐: ● ⚡ ZONES VARY
Syringa   p. 391

Mahonia
NEEDS, ZONES VARY
                                p. 288

Mock orange
:☼: :◐: ● ● ⚡ ZONES VARY   p. 323
Philadelphus (single-flowering)

Rhododendron
:◐: ● ● ● ◊ ⚡ ZONES VARY
                                p. 353

Rosemary
:☼: ● ⚡ MS, LS, CS
Rosmarinus officinalis   p. 366

Spiraea
:☼: ● ● ● ⚡ ZONES VARY
                                p. 383

Sweet pepperbush
:◐: ● ● ● ⚡ US, MS, LS, CS
Clethra alnifolia   p. 186

Viburnum
:☼: :◐: ● ⚡ ZONES VARY
                                p. 407

ADULT BUTTERFLIES
Trees

Apple
:☼: ● ⚡ ZONES VARY
                                p. 130

Chaste tree
:☼: ● ● ⚡ ZONES VARY
Vitex   p. 410

Cherry, plum, peach
:☼: ● ● ⚡ ZONES VARY
Prunus   p. 342

Citrus
:☼: ● ⚡ CS, TS
                                p. 181

Glossy privet
:☼: :◐: ● ● ◊ ⚡ LS, CS, TS
Ligustrum lucidum   p. 275

Mimosa
:☼: ● ● ● ⚡ US, MS, LS, CS
Albizia julibrissin   p. 122

Palmetto
:☼: :◐: ● ⚡ ZONES VARY
Sabal   p. 368

Mahonia

Mock orange
Philadelphus

Rhododendron

Spiraea, Bumalda
Spiraea bumalda

For growing symbol explanations, please see page 38.

Plants that
TOLERATE SHADE

A lot of folks think of shade as a problem. But actually, shade presents a great opportunity to use a wide range of plants that offer stunning flowers, fruits, or foliage in the absence of bright sun. And because fewer weeds plague shady gardens, these leafy retreats usually need less maintenance. The lists below contain trees, shrubs, vines, ground covers, perennials, bulbs, and annuals that prefer or accept some degree of shade. Those plants with the symbol ✳ have showy flowers.

Hydrangea, French
Hydrangea macrophylla

Franklin tree
Franklinia alatamaha

American beech
Fagus grandifolia

Holly
Ilex

Japanese maple
Acer palmatum

TREES

American beech
☀ ◐ ⬥ ⚡ US, MS, LS, CS
Fagus grandifolia   p. 222

Black gum
☀ ◐ ⬥ ⬥ ⚡ US, MS, LS, CS
Nyssa sylvatica   p. 304

Dwarf palmetto
☀ ◐ ⬥ ⚡ MS, LS, CS, TS
Sabal minor   p. 368

Eastern redbud   ✳
☀ ◐ ⬥ ⚡ US, MS, LS, CS
Cercis canadensis   p. 173

Flowering dogwood   ✳
☀ ◐ ⬥ ⚡ US, MS, LS, CS
Cornus florida   p. 192

Franklin tree   ✳
☀ ◐ ⬥ ⚡ US, MS, LS
Franklinia alatamaha   p. 227

Grancy graybeard   ✳
☀ ◐ ⬥ ⚡ US, MS, LS, CS
Chionanthus virginicus   p. 177

Handkerchief tree   ✳
☀ ◐ ⬥ ⚡ US, MS, LS
Davidia involucrata   p. 204

Hemlock
☀ ◐ ⬥ ⚡ ZONES VARY
Tsuga   p. 402

Holly
☀ ◐ ⬥ ⚡ ZONES VARY
Ilex   p. 253

Ironwood
☀ ◐ ⬥ ⬥ ⚡ US, MS, LS, CS
Carpinus caroliniana   p. 166

Japanese maple
☀ ◐ ⬥ ⬥ ⚡ US, MS, LS, CS
Acer palmatum   p. 116

Katsura tree
☀ ◐ ⬥ ⚡ US, MS
Cercidiphyllum japonicum   p. 173

Mountain ash   ✳
☀ ◐ ⬥ ⬥ ⚡ ZONES VARY
Sorbus   p. 381

Palms (some)
NEEDS, ZONES VARY
                                     p. 310

Pawpaw
☀ ◐ ⬥ ⚡ US, MS, LS, CS
Asimina triloba   p. 139

Podocarpus
☀ ◐ ⬥ ⬥ ⚡ ZONES VARY
                                     p. 336

Sassafras
☀ ◐ ⬥ ⚡ US, MS, LS, CS
Sassafras albidum   p. 373

Schefflera
☀ ◐ ⬥ ⚡ TS
                                     p. 374

Silver bell
☀ ◐ ⬥ ⚡ US, MS, LS
Halesia   p. 240

Serviceberry   ✳
☀ ◐ ⬥ ⬥ ⚡ US, MS, LS
Amelanchier   p. 126

Sourwood   ✳
☀ ◐ ⬥ ⚡ US, MS, LS, CS
Oxydendrum arboreum   p. 308

Snowbell   ✳
☀ ◐ ⬥ ⚡ ZONES VARY
Styrax   p. 389

Stewartia   ✳
☀ ◐ ⬥ ⚡ ZONES VARY
                                     p. 385

Sweet bay   ✳
☀ ◐ ⬥ ⚡ US, MS, LS, CS
Magnolia virginiana   p. 287

Podocarpus

Sassafras
Sassafras albidum

Sourwood
Oxydendrum aboreum

Plant listings continue ▶

Boxwood, edging
Buxus sempervirens 'Suffruticosa'

Brunfelsia pauciflora

Daphne
Daphne odora 'Marginata'

Gardenia
Gardenia jasminoides

Hybrid fuchsia

Tree ferns
☼ ◑ ● ▲ ✿ ✿ TS
Dicksonia — p. 207

Trumpet tree ✳
☼ ◑ ● ▲ ✿ TS
Tabebuia — p. 392

SHRUBS

Anise tree
◑ ● ▲ ▲▲ ✿ ✿ ZONES VARY
Illicium — p. 255

Azalea, native ✳
☼ ● ▲▲ ▲✿ ✿ ZONES VARY
Rhododendron — p. 353

Banana shrub ✳
☼ ◑ ● ✿ LS, CS
Michelia figo — p. 294

Bottlebrush buckeye
☼ ◑ ● ▲ ✿ ✿ US, MS, LS, CS
Aesculus parviflora — p. 120

Boxwood
☼ ◑ ● ▲ ✿ ✿ ZONES VARY
Buxus — p. 157

Brunfelsia pauciflora ✳
◑ ● ▲ ✿ CS, TS
— p. 155

Butcher's broom
◑ ● ▲ ▲ ✿ MS, LS, CS
Ruscus aculeatus — p. 367

Camellia (most) ✳
◑ ● ▲ ✿ ✿ US, MS, LS, CS
— p. 161

Chinese fringe ✳
☼ ◑ ● ✿ ✿ MS, LS, CS
Loropetalum chinense — p. 281

Daphne ✳
☼ ◑ ● ▲ ✿ ✿ ZONES VARY
— p. 203

Farkleberry
☼ ◑ ● ▲ ✿ ✿ MS, LS, CS
Vaccinium arboreum — p. 405

Fiveleaf aralia
☼ ◑ ● ▲ ● ▲▲ ✿ US, MS, LS, CS
Acanthopanax sieboldianus — p. 115

Fothergilla ✳
☼ ◑ ● ✿ ✿ US, MS, LS
— p. 227

Gardenia, common ✳
☼ ◑ ● ✿ ✿ MS, LS, CS
Gardenia jasminoides — p. 230

Heavenly bamboo
☼ ◑ ● ▲ ● ▲ ✿ US, MS, LS, CS
Nandina domestica — p. 299

Holly
☼ ◑ ● ▲ ✿ ✿ ZONES VARY
Ilex — p. 253

Hybrid fuchsia ✳
◑ ▲ ✿ US
Fuchsia hybrida — p. 228

Hydrangea ✳
☼ ◑ ● ✿ ZONES VARY
— p. 251

Japanese aucuba
☼ ◑ ● ▲ ✿ ALL ZONES
Aucuba japonica — p. 142

Japanese cleyera
☼ ◑ ● ▲ ✿ ✿ MS, LS, CS, TS
Ternstroemia gymnanthera — p. 395

Japanese fatsia
◑ ● ▲ ✿ LS, CS, TS
Fatsia japonica — p. 222

Japanese kerria ✳
☼ ◑ ● ▲ ✿ US, MS, LS
Kerria japonica — p. 266

Japanese pittosporum ✳
☼ ◑ ● ▲ ▲ ✿ LS, CS, TS
Pittosporum tobira — p. 329

Japanese skimmia
◑ ● ▲ ✿ US
Skimmia japonica — p. 379

Lady palm
◑ ● ▲ ✿ ZONES VARY
Rhapis — p. 353

Leucothoe ✳
◑ ● ▲ ▲ ▲✿ ✿ ZONES VARY
— p. 273

Mahonia ✳
NEEDS, ZONES VARY
— p. 288

Mountain laurel ✳
☼ ◑ ● ▲ ▲✿ ✿ US, MS, LS, CS
Kalmia latifolia — p. 265

Osmanthus
☼ ◑ ● ▲ ✿ ZONES VARY
— p. 307

Pieris ✳
◑ ● ▲✿ ✿ ZONES VARY
— p. 328

Redvein enkianthus ✳
☼ ◑ ● ▲ ✿ US, MS, LS
Enkianthus campanulatus — p. 213

Saddle-leaf philodendron
☼ ◑ ● ▲ ▲▲ ✿ TS
Philodendron selloum — p. 324

Sago palm
◑ ▲ ✿ CS, TS
Cycas revoluta — p. 199

Spicebush
☼ ◑ ● ▲ ✿ US, MS, LS
Lindera benzoin — p. 277

Sweet box
◑ ● ▲ ▲✿ ✿ LS
Sarcococca — p. 372

Japanese pittosporum
Pittosporum tobira 'Wheeler's Dwarf'

Sago palm
Cycas revoluta

Spicebush
Lindera benzoin

Sweet pepperbush
Clethra alnifolia

For growing symbol explanations, please see page 38.

Actinidia kolomikta

Bishop's weed
Aegopodium podagraria 'Variegata'

Boston ivy
Parthenocissus tricuspidata

Carpet bugleweed
Ajuga reptans

Mazus
Mazus reptans

Sweet pepperbush ☀
☀ ◐ ◕ ◔ US, MS, LS, CS
Clethra alnifolia   p. 186

Viburnum ☀
☼ ◑ ◕ ◔ ZONES VARY
    p. 407

Witch hazel ☀
☼ ◑ ◕ ◔ US, MS, LS
Hamamelis   p. 240

Yew
☼ ◑ ● ◕ ◔ ◔ ◔ US, MS
Taxus   p. 394

GROUND COVERS, VINES

Actinidia kolomikta
☼ ◑ ◕ ◔ US, MS, LS
    p. 119

Bishop's weed
☼ ◑ ◕ ◔ US, MS, LS
Aegopodium podagraria   p. 120

Boston ivy
☼ ◑ ● ◕ ◔ US, MS, LS
Parthenocissus tricuspidata   p. 313

Carolina jessamine ☀
☼ ◑ ● ◕ ◔ MS, LS, CS
Gelsemium sempervirens   p. 231

Carpet bugleweed ☀
☼ ◑ ● ◕ ◔ US, MS, LS
Ajuga reptans   p. 122

Confederate jasmine ☀
☼ ◑ ● ◕ ◔ LS, CS, TS   p. 400
Trachelospermum jasminoides

Creeping fig ☀
☼ ◑ ● ◕ ◔ LS, CS, TS
Ficus pumila   p. 224

English ivy
☼ ◑ ● ◕ ◔ ◔ ALL ZONES
Hedera helix   p. 241

Fatshedera lizei
☼ ● ◕ ◔ LS, CS, TS
    p. 222

Fiveleaf akebia
☼ ◑ ● ◕ ◔ US, MS, LS, CS
Akebia quinata   p. 122

Grape ivy
☼ ◑ ● ◕ ◔ LS, CS, TS
Cissus rhombifolia   p. 181

Hellebore ☀
☼ ◑ ● ◕ ◔ ◔ ZONES VARY
Helleborus   p. 244

Honeysuckle ☀
☼ ◑ ● ◕ ◔ ZONES VARY
Lonicera (some)   p. 280

Houttuynia cordata
☼ ◑ ● ◕ ◔ US, MS, LS
    p. 250

Japanese ardisia
◑ ● ◕ ◔ LS, CS
Ardisia japonica   p. 136

Japanese pachysandra ☀
◑ ● ◕ ◔ US, MS, LS
Pachysandra terminalis   p. 309

Lily-of-the-valley ☀
☼ ◑ ● ◕ ◔ US, MS, LS
Convallaria majalis   p. 189

Lily turf ☀
☼ ◑ ● ◕ ◔ ◔ ZONES VARY
Liriope   p. 278

Lysimachia
☼ ◑ ● ◕ ◔ ZONES VARY
    p. 283

Mazus ☀
☼ ◑ ● ◕ ◔ US, MS, LS, CS
Mazus reptans   p. 292

Mondo grass
◑ ● ◕ ◔ MS, LS, CS, TS
Ophiopogon japonicus   p. 279

Partridgeberry
● ◕ ◔ ◔ US, MS, LS
Mitchella repens   p. 295

Periwinkle ☀
◑ ● ◕ ◔ ZONES VARY
Vinca   p. 409

Porcelain berry
☼ ◑ ● ◕ ◔ US, MS, LS, CS   p. 126
Ampelopsis brevipedunculata

Split-leaf philodendron
◑ ◕ ◔ TS
Monstera deliciosa   p. 296

Spotted dead nettle
◑ ● ◕ ◔ US, MS, LS
Lamium maculatum   p. 269

Sweet woodruff ☀
◑ ● ◕ ◕ ◔ US, MS, LS
Galium odoratum   p. 229

Virginia creeper
☼ ◑ ● ◕ ◔ US, MS, LS, CS
Parthenocissus quinquefolia   p. 313

Wintercreeper euonymus
☼ ◑ ● ◕ ◔ US, MS, LS, CS
Euonymus fortunei   p. 218

PERENNIALS, BULBS, ANNUALS

Amethyst flower ☀
◑ ◕ ◔ ALL ZONES
Browallia   p. 155

Astilbe ☀
☼ ◑ ◕ ◔ US, MS
    p. 141

Bear's breech ☀
☼ ◑ ● ◕ ◔ US, MS, LS, CS
Acanthus mollis   p. 115

Astilbe

Bear's breech
Acanthus mollis

Begonia
Begonia foliosa 'Miniata'

Bergenia

Bleeding heart, common
Dicentra spectabilis

Plant listings continue ▶

SPECIAL SITUATIONS

Chinese foxglove
Rehmannia elata

Coral bells
Heuchera 'Pewter Veil'

Corydalis
Corydalis cheilanthifolia

Cranesbill
Geranium 'Johnson's Blue'

Foxglove
Digitalis purpurea Foxy strain

Begonia ✳
TS
p. 147

Bergenia ✳
US, MS, LS
p. 149

Black snakeroot ✳
US, MS
Cimicifuga racemosa   p. 181

Bleeding heart ✳
ZONES VARY
Dicentra (most)   p. 207

Bloodroot ✳
US, MS, LS
Sanguinaria canadensis   p. 369

Blue-eyed grass ✳
ZONES VARY
Sisyrinchium   p. 379

Blue phlox ✳
US, MS, LS, CS
Phlox divaricata   p. 325

Blue star ✳
US, MS, LS
Amsonia tabernaemontana   p. 126

Cardinal flower ✳
US, MS, LS, CS
Lobelia cardinalis   p. 278

Cast-iron plant
LS, CS, TS
Aspidistra elatior   p. 140

Chinese foxglove ✳
MS, LS, CS
Rehmannia elata   p. 352

Chinese ground orchid ✳
MS, LS, CS
Bletilla striata   p. 151

Coleus ✳
TS
Coleus hybridus   p. 188

Columbine ✳
ZONES VARY
Aquilegia   p. 134

Coral bells ✳
ZONES VARY
Heuchera   p. 246

Corydalis ✳
US, MS, LS
p. 193

Cranesbill ✳
US, MS, LS
Geranium (some)   p. 231

Crassula
TS
p. 195

Creeping phlox ✳
US, MS, LS
Phlox stolonifera   p. 325

Cyclamen ✳
ZONES VARY
p. 199

Elephant's ear ✳
LS, CS, TS
Colocasia esculenta   p. 189

Epimedium ✳
US, MS, LS
p. 213

Erythronium ✳
ZONES VARY
p. 217

False solomon's seal ✳
US, MS, LS
Smilacina racemosa   p. 379

Fancy-leafed caladium ✳
TS
Caladium bicolor   p. 158

Ferns
NEEDS, ZONES VARY
p. 223

Filipendula ✳
US, MS, LS
p. 225

Fire pink ✳
US, MS, LS
Silene virginica   p. 378

Flowering tobacco ✳
ALL ZONES
Nicotiana alata   p. 303

Foamflower ✳
US, MS, LS
Tiarella   p. 397

Forget-me-not ✳
US, MS, LS
Myosotis scorpioides   p. 298

Foxglove ✳
US, MS, LS, CS
Digitalis   p. 208

Galax ✳
US, MS, LS
Galax urceolata   p. 229

Ginger lily ✳
ZONES VARY
Hedychium   p. 241

Globeflower ✳
US, MS
Trollius   p. 402

Goat's beard ✳
US, MS
Aruncus   p. 138

Golden ray ✳
ZONES VARY
Ligularia   p. 274

Greater celandine ✳
US, MS, LS
Chelidonium majus   p. 175

Goat's beard
Aruncus dioicus

Hosta

Impatiens
Impatiens wallerana

Indian pink
Spigelia marilandica

Monkshood
Aconitum

For growing symbol explanations, please see page 38.

Kaffir lily
Clivia miniata

Lady's-mantle
Alchemilla mollis

Oxalis

Pansy
Viola

Creeping phlox
Phlox stolonifera

Heliconia ☼
☼ ☼ ◑ ◑ ⚡ TS
p. 243

Heucherella tiarelloides ☼
◑ ◑ ⚡ US, MS, LS
p. 246

Hosta ☼
◑ ◑ ◑ ⚡ US, MS, LS
p. 249

Impatiens (most) ☼
☼ ☼ ◑ ◑ ⚡ ALL ZONES
p. 255

Indian pink ☼
◑ ◑ ◑ ◑ ⚡ US, MS, LS, CS
Spigelia marilandica   p. 382

Iris, crested ☼
◑ ◑ ⚡ CS
p. 259

Italian arum
◑ ◑ ◑ ◑ ⚡ US, MS, LS, CS
Arum italicum   p. 138

Jack-in-the-pulpit ☼
◑ ◑ ◑ ◑ ⚡ US, MS, LS
Arisaema triphyllum   p. 136

Jacob's ladder ☼
◑ ◑ ◑ ⚡ US, MS, LS
Polemonium caeruleum   p. 337

Kaffir lily ☼
◑ ◑ ◑ ⚡ TS
Clivia miniata   p. 187

Lady's-mantle
◑ ◑ ⚡ US, MS, LS
Alchemilla mollis   p. 123

Liverwort ☼
◑ ◑ ◑ ⚡ US, MS, LS
Hepatica   p. 245

Lobelia (most) ☼
◑ ◑ ◑ ◑ ◑ ⚡ ZONES VARY
p. 278

Lungwort ☼
◑ ◑ ◑ ⚡ US, MS, LS
Pulmonaria   p. 345

May apple
◑ ◑ ◑ ◑ ⚡ US, MS, LS, CS
Podophyllum peltatum   p. 336

Meadow rue ☼
◑ ◑ ⚡ ZONES VARY
Thalictrum   p. 395

Mexican petunia ☼
☼ ☼ ◑ ◑ ⚡ MS, LS, CS
Ruellia brittoniana   p. 367

Monkshood ☼
☼ ◑ ◑ ◑ ⚡ US
Aconitum   p. 118

Oxalis ☼
☼ ☼ ◑ ⚡ ZONES VARY
p. 308

Palm grass
☼ ☼ ◑ ⚡ CS, TS
Setaria palmifolia   p. 377

Peace lily
◑ ◑ ◑ ◑ ◑ ⚡ TS
Spathiphyllum   p. 382

Piggyback plant
◑ ◑ ◑ ◑ ⚡ US
Tolmiea menziesii   p. 399

Primrose ☼
◑ ◑ ◑ ◑ ⚡ ZONES VARY
Primula   p. 341

River oats
☼ ☼ ◑ ⚡ US, MS, LS, CS
Chasmanthium lalifolium   p. 175

Rodgersia
◑ ◑ ⚡ US
p. 359

Sedge
◑ ◑ ◑ ◑ ⚡ US, MS, LS, CS
Carex   p. 165

Siberian bugloss ☼
◑ ◑ ◑ ⚡ US, MS, LS
Brunnera macrophylla   p. 155

Solomon's seal
◑ ◑ ◑ ⚡ US, MS, LS, CS
Polygonatum   p. 337

Spanish bluebell ☼
☼ ☼ ◑ ⚡ US, MS, LS, CS
Endymion hispanicus   p. 213

Strawberry geranium ☼
☼ ◑ ◑ ◑ ⚡ MS, LS, CS
Saxifraga stolonifera   p. 373

Toad lily ☼
◑ ◑ ◑ ◑ ⚡ US, MS, LS
Tricyrtis   p. 401

Tradescantia ☼
◑ ◑ ◑ ◑ ◑ ⚡ ZONES VARY
p. 401

Viola, violet, pansy ☼
☼ ◑ ◑ ◑ ⚡ ZONES VARY
Viola   p. 409

Virginia bluebells ☼
◑ ◑ ◑ ⚡ US, MS, LS
Mertensia virginica   p. 293

Wake robin ☼
◑ ◑ ◑ ⚡ US, MS, LS
Trillium   p. 401

Wild ginger ☼
◑ ◑ ◑ ◑ ⚡ ZONES VARY
Asarum   p. 138

Windflower ☼
☼ ☼ ◑ ◑ ◑ ⚡ US, MS, LS
Anemone   p. 127

Wishbone flower ☼
◑ ◑ ⚡ ALL ZONES
Torenia fournieri   p. 400

Siberian bugloss
Brunnera macrophylla

Solomon's seal
Polygonatum

Tradescantia

Virginia bluebells
Mertensia virginica

Wake robin
Trillium

SPECIAL SITUATIONS

Plants for

DAMP SOIL

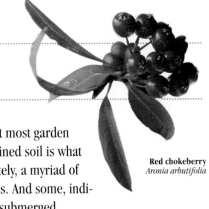

Red chokeberry
Aronia arbutifolia

S wamps and marshes may be heaven to alligators, but most garden plants have a devil of a time growing there. Well-drained soil is what they want, but providing it can be a labor of Job. Fortunately, a myriad of attractive plants flourish in heavy, soggy, oxygen-poor soils. And some, indicated by the symbol 👑, will grow with their roots totally submerged.

Bald cypress
Taxodium distichum

Black gum
Nyssa sylvatica

Cabbage palm
Sabal palmetto

Red maple
Acer rubrum and birches

TREES

American ironwood
☼ ◐ ● ◑ ⚡ US, MS, LS, CS
Carpinus caroliniana   p. 166

Bald cypress   👑
☼ ◐ ◐ ◑ ⚡ US, MS, LS, CS
Taxodium distichum   p. 394

Bigleaf magnolia
☼ ◐ ◑ ⚡ US, MS, LS, CS
Magnolia macrophylla   p. 286

Black gum
☼ ◐ ◐ ◑ ⚡ US, MS, LS, CS
Nyssa sylvatica   p. 304

Box elder
☼ ◐ ◑ ◐ ⚡ US, MS, LS, CS
Acer negundo   p. 116

Cabbage palm
☼ ◐ ◑ ⚡ LS, CS, TS
Sabal palmetto   p. 368

Dahoon
☼ ◐ ◑ ⚡ MS, LS, CS
Ilex cassine   p. 254

Juneberry
☼ ◐ ◑ ◑ ⚡ US, MS, LS
Amelanchier arborea   p. 126

Loblolly bay
☼ ◐ ◐ ◑ ⚡ LS, CS, TS
Gordonia lasianthus   p. 235

Laurel oak
☼ ◐ ⚡ ALL ZONES
Quercus laurifolia   p. 349

Mayhaw
☼ ◐ ◐ ◑ ⚡ MS, LS, CS
Crataegus opaca   p. 196

Pond cypress   👑
☼ ◐ ◑ ◐ ⚡ US, MS, LS, CS
Taxodium ascendens   p. 394

Possumhaw
☼ ◐ ◑ ⚡ US, MS, LS, CS
Ilex decidua   p. 254

Red maple
☼ ◐ ◐ ◑ ⚡ US, MS, LS, CS
Acer rubrum   p. 117

River birch
☼ ◐ ◑ ◐ ⚡ US, MS, LS, CS
Betula nigra   p. 150

Southern magnolia
☼ ◐ ◑ ⚡ US, MS, LS, CS
Magnolia grandiflora   p. 285

Sugarberry
☼ ◐ ◑ ⚡ US, MS, LS
Celtis laevigata   p. 171

Swamp white oak
☼ ◐ ◑ ⚡ US, MS, LS
Quercus bicolor   p. 348

Sweet bay
☼ ◐ ◐ ◑ ⚡ US, MS, LS, CS
Magnolia virginiana   p. 287

Sweet gum
☼ ◐ ◑ ⚡ ALL ZONES
Liquidambar styraciflua   p. 277

Sycamore
☼ ◐ ◑ ⚡ US, MS, LS, CS
Platanus occidentalis   p. 332

Water oak
☼ ◐ ◐ ⚡ US, MS, LS, CS
Quercus nigra   p. 349

Water tupelo   👑
☼ ◐ ◑ ◐ ⚡ US, MS, LS, CS
Nyssa aquatica   p. 304

White cedar
☼ ◐ ◑ ⚡ US, MS, LS
Chamaecyparis thyoides   p. 174

Weeping willow
☼ ◐◑ ⚡ US, MS, LS, CS
Salix babylonica   p. 369

SHRUBS

American elderberry
☼ ◐ ◐ ⚡ US, MS, LS, CS
Sambucus canadensis   p. 369

Swamp white oak
Quercus bicolor

Sweet bay
Magnolia virginiana

Bottlebrush buckeye
Aesculus parviflora

For growing symbol explanations, please see page 38.

Leucothoe

Spicebush
Lindera

Virginia sweetspire
Itea virginica

Winterberry
Ilex verticillata

Bee balm
Monarda didyma

American arborvitae
☼ ◑ ◐ ⬦ ⬦ ✂ US, MS
Thuja occidentalis — p. 396

Bamboo
☼ ◑ ◐ ⬦ ⬦ ✂ ZONES VARY
Phyllostachys (most) — p. 144

Bottlebrush buckeye
☼ ◑ ◐ ⬦ ⬦ US, MS, LS, CS
Aesculus parviflora — p. 120

Buttonbush ♛
☼ ◑ ◐ ⬦ ⬦⬦ ✂ ALL ZONES
Cephalanthus occidentalis — p. 172

Dusty zenobia
◑ ◐ ⬦ ⬦⬦ ✂ US, MS, LS, CS
Zenobia pulverulenta — p. 415

Dwarf palmetto
☼ ◑ ◐ ⬦ ⬦ ✂ MS, LS, CS, TS
Sabal minor — p. 368

Florida anise
◑ ◐ ⬦ ⬦ ⬦ ✂ MS, LS, CS
Illicium floridanum — p. 255

Florida leucothoe
◑ ◐ ⬦ ⬦⬦ ✂ MS, LS, CS
Agarista populifolia — p. 120

Inkberry
☼ ◑ ◐ ⬦ ⬦⬦ ✂ ALL ZONES
Ilex glabra — p. 254

Leucothoe
⬦ NEEDS, ZONES VARY
— p. 273

Red chokeberry
☼ ◑ ◐ ⬦ ⬦ ✂ US, MS, LS
Aronia arbutifolia — p. 137

Redtwig dogwood
☼ ◑ ◐ ⬦ ⬦✂ US, MS, LS
Cornus stolonifera — p. 192

Sea buckthorn
☼ ⬦ ⬦ ✂ US
Hippophae rhamnoides — p. 248

Spicebush
☼ ◑ ◐ ⬦ ⬦ ✂ US, MS, LS
Lindera — p. 277

Sweet pepperbush
◑ ◐ ⬦ ⬦⬦ ✂ US, MS, LS, CS
Clethra alnifolia — p. 186

Sweetshrub, common
☼ ◑ ◐ ⬦ ⬦ ⬦ ✂ US, MS, LS
Calycanthus floridus — p. 161

Turk's-cap
◑ ◐ ⬦ ⬦ ✂ LS, CS, TS
Malvaviscus arboreus — p. 290

Virginia sweetspire
☼ ◑ ◐ ⬦ ⬦⬦ ✂ US, MS, LS, CS
Itea virginica — p. 260

Wax myrtle
☼ ◑ ◐ ⬦ ✂ MS, LS, CS, TS
Myrica cerifera — p. 298

Winterberry ♛
☼ ◑ ◐ ⬦ ⬦ ✂ US, MS, LS, CS
Ilex verticillata — p. 255

PERENNIALS, BULBS

Astilbe
☼ ◑ ◐ ⬦ ✂ US, MS
— p. 141

Bee balm
☼ ◑ ◐ ⬦ ⬦⬦ ✂ US, MS, LS
Monarda didyma — p. 296

Black snakeroot
◑ ◐ ⬦ ✂ US, MS
Cimicifuga racemosa — p. 181

Bloodroot
◑ ◐ ⬦ ⬦ ✂ US, MS, LS
Sanguinaria canadensis — p. 369

Blue cardinal flower
◑ ◐ ⬦ ⬦⬦ ⬦ ✂ US, MS, LS
Lobelia syphilitica — p. 280

Blue flag iris ♛
☼ ◑ ◐ ⬦ ⬦⬦ ✂ US, MS, LS, CS
Iris brevicaulis — p. 259

Bluets
◑ ◐ ⬦ ✂ US, MS, LS
Houstonia caerulea — p. 250

Calla, common ♛
☼ ◑ ◐ ⬦ ✂ CS, TS
Zantedeschia aethiopica — p. 414

Canna ♛
☼ ⬦ ⬦⬦ ✂ LS, CS, TS
— p. 164

Cardinal flower ♛
◑ ◐ ⬦ ⬦⬦ ⬦ ✂ US, MS, LS, CS
Lobelia cardinalis — p. 278

Cinnamon fern
◑ ◐ ⬦ ⬦⬦ ✂ US, MS, LS
Osmunda cinnamomea — p. 308

Crinum
☼ ◑ ◐ ⬦ ⬦⬦ ⬦ ✂ ZONES VARY
— p. 196

Daylily
☼ ◑ ◐ ⬦ ✂ ALL ZONES
Hemerocallis — p. 244

Elephant's ear ♛
◑ ◐⬦ ⬦ ✂ LS, CS, TS
Colocasia esculenta — p. 189

Filipendula
◑ ◐ ⬦ ⬦ ✂ US, MS, LS
— p. 225

Forget-me-not
◑ ◐ ⬦ ⬦⬦ ✂ US, MS, LS
Myosotis scorpioides — p. 298

Globeflower
◑ ◐ ⬦ ⬦⬦ ✂ US, MS
Trollius — p. 402

Astilbe

Black snakeroot
Cimicifuga racemosa

Cardinal flower
Lobelia cardinalis

Filipendula

Plant listings continue ▶

Globeflower
Trollius

Goat's beard
Aruncus dioicus

Horsetail
Equisetum hyemale

Japanese iris
Iris ensata

Goat's beard
☀ ◑ ◐ ✿ US, MS
Aruncus dioicus p. 138

Golden ray
☀ ◑ ● ◑◑ ✿ ZONES VARY
Ligularia p. 274

Gooseneck loosestrife
☀ ◑ ● ◐ ✿ US, MS, LS
Lysimachia clethroides p. 283

Greater celandine
☀ ◑ ● ◐ ◈ ✿ US, MS, LS
Chelidonium majus p. 175

Horsetail 👑
☀ ◑ ◐◐ ✿ ALL ZONES
Equisetum hyemale p. 214

Houttuynia cordata 👑
☀ ◑ ◐ ◐◐ ✿ US, MS, LS
p. 250

Iris laevigata 👑
☀ ◑ ◐ ● ✿ US, MS, LS
p. 259

Ironweed
☀ ◑ ● ◐ ◐◐ ✿ US, MS, LS
Vernonia noveboracensis p. 406

Jack-in-the-pulpit
◑ ● ◐ ◐◐ ✿ US, MS, LS
Arisaema triphyllum p. 136

Japanese iris 👑
☀ ◑ ◐ ● ◐ ✿ US, MS, LS
Iris ensata p. 258

Japanese primrose
◑ ◐◐ ✿ US
Primula japonica p. 341

Joe-Pye weed
☀ ◑ ◐◐ ✿ US, MS, LS, CS
Eupatorium purpureum p. 219

Lady fern
◑ ● ◐◐ ✿ US, MS, LS
Athyrium filix-femina p. 142

Louisiana iris 👑
☀ ◑ ◐◐ ✿ US, MS, LS, CS
p. 258

Marsh marigold 👑
☀ ◑ ● ◐ ◐◐ ◈ ✿ US, MS, LS
Caltha palustris p. 160

Marsh fern 👑
☀ ◑ ● ◐◐ ✿ US, MS, LS
Thelypteris palustris p. 396

Mint
☀ ◑ ◑ ● ✿ ZONES VARY
Mentha p. 293

Monkshood
☀ ◑ ◐ ● ◈ ✿ US
Aconitum p. 118

Moor grass
☀ ◑ ◐ ● ✿ US, MS
Molinia caerulea p. 295

New England aster
☀ ◑ ✿ US, MS, LS
Aster novae-angliae p. 141

Pentas
☀ ◑ ◐ ◐◐ ✿ ALL ZONES
Pentas lanceolata p. 321

Perennial hibiscus
☀ ◑ ◐◐ ✿ ALL ZONES
Hibiscus moscheutos p. 247

River oats
☀ ◑ ◐ ● ✿ US, MS, LS, CS
Chasmanthium latifolium p. 175

Rodgersia
☀ ◑ ◐ ✿ US
p. 359

Royal fern 👑
☀ ◑ ◐ ● ✿ US, MS, LS, CS
Osmunda regalis p. 308

Sedge
☀ ◑ ● ◐ ✿ US, MS, LS, CS
Carex p. 165

Sensitive fern
☀ ◑ ◐◐ ✿ US, MS, LS
Onoclea sensibilis p. 305

Siberian iris
☀ ◑ ◐ ● ✿ US, MS, LS
p. 259

Southern blue flag 👑
☀ ◑ ◐ ● ◐ ✿ US, MS, LS, CS
Iris virginica p. 259

Spiderwort
☀ ◑ ◐ ● ◐ ✿ US, MS, LS, CS
Tradescantia virginiana p. 401

Swamp milkweed 👑
☀ ◑ ◐◐ ◈ ✿ ALL ZONES
Asclepias incarnata p. 139

Swamp sunflower
☀ ◑ ◐ ◐◐ ✿ US, MS, LS, CS
Helianthus angustifolius p. 242

Sweet flag
☀ ◑ ◐ ◐◐ ✿ ALL ZONES
Acorus gramineus p. 118

Sweet woodruff
☀ ◑ ● ◐ ◐◐ ✿ US, MS, LS
Galium odoratum p. 229

Texas star 👑
☀ ◑ ◐ ◐◐ ✿ MS, LS, CS, TS
Hibiscus coccineus p. 246

Wand loosestrife 👑
☀ ◑ ✿ US, MS, LS
Lythrum virgatum p. 283

White turtlehead
☀ ◑ ◑ ● ◐◐ ✿ US, MS, LS, CS
Chelone glabra p. 175

Yellow flag 👑
☀ ◑ ◐ ◐◐ ✿ US, MS, LS, CS
Iris pseudacorus p. 259

Golden ray
Ligularia

Monkshood
Aconitum

Perennial hibiscus
Hibiscus moscheutos

Sedge
Carex

Spiderwort
Tradescantia virginiana

For growing symbol explanations, please see page 38.

Plants that tolerate
DROUGHT

Butterfly bush
Buddleia

Despite our best wishes and fervent prayers, not all of our gardens receive that magical "one inch of rainfall per week." Long, dry summers inevitably hit; and some years it seems that it doesn't rain at all. But the good news is, many plants, once established, grow just fine with far less than ample water. Here are some proven performers. The symbol ✲ indicates plants that even have showy flowers.

Goldenrain tree
Koelreuteria paniculata

Cedar of Lebanon
Cedrus libani

Chinese pistache
Pistacia chinensis

Crepe myrtle
Lagerstroemia indica

TREES

Ash
☼ ◐ ● ⬝ ZONES VARY
Fraxinus (most)   p. 227

Black locust   ✲
☼ ◐ ● ⬝ ⬝ US, MS, LS, CS
Robinia pseudoacacia   p. 359

Bottlebrush   ✲
☼ ◐ ● ⬝ CS, TS
Callistemon   p. 160

Caddo maple
☼ ◐ ◐ ● ⬝ US, MS, LS
Acer saccharum 'Caddo'   p. 117

Cedar
☼ ◐ ● ⬝ ZONES VARY
Cedrus   p. 170

Chaste tree   ✲
☼ ◐ ● ⬝ ALL ZONES
Vitex agnus-castus   p. 410

Chinese elm
☼ ◐ ● ⬝ US, MS, LS, CS
Ulmus parvifolia   p. 404

Chinese pistache
☼ ◐ ● ⬝ US, MS, LS, CS
Pistacia chinensis   p. 329

Chitalpa   ✲
☼ ◐ ⬝ MS, LS, CS
Chitalpa tashkentensis   p. 177

Crepe myrtle   ✲
☼ ◐ ● ⬝ US, MS, LS, CS
Lagerstroemia indica   p. 267

Desert willow   ✲
☼ ◐ ● ⬝ MS, LS, CS
Chilopsis linearis   p. 176

Eastern redbud   ✲
☼ ◐ ◐ ● ⬝ US, MS, LS, CS
Cercis canadensis   p. 173

Eastern red cedar
☼ ◐ ◐ ● ⬝ ⬝ US, MS, LS, CS
Juniperus virginiana   p. 264

Gold medallion tree   ✲
☼ ◐ ● ⬝ TS
Cassia leptophylla   p. 168

Goldenrain tree   ✲
☼ ◐ ● ⬝ US, MS, LS, CS
Koelreuteria paniculata   p. 267

Hackberry
☼ ◐ ● ⬝ US, MS, LS
Celtis   p. 171

Italian cypress
☼ ◐ ● ⬝ MS, LS, CS
Cupressus sempervirens   p. 199

Japanese pagoda tree   ✲
☼ ◐ ◐ ● ⬝ US, MS, LS
Sophora japonica   p. 381

Jerusalem thorn   ✲
☼ ● ⬝ CS, TS
Parkinsonia aculeata   p. 312

Kentucky coffee tree
☼ ◐ ● ⬝ US, MS, LS
Gymnocladus dioica   p. 236

Mesquite
☼ ● ⬝ MS, LS, CS, TS
Prosopis glandulosa   p. 342

Oak
☼ ● ● ⬝ ZONES VARY
Quercus (some)   p. 348

Pine
☼ ● ● ⬝ ZONES VARY
Pinus (many)   p. 329

Russian olive
☼ ◐ ◐ ● ⬝ US, MS
Elaeagnus angustifolia   p. 212

Sumac
☼ ● ● ⬝ ZONES VARY
Rhus   p. 358

Japanese pagoda tree
Sophora japonica

Jerusalem thorn
Parkinsonia aculeata

Sumac
Rhus

Plant listings continue ▸

Broom
Cytisus

Cape plumbago
Plumbago auriculata

Juniper
Juniperus chinensis

Lemon bottlebrush
Callistemon citrinus

Texas persimmon
ALL ZONES
Diospyros texana p. 209

SHRUBS

Barberry
US, MS, LS, CS
Berberis p. 149

Bay
LS, CS, TS
Laurus nobilis p. 271

Blue mist
US, MS, LS, CS
Caryopteris clandonensis p. 167

Broom
US, MS, LS
Cytisus p. 201

Butterfly bush
ZONES VARY
Buddleia p. 156

Cape plumbago
CS, TS
Plumbago auriculata p. 335

Carolina buckthorn
US, MS, LS, CS
Rhamnus caroliniana p. 352

Chinese photinia
US, MS, LS, CS
Photinia serrulata p. 326

Cotoneaster
ZONES VARY
p. 194

Elaeagnus (some)
ZONES VARY
p. 212

European fan palm
LS, CS, TS
Chamaerops humilis p. 175

Euryops
ZONES VARY
p. 220

Firethorn
ZONES VARY
Pyracantha p. 347

Flowering quince
US, MS, LS, CS
Chaenomeles p. 174

Germander
US, MS, LS, CS
Teucrium chamaedrys p. 395

Holly
ZONES VARY
Ilex p. 253

Japanese fatsia
LS, CS, TS
Fatsia japonica p. 222

Japanese pittosporum
LS, CS, TS
Pittosporum tobira p. 329

Juniper
ZONES VARY
Juniperus (some) p. 262

Lemon bottlebrush
CS, TS
Callistemon citrinus p. 160

Mahonia (most)
NEEDS, ZONES VARY
p. 288

Myrtle
CS
Myrtus communis p. 299

Nandina
US, MS, LS, CS
Nandina domestica p. 299

Needle palm
ALL ZONES
Rhapidophyllum hystrix p. 352

Oleander, common
LS, CS, TS
Nerium oleander p. 302

Pineapple guava
LS, CS, TS
Feijoa sellowiana p. 223

Pomegranate
MS, LS, CS, TS
Punica granatum p. 346

Prickly pear cactus
ZONES VARY
Opuntia p. 306

Rose of Sharon
US, MS, LS, CS
Hibiscus syriacus p. 247

Rosemary
MS, LS, CS
Rosmarinus officinalis p. 366

Rugosa rose
US, MS, LS
Rosa rugosa p. 365

Sage
NEEDS, ZONES VARY
Salvia (some) p. 369

Sago palm
CS, TS
Cycas revoluta p. 199

Senna
ZONES VARY
Cassia (some) p. 167

Smoke tree
US, MS, LS
Cotinus coggygria p. 194

Spiraea
ZONES VARY
p. 383

Myrtle
Myrtus communis

Nandina
Nandina domestica

Oleander, common
Nerium oleander

Rosemary
Rosmarinus officinalis

Sago palm
Cycas revoluta

For growing symbol explanations, please see page 38.

Sage, Mexican bush
Salvia leucantha

Yellow bells
Tecoma stans

Bougainvillea

Crossvine
Bignonia capreolata

Wisteria, Chinese
Wisteria sinensis

Sumac
☼ ◐ ● ◊ ✘ ZONES VARY
Rhus — p. 358

Texas sage ✳
☼ ● ◊ ✘ MS, LS, CS
Leucophyllum frutescens — p. 273

Windmill palm
☼ ◐ ● ✘ LS, CS, TS
Trachycarpus fortunei — p. 401

Yellow bells ✳
☼ ● ◊ ✘ CS, TS
Tecoma stans — p. 394

VINES

Beach morning glory ✳
☼ ● ◊ ✘ CS, TS
Ipomoea pes-caprae — p. 256

Bittersweet
☼ ● ✘ US, MS, LS
Celastrus — p. 170

Boston ivy
☼ ◐ ● ◊ ● ✘ US, MS, LS
Parthenocissus tricuspidata — p. 313

Bougainvillea ✳
☼ ◐ ● ◊ ✘ CS, TS
— p. 153

Carolina jessamine ✳
☼ ◐ ● ◊ ● ✘ MS, LS, CS
Gelsemium sempervirens — p. 231

Coral vine ✳
☼ ● ◊ ● ✘ LS, CS, TS
Antigonon leptopus — p. 129

Crossvine ✳
☼ ◐ ● ◊ ✘ ALL ZONES
Bignonia capreolata — p. 150

Pink trumpet vine ✳
☼ ◐ ● ◊ ✘ CS, TS
Podranea ricasoliana — p. 336

Porcelain berry
☼ ◐ ● ◊ ● ✘ US, MS, LS, CS — p. 126
Ampelopsis brevipedunculata

Potato vine ✳
☼ ◐ ● ◊ ● ✘ CS, TS
Solanum jasminoides — p. 380

Silver lace vine ✳
☼ ● ✘ US, MS, LS
Polygonum aubertii — p. 337

Sweet autumn clematis ✳
☼ ● ✘ US, MS, LS, CS
Clematis dioscoreifolia — p. 185

Trumpet creeper, common ✳
☼ ◐ ● ◊ ● ✘ ALL ZONES
Campsis radicans — p. 164

Virginia creeper
☼ ◐ ● ◊ ● ✘ US, MS, LS, CS
Parthenocissus quinquefolia — p. 313

Wisteria ✳
☼ ◐ ● ◊ ✘ US, MS, LS, CS
— p. 412

GROUND COVERS

Calylophus ✳
☼ ◐ ● ◊ ✘ US, MS, LS
— p. 161

Ceratostigma ✳
☼ ◐ ● ◊ ✘ US, MS, LS, CS — p. 172
Ceratostigma plumbaginoides

Lady Banks's Rose ✳
☼ ◐ ● ◊ ✘ LS, CS, TS
Rosa banksiae — p. 364

Lamb's ears ✳
☼ ◐ ● ◊ ✘ US, MS, LS
Stachys byzantina — p. 384

Lantana ✳
☼ ● ◊ ✘ MS, LS, CS, TS
— p. 269

Snow-in-summer ✳
☼ ◐ ● ◊ ✘ US, MS, LS
Cerastium tomentosum — p. 172

Stonecrop ✳
☼ ◐ ● ◊ ✘ US, MS, LS
Sedum — p. 375

PERENNIALS, BULBS, ANNUALS, ACCENTS

Agave ✳
☼ ◐ ● ◊ ✘ CS, TS
— p. 121

Aloe (most) ✳
☼ ◐ ● ◊ ● ✘ TS
— p. 124

Artemisia
☼ ● ◊ ✘ ZONES VARY
— p. 137

Baby's breath ✳
☼ ● ◊ ✘ US, MS
Gypsophila paniculata — p. 239

Blackfoot daisy ✳
☼ ● ◊ ✘ US, MS, LS
Melampodium leucanthum — p. 292

Blanket flower ✳
☼ ● ◊ ✘ ALL ZONES
Gaillardia — p. 229

Blazing star ✳
☼ ● ◊ ✘ US, MS, LS, CS
Liatris — p. 274

Blue fescue
☼ ◐ ● ◊ ✘ US, MS
Festuca ovina 'Glauca' — p. 223

Butterfly weed ✳
☼ ● ◊ ✘ ALL ZONES
Asclepias tuberosa — p. 139

Lamb's ears
Stachys byzantina

Agave

Artemisia
Artemisia 'Powis Castle'

Blanket flower
Gaillardia

Coreopsis
Coreopsis lanceolata

Plant listings continue ▸

SPECIAL SITUATIONS

Echeveria

Jerusalem sage
Phlomis

Madagascar periwinkle
Catharanthus roseus

Mexican sunflower
Tithonia rotundifolia

Red-hot poker
Kniphofia uvaria

Cockscomb ✻
☼ ◐ ◑ ✓ ALL ZONES
Celosia argentea ⁣ p. 171

Coreopsis ✻
☼ ◐ ◑ ✓ US, MS, LS, CS
⁣ p. 190

Echeveria (most) ✻
☼ ◐ ◑ ✓ LS, CS, TS
⁣ p. 211

Euphorbia (most) ✻
◐ NEEDS, ZONES VARY
⁣ p. 219

False indigo ✻
☼ ◐ ◑ ✓ US, MS, LS, CS
Baptisia ⁣ p. 145

Feather grass ✻
☼ ◑ ◐ ◑ ✓ US, MS, LS
Stipa ⁣ p. 386

Fountain grass ✻
☼ ◐ ◑ ◑ ✓ CS, TS
Pennisetum setaceum ⁣ p. 320

Gaura ✻
☼ ◐ ◑ ◑ ✓ US, MS, LS, CS
Gaura lindheimeri ⁣ p. 230

Geranium ✻
☼ ◑ ◐ ◑ ◑ ✓ CS, TS
Pelargonium ⁣ p. 318

Globe amaranth ✻
☼ ◑ ◐ ◑ ✓ ALL ZONES
Gomphrena globosa ⁣ p. 235

Iris, bearded ✻
☼ ◑ ◐ ◑ ◑ ✓ US, MS, LS
⁣ p. 258

Jerusalem sage ✻
☼ ◐ ◑ ✓ US, MS, LS
Phlomis ⁣ p. 324

Lamb's ears ✻
☼ ◑ ◐ ◑ ✓ US, MS, LS
Stachys byzantina ⁣ p. 384

Lantana ✻
☼ ◐ ◑ ◑ ✓ MS, LS, CS, TS
⁣ p. 269

Lavender cotton ✻
☼ ◐ ◑ ◑ ✓ US, MS, LS
Santolina chamaecyparissus ⁣ p. 371

Lemon marigold ✻
☼ ◑ ✓ LS, CS
Tagetes lemmonii ⁣ p. 393

Lily-of-the-Nile ✻
☼ ◐ ◑ ◑ ✓ ZONES VARY
Agapanthus ⁣ p. 120

Madagascar periwinkle ✻
☼ ◑ ◐ ◑ ✓ ALL ZONES
Catharanthus roseus ⁣ p. 169

Maiden grass ✻
☼ ◑ ◐ ◑ ◑ ✓ US, MS, LS, CS
Miscanthus ⁣ p. 295

Mexican petunia ✻
☼ ◑ ◐ ◑ ✓ MS, LS, CS
Ruellia brittoniana ⁣ p. 367

Mexican sunflower ✻
☼ ◐ ◑ ✓ ALL ZONES
Tithonia rotundifolia ⁣ p. 398

Morea iris ✻
☼ ◐ ◑ ◑ ✓ LS, CS, TS
Dietes ⁣ p. 208

Mullein ✻
☼ ◐ ◑ ✓ US, MS, LS
Verbascum ⁣ p. 405

Narrow-leaf zinnia ✻
☼ ◐ ◑ ✓ ALL ZONES
Zinnia angustifolia ⁣ p. 416

Orange coneflower ✻
☼ ◑ ◐ ◑ ✓ US, MS, LS, CS
Rudbeckia fulgida ⁣ p. 366

Purple coneflower ✻
☼ ◐ ◑ ✓ US, MS, LS, CS
Echinacea purpurea ⁣ p. 211

Red-hot poker ✻
☼ ◑ ◐ ◑ ✓ US, MS, LS, CS
Kniphofia uvaria ⁣ p. 266

Red yucca ✻
☼ ◐ ◑ ✓ US, MS, LS, CS
Hesperaloe parviflora ⁣ p. 246

Russian sage ✻
☼ ◐ ✓ US, MS, LS, CS
Perovskia ⁣ p. 321

Sage ✻
NEEDS, ZONES VARY
Salvia (most) ⁣ p. 369

Stonecrop ✻
☼ ◑ ◐ ◑ ✓ US, MS, LS
Sedum (many) ⁣ p. 375

Valerian ✻
☼ ◑ ◐ ✓ US, MS, LS
Centranthus ruber ⁣ p. 172

Verbena (most) ✻
☼ ◐ ✓ ZONES VARY
⁣ p. 406

Wild ageratum ✻
☼ ◑ ◐ ◑ ◐ ◑ ✓ ALL ZONES
Eupatorium coelestinum ⁣ p. 219

Wild foxglove ✻
☼ ◑ ◐ ◑ ✓ US, MS, LS, CS
Penstemon cobaea ⁣ p. 320

Yarrow ✻
☼ ◐ ✓ US, MS, LS
Achillea ⁣ p. 117

Yucca (most) ✻
☼ ◐ ◑ ✓ ZONES VARY
⁣ p. 413

Zinnia, common ✻
☼ ◐ ✓ ALL ZONES
Zinnia elegans ⁣ p. 416

Russian sage
Perovskia 'Blue Spire'

Sage, Texas
Salvia coccinea

Wild foxglove
Penstemon cobaea

Yarrow
Achillea taygetea

For growing symbol explanations, please see page 38.

Plants for
COASTAL GARDENS

Life is no walk on the beach for most plants near the coast. They must endure constant wind, salt-laden air, and poor, sandy soil. Fortunately however, many plants thrive under such demanding conditions. And some, indicated by the symbol ♛, are suitable for planting right on the frontline dunes. Keep in mind though, that groupings of plants usually take coastal conditions better than single specimens.

A garden by the beach

American holly
Ilex opaca

Cabbage palm
Sabal palmetto

Japanese cryptomeria
Cryptomeria japonica

TREES

American arborvitae
☼ ◗ ◖ ◗ ✂ US, MS
Thuja occidentalis — p. 396

American holly
☼ ◗ ◖ ✂ US, MS, LS, CS
Ilex opaca — p. 254

Beach plum
☼ ◗ ◖ ◗ ✂ US, MS
Prunus maritima — p. 344

Cabbage palm ♛
☼ ◗ ◖ ✂ LS, CS, TS
Sabal palmetto — p. 368

Canary Island date palm
☼ ◖ ✂ CS, TS
Phoenix canariensis — p. 325

Chinese elm
☼ ◖ ✂ US, MS, LS, CS
Ulmus parvifolia — p. 404

Coconut palm ♛
☼ ◖ ✂ TS
Cocos nucifera — p. 188

Dahoon
☼ ◗ ◖ ✂ MS, LS, CS
Ilex cassine — p. 254

Eastern red cedar
☼ ◗ ◖ ◗ ✂ US, MS, LS, CS
Juniperus virginiana — p. 264

Glossy privet
☼ ◗ ◖ ◗ ✂ LS, CS, TS
Ligustrum lucidum — p. 275

Japanese black pine
☼ ◖ ◗ ✂ US, MS, LS, CS
Pinus thunbergiana — p. 331

Japanese cryptomeria
☼ ◖ ◗ ✂ US, MS, LS
Cryptomeria japonica — p. 197

Jerusalem thorn
☼ ◖ ◗ ✂ CS, TS
Parkinsonia aculeata — p. 312

Live oak
☼ ◖ ◗ ✂ LS, CS, TS
Quercus virginiana — p. 350

Marlberry ♛
☼ ◗ ◖ ◗ ✂ TS
Ardisia paniculata — p. 136

Norfolk Island pine
☼ ◖ ✂ TS
Araucaria heterophylla — p. 135

Norway maple
☼ ◗ ◖ ◗ ✂ US, MS
Acer platanoides — p. 116

Pindo palm
☼ ◗ ◖ ◗ ✂ CS, TS
Butia capitata — p. 157

Royal palm
☼ ◖ ◗ ✂ TS
Roystonea — p. 366

Sand pine
☼ ◖ ◗ ✂ CS, TS
Pinus clausa — p. 330

Sawara false cypress
☼ ◗ ◖ ✂ US, MS
Chamaecyparis pisifera — p. 174

Sea grape ♛
☼ ◖ ✂ TS
Coccoloba uvifera — p. 187

Slash pine
☼ ◖ ◗ ✂ MS, LS, CS
Pinus elliottii — p. 330

Southern magnolia
☼ ◗ ◖ ✂ US, MS, LS, CS
Magnolia grandiflora — p. 285

Southern red cedar ♛
☼ ◗ ◖ ◗ ✂ CS, TS
Juniperus siliciocola — p. 264

Tamarisk
☼ ◖ ✂ ZONES VARY
Tamarix — p. 393

Windmill palm
☼ ◗ ◖ ✂ LS, CS, TS
Trachycarpus fortunei — p. 401

Live oak
Quercus virginiana

Norway maple
Acer platanoides

Sawara false cypress
Chamaecyparis pisifera

Sea grape
Coccoloba uvifera

Plant listings continue ▷

Cotoneaster, rock
Cotoneaster horizontalis

Indian hawthorn
Raphiolepis indica

Japanese pittosporum
Pittosporum tobira

Juniper
Juniperus chinensis

Oleander, common
Nerium oleander

Yaupon
☼ ◐ ◐ ● ⚡ MS, LS, CS
Ilex vomitoria   p. 255

SHRUBS

Arrowwood
☼ ◐ ◐ ● ⚡ US, MS, LS
Viburnum dentatum   p. 407

Box honeysuckle
☼ ◐ ◐ ● ⚡ US, MS, LS, CS
Lonicera nitida   p. 281

Broom
☼ ● ⚡ US, MS, LS
Cytisus   p. 201

Butcher's broom
◐ ◐ ● ◐ ● ⚡ MS, LS, CS
Ruscus aculeatus   p. 367

Century plant   ♛
☼ ◐ ◐ ● ⚡ CS, TS
Agave americana   p. 121

Coontie   ♛
◐ ◐ ● ⚡ CS, TS
Zamia pumila   p. 414

Cotoneaster
☼ ◐ ● ⚡ ZONES VARY
                                  p. 194

Croton
NEEDS VARY ⚡ TS
Codiaeum variegatum   p. 188

Dwarf palmetto   ♛
☼ ◐ ◐ ● ⚡ MS, LS, CS, TS
Sabal minor   p. 368

Flame of the woods
☼ ● ⚡ CS, TS
Ixora coccinea   p. 260

Flowering quince
☼ ◐ ● ● ⚡ US, MS, LS, CS
Chaenomeles   p. 174

Heliconia
☼ ◐ ◐● ⚡ TS
                                  p. 243

Indian hawthorn   ♛
☼ ◐ ◐ ● ⚡ LS, CS
Raphiolepis indica   p. 351

Inkberry
☼ ◐ ◐ ● ⚡ ALL ZONES
Ilex glabra   p. 254

Japanese barberry
☼ ◐ ◐ ● ● ⚡ US, MS, LS, CS
Berberis thunbergii   p. 149

Japanese fatsia
◐ ● ◐ ● ⚡ CS, TS
Fatsia japonica   p. 222

Japanese pittosporum   ♛
☼ ◐ ◐ ● ⚡ LS, CS, TS
Pittosporum tobira   p. 329

Juniper
☼ ◐ ◐ ● ⚡ ZONES VARY
Juniperus   p. 262

Lemon bottlebrush
☼ ◐ ● ⚡ CS, TS
Callistemon citrinus   p. 160

Mound-lily yucca
☼ ◐ ◐ ● ⚡ US, MS, LS, CS
Yucca gloriosa   p. 414

Myrtle
☼ ◐ ◐ ● ⚡ CS
Myrtus communis   p. 299

Natal plum   ♛
☼ ◐ ◐ ● ⚡ TS
Carissa macrocarpa   p. 166

Oleander, common
☼ ◐ ◐ ● ◐ ⚡ LS, CS, TS
Nerium oleander   p. 302

Pampas grass
☼ ◐ ◐ ● ◐● ⚡ MS, LS, CS, TS
Cortaderia selloana   p. 192

Pineapple guava
☼ ◐ ● ⚡ LS, CS, TS
Feijoa sellowiana   p. 223

Red chokeberry
☼ ◐ ◐ ● ◐ ● ⚡ US, MS, LS
Aronia arbutifolia   p. 137

Redtwig dogwood
☼ ◐ ● ⚡ US, MS, LS
Cornus stolonifera   p. 192

Rose of Sharon
☼ ● ◐ ● ⚡ US, MS, LS, CS
Hibiscus syriacus   p. 247

Rosemary
☼ ◐ ● ⚡ MS, LS, CS
Rosmarinus officinalis   p. 366

Rugosa rose
☼ ◐ ● ⚡ US, MS, LS
Rosa rugosa   p. 365

Sea buckthorn   ♛
☼ ◐ ● ● ⚡ US
Hippophae rhamnoides   p. 248

Southern yew
☼ ◐ ◐ ● ⚡ LS, CS, TS
Podocarpus macrophyllus   p. 336

Stokes' dwarf yaupon
☼ ◐ ◐ ● ⚡ MS, LS, CS
Ilex vomitoria 'Stokes'   p. 255

Sumac
☼ ◐ ● ⚡ ZONES VARY
Rhus   p. 358

Thorny elaeagnus   ♛
☼ ◐ ◐ ● ⚡ US, MS, LS, CS
Elaeagnus pungens   p. 212

Wax myrtle
☼ ◐ ◐ ● ⚡ MS, LS, CS, TS
Myrica cerifera   p. 298

Yellowtwig dogwood
Cornus stolonifera 'Flaviramea'

Redtwig dogwood
Cornus stolonifera

Rose of Sharon
Hibiscus syriacus

Rugosa rose
Rosa rugosa

Thorny elaeagnus
Elaeagnus pungens

For growing symbol explanations, please see page 38.

Cape honeysuckle
Tecomaria capensis

Confederate jasmine
Trachelospermum jasminoides

Trumpet creeper, common
Campsis radicans

Artemisia
Artemisia 'Powis Castle'

Daylily
Hemerocallis

VINES

Allamanda, common
☼ ◐ ◊ ⚡ TS
Allamanda cathartica   p. 123

Beach morning glory   ♔
☼ ◐ ◊ ⚡ CS, TS
Ipomoea pes-caprae   p. 256

Bittersweet
☼ ◊ ⚡ US, MS, LS
Celastrus   p. 170

Cape honeysuckle
☼ ◐ ◊ ◊ ⚡ CS, TS
Tecomaria capensis   p. 395

Confederate jasmine
☼ ◐ ● ◊ ◊ ⚡ LS, CS, TS   p. 400
Trachelospermum jasminoides

Trumpet creeper, common
☼ ◐ ● ◊ ⚡ ALL ZONES
Campsis radicans   p. 164

Virginia creeper
☼ ◐ ● ◊ ⚡ US, MS, LS, CS
Parthenocissus quinquefolia p. 313

Wedelia   ♔
☼ ◐ ◊ ⚡ CS, TS
Wedelia trilobata   p. 411

ANNUALS, PERENNIALS, BULBS

Artemisia (most)
☼ ◊ ⚡ ZONES VARY
                                     p. 137

Blue wild indigo
☼ ◊ ⚡ US, MS, LS, CS
Baptisia australis   p. 145

Blue lyme grass
☼ ◐ ◊ ◊ ⚡ US, MS, LS, CS
Elymus arenarius 'Glaucus' p. 213

Butterfly weed
☼ ◊ ◊ ◐ ◊ ⚡ ALL ZONES
Asclepias tuberosa   p. 139

Cape plumbago
☼ ◊ ⚡ CS, TS
Plumbago auriculata   p. 335

Chinese pennisetum
☼ ◐ ◊ ◊ ⚡ US, MS, LS, CS
Pennisetum alopecuroides   p. 320

Crinum
☼ ◐ ◊ ◊ ◐ ◊ ⚡ ZONES VARY
                                     p. 196

Daylily
☼ ◐ ◊ ⚡ ALL ZONES
Hemerocallis   p. 244

Dusty miller
☼ ◊ ⚡ MS, LS, CS
Senecio cineraria   p. 376

Euryops
☼ ◊ ⚡ ZONES VARY
                                     p. 220

Evergreen candytuft
☼ ◊ ⚡ US, MS, LS
Iberis sempervirens   p. 253

Fernleaf yarrow
☼ ◊ ⚡ US, MS, LS
Achillea filipendula   p. 117

Indian blanket   ♔
☼ ◊ ⚡ ALL ZONES
Gaillardia pulchella   p. 229

Lamb's ears
☼ ◊ ⚡ US, MS, LS
Stachys byzantina   p. 384

Lantana
☼ ◊ ◊ ⚡ MS, LS, CS, TS
                                     p. 269

Lily-of-the-Nile
☼ ◐ ◊ ◊ ⚡ LS, CS, TS
Agapanthus africanus   p. 120

Perennial hibiscus
☼ ◊ ◊ ◐ ⚡ ALL ZONES
Hibiscus moscheutos   p. 247

Pine cone ginger
◊ ◐ ◊ ⚡ CS, TS
Zingiber zerumbet   p. 416

Prickly pear cactus   ♔
☼ ◊ ⚡ ZONES VARY
Opuntia   p. 306

Purple heart
☼ ◊ ⚡ MS, LS, CS, TS   p. 377
Setcreasea pallida 'Purple Heart'

Red-hot poker
☼ ◐ ◊ ◊ ⚡ US, MS, LS, CS
Kniphofia uvaria   p. 266

River oats
☼ ◐ ◊ ⚡ US, MS, LS, CS
Chasmanthium latifolium   p. 175

Santolina
☼ ◊ ◊ ⚡ US, MS, LS
                                     p. 371

Spanish bayonet   ♔
☼ ◊ ⚡ LS, CS, TS
Yucca aloifolia   p. 413

Sea holly
☼ ◊ ⚡ US, MS, LS, CS
Eryngium alpinum   p. 216

Snow-in-summer
☼ ◐ ◊ ⚡ US, MS, LS
Cerastium tomentosum   p. 172

Society garlic
☼ ◐ ◊ ⚡ LS, CS, TS
Tulbaghia violacea   p. 402

Stonecrop
☼ ◐ ◊ ⚡ US, MS, LS
Sedum   p. 375

Indian blanket
Gaillardia pulchella

Perennial hibiscus
Hibiscus moscheutos

Santolina
Santolina chamaecyparissus

Sea holly
Eryngium alpinum

Stonecrop
Sedum

SPECIAL SITUATIONS

CAREFREE PLANTS

Bald cypress
Taxodium distichum

Texas star
Hibiscus coccineus

For many gardeners today, time is of the essence. We can't spare an hour or three to fuss over plants that need constant watering, fertilizing, and spraying for insects and diseases. The following plants make life easier. Most tolerate drought, adapt to different soils, and seldom fall victim to serious pests. (An ∾ by the plant's name indicates that you should plant a disease-resistant selection.) So plant them, relax, and enjoy.

Cabbage palm
Sabal palmetto

Chaste tree
Vitex agnus-castus

Chinese pistache
Pistacia chinensis

TREES

Bald cypress
☼ ◐ ◑ ◑ ✿ US, MS, LS, CS
Taxodium distichum   p. 394

Cabbage palm
☼ ◐ ◑ ✿ LS, CS, TS
Sabal palmetto   p. 368

Chaste tree
☼ ◑ ◑ ✿ ALL ZONES
Vitex agnus-castus   p. 410

Chinaberry
☼ ◑ ◓ ✿ MS, LS, CS
Melia azedarach   p. 292

Chinese elm
☼ ◑ ✿ US, MS, LS, CS
Ulmus parvifolia   p. 404

Chinese pistache
☼ ◐ ◑ ✿ US, MS, LS, CS
Pistacia chinensis   p. 329

Crabapple   ∾
☼ ◑ ◑ ✿ US, MS, LS
Malus   p. 288

Crepe myrtle   ∾
☼ ◑ ✿ US, MS, LS, CS
Lagerstroemia indica   p. 267

Eastern red cedar
☼ ◐ ◑ ◑ ✿ US, MS, LS, CS
Juniperus virginiana   p. 264

Goldenrain tree
☼ ◑ ◑ ✿ US, MS, LS, CS
Koelreuteria paniculata   p. 267

Grancy graybeard
☼ ◑ ◑ ✿ US, MS, LS, CS
Chionanthus virginicus   p. 177

Japanese pagoda tree
☼ ◐ ◑ ◑ ✿ US, MS, LS
Sophora japonica   p. 381

Lemon bottlebrush
☼ ◑ ◑ ✿ CS, TS
Callistemon citrinus   p. 160

Live oak
☼ ◑ ✿ LS, CS, TS
Quercus virginiana   p. 350

Longleaf pine
☼ ◑ ◑ ✿ MS, LS, CS, TS
Pinus palustris   p. 331

Maidenhair tree
☼ ◑ ◑ ✿ US, MS, LS, CS
Ginkgo biloba (male)   p. 233

Mesquite
☼ ◑ ✿ MS, LS, CS, TS
Prosopis glandulosa   p. 342

Mexican buckeye
☼ ◐ ◑ ◑ ◑ ✿ MS, LS, CS
Ungnadia speciosa   p. 405

Pawpaw
☼ ◐ ◑ ◑ ✿ US, MS, LS, CS
Asimina triloba   p. 139

Possumhaw
☼ ◐ ◑ ✿ US, MS, LS, CS
Ilex decidua   p. 254

Redbud
☼ ◐ ◑ ◑ ✿ ZONES VARY
Cercis   p. 173

Sawtooth oak
☼ ◑ ✿ US, MS, LS, CS
Quercus acutissima   p. 348

Shumard red oak
☼ ◑ ✿ US, MS, LS, CS
Quercus shumardii   p. 349

Sourwood
☼ ◐ ◑ ✿ US, MS, LS, CS
Oxydendrum arboreum   p. 308

Texas mountain laurel
☼ ◐ ◑ ◑ ✿ LS, CS
Sophora secundiflora   p. 381

Maidenhair tree
Ginkgo biloba

Possumhaw
Ilex decidua

Redbud
Cercis

Texas mountain laurel
Sophora secundiflora

For growing symbol explanations, please see page 38.

Beauty bush
Kolkwitzia amabilis

Firethorn
Pyracantha

Holly
Ilex

Japanese cleyera
Ternstroemia gymnanthera

Pomegranate
Punica granatum

Trumpet tree
☼ ◐ ◌ ❋ TS
Tabebuia   p. 392

Windmill palm
☼ ◐ ◌ ❋ LS, CS, TS
Trachycarpus fortunei   p. 401

Yaupon
☼ ◐ ◌ ❋ MS, LS, CS
Ilex vomitoria   p. 255

SHRUBS

Beautyberry
☼ ◐ ◌ ◌ ❋ US, MS, LS, CS
Callicarpa   p. 160

Beauty bush
☼ ◐ ◌ ◌ ❋ US, MS, LS
Kolkwitzia amabilis   p. 267

Border forsythia
☼ ◌ ◌ ❋ US, MS, LS
Forsythia intermedia   p. 227

Butterfly bush
☼ ◐ ◌ ◌ ❋ ZONES VARY
Buddleia   p. 156

Common sweetshrub
☼ ◐ ◌ ◌ ◌ ❋ US, MS. LS
Calycanthus floridus   p. 161

Dwarf palmetto
☼ ◐ ◌ ❋ MS, LS, CS, TS
Sabal minor   p. 368

Firethorn   ∾
☼ ◌ ❋ ZONES VARY
Pyracantha   p. 347

Flowering quince
☼ ◐ ◌ ◌ ❋ US, MS, LS, CS
Chaenomeles   p. 174

Fuzzy deutzia
☼ ◐ ◌ ◌ ❋ US, MS, LS
Deutzia scabra   p. 205

Holly
☼ ◐ ◌ ❋ ZONES VARY
Ilex   p. 253

Japanese cleyera
☼ ◐ ◌ ◌ ❋ MS, LS, CS, TS
Ternstroemia gymnanthera   p. 395

Juniper
☼ ◐ ◌ ◌ ❋ ZONES VARY
Juniperus   p. 262

Nandina
☼ ◐ ◌ ◌ ◌ ❋ US, MS, LS, CS
Nandina domestica   p. 299

Oakleaf hydrangea
☼ ◐ ◌ ❋ US, MS, LS, CS
Hydrangea quercifolia   p. 251

Oleander, common
☼ ◐ ◌ ◌ ❋ LS, CS, TS
Nerium oleander   p. 302

Pomegranate
☼ ◐ ◌ ◌ ❋ MS, LS, CS, TS
Punica granatum   p. 346

Rosemary
☼ ◌ ❋ MS, LS, CS
Rosmarinus officinalis   p. 366

Rose of Sharon
☼ ◐ ◌ ◌ ❋ US, MS, LS, CS
Hibiscus syriacus   p. 247

Sea grape
☼ ◌ ❋ TS
Coccoloba   p. 187

Spiraea
☼ ◐ ◌ ◌ ❋ ZONES VARY
                                   p. 383

Sumac
☼ ◌ ◌ ❋ ZONES VARY
Rhus   p. 358

Sweet mock orange
☼ ◐ ◌ ❋ US, MS, LS, CS
Philadelphus coronarius   p. 323

Thorny elaeagnus
☼ ◐ ◌ ◌ ❋ US, MS, LS, CS
Elaeagnus pungens   p. 212

Titi
☼ ◐ ◌ ◌ ❋ ALL ZONES
Cyrilla racemiflora   p. 201

Viburnum
☼ ◌ ◌ ❋ ZONES VARY
                                   p. 407

Virginia sweetspire
☼ ◐ ◌ ◌ ❋ US, MS. LS, CS
Itea virginica   p. 260

Wax myrtle
☼ ◐ ◌ ❋ MS, LS, CS, TS
Myrica cerifera   p. 298

Weigela
☼ ◐ ◌ ❋ US, MS, LS
Weigela florida   p. 411

Winter honeysuckle
☼ ◐ ◌ ❋ US, MS, LS, CS
Lonicera fragrantissima   p. 280

Winter jasmine
☼ ◐ ◌ ❋ US, MS, LS, CS
Jasminum nudiflorum   p. 261

Witch hazel
☼ ◐ ◌ ❋ US, MS, LS
Hamamelis   p. 240

ROSES

'Abraham Darby'
☼ ☼ ◌ ❋ ALL ZONES
(English)   p. 363

'Bonica'
☼ ◐ ◌ ❋ ALL ZONES
(Shrub)   p. 363

Rose of Sharon
Hibiscus syriacus

Viburnum

Virginia sweetspire
Itea virginica

Weigela
Weigela florida

'Bonica'
Shrub rose

Plant listings continue ▸

'Carefree Wonder'
Shrub rose

'New Dawn'
Climber rose

'Zéphirine Drouhin'
Bourbon rose

'Perle d'Or'
Polyantha rose

Algerian ivy
Hedera canariensis

'Carefree Wonder'
☼ ◐ ♦ ⚡ ALL ZONES
(Shrub) p. 363

'Duchesse de Brabant'
☼ ◐ ♦ ⚡ MS, LS, CS, TS
(Tea) p. 364

Lady Banks's rose
☼ ◐ ♦ ⚡ LS, CS, TS
Rosa banksiae p. 364

'Lamarque'
☼ ◐ ♦ ⚡ LS, CS, TS
(Tea-Noisette) p. 364

'Louis Philippe'
☼ ◐ ♦ ⚡ MS, LS, CS, TS
(China) p. 364

'Marie van Houtte'
☼ ◐ ♦ ⚡ MS, LS, CS, TS
(Tea) p. 364

'Mary Rose'
☼ ◐ ♦ ⚡ ALL ZONES
(English) p. 363

'Mr. Lincoln'
☼ ◐ ♦ ⚡ ALL ZONES
(Hybrid tea) p. 362

'Mrs. B. R. Cant'
☼ ◐ ♦ ⚡ MS, LS, CS, TS
(Tea) p. 364

'New Dawn'
☼ ◐ ♦ ⚡ ALL ZONES
(Climber) p. 363

'Old Blush'
☼ ◐ ♦ ⚡ ALL ZONES
(China) p. 364

'Perle d'Or'
☼ ◐ ♦ ⚡ ALL ZONES
(Polyantha) p. 362

'Souvenir de la Malmaison'
☼ ◐ ♦ ⚡ ALL ZONES
(Bourbon) p. 364

'The Fairy'
☼ ◐ ♦ ⚡ ALL ZONES
(Polyantha) p. 362

'Zéphirine Drouhin'
☼ ◐ ♦ ⚡ ALL ZONES
(Bourbon) p. 364

GROUND COVERS, VINES

Asian star jasmine
☼ ◐ ● ♦ ♦ ⚡ LS, CS, TS
Trachelospermum asiaticum p. 400

Boston ivy
☼ ◐ ♦ ⚡ US, MS, LS
Parthenocissus tricuspidata p. 313

Bougainvillea
☼ ◐ ♦ ♦ ⚡ CS, TS
p. 153

Cape honeysuckle
☼ ◐ ♦ ⚡ CS, TS
Tecomaria capensis p. 395

Carolina jessamine
☼ ◐ ● ♦ ♦ ⚡ MS, LS, CS
Gelsemium sempervirens p. 231

Common trumpet creeper
☼ ◐ ● ♦ ♦ ⚡ ALL ZONES
Campsis radicans p. 164

Confederate jasmine
☼ ◐ ● ♦ ♦ ⚡ LS, CS, TS p. 400
Trachelospermum jasminoides

Coral vine
☼ ♦ ♦ ⚡ LS, CS, TS
Antigonon leptopus p. 129

Creeping fig
☼ ◐ ● ♦ ⚡ LS, CS, TS
Ficus pumila p. 224

Creeping juniper
☼ ◐ ♦ ♦ ⚡ US, MS, LS, CS
Juniperus horizontalis p. 263

Crossvine
☼ ◐ ♦ ⚡ US, MS, LS, CS
Bignonia capreolata p. 150

English ivy, Algerian ivy
☼ ◐ ● ♦ ♦ ⚡ ZONES VARY
Hedera helix, canariensis p. 241

Fiveleaf akebia
☼ ◐ ● ♦ ⚡ US, MS, LS, CS
Akebia quinata p. 122

Goldmoss sedum
☼ ◐ ♦ ⚡ US, MS, LS, CS
Sedum acre p. 375

Greenbrier smilax
☼ ◐ ♦ ♦ ⚡ MS, LS, CS
Smilax lanceolata p. 379

Lily turf
◐ ● ♦ ♦ ⚡ ZONES VARY
Liriope p. 278

Mondo grass
◐ ● ♦ ♦ ⚡ ZONES VARY
Ophiopogon japonicus p. 278

Morning glory
☼ ♦ ♦ ⚡ ZONES VARY
Ipomoea p. 256

Silver lace vine
☼ ♦ ⚡ US, MS, LS
Polygonum aubertii p. 337

Sweet autumn clematis
☼ ♦ ⚡ US, MS, LS, CS
Clematis dioscoreifolia p. 185

Trumpet honeysuckle
☼ ◐ ♦ ⚡ US, MS, LS, CS
Lonicera sempervirens p. 281

Wedelia
☼ ◐ ♦ ⚡ CS, TS
Wedelia trilobata p. 411

Asian star jasmine
Trachelospermum asiaticum

Morning glory
Ipomoea

Wedelia
Wedelia trilobata

Blue star
Amsonia tabernaemontana

For growing symbol explanations, please see page 38.

Crinum

Daylily
Hemerocallis

Ginger lily, common
Hedychium coronarium

Louisiana iris

PERENNIALS, BULBS

Blackberry lily
☼ ◑ ◐ ⚡ US, MS, LS, CS
Belamcanda   p. 148

Blue star
☼ ◑ ◐ ◐ ⚡ US, MS, LS
Amsonia tabernaemontana   p. 126

Butterfly weed
☼ ◐ ⚡ ALL ZONES
Asclepias tuberosa   p. 139

Canna
☼ ◐ ◐ ◑ ⚡ LS, CS, TS
                              p. 164

Cast-iron plant
◑ ● ◐ ⚡ LS, CS, TS
Aspidistra elatior   p. 140

Coneflower
☼ ◑ ◐ ◐ ⚡ ZONES VARY
Rudbeckia   p. 366

Crinum
☼ ◑ ◐ ◑ ◐ ⚡ ZONES VARY
                              p. 196

Daffodil
☼ ◑ ◐ ⚡ US, MS, LS, CS
Narcissus   p. 299

Daylily
☼ ◑ ◐ ◐ ⚡ ZONES VARY
Hemerocallis   p. 244

Fernleaf yarrow
☼ ◐ ⚡ US, MS, LS
Achillea filipendulina   p. 117

Four o'clock
☼ ◐ ◐ ◐ ⚡ MS, LS, CS, TS
Mirabilis jalapa   p. 295

Gaura
☼ ◐ ◐ ⚡ US, MS, LS, CS
Gaura lindheimeri   p. 230

Ginger lily, common
☼ ◑ ◐ ⚡ MS, LS, CS, TS
Hedychium coronarium   p. 242

Goldenrod
☼ ◑ ◐ ◐ ⚡ US, MS, LS, CS
Solidago and Solidaster   p. 380

Hen and chickens
☼ ◐ ◐ ⚡ US, MS, LS, CS
Sempervivum tectorum   p. 376

Japanese silver grass
☼ ◑ ◐ ◐ ⚡ US, MS, LS, CS
Miscanthus sinensis   p. 295

Louisiana iris
☼ ◑ ◐ ◑ ⚡ US, MS, LS, CS
                              p. 258

Mexican bush sage
☼ ◑ ◐ ◐ ⚡ LS, CS, TS
Salvia leucantha   p. 370

Montbretia
☼ ◑ ◐ ◐ ⚡ US, MS, LS, CS
Crocosmia crocosmiiflora   p. 197

Morea iris
☼ ◑ ◐ ◐ ⚡ LS, CS, TS
Dietes vegeta   p. 208

Parrot lily
☼ ◑ ◐ ◐ ⚡ MS, LS, CS
Alstroemeria psittacina   p. 125

Prickly pear cactus
☼ ◐ ⚡ ZONES VARY
Opuntia   p. 306

Purple coneflower
☼ ◐ ◐ ⚡ US, MS, LS, CS
Echinacea purpurea   p. 211

Purple heart
☼ ◐ ◐ ⚡ MS, LS, CS, TS   p. 377
Setcreasea pallida 'Purple Heart'

Ruellia
☼ ◐ ◐ ◐ ⚡ MS, LS, CS
Ruellia malacosperma   p. 367

Russian sage
☼ ◐ ◐ ⚡ US, MS, LS, CS
Perovskia artriplicifolia   p. 321

Showy sedum
☼ ◑ ◐ ◐ ⚡ US, MS, LS, CS
Sedum spectabile   p. 376

Southern shield fern
◑ ◐ ◐ ◑ ⚡ MS, LS, CS
Thelypteris kunthii   p. 396

Spider lily
☼ ◑ ◐ ⚡ ALL ZONES
Lycoris radiata   p. 282

Stokesia
☼ ◐ ⚡ ALL ZONES
Stokesia laevis   p. 386

Texas star
☼ ◐ ◐ ⚡ MS, LS, CS, TS
Hibiscus coccineus   p. 246

Threadleaf coreopsis
☼ ◐ ⚡ US, MS, LS, CS
Coreopsis verticillata   p. 190

Turk's cap
◑ ● ◐ ◐ ⚡ LS, CS, TS   p. 290
Malvaviscus arboreus drummondii

Wild ageratum
☼ ◑ ◐ ⚡ ALL ZONES
Eupatorium coelestinum   p. 219

Wine cups
☼ ◐ ⚡ US, MS, LS
Callirhoe   p. 160

Yellow flag
☼ ◑ ◐ ⚡ US, MS, LS, CS
Iris pseudacorus   p. 259

Yucca
NEEDS, ZONES VARY
                              p. 413

Prickly pear cactus
Opuntia

Purple coneflower
Echinacea purpurea

Wine cups
Callirhoe

Yellow flag
Iris pseudacorus

SPECIAL SITUATIONS

PLANTS EASY TO PROPAGATE

Azalea
Rhododendron

O nce you grow a beautiful plant, it's only natural to want a few more of the same. Maybe you'd like to give some starts to friends and neighbors. The following plants make it easy. You can propagate them by rooting cuttings (indicated by ♦️⚘), layering (⚘), or separating a sucker from the mother plant (♛). For more information on cuttings, see p. 426; for layering, see p. 439; for suckers, see p. 464.

Boxwood
Buxus

Chaste tree
Vitex agnus-castus

Dwarf flowering almond
Prunus glandulosa

Forsythia

SHRUBS

American beautyberry ♦️⚘ ⚘
☼ ◐ ◌ ◌ ✂ MS, LS, CS
Callicarpa americana p. 160

Angel's trumpet ♦️⚘
☼ ◐ ◌ ◌ ◌ ✂ CS, TS
Brugmansia candida p. 155

Azalea ♦️⚘ ⚘
◌ ◌ ◌ ◌ ✂ ALL ZONES
Rhododendron p. 353

Beauty bush ♦️⚘ ⚘
☼ ◌ ◌ ◌ ✂ US, MS, LS
Kolkwitzia amabilis p. 267

Boxwood ♦️⚘
☼ ◐ ◌ ◌ ✂ ZONES VARY
Buxus p. 157

Chaste tree ♦️⚘ ⚘
☼ ◌ ◌ ✂ ALL ZONES
Vitex agnus-castus p. 410

Confederate rose ♦️⚘ ⚘
☼ ◌ ◌ ✂ LS, CS, TS
Hibiscus mutabilis p. 247

Doublefile viburnum ♦️⚘
☼ ◐ ◌ ✂ US, MS, LS
Viburnum plicatum tomentosum p. 408

Dwarf flowering almond ♦️⚘ ♛
☼ ◌ ◌ ✂ US, MS, LS
Prunus glandulosa p. 344

Flowering quince ♦️⚘ ⚘
☼ ◌ ◌ ✂ US, MS, LS, CS
Chaenomeles p. 174

Forsythia ♦️⚘ ⚘
☼ ◌ ◌ ✂ US, MS, LS
p. 226

French hydrangea ♦️⚘ ⚘ ♛
☼ ◐ ◌ ✂ US, MS, LS, CS
Hydrangea macrophylla p. 251

Fuzzy deutzia ♦️⚘
☼ ◐ ◌ ◌ ✂ US, MS, LS
Deutzia scabra p. 205

Gardenia, common ♦️⚘
☼ ◐ ◌ ◌ ✂ MS, LS, CS
Gardenia jasminoides p. 230

Harlequin glorybower ♛
☼ ◌ ◌ ✂ MS, LS, CS, TS
Clerodendrum trichotomum p. 186

Japanese aucuba ♦️⚘ ⚘
☼ ◐ ◌ ◌ ✂ ALL ZONES
Aucuba japonica p. 142

Japanese kerria ♦️⚘ ⚘ ♛
☼ ◐ ◌ ✂ US, MS, LS
Kerria japonica p. 266

Leatherleaf viburnum ♦️⚘
☼ ◐ ◌ ◌ ✂ US, MS, LS
Viburnum rhytidophyllum p. 408

Nandina ♦️⚘ ♛
☼ ◐ ◌ ◌ ◌ ✂ US, MS, LS, CS
Nandina domestica p. 299

Oakleaf hydrangea ♦️⚘ ⚘ ♛
☼ ◐ ◌ ✂ US, MS, LS, CS
Hydrangea quercifolia p. 251

Oleander, common ♦️⚘
◌ ◌ ◌ ✂ LS, CS, TS
Nerium oleander p. 302

Orange-eye butterfly bush ♦️⚘
☼ ◐ ◌ ◌ ✂ US, MS, LS, CS
Buddleia davidii p. 156

Prickly pear cactus ♦️⚘
☼ ◌ ✂ ZONES VARY
Opuntia p. 306

Pussy willow ♦️⚘
☼ ◌ ◌ ✂ US, MS, LS
Salix discolor p. 369

Red chokeberry ♦️⚘ ♛
☼ ◐ ◌ ◌ ◌ ✂ US, MS, LS
Aronia arbutifolia p. 137

Rice paper plant ♛
☼ ◐ ◌ ◌ ✂ LS, CS, TS
Tetrapanax papyriferus p. 395

Rose ♦️⚘ ⚘
☼ ◐ ◌ ✂ ALL ZONES
Rosa p. 359

Japanese kerria
Kerria japonica

Oakleaf hydrangea
Hydrangea quercifolia

Oleander, common
Nerium oleander

Red chokeberry
Aronia arbutifolia

For growing symbol explanations, please see page 38.

Rose
Rosa

Sumac
Rhus

Virginia sweetspire
Itea virginica

Yellow shrimp plant
Pachystachys lutea

Lantana

Rose of Sharon ✤✿
☼ ◑ ✿ US, MS, LS, CS
Hibiscus syriacus p. 247

Slender deutzia ✤✿ ✾
☼ ◑ ◑ ◑ ✿ US, MS, LS
Deutzia gracilis p. 205

Spanish bayonet ✤✿
☼ ◑ ✿ MS, LS, CS, TS
Yucca aloifolia p. 413

Spiraea ✤✿ ✾
☼ ◑ ◑ ◑ ✿ ZONES VARY
 p. 383

Sumac ✾
☼ ◑ ◑ ✿ ZONES VARY
Rhus p. 358

Sweet mock orange ✤✿ ✾ ✾
☼ ◑ ◑ ◑ ✿ US, MS, LS, CS
Philadelphus coronarius p. 323

Sweet pepperbush ✤✿ ✾
☼ ◑ ◑ ◑ US, MS, LS, CS
Clethra alnifolia p. 186

Tatarian dogwood ✤✿ ✾
☼ ◑ ◑ ✿ US, MS
Cornus alba p. 191

Virginia sweetspire ✤✿ ✾ ✾
☼ ◑ ◑ ◑ ✿ US, MS, LS, CS
Itea virginica p. 260

Weigela florida ✤✿ ✾ ✾
☼ ◑ ◑ ✿ US, MS, LS
 p. 411

Winterberry ✤✿ ✾
☼ ◑ ◑ ◑ ✿ US, MS, LS, CS
Ilex verticillata p. 255

Winter honeysuckle ✤✿ ✾
☼ ◑ ◑ ✿ US, MS, LS, CS
Lonicera fragrantissima p. 280

Winter jasmine ✤✿ ✾ ✾
☼ ◑ ◑ ✿ US, MS, LS, CS
Jasminum nudiflorum p. 261

Yellow shrimp plant ✤✿
☼ ◑ ◑ ✿ CS, TS
Pachystachys lutea p. 309

PERENNIALS

Lantana ✤✿ ✾
☼ ◑ ◑ ✿ MS, LS, CS, TS
 p. 269

Mexican petunia ✤✿
☼ ◑ ◑ ◑ ✿ MS, LS, CS
Ruellia brittoniana p. 367

Night-blooming cereus ✤✿
☼ ◑ ◑ ◑ ✿ TS
Hylocereus undatus p. 252

Perennial hibiscus ✤✿
☼ ◑ ◑ ✿ ALL ZONES
Hibiscus moscheutos p. 247

Purple heart ✤✿
☼ ◑ ✿ MS, LS, CS, TS p. 377
Setcreasea pallida 'Purple Heart'

Texas star ✤✿
☼ ◑ ◑ ✿ MS, LS, CS, TS
Hibiscus coccineus p. 246

Toad lily ✤✿
☼ ◑ ◑ ◑ ✿ US, MS, LS
Tricyrtis p. 401

Walking iris ✤✿ ✾
☼ ◑ ◑ ✿ CS, TS
Neomarica gracilis p. 301

Wedelia ✤✿ ✾
☼ ◑ ✿ CS, TS
Wedelia trilobata p. 411

VINES

American bittersweet ✤✿
☼ ◑ ✿ US, MS, LS
Celastrus scandens p. 171

Boston ivy ✤✿
☼ ◑ ◑ ◑ ✿ US, MS, LS
Parthenocissus tricuspidata p. 313

Carolina jessamine ✤✿ ✾
☼ ◑ ◑ ◑ ◑ ✿ MS, LS, CS
Gelsemium sempervirens p. 231

Coral vine ✤✿ ✾
☼ ◑ ◑ ✿ LS, CS, TS
Antigonon leptopus p. 129

Crossvine ✤✿ ✾ ✾
☼ ◑ ◑ ✿ MS, LS, CS, TS
Bignonia capreolata p. 150

English ivy ✤✿ ✾
☼ ◑ ◑ ◑ ◑ ✿ ALL ZONES
Hedera helix p. 241

Fiveleaf akebia ✤✿
☼ ◑ ◑ ✿ US, MS, LS, CS
Akebia quinata p. 122

Flame vine ✤✿ ✾
☼ ◑ ◑ ✿ CS, TS
Pyrostegia venusta p. 347

Porcelain berry ✤✿
☼ ◑ ◑ ◑ ◑ ✿ US, MS, LS, CS p. 126
Ampelopsis brevipedunculata

Silver lace vine ✤✿
☼ ◑ ◑ ✿ US, MS, LS
Polygonum aubertii p. 337

Trumpet creeper, common ✤✿ ✾
☼ ◑ ◑ ◑ ✿ ALL ZONES
Campsis radicans p. 164

Trumpet honeysuckle ✤✿
☼ ◑ ◑ ✿ US, MS, LS, CS
Lonicera sempervirens p. 281

Virginia creeper ✤✿
☼ ◑ ◑ ◑ ◑ ✿ US, MS, LS, CS
Parthenocissus quinquefolia p. 313

Mexican petunia
Ruellia brittoniana

Texas star
Hibiscus coccineus

Boston ivy
Parthenocissus tricuspidata

Fiveleaf akebia
Akebia quinata

Virginia creeper
Parthenocissus quinquefolia

Epimedium at base of tree

Plants for
GROUND COVER

Artemisia
Artemisia stellerana 'Silver Brocade'

Bergenia

Bishop's weed
Aegopodium podagraria 'Variegatum'

Blue fescue
Festuca ovina 'Glauca'

Rosemary
Rosmarinus officinalis 'Prostratus'

W hile a lawn is often the best ground cover, not every place is suited to one. Some sites are too shady; others too steep. Sometimes you just don't feel like mowing. That's when you should consider the following plants. These ground covers shelter the soil, prevent erosion, and many offer considerable ornamental appeal with striking flowers, foliage, or berries. Some spread by underground runners, or root as they grow. Others sprawl over the soil and become a true ground cover only when planted in masses.

Algerian ivy
☼ ☽ ● ◗ ◗ ✂ CS, TS
Hedera canariensis   p. 241

Artemisia (several)
☼ ◗ ✂ ZONES VARY
                            p. 137

Asian star jasmine
☼ ☽ ● ◗ ◗ ✂ LS, CS, TS
Trachelospermum asiaticum p. 400

Bamboo (dwarf types)
☼ ☽ ◗ ◗ ✂ ZONES VARY
                            p. 143

Bergenia
☽ ◗ ◗ ✂ US, MS, LS
                            p. 149

Big blue liriope
☽ ● ◗ ◗ ✂ ALL ZONES
Liriope muscari   p. 279

Bishop's weed
☼ ☽ ● ◗ ✂ US, MS, LS
Aegopodium podagraria   p. 120

Blue fescue
☼ ◗ ✂ US, MS
Festuca ovina 'Glauca'   p. 223

Carpet bugleweed
☼ ☽ ● ◗ ✂ US, MS, LS
Ajuga reptans   p. 122

Catmint
☼ ☽ ◗ ✂ US, MS, LS
Nepeta faassenii   p. 302

Cerastostigma
☼ ☽ ◗ ✂ US, MS, LS, CS   p. 192
Ceratostigma plumbaginoides

Cinquefoil
☽ ◗ ✂ ZONES VARY
Potentilla (several)   p. 340

Cotoneaster (some)
☼ ◗ ✂ ZONES VARY
                            p. 194

Creeping buttercup
☼ ☽ ● ◗ ✂ US, MS, LS, CS   p. 351
Ranunculus repens 'Pleniflorus'

Creeping liriope
☽ ● ◗ ◗ ✂ ALL ZONES
Liriope spicata   p. 279

Cumberland rosemary
☼ ◗ ✂ MS, LS
Conradina verticillata   p. 189

Dwarf-eared coreopsis
☼ ◗ ✂ US, MS, LS, CS
Coreopsis auriculata 'Nana' p. 190

English ivy
☼ ☽ ● ◗ ◗ ✂ ALL ZONES
Hedera helix   p. 241

Epimedium
☽ ◗ ✂ US, MS, LS
                            p. 213

Evergreen candytuft
☼ ◗ ✂ US, MS, LS
Iberis sempervirens   p. 253

Galax
☽ ● ◗ ✂ US, MS, LS
Galax urceolata   p. 229

Germander
☼ ◗ ✂ US, MS, LS, CS
Teucrium chamaedrys   p. 395

Golden globes
☼ ☽ ◗ ✂ MS, LS, CS
Lysimachia congestiflora   p. 283

Golden star
☽ ◗ ✂ US, MS, LS, CS
Chrysogonum virginianum   p. 180

Grape ivy
☼ ☽ ● ◗ ✂ LS, CS, TS
Cissus rhombifolia   p. 181

Himalayan sweet box
☽ ● ◗ ◗ ✂ US, MS, LS   p. 373
Sarcococca hookerana humilis

Catmint
Nepeta faassenii

Cinquefoil
Potentilla

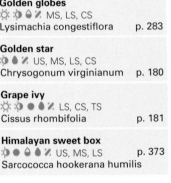

Carpet bugleweed
Ajuga reptans

For growing symbol explanations, please see page 38.

Creeping liriope
Liriope spicata

Epimedium

Germander
Teucrium chamaedrys

Houttuynia cordata 'Variegata'

Lady's-mantle
Alchemilla mollis

Holly fern
☼ ◑ ◖ ⬙ ⬕ LS, CS, TS
Cyrtomium falcatum   p. 201

Hosta
☼ ◑ ● ◖ ⬕ US, MS, LS
                            p. 249

Houttuynia cordata
☼ ◑ ● ◖ ⬙ ⬕ US, MS, LS
                            p. 250

Japanese ardisia
◑ ● ◖ ⬕ LS, CS
Ardisia japonica   p. 136

Japanese pachysandra
◑ ● ◖ ⬕ US, MS, LS
Pachysandra terminalis   p. 309

Jasmine
☼ ◑ ⬙ ⬕ ZONES VARY
Jasminum (some)   p. 261

Juniper
☼ ◑ ⬙ ● ◖ ⬕ ZONES VARY
Juniperus (low-growing)   p. 262

Lady's-mantle
● ◖ ⬕ US, MS, LS
Alchemilla mollis   p. 123

Lamb's ears
☼ ◖ ⬕ US, MS, LS
Stachys byzantina   p. 384

Lavender cotton
☼ ⬙ ◖ ⬕ US, MS, LS
Santolina chamaecyparissus p. 371

Lenten rose
◑ ● ◖ ⬙ ◖ ⬕ US, MS, LS
Helleborus orientalis   p. 244

Lily-of-the-valley
◑ ◖ ⬙ ⬕ US, MS, LS
Convallaria majalis   p. 189

Lungwort
◑ ● ◖ ⬙ ⬕ US, MS, LS
Pulmonaria (several)   p. 345

Marjoram
☼ ◖ ⬕ ZONES VARY
Origanum (several)   p. 307

Mazus
☼ ◑ ◖ ⬕ US, MS, LS, CS
Mazus reptans   p. 292

Memorial rose
☼ ◑ ◖ ⬕ US, MS, LS, CS
Rosa wichuraiana   p. 365

Mondo grass
◑ ● ◖ ⬕ MS, LS, CS, TS
Ophiopogon japonicus   p. 279

Moneywort
☼ ◑ ◖ ⬕ US, MS, LS
Lysimachia nummularia   p. 283

Mountain rockcress
☼ ◖ ⬕ US
Arabis alpina   p. 135

Partridgeberry
● ◖ ⬙ ⬕ US, MS, LS
Mitchella repens   p. 295

Paxistima canbyi
◑ ◑ ◖ ⬕ US, MS
                            p. 314

Periwinkle
☼ ◑ ● ◖ ⬕ ZONES VARY
Vinca   p. 409

Pussy toes
☼ ◖ ⬕ US
Antennaria   p. 128

Rock soapwort
☼ ◖ ⬙ ⬕ US
Saponaria ocymoides   p. 372

Rosemary
☼ ◖ ⬕ MS, LS, CS
Rosmarinus officinalis (low) p. 366

Strawberry geranium
◑ ● ◖ ⬕ MS, LS, CS
Saxifraga stolonifera   p. 373

Snow-in-summer
☼ ◑ ◖ ⬙ ⬕ US, MS, LS
Cerastium tomentosum   p. 172

Spotted dead nettle
◑ ◖ ⬙ ⬕ US, MS, LS
Lamium maculatum   p. 269

Sprenger asparagus
☼ ◑ ◖ ⬕ TS   p. 140
Asparagus densiflorus 'Sprengeri'

St. Johnswort
☼ ◑ ◖ ● ⬕ ZONES VARY
Hypericum (low-growing)   p. 252

Stonecrop
☼ ◑ ◖ ⬙ ⬕ US, MS, LS
Sedum (many)   p. 375

Sweet woodruff
☼ ◑ ◖ ⬙ ● ⬕ US, MS, LS
Galium odoratum   p. 229

Thrift
☼ ◑ ◖ ⬙ ⬕ US, MS, LS, CS
Phlox subulata   p. 325

Thrift, common
☼ ◑ ◖ ⬙ ⬕ US, MS
Armeria maritima   p. 137

Thyme
☼ ◑ ◖ ⬙ ⬕ ZONES VARY
Thymus   p. 397

Wedelia
☼ ◑ ◖ ⬙ ⬕ CS, TS
Wedelia trilobata   p. 411

Wild ginger
◑ ● ◖ ⬙ ● ⬕ US, MS, LS
Asarum canadense   p. 138

Wintercreeper euonymus
☼ ◑ ● ◖ ⬙ ● ⬕ US, MS, LS, CS
Euonymus fortunei   p. 218

Lamb's ears
Stachys byzantina

Mondo grass
Ophiopogon japonicus

Periwinkle, common
Vinca minor

Thrift
Phlox subulata

Wintercreeper euonymus
Euonymus fortunei

VINES
and Vinelike Plants

Bougainvillea and nasturtium

V ines are the garden's most flexible members. Unlike trees and shrubs, which have fairly rigid stems, the stems of most vines can be guided to grow where you want them. You can train them to grow upward or outward on a flat, vertical surface; up and around a tree trunk; or up and over an arbor. Many perform alternative duty as a ground cover.

Some vines climb with tendrils, some use aerial roots, and some employ suction-cuplike holdfasts. Some twine; others cling. Some simply laze about; they only climb if tied to a support. On the following chart, the symbol ❋, indicates vines with showy flowers.

Cape honeysuckle
Tecomaria capensis

Confederate jasmine
Trachelospermum jasminoides

Gold flame honeysuckle
Lonicera heckrottii

Fiveleaf akebia
Akebia quinata

Ivy, English
Hedera helix 'Buttercup'

Madagascar jasmine
Stephanotis floribunda

Passion vine
Passiflora

EVERGREEN

Allamanda, common ❋
☀ ◑ ♦ ✿ TS
Allamanda cathartica — p. 123

Armand clematis ❋
☀ ♦ ✿ MS, LS, CS
Clematis armandii — p. 184

Bleeding heart vine ❋
◑ ♦ ✿ CS, TS
Clerodendrum thomsoniae — p. 186

Bougainvillea ❋
☀ ◑ ♦ ✿ CS, TS
— p. 153

Cape honeysuckle ❋
☀ ◑ ♦ ♦ ✿ CS, TS
Tecomaria capensis — p. 395

Carolina jessamine ❋
☀ ◑ ♦ ♦ ♦ ✿ MS, LS, CS
Gelsemium sempervirens — p. 231

Cat's claw ❋
☀ ◑ ♦ ✿ LS, CS
Macfadyena unguis-cati — p. 283

Confederate jasmine ❋
☀ ♦ ◑ ♦ ✿ LS, CS, TS — p. 400
Trachelospermum jasminoides

Creeping fig
☀ ◑ ♦ ♦ ✿ LS, CS, TS
Ficus pumila — p. 224

Crossvine ❋
☀ ◑ ♦ ✿ ALL ZONES
Bignonia capreolata — p. 150

Cup-of-gold vine ❋
☀ ♦ ✿ TS
Solandra maxima — p. 380

Fatshedera lizei
◑ ♦ ◑ ♦ ✿ LS, CS, TS
— p. 222

Fiveleaf akebia
☀ ◑ ♦ ✿ US, MS, LS, CS
Akebia quinata — p. 122

Flame vine ❋
☀ ◑ ♦ ✿ CS, TS
Pyrostegia venusta — p. 347

Grape ivy
☀ ◑ ♦ ♦ ✿ LS, CS, TS
Cissus rhombifolia — p. 181

Greenbrier smilax
☀ ◑ ♦ ♦ ✿ MS, LS, CS
Smilax lanceolata — p. 379

Herald's trumpet ❋
☀ ◑ ♦ ♦ ✿ TS
Beaumontia grandiflora — p. 147

Honeysuckle ❋
☀ ◑ ♦ ✿ ZONES VARY
Lonicera (several) — p. 280

Ivy
☀ ◑ ♦ ♦ ♦ ✿ ZONES VARY
Hedera — p. 241

Jackson vine
☀ ◑ ♦ ♦ ✿ MS, LS, CS
Smilax smallii — p. 379

Jasmine ❋
☀ ♦ ◑ ♦ ✿ ZONES VARY
Jasminum (several) — p. 261

Madagascar jasmine ❋
◑ ♦ ✿ TS
Stephanotis floribunda — p. 385

Mandevilla 'Alice du Pont' ❋
☀ ◑ ♦ ✿ CS, TS
— p. 291

Mandevilla splendens ❋
☀ ◑ ♦ ✿ CS, TS
— p. 291

Mexican flame vine ❋
☀ ◑ ♦ ✿ CS, TS
Senecio confusus — p. 376

Plant listings continue ▶

96

Pandorea

Night-blooming jasmine ❋
◐ ◌ ◑ ◿ TS
Cestrum nocturnum   p. 173

Pandorea ❋
☼ ◐ ◌ ◑ ◿ CS, TS
                                      p. 311

Passion vine ❋
☼ ◐ ◌ ◑ ◿ ZONES VARY
Passiflora   p. 313

Pink trumpet vine ❋
☼ ◐ ◌ ◑ ◿ CS, TS
Podranea ricasoliana   p. 336

Potato vine ❋
☼ ◐ ◌ ◑ ◑ ◿ CS, TS
Solanum jasminoides   p. 380

Queen's wreath ❋
☼ ◐ ◑ ◿ TS
Petrea volubilis   p. 322

Sky flower ❋
☼ ◐ ◑ ◿ TS
Thunbergia grandiflora   p. 397

Trumpet honeysuckle ❋
☼ ◐ ◌ ◑ ◿ US, MS, LS, CS
Lonicera sempervirens   p. 281

Violet trumpet vine ❋
☼ ◐ ◌ ◑ ◿ CS, TS
Clytostoma callistegioides   p. 187

Wintercreeper euonymus
☼ ◐ ◑ ◌ ◑ ◿ US, MS, LS, CS
Euonymus fortunei   p. 218

DECIDUOUS

Bittersweet
☼ ◑ ◿ US, MS, LS
Celastrus   p. 170

Chilean jasmine ❋
☼ ◐ ◑ ◿ LS, CS, TS
Mandevilla laxa   p. 291

Clematis (most) ❋
☼ ◑ ◿ ZONES VARY
                                      p. 184

Climbing hydrangea ❋
☼ ◐ ◑ ◿ US, MS, LS
Hydrangea anomala   p. 251

Coral vine ❋
☼ ◑ ◌ ◿ LS, CS, TS
Antigonon leptopus   p. 129

Costa Rican nightshade ❋
☼ ◐ ◌ ◑ ◑ ◿ TS
Solanum wendlandii   p.380

Dutchman's pipe
☼ ◐ ◌ ◑ ◑ ◿ US, MS, LS, CS
Aristolochia durior   p. 137

Grape
☼ ◑ ◿ ZONES VARY
                                      p. 236

Japanese hydrangea vine ❋
◐ ◑ ◿ US, MS, LS   p. 374
Schizophragma hydrangeoides

Kiwi vine
☼ ◐ ◑ ◌ ◿ LS, CS
Actinidia deliciosa   p. 118

Maypop ❋
☼ ◑ ◌ ◿ ALL ZONES
Passiflora incarnata   p. 314

Morning glory ❋
☼ ◑ ◌ ◿ ZONES VARY
Ipomoea   p. 256

Porcelain berry
☼ ◐ ◑ ◌ ◿ US, MS, LS, CS   p. 126
Ampelopsis brevipedunculata

Rose ❋
☼ ◐ ◑ ◿ ZONES VARY
Rosa (climbers)   p. 359

Silver lace vine ❋
☼ ◑ ◿ US, MS, LS
Polygonum aubertii   p. 337

Trumpet creeper, common ❋
☼ ◐ ◑ ◌ ◿ ALL ZONES
Campsis radicans   p. 164

Virginia creeper
☼ ◐ ◑ ◌ ◿ US, MS, LS, CS
Parthenocissus quinquefolia p. 313

Wisteria ❋
☼ ◑ ◌ ◿ US, MS, LS, CS
                                      p. 412

ANNUAL

Bean, scarlet runner ❋
☼ ◑ ◿ ALL ZONES
                                      p. 146

Cup-and-saucer vine ❋
☼ ◑ ◿ ALL ZONES
Cobaea scandens   p. 187

Cypress vine ❋
☼ ◑ ◌ ◿ ALL ZONES
Ipomoea quamoclit   p. 257

Garden nasturtium ❋
☼ ◐ ◑ ◌
Tropaeolum majus   p. 402

Hyacinth bean ❋
☼ ◑ ◌ ◿ LS, CS, TS
Dolichos lablab   p. 209

Moonflower ❋
☼ ◑ ◌ ◿ ALL ZONES
Ipomoea alba   p. 256

Morning glory ❋
☼ ◑ ◌ ◿ ZONES VARY
Ipomoea (some)   p. 256

Sweet pea ❋
☼ ◑ ◌ ◿ ALL ZONES
Lathyrus odoratus   p. 270

Clematis

Morning glory
Ipomoea

Virginia creeper
Parthenocissus quinquefolia

Wisteria

Garden nasturtium
Tropaeolum majus

Sky flower
Thunbergia grandiflora

Violet trumpet vine
Clytostoma callistegioides

Trumpet honeysuckle
Lonicera sempervirens

For growing symbol explanations, please see page 38.

Nandina
Nandina domestica

Plants for
HEDGES AND SCREENS

When Robert Frost wrote, "Good fences make good neighbors," he might have added, "And so do hedges and screens." Shrubs and trees with dense foliage from top to bottom can block unwanted views, create privacy, edge a walk or path, lessen the effects of noise and wind, and provide a pleasant background for flowering plants. Some plants, indicated by the symbol ♦♦♦, can be sheared into formal hedges.

Japanese barberry
Berberis thunbergii

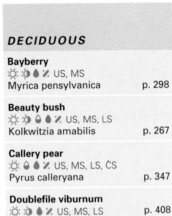

Flowering quince
Chaenomeles

Rose
Rosa 'Showbiz'

Russian olive
Elaeagnus angustifolia

DECIDUOUS

Bayberry
☼ ◑ ◐ ✂ US, MS
Myrica pensylvanica   p. 298

Beauty bush
☼ ◑ ◐ ◐ ✂ US, MS, LS
Kolkwitzia amabilis   p. 267

Callery pear
☼ ◐ ◐ ✂ US, MS, LS, CS
Pyrus calleryana   p. 347

Doublefile viburnum
☼ ◑ ◐ ✂ US, MS, LS   p. 408
Viburnum plicatum tomentosum

English oak
☼ ◐ ✂ US, MS, LS
Quercus robur   p. 349

European beech   ♦♦♦
☼ ◑ ◐ ✂ US, MS
Fagus sylvatica   p. 222

European hornbeam   ♦♦♦
☼ ◑ ◐ ✂ US, MS, LS
Carpinus betulus   p. 166

Fiveleaf aralia   ♦♦♦
☼ ◑ ◐ ◐ ◐ ◐ ✂ US, MS, LS, CS
Acanthopanax sieboldianus p. 115

Flowering quince   ♦♦♦
☼ ◐ ◐ ✂ US, MS, LS, CS
Chaenomeles   p. 174

Hardy orange   ♦♦♦
☼ ◐ ✂ ALL ZONES
Poncirus trifoliata   p. 184

Hawthorn
☼ ◐ ✂ ZONES VARY
Crataegus   p. 195

Hedge maple   ♦♦♦
☼ ◑ ◐ ◐ ✂ US, MS, LS
Acer campestre   p. 116

Japanese barberry   ♦♦♦
☼ ◑ ◐ ◐ ✂ US, MS, LS, CS
Berberis thunbergii   p. 149

Osage orange
☼ ◐ ◐ ✂ US, MS, LS
Maclura pomifera   p. 284

'PJM' rhododendron   ♦♦♦
☼ ◐ ◐ ◐ ✂ US, MS, LS   p. 355
Rhododendron mucronulatum 'PJM'

Rose
☼ ◑ ◐ ✂ ZONES VARY
Rosa (shrub)   p. 359

Russian olive
☼ ◑ ◐ ◐ ✂ US, MS
Elaeagnus angustifolia   p. 212

Spiraea
☼ ◑ ◐ ◐ ✂ ZONES VARY
                                       p. 383

Weigela
☼ ◑ ◐ ✂ US, MS, LS
Weigela florida   p. 411

Winged euonymus (some)   ♦♦♦
☼ ◑ ◐ ◐ ◐ ✂ US, MS, LS
Euonymus alata   p. 218

Winter honeysuckle   ♦♦♦
☼ ◑ ◐ ✂ US, MS, LS, CS
Lonicera fragrantissima   p. 280

EVERGREEN

Arborvitae   ♦♦♦
☼ ◑ ◐ ◐ ✂ ZONES VARY
Thuja   p. 396

Banana shrub
☼ ◑ ◐ ✂ LS, CS
Michelia figo   p. 294

Bamboo
☼ ◑ ◐ ◐ ✂ ZONES VARY
                                       p. 143

Barberry   ♦♦♦
☼ ◑ ◐ ◐ ◐ ✂ US, MS, LS, CS
Berberis (some)   p. 149

Bay   ♦♦♦
☼ ◑ ◐ ◐ ✂ LS, CS, TS
Laurus nobilis   p. 271

Spiraea

Beauty bush
Kolkwitzia amabilis

Boxwood
Buxus

Canadian hemlock
Tsuga canadensis

For growing symbol explanations, please see page 38.

Cape honeysuckle
Tecomaria capensis

Chinese hibiscus
Hibiscus rosa-sinensis

Elaeagnus, thorny
Elaeagnus pungens

Glossy abelia
Abelia grandiflora

Holly
Ilex

Boxwood ♦♦♦
☼ ◐ ● ◗ ∥ ZONES VARY
Buxus   p. 157

Camellia
◐ ● ◗ ∥ US, MS, LS, CS
                         p. 161

Canadian hemlock ♦♦♦
☼ ◐ ● ∥ US, MS, LS
Tsuga canadensis   p. 402

Cape honeysuckle
☼ ◐ ● ◗ ∥ CS, TS
Tecomaria capensis   p. 395

Carolina cherry laurel ♦♦♦
☼ ◐ ● ◗ ∥ US, MS, LS, CS
Prunus caroliniana   p. 342

Chinese fringe
☼ ◐ ● ∥ MS, LS, CS
Loropetalum chinense   p. 281

Chinese hibiscus
☼ ● ◗ ∥ CS, TS
Hibiscus rosa-sinensis   p. 247

Colorado blue spruce
☼ ◐ ● ◗ ∥ US, MS
Picea pungens   p. 327

Elaeagnus (some)
☼ ◐ ● ◗ ∥ ZONES VARY
                         p. 212

Firethorn ♦♦♦
☼ ● ◗ ∥ ZONES VARY
Pyracantha   p. 347

Gardenia, common
☼ ◐ ● ◗ ∥ MS, LS, CS
Gardenia jasminoides   p. 230

Germander ♦♦♦
☼ ● ◗ ∥ US, MS, LS, CS
Teucrium chamaedrys   p. 395

Glossy abelia ♦♦♦
☼ ◐ ● ∥ US, MS, LS
Abelia grandiflora   p. 114

Holly ♦♦♦
☼ ◐ ● ◗ ∥ ZONES VARY
Ilex   p. 253

Indian hawthorn ♦♦♦
☼ ◐ ● ◗ ∥ LS, CS
Raphiolepis indica   p. 351

Japanese anise
◐ ● ◗ ∥ LS, CS
Illicium anisatum   p. 255

Japanese aucuba
☼ ◐ ● ◗ ∥ ALL ZONES
Aucuba japonica   p. 142

Japanese black pine
☼ ● ◗ ∥ US, MS, LS, CS
Pinus thunbergiana   p. 331

Japanese cleyera ♦♦♦
☼ ◐ ● ◗ ∥ MS, LS, CS, TS
Ternstroemia gymnanthera p. 395

Japanese pittosporum ♦♦♦
☼ ◐ ● ◗ ∥ LS, CS, TS
Pittosporum tobira   p. 329

Juniper ♦♦♦
☼ ◐ ● ◗ ∥ ZONES VARY
Juniperus (shrub, columnar) p. 262

Lemon bottlebrush ♦♦♦
☼ ● ◗ ∥ CS, TS
Callistemon citrinus   p. 160

Leyland cypress ♦♦♦
☼ ● ◗ ∥ US, MS, LS, CS
Cupressocyparis leylandii p. 198

Mahonia ♦♦♦
NEEDS, ZONES VARY
                         p. 288

Nandina
☼ ◐ ● ● ◗ ∥ US, MS, LS, CS
Nandina domestica   p. 299

Natal plum ♦♦♦
☼ ◐ ● ∥ TS
Carissa macrocarpa   p. 166

Oleander, common
☼ ● ◗ ◈ ∥ LS, CS, TS
Nerium oleander   p. 302

Orange jessamine
☼ ◐ ● ∥ CS, TS
Murraya paniculata   p. 297

Osmanthus (several) ♦♦♦
☼ ◐ ● ◗ ∥ ZONES VARY
                         p. 307

Pineapple guava
☼ ● ∥ LS, CS, TS
Feijoa sellowiana   p. 223

Podocarpus ♦♦♦
☼ ◐ ● ◗ ∥ ZONES VARY
                         p. 336

Privet ♦♦♦
☼ ◐ ● ◈ ∥ ZONES VARY
Ligustrum (some)   p. 274

Texas sage
☼ ● ∥ MS, LS, CS
Leucophyllum frutescens p. 273

Viburnum (several)
☼ ◐ ● ∥ ZONES VARY
                         p. 407

Wax myrtle ♦♦♦
☼ ◐ ● ● ◗ ∥ MS, LS, CS, TS
Myrica cerifera   p. 298

White pine
☼ ● ◗ ∥ US, MS
Pinus strobus   p. 331

Yellow bells
☼ ● ◗ ∥ CS, TS
Tecoma stans   p. 394

Yew ♦♦♦
☼ ◐ ● ● ◗ ◈ ∥ US, MS
Taxus   p. 394

Leyland cypress
Cupressocyparis leylandii

Pineapple guava
Feijoa sellowiana

Privet
Ligustrum

Viburnum

Oleander, common
Nerium oleander

TREES

Woodland at Butchart Gardens

Crepe myrtle
Lagerstroemia indica

Desert willow
Chilopsis linearis

Fringe tree
Chionanthus

T rees are the backbone of a garden, whether they shade the
yard, buffer the wind, frame the house, or flaunt blazing autumn
foliage. You'll save yourself time, money, and trouble by selecting trees that
are long-lived, strong-wooded, and not susceptible to insects and disease.
Lawn trees should have deep roots. Trees that shade decks, terraces, and
parking areas shouldn't drop messy fruits. Always consider a tree's mature size; here, small trees
are up to 30 feet tall; medium trees 30 to 60 feet; and large trees are taller than 60 feet (mature
sizes may vary somewhat across the South).

Japanese maple
Acer palmatum 'Dissectum'

SMALL TREES
Deciduous

Amur maple
☼ ◐ ◌ ◑ ✄ US, MS, LS
Acer ginnala   p. 116

Brazilian butterfly tree
☼ ◐ ◌ ◑ ✄ TS
Bauhinia forficata   p. 145

Carolina silver bell
◐ ◑ ✄ US, MS, LS
Halesia carolina   p. 240

Chaste tree
☼ ◑ ◌ ✄ ALL ZONES
Vitex agnus-castus   p. 410

Crabapple
☼ ◑ ◌ ✄ US, MS, LS
Malus   p. 288

Crepe myrtle
☼ ◑ ✄ US, MS, LS, CS
Lagerstroemia indica   p. 267

Desert willow
☼ ◑ ✄ MS, LS, CS
Chilopsis linearis   p. 176

Flowering dogwood
☼ ◐ ◑ ✄ US, MS, LS, CS
Cornus florida   p. 192

Franklin tree
☼ ◐ ◑ ✄ US, MS, LS
Franklinia alatamaha   p. 227

Fringe tree
☼ ◑ ◌ ✄ US, MS, LS, CS
Chionanthus   p. 177

Harlequin glorybower
◐ ◑ ✄ MS, LS, CS, TS
Clerodendrum trichotomum p. 186

Hawthorn
☼ ◑ ✄ ZONES VARY
Crataegus   p. 195

Hong Kong orchid tree
☼ ◑ ◌ ◑ ✄ TS
Bauhinia blakeana   p. 145

Japanese flowering apricot
☼ ◑ ◌ ◑ ✄ US, MS, LS, CS
Prunus mume   p. 344

Japanese maple
☼ ◑ ◌ ◑ ✄ US, MS, LS, CS
Acer palmatum   p. 116

Japanese persimmon
☼ ◑ ◌ ✄ US, MS, LS, CS
Diospyros kaki   p. 322

Japanese stewartia
☼ ◑ ◌ ✄ US, MS
Stewartia pseudocamellia   p. 386

Jerusalem thorn
☼ ◑ ◌ ✄ CS, TS
Parkinsonia aculeata   p. 312

Juneberry
☼ ◐ ◌ ◑ ✄ US, MS, LS
Amelanchier arborea   p. 126

Kousa dogwood
☼ ◑ ◌ ✄ US, MS, LS
Cornus kousa   p. 192

Paperbark maple
☼ ◐ ◌ ◑ ✄ US, MS
Acer griseum   p. 116

Persian parrotia
☼ ◑ ◌ ◑ ✄ US, MS, LS
Parrotia persica   p. 312

Purple orchid tree
☼ ◑ ◌ ✄ TS
Bauhinia variegata   p. 145

Redbud
☼ ◐ ◑ ◌ ✄ ZONES VARY
Cercis   p. 173

Silky stewartia
☼ ◐ ◑ ◌ ✄ MS, LS, CS
Stewartia malacodendron   p. 386

Silver trumpet tree
☼ ◐ ◑ ✄ TS
Tabebuia argentea   p. 392

Smoke tree
☼ ◑ ◌ ✄ US, MS, LS
Cotinus coggygria   p. 194

Hawthorn
Crataegus

Hong Kong orchid tree
Bauhinia blakeana

Japanese maple
Acer palmatum

For growing symbol explanations, please see page 38.

Paperbark maple
Acer griseum

Smoke tree
Cotinus coggygria

Snowbell
Styrax

Bottlebrush, lemon
Callistemon citrinus

Giant thevetia
Thevetia thevetioides

Snowbell
☀ ◐ ♦ ✂ ZONES VARY
Styrax   p. 389

Sourwood
☀ ◐ ♦ ✂ US, MS, LS, CS
Oxydendrum arboreum   p. 308

Star magnolia
☀ ◐ ♦ ✂ US, MS, LS, CS
Magnolia stellata   p. 287

Sweet acacia
☀ ♦ ✂ TS
Acacia farnesiana   p. 115

Texas mountain laurel
☀ ◐ ♦ ♦ ✂ LS, CS
Sophora secundiflora   p. 381

Trident maple
☀ ◐ ♦ ♦ ✂ US, MS, LS
Acer buergeranum   p. 116

Yellow wood
☀ ♦ ✂ US, MS, LS
Cladrastis lutea   p. 184

SMALL TREES
Evergreen

Bottlebrush
☀ ♦ ✂ CS, TS
Callistemon   p. 160

Citrus
☀ ♦ ✂ CS, TS
                                            p. 181

Cordyline
☀ ♦ ✂ CS, TS
Cordyline australis   p. 190

Fern podocarpus
☀ ◐ ♦ ♦ ✂ TS
Podocarpus gracilior   p. 336

Giant thevetia
☀ ♦ ♦ ✂ TS
Thevetia thevetioides   p. 396

Glossy privet
☀ ◐ ♦ ♦ ✂ LS, CS, TS
Ligustrum lucidum   p. 275

Gold medallion tree
☀ ♦ ♦ ✂ TS
Cassia leptophylla   p. 168

'Little Gem' Southern magnolia
☀ ◐ ♦ ♦ ✂ US, MS, LS, CS
Magnolia grandiflora   p. 285

Loquat
☀ ◐ ♦ ♦ ✂ LS, CS, TS
Eriobotrya japonica   p. 216

Palms (some)
NEEDS, ZONES VARY
                                            p. 310

Sweet bay
☀ ◐ ♦ ✂ US, MS, LS, CS
Magnolia virginiana   p. 287

Sweet olive
☀ ◐ ♦ ♦ ✂ LS, CS, TS
Osmanthus fragrans   p. 307

MEDIUM TREES
Deciduous

Birch
☀ ♦ ♦ ✂ ZONES VARY
Betula   p. 149

Callery pear
☀ ♦ ♦ ✂ US, MS, LS, CS
Pyrus calleryana   p. 347

Chinese pistache
☀ ♦ ✂ US, MS, LS, CS
Pistacia chinensis   p. 329

Chinese tallow
☀ ♦ ♦ ✂ LS, CS, TS
Sapium sebiferum   p. 372

Chitalpa
☀ ♦ ✂ MS, LS, CS
Chitalpa tashkentensis   p. 177

Handkerchief tree
☀ ◐ ♦ ✂ US, MS, LS
Davidia involucrata   p. 204

Honey locust
☀ ◐ ♦ ✂ US, MS, LS
Gleditsia triacanthos   p. 234

Ironwood
☀ ◐ ♦ ♦ ✂ US, MS, LS, CS
Carpinus caroliniana   p. 166

Jacaranda
☀ ♦ ✂ CS, TS
Jacaranda mimosifolia   p. 260

Japanese pagoda tree
☀ ◐ ♦ ✂ US, MS, LS
Sophora japonica   p. 381

Katsura tree
☀ ◐ ♦ ✂ US, MS
Cercidiphyllum japonicum   p. 173

Koelreuteria
☀ ♦ ♦ ✂ ZONES VARY
                                            p. 266

Littleleaf linden
☀ ♦ ✂ US, MS
Tilia cordata   p. 398

Mesquite
☀ ♦ ✂ MS, LS, CS, TS
Prosopis glandulosa   p. 342

Oriental magnolia (many)
☀ ◐ ♦ ✂ ZONES VARY
Magnolia   p. 284

Texas persimmon
☀ ◐ ♦ ✂ ALL ZONES
Diospyros texana   p. 209

Willow
☀ ♦ ✂ US, MS, LS
Salix   p. 368

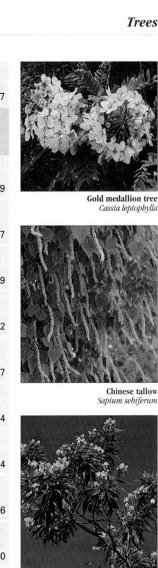

Gold medallion tree
Cassia leptophylla

Chinese tallow
Sapium sebiferum

Chitalpa
Chitalpa tashkentensis

Littleleaf linden
Tilia cordata

Plant listings continue ▶

Yoshino flowering cherry
Prunus yedoensis

Bailey acacia
Acacia baileyana

Canary Island date palm
Phoenix canariensis

Eastern red cedar
Juniperus virginica

White ash
Fraxinus americana

Yoshino flowering cherry
☼ ◐ ● ⚡ US, MS, LS
Prunus yedoensis   p. 343

MEDIUM TREES
Evergreen

Bailey acacia
☼ ● ⚡ CS, TS
Acacia baileyana   p. 114

Chinese elm
☼ ● ⚡ US, MS, LS, CS
Ulmus parvifolia   p. 404

Eastern red cedar
☼ ◐ ● ● ⚡ US, MS, LS, CS
Juniperus virginiana   p. 264

Holly
☼ ◐ ● ⚡ ZONES VARY
Ilex (many)   p. 253

Loblolly bay
☼ ◐ ● ● ⚡ LS, CS, TS
Gordonia lasianthus   p. 235

Palms (some)
NEEDS, ZONES VARY
                                    p. 310

Southern sweet bay
☼ ◐ ● ⚡ MS, LS, CS, TS
Magnolia virginiana australis p. 287

LARGE TREES
Deciduous

American beech
☼ ◐ ● ● ⚡ US, MS, LS, CS
Fagus grandifolia   p. 222

Ash, White and Green
☼ ● ● ⚡ US, MS, LS, CS
Fraxinus   p. 227

Bald cypress
☼ ● ● ● ● ⚡ US, MS, LS, CS
Taxodium distichum   p. 394

Black gum
☼ ◐ ● ● ● ⚡ US, MS, LS, CS
Nyssa sylvatica   p. 304

Catalpa
☼ ◐ ● ● ⚡ US, MS, LS, CS
                                    p. 169

Dawn redwood
☼ ● ⚡ US, MS, LS   p. 294
Metasequoia glyptostroboides

Hackberry
☼ ◐ ● ● ⚡ US, MS, LS
Celtis   p. 171

Japanese zelkova
☼ ◐ ● ● ⚡ US, MS, LS
Zelkova serrata   p. 415

Kentucky coffee tree
☼ ● ● ⚡ US, MS, LS
Gymnocladus dioica   p. 236

Maidenhair tree
☼ ● ● ⚡ US, MS, LS, CS
Ginkgo biloba   p. 233

Oak
☼ ● ⚡ ZONES VARY
Quercus (many)   p. 348

Pecan
☼ ● ● ⚡ US, MS, LS, CS
Carya illinoensis   p. 167

Red maple
☼ ◐ ● ● ⚡ US, MS, LS, CS
Acer rubrum   p. 117

River birch
☼ ● ● ⚡ US, MS, LS, CS
Betula nigra   p. 150

Shagbark hickory
☼ ● ● ⚡ US, MS, LS, CS
Carya ovata   p. 167

Sugar maple
☼ ◐ ● ● ⚡ US, MS, LS
Acer saccharum   p. 117

Sweet gum
☼ ● ● ⚡ ZONES VARY
Liquidambar   p. 277

Sycamore
☼ ● ● ⚡ US, MS, LS, CS
Platanus occidentalis   p. 332

Tulip poplar
☼ ● ⚡ US, MS, LS, CS
Liriodendron tulipifera   p. 278

LARGE TREES
Evergreen

Camphor tree
☼ ◐ ● ● ⚡ CS, TS
Cinnamomum camphora   p. 181

Canadian hemlock
☼ ● ● ⚡ US, MS, LS
Tsuga canadensis   p. 402

Cedar
☼ ● ⚡ ZONES VARY
Cedrus   p. 170

Laurel oak
☼ ● ⚡ CS, TS
Quercus laurifolia   p. 349

Live oak
☼ ● ⚡ LS, CS, TS
Quercus virginiana   p. 350

Pines (most)
☼ ● ● ⚡ ZONES VARY
Pinus   p. 329

Southern magnolia
☼ ◐ ● ⚡ US, MS, LS, CS
Magnolia grandiflora   p. 285

Spruce
☼ ● ● ● ⚡ US, MS
Picea   p. 327

Maidenhair tree
Ginkgo biloba

Red maple
Acer rubrum

Camphor tree
Cinnamomum camphora

Sweet gum
Liquidambar

For growing symbol explanations, please see page 38.

Holly
Ilex

Laurel oak
Quercus laurifolia

Loquat
Eriobotrya japonica

Southern magnolia
Magnolia grandiflora

Canadian hemlock
Tsuga canadenses

EVERGREEN PLANTS

No doubt about it—Southerners prefer evergreens. We figure if we spend good money for a plant, we deserve a full twelve months of green. Whether broad-leafed or needle-leafed plants, evergreens form the backbone of the garden, leaving the seasonal show to annuals, perennials, and deciduous shrubs and trees. Of course, many evergreens also provide the garden with colorful flowers and foliage. The following list includes just a few of the myriad evergreens that grow well in our region.

BROAD-LEAFED TREES

Bailey acacia
☼ ◔ ◑ ⚡ CS, TS
Acacia baileyana   p. 114

Carolina cherry laurel
☼ ◑ ◕ ⚡ US, MS, LS, CS
Prunus caroliniana   p. 342

Glossy privet
☼ ◔ ◑ ◕ ⚡ LS, CS, TS
Ligustrum lucidum   p. 275

Holly
☼ ◔ ◑ ⚡ ZONES VARY
Ilex (several)   p. 253

Laurel oak
☼ ◑ ◕ ⚡ ALL ZONES
Quercus laurifolia   p. 349

Live oak
☼ ◑ ◕ ⚡ LS, CS, TS
Quercus virginiana   p. 350

Loblolly bay
☼ ◔ ◑ ◕ ⚡ LS, CS, TS
Gordonia lasianthus   p. 235

Loquat
☼ ◔ ◑ ⚡ LS, CS, TS
Eriobotrya japonica   p. 216

Palms (some)
NEEDS, ZONES VARY
                                    p. 310

Southern magnolia
☼ ◔ ◑ ⚡ US, MS, LS, CS
Magnolia grandiflora   p. 285

NEEDLE-LEAFED TREES

American arborvitae
☼ ◔ ◑ ◕ ⚡ US, MS
Thuja occidentalis   p. 396

Canadian hemlock
☼ ◔ ◑ ⚡ US, MS, LS
Tsuga canadensis   p. 402

Cedar
☼ ◔ ◑ ⚡ ZONES VARY
Cedrus   p. 170

Cypress
☼ ◔ ◑ ⚡ ZONES VARY
Cupressus   p. 199

Douglas fir
☼ ◔ ◑ ◕ ⚡ US, MS
Pseudotsuga menziesii   p. 345

Eastern red cedar
☼ ◔ ◑ ◕ ⚡ US, MS, LS, CS
Juniperus virginiana   p. 264

Fir
☼ ◔ ◑ ◕ ⚡ ZONES VARY
Abies   p. 114

Japanese cryptomeria
☼ ◑ ◕ ⚡ US, MS, LS
Cryptomeria japonica   p. 197

Leyland cypress
☼ ◑ ◕ ⚡ US, MS, LS, CS
Cupressocyparis leylandii   p. 198

Pine
☼ ◑ ◕ ⚡ ZONES VARY
Pinus (many)   p. 329

Spruce
☼ ◔ ◑ ◕ ⚡ US, MS
Picea   p. 327

White cedar
☼ ◔ ◑ ⚡ US, MS, LS
Chamaecyparis thyoides   p. 174

BROAD-LEAFED SHRUBS

Anise tree
◔ ◑ ◕ ◑ ⚡ ZONES VARY
Illicium   p. 255

Plant listings continue ▶

Cedar, Atlas
Cedrus atlantica

Eastern red cedar
Juniperus virginiana

Leyland cypress
Cupressocyparis leylandii

Pine, white
Pinus strobus

Anise tree (Florida anise)
Illicium floridanum

Camellia

Chinese fringe
Loropetalum chinense

Glossy abelia
Abelia grandiflora

Japanese aucuba
Aucuba japonica

Japanese fatsia
Fatsia japonica

Banana shrub
☼ ◐ ◕ ⬥ ⚡ LS, CS
Michelia figo   p. 294

Barberry
☼ ◐ ◕ ⬥ ⚡ US, MS, LS, CS
Berberis   p. 149

Boxwood
☼ ◐ ● ⬥ ⚡ ZONES VARY
Buxus   p. 157

Camellia
◐ ◕ ⬥ ⚡ US, MS, LS, CS
                                 p. 161

Chinese fringe
☼ ◐ ⬥ ⚡ MS, LS, CS
Loropetalum chinense   p. 281

Citrus
☼ ⬥ ⚡ CS, TS
                                 p. 181

Coastal leucothoe
◐ ● ⬥ ◕ ⚡ US, MS, LS
Leucothoe axillaris   p. 273

Firethorn
☼ ◕ ⬥ ⚡ ZONES VARY
Pyracantha   p. 347

Florida leucothoe
☼ ◕ ⬥ ◕ ⚡ MS, LS, CS
Agarista populifolia   p. 120

Gardenia
☼ ◐ ⬥ ⚡ MS, LS, CS
                                 p. 230

Germander
☼ ⬥ ⚡ US, MS, LS, CS
Teucrium chamaedrys   p. 395

Glossy abelia
☼ ◐ ⬥ ⚡ US, MS, LS
Abelia grandiflora   p. 114

Golden dewdrop
☼ ⬥ ◕ ⚡ TS
Duranta repens   p. 210

Holly
☼ ◐ ◕ ⬥ ⚡ ZONES VARY
Ilex (most)   p. 253

Indian hawthorn
☼ ◐ ◕ ⬥◕ ⚡ LS, CS
Raphiolepis indica   p. 351

Ixora
☼ ⬥ ⚡ CS, TS
                                 p. 260

Japanese andromeda
◐ ⬥ ◕ ⚡ US, MS, LS
Pieris japonica   p. 328

Japanese aucuba
☼ ◐ ● ⬥ ◕ ⚡ ALL ZONES
Aucuba japonica   p. 142

Japanese cleyera
☼ ◐ ● ⬥ ⚡ MS, LS, CS, TS
Ternstroemia gymnanthera   p. 395

Japanese fatsia
◐ ● ⬥ ⚡ LS, CS, TS
Fatsia japonica   p. 222

Japanese pittosporum
☼ ◐ ◕ ⬥ ⚡ LS, CS, TS
Pittosporum tobira   p. 329

Mahonia
NEEDS AND ZONES VARY
                                 p. 288

Mexican orange
☼ ◐ ⬥ ⚡ LS, CS, TS
Choisya ternata   p. 178

Mountain laurel
☼ ◐ ◕ ⬥ ◕ ⚡ US, MS, LS, CS
Kalmia latifolia   p. 265

Nandina
☼ ◐ ● ◕ ⬥ ● ⚡ US, MS, LS, CS
Nandina domestica   p. 299

Natal plum
☼ ◐ ⬥ ◕ ⚡ TS
Carissa macrocarpa   p. 166

Oleander, common
☼ ◕ ⬥ ◕ ⚡ LS, CS, TS
Nerium oleander   p. 302

Osmanthus (several)
☼ ◐ ◕ ⬥ ⚡ ZONES VARY
                                 p. 307

Pineapple guava
☼ ◕ ⬥ ⚡ LS, CS, TS
Feijoa sellowiana   p. 223

Rhododendron and azalea
◐ ◕ ● ◕ ⬥ ⚡ ZONES VARY
Rhododendron (some)   p. 353

Sago palm
◕ ⬥ ⚡ CS, TS
Cycas revoluta   p. 199

Sweet bay
☼ ◐ ⬥ ◕ ⚡ US, MS, LS, CS
Magnolia virginiana   p. 287

Texas mountain laurel
☼ ◐ ◕ ⬥ ◕ ⚡ LS, CS
Sophora secundiflora   p. 381

Texas sage
☼ ◕ ⬥ ⚡ MS, LS, CS
Leucophyllum frutescens   p. 273

Thorny elaeagnus
☼ ◐ ◕ ⬥ ◕ ⚡ US, MS, LS, CS
Elaeagnus pungens   p. 212

Viburnum (several)
☼ ◐ ◕ ⬥ ⚡ ZONES VARY
                                 p. 407

Wax myrtle
☼ ◐ ◕ ⬥ ◕ ⚡ MS, LS, CS, TS
Myrica cerifera   p. 298

Winter daphne
◕ ◕ ⬥ ◕ ⚡ MS, LS
Daphne odora   p. 203

Mahonia

Rhododendron

Sweet bay
Magnolia virginiana

Juniper
Juiperus

Carpet bugleweed
Ajuga reptans

For growing symbol explanations, please see page 38.

Asian star jasmine
Trachelospermum asiaticum

English ivy
Hedera helix

Liriope

Japanese pachysandra
Pachysandra terminalis

Mondo grass
Ophiopogon japonicus

NEEDLE-LEAFED SHRUBS

Juniper
☼ ◐ ◗ ♦ ✄ ZONES VARY
Juniperus (several)   p. 262

Mugho pine
☼ ◗ ♦ ✄ US, MS
Pinus mugo mugo   p. 330

Plum yew
☼ ◐ ◗ ♦ ✄ US, MS, LS, CS
Cephalotaxus   p. 172

Yew
☼ ◐ ● ◗ ♦ ♦ ✄ US, MS
Taxus   p. 394

GROUND COVERS

Carpet bugleweed
☼ ◐ ● ◗ ✄ US, MS, LS
Ajuga reptans   p. 122

Algerian ivy
☼ ◗ ● ◗ ✄ CS, TS
Hedera canariensis   p. 241

Asian star jasmine
☼ ◗ ● ◗ ♦ ✄ LS, CS, TS
Trachelospermum asiaticum p. 400

Cotoneaster (several)
☼ ◗ ✄ ZONES VARY
          p. 194

English ivy
☼ ◗ ● ◗ ♦ ✄ ALL ZONES
Hedera helix   p. 241

Evergreen candytuft
☼ ● ◗ ✄ US, MS, LS
Iberis sempervirens   p. 253

Liriope
◗ ● ◗ ♦ ✄ ZONES VARY
          p. 278

Japanese ardisia
◗ ● ◗ ✄ LS, CS
Ardisia japonica   p. 136

Japanese pachysandra
◗ ● ◗ ✄ US, MS, LS
Pachysandra terminalis   p. 309

Juniper
☼ ◗ ● ◗ ♦ ✄ ZONES VARY
Juniperus (prostrate forms) p. 262

Mazus
☼ ◗ ● ◗ ✄ US, MS, LS, CS
Mazus reptans   p. 292

Mondo grass
◗ ● ◗ ♦ ◗ ✄ MS, LS, CS, TS
Ophiopogon japonicus   p. 279

Periwinkle
◗ ● ◗ ✄ ZONES VARY
Vinca   p. 409

VINES

Allamanda, common
☼ ◗ ♦ ✄ TS
Allamanda cathartica   p. 123

Armand clematis
☼ ◗ ✄ MS, LS, CS
Clematis armandii   p. 184

Bougainvillea
☼ ◗ ● ◗ ♦ ✄ CS, TS
          p. 153

Cape honeysuckle
☼ ◗ ● ◗ ✄ CS, TS
Tecomaria capensis   p. 395

Carolina jessamine
☼ ◗ ● ◗ ♦ ✄ MS, LS, CS
Gelsemium sempervirens p. 231

Confederate jasmine
☼ ◗ ● ◗ ♦ ✄ LS, CS, TS p. 400
Trachelospermum jasminoides

Creeping fig
☼ ◗ ● ◗ ✄ LS, CS, TS
Ficus pumila   p. 224

Crossvine
☼ ◗ ◗ ✄ ALL ZONES
Bignonia capreolata   p. 150

Cup-of-gold vine
☼ ◗ ✄ TS
Solandra maxima   p. 380

Fiveleaf akebia
☼ ◗ ● ◗ ✄ US, MS, LS, CS
Akebia quinata   p. 122

Flame vine
☼ ◗ ♦ ✄ CS, TS
Pyrostegia venusta   p. 347

Jasmine
☼ ◗ ◗ ✄ ZONES VARY
Jasminum (some)   p. 261

Passion vine
☼ ◗ ♦ ✄ ZONES VARY
Passiflora (most)   p. 313

Potato vine
☼ ◗ ◗ ♦ ◗ ✄ CS, TS
Solanum jasminoides   p. 380

Smilax
☼ ◗ ◗ ♦ ✄ MS, LS, CS
          p. 379

Trumpet honeysuckle
☼ ◗ ◗ ♦ ✄ US, MS, LS, CS
Lonicera sempervirens   p. 281

Violet trumpet vine
☼ ◗ ♦ ✄ CS, TS
Clytostoma callistegioides p. 187

Wintercreeper euonymus
☼ ◗ ● ◗ ♦ ✄ US, MS, LS, CS
Euonymus fortunei   p. 218

Periwinkle
Vinca

Allamanda, common
Allamanda cathartica

Creeping fig
Ficus pumila

Passion vine
Passiflora

Trumpet honeysuckle
Lonicera sempervirens

SOUTHERN NATIVES

American beech
Fagus grandifolia

Interest in native plants has skyrocketed in recent years. Here's just a few of the plants that are native to the South. But before you rush out to create a completely native garden, keep in mind a couple of points. First, the South is a big, big place. Just because a plant is native to the Southeast doesn't mean it will grow well in the Southwest. Second, native plants aren't always easier to grow than exotics. The key to any successful garden is choosing the right plant for the right spot. The encyclopedia entries for each plant will help you do just that.

Live oak
Quercus virginiana

Eastern redbud
Cercis canadensis

Flowering dogwood
Cornus florida

Grancy graybeard
Chionanthus virginicus

Juneberry
Amelanchier arborea

TREES

American beech
☀ ◑ ◐ ◆ ✓ US, MS, LS, CS
Fagus grandifolia   p. 222

American holly
☀ ◑ ◆ ✓ US, MS, LS, CS
Ilex opaca   p. 254

Bald cypress
☀ ◆ ◆ ◆◆ ✓ US, MS, LS, CS
Taxodium distichum   p. 394

Black gum
☀ ◑ ◆ ◆◆ ✓ US, MS, LS, CS
Nyssa sylvatica   p. 304

Cabbage palm
☀ ◑ ◆ ✓ LS, CS, TS
Sabal palmetto   p. 368

Canadian hemlock
☀ ◑ ◆ ✓ US, MS, LS
Tsuga canadensis   p. 402

Carolina silver bell
◑ ◆ ✓ US, MS, LS
Halesia carolina   p. 240

Eastern redbud
☀ ◑ ◆ ✓ US, MS, LS, CS
Cercis canadensis   p. 173

Eastern red cedar
☀ ◑ ◆ ◆ ✓ US, MS, LS, CS
Juniperus virginiana   p. 264

Flowering dogwood
☀ ◑ ◆ ✓ US, MS, LS, CS
Cornus florida   p. 192

Grancy graybeard
☀ ◑ ◆ ✓ US, MS, LS, CS
Chionanthus virginicus   p. 171

Ironwood
☀ ◑ ◆ ◆ ✓ US, MS, LS, CS
Carpinus caroliniana   p. 166

Juneberry
☀ ◑ ◆ ◆ ✓ US, MS, LS
Amelanchier arborea   p. 126

Live oak
☀ ◆ ✓ LS, CS, TS
Quercus virginiana   p. 350

Loblolly bay
☀ ◑ ◆ ◆ ✓ LS, CS, TS
Gordonia lasianthus   p. 235

Loblolly pine
☀ ◆ ◆ ✓ US, MS, LS, CS
Pinus taeda   p. 331

Longleaf pine
☀ ◆ ◆ ✓ MS, LS, CS, TS
Pinus palustris   p. 331

Mesquite
☀ ◆ ✓ MS, LS, CS, TS
Prosopis glandulosa   p. 342

Pecan
☀ ◆ ◆ ✓ US, MS, LS, CS
Carya illinoensis   p. 167

Red buckeye
◑ ◆ ◆ ✓ US, MS, LS, CS
Aesculus pavia   p. 120

Red maple
☀ ◑ ◆ ◆ ✓ US, MS, LS, CS
Acer rubrum   p. 117

Red oak
☀ ◆ ✓ US, MS, LS
Quercus rubra   p. 349

River birch
☀ ◆ ◆ ✓ US, MS, LS, CS
Betula nigra   p. 150

River birch
Betula nigra

Sassafras
Sassafras albidum

Sourwood
Oxydendrum arboreum

For growing symbol explanations, please see page 38.

Southern sugar maple
Acer barbatum

American beautyberry
Callicarpa americana

Mountain laurel
Kalmia latifolia

Sassafras
☼ ◑ ◔ ✻ US, MS, LS, CS
Sassafras albidum   p. 373

Shumard red oak
☼ ◑ ◔ ✻ US, MS, LS, CS
Quercus shumardii   p. 349

Sourwood
☼ ◑ ◔ ✻ US, MS, LS, CS
Oxydendrum arboreum   p. 308

Southern magnolia
☼ ◑ ◔ ✻ US, MS, LS, CS
Magnolia grandiflora   p. 285

Southern sugar maple
☼ ◑ ◔ ◑ ✻ MS, LS, CS
Acer barbatum   p. 115

Sweet bay
◑ ◔ ✻ US, MS, LS, CS
Magnolia virginiana   p. 287

Sweet gum
☼ ◑ ◔ ◑ ✻ ALL ZONES
Liquidambar styraciflua   p. 277

Sycamore
☼ ◑ ◔ ✻ US, MS, LS, CS
Platanus occidentalis   p. 332

Texas persimmon
☼ ◑ ◔ ✻ ALL ZONES
Diospyros texana   p. 209

Tulip poplar
☼ ◔ ✻ US, MS, LS, CS
Liriodendron tulipifera   p. 278

Virginia pine
☼ ◔ ◑ ✻ US, MS, LS, CS
Pinus virginiana   p. 331

Western soapberry
☼ ◔ ✻ US, MS, LS, CS
Sapindus drummondii   p. 372

White oak
☼ ◔ ✻ US, MS, LS, CS
Quercus alba   p. 348

Willow oak
☼ ◔ ✻ US, MS, LS, CS
Quercus phellos   p. 349

Yellow wood
☼ ◔ ✻ US, MS, LS
Cladrastis lutea   p. 184

SHRUBS

American beautyberry
☼ ◑ ◔ ◑ ✻ MS, LS, CS
Callicarpa americana   p. 160

Bottlebrush buckeye
◑ ◔ ◑ ✻ US, MS, LS, CS
Aesculus parviflora   p. 120

Buttonbush
☼ ◑ ◔ ◑ ◑ ✻ ALL ZONES
Cephalanthus occidentalis   p. 172

Coontie
◑ ◔ ◑ ✻ CS, TS
Zamia pumila   p. 414

Florida flame azalea
☼ ◑ ◔ ◑ ◑ ◔ ✻ US, MS, LS, CS
Rhododendron austrinum   p. 356

Heart's-a-bustin'
☼ ◑ ◔ ◑ ✻ US, MS, LS, CS
Euonymus americana   p. 218

Indigo bush
☼ ◔ ◑ ✻ US, MS, LS, CS
Amorpha fruticosa   p. 126

Inkberry
☼ ◑ ◔ ✻ ALL ZONES
Ilex glabra   p. 254

Mountain laurel
☼ ◑ ◔ ◑ ✻ US, MS, LS, CS
Kalmia latifolia   p. 265

Oakleaf hydrangea
☼ ◑ ◔ ◑ ✻ US, MS, LS, CS
Hydrangea quercifolia   p. 251

Piedmont azalea
☼ ◑ ◔ ◑ ◑ ◔ ✻ US, MS, LS, CS
Rhododendron canescens   p. 356

Plumleaf azalea
◑ ◔ ◑ ◑ ◔ ✻ US, MS, LS, CS
Rhododendron prunifolium   p. 357

Possumhaw
☼ ◔ ✻ US, MS, LS, CS
Ilex decidua   p. 254

Red chokeberry
☼ ◑ ◔ ◑ ◑ ✻ US, MS, LS
Aronia arbutifolia   p. 137

Red yucca
☼ ◔ ✻ US, MS, LS, CS
Hesperaloe parviflora   p. 246

Staghorn sumac
☼ ◔ ◑ ✻ US, MS, LS
Rhus typhina   p. 358

Sweet pepperbush
◑ ◔ ◑ ✻ US, MS, LS, CS
Clethra alnifolia   p. 186

Texas sage
☼ ◔ ✻ MS, LS, CS
Leucophyllum frutescens   p. 273

Virginia sweetspire
☼ ◑ ◔ ◑ ◑ ✻ US, MS, LS, CS
Itea virginica   p. 260

Wax myrtle
☼ ◑ ◔ ◑ ✻ MS, LS, CS, TS
Myrica cerifera   p. 298

Witch hazel, common
☼ ◑ ◔ ✻ US, MS, LS, CS
Hamamelis virginiana   p. 240

Yaupon
☼ ◔ ◑ ✻ MS, LS, CS
Ilex vomitoria   p. 255

Oakleaf hydrangea
Hydrangea quercifolia

Plumleaf azalea
Rhododendron prunifolium

Possumhaw
Ilex decidua

Red chokeberry
Aronia arbutifolia

Sweet pepperbush
Clethra alnifolia

Plant listings continue ▶

107

Bloodroot
Sanguinaria canadensis

Blue phlox
Phlox divaricata

Cardinal flower
Lobelia cardinalis

Goldenrod
Solidago

Hardy begonia
Begonia grandis

PERENNIALS, ANNUALS

Bloodroot
☼ ◐ ◖ ◖ ◖ ⚡ US, MS, LS
Sanguinaria canadensis   p. 369

Blue phlox
◐ ◖ ⚡ US, MS, LS, CS
Phlox divaricata   p. 325

Blue star
☼ ◐ ◖ ◖ ⚡ US, MS, LS
Amsonia tabernaemontana   p. 126

Butterfly weed
☼ ◖ ◖ ◖ ⚡ ALL ZONES
Asclepias tuberosa   p. 139

Cardinal flower
◐ ● ◖ ◖ ◖ ⚡ US, MS, LS, CS
Lobelia cardinalis   p. 278

Carolina bush pea
☼ ◐ ◖ ⚡ US, MS, LS
Thermopsis caroliniana   p. 396

Foamflower
◐ ● ◖ ⚡ US, MS, LS
Tiarella   p. 397

Galax
◐ ● ◖ ⚡ US, MS, LS
Galax urceolata   p. 229

Gaura
☼ ◖ ◖ ⚡ US, MS, LS, CS
Gaura lindheimeri   p. 230

Goldenrod
☼ ◐ ◖ ⚡ US, MS, LS, CS
Solidago and Solidaster   p. 380

Hardy begonia
◐ ● ◖ ◖ ⚡ ALL ZONES
Begonia grandis   p. 147

Hinckley's columbine
☼ ◐ ◖ ⚡ US, MS, LS
Aquilegia hinckleyana   p. 134

Indian blanket
☼ ◖ ⚡ ALL ZONES
Gaillardia pulchella   p. 229

Indian pink
◐ ● ◖ ⚡ US, MS, LS, CS
Spigelia marilandica   p. 382

Joe-Pye weed
☼ ◐ ◖◖ ⚡ US, MS, LS, CS
Eupatorium purpureum   p. 219

May apple
◐ ● ◖ ◖ ⚡ US, MS, LS, CS
Podophyllum peltatum   p. 336

Purple coneflower
☼ ◖ ⚡ US, MS, LS, CS
Echinacea purpurea   p. 211

Virginia bluebells
◐ ● ◖ ⚡ US, MS, LS
Mertensia virginica   p. 293

Wake robin
◐ ● ◖ ⚡ US, MS, LS
Trillium   p. 401

Wild columbine
☼ ◐ ◖ ⚡ US, MS, LS
Aquilegia canadensis   p. 134

Wild ginger
◐ ● ◖ ◖◖ ⚡ ZONES VARY
Asarum   p. 138

Wine cups
☼ ◖ ⚡ US, MS, LS
Callirhoe involucrata   p. 160

VINES

Carolina jessamine
☼ ◐ ◖ ◖ ⚡ MS, LS, CS
Gelsemium sempervirens   p. 231

Crossvine
☼ ◐ ◖ ⚡ ALL ZONES
Bignonia capreolata   p. 150

Greenbrier smilax
☼ ◐ ◖ ◖ ⚡ MS, LS, CS
Smilax lanceolata   p. 379

Maypop
☼ ◖ ◖ ⚡ ALL ZONES
Passiflora incarnata   p. 314

Trumpet creeper, common
☼ ◐ ◖ ◖ ⚡ ALL ZONES
Campsis radicans   p. 164

Trumpet honeysuckle
☼ ◐ ◖ ⚡ US, MS, LS, CS
Lonicera sempervirens   p. 281

Virginia creeper
☼ ◐ ● ◖ ⚡ US, MS, LS, CS
Parthenocissus quinquefolia p. 313

FRUITS

American persimmon
☼ ◖ ◖ ⚡ US, MS, LS, CS
Diospyros virginiana   p. 322

Blackberry
☼ ◖ ⚡ US, MS, LS, CS
        p. 150

Blueberry
☼ ◖◖ ⚡ ZONES VARY
Vaccinium (some)   p. 151

Mayhaw
☼ ◐ ◖ ⚡ MS, LS, CS
Crataegus opaca   p. 196

Muscadine grape
☼ ◖ ⚡ ZONES VARY
        p. 238

Pawpaw
☼ ◐ ● ◖ ⚡ US, MS, LS, CS
Asimina triloba   p. 139

Virginia bluebells
Mertensia virginica

Trumpet creeper, common
Campsis radicans

Trumpet honeysuckle
Lonicera sempervirens

Blueberry
Vaccinium

Muscadine grapes

For growing symbol explanations, please see page 38.

Big blue lily turf
Liriope muscari

Canna

Cosmos, common
Cosmos bipinnatus

Four o'clock
Mirabilis jalapa

Foxglove, common
Digitalis purpurea

Coleus
Coleus hybridus

SOUTHERN HERITAGE PLANTS

Certain plants can define a region. They shape its character, infiltrate its culture, influence its aesthetics, and even affect its industry. Daily life wouldn't be the same without them. This chart represents a thin slice of the pie of the cherished Southern plants we grew up with, handed down, and expect to see in our beds and borders today. When you encounter one in either a fancy garden or a simple swept yard, you know you're in the South.

Ginger lily, common
Hedychium coronarium

Larkspur
Consolida ambigua

Lenten rose
Helleborus orientalis

Money plant
Lunaria annua

ANNUALS, PERENNIALS

African violet
☼ ◑ ◕ 🌢 🗲 INDOORS
Saintpaulia ionantha — p. 368

Bee balm
☼ ◑ 🌢 🌢 🗲 US, MS, LS
Monarda didyma — p. 296

Big blue lily turf
◑ ◕ 🌢 🌢 🗲 ZONES VARY
Liriope muscari — p. 279

Bird of paradise
☼ ◑ 🌢 🗲 CS, TS
Strelitzia reginae — p. 388

Blackberry lily
☼ ◑ 🌢 🌢 🗲 US, MS, LS, CS
Belamcanda chinensis — p. 148

Canna
☼ 🌢 🌢 🗲 LS, CS, TS
— p. 164

Carpet bugleweed
☼ ◑ ◕ 🌢 🗲 US, MS, LS
Ajuga reptans — p. 122

Chinese ground orchid
◑ 🌢 🗲 US, MS, LS, CS
Bletilla striata — p. 151

Coleus
☼ ◑ 🌢 🌢 🗲 ALL ZONES
Coleus hybridus — p. 188

Cosmos, common
☼ 🌢 🌢 🗲 ALL ZONES
Cosmos bipinnatus — p. 194

Dame's rocket
☼ ◑ 🌢 🗲 ALL ZONES
Hesperis matronalis — p. 246

Four o'clock
☼ 🌢 🌢 🗲 ALL ZONES
Mirabilis jalapa — p. 295

Foxglove, common
◑ 🌢 🌢 🗲 US, MS, LS, CS
Digitalis purpurea — p. 208

Giant reed
☼ 🌢 🌢 🗲 ALL ZONES
Arundo donax — p. 138

Ginger lily, common
☼ ◑ 🌢 🌢 🗲 MS, LS, CS, TS
Hedychium coronarium — p. 242

Hen and chickens
☼ 🌢 🌢 🗲 US, MS, LS, CS
Sempervivum tectorum — p. 376

Horsetail
☼ ◑ 🌢 🌢 🗲 ALL ZONES
Equisetum hyemale — p. 214

Larkspur
☼ 🌢 🌢 🗲 ALL ZONES
Consolida ambigua — p. 189

Lemon daylily
☼ 🌢 🌢 🗲 US, MS, LS, CS
Hemerocallis lilio-asphodelus — p. 245

Lenten rose
◑ ◕ 🌢 🌢 ◕ 🗲 US, MS, LS
Helleborus orientalis — p. 244

Lily-of-the-valley
◑ 🌢 ◕ 🌢 🗲 US, MS, LS
Convallaria majalis — p. 189

Mexican petunia
☼ ◑ 🌢 🌢 🗲 MS, LS, CS
Ruellia brittoniana — p. 367

Mondo grass
◑ ◕ 🌢 🌢 🗲 MS, LS, CS, TS
Ophiopogon japonicus — p. 279

Money plant
☼ ◑ 🌢 🌢 🗲 US, MS, LS, CS
Lunaria annua — p. 281

Moraea iris
☼ ◑ 🌢 🌢 🌢 🗲 LS, CS, TS
Dietes vegeta — p. 208

Plant listings continue ▸

Perennial hibiscus
Hibiscus moscheutos

Perennial phlox
Phlox paniculata

Spanish moss
Tillandsia usneoides

Spider flower
Cleome hasslerana

Sundrops
Oenothera fruticosa

Moses-in-the-cradle
☼ ◑ ◐ ⬥ ⚡ CS, TS
Rhoeo spathecea   p. 357

Night-blooming cereus
☼ ◑ ◐ ◐ ⚡ TS
Hylocereus undatus   p. 252

Opium poppy
☼ ◐ ◐ ⚡ ALL ZONES
Papaver somniferum   p. 312

Orange daylily
☼ ◑ ◐ ⚡ ALL ZONES
Hemerocallis fulva   p. 244

Pampas grass
☼ ◐ ◐ ◐⬥ ⚡ MS, LS, CS, TS
Cortaderia selloana   p. 192

Parrot lily
☼ ◑ ◐ ◐⚡ MS, LS, CS
Alstroemaria psittacina   p. 125

Peony 'Festiva Maxima'
☼ ◐ ◐⚡ US, MS, LS
Paeonia   p. 310

Perennial hibiscus
☼ ◐ ◐⬥ ⚡ ALL ZONES
Hibiscus moscheutos   p. 247

Perennial phlox
☼ ◑ ◐⚡ US, MS, LS, CS
Phlox paniculata   p. 325

Perilla
☼ ◑ ◐ ◐⚡ ALL ZONES
Perilla frutescens   p. 321

Purple heart
☼ ◐ ⚡ MS, LS, CS, TS   p. 377
Setcreasea pallida 'Purple Heart'

Ribbon grass
☼ ◑ ◐ ◐ ◐⬥ ⚡ US, MS, LS, CS
Phalaris arundinacea   p. 323

Snake plant
◑ ◐ ⚡ TS
Sansevieria trifasciata   p. 371

Soapwort
☼ ◐ ◐⚡ US, MS, LS, CS
Saponaria officinalis   p. 372

Spanish moss
◑ ◐ ◐ ◐⚡ LS, CS, TS
Tillandsia usneoides   p. 398

Spider flower
☼ ◐ ◐⚡ ALL ZONES
Cleome hasslerana   p. 185

Spiderwort
☼ ◑ ◐ ◐⬥ ⚡ US, MS, LS, CS
Tradescantia virginiana   p. 401

Strawberry geranium
◑ ◐ ◐⚡ MS, LS, CS
Saxifraga stolonifera   p. 373

Sundrops
☼ ◑ ◐⚡ US, MS, LS
Oenothera fruticosa   p. 304

Sweet pea
☼ ◐ ◐⬥ ⚡ ALL ZONES
Lathyrus odoratus   p. 270

Sweet William
☼ ◐ ◐⚡ US, MS, LS
Dianthus barbatus   p. 206

Texas bluebonnet
☼ ◐ ◐⚡ MS, LS, CS
Lupinus texensis   p. 282

Texas star
☼ ◐ ◐ ◐⬥ ⚡ MS, LS, CS, TS
Hibiscus coccineus   p. 246

Thrift
☼ ◑ ◐ ◐⚡ US, MS, LS, CS
Phlox subulata   p. 325

Tuberose
☼ ◑ ◐ ◐⚡ ALL ZONES
Polianthes tuberosa   p. 337

Walking iris
☼ ◐ ◐ ◐⚡ CS, TS
Neomarica gracilis   p. 301

Zebra grass
☼ ◑ ◐ ◐ ◐⚡ US, MS, LS, CS   p. 295
Miscanthus sinensis 'Zebrinus'

Zinnia, common
☼ ◐ ◐⚡ ALL ZONES
Zinnia elegans   p. 416

BULBS, BULBLIKE PLANTS

Crinum
☼ ◑ ◐ ◐ ◐⬥ ◐⚡ ZONES VARY   p. 196

Daffodil
☼ ◑ ◐ ◐⚡ US, MS, LS, CS
Narcissus   p. 299

Elephant's ear
◐ ◐⬥ ◐⚡ LS, CS, TS
Colocasia esculenta   p. 189

Grape hyacinth, common
☼ ◐ ◐ ◐⚡ US, MS, LS
Muscari botryoides   p. 298

Hardy gladiolus
☼ ◐⚡ MS, LS, CS, TS
Gladiolus byzantinum   p. 233

Iris
NEEDS, ZONES VARY
                                   p. 257

Lily-of-the-Nile
☼ ◐ ◐ ◐⚡ LS, CS, TS
Agapanthus africanus   p. 120

Magic lily
☼ ◐ ◐ ◐⚡ US, MS, LS, CS
Lycoris squamigera   p. 283

Montbretia
☼ ◑ ◐ ◐⚡ US, MS, LS, CS
Crocosmia crocosmiiflora   p. 197

Sweet William
Dianthus barbatus

Texas bluebonnet
Lupinus texensis

Zinnia, common
Zinnia elegans

Crinum

Hardy gladiolus
Gladiolus byzantinum

For growing symbol explanations, please see page 38.

Spider lily
Lycoris radiata

Angel's trumpet
Brugmansia arborea

French hydrangea
Hydrangea macrophylla

Japanese kerria
Kerria japonica

Camellia
Camellia japonica

Oxalis crassipes
☼ ◑ ◐ ✿ MS, LS, CS
p. 308

Pregnant onion
☼ ◐ ◈ ✿ TS
Ornithogalum caudatum   p. 307

Rain lily
☼ ◐ ✿ ZONES VARY
Zephyranthes   p. 415

Society garlic
☼ ◐ ✿ LS, CS, TS
Tulbaghia violacea   p. 402

Spider lily
☼ ◑ ◐ ✿ ALL ZONES
Lycoris radiata   p. 282

Spring star flower
☼ ◑ ◐ ✿ US, MS, LS, CS
Ipheion uniflorum   p. 256

Star of Bethlehem
☼ ◐ ◈ ✿ US, MS, LS, CS
Ornithogalum umbellatum   p. 307

Saint Joseph's lily
☼ ◑ ◐ ✿ LS, CS, TS
Hippeastrum johnsonii   p. 248

Summer snowflake
☼ ◑ ◐ ✿ US, MS, LS, CS
Leucojum aestivum   p. 273

SHRUBS

American beautyberry
☼ ◑ ◐ ◈ ✿ MS, LS, CS
Callicarpa americana   p. 160

Angel's trumpet
☼ ◑ ◐ ◈ ◈ ✿ LS, CS, TS
Brugmansia   p. 155

Baby's breath spiraea
☼ ◑ ◐ ◈ ✿ US, MS, LS, CS
Spiraea thunbergii   p. 383

Banana shrub
☼ ◐ ◈ ✿ LS, CS
Michelia figo   p. 294

Beauty bush
☼ ◑ ◐ ◈ ✿ US, MS, LS
Kolkwitzia amabilis   p. 267

Border forsythia
☼ ◐ ◈ ✿ US, MS, LS
Forsythia intermedia   p. 227

Bridal wreath
☼ ◑ ◐ ◈ ✿ US, MS, LS
Spiraea prunifolia 'Plena'   p. 383

Butcher's broom
◑ ◐ ◈ ◈ ✿ MS, LS, CS
Ruscus   p. 367

Camellia, common
◑ ◐ ◈ ✿ US, MS, LS, CS
Camellia japonica   p. 162

China rose
☼ ◑ ◐ ◈ ✿ ALL ZONES
Rosa chinensis   p. 364

Chinese hibiscus
☼ ◐ ◈ ✿ CS, TS
Hibiscus rosa-sinensis   p. 247

Confederate rose
☼ ◐ ◐ ✿ LS, CS, TS
Hibiscus mutabilis   p. 247

Coontie
◑ ◐ ◈ ✿ CS, TS
Zamia pumila   p. 414

Flowering quince
☼ ◐ ◈ ✿ US, MS, LS, CS
Chaenomeles   p. 174

French hydrangea
☼ ◑ ◐ ✿ US, MS, LS, CS
Hydrangea macrophylla   p. 251

Fuzzy deutzia
☼ ◑ ◐ ◈ ✿ US, MS, LS, CS
Deutzia scabra   p. 205

Harison's yellow rose
☼ ◑ ◐ ✿ US, MS, LS
Rosa harisonii   p. 365

Japanese kerria
☼ ◑ ◐ ✿ US, MS, LS
Kerria japonica   p. 266

Lady Banks's rose
☼ ◑ ◐ ✿ LS, CS, TS
Rosa banksiae   p. 364

Lantana, common
☼ ◐ ◈ ✿ MS, LS, CS, TS
Lantana camara   p. 270

Lemon verbena
☼ ◐ ✿ LS, CS, TS
Aloysia triphylla   p. 124

Musk rose
☼ ◑ ◐ ✿ ALL ZONES
Rosa moschata   p. 365

Nandina
☼ ◑ ◐ ◐ ◈ ✿ US, MS, LS, CS
Nandina domestica   p. 299

Oleander, common
☼ ◐ ◈ ✿ LS, CS, TS
Nerium oleander   p. 302

Orange-eye butterfly bush
☼ ◑ ◐ ✿ US, MS, LS, CS
Buddleia davidii   p. 156

Pomegranate
☼ ◐ ◈ ✿ MS, LS, CS, TS
Punica granatum   p. 346

Prickly pear
☼ ◐ ◈ ✿ ALL ZONES
Opuntia humifusa   p. 306

Rice paper plant
☼ ◑ ◐ ✿ LS, CS, TS
Tetrapanax papyriferus   p. 395

Plant listings continue ▶

Nandina
Nandina domestica

Oleander, common
Nerium oleander

Orange-eye butterfly bush
Buddleia davidii

Weigela
Weigela florida

Chinese tallow
Sapium sebiferum

Crabapple
Malus

Crepe myrtle
Lagerstroemia indica

Live oak
Quercus virginiana

Mimosa
Albizia julibrissin

Rose of Sharon
☼ ◐ ◑ ◉ ⚡ US, MS, LS, CS
Hibiscus syriacus   p. 247

Sago palm
◐ ◉ ⚡ CS, TS
Cycas revoluta   p. 199

Sweet mock orange
☼ ◐ ◉ ◉ ⚡ US, MS, LS, CS
Philadelphus coronarius   p. 323

Sweetshrub, common
☼ ◐ ● ◉ ◉ ⚡ US, MS, LS
Calycanthus floridus   p. 161

Van Houtte spiraea
☼ ◐ ◉ ◉ ⚡ US, MS, LS, CS
Spiraea vanhouttei   p. 383

Weigela
☼ ◐ ◉ ⚡ US, MS, LS
Weigela florida   p. 411

TREES

Cabbage palmetto
☼ ◐ ◉ ⚡ LS, CS, TS
Sabal palmetto   p. 368

Catalpa, common
☼ ◐ ◉ ◉ ⚡ US, MS, LS, CS
Catalpa bignonioides   p. 169

Chaste tree
☼ ◉ ◉ ⚡ ALL ZONES
Vitex agnus-castus   p. 410

Chinaberry
☼ ◉ ◉ ⚡ MS, LS, CS
Melia azedarach   p. 292

Chinese parasol tree
☼ ◐ ◉ ◉ ⚡ MS, LS, CS, TS
Firmiana simplex   p. 226

Chinese tallow
☼ ◉ ◉ ⚡ LS, CS, TS
Sapium sebiferum   p. 372

Crabapple
☼ ◉ ◉ ⚡ US, MS, LS
Malus   p. 288

Crepe myrtle
☼ ◉ ⚡ US, MS, LS, CS
Lagerstroemia indica   p. 267

Empress tree
☼ ◐ ◉ ◉ ⚡ US, MS, LS
Paulownia tomentosa   p. 314

Grancy graybeard
☼ ◉ ◉ ⚡ US, MS, LS, CS
Chionanthus virginicus   p. 177

Live oak
☼ ◉ ⚡ LS, CS, TS
Quercus virginiana   p. 350

Mimosa
☼ ◐ ◉ ⚡ US, MS, LS, CS
Albizia julibrissin   p. 122

Pecan
☼ ◉ ◉ ⚡ US, MS, LS, CS
Carya illinoensis   p. 167

Southern magnolia
☼ ◐ ◉ ⚡ US, MS, LS, CS
Magnolia grandiflora   p. 285

Texas mountain laurel
☼ ◉ ◉ ⚡ LS, CS
Sophora secundiflora   p. 381

VINES

Bougainvillea
☼ ◐ ◉ ◉ ⚡ CS, TS
    p. 153

Cape plumbago
☼ ◉ ⚡ CS, TS
Plumbago auriculata   p. 335

Carolina jessamine
☼ ◐ ● ◉ ◉ ⚡ MS, LS, CS
Gelsemium sempervirens   p. 231

Cherokee rose
☼ ◐ ◉ ⚡ LS, CS, TS
Rosa laevigata   p. 365

Chinese wisteria
☼ ◉ ◉ ⚡ US, MS, LS, CS
Wisteria sinensis   p. 412

Coral vine
☼ ◉ ⚡ LS, CS, TS
Antigonon leptopus   p. 129

Creeping fig
☼ ◐ ● ◉ ⚡ LS, CS, TS
Ficus pumila   p. 224

Crossvine
☼ ◐ ◉ ⚡ ALL ZONES
Bignonia capreolata   p. 150

Gourd
☼ ◉ ⚡ ALL ZONES
    p. 235

Heart-leaf philodendron
◐ ● ◉ ◉ ⚡ TS
Philodendron scandens oxycardium   p. 324

Japanese honeysuckle
☼ ◐ ◉ ⚡ US, MS, LS, CS
Lonicera japonica   p. 280

Kudzu
☼ ◉ ⚡ MS, LS, CS, TS
Pueraria lobata   p. 345

Maypop
☼ ◉ ◉ ⚡ ALL ZONES
Passiflora incarnata   p. 314

Moonflower
☼ ◉ ◉ ⚡ ALL ZONES
Ipomoea alba   p. 256

Trumpet honeysuckle
☼ ◐ ◉ ⚡ US, MS, LS, CS
Lonicera sempervirens   p. 281

Southern magnolia
Magnolia grandiflora

Cape plumbago
Plumbago auriculata

Carolina jessamine
Gelsemium sempervirens

Creeping fig
Ficus pumila

Kudzu
Pueraria lobata

For growing symbol explanations, please see page 38.

The A to Z Plant ENCYCLOPEDIA

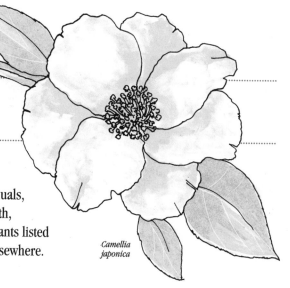

Camellia japonica

This encyclopedia describes more than 5,000 plants—from magnificent shade trees to diminutive succulents, from familiar annuals, fruits, and vegetables to such little-known natives as Alabama snow-wreath, Tennessee coneflower, Florida anise, and Texas madrone. Many of the plants listed here are widely available. Others are common in some states, but rare elsewhere.

Plants are listed alphabetically by botanical name (genus and species). Familiar fruits, vegetables, and berries are exceptions—these are listed by common name (apple or pumpkin, for example). If you know only the common name of a particular plant, look that up either in this encyclopedia section or in the Index of Botanical and Common Names (beginning on page 496) to find a reference to the plant entry.

The botanical names we use for the plants and their families are based mainly on *Hortus Third* (New York: Macmillan, 1976) and the more recent *New Royal Horticultural Society Dictionary of Gardening* (London: Macmillan; New York: Stockton Press, 1992). Where these two authoritative sources differ (plant taxonomists continually change plant names), we give both names with cross-references. Although some botanical names are not familiar to every reader, their use makes it easier for gardeners to speak a common language. (For help in deciphering botanical names, see pages 492 and 493.)

The sample plant entry that follows below, right, illustrates the format used throughout the encyclopedia. The 🏛 symbol identifies the entry as a Southern heritage plant. For the convenience of weekend gardeners, former (and perhaps better-known) botanical names are shown in parentheses after the botanical name and are indexed or may be cross-referenced. (Several family names also are cross-referenced in the encyclopedia.) Next comes the plant's common name or names, followed by the family name in italics. Plant type is described on the next line (note that some plants described as annuals in areas with cold winters may grow as perennials in warmer climates). The next three lines provide cultural information for the genus or species, and the last line indicates toxicity.

CLIMATE

✍ Refers to climate zones (see pages 26–37) where the plant grows best. "Zones MS, LS, CS," for example, means it is best suited to the Middle South, Lower South, and Coastal South. "All zones" means it will grow anywhere in the South

EXPOSURE

☼ Grows best with unobstructed sunlight all day long or almost all day; you can overlook an hour or so of shade at the start or end of a summer day

◑ Needs partial shade—shade for half the day or for at least 3 hours during the hottest part of the day

● Prefers little or no direct sunlight—for example, does best on the north side of a house or beneath a broad, densely foliaged tree

MOISTURE

◖ Thrives with less than regular moisture—moderate amounts for some plants, little for those with more drought tolerance

◗ Needs regular moisture—soil shouldn't become too dry

◖◗ Takes more than regular moisture—includes plants needing constantly moist soil, bog plants, and aquatic plants

TOXICITY

◆ Plant or its parts are known to have toxic or irritant properties

The drawings that accompany the entries illustrate the general appearance of one or more members of a genus, but be sure to read the individual species descriptions; not all look alike.

🏛 GELSEMIUM sempervirens

CAROLINA JESSAMINE, YELLOW JESSAMINE

Loganiaceae

EVERGREEN VINE

✍ ZONES MS, LS, CS

☼ ◑ ● BEST IN FULL SUN; TOLERATES SHADE

◗ REGULAR WATER

◆ ALL PARTS ARE POISONOUS IF INGESTED

Gelsemium sempervirens

A

ABELIA

Caprifoliaceae
EVERGREEN OR DECIDUOUS SHRUBS
🗓 ZONES US, MS, LS
☼ ◑ BEST IN SUN, TOLERATE SOME SHADE
💧 REGULAR WATER

Abelia grandiflora

Graceful, arching branches densely clothed with oval, usually glossy leaves ½–1½ in. long; bronzy new growth. Tubular or bell-shaped flowers in clusters at ends of branches or among leaves. Though small, the blossoms are plentiful enough to put on a good show, mostly during summer and early autumn. When blooms drop, they usually leave purplish or copper-colored sepals that continue to provide color into the fall months. Leaves also may take on bronzy tints in fall.

To keep the shrub's graceful form, prune selectively; don't shear. The more stems you cut to the ground in winter or early spring, the more open and arching next year's growth will be.

Abelias are adaptable plants, useful in shrub borders, as space dividers and visual barriers, and near house walls; lower kinds are good bank or ground covers.

A. chinensis. Deciduous. Grows to 4–5 ft. tall with fragrant, pink-tinted white flowers. Exceptionally attractive to butterflies.

A. grandiflora. GLOSSY ABELIA. Evergreen to semievergreen. Hybrid of two species from China. Best known and most popular of the abelias. Grows to 8 ft. or taller; spreads to 5 ft. or wider. Flowers white or faintly tinged pink. Stems freeze at about 0°F, but the plant will usually recover and bloom the same year, making a graceful border plant that grows to 10–15 in. tall.

'Francis Mason' is a compact (3–4 ft. high and wide), densely branched selection, with pink flowers and yellow-variegated leaves. 'Golden Glow' is similar, but with entirely yellow foliage. 'Prostrata' is a low-growing (1½–2-ft.), smaller-leafed type useful as ground cover, bank planting, low foreground shrub. 'Sherwoodii' grows 3–4 ft. tall, 5 ft. wide. Hybrid 'Edward Goucher' is less hardy, lower growing (to 3–5 ft.), and lacier than its *A. grandiflora* parent, with small, orange-throated, lilac-pink flowers.

ABELMOSCHUS moschatus

SILK FLOWER
Malvaceae
ANNUAL
🗓 ALL ZONES
☼ FULL SUN
💧 REGULAR WATER

Abelmoschus moschatus

Bushy plant about 1½ ft. tall and wide, with deep green, deeply cut leaves. The five-petaled, 3–4½-in. flowers, cherry red or pink with white centers, look similar to tropical hibiscus blossoms. Likes good garden soil, heat, and a sunny location; will produce a greater profusion of blooms in areas of the South that have long summers. Grow from seed sown outdoors as soon as ground is warm (or start indoors 6 to 8 weeks before transplanting outdoors). Flowering begins 100 days after sowing and continues to frost or cold weather. Silk flower also can be grown as a house plant in a 6-in. container; set on a windowsill in bright light.

SOUTHERN HERITAGE PLANTS
IDENTIFIED BY SYMBOL 🌡

ABIES

FIR
Pinaceae
EVERGREEN TREES
🗓 ZONES VARY BY SPECIES
☼ ◑ FULL SUN OR LIGHT SHADE
💧 REGULAR TO MODERATE WATER

Abies concolor

In nature, firs are tall, erect, symmetrical trees with uniformly spaced branch whorls. Though sometimes confused with spruces *(Picea)*, they have softer needles that fall directly from the stems (spruces leave short pegs behind), and their large cones grow up rather than down. The cones shatter after ripening, leaving a spiky stalk. Most (but not all) native firs are high-mountain plants that grow best in or near their natural environments. Some species adapt well to warmer, drier conditions.

Christmas tree farms grow native firs for cutting, and nurseries in "fir country" grow a few species for the living Christmas tree trade. Primary use in the South for most species is as cut Christmas tree.

A. balsamea. BALSAM FIR. Zone US. Native to Northeast. Pyramidal tree to 50 ft.; dark green needles. Legendary fragrance makes it a favorite for Christmas trees, wreaths. Use dwarf 'Nana' in rock gardens, containers.

A. concolor. WHITE FIR. Zones US, MS. Native to mountain regions of West and Southwest but tolerates hot, humid summers better than most firs. Grows 50–70 ft. tall in gardens. Bluish green, 1–2-in.-long needles; 'Candicans' is bluish white.

A. firma. JAPANESE FIR, MOMI FIR. Zones US, MS. Native to Japan. Broadly pyramidal to 40–50 ft., branches just above horizontal. Needles dark green above, lighter beneath. Can tolerate hot, moist climates.

A. fraseri. FRASER FIR, SOUTHERN FIR. Zone US. Native to higher, cooler elevations of the Appalachian Mountains. Attractive pyramidal tree resembling *A. balsamea* in both looks and fragrance. Widely grown as a Christmas tree where summers are not too hot.

A. homolepis. NIKKO FIR. Zones US, MS. Native to Japan. Broad, dense, rather formal fir to 80 ft. Needles are densely arranged, forward pointing. Adapted to warm, moist regions.

A. procera (A. nobilis). NOBLE FIR. Zone US. Native to Northwest. Narrow, graceful tree to 100 ft. or more. Blue-green, inch-long needles; short, stiff branches. Cones 6–10 in. long, 3 in. wide, with extended bracts.

ACACIA

Fabaceae (Leguminosae)
EVERGREEN OR DECIDUOUS SHRUBS OR TREES
🗓 ZONES VARY BY SPECIES
☼ FULL SUN
💧 MODERATE TO LITTLE WATER

Acacia baileyana

Large group of shrubs or small trees native to tropics or warm regions of the world, notably Australia, Mexico, and southwestern U.S. Some have enjoyed use in the warmest southeastern climates. Acacias are relatively short lived (20 to 30 years on average), but all grow so rapidly that they reach good size in a few years. The various species produce yellow, cream, or white flowers; the blossoms of some are quite fragrant. All acacias are attractive to birds.

A. baileyana. BAILEY ACACIA (often called mimosa as cut flowers). Evergreen. Zones CS, TS. Most widely planted acacia and among the hardiest to cold. Often grown as a multitrunked plant 20–30 ft. high. Feathery, finely cut, blue-gray leaves; thornless. Starts blooming when young, producing profuse, fragrant yellow flowers early in the year.

'Purpurea'. PURPLE-LEAF ACACIA. Same as *A. baileyana* except for purple new growth.

A. berlandieri. GUAJILLO. Deciduous. Zones CS, TS. Southwestern native planted as a shrub, hedge, or small tree. Thornless growth to about 15 ft. high. Fernlike foliage. Fragrant white flowers, rich in nectar, bloom winter to spring.

A. farnesiana. SWEET ACACIA. Deciduous. Zone TS. To 20 ft. high, with feathery foliage and thorny branches. Fragrant, deep yellow blossoms, borne nearly year-round, may freeze in a cold snap. Garden centers often sell the more cold-tolerant *A. smallii* under this name.

A. schaffneri. Deciduous. Zones CS, TS. To about 18 ft., with curving branches like green tentacles and finely divided leaves hiding short thorns. Perfumed yellow balls in spring.

A. wrightii. WRIGHT ACACIA. Deciduous. Zones LS, CS, TS. Cold-hardy acacia native to Texas, survives winter as far north as Dallas–Fort Worth. Usually grows to 6–10 ft., occasionally to 20 ft. Pale yellow flowers bloom in spring on 2-in. spikes. Delicate foliage sometimes persists through winter. Thorns on branches have sharp hooks. Does best in dry, well-drained soil. Not well adapted to Southeast.

ACALYPHA

Euphorbiaceae

EVERGREEN TROPICAL SHRUBS

✂ ZONE TS; OR INDOORS

☼ ◑ FULL SUN OR PARTIAL SHADE

◐ ● REGULAR TO MODERATE WATER

All three of the species described here are tropical and quite tender; *A. wilkesiana* can be used as an annual. All need well-drained soil, bloom intermittently during warm months.

Acalypha hispida

A. hispida. CHENILLE PLANT. Native to the East Indies. Grows outdoors only in the mildest frost-free climates; elsewhere, good in greenhouse or enclosed patio or, with heavy pruning, as house plant. Can grow to a bulky 15 ft. Heavy, rich green leaves to 8 in. wide. Flowers hang in 1½-ft.-long clusters resembling tassels of crimson chenille.

A. pendula. FIRETAIL. Resembles *A. hispida* in flower form but plant is much smaller; shorter tassels droop from trailing branches. Good in hanging basket.

A. wilkesiana (A. tricolor). COPPER LEAF. Native to South Pacific islands. Foliage more colorful than many flowers. Provides year-round interest in southern Florida, where it is an outdoor plant. Elsewhere, it is used as an annual, substituting for flowers from late summer to frost. Leaves grow to 8 in.; may be bronzy green mottled with shades of red and purple, red with crimson and bronze, or green edged with crimson and stippled with orange and red. In a warm, sheltered spot it can grow as a shrub to 6 ft. or more. Container plants need fast-draining potting mix, kept slightly dry through winter.

Acanthaceae. The acanthus family of herbs and shrubs generally come from warm or tropical areas. Many have showy flowers or foliage. Examples are bear's breech (*Acanthus*), *Aphelandra*, and *Thunbergia*.

ACANTHOPANAX sieboldianus (Eleutherococcus sieboldianus)

FIVELEAF ARALIA

Araliaceae

DECIDUOUS SHRUB

✂ ZONES US, MS, LS, CS

☼ ◑ ● SUN OR SHADE

◐ ◑ ● MUCH OR LITTLE WATER

Acanthopanax sieboldianus

Grows 8–10 ft. tall and wide; erect, eventually arching stems have short thorns below each

leaf. Leaves bright green, with five to seven leaflets 1–2½ inches long arranged like fingers on a hand. Clustered white flowers are small and inconspicuous, only rarely followed by clusters of small black berries. This plant's great virtues are its somewhat tropical appearance and high tolerance for difficult conditions. It can thrive in bright sun or dense shade, with much or little water, in rich or poor soil. It is remarkably tolerant of urban air pollution. 'Variegatus', a showy 6–8-ft. plant with white-bordered leaflets, is grown more often than the species.

ACANTHUS mollis

BEAR'S BREECH

Acanthaceae

PERENNIAL

✂ ZONES US, MS, LS, CS

☼ ◑ FULL SUN OR PARTIAL SHADE

◐ ● REGULAR TO MODERATE WATER

Acanthus mollis

Native to southern Europe. Fast-growing, spreading plant with basal clusters of handsome, deeply lobed and cut, shining dark green leaves to 2 ft. long. Rigid 1½-ft. spikes of tubular whitish, lilac, or rose flowers with spiny green or purplish bracts top 2–3-ft. stems. Blooms late spring or early summer. 'Oak Leaf' is very similar to species; 'Latifolius' has larger leaves, is hardier and less aggressive than species.

Cut back after flowering. To keep foliage through the summer, cut off flower stalks and soak roots occasionally. Best time to divide the clumps is between October and March. Plant where it can be confined; roots travel underground, making the plant difficult to eradicate. Effective with bamboo and large-leafed ferns.

ACCA sellowiana. See FEIJOA sellowiana

ACER

MAPLE

Aceraceae

DECIDUOUS TREES OR SHRUBS

✂ ZONES VARY BY SPECIES

☼ ◑ FULL SUN OR PARTIAL SHADE

◐ ● REGULAR TO MODERATE WATER

Acer saccharum

When you talk about maples, you're talking about many trees—large and midsize deciduous shade trees; small deciduous trees; and dainty, picturesque shrub-trees. Maples of one type or another will grow over much of the country, the limiting factors being heat, dryness, and lack of winter cold. Only very tough or drought-tolerant types are worth trying in the Southwest. For a good fall leaf display, look for a maple that colors well in your area; visit local garden centers while the foliage is changing hue.

All maples prefer well-drained soil but must have moisture available in the root zone throughout their leafy period. Most have shallow, competitive roots, and the sizable ones cast dense shade; it's not easy to maintain a garden beneath them. They are subject to various problems, including anthracnose and verticillium wilt.

A. barbatum (A. floridanum). SOUTHERN SUGAR MAPLE, FLORIDA MAPLE. Deciduous tree. Zones MS, LS, CS. Native to Virginia and south to Florida and west to Oklahoma and Texas. Grows to 25–30 ft. Usually turns the same rich yellow and occasionally red in fall as *A. saccharum*, the sugar maple, but is smaller in stature with smaller leaves, paler bark, a more open habit of growth, and is better adapted to the low, wet coastal plains of the South. Often found in forest understory alongside streams.

A. buergeranum. TRIDENT MAPLE. Deciduous tree. Zones US, MS, LS. Native to China, Japan. Grows 20–25 ft. high. Roundish crown of 3-in.-wide, glossy, three-lobed leaves that are pale beneath. Fall color usually red, sometimes orange or yellow. Attractive flaking bark on older wood. Low, spreading growth; stake and prune to make it branch high. A decorative, useful patio tree and favorite bonsai subject.

A. campestre. HEDGE MAPLE. Deciduous tree. Zones US, MS, LS. Native to Europe, western Asia. Slow growing to 70 ft., seldom over 30 ft. in cultivation. Usually rounded, dense habit. Leaves 2–4 in. wide, with three to five lobes, dull green above; turn yellow in fall. 'Queen Elizabeth' has glossier foliage, more erect habit.

A. ginnala. AMUR MAPLE. Deciduous shrub or small tree. Zones US, MS, LS. Native to Manchuria, north China, Japan. To 20 ft. high. Three-lobed, toothed leaves to 3 in. long, 2 in. wide. Striking red fall color. Clusters of small, fragrant yellowish flowers in early spring are followed by handsome bright red, winged seeds. Grown as staked, trained single-trunked tree or multiple-trunked tall shrub. 'Flame', 15–20 ft. tall, shows fiery red fall color. Tough trees, tolerating heat and cold.

A. griseum. PAPERBARK MAPLE. Deciduous tree. Zones US, MS; will grow in LS, but unhappy there. Native to China. Grows to 25 ft. or higher with narrow to rounded crown. In the winter it makes a striking silhouette with bare branches angling out and up from main trunk, and cinnamon-colored bark peeling away in paper-thin sheets. Late to leaf out in spring; leaves are divided into three coarsely toothed leaflets 1½–2½ in. long, dark green above, silvery below. Inconspicuous red flowers in spring develop into showy winged seeds. Foliage turns brilliant red in fall unless caught by early frosts. Not drought tolerant.

A. japonicum. FULLMOON MAPLE. Deciduous shrub or small tree. Zones US, MS. Native to Japan. To 20–30 ft. Nearly round, 2–5-in.-long leaves cut into 7 to 11 lobes. Give regular moisture, part shade in warm regions. 'Aconitifolium', fernleaf fullmoon maple, is small, slow growing, and best placed as a shrub. Leaves are deeply cut, almost to leafstalk; each lobe is also cut and toothed. Fine fall color where adapted.

A. leucoderme (A. saccharum leucoderme). CHALK MAPLE. Deciduous tree. Zones US, MS, LS, CS. Native to southeastern U.S. Grows to 25–30 ft. Quite similar to southern sugar maple, *A. barbatum,* but prefers drier, upland sites and tolerates chalky, limestone soils.

A. macrophyllum. BIGLEAF MAPLE. Deciduous tree. Zones US, MS. Native to stream banks, moist canyons. Broad-topped, dense shade tree 30–95 ft. tall—too big for small garden or street tree. Large (6–15-in.-wide) medium green leaves with three to five lobes; turn bright yellow to orange in fall. Small greenish yellow spring flowers are followed by tawny winged seeds hanging in long, chainlike clusters.

A. negundo. BOX ELDER. Deciduous tree. Zones US, MS, LS, CS. Native to most of U.S. Where you can grow other maples of your choice, do so. This is a weed tree of many faults—it seeds readily, hosts box elder bugs, suckers badly, and is subject to breakage. Fast growing to 60 ft., usually less. Leaves divided into three to five (or seven to nine) oval, 2–5-in.-long leaflets with toothed margins; yellow in fall.

'Flamingo'. Has white and pink leaf markings.

'Variegatum'. VARIEGATED BOX ELDER. Not as large or weedy as the species. Combination of green and creamy white leaves stands out in any situation. Large, pendent clusters of white fruit are spectacular.

A. nigrum. BLACK MAPLE. Deciduous tree. Zones US, MS, LS. Similar to sugar maple *(A. saccharum),* but more resistant to heat and drought. Light green leaves turn yellow in fall. 'Greencolumn' can reach 65 ft. tall, 25 ft. wide.

A. palmatum. JAPANESE MAPLE. Deciduous shrub or tree. Zones US, MS, LS, CS. Native to Japan and Korea. Slow growing to 20 ft.; normally many stemmed. Most airy and delicate of all maples. Leaves 2–4 in. long, deeply cut into five to nine toothed lobes. All-year interest: Young spring growth is glowing red; summer's leaves are soft green; fall foliage is scarlet, orange, or yellow. Slender leafless branches in greens and reds provide winter interest. Japanese maples tend to grow

Acer palmatum

in flat, horizontal planes, so pruning to accentuate this growth habit is easy. Plants fare best in filtered shade, though full sun can be satisfactory in Upper and Middle South.

Grafted garden forms are popular, but common seedlings have uncommon grace and usefulness: They are more rugged, faster growing, and more drought tolerant than named forms; they also tolerate more sun and wind. Grafted forms are usually smaller, more weeping and spreading in form, brighter in foliage color, and more finely cut in leaf. The following list includes the best known of the numerous selections available:

'Atropurpureum'. RED JAPANESE MAPLE. Purplish or bronze to bronzy green leaves, brighter in sun. Color tends to fade in summer heat.

'Bloodgood'. Vigorous, upright growth to 15 ft. Deep red spring and summer foliage, scarlet in fall. Bark blackish red.

'Bonfire'. Orange-pink spring and fall foliage; twisted trunk, short branches, drooping branchlets.

'Burgundy Lace'. Leaves purplish, more deeply cut than those of 'Atropurpureum'; branchlets bright green.

'Butterfly'. Small (to 7-ft.) shrub with small bluish green leaves edged in white. Cut out growth that reverts to plain green. Needs some shade.

'Crimson Queen'. Small, shrubby, with finely cut reddish leaves that hold color all summer, turn scarlet before dropping off in fall.

'Dissectum' ('Dissectum Viridis'). LACELEAF JAPANESE MAPLE. Small tree with drooping branches, green bark; pale green, finely divided leaves turn gold in autumn.

'Ever Red' ('Dissectum Atropurpureum'). Small mounding shrub with weeping branches. Finely divided, purple-tinged, lacy foliage turns crimson in the fall.

'Filiferum Purpureum'. Mounding shrub to 10 ft. with threadlike leaf segments opening dark red and aging bronzy green.

'Garnet'. Similar to 'Crimson Queen' and 'Ever Red'; somewhat more vigorous grower.

'Hogyoku'. Upright growth to 15 ft. Sturdy and easy to grow in most situations. Leaves turn a deep yellow-orange pumpkin color in fall.

'Ornatum' ('Dissectum Atropurpureum'). RED LACELEAF JAPANESE MAPLE. Like 'Dissectum' but with red leaves turning brighter red in fall.

'Osakazuki'. Large leaves, to 5 in. wide, turn from a rich green in summer to brilliant crimson red in fall. Often considered the Japanese maple with the best fall color. Grows upright, becomes wider with age; eventually makes a 20–25 ft. round-topped tree. Sun, heat, and drought tolerant.

'Oshio Beni'. Like 'Atropurpureum' but more vigorous; has long, arching branches.

'Sango Kaku' ('Senkaki'). CORAL BARK MAPLE. Vigorous, upright, treelike. Fall foliage yellow. Twigs, branches a striking coral red in winter.

'Tamukeyama'. Leaves open deep crimson red in spring and turn quickly to dark purple red, which holds well through summer, even in high heat and humidity. Scarlet fall color. Leaves less lacy than 'Crimson Queen', branches more cascading.

'Waterfall'. Very similar to 'Dissectum'. Branches cascade. Leaves deeply divided, fernlike, flowing and elegant. Fall color brilliant yellow, gold. Takes full sun quite well.

A. platanoides. NORWAY MAPLE. Deciduous tree. Zones US, MS. Native to Europe, western Asia. Broad-crowned, densely foliaged tree to 50–60 ft. Leaves five-lobed, 3–5 in. wide, deep green above, paler beneath; turn yellow in late fall. Showy clusters of small, greenish yellow flowers in early spring. Very adaptable, tolerating many soil and environmental conditions. Once widely recommended, especially as street tree, but now strongly objected to in some areas because of voracious roots, self-sown seedlings, and aphid-caused honeydew drip and sooty mold. Here are some of the best selections:

'Cavalier'. Compact, round headed, to 30 ft.

'Cleveland' and 'Cleveland II'. Shapely, compact, well-formed trees about 50 ft. tall.

'Columnare'. Slower growing and narrower in form than the species.

'Crimson King'. Holds purple foliage color until leaves drop. Slower growing, more compact than the species.

'Deborah'. Like 'Schwedler' but faster growing, straighter.

'Drummondii'. Leaves are edged with silvery white; unusual and striking. Some shade in warm areas.

'Emerald Queen'. Fast-growing, upright tree, grows to 50 ft.; similar to 'Summershade'.

'Faassen's Black'. Pyramidal in shape, with dark purple leaves.

'Globe'. Slow growing to 20–25 ft., with dense, round crown.

'Green Lace'. Finely cut, dark green leaves; moderate growth rate to 40 ft.

'Jade Glen'. Vigorous, straight-growing form with bright yellow fall color.

'Parkway'. A broader tree than 'Columnare', with a dense canopy.

'Royal Red Leaf'. Another good red- or purple-leafed form.

'Schwedler' ('Schwedleri'). Purplish red leaves in spring turn to dark bronzy green, gold in autumn.

'Summershade'. Fast-growing, upright, heat-resistant selection.

A. rubrum. RED MAPLE, SCARLET MAPLE, SWAMP MAPLE. Deciduous tree. Zones US, MS, LS, CS. Native to low, wet areas of eastern North America. Fairly fast growth to 60 ft. or more, 40 ft. or wider. Faster growing than Norway or sugar maples. Red twigs, branchlets, and buds; quite showy flowers. Fruit dull red. Leaves 2–4 in. long, with three to five lobes, shiny green above, pale beneath; brilliant scarlet fall color in frosty areas. Often among the first trees to color up in fall. Tolerates most soils. Not at its best in urban pollution. Selected forms include the following:

'Autumn Flame'. Rounded form, 60 ft., excellent early red fall color.

'Autumn Radiance'. Broad oval form, 50 ft., orange-red fall color.

'Bowhall'. Tall, narrow, cone shaped, with orange-red foliage color in fall.

'Columnare'. Tall, broadly columnar. 70 ft.

'October Glory'. Tall, round-headed tree; last to turn color in fall. Good scarlet fall color even in the Lower South. 50–60 ft.

'Red Sunset'. Upright, vigorous, fast growing, 50–60 ft. Early orange-red fall color.

Acer rubrum

'Scarlet Sentinel'. Hybrid between red and silver maples. Columnar, fast-growing form. 50 ft.

'Schlesingeri'. Tall, broad, fast growing, with regular form; orange-red fall color. 60–70 ft.

'Shade King'. Very fast grower to 50 ft. Pale green foliage turns bright red in fall.

'Tilford'. Nearly globe-shaped crown if grown in the open; pyramidal when crowded. 40 ft.

A. saccharinum. SILVER MAPLE. Deciduous tree. Zones US, MS, LS, CS. Native to eastern North America. Grows fast to 40–100 ft. with equal spread. Open form, with semipendulous branches; casts fairly open shade. Silvery gray bark peels in long strips on old trees. Leaves 3–6 in. wide, five lobed, light green above, silvery beneath. Autumn color is usually poor, pale yellow. Aggressive roots are hard on sidewalks, sewers.

You pay a penalty for the benefit of fast growth: Weak wood and narrow crotch angles make this tree break easily. Unusually susceptible to aphids and cottony-cushion scale. Many rate it among least desirable of maples. Nevertheless, it is often planted for fast growth, graceful habit.

A. saccharum. SUGAR MAPLE. Deciduous tree. Zones US, MS, LS. Native to eastern North America. The source of maple sugar in the Northeast, this tree is renowned for spectacular fall color in the Upper South. Moderate growth to 60 ft. and more, with stout branches and upright oval to rounded canopy. Leaves 3–6 in. wide, with three to five lobes, green above, pale below. Brilliant autumn foliage ranges from yellow and orange to deep red and scarlet. Intolerant of road salt; also not suited to humid heat of the Lower South (though some selections succeed there). These are some of the most commonly available selections:

'Arrowhead'. Erect pyramid, 60 ft., with yellow to orange leaves in fall.

'Bonfire'. Tall, spreading tree with bright red fall foliage. To 50 ft.

'Caddo'. CADDO MAPLE. Native to Oklahoma. To 50 ft. More tolerant of alkaline soils than eastern maples. Yellow and orange fall color. Good choice for Southwest areas.

'Commemoration'. Heavy leaf texture; orange, yellow, and red fall color.

'Green Mountain'. Tolerant of heat and drought; autumn leaves are yellow to orange to reddish orange. 70 ft.

'Legacy'. Fast growing, to 60 ft., drought tolerant, and multihued in fall; best selection for the South.

'Monumentale' ('Temple's Upright'). Narrow, erect form with yellow-orange fall leaves.

'Seneca Chief'. Narrow form, orange to yellow fall color.

A. s. grandidentatum (*A. grandidentatum*). BIG-TOOTH MAPLE. Leaves with three to five lobes and large blunt teeth. Grows as shrub or 20–30-ft. tree. Brilliant fall color in tones of yellow, orange, rose red. In nature, it grows in canyons and on stream banks. In gardens, it requires well-drained soil on the dry side. Good maple for Southwest areas.

Aceraceae. The maple family consists of deciduous, rarely evergreen, trees and shrubs with paired opposite leaves and paired, winged seeds.

ACHILLEA

YARROW

Asteraceae (Compositae)

PERENNIALS

☀ ZONES US, MS, LS

☼ FULL SUN

💧 MODERATE WATER

Yarrows are among the most carefree and generously blooming perennials for summer and early fall; several are useful as cut flowers (cut and dry taller kinds for winter bouquets). Leaves are gray or green, bitter-aromatic, usually finely divided (some with toothed edges). Flower heads usually in flattish clusters. Drought tolerant once established. Cut back after bloom; divide crowded clumps. Need excellent drainage. Tend to rot in high-humidity, high-rainfall areas if soil is wet and heavy.

Achillea tomentosa

A. clavennae. SILVERY YARROW. Mats of lobed, silvery gray, silky leaves. Loose, flat-topped clusters of ½–¾-in.-wide ivory white flower heads on 5–10-in.-high stems. Often sold as *A. argentea*.

A. filipendulina. FERNLEAF YARROW. Tall, erect plants 4–5 ft. high, with deep green, fernlike leaves. Bright yellow flower heads. Good for flower arrangements. Several selections are available. 'Gold Plate', a tall plant, has flower clusters up to 6 in. wide; 'Coronation Gold', to about 3 ft., also has large flower clusters. All types are less successful in Gulf Coast states than the species *A. millefolium*.

A. millefolium. COMMON YARROW, MILFOIL. This aggressively spreading species grows to 3 ft. Narrow, fernlike, green or gray-green leaves on 3-ft. stems. White flower clusters grow on long stems. 'Rosea' has rosy flower heads. One of the more successful selections is 'Fire King', about 3 ft. tall with gray foliage and dark reddish flowers. 'Cerise Queen' has brighter red flowers. Hybrids, many of them named, have extended the color range and are less invasive. Summer Pastels and Debutante strains show white and cream to lighter shades of yellow and red; they can grow from seed. Galaxy exhibits deeper colors.

A. 'Moonshine'. Upright growth to 2 ft. Gray-green foliage and light yellow flowers. Like *A. taygetea*, but flowers are deeper yellow.

A. ptarmica. SNEEZEWORT YARROW. Erect plant up to 2 ft. high. Narrow leaves with finely toothed edges. White flower heads in rather open, flattish clusters. 'The Pearl' has double flowers.

A. taygetea. Native to the eastern Mediterranean. Grows to 1½ ft. Gray-green, divided leaves 3–4 in. long. Dense clusters of bright yellow flower heads fade to primrose yellow. Good cut flowers. Shear off old stalks.

A. tomentosa. WOOLLY YARROW. Spreading mat of fernlike, deep green, hairy leaves. Golden flower heads top 6–10-in. stems in summer. 'Primrose Beauty' has pale yellow flowers; 'King George' has cream flowers. Good for edging; neat ground cover. Shear off dead flowers.

117

ACHIMENES

Gesneriaceae

PERENNIALS, MOST TENDER AND GROWN IN POTS

✿ ZONES CS, TS, EXCEPT AS NOTED; IN CONTAINERS OUTDOORS; OR INDOORS OR IN GREENHOUSE

☀ ◐ ● SHADE OUTDOORS; BRIGHT LIGHT INDOORS

● REGULAR WATER

Achimenes

Native to tropical America. Related to African violet and gloxinia. Plants 1–2 ft. high, some trailing. Slender stems; roundish, crisp, bright to dark green, hairy leaves. Flaring tubular flowers, 1–3 in. across, in pink, blue, lavender, orchid, purple.

Sometimes grown in beds as ground cover in Coastal and Tropical South, but more commonly used in containers—outdoors (protected from direct sun and wind) in window box, on porch or patio, under lath; or indoors (in bright light) in house or greenhouse. Plant rhizomes March–April, placing ½–1 in. deep in moist peat moss and sand. Keep in light shade at 60°F. When 3 in. high, set 6–12 plants in 6–7-in. fern pot or hanging basket, in potting mix of equal parts peat moss, perlite, leaf mold. In fall, dig rhizomes and let dry. Store in cool, dry place over winter; repot in spring.

'Purple King', Zones MS, LS, CS, TS, is unusually hardy. Can be brought back from 0°F. Grows to 6 in. tall. Flowers deep purple, 2 in. across, on trailing stems. Breaks dormancy late, not appearing until late May. Blooms intermittently throughout summer.

ACIDANTHERA bicolor. See GLADIOLUS callianthus

ACOELORRHAPHE wrightii (Paurotis wrightii)

Arecaceae (Palmae)

PALM

✿ ZONE TS; OR INDOORS

☀ ◐ FULL SUN OR PARTIAL SHADE

● ●● AMPLE TO REGULAR WATER

Acoelorrhaphe wrightii

Native to the Florida Everglades, West Indies. Hardy to 20°F. Handsome fan palm with several slender trunks topped by 2–3-ft.-wide leaves, green above, silvery below. Spines on leafstalks. Grows to 25 ft. tall in Florida, considerably less in extreme south Texas, where plant is somewhat difficult to establish. Tolerant of many soils. Can be grown as a house plant.

ACONITUM

MONKSHOOD, ACONITE

Ranunculaceae

PERENNIALS

✿ ZONE US

☀ ◐ FULL SUN OR PARTIAL SHADE

● REGULAR WATER

☠ ALL PARTS ARE POISONOUS IF INGESTED

Aconitum napellus

Leaves, usually lobed, in basal clusters. Flowers shaped like hoods or helmets, along tall, leafy spikes. Monkshood has a definite place in rich soil under trees, at the back of flower beds, or even at the edge of a bog garden. Substitute for delphinium in shade. Combines effectively with ferns, meadow rue, astilbe, and hosta.

Suited to Upper South. Needs some winter chill. Hard to establish in warm, dry climates. Sow seeds in spring; or sow in late summer or early fall for bloom the next year. Moist, fertile soil for best growth and bloom. Divide in early spring or late fall, or leave undivided for years. Completely dormant in winter; mark site.

A. cammarum 'Bicolor'. Grows to 3 ft., with broad, branching spires of blue-and-white flowers in summer.

A. carmichaelii (A. fischeri). Native to central China. Densely leafy stems 2–4 ft. high. Leaves leathery, dark green, lobed and coarsely toothed. Blooms late summer into fall; deep purple-blue flowers form dense, branching clusters 4–8 in. long. 'Wilsonii' grows 6–8 ft. high, has more open flower clusters 10–18 in. long.

A. henryi (A. bicolor) 'Sparks'. Grows 4–5 ft. tall, with dark purple-blue flowers on a widely branching plant. Summer bloom.

A. napellus. GARDEN MONKSHOOD. Native to Europe. Upright leafy plants 2–5 ft. high. Leaves 2–5 in. wide, divided into narrow lobes. Flowers usually blue or violet, in spikelike clusters in late summer.

ACORUS gramineus

SWEET FLAG

Araceae

PERENNIAL

✿ ALL ZONES

☀ FULL SUN

●● MUCH WATER

Acorus gramineus

Native to Japan, northern Asia. Related to callas, but fans of grasslike leaves more nearly resemble miniature tufts of iris. Flowers are inconspicuous. 'Ogon' has rich golden yellow leaves. 'Pusillus' is tiny, its green leaves seldom more than 1 in. long. It is used in planting miniature landscapes and dish gardens. 'Variegatus', with white-edged, ¼-in.-wide leaves to 1½ ft. long, can be planted in bog gardens or at pond edges. 'Variegatus' is also useful with collections of grasses, bamboos, or sword-leafed plants among gravel and boulders.

ACTINIDIA

Actinidiaceae

DECIDUOUS VINES

✿ ZONES VARY BY SPECIES

☀ ◐ FULL SUN OR PARTIAL SHADE

● ●● REGULAR TO MODERATE WATER

Actinidia deliciosa

Native to eastern Asia. Handsome foliage. Plant in rich soil. Supply sturdy supports for them to twine upon, such as a trellis, an arbor, or a patio overhead. You can also train them to cover walls and fences; guide and tie vines to the support as necessary. Thin occasionally to shape or to control pattern.

In winter, prune and shape plant for form and fruit production. Shape to one or two main trunks; cut out closely parallel or crossing branches. Fruit is borne on shoots from year-old or older wood; cut out shoots that have fruited for 3 years and shorten younger shoots, leaving from three to seven buds beyond previous summer's fruit. In summer, shorten overlong shoots and unwind shoots that twine around main branches.

A. arguta. HARDY KIWI. Zones US, MS, LS, CS. Much like *A. deliciosa* but with smaller leaves, flowers; fruit 1–1½ in. long, fuzzless (you can eat skin and all). Female selections 'Ananasnaja' and 'Hood River' need male plants for pollen. The rare selection 'Issai' is self-fertile. Fruiting is satisfactory even in mild winters.

A. deliciosa (A. chinensis). KIWI VINE. Zones LS, CS. Twines and leans to 30 ft. if not curbed. Leaves 5–8 in. long, roundish, rich dark green above, velvety white below. New growth often has rich red fuzz. Flowers 1–1½ in. wide, opening creamy and fading to buff. Fruit is egg size, roughly egg shaped, covered with brown fuzz. Green flesh edible and delicious, with hints of melon, strawberry, banana. Although single plants are ornamental, you need both a male and a female plant for fruit. The best female (fruiting) selections are 'Chico' and 'Hayward' (similar, possibly identical selections); 'Vincent' needs little winter chill and is a good choice for the mildest winter climates. 'Tomuri' is pollinator for 'Vincent'.

Harvest fruit in late October or November. Store at refrigerator temperature in plastic bags. Ripen fruit at room temperature as needed.

A. kolomikta. Zones US, MS, LS. Rapid growth to 15 ft. or more to produce a wondrous foliage mass made up of heart-shaped, 3–5-in.-long, variegated leaves. Male selections are generally sold, since they are said to have better color than females. Some leaves are all white, some are green splashed with white, and others have rose, pink, or even red variegation. Color is best in cool spring weather; otherwise, color is apparent only in light shade. Clusters of fragrant, small white flowers in early summer.

ADAM'S NEEDLE. See YUCCA

ADENIUM obesum

DESERT ROSE

Apocynaceae

SHRUB, OFTEN GROWN AS HOUSE PLANT

🌡 ZONE TS; OR INDOORS

☼ FULL SUN

💧 REGULAR WATER DURING GROWTH

🜄 MILKY SAP IS POISONOUS IF INGESTED

Adenium obesum

Twisted branches grow from huge, fleshy, half-buried trunk or rootstock. Can reach 9 ft. tall outdoors. Leaves sparse; plant leafless for long periods. Clustered saucer-shaped blossoms are deep pink, 2 in. or more across. Cannot take frost or winter chill and cold soil. Relocate container plants to warm area when temperatures dip below 50°F. Needs heat, light, perfect drainage, regular water during growth, dryness during dormancy; in short, this is a plant for careful enthusiasts and collectors. In bloom, extremely showy; in eastern tropical Africa, where it is native, it is known as desert rose or desert azalea.

ADENOPHORA

LADYBELLS

Campanulaceae (Lobeliaceae)

PERENNIALS

🌡 ZONES US, MS

☼ ◑ FULL SUN OR LIGHT SHADE

💧 💧 REGULAR TO MODERATE WATER

Adenophora liliifolia

Campanula relatives, mostly from the Far East; erect plants with narrow, leafy stems bearing fragrant blue bell flowers along their upper portions. Useful in the shade garden but tolerate sun as well. Long lived, they resent moving once well established. Provide well-drained soil.

A. confusa. PURPLE LADYBELLS. To 2½ ft., with deep blue flowers in mid- to late summer.

A. liliifolia. To 1½ ft., with pale blue (rarely white) flowers.

ADIANTUM

MAIDENHAIR FERN

Polypodiaceae

FERNS

🌡 ZONES VARY BY SPECIES

◑ ● PARTIAL OR FULL SHADE

💧 💧 AMPLE TO REGULAR WATER

Adiantum pedatum

Most are native to tropics; some originate in North America. Stems thin, wiry, and dark;

fronds finely cut; leaflets mostly fan shaped, bright green, thin textured. Plants need shade, steady moisture, and soil rich in organic matter. Leaves of even hardy kinds die back in hard frosts. Those listed as tender or indoor plants sometimes succeed in sheltered places in mild-winter areas.

A. capillus-veneris. SOUTHERN MAIDENHAIR. Zones US, MS, LS. Native to North America. To 1½ ft. tall, fronds twice divided but not forked. Easy to grow.

A. hispidulum. ROSY MAIDENHAIR. Zone TS. Native to tropics of Asia, Africa. Indoor or greenhouse plant. To 1 ft. tall. Young fronds rosy brown, turning medium green, shaped somewhat like American maidenhair fern.

A. pedatum (A. aleuticum). AMERICAN MAIDENHAIR FERN, NORTHERN MAIDENHAIR. Zones US, MS. Native to North America. Fronds fork to make a fingerlike pattern atop slender 1–2½-ft. stems. General effect airy and fresh; excellent in containers or shaded beds.

A. peruvianum. SILVER DOLLAR MAIDENHAIR. Native to Peru. Indoor or greenhouse plant. To 1½ ft. or more in height. Segments of fronds quite large, to 2 in. wide.

A. raddianum (A. cuneatum, A. decorum). Native to Brazil. Tender fern for indoors or greenhouse. Fronds cut three or four times, 15–18 in. long. Many named types differing in texture and compactness. Grow in pots; move outdoors to a sheltered, shaded patio in summer. Selections commonly sold are 'Fritz-Luthii', 'Gracillimum' (most finely cut), and 'Pacific Maid'.

A. tenerum. Native to New World tropics. Indoors or greenhouse. Long, broad fronds arch gracefully, are finely divided into many deeply cut segments ½–¾ in. wide. 'Wrightii' is similar or identical.

AECHMEA

Bromeliaceae

BROMELIADS

🌡 ZONE TS; OR INDOORS

◑ PARTIAL SHADE

🜄 UNIQUE WATER NEEDS AND METHODS

Aechmea fasciata

In frost-free areas, grow in pots, in hanging baskets, or in moss fastened in crotches of trees—always in shaded places with good air circulation. Can grow in ground, but be ready to bring indoors or cover during cold spells. Indoors or outdoors, soil should be fast draining but moisture retentive. Apply water regularly into cups within leaves. Put water on soil when it's really dry to the touch. Bromeliad specialists list dozens of species and selections, and new hybrids appear frequently.

A. chantinii. Rosettes of leaves 1–3 ft. long, green to gray green banded with silver or darker green. Tall flower clusters have orange, pink, or red bracts; yellow-and-red flowers; white or blue fruit.

A. fasciata. Gray-green leaves crossbanded with silvery white. From the center grows a cluster of rosy pink flower bracts in which nestle pale blue flowers that change to deep rose. 'Silver King' has unusually silvery leaves; 'Marginata' has leaves edged with creamy white bands.

A. 'Foster's Favorite'. Hybrid with bright wine red, lacquered leaves about 1 ft. long. Drooping, spikelike flower clusters in coral red and blue. 'Royal Wine', another hybrid, forms an open rosette of somewhat leathery, glossy, light green leaves that are burgundy red beneath. Orange-and-blue flowers are borne in drooping clusters.

A. fulgens. Green leaves dusted with gray, 12–16 in. long, 2–3 in. wide. Flower cluster usually above the leaves; blossoms red, blue, and blue violet. *A. f. discolor* has brownish red or violet red leaves, usually faintly striped. Many hybrids.

A. pectinata. Stiff rosettes up to 3 ft.; leaves to 3 in. wide, strongly marked pink or red at bloom time. Flowers whitish and green.

A. weilbachii. Shiny leaves, green or suffused with red tones, in rosettes 2–3 ft. wide. Dull red, 1½-ft. flower stalk has orange-red berries tipped with lilac.

A

AEGOPODIUM podagraria

BISHOP'S WEED, GOUT WEED

Apiaceae (Umbelliferae)

DECIDUOUS PERENNIAL

☘ ZONES US, MS, LS

☼ ◗ ● SUN OR SHADE

◖ MODERATE WATER

Agegopodium podagraria
'Variegatum'

Very vigorous ground cover, especially in rich soil. Spreads by creeping roots; best if contained behind underground barrier of heavy tar paper, wood, or concrete. Many light green, divided leaves make a low (to 6-in.), dense mass; leaflets are ½–3 in. long. To keep it low and even, mow it two or three times a year.

'Variegatum' is the most widely planted form. Leaflets are edged white, giving a luminous effect in shade. Pull plants that revert to solid green leaves. Can become invasive but takes longer to do so than the species.

AESCULUS

HORSECHESTNUT, BUCKEYE

Hippocastanaceae

DECIDUOUS TREES OR LARGE SHRUBS

☘ ZONES VARY BY SPECIES

☼ ◗ FULL SUN OR LIGHT SHADE

● REGULAR WATER, EXCEPT AS NOTED

◈ SEEDS OF ALL ARE SLIGHTLY TOXIC IF INGESTED

Aesculus carnea

Leaves are divided fanwise into large, toothed leaflets. Springtime flowers, in long, dense, showy clusters at the ends of branches, attract hummingbirds. Leathery fruit capsules enclose glossy seeds.

A. carnea. RED HORSECHESTNUT. Zones US, MS, LS. Hybrid between *A. hippocastanum* and *A. pavia*. To 40 ft. high and 30 ft. wide—smaller than *A. hippocastanum* and a better fit for small gardens. Round headed with large, dark green leaves, each divided into five leaflets; casts dense shade. Gets leaf scorch, defoliates in warmest, most humid areas. Bears hundreds of 8-in.-long plumes of soft pink to red flowers. 'Briotii' has rosy crimson flowers; 'O'Neill Red' has bright red blooms.

A. glabra. OHIO BUCKEYE. Zones US, MS. To 40 ft., possibly taller, with dense, rounded form. Low branching, casts dense shade. Early to leaf out. Bright green expanding leaves mature to dark green, then turn yellow to orange in autumn. Flowers greenish yellow in 4–7-in. clusters. Prickly seed capsules enclose shiny brown buckeyes.

A. g. arguta (A. arguta). TEXAS BUCKEYE. Zones US, MS, LS. Native to southern U.S. Attractive small tree, to 15–20 ft., sometimes taller. Leaves have seven to nine narrow 3–5-in.-long pointed leaflets. Pale yellow flowers in late spring. Weight of fruit may bend branches in fall.

A. hippocastanum. COMMON HORSECHESTNUT. Zones US, MS. Native to Europe. To 60 ft. high and 40 ft. wide. Bulky, densely foliaged tree gives heavy shade. Leaves divided into five to seven toothed, 4–10-in.-long leaflets. Can get leaf scorch, defoliate. Spectacular flower show: ivory blooms with pink markings in 1-ft.-long plumes. Invasive roots can break up walks. 'Baumannii' has double flowers, sets no seeds.

A. octandra (A. flava). YELLOW BUCKEYE, SWEET BUCKEYE. Zones US, MS, LS. Native to South. Most majestic of the North American native species. Grows to 90 ft. Dark green foliage, with five to seven 5–8-in.-long finely toothed leaflets, makes a handsome round crown. Yellow flowers form on erect panicles, less showy than those of *A. hippocastanum*. Smooth brown bark. No resinous sticky coating on buds.

A. parviflora. BOTTLEBRUSH BUCKEYE. Zones US, MS, LS, CS. Native to southeastern U.S. Shrub to 12–15 ft. tall, spreading by suckers, with dark green leaves divided into five to seven 3–8-in.-long leaflets. Very showy white flower clusters (8–12 in. tall, 2–4 in. wide). Blooms in light

shade. Bright yellow fall foliage. Good choice for massing, shrub borders, or specimen or understory planting.

A. pavia. RED BUCKEYE. Zones US, MS, LS, CS. Native to eastern U.S. Bulky shrub or tree to 12–20 ft., with irregular rounded crown. Narrow, erect 10-in. clusters of bright red or orange-red (rarely yellow) flowers. Blooms in light shade. Best foliage for warm, humid climates.

AFRICAN DAISY. See DIMORPHOTHECA

AFRICAN LILY. See AGAPANTHUS africanus

AFRICAN MASK. See ALOCASIA amazonica

AFRICAN VIOLET. See SAINTPAULIA ionantha

AGAPANTHUS

LILY-OF-THE-NILE

Amaryllidaceae

EVERGREEN OR DECIDUOUS PERENNIALS

☘ ZONES VARY BY SPECIES

☼ ◗ FULL SUN OR LIGHT SHADE

◖◖ REGULAR TO MODERATE WATER

Agapanthus africanus

All form fountainlike clumps of strap-shaped leaves, from which rise bare stems ending in spherical clusters of funnel-shaped flowers in summer. Each blue (sometimes white) bloom cluster resembles a burst of fireworks.

These plants are very adaptable. Will bloom in either full sun or light shade. Grow best in loamy soil but will grow in heavy soils. Plants thrive with regular water, but those established in the ground year-round can grow and bloom without watering during prolonged dry periods. Divide infrequently; every 5 or 6 years is usually sufficient. In colder-winter areas, lift and store over winter and replant in spring. Superb container plants. Good near ponds and pools.

☙ **A. africanus.** LILY-OF-THE-NILE, AFRICAN LILY. Evergreen. Zones LS, CS, TS. Leaves shorter, narrower than those of *A. orientalis;* flower stalks shorter (to 1½ ft. tall) with blue flowers in fewer numbers (20–50 to a cluster). Often sold as *A. umbellatus.*

A. Headbourne Hybrids. Deciduous. Zones MS, LS, CS, TS. Flowers come in a range of blues and in white on 2–2½-ft.-tall stems above fairly narrow, rather upright foliage. Surprisingly cold hardy.

A. inapertus. Deciduous. Zones LS, CS, TS. Deep blue blossoms in drooping clusters atop 4–5-ft. stems.

A. orientalis. Evergreen. Zones LS, CS, TS. This species is most commonly planted. Produces broad, arching leaves in big clumps. Stems to 4–5 ft. tall bear up to 100 blue flowers. White ('Albus'), double ('Flore Pleno'), and giant blue forms are also available. Often sold as *A. africanus, A. umbellatus.*

A. 'Peter Pan'. Evergreen. Zones LS, CS, TS. Outstanding dwarf. Foliage clumps 8–12 in. tall; profuse blue flowers top 1–1½-ft. stems.

AGARISTA populifolia
(Leucothoe populifolia)

FLORIDA LEUCOTHOE

Ericaceae

EVERGREEN SHRUB

☘ ZONES MS, LS, CS

◗ ● PARTIAL TO FULL SHADE

◖◖ REGULAR WATER, KEEP MOIST

Agarista populifolia

Attractive arching evergreen shrub native to South Carolina and south to Florida. Grows to 8–12 ft. Oval leaves to

4 in. long are glossy, rich green. Cream flowers borne in early summer are fragrant but not showy. Its open, multistemmed form makes an excellent addition to the woodland garden; it likes shade and moist, acid soil. Good companion to azaleas, rhododendrons, mountain laurels, and ferns. Prune out old branches periodically to retain its handsome open habit.

AGASTACHE

GIANT HYSSOP

Lamiaceae (Labiatae)

PERENNIALS

🗺 ZONES VARY BY SPECIES

☼ ◐ FULL SUN OR PARTIAL SHADE

💧 MODERATE WATER

Agastache foeniculum

Aromatic summer-blooming perennials somewhat resembling salvias, with whorls of blue, purple, or yellow flowers forming spikelike clusters. Provide well-drained soil. Not good choices for high-humidity, high-rainfall areas.

A. barberi. Zones LS, CS. Woody-based perennial to 2 ft., with 2-in. leaves and reddish purple flowers on 6–12-in. spikes. 'Firebird' has coppery orange-red flowers. Purple-flowered 'Tutti-Frutti' is a good substitute for purple loosestrife *(Lythrum)*.

A. foeniculum. ANISE HYSSOP. Zones US, MS, LS, CS. Erect, narrow clumping perennial to 5 ft., with anise- or licorice-scented foliage and dense clusters of lilac blue flowers on 4-in. spikes. Decorative and useful in perennial borders or herb gardens.

A. mexicana. MEXICAN GIANT HYSSOP. Zones CS, TS. Grows to 2 ft., with 2½-in. toothed leaves and rose pink inch-long flowers on spikes to 1 ft. long. 'Champagne' has apricot flowers.

Agavaceae. The agave family contains rosette-forming, sometimes treelike plants generally from dry regions. Flower clusters are spikes or spikelike; leaves often contain tough fibers.

AGAVE

Agavaceae

SUCCULENTS

🗺 ZONES CS, TS

☼ ◐ FULL SUN OR PARTIAL SHADE

💧 MODERATE TO LITTLE WATER, EXCEPT AS NOTED

Agave attenuata

Succulents, mostly gigantic, with large clumps of fleshy, strap-shaped leaves. The flower clusters are big but not colorful. After flowering—which may not occur for years—the foliage clump dies, usually leaving behind suckers that make new plants. The plants shrivel from serious drought but plump up again when watered or rained on. In rainy climates, they must have good drainage.

A. americana. CENTURY PLANT. Leaves to 6 ft. long, with hooked spines along the edges and a wicked spine at the tip; blue green in color. Be sure you really want one before planting it: The bulk and spines make it formidable to remove. After 10 years or more, the plant produces a branched, 15–40-ft. flower stalk bearing yellowish green flowers. There are several selections with yellow- or white-striped leaves.

A. attenuata. CENTURY PLANT. Leaves 2½ ft. long, soft green or gray green, fleshy, somewhat translucent, without spines. Makes clumps to 5 ft. across; older plants develop a stout trunk to 5 ft. tall. Greenish yellow flowers dense on arching spikes to 12–14 ft. long. Will take poor soil but does best in rich soil with regular water. Protect from frost and hot sun. Statuesque container plant. Good near ocean or pool.

A. filifera. Rosettes less than 2 ft. wide; leaves are narrow, dark green, lined with white, and edged with long white threads.

A. parryi huachucensis. Gray-green, 2–3-ft.-wide rosettes resemble giant artichokes. Tips of leaves fiercely spined. Makes offsets freely.

A. victoriae-reginae. Clumps only a foot or so across. The many dark green leaves are 6 in. long, 2 in. wide, stiff, thick, with narrow white lines. Slow growing; will stand in pot or ground 20 years before flowering (greenish flowers on tall stalks), and then die.

AGERATUM, HARDY. See EUPATORIUM coelestinum

AGERATUM houstonianum

AGERATUM, FLOSS FLOWER

Asteraceae (Compositae)

ANNUAL

🗺 ALL ZONES

☼ FULL SUN

💧 REGULAR WATER

Ageratum houstonianum

Reliable favorite for summer and fall in borders and containers. Leaves roundish, usually heart shaped at the base, soft green, hairy. Tiny blue, white, or pink tassel-like flowers in dense clusters. A few tall types, such as 2½-ft. 'Blue Horizon', are sold, but most selections offered are low growers. Dwarf kinds (4–6 in. high) with blue flowers include 'Blue Blazer', 'Blue Danube' ('Blue Puffs'), 'Blue Surf', and 'Royal Delft'. Somewhat taller (9–12-in.) blues include 'Blue Mink' and 'North Sea'. Good selections in other colors are 'Pink Powder-puffs' and white-blooming 'Summer Snow', both 9 in. high.

Best in rich, moist soil. Easy to transplant even when in bloom. Low growers make excellent edgings or pattern plantings with other similar-size annuals. Tall types provide good cut flowers.

AGLAONEMA

Araceae

PERENNIALS

🗺 ZONE TS; OR INDOORS

◐ ● TOLERATE VERY LOW LIGHT

💧 💧 AMPLE TO REGULAR WATER

Aglaonema modestum

Tropical plants valued for their ornamental foliage. Flowers resemble small, greenish white callas. Often used outdoors in containers or in north-side foundation plantings in mildest frost-free areas; elsewhere, they're house plants. Among the best plants for poorly lighted situations. In fact, few plants can get by on as little light as aglaonemas; *A. modestum* is especially tolerant of low light.

Potted plants need a rich, porous potting mix; they thrive with lots of water but will get along with small amounts. Cut stems will grow for a long time in a glass of water. Exudation from leaf tips (especially those of *A. modestum*) spots wood finishes (as on tabletops).

A. commutatum. Grows to 2 ft. Deep green leaves to 6 in. long, 2 in. across, with pale green markings on veins. Flowers followed by inch-long clusters of yellow to red berries. *A. c. maculatum*, with many irregular, gray-green stripes on leaves, is the most common. 'Pseudobracteatum', 1–2 ft. tall, has white leafstalks and deep green leaves marked with pale green and creamy yellow. 'Treubii' has narrow leaves heavily marked with silvery gray.

A. costatum. Slow-growing, low plant with leaves to 8 in. long, 4 in. wide. Bright green spotted white and a broad white stripe along the midrib. 'Foxii' is similar or identical.

A. crispum (A. roebelenii). PAINTED DROP-TONGUE. Robust plant with leathery leaves to 10 in. long, 5 in. wide, dark green with pale green markings. Sometimes sold as *A.* 'Pewter'.

▶

A. modestum. CHINESE EVERGREEN. A serviceable, easily grown plant, in time forming substantial clumps with several stems 2–3 ft. high. Shiny dark green leaves to 1½ ft. long, 5 in. wide. Often sold as *A. simplex.*

A. 'Silver King' and **'Silver Queen'.** Both are heavy producers of narrow, dark green leaves strongly marked with silver. Both grow to 2 ft. 'Silver King' has larger leaves than 'Silver Queen'.

AIR PLANT. See KALANCHOE pinnata

AJUGA

CARPET BUGLEWEED

Lamiaceae (Labiatae)

PERENNIALS

ZONES US, MS, LS

FULL SUN OR SHADE

REGULAR WATER

Ajuga reptans

One species is a rock garden plant; the others are ground covers. Of the latter, the highly variable *A. reptans* is better known and more useful, though it will escape into lawns unless contained. All bloom from spring to early summer.

A. genevensis. GENEVA CARPET BUGLEWEED. Rock garden plant 5–14 in. high, does not spread by runners. Grayish, hairy stems and coarse-toothed leaves to 3 in. long. Flowers in blue spikes; rose and white forms are also sold.

A. pyramidalis. Erect plant 2–10 in. high; does not spread by runners. Stems, with long grayish hairs, have many roundish, 1½–4-in.-long leaves. Violet blue flowers are not obvious among the large leaves. 'Metallica Crispa' has reddish brown leaves with a metallic glint.

A. reptans. CARPET BUGLEWEED. The popular ground cover ajuga. Spreads quickly by runners, making a mat of dark green leaves that grow 2–3 in. wide in full sun, 3–4 in. wide in part shade. Selections with bronze- or metallic-tinted leaves keep color best in full sun. Flowers, usually blue, are borne on 4–5-in.-high spikes. Plant in the spring or early fall 6–12 in. apart. Mow or trim off old flower spikes. Subject to root-knot nematodes; also susceptible to rot and fungal diseases where drainage or air circulation is poor. Many selections of this species are offered, some sold under several names. The following selections are among the best choices available:

'Alba'. Flowers are white.

'Burgundy Glow'. Green and pink leaves edged in white; blue flowers.

'Purpurea'. Usually has somewhat larger leaves tinted bronze or purple. Often sold as 'Atropurpurea'.

'Rosea'. Pink flowers.

'Variegata'. Leaves edged and splotched with creamy yellow.

AKEBIA quinata

FIVELEAF AKEBIA

Lardizabalaceae

EVERGREEN VINE

ZONES US, MS, LS, CS

SUN OR SHADE

REGULAR WATER

Akebia quinata

Native to Japan, China, and Korea. Plant twines to 15–20 ft. Grows fast in the Lower and Coastal South, slower elsewhere. Dainty leaves on 3–5-in. stalks, each divided into five deep green leaflets 2–3 in. long and notched at tips. Bears clusters of dull purple flowers in spring that are more a surprise than a

show. Edible fruit, if produced, looks like a thick, 2½–4-in.-long, purplish sausage.

Give support for climbing; keep plant under control to prevent it from becoming rampant. Benefits from annual pruning. Recovers quickly when cut to the ground. For a tracery effect on post or column, prune out all but two or three basal stems.

A. trifoliata. THREELEAF AKEBIA. Like the above but with three instead of five leaflets per leaf.

ALABAMA SNOW-WREATH. See NEVIUSIA alabamensis

ALBIZIA julibrissin

MIMOSA

Fabaceae (Leguminosae)

DECIDUOUS TREE

ZONES US, MS, LS, CS

FULL SUN OR PARTIAL SHADE

REGULAR WATER

Albizia julibrissin

Native to Asia from Iran to Japan. Rapid growth to 40 ft. with wider spread. Fluffy pink flowers like pincushions on ferny-leafed branches in summer. Blooms carry a delicate gardenia scent. Flowers attract hummingbirds and butterflies. 'Rosea' has richer pink flowers and is considered hardier. Mimosa does best with high summer heat. Tolerates constant wind, salt spray, and alkaline soil. With regular watering, it grows fast; on skimpy moisture, it usually survives but grows slowly, looks yellowish.

A favorite climbing tree of Southern children, mimosa is unfortunately beset by a host of problems, including short life, susceptibility to wilt disease and webworm, unattractive seed pods in winter, and weak, brittle branches. It also reseeds prolifically.

> **MAKE HOLLYHOCKS BLOOM TWICE**
>
> In July, after blooms fade, cut off flower stems just above the ground. Continue to feed and water the plants. Roots will push out another flush of growth, which will rebloom in September. This technique demands a lot from the plants, so feed two or three times during the regular growing season, and water as needed all along.

ALCEA rosea (Althaea rosea)

HOLLYHOCK

Malvaceae

BIENNIAL OR SHORT-LIVED PERENNIAL

ALL ZONES

FULL SUN

REGULAR WATER

Alcea rosea

This old-fashioned favorite has its place against a fence or wall or at the back of a border. Old single types can reach 9 ft.; newer strains and selections are shorter. Big, rough, roundish heart-shaped leaves more or less lobed; single, semidouble, or double flowers 3–6 in. wide in white, pink, rose, red, purple, creamy yellow, apricot. Summer bloom. Destroy rust-infected leaves as soon as the telltale yellow, orange, and reddish-brown spots appear.

Chater's Double is a fine perennial strain; 6-ft. spires have 5–6-in. flowers. So-called annual strains (biennials treated as annuals) bloom first year from seed sown in early spring: Summer Carnival strain is 5–6 ft. tall with double 4-in. flowers; Majorette strain is 2½ ft. tall with 3–4-in. flowers; Pinafore strain (mixed colors) branches freely from base, has five to eight bloom stalks per plant. Sow seeds in ground in August or September for next season's bloom.

ALCHEMILLA

LADY'S-MANTLE

Rosaceae

PERENNIALS

ZONES VARY BY SPECIES

● SHADE

● REGULAR WATER

Alchemilla mollis

Rounded pale green lobed leaves have a silvery look; after rain or overhead watering they hold beads of water on their surfaces. Summer flowers are yellowish green, in large branched clusters, individually inconspicuous but attractive as a mass. Useful for edgings in shady places, as ground cover and as soothing contrast to brightly colored flowers.

A. alpina. Zones US, MS. Mat-forming plant creeping by runners, with flowering stems 6–8 in. tall. Leaves 2 in. wide, divided into either five or seven leaflets.

A. erythropoda. Zones US, MS. Resembles *A. glaucescens* but has more deeply lobed leaves and red-tinted flowering stems.

A. glaucescens (A. pubescens). Zones US, MS. Dense grower. Flowering stems to 8 in. tall. Leaves nearly round; seven to nine lobes.

A. mollis. Zones US, MS, LS. To 2 ft. or more, with equal spread, and nearly circular, scallop-edged leaves to 6 in. across.

ALEXANDER PALM. See PTYCHOSPERMA elegans

ALEXANDRA PALM. See ARCHONTOPHOENIX alexandrae

ALGERIAN IVY. See HEDERA canariensis

ALLAMANDA

Apocynaceae

EVERGREEN VINES OR SHRUBS

ZONE TS; OR ANNUAL, GREENHOUSE PLANTS

FULL SUN

● REGULAR WATER

◊ ALL PARTS ARE POISONOUS IF INGESTED

Allamanda cathartica

These handsome plants produce showy flowers nearly continuously during warm weather. They are year-round outdoor plants only in the Tropical South. Will succeed as annual vines anywhere with a long growing season; otherwise, grow in greenhouse.

A. cathartica. COMMON ALLAMANDA, GOLDEN TRUMPET. Can grow to great heights as a vine, but often pinched back as a large free-standing shrub. Leaves are glossy, leathery, 4–6 in. long. Trumpet-shaped yellow flowers are 5 in. wide, 3 in. long. 'Hendersonii' has exceptionally attractive orange-yellow flowers.

A. schottii (A. neriifolia). BUSH ALLAMANDA. Shrubby, to 5 ft., with occasional climbing stems. Flowers 3 in. wide, tinted orange or reddish.

ALLIUM

ORNAMENTAL ALLIUM

Liliaceae

BULBS

ZONES VARY; OR DIG AND STORE; OR GROW IN POTS

FULL SUN OR PARTIAL SHADE

● REGULAR WATER DURING GROWTH AND BLOOM

Allium tuberosum

About 500 species, all from the Northern Hemisphere. Relatives of the edible onion, peerless as cut flowers (fresh or dried), useful in borders; smaller kinds are effective in rock gardens. Most ornamental alliums are hardy, sun loving, easy to grow; they thrive in deep, rich, sandy loam. Plant bulbs in fall. Lift and divide only after they become crowded. Alliums bear small flowers in compact or loose roundish clusters at ends of leafless stems 6 in.–5 ft. tall or more. Many are delightfully fragrant; those with onion odor must be bruised or cut to give it off. Various species provide flowers from late spring through summer, in white and shades of pink, rose, violet, red, blue, yellow. All alliums die to the ground after bloom, even in mild climates. In areas colder than stated hardiness, dig and store; or grow in pots and protect during winter.

A. aflatunense. Zones US, MS, LS. Round clusters of lilac flowers on stems 2½–5 ft. tall. Resembles *A. giganteum* but with smaller (2–3-in.) flower clusters; blooms in late spring.

A. atropurpureum. Zones US, MS, LS. Stems to 2½ ft. tall carry 2-in. clusters of dark purple to nearly black flowers in late spring.

A. caeruleum (A. azureum). BLUE ALLIUM. Zones US, MS, LS. Cornflower blue flowers in dense, round clusters 2 in. across on 1-ft. stems. Late spring bloom.

A. carinatum pulchellum (A. pulchellum). Zones US, MS, LS. Tight clusters of reddish purple flowers on 2-ft. stems, late spring.

A. cepa. See Onion

A. christophii (A. albopilosum). STAR OF PERSIA. Zones US, MS, LS. Distinctive. Very large clusters (6–12 in. across) of lavender to deep lilac starlike flowers with metallic sheen. Late spring bloom. Stems are 12–15 in. tall. Leaves to 1½ ft. long, white and hairy beneath. Dried flower cluster looks like an elegant ornament.

A. giganteum. GIANT ALLIUM. Zones US, MS, LS. Spectacular ball-like clusters of bright lilac flowers on stems 5 ft. tall or more. Summer bloom. Leaves 1½ ft. long, 2 in. wide.

A. karataviense. TURKESTAN ALLIUM. Zones US, MS, LS. Large, dense, round flower clusters in midspring, varying in color from pinkish to beige to reddish lilac. Broad, flat, recurved leaves, 2–5 in. across.

Allium giganteum

A. moly. GOLDEN GARLIC. Zones US, MS, LS. Bright, shining, yellow flowers in open clusters on 9–18-in.-tall stems. Late spring bloom. Flat leaves 2 in. wide, almost as long as flower stems.

A. narcissiflorum. Zones US, MS, LS. Foot-tall stems with loose clusters of ½-in. bell-shaped, bright rose flowers in summer.

A. neapolitanum. Zones US, MS, LS, CS. Spreading clusters of large white flowers on 1-ft. stems bloom in midspring. Leaves 1 in. wide. 'Grandiflorum' is larger, blooms earlier. A form of 'Grandiflorum' listed as 'Cowanii' is considered superior. Grown commercially as cut flowers.

A. ostrowskianum (A. oreophilum ostrowskianum). Zones US, MS, LS, CS. Large, loose clusters of rose-colored flowers on 8–12-in. stems in late spring; two or three narrow, gray-green leaves. 'Zwanenburg' has deep carmine red flowers, 6-in. stems. Good for rock gardens, cutting.

A. porrum. See Leek

A. rosenbachianum. Zones US, MS, LS. Similar to *A. giganteum* but slightly smaller; blooms in late spring.

A. sativum. See Garlic

▶

A. schoenoprasum. See Chives

A. scorodoprasum. See Garlic

A. sphaerocephalum. DRUMSTICKS, ROUND-HEADED GARLIC. Zones US, MS, LS. Tight, dense, spherical red-purple flower clusters on 2-ft. stems, early summer. Spreads freely.

A. tuberosum. GARLIC CHIVES, CHINESE CHIVES, ORIENTAL GARLIC. Zones US, MS, LS, CS. Spreads by tuberous rootstocks and by seeds. Plant grows in clumps of gray-green, flat leaves ¼ in. wide, 1 ft. long or less. Abundance of 1–1½-ft.-tall stalks bear clusters of white flowers in summer. Flowers have scent of violets, are excellent for fresh or dry arrangements. Leaves have mild garlic flavor, are useful in salads and cooked dishes. Grow like chives.

ALLSPICE, CAROLINA. See CALYCANTHUS floridus

ALMOND, FLOWERING. See PRUNUS triloba

ALOCASIA

ELEPHANT'S EAR

Araceae

PERENNIALS

ZONE TS UNLESS NOTED; OR INDOORS

FILTERED SUNLIGHT

AMPLE TO REGULAR WATER

PLANT JUICES ARE POISONOUS IF INGESTED

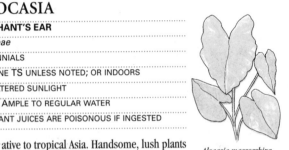
Alocasia macrorrhiza

Native to tropical Asia. Handsome, lush plants for tropical effects. Plant in wind-protected places or indoors. Provide ample organic matter in soil and light, frequent feedings. Tropical plant specialists sell many kinds with leaves in coppery and purplish tones, often with striking white veins.

A. amazonica. AFRICAN MASK. Leathery, deep bronzy green leaves to 16 in. long have wavy edges, heavy white main veins. This species is the one most commonly available as a house plant.

A. macrorrhiza. GIANT ALOCASIA. Zones LS (protected), CS, TS. Evergreen at 29°F; loses leaves at lower temperatures but comes back in spring if frosts not too severe. Large, arrow-shaped leaves to 2 ft. or longer, on stalks to 5 ft. tall, form a dome-shaped plant 4 ft. across. Tiny flowers on spike surrounded by greenish white bract. Flowers followed by reddish fruit, giving spike the look of corn on the cob.

A. odora. Similar to *A. macrorrhiza* but not quite as hardy. Flowers are fragrant.

ALOE

Liliaceae

SUCCULENTS

ZONE TS

FULL SUN OR LIGHT SHADE

REGULAR TO LITTLE WATER

LATEX BENEATH PLANT SKIN IS AN IRRITANT

Aloe vera

Aloes range from 6-in. miniatures to trees; all form clumps of fleshy, pointed leaves and bear branched or unbranched clusters of orange, yellow, cream, or red flowers. Most are South African. Showy, easy to grow in well-drained soil in reasonably frost-free areas. Need little water but can take more. Most kinds make outstanding container plants. Some species in bloom every month; biggest show midwinter through summer. Leaves may be green or gray green, often strikingly banded or streaked with contrasting colors. Where winters are too cool, grow in pots and shelter from frosts. Aloes listed here are only a few of the many kinds.

A. arborescens. TREE ALOE. Older clumps may reach 18 ft. Branching stems carry big clumps of gray-green, spiny-edged leaves. Flowers (early to midwinter) in long, spiky clusters, bright vermilion to clear yellow. Withstands salt spray. Tolerates shade. Foliage damaged at 29°F, but plants have survived 17°F.

A. barbadensis. See A. vera

A. saponaria. Short-stemmed, broad clumps. Broad, thick, 8-in.-long leaves with white spots. Clumps spread rapidly and may become bound together—dig up too-thick clumps and separate them. Branched flower stalk 1½–2½ ft. tall. Orange-red to shrimp pink flowers over long period.

Aloe arborescens

A. variegata. PARTRIDGE-BREAST ALOE, TIGER ALOE. Foot-high, triangular rosette of fleshy, triangular, dark green, 5-in.-long leaves strikingly banded and edged with white. Loose clusters of pink to dull red flowers intermittent all year.

A. vera (A. barbadensis). MEDICINAL ALOE, BARBADOS ALOE. Clustering rosettes of narrow, fleshy, stiffly upright leaves 1–2 ft. long. Yellow flowers in dense spike atop 3-ft. stalk, spring and summer. Favorite folk medicine plant used to treat burns, bites, inflammation, and a host of other ills.

> **LEMON VERBENA LEAVES FOR FRAGRANCE AND FLAVOR**
> This plant is prized for its leaves, which scent the area around them with a citruslike fragrance. The long, shiny leaves add lemony flavor to teas and iced drinks. Dry the leaves for potpourri. When making apple jelly, try placing a big fresh leaf in the bottom of each glass or jar. For all these purposes, pick the fresh-looking leaves from near top of stem.

ALOYSIA triphylla (Lippia citriodora)

LEMON VERBENA

Verbenaceae

DECIDUOUS OR PARTIALLY EVERGREEN HERB-SHRUB

ZONES LS, CS, TS

FULL SUN

REGULAR WATER

Aloysia triphylla

May succeed outdoors north of its usual range if planted against warm wall; otherwise, can be grown as house plant. Legginess is the natural state of this plant; it's the herb that grew like a gangling shrub in grandmother's garden. Prized for its lemon-scented leaves. When you read of the scent of verbena in literature about the antebellum South, lemon verbena is the plant being described. Grows to 6 ft. or taller; narrow leaves to 3 in. long are arranged in whorls of three or four along branches. Bears open clusters of very small lilac or whitish flowers in summer. By pinch-pruning you can shape it to give interesting tracery against wall. Or let it grow among lower plants to hide its legginess. Needs well-drained soil.

ALPINIA

Zingiberaceae

PERENNIALS WITH RHIZOMES

ZONE TS UNLESS NOTED

LIGHT SHADE

AMPLE TO REGULAR WATER

Alpinia zerumbet

Evergreen in the Tropical South. Roots hardy to about 15°F. Need wind-free exposure, good soil. In order to bloom, alpinias must be established at least 2 years. Remove flowered canes yearly.

A

A. purpurata. RED GINGER. Native to the Pacific Islands. Grows in clumps to 6–12 ft., possibly taller, with leaves 2½ ft. long, 6 in. wide. Flower stems are 1–2-ft. upright spikes of brilliant purplish red boat-shaped bracts; they last well in indoor arrangements. Small white flowers bloom inconspicuously among the bracts, and seeds sometimes germinate there, forming plantlets that can be removed and rooted as cuttings.

A. sanderae. VARIEGATED GINGER. To 3–4 ft. tall, with 8-in.-long leaves striped with white. Rarely blooms. A good container plant.

A. zerumbet (A. nutans, A. speciosa). SHELL GINGER, SHELL FLOWER. Zones LS, CS, TS. Native to tropical Asia and Polynesia. Grandest of gingers, best all-year appearance. To 8–9 ft. tall. Leaves shiny, 2 ft. long, 5 in. wide, with distinct parallel veins; grow on stems that are maroon at maturity. Waxy white or pinkish, shell-like, fragrant flowers marked red, purple, brown, in pendent clusters on arching stems in late summer. Most popular of the alpinias grown in Florida. 'Variegata' has striking yellow or cream bands on foliage.

ALSOPHILA australis, A. cooperi. See CYATHEA cooperi

ALSTROEMERIA

Liliaceae

PERENNIALS

✄ ZONES MS, LS, CS

☼ ◑ AFTERNOON SHADE

● REGULAR WATER

◈ CAUSES DERMATITIS IN ALLERGIC PEOPLE

Alstroemeria psittacina

Old Southern gardens often have plantings of a species *Alstroemeria*, 🏛 *A. psittacina* (formerly *A. pulchella*), called parrot lily. This species is hardy to 0°F; grows to 2–3 ft.; has narrow red flowers tipped green and spotted deep purple, interesting rather than showy. It's a steady spreader, can be invasive. In contrast, the butterfly-flowered hybrids with delicate streaks and speckles, most like the cut flowers sold by florists, are expensive and sometimes difficult to find.

The new hybrids that are widely available include a Connecticut-bred group called the Constitution Series. The plants in this group have proved fairly hardy (with heavy mulching), flower from spring to fall (though flowering may slow or stop in midsummer because of heat), and are not invasive. They grow to 2½ ft., don't require staking, and produce 10 to 20 blossoms per stem and 30 to 40 stems per plant. Colors are white, pink, red, purple, yellow; some are heavily streaked and spotted. Selections include 'Freedom' (pink), 'Redcoat' (red), and lightly fragrant 'Sweet Laura' (yellow).

Cordu and Meyer hybrids have a long bloom season if spent flowering stems are pulled up from the ground, not cut. Colors include white to pink, red, lilac, and purple, usually bicolored and spotted. Ligtu hybrids, the oldest hybrids available, are tall (need staking), and the flowers are fewer, less brightly colored, and less delicately streaked and spotted than the newest hybrids, though these older hybrids are often available as seed. Examples include Dr. Salter's hybrids.

All types grow best in cool, moist, deep, sandy to medium loam. Plant roots in fall; if you buy alstroemeria in a pot, you can plant outdoors any time in mild-winter climates. Set roots 6–8 in. deep, 1 ft. apart; handle brittle roots gently. Leave clumps undisturbed for many years because they reestablish slowly after transplanting. You can easily start alstroemeria by sowing seed where the plants are to grow or in individual pots for later transplanting. Sow in fall, winter, or earliest spring. Hardy in the Middle South if planted at proper depth and kept mulched in winter. Ligtu hybrids can be allowed to dry off after bloom. Evergreen kinds need moisture for continued bloom; cool summers also prolong bloom.

ALTERNANTHERA ficoidea

Amaranthaceae

PERENNIAL TREATED AS ANNUAL

✄ ZONE TS

☼ FULL SUN

● REGULAR WATER

Alternanthera ficoidea 'Bettzickiana'

Colorful foliage somewhat resembles that of coleus. Often sold as 'Joseph's Coat'. Plants grow 6–12 in. tall and should be planted 4–10 in. apart for colorful effect. Where winters are cold, plant only after the soil warms up. Tolerates heat well. Keep low and compact by shearing. Grow from cuttings. Often sold as *A. bettzickiana.* 'Aurea Nana' is low grower with yellow-splotched foliage. 'Bettzickiana' has spoon-shaped leaves with red and yellow markings. 'Magnifica' is a red-bronze dwarf. 'Parrot Feather' and 'Versicolor' have broad green leaves with yellow markings and pink veins.

ALTHAEA rosea. See ALCEA rosea

ALUM ROOT. See HEUCHERA

ALYSSUM, SWEET. See LOBULARIA maritima

AMARACUS dictamnus. See ORIGANUM dictamnus

Amaranthaceae. The amaranth family largely consists of herbaceous plants, many of them weedy. Flowers are small and chaffy, but very effective when massed.

AMARANTHUS

AMARANTH

Amaranthaceae

ANNUALS

✄ ALL ZONES

☼ ◑ FULL SUN OR PARTIAL SHADE

● REGULAR WATER

Amaranthus caudatus

Coarse, sometimes weedy plants; a few ornamental kinds are grown for their brightly colored foliage or flowers. Sow seed in early summer—soil temperature must be above 70°F for germination.

Picked when young and tender, leaves and stems of many species (even some of the weedy ones) can be cooked like spinach, taking its place in hot weather. Some species have seeds that look like sesame seeds, have a high protein content, and can be used as grain.

A. caudatus. LOVE-LIES-BLEEDING, TASSEL FLOWER. Sturdy, branching plant 3–8 ft. high; leaves 2–10 in. long, ½–4 in. wide. Red flowers in drooping, tassel-like clusters. A curiosity rather than a pretty plant. One of the amaranths that produce grain.

A. hybridus erythrostachys. PRINCE'S FEATHER. To 5 ft. high with leaves 1–6 in. long, ½–3 in. wide, usually reddish. Flowers red or brownish red in many-branched clusters. Some strains grown as spinach substitute or for grain.

A. tricolor. JOSEPH'S COAT. Branching plant 1–4 ft. high. Leaves 2½–6 in. long, 2–4 in. wide, blotched in shades of red and green. 'Early Splendor', 'Flaming Fountain', and 'Molten Fire' bear masses of yellow to scarlet foliage at tops of main stems and principal branches. Green-leafed strains used as spinach substitute under the name "tampala."

Amaryllidaceae. Plants of the amaryllis family have strap-shaped leaves, bulbous or rhizomatous rootstocks, and flowers atop leafless stems. Examples include crinum, *Hymenocallis,* lily-of-the-Nile (*Agapanthus*), snowdrop (*Galanthus*), snowflake (*Leucojum*), society garlic (*Tulbaghia*), spider lily (*Lycoris*), and spring star flower (*Ipheion*).

A

AMARYLLIS. See HIPPEASTRUM

AMARYLLIS hallii. See LYCORIS squamigera

AMAZON VINE. See STIGMAPHYLLON

AMELANCHIER

SERVICEBERRY, JUNEBERRY, SHADBLOW

Rosaceae

DECIDUOUS SHRUBS OR SMALL TREES

✧ ZONES US, MS, LS

☼ ◐ FULL SUN OR PARTIAL SHADE

◔ ◕ REGULAR TO MODERATE WATER

Amelanchier laevis

Graceful, airy trees provide year-round interest. Drooping clusters of white or pinkish flowers in early spring, just before or during leaf-out, are showy, though short lived. These are followed in early summer by edible blueberry-flavored fruits excellent in pies—if you can get to them before the birds do. Purplish new spring foliage turns deep green in summer, then fiery in fall; drops to reveal attractive silhouette in winter.

Plant against dark background to show off form, flowers, fall color. Noninvasive roots and light shade make these good trees to garden under. Especially lovely in woodland gardens. All need a definite period of winter chill. Serviceberry is often pronounced "sarvisberry."

A. alnifolia. SASKATOON. Native to western Canada and mountainous parts of the western U.S. To 20 ft., spreading by rhizomes. 'Regent', 4–6 ft. tall, bears heavy crop of fruit in early summer. Red-and-yellow fall foliage.

A. arborea. JUNEBERRY. Native to eastern and southern U.S. Narrow tree, similar to *A. canadensis* but sometimes taller, more often forms a nice round-headed tree, and has larger, pendulous loose racemes of white flowers that bloom as the leaves unfold. Delicious dark red–purple fruit tastes like blueberries.

A. canadensis. SHADBLOW SERVICEBERRY. Narrowish, to 25 ft. tall, with short, erect flower clusters. Plants offered under this name may actually belong to other species. Often suckering and multitrunked.

A. grandiflora. APPLE SERVICEBERRY. Hybrid between *A. arborea* and *A. laevis.* Named selections may be sold under any of these species names. Most grow to 25 ft., with drooping clusters of white flowers opening from pinkish buds. 'Autumn Brilliance' has blue-green foliage that turns orange red in fall. 'Cole's Selection' and 'Princess Diana' are similar.

A. laevis. ALLEGHENY SERVICEBERRY. Native to eastern North America. Narrow shrub or small tree to 40 ft. with nodding or drooping, 4-in. white flower clusters. Leaves are bronzy purple when new, dark green in summer, yellow to red in autumn. Small black-purple fruit is very sweet.

AMERICAN CRANBERRY BUSH. See VIBURNUM trilobum

AMERICAN MAIDENHAIR FERN. See ADIANTUM pedatum

AMETHYST FLOWER. See BROWALLIA

AMORPHA

Fabaceae (Leguminosae)

DECIDUOUS SHRUBS

✧ ZONES US, MS, LS, CS

☼ FULL SUN

◔ ◕ REGULAR TO MODERATE WATER, UNLESS NOTED

Amorpha fruticosa

Shrubs with leaves divided featherwise into many leaflets; 3–6-in.-long spikelike clusters of single-petaled flowers in early summer are blue or purple. In cold weather, plants may die back nearly to the ground; in warmer areas, they should be cut back severely to

prevent lankiness. Tough and undemanding, withstanding heat and wind. Need at least moderate amount of water in dry climates, except the Texas native, *A. texana,* which is like *A. canescens,* but drought tolerant.

A. canescens. LEAD PLANT. Native to the High Plains from Canada to Texas. About 3 ft. tall and wide, with silvery, downy foliage.

A. fruticosa. INDIGO BUSH, FALSE INDIGO. Native to eastern U.S. Lanky growth to 10–15 ft. tall, with light green foliage. Needs hard pruning in winter or early spring to maintain some degree of compactness.

AMPELOPSIS
brevipedunculata

PORCELAIN BERRY, PORCELAIN AMPELOPSIS

Vitaceae

DECIDUOUS VINE

✧ ZONES US, MS, LS, CS

☼ ◐ SUN OR PARTIAL SHADE

◔ ◕ REGULAR TO MODERATE WATER

Ampelopsis brevipedunculata

Rampant climber with twining tendrils. Grows to 20 ft. Large, handsome, three-lobed, 2½–5-in.-wide leaves are dark green. In warmer areas of range, leaves turn red and partially drop in fall; more leaves come out, redden, and drop all winter. Many clusters of small grapelike berries turn from greenish ivory to brilliant metallic blue in late summer and fall. Needs strong support. Superb on concrete and rock walls or as shade plant on arbors. Invasive from seed; use with extreme caution near woods, natural areas. Attracts birds. Japanese beetles can be a problem. 'Elegans' has leaves variegated with white and pink. Although smaller, less vigorous, and less hardy than the species, it is a splendid hanging basket plant.

Boston ivy and Virginia creeper, formerly included in genus *Ampelopsis,* are now listed under *Parthenocissus* because, unlike *Ampelopsis,* both have disks at ends of their tendrils.

AMSONIA

BLUE STAR FLOWER

Apocynaceae

PERENNIALS

✧ ZONES US, MS, LS

☼ ◐ FULL SUN OR LIGHT SHADE

◔ ◕ REGULAR TO MODERATE WATER

Amsonia tabernaemontana

Elegant milkweed relatives with narrow leaves and erect stems topped by clusters of small, star-shaped, pale blue flowers. Most bloom in late spring. All are tough plants that tolerate ordinary soil and occasional lapses in watering. Bright yellow fall foliage color is a bonus.

A. hubrectii (A. ciliata). To 2½–3 ft. tall, with crowded, needlelike (but soft), 2-in. leaves; has exceptional fall color.

A. illustris. Like *A. tabernaemontana* but has shiny, leathery leaves.

A. tabernaemontana. BLUE STAR. Reaches to 2–2½ ft. tall, with narrow, willowlike foliage. 'Montana' is more compact and blooms earlier.

AMUR CHOKECHERRY. See Prunus maackii

AMUR MAPLE. See ACER ginnala

Anacardiaceae. The cashew family includes trees, shrubs, and vines with small, often profuse flowers. Foliage is attractive; fruits are sometimes showy or edible. Many have poisonous or irritating sap. Mango (*Mangifera*) and poison ivy (*Toxicodendron*) indicate the diversity of the family.

ANDROPOGON

BLUESTEM

Poaceae (Gramineae)

PERENNIAL GRASSES

ZONES US, MS, LS, UNLESS NOTED

FULL SUN OR LIGHT SHADE

WATER NEEDS VARY BY SPECIES

Andropogon gerardii

These slender-leafed, upright native grasses formed a predominant part of old tall- and short-grass prairies. Big bluestem made waves of rippling green sometimes nearly twice as tall as the settlers. The bluestems were once found in most of the continental states of the U.S.

Plant these clumping grasses in drifts or masses, for erosion control, as airy vertical accents in flower or shrub borders, or in a natural garden with sunflowers, goldenrod, and coreopsis. Be sure to divide clumps every few years when centers start to die; discard the center and replant vigorous young clumps from the edge. Every year, shear dried stems to base before new growth begins in spring.

A. gerardii. BIG BLUESTEM, TURKEYFOOT. Variable growth, 3–7 ft., sometimes to 10 ft. in moist, warm soil. Often tall enough to make a screen or dramatic specimen in large perennial borders. Thin blades are blue green or silvery in summer, bronze red in fall. Smoky purple flower spikes and seed heads form at stem end in elegant sets of three, like the toes of a turkey foot. Prefers moisture throughout the growing season; tolerates drought but grows much less vigorously. Tolerates wide range of soils, including clay soils and acid or alkaline soils.

A. scoparius (Schizachyrium scoparium). LITTLE BLUESTEM. To 1–2 ft., possibly 5 ft. in moist situation. Slender, compact clump, usually less than 1 ft. across. Foliage light green to blue green during summer, turning to warm coppery red in fall. Tough grass, tolerant of wet soil and drought. May self-sow in warm soil and become a nuisance if planted in flower borders.

A. virginicus. BROOM SEDGE. Zones US, MS, LS, CS. Small clumping grass similar to little bluestem in size and summer foliage color, but blades turn showy orange in fall. Tolerates poor, dry, clay, or rocky soil. Often colonizes abandoned farm fields, roadsides, and disturbed areas.

ANEMONE

WINDFLOWER, ANEMONE

Ranunculaceae

PERENNIALS WITH TUBEROUS OR FIBROUS ROOTS

ZONES US, MS, LS, UNLESS NOTED

EXPOSURE NEEDS VARY BY SPECIES

REGULAR WATER

ALL PARTS ARE POISONOUS IF INGESTED

Anemone coronaria

A rich and varied group of plants ranging in size from alpine rock garden miniatures to tall Japanese anemones grown in borders; bloom extends from very early spring to fall, depending on species or selection.

Of the species listed here, *A. blanda* and *A. coronaria* are grown from tubers; in general, tuberous types are short lived in warmest areas, where they may best be treated as annuals. Plant them in a spot that gets some shade every day. Set out tubers October or November. Some gardeners soak tubers of *A. coronaria* for a few hours before planting.

Plant tubers 1–2 in. deep, 8–12 in. apart, in rich, light, well-drained garden loam. Or start in flats of damp sand; set out in garden when the leaves are a few inches tall. Keep soil moist. Protect from birds until leaves toughen. In high-rainfall areas, excess moisture induces rot.

A. blanda. GREEK ANEMONE, GREEK WINDFLOWER. Stems rise 2–8 in. from tuberous roots. Finely divided leaves covered with soft hairs. In spring, one sky blue flower, 1–1½ in. across, on each stem. Grow with and among

Japanese maples, azaleas, and other light shrubbery in partial shade. Associate with miniature daffodils, tulips, and scillas; or grow in pots. Types with 2-in. flowers (in blue and other colors) on 10–12-in. plants include 'Blue Star', 'Pink Star', 'White Splendor', and purplish red 'Radar'.

Anemone blanda

A. canadensis. Grows 1–2 ft. tall, with divided leaves and inch-wide white flowers springing in twos and threes from the upper leaf joints; summer bloom. Partial shade.

A. coronaria. POPPY ANEMONE. Tuberous rooted. Common large-flowered, showy anemone valued for cutting and for spectacular color in spring borders. Finely divided green leaves. Flowers red, blue, tones and mixtures of these colors, and white, 1½–2½ in. across, borne singly on 6–18-in. stems. Most popular strains are De Caen (single flowers) and St. Brigid (semidouble to double flowers). Full sun or partial shade.

A. hybrida (A. japonica, A. hupehensis japonica). JAPANESE ANEMONE. A long-lived, fibrous-rooted perennial indispensable for fall color in partial shade. Graceful, branching stems 2–4 ft. high rise from clump of dark green, three- to five-lobed leaves covered with soft hairs. Flowers single, semidouble, and double, in white, silvery pink, or rose. Many named selections, including 'Honorine Jobert', with single white flowers on 2–3-ft. stems, which blooms reliably in Lower South; 'Margarete', semidouble or double rose pink flowers, 2–3-ft. stems; 'Prinz Heinrich', rosy red semidouble flowers, 18–24-in. stems; 'Queen Charlotte', pink single flowers, 3-ft. stems; 'September Charm', soft silver pink flowers, 2-ft. stems; 'Whirlwind', semidouble large white flowers, 3-ft. stems.

Slow to establish but once started spreads readily if roots not disturbed. Mulch in fall where winters are extremely severe. Increase by divisions in fall or early spring or by root cuttings in spring. May need staking. Effective in clumps in front of tall shrubbery or under high-branching trees.

A. nemorosa. WOOD ANEMONE. To 1 ft., with creeping rhizomes, deeply cut leaves, and inch-wide white (rarely pinkish or blue) spring flowers held above the foliage. Spreads slowly to make an attractive woodland ground cover. Many named selections exist; 'Allenii' has large blue flowers, and there are double forms. Partial to full shade.

A. quinquefolia. Zones US, MS. American native. Attractive woodland ground cover resembling *A. nemorosa*, with inch-wide white flowers in spring. *A. q. oregana* is similar, but blooms are sometimes blue or pink.

A. sylvestris. SNOWDROP ANEMONE. European native grows to 1½ ft. tall. White, fragrant, 1½–3-in. flowers appear in spring; attractive cottony seed heads follow. Partial to full shade.

A. vitifolia robustissima. GRAPELEAF ANEMONE. Vigorous plant grows to 6 ft. tall with single pink flowers in fall. Resembles *A. hybrida* on a larger scale. Partial shade. True name is probably *A. tomentosa*.

WHICH SIDE OF AN ANEMONE TUBER IS UP?

Locating the top side of an anemone tuber can be difficult because of its irregular shape. The important sign to look for is the depressed scar left by the base of last year's stem (sometimes you really have to search for it); plant the tuber with the scarred side up.

ANEMONELLA thalictroides

RUE ANEMONE

Ranunculaceae

PERENNIAL

ZONES US, MS, LS

PARTIAL OR FULL SHADE

REGULAR WATER

Anemonella thalictroides

Delicate woodland plant native to eastern North America. To 9 in. high, with finely divided leaves resembling those of meadow rue (*Thalictrum*). Loose clusters of inch-wide white

A

(usually) or pink flowers appear in early spring. Attractive for close-up viewing. Selection known as either 'Rosea Plena' or 'Schoaff's Double Pink' has long-lasting, fully double pink flowers like tiny roses.

ANETHUM graveolens

DILL

Apiaceae (Umbelliferae)

ANNUAL HERB

☘ ALL ZONES

☼ FULL SUN

◑ REGULAR WATER

Anethum graveolens

Aromatic herb, grows to 3–4 ft. Soft and feathery leaves; umbrellalike, 6-in.-wide clusters of small yellow flowers. The seeds and leaves have pungent fragrance. Sow seed where the plants are to be grown; for a constant supply, sow them several times during spring and summer. Thin the seedlings to about 1½ ft. apart. Plant sprouts and grows better in the spring than in summer. An easy way to grow it in a casual garden is to let a few plants go to seed. Seedlings appear here and there at odd times and can be pulled and chopped as "dill weed." Use seeds in pickling and vinegar; use fresh or dried leaves when preparing fish or lamb, in salads, stews, sauces, as garnish.

ANGEL'S HAIR. See ARTEMISIA schmidtiana

ANGEL'S TEARS. See NARCISSUS triandrus

ANGEL'S TRUMPET. See BRUGMANSIA

ANISACANTHUS

Acanthaceae

EVERGREEN OR DECIDUOUS SHRUBS

☘ ZONES LS, CS

☼ FULL SUN

◑ INFREQUENT, DEEP WATERING

Anisacanthus wrightii

Small shrubs native to Texas, parts of Southwest, and northern Mexico. Growth is twiggy, to 3–4 ft. Although plants may be evergreen in recommended zones, they look best if treated as herbaceous perennials and cut back to ground in winter. Spikes of tubular bright flowers open over a very long blooming season. Make good container plants.

A. thurberi. DESERT HONEYSUCKLE, CHUPAROSA. Yellow-orange flowers, 1½ in. long, cover plant from spring through summer. Leaves light green, 1½–2 in. long and ½ in. wide. Plants sold under this name may be *Justicia leonardii;* these have bright red flowers and leaves to 6 in. long.

A. wrightii. HUMMINGBIRD BUSH. Orange-red flowers, 2 in. long, from June to frost. Glossy green leaves, 2 in. long.

ANISE HYSSOP. See AGASTACHE foeniculum

ANISE TREE. See ILLICIUM

Annonaceae. The annona family consists primarily of tropical trees and shrubs, many with edible fruit, such as pawpaw (*Asimina triloba*).

ANNUAL BLUEGRASS. See POA annua

ANNUAL MALLOW. See LAVATERA trimestris

ANNUAL PHLOX. See PHLOX drummondii

ANNUAL RYEGRASS. See LOLIUM multiflorum

ANREDERA cordifolia (Boussingaultia baselloides)

MADEIRA VINE

Basellaceae

PERENNIAL VINE

☘ ZONES CS, TS; FARTHER NORTH, DIG AND STORE

☼ FULL SUN

◑ MODERATE WATER

Anredera cordifolia

Heart-shaped green leaves 1–3 in. long. Fragrant white flowers in foot-long spikes in late summer, fall. Climbs by twining; may reach 20 ft. in one season. Small tubers form where leaves join stems. Old-fashioned plant useful for summer screening of decks or other sitting areas. Can run rampant in the Coastal and Tropical South. In areas farther north, treat as you would dahlias: Dig in fall and store tubers over winter.

ANTENNARIA

PUSSY TOES

Asteraceae (Compositae)

PERENNIALS

☘ ZONE US

☼ FULL SUN

◑ REGULAR TO LITTLE WATER

Antennaria dioica

Mat-forming plants with rosettes of woolly foliage and small furry puffs of flower heads. Tough and tolerant of heat and poor soil, they spread slowly but surely among rocks or along crevices in paving. Useful small-scale bulb cover or ground cover. Accept regular water if soil is well drained.

A. dioica. Inch-high gray mats produce pinkish white flower puffs. 'Rubra' has deep pink flowers.

A. neglecta. White flower puffs atop 3-in. stems.

ANTHEMIS tinctoria

GOLDEN MARGUERITE

Asteraceae (Compositae)

PERENNIAL

☘ ZONES US, MS, LS

☼ FULL SUN

◑ REGULAR TO MODERATE WATER

Anthemis tinctoria

Erect, shrubby plant with angular stems. Grows to 2–3 ft. Foliage is aromatic, especially when bruised. Leaves are light green, divided into many segments. Golden yellow, daisylike flowers, to 2 in. across, bloom in summer and fall. Plant is short lived and requires replanting often. Needs good drainage. Grow from seed, stem cuttings, or divisions in fall or spring. Golden marguerite is a choice garden plant. Selections include 'Beauty of Grallagh', with golden orange flowers; 'E. C. Buxton', white with yellow centers; 'Kelwayi', golden yellow; 'Moonlight', soft pale yellow.

ANTHURIUM

Araceae

PERENNIALS

🌿 ZONE TS; OR INDOORS

● NO DIRECT SUN

◐ ◑ AMPLE TO REGULAR WATER; NEED HUMIDITY

Anthurium andraeanum

Native to tropical rain forests of the Americas. Exotic plants with handsome dark green leaves and lustrous flower bracts in vivid red, luscious pinks, or white. In southern Florida, they thrive outdoors in frost-free, shady spots, either in the ground or in pots. In all zones, they're no more difficult to grow as house plants than are some orchids.

The higher the humidity, the better. Anthurium leaves lose shiny texture and may die if humidity drops below 50 percent for more than a few days. Keep pots on trays of moist gravel, in bathroom, or under polyethylene cover. Sponge or spray leaves several times daily. For good bloom, plant by window with good light but no direct sun. Generally grow best at 80–90°F but will get along at normal house temperatures. Growth stops below 65°F, is damaged below 50°F. Protect from drafts. Pot anthuriums in coarse, porous mix of leaf mold, sandy soil, and shredded osmunda. Give light feeding every 4 weeks.

A. andraeanum. FLAMING ANTHURIUM. Dark green, oblong leaves to 1 ft. long and 6 in. wide, heart shaped at base. Flower bracts spreading, heart shaped, to 6 in. long, surrounding yellow, callalike flower spike. Flower bracts, in shades of red, rose, pink, and white, shine as though lacquered. Bloom more or less continuously—plant may have from four to six flowers during the year. Flowers last 6 weeks on plant, 4 weeks after cut.

A. crystallinum. Leaves, up to 1½ ft. long, 1 ft. wide, are deep green with striking white veining. Flowers are not exciting, with small, narrow, greenish bracts. Many similar anthuriums exist in the florist trade; plants offered as *A. crystallinum* may be *A. clarinervium*, *A. magnificum*, or some other species.

A. scandens. Climbing or trailing plant to 2 ft., with 3-in.-long tapered oval leaves, small, fragrant greenish flowers, and translucent lilac berries.

A. scherzeranum. Slow growing, to 2 ft., compact. Dark green leaves 8 in. long, 2 in. wide. Flower bracts broad, 3 in. long, deep red varying to rose, salmon, white. Yellow flower spikes spirally coiled. Easier to handle than *A. andraeanum*; often thrives under good house plant conditions.

🏛 ANTIGONON leptopus

CORAL VINE, QUEEN'S WREATH, ROSA DE MONTANA

Polygonaceae

DECIDUOUS VINE

🌿 ZONES LS, CS, TS

☼ FULL SUN

◐ ● REGULAR TO LITTLE WATER

Antigonon leptopus

This native of Mexico revels in high summer heat, sun. Evergreen in the Tropical South. A fast-growing vine, climbing by tendrils to 40 ft. Foliage—dark green, 3–5-in.-long, heart-shaped or arrow-shaped leaves—is open and airy. Small rose pink flowers 1½ in. long are carried in long, trailing sprays from midsummer to fall. In cold winters, leaves fall and most of top dies. Recovers quickly. Treat as perennial. Where winter temperatures drop below 25°F, protect roots with mulch. There is a rare white selection 'Album', and a hot rose pink—nearly red—type named 'Baja Red'; from seed the color of the latter is variable, but the best are as red as 'Barbara Karst' bougainvillea.

Widespread in Florida and parts of Central and Southeast Texas. Use the vine to shade patio or terrace, or let it drape its foliage and blossom sprays along eaves, fence, or garden wall.

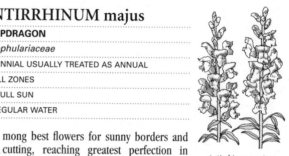

> ### FIVE WAYS TO AVOID SNAPDRAGON RUST
>
> Snapdragons, like lawns, roses, and hollyhocks, can fall victim to rust (orange pustules on undersides of leaves). Here are five ways to avoid or minimize it: Start with rust-resistant selections (even that's not foolproof). Keep plants well watered. Avoid overhead watering (or do it only in the morning or on sunny days). Feed regularly. If necessary, change planting locations from one year to the next.

ANTIRRHINUM majus

SNAPDRAGON

Scrophulariaceae

PERENNIAL USUALLY TREATED AS ANNUAL

🌿 ALL ZONES

☼ FULL SUN

● REGULAR WATER

Antirrhinum majus

Among best flowers for sunny borders and cutting, reaching greatest perfection in spring and early summer. In the Lower, Coastal, and Tropical South, will bloom in winter and spring. Individual flower of basic snapdragon has five lobes, which are divided into unequal upper and lower "jaws"; slight pinch at sides of flower will make dragon open its jaws. Later developments include double flowers; the bell-shaped kind, with round, open flowers; and the azalea-shaped bloom, which is a double bell flower.

Snapping snapdragons in tall (2½–3-ft.) range include Rocket and Topper strains (single flowers) and Double Supreme strain. Intermediate (12–20 in.) are Cinderella, Coronette, Minaret, selection 'Princess White with Purple Eye', Sprite, and Tahiti. Dwarfs (6–8 in.) include Dwarf Bedding Floral Carpet, Kim, Kolibri, and Royal Carpet.

Bell-flowered strains include Bright Butterflies and Wedding Bells (both 2½ ft.); Little Darling and Liberty Bell (both 15 in.); and Pixie (6–8 in.). Among the azalea-flowered strains are Madame Butterfly (2½ ft.) and Sweetheart (1 ft.).

Sow seed in flats from late summer to early spring for later transplanting or buy started plants at a garden center. Set out plants in early fall in the Lower, Coastal, and Tropical South, spring in the Upper and Middle South. If snapdragons set out in early fall reach bud stage before night temperatures drop below 50°F, they will start blooming in winter and continue until weather gets hot.

Valuable cut flowers. Tall and intermediate forms are splendid vertical accents in borders with delphinium, iris, daylily, peach-leafed bluebell *(Campanula persicifolia)*, and foxgloves. Dwarf kinds are effective as edgings and in rock gardens and raised beds, or pots.

APHELANDRA squarrosa

ZEBRA PLANT

Acanthaceae

EVERGREEN SHRUB

🌿 ZONE TS; OR INDOORS

◐ ● PARTIAL OR FULL SHADE

● REGULAR WATER

Aphelandra squarrosa

Native to Mexico, South America. Popular for leaves and flowers. Large, 8–12-in.-long, dark green leaves strikingly veined with white. Green-tipped yellow flowers and waxy, golden yellow flower bracts make colorful upright spikes at tips of stems. 'Louisae' is best known, but newer selections 'Apollo White' and 'Dania' are more compact and show more white venation. To make plant bushy, cut stems back to one or two pairs of leaves after flowering.

Grown as an accent with other tender shrubs in sheltered borders in warmest parts of Florida. If plant freezes, cut it to the ground; new shoots will appear when weather warms up. Indoors, provide morning (or filtered) sun and routine house plant care.

Apiaceae. This family, formerly known as Umbelliferae, comprises nearly 3,000 plants, most of them annuals and perennials. All have flowers in umbels—flat- or round-topped clusters whose individual flower stems all originate at a single point. Many are vegetables (carrot, parsnip, celery, fennel) or aromatic herbs (parsley, coriander, dill). Others are grown for ornament, such as sea holly *(Eryngium)*.

Apocynaceae. The dogbane family contains shrubs, trees, and vines with milky, often poisonous sap. Flowers are often showy and fragrant, as in *Plumeria* and common oleander *(Nerium)*.

APOTHECARY ROSE. See ROSA gallica 'Officinalis'

☖ APPLE

Rosaceae

DECIDUOUS FRUIT TREES

⚡ ZONES VARY BY SELECTION

☼ FULL SUN

◐ REGULAR WATER DURING FRUIT DEVELOPMENT

▷ SEE CHART

Apple

Most widely adapted deciduous fruit tree. Grows in home gardens and orchards from central Florida all the way north into Canada. The apple blossom is the state flower of Arkansas. Fruit ripens from June to early November, depending on type. To grow and fruit properly, most selections require between 900 and 1,200 hours of 45°F or lower temperatures. In the Coastal South, it's important to choose types with low winter-chill requirement. Apples will not grow in the Tropical South.

All apples except 'Golden Delicious' require cross-pollination for good fruit set. Certain types (triploids) do not produce fertile pollen and will not fertilize either their own flowers or those of other apples. If you have a tree that is not bearing, graft a branch of another selection onto it or place fresh flower bouquets from another selection (in can of water) at base of tree. Don't use 'Stayman' or any other triploid (pollen-sterile) tree to pollinate an unfruitful tree.

An apple tree needs regular moisture while fruit is developing; you will have to make up for any lack of rainfall at this time with periodic deep soakings. The tree also needs full sun for best production, so don't crowd it into a partially shaded site. To have more than one type in limited space, buy multiple-selection trees or dwarf trees. Multiple-selection trees have three to five types grafted onto a single trunk and rootstock, providing a variety of selections and pollination, if needed.

In choosing selections, remember that good apples are not necessarily red. Skin color is not an indicator of quality or taste. Make sure that eye appeal, slight taste preference, or name doesn't influence you to choose a difficult-to-grow type. For example, if to your taste 'Golden Delicious' and 'Red Delicious' are nearly equal, consider differences in growing them. 'Golden Delicious' produces fruit without pollinator and comes into bearing earlier. It keeps well, while 'Red Delicious' becomes mealy if not stored

at 35–40°F or lower. And 'Golden Delicious' can be used for cooking, while 'Red Delicious' is principally an eating apple.

If you want nearly perfect fruit, the apple tree will need much care; however, as an ornamental tree it has more character, better form, and longer life than most deciduous fruit trees. It does best in deep, well-drained soil, but gets by in many imperfect situations.

The main insect pests are apple maggot, codling moth, and plum curculio, all of which infest the fruit. Scented traps may be enough to control these insects in a home garden. Diseases of apple are prevalent—and good reason to plant resistant types (see chart). Apple scab causes hard, corky spots on fruit. Cedar-apple rust (spread from red cedars to apples) is responsible for orange spots on leaves and fruit, and subsequent defoliation and stunting of fruit. Powdery mildew causes twig dieback and russeting of fruit. Fungicidal sprays will help prevent all of these diseases. The bacterial disease fireblight produces blackening and dieback of growth. For timing of insect traps and fungicide sprays, consult your Cooperative Extension Office or a good local garden center.

Dwarf and spur apples. True dwarf apples (5–8 ft. in height and spread) are made by grafting standard apples on dwarfing rootstocks such as M9 and Bud 9. These trees take up little room and bear at a younger age than standard apples, but have shallow roots; they need the support of a post, fence, wall, or sturdy trellis to stand against wind and rain. They also need good soil and extra care in feeding and watering.

Semidwarf trees are larger than true dwarfs but smaller than standard trees. They bear bigger crops than dwarfs and take up less space than standards. Many commercial orchards get high yields by using semidwarf trees and planting them close together. Semidwarf rootstocks reduce tree size by approximately the following factors: M26 and M7A are about half normal size; they may be espaliered or trellised if planted 12–16 ft. apart and allowed to grow 10–12 ft. tall. Trees on MM106 are approximately 65 percent of normal height; those on MM111 are 75 percent of normal height.

Rarely, growers offer trees dwarfed by double-working—grafting a piece of M9 trunk on vigorous rootstock, then grafting a bearing selection on this "interstock." The resulting dwarf is somewhat larger than a true dwarf tree and similar in size to a tree grown on an M26 rootstock.

Apples bear flowers and fruit on spurs—short branches that grow from 2-year or older wood. On spur-type apples, spurs form earlier (within 2 years after planting) and grow closer together on shorter branches, giving more apples per foot of branch. Spur apples are natural or genetic semidwarfs about two-thirds the size of normal apple trees when they are grafted onto ordinary rootstocks. They can be further dwarfed by grafting onto dwarfing rootstocks; M7A and M26 give smallest trees, MM106 and MM111 somewhat larger ones.

Training and pruning apple trees. For most home use, plant dwarf or semidwarf trees for ease in maintenance and picking. Even commercial growers favor these smaller trees: Closer spacing permits more trees to the acre and a heavier crop. Preferred style is pyramidal or modified leader, in which widely angled branches are encouraged to grow in spiral placement around trunk. Prune as little as possible during first 5 or 6 years—just keep narrow-angled crotches from developing, and don't let side branches outgrow leader, or secondary branches outgrow primary branches.

Pruning of mature trees consists of removing weak, dead, or poorly placed branches and twigs, especially those growing toward the center of the tree (bearing is heaviest when some sun can reach the middle). Removing such growth will encourage development of strong new wood with new fruiting spurs (on apples, spurs are productive for about 3 years) and discourage mildew. If you have inherited an old tree, selective thinning of branches will accomplish the same goal.

Dwarf trees can be grown as espaliers tied to wood or wire frames, fences, or other supports. The technique requires manipulating the branches to the desired pattern and pruning out excess growth.

Recent arrivals are the colonnade apples. These develop a single spire-like trunk to 8 ft. tall, with fruiting spurs directly on the trunk or on very short branchlets. Total width does not exceed 2 ft. Five selections are currently available: 'Emeraldspire', green-tinted yellow; 'Scarletspire', red and

▶ page 134

APPLE

SELECTION	ZONES	RIPENING TIME	FRUIT	COMMENTS
'Adina'	LS, CS	Midseason	Large, round, fragrant, dark red. Firm, sweet, creamy white flesh with cinnamon overtones	Needs only 350 hours of winter chill. Pollinate with 'Anna', 'Dorsett Golden', 'Ein Shemer'
'Anna'	LS, CS	Early. Sometimes a light second crop late in the season	Large. Pale green blushed red. Crisp, sweet with some acid	Begins producing at a young age. Needs very little winter chill. Good annual bearer. Use 'Dorsett Golden' as pollinator
'Arkansas Black' 🏛	US, MS, LS	Late	Medium size. Dark, deep red. Hard-crisp. Excellent keeper. Good for cooking, fresh eating	Best flavor after storage for 2 months. Born 1870 in Benton County, Arkansas. 'Arkansas Black Spur' is spurred variation
'Ashmead's Kernel' 🏛	US, MS	Late	Medium size. Red-orange blush over rough yellow-green skin. Crisp, juicy, aromatic	Good disease resistance. Best flavor after a few months' storage. Good keeper. Originated in Gloucester, England, around 1700
'Black Twig' 🏛	US, MS, LS	Late	Large to medium. Green to yellow flushed with red. Tart, fine-grained flesh. Good for fresh eating, cooking, and for cider	Good disease resistance. One of the best keepers. Originated near Fayetteville, Tennessee, in the early 1800s. Best flavor develops in storage
'Braeburn'	US, MS, LS	Late	Medium size. Orange red over yellow ground. Crisp, sweet-tart flavor. From New Zealand	Thin fruit to prevent bearing in alternate years. Susceptible to mites. Stores well
'Calville Blanc d'Hiver'	US, MS	Late	Medium to large. Light green spotted with red; flattish shape. One of the best for making cider or vinegar	Susceptible to cedar-apple rust, powdery mildew, and scab. Bears early. Grown in France since 1627
'Carolina Red June' 🏛	US, MS, LS	Early	Pale yellow flushed with purplish red. Juicy, aromatic. Good for eating, pies, cider	Originated in North Carolina. Not a good keeper, but ripens fruit over a long period. Heavy bearer. Thin crop for bigger fruit
'Cortland' 🏛	US, MS	Early midseason	Large. Dark bluish red skin streaked with yellow. Excellent all-purpose fruit	Vigorous, early bearer. Produces annually. Holds fruit better than 'McIntosh'. Excellent pollinator. Sliced apples don't turn brown
'Delicious' ('Red Delicious')	US, MS, LS	Midseason to late	Easily recognized pointed blossom end with five knobs. Color varies with strain and garden climate; best where days are sunny and warm, nights cool. Often older, striped kinds have better flavor than highly colored commercial strains	Many strains vary in depth and uniformity of coloring. 'Crimson Spur' is a popular home selection. All types susceptible to scab
'Dorsett Golden'	LS, CS	Early	Medium to large. Yellow or greenish yellow, sweet flavor. Good for eating fresh or cooking. Keeps a few weeks	Seedling of 'Golden Delicious' from Bermuda. Needs very little winter chill. Good pollinator for 'Adina', 'Anna', 'Ein Shemer'
'Ein Shemer'	LS, CS	Early	Medium size. Yellow to greenish yellow. Juicy, crisp, mildly acid	Needs very little winter chill. Pollinates 'Adina', 'Anna', 'Dorsett Golden'
'Empire'	US, MS, LS	Late midseason	Small to medium, roundish, dark red. Flesh creamy white, juicy, crisp, mildly tart	Cross between 'McIntosh' and 'Delicious'. Semispur growth habit. Good tree structure. Susceptible to spring frost damage
'Freedom'	US, MS, LS	Midseason	Medium to large. Round, red fruit. Good for eating and cooking	Disease resistant. Excellent pollinator for 'Liberty', another disease-resistant selection
'Fuji'	US, MS, LS	Late	Medium to large. Yellow-green ground with red stripes; firm, very sweet, excellent flavor. Stores exceptionally well	Tends to bear heavy crops in alternate years. A cross between 'Ralls' and 'Delicious' made in Japan in 1939
'Gala'	US, MS, LS	Early to midseason	Medium size. Beautiful red-on-yellow color. Highly aromatic, firm, crisp, juicy, sweet, yellow flesh. Loses flavor in storage. From New Zealand	Vigorous, heavy bearer with long, supple branches that break easily; may need support. Several color strains are available. Very susceptible to fireblight

A

APPLE

SELECTION	ZONES	RIPENING TIME	FRUIT	COMMENTS
'Ginger Gold'	US, MS, LS	Early midseason	Medium to large. Yellow, firm, crisp, mild flavor. Resembles 'Golden Delicious'. Good keeper	One of best early yellow apples. Ripens over 2–3 weeks. Susceptible to mildew. Resistant to sunburn. Chance seedling from the orchard of Ginger Harvey in Livingston, Virginia
'Golden Delicious' ('Yellow Delicious')	US, MS, LS	Late midseason	Medium to large. Clear yellow, may develop skin russeting in some areas. Similar in shape to 'Delicious', with less prominent knobs. Highly aromatic, crisp. Excellent for eating fresh and cooking	Not related to 'Red Delicious'; different taste, habit. Long bloom season, heavy pollen production make it a good pollinator. Various strains available. Spurred types include 'Goldspur', 'Yelospur'. Self-pollinating
'Golden Russet' 🏛	US, MS, LS	Late	Medium size. Greenish yellow to gold, marked with russet. Fine-grained, yellow flesh. Excellent for cider, fresh eating, and cooking	Vigorous; resistant to scab but susceptible to rust and fireblight. Good pollinator for other selections
'Gold Rush'	US, MS, LS	Late	Medium size. Yellow, often with some russeting. Best after storage. Good for pies, fresh eating	Immune to scab; good resistance to powdery mildew; some resistance to fireblight
'Granny Smith'	US, MS, LS, CS	Early midseason	Large. Bright to yellowish green, firm and tart. Good quality. Stores well, good for pies, sauce	Australian favorite before it came to U.S. Resistant to rust. Good pollinator
'Grimes Golden' 🏛	US, MS, LS	Midseason	Medium size. Round, golden. Crisp, yellow fruit, spicy sweet. Good for fresh eating, cider, desserts. Moderate for keeping	Bears young. Discovered in West Virginia by Thomas Grimes around 1804. No pollinator required. Good pollinator for other selections
'Horse' 🏛	US, MS, LS	Early midseason	Greenish yellow, blushed pink. Tart flavor. Excellent for jelly or making vinegar	Slow to bear. Allow to ripen fully for good flavor. Probably originated in North Carolina
'Jonagold'	US, MS, LS	Late midseason	Large. Heavy red striping over yellow ground. Firm, mildly tart, juicy, fine flavor. A frequent taste-test favorite	Productive, medium-size tree. Heavy bearer. Pollen-sterile, won't pollinate others. Not pollinated by 'Golden Delicious'
'Jonathan'	US, MS, LS	Midseason	Small to medium, round oblong. High-colored red. Juicy, moderately tart, crackling crisp, sprightly. All-purpose apple, good keeper	Subject to mildew. Somewhat resistant to scab
'Kinnard's Choice' ('Kinnaird', 'Red Winter Cluster') 🏛	US, MS, LS	Early midseason	Smooth-skinned yellow flushed with red, deep red in sun. Crisp, white flesh, good for fresh eating, making cider	Old favorite in north Georgia. Originated in Franklin, Tennessee. Will bear heavily one year and lightly the next unless heavy crop is thinned
'Liberty'	US, MS	Late midseason	Medium size. Heavy red blush. Crisp, fine sweet-tart flavor, dessert quality	Productive annual bearer One of the best disease-resistant selections. Immune to scab; resists cedar-apple rust, fireblight
'Limbertwig' 🏛	US, MS, LS	Late	Medium size. Greenish yellow flushed red. Hard yellow flesh. Excellent for cider	Old Southern favorite with many regional forms. Among the best keepers
'Lodi'	US, MS, LS	Very early	Large. Green to greenish yellow. Crisp, tart flesh good for pies, sauce	Vigorous tree, heavy bearer
'Magnum Bonum' 🏛	US, MS, LS	Midseason	Red and greenish yellow fruit. Crisp flesh, juicy and aromatic. Excellent for fresh eating	Stores well. North Carolina heirloom originating in Davidson County, about 1828. Bears at early age
'McIntosh'	US	Midseason	Medium to large. Bright red, nearly round. Snowy white, tender flesh. Excellent, tart flavor. 'Marshall' and 'Redmax' have high color	Very susceptible to scab and preharvest drop. Not a good choice for the South; doesn't like long, hot summers
'Mollie's Delicious'	US, MS, LS	Midseason	Large, light yellow blushed red. Light yellow flesh, aromatic, juicy, sweet. Stores well	Bears early, well adapted to Southeast

APPLE

SELECTION	ZONES	RIPENING TIME	FRUIT	COMMENTS
'Mutsu' ('Crispin')	US, MS, LS, CS	Late	Very large. Greenish yellow to yellow blushed red. Flesh cream colored, very crisp, more tart than 'Golden Delicious'. Frequent taste-test winner. Excellent dessert, cooking apple with long storage life; fruit won't shrivel	Exceptionally large and vigorous tree. Pollen-sterile, won't pollinate other selections. Resists powdery mildew
'Newtown Pippin' ('Albemarle Pippin')	US, MS, LS	Late	Large. Greenish yellow or clear yellow. Crisp, firm, juicy, slightly tart. Good all-purpose apple. Excellent keeper. Flavor improves in storage	Large, vigorous tree. Self-pollinating. Originated in Newtown, Long Island, early 1700s
'Northern Spy' ('Red Spy')	US	Late	Large, red skinned. Tender, fine-grained flesh. Apple epicure's delight for sprightly flavor. Not attractive but excellent dessert, cooking apple. Keeps well	Slow to reach bearing age. 'Prairie Spy' is similar selection
'Ozark Gold'	US, MS, LS	Midseason	Medium to large, yellow fruit with pointed blossom end	Bears young. Spreading habit. Similar to 'Golden Delicious', but 2–3 weeks earlier. Disease resistant
'Paulared'	US	Early	Large, red skinned, mild flavored. One of the best early apples	Good branch structure. Has some resistance to scab
'Pound Sweet' ('Pumpkin Sweet')	US, MS	Midseason	Very large, golden fruit. Crisp and sweet. Excellent fresh or baked	Vigorous grower. Originated in Manchester, Connecticut, around 1834
'Pristine'	US	Early	Medium size. Bright yellow skin, mildly tart white flesh. Good for eating, baking, sauce	Immune to scab; resistant to cedar-apple rust; has some resistance to powdery mildew and fireblight
'Rall's Janet' ('Ralls')	US, MS	Late	Small to medium. Greenish yellow, streaked with red. Crisp white flesh, good for eating. Keeps well	Late to bloom; good in areas with late frosts. Probably originated in Amherst County, Virginia, on farm of Caleb Ralls
'Rome Beauty' ('Red Rome')	US, MS, LS	Late	Large. Round, smooth, red with greenish white flesh. Original 'Rome Beauty' supplanted by more uniformly red-skinned types like 'Red Rome'. Outstanding baking apple, good for cider, only fair for eating fresh	Bears at early age. Self-pollinating. Several regional strains
'Roxbury Russet' ('Shipper's Russet', 'Hewe's Russet')	US, MS, LS	Late	Large, green, with brown russet. Firm, yellowish flesh. Good for eating and cooking. Superior for cider. Good keeper	Blooms late. Resistant to scab and mildew. Oldest named American apple, originating in Roxbury, Massachusetts, early 1600s
'Spitzenberg' ('Esopus Spitzenberg')	US, MS	Midseason	Medium to large. Red-dotted yellow. Crisp, fine grained, tangy, spicy. Eat fresh	Old favorite; best in Upper South. Subject to fireblight, mildew. Not a good keeper
'Stayman' (often called 'Winesap')	US, MS, LS	Late	'Stayman' and 'Winesap' are actually two different apples. 'Stayman' (a 'Winesap' cross) is large, greenish yellow with red stripes. Fine grained, firm, aromatic "winey" flavor. Good for fresh eating, applesauce, cider, baking	Pollinate with 'Golden Delicious', 'Grimes Golden', 'Lodi', 'Golden Russet'. Good keeper. Early bearer. Sterile pollen cannot pollinate other selections
'Westfield Seek-No-Further' ('Red Winter Pearmain')	US, MS	Late	Greenish yellow flushed with orange red. Crisp, juicy fruit, best for fresh eating	Average keeper
'Winter Banana'	US, MS, LS	Late midseason	Large. Attractive, pale yellow blushed pink, with waxy finish. Tender, aromatic	Good pollinator and keeper. Ripe fruit has bananalike aroma

▶

APPLE

SELECTION	ZONES	RIPENING TIME	FRUIT	COMMENTS
'Winter Pearmain' **('White Winter Pearmain')** 🏛	US, MS	Midseason	Medium to large. Pale greenish yellow skin with pink blush. Excellent flavor, tender flesh, fine grained. All-purpose	Good keeper
'Yates' ('Jates') 🏛	US, MS, LS, CS	Late	Small, bright red, spotted fruit; spicy, aromatic, good flavor. Keeps well. Best flavor after a frost	Originated in Georgia in 1813. Heavy bearer; vigorous grower. Good pollinator for other selections
'York Imperial' **('York', 'Johnson's Fine Winter')** 🏛	US, MS, LS	Late	Medium to large. Yellow or green flushed pink. Firm, yellowish flesh, juicy. Great for cooking, baking. Best flavor if kept till Christmas	One of the best old-time selections for winter keeping. Discovered around 1830 by Mr. Johnson in York, Pennsylvania

green; 'Crimsonspire', dark red; 'Ultraspire', red-blushed yellow green; and 'Maypole', a crabapple with deep pink blossoms and red fruit. Two selections are needed for pollination. Easy to maintain, colonnade trees are attractive as accents or screen plants, or in containers.

For ornamental relatives, see *Malus*.

Aquifoliaceae. The holly family contains evergreen trees or shrubs with berrylike fruit. *Ilex* (holly) is the only important genus.

AQUILEGIA

COLUMBINE

Ranunculaceae

PERENNIALS

🌢 ZONES VARY BY SPECIES

☼ ◑ FULL SUN OR FILTERED SHADE

🌢 REGULAR WATER

Aquilegia canadensis

Columbines have a fairylike, woodland quality with their lacy foliage and beautifully posed flowers in exquisite pastels, deeper shades, and white. Erect, 2 in.–4 ft. high, depending on species or hybrid. Fresh green, blue-green, or gray-green divided leaves reminiscent of maidenhair fern. Slender, branching stems carry flowers to 3 in. across, erect or nodding, often with sepals and petals in contrasting colors; they usually have backward-projecting, nectar-bearing spurs. Some columbines have large flowers and very long spurs; these have an airier look than short-spurred and spurless kinds. Double-flowered types lack the delicacy of those with single blossoms, but they make a bolder color mass. Bloom season for columbines is spring, early summer.

Plants are not fussy about soil as long as it is well drained. On all columbines, cut back old stems for second crop of flowers. All kinds attract hummingbirds. Most columbines are not long-lived perennials; replace plants every 3 or 4 years. If you allow spent flowers to form seed capsules, you'll ensure a crop of volunteer seedlings. If you're growing hybrids, the seedlings won't necessarily duplicate the parent plants; seedlings from species (if grown isolated from other columbines) should closely resemble the originals. Leaf miners are a potential pest, especially on hybrids.

A. alpina. ALPINE COLUMBINE. Zones US, MS. Native to the Alps. Grows 1–2 ft. tall. Nodding, bright blue flowers to 2 in. across, with curved spurs to 1 in. long. Good rock garden plant. 'Hensol Harebell' is a cross between this species and *A. vulgaris;* flowers are deep blue on stems that may reach 3 ft. tall.

A. caerulea. COLORADO COLUMBINE. Zones US, MS. Grows 1½–3 ft. high. Flowers upright, 2 in. or more across, blue and white. Spurs straight or spreading, to 2 in. long. This species is an important parent of many long-spurred hybrids.

A. canadensis. WILD COLUMBINE. Zones US, MS, LS. Native to much of eastern and central North America. Grows 1–2 ft. tall, occasionally taller. Red-and-yellow, 1½-in., nodding flowers have slightly curved, 1-in. spurs. Red color may wash out to pink in areas with warm nighttime temperatures. Less susceptible to leaf miners than most columbines. 'Corbett' (*A. c. flavescens*) has creamy yellow flowers.

A. chrysantha. GOLDEN COLUMBINE, GOLDEN-SPURRED COLUMBINE. Zones US, MS. Native to Arizona, New Mexico, and adjacent Mexico. One of showiest species. Large, many-branched plant to 3–4 ft. tall. Leaflets densely covered with soft hairs beneath. Upright, clear yellow, 1½–3 in. flowers, with slender, hooked spurs 2–2½ in. long. 'Silver Queen' has white flowers; double-flowered forms are white (sometimes pink-tinged) 'Alba Plena' and yellow 'Flore Pleno'.

A. flabellata. FAN COLUMBINE. Zones US, MS. Native to Japan. Stocky, 9-in. plant with nodding lilac blue and creamy white flowers and hooked spurs to 1 in. long. Differs from most other columbines in having thicker, darker leaves with often overlapping segments. *A. f. pumila* is a very dwarf (4-in.) form. Good rock garden plants.

A. hinckleyana. HINCKLEY'S COLUMBINE. Zones US, MS, LS. Native to Big Bend country of Texas. To 1½–2 ft. high, with blue-gray foliage and long-spurred, chartreuse yellow flowers.

A. hybrids. Zones US, MS, LS. Derived from several species. Preferred tall hybrid strains are graceful, long-spurred McKana Giants and double-flowering Spring Song (both to 3 ft.). Lower-growing strains include Biedermeier and Dragonfly (1 ft.); long-spurred Music (1½ ft.); and single to double, upward-facing Fairyland (15 in.). One of the most unusual hybrids is 2–2½-ft.-tall 'Nora Barlow', which has spurless, double, dahlialike flowers of reddish pink with a white margin.

A. longissima. Zones US, MS, LS. Native to Southwest Texas and northern Mexico. Grows to 2½–3 ft. tall. Similar to *A. chrysantha*. Flowers numerous, erect, pale yellow, spurs very narrow, drooping, 4–6 in. long. 'Maxistar' is most commonly offered.

A. saximontana. Zones US, MS. In effect, a miniature *A. caerulea*, 4–8 in. high.

A. vulgaris. EUROPEAN COLUMBINE. Zones US, MS. Naturalized in eastern U.S. Grows to 1–2½ ft. tall. Nodding, blue or violet flowers to 2 in. across; short, knobby spurs are about ¾ in. long. Many selections and hybrids, from single to fully double and either short spurred or spurless. Some garden centers offer a mix of flower forms in white and shades of pink, red, and violet.

ARABIS alpina

MOUNTAIN ROCKCRESS

Brassicaceae (Cruciferae)

PERENNIAL

ZONE US

FULL SUN

MODERATE WATER

Arabis alpina

Low-growing, tufted plant for edgings, rock gardens, ground covers, and pattern plantings. Rough-hairy foliage, with leafy stems 4–10 in. high and basal leaves in clusters. White flowers in dense, short clusters bloom in spring. Provide good drainage. 'Rosea', 6 in. high, has pink flowers; 'Variegata' has variegated leaves.

Araceae. The arum family contains plants ranging from tuberous or rhizomatous perennials to shrubby or climbing tropical foliage plants. Leaves are often highly ornamental; while variable in shape, they tend to be arrow-like. Inconspicuous flowers cluster tightly on a club-shaped spadix within an often showy leaflike bract (spathe). Examples are *Anthurium*, calla *(Zantedeschia)*, and *Philodendron*. Sap of many is highly irritating to mouth and throat.

ARALIA

Araliaceae

DECIDUOUS SHRUB-TREES OR PERENNIALS

ZONES VARY BY SPECIES

FULL SUN OR PARTIAL SHADE

REGULAR TO MODERATE WATER

Aralia spinosa

Most are striking bold-leafed plants that may eventually grow to 25–30 ft. under ideal conditions. Branches are nearly vertical or slightly spreading, usually very spiny. Huge leaves, clustered at ends of branches and divided into many leaflets, have effective pattern value. White flowers, small but in such large, branched clusters that they are showy in midsummer, are followed by purplish berrylike fruit.

Grow in well-drained soil. Not good near swimming pools because of spines; even leafstalks are sometimes prickly. Protect plants from wind to avoid burning foliage.

A. elata. JAPANESE ANGELICA TREE. Zones US, MS. Native to northeast Asia. Moderately spiny. Leaves 2–3 ft. long, divided into 2–6-in.-long toothed leaflets. Selection 'Variegata' has leaflets strikingly bordered with creamy white.

A. elegantissima. See Schefflera elegantissima

A. papyrifera. See Tetrapanax papyriferus

A. racemosa. SPIKENARD. Zones US, MS, LS. Native to eastern U.S. Unlike other species, a rhizomatous perennial to 6 ft., with leaves 2½ ft. long, divided into many coarse leaflets. Tiny white flowers are clustered into balls on branching stems. Tiny fruits are black or brown.

A. sieboldii. JAPANESE FATSIA. See Fatsia japonica

A. spinosa. DEVIL'S WALKING STICK, HERCULES'S CLUB. Zones US, MS, LS, CS. Native to eastern U.S. Has a few usually unbranched spiny stems, each crowned by 2–6-ft. leaves. Tiny flowers form huge, branched clusters. Blue-black fruits prized by birds. Spreads by suckers. One of the most tropical-looking, genuinely hardy trees.

Araliaceae. The aralia family of herbaceous and woody plants is marked by leaves that are divided fanwise into leaflets or veined in pattern like the fingers of a hand. Individually tiny flowers are in round clusters or in large compound clusters. Examples are *Aralia*, English ivy *(Hedera helix)*, Japanese fatsia *(Fatsia japonica)*, and *Schefflera*.

ARAUCARIA

Araucariaceae

EVERGREEN TREES

ZONES VARY BY SPECIES

FULL SUN

REGULAR WATER

Araucaria araucana

These strange-looking conifers provide distinctive silhouette with their evenly spread tiers of stiff branches. Most have stiff, closely overlapping, dark to bright green leaves. All do well in a wide range of soils with adequate drainage.

These trees serve well as skyline trees, but they become so towering that they need the space they would have in a park. They are not trees to sit under—with age they bear large, spiny, 10–15-lb. cones that fall with a crash. The trees thrive in containers for years.

A. araucana (A. imbricata). MONKEY PUZZLE TREE. Zones US, MS, LS, CS. Native to Chile. Arboreal oddity with heavy, spreading branches and ropelike branchlets closely set with sharp-pointed dark green leaves. Hardiest of araucarias. Slow growing in youth, it eventually reaches 70–90 ft.

A. bidwillii. BUNYA-BUNYA. Zones CS, TS. Native to Australia. Moderate growth to 80 ft.; broadly rounded crown supplies dense shade. Two kinds of leaves: Juvenile leaves are glossy, rather narrow, ¾–2 in. long, stiff, more or less

Araucaria heterophylla

spreading in two rows; mature leaves are oval, ½ in. long, rather woody, spirally arranged and overlapping along branches. Unusual house plant; very tough and tolerant of low light.

A. heterophylla (A. excelsa). NORFOLK ISLAND PINE. Zone TS; indoors anywhere. Moderate growth rate to 100 ft., of pyramidal shape. Juvenile leaves rather narrow, ½ in. long, curved and with sharp points; mature leaves somewhat triangular and densely overlapping. Can be held in containers for many years.

Araucariaceae. Coniferous trees with symmetrical branching habit and leaves that vary from needlelike to broad and leathery. *Araucaria* is the only representative in this book.

ARBORVITAE. See THUJA

ARBUTUS

Ericaceae

EVERGREEN TREES AND SHRUB-TREES

ZONES VARY BY SPECIES

FULL SUN, EXCEPT AS NOTED

REGULAR TO LITTLE WATER

Arbutus xalapensis

All types have ornamental bark, clusters of little urn-shaped flowers, decorative (and edible) fruit, and handsome foliage. Provide good drainage, especially if plant receives regular water. Best in low-humidity, low-rainfall areas, such as Southwest Texas.

A. unedo. STRAWBERRY TREE. Zones MS, LS, CS. Native to southern Europe, Ireland. Slow to moderate growth to 8–35 ft. tall and wide; tends to be a small shrub in Southeast. Trunk and branches have shreddy red-brown bark, become twisted and gnarled in age. Dark green, red-stemmed leaves 2–3 in. long. Clusters of flowers and fruit often appear simultaneously in fall and winter. Small, white or greenish white flowers; red-and-yellow, ¾-in. fruits resemble strawberries but are mealy and bland tasting. Selections include 'Elfin King', a dwarf form (not over 5 ft. tall at 10 years

A

old) that flowers and fruits nearly continuously; 'Compacta', seldom exceeding 10 ft.; and 'Oktoberfest', a 6–8-ft. form with deep pink flowers. Sun or part shade.

A. xalapensis (A. texana). TEXAS MADRONE. Zones MS, LS, CS. Native to Texas, New Mexico, Mexico to Guatemala. Striking multitrunked small tree, to 20–30 ft. with handsome deep green leaves, clusters of small white or pale pink flowers in spring, raspberrylike fruit in fall. Bark extremely showy: changes in color through the year, from cream, when young, to pink, and then to brown before it peels, revealing new bark beneath. Requires careful attention to get established; provide light shade, and water consistently for several years but never allow soil to become waterlogged. Grows well in chalky soil.

ARCHONTOPHOENIX

Arecaceae (Palmae)

PALMS

✂ ZONE TS; OR INDOORS

☼ ◐ FULL SUN OR PARTIAL SHADE

◌ ● REGULAR TO MODERATE WATER

Archontophoenix cunninghamiana

Called bangalow or piccabeen palms in Australia. They grow to 50 ft. or more, with 10–15-ft. spread. Handsome, stately, difficult to transplant when large. Where winds are strong, plant in lee of buildings to prevent damage. Young trees can't take frost; mature plants may stand 28°F. They tolerate shade and can grow many years grouped under tall trees. Old leaves shed cleanly, leaving smooth green trunks. Feathery leaves on mature trees 8–10 ft. long, green above, gray green beneath. Good pot plant indoors or out.

A. alexandrae. ALEXANDRA PALM. Trunk enlarged toward base.

A. cunninghamiana (Seaforthia elegans). KING PALM. More common than *A. alexandrae.* Trunk not prominently enlarged at base. Clustered amethyst flowers are handsome. Highly recommended for nearly frost-free areas.

ARDISIA

MARLBERRY

Myrsinaceae

EVERGREEN SHRUBS AND SHRUBLETS

✂ ZONES VARY BY SPECIES

☼ ◐ ● EXPOSURE NEEDS VARY BY SPECIES

● REGULAR WATER, EXCEPT AS NOTED

Ardisia japonica

Of the 150 species of evergreen shrubs in this genus, only the following three are commonly grown. Valued for foliage, beadlike fruits.

A. crenata (A. crenulata, A. crispa). CORAL ARDISIA. Zones CS, TS; or indoors. In Florida, plant often grown in the ground on the north side of houses or in planters. Most familiar as 1½-ft. single-stemmed potted plant needing only routine house plant care. In large tub it can reach 4 ft. with nearly equal spread. In spring, spirelike clusters of tiny, ¼-in. white or pinkish flowers are carried above shiny, wavy-edged, 3-in.-long leaves. Flowers are followed in autumn by brilliant scarlet fruit that usually hangs on through winter. Outdoors, plant in partial or full shade.

A. japonica. JAPANESE ARDISIA. Zones LS, CS. Low shrub that spreads as ground cover by rhizomes to produce succession of upright branches 6–12 in. high. Makes quality ground cover in partial or full shade. Leathery, bright green leaves, 4 in. long, are clustered at tips of branches. Forms with white or gold leaf variegation are sometimes sold. White, ¼-in. flowers, two to six in cluster, appear in fall, followed by small, round, bright red fruits that last into winter.

A. paniculata. MARLBERRY. Zone TS. Slender shrub or small tree, to 20–25 ft. Native to southern Florida. Coarse, dark green leaves, lance shaped, to 6 in. Fragrant white flowers with purple marks appear at intervals through most of the year. Fruits glossy black. Both flowers and fruits ¼ in. Excellent for coastal gardens; takes salt spray, and full sun or light shade. Tolerates clay, alkaline soils. Needs less water than other two species.

Arecaceae. It's difficult to generalize about any plant family as large and widespread as palms. Generally speaking, they have single, unbranched trunks of considerable height; some grow in clusters, though, and some are dwarf or stemless. The leaves are usually (but not always) divided into many leaflets, either like ribs of a fan (fan palms) or like a feather, with many parallel leaflets growing outward from a long central stem (feather palms). This family was formerly called Palmae. See also Palms.

ARECA lutescens. See CHRYSALIDOCARPUS lutescens

ARECA PALM. See CHRYSALIDOCARPUS lutescens

ARECASTRUM romanzoffianum. See SYAGRUS romanzoffianum

ARGYRANTHEMUM. See CHRYSANTHEMUM frutescens

ARISAEMA

Araceae

TUBEROUS-ROOTED PERENNIALS

✂ ZONES VARY BY SPECIES

◐ ● PARTIAL OR FULL SHADE

◌ ◌◌ AMPLE WATER DURING ACTIVE GROWTH

Arisaema triphyllum

Eerie-looking woodland plants from the eastern U.S. and the Far East. All have segmented leaves and summer flowers somewhat resembling otherworldly callas, with a much-modified leaflike bract (spathe) surrounding a spike of minute flowers on a fleshy stalk (spadix). The native Jack-in-the-pulpit is a familiar example, but species from Asia attract connoisseurs of the odd. Fruits resemble small, bright red ears of corn. All die down in winter and tend to reappear late in spring. Use in the woodland garden or grow in pots for close-up viewing. All like rich soil, with abundant organic matter and plenty of water.

A. sikokianum. Zones US, MS, LS. Native to Japan. Grows to 20 in. Plant has two leaves, one with three leaflets, the other with five; leaflets grow 6 in. long, 4 in. wide. Flower stem, as tall (or nearly) as leafstalks, bears a 6-in. spathe—deep purple outside, yellowish within. Tip of spathe curves over a white spadix with a rounded, club-shaped tip.

A. speciosum. SHOWY COBRA LILY. Zone LS. Native to Himalayas, western China. Grows 2–3 ft., with a single 1½-ft. leaf bearing three leaflets with reddish edges. Leafstalk marbled dark purple. Spathe to 8 in., dark purple striped white. Whitish spadix terminates in a slender 2-ft. tail.

A. tortuosum. Zones MS, LS. Native to Himalayas, western China. Grows 3–4 ft. tall. Each leaf has 5 to 15 narrow leaflets. Green or purplish, 6-in. spathe is strongly curved downward at tip; green or purplish spadix thrusts out and upward in a strong curve.

A. triphyllum. JACK-IN-THE-PULPIT, INDIAN TURNIP. Zones US, MS, LS. Native to eastern North America. Each of the two 2-ft. leafstalks bears three 6-in. leaflets. Flowering stems, usually taller than leaves, carry a hooded spathe to 6 in., green or purple with white stripes (the pulpit), and a green or purple spadix (Jack). A common woodland plant. The name "Indian turnip" refers to the root. It contains calcium oxalate crystals that sting the tongue and throat, but is edible if thoroughly boiled.

ARISTOLOCHIA durior (A. macrophylla)

DUTCHMAN'S PIPE

Aristolochiaceae

DECIDUOUS VINE

ZONES US, MS, LS, CS

SUN OR SHADE

AMPLE TO REGULAR WATER

Aristolochia durior

Native to eastern U.S. Broad heart-shaped, deep green, glossy leaves, 6–14 in. long, are carried in shinglelike pattern, form dense cover on trellis. Vine covers 15 by 20 ft. in one season. Often used to provide summer shade to south- or west-facing porches. Blossom is yellowish green, 3-in. curved tube that flares into three brownish purple lobes about 1 in. wide; shape gives plant its name. Flowers nearly hidden by leaves. Blooms late spring to early summer. Easily grown from seed. Will not stand strong winds.

Aristolochiaceae. This family includes *Aristolochia* and wild ginger (*Asarum*). All display odd-shaped flowers in low-key colors.

ARMERIA

THRIFT, SEA PINK

Plumbaginaceae

PERENNIALS

ZONES VARY BY SPECIES

FULL SUN

REGULAR TO LITTLE WATER

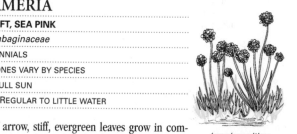

Armeria maritima

Narrow, stiff, evergreen leaves grow in compact tufts or basal rosettes; small white, pink, rose, or red flowers in dense globular heads. Main bloom period is spring to early summer, but removing faded flowers may prolong blooming into fall. Sturdy, dependable plants for edging walks or borders and for tidy mounds in rock gardens or raised beds. Attractive in containers. Need excellent drainage. Propagate by divisions or from seeds in spring or fall.

A. arenaria (A. plantaginea). Zones US, MS. Leaves narrow, 2–6 in. long. Flowering stems 8–24 in. tall, with purplish pink or white blossoms.

A. girardii (A. juncea, A. setacea). Zone MS. Low, dense mounds of narrow, needlelike foliage produce lavender pink flowers.

A. maritima (Statice armeria, Armeria vulgaris). COMMON THRIFT. Zones US, MS. Tufted mounds spreading to 1 ft. with 6-in.-long, stiff, grasslike leaves. Small white to rose pink flowers in tight clusters at top of 6–10-in. stalks. 'Bloodstone' is rose red; 'Cotton Tail' is white.

ARONIA

CHOKEBERRY

Rosaceae

DECIDUOUS SHRUBS

ZONES US, MS, LS

FULL SUN OR LIGHT SHADE

MUCH OR LITTLE WATER

Aronia arbutifolia

Chokeberries, native to southern Canada and the eastern U.S., are tough, undemanding shrubs useful as fillers or background plantings. They tolerate a wide variety of soils and can thrive on much or little water. All tend to spread by suckering, but are somewhat leggy (good for planting beneath). Small white or pinkish flowers are followed by showy fruits that last well into winter. Fall foliage is brightly colored.

A. arbutifolia. RED CHOKEBERRY. Clumping shrub to 6–8 ft., with many erect stems bearing shiny foliage that is rich green above, paler beneath. Fruits are clustered, ¼ in. wide, brilliant red, long lasting. Fall foliage is also bright red; plants tend to color early. 'Brilliant' ('Brilliantissima') is a selected form with exceptionally fine fall color.

A. melanocarpa. BLACK CHOKEBERRY. Shrub is lower growing than *A. arbutifolia*, to just 3–5 ft. tall, rarely taller. Foliage features purple-red fall color; shiny black ½-in. fruits.

ARROWHEAD VINE. See SYNGONIUM

ARTEMISIA

Asteraceae (Compositae)

PERENNIALS

ZONES VARY BY SPECIES

FULL SUN

MODERATE WATER

Artemisia abrotanum

Several species are valuable for interesting leaf patterns and silvery gray or white aromatic foliage. Most of those described here have woody stems; *A. dracunculus, A. lactiflora, A. ludoviciana albula,* and *A. stellerana* are herbaceous. Most need excellent drainage. Not the best choice for high-rainfall areas, particularly along the Gulf Coast and in Florida. Most kinds excellent for use in mixed border where white or silvery leaves soften harsh reds or oranges and blend beautifully with blues, lavenders, and pinks. Divide in spring and fall.

A. abrotanum. SOUTHERNWOOD, OLD MAN. Zones US, MS, LS, CS. To 3–5 ft. Beautiful lemon-scented, green, feathery foliage; yellowish white flower heads. Use for pleasantly scented foliage in shrub border. Hang sprigs in closet to discourage moths. Burn a few leaves on stove to kill cooking odors.

A. absinthium. COMMON WORMWOOD. Zones US, MS, LS. To 2–4 ft. Silvery gray, finely divided leaves with pungent odor. Tiny yellow flowers. Prune for better-shaped plant. Divide every 3 years. Background shrub; good gray feature in flower border, particularly fine with delphiniums. 'Lambrook Silver' is a 1½-ft. form with especially finely cut, silvery white leaves.

A. arborescens. Zone CS. To 3 ft. or a little more in height, 2 ft. wide, with silvery white, very finely cut foliage. Most attractive but more tender than other artemisias.

Artemisia dracunculus

A. caucasica. SILVER SPREADER. Zones US, MS, LS. To 3–6 in. tall, spreading to 2 ft. in width. Silky, silvery green foliage; small yellow flowers. Bank or ground cover; plant 1–2 ft. apart. Needs good drainage. Takes extremes of heat and cold.

A. dracunculus. FRENCH TARRAGON, TRUE TARRAGON. Zones US, MS. Doesn't do well in warmer areas. Mexican mint marigold (*Tagetes lucida*) is a good substitute. To 1–2 ft.; spreads slowly by creeping rhizomes. Shiny dark green, narrow leaves are very aromatic. Flowers greenish white in branched clusters. Attractive container plant. Cut sprigs in June for seasoning vinegar. Use fresh or dried leaves to season salads, egg and cheese dishes, fish. Divide plant every 3 or 4 years to keep it vigorous. Propagate by divisions or by cuttings. Plants grown from seed are not true culinary tarragon.

A. lactiflora. WHITE MUGWORT. Zones US, MS, LS. Tall, straight column to 4–5 ft. One of few artemisias with attractive flowers: creamy white in large, branched, 1½-ft. sprays in late summer. Leaves dark green with broad, tooth-edged lobes.

▶

A. ludoviciana albula (A. albula). SILVER KING ARTEMISIA. Zones US, MS, LS, CS. Bushy growth to 2–3½ ft., with slender, spreading branches and silvery white, 2-in. leaves. The lower leaves have three to five lobes; the upper ones are narrow and unlobed. Cut foliage useful in arrangements. 'Valerie Finnis' is a compact grower (to 2 ft. tall), with broader silvery leaves slightly lobed toward the tips.

A. pontica. ROMAN WORMWOOD. Zones US, MS, LS, CS. To 4 ft. Feathery, silver-gray leaves. Heads of nodding, whitish yellow flowers in long, open, branched clusters. Leaves used in sachets.

A. 'Powis Castle'. Zones US, MS, LS. A hybrid, with *A. absinthium* as a probable parent. Silvery, lacy mound to 3 ft. tall, 6 ft. wide. Unlike most other artemisias, does not "melt" during hot, humid summers; retains dense shape, and is not invasive. Don't prune in fall; wait until new growth sprouts near crown in spring to cut back.

A. schmidtiana. ANGEL'S HAIR. Zones US, MS, LS. Forms dome, 2 ft. high and 1 ft. wide, of woolly, silvery white, finely cut leaves. Flowers insignificant. 'Silver Mound' is 1 ft. high.

A. stellerana. BEACH WORMWOOD, OLD WOMAN, DUSTY MILLER. Zones US, MS, LS. Dense, silvery gray plant to 2½ ft. with 1–4-in. lobed leaves. Hardier than *Senecio cineraria* (another dusty miller), this artemisia is often used in its place in colder climates. Yellow flowers in spikelike clusters. 'Silver Brocade' is a superior, densely growing selection.

ARUM

Araceae

PERENNIALS WITH TUBEROUS ROOTS

� ZONES VARY BY SPECIES

☼ ● PARTIAL OR FULL SHADE

● REGULAR WATER DURING ACTIVE GROWTH

◊ SAP IS AN IRRITANT IF INGESTED

Arum italicum

Arrow-shaped or heart-shaped leaves. Curious callalike blossoms on short stalks. Flower bract (spathe) half encloses thick, fleshy spike (spadix), which bears tiny flowers. Use in shady flower borders where hardy; *A. pictum* is sometimes used as indoor plant in colder climates.

A. italicum. ITALIAN ARUM. Zones US, MS, LS, CS. Arrow-shaped leaves, 8 in. long and wide, emerge in fall or early winter. Very short stem; white or greenish white (sometimes purple-spotted) flowers in spring and early summer. Spathe first stands erect, then folds over and conceals short yellow spadix. Dense clusters of bright red fruit follow. Lasting long after leaves have faded, these are the most conspicuous feature of the plant. They resemble small, bright red ears of shucked corn. In the selection 'Pictum', leaves are veined with white.

A. pictum. Zones LS, CS. Light green, heart-shaped, 10-in.-long leaves on 10-in. stalks appear in autumn, with or just after the flowers. Spathe is violet, green at base; spadix purplish black.

ARUNCUS

GOAT'S BEARD

Rosaceae

PERENNIALS

� ZONES US, MS

☼ LIGHT SHADE

● REGULAR WATER

Aruncus dioicus

Resemble *Astilbe*, with slowly spreading clumps of finely divided leaves topped in summer by plumy branched clusters of tiny white or creamy flowers. Good in perennial borders or at edge of woodland; especially handsome against a dark background. Require moist but not boggy soil.

A. aethusifolius. Deep green, finely divided leaves make foot-tall mounds. White flower plumes reach 16 in. Useful in rock garden, as edging or small-scale ground cover.

A. dioicus (A. sylvester). Grows to 6 ft., with a foam of white flowers in 20-in., much-branched clusters. 'Kneiffii' is half as tall, with more finely divided, almost ferny, leaves. 'Child of Two Worlds' ('Zweiweltenkind'), often sold as *A. chinensis,* grows to 5 ft.; branched flower clusters droop gracefully.

ARUNDINARIA. See BAMBOO

ARUNDO donax

GIANT REED

Poaceae (Gramineae)

PERENNIAL

� ALL ZONES

☼ FULL SUN

● ●● AMPLE TO REGULAR WATER

Arundo donax

One of largest grasses, planted for bold effects in garden fringe areas or by watersides. Also planted as quick windbreak or for erosion control. Often called a bamboo. Strong, somewhat woody stems, 6–20 ft. high. Leaves 2 ft. long, flat, 3 in. wide. Flowers in rather narrow, erect clusters to 2 ft. high. 'Versicolor' ('Variegata'), less hardy than species (Zones MS, LS, CS, TS), has leaves with white or yellowish stripes. Plants need rich soil. Protect roots with mulch in cold-winter areas. Cut out dead stems and thin occasionally to get look-through quality. Extremely invasive; plant only where you can control it. Can become a pest in irrigation ditches. Stems have some utility as plant stakes or, if woven together with wire, as fencing or shade canopy.

ASARUM

WILD GINGER

Aristolochiaceae

PERENNIALS

� ZONES VARY BY SPECIES

☼ ● PARTIAL OR FULL SHADE

● ●● AMPLE TO REGULAR WATER

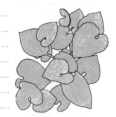

Asarum caudatum

Roots and leaves of the wild gingers have a scent somewhat like that of ginger, but are not used as seasoning. Low, creeping plants with roundish or heart-shaped leaves, they make attractive woodland ground covers. Flowers are oddly shaped, with three spreading, leathery lobes that may be brownish, purplish, or greenish; hidden among the leaves, blossoms are curious rather than showy. Of the many species, only a few are available to gardeners. Asiatic species with fancily variegated leaves, now grown as connoisseur's plants in Japan, may eventually make their way here.

A. canadense. Zones US, MS, LS. Native to eastern North America. Deciduous, kidney-shaped, dark green leaves to 6 in. wide. Flowers are purplish brown. The hardiest species.

A. caudatum. Zones US, MS. Native to the West Coast. Evergreen in warmest areas of zones. Heart-shaped leaves are 2–7 in. wide. Flowers reddish brown, lobes elongated into tails. Where adapted, a valuable, quick-growing ground cover for shady places.

A. europaeum. EUROPEAN WILD GINGER. Zones US, MS. Native to Europe. Evergreen, shiny, kidney-shaped, dark green leaves 2–3 in. wide. Small brown flowers. Slow spreader.

Asarum shuttleworthii

A. shuttleworthii. Zones US, MS, LS. Native to the Appalachians. Evergreen, 4-in. heart-shaped or roundish leaves usually variegated with silvery markings. Brown flowers with red spots. Slow growing. 'Callaway' spreads more quickly and has extremely handsome, mottled foliage.

Asclepiadaceae. The best-known family members are the milkweeds *(Asclepias)*, but other garden plants belong to this group, among them many succulents and some perennials and vines, including *Stephanotis*.

ASCLEPIAS

Asclepiadaceae

PERENNIALS

☘ ALL ZONES

☼ FULL SUN

◐ ◐ ◖ WATER NEEDS VARY BY SPECIES

⬧ ALL PARTS OF MANY SPECIES ARE POISONOUS IF INGESTED

Asclepias tuberosa

Milkweeds are the most well known representatives of this group of plants. Just a few are cultivated in gardens; both of the following are native to eastern U.S.

A. incarnata. SWAMP MILKWEED. Grows 3–5 ft. tall, with narrow, long-pointed leaves and clustered pink flowers in joints of upper leaves. Needs plenty of moisture, even withstands wet soil. 'Ice Ballet', with white flowers, is a more compact, 3½-ft. plant.

A. tuberosa. BUTTERFLY WEED. Many stems to 3 ft. rise every year from perennial root. Broad clusters of bright orange flowers appear in midsummer, attracting swarms of butterflies. Prefers good drainage and moderate water. Flowers of Gay Butterflies strain are yellow to red. 'Hello Yellow' is a selected form with bright yellow flowers.

ASH. See FRAXINUS

ASH, MOUNTAIN. See SORBUS

🏛 ASIMINA triloba

PAWPAW

Annonaceae

DECIDUOUS TREE

☘ ZONES US, MS, LS, CS

☼ ◐ ● SUN OR SHADE

◐ REGULAR WATER

Asimina triloba

The pawpaw (sometimes known as Indian banana) is the only hardy representative of a tropical family that has given us the heat-sensitive and less hardy cherimoya *(Annona cherimola)*. Pest-resistant plant doesn't need spraying. Will fruit well in shade. Only major drawback is perishability of fruit, which won't keep more than a week unless frozen. The plant grows to 30 ft., generally broad and spreading when grown alone, but often narrow and erect in thickets that arise from suckering. In most areas, pawpaw suffers in full sun while very young and should have some shade in the first years. Leaves are oval, somewhat drooping, 4–10 in. long, medium green, turning bright yellow in fall. Foliage has an unpleasant odor when crushed. Flowers are large but not showy, purplish or brownish (sometimes green), with three prominent petals. Fruits are roughly oval, yellowish green turning brown, 3–5 in. long. The soft, custardlike flesh has a flavor between banana and mango, and a number of large brown seeds.

If possible, get grafted plants of named selections such as 'Mango', 'Overleese', 'Prolific', 'Rebecca's Gold', 'Sunflower', and 'Taylor'. Plant two selections or more for cross-pollination. Seedlings are highly variable.

SOUTHERN HERITAGE PLANTS
IDENTIFIED BY SYMBOL 🏛

ASPARAGUS, EDIBLE

Liliaceae

PERENNIAL VEGETABLE

☘ ZONES US, MS, LS

☼ FULL SUN

◐ ◖ AMPLE TO REGULAR WATER

Edible Asparagus

One of most permanent and dependable of home garden vegetables. Plants take 2 to 3 years to come into full production but then furnish delicious spears every spring for 10 to 15 years. They take up considerable space but do so in the grand manner: Plants are tall, feathery, graceful, highly ornamental. Use asparagus along sunny fence or as background for flowers or vegetables.

Seeds grow into strong young plants in one season (sow in spring), but roots are far more widely used. Set out seedlings or roots (not wilted, no smaller than an adult's hand) in fall or winter, or in early spring in Upper South. Make trenches 1 ft. wide and 8–10 in. deep. Space trenches 4–6 ft. apart. Heap loose, manure-enriched soil at bottoms of trenches, and soak. Space plants 1 ft. apart, setting them so that tops are 6–8 in. below top of trench. Spread roots out evenly. Cover with 2 in. of soil and water again.

As young plants grow, gradually fill in trench, taking care not to cover growing tips. Soak deeply whenever soil begins to dry out at root depth. Don't harvest spears the first year; object is to build big root mass. When plants turn brown in late fall or early winter, cut stems to ground.

The following spring you can cut your first spears; cut only for 4 to 6 weeks or until appearance of thin spears indicates that roots are nearing exhaustion. Then permit plants to grow. Cultivate, feed, and irrigate heavily. The third year you should be able to cut spears for 8 to 10 weeks. Spears are ready to cut when they are 5–8 in. long. Thrust knife down at 45° angle to soil; flat cutting may injure adjacent developing spears. If asparagus beetles appear during cutting season, hand-pick them, knock them off the plant with water jets, or spray with rotenone or (carefully noting label precautions) malathion (see page 445).

Asparagus seed and roots are sold as "traditional" ('Martha Washington' and others) and "all-male" ('Jersey Giant' and others). The latter kinds are bred to produce more and larger spears because they don't have to put energy into seed production. Such selections still produce an occasional female plant.

ASPARAGUS, ORNAMENTAL

Liliaceae

PERENNIAL SHRUBS OR VINES

☘ ZONE TS; OR INDOORS

☼ ◐ FULL SUN OR PARTIAL SHADE

◐ REGULAR WATER

Asparagus densiflorus
'Sprengeri'

There are about 150 kinds of asparagus besides the edible one—all members of the lily family. Best known of the ornamental types is asparagus fern *(A. setaceus)*, which is not a true fern. Although valued mostly for handsome foliage of unusual textural quality, some of these species have small but fragrant flowers and colorful berries. Green foliage sprays are made up of what look like leaves. Needle-like or broader, these are actually short branches called cladodes. The true leaves are inconspicuous dry scales.

Most ornamental asparagus look greenest in partial shade. Leaves turn yellow in dense shade. Plant in well-drained soil to which peat moss or ground bark has been added. Because of fleshy roots, plants can go for periods without water but grow better when it comes regularly. Feed in spring with complete fertilizer. Trim out old shoots to make room for new growth. Will survive light frosts but may be killed to ground by severe cold. After frost, plants often come back from roots.

A. asparagoides. SMILAX ASPARAGUS. Much-branched vine with spineless stems to 20 ft. or more. Leaves to 1 in. long, sharp pointed, stiffish, glossy grass green. Small, fragrant white flowers in spring followed by blue berries. Birds feed on berries, drop seeds that sprout at random about the garden. (Plant also self-sows readily.) Roots are clusters of fleshy thongs and are nearly immortal, surviving long drought. Foliage sprays prized for table decoration. Becomes tangled mass unless trained. 'Myrtifolius', commonly called baby smilax, is a more graceful form with smaller leaves.

A. densiflorus. The species is less commonly grown than its forms. The following are the two most popular:

'Myers'. MYERS ASPARAGUS. Plants send up several to many stiffly upright stems to 2 ft. or more, densely clothed with needlelike deep green leaves. Plants have fluffy look. Good in containers. A little less hardy than Sprenger asparagus. Sometimes sold as *A. meyeri* or *A. myersii*.

'Sprengeri'. SPRENGER ASPARAGUS. Arching or drooping stems 3–6 ft. long. Shiny, bright green needlelike leaves, 1 in. long, in bundles. Bright red berries. Popular for hanging baskets or containers, indoors and out. Train on trellis; climbs by means of small hooked prickles. Used as billowy ground cover where temperatures stay above 24°F. Takes full sun as well as partial shade; grows in ordinary or even poor soil. Will tolerate dryness of indoors but needs bright light. Sometimes sold as *A. sprengeri*. Form sold as 'Sprengeri Compacta' or *A. sarmentosus* 'Compacta' is denser with shorter stems.

A. meyeri, A. myersii. See A. densiflorus 'Myers'

A. plumosus. See A. setaceus

A. sarmentosus. See A. densiflorus 'Sprengeri'

A. setaceus (A. plumosus). ASPARAGUS FERN. Branching woody vine climbs by wiry, spiny stems to 10–20 ft. Tiny threadlike leaves form feathery dark green sprays that resemble fern fronds. Tiny white flowers. Berries purple black. Dense, fine-textured foliage mass useful as screen against walls, fences. Florists use foliage as fillers in bouquets; holds up better than delicate ferns. Sometimes called emerald feather. Dwarf type 'Nanus' is good in containers. 'Pyramidalis' has upswept, windblown look, is less vigorous than common asparagus fern.

A. sprengeri. See A. densiflorus 'Sprengeri'

ASPEN. See POPULUS

ASPERULA odorata. See GALIUM odoratum

ASPIDISTRA elatior
(A. lurida)

CAST-IRON PLANT

Liliaceae

PERENNIAL

⚘ ZONES LS, CS, TS; OR INDOORS

☼ ● TOLERATES VERY LOW LIGHT

💧 MODERATE WATER

Aspidistra elatior

Sturdy, long-lived evergreen foliage plant is remarkable for its ability to thrive under conditions unacceptable to most kinds of plants. Leaf blades 1–2½ ft. long, 3–4 in. wide, tough, glossy dark green and arching, with distinct parallel veins; each blade is supported by a 6–8-in.-long grooved leafstalk. Inconspicuous brownish flowers bloom in spring close to ground. Although extremely tolerant, requiring minimal care, cast-iron plant grows best in porous soil enriched with organic matter and responds to feeding in spring and summer. Will grow in dark, shaded areas (under decks or stairs) anywhere, as well as in filtered sun—except in hot, dry areas, where it takes full shade only. A good porch plant. Keep leaves dust-free and glossy by hosing them off or cleaning them with a soft brush or cloth. Variegated form ('Variegata'), with leaves striped with white, loses its variegation if it is planted in soil that's too rich.

ASPLENIUM

Polypodiaceae

FERNS

⚘ ZONES VARY BY SPECIES

☼ ● PARTIAL OR FULL SHADE

💧 AMPLE TO REGULAR WATER

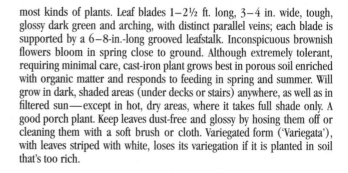
Asplenium nidus

Widespread and variable group of plants. These resemble each other only in botanical details and need for shade and liberal watering. Common name "spleenwort" refers to alleged medicinal value.

A. bulbiferum. MOTHER FERN. Zone TS, or house plant. From New Zealand. Graceful, very finely cut light green fronds to 4 ft. tall. Fronds produce plantlets that can be removed and planted. Hardy to 26°F.

A. ebenoides (Asplenosorus ebenoides). SCOTT'S SPLEENWORT. Zones US, MS, LS. Hybrid between *A. platyneuron* and *A. rhizophyllum*. Small evergreen fern of variable appearance, with unevenly divided leaves.

A. nidus (A. nidus-avis). BIRD'S NEST FERN. Zone TS, or house plant. Native to Old World tropics. Tender fern with showy, apple green, undivided fronds 4 ft. by 8 in., growing upright in cluster. Striking foliage. Grow potted plant indoors in winter, move to shady patio in summer.

Asplenium platyneuron

A. platyneuron. EBONY SPLEENWORT. Zones US, MS, LS. Native to eastern U.S. Evergreen, to 1½ ft. tall. Erect, once-divided dark green fronds have blackish brown midribs.

A. rhizophyllum (Camptosorus rhizophyllum). WALKING FERN. Zones US, MS, LS. Native to North America. An oddity with long, slender undivided fronds that taper to the tips; where they touch soil, tips take root and produce new plantlets. Needs some lime in the soil.

A. scolopendrium (Phyllitis scolopendrium). HART'S TONGUE FERN. Zones US, MS, LS. Native to Europe (rare native in eastern U.S.). Strap-shaped leaves 9–18 in. long. Dwarf, crested, puckered, and forked kinds are collector's items. Plant needs humus; add limestone chips to acid soil. Good woodland plant, rhododendron and azalea companion; also fine pot plant.

A. trichomanes. MAIDENHAIR SPLEENWORT. Zones US, MS. Native to much of the Northern Hemisphere. Delicate evergreen fern with narrow, bright green fronds 8–12 in. long. Leaflets are round or nearly so, only ½ in. long. Likes lime. Attractive in shady rock garden or on a wall where it can be seen close up.

Asplenium scolopendrium

ASTER

Asteraceae (Compositae)

PERENNIALS

❀ ZONES US, MS, LS, EXCEPT AS NOTED

☼ FULL SUN, EXCEPT AS NOTED

◐ ◑ REGULAR TO MODERATE WATER

Aster frikartii

There are more than 600 species of true
asters, ranging from alpine kinds forming compact mounds 6 in.
high, to open-branching plants 6 ft. tall, to the odd tall climber. Flowers
come in white or shades of blue, red, pink, lavender, or purple, mostly
with yellow centers. Bloom is late summer to early fall, except as noted.
Taller asters are invaluable for abundant color in large borders or among
shrubs. Large sprays are effective in arrangements. Compact dwarf or
cushion types make tidy edgings, mounds of color in rock gardens, good
container plants.

Adapted to most soils. Most luxuriant in fertile soil. Few problems
except for mildew on leaves in late fall. Strong-growing asters have invasive
roots, need control. Divide clumps yearly in late fall or early spring.
Replant vigorous young divisions from outside of clump; discard old center. Divide smaller, tufted, less vigorously growing kinds every 2 years.

A. alpinus. ALPINE ASTER. Zones US, MS. Mounding plant 6–12 in.
tall. Leaves ½–5 in. long, mostly in basal tuft. Several stems grow from
basal clump, each carrying one violet blue flower 1½–2 in. across. Late
spring to early summer bloom. White and pink forms are uncommon.

A. amellus. ITALIAN ASTER. Sturdy, hairy plant to 2 ft. Branching stems
with violet, yellow-centered flowers 2 in. across.

A. frikartii. FRIKART ASTER. One of the finest, most useful, and widely
adapted perennials. Requires excellent drainage, or it rots. Hybrid between
A. amellus and *A. thomsonii*, a hairy-leafed, lilac-flowered, 3-ft. species
native to the Himalayas. Abundant clear lavender to violet blue single flowers are 2½ in. across. Open, spreading growth to 2 ft. high. Blooms early
summer to fall—almost all year in mild-winter areas if dead flowers are
removed regularly. May be short lived. Selections 'Wonder of Staffa' and
'Mönch' are lavender blue favorites.

A. laevis. SMOOTH ASTER. To 3½ ft., with smooth, mildew-free
foliage. Clustered, 1-in. flower heads of deep purple blue.

A. lateriflorus. Species grows to 4 ft.; garden selections are smaller, to
2½ ft. 'Horizontalis' is a twiggy, mounding plant with spreading branches
bearing small pale blue flowers. Foliage turns purplish in fall, at height of
bloom. 'Prince' is similar in form, with dark purple foliage and white
flower heads centered in dark red.

A. novae-angliae. NEW ENGLAND ASTER. Stout-stemmed plant to
3–5 ft. with hairy leaves 5 in. long. Flowers are variable in color, from
pink to deep purple, 2 in. across. Good in wet areas.

A. novi-belgii. NEW YORK ASTER. To 3 ft., similar to New England
aster but with smooth leaves. Full clusters of bright blue-violet flowers.

Michaelmas daisy is the name applied to the selections and hybrids of
A. novae-angliae and *A. novi-belgii*. They are tall (3–4-ft.), graceful,
branching plants. Flowers in white, pale to deep pink, rose, red, and many
shades of blue, violet, and purple. Here are a few of the many selections:

'Alma Potschke'. Midseason. Rose, 3 ft.

'Barr's Blue'. Late season. Deep violet, 4 ft.

'Eventide'. Late summer–early fall. Very showy semidouble, deep purple, 3 ft.

'Fanny's Aster'. Very late season. Purple blue, 2–4 ft.

'Harrington's Pink'. Late season. Large, good cut flowers, clear pink,
3–4 ft.

'Hella Lacy'. Midseason. Lavender with yellow center, 3 ft.

'September Ruby'. Late September. Cerise with yellow center, 3–4 ft.

A. dumosus hybrids, sometimes known as Oregon-Pacific hybrids, are
splendid garden plants developed by crossing some well-known Michaelmas daisies with a dwarf aster species native to the West. Dwarf, intermediate, and taller forms range in height from under 1 ft. to 2½ ft. Compact,
floriferous, blooming late spring to fall. Many named selections are available in white, blue, lavender, purple, rose, pink, cream.

A. oblongifolius. AROMATIC ASTER. To 2 ft., with light blue-violet
flowers that last through heavy frosts into late fall. Prefers a dry, open site.
Tolerates harsh conditions, including heat, cold, poor or alkaline soil, and
strong winds. Foliage pale green, aromatic when crushed.

A. patens. LATE PURPLE ASTER. To 3 ft. Prolific flowers are bright violet blue. Tolerates drought and partial shade.

A. pringlei. Eastern U.S. native known in cultivation through its selection 'Monte Cassino', a familiar florists' cut flower. Stems are long (sometimes to 5 ft.) and narrowish, freely set with very short branches bearing
starry white, ¾-in. flower heads. Plant is usually sold as *A. ericoides*
'Monte Cassino'.

A. tataricus. TATARIAN ASTER. A giant (to 5–7 ft.) with 2-ft. leaves and
sheaves of inch-wide blue flower heads in flat clusters in fall. Sun or shade.
'Jindai', a compact selection, grows 4 ft. tall.

Asteraceae. The sunflower or daisy family, one of the largest plant families, is characterized by flowers borne in tight clusters (heads). In the most
familiar form, these heads contain two types of flowers—small, tightly
clustered disk flowers in the center of the head, and larger, strap-shaped
ray flowers around the edge. The sunflower *(Helianthus)* is a familiar
example. The family was formerly called Compositae.

ASTERMOEA mongolica. See KALIMERIS pinnatifida

ASTILBE

ASTILBE, FALSE SPIRAEA, MEADOW SWEET

Saxifragaceae

PERENNIALS

❀ ZONES US, MS

☼ ◐ FULL SUN OR PARTIAL SHADE

◑ MOIST BUT NOT BOGGY SOIL

Astilbe arendsii

Valued for light, airy quality of plumelike flower clusters and attractive
foliage, ability to provide color from late spring through summer.
Leaves divided, with toothed or cut leaflets; leaves in some species simply
lobed with cut margins. Small white, pink, or red flowers are carried in
graceful, branching, feathery plumes held on slender, wiry stems ranging
from 6 in. to 3 ft. or taller.

Astilbes are the mainstay of the shady perennial border, although in the
Upper South they can take quite a bit of sun if given plenty of moisture.
Combine them with columbine, meadow rue, hosta, and epimedium in
shady borders; with peonies, delphinium, and iris in sunnier situations.
Effective at the edge of ponds, along shady paths, and in containers. They
require rich soil with ample humus. Cut off faded flowering stems and
divide clumps every 4 or 5 years.

A. arendsii. Most astilbes sold belong to this hybrid group or are sold
as such. Most earliest blooming selections belong to species *A. japonica*,
some later bloomers to *A. chinensis* or *A. thunbergii*. The plants differ
chiefly in technical details. Here are some of the many selections in use:

'Amethyst'. Late. Lavender, 3–4 ft.

'Bonn'. Early. Medium pink, 1½–2 ft.

'Bremen'. Midseason. Dark rose, 1½–2 ft.

'Bressingham Beauty'. Late midseason. Drooping pink clusters, 3 ft.

'Bridal Veil'. Midseason to late. Full white plumes, 3 ft.

'Deutschland'. Early. White, 1½ ft.

'Erica'. Midseason. Slender pink plumes, 2½–3 ft.

'Fanal'. Early. Blood red flowers, bronzy foliage, 1½–2½ ft.

'Hyacinth'. Midseason. Purplish pink, 2–3 ft.

'Koblenz'. Early to midseason. Bright red, 1½–2½ ft.

'Ostrich Plume' ('Straussenfeder'). Midseason to late. Drooping pink
clusters, 3–3½ ft.

'Peach Blossom'. Midseason. Light salmon pink, 2 ft.

'Rheinland'. Early. Deep pink, 2–2½ ft.

'White Gloria'. Early to midseason. Creamy white, 2 ft.

A

141

A. chinensis. CHINESE ASTILBE. Resembles the *A. arendsii* hybrids, but generally blooms in late summer, grows taller, and tolerates dryness a little better. Varieties and selections include:

A. c. davidii. Late, with dense, narrow pink plumes 3 ft. tall. Pink-flowered 'Finale' blooms latest, grows 18–20 in. tall.

A. c. taquetii 'Superba'. Bright pinkish purple flowers in spikelike clusters 4–5 ft. tall. 'Purple Candles' is deeper purple, slightly shorter.

A. simplicifolia. Grows to 16 in., with leaves merely cut or lobed instead of divided into leaflets. Known for its selections. 'Sprite', the best known, is a low, compact plant with abundant pink, drooping, 1-ft. spires above bronze-tinted foliage; summer bloomer. 'Hennie Graefland' is similar, but grows a few inches taller and blooms somewhat earlier.

A. taquetii 'Superba'. See *A. chinensis taquetii* 'Superba'

ATAMASCO LILY. See ZEPHYRANTHES atamasco

ATHYRIUM

Polypodiaceae

FERNS

🌿 ZONES US, MS, LS

◐ ● PARTIAL OR FULL SHADE, EXCEPT AS NOTED

💧 AMPLE WATER

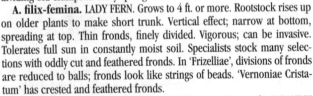
Athyrium filix-femina

Evergreen in mildest areas, these ferns turn brown after repeated frosts. Leave dead fronds on plant to provide mulch and to shelter emerging fronds in early spring, then cut back. Prefer rich, damp soil and shade. Propagate by dividing old clumps in early spring.

A. filix-femina. LADY FERN. Grows to 4 ft. or more. Rootstock rises up on older plants to make short trunk. Vertical effect; narrow at bottom, spreading at top. Thin fronds, finely divided. Vigorous; can be invasive. Tolerates full sun in constantly moist soil. Specialists stock many selections with oddly cut and feathered fronds. In 'Frizelliae', divisions of fronds are reduced to balls; fronds look like strings of beads. 'Vernoniae Cristatum' has crested and feathered fronds.

A. nipponicum 'Pictum' (A. goeringianum 'Pictum'). JAPANESE PAINTED FERN. Fronds grow to 1½ ft. long, making a tight, slowly spreading clump. Leaflets are purplish at base, then lavender, then silvery greenish gray toward ends. The South's most beautiful outdoor fern.

A. otophorum. ENGLISH PAINTED FERN. Actually a native of the Orient. It resembles Japanese painted fern, but its dark green fronds have a reddish or purple midrib.

A. pycnocarpon. GLADE FERN, SILVERY SPLEENWORT. Attractive rosette-forming deciduous fern with once-divided fronds to 4 ft. long. New spring fronds are silvery light green; they turn darker in summer, then russet before dying back. Tolerates full sun in constantly moist soil.

AUCUBA japonica

JAPANESE AUCUBA

Cornaceae

EVERGREEN SHRUB

🌿 ALL ZONES

◐ ◑ ● SUN OR SHADE

💧 MODERATE WATER

Aucuba japonica

Native from Himalayas to Japan. Seedlings vary in leaf form and variegations; many selections offered. Standard green-leafed aucuba grows at moderate rate to 6–10 ft. (sometimes 15 ft.) tall and almost as wide. Can be kept lower by pruning. Buxom shrub, densely clothed with polished, dark green, toothed leaves 3–8 in. long, 1½–3 in. wide.

Minute, dark maroon flowers in spring are followed by clusters of bright red, ¾-in. berries hidden in leaves in fall and winter. Both sexes

must be planted to ensure fruit crop. Green-leafed 'Rozannie' is reportedly self-fertile.

Other green-leafed kinds include 'Longifolia' ('Salicifolia'), narrow and willowlike leaves (female); 'Nana', dwarf shrub to about 3 ft. (female); 'Serratifolia', long leaves, coarsely toothed edges (female).

Variegated selections (usually slower growing) include 'Crotonifolia', leaves heavily splashed with white and gold (male); 'Fructu Albo', leaves variegated with white, berries pale pinkish buff (female); 'Picturata' ('Aureo-maculata'), leaves centered with golden yellow, edged with dark green dotted yellow (female); 'Sulphur', green leaves with broad yellow edge (female); and 'Variegata', gold dust plant, best-known aucuba, dark green leaves spotted with yellow (male or female). Selection 'Mr. Goldstrike' has heavier gold splashings.

Tolerant of wide range of soils. Requires shade from hot sun, accepts deep shade. Tolerates low light level under trees, competes successfully with tree roots. Gets mealybug and mites. Prune to control height or form by cutting back to a leaf joint (node).

All aucubas make choice container plants for shady patio or in the house. Use variegated forms to light up dark corners. Associate with ferns, hydrangeas.

AURICULA. See PRIMULA auricula

AURINIA saxatilis
(Alyssum saxatile)

BASKET-OF-GOLD

Brassicaceae (Cruciferae)

PERENNIAL

🌿 ZONES US, MS

◐ ◑ FULL SUN OR LIGHT SHADE

💧 MODERATE WATER

Aurinia saxatilis

Stems 8–12 in. high; leaves gray, 2–5 in. long. Dense clusters of tiny golden yellow flowers in spring and early summer. Use as foreground plant in borders, in rock gardens, atop walls. Shear (not more than half) immediately after bloom. Generally hardy but may be killed in extremely cold winters. Self-sows readily. Short lived in hottest, most humid areas. Selections include 'Citrina' ('Lutea'), pale yellow flowers; 'Compacta', dwarf, tight growing; 'Plena' ('Flore Pleno'), double flowered; 'Silver Queen', compact, with pale yellow flowers; 'Sunnyborder Apricot', apricot-shaded flowers; and 'Dudley Neville Variegated', with flower color similar to that of 'Sunnyborder Apricot' but leaves with whitish or creamy edges.

AUSTRALIAN FAN PALM. See LIVISTONA australis

AUSTRALIAN TREE FERN. See CYATHEA cooperi

AUSTRIAN BRIER. See ROSA foetida

AUTUMN CROCUS. See COLCHICUM

AUTUMN FERN. See DRYOPTERIS erythrasora

AVOCADO (Persea americana)

Lauraceae

EVERGREEN TREES

🌿 ZONES CS (MILDER PARTS), TS

◐ FULL SUN

💧 LIGHT, FREQUENT WATERING

Avocado

Delicious and popular tropical fruit, native to Mexico, Central and South America. There are three races of avocado that are grown, and numerous hybrids among them exist. In Florida, the Mexican (the hardiest, often surviving to 18°F) is grown in the colder parts of central Florida, while the Guatemalan (hardy to 21–25°F) and the West Indian (the most tropical type, often perishing at temperatures below 25°F) and their hybrids are cultivated southward. Mexican race seedlings are often grown in home gardens across South Texas. For this plant's ornamental relative, see *Persea borbonia*.

Plants bloom in late winter, and pollination is complex. Most types will produce some fruit if grown alone, but production is heavier when two or more selections are planted. Fruit ripens from summer into winter, depending on selection. Guatemalan and West Indian fruits differ from Mexican in generally being larger with a lower oil content.

All avocado trees require good drainage; constantly wet soil encourages fatal root rot. Tree is shallow rooted; do not cultivate deeply. In the absence of rainfall, irrigate lightly and frequently enough to keep soil moist but not wet. A mulch is helpful; the tree's own fallen leaves can provide this. Scab disease can be a problem in Florida; choose resistant varieties.

When using avocado in the landscape, consider that most selections will eventually grow quite large (to 40 ft.), produce dense shade, and shed leaves constantly throughout the year. Growth is rapid, but plants may be shaped by pinching terminal shoots. Avocado takes well to container culture, and selections in marginal climates can be moved to protection during cold spells.

Florida selections include the hardy 'Brogdon', 'Gainesville', 'Mexicola', and 'Tonnage' (all moderately scab resistant); the somewhat less hardy 'Booth', 'Hall', 'Monroe' (all moderately scab resistant), and 'Choquette' (very scab resistant); and the least hardy 'Pollock', 'Ruehle', 'Simmonds', and 'Waldin' (all very scab resistant). Two hardy types setting good crops without cross-pollination are the commercial selection 'Lula' (susceptible to scab) and 'Taylor' (very scab resistant).

In Texas, 'Lula' is grown commercially in the lower Rio Grande Valley. Most avocado trees in home gardens are selections developed from Mexican race seedlings that survived cold winters. For the selections that grow best in your area, check with a local garden center.

AXONOPUS affinis

CARPET GRASS
Poaceae (Gramineae)
LAWN GRASS
🗡 ZONES CS, TS
☼ FULL SUN
💧 REGULAR WATER

Axonopus affinis

P asture grass native from North Carolina to Florida, and west to Oklahoma and Texas. Makes a medium coarse–textured lawn. Fertilize each spring with a balanced, slow-release fertilizer such as 16-4-8. Mow every 10 to 14 days at 1–2 in., or let grow taller in informal areas. Good for wet, acid soil; does not tolerate drought, alkaline soil, or salt spray. Produces numerous seed heads. Turns brown in winter. This is a lawn grass of last resort.

AZALEA. See RHODODENDRON

AZTEC LILY. See SPREKELIA formosissima

BABY'S BREATH. See GYPSOPHILA paniculata

BACHELOR'S BUTTON. See CENTAUREA cyanus

BAHIA GRASS. See PASPALUM notatum

BALD CYPRESS. See TAXODIUM distichum

BALLOON FLOWER. See PLATYCODON grandiflorus

BALM-OF-GILEAD. See POPULUS balsamifera

BALSAM. See IMPATIENS balsamina

Balsaminaceae. The touch-me-not family embraces herbaceous or shrubby plants with juicy stems, irregular flowers with spurs, and explosive seed capsules. *Impatiens* is the only important member.

BAMBOO

Poaceae (Gramineae)
GIANT GRASSES
🗡 SEE CHART FOR HARDINESS
☼ :◐ FULL SUN OR LIGHT SHADE
💧 💧 REGULAR TO LITTLE WATER
▶ SEE CHART NEXT PAGE

Bambusa multiplex

L arge, woody stems (culms) divided into sections (internodes) by obvious joints (nodes). Upper nodes produce buds that develop into branches; these, in larger bamboos, divide into secondary branches that bear leaves. Bamboos spread by underground stems (rhizomes) that, like the aboveground culms, are jointed and carry buds. Manner in which rhizomes grow explains difference between running and clump bamboos.

In the running bamboos (*Arundinaria, Phyllostachys, Pleioblastus, Pseudosasa,* and *Sasa*), underground stems grow rapidly to varying distances from parent plant before sending up new vertical shoots. These bamboos eventually form large patches or groves unless spread is curbed. They are generally fairly hardy plants from temperate regions in China and Japan, and they are tolerant of a wide variety of soils.

In clump bamboos (*Bambusa, Fargesia*), underground stems grow only a short distance before sending up new stems. These form clumps that slowly expand around the edges. Most are tropical or subtropical.

See chart for hardiness. Figures indicate temperatures at which leaf damage occurs. Stems and rhizomes may be considerably hardier.

Plant container-grown bamboos at any time of year. Best time to propagate from existing clumps is just before growth begins in spring; divide hardy kinds in March or early April, tropical ones in May or early June. (Transplanting at other times is possible, but risk of losing divisions is high in summer heat or winter chill and wet soil.) Cut or saw out divisions with roots and at least three connected culms. If divisions are large, cut back tops to balance loss of roots and rhizomes. Foliage may wilt or wither, but culms will send out new leaves.

Rhizome cutting is another means of propagation. In clump bamboos, this cutting consists of the rooted base of a culm; in running bamboos, it is a foot-long length of rhizome with roots and buds. Plant in rich mix with ample organic material added.

Culms of all bamboos have already attained their maximum diameter when they poke through ground; in mature plants, they usually reach their maximum height within a month. Many do become increasingly leafy in subsequent years, but not taller. Plants are evergreen, but there is considerable dropping of older leaves; old plantings develop nearly weedproof mulch of dead leaves. Individual culms live for several years but eventually die and should be cut out.

Mature bamboos grow phenomenally fast during their brief growth period—culms of giant types may increase in length by several feet a day. Don't expect such quick growth the first year after transplanting, though. Giant timber bamboo, for example, needs 3 to 5 years to build up a rhizome system capable of supporting culms that grow several feet a day; growth during early years will be less impressive. To get fast growth and great size, water frequently and feed once a month with high-nitrogen or lawn fertilizer; to restrict size and spread, water and feed less. Once established, plants tolerate considerable drought, but rhizomes will not spread into dry soil (or into water). The accompanying chart lists two heights for each bamboo. "Controlled Height" means average height under dry conditions with little feeding, or with rhizome spread controlled by barriers. "Uncontrolled Height" refers to plants growing under best conditions without confinement.

In the case of bamboo, disregard the rule of never buying root-bound plants: The more crowded the plant in the container, the faster its growth

▶ page 145

BAMBOO

For explanation of height, see page 143; for Roman numerals I, II, III, and IV, see page 145. Hardiness is temperature at which leaf damage occurs.

NAME	ALSO SOLD AS	ZONES	CONTROLLED (UNCONTROLLED) HEIGHT	GROWTH HABIT	STEM DIAMETER	COMMENTS (FORM, CHARACTERISTICS, USES)
Arundinaria amabilis TONKIN CANE, TEASTICK BAMBOO		LS, CS, TS. Hardy to 10°F	20–25 ft. (50 ft.)	Running	2½ in.	III. Erect, thick-walled culms with small nodes. Beautiful, useful for wood
Bambusa multiplex	*B. glaucescens*	CS, TS. Hardy to 15°F	8–10 ft. (15–25 ft.)	Clump	1½ in.	II. Branches from base to top. Dense growth. Good for hedges, screens
B. oldhamii OLDHAM BAMBOO, CLUMPING GIANT TIMBER BAMBOO	*Sinocalamus oldhamii*	CS, TS. Hardy to 15°F	15–25 ft. (20–55 ft.)	Clump	4 in.	IV. Densely foliaged, erect clumps make it good plant for big, dense screens. Or use single plant for imposing vertical mass
Fargesia murielae	*Sinarundinaria murielae*	US, MS, LS. Hardy to −20°F	6–8 ft. (15 ft.)	Clump	¾ in.	II. One of two hardiest bamboos listed here. Light, airy, narrow clump, arching and drooping at top. Needs shade to look best. Rare
Phyllostachys aurea GOLDEN BAMBOO		MS, LS, CS, TS. Hardy to 0°F	6–10 ft. (10–20 ft.)	Running	2 in.	III. Erect, stiff culms, usually with crowded joints at base—good identifying mark. Its dense foliage makes a good screen or hedge. Can take much drought but looks better with regular water. Good for containers
P. aureosulcata YELLOW GROOVE BAMBOO		US, MS, LS, CS. Hardy to −20°F	12–15 ft. (15–25 ft.)	Running	1½ in.	III. Like more slender, more open golden bamboo. Young culms green with pronounced yellowish groove. One of two hardiest listed
P. bambusoides GIANT TIMBER BAMBOO, JAPANESE TIMBER BAMBOO	*P. reticulata*	MS, LS, CS, TS. Hardy to 0°F	15–35 ft. (25–45 ft.)	Running	6 in.	IV. Once commonest of large, hardy timber bamboos. Most perished during blooming period in 1960s–1970s. New plants from seed are available. Makes beautiful groves if lowest branches are trimmed off
P. nigra BLACK BAMBOO		MS, LS, CS, TS. Hardy to 0°F	4–8 ft. (10–15 ft.)	Running	1½ in.	III. New culms green, turning black in second year (rarely olive green dotted black). Best in afternoon shade
P. n. 'Henon' HENON BAMBOO		MS, LS, CS, TS. Hardy to 0°F	50 ft. (54 ft.)	Running	3½ in.	III. Larger than black bamboo. Culms whitish green, don't blacken; rough to touch
Pleioblastus argenteostriata		LS, CS, TS. Hardy to 10°F	2–3 ft. (3–4 ft.)	Running	¼ in.	I. Good light-colored ground cover for shade. Cut back every year. White stripes on leaves
P. pygmaea PYGMY BAMBOO	*Sasa pygmaea*	MS, LS, CS, TS. Hardy to 0°F	½–1 ft. (1–1½ ft.)	Running	⅛ in.	I. Aggressive spreader; good bank holder and erosion control. Mow every few years to keep it from growing stemmy, unattractive
P. variegata DWARF WHITESTRIPE BAMBOO	*Sasa variegata, S. fortunei*	All zones. Hardy to −10°F	1–2 ft. (2–3 ft.)	Running	¼ in.	I. Fast spreader; curb rhizomes. Use in tubs or as deep ground cover
Pseudosasa japonica ARROW BAMBOO	*Arundinaria japonica*	MS, LS, CS, TS. Hardy to 0°F	6–10 ft. (10–18 ft.)	Running	¾ in.	III. Stiffly erect culms with one branch at each joint. Leaves large, with long, pointed tails. Rampant thick hedge; slow spreader in Upper South, making dense clumps
Sasa palmata PALMATE BAMBOO	Sometimes sold as *S. senanensis*	MS, LS, CS. Hardy to 0°F	4–5 ft. (8–12 ft.)	Running	⅜ in.	In class by itself. Broad, handsome leaves (to 15 in. long by 4 in. wide) spread fingerlike from stem and branch tips. Rampant spreader

when planted. Both running and clump types grow well when roots are confined.

Scale, mealybugs, and aphids are occasionally found on bamboo but seldom do any harm; if they excrete honeydew in bothersome amounts, spray with insecticidal soap or summer oil. To control mites, release predatory mites.

The chart classifies each bamboo by habit of growth, which, of course, determines its use in the garden. In Group I are the dwarf or low-growing ground cover types. These can be used for erosion control or, in small clumps (carefully confined in a long section of flue tile), in a border or rock garden. Group II includes clump bamboos with fountainlike habit of growth. These have widest use in landscaping. They require no more space than the average strong-growing shrub. Clipped, they make hedges or screens that won't spread much into surrounding soil. Unclipped, they create informal screens or grow singly to show off their graceful form.

Phyllostachys nigra

Bamboos in Group III are running bamboos of moderate size and more or less vertical growth. Use them as screens, hedges, or (if curbed) alone. Group IV includes the giant bamboos. Use running kinds for groves or for oriental effects on a grand scale. Clumping kinds have a tropical look, especially if they are used with broad-leafed tropical plants. All may be thinned and clipped to show off culms. Thin clumps or groves by cutting out old or dead culms at the base.

Some smaller bamboos bloom on some of their stalks every year and continue to grow. Some bloom partially, at erratic intervals. Some have never been known to bloom. Others bloom heavily, set seed, and die. Giant timber bamboo (*Phyllostachys bambusoides*) and other species of *Phyllostachys* bloom at rare intervals of 30 to 60 years, produce flowers for a long period, and become enfeebled. They may recover slowly or die. There is evidence that very heavy feeding and watering may speed recovery.

Bamboos are not recommended for year-round indoor culture, but container-grown plants can spend extended periods indoors in cool, bright rooms. You can revive plants by taking them outdoors, but it is important to avoid sudden changes in temperature and light.

There are several ways to eliminate unwanted bamboo. Digging it out with mattock and spade is the surest method, though sometimes difficult. Rhizomes are generally not deep, but they may be widespread. Remove them all or regrowth will occur. Starve out roots by cutting off all shoots before they exceed 2 ft. in height; repeat as needed—probably many times over the course of a year. Contact herbicide sprays that kill leaves have the same effect as removing culms. Full-strength glyphosate weed killer poured into freshly cut stumps is another good control.

BAMBUSA. See BAMBOO

BANANA. See MUSA

BANANA SHRUB. See MICHELIA figo

BANYAN TREE. See FICUS benghalensis

BAPTISIA

FALSE INDIGO, WILD INDIGO

Fabaceae (Leguminosae)

PERENNIALS

⚟ ZONES US, MS, LS, CS

☀ FULL SUN

💧 MODERATE WATER

Baptisia australis

Native to eastern and midwestern U.S. The false indigos somewhat resemble lupines, but have deep taproots that enable them to survive difficult conditions. Long lived, they become large clumps with many stems and bloom spikes. They resent transplanting once

established. Bluish green leaves are divided into three leaflets. Flower spikes to 1 ft. long top the plants in late spring or early summer. Flowers resemble small sweet peas and are followed by inflated seedpods; both flowers and pods are interesting in arrangements. Remove spent flowers to encourage repeat bloom.

B. alba. WHITE FALSE INDIGO. To 3 ft. tall; clusters of white flowers.

B. australis. BLUE WILD INDIGO. Grows 3–6 ft. tall; flowers are indigo blue. 'Purple Smoke', a hybrid between this species and *B. alba*, grows 4½ ft. tall and has violet flowers with dark purple centers.

BARBERRY. See BERBERIS

BASIL. See OCIMUM

BASKET FLOWER. See CENTAUREA americana, HYMENOCALLIS narcissiflora

BASKET-OF-GOLD. See AURINIA saxatilis

BASSWOOD. See TILIA americana

BAUHINIA

ORCHID TREE

Fabaceae (Leguminosae)

EVERGREEN, SEMIEVERGREEN, OR DECIDUOUS TREES OR SHRUBS

⚟ ZONE TS, EXCEPT AS NOTED

☀ B. FORFICATA TOLERATES JUST A LITTLE SHADE

💧💧 REGULAR TO MODERATE WATER

These flamboyant flowering plants have a very special place in central and southern Florida. Common to all garden bauhinias are twin "leaves," actually twin lobes. Not fussy about soil as long as it is reasonably well drained.

B. blakeana. HONG KONG ORCHID TREE. Partially deciduous for short period. Native to southern China. Grows to 20 ft. high; umbrella-type habit. Flowers are shaped like some orchids; colors range from cranberry maroon through purple and rose to orchid pink, often in same blossom. Flowers are much larger (5½–6 in. wide) than those of other bauhinias; they appear in late fall to spring. Gray-green leaves tend to drop off around bloom time, but the tree does not lose all of its foliage.

Bauhinia blakeana

B. forficata. BRAZILIAN BUTTERFLY TREE. Evergreen to deciduous large shrub or tree. Native to Brazil. Probably hardiest bauhinia, though chancy in the Coastal South. In spring and through summer, bears narrow-petaled, creamy white flowers to 3 in. wide. Deep green leaves, with more pointed lobes than those of other species. Grows to 20 ft., often with twisting, leaning trunk, picturesque angled branches. Short, sharp thorns at branch joints. Good canopy for patio. In the Tropical South, give some afternoon shade; when unshaded, blooms tend to shrivel during the day. Often sold as *B. corniculata* or *B. candicans*.

B. galpinii (B. punctata). RED BAUHINIA. Evergreen to semievergreen shrub. Native to tropical and South Africa. Brick red to orange flowers, as spectacular as those of bougainvillea, spring to fall. Sprawling, half-climbing, with 15-ft. spread. Best as espalier on warm wall. With hard pruning, can make splendid flowering bonsai for large pot or box.

B. monandra. BUTTERFLY FLOWER, JERUSALEM DATE. Deciduous shrub or small tree. Native to tropical Asia. Similar to *B. variegata*, but smaller, to 20 ft. Flowers in summer, from April to November in Florida. Blooms pale pink to magenta, streaked or spotted with purple, in clusters at ends of branches.

B. purpurea. See B. variegata

B. variegata. PURPLE ORCHID TREE. Partially to wholly deciduous large shrub or tree. Native to India, China. The most frequently planted species. Hardy to 22°F. Spectacular street tree where spring is warm and stays warm. Wonderful show of light pink to orchid purple, broad-petaled,

2–3-in.-wide flowers, usually January to April. Light green, broad-lobed leaves generally drop in midwinter. Produces huge crop of messy-looking beans after blooming. Trim beans off if you wish—trimming brings new growth earlier. Inclined to grow as shrub with many stems. Staked and pruned, becomes attractive 20–35-ft. tree. 'Candida' is the same, but with white flowers. The species is commonly sold as *B. purpurea*.

BAY. See LAURUS nobilis

BAYBERRY. See MYRICA

BEACH PLUM. See PRUNUS maritima

BEACH WORMWOOD. See ARTEMISIA stellerana

BEAN, GREEN. See BEAN, SNAP

BEAN, LIMA

Fabaceae (Leguminosae)

ANNUAL

✄ ALL ZONES

☼ FULL SUN

💧 REGULAR WATER AFTER SEEDLINGS EMERGE

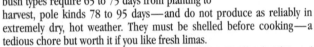
Lima Bean

Like snap beans (which they resemble), limas come in either bush or vine (pole) form. They develop more slowly than string beans— bush types require 65 to 75 days from planting to harvest, pole kinds 78 to 95 days—and do not produce as reliably in extremely dry, hot weather. They must be shelled before cooking—a tedious chore but worth it if you like fresh limas.

Among bush types, 'Burpee's Improved Bush', 'Fordhook 242', and 'Henderson Bush' are outstanding; the last two are especially good in hot weather. 'King of the Garden' and 'Prizetaker' are fine, large-seeded climbing forms; 'Small White Lima' ('Sieva'), usually grown for drying, gives heavy yields of shelled beans. Grow like snap beans.

GROW A BEAN TEPEE

From July to September, children can play in the cool, shady confines of a bean tepee (it will be especially colorful if scarlet runner beans are used). Place a vertical 10-ft. center pole 1½ ft. deep in the soil. Pack it in well. Place bases of at least four 10-ft.-long bamboo poles (or other skinny wooden sticks) 4½ ft. out from base of center pole and tie their tops together 6–12 in. below top of center pole. In a circle just outside pole bases, plant the beans 1 in. deep and 1–3 in. apart. Train the vines up the outside of the tepee, keeping main stems out of its interior.

BEAN, SCARLET RUNNER

Fabaceae (Leguminosae)

PERENNIAL TWINING VINE GROWN AS ANNUAL

✄ ALL ZONES

☼ FULL SUN

💧 REGULAR WATER AFTER SEEDLINGS EMERGE

Scarlet Runner Bean

Showy and ornamental with bright scarlet flowers in slender clusters and with bright green leaves divided into three roundish, 3–5-in.-long leaflets. Use to cover fences, arbors, outbuildings; provides quick shade on porches. Pink- and white-flowered types exist.

Flowers are followed by flattened, very dark green pods that are edible and tasty when young but toughen as they reach full size. Beans from older

---

pods can be shelled for cooking like green limas. Culture is same as for snap beans.

BEAN, SNAP

STRING BEAN, GREEN BEAN

Fabaceae (Leguminosae)

ANNUAL

✄ ALL ZONES

☼ FULL SUN

💧 REGULAR WATER AFTER SEEDLINGS EMERGE

Snap Bean

Of all beans, the snap bean is the most widely planted and most useful for home gardens. Snap beans have tender, fleshy pods with little fiber; they may be green, yellow (wax beans), or purple. Purple kinds turn green in cooking. Plants grow as self-supporting bushes (bush beans) or as climbing vines (pole beans). Bush types bear earlier, but vines are more productive. Plants resemble scarlet runner bean, but white or purple flowers are not showy.

Plant seeds as soon as soil is warm, in full sun and good soil. The seeds must push heavy seed leaves through soil, so see that soil is reasonably loose and open. Plant seeds of bush types 1 in. deep and 1–3 in. apart in rows, with 2–3 ft. between rows. Pole beans can be managed in a number of ways: set three or four 8-ft. poles in the ground and tie together at top in tepee fashion; or set single poles 3–4 ft. apart and sow six or eight beans around each, thinning to three or four strongest seedlings; or insert poles 1–2 ft. apart in rows and sow seeds as you would bush beans; or sow along sunny wall, fence, or trellis and train vines on web of light string supported by wire or heavy twine. Moisten ground thoroughly before planting; do not water again until seedlings have emerged.

Once growth starts, keep soil moist. In absence of rainfall, occasional deep soaking is preferable to frequent light sprinklings, which may encourage mildew. Feed after plants are in active growth and again when pods start to form. Pods are ready in 50 to 70 days, depending on selection. Pick every 5 to 7 days; if pods mature, plants will stop bearing. Mexican bean beetles are often a problem. A trap crop is an effective control: Set out a few bean plants earlier than the bean crop you intend to harvest, wait until the trap beans are infested, then dispose of them, pests and all. Other controls include spraying plants with rotenone or pyrethrin, or protecting plants with floating row covers. Control aphids, cucumber beetles, and whiteflies as needed.

BEAN, STRING. See BEAN, SNAP

BEAR GRASS. See NOLINA erumpens

BEARD TONGUE. See PENSTEMON

BEAR'S BREECH. See ACANTHUS mollis

BEAUCARNEA recurvata

PONYTAIL, BOTTLE PALM

Agavaceae

SUCCULENT SHRUB OR TREE

✄ ZONE TS; OR INDOORS

☼ FULL SUN

💧 MODERATE WATER

Beaucarnea recurvata

Base of trunk is greatly swollen. On young plant, it resembles a big onion sitting on soil; on mature tree in the ground, it can be a woody mass several feet across. Old plants can reach 15 ft. tall. Leaves cluster at ends of branches in dense tufts; arching and drooping, they measure 3 ft. or more in length,

¾ in. wide. Very old trees may produce large clusters of tiny, creamy white flowers.

Outdoors, give plant sun, well-drained soil, and infrequent deep watering during prolonged dry periods. Does exceptionally well as house plant if given good light and not overwatered. A mature plant can endure temperatures to 18°F; a young plant in container will freeze to death at a few degrees higher.

BEAUMONTIA grandiflora

HERALD'S TRUMPET, EASTER LILY VINE

Apocynaceae

EVERGREEN VINE

🗡 ZONE TS

☀ ◑ FULL SUN OR LIGHT SHADE

💧 💧 AMPLE TO REGULAR WATER

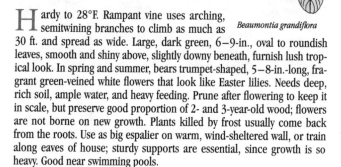

Beaumontia grandiflora

H ardy to 28°F. Rampant vine uses arching, semitwining branches to climb as much as 30 ft. and spread as wide. Large, dark green, 6–9-in., oval to roundish leaves, smooth and shiny above, slightly downy beneath, furnish lush tropical look. In spring and summer, bears trumpet-shaped, 5–8-in.-long, fragrant green-veined white flowers that look like Easter lilies. Needs deep, rich soil, ample water, and heavy feeding. Prune after flowering to keep it in scale, but preserve good proportion of 2- and 3-year-old wood; flowers are not borne on new growth. Plants killed by frost usually come back from the roots. Use as big espalier on warm, wind-sheltered wall, or train along eaves of house; sturdy supports are essential, since growth is so heavy. Good near swimming pools.

BEAUTYBERRY. See CALLICARPA

BEAUTY BUSH. See KOLKWITZIA amabilis

BEE BALM. See MONARDA didyma

BEECH. See FAGUS

BEEFWOOD. See CASUARINA

BEET

Chenopodiaceae

BIENNIAL GROWN AS ANNUAL

🗡 ALL ZONES

☀ FULL SUN

💧 REGULAR WATER

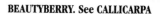

R aised for edible root and tender young leaves, beet grows best in relatively cool weather. In most areas, sow in early spring or late summer. In the Coastal and Tropical South, can be grown in fall and winter. Crop is ready to harvest 45 to 65 days after seeding; sow at monthly intervals to have beets over a long season.

Grow in fertile, well-drained soil without lumps or rocks. Sow seed 1 in. apart and cover with ¼ in. of compost, sand, or vermiculite. Thin to about 2 in. apart while plants are small—the thinnings (tops as well as roots) are edible. To keep roots tender, keep soil evenly moist. Begin harvesting when roots are 1 in. wide; complete harvesting before they exceed 3 in. (they will be woody if allowed to grow bigger).

Types with round, red roots include 'Crosby's Egyptian' and 'Detroit Dark Red' (old favorites) as well as many newer selections. Novelties include 'Cylindra' and 'Forma Nova' (with long, cylindrical roots); there are also selections with golden yellow or white roots.

Beet

SOUTHERN HERITAGE PLANTS
IDENTIFIED BY SYMBOL 🌿

BEGONIA

Begoniaceae

ANNUALS AND TENDER PERENNIALS

🗡 ZONE TS, EXCEPT AS NOTED; OR OVERWINTER INDOORS OR TREAT AS ANNUALS

☀ ● BEST IN FILTERED SHADE

💧 MOIST SOIL AND HUMID AIR

Begonia grandis

T ender perennials, sometimes shrubby, grown for textured, multicolored foliage, saucer-sized flowers, or lacy clusters of smaller flowers. Outdoors, most grow well in pots, in the ground, or in hanging baskets in filtered shade with rich, porous, fast-draining soil, consistent but light feeding, and enough water to keep soil moist but not soggy. Most thrive as indoor plants, in greenhouse, or under lath. Some prefer terrarium conditions. Almost all require at least moderate humidity. (In dry-summer areas or indoors during winter, set pots in saucers filled with wet pebbles.)

Most can be propagated easily from leaf, stem, or rhizome cuttings. They also grow from dust-fine seed. Of the many hundreds of species and selections, relatively few are sold widely.

Begonia enthusiasts group or classify the different kinds by growth habit, which coincidentally groups them by their care needs.

Hardy begonia. Unique among begonias is *B. grandis (B. evansiana, B. grandis evansiana)*. Suitable for all areas, it is the only begonia that is hardy outside the Coastal and Tropical South. Grows from a tuber; reaches 2–3 ft. tall, with branching red stems carrying large, smooth coppery green leaves with red undersides. Summer flowers are pink or white, borne in drooping clusters. Tops die down after frost; mulch to protect roots. Grow with ferns, hostas, hellebores, and similar shade plants.

Cane-type begonias. They get their name from their stems, which grow tall and woody and have prominent bamboolike joints. The group includes so-called angel-wing begonias. These erect plants have multiple stems, some reaching 5 ft. or more under the right conditions. Most bloom profusely with large clusters of white, pink, orange, or red flowers, early spring through autumn. Some are everblooming. When roots fill 4-in. pots, plants can be placed in larger containers or in the ground. Position plants where they will get plenty of light, some sun, and no wind. They may require staking. Protect them from heavy frosts. Old canes that have grown barren should be pruned to two leaf joints in early spring to stimulate new growth.

B. 'Irene Nuss'. Dark red-and-green leaves and huge drooping clusters of coral pink flowers.

Hiemalis begonias. Usually sold as Rieger begonias. Bushy, compact; profuse bloomers and outstanding outdoor or indoor plants. Flowers average about 2 in. across and appear over a long season that includes winter. On well-grown plants, green leaves and stems are all but invisible beneath a blanket of bloom. Give indoor plants plenty of light in winter. In summer, keep out of hot noonday sun. Water thoroughly when top inch of soil is dry. Don't mist leaves. Plants may get rangy, an indication of approaching dormancy; if they do, cut stems to 4-in. stubs.

Multiflora begonias. Bushy, compact plants 1–1½ ft. tall. Abundant summer and fall blooms in carmine, scarlet, orange, yellow, apricot, salmon, pink. Includes Nonstop strain. All are essentially small-flowered, profuse-blooming tuberous begonias; for care, see Tuberous begonias.

Rex begonias. With their bold, multicolored leaves, these are probably the most striking of all foliage begonias. While many named selections are grown by collectors, easier-to-find unnamed seedling plants are almost as decorative. The leaves grow from a rhizome; see Rhizomatous begonias for care. In addition, rex begonias should get high humidity (at least 50 percent) to do their best. In dry climates or indoors in winter, provide it by misting with a spray bottle, placing pots on wet pebbles in a

Rex Begonia

tray, or keeping plants in greenhouse. When rhizome grows too far past edge of pot for your taste, either repot into slightly larger container or cut off rhizome end inside pot edge. Old rhizome will branch and grow new leaves. Make rhizome cuttings of the piece you remove and root in mixture of half peat moss, half perlite.

Rhizomatous begonias. Like rex begonias, these grow from a rhizome, a usually creeping stem-type structure at or near soil level. Although some have handsome flowers, they are grown primarily for foliage, which varies in color and texture among species and varieties. The group includes so-called star begonias, named for their leaf shape. Rhizomatous begonias perform well as house plants: Give them bright light through a window and water only when the top inch or so of soil is dry. Plant them in wide, shallow pots. They flower from winter through summer, the season varying among specific plants. White to pink flowers appear in clusters on erect stems above the foliage. Rhizomes will grow over edge of pot, eventually forming a ball-shaped plant; if you wish, cut rhizomes back to pot. (For care of rhizomes, see rex begonias, page 147.)

B. masoniana. IRON CROSS BEGONIA. Large puckered leaves; known for chocolate brown pattern resembling Maltese cross on green background. Flowers insignificant.

Semperflorens begonias. (Also known as wax begonias.) Fibrous or bedding begonias. Dwarf (6–8-in.) and taller (10–12-in.) strains grown in garden beds or containers as if annuals, producing lots of small flowers spring through fall in a white through red range. Foliage can be green, red, bronze, or variegated. In mild climates, can overwinter and live for years. Thrives in full sun in the Upper South. Prefers broken shade elsewhere, but dark-foliaged kinds will take sun if well watered.

Shrublike begonias. This large class is marked by multiple stems that are soft and green rather than bamboolike as in the cane-type group. Grown for both foliage and flowers. Leaves are very interesting—some are heavily textured; others grow white or red "hairs"; still others develop a soft, feltlike coating. Most grow upright and bushy, but others are less erect and make suitable subjects for hanging baskets. Flowers in shades of pink, red, white, and peach can come any time, depending on species or selection. Care consists of repotting into larger container as the plant outgrows its pot. Some shrublike begonias can get very large—as tall as 8 ft. They require ample moisture—water when soil begins to dry on surface. Prune to shape; pinch tips to encourage branching.

B. 'Digswelliana'. Shrublike plant, 2–3 ft. high; glossy leaves 2–4 in. long. Red flowers in clusters bloom almost continuously spring–fall.

B. foliosa. Inch-long leaves packed tightly on twiggy plant give fernlike look. Stems arch or droop to 3 ft. Flowers are small, white to red, everblooming in mild weather. 'Miniata' has rose pink to rose red flowers.

B. 'Richmondensis'. Exceeds 2 ft. tall, with arching stems carrying deep green, shiny, crisp leaves with red undersides. Vivid pink to crimson flowers develop from darker buds; nearly year-round bloom. Big and sturdy. Tolerant of sun and wind.

Trailing or climbing begonias. These have stems that trail or climb, depending on how you train them. They are suited to hanging basket culture or planting in the ground where well protected. Growing conditions similar to those for tuberous begonias, though trailing types are not lifted. Sporadic bloom during warm weather.

B. solananthera. Glossy light green leaves; fragrant white flowers with red centers.

Tuberous begonias. These magnificent large-flowered hybrids grow from tubers. Types range from plants with saucer-size blooms and a few upright stems to multistemmed hanging basket types covered with flowers. Except for some rare kinds, they are summer and fall blooming in almost any flower color except blue.

Grow tuberous begonias in filtered shade, such as under lath or in the open with eastern exposure. Best for the Upper South; not suited to areas of extreme heat and humidity. For best bloom in northern Texas and in Oklahoma, mist with water several times a day. Watch for fuzzy white spots on leaves, which signal powdery mildew. In fall, when leaves begin to

yellow and wilt, reduce watering. When stems have fallen off the plant on their own, lift tuber, shake off dirt, dry tuber in the sun for 3 days, and store in cool, dry place, such as a garden shed or garage, with its label, until spring, when little pink buds will become visible. In April and May you can buy small seedling plants and plant them directly in pots.

Strains are sold as hanging or upright. The former bloom more profusely; the latter have larger flowers. Colors are white, red, pink, yellow, and peach; shapes are frilly (carnation), formal double (camellia), and tight-centered (rose). Some have petal edges in contrasting colors (picotee). Popular strains are Double Trumpet (improved rose form), Prima Donna (improved camellia), and Hanging Sensation.

HOW AND WHEN TO START BEGONIA TUBERS

In early February, place dormant tubers in shallow flats and cover ½–1 in. deep with coarse organic matter such as leaf mold. Water the flats regularly and keep them in broken shade (in Tropical South) or under lights indoors. As each plant reaches 3 in. high, repot into 8–10-in. pot with humus-rich, fast-draining potting mix. Stake upright types. Keep potting mix moist but not soggy. Feed weekly with quarter-strength high-nitrogen fertilizer until mid-May, then with bloom-producing fertilizer.

BELAMCANDA

BLACKBERRY LILY

Iridaceae

PERENNIALS WITH RHIZOME

ZONES US, MS, LS, CS

FULL SUN OR PARTIAL SHADE

REGULAR WATER

Belamcanda chinensis

Like its iris relatives, forms clumps of sword-shaped leaves in fanlike sheaves from slowly creeping rhizomes. In summer, zigzagging stems carry flowers that last only a day, but new blossoms keep opening for weeks. As blooms fade, rounded seed capsules develop; they split open to expose shiny black seeds that look like blackberries (hence the plant's common name). Cut seed-bearing stems for unique dried arrangements. Plant is effective in clumps in border. Plant rhizomes in porous soil, 1 in. deep.

B. chinensis. Sprays of 1½-in. yellowish orange flowers dotted with red, on 3–4-ft. stems.

B. flabellata 'Hello Yellow'. Dwarf blackberry lily, under 2 ft., with yellow flowers.

Blackberry lily was crossed with vesper iris (*Pardanthopsis dichotoma*, formerly *Iris dichotoma*) to create a group of hybrids, *Pardancanda norrisii*, sometimes called candy lily. These plants produce the same general effect as blackberry lily but bear flowers in an expanded color range, including white, yellow, red, pink, and purple.

BELLFLOWER. See CAMPANULA

BELLIS perennis

ENGLISH DAISY

Asteraceae (Compositae)

PERENNIAL OFTEN TREATED AS ANNUAL

ZONE US

LIGHT SHADE IN WARM AREAS

MODERATE TO LOTS OF WATER

Bellis perennis

Native to Europe and Mediterranean region. The original English daisies are the kind you sometimes see growing in winter lawns. Plump, fully double ones sold in garden centers are horticultural selections. Rosettes of dark green leaves 1–2 in. long. Pink, rose, red, or white double flowers on 3–6-in. stems, in spring and early summer. Edging or bedding plant; effective with bulbs. In the South, usually a cool-weather annual planted in fall, then allowed to overwinter; blooms in spring.

BELLS-OF-IRELAND. See MOLUCCELLA laevis

BELOPERONE. See JUSTICIA

BENJAMIN FIG. See FICUS benjamina

Berberidaceae. The barberry family contains both shrubs and herbaceous perennials. Barberry (*Berberis*) and nandina are typical of the former; *Epimedium* of the latter.

BERBERIS

BARBERRY
Berberidaceae

EVERGREEN, SEMIEVERGREEN, DECIDUOUS SHRUBS

☀ ZONES US, MS, LS, CS, EXCEPT AS NOTED

☼ ☽ FULL SUN OR LIGHT SHADE

◐ ◑ REGULAR TO MODERATE WATER

Berberis thunbergii

The ability of barberries, especially the deciduous species, to take punishment from climate and soil extremes makes them worth attention in all "hard" climates. They require no more than ordinary garden care. Vigorous growers can take a lot of cutting back; if plants are left to their own devices, some inner branches die and plants become ratty. The following species all bear yellow spring flowers and spiny branches typical of the genus. (Barberries with much-divided leaves are classified under *Mahonia* in this book.)

B. gladwynensis 'William Penn'. Evergreen; loses some of its leaves at 0–10°F. Hardy to about −10°F. Resembles *B. julianae* in general effect but is faster growing, with denser growth to 4 ft. high and broader, glossier leaves. Good show of bright yellow flowers.

B. julianae. WINTERGREEN BARBERRY. Evergreen or semievergreen. Hardy to 0°F, but foliage damaged by winter cold. Dense, upright, to 6 ft., with slightly angled branches. Leathery, spine-toothed, 3-in.-long, dark green leaves. Fruit bluish black. Reddish fall color. One of the thorniest—formidable as barrier hedge.

B. mentorensis. MENTOR BARBERRY. Evergreen; loses some or all leaves below about −5°F. Hardy to −20°F. Hybrid with rather compact growth to 7 ft. and as wide. Leaves dark green, 1 in. long; beautiful red fall color in the Upper South. Berries dull dark red. Easy to maintain as hedge at any height. Tolerates hot, dry weather.

B. swaseyi. TEXAS BARBERRY. Evergreen or semievergreen. Zones MS, LS. Grows slowly, to 3–5 ft. Leaves light green gray, turning pale purple and red in fall. Fragrant golden yellow flowers, small amber to red berries, very thorny branches. Grows very well in limy soil.

B. thunbergii. JAPANESE BARBERRY. Deciduous. Hardy to −20°F. Graceful growth habit with slender, arching, spiny branches; if not sheared, usually reaches 4–6 ft. tall with equal spread. Dense foliage with roundish, ½–1½-in.-long leaves, deep green above, paler beneath, turning to yellow, orange, and red before they fall. Beadlike, bright red berries stud branches in fall and through winter. Hedge, barrier planting, or single shrub. Many attractive selections include the following:

'Atropurpurea'. RED-LEAF JAPANESE BARBERRY. Plants sold as such vary in size and leaf color, from bronzy red to purplish red. Hold color all summer. Must have sun to develop color.

'Aurea'. Bright golden yellow foliage, best in full sun. Will tolerate light shade. Slow growing to 2½–3 ft.

'Cherry Bomb'. Resembles 'Crimson Pygmy', but taller (to 4 ft.), with large leaves and more open growth.

'Crimson Pygmy' ('Atropurpurea Nana'). Selected miniature form, generally less than 1½ ft. high and 2½ ft. wide as 10-year-old. Mature leaves bronzy blood red; new leaves bright red. Must have sun to develop color.

'Helmond Pillar'. Resembles 'Atropurpurea' but columnar in form; grows to 6 ft. tall, less than 1 ft. wide.

'Kobold'. Extra-dwarf bright green selection. Like 'Crimson Pygmy' in habit but fuller and rounder.

'Rose Glow'. New foliage marbled bronzy red and pinkish white, deepening to rose and bronze. Colors best in full sun or lightest shade.

'Sparkle'. To 5 ft. tall and 4–6 ft. wide, with rich green foliage that turns vivid yellow, orange, and red in fall.

BERCKMAN DWARF ARBORVITAE. See PLATYCLADUS orientalis 'Aureus'

BERGAMOT. See MONARDA fistulosa

BERGENIA

Saxifragaceae

PERENNIALS

☀ ZONES US, MS, LS

◐ ● PARTIAL SUN OR SHADE

◑ REGULAR WATER FOR BEST APPEARANCE

Bergenia cordifolia

Native to Himalayas and mountains of China. Thick rootstocks; large, ornamental, glossy green leaves, evergreen except in coldest areas. Thick leafless stalks, 1–1½ ft. high, bear graceful nodding clusters of small white, pink, or rose flowers. Strong, substantial textural quality in borders, under trees, as bold-patterned ground cover. Effective with ferns, hellebores, hostas, and as foreground planting for aucubas, rhododendrons, Japanese yew.

Does well in part shade in Upper and Middle South, full shade in Lower South. *B. cordifolia* endures neglect, poor soil, and cold, but responds to good soil, regular watering, feeding, and grooming. Cut back yearly to prevent legginess. Divide crowded clumps, replant vigorous divisions.

B. ciliata (B. ligulata). HAIRY BERGENIA. Choicest, most elegant. To 1 ft. Lustrous, light green leaves to 1 ft. across, smooth on edges but fringed with soft hairs; young leaves bronzy. White, rose, or purplish flowers bloom late spring, summer. Slightly tender; leaves burn in severe frost. Plants sold under this name may be garden hybrids.

B. cordifolia. HEARTLEAF BERGENIA. Leaves, to 1 ft. across, are glossy, roundish, heart shaped at base, with wavy, toothed edges. In spring, rose or lilac flowers in pendulous clusters partially hidden by leaves. Plant grows to 20 in. 'Morning Red' ('Morgenrote') has leaves with bronzy tones, dark red flowers.

BERMUDA, BERMUDA GRASS. See CYNODON dactylon

BETHLEHEM LUNGWORT. See PULMONARIA saccharata

BETONY. See STACHYS officinalis

BETULA

BIRCH
Betulaceae

DECIDUOUS TREES

☀ ZONES VARY BY SPECIES

☼ FULL SUN

◑ ◐ AMPLE TO REGULAR WATER

The white-barked European white birch—the tree that comes to mind when most people think of birches—has relatives that resemble it in graceful habit, thin bark that peels in layers, and

Betula pendula

small-scale, finely toothed leaves that turn from green to glowing yellow in fall. After leaf drop, the delicate limb structure, handsome bark, and small conelike fruit of birches provide a winter display.

All birches need ample moisture at all times. They are generally too greedy for lawns. All are susceptible to aphids that drip honeydew; for that reason, these are not trees for a patio or to park a car under. Susceptibility to heat and bronze birch borer restricts birches to the Upper South and the Appalachians; exceptions are *B. nigra* and *B. platyphylla japonica*.

B. lenta. SWEET BIRCH, CHERRY BIRCH, BLACK BIRCH. Zone US. Native to eastern U.S. Seldom sold. An attractive tree with shiny reddish to blackish brown bark; grows to 40–50 ft. tall. Rich yellow fall foliage color. Many country children have tasted the bark of this tree, which has a sweet wintergreen flavor and was once routinely used to make a tasty soft drink known as birch beer.

B. maximowicziana. MONARCH BIRCH. Zones US, MS. Native to Japan. Fast growing; open growth when young. Can reach 80–100 ft. Bark flaking, orange brown, eventually gray or white. Leaves up to 6 in. long. Plants sold under this name are not always the true species.

B. nigra. RIVER BIRCH, RED BIRCH. Zones US, MS, LS, CS. Native to eastern U.S. Very fast growth in first years; eventually reaches 50–90 ft. Trunk often forks near ground, but tree can be trained to single stem. Young bark is apricot to pinkish, very smooth, and shiny. On older trees bark flakes and curls in cinnamon brown to blackish sheets. Diamond-shaped leaves, 1–3 in. long, are bright glossy green above, silvery below. 'Heritage' has darker leaves and tan-and-apricot bark; keeps apricot color longer than the species. These are the best birches for hot, humid climates; drop leaves in hot, dry weather. Tolerate poor drainage.

B. papyrifera. PAPER BIRCH, CANOE BIRCH. Zone US. Native to northern part of North America. Similar to *B. pendula* but taller (to 100 ft.), less weeping, with a stouter trunk that is creamy white. Bark peels off in papery layers. Leaves are larger (to 4 in. long), more sparse. Excellent fall color. More resistant to bronze birch borer than *B. pendula*.

B. pendula. EUROPEAN WHITE BIRCH. Zone US. Native from Europe to Asia Minor. Delicate and lacy. Upright branching with weeping side branches. Average mature tree 30–40 ft. high, spreading to half its height. Bark on twigs and young branches is golden brown. Bark on trunk and main limbs becomes white, marked with black clefts; oldest bark at base is blackish gray. Rich green, glossy leaves to 2½ in. long, diamond shaped, with slender tapered point. Often sold as weeping birch, although trees vary somewhat in habit, and young trees show little inclination to weep. Very susceptible to bronze birch borer. The following are some of the selections offered:

'Dalecarlica' ('Laciniata'). CUTLEAF WEEPING BIRCH. Leaves deeply cut. Branches strongly weeping; graceful open tree. Weeping forms are more affected by dry, hot weather than is the species. Foliage shows stress by late summer.

'Fastigiata' (*B. alba* 'Fastigiata'). PYRAMIDAL WHITE BIRCH. Branches upright; habit somewhat like Lombardy poplar. Excellent screening tree.

'Purpurea' (*B. alba* 'Purpurea'). PURPLE BIRCH. Twigs purple black. New foliage rich purple maroon, fading to purplish green in summer; striking effect against white bark.

'Youngii'. YOUNG'S WEEPING BIRCH. Slender branches hang straight down. Form like weeping mulberry's, but tree is more graceful. Decorative display tree. Trunk must be staked to desired height. Same climate limitations as those of 'Dalecarlica'.

B. platyphylla japonica. JAPANESE WHITE BIRCH. Zones US, MS, LS. Native to Japan. Fast growth to 40–50 ft.; narrow, open habit. Leaves glossy green, to 3 in. long. Bark white. 'Whitespire' is a narrowly pyramidal, heat-tolerant selection resistant to bronze birch borer.

Betulaceae. The birch family includes deciduous trees and shrubs with inconspicuous flowers in tight clusters (catkins). Some representatives are birch *(Betula)*, filbert *(Corylus)*, and hornbeam *(Carpinus)*.

BIG BETONY. See STACHYS macrantha

BIG EARS. See STACHYS byzantina 'Countess Helene von Stein'

BIGLEAF SNOWBELL. See STYRAX grandifolius

🏛 BIGNONIA capreolata

Bignonia capreolata

CROSSVINE

Bignoniaceae

EVERGREEN OR SEMIEVERGREEN VINE

🖉 ZONES US (MILDER PARTS), MS, LS, CS, TS

☼ ◑ FULL SUN OR LIGHT SHADE

💧 REGULAR WATER

Native to the South and Southern Midwest. Climbs rapidly to 30 ft. or more by tendrils and holdfast disks; useful for covering fences, masonry walls. Shiny dark green leaves consist of two 2–6-in. leaflets and a branching tendril. In winter, leaves turn purplish, will fall off in severe weather. Clustered, 2-in., trumpet-shaped flowers, typically brownish red or brownish orange, in spring. 'Tangerine Beauty', with apricot orange flowers, is exceptionally bright colored and free blooming.

Bignoniaceae. The bignonia family includes vines (mostly), trees, shrubs, and (rarely) perennials or annuals—all with trumpet-shaped, often two-lipped flowers. The family gets its name from the genus *Bignonia*, which once included most of the trumpet vines; though most of these have been reclassified, they are often still sold as *Bignonia*. Listed below are the older names, followed by the new:

B. chinensis. See Campsis grandiflora

B. jasminoides. See Pandorea jasminoides

B. radicans. See Campsis radicans

B. speciosa. See Clytostoma callistegioides

B. tweediana. See Macfadyena unguis-cati

B. venusta. See Pyrostegia venusta

B. violacea. See Clytostoma callistegioides

BIRCH. See BETULA

BIRD OF PARADISE. See CAESALPINIA, STRELITZIA

BIRD OF PARADISE, FALSE. See HELICONIA brasiliensis

BIRD OF PARADISE BUSH. See CAESALPINIA gilliesii

BIRD'S NEST FERN. See ASPLENIUM nidus

BISHOP'S HAT. See EPIMEDIUM grandiflorum

BISHOP'S WEED. See AEGOPODIUM podagraria

BITTERSWEET. See CELASTRUS

BLACKBERRY

Rosaceae

DECIDUOUS SHRUBS OR VINES

🖉 ZONES US, MS, LS, CS

☼ FULL SUN

💧 REGULAR WATER

Blackberries grow in areas of the South where summers are not too dry and winters not too harsh. They thrive along the eastern coast, as well as in the cool-night areas of the Appalachians, Ozarks, and Blue Ridge.

Blackberry

Upright types tend to be hardy and stiff caned; they usually grow to 4–6 ft. Trailing kinds known as dewberries (also boysenberries) are usually grown in the South. Crosses between upright and trailing types are termed semierect.

All types bear fruit in summer. The fruit clusters of trailing plants ripen earlier and are smaller and more open than those of erect or semierect types. For good crops, all blackberries need full sun, deep, well-drained soil, and regular water throughout the growing season. The fruit makes excellent pies, fine jams and jellies, tangy syrups, and even good wines.

Blackberries are subject to many pests and diseases, so start with healthy, resistant selections from a reputable supplier. Because of their susceptibility to verticillium wilt, blackberries should not be planted where potatoes, tomatoes, eggplants, or peppers have grown in the last 2 years.

Blackberries are usually planted in spring. Set new bare-root plants an inch deeper than they grew at the garden center, their crowns covered with an inch of soil.

In general, blackberries will grow in the Upper, Middle, Lower, and Coastal South. The plants are best located on slight slopes with good air drainage. Northern exposures help keep plants dormant until spring freezes are past. Don't put plants where they will get standing water during the dormant season.

Although blackberry roots are perennial, the canes are biennial; they develop and grow one year, flower and fruit the second. Erect types can be tied to wire, though they don't need support. First-year canes can be headed back a little in midsummer to encourage side branches; the lateral branches can then be cut to 1 ft. long in early spring.

Trailing and semierect types are best grown on some kind of trellis. Train 1-year-old canes on the structure; after harvest, cut to the ground all canes that have fruited. The canes of the current season, those growing beneath the trellis, should now be trained onto it; thin to desired number of canes and prune to 6–8 ft., spreading them fanwise on trellis. Canes of semierect types often become more upright as plants mature.

The following are some of the best blackberry selections:

'Arapaho'. Erect, thornless. Large, firm berries ripen at least 3 weeks before 'Navaho'. Disease resistant. Will grow in north Florida.

'Black Satin'. Semierect, thornless, vigorous. Shiny black, very tart fruit. Does best in Upper South.

'Boysen' and 'Thornless Boysen'. Trailing types most commonly grown. Large reddish berries with sweet-tart flavor, delightful aroma.

'Brazos'. Erect. Productive, disease resistant, with large, fairly firm, tart fruit. Well adapted to Texas, Gulf Coast states, north Florida.

'Cherokee'. Erect, thorny. Firm berries with excellent flavor. Resists anthracnose. Heat tolerant. Good kind for Gulf Coast, north Florida.

'Chester'. Semierect, thornless, heavy bearing, and resistant to cane blight. Very cold tolerant.

'Choctaw'. Erect. Berries have excellent flavor and very small seeds; ripens early. Heat tolerant.

'Darrow'. Erect. A heavy bearer, with large fruit ripening over a long season. Reliable in Virginia.

'Dirksen'. Semierect. Resistant to anthracnose, leaf spot, and mildew. Good selection for Delaware, Maryland, and Virginia.

'Hull'. Erect. Heavy bearing, with large glossy black fruit that holds up well in heat.

'Illini Hardy'. Erect, very thorny. Cold-hardy. Introduced by University of Illinois. Good in southern Midwest.

'Navaho'. Erect, thornless. Firm, sweet fruit that ripens late. Disease resistant. Heat tolerant. Will grow in north Florida.

'Rosborough'. Erect. Resembles 'Brazos', but fruit is smaller, sweeter, ripens early. Heat tolerant. Good choice for Texas.

'Shawnee'. Erect. Heavy crop ripens late, over long period. Fruit large, glossy black, sweet.

'Thornfree'. Semierect, thornless canes bearing large crop of tart berries. Productive from Maryland south to North Carolina and west to Arkansas.

BLACKBERRY LILY. See BELAMCANDA

BLACK CHERRY. See PRUNUS serotina

BLACK-EYED SUSAN. See RUDBECKIA hirta

BLACK-EYED SUSAN VINE. See THUNBERGIA alata

BLACKFOOT DAISY. See MELAMPODIUM

BLACK GUM. See NYSSA sylvatica

BLACK HAW. See VIBURNUM prunifolium

BLACK JETBEAD. See RHODOTYPOS scandens

BLACK SNAKEROOT. See CIMICIFUGA racemosa

BLANKET FLOWER. See GAILLARDIA

BLAZING STAR. See LIATRUS

BLEEDING HEART. See DICENTRA

BLEEDING HEART VINE. See CLERODENDRUM thomsoniae

BLETILLA striata (B. hyacinthina)

CHINESE GROUND ORCHID, HARDY ORCHID

Orchidaceae

TERRESTRIAL ORCHID

ZONES US, MS, LS, CS

UNDER HIGH-BRANCHING TREES

FREQUENT WATER DURING GROWTH

Bletilla striata

A terrestrial orchid native to China and Japan. Lavender, cattleya-like, 1–2-in. flowers, up to a dozen on 1½–2-ft. stem, produced for about 6 weeks beginning in May or June. Pale green leaves, three to six to a plant. 'Alba' is a white-flowered form.

Plant the tuberlike roots outdoors in early spring for spring and early summer bloom. Grow in pot or in ground under high-branching trees. Hardy to about –10°F. Dies back to ground each winter. In time will develop large clumps if grown in light shade and in a moist soil rich in humus. Can be divided in early spring before growth starts, but don't do it too often; blooms best when crowded.

BLOODLEAF. See IRESINE

BLOODROOT. See SANGUINARIA canadensis

BLOODY BUTCHER. See TRILLIUM recurvatum

BLUEBEARD. See CARYOPTERIS

BLUEBELL. See SCILLA

BLUEBERRY

Ericaceae

DECIDUOUS SHRUBS

ZONES VARY BY TYPE

FULL SUN

DON'T LET SOIL SURFACE DRY OUT

Native to eastern North America, blueberries thrive in soil conditions that suit rhododendrons and azaleas, to which they are related. Plants require sun and moist, well-drained acid soil (pH 4.5–5.5). Outside their favored regions, create proper soil conditions or grow plants in containers.

Most blueberries grown for fruit are also handsome plants suitable for hedges or shrub borders. Dark green or blue-green leaves change to red, orange, or yellow combinations in autumn. Spring flowers are tiny, white or pinkish, urn shaped. Summer fruit is very decorative. ▶

Blueberry

Blueberries are available bare-root or in containers. Plant in autumn or spring. Position crown so that it is ½ in. above the ground. Grow at least two kinds for better pollination, resulting in larger berries and bigger yields per plant. Choose types that ripen at different times, for a long harvest season. Blueberries have fine roots near the soil surface; keep them moist but don't subject them to standing water. A 4–6-in.-thick mulch of pine straw, ground bark, or the like will protect roots and help conserve soil moisture. Don't cultivate around the plants.

Prune to prevent overbearing. Plants often produce so many fruit buds that berries are undersize and growth of plants slows down. Keep first-year plants from bearing by stripping off flowers. On older plants, cut back ends of twigs until fruit buds are widely spaced. Or simply remove some of oldest branches each year. Also get rid of all weak shoots. Plants don't usually have serious problems requiring regular controls in home gardens. Netting will keep birds from getting the berries before you do.

The following are some of the major types of blueberries grown. (For ornamental relatives, see *Vaccinium*.)

Highbush blueberries. Suited to Upper and Middle South. Selections of *Vaccinium corymbosum* are the blueberries usually found in grocery stores. Most grow upright to 6 ft. or more; a few are rather sprawling, under 5 ft. The majority are northern types, requiring definite winter cold and ripening their berries between June and late August. The relatively new southern highbush types will also grow in the Lower and Coastal South; they ripen their fruit in April or May, even before rabbiteye blueberries. Except as noted, those listed below are northern types.

'Bluecrop'. Midseason. Erect, tall growth. Large berries. Excellent flavor. Attractive shrub.

'Blueray'. Midseason. Vigorous, tall. Large, highly flavored, crisp berries. Attractive shrub.

'Coville'. Late. Tall, open, spreading. Unusually large leaves. Very attractive. Long clusters of very large light blue berries.

'Earliblue'. Early. Tall, erect. Large, heavy leaves. Large berries of excellent flavor.

'Elliott'. Late. Tall, upright. Medium to large berries of excellent flavor.

'Georgiagem'. Southern highbush. Very early. Moderately vigorous, upright. Medium-size, firm fruit of good flavor.

'Herbert'. Late. Vigorous, open, spreading. Among the biggest, best-flavored berries.

'O'Neal'. Southern highbush. Very early. Large, flavorful berries.

'Sharpblue'. Southern highbush. Very early. Flavorful berries prone to bird damage. Attractive landscape plant. Does well in central Florida.

Rabbiteye blueberries. Zones MS, LS, CS. Like southern highbush blueberries, these selections of the Southeast native *Vaccinium ashei* are adapted to hot, humid summers and mild winters. They are often taller than highbush plants, and they ripen their large light blue berries a little earlier—in May and June. Plant two or three kinds for good cross-pollination. Good fall color. The following list includes some of the most flavorful selections:

'Brightwell'. Midseason. Tolerant of spring freezes. Large, sweet, light blue berries.

'Climax'. Early. Upright and spreading. Good pollinator. Medium dark blue berries.

'Delite'. Midseason. Medium-large fruit. Excellent flavor.

'Premier'. Early. Large, good-quality fruit.

'Tifblue'. Midseason to late. Vigorous, upright. Good commercial selection. Firm, excellent flavor. Tart until completely ripe. The most cold-hardy. Light blue berries.

'Woodward'. Early. Shorter, more spreading than other rabbiteyes. Rather soft berries, tart until fully ripe.

BLUE CURLS. See PHACELIA congesta

BLUE DAZE. See EVOLVULUS glomeratus

BLUE-EYED GRASS. See SISYRINCHIUM

BLUE FAN PALM. See BRAHEA armata

BLUE FESCUE. See FESTUCA ovina 'Glauca'

BLUE FLAG. See IRIS versicolor

BLUE GINGER. See DICHORISANDRA thyrsiflora

BLUEGRASS. See POA

BLUE LYME GRASS. See ELYMUS arenarius 'Glaucus'

BLUE MIST. See CARYOPTERIS clandonensis

BLUE OAT GRASS. See HELICTOTRICHON sempervirens

BLUE SPIRAEA. See CARYOPTERIS incana

BLUE STAR FLOWER. See AMSONIA

BLUESTEM. See ANDROPOGON

BLUETS. See HOUSTONIA caerulea

BLUE WILD RYE. See ELYMUS glaucus

BOCCONIA. See MACLEAYA

BOLTONIA asteroides

BOLTONIA

Asteraceae (Compositae)

PERENNIAL

✂ ZONES US, MS, LS, CS

☼ ◐ FULL SUN OR LIGHT SHADE

◖ REGULAR WATER

Boltonia asteroides

In late summer, tall stems bear broad and mounded clusters of small, yellow-centered white to pink flowers that much resemble Michaelmas daisies. Plant grows to 6 ft. or more; may be floppy with overhead watering. 'Snowbank' is more compact (to 5 ft. tall) and upright, with larger flowers of a clearer white. 'Pink Beauty' has lilac-pink flowers. Plant will survive in poor soil and with reduced water, but it may bloom feebly on 2-ft. stems as a result.

Bombacaceae. This tropical family of trees and shrubs includes *Chorisia*, a genus with very showy flowers.

BONESET. See EUPATORIUM perfoliatum

Boraginaceae. The borage family consists of annuals and perennials, most of which have small flowers in coiled clusters that straighten as bloom progresses. Forget-me-not *(Myosotis)* is a familiar example.

BORAGO officinalis

BORAGE

Boraginaceae

ANNUAL HERB

✂ ALL ZONES

☼ ◐ ◖ SUN OR SHADE

◓ ◖ REGULAR TO MODERATE WATER

Borago officinalis

Grows 1–3 ft. high. Bristly, gray-green leaves, 4–6 in. long, are edible, with a cucumber-like flavor. Blue, saucer-shaped, nodding flowers in leafy clusters on branched stems.

Usually sown in spring after frost danger; best as a fall–spring crop in the Coastal and Tropical South. Tolerates poor soil. Seeds itself but doesn't transplant easily. Use small tender leaves in salads; you can also pickle them or cook them as greens. Cut flowers for arrangements or use as an attractive garnish.

BOSTON FERN. See NEPHROLEPIS exaltata 'Bostoniensis'

BOSTON IVY. See PARTHENOCISSUS tricuspidata

BO-TREE. See FICUS religiosa

BOTTLEBRUSH. See CALLISTEMON

BOTTLE PALM. See BEAUCARNEA recurvata

⌂ BOUGAINVILLEA

Nyctaginaceae

EVERGREEN SHRUBBY VINES

✂ ZONES CS, TS; OR GROW IN CONTAINERS

☼ ◐ LIGHT SHADE IN HOTTEST AREAS

◒ ◓ REGULAR TO MODERATE WATER

Bougainvillea
'San Diego Red'

No longer restricted to the Coastal and Tropical South, thanks to low-growing shrubby types that can be purchased in full bloom in gallon cans and grown as container plants. They are used on terrace or patio as summer annuals and moved to a protected area over winter. Where frosts are routine, vines should be given protected warm wall or warmest spot in garden. If vines get by first winter or two, they will be big enough to take most winter damage and recover. In any case, flower production comes so quickly that replacement is not a real deterrent.

Bougainvillea's vibrant colors come not from its small inconspicuous flowers, but from the three large bracts that surround them. Vines make dense cover of medium-size, medium green leaves. Vigor and growth habit vary by species and selection. Plant in sun (in light shade in hottest areas) in early spring (after frosts), to give longest possible growing time before next frost.

Supply sturdy supports and keep shoots tied up so they won't whip in wind and strong gusts won't shred leaves against sharp thorns along stems.

Fertilize in spring and summer. Water normally while plants are growing fast; then ease off temporarily in midsummer to promote better flowering. Don't be afraid to prune—to renew plant, shape, or direct growth. Prune heavily after bloom. On wall-grown plants, nip back long stems during growing season to produce more flowering wood. Shrubby kinds or heavily pruned plants make good self-supporting container shrubs for terrace or patio. Without support and with occasional corrective pruning, bougainvillea can make broad, sprawling shrub, bank and ground cover, or hanging basket plant.

All of the following are tall-growing vines except those noted as shrubs. Double-flowering kinds can look messy because they hold faded flowers for a long time.

'Afterglow'. Yellow orange; heavy bloom. Open growth, sparse foliage.

'Barbara Karst'. Bright red in sun, bluish crimson in shade; blooms young and for long period. Vigorous growth. Fast comeback after frost.

'Betty Hendry' ('Indian Maid'). Basically red but with touches of yellow and purple. Blooms young and for a long period.

B. brasiliensis. See B. spectabilis

'Brilliant Variegated'. Spreading, mounding shrub. Leaves variegated with gray green and silver. Brick red bracts. Often used in hanging baskets, containers.

'California Gold' ('Sunset'). Deep golden yellow. Blooms young.

'Camarillo Festival'. Hot pink to gold blend.

'Cherry Blossom'. Double-flowered rose pink, with centers of white to pale green.

'Crimson Jewel'. Vigorous shrubby, sprawling plant. Good in containers, as shrub, or as sunny bank cover. Lower growth, better color than 'Temple Fire'. Heavy bloom, long season.

'Crimson Lake'. See 'Mrs. Butt'

'Don Mario'. Large and vigorous vine with huge clusters of deep purple-red blooms.

'Hawaii'. ('Raspberry Ice'). Shrubby, mounding, spreading. Leaves have golden yellow margins. New leaves tinged red. Bracts red. Good hanging basket plant. Regardless of its tropical name, it's one of the hardiest.

'Isabel Greensmith'. Bracts variously described as orange, red orange, or red with yellow tinting.

'Jamaica White'. Bracts white, veined light green. Blooms young. Moderately vigorous.

'James Walker'. Big reddish purple bracts on big vine.

'La Jolla'. Bright red bracts, compact, shrubby habit. Good shrub, container plant.

'Lavender Queen'. An improved *B. spectabilis*, with bigger bracts, heavier bloom.

'Manila Red'. Many rows of magenta red bracts make heavy clusters of double-looking bloom.

'Mary Palmer's Enchantment'. Very vigorous, large-growing vine with pure white bracts.

'Mrs. Butt' ('Crimson Lake'). Old-fashioned type with good crimson color. Needs lots of heat for bloom. Moderately vigorous.

'Orange King'. Bronzy orange. Open growth. Needs long summer, and no frost.

'Pink Tiara'. Abundant pale pink to rose bracts over long season.

'Raspberry Ice'. See 'Hawaii'

'Rosea'. Large rose red bracts on large vine.

'Rosenka'. Can be held to shrub proportions if occasional wild shoot is pruned out. Gold bracts age pink.

'San Diego Red' ('San Diego', 'Scarlett O'Hara'). One of best on all counts: large, deep green leaves that hold well in mild winters; deep red bracts over long season; hardiness equal to old-fashioned purple kind. Vigorous, high climbing. Can be trained to tree form by staking and pruning.

'Southern Rose'. Lavender rose to pink.

B. spectabilis (B. brasiliensis). Hardy and vigorous. Blooms well in cool summers. Purple bracts.

'Tahitian Dawn'. Big vine with gold bracts aging to rosy purple.

'Tahitian Maid'. Extra rows of bracts give double effect to blush pink clusters.

'Temple Fire'. Shrublike growth to 4 ft. high, 6 ft. wide. Partially deciduous. Bronze red.

'Texas Dawn'. Choice, vigorous plant. Purplish pink bracts form large sprays of color.

'Torch Glow'. An oddity: an erect, multistemmed plant to 6 ft. Needs no support. Reddish pink bracts growing close to the stems are partially hidden by foliage.

'White Madonna'. Pure white bracts.

PLANTING A BOUGAINVILLEA?

Watch those roots—they're fragile and do not knit easily. Here is how to keep the root ball intact during planting. Put the plant in an extra-wide planting hole, can and all. Insert blades of sharp, needle-nose shears into one of the drain holes and cut all the way around the can's bottom. Slide the detached bottom out from under the can. Then, make a cut down one side of can from the top to bottom. Make another cut on the opposite side. Fill in with soil around the root ball. Slide the two detached pieces up and out.

BOUGAINVILLEA GOLDENRAIN TREE. See KOELREUTERIA bipinnata

BOUNCING BET. See SAPONARIA officinalis

BOUSSINGAULTIA baselloides. See ANREDERA cordifolia

BOWER VINE. See PANDOREA jasminoides

BOX, BOXWOOD. See BUXUS

BOX ELDER. See ACER negundo

BOYSENBERRY. See BLACKBERRY

BRADFORD PEAR. See PYRUS calleryana 'Bradford'

BRAHEA (Erythea)

Arecaceae (Palmae)
PALMS
ZONE TS
FULL SUN
VERY DROUGHT TOLERANT

Brahea armata

These fan palms from Mexico are somewhat like washingtonias in appearance, but with important differences. All can tolerate drought.

B. armata. BLUE FAN PALM. Hardy to 18°F. Grows slowly to 40 ft. tall, with top spreading to 6–8 ft. Leaves silvery blue in color, almost white. Conspicuous creamy flowers. Takes heat and wind.

B. brandegeei. SAN JOSE HESPER PALM. Hardy to 26°F. Slow grower with slender, flexible trunk. Eventually reaches to 125 ft. in its native environment. Trunk sheds leaves when old. Leaves 3 ft. long, light gray green.

BRASSAIA actinophylla. See SCHEFFLERA actinophylla

Brassicaceae. The mustard, or cress, family contains many food plants and ornamentals as well as a number of weeds. The notable characteristic is a four-petaled flower resembling a cross. Familiar members include all the cabbage group, radishes, turnips, stock *(Matthiola)*, and sweet alyssum *(Lobularia)*. This family was formerly called Cruciferae.

BRAUN'S HOLLY FERN. See POLYSTICHUM braunii

BRAZILIAN BUTTERFLY TREE. See BAUHINIA forficata

BRAZILIAN GOLDEN VINE. See STIGMAPHYLLON littorale

BRAZILIAN NIGHTSHADE. See SOLANUM seaforthianum

BRAZILIAN PLUME. See JUSTICIA carnea

BRAZILIAN SKY FLOWER. See DURANTA stenostachya

BRIDAL WREATH. See SPIRAEA prunifolia 'Plena'

BRIZA maxima

RATTLESNAKE GRASS, QUAKING GRASS
Poaceae (Gramineae)
ANNUAL
ALL ZONES
FULL SUN
MUCH TO LITTLE WATER

Briza maxima

Native to Mediterranean region. Ornamental grass of delicate, graceful form; attractive in bouquets, dry arrangements. Grows 1–2 ft. high. Leaves are ¼ in. wide, to 6 in. long. Clusters of nodding, seed-bearing spikelets, ½ in. long (or longer), papery and straw colored when dry, dangle on threadlike stems. Spikelets resemble rattlesnake rattles. Scatter seed where plants are to grow; thin seedlings to 1 ft. apart. Often grows wild along roadsides, in fields. *B. media* is similar but perennial.

BROAD BEECH FERN. See THELYPTERIS hexagonoptera

BROAD BUCKLER FERN. See DRYOPTERIS dilatata

BROCCOLI

Brassicaceae (Cruciferae)
BIENNIAL GROWN AS ANNUAL
ALL ZONES
FULL SUN
REGULAR WATER

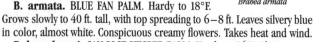

Broccoli

Of the cole crops (cabbage and its close relatives), broccoli is among the easiest to grow. Grows to 4 ft. and has branching habit. Central stalk bears cluster of green flower buds that may reach 6 in. in diameter. When central cluster is removed, side branches will lengthen and produce smaller clusters. Good selections are 'Emperor', 'Green Comet', 'Green Goliath', 'Parkman', 'Premium', and 'Saga'.

Broccoli is a cool-season plant that tends to bolt into flower in high heat; plant it to mature in cool weather in spring or fall. In the Coastal South, also plant in late summer, fall, or winter for winter or early spring crops.

Young plants resist frost but not hard freezes. A good guide to planting time is the appearance of young plants in garden centers. Young plants ready to be planted take 4 to 6 weeks to develop from seed. One pack of seed will produce far more plants than most home gardens can handle, so save surplus seed for later plantings. A dozen plants will supply a family of four.

Choose a sunny spot; set plants 1½–2 ft. apart in rows and leave 3 ft. between rows. Provide regular deep irrigation during dry periods and one or two fertilizer applications before heads start to form. Harvest 50 to 100 days after planting. Cut heads before clustered buds begin to open, including 5–6 in. of edible stalk and leaves. Subject to same pests as cabbage.

Bromeliaceae. All the members of the bromelia, or pineapple, family are called bromeliads. Most are stemless perennials with clustered leaves and showy flowers in unbranched or branched clusters. Leaves of many kinds are handsomely marked, and flower clusters gain beauty from colorful bracts. Examples are *Aechmea, Tillandsia, Vriesa,* as well as the pineapple.

Bromeliads are considered choice house plants. The kinds most often grown indoors are, in their native homes, epiphytes: plants that perch on trees or rocks and gain their sustenance from rain and from whatever leaf mold gathers around their roots. In mildest climates, many of these epiphytes grow well outdoors in sheltered places.

BRONZE DRACAENA. See CORDYLINE australis 'Atropurpurea'

BROOM. See CYTISUS

BROOM SEDGE. See ANDROPOGON virginicus

BROUSSONETIA papyrifera

PAPER MULBERRY
Moraceae
DECIDUOUS TREE
ZONES MS, LS, CS
FULL SUN
MUCH TO LITTLE WATER

Broussonetia papyrifera

Native to China and Japan. Common name comes from inner bark, used for making paper and Polynesian tapa cloth. Has been sold as *Morus papyrifera.* Valuable as shade tree where soil and climate limit choices. Tolerates heat, drought, strong winds, city pollution, and stony, sterile, or alkaline soils.

Moderate to fast growth to 50 ft., with dense, broad crown to 40 ft. across. Often considerably smaller and more shrublike in gardens. Suckering habit can be problem in rainy climates and highly cultivated gardens; very weedy. Good in rough bank plantings. Smooth gray bark can become ridged and furrowed with age, creating handsome old specimens. Heart-shaped, 4–8-in., rough leaves, gray and velvety beneath; edges toothed, often lobed when young. Flowers on male trees are catkins; on female trees, rounded flower heads are followed by red fruits if a male tree is growing nearby.

BROWALLIA

AMETHYST FLOWER

Solanaceae

ANNUALS

☀ ALL ZONES

☽ WARM SHADE OR FILTERED SUNLIGHT

💧 REGULAR WATER

Browallia speciosa

Choice plants for connoisseur of blue flowers. Bear one-sided clusters of lobelia-like blooms in brilliant blue, violet, or white; blue flowers are more striking because of contrasting white eye or throat. Bloom profusely in warm shade or filtered sunlight. Graceful in hanging basket or container. Fine cut flowers.

Sow seeds in early spring for summer bloom, in fall for winter color indoors or in greenhouses. Plants need warmth, regular moisture. You can lift vigorous plants in fall, cut back, and pot; new growth will produce flowers through winter in warm spot. Often sold in garden centers. Less common elsewhere.

B. americana. Branching, 1–2 ft. high; roundish leaves. Violet or blue flowers ½ in. long, ½ in. across, borne among leaves. 'Sapphire', a compact dwarf, dark blue with white eye, is very free blooming. Species and selections are often listed in catalogs as *B. elata* or *B. e.* 'Sapphire'.

B. speciosa. BLUE BELLS. Sprawling, to 1–2 ft. high. Flowers dark purple above, pale lilac beneath, 1½–2 in. across. 'Blue Bells Improved', lavender blue, grows 10 in. tall, needs no pinching to make it branch. 'Marine Bells' has deep indigo flowers. 'Silver Bells' has white flowers.

🕎 BRUGMANSIA (Datura)

ANGEL'S TRUMPET

Solanaceae

EVERGREEN TO SEMIEVERGREEN SHRUBS

☀ ZONES LS (PROTECTED), CS, TS

☼ ☽ ● SUN OR SHADE

💧 REGULAR WATER

☤ ALL PARTS ARE POISONOUS IF INGESTED

Brugmansia candida

Related to the annual or perennial jimsonweeds. All are large shrubs that can be trained as small trees. With their outsize leaves and big tubular flowers, they are dominating plants that will astonish your visitors. Main bloom period is summer and fall.

Provide sheltered position; wind tatters the foliage. Expect frost damage and unattractive winter appearance. Prune in early spring after last frost; cut back branchlets to one or two buds. Beyond hardiness range, grow in containers and move to a frost-free site in cold weather. Potted plants can be wintered indoors with a little light and very little water.

B. arborea. Plants often sold under this name are either *B. candida* or *B. suaveolens.* The true *B. arborea* has smaller flowers.

B. candida. Native to Peru. Fast and rank growing with soft, pulpy growth to 10–15 ft. (6 ft. or more in one season). Dull green, large leaves

in the 8–12-in. range. Heavy, single or double white trumpets, to 8 in. long or more, are fragrant, especially at night. Shrub is showy in moonlight.

B. sanguinea. Native to Peru. Fast growing to 12–15 ft. Leaves, bright green, to 8 in. long. Trumpets, orange red with yellow veinings, to 10 in. long, hang straight down like bells from new growth. Rare.

B. suaveolens. Native to Brazil. Similar to *B. candida*, but leaves and flowers are somewhat larger and flowers less fragrant.

B. versicolor. To 15 ft. tall. Flowers white or peach colored. Named versions of uncertain origin include 'Charles Grimaldi' (pale orange yellow) and 'Frosty Pink' (cream deepening to pink).

BRUNFELSIA pauciflora
(B. calycina)

Solanaceae

EVERGREEN SHRUBS

☀ ZONES CS, TS

☽ PARTIAL SHADE

💧 REGULAR WATER

Brunfelsia pauciflora
'Floribunda'

Grown for showy clusters of white-throated, rich dark purple tubular flowers opening to a flat disk; spring and early summer bloom. In all but the warmest locations they lose most of their foliage for a short period. These handsome plants deserve extra attention—give them rich, well-drained soil, a constant supply of moisture, and regular feedings through the growing season. Prune in spring to remove scraggly growth and to shape. Use where you can admire the flower show. Good in containers; can also be grown in a greenhouse. The following are the forms available:

'Eximia' (*B. calycina eximia*). Somewhat dwarfed, compact version of 'Floribunda', a more widely planted selection. Flowers are a bit smaller but more generously produced.

'Floribunda'. YESTERDAY-TODAY-AND-TOMORROW. Common name comes from quick color change of blossoms: purple ("yesterday"), lavender ("today"), white ("tomorrow"). Flowers, several in a cluster and each flaring to 2 in. wide, profusely displayed all over plant. Oval leaves, 3–4 in. long, dark green above, pale green below. In partial shade, plant will reach 10 ft. or more with several stems from base, but can be held to 3 ft. by pruning. Rather spreading habit.

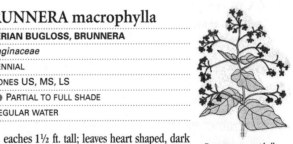
Brunfelsia pauciflora
'Floribunda'

'Macrantha' (*B. floribunda* 'Lindeniana', *B. grandiflora*). In addition to being less cold-hardy, differs from the above in having fewer but larger flowers, 2–4 in. across. Also has a more slender growth habit and bigger leaves, to 8 in. long, 2½ in. wide.

BRUNNERA macrophylla

SIBERIAN BUGLOSS, BRUNNERA

Boraginaceae

PERENNIAL

☀ ZONES US, MS, LS

☽ ● PARTIAL TO FULL SHADE

💧 REGULAR WATER

Reaches 1½ ft. tall; leaves heart shaped, dark green, 3–4 in. wide. Variegated forms also available. In spring, plants produce airy clusters of tiny clear blue forget-me-not flowers with yellow centers. Uses include informal ground cover under high-branching deciduous trees; among spring-flowering shrubs such as forsythia, deciduous magnolias; filler between newly planted evergreen shrubs. Freely self-sows once established. Planted seeds often difficult to germinate (try freezing them before sowing). Needs well-drained, moisture-retentive soil. Increase by dividing clumps in fall.

Brunnera macrophylla

BRUSSELS SPROUTS

Brassicaceae (Cruciferae)

BIENNIAL GROWN AS ANNUAL

ALL ZONES

FULL SUN

REGULAR WATER

Brussels Sprouts

A cabbage relative of unusual appearance. Mature plant has crown of fairly large leaves, and its tall stem is completely covered with tiny sprouts. 'Jade Cross Hybrid' is easiest to grow and most heat tolerant; 'Long Island Improved' ('Catskill') is standard market type. You may have to grow your own from seed. Sow outdoors or in flats in April; transplant young plants in June to sunny place. Sprouts are ready in fall. In the Coastal and Tropical South, plant in fall or winter for winter and spring use.

Treat the same as broccoli. When big leaves start to turn yellow, begin harvesting this plant. Snap off little sprouts from the bottom of stem first—best when slightly smaller than a golf ball. Leave the smaller sprouts on upper stem to mature. After picking, remove only leaves below harvested sprouts. A single plant may yield from 50 to 100 sprouts. Plant is subject to same pests as cabbage.

BUCHLOE dactyloides

BUFFALO GRASS

Poaceae (Gramineae)

PERENNIAL GRASS

ZONES US, MS, LS

FULL SUN

LITTLE WATER ONCE ESTABLISHED

Buchloe dactyloides

Makes a relatively low-maintenance lawn that takes hard wear and looks fairly good with very little irrigation during dry periods. Green from late spring to hard frost, straw colored through late fall and winter. Not well adapted to Florida or Gulf Coast. Buffalo grass is at its best when allowed to grow tall, but needs mowing three times a year to form a good thick turf: Cut it short (to about 1 in.) in late winter or very early spring; then cut it to 2 in. in mid-June and again to 2 in. in early fall. Between mowings, it will grow to 4–6 in.

Sodded lawns look best, but seed and plugs are less expensive. Sow seed at the rate of 2 lb. per 1,000 sq. ft. In absence of rain, soak occasionally to 1 ft. while grass is getting started. Slow to sprout and fill in, but will spread rapidly, even invasively, by surface runners once established. Plant 4-in.-wide plugs 3–4 ft. apart in prepared soil in spring; cover should be complete in two seasons.

Selections include the following:

'Bison'. Very cold-hardy. Produces seed heads. Summer color and thickness not as good as '609' or 'Prairie'. Available as seed.

'Prairie'. Spreads more aggressively than selection '609', but summer color is not quite as good. Produces thick turf, without seed heads. Available as sod or plugs.

'609'. Lovely blue-green summer color. Makes thick lawn, no seed heads. Available as sod or plugs.

'Texoka'. Produces lots of seed heads. Inferior quality for home-lawn use; much better suited to roadsides and industrial parks. An old selection, available as seed.

'Top Gun'. Superior to 'Bison' in appearance and thickness. Produces seed heads. Available as seed.

BUCKEYE. See AESCULUS

BUCKWHEAT TREE. See CLIFTONIA monophylla

BUDDLEIA

BUTTERFLY BUSH

Loganiaceae

EVERGREEN, SEMIEVERGREEN, OR DECIDUOUS SHRUBS

ZONES VARY BY SPECIES

FULL SUN OR LIGHT SHADE

REGULAR TO MODERATE WATER

Buddleia davidii

Of the many species and selections—all notable for flower color or fragrance, or both—these are the most commonly available. Buddleias look best if pruned hard each year. May die to ground in winter in Upper South. Need well-drained soil.

B. alternifolia. FOUNTAIN BUTTERFLY BUSH. Deciduous. Zones US, MS, LS, CS. It can reach 12 ft. or more, with arching, willowlike branches rather thinly clothed with 1–4-in.-long leaves, dark dull green above, gray and hairy beneath. Blooms in spring from previous year's growth; profuse small clusters of mildly fragrant, lilac purple flowers make sweeping wands of color. Tolerates many soils; does very well in poor, dry gravels. Prune after bloom: Remove some of oldest wood down to within few inches of ground. Or train up into small single- or multiple-trunked tree. So trained, it somewhat resembles a small weeping willow.

B. davidii. ORANGE-EYE BUTTERFLY BUSH, SUMMER LILAC. Deciduous or semievergreen. Zones US, MS, LS, CS. Fast, rank growth each spring and summer to 5, 6, or even 10 ft. Leaves tapering, 4–12 in. long, dark green above, white and felted beneath. In midsummer, branch ends adorned with small, fragrant flowers in dense, arching, spikelike, slender clusters 6–12 in. long or more. Needs good drainage and enough water to maintain growth but little else. Cut back plants heavily in late winter to early spring to promote strong new growth for good flowering. In Upper South, plants may freeze to the ground but will regrow each year from the roots. Butterflies often visit flowers. Here are a few of the many types available:

'Black Knight'. Darkest flower, almost grape violet. Small leaves. Grows to 6–7 ft. A superior selection.

'Charming'. Lots of large lavender-pink flowers. Large bush, to 7 ft., and 10 ft. across.

'Dartmoor'. Very fragrant purple flowers, on side shoots as well as main branches. To 6 ft.

'Empire Blue'. Truest blue flowers. Silvery green foliage. Vigorous, upright growth, to 10–12 ft.

'Harlequin'. Cream variegation on leaves. Reddish purple flowers. Slower growing. To 7–8 ft.

'Pink Delight'. Clear pink flowers. Silvery foliage. To 6–8 ft.

'Potters Purple'. Long violet flower spikes. Vigorous, upright. To 7 ft.

'Purple Prince'. Very fragrant violet flowers. Upright form, to 6 ft.

'White Bouquet'. Lots of white flower spikes. Dense growth, to 6 ft.

B. fallowiana 'Alba'. Deciduous or semievergreen. Zones US, MS, LS, CS. To 5 ft. tall. Similar to *B.* 'Lochinch', but long panicles of white flowers. Felty gray leaves. Prune as you would *B. davidii*.

B. globosa. ORANGE BUTTERFLY BUSH. Evergreen or semievergreen. Zones LS, CS. Grows 10–15 ft. tall. Fragrant orange-yellow flowers are tightly clustered in ¾-in. balls, which in turn are carried in narrow, spikelike 6–8-in. clusters. Blooms late spring or early summer. Flowers produced on previous year's wood, so prune as for *B. alternifolia*.

B. 'Lochinch'. Deciduous. Zones US, MS, LS, CS. A hybrid between *B. davidii* and *B. fallowiana*. To 5–6 ft. tall. Displays woolly white new growth and branching foot-long clusters of intensely fragrant lilac blossoms with orange eyes. Produces summer flowers on current year's growth, so prune as for *B. davidii*. Excellent flowers and foliage.

B. 'Nanho Alba'. Deciduous or semievergreen. Zones US, MS, LS, CS. To 4–6 ft. White flower spikes. Fast growing. Prune as for *B. davidii*.

B. 'Nanho Blue'. Deciduous or semievergreen. Zones US, MS, LS, CS. To 4–6 ft. Lots of blue flowers. Slender, silvery, small leaves. Prune as for *B. davidii*.

B. 'Nanho Purple'. Deciduous or semievergreen. Zones US, MS, LS, CS. To 4–6 ft. Dark violet flower panicles. Narrow leaves. Prune as you would *B. davidii.*

B. pikei 'Hever' ('Hever Castle'). Deciduous. Zones LS, CS. Hybrid between *B. alternifolia* and a Himalayan species. Resembles a smaller *B. alternifolia*, with a profusion of fragrant, orange-centered lilac flowers in mid- to late spring. Leaves gray green. Prune as for *B. alternifolia.*

B. weyeriana 'Sungold'. Zones MS, LS, CS. Hybrid between *B. davidii* and *B. globosa.* Resembles latter parent but deciduous and probably hardier, with orange-yellow flower clusters that are somewhat less globular. To 8–10 ft. Blooms on old wood, so cut back after flowering as for *B. alternifolia.* (In coldest part of range, however, it freezes to the ground and so blooms on new wood.)

BUFFALO GRASS. See BUCHLOE dactyloides

BUGBANE. See CIMICIFUGA

BULRUSH. See CYPERUS papyrus

BUNNY EARS. See OPUNTIA microdasys

BUNYA-BUNYA. See ARAUCARIA bidwillii

BURMESE FISHTAIL PALM. See CARYOTA mitis

BURNET. See SANGUISORBA

BURRO TAIL. See SEDUM morganianum

BUSH PEA. See THERMOPSIS

BUSY LIZZIE. See IMPATIENS wallerana

BUTCHER'S BROOM. See RUSCUS

BUTIA capitata

PINDO PALM
Arecaceae (Palmae)
PALM
☀ ZONES CS, TS
☀ ◑ FULL SUN OR LIGHT SHADE
● REGULAR WATER

Butia capitata

Native to Brazil, Uruguay, Argentina. This is a slow-growing, very hardy palm. Eventually reaches to 10–20 ft. Trunk heavy, patterned with the stubs of old leaves; tree is more attractive if the stubs are trimmed to the same length. Produces feathery, arching gray-green leaves and long spikes of small flowers. Blooms are followed by showy clusters of yellow to red edible dates in summer.

BUTTERCUP WINTER HAZEL. See CORYLOPSIS pauciflora

BUTTER DAISY. See MELAMPODIUM paludosum

BUTTERFLY BUSH. See BUDDLEIA

BUTTERFLY FLOWER. See BAUHINIA monandra

BUTTERFLY WEED. See ASCLEPIAS tuberosa

BUTTERNUT. See WALNUT

BUTTONBUSH. See CEPHALANTHUS occidentalis

Buxaceae. The boxwood family comprises principally evergreen shrubs with inconspicuous flowers (fragrant in *Sarcococca*). Other members include boxwood *(Buxus)* and *Pachysandra.*

SOUTHERN HERITAGE PLANTS
IDENTIFIED BY SYMBOL 🏛

BUXUS

BOXWOOD, BOX
Buxaceae
EVERGREEN SHRUBS
☀ ZONES VARY BY SPECIES
☀ ◑ ● SUN OR SHADE
● REGULAR WATER

Buxus microphylla japonica

Widely used for edging and hedging. Left unclipped, usually grow soft and billowing. Provide fertile, moist soil, either acid or alkaline. Need excellent drainage. Often attacked by nematodes in sandy soil of Florida.

B. microphylla. LITTLELEAF BOXWOOD. Zones US, MS, LS, CS. Hardy to 10°F. Slow-growing species, reaches 3–4 ft. tall and wide. Rarely planted. The following varieties and selections are much more common:

'Compacta'. Small, dense form with tiny, dark green leaves. Extremely slow-growing; 50-year-old plants may reach only 1 ft. tall.

B. m. japonica. JAPANESE BOXWOOD. Zones MS, LS, CS. Faster growing than species, to 6 ft. tall. Well suited to Coastal South; tolerates heat, humidity, and nematodes better than most boxwoods. Leaves ⅓–1 in., round tipped. Foliage may bronze in cold winters. Often used as clipped hedge in Gulf Coast areas.

'Green Beauty'. Compact, with glossy, deep green leaves; holds color even in coldest winters.

'Kingsville Dwarf'. Exceptionally compact and low growing.

B. m. koreana. KOREAN BOXWOOD. Zones US, MS, LS, CS. Hardy to −25°F. Slower and lower growing than Japanese boxwood, with smaller leaves. Good choice for severe winters of Upper South.

'Winter Gem'. Very cold-hardy. Foliage retains its deep green color through the winter.

🏛 **B. sempervirens.** COMMON BOXWOOD, AMERICAN BOXWOOD. Zones US, MS, LS. Hardy to −10°F. A true garden aristocrat, nearly indispensable in formal garden settings. Slowly grows to 15–20 ft. tall and wide. Dense foliage; dark green, oval leaves. Can be used in foundation plantings, for hedges, or pruned into a small tree. Control leaf miner by spraying with Cygon (see page 445) in May. To prevent common diseases of canker and root rot, avoid planting in low, wet areas. Clean out dead leaves and other debris that accumulate in center of plant.

Of the many selections available, the following are most common:

'Newport Blue'. Dense, low grower with bluish green foliage.

🏛 'Suffruticosa'. EDGING BOXWOOD. Dense, compact, very slow growing; 150-year-old plants reach 3 ft. high. Often used for edging in formal garden settings. Also commonly known as English boxwood.

'Vardar Valley'. Becomes a flat-topped mound, 2–3 ft. tall, nearly twice as wide. Dark blue-green foliage. Discovered in the Vardar Valley of Macedonia. Hardy to about −15°F.

CABBAGE

Brassicaceae (Cruciferae)
BIENNIAL GROWN AS ANNUAL
☀ ALL ZONES
☀ ◑ TOLERATES LIGHT SHADE IN HOT CLIMATES
● NEVER LET PLANTS WILT

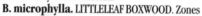
Cabbage

Early selections mature in 7 to 8 weeks from transplanting into garden; late types require 3 to 4 months. In addition to green cabbage you can get red and curly-leafed (Savoy) forms. To avoid overproduction, set out a few plants every week or two or plant both early and late kinds. Time plantings so heads will form either before or after hot summer months. Sow seeds ½ in. deep about 6 weeks before planting-out time. Transplant to rich, moist soil, spacing plants 2–2½ ft. apart. Give frequent light applications of nitrogen fertilizer. Mulch helps keep soil moist and cool. Light frost doesn't hurt cabbage, but harvest and store before heavy freezes.

To avoid pest buildup, change planting site each year. Row covers protect plants from some pests such as cabbage loopers, imported cabbageworms, root maggots. Another way to prevent root maggots is by ringing the base of the plant with a tar paper collar; the adult flies don't like to lay eggs on it. Collars also deter cutworms, which chew seedlings off at the base. *Bacillus thuringiensis* will control young larvae of loopers and cabbageworms if they get on the plants. Pests are less of a problem for fall crops than for spring ones.

For ornamental relatives, see Cabbage, Flowering.

CABBAGE, FLOWERING

Brassicaceae (Cruciferae)

BIENNIALS GROWN AS ANNUALS

✔ ALL ZONES

☼ ☼ ◑ BEST IN FULL SUN, TOLERATE SOME SHADE

◐ REGULAR WATER

Flowering cabbage and flowering kale are grown for their very ornamental, highly colored leaf rosettes, which look like giant peonies in deep blue green, marbled and edged with white, cream, rose, or purple. Kale differs from cabbage in that its head is slightly

Flowering Cabbage

looser and its leaf edges are more heavily fringed. Both are spectacular in the cool-season garden. They appreciate the same soil, care, and timing as conventional cabbage. Plant 15–18 in. apart in open-ground beds, singly in 8-in. pots, or several in a large container. Colors are strongest after first frosts touch plants. Single rosette cut and placed on spike holder in bowl makes striking harvest arrangement. Foliage is edible raw or cooked and is highly decorative as a salad garnish.

CABBAGE PALM. See SABAL palmetto

CABBAGE ROSE. See ROSA centifolia

Cactaceae. The cactus family contains a huge number of succulent plants (see also Succulents). Generally leafless, they have stems modified into cylinders, pads, or joints that store water in times of drought. Thick skin reduces evaporation, and most species have spines to protect plants against browsing animals. Flowers are usually large and brightly colored; fruit also may be colorful and is sometimes edible.

All (with one doubtful exception) are native to the Americas—from Canada to Argentina, from sea level into high mountains, in deserts or in dripping tropical rain forests.

Cacti range in height from a few inches to 50 ft. Larger species are used to create desert landscapes. Smaller species are grown in pots or, if sufficiently hardy, in rock gardens. Many are easy-care, showy house or greenhouse plants. Large landscaping types require full sun, well-drained soil. Water newly planted cacti very little; roots are subject to rot before they begin active growth. In 4 to 6 weeks, when new roots are active, water thoroughly; then let soil dry before watering again. Reduce watering in fall to allow plants to go dormant. Feed monthly in spring, summer. For some larger kinds appropriate for garden use, see *Echinocereus* and *Opuntia*.

Showiest in flower are tropical cacti that grow as epiphytes on trees or rocks. These plants need rich soil with much humus, frequent feeding and watering, partial shade, and protection from frost. In all but the mildest climates, grow them in a greenhouse, or use as outdoor/indoor plants. See *Epiphyllum*, *Rhipsalidopsis*, and *Schlumbergera*.

SOUTHERN HERITAGE PLANTS
IDENTIFIED BY SYMBOL 🏛

CAESALPINIA (Poinciana)

Fabaceae (Leguminosae)

✔ EVERGREEN OR DECIDUOUS SHRUBS OR SMALL TREES

✔ ZONES VARY BY SPECIES

☼ FULL SUN

◐ MODERATE TO LITTLE WATER

◆ PODS AND SEEDS CAUSE SERIOUS ILLNESS

Caesalpinias grow quickly and easily in hot sun with light, well-drained soil and occasional, deep watering during periods of drought.

Caesalpinia gilliesii

C. gilliesii (Poinciana gilliesii). BIRD OF PARADISE BUSH. Evergreen shrub or small tree; drops leaves in cold winters. Zones CS, TS. Tough, interesting, fast growing to 10 ft., with finely cut, filmy foliage on rather open, angular branch structure. Blooms all summer; clusters of yellow flowers adorned with protruding, bright red, 4–5-in.-long stamens. Flowers attract hummingbirds.

C. mexicana. MEXICAN BIRD OF PARADISE. Evergreen shrub or small tree; blooms year-round except in coldest months. Zone TS. Moderately fast growth to 10–12 ft.; may be pruned to 6–8 ft. Foliage coarser than that of *C. pulcherrima*. Lemon yellow flower clusters are 6 in. long, 4 in. thick.

C. pulcherrima (Poinciana pulcherrima). RED BIRD OF PARADISE, DWARF POINCIANA. Deciduous shrub; may be evergreen in mild winters. Zone TS. Fast, dense growth to 10 ft. tall and as wide. Dark green leaves with many ¾-in.-long leaflets. Blooms throughout warm weather; flowers orange or red (rarely yellow), clustered, with long red stamens. Useful for quick screening. Acts as herbaceous perennial in colder part of growing range—freezes to ground but rebounds quickly in spring. Even if it doesn't freeze back, you can cut it back to ground in early spring to make more compact mound.

🏛 CALADIUM bicolor

FANCY-LEAFED CALADIUM

Araceae

TUBEROUS-ROOTED PERENNIAL

✔ ZONE TS; OR DIG AND STORE OR GROW IN POTS

☼ ◑ ◐ SOME TYPES ARE BRED FOR SUN

◐◐ CAREFUL, FREQUENT WATERING

◆ JUICES CAN CAUSE SWELLING IN MOUTH, THROAT

Caladium bicolor

Native to tropical America. Not grown for flowers. Entire show comes from large (to 1½-ft.-long), heart- and arrow-shaped, long-stalked, almost translucent leaves colored in bands and blotches of red, rose, pink, white, silver, bronze, and green. Most selections sold in garden centers are derived from *C. bicolor*—usually 2 ft. tall, occasionally 4 ft. They include 'Candidum', 'Candidum Junior', 'Fanny Munson', 'Frieda Hemple', 'Pink Beauty', and 'Pink Symphony'. Most require shade. New sun-tolerant types, with thicker leaves, include 'Aaron', 'Fire Chief', 'Lance Whorton', 'Pink Cloud', 'Red Flash', 'Red Frill', 'Rose Bud', and 'White Queen'.

Caladiums need rich soil, high humidity, heat (above 70°F during days and rarely below 60°F at night), and ample water. In warmest parts of Florida and Texas, tubers can remain in the ground all year. Elsewhere, dig and store after leaf dieback, or grow in pots and bring indoors during cold weather.

To grow in ground, plant tubers when days lengthen in spring; place tubers with knobby side up so tops are even with soil surface. Keep well watered and feed lightly throughout growing season. Foliage may be cut back in autumn. Where freezes are likely, dig tubers, removing most soil from them, dry in semishade for 10 days, and store in dry peat moss or vermiculite at 50–60°F.

To grow in pots, start tubers indoors in March, outdoors in May. Pot in mix of equal parts coarse sand, leaf mold, and ground bark or peat moss.

Use 5-in. pot for 2½-in. tuber, 7-in. pot for one or two large tubers. Fill pot halfway with mix; stir in heaping teaspoon of fish meal. Add 1 in. of mix, place tuber on top, cover with 2 in. of mix. Water thoroughly.

C. esculentum. See Colocasia esculenta

CALAMAGROSTIS
acutifolia 'Stricta'

FEATHER REED GRASS

Poaceae (Gramineae)

PERENNIAL

✿ ZONES US, MS, LS

☼ FULL SUN

💧 REGULAR WATER

Calamagrostis acutifolia 'Stricta'

One of the most effective and handsome ornamental grasses. Erect, somewhat arching clumps of narrow, bright green leaves grow 1½–4 ft. in height. Blooms well in the Upper and Middle South, less well in the Lower South. Upright flowering stems rise 3–4 ft. above foliage in late spring or early summer, remain upright until first snow. Green with purplish tones, they age to golden yellow, turn buff by winter.

CALAMONDIN. See CITRUS, Sour-Acid Mandarin

CALATHEA

Marantaceae

PERENNIALS

✿ ZONE TS; OR INDOOR OR GREENHOUSE PLANTS

◖ ● PARTIAL OR FULL SHADE

💧 REGULAR WATER

Calathea zebrina

Native to tropical America or Africa. Ornamental leaves, beautifully marked in shades of green, white, and pink, arranged in basal tufts. Flowers of most are inconspicuous and of no consequence. Need high humidity and warm air (not under 55°F). Succeed outdoors in south Florida; elsewhere, they are greenhouse or indoor plants that can be brought outdoors in summer. Need porous soil, perfect drainage, frequent misting in dry air. Repot as often as necessary to avoid root-bound condition. Calatheas are often mistakenly called marantas.

C. crocata. ETERNAL FLAME. Grows to 10 in. high. Leaves to 6 in. long, 1–1½ in. wide, dark green above, purple beneath. Spikes 2 in. long, consisting of bright orange flower bracts that look like little torches. Clump has several shoots; each shoot dies after blooming, but new ones appear to keep up the show. Variable performance as house plant; subject to mites in low humidity. Does better in greenhouse.

C. insignis. RATTLESNAKE PLANT. Striking plant to 3–7 ft. in native rain forest, lower in cultivation, with 1–1½-ft.-long, yellow-green leaves striped olive green.

C. lancifolia. Grows to 1½ ft. tall. Long (1–1½-ft.), narrow, wavy-edged leaves are yellow green, banded with dark olive green. Usually sold as *C. insignis*.

C. louisae. To 3 ft. Foot-long dark green leaves heavily feathered with gray green along midrib.

C. makoyana. PEACOCK PLANT. Showy, 2–4 ft. high. Leaves have areas of olive green or cream above, pink blotches beneath. Silver featherings on rest of upper surface, corresponding cream-colored areas underneath.

C. ornata (C. majestica). Sturdy, 1½–3 ft. high. Leaves 2–3 ft. long, rich green above, purplish red beneath. Juvenile leaves usually pink striped between veins; intermediate foliage striped white. 'Roseo-lineata' has pink and white stripes at angle to midrib.

C. zebrina. ZEBRA PLANT. Compact plant to 1–3 ft. high. Elliptic leaves reach 1–2 ft. long, almost half as wide. Upper surfaces are velvety green with alternating bars of pale yellow green and olive green extending outward from midrib; undersides are purplish red.

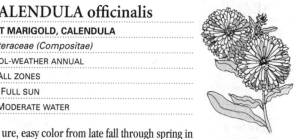

CALENDULAS IN COOKING

In times past, calendula leaves and flowers went into vegetable stews, and the vivid petals are still popular today for the tangy flavor they bring to salads, fish, and egg dishes. If cooked with rice, they give the grain a saffron color.

CALENDULA officinalis

POT MARIGOLD, CALENDULA

Asteraceae (Compositae)

COOL-WEATHER ANNUAL

✿ ALL ZONES

☼ FULL SUN

💧 MODERATE WATER

Calendula officinalis

Sure, easy color from late fall through spring in the Lower and Tropical South; spring to early summer in the Upper and Middle South. Besides familiar daisylike, orange and bright yellow double blooms 2½–4½ in. across, calendulas come in more subtle shades of apricot, cream, and soft yellow. Plants somewhat branching, 1–2 ft. high. Leaves are long, narrow, round on ends, slightly sticky, and aromatic. Plants effective in masses of single colors in borders and parking strips, along drives, in containers. Long-lasting cut flowers.

Sow seed in place or in flats in late summer or early fall in mild-winter areas, spring elsewhere. Or buy seedlings at garden centers. Plant adapts well to most soils if drainage is fast. Remove spent flowers to prolong bloom. Although it is an excellent pot plant, the common name is actually derived from the plant's earlier use as a "pot herb"—a vegetable to be used in the cooking pot.

Dwarf strains (12–15 in.) include Bon Bon (earliest), Dwarf Gem, and Fiesta (Fiesta Gitana). Taller (1½–2 ft.) are Kablouna (pompom centers with looser edges), Pacific Beauty, and Radio (quilled, "cactus" blooms).

CALIFORNIA PRIVET. See LIGUSTRUM ovalifolium

CALLA. See ZANTEDESCHIA

CALLERY PEAR. See PYRUS calleryana

CALLIANDRA

Fabaceae (Leguminosae)

EVERGREEN SHRUBS

✿ ZONES VARY BY SPECIES

☼ FULL SUN

💧 💧 WATER NEEDS VARY BY SPECIES

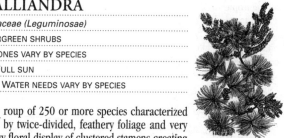

Calliandra tweedii

Group of 250 or more species characterized by twice-divided, feathery foliage and very showy floral display of clustered stamens creating a powder-puff effect. Grown as landscape plants in the Coastal and Tropical South, in greenhouses elsewhere.

C. haematocephala (C. inaequilatera). PINK POWDER PUFF, RED POWDER PUFF. Zones CS, TS. Native to Bolivia. Grows fast to 10 ft. or more with equal spread. Among the most popular large flowering shrubs in central Florida. Its beauty has carried it into areas harsher than those to which it is adapted; it will grow in the Coastal South if given special protection of overhang or warm, sunny wall. In form, it's a natural espalier. Foliage not as feathery as that of *C. tweedii;* leaflets longer, broader, and darker—glossy copper when new, turning to dark metallic green. Big puffs (2–3 in. across) of silky, watermelon pink stamens are produced in fall and winter. There is a rare white-flowered form. Needs light soil and regular water.

C. tweedii. TRINIDAD FLAME BUSH, BRAZILIAN FLAME BUSH. Best in the Tropical South. Freezes back but recovers in the Coastal South. Graceful, picturesque structure to 6–8 ft. tall, 5–8 ft. wide. Lacy, fernlike leaves, divided into many tiny leaflets, scarcely hide branches. Flower clusters show as bright crimson pompoms at branch ends, midwinter to fall. Not fussy about soil. Takes regular to little water. Prune to thin and also to retain an interesting branch pattern. Often sold as *C. guildingii.*

CALLICARPA

BEAUTYBERRY

Verbenaceae

DECIDUOUS SHRUBS

ZONES US, MS, LS, CS, EXCEPT AS NOTED

FULL SUN OR LIGHT SHADE

REGULAR TO MODERATE WATER

Callicarpa bodinieri

These graceful shrubs with arching branches are cultivated for their pleasing fruit display. Small lilac flowers in summer are followed by tight clusters of small, round, lavender to violet purple fruits persisting into winter. Plants bloom and fruit on new wood, so prune in spring. In very cold winters, plants may freeze to the ground, but they come back from roots. Beautyberry is effective in woodland gardens or massed in shrub borders.

C. americana. AMERICAN BEAUTYBERRY. Zones MS, LS, CS. To 6 ft. tall, with leaves to 6 in. long that turn yellowish in fall. Fruits are purple. Biggest, coarsest foliage of the species listed here.

C. bodinieri. BODINIER BEAUTYBERRY. Grows to 6 ft. or more, with willowlike leaves to 5 in. long that turn purple in fall. Berries are violet. 'Profusion' is a heavy-fruiting selection.

C. dichotoma. PURPLE BEAUTYBERRY. To 4–5 ft. tall and slightly wider in sun (as tall as 8 ft. in shade), with slender branches sweeping the ground. Lilac purple berries. Resembles a finer-textured *C. bodinieri.* Leaves to 3 in. long. *C. d. albifructus* is a white-fruited form. The best, most refined beautyberry for the home garden.

C. japonica. JAPANESE BEAUTYBERRY. Upright, to 3–5 ft., with pink flowers, purple fruits. Leaves to 5 in. long; fall color varies from yellowish to deep reddish purple. 'Leucocarpa' has white fruits.

CALLIOPSIS. See COREOPSIS tinctoria

CALLIRHOE

WINE CUPS, POPPY MALLOW

Malvaceae

PERENNIALS AND ANNUALS

ZONES US, MS, LS

FULL SUN

MODERATE TO LITTLE WATER

Callirhoe involucrata

Thick, fleshy root produces a spreading plant with roundish, deeply cut leaves and quantities of cupped flowers during hot weather. Needs superb drainage but survives in infertile soil and intense heat. Useful on hot slopes or in areas that get little attention.

C. involucrata. Perennial. To 6 in. tall by 2–3 ft. wide. Flowers 2 in. across, purplish red.

C. leicocarpa. Annual. To 6 in. tall. Flowers pale pink, white, and rose.

CALLISTEMON

BOTTLEBRUSH

Myrtaceae

EVERGREEN SHRUBS OR TREES

ZONES CS (WARMER PARTS), TS

FULL SUN

REGULAR TO MODERATE WATER

Callistemon citrinus

Fast-growing plants native to Australia. Colorful flowers, carried in dense spikes or round clusters, consist principally of long, bristlelike stamens—hence the common name "bottlebrush." Flowers followed by persistent woody capsules that sometimes look like bands of beads pressed into bark. Plants often severely damaged at 20°F.

C. citrinus (C. lanceolatus). LEMON BOTTLEBRUSH. Most commonly grown bottlebrush; most tolerant of heat, cold, and adverse soils. Massive shrub to 10–15 ft., but with staking and pruning in youth easily trained into narrowish, round-headed, 20–25-ft. tree. Garden centers offer it as shrub, espalier, or tree. Narrow, 3-in.-long leaves coppery when new, green at maturity. Bruised leaves smell lemony. Bright red, 6-in.-long brushes attract hummingbirds, appear in cycles throughout the year.

Variable plant when grown from seed. Cutting-grown selections with good flower size and color include 'Improved' and 'Splendens'. 'Compacta' makes a 4-ft. mound with smaller spikes. 'Violaceus' ('Jeffersii'), to 6 ft. tall and 4 ft. wide, has stiffer branching, narrower, shorter leaves, and reddish purple flowers fading to lavender. 'Mauve Mist' has the same flower color but grows taller, to about 10 ft.

C. rigidus. STIFF BOTTLEBRUSH. Erect, sparse, rigid shrub or small tree to 20 ft. with 10-ft. spread. Leaves sharp pointed, gray green (sometimes purplish). Red flower brushes 2½–4½ in. long, spring and summer. Seed capsules prominent. Least graceful bottlebrush.

C. viminalis. WEEPING BOTTLEBRUSH. Shrub or small tree with pendulous branches. Fast growing to 20–30 ft. with 15-ft. spread. Leaves narrow, light green, 6 in. long. Bright red brushes late spring into summer, scattered bloom throughout year. As with tree, needs staking, thinning of surplus branches to prevent tangled, top-heavy growth. Leaves tend to grow only at ends of long, hanging branches. 'Little John' is a superior dwarf form, 3 ft. tall and wide, with dense growth pattern and blood red flowers in fall, winter, spring. 'Captain Cook' is a dense, rounded form to 6 ft. high,

Callistemon viminalis

suitable for border, low hedge, screen. 'McCaskillii' is denser than others, more vigorous (to 20 ft. tall), and better in flower color and form.

CALONYCTION aculeatum. See IPOMOEA alba

CALTHA palustris

MARSH MARIGOLD

Ranunculaceae

PERENNIAL

ZONES US, MS, LS

SUN OR SHADE

BOG OR MARSH PLANT IN NATURE

SAP IS AN IRRITANT

Caltha palustris

Native to eastern U.S., Europe, Asia. To 2 ft. tall. Well adapted to edges of pools, ponds, streams, other moist situations. With sufficient water it can be grown in borders; good with bog irises, moisture-loving ferns. Green leaves 2–7 in. across, rounded with a heart-shaped base. Vivid yellow flowers are 2 in. across, in clusters. Lush, glossy foliage gives an almost tropical effect. Plant is vigorous; increase by divisions or sow seed in boggy soil. There is a double-flowered form.

Calycanthaceae. The calycanthus family contains shrubs with paired opposite leaves and flowers that somewhat resemble small water lilies—each bloom has an indefinite number of segments not easily defined as petals or sepals. Typical examples are sweetshrub (*Calycanthus*) and wintersweet (*Chimonanthus praecox*).

CALYCANTHUS

Calycanthaceae

DECIDUOUS SHRUBS

✓ ZONES US, MS, LS

☼ ◑ ● SUN OR SHADE

● REGULAR WATER

✿ SEEDS CAN PRODUCE CONVULSIONS

Calycanthus floridus

Deciduous shrubs, represented here by two U.S. natives. Both of these are bulky plants with lush foliage and flowers worthwhile for their fragrance and form.

🏛 **C. floridus.** COMMON SWEETSHRUB, CAROLINA ALLSPICE. Native Virginia to Florida. Stiffly branched to 6–10 ft. tall and as wide or wider. Suckering, fast spreading. Leaves are oval, to 5 in., glossy dark green above, grayish green beneath. Plant blooms most heavily April–May, and then sporadically to July. Flowers are reddish brown, 2 in. wide, often with heady strawberry fragrance. Blossoms are carried at ends of leafy branchlets. Blooms are followed by brownish, pear-shaped capsules that are very fragrant when crushed.

Plant in shrub border or around outdoor living space where its flower scent can be appreciated. Aroma varies, so buy when plants are in bloom. Selection 'Athens' has yellow flowers and an outstanding fragrance reminiscent of cantaloupe.

C. occidentalis. SPICE BUSH. Native to California. Grows to 4–12 ft. high. Leaves are 2–6 in. long and 1–2 in. wide, bright green, turning yellow in autumn. Reddish brown flowers to 2 in. across resemble small water lilies. Blossoms appear April–August, depending on the climate and the exposure. Both flowers and bruised leaves have a pleasing fragrance of old wine barrel. Shrub can be trained into a multistemmed small tree but is most useful as a background shrub or medium to tall screen. Easily grown from seed.

CALYLOPHUS

Onagraceae

PERENNIALS

✓ ZONES US, MS, LS

☼ ◑ FULL SUN OR PARTIAL SHADE

◔ MODERATE WATER

Calylophus hartwegii

Evening primrose look-alikes, these perennials grow 8–15 in. tall, 2 ft. across, and spread by underground rhizomes. Flowers appear over a long season, from spring well into fall. Plants are dormant in winter, when stems can be cut back.

C. hartwegii has pale yellow, 1-in. flowers. *C. drummondii* spreads less rapidly and has golden yellow blooms. Flowers of both species fade to orange pink. Remove old flowers and water during summer to prolong bloom period.

CAMASSIA

CAMASS

Liliaceae

BULBS

✓ ZONES US, MS, LS

☼ FULL SUN

◔ ◑ AMPLE WATER DURING GROWTH AND BLOOM

Camassia quamash

Starlike, slender-petaled blossoms are carried on spikes in late spring, early summer; grasslike basal leaves dry quickly after bloom. Plant in moist situation, fairly heavy soil, where bulbs can remain undisturbed for many years. Set bulbs 4 in. deep, 6 in. apart. To avoid premature sprouting, plant after weather cools in fall.

C. cusickii. Dense clusters of pale blue flowers on stems 2–3 ft. tall.

C. leichtlinii. Large, handsome clusters of creamy white flowers on stems 2–4 ft. tall. 'Alba' has whiter flowers than species; 'Blue Danube' is attractive blue form, 2½–3 ft. tall; 'Plena' has greenish yellow double blooms; 'Semiplena' has cream white semidouble flowers.

C. quamash (C. esculenta). Loose clusters of deep blue flowers on 1–2-ft. stems; flowers of 'Orion' are deeper blue, those of 'San Juan Form' deeper still.

C. scilloides. WILD HYACINTH. Native to Texas, north to Canada, east to Appalachians. Lightly fragrant flowers on 5–7-in. spikes, from pale lavender to violet or white, on 6-in.–2-ft. stems. Not striking unless planted in masses, among green grasses, or against green background.

CAMELLIA

Theaceae

EVERGREEN SHRUBS OR SMALL TREES

✓ ZONES US (MILDER PARTS, PROTECTED), MS, LS, CS

◑ BEST OUT OF STRONG SUN, EXCEPT AS NOTED

◔ ◑ REGULAR TO MODERATE WATER

Camellia hiemalis

Native to eastern and southern Asia. More than 3,000 named kinds exist; their range in color, size, and form is quite remarkable.

If you live in traditional camellia country, you are already aware of these splendid shrubs. If you live in the Upper South, take heart; although a few of the hardiest *C. japonica* selections noted here can be grown there if given careful attention to proper siting and winter protection, the newer hardy hybrids (see page 163) from *C. oleifera* are a safer choice.

The following pages briefly discuss the cultural requirements of camellias and describe some of the lesser-known species as well as the widely distributed old favorites and new selections. The plant descriptions include the unique cultural needs of species and selections; general cultural requirements appear below.

Camellias need well-drained soil rich in organic material. Never plant camellias so trunk base is below soil line, and never permit soil to wash over and cover this base. Keep roots cool with 2-in.-thick mulch.

These make outstanding container plants—especially in wooden tubs and barrel halves. As a general rule, plant gallon-size camellias into 12–14-in.-wide tubs, 5-gallon ones into 16–18-in. tubs. Fill with a planting mix containing 50 percent or more organic material.

Camellias thrive and bloom best when sheltered from strong, hot sun and drying winds, though some species and selections are more sun tolerant than others. Tall old plants in old gardens prove that camellias can thrive in full sun when they are mature enough to have roots shaded by heavy canopy of leaves. Young plants will grow better and bear more attractive flowers if grown under partial shade of tall trees, under lath cover, or on north side of a building. A few camellias need shade at any age.

Give regular to moderate water. Established plants (over 3 years old and vigorous) can survive on natural rainfall. Fertilize with a commercial

C

acid plant food; read fertilizer label for complete instructions. Don't use more than called for. Better to cut amounts in half and feed twice as frequently. Don't feed sick plants. Poor drainage and excessive salts in water or soil are the main troublemakers. Best cure is to move plant into raised bed of pure ground bark or peat moss until it recovers.

Scorched or yellowed areas in center of leaves are usually due to sunburn. Burned leaf edges, excessive leaf drop, or corky spots usually indicate overfertilizing. Yellow leaves with green veins are signs of chlorosis; check drainage, leach, and treat with iron or iron chelates.

One disease may be serious: camellia petal blight. Flowers rapidly turn ugly brown. Browning at edges of petals (especially whites and pale pinks) may be caused by sun or wind, but if brown rapidly runs into center of flower, suspect petal blight. Sanitation is the best control. Pick up all fallen flowers and petals, pick off all infected flowers from plants, and dispose of in covered trash bin; encourage neighbors to do the same. Remove mulch, haul it away, and replace with fresh one; a deep mulch (4–5 in.) helps keep spores of fungus from reaching the air.

Some flower bud dropping may be natural phenomenon; many camellias set more buds than they can open. Bud drop can be caused by overwatering, but more often by underwatering, especially during summer. It can also be caused by spells of very low humidity.

Some kinds bear too many flowers. To get nicest display from them, remove buds in midsummer like this: From branch-end clusters remove all but one or two round flower buds (leaf buds are slender); along stems, remove enough to leave single flower bud for each 2–4 in. of branch.

Prune after flowering. Remove dead or weak wood and thin when growth is so dense that flowers have no room to open properly. Prune at will to get form you want. Shorten lower branches to encourage upright growth. Cut back top growth to flatten lanky shrubs. Make cut just above scar that terminates previous year's growth (often a slightly thickened, somewhat rough area where bark texture and color change slightly). A cut just above this point will usually force three or four dormant buds into growth.

C. hiemalis. This species includes a number of selections formerly listed as sasanquas but differing in their later and longer bloom and their heavier-textured flowers. Four good examples:

'Chansonette'. Vigorous, spreading growth. Large, bright pink, formal double flowers with frilled petals.

'Shishi-Gashira'. One of the most useful and ornamental shrubs. Low growing with arching branches that in time pile up tier on tier to make compact, dark green, glossy-leafed plant. Leaves rather small for camellia, giving medium-fine foliage texture. Flowers rose red, semidouble to double, 2–2½ in. wide, heavily borne over long season—October–March in good year. Full sun or shade.

'Showa-No-Sakae'. Faster growing, more open than 'Shishi-Gashira'; willowy, arching branches. Semidouble to double flowers of soft pink, occasionally marked with white. Try this as espalier or in hanging basket.

'Showa Supreme'. Very similar to above but has somewhat larger flowers of peony form.

🌳 **C. japonica.** COMMON CAMELLIA. Blossom of this plant is Alabama state flower. Most gardeners have *C. japonica* in mind when they mention camellias. Naturally a large shrub or small tree, but variable in size, growth rate, and habit. Hundred-year-old plants may reach 25 ft. high and as wide, but most gardeners can consider camellias to be 6–12-ft. shrubs. Many are lower growing.

Following is a list of 17 selections that are old standbys. Easily obtainable and handsome even in comparison with some of the newest introduc-

tions, they are plants for both beginners and advanced gardeners. The list specifies season of bloom as early, midseason, or late. The earliest types start blooming in November; the latest put on a show as late as May. Flower size is noted for each selection. Very large blossoms are over 5 in. across; large, 4–5 in.; medium large, 3½–4 in.; medium, 3–3½ in.; small, 2½–3 in.; and miniature, 2½ in. or less.

'Adolphe Audusson'. Midseason. Very large, dark red, semidouble flowers, heavily borne on a medium-size, symmetrical, vigorous shrub. Hardy. 'Adolphe Audusson Variegated' is identical but heavily marbled white on red.

'Alba Plena.' Early. Brought from China in 1792 and still a favorite large, white, formal double. Slow, bushy growth. Early bloom a disadvantage in cold or rainy areas. Protect flowers from rain and wind.

'Berenice Boddy'. Midseason. Medium semidouble, light pink with deeper shading. Vigorous upright growth. One of the most cold-hardy.

'Covina'. Midseason–late. Medium, rose red, semidouble to rose-form flowers on a compact plant. Highly sun tolerant.

'Daikagura'. Early–late. Large, rose red, peony-form flowers on a dense, upright bush. Very long bloom season. 'Daikagura Variegated' is similar but has rose red flowers marbled with white.

'Debutante'. Early–midseason. Medium-large, peony-form flowers of light pink. Profuse bloom. Vigorous upright growth.

'Elegans' ('Chandler'). Early–midseason. Very large anemone-form camellia with rose pink petals and smaller petals called petaloids, the latter often marked white. Slow growth and spreading, arching branches make it a natural for espalier. Stake to provide height, and don't remove main shoot; it may be very slow to resume upward growth. Also known as 'Chandleri Elegans'. A 100-year-old-plus selection that remains a favorite. Its offspring resemble it in every way except flower color: 'C. M. Wilson', pale pink; 'Shiro Chan', white, sometimes faintly marked with pink; and 'Elegans Variegated' (Chandler Variegated'), heavily marbled rose pink and white. Also available is a solid rose pink form called 'Francine'. 'Elegans Champagne' has creamy-centered white flowers. 'Elegans Splendor' is blush pink edged with white.

'Glen 40' ('Coquetti'). Midseason–late. Large formal double of deep red. One of best reds for corsages. Slow, compact, upright growth. Handsome even out of flower. Very good in containers.

'Herme' ('Jordan's Pride'). Midseason. Medium-large, semidouble flowers are pink, irregularly bordered white and streaked deep pink. Sometimes has all solid pink flowers on certain branches. Free blooming, dependable.

'Kramer's Supreme'. Midseason. Very large, deep, full peony-form flowers of deep, clear red. Some people can detect a faint fragrance. Unusually vigorous, compact, upright. Takes some sun.

'Kumasaka'. Midseason–late. Medium large, rose form to peony form, rose pink. Vigorous, compact, upright growth and remarkably heavy flower production make it choice landscape plant. Good cold-hardiness. Takes morning sun.

'Magnoliaeflora'. Midseason. Medium semidouble flowers of pale pink. Many blossoms, good cut flower. Medium grower of compact yet spreading form. Hardy.

'Mathotiana'. Midseason–late. Very large, rose form to formal double, deep crimson, sometimes with purplish cast. Vigorous, upright. Hardy.

'Mrs. Charles Cobb'. Midseason–late. Large semidouble to peony-form flowers in deep red. Freely flowering. Compact plant with dense foliage. Best in warmer areas.

'Pope Pius IX' ('Prince Eugene Napoleon'). Midseason. A cherry red, medium-large formal double. Medium, compact, upright growth.

Flower Forms of *Camellia japonica*

Single

Semidouble

Formal Double

Peony Form

Anemone Form

Rose Form

'Purity'. Late. White, medium, rose form to formal double, usually showing a few stamens. Vigorous upright plant. Late bloom often means flowers escape rain damage.

'Wildfire'. Early–midseason. Medium, semidouble, orange-red flowers. Vigorous, upright plant.

The preceding 17 are the old classics in the camellia world. The following, all introduced since 1950, may supplant them in time:

'Carter's Sunburst'. Early–late. Large to very large pale pink blooms striped deeper pink. Semidouble to peony-form to formal double flowers on medium, compact plants.

'Drama Girl'. Midseason. Huge semidouble flowers of deep salmon rose pink. Vigorous, open, pendulous growth.

'Grand Slam'. Midseason. Large to very large flowers in glowing deep red. Semidouble to peony form. There is a form with variegated flowers.

'Guilio Nuccio'. Midseason. Coral rose, very large semidouble flowers with inner petals fluted in "rabbit-ear" effect. Unusual depth and substance. Vigorous upright growth. Many consider this to be the world's finest camellia. Variegated, fringed forms are available.

'Mrs. D. W. Davis'. Midseason. Spectacular, very large, somewhat cup-shaped flowers of palest blush pink open from egg-size buds. Vigorous, upright, compact plant with very handsome broad leaves.

'Nuccio's Gem'. Midseason. Medium-large, perfectly formed full formal double, white. Strong, full, upright grower.

'Nuccio's Jewel'. Midseason–late. Large, loose to full peony-form flowers are white with pink edging on petals.

'Nuccio's Pearl'. Midseason. Medium-size, full formal double flowers are white, with a rim of deep pink outer petals.

'Silver Waves'. Early–midseason. Large, semidouble white flowers have wavy-edged petals.

'Swan Lake'. Midseason–late. Very large, white, formal double to peony-form flowers. Vigorous upright growth.

'Tiffany'. Midseason–late. Very large, warm pink flowers. Rose form to loose, irregular semidouble. Vigorous, upright shrub.

'Tom Knudsen'. Early–midseason. Medium to large dark red flowers with deeper red veining. Formal double to peony form to rose form.

C. oleifera. Large shrub or small tree to 20 ft. tall, with glossy, dark green leaves and fragrant, 2-in. white flowers in fall. Name means "oil bearing"; oil extracted from the large seeds has been used in China for cooking or as a hair conditioner. Possibly the hardiest of all camellias. A parent of hardy hybrids (see listing this page).

C. reticulata. Some of the biggest and most spectacular camellia flowers occur in this species, and likely as not they appear on some of the lankiest and least graceful plants.

Plants differ somewhat according to selection, but generally speaking they are rather gaunt and open shrubs that eventually become trees of considerable size—possibly 35–50 ft. tall. In gardens consider them 10-ft.-tall shrubs, 8 ft. wide. Leaves also variable but tend to be dull green, leathery, and strongly net-veined.

Camellia reticulata

Culture is similar to that of other camellias, except that these plants seem intolerant of heavy pruning. This, with their natural lankiness and size, makes them difficult to place in garden. They are at their best in light shade of old oaks, where they should stand alone with plenty of room to develop. Good container subjects while young, but not handsome there out of bloom. Develop better form and heavier foliage in open ground. They are less hardy than *C. japonica* (not recommended for the Upper or Middle South). In Lower South, grow in containers so you can move them into winter protection, or plant beneath overhang or near wall.

Best-known kinds have very large, semidouble flowers with deeply fluted and curled inner petals. These inner petals give great depth to flower. All bloom late winter to early spring. The following are best choices for garden use:

'Buddha'. Rose pink flower of very large size; inner petals unusually erect and wavy. Gaunt, open; fast growth.

'Butterfly Wings'. Loose, semidouble flower of great size (reported up to 9 in. across), rose pink; petals broad and wavy. Growth open, rather narrow.

'Captain Rawes'. Reddish rose pink semidouble flowers of large size. Vigorous bushy plant with good foliage. Hardiest of reticulatas.

'Chang's Temple'. True selection is large, open-centered, deep rose flower, with center petals notched and fluted. 'Cornelian' is sometimes sold as 'Chang's Temple'.

'Cornelian'. Large, deep, irregular peony-form flowers with wavy petals, rosy pink to red, heavily variegated with white. Vigorous plant with big leaves; leaves are usually marked with white. This plant is often sold as 'Chang's Temple' or as 'Lion Head'. (The true 'Lion Head' is not found in American gardens.)

'Crimson Robe'. Very large, bright red, semidouble flowers. Petals firm textured and wavy. Vigorous plant of better appearance than most reticulatas.

'Purple Gown'. Large, purplish red, peony-form to formal double flowers. Compact plant with best growth habit and foliage in the group.

'Shot Silk'. Large, loose, semidouble flowers of brilliant pink with iridescent finish that sparkles in sunlight. Fast, rather open growth.

'Tali Queen'. Very large, deep reddish pink flowers of loose semidouble form with heavily crinkled petals. Plant form and foliage very good. This plant is often sold as 'Noble Pearl'; true 'Noble Pearl' is not available in the U.S.

C. sasanqua. SASANQUA CAMELLIA. Useful broad-leafed evergreens for espaliers, ground covers, informal hedges, screening, containers, bonsai. Vary in form from upright and densely bushy to spreading and vinelike. Heights range from 1½ to 12 ft. tall. Leaves dark green, shiny, 1½–3½ in. long, a third as wide. Flowers heavily produced in autumn and early winter, short lived, rather flimsy, but so numerous that plants make a show for months. Some are lightly fragrant.

Most sasanquas tolerate much sun, and some will thrive in full hot sun if soil is right and watering is plentiful. They also take drought very well. May be slightly less cold-hardy than *C. japonica*, but garden conditions will determine survival.

'Apple Blossom'. Single white flowers blushed with pink, from pink buds. Spreading plant.

'Cleopatra'. Rose pink semidouble flowers with narrow, curving petals. Growth is erect, fairly compact. Takes clipping well. Very cold-hardy.

'Hana Jiman'. Large semidouble flowers white, edged pink. Fast, open growth; good espalier.

'Jean May'. Large double, shell pink. Compact, upright grower with exceptionally glossy foliage.

'Kanjiro'. Large semidouble flowers of rose pink shading to rose red at petal edges. Erect growth habit.

'Mine-No-Yuki' ('White Doves'). Large, white, peony-form double. Drops many buds. Spreading, willowy growth; effective espalier.

'Momozono-Nishiki'. Large semidouble flowers are rose, shaded white. Twisted petals.

'Narumigata'. Large, single, cupped flowers, white tinged pink.

'Setsugekka'. Large, white, semidouble flowers with fluted petals. Considerable substance to flowers; cut sprays hold well in water. Shrub's growth is upright and rather bushy.

'Tanya'. Deep rose pink single flowers. Tolerates much sun. Good ground cover.

'Yuletide'. Profusion of small, single, bright red flowers on dense, compact, upright plant.

C. sinensis (Thea sinensis). TEA PLANT. Dense, round shrub to 15 ft. with leathery, dull, dark green leaves to 5 in. long. Grown commercially in Asia, but an ornamental in the U.S. Fall flowers white, small (1½ in. across), and fragrant. Takes well to pruning and can be trimmed as a hedge. Somewhat more cold-hardy than *C. japonica*.

Hardy hybrids. Dr. William Ackerman, National Arboretum, Washington, D.C., and Dr. Clifford Parks, University of North Carolina, Chapel Hill, bred a number of species, notably the hardy *C. oleifera* to produce hardy camellias. These hybrids withstand temperatures as low as −15°F with little or no damage, provided they have some shelter from winter sun and wind. Bear 3½–4-in. flowers, October–November. Selections include 'Polar Ice' and 'Snow Flurry', white, anemone form; 'Winter's Charm', pink, peony form; 'Winter's Dream', pink, semidouble; 'Winter's Star', lavender pink, single; and 'Winter's Waterlily', white, formal double. ▶

April Series of hardy camellias developed by Camellia Forest Nursery, Chapel Hill, North Carolina, includes 'April Dawn', variegated pink and white, formal form; 'April Rose', double rose red, formal form; 'April Snow', double white, rose form; and 'April Tryst', bright red, anemone form.

CHOCOLATE CAMELLIA LEAVES

Camellia leaves make perfect "molds" for a pretty dessert garnish. Spread melted semisweet chocolate over undersides of washed, dried leaves; refrigerate or freeze until chocolate is hard, then carefully peel off leaves. Keep chocolate leaves chilled or frozen until you're ready to use them.

CAMPANULA

BELLFLOWER

Campanulaceae (Lobeliaceae)

MOSTLY PERENNIALS; SOME BIENNIALS OR ANNUALS

☀ ZONES US, MS, LS

☼ ◐ TOLERATE FULL SUN IN COOLEST AREAS

◖◗ REGULAR TO MODERATE WATER

Campanula persicifolia

Vast and varied group (nearly 300 species) encompassing trailers, creeping or tufted miniatures, and erect kinds 1–6 ft. tall. Flowers generally bell shaped, but some star shaped, cup shaped, or round and flat. Usually blue, lavender, violet, purple, or white; some pink. Bloom period from spring to fall.

Uses are as varied as the plants. Gemlike miniatures deserve special settings—close-up situations in rock gardens, niches in dry walls, raised beds, containers. Trailing kinds are ideal for hanging pots or baskets, wall crevices; vigorous spreading growers serve well as ground covers. Upright growers are valuable in borders, for cutting, occasionally in containers.

In general, campanulas grow best in good, well-drained soil and the cooler climates of the Upper and Middle South. Most species are fairly easy to grow from seed sown in flats in spring or early summer, transplanted to garden in fall for bloom the following year; also may be increased by cuttings or divisions. Divide clumps in fall every 3 or 4 years; some may need yearly division.

C. carpatica (C. turbinata). TUSSOCK BELLFLOWER. Perennial. Compact plant, leafy tufts, stems branching and spreading. About 8 in. tall but may reach 1–1½ ft. Leaves smooth, bright green, wavy, toothed, 1–1½ in. long. Flowers, 1–2 in. across, open to bell or cup shapes, single, blue or white. Blooms late spring. Use in rock gardens, borders, edging. 'Blue Chips' and 'White Chips' are good dwarf selections. Easily grown from seed; sometimes sold as 'Blue Clips', 'White Clips'.

C. glomerata. Perennial. Upright, with erect side branches to 1–2 ft. Basal leaves broad, wavy edged; stem leaves broad, toothed. Both somewhat hairy. Narrow, bell-shaped flowers, 1 in. long, blue violet, tightly clustered at stem tops. Summer bloom. Plant in shaded borders. Seed-grown strains Superba and Alba are deepest purple and white, respectively. 'Joan Elliott' is deep violet blue.

C. lactiflora. Perennial. Erect, branching, to 3½–5 ft. tall. Leaves oblong, toothed, 2–3 in. long. Flowers broadly bell shaped to star shaped, 1 in. long, white to pale blue in drooping clusters at ends of branches. Summer bloom. Plant in back of borders in sun or partial shade. Endures even dry shade and is long lived. 'Loddon Anna' has pale pink flowers.

C. persicifolia. PEACH-LEAFED BLUEBELL. Perennial. Strong-growing, slender, erect stems. Plants leafy at base; 2–3 ft. tall. Basal leaves smooth-edged, green, 4–8 in. long; stem leaves 2–4 in. long, shaped like leaves of peach tree. Open, cup-shaped flowers in blue, pink, or white, about 1 in. across, held erect on short side shoots or sturdy stems, bloom in summer.

SOUTHERN HERITAGE PLANTS
IDENTIFIED BY SYMBOL ⌂

Choice plants for borders. Easy to grow from seed sown in late spring. Long-time favorite 'Telham Beauty' has 3-in. blue flowers. 'Blue Gardenia' and 'White Pearl' have double flowers.

Campanulaceae. The campanula, or bellflower, family contains perennials and biennials, typically with bell-shaped or saucer-shaped flowers in shades of blue to purple, lilac, and white. This family includes plants formerly grouped under Lobeliaceae.

CAMPERNELLE JONQUIL. See NARCISSUS odorus

CAMPHOR TREE. See CINNAMOMUM camphora

CAMPSIS

TRUMPET CREEPER, TRUMPET VINE

Bignoniaceae

DECIDUOUS VINES

☀ ZONES VARY BY SPECIES

☼ ◐ FULL SUN OR PARTIAL SHADE

◖◗ REGULAR TO MODERATE WATER

Campsis radicans

Vigorous climbers that cling to wood, brick, and stucco surfaces with aerial rootlets. Unless thinned, old plants sometimes become top-heavy and pull away from supporting surface. Spreads by suckering roots. If you try to dig up suckers, any remaining piece of root will grow another plant. Vine can be trained as big shrub or flowering hedge after first year's growth. Use for quick summer screen. All produce open, arching sprays of trumpet-shaped flowers in summer.

C. grandiflora (Bignonia chinensis). CHINESE TRUMPET CREEPER. Zones LS, CS. Not as vigorous, large, or hardy as the American native *C. radicans*, but with slightly larger, more open scarlet flowers. Leaves divided into seven to nine leaflets, each 2½ in. long. 'Morning Calm' has peach-colored flowers.

⌂ **C. radicans (Bignonia radicans).** COMMON TRUMPET CREEPER. All zones. Native to Southeast. Leaves divided into 9 to 11 toothed leaflets, each 2½ in. long. Flowers, growing in clusters of 6–12, are 3-in.-long orange tubes with scarlet lobes that flare to 2 in. wide. Grows fast to 40 ft. or more, bursting with health and vigor. Blossoms of 'Flava' are yellow to pale orange.

C. tagliabuana. HYBRID TRUMPET CREEPER. All zones. Hybrid between two above species. 'Mme Galen', best-known selection, has attractive salmon red flowers. 'Crimson Trumpet' bears pure red blooms.

CANARY ISLAND DATE PALM. See PHOENIX canariensis

CANDLE DELPHINIUM. See DELPHINIUM elatum

CANDLESTICK SENNA. See CASSIA alata

CANDYTUFT. See IBERIS

⌂ CANNA

Cannaceae

TUBEROUS-ROOTED PERENNIALS

☀ ZONES LS, CS, TS; OR DIG AND STORE

☼ FULL SUN

◖◗ AMPLE WATER DURING GROWTH AND BLOOM

Canna

Native to tropics, subtropics. Old Southern favorite. Plants add a tropical touch. Large, rich green to bronzy red leaves resemble those of banana *(Musa)* or ti *(Cordyline terminalis)*. Spikes of large, showy, irregularly shaped flowers bloom on 3–6-ft. stalks in summer, fall. Many kinds in a wide range of sizes and shapes, in near-white, ivory, yellow, orange, pink, apricot, coral, salmon, and red.

Bicolors include 'Cleopatra', with flowers strikingly streaked and spotted red on yellow, and 'Yellow King Humbert', with bright yellow flowers spotted with crimson.

Low-growing strains include 'Ambrosia' (2–2½ ft.), 'Bankock Yellow' (2 ft.), 'China Lady' (2–3 ft.), 'Eureka' (4 ft.), 'Grand Opera' (2 ft.), 'Pfitzer's Chinese Coral' (2½ ft.), 'Pfitzer's Crimson Beauty' (2 ft.), 'Pfitzer's Dwarf' (2½–3 ft.), 'Pfitzer's Primrose Yellow' (2–2½ ft.), 'Pfitzer's Salmon Pink' (2½ ft.), 'Seven Dwarfs' (1½ ft.), and 'Tropical Rose' (2½ ft.). Grow 'Seven Dwarfs' from seed, and also 'Tropical Rose' from seed if you like; they'll bloom 90 days after sowing.

Some forms with variegated leaves include 6-ft. 'Bengal Tiger', green-and-yellow-striped leaves with maroon margin, bright orange flowers, will grow in standing water; 4-ft. 'Minerva', green-and-white-striped leaves, prolific red buds, yellow flowers; and 4-ft. 'Pink Sunburst', green-and-yellow-striped leaves with reddish cast, large salmon pink flowers.

Selections with dark foliage include 'Red King Humbert', with reddish bronze leaves, orange-scarlet to red flowers, and 'Wyoming', with bronze leaves with purple tint, bright orange flowers. Both are 4 ft. tall.

Most effective in groups of single colors against plain background. Grow in borders, near poolside, in large pots or tubs on terrace or patio. Leaves useful in arrangements; cut flowers do not keep well. Plant rootstocks in spring after frost danger is past, in rich, loose soil. Set 5 in. deep, 10 in. apart. Remove faded flowers after bloom. After all flower clusters have bloomed, cut stalk to ground. Can be left in ground in Lower, Coastal, and Tropical South. Elsewhere, lift tubers in fall and store over winter.

CANTALOUPE. See MELON, MUSKMELON, CANTALOUPE

CAPE FUCHSIA. See PHYGELIUS

CAPE HONEYSUCKLE. See TECOMARIA capensis

CAPE JASMINE. See GARDENIA jasminoides

CAPE MARIGOLD. See DIMORPHOTHECA

CAPE PLUMBAGO. See PLUMBAGO auriculata

CAPE PRIMROSE. See STREPTOCARPUS

Capparaceae. The caper family includes *Cleome hasslerana,* commonly known as spider flower.

Caprifoliaceae. The honeysuckle family of shrubs and vines contains many ornamentals in addition to honeysuckle *(Lonicera);* among them are *Abelia, Viburnum,* and *Weigela.*

CARDBOARD PALM. See ZAMIA furfuracea

CARDINAL FLOWER. See LOBELIA cardinalis

CARDINAL'S-GUARD. See PACHYSTACHYS coccinea

CAREX

SEDGE

Cyperaceae

PERENNIALS

ZONES US, MS, LS, CS

PART SHADE TO SHADE

CONSTANTLY MOIST SOIL

Carex buchananii

Grasslike, clumping plants grown for foliage effect in borders, rock gardens, containers, water gardens. Long, narrow evergreen leaves are often striped or oddly colored. Specialists offer many selections.

C. buchananii. LEATHER LEAF SEDGE. Curly-tipped, arching blades 2–3 ft. tall make clumps of striking reddish bronze. Use with gray foliage or with deep greens.

C. comans (C. albula). NEW ZEALAND HAIR SEDGE. Dense, finely textured clumps of narrow leaves are silvery green. Leaves, usually 1 ft. long, may reach 6 ft.; on slopes, they look like flowing water. Also sold as 'Frosty Curls'. 'Bronze' is similar but has coppery brown leaves.

C. conica 'Marginata'. A 6-in. dwarf sedge with white-margined leaves.

C. elata 'Bowles Golden'. Clumps up to 2 ft. have narrow leaves that emerge bright yellow in spring and hold some color until late summer. Needs much moisture; will grow in water.

C. flacca (C. glauca). BLUE SEDGE. Creeping perennial with blue-gray grasslike foliage 6–12 in. tall; evergreen only in mildest climates. Tolerant of many soils and irrigation schemes; best in moist soil. Not invasive; spreads slowly and can be clipped like a lawn. Endures light foot traffic, moderate shade, competition with tree roots.

C. morrowii expallida (C. m. 'Variegata'). SILVER VARIEGATED JAPANESE SEDGE. Drooping leaves striped with green and white make 1-ft. mound. Useful as edging plant; single clumps are attractive among rocks. 'Aurea-variegata' ('Goldband') has gold-striped leaves.

CARICA papaya

PAPAYA

Caricaceae

EVERGREEN TREE

ZONE TS; OR IN GREENHOUSE

BENEFITS FROM REFLECTED HEAT IN WINTER

REGULAR WATER

Carica papaya

Native to tropical America. Grows 20–25 ft. tall, with a straight trunk topped by crown of broad (to 2-ft.), fanlike, deeply lobed leaves on 2-ft.-long stems. Cream-colored flowers are inconspicuous; tree bears fruit when young. Self-fertile forms are sometimes available; otherwise, need both male and female trees to produce fruit. To get the most fruit, don't attempt to grow papaya as permanent tree. Keep a few plants coming along each year and destroy old ones. Give plants regular supply of water and fertilizer in warm weather. Grow from seeds saved from fruit, or start with purchased plants.

CARISSA'S TASTY FRUIT

Carissa macrocarpa, a plant of considerable beauty and function, also offers tasty and useful oval fruits. Pick them when they are 1–2 in. long and red. They're good eaten out of hand or in salads (skin and all). When people describe the taste, they most often use the word "cranberry." If you can pick enough at one time, you can make jelly, sauce, or pie from them. While picking, be wary of the plant's spines.

CARISSA

Apocynaceae

EVERGREEN SHRUBS

ZONE TS; SEE BELOW

TOLERATE SOME SHADE; FRUIT BEST IN SUN

REGULAR WATER

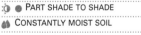

Carissa macrocarpa

Their rightful home is the Tropical South, but so many gardeners find carissas appealing that these shrubs are grown in the Coastal South—far beyond safe limits. Excellent in ocean wind, salt spray. Easy to grow. Accept variety of soils. Prune to control erratic growth.

C. edulis. Native to Africa. Differs from widely grown *C. macrocarpa* in several ways. Shrubby or somewhat vinelike to 10 ft.; will grow to 30 ft. high and as wide. Glossy, bright green, red-tinged leaves to 2 in. long. Bears large clusters of pure white, fragrant flowers, opening from pink buds. Cherry-size fruit changes from green to red to purplish black as it ripens.

C. macrocarpa (C. grandiflora). NATAL PLUM. Native to South Africa. Fast-growing, strong, upright, rounded shrub of rather loose habit to 5–7 ft. (occasionally to 18 ft.). Lustrous, leathery, rich green, 3-in. oval leaves. Spines along branches and at end of each twig. White flowers, almost as fragrant as star jasmine and of same five-petaled star shape but larger (to 2 in. wide), appear throughout year, followed by fruit. Flowers, green fruit, and ripe fruit often appear together. Use as screen or hedge. Prune heavily for formal hedges, lightly for informal screen. Strong growth, spines discourage trespassers. Don't plant near walkways, where spines can be annoying to passersby. Widely used as an oceanfront plant in Florida. If you grow Natal plum outside the Tropical South, give it the same favorite spot you'd give bougainvillea—a warm wall facing south or west, preferably with overhang to keep off frost. It may also be grown as an indoor plant in good light. Many selections are available.

'Boxwood Beauty'. Exceptionally compact growth to 2 ft. and as wide. Deep green leaves, like a large-leafed boxwood. Excellent for hedging and shaping. No thorns.

'Fancy'. Upright grower to 6 ft. Unusually large fruit, good show of flowers. Use as lightly pruned screen.

'Green Carpet'. Low growing to 1–1½ ft., spreading to 4 ft. or more. Smaller leaves than those of the species. Excellent ground cover.

'Horizontalis'. To 1½–2 ft., spreading, trailing. Dense foliage.

'Minima'. Slow growth to 1–1½ ft. tall, 2 ft. wide. Leaves and flowers both tiny.

'Prostrata'. Vigorous, to about 2 ft. and spreading. Good ground cover. Prune out growth that tends to grow upright. Can be trained as espalier.

'Ruby Point'. Upright grower to 6 ft. New leaves hold their red color through the growing season.

'Tomlinson'. Dwarf, compact growth to 2–2½ ft. high, 3 ft. wide. Shiny mahogany-tinted foliage, large flowers, wine-colored fruit. No thorns. Slow growing. Use as tub plant or for foundation plantings.

'Tuttle' ('Nana Compacta Tuttlei'). To 2–3 ft. high, 3–5 ft. wide. Compact, dense foliage. Heavy producer of flowers and fruit. Use as ground cover.

CARNATION. See DIANTHUS caryophyllus

CAROLINA ALLSPICE. See CALYCANTHUS floridus

CAROLINA BUCKTHORN. See RHAMNUS caroliniana

CAROLINA JESSAMINE. See GELSEMIUM sempervirens

CAROLINA LAUREL CHERRY. See PRUNUS caroliniana

CAROLINA MOONSEED. See COCCULUS carolinus

CAROLINA SILVER BELL. See HALESIA carolina

CARPET BUGLEWEED. See AJUGA

CARPET GRASS. See AXONOPUS affinis

CARPINUS

HORNBEAM

Betulaceae

DECIDUOUS TREES

✴ ZONES VARY BY SPECIES

☀ ◑ ● EXPOSURE NEEDS VARY BY SPECIES

💧 REGULAR WATER

These are well-behaved, relatively small shade trees. They have good habits as street trees, and are long lived. Growth rate is slow to moderate. Very hard, tough wood. Dark green, sawtooth-edged leaves color up agreeably in the Upper and Middle South, hang on late in season. Fruits

Carpinus caroliniana

(small, hard nutlets in leaflike bracts) are carried in attractive drooping clusters to 5 in. long.

C. betulus. EUROPEAN HORNBEAM. Zones US, MS, LS. Excellent landscape tree to 40 ft. tall. Dense pyramidal form, eventually becoming broad with drooping outer branches. Handsome, furrowed gray bark somewhat similar to that of *C. caroliniana*. Very clean leaves, 2–5 in. long, turn yellow or dark red in autumn. Best in full sun, but tolerates light shade. 'Fastigiata' is the selection commonly sold; though name implies very upright growth, tree develops an oval-vase shape with age.

C. caroliniana. IRONWOOD. Zones US, MS, LS, CS. Native from Nova Scotia to Minnesota, southward to Texas and Florida. Species also known as blue beech and musclewood in its native range, where it is often found at forest edges or as an understory plant along rivers and streams (in this location, it can withstand periodic flooding). Those common names refer to the tree trunk, which is blue gray and smooth, with undulations that look like muscles flexing beneath the surface. Grows to 25–30 ft. tall with round head; can be grown as single- or multitrunked tree. Leaves, 1–3 in. long, turn mottled yellow and red in fall. Drops leaves before *C. betulus*. Ironwood does well in a broad range of exposures from full sun to heavy shade. Best in natural gardens.

CARRION FLOWER. See STAPELIA

CARROT THINNINGS TO EAT

Carrot harvesting actually starts with thinning—the removal of excess seedlings when the tops are about 1–2 in. tall to make space for others to grow. Steam the tiny carrots in butter. Or chop the entire miniature plants, tops and all; add to tossed salads for a fresh surprise.

CARROT

Apiaceae (Umbelliferae)

BIENNIAL GROWN AS ANNUAL

✴ ALL ZONES

☀ FULL SUN

💧 MAINTAIN EVEN SOIL MOISTURE

Carrot

The type to plant depends on the soil's condition: Carrots reach smooth perfection only in good-textured soil free of stones and clods. Plant long market kinds, such as 'A+', 'Kuroda' (early, heat resistant), and 'Nantes Scarlet', only if you can give them a foot of this ideal, light soil. If you can provide only a few inches, plant half-long selections, such as 'Chantenay', 'Danvers Half Long' (heirloom variety, grows well in clay soil), and 'Nantes'; or short round types, such as 'Parmex', 'Planet', and 'Thumbelina'; or miniatures 'Amstel', 'Babette', Lady Finger', 'Minicor', and 'Short 'n Sweet'.

Sow thickly in rows at least 1 ft. apart. Soil should be fine enough for root development and loose enough so crusting can't check sprouting of seeds. If crust should form, keep soil soft by sprinkling. Too much nitrogen or a lot of manure will make excessive top growth and cause forking of roots. Maintain even soil moisture; alternating dry and wet conditions causes split roots. To grow successive plantings, sow seed when previous planting is up and growing; in cold-winter climates, make the last sowing 70 days before anticipated killing frost. When tops are 1–2 in. high, thin plants to 1½ in. apart; thin again if roots begin to crowd. After first thinning, apply narrow band of commercial fertilizer 2 in. out from the row. Begin harvest when carrots reach finger size, usually 30 to 40 days after sowing; most types reach maturity in 60 to 70 days. In mild-winter climates, carrots store well in the ground; dig as needed.

CARYA

PECAN, HICKORY

Juglandaceae

DECIDUOUS TREES

ZONES VARY BY SPECIES

FULL SUN

REGULAR TO MODERATE WATER

Carya illinoensis

Large trees with leaves divided featherwise into many leaflets, inconspicuous flowers, and nuts enclosed in husks that usually break away at maturity. Nuts of pecan and hickory are delicious, and the former is an important commercial crop. Trees are too large for smaller home plots but are attractive where space is available. All develop deep taproots and should be planted while young and not moved later.

C. glabra. PIGNUT HICKORY. Native to southern and eastern U.S. Zones US, MS, LS, CS. Grows to 50–60 ft., sometimes 100 ft., and has broad canopy. Leaves, 8–10 in. long, with five to nine leaflets, are retained into late fall and turn a beautiful orange, brown, and yellow, even in the Lower South. Bark is not shaggy; seeds are bitter.

C. illinoensis. PECAN. Native to southern and central U.S. While commercial nut production is largely limited to the Lower and Coastal South, hardy selections do quite well in the Upper and Middle South. Graceful, shapely tree to 70 ft. tall and equally wide. Foliage like that of English walnut but prettier, with more (11 to 17) leaflets that are narrower and longer (4–7 in.); foliage pattern is finer textured, casts less shade. Trees need well-drained, deep soils (6–10 ft. deep); won't stand salinity. Prune to shape or remove dead wood.

Papershell pecans need a 210-day growing season to ripen. 'Caddo', 'Elliot', 'Houma', 'Melrose', 'Stuart', and 'Sumner' are scab resistant and suitable for Southeast. Western papershells, recommended for drier areas of West Texas, include 'Western Schley' and 'Wichita'. Hardy northern types suitable for the southern Midwest include the prevalent 'Major' as well as 'Fritz', 'Greenriver', and 'Peruque'. Most selections need pollinators.

C. ovata. SHAGBARK HICKORY. Zones US, MS, LS, CS. Typically grows to 60–100 ft. Most conspicuous feature is bark, which is gray and shaggy, with large plates curving out and away from the trunk. The hard-shelled nuts are sweet. Autumn foliage is an attractive bright yellow. Wood is proverbially tough and hard. *C. laciniosa*, shellbark hickory, is a similar but smaller tree.

Caryophyllaceae. The pink family includes many garden annuals and perennials as well as a few weeds. Leaves are borne in opposite pairs at joints that are often swollen; leaves are often joined together at their bases. Pinks and carnations are typical representatives, along with snow-in-summer (*Cerastium*) and *Lychnis*.

CARYOPTERIS

BLUEBEARD

Verbenaceae

DECIDUOUS SHRUBS

ZONES US, MS, LS, CS

FULL SUN

MODERATE WATER

Caryopteris clandonensis

Valued for contribution of cool blue to flower borders from August to frost. Generally grown as shrubby perennials. If plant is not frozen back in winter, cut nearly to ground in spring. Cut back growth after each wave of bloom to encourage more flowers. Provide good drainage; can rot in wet soils.

C. clandonensis. BLUE MIST. Low-growing mound (to 2 ft. tall and wide) of narrow, 3-in.-long leaves. Clusters of small blue flowers top upper parts of stems. Selected forms 'Azure' and 'Heavenly Blue' have deep blue flowers. 'Dark Knight' and 'Longwood Blue' have deep blue flowers and silvery foliage. 'Worcester Gold' has yellow leaves, blue flowers.

C. incana (C. mastacanthus). BLUE SPIRAEA, COMMON BLUE-BEARD. Taller than *C. clandonensis*, with looser, more open growth to 3–4 ft. Lavender blue flowers.

CARYOTA

FISHTAIL PALM

Arecaceae (Palmae)

PALMS

ZONE TS; OR INDOORS

FULL SUN OR PARTIAL SHADE

REGULAR WATER

Caryota ochlandra

Feather palms with finely divided leaves, the leaflets flattened and split at tips like fish tails. Tender. Native to Southeast Asia, where they grow in full sun. Indoors, need as much light as possible.

C. mitis. BURMESE FISHTAIL PALM. Slow grower to 20–25 ft. Basal offshoots eventually form clustered trunks. Foliage light green. Very tender; thrives only in ideal environment.

C. ochlandra. CANTON FISHTAIL PALM. Will probably reach 25 ft. Medium dark green leaves. Hardiest of the caryotas; has survived to 26°F.

C. urens. WINE PALM. Single-stemmed palm to 100 ft. in Asia, to 15–20 ft. in Tropical South with careful protection. If temperatures go below 32°F, it's certain to die. Dark green leaves. Avoid handling fruit with bare hands; invisible crystals can cause severe itching.

CASHMERE BOUQUET. See CLERODENDRUM bungei

CASSIA

SENNA

Fabaceae (Leguminosae)

EVERGREEN OR DECIDUOUS SHRUBS AND TREES, AND PERENNIALS

ZONES VARY BY SPECIES

FULL SUN, EXCEPT AS NOTED

REGULAR TO MODERATE WATER

Cassia splendida

The following tropical flowering shrubs and trees from many lands provide numerous landscaping choices for gardeners. "Yellow" and "golden" are the words associated with cassia. Blossoms may be yellow, bright yellow, egg-yolk yellow, deep yellow gold. Flowering dates are approximate, since plants may bloom at any time or scatter bloom over a long period. Many species have been reclassified as *Senna*.

C. alata (Senna alata). CANDLESTICK SENNA. Deciduous shrub. Zone TS. Native to tropics. Grows 8–12 ft. tall and spreads wider. Golden yellow flowers (1 in. wide) in big spikelike clusters, November–January. Leaves divided into 12 to 28 leaflets 2½ in. long. Prune hard after bloom.

C. artemisioides (Senna artemisioides). FEATHERY CASSIA. Evergreen shrub. Zone TS. Native to Australia. To 3–5 ft.; attractive light, airy structure. Gray leaves divided into six to eight needlelike, 1-in.-long leaflets. Sulfur yellow, ¾-in. flowers, five to eight in a cluster, bloom January–April, often into summer. Prune lightly after flowering to eliminate heavy setting of seed. More drought tolerant than other species.

C. bicapsularis (Senna bicapsularis). Evergreen shrub. Zones CS, TS. Native to tropics. To 10 ft. Recovers after being killed to ground by frost. Yellow, ½-in.-wide flowers in spikelike clusters, October–February, if not cut short by frost. Leaflets roundish, rather thick, six to ten to a leaf. Prune severely after flowering.

C. corymbosa (Senna corymbosa). FLOWERY SENNA. Evergreen shrub. Zones CS, TS. Native to Argentina. Naturalizes. To 10 ft. Yellow flowers in rounded clusters, spring to fall. Dark green leaves with six narrow, oblong, 1–2-in. leaflets. Prune severely after flowering.

C. excelsa. CROWN OF GOLD TREE. Partially evergreen tree. Zone TS. Native to Argentina. Grows fast to 25–30 ft. Leaves divided into 10 to 20 pairs of 1-in.-long leaflets. Large bright yellow flowers in 12–16-in.-long clusters, late summer, early fall. Prune hard after flowering.

C. fistula. SHOWER OF GOLD, GOLDEN SHOWER. Deciduous or partly evergreen tree. Zone TS. To 30–40 ft., with 2-ft. leaves divided into 3-in. leaflets. Summer flowers are bright yellow, 2 in. wide, in drooping, nearly 2-ft.-long clusters of 50 or more. Prune hard after bloom. Extremely showy, but suitable only for the Tropical South.

C. leptophylla. GOLD MEDALLION TREE. Nearly evergreen tree. Zone TS. Native to Brazil. Most shapely, graceful of the cassias. Fast growing to 20–25 ft.; open headed, low spreading, tending to weep. Shape to single trunk, or plant becomes very sprawling. Leaves with up to 12 pairs of narrow leaflets. Deep yellow flowers to 3 in. wide, in 6–8-in. clusters in July–August; scattered blooms later. Prune hard after flowering.

C. lindheimeriana (Senna lindheimeriana). VELVET-LEAF SENNA. Zones LS, CS, TS. Native to Texas, Arizona, Mexico. Perennial, usually 2 ft. or less, possibly 6 ft. Velvety gray leaves. Flowers late summer and fall. Partial shade or full sun. Grows well in caliche soils. Do not overwater or it will rot. Not a good choice for high-rainfall areas.

C. marilandica (Senna marilandica). WILD SENNA. Zones US, MS, LS, CS. Unlike most of its relatives, *C. marilandica* is a perennial, dying back to the ground in winter. Grows 4–6 ft. tall. Feathery bright green leaves; tall clusters of brownish yellow flowers at stalk ends in summer.

C. splendida (Senna splendida). GOLDEN WONDER SENNA. Evergreen shrub. Zones CS, TS. Native to Brazil. This name has been applied to a number of cassias of varying growth habits. This species grows to 10–12 ft. high and about as wide. Flowers are orange yellow, 1½ in. wide, in loose clusters at branch ends, November–January. Other cassias with this name, with bright yellow flowers, are strongly horizontal in branch pattern, 5–8 ft. high, spreading to 12 ft. wide. All cassias of this name must be severely pruned after flowering.

C. wislizenii. CANYON SENNA. Deciduous shrub. Zones LS, CS, TS. Native to Texas, Southwest, Mexico. To 4–6 ft., sometimes 10 ft., with attractive arching branches. Blooms through summer. Partial shade or full sun. Prefers dry conditions.

CASTANEA

CHESTNUT
Fagaceae
DECIDUOUS TREES
✿ ZONES US, MS, LS, CS
☼ FULL SUN
💧 REGULAR WATER

Castanea mollissima

The American chestnut (*C. dentata*) has become nearly extinct as a result of chestnut blight, but other chestnuts are available. They make wonderful, dense shade trees where there is space to accommodate them and where their litter and rank-smelling pollen won't be as noticeable—in large country gardens, for example. All chestnuts have handsome dark to bright green foliage. Small, creamy white flowers in long (8–10-in.), slim catkins make an impressive display in early summer. The large edible nuts are enclosed in prickly burrs. Plant two or more kinds to ensure cross-pollination and a substantial crop. Single trees bear lightly or not at all. Somewhat drought tolerant.

C. mollissima. CHINESE CHESTNUT. Grows to 60 ft. with rounded crown that may spread to 40 ft. Leaves 3–7 in. long, with coarsely toothed

edges. Most nursery trees are grown from seed rather than from cuttings; hence, nuts are variable but generally of good quality. Tree does not tolerate alkaline soil.

Dunstan hybrid chestnuts. These are offspring of American and Chinese chestnut parents, with characteristics intermediate between the two (the American chestnut is—or was—a tall, broad timber tree with small but very sweet nuts). The hybrids seem resistant to the blight.

CASTILLEJA

INDIAN PAINTBRUSH
Scrophulariaceae
BIENNIALS, ANNUALS, PERENNIALS
✿ ZONES US, MS, LS
☼ ◐ FULL SUN OR PARTIAL SHADE
💧 WATER DURING DRY SEASON

Castilleja indivisa

Native to the Southeast, the Midwest, and Texas, Indian paintbrushes are among some of the hardest wildflowers to get established in garden conditions, but once growing, they are quite tough. Plants typically grow to 2 ft. or less. Small inconspicuous flowers appear in spring among showy fan-shaped bracts that range in color from pink and purple to yellow, orange, and flame red. Sow seeds thickly among other plants, such as grasses or perennials, because during germination these plants may be parasitic on the roots of other plants.

C. indivisa. INDIAN PAINTBRUSH. Annual or biennial. Native to southeastern Oklahoma, eastern Texas, and the Coastal Plains. Plant height varies, from 6 to 16 in. Flower spikes are 3–8 in. long, orange to red, and bloom through spring.

C. purpurea. PURPLE PAINTBRUSH. Perennial. Native to Midwest and Texas. To 9 in. tall. Flowers vary widely in color: purple, but just as often pink, red, or yellow. Also known as lemon paintbrush. Blooms late spring.

CAST-IRON PLANT. See ASPIDISTRA elatior

CASTOR ARALIA. See KALOPANAX septemlobus

CASTOR BEAN. See RICINUS communis

CASUARINA

BEEFWOOD, SHE-OAK
Casuarinaceae
EVERGREEN TREES
✿ ZONE TS
☼ FULL SUN
💧 💧 REGULAR TO LITTLE WATER

Casuarina equisetifolia

Native mostly to Australia. Long, thin, jointed, green branches look like long pine needles; true leaves are inconspicuous. Sturdy root system and ability, when damaged, to send up suckers from roots help these plants stabilize sandy soil near beaches, where tolerance of wind and salt makes them useful windbreaks as well. Also tolerate heat and wet or dry soils.

C. cunninghamiana. RIVER SHE-OAK. Tallest and largest. To 70 ft. Finest texture, with dark green branches.

C. equisetifolia. HORSETAIL TREE. Fast grower to 40–60 ft., 20 ft. wide. Has pendulous gray-green branches. This is the species widely used for oceanfront windbreaks, clipped hedges, and topiary in south Florida. Plants sold under this name may be *C. cunninghamiana* or hybrids between it and *C. glauca*.

CATALPA

Bignoniaceae

DECIDUOUS TREES

ZONES US, MS, LS, CS

FULL SUN OR LIGHT SHADE

REGULAR TO MODERATE WATER

atalpas are among the few truly deciduous trees that can compete in flower and leaf with subtropical species. Bloom in late spring and summer, bearing large, upright clusters of trumpet-shaped, 2-in.-wide flowers in pure white, striped and marked with yellow and soft brown; flowers are held above large, bold, heart-shaped leaves. Long, bean-shaped seed capsules, sometimes called Indian beans or Indian stogies, follow the blossoms.

Catalpa bignonioides

Unusually well adapted to extremes of heat and cold, and to all soils. Where winds are strong, plant in lee of taller trees or buildings to protect leaves from damage. Some gardeners object to litter of fallen flowers in summer and seed capsules in autumn. Plants need shaping while young, seldom develop a well-established dominant shoot. Shorten side branches as tree grows. When branching begins at desired height, remove lower branches.

For the tree sometimes called desert catalpa, see *Chilopsis linearis*. Another tree sometimes mistakenly called catalpa is the very similar *Paulownia tomentosa*, or empress tree, with lavender flowers. *Paulownia* shows flower buds in winter; catalpa does not.

🎵 **C. bignonioides.** COMMON CATALPA, INDIAN BEAN. Native to southeastern U.S. Generally smaller than *C. speciosa*, 20–50 ft. according to climate or soil, with somewhat smaller spread. Leaves are 5–8 in. long, often in whorls, and give off an odd odor when crushed. Chlorotic in alkaline soil. Yellow leaves of 'Aurea' are showier in the Upper South.

Catalpa bignonioides

'Nana'. UMBRELLA CATALPA. A dense globe form usually grafted high on *C. bignonioides*. Almost always sold as *C. bungei*. It never blooms. Cut it back to keep it in scale.

C. speciosa. NORTHERN CATALPA. Native to central and southern Midwest. Round headed; 40–70 ft. tall. Leaves 6–12 in. long; no odor when crushed. Fewer flowers per cluster than for *C. bignonioides*. Early training and pruning will give tall trunk and umbrella-shaped crown.

CATANANCHE caerulea

CUPID'S DART

Asteraceae (Compositae)

PERENNIAL

ZONES US, MS, LS

FULL SUN

MODERATE WATER

Catananche caerulea

turdy, free-flowering plant for summer borders and arrangements. Needs well-drained soil, not too much moisture; self-sows freely. Narrow gray-green leaves are 8–12 in. long, grow mostly at base of stem. Leafless, 2-ft. stems carry lavender blue, 2-in. flower heads reminiscent of cornflowers and surrounded by strawlike, shining bracts. Flowers dry well for everlasting bouquets. Remove faded flowers to prolong bloom. 'Alba' is white flowered.

CATHARANTHUS roseus (Vinca rosea)

MADAGASCAR PERIWINKLE

Apocynaceae

ANNUAL SOMETIMES GROWN AS PERENNIAL

ALL ZONES

FULL SUN OR PARTIAL SHADE

MODERATE WATER

Catharanthus roseus

rought resistant and showy, blooms continuously in hot weather. Glossy leaves 1–3 in. long cover bushy plant 1–2 ft. high. Phloxlike flowers 1½ in. wide in pure white, white with rose or red eye, blush pink, clear cotton-candy pink, or bright rose. The Little series grows 8–10 in. high. Pacific and Cooler series are compact, 15-in. plants with large (2-in. or wider) flowers. The Tropicana series is early blooming (60 days from seed). Creeping strains, including the Carpet series, grow 4–8 in. tall and 1½ ft. wide. All types will bloom first season from seed sown early indoors, in greenhouse or cold frame. Garden centers sell plants in late spring.

Blooms all summer and keeps flowering after zinnias and marigolds have gone, until Thanksgiving if weather stays mild. Lives over in frost-free areas but may look ragged in winter. Self-sows readily. Provide good drainage and avoid overwatering. Susceptible to wilt disease and rot if planted in heavy, wet soil.

> **USEFUL IN MORE WAYS THAN ONE**
>
> Madagascar periwinkle is a workhorse in the garden, bearing its colorful blooms over a long season and outlasting other summer annuals. It doesn't even need deadheading to keep the show going; the blossoms drop cleanly on their own. The plant's usefulness goes beyond the garden: In the 1950s, its alkaloids were discovered to be valuable in treating leukemia.

CATMINT. See NEPETA faassenii

CATNIP. See NEPETA cataria

CAT'S CLAW. See MACFADYENA unguis-cati

CATTLEYA

Orchidaceae

EPIPHYTIC ORCHIDS

ZONE TS; OR GREENHOUSE OR INDOOR PLANTS

LIGHT SHADE

REGULAR WATER

ative to tropical America. Most popular and best known of orchids. Showy flowers are used for corsages.

Species, selections, hybrids are too numerous to list here. All have pseudobulbs, 1–3 in. thick, bearing leathery leaves and a stem topped with

Cattleya

one to four or more flowers. Plants range from a few inches tall to 2 ft. or more. Commercial growers offer wide range of flower colors—lavender and purple; white; semialbas (white with colored lip), including some novelties such as yellow, orange, red, green, bronze (many of these are crosses between *Cattleya* and other genera).

In mildest parts of Florida and Texas, potted plants are often left on terraces or under trees year-round; in central Florida, they should be brought indoors during the few cold nights. Indoors, cattleyas grow best in greenhouse where temperature, humidity, and light can be readily controlled. However, they can be grown as house plants. The main requirements: (1) warm temperature (60°F at night, 70°F or higher during the day);

(2) relatively high humidity (50–60 percent or more); (3) good light (20–40 percent of outside light with protection from hot midday sun). Color of orchid foliage should be light green, and leaves should be erect. When light intensity is too low, leaves turn dark green and new growth becomes soft. Also see Orchidaceae.

CAULIFLOWER

Brassicaceae (Cruciferae)

ANNUAL OR BIENNIAL GROWN AS ANNUAL

✎ ALL ZONES

☼ FULL SUN

💧 REGULAR WATER

Cauliflower

R elated to broccoli and cabbage; has similar cultural requirements but is more difficult to grow. Easiest in the Upper South. Elsewhere grow it to harvest well before or well after midsummer; also look for heat-tolerant kinds. Home gardeners usually plant one of the several 'Snowball' selections or hybrids such as 'Early White Hybrid' and 'Snow Crown Hybrid'. An unusual type is 'Purple Head', a large plant with a deep purple head that turns green in cooking. 'Romanesco' makes cone-shaped heads of light green flowerets that are less tightly packed than those of other cauliflowers. Considered to have a fine flavor.

Grow cauliflower like broccoli. Start with small plants; space them 1½–2 ft. apart in rows and leave 3 ft. between rows. Be sure to keep plants actively growing; any check during transplanting or later growth is likely to cause premature setting of undersize heads. When heads first appear, tie up the large leaves around them to keep them white. On self-blanching types, leaves curl over developing heads without assistance. Harvest heads as soon as they reach full size. Most kinds are ready in 50 to 100 days after transplanting; overwintering types may take 6 months. Cauliflower is subject to same pests as cabbage.

CEDAR. See CEDRUS

CEDAR, EASTERN RED. See JUNIPERUS virginiana

CEDAR OF LEBANON. See CEDRUS libani

CEDRUS

CEDAR

Pinaceae

EVERGREEN TREES

✎ ZONES VARY BY SPECIES

☼ FULL SUN

💧 MODERATE WATER

Cedrus atlantica

T hese conifers, the true cedars, are stately specimen trees that look best when given plenty of room. Needles are borne in tufted clusters. Cone scales, like those of firs, fall from tree, leaving a spiky core behind. Male catkins produce prodigious amounts of pollen that may cover you with yellow dust on a windy day. Plant in deep, well-drained soil. All species are deep rooted and drought tolerant once established.

C. atlantica (C. libani atlantica). ATLAS CEDAR. Zones US, MS. Native to North Africa. Slow to moderate growth to 60 ft. or more. Open, angular in youth. Branches usually get too long and heavy on young trees unless tips are pinched or cut back. Growth naturally less open with age. Less spreading than other true cedars, but still needs 30-ft. circle.

Needles, less than 1 in. long, are bluish green. Selections include: 'Aurea', needles with yellowish tint; 'Glauca', silvery blue; 'Glauca Pendula', weeping form with blue needles; 'Pendula', vertically drooping branches. Untrained, spreading, informally branching plants are sold as "rustics." All types stand up well to hot, humid weather.

C. deodara. DEODAR CEDAR. Zones MS, LS, CS, protected sites in US. (In Upper South, best bet is an extra-hardy selection such as 'Shalimar'.) Native to the Himalayas. Fast growing to 80 ft., with 40-ft. spread at ground level. Lower branches sweep down to ground, then upward. Upper branches openly spaced, graceful. Nodding tip identifies it in skyline. Softer, lighter texture than other cedars. Planted in small lawn, it soon overpowers area. You can control spread of tree by cutting new growth of side branches halfway back in late spring. This pruning also makes tree more dense.

Although deodars sold by garden centers are very similar in form, many variations occur in a group of seedlings—from scarecrowlike forms to compact low shrubs. Needles, to 2 in. long, may be green or have blue, gray, or yellow cast. The following three variations are propagated by cuttings or grafting: 'Aurea', with yellow new foliage turning golden green in summer; 'Descanso Dwarf' ('Compacta'), a slow-growing form reaching 15 ft. in 20 years; and 'Pendula' ('Prostrata'), which grows flat on ground or will drape over rock or wall. Deodar cedar can be pruned to grow as spreading low or high shrub. Annual late-spring pruning will keep it in the shape you want. This is the best species for hot, humid climates.

Cedrus deodara

C. libani. CEDAR OF LEBANON. Zones US, MS. Native to Asia Minor. To 80 ft., but slow—to 15 ft. in 15 years. Variable in habit. Usually a dense, narrow pyramid in youth. Spreads picturesquely as it matures to become majestic skyline tree with long horizontal arms and irregular crown. In young trees, needles, less than 1 in. long, are brightest green of the cedars; in old trees, they are dark gray green. Rather scarce and expensive because of time it requires to reach salable size. Routine garden care. No pruning needed. 'Sargentii' ('Pendula Sargentii') grows even more slowly, has a short trunk and crowded, pendulous branches; choice container or rock garden plant. 'Pendula' is a weeping form.

C. l. stenocoma. Zones US, MS. Hardiest of the cedars. More stiffly branched than species, with good green color.

CELANDINE POPPY. See STYLOPHORUM diphyllum

Celastraceae. This family of evergreen or deciduous woody plants has undistinguished flowers, but fruit is often brightly colored. Bittersweet (*Celastrus*) and *Euonymus* are examples.

CELASTRUS

BITTERSWEET

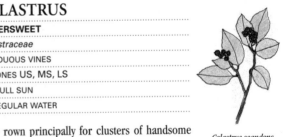

Celastraceae

DECIDUOUS VINES

✎ ZONES US, MS, LS

☼ FULL SUN

💧 REGULAR WATER

Celastrus scandens

G rown principally for clusters of handsome summer fruit—yellow to orange capsules that split open to display brilliant red-coated seeds inside. Branches bearing fruit are much prized for indoor arrangements. Since birds seem uninterested in fruit, display extends into winter. To get fruit, you need a male plant near the female; self-fertile forms of *C. orbiculatus* are available.

Vigorous and twining with ropelike branches; need support. Will become tangled mass of intertwining branches unless pruned constantly. Cut out fruiting branches in winter; pinch out tips of vigorous branches in summer.

C. orbiculatus. ORIENTAL BITTERSWEET. To 30–40 ft. Leaves roundish, toothed, to 4 in. Fruit on short side shoots is partially obscured until leaves drop. Foliage may turn an attractive yellow in fall. A very aggressive grower that has escaped gardens and become a weed in the Upper South.

C. rosthornianus (C. loeseneri). LOESENER BITTERSWEET. Grows to 20 ft. Dark green, oval leaves to 5 in. long. Fruit heavily borne. Similar to *C. orbiculatus* but not as rampant.

C. scandens. AMERICAN BITTERSWEET. Native to eastern U.S. To 20 ft.; even higher if plant has something to grow on. If allowed to climb shrubs or small trees, it can kill them by girdling the stems. Leaves very light green, oval, toothed, to 4 in. Fruit in scattered dense clusters is held above leaves, looks showy before foliage falls.

CELOSIA

Amaranthaceae

ANNUALS

✂ ALL ZONES

☼ FULL SUN

💧 MODERATE WATER

Celosia 'Cristata'

Richly colored tropical plants, some with flower clusters in bizarre shapes. Although attractive in cut arrangements with other flowers, in gardens celosias are most effective by themselves. Dry cut blooms for winter bouquets. Sow seed in place in late spring or early summer, or set out started plants.

C. argentea. COCKSCOMB. Two kinds of cockscombs are derived from this species, which has silvery white flowers and narrow leaves to 2 in. or longer. One group, the plume cockscombs (often sold as *C.* 'Plumosa'), has plumy flower clusters. Some of these (sometimes sold as Chinese woolflower or *C.* 'Childsii'), have flower clusters that look like tangled masses of yarn. Flowers come in brilliant shades of pink, orange red, gold, crimson. You can get 2½–3-ft.-high forms or dwarf, more compact selections. The latter grow about 1 ft. high and bear heavily branched plumes.

The other group is the crested cockscombs (often sold as *C.* 'Cristata'). These have velvety, fan-shaped flower clusters, often much contorted and fluted. Flowers are yellow, orange, crimson, purple, and red. Tall kinds grow to 3 ft., dwarf types to 10 in. high.

C. spicata. WHEAT CELOSIA. Plant is covered in small silvery pink and purple spikes; it looks like a tall wild grass with elegant flowers. Ideal for a natural planting or rock garden and good for drying. Reseeds readily. Stems to 3½ ft. Selections include 'Flamingo Feather' (soft pink to white), 'Flamingo Purple' (purple spikes and dark reddish green leaves) 'Pink Candle' (rose pink spikes).

CELTIS

HACKBERRY

Ulmaceae

DECIDUOUS TREES

✂ ZONES US, MS, LS

☼ ◐ FULL SUN OR PARTIAL SHADE

💧 MODERATE WATER

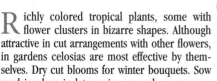

Celtis occidentalis

Related to elms and similar to them in most details, but smaller. All have virtue of deep rooting; old trees in narrow planting strips expand in trunk diameter and nearly fill strips without surface roots or any sign of heaving the sidewalk or curb. Good choice for street or lawn tree, even near buildings or paving. Canopy casts moderate shade in spring and summer; leaves turn yellow in fall. Mature trees have picturesque gray bark with corky warts and ridges. Small berrylike fruit attracts birds.

Hackberry is exceptionally tough, taking strong winds (stake young trees until well established), dry heat, and dry, alkaline soils. Bare-root plants, especially in larger sizes, sometimes fail to leaf out. Buy in containers or try for small bare-root trees with big root systems.

C. laevigata. SUGARBERRY, SUGAR HACKBERRY. Native to southern Midwest and South. Grows to 60 ft. or more, with rounded crown. Similar to *C. occidentalis,* but resistant to witches'-broom (ugly clusters of dwarfed twigs). A desirable street or park tree.

C. occidentalis. COMMON HACKBERRY. Native from Rocky Mountains to the Atlantic, north to Quebec and south to Alabama. Grows to form rounded crown 50 ft. high or more and nearly as wide. Branches are spreading and sometimes pendulous. Leaves oval, light green, 2–5 in. long, finely toothed on edges. Tree leafs out fairly late. Withstands urban pollution. Widely used in plains and prairie states, since it endures adverse conditions, including extreme cold, winds, soggy soil. Sometimes disfigured by witches'-broom.

CENIZO. See LEUCOPHYLLUM frutescens

CENTAUREA

Asteraceae (Compositae)

PERENNIALS AND ANNUALS

✂ ZONES VARY BY SPECIES

☼ FULL SUN

💧 MODERATE WATER, EXCEPT AS NOTED

Centaurea cineraria

Out of some 500 species, only a dozen or so are widely cultivated. Of these, annuals are grown mainly for cut flowers; perennial kinds are used principally for soft, silvery foliage. All are relatively easy to grow. For best performance, add lime to acid soils. Sow seeds of annuals or set out plants of perennial kinds in spring (or in fall, in mild-winter areas).

C. americana. BASKET FLOWER. Annual. All zones. Native to central and southwestern U.S. Grows to 5–6 ft. high, with rather rough, oval leaves to 4 in. long. Flower heads to 4 in. wide are rose pink, paler toward center. Good in arrangements, fresh or dried.

C. cineraria (C. candidissima). DUSTY MILLER. Perennial in Zones LS, CS, TS; annual anywhere. (This common name applies to many plants with whitish to silvery white foliage.) Compact plant grows to 1 ft. or more. Velvety white leaves, mostly in basal clump, are strap shaped, with broad, roundish lobes. Solitary 1-in. flower heads (purple, occasionally yellow) in summer. Trim back after flowering. Attracts bees.

C. cyanus. BACHELOR'S BUTTON, CORNFLOWER. Annual. All zones. To 1–2½ ft., branching if given sufficient space. Narrow gray-green leaves, 2–3 in. long. Flower heads 1–1½ in. across, blue, pink, rose, wine red, or white. Blue forms are traditional favorites for boutonnieres. 'Jubilee Gem' is bushy, compact, 1 ft. tall, with deep blue flowers; Polka Dot strain has all cornflower colors on 16-in. plants. Sow seed in late summer or fall.

C. gymnocarpa. DUSTY MILLER. Perennial. Zones LS, CS, TS. Now considered a form of *C. cineraria.* To 1–3 ft.; white, feltlike leaves, somewhat resembling those of *C. cineraria* but more finely divided. Usually two or three purple flower heads at ends of leafy branches. Trim plants after bloom. Very drought tolerant.

C. hypoleuca 'John Coutts'. Perennial. Zones US, MS, LS. Somewhat resembles *C. montana* but has deeply lobed leaves and deep rose flower heads. Sometimes offered as a selection of *C. dealbata.*

C. macrocephala. GLOBE CENTAUREA. Perennial. Zones US, MS, LS. Coarse-foliaged, leafy plant 3–4 ft. tall, with 2-in. clusters of yellow flowers tightly enclosed at the base by papery, overlapping, shiny brown bracts. Flower heads resemble thistles. Use in fresh or dried arrangements.

C. montana. Perennial. Zones US, MS, LS. Clumps 1½–2 ft. tall and as wide, with grayish green leaves to 7 in. long. Flowers resembling ragged 3-in. blue cornflowers top the stems. Divide every other year. Cool-season plant, less vigorous in warmer climates. Regular water. ▶

C. moschata. SWEET SULTAN. Annual. All zones. Erect, branching at base, to 2 ft.; Imperialis strain to 3 ft. Green, deeply toothed leaves; thistle-like, 2-in. flower heads mostly in shades of lilac through rose, sometimes white or yellow. Musklike fragrance. Splendid cut flower. Sow seed directly on soil in spring or set out as transplants. Needs lots of heat.

CENTIPEDE GRASS. See EREMOCHLOA ophiuroides

CENTRANTHUS ruber (Valeriana rubra)

VALERIAN, JUPITER'S BEARD

Valerianaceae

PERENNIAL

ZONES US, MS, LS

FULL SUN OR PARTIAL SHADE

MODERATE TO LITTLE WATER

Centranthus ruber

Trouble-free plant. Self-sows prolifically because of small dandelion-like parachutes on seeds. Forms a bushy clump with upright stems to 3 ft. high bearing 4-in.-long bluish green leaves. Small, dusty crimson or rose pink flowers about ½ in. long in dense terminal clusters in late spring, early summer. 'Albus' is white. Plants give long, showy bloom in difficult situations. Will grow in poor, dry soils; accept almost any condition except damp shade. Cut off old flowering stems to shape plants, prolong bloom, and prevent seeding.

CENTURY PLANT. See AGAVE

CEPHALANTHUS occidentalis

BUTTONBUSH

Rubiaceae

DECIDUOUS SHRUB OR SMALL TREE

ALL ZONES

FULL SUN OR LIGHT SHADE

MOIST TO WET SOIL

Cephalanthus occidentalis

Remarkable for wide distribution—eastern Canada to Florida, Minnesota south through Oklahoma. To 3–15 ft. or taller; rounded, open habit and bright green paired or whorled leaves 2–6 in. long. Leafs out late in spring. Creamy white, slender-tubed flowers crowded in rounded, 1–1½-in.-wide heads in late summer. Projecting stigmas produce a pincushion effect. Attracts butterflies. Useful for naturalizing in wet areas.

CEPHALOTAXUS

PLUM YEW

Cephalotaxaceae

EVERGREEN SHRUBS OR TREES

ZONES US, MS, LS, CS

SUN OR LIGHT SHADE

MODERATE WATER

Cephalotaxus harringtonia

Slow-growing plants related to yews *(Taxus);* differ from yews in larger, brighter green needles and (on female plants only) larger fruit that resembles small green or brown plums. May not bear fruit in all areas. Very heat tolerant.

C. fortunei. CHINESE PLUM YEW. Big shrub or small tree to 10 ft. tall (rarely more), with soft, needlelike leaves up to 3½ in. long.

C. harringtonia. JAPANESE PLUM YEW. Spreading shrub or small tree to 10 ft. (possibly 20 ft.) tall, with needles 1–2½ in. long. Spreading ('Prostrata') and columnar ('Fastigiata') forms are sometimes seen. When young, the latter resembles Irish yew (*Taxus baccata* 'Fastigiata'). 'Korean Gold' has golden new foliage, columnar habit.

CERASTIUM tomentosum

SNOW-IN-SUMMER

Caryophyllaceae

PERENNIAL

ZONES US, MS, LS

PARTIAL SHADE IN LOWER SOUTH

REGULAR MOISTURE FOR FAST GROWTH

Cerastium tomentosum

Low-growing plant. Spreading, dense, tufty mats of silvery gray, with leaves ¾ in. long. Masses of snow white flowers, ½–¾ in. across, in early summer. Plant grows 6–8 in. high, spreads 2–3 ft. in a year. Use as ground cover on slopes or level ground, as bulb cover, in rock gardens, as edging for paths, between stepping-stones. Avoid extensive planting in prominent situations, since plant is not long lived.

In warmest areas of range, provide some shade. Takes any soil as long as drainage is good: Standing water causes root rot. Set divisions or plants 1–1½ ft. apart, or sow seed. Feed two or three times a year to speed growth. Shear off faded flower clusters. May look a bit shabby in winter but revives rapidly in spring. Divide in autumn or early spring.

CERATOSTIGMA plumbaginoides

CERATOSTIGMA, DWARF PLUMBAGO

Plumbaginaceae

PERENNIAL GROUND COVER

ZONES US, MS, LS, CS

FULL SUN OR PARTIAL SHADE

MODERATE WATER

Ceratostigma plumbaginoides

Wiry-stemmed ground cover 6–12 in. high. In loose soil and where growing season is long, plant spreads rapidly by underground stems, eventually covering large areas. Bronzy green to dark green, 3-in.-long leaves turn reddish brown with frosts. Bears intense blue, ½-in. phloxlike flowers from July until first frosts. Most effective in early or midautumn, when blue flowers contrast with red autumn foliage. Semievergreen only in the mildest-winter areas; best to cut back after bloom. Dies back elsewhere; leafs out late in spring. When plants show signs of aging, remove old crowns and replace with rooted stems. Often sold as *Plumbago larpentae*.

For Cape plumbago, see *Plumbago auriculata*

CERATOZAMIA mexicana

Zamiaceae

CYCAD

ZONE TS

PARTIAL SHADE

REGULAR TO MODERATE WATER

Ceratozamia mexicana

Related to sago palm (*Cycas revoluta*) and similar in appearance. Trunk usually a foot high, 4–6 ft. in great age, a foot thick. Very slow growing. Leaves in whorl, 3–6 ft. long, divided featherwise into 15 to 20 pairs of foot-long, inch-wide leaflets. Striking in container or protected place in open ground. Protect from frosts.

CERCIDIPHYLLUM
japonicum

KATSURA TREE

Cercidiphyllaceae

DECIDUOUS TREE

ZONES US, MS

FULL SUN OR LIGHT SHADE

REGULAR WATER

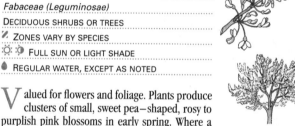

Cercidiphyllum japonicum

Native to Japan. A specimen tree of many virtues if given regular moisture, especially during youth, and sheltered from intense sun and wind. Light, dainty branch and leaf pattern. Foliage, always fresh looking, changes color during the growing season: New growth emerges reddish purple, becomes bluish green in summer, then turns yellow to apricot in autumn. To enhance fall color, water less frequently in late summer. Trees grown in acid soil will have the best color. Foliage of some katsura trees smells like burnt sugar on warm autumn days during leaf fall.

Rather slow growing, katsura trees will eventually reach 40 ft. or more. They have a pyramidal form when young; growth may remain upright or become more spreading with maturity. Some specimens have a single trunk, but multiple trunks are more commonplace. Growth habit is nearly round, with 2–4-in. leaves neatly spaced in pairs along arching branches. Flowers are inconspicuous. Brown bark is somewhat shaggy on old trees. No serious pest or disease problems. There is a weeping form known as 'Pendulum' or 'Pendula'.

CERCIS

REDBUD

Fabaceae (Leguminosae)

DECIDUOUS SHRUBS OR TREES

ZONES VARY BY SPECIES

FULL SUN OR LIGHT SHADE

REGULAR WATER, EXCEPT AS NOTED

Cercis canadensis

Valued for flowers and foliage. Plants produce clusters of small, sweet pea–shaped, rosy to purplish pink blossoms in early spring. Where a plant is adapted, blooms are borne in great showy profusion on bare twigs, branches, and sometimes even on the plant's main trunk. Flowers are followed by clusters of flat, beanlike pods that persist into winter. Attractive broad, rounded leaves are heart shaped at the base. All species and selections provide fall color with first frosts. All are attractive in naturalized settings.

C. canadensis. EASTERN REDBUD. Zones US, MS, LS, CS. Native to eastern U.S. The largest (grows to 25–35 ft. tall) and fastest growing of the redbuds, and the most apt to take tree form. Round-headed growth habit but with horizontally tiered branches in age. Leaves are rich green, 3–6 in. long, with pointed tips. Flowers are small (½ in. long), rosy pink or lavender. Needs some winter chill to flower profusely.

Eastern redbud is valuable for bridging the color gap between the early-flowering fruit trees (flowering peach, flowering plum) and the crabapples and late-flowering dogwoods and cherries. Effective as a specimen or understory tree. Selections include 'Alba' (white flowers); 'Flame' (double pink flowers); 'Forest Pansy' (purple foliage, needs some shade in hot climates); 'Rubye Atkinson' (pure pink flowers); and 'Silver Cloud' (leaves marbled with white).

C. c. mexicana (C. mexicana). Zones US, MS, LS, CS. Includes plants from many sources in Mexico. The most widely distributed is a form with a single trunk to 15 ft., and leathery blue-green leaves and pinkish purple flowers. Drought tolerant.

C. chinensis. CHINESE REDBUD. Zones US, MS, LS. Native to China, Japan. Seen mostly as light, open shrub to 10–12 ft. Flower clusters are deep rose, almost rosy purple, and 3–5 in. long. Leaves are sometimes glossier and brighter green than those of *C. canadensis*, with transparent line around the edge. 'Avondale' is a superior form with deep purple flowers. Full sun.

C. occidentalis. WESTERN REDBUD. Zones US, MS, LS. Shrub or small tree 10–18 ft. tall and wide, usually multitrunked. All-year interest: magenta flowers in spring, handsome blue-green leaves and newly forming magenta seedpods in summer, light yellow or red foliage in fall, and picturesque bare branches holding reddish brown seedpods in winter. Best floral display with some winter chill. Very drought tolerant; excellent for seldom-watered banks.

Cercis occidentalis

C. reniformis. Zones US, MS, LS. A Southwest native the equivalent of eastern redbud (*C. canadensis*). Leaves are leathery, blue green, 2–3 in. wide, with rounded or notched tips. Selection 'Alba' has white flowers. 'Oklahoma' has wine red flowers and thick, glossy, heat-resistant leaves. Drought tolerant.

C. siliquastrum. JUDAS TREE. Zones US, MS, LS. Native to Europe and western Asia. Performs best with some winter chill. Generally of shrubby habit to 25 ft., occasionally a taller, slender tree with single trunk. Purplish rose, ½-in.-long flowers; 3–5-in. leaves, deeply heart shaped at base, rounded or notched at tip. Fairly drought tolerant.

CESTRUM

Solanaceae

EVERGREEN SHRUBS

ZONES VARY BY SPECIES

PARTIAL SHADE

REGULAR WATER

FRUIT AND SAP ARE POISONOUS IF INGESTED

Cestrum elegans

All have showy, tubular flowers. Flowers and fruit attract birds. Fast growing, inclined to be rangy and top-heavy unless consistently pruned. Best in warm, sheltered spot. Feed generously. Add organic soil amendments before planting. Nip back consistently to maintain compact form; cut back severely after flowering or fruiting. In the Coastal South, plants may freeze back in heavy frosts but will recover quickly.

C. aurantiacum. ORANGE CESTRUM. Zone TS. Native to Guatemala. Rare and handsome. To 8 ft. Brilliant show of clustered, 1-in.-long, orange flowers in late spring and summer, followed by white berries. Deep green, oval, 4-in. leaves.

C. elegans (C. purpureum). RED CESTRUM. Zone TS. Shrub or semi-climber to 10 ft. or higher, with arching branches, deep green, 4-in. leaves. Plant produces masses of purplish red, 1-in.-long flowers in spring and summer, followed by red berries. Good plant for espalier. 'Smithii' selection has pink flowers.

C. nocturnum. NIGHT-BLOOMING JASMINE. Zone TS. Native to West Indies. To 12 ft., with 4–8-in.-long leaves and clusters of creamy white flowers in summer; white berries. Powerfully fragrant at night—too powerful for some people.

C. parqui. CHILEAN CESTRUM, WILLOW-LEAFED JESSAMINE. Zones CS, TS. Native to Chile. To 6–10 ft. tall with many branches from base. Dense foliage of willowlike leaves, 3–6 in. long. Greenish yellow, 1-in.-long summer flowers in clusters. Berries dark violet brown. Not as attractive as other species in form, flowers, or fruit, but its perfume is potent. Leaves blacken in light frost. Best used where winter appearance is unimportant. In Coastal South, protect roots with mulch, treat as perennial.

C

 CHAENOMELES

FLOWERING QUINCE

Rosaceae

DECIDUOUS SHRUBS

ZONES US, MS, LS, CS

FULL SUN

REGULAR TO MODERATE WATER

Chaenomeles

Bloom time—as early as January where winters are mild—is the only time flowering quince calls attention to itself. The plant is bland-looking the remainder of the year, though judicious pruning improves its looks. Blossoms are 1½–2½ in. across, single to semidouble or double, in colors ranging from soft to vibrant.

Practically indestructible shrubs with shiny green leaves (red tinged when young) and varying growth habit. Some grow to 10 ft. and spread wider; others are compact and low growing. Most are thorny, a few thornless. Some bear small, 2–4-in. fruits. Although not as tasty as those of common quince, they contain lots of pectin, making them good for adding to jelly and preserves. If your plant never fruits, it's probably because it needs cross-pollination with another selection. All flowering quince are useful as hedges and barriers. Easy to grow; tolerant of extremes in cold and heat, light to heavy soil. In the more humid areas, lower leaves may drop in summer. May bloom reluctantly in Coastal South. Prune any time to shape, limit growth, or gain special effects. Good time to prune is in bud and bloom season—use cut branches for indoor arrangements. New growth that follows will bear next year's flowers. Blossoms attract birds.

The following list of choice selections notes both height and flower color. Tall types are 6 ft. and over; low types are 2–3 ft. All are garden hybrids (some formerly called *Cydonia*); specialists can furnish even more selections.

'Apple Blossom'. Tall. White and pink. Good for fruit.
'Cameo'. Low, compact. Double, soft apricot pink. Good for fruit.
'Contorta'. Low. White to pink; twisted branches. Good as bonsai.
'Corallina' ('Coral Glow'). Tall. Reddish orange.
'Coral Sea'. Tall. Large, coral pink.
'Enchantress'. Tall. Large, shell pink.
'Falconet Charlot'. Tall, thornless. Double, salmon pink.
'Hollandia'. Tall. Large red flowers; reblooms in fall.
'Jet Trail'. Low. Pure white.
'Low-n-White'. Low, spreading. White.
'Minerva'. Low, spreading. Cherry red.
'Nivalis'. Tall. Large, pure white. Good for fruit.
'Orange Delight' ('Maulei'). Low, spreading. Orange to orange red.
'Pink Beauty'. Tall. Purplish pink.
'Pink Lady'. Low. Rose pink blooms from deeper-colored buds.
'Red Ruffles'. Tall, almost thornless. Large, ruffled, red.
'Rowallane'. Low. Darkest red.
'Snow'. Tall. Large, pure white.
'Stanford Red'. Low, almost thornless. Tomato red. Good for fruit.
'Super Red'. Tall, upright. Large, bright red.
'Texas Scarlet'. Low. Tomato red. Good for fruit.
'Toyo Nishiki'. Tall. Pink, white, pink and white, red all on same branch. Good for fruit.

CHAIN FERN. See WOODWARDIA

CHAIN-LINK CACTUS. See OPUNTIA imbricata

CHALK MAPLE. See ACER leucoderme

CHAMAECYPARIS

FALSE CYPRESS

Cupressaceae

EVERGREEN SHRUBS OR TREES

ZONES US, MS, EXCEPT AS NOTED

FULL SUN OR PARTIAL SHADE

REGULAR WATER

Chamaecyparis obtusa

False cypress is sometimes mistaken for arborvitae (*Thuja*), but the leaf undersides of false cypress have white lines, while the leaves of arborvitae are entirely green. Most false cypresses have two distinct types of leaves: juvenile and mature. Juvenile leaves (short, needlelike, soft but often prickly) appear on young plants and some new growth of larger trees. Mature foliage consists of tiny, scalelike, overlapping leaves. Cones are small and round.

All of the many selections sold are forms of a few species—one from the eastern U.S. and two from Japan. Many closely resemble one another and are often mislabeled. Dwarf and variegated kinds are available, providing rich source of bonsai and rock garden material. All need good drainage and protection from wind.

C. obtusa. HINOKI FALSE CYPRESS. There are dozens of golden, dwarf, and fern-leafed forms, but two selections are the most important in landscaping. 'Gracilis', slender hinoki cypress, has slender, upright growth to 20 ft. with nodding branch tips; 'Nana Gracilis' is a miniature of the former to 4 ft. in height.

C. pisifera. SAWARA FALSE CYPRESS. Japanese tree grows to 20–30 ft., rarely seen except in its garden forms. Selections include 'Cyano-Viridis' ('Boulevard'), a slow, dense bush to 6–8 ft., silvery blue-green foliage; 'Filifera', to 8 ft., drooping, threadlike branchlets; 'Filifera Aurea', similar branchlets in yellow.

C. thyoides. WHITE CEDAR. Zones US, MS, LS. Eastern U.S. timber tree, columnar to 75 ft. tall, found in wet sites in the wild. Garden forms include 'Andelyensis', dense, columnar, gray-green shrub to 10 ft., turning bronze in cold weather; and 'Heather Bun', broader than 'Andelyensis', turning intense plum purple in winter.

CHAMAEDOREA

Arecaceae (Palmae)

PALMS

ZONE TS; OR INDOORS

PARTIAL OR FULL SHADE

REGULAR WATER

Chamaedorea elegans

Generally slow-growing, small, feather-type palms. Some have single trunks, others clustered trunks. Leaves variable in shape. Good on shaded patio.

C. cataractarum. Single-stemmed palm growing slowly to 4–5 ft.; trunk speckled. Older plants take some frost.

C. costaricana. If well fed and liberally watered, develops fairly fast into bamboolike clumps of 8–10-ft. trunks. Good pot palm; will eventually need good-sized container. Lacy, feathery leaves 3–4 ft. long.

C. elegans. PARLOR PALM. The best indoor chamaedorea, tolerating crowded roots, poor light. Single stemmed; grows very slowly to eventual 3–4 ft. Occasionally douse tops of potted plants with water. Feed regularly. Groom by removing old leafstalks. Repot every 2 to 3 years, carefully washing off old soil and replacing with good potting mix. Plant three or more in container for effective display. Widely sold as *Neanthe bella*.

C. tenella. Single trunk to 3–4 ft. Dark bluish green leaves are exceptionally strong, large, and broad; undivided but deeply cleft at ends.

C. tepejilote. Single trunk ringed with swollen joints like those of bamboo. Moderate growth to 10 ft.; leaves 4 ft. long, feathery.

CHAMAEROPS humilis

EUROPEAN FAN PALM

Arecaceae (Palmae)

PALM

🌡 ZONES LS, CS, TS

☼ ◑ FULL SUN OR PARTIAL SHADE

💧 💧 REGULAR TO MODERATE WATER

Chamaerops humilis

Among the hardiest palms; has survived 6°F. Clumps develop slowly from offshoots, curving to 20 ft. tall and as wide. Extremely slow rate of growth in northern part of climate range. Leaves green to bluish green. Grow in containers, under trees, as impenetrable hedge. Wind resistant.

CHARD. See SWISS CHARD

CHASMANTHIUM latifolium (Uniola latifolia)

RIVER OATS, INLAND SEA OATS

Poaceae (Gramineae)

PERENNIAL GRASS

🌡 ZONES US, MS, LS, CS

☼ ◑ SUN OR LIGHT SHADE

💧 REGULAR WATER

Chasmanthium latifolium

Ornamental clump-forming grass. Broad, bamboolike leaves are topped by arching flowering stems, 2–5 ft. tall, carrying showers of silvery green flower spikelets that resemble flattened clusters of oats (or flattened armadillos). Flowering stems dry to an attractive greenish straw color and look good in dried arrangements. Clumps broaden slowly and are not aggressive like bamboo. Leaves turn brown in winter, when plants should be cut back almost to ground. Divide clumps when they become overgrown and flowering diminishes. Stake if flowering stems sprawl too far. Self-sows extensively and can become invasive.

CHASTE TREE. See VITEX

CHECKERBLOOM. See SIDALCEA

CHECKERED LILY. See FRITILLARIA meleagris

CHEIRANTHUS. See ERYSIMUM

CHELIDONIUM majus

GREATER CELANDINE

Papaveraceae

PERENNIAL OR BIENNIAL

🌡 ZONES US, MS, LS

◑ ● PART SHADE OR SHADE

💧 REGULAR WATER

⬦ SAP IS IRRITATING TO THE SKIN

Chelidonium majus

Native to Europe. Grows to 2–3 ft. tall, with several erect stems rising from the rootstock. Leaves are attractively cut and lobed, smooth bright green. Profuse yellow to orange-yellow flowers grow to 1 in. wide; summer bloom. Self-sows freely and naturalizes (sometimes too well). Double-flowered 'Flore Pleno' also seeds itself freely. Both forms are best in wild gardens.

CHELONE

TURTLEHEAD

Scrophulariaceae

PERENNIALS

🌡 ZONES US, MS, LS, CS

◑ LIGHT SHADE

💧 💧 AMPLE TO REGULAR WATER

Chelone lyonii

Leafy, clump-forming perennials related to penstemon. All are native to the eastern U.S. and grow in damp places in sun or light shade. Frequently used in bog gardens. All bloom in late summer and autumn. Common name comes from the oddly formed flowers—inch-long, puffy, and two lipped, with a fancied resemblance to a turtle's or snake's head. Useful for cut flowers, shade gardens, wild gardens.

C. glabra. WHITE TURTLEHEAD. Grows 2–3 ft. tall, occasionally much taller. Flowers are white or palest pink.

C. lyonii. PINK TURTLEHEAD. Reaches 3 ft. tall. Rose pink flowers.

C. obliqua. ROSE TURTLEHEAD. To 2–2½ ft.; deep pink flowers. Latest bloomer among species listed. 'Alba' compact, white-flowered form.

CHENILLE PLANT. See ACALYPHA hispida

CHEROKEE ROSE. See ROSA laevigata

CHERRY

Rosaceae

DECIDUOUS FRUIT TREES

🌡 ZONES VARY BY TYPE

☼ FULL SUN

💧 REGULAR, DEEP WATERING

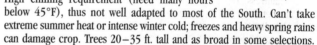

Fruiting Cherry

Both the sweet and sour cherries are useful and attractive trees in the home garden, but they are hard to grow there.

Sweet cherries. Most common market type. High chilling requirement (need many hours below 45°F), thus not well adapted to most of the South. Can't take extreme summer heat or intense winter cold; freezes and heavy spring rains can damage crop. Trees 20–35 ft. tall and as broad in some selections.

Two trees are usually needed to produce fruit, and second tree must be chosen with care. No combination of these will produce fruit: 'Bing', 'Lambert', 'Royal Ann'. However, the following selections will pollinate these and any other cherry: 'Black Tartarian', 'Corum', 'Deacon', 'Hedelfingen', 'Republican', 'Sam', 'Stella', and 'Van'. Because 'Lambert' blooms late, it is pollinated best by 'Republican'. 'Glacier', 'Lapins', 'Stella', and 'Sunburst' are self-fertile (a lone tree will bear).

Fruiting spurs are long lived, do not need to be renewed by pruning. Prune trees only to maintain good structure and shape. Fruit appears in late spring to early summer. Use netting to keep birds from eating the crop. For control of brown rot and blossom blight, apply a copper spray just as leaves fall in autumn, then a fungicide when first blooms appear and weekly during bloom. Resume fungicide program about 2 weeks before harvest. Dormant oil spray will control various pests, including scale insects and mites. Selections include the following:

'Bing'. Top quality. Large, dark red, meaty fruit of fine flavor. Midseason.

'Black Tartarian'. Fruit smaller than 'Bing', purplish black, firm and sweet. Early.

'Hedelfingen'. Medium-large black cherry. Ripens with 'Van', but fruit colors before maturity, needs early protection from birds. Early-bearing, productive tree.

'Lambert'. Large, firm, black fruit. Flavor more sprightly than 'Bing'. Late.

'Olympus'. Dark cherry, ripens after 'Bing'. Smaller fruit, larger crop. Pollinate with sour cherry 'Montmorency'.

▶

'Stella'. Dark fruit like 'Lambert'; ripens a few days later. Self-fertile and good pollinator for other cherries.

'Van'. Heavy-bearing tree. Shiny black fruit, firmer and slightly smaller than 'Bing'. Ripens slightly earlier than or at the same time as 'Bing'.

Sour cherries. Also known as pie cherries. More widely adapted than sweet cherries; succeed along the Atlantic Coast and farther north and south than sweet cherries do. In home gardens and orchards, grow in Upper and Middle South in well-drained soil.

Sour cherry trees are smaller than sweet cherry trees—to about 20 ft. tall and spreading. They are self-fertile. There are far fewer types of sour cherries than sweet ones. 'Early Richmond' and 'Montmorency' are the preferred kinds, bearing small, bright red, soft, juicy, sweet-tart fruit. 'English Morello' is darker, with tarter fruit and red juice. 'Meteor' has fruit like 'Montmorency' but is a smaller tree. 'North Star', with red to dark red skin and yellow, sour flesh, is a small, very hardy tree.

CHERRY, FLOWERING. See PRUNUS

CHERRY LAUREL. See PRUNUS laurocerasus

CHERRY PLUM. See PRUNUS cerasifera

CHESTNUT. See CASTANEA

CHICKASAW PLUM. See PRUNUS angustifolia

CHICKWEED. See STELLARIA pubera

CHICORY

Asteraceae (Compositae)

PERENNIAL

ZONES US, MS, LS

FULL SUN

REGULAR TO MODERATE WATER

Chicory

Botanically known as *Cichorium intybus*. Dried ground roots can be roasted and used as substitute for coffee. Wild form grows as 3–6-ft. perennial roadside weed and is recognized by its pretty sky blue flowers that close by midday. Grown for its leaves, it is known as chicory, endive, or curly endive; grown for its blanched sprouts, it's known as Belgian or French endive, endive hearts, or witloof ("white leaf"). Matures in 90 to 95 days. In cold-winter areas, sow seed in summer; elsewhere, sow so that plants mature after summer heat. To blanch center leaves of full-size plant, pull outer leaves over center and tie.

Radicchio is the name given to a number of red-leafed chicories grown for salads. 'Rossa de Verona', or 'Rouge de Verone', is the best known. Best in Coastal South. Sow seed in summer for a winter harvest.

CHIHUAHUAN SAGE. See LEUCOPHYLLUM laevigatum

CHILEAN JASMINE. See MANDEVILLA laxa

CHILOPSIS linearis

DESERT WILLOW, DESERT CATALPA

Bignoniaceae

DECIDUOUS SHRUB OR SMALL TREE

ZONES MS, LS, CS

FULL SUN

MODERATE TO LITTLE WATER

Chilopsis linearis

Native to desert washes and stream beds below 5,000 ft. Open and airy when trained as small tree. At first grows fast (3 ft. in a season), then slows down, leveling off at about 25 ft. With age it develops shaggy bark and twisting trunks. Drops leaves early,

holds a heavy crop of catalpa-like fruit through winter, and can look messy. But pruning can make it very handsome.

Chilopsis linearis

Narrow, 2–5-in.-long leaves. Trumpet-shaped flowers with crimped lobes look somewhat like those of catalpa. Flower color—pink, white, rose, or lavender, marked with purple—varies among seedlings; garden centers select the most colorful. 'Burgundy' ('Burgundy Lace') has deep purplish red flowers. 'Cameo' is pure white with a yellow-striped throat. 'Pink Star' is light pink with some purple striping. All bloom in spring and often through fall. Attract birds. Like dry, limy soil. Not for humid, high-rainfall areas.

CHIMONANTHUS praecox
(C. fragrans, Meratia praecox)

WINTERSWEET

Calycanthaceae

DECIDUOUS SHRUB

ZONES US, MS, LS, CS

FULL SUN OR PARTIAL SHADE

MODERATE WATER

Chimonanthus praecox

Native to China and Japan. Winter-blooming shrub with wonderfully spicy-scented blossoms. Needs some winter cold. Tall, open, slow growing to 10–15 ft. high and 6–8 ft. wide, with many basal stems. Flowers appear on leafless branches late winter to early spring, depending on climate. Blossoms are 1 in. wide, with pale yellow outer sepals and smaller, chocolate-colored inner sepals. Tapered leaves are rough to the touch, medium green, 3–6 in. long and half that wide; turn yellow green in fall.

In the Upper South, plant in sheltered site to prevent frost damage. In all areas, locate plant where its winter fragrance can be enjoyed. Possible locations: near an entrance or path, under a bedroom window. Keep plant lower by cutting back after bloom; shape as a small tree by removing excess basal stems; rejuvenate leggy plant by trimming to within a foot of the ground in spring. Needs good drainage.

CHINABERRY. See MELIA azedarach

CHINA FIR. See CUNNINGHAMIA lanceolata

CHINA ROSE. See ROSA chinensis

CHINCHERINCHEE. See ORNITHOGALUM thyrsoides

CHINESE CABBAGE

Brassicaceae (Cruciferae)

BIENNIAL GROWN AS ANNUAL

ALL ZONES

TOLERATES LIGHT SHADE

REGULAR WATER

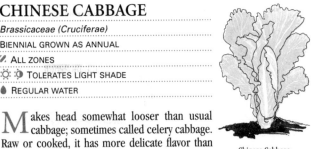

Chinese Cabbage

Makes head somewhat looser than usual cabbage; sometimes called celery cabbage. Raw or cooked, it has more delicate flavor than cabbage. There are two kinds: pe-tsai, with tall, narrow heads; and wong bok, with short, broad heads. Favored pe-tsai type is 'Michihli'; wong bok selections include 'Springtime', 'Summertime', and 'Wintertime' (early to late maturing). Definitely cool-season crop; very prone to bolt to seed in hot weather or in long days of spring and early summer. In colder-winter areas, plant seeds directly in open ground in July; in August or September in milder climates. Sow seeds thinly in rows 2–2½ ft. apart and thin plants to 1½–2 ft. apart. Heads should be ready in 70 to 80 days. Subject to same pests as cabbage.

CHINESE CHESTNUT. See **CASTANEA mollissima**

CHINESE CHIVES. See **ALLIUM tuberosum**

CHINESE ELM. See **ULMUS parvifolia**

CHINESE EVERGREEN. See **AGLAONEMA modestum**

CHINESE FAN PALM. See **LIVISTONA chinensis**

CHINESE FLAME TREE. See **KOELREUTERIA bipinnata**

CHINESE FOUNTAIN PALM. See **LIVISTONA chinensis**

CHINESE FOXGLOVE. See **REHMANNIA elata**

CHINESE FRINGE. See **LOROPETALUM chinense**

CHINESE GROUND ORCHID. See **BLETILLA striata**

CHINESE JUJUBE. See **ZIZIPHUS jujuba**

CHINESE LANTERN PLANT. See **PHYSALIS alkekengi**

CHINESE PARASOL TREE. See **FIRMIANA simplex**

CHINESE PARSLEY. See **CORIANDRUM sativum**

CHINESE PISTACHE. See **PISTACIA chinensis**

CHINESE QUINCE. See **PSEUDOCYDONIA sinense**

CHINESE REDBUD. See **CERCIS chinensis**

CHINESE SCHOLAR TREE. See **SOPHORA japonica**

CHINESE SNOWBALL. See **VIBURNUM macrocephalum macrocephalum**

CHINESE SWEET GUM. See **LIQUIDAMBAR formosana**

CHINESE TALLOW. See **SAPIUM sebiferum**

CHINESE WITCH HAZEL. See **HAMAMELIS mollis**

CHIONANTHUS

FRINGE TREE

Oleaceae

DECIDUOUS SHRUBS OR SMALL TREES

ZONES US, MS, LS, CS

FULL SUN

REGULAR TO MODERATE WATER

Chionanthus virginicus

Spectacular flowering plants requiring some winter chill. Earn common name from narrow, fringelike white petals on flowers that are borne in impressive, ample, lacy clusters. There are male and female plants. Males have larger flowers. If both are present, female plants produce fruit like clusters of small dark olives, favored by birds. Broad leaves turn bright to deep yellow in fall. Both species tolerate city pollution.

C. retusus. CHINESE FRINGE TREE. Grows to about 20 ft. tall; not quite as wide spreading as *C. virginicus.* Usually seen as a big multistemmed shrub, but can also be grown as small tree. Produces pure white flower clusters to 4 in. long in late spring or early summer, 2 to 3 weeks before *C. virginicus.* Magnificent in bloom, something like a tremendous white lilac. Handsome gray-brown bark (sometimes golden on young stems) provides winter interest.

C. virginicus. GRANCY GRAYBEARD, FRINGE TREE, OLD MAN'S BEARD. Native from Pennsylvania to Florida, and Texas. Leaves and flower

clusters often twice as big as those of *C. retusus,* and the blooms appear a little later. White, slightly fragrant flowers. Can reach 30 ft., but in cultivation usually 12–20 ft. high with equal spread. Variation in habit, from very shrubby and open to more treelike.

CHIONODOXA

GLORY-OF-THE-SNOW

Liliaceae

BULBS

ZONES US, MS

PARTIAL SHADE

REGULAR WATER DURING GROWTH AND BLOOM

Chionodoxa luciliae

Native to alpine meadows in Asia Minor. Charming small bulbous plants 4–6 in. high; among first to bloom in spring. Narrow basal leaves, two or three to each flower stalk. Blue or white, short, tubular, open flowers in loose spikes. Plant bulbs 3 in. deep in September or October in half shade; keep moist. Under favorable conditions, plants self-sow freely.

C. luciliae. This species and its selections are most generally available. Species produces brilliant blue, white-centered, starlike flowers. 'Alba' offers larger white flowers; 'Gigantea' has larger leaves, larger flowers of violet blue with white throat.

C. sardensis. Deep, true gentian blue flowers with very small white eye.

CHITALPA tashkentensis

CHITALPA

Bignoniaceae

DECIDUOUS TREE

ZONES MS, LS, CS

FULL SUN

MODERATE TO LITTLE WATER

Chitalpa tashkentensis

Fast growing to 20–30 ft. and as wide, this tree combines the larger flowers of its *Catalpa bignonioides* parent with the desert toughness and flower color of *Chilopsis linearis,* its other parent. Leaves are 4–5 in. long, an inch wide. Produces clusters of frilly trumpet-shaped flowers that appear late spring to fall. 'Pink Dawn' has pink flowers, 'Morning Cloud' white ones. Culture is the same as for *Catalpa,* but even more tolerant of dry, limy soil.

CHIVES

Liliaceae

PERENNIAL HERB

ALL ZONES

FULL SUN OR LIGHT SHADE

REGULAR WATER

Chives

Leaves are grasslike in general appearance but round and hollow in cross section. Clumps may reach 2 ft. tall but are usually shorter. Cloverlike, rose purple spring flowers are carried in clusters atop thin stems. Plant is pretty enough to use as edging in sunny or lightly shaded flower border or herb garden. Does best in moist, fairly rich soil. May be increased by divisions or grown from seed. Evergreen (or nearly so) in mild regions; goes dormant where winters are severe, but small divisions may be potted in rich soil and grown on kitchen windowsill. Chop or snip leaves; use as garnish or add to salads, cream cheese, cottage cheese, egg dishes, gravies, and soups for delicate onionlike flavor. For garlic chives, see *Allium tuberosum.*

C

🏛 CHLOROPHYTUM
comosum

SPIDER PLANT

Liliaceae

PERENNIAL

✂ ZONE TS; OR INDOORS

◑ PARTIAL SHADE

💧 REGULAR WATER

Chlorophytum comosum

Lily relative, native to Africa. Forms 1–3-ft.-high clumps of soft, curving leaves like long, broad grass blades. 'Variegatum' and 'Vittatum', both striped white, are popular. Flowers white, ½ in. long, in loose, leafy-tipped spikes standing above foliage. Greatest attraction: miniature duplicates of mother plant, complete with root, at end of curved stems (as with strawberry plant offsets); these offsets can be cut off, potted individually. Excellent, easily grown house plant for fully lighted window, greenhouse. Ground cover or outdoor hanging basket plant in partial shade. As ground cover, set 2 ft. apart in diamond pattern. Plants will fill in area in same year. Often sold as *C. capense*.

CHOISYA ternata

MEXICAN ORANGE

Rutaceae

EVERGREEN SHRUB

✂ ZONES LS, CS, TS

◔◑ LIGHT SHADE IN TROPICAL SOUTH

💧 MODERATE WATER

Choisya ternata

Fast growing to 6–8 ft. high and wide. Lustrous rich green leaves, held toward ends of branches, are divided into fans of three leaflets to 3 in. long. Clusters of fragrant white flowers, somewhat like small orange blossoms, open in very early spring and bloom continuously for a couple of months, then intermittently through summer. Sometimes called mock orange. Appealing to bees. Attractive informal hedge or screen. Needs fast drainage, neutral to acid soil. Hardy to about 10°F. Subject to damage from sucking insects and mites. Foliage of 'Sundance' is yellow, gradually turning green.

CHOKEBERRY. See ARONIA

CHOKECHERRY. See PRUNUS virginiana

CHORISIA

FLOSS SILK TREE

Bombacaceae

EVERGREEN TO BRIEFLY DECIDUOUS TREES

✂ ZONE TS

◯ FULL SUN

💧◐ REGULAR TO MODERATE WATER

Chorisia speciosa

Native to South America. Heavy trunks studded with thick, heavy spines. Young trunks are green, becoming gray with age. Leaves divided into leaflets like fingers of a hand; leaves fall during autumn flowering or whenever winter temperatures drop below 27°F. Flowers large and showy, somewhat resembling narrow-petaled hibiscus blossoms. Needs good drainage.

  C. insignis. WHITE FLOSS SILK TREE. To 50 ft. tall. Flowers white to pale yellow, 5–6 in. across.

  C. speciosa. Grows 3–5 ft. a year for the first few years, then slowly to 30–60 ft. tall. Flowers are pink, purplish rose, or burgundy. 'Los

Angeles Beautiful', with wine red flowers, and 'Majestic Beauty', with rich pink flowers, are both grafted selections.

CHRISTMAS CACTUS. See SCHLUMBERGERA bridgesii

CHRISTMAS FERN. See POLYSTICHUM acrostichoides

CHRISTMAS ROSE. See HELLEBORUS niger

CHRYSALIDOCARPUS
lutescens

ARECA PALM, CANE PALM, YELLOW PALM

Arecaceae (Palmae)

PALM

✂ ZONE TS; OR INDOORS

◯◑● SUN OR SHADE

💧 REGULAR WATER

Chrysalidocarpus lutescens

Clumping feather palm of slow growth to 10–15 ft. or even taller. Graceful plant with smooth trunks and yellowish green leaves. Can take dense shade; intolerant of salt. Used in foundation plantings and as a patio plant in the Tropical South; house plant elsewhere. Tricky to maintain indoors, but a lovely palm. Prone to spider mites as a house plant. Often sold as *Areca lutescens*.

CHRYSANTHEMUM

Asteraceae (Compositae)

PERENNIALS AND ANNUALS

✂ ZONES VARY BY SPECIES

◯ BEST IN FULL SUN, EXCEPT AS NOTED

💧 REGULAR WATER, EXCEPT AS NOTED

Chrysanthemum maximum 'Wirral Supreme'

There are about 160 species of chrysanthemum, mostly native to China, Japan, and Europe. Included are some of most popular and useful of garden plants—top favorite being *C. morifolium*, whose modern descendants are known as florists' chrysanthemums. Botanists have split *Chrysanthemum* into many new genera. Growers may be slow to use new names, but some have begun to do so. The new names are listed immediately after the old.

  C. coccineum (Pyrethrum roseum, Tanacetum coccineum). PAINTED DAISY, PYRETHRUM. Perennial. Zones US, MS. Bushy plant to 2–3 ft., with very finely divided, bright green leaves and single, daisylike, long-stemmed flowers in pink, red, or white. Also available in double and anemone-flowered forms. Starts blooming in April, May, or June; if cut back, blooms again in late summer. Excellent for cutting, borders. Needs summer heat to perform well (but does not take high humidity). Divide clumps or sow seeds in spring. Double forms may not come true from seed; they may revert to single forms.

  C. frutescens (Argyranthemum frutescens). MARGUERITE, PARIS DAISY. Short-lived shrubby perennial in Zones CS, TS; grown as summer annual elsewhere. Bright green, coarsely divided leaves; abundant daisies 1½–2½ in. across in white, yellow, or pink. 'Pink Lady' and 'White Lady' produce buttonlike flower heads; 'Silver Leaf' has gray-green leaves and masses of very small white flowers; 'Snow White', double anemone type, has pure white flowers, more restrained growth habit. Dwarf selections also available. All types are splendid in containers and for quick effects in borders, mass displays in new gardens. For continued bloom, prune lightly at frequent intervals. In Coastal and Tropical South, do not prune severely, since plants seldom produce new growth from hardened wood; replace every 2 to 3 years.

C. leucanthemum (Leucanthemum vulgare). OX-EYE DAISY, COMMON DAISY. Perennial. Zones US, MS, LS, CS. European native naturalized in many places. To 2 ft., with bright green foliage, yellow-centered daisies from late spring through fall. 'May Queen' begins blooming in early spring.

C. maximum (C. superbum, Leucanthemum maximum, L. superbum). SHASTA DAISY. Perennial. Zones US, MS, LS, CS. Summer and fall bloomer. Original 2–4-ft.-tall Shasta daisy, with coarse, leathery leaves and gold-centered, white flower heads 2–4 in. across, has been largely superseded by types with larger, better-formed, longer-blooming flowers. These are available in single, double, quilled, and shaggy-flowered forms. All are white, but two show a touch of yellow. Some bloom May–October. Shasta daisies are splendid in borders and cut arrangements.

Following are some of the selections available in garden centers:

'Esther Read', most popular double white, long bloom; 'Marconi', large frilly double; 'Aglaya', similar to 'Marconi', long blooming season; 'Wirral Supreme', double white with short, white central petals; 'Alaska', big, old-fashioned single; 'Horace Read', 4-in.-wide dahlia-like flower; 'Majestic', large yellow-centered flower; 'Thomas Killin', 6-in.-wide (largest) yellow-centered flower.

'Cobham's Gold' has distinctive flowers in yellow-tinted, off-white shade. 'Canarybird', another yellow, is dwarf, with attractive dark green foliage.

Most popular selections for cut flowers are 'Esther Read', 'Majestic', 'Aglaya', and 'Thomas Killin'.

Shasta daisies are easy to grow from seed. Catalogs offer many strains, including Diener's Strain (double) and Roggli Super Giant (single). 'Marconi' (double), also available in seed, nearly always blooms double. 'Silver Princess' (also called 'Little Princess' and 'Little Miss Muffet') is 12–15-in. dwarf single. 'Snow Lady' (single), an All-America winner, 10–12 in. tall, begins to bloom in 5 months from seed, then blooms nearly continuously.

Set out divisions of Shasta daisies in fall or early spring, container-grown plants any time. Thrive in fairly rich, moist, well-drained soil. Prefer sun, but do well in partial shade in Lower and Coastal South; double-flowered kinds hold up better in very light shade. Divide clumps every 2 or 3 years in early spring (or in fall in Lower and Coastal South). Shasta daisies are generally easy to grow but have a few problems. Disease called gall causes root crown to split into many weak, poorly rooted growing points that soon die. Dig out and dispose of affected plants; don't replant Shasta daisies in the same spot.

Chrysanthemum morifolium

C. morifolium (Dendranthema grandiflorum). FLORISTS' CHRYSANTHEMUM. Perennial. Zones US, MS, LS, CS. The most useful of all autumn-blooming perennials for borders, containers, and cutting, and the most versatile and varied of all chrysanthemum species, available in many flower forms, colors, plant and flower sizes, and growth habits. Colors include white, yellow, red, pink, orange, bronze, purple, and lavender, as well as multicolors. Following are flower forms as designated by chrysanthemum hobbyists:

Anemone. One or more rows of rays with large raised center disk or cushion. Center disk may be same color as rays or different. (Disbud to encourage very large flowers.)

Brush. Narrow, rolled rays give brush or soft cactus dahlia effect.

Decorative. Long, broad rays overlap like shingles to form full flower.

Incurve. Big double flowers with broad rays curving upward and inward.

Irregular curve. Like above, but with looser, more softly curving rays.

Laciniated. Fully double, with rays fringed and cut at tips in carnation effect.

Pompom. Globular, neat, compact flowers with flat, fluted, or quilled rays. Usually small, they can reach 5 in. with disbudding.

Quill. Long, narrow rolled rays; like spider but less droopy.

Reflex. Big double flowers with rays that curl in, out, and sideways, creating shaggy effect.

Semidouble. Somewhat like single or daisy, but with two, three, or four rows of rays around a yellow center.

Single or daisy. Single row of rays around a yellow center. May be large or small, with broad or narrow rays.

Spider. Long, curling, tubular rays ending in fishhook curved tips.

Spoon. Tubular rays flatten at tip to make little disks, sometimes in colors that contrast with body of flower.

Garden culture. It's easy to grow chrysanthemums, not so easy to grow prize-winning chrysanthemums. The latter need more water, feeding, pinching, pruning, grooming, and pest control than most perennials.

Plant in well-drained garden soil improved by organic matter and a complete fertilizer dug in 2 to 3 weeks before planting. In Lower and Coastal South, provide shade from afternoon sun. Don't plant near large trees or hedges with invasive roots.

Set out young plants (rooted cuttings or vigorous, single-stem divisions) in early spring. When dividing clumps, take divisions from outside; discard woody centers. Water deeply at intervals determined by your soil structure—frequently in porous soils, less often in heavy soils. Too little water causes woody stems and loss of lower leaves; overwatering causes leaves to yellow, then blacken and drop. Aphids are the only notable pest in all areas. Feed plants in ground two or three times during the growing season; make last application with low-nitrogen fertilizer not less than 2 weeks before bloom.

Sturdy plants and big flowers are result of frequent pinching, which should begin at planting time with removal of new plant's tip. Lateral shoots will form; select one to four of these for continued growth. Continue pinching all summer, nipping top pair of leaves on every shoot that reaches 5 in. in length. On some early-blooming cushion types, or in the Upper South, pinching should be stopped earlier. Stake plants to keep them upright. To produce huge blooms, remove all flower buds except for one or two in each cluster—this is called disbudding. ▶

Flower Forms of *Chrysanthemum*

Anenome

Brush

Decorative

Incurve

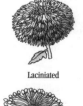

Laciniated

Pompom

Reflex

Semidouble

Single

Spider

Spoon

Pot culture. Pot rooted cuttings February–April, using porous, fibrous, moisture-holding planting mix. Move plants to larger pots as growth requires—don't let them become root-bound. Pinch as directed above; stake as required. Plants need water daily in warm weather, every other day in cool conditions. Feed with liquid fertilizer every 7 to 10 days until buds show color.

Care after bloom. Cut back plants to within 8 in. of ground. Where soils are heavy and likely to remain wet in winter, dig clumps with soil intact and set on top of ground in inconspicuous place. Cover with sand or sawdust if you wish. Take cuttings from early to late spring (up until May for some types), or when shoots are 3–4 in. long. As new shoots develop, you can make additional cuttings of them.

C. nipponicum (Nipponanthemum nipponicum). NIPPON DAISY. Perennial. Zones US, MS, LS, CS. Resembles a large (up to 3-ft.), rounded, shrubby Shasta daisy with a dense mass of nearly succulent bright green leaves. White daisy flowers on long stems form in fall. In Lower and Coastal South, you may cut back after bloom. In Upper and Middle South, do not disturb plants until they put on strong new growth in spring; at that time, you may cut back partway to maintain compactness.

C. pacificum (Pyrethrum marginatum, Dendranthema pacificum). GOLD AND SILVER CHRYSANTHEMUM. Perennial. Zones US, MS, LS, CS. Semitrailing and semishrubby, with stems to 2–3 ft. densely clad in lobed, dark green leaves apparently edged white (woolly white undersides show at edges). Broad clusters of yellow flowers appear in fall; lacking rays, they resemble clustered brass buttons. 'Pink Ice' is a pale pink–flowered type with short petals. Use as bank or ground cover or at front of perennial border. In most areas, you may cut back after bloom. In Upper and Middle South, do not disturb plants until they put on strong new growth in spring; at that time, cut back partway to maintain compactness.

C. paludosum (Leucanthemum paludosum). SWAMP CHRYSANTHEMUM. Annual, sometimes living over for a second bloom season. All zones. In summer, bears white daisies 1–1½ in. wide on 8–10-in. stems above dark green, deeply toothed leaves. Flowers look like miniature Shasta daisies.

C. parthenium (Tanacetum parthenium). FEVERFEW. Perennial. Zones US, MS, LS, CS. Compact, leafy, aggressive; once favored in Victorian gardens. Leaves have strong odor, offensive to some. Named selections range from 1 to 3 ft. tall. 'Golden Ball' has bright yellow flower heads and no rays; 'Silver Ball' is completely double with only the white rays showing. In 'Aureum', often sold in flats as 'Golden Feather', chartreuse-colored foliage is principal attraction. Sow seeds in spring for bloom by midsummer, or plant from divisions in fall or spring. Can also grow from cuttings. Full sun or light shade.

C. serotinum (C. uliginosum). GIANT DAISY. Perennial. Zones US, MS, LS, CS. Grows 5–6 ft. tall, producing sheaves of 3-in., yellow-eyed white daisies in late summer. Useful for late flowers in back of perennial border. Can tolerate damp soil better than most daisies.

CHRYSOGONUM virginianum

GOLDEN STAR, GREEN AND GOLD

Asteraceae (Compositae)

PERENNIAL

ZONES US, MS, LS, CS

PARTIAL SHADE

REGULAR WATER

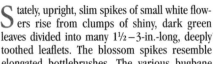
Chrysogonum virginianum

Native to eastern U.S. Useful and attractive native plant for ground cover or foreground planting. Grows 8 in. tall and spreads freely. Bright green, toothed leaves, 1–3 in. long, make a good background for its bright yellow flower heads. Blossoms have five rays, resemble stars more than daisies. Bloom is heavy in spring and fall, sporadic through summer

months. Plant 1 ft. apart in rich soil high in organic matter for quick ground cover.

CHRYSOPSIS

GOLDEN ASTER

Asteraceae (Compositae)

PERENNIALS

ZONES US, MS, LS

FULL SUN

REGULAR TO MODERATE WATER

Chrysopsis villosa

Perennials native to eastern and central U.S. Tough, somewhat coarse plants. Drought and heat tolerance makes them useful for poor, dry soils and hot situations, yet bright yellow daisylike flowers are showy enough for garden use. Late summer and fall bloom.

C. mariana. MARYLAND GOLDEN ASTER. Grows to 2 ft. or possibly 3 ft. high, with large (9-in.) basal leaves, smaller stem leaves, tight clusters of 1½-in. flowers.

C. villosa. GOLDEN ASTER. Taller than *C. mariana* (to 4–5 ft.), with smaller, somewhat more scattered flowers. Blooms for a long time; excellent cut flower. Good to combine with ironweed, fall asters, and any of the blue salvias.

CHUPAROSA. See ANISACANTHUS thurberi

CIBOTIUM chamissoi

HAWAIIAN TREE FERN

Dicksoniaceae

TREE FERN

ZONE TS

SHADE OUTDOORS, BRIGHT LIGHT INDOORS

KEEP SOIL MOIST AND HUMIDITY HIGH

Cibotium chamissoi

Native to Hawaii, this tropical evergreen tree fern has a stiff fibrous trunk, to 6 ft., possibly 20 ft., and a crown of long, lacy, yellow-green fronds with overall spread to about 10 ft. The overall effect is delicate and feathery. Requires moist soil and high humidity; mist frequently in dry air, especially the trunk, because it is a mass of aerial roots. Plant will grow indoors in areas with high light, but tips burn quickly if humidity is low.

CICHORIUM intybus. See CHICORY

CIDER GUM. See EUCALYPTUS gunnii

CIGAR PLANT. See CUPHEA ignea

CILANTRO. See CORIANDRUM sativum

CIMICIFUGA

BUGBANE

Ranunculaceae

PERENNIALS

ZONES US, MS

PARTIAL SHADE

REGULAR WATER

Cimicifuga racemosa

Stately, upright, slim spikes of small white flowers rise from clumps of shiny, dark green leaves divided into many 1½–3-in.-long, deeply toothed leaflets. The blossom spikes resemble elongated bottlebrushes. The various bugbane species bloom midsummer into fall. All are handsome planted among large ferns in woodland gardens; use the tallest types at the back of borders. Delicate, airy effect.

Best in rich, well-drained, moist soil. Will take considerable sun with plentiful water. Need some winter chill for best blooming. Clumps can remain undisturbed for many years. Divide in early spring before growth starts in colder-winter areas, in fall in milder climates. Dried seed clusters useful in flower arrangements.

C. japonica. JAPANESE BUGBANE. Native to Japan. White flowers on purplish black, leafless stalks in autumn. About 3–4 ft. tall when in bloom. 'Acerina' has white flowers opening from pink buds.

C. racemosa. BLACK SNAKEROOT. Native from Massachusetts south to Georgia and west to Missouri. Plant was once used medicinally by Native Americans. Flowering stems to 7 ft. tall. Starts blooming in midsummer in southern part of range, in late summer or early fall farther north.

C. ramosa. Fall bloomer. Flowers on branched stems to 7 ft. tall. Narrow 1-ft. spires on each branch give a long floral display. 'Atropurpurea' is lower growing (to 5 ft.), with dark reddish purple foliage.

C. simplex. KAMCHATKA BUGBANE. Native to Siberia and Japan. Fall bloomer, with plumes reaching 3–5 ft. high. 'White Pearl' has especially large flower spikes.

CINERARIA. See SENECIO hybridus

CINNAMOMUM camphora

CAMPHOR TREE

Lauraceae

EVERGREEN TREE

⚡ ZONES CS, TS

☼ ◑ FULL SUN OR LIGHT SHADE

◐ ● REGULAR OR MODERATE WATER

Cinnamomum camphora

Native to China, Japan. Grows slowly to 50 ft. or more with wider spread. Aromatic foliage smells like camphor when crushed. Winter leaves are shiny yellow green. New foliage in early spring may be pink, red, or bronze, depending on tree. Usually strong structure, heavy trunk, and heavy, upright, spreading limbs. Beautiful in rain, when trunk looks black. Inconspicuous, fragrant yellow flowers in profusion in May, followed by small blackish fruits. Drops leaves quite heavily in March; flowers, fruits, and twigs drop later. Competitive roots make this tree a poor choice near garden beds. Most prone to a root rot (verticillium wilt) after wet winter or if planted in poorly drained soil.

CINNAMON FERN. See OSMUNDA cinnamomea

CINQUEFOIL. See POTENTILLA

CISSUS rhombifolia

GRAPE IVY

Vitaceae

EVERGREEN VINE

⚡ ZONES LS (PROTECTED), CS, TS; OR INDOORS

☼ ◑ ● SUN OR SHADE

● REGULAR WATER

Cissus rhombifolia

Native to South America. Related to Virginia creeper, Boston ivy, and grape, this plant is distinguished for its handsome, evergreen foliage. Grows to 20 ft. Leaves, dark green, divided into diamond-shaped leaflets 1–4 in. long, with sharp-toothed edges; show bronze overtones because of reddish hairs on veins beneath. Widely used

indoors. Outdoors, it grows to good size and can be trained on trellis, pergola, or wall. Grape ivy is very easy to grow. Particularly useful near swimming pools. Takes sun or shade outdoors, indirect light indoors. Selection 'Mandaiana' is more upright and compact than the species, with larger, more substantial leaflets. 'Ellen Danica' has leaflets shallowly lobed like an oak leaf; it grows more compactly than does the species and has darker green, less lustrous leaves.

Cistaceae. Members of the rockrose family, grown primarily in the West, are evergreen shrubs with flowers that look something like single roses—large in rockrose (*Cistus*), small in sunrose (*Helianthemum*). Individual flowers are short lived, but plants bloom over a long season.

CISTUS

ROCKROSE

Cistaceae

EVERGREEN SHRUBS

⚡ ZONES MS, LS, CS

☼ FULL SUN

◌ VERY LITTLE WATER

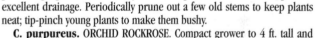
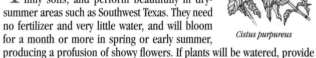
Cistus purpureus

These are carefree shrubs that grow well in limy soils, and perform beautifully in dry-summer areas such as Southwest Texas. They need no fertilizer and very little water, and will bloom for a month or more in spring or early summer, producing a profusion of showy flowers. If plants will be watered, provide excellent drainage. Periodically prune out a few old stems to keep plants neat; tip-pinch young plants to make them bushy.

C. purpureus. ORCHID ROCKROSE. Compact grower to 4 ft. tall and wide. Leaves 1–2 in. long, dark green above, gray and hairy beneath. Reddish purple, 3-in. flowers with red spot at base of each petal.

C. skanbergii. Low, broad bush 3 ft. tall and 8 ft. wide. Gray-green leaves; pure pink, 1-in. flowers in great profusion in spring.

CITRUS

Rutaceae

EVERGREEN TREES AND SHRUBS

⚡ ZONES CS FOR HARDIER TYPES, TS FOR MOST; OR INDOORS

☼ FULL SUN

● DO NOT LET ROOT ZONE BECOME DRY OR SOGGY

Orange

As landscaping plants, they offer year-round attractive form and glossy deep green foliage. Citrus plants also produce fragrant flowers and brightly colored decorative fruit in season. If you want quality fruit, your choice of plants will largely depend on the amount of winter cold in your area.

Hardiness. Citrus plants of one type or another are grown outdoors year-round in the Tropical South and mildest parts of the Coastal South. Lemons and limes are most sensitive to freezes. Sweet oranges, grapefruit, and most mandarins and their hybrids are intermediate. Kumquats, satsuma mandarins, and calamondins are most cold resistant, withstanding temperatures in the high teens. Hardy citrus (see page 184) is available to gardeners just beyond the citrus belt.

Other factors affecting a tree's cold tolerance include preconditioning to cold (more endurance if exposed to cold slowly and if first freeze comes late), type of rootstock, location in garden. Prolonged exposure to freezing weather is more damaging than a brief plunge in temperature. All citrus fruit is damaged at several degrees below freezing, so in freeze-prone areas choose early-ripening types.

▶

C

Anatomy. A citrus tree consists of two parts: scion (upper part of tree producing desirable fruit) and rootstock (lower few inches of trunk and the roots). These are joined at the bud union. Grafted trees begin bearing fruit in just a few years, contrasted with 10 to 15 years for seedling trees. Most kinds produce a single crop in fall or winter. Everbearing types (lemons, limes, calamondins) can produce throughout the year, though they fruit most heavily in spring. Plants don't go completely dormant, but their growth does slow in winter. Citrus fruit ripens only on the tree.

Tree size depends on category of citrus and on selection within category. Standard tree grows full size; dwarf is grafted onto rootstock that reduces size of tree but not of fruit. Dwarf trees are sold through mail-order suppliers (these can't ship to commercial citrus-producing states). Standard trees are the norm in Florida, Texas, and along the Gulf Coast.

Drainage. Fast drainage is essential. In poorly drained soils or in areas with heavy rainfall or a high water table, plant above soil level in raised beds or on soil mound. To improve drainage in average soil and water retention in sandy soil, dig in a 4–6-in. layer of organic matter (such as garden compost or aged sawdust) to depth of 1 ft.

Watering. Citrus trees need moist soil but never standing water. Though they require moisture all year, greatest demand is during active growth, usually from late winter or early spring through summer. Most critical when fruit is developing. Irrigate when top few inches of soil are dry but rest of root zone is still slightly moist. To check soil moisture, simply stick your finger in the soil; or use a moisture meter.

Fertilizing. Nitrogen is the main nutrient that must be supplied in all regions; if you garden in sandy soil, choose a complete fertilizer containing a full range of nutrients. Apply 2 oz. actual nitrogen the first year after newly planted tree puts on new growth; increase by 4 oz. each year for the next few years; after the fifth year, apply 1–1½ lb. yearly (use higher end of range for rainy-summer areas). To calculate pounds of actual nitrogen, multiply percentage of total nitrogen (as stated by first number on fertilizer label) by weight of fertilizer.

Divide into several feedings throughout growing season (slow-release fertilizers, however, can be applied all at once). In freeze-prone areas, start feeding after last spring frost and stop in late summer.

Pests and diseases. Most problems are minor or can be solved by improving growing conditions. Unlike deciduous fruit trees, such as apples or peaches, citrus trees do not need regular spraying. Treat citrus leaf miner and scale insects with horticultural oil spray, and greasy spot with either oil spray or copper fungicide spray (and remove fallen leaves to prevent disease from spreading). Check with Cooperative Extension Office or local garden centers for problems you may encounter in your area.

Pruning. Commercial trees are allowed to carry branches right to ground. Production is heaviest on lower branches. Growers prune only to remove twiggy growth and weak branches or, in young plant, to nip back wild growth and balance plant. You can prune garden trees to shape as desired; espaliers of citrus are traditional. Lemons and sour oranges are often planted close and pruned as hedges. Many citrus plants are thorny, so wear gloves and long-sleeved shirt when picking fruit or pruning. In freeze-prone areas, don't prune in fall or winter.

Citrus in containers. Use containers at least 1½ ft. in diameter, though calamondin can stay in 8–10-in. pots for years. Plant in light, well-drained soil mix. Daily watering may be necessary in hot weather. Use a slow-release fertilizer to keep nutrients from washing out with each watering.

Potted citrus can stay outdoors most or all year in mild-winter climates, but should be moved to protection if a freeze is predicted. In the Upper, Middle, and Lower South, shelter plants in winter: A cool greenhouse is best, but a basement area or garage with good bright light is satisfactory.

Citrus as house plants. No guarantee of flowering or fruiting indoors (though plants are still appealing). 'Improved Meyer' and 'Ponderosa' lemons, 'Persian', or 'Bearss', lime, kumquats, calamondins, 'Rangpur' sour-acid mandarin most likely to produce good fruit. Locate no more than 6 ft. from sunny window, away from radiator or other heat source. Ideal humidity level is 50 percent. Increase air moisture by misting tree; also ring tree with pebble-filled trays of water. Water sparingly in winter.

SWEET ORANGE

Dense globes to about 25 ft. tall. Fruit usually stores on the tree for a few months. The orange blossom is Florida's state flower.

'Washington'. Original navel selection from which the other navels developed. Seedless eating orange ripens early, fall into winter. In Texas and Florida, local selections sold simply as "navel" have better flavor.

'Cara Cara'. First rosy-fleshed navel, bearing at about same time as 'Washington'. Red in Florida.

'Hamlin'. Early juice orange, nearly seedless, maturing fall into winter. Best in South Texas, Florida.

'Jaffa' ('Shamouti'). Midseason (ripens winter into spring), nearly seedless eating orange from Israel. Grown in South Texas.

'Marrs'. Low-acid, few seeds, ripening fall into winter. Grows well in South Texas.

'Parson Brown'. Early-ripening small juice orange, seedy fruit. Best in Florida.

'Pineapple'. Leading midseason orange in Florida; also grown in South Texas. Fairly seedy but excellent for juicing. Fruit tends to drop from tree after ripening.

'Trovita'. Midseason eating and juice orange.

'Valencia.' This is the premier juice orange. Widely adapted, bearing nearly seedless fruit in midwinter and spring. 'Delta' and 'Midknight' are seedless selections ripening a little earlier. If grown in Florida, 'Rohde Red' has more highly colored flesh than the plain 'Valencia'.

Blood oranges. These are characterized by red pigmentation in flesh, juice, and (to a lesser degree) rind. Flavor has raspberry overtones. Need chilly nights during ripening. Main kinds grown are 'Moro', 'Sanguinelli', and 'Tarocco'.

MANDARIN

Small to medium-size trees (10–20 ft. tall) bearing juicy, loose-skinned, and often flattened fruit; most produce in winter. Selections with red-orange peel are usually called tangerines. Many mandarins tend to bear heavily in alternate years.

'Clementine' (Algerian tangerine). Sweet, variably seedy flesh. Ripens early from fall into winter, holds well on tree. Light crop without a pollinator. Good for Texas Gulf Coast.

'Dancy'. Small, seedy fruit is traditional Christmas "tangerine." Needs high heat; best in Florida. Also grows in desert. Alternate bearer.

'Encore'. Very late, ripening spring into summer and holding on tree until fall. Sweet-tart, seedy fruit. Alternate bearer. Good for South Texas.

'Fremont.' Early type with seedy, richly sweet fruit. Alternate bearer. Does well along Upper Gulf Coast.

'Honey'. Midseason, seedy, very sweet fruit. Different from 'Murcott' tangor, which is marketed as Honey tangerine. Alternate bearer. Does well in South Texas, Gulf Coast.

'Kara'. Springtime crop of sweet-tart fruit with varying seediness. Gets puffy soon after ripening. Alternate bearer.

'Kinnow'. Midseason type with seedy fruit too sweet for some people. Holds fairly well on tree. Alternate bearer.

'Mediterranean' ('Willow Leaf'). Midseason crop of sweet, aromatic, very juicy fruit gets puffy soon after ripening. Needs high heat. Alternate bearer. Good for South Texas, Gulf Coast.

'Pixie'. Late selection with seedless, mild, sweet fruit. Alternate bearer. Recommended for South Texas.

'Ponkan' (Chinese honey mandarin). Early crop of seedy, very sweet fruit. Alternate bearer. Good for both South Texas, Florida.

🌳 Satsuma. Very early mandarin with mild, sweet fruit that begins ripening in fall. Succeeds in areas too cold for most citrus. Ripe fruit deteriorates quickly on tree but keeps well in cool storage. Selections include

'Dobashi Beni', 'Kimbrough', 'Okitsu Wase', and 'Owari'. Does well in South Texas, Gulf Coast, north Florida.

'Wilking'. Midseason selection with juicy, rich, distinctive flavor. Holds fairly well on tree. Alternate bearer. Recommended for South Texas.

MULTIPLE-SELECTION CITRUS PLANTS

The garden center offerings go by such names as cocktail citrus, salad citrus, and citrus medley. On these plants, which bear multiple kinds of fruit, several selections (usually two or three) have been budded onto one stem. Such plants save space, but you must continually cut back the vigorous growers (limes, lemons, grapefruit) so the weaker ones (oranges, mandarins) can survive.

MANDARIN HYBRIDS

These hybrids generally perform best in hot weather. Many were developed in Florida, where they produce outstanding crops.

Tangelo. Hybrid between mandarin and grapefruit. Best with a pollinator. Two main selections. 'Minneola' bears winter crop of bright orange-red fruit (often with a noticeable "neck") with rich, tart flavor and some seeds. 'Orlando' produces mild, sweet, fairly seedy fruit about a month earlier than 'Minneola'.

Tangor. Hybrid between mandarin and sweet orange. Especially well adapted to sweet orange–growing areas of Florida. 'Murcott' is an alternate bearer with very sweet, seedy, yellowish orange fruit winter into spring; it's marketed under the name "Honey tangerine." 'Ortanique' has sweet, juicy, variably seedy fruit ripening spring to summer. 'Temple' bears winter to spring crop of sweet to tart, seedy fruit; needs high heat and is more cold sensitive than other tangors.

Other mandarin hybrids include the following:

'Ambersweet'. Result of crossing a hybrid of 'Clementine' mandarin and 'Orlando' tangelo with a midseason orange. Juicy fruit, borne fall to winter, is classified as an orange by fresh fruit marketers. Very seedy when grown near another selection.

'Fairchild'. Hybrid between 'Clementine' and 'Orlando'. Juicy, sweet fruit in winter. Best in desert. Bigger crop with a pollinator.

'Fallglo'. Somewhat cold sensitive, like its 'Temple' tangor parent. Juicy, tart, very seedy fruit ripening in fall.

'Lee'. Hybrid between 'Clementine' and unknown pollen parent. Fairly seedy fruit matures fall to winter. Has best flavor if grown in Florida.

'Nova'. Cross between 'Clementine' and 'Orlando'. Juicy, richly sweet fruit fall to winter. Needs a pollinator.

'Page'. Parents are 'Clementine' and 'Minneola' tangelo. Many small, juicy, sweet fruits fall into winter. Few seeds, even with pollinator to improve fruit set.

'Robinson'. Hybrid between 'Clementine' and 'Orlando'. Very sweet fruit in fall. Quite seedy with a pollinator. Best flavor if grown in Florida.

'Sunburst'. Cross between 'Robinson' and 'Osceola' (an infrequently grown mandarin hybrid from Florida). Big, sweet, red-orange fruit in late fall. Nearly seedless without a pollinator. Best flavor in Florida.

'Wekiwa' (pink tangelo, 'Lavender Gem'). A cross between a tangelo and a grapefruit: looks like a small grapefruit but is eaten like a mandarin. Juicy, mild, sweet flesh is purplish rose in hot climates. Ripens late fall into winter.

SOUR-ACID MANDARIN

Both of these bear throughout the year in mild-winter climates; also fruit very well indoors.

Calamondin. A mandarin-kumquat hybrid with fruit like a very small orange but a sweet, edible rind. Juicy, tart flesh has some seeds. Variegated form is especially ornamental.

'Rangpur'. Often called Rangpur lime, though it's not a lime and doesn't taste like one. Fruit looks and peels like a mandarin. Less acid than lemon;

flavor overtones make it a good base for punches and mixed drinks. 'Otaheite' (Tahiti orange) is an acidless form sold as a house plant.

GRAPEFRUIT

Trees to about 30 ft. tall. Best in Florida and South Texas.

'Duncan'. Oldest known grapefruit variety in Florida and the one from which all the others developed. Extremely seedy, white flesh with better flavor than modern seedless types. Good for juice.

'Flame'. Red flesh similar to that of 'Rio Red', slight rind blush, and few to no seeds. Now widely planted in Florida.

'Marsh' ('Marsh Seedless'). Main white-fleshed commercial kind. Seedless offspring of 'Duncan'. A pigmented form, 'Pink Marsh' ('Thompson'), doesn't hold its color well.

'Melogold'. Grapefruit-pummelo hybrid. Seedless white flesh is sweeter than fruit of its sister selection 'Oroblanco'; tree tolerates slightly more cold than 'Oroblanco'.

'Oroblanco'. Grapefruit-pummelo hybrid. Fruit containing few to no seeds has a thicker rind and more sweet-tart flavor than 'Melogold'.

'Ray Ruby' and 'Henderson'. Almost identical seedless types that have good rind blush and flesh pigmentation.

'Redblush' ('Ruby', 'Ruby Red'). Seedless with red-tinted flesh. Red internal color fades to pink, then buff by end of season.

'Rio Red'. Seedless type with good rind blush and flesh nearly as red as that of 'Star Ruby'. More dependable fruit producer than 'Star Ruby'.

'Star Ruby'. Seedless selection with the reddest color. Tree is subject to cold damage, erratic bearing, and other growing problems. Doesn't withstand dry heat.

LEMON

Low heat requirement; will even produce indoors.

'Bearss'. Selection of a Sicilian variety grown in Florida; no relation to 'Bearss' ('Persian' or 'Tahiti') lime. Fruit similar to 'Eureka'. Some fruit all year, but main crop comes in fall and winter.

'Eureka'. Familiar lemon sold in grocery stores. Some fruit all year in mild climates. Big, vigorous, nearly thornless tree needs periodic pruning.

'Improved Meyer'. Hybrid between lemon and sweet orange or mandarin. More cold tolerant

Lemon

than true lemon. Yellow-orange, juicy fruit with few seeds, throughout year. Can grow to 15 ft. tall, but is usually considerably shorter.

'Lisbon'. Fruit is similar to 'Eureka' (and is also sold in markets), but tree is bigger, thornier, and more cold tolerant. 'Lisbon Seedless' is the same without seeds. These are the best lemons for hot, dry areas. Some fruit all year in mild climates.

'Ponderosa' ('American Wonder'). Thorny lemon-citron hybrid, naturally dwarf. Seedy, thick-skinned, moderately juicy fruit weighing up to 2 lb. apiece. Some fruit all year. More susceptible to cold than true lemon. Thrives indoors.

'Variegated Pink' ('Pink Lemonade'). Sport of 'Eureka' with green-and-white leaves and green stripes on immature fruit. Light pink flesh doesn't need heat to develop color. Grows to about 8 ft. tall.

LIME

There's a lime for just about every area of the citrus belt warm enough for sweet oranges. Limes outperform lemons in Florida.

'Kieffer'. Leaves are used in Thai and Cambodian cooking, as is bumpy, sour spring fruit.

'Mexican' ('Key', West Indian lime, bartender's lime). Very thorny plant to about 15 ft. high, bearing small, rounded, intensely flavored fruit all year. 'Mexican Thornless' is the same, minus the spines. Plants need high heat and are very cold sensitive.

'Palestine Sweet'. Shrubby plant with acidless fruit resembling that of 'Persian' or 'Tahiti' and used in Middle Eastern, Indian, and Latin American cooking. Ripens fall or winter.

'Persian' or 'Tahiti' ('Bearss'). Big-fruited, seedless lime sold in grocery stores. Some fruit all year. Needs less heat for fruiting and tolerates more cold than 'Mexican'. Plant grows 15–20 ft. tall. ▶

KUMQUAT

Shrubby plants 6–15 ft. or taller bear yellow to reddish orange fruits that look like tiny oranges. Eat whole and unpeeled—spongy rind is sweet, pulp is tangy. Best in areas with warm to hot summers and chilly nights during fall or winter ripening. Hardy to at least 18°F.

'Marumi'. Slightly thorny plant with round fruit. Peel is sweeter than that of 'Nagami', but slightly seedy flesh is more acidic.

'Meiwa'. Round fruit is sweeter, juicier, and less seedy than that of other forms. Considered the best kumquat for eating fresh. Nearly thornless.

'Nagami'. Main commercial type. Oval-shaped, slightly seedy fruit is more abundant and sweeter in hot-summer climates. Thornless.

HARDY CITRUS

For areas beyond citrus belt. Most are good choices for Lower and Coastal South; some can be grown in chillier areas. Hardiness figures apply to established plants conditioned to cold by the time freezes arrive.

'Changsha' mandarin. Small tree with fruit similar to satsuma mandarin but not as tasty. Ripens from fall into winter. Sometimes grown in regions of Texas, Gulf Coast, and Southwest too cold for regular mandarin selections. Hardy to about 5°F.

Citrange. Hybrid between sweet orange and hardy orange. 'Morton' has fruit like slightly tart sweet orange. 'US-119' is newer and sweeter. Ripens late fall. Hardy to 5–10°F.

Hardy orange *(Poncirus trifoliata)*. Extremely thorny deciduous shrub or small tree with fragrant flowers and inedible fruit makes an unusual specimen or barrier hedge. Hardy to about –20°F. 'Flying Dragon', a natural dwarf with curved thorns and twisted branches, survives to about –15°F. Used as a dwarfing understock.

'Thomasville' orangequat. Developed from a hardy orange, kumquat, and sweet orange. Small, nearly seedless fruit used as lime substitute if picked soon after ripening in fall. Left on tree, may become sweet enough to eat fresh. Hardy to about 0°F.

CLADRASTIS lutea

YELLOW WOOD

Fabaceae (Leguminosae)

DECIDUOUS TREE

ZONES US, MS, LS

FULL SUN

REGULAR WATER

Cladrastis lutea

Native to Kentucky, Tennessee, and North Carolina. Slow growing to 30–50 ft. with broad, rounded head. Big leaves, 8–12 in. long, divided into many (usually 7 to 11) oval leaflets. Yellowish green new foliage turns to beautiful bright green in summer, then brilliant yellow in fall. Mature trees have handsome smooth gray bark; common name refers to color of freshly cut heartwood.

Tree may not flower until 10 years old and may skip bloom some years, but when floral display does come (possibly every 2 to 3 years), it's quite spectacular. In late spring to early summer, the tree produces big clusters (to 14 in. long) of fragrant white flowers that look somewhat like wisteria blossoms. ('Rosea' is pink-flowered form.) Blooms are followed by flat, 3–4-in.-long seedpods.

Even if it never blooms, yellow wood is useful and attractive as a terrace, patio, or lawn tree. It's deep rooted, so you can grow other plants beneath it. Tolerates alkaline soils. Established trees withstand some drought.

Prune when young to shorten side branches or to correct narrow, weak branch crotches, which are susceptible to breakage in ice storms. Usually low branching; you can remove lower branches entirely when tree reaches the height you want. Confine any pruning to summer, since cuts made in winter or spring bleed profusely.

SOUTHERN HERITAGE PLANTS
IDENTIFIED BY SYMBOL

CLARET CUP. See ECHINOCEREUS triglochidiatus

CLARY. See SALVIA sclarea

CLASPING CONEFLOWER. See DRACOPIS amplexicaulis

CLEMATIS

Ranunculaceae

DECIDUOUS OR EVERGREEN VINES AND PERENNIALS

ZONES VARY BY SPECIES

ROOTS NEED TO BE COOL; TOPS IN SUN

REGULAR WATER

Clematis armandii

Most of the 200-odd species are deciduous vines; the evergreen *C. armandii* and a few interesting freestanding or sprawling perennials and small shrubs are exceptions. All have attractive flowers, and most are spectacular. The flowers are followed by fluffy clusters of seeds with tails, often quite effective in flower arrangements. Leaves of vining kinds are dark green, usually divided into leaflets; leafstalks twist and curl to hold plant to its support.

Clematis are not demanding, but their few specific requirements should be met. Plant vining types next to trellis, tree trunk, or open framework to give stems support for twining. Provide rich, loose, fast-draining soil; add generous quantities of organic matter such as decomposed ground bark. Add lime only where soil tests indicate calcium deficiency.

To provide cool area for roots, add mulch, place large flat rock over soil, or plant shallow-rooted ground cover over the root area. Put in support when planting, and tie up stems at once. Stems are easily broken, so protect them with wire netting if child or dog traffic is heavy. Clematis need constant moisture and nutrients to make their great rush of growth; apply a complete liquid fertilizer monthly during the growing season.

When pruning clematis, remember that dormant wood can look dead, so take care not to make accidental cuts. Watch for healthy buds at leaf bases and preserve them. The basic objective is to get the greatest number of flowers on the shapeliest plant.

The type of pruning you do depends on when your plants flower. If you don't know what kind you have, watch them for a year to see when they bloom; then prune accordingly.

Spring-blooming clematis bloom only on the previous year's wood. Cut back a month after flowering to restrict sprawl, preserving main branches.

Summer- and fall-blooming clematis bloom on wood produced in the spring. In the Lower and Coastal South, cut back in late fall after flowering or in early spring as buds swell; wait until spring in the Upper and Middle South. For the first 2 to 3 years, cut to within 6–12 in. of the ground, or to two or three buds; cut to 2 ft. or less on older plants.

Clematis that bloom in spring and again in summer or fall bloom on old wood in spring, new wood later. Do only light, corrective pruning in fall or early spring; pinch or lightly shape portions that have bloomed to stimulate low branching and avoid a bare base.

Cut flowers are choice for indoors (float in bowl). Burn cut stems with match to make flowers last longer. Unless otherwise specified, flowers are 4–6 in. across.

C. armandii. ARMAND CLEMATIS, EVERGREEN CLEMATIS. Zones LS, CS. Native to China. Fast growing to 20 ft. Leaves divided into three glossy dark green leaflets, 3–5 in. long; they droop downward to create strongly textured pattern. Glistening white, $2\frac{1}{2}$-in.-wide, fragrant flowers in large, branched clusters in spring. 'Hendersoni Rubra' has light pink flowers.

Slow to start; races when established. Needs constant pruning after flowering to prevent tangling and buildup of dead thatch on inner parts of vine. Keep and tie up stems you want, and cut out all others. Frequent pinching will hold foliage to eye level. Train along fence tops or rails, roof gables. Allow to climb tall trees. Trained on substantial frame, makes privacy screen if not allowed to become bare at base.

C. davidiana. See C. heracleifolia davidiana

C. dioscoreifolia (C. terniflora, C. paniculata, C. maximow-icziana). SWEET AUTUMN CLEMATIS. Zones US, MS, LS, CS. Native to Japan. Tall and vigorous (some would say rampant), forming billowy masses of 1-in.-wide, creamy white, fragrant flowers in late summer, fall. Attractive plumed seeds; self-sows freely. Dark green, glossy leaves divided into three to five oval leaflets, 1–2½ in. long. After bloom or in early spring, prune growth that has bloomed most recently to one or two buds. Good privacy screen, arbor cover.

C. florida 'Sieboldii' (C. f. 'Bicolor'). Zones US, MS, LS. Flowers 3–4 in. across, with a central puff of purple petal-like stamens, in summer. Vine is a somewhat delicate 8–12 ft. Not as rugged as other clematis, but bears striking flowers. 'Alba Plena' has double greenish white blooms.

C. heracleifolia davidiana (C. davidiana). Zones US, MS, LS. Native to China. Woody-based perennial to 4 ft. high. Deep green leaves divided into three broad, oval, 3–6-in.-long leaflets. Dense clusters of 1-in.-long, tubular, medium to deep blue, fragrant flowers in summer. Use in perennial or shrub border.

C. integrifolia. Zones US, MS, LS. Native to Europe and Asia. Woody-based perennial to 3 ft. with dark green, undivided, 2–4-in.-long leaves and nodding, urn-shaped, 1½-in.-long blue flowers in summer. 'Hendersonii' has larger flowers.

C. jackmanii. JACKMAN CLEMATIS. Zones US, MS, LS. A series of hybrids between forms of *C. lanuginosa* and *C. viticella*. All are vigorous plants of rapid growth to 10 ft. or more in one season. *C. jackmanii* is the best known of the older large-flowered hybrids. It bears a profusion of 4–5-in. rich purple flowers with four sepals. Blooms from early summer through fall, with heaviest bloom early in the season. Newer hybrids have larger flowers with more sepals, but none blooms as profusely. 'Comtesse de Bouchard' has silvery rose pink flowers; 'Mme Edouard Andre' has purplish red blossoms. All flower on new wood; do best with severe pruning in early spring as buds begin to swell. May freeze to the ground in cold-winter areas. (For more on large-flowered hybrid clematis, see discussion this page.)

C. lanuginosa. Zones US, MS, LS. Native to China. A parent of many of the finest large-flowered hybrids. Grows to only about 6–9 ft. but produces magnificent display of large (6-in.) lilac to white flowers, May–July. Best known for its selection 'Candida', with 8-in. white flowers and light yellow stamens. Blooms on new and old wood. Prune only to remove dead or weak growth in early spring. Then, after first flush of flowers (March–April in favorable climates), cut back flowered portions promptly for another crop later in the summer.

C. macropetala. DOWNY CLEMATIS. Zones US, MS, LS. Native to China, Siberia. Size variable, 6–10 ft. high. In early spring, produces 4-in. lavender to powder blue flowers that look double, resembling a dancer's tutu. Blooms are followed by bronzy pink, silvery-tailed seed clusters. 'Markham Pink' has lavender-pink flowers. Prune lightly in late winter to remove weak shoots and limit vigorous growth to sound wood.

C. montana. ANEMONE CLEMATIS. Zones US, MS, LS. Native to the Himalayas, China. Vigorous to 20 ft. or more. Easy to grow. Massive early spring display of 2–2½-in. anemone-like flowers, opening white, turning pink. Flowers on old wood, so can be heavily thinned or pruned immediately after flowering to rejuvenate or reduce size.

'Tetrarose' has large, rich mauve flowers. 'Elizabeth' has pale pink blooms with fragrance of vanilla. 'Grandiflora', vigorous growth to 40 ft., bears abundant pure white blooms. *C. m. rubens*, to 15–25 ft., has crimson new leaves maturing to bronzy green; fragrant rose red to pink flowers are carried throughout vine. In *C. m. rubens* 'Odorata', the blossoms are vanilla scented.

C. paniculata. See C. dioscoreifolia

C. tangutica. GOLDEN CLEMATIS. Zones US, MS, LS. Native to Mongolia, northern China. To 10–15 ft., with gray-green, finely divided leaves. Bright yellow, 2–4-in., nodding, lantern-shaped flowers in great profusion

Clematis montana

from July to fall. They are followed by handsome, silvery-tailed seed clusters. Prune as for *C. dioscoreifolia*.

C. terniflora. See C. dioscoreifolia

C. texensis. SCARLET CLEMATIS. Zones US, MS, LS. Native to Texas. Fast growing to 6–10 ft. Dense bluish green foliage. Bright scarlet, urn-shaped flowers to 1 in. long, early summer until frost. More tolerant of dry soils than most clematis. Hybrid 'Duchess of Albany' has flowers of bright pink shading to lilac at the edges.

C. viticella. ITALIAN CLEMATIS. Zones US, MS, LS. Native to southern Europe, western Asia. To 12–15 ft. Purple or rose purple, 2-in. flowers in summer. Selections include 'Mme Julia Correvon', rosy red, and 'Polish Spirit', deep purple blue with red center.

Large-flowered hybrid clematis. Best in Zones US, MS, LS, CS. Although well over a hundred selections of large-flowered hybrid clematis are being grown today, your local garden center is not likely to offer more than a dozen of the old favorites. Mail-order catalogs remain the best source for collectors seeking the newest. Flowers on some of these may reach 10 in. wide. Most are summer bloomers.

Here are some selections to choose from—old favorites first, then newer offerings:

White. 'Candida' and 'Henryi' are standard. 'Marie Boisselot' or 'Mme Le Coultre' (large, flat, round flowers) and 'Gillian Blades' (huge, star-shaped flowers) are newer.

Pink. 'Comtesse de Bouchard', the standard pink, has these rivals: 'Charissima' (veined pink with deeper bars); 'Hagley Hybrid' ('Pink Chiffon'), shell pink with pointed sepals; and 'Lincoln Star' (pink with paler edges).

Red. Red clematis have deep purplish red flowers that are best displayed where the sun can shine through them, as on the top of a fence. 'Mme Edouard Andre', 'Ernest Markham', and 'Red Cardinal' are standards. 'Ville de Lyon' has full, rounded, velvety flowers; 'Niobe' is the darkest red of all.

Blue violet. Mid-blue 'Ramona' is always popular. Other selections are 'Edo Murasaki' (deep blue); 'General Sikorski' (huge, with faint red bar); 'Lady Betty Balfour' (dark blue); 'Mrs. Cholmondeley' (big, veined sky blue); 'Piccadilly' (purplish blue); 'Prince Philip' (huge, purplish blue with ruffled edges); and 'Will Goodwin' (lavender to sky blue).

Purple. Classic *C. jackmanii* is the most popular. 'Purpureus Superba' ('Jackmanii Superba') is larger, somewhat redder. Others include 'Gypsy Queen' (deepest purple); 'Mrs. M. Thompson' (deep bluish purple with red bar); and 'Richard Pennell' (rosy purple).

Bicolor. 'Nelly Moser' (purplish pink with reddish center bar) is deservedly one of the most popular clematis. 'Carnaby' (white with red bar) and 'Dr. Ruppel' (pink with red bar) are newer and splashier.

Double. Fully double, roselike blooms in early summer on old wood are usually followed later by single or semidouble flowers on new wood. 'Belle of Woking' is silvery blue; 'Duchess of Edinburgh', white; 'Mrs. P. T. James', deep blue; 'Teshio', lavender; and 'Vyvyan Pennell', deep blue with lavender blue center.

CLEOME hasslerana (C. spinosa)

SPIDER FLOWER, CLEOME

Capparaceae

ANNUAL

ALL ZONES

FULL SUN

REGULAR TO MODERATE WATER

Cleome hasslerana

Shrubby, branching plant topped in summer and fall with many open, fluffy clusters of pink or white flowers with extremely long, protruding stamens. Slender seed capsules follow blossoms. Short, strong spines on stems; lower leaves divided, upper ones undivided. Leaves and stems feel clammy to the touch, have a strong but not unpleasant smell. Reaches 4–6 ft. tall, 4–5 ft. wide. Thrives in heat, tolerates some drought. Grow in background, as summer hedge, against walls or fences, in large containers. Flowers and dry seed capsules are useful in arrangements.

Sow seeds in place in spring. Many kinds can be grown from seed. In most cases, selection name indicates color: 'Cherry Queen', 'Mauve Queen', 'Pink Queen', 'Purple Queen', 'Rose Queen', and 'Ruby Queen'. 'Helen Campbell' is snow white. Plants self-sow to a fault.

CLERODENDRUM

GLORYBOWER
Verbenaceae
EVERGREEN OR DECIDUOUS SHRUBS OR TREES
🌡 ZONES VARY BY SPECIES
◐ PARTIAL SHADE
💧 REGULAR WATER

Clerodendrum thomsoniae

This relatively little known group of small trees, shrubs, and shrubby vines is cultivated for big clusters of showy, brightly colored flowers.

C. bungei (C. foetidum). CASHMERE BOUQUET. Deciduous shrub. Zones LS, CS, TS. Native to China. Grows rapidly to 6 ft. tall; soft wooded. Prune severely in spring and pinch back through growing season to make 2–3-ft. compact shrub. Spreads by suckers, eventually forming thicket if not restrained. Big leaves (to 1 ft.), broadly oval with toothed edges, dark green above, with rusty fuzz beneath; ill smelling when crushed. Delightfully fragrant flowers in summer: ¾ in. wide, rosy red, in loose clusters to 8 in. across. Plant where it will be inconspicuous when out of bloom.

C. fragrans pleniflorum (C. philippinum pleniflorum). Evergreen to partly deciduous shrub. Zones CS, TS. Coarse shrub spreading freely by root suckers unless confined. To 5–8 ft. (much less in containers), 10-in. leaves like those of *C. bungei*. Flowers pale pink, double, in broad clusters that resemble florists' hydrangea; sweet, clean fragrance. Summer bloom.

C. paniculatum. PAGODA FLOWER. Evergreen shrub. Zone TS. To 4 ft. or more, with roundish or oval leaves to 16 in. long and foot-long, branched, pyramidal clusters of small scarlet flowers.

C. speciosissimum. JAVA GLORYBOWER. Evergreen shrub. Zones CS, TS. Dense-growing and tall (to 12 ft.); can be kept to 4–5 ft. with pruning. Large, velvety leaves. Pyramidal, 1–1½-ft.-long clusters of small brilliant red flowers can appear at any time of year.

C. thomsoniae (C. balfouri). BLEEDING HEART VINE. Evergreen vining shrub. In most protected spots of Zones CS, TS; indoor/outdoor container plant elsewhere. Native to West Africa. Leaves are oval, 4–7 in. long, dark green, shiny, and distinctly ribbed. Flowers are a study in color contrast—scarlet, 1-in. tubes surrounded by large (¾-in.-long) white calyxes, carried in flattish, 5-in.-wide clusters, late summer to fall. Will flower in 6-in. container. Can grow to 6 ft. or more if left untrimmed. Give support for twining. Needs rich, loose soil mix, plenty of water with good drainage. Prune after flowering.

🌲 **C. trichotomum.** HARLEQUIN GLORYBOWER. Deciduous shrub-tree in Zones LS, CS, TS; treat as herbaceous perennial in Zone MS. Native to Japan. Grows with many stems from base to 10–15 ft. or more; suckers freely. Leaves oval, to 5 in. long, dark green, soft, hairy. Fragrant clusters of white, tubular flowers almost twice as long as prominent, fleshy, scarlet calyxes, ½ in. Late-summer bloom. Calyxes hang on and contrast nicely with turquoise or blue-green, metallic-looking fruit. Give room to spread at top; plant under it to hide its legginess. *C. t. fargesii*, from China, is somewhat hardier and smaller; it has smooth leaves and green calyxes that later turn pink.

C. ugandense. Evergreen shrub. Zones CS, TS. To 10 ft. (usually much less), with glossy dark green, 4-in.-long leaves and 1-in.-long flowers with one violet blue petal and four pale blue ones. Pistil and stamens arch outward and upward. Summer bloom.

CLETHRA

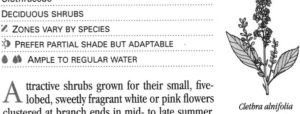

Clethraceae
DECIDUOUS SHRUBS
🌡 ZONES VARY BY SPECIES
◐ PREFER PARTIAL SHADE BUT ADAPTABLE
💧 AMPLE TO REGULAR WATER

Attractive shrubs grown for their small, five-lobed, sweetly fragrant white or pink flowers clustered at branch ends in mid- to late summer.

Clethra alnifolia

Fairly soil tolerant, but do best in moist, organic, slightly acid soil. Prefer partial shade but adapt well to less light, or to full sun. No serious pest or disease problems. Routine pruning not required.

C. acuminata. CINNAMON CLETHRA. Zones US, MS, LS. Native to mountain areas of Virginia, Georgia, and Alabama. Grows to 8–12 ft., rarely 20 ft. Habit is open, gaunt even, so polished brown bark, in various shades of tan, cinnamon, reddish brown, shows beautifully. Fragrant white flowers. Leaves golden yellow in fall.

C. alnifolia. SWEET PEPPERBUSH, SUMMERSWEET. Zones US, MS, LS, CS. Native to eastern U.S. As the common names imply, this shrub's outstanding feature is its display of flowers with a sweet, spicy scent. Sweet pepperbush grows 4–10 ft. tall (it's more apt to reach the upper end of the range in moist soil and in shade), with thin, strong branches forming a vertical pattern. The toothed, dark green, 2–4-in.-long leaves appear late in spring. In summer, each branch tip carries several 4–6-in.-long spires of tiny, gleaming white, perfumed blossoms. Fall foliage color ranges from golden yellow to brownish and can last for several weeks; old flower spikes hang on while the leaves are changing. Several types are commonly grown. 'Hummingbird' is a dense, compact plant; 'Paniculata' has clustered flower spires; 'Pink Spires' produces pale pink flowers from rose pink buds; 'Rosea' has pink buds opening pinkish white.

'Ruby Spice' has dark pink blooms. Tolerates coast conditions. Wonderful for borders, shade plantings. Prune in early spring, since flowers are produced on new growth. Spreads by suckers into a broad clump.

C. barbinervis. JAPANESE CLETHRA. Zones US, MS, LS. Slow grower to 15–18 ft., with sharply toothed leaves that turn bright yellow in fall. Drooping, 4–6-in. clusters of fragrant white flowers. Attractive glossy gray to brown bark. Beautiful plant, but rarely grown in U.S.

CLEYERA japonica
(Eurya ochnacea)

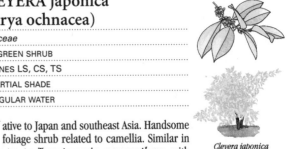

Theaceae
EVERGREEN SHRUB
🌡 ZONES LS, CS, TS
◐ PARTIAL SHADE
💧 REGULAR WATER

Native to Japan and southeast Asia. Handsome foliage shrub related to camellia. Similar in character to *Ternstroemia gymnanthera*, with

Cleyera japonica

which it is often confused in the nursery trade. Grows at moderate rate to 20 ft. tall, with graceful, arching branches. New leaves are beautiful deep brownish red. Mature leaves, 3–6 in. long, are glossy dark green with reddish midrib. Small clusters of fragrant, creamy white flowers in summer are followed by small, dark red, puffy berries that last through winter. Flowers and berries are attractive but not showy. 'Tricolor' (*C. fortunei*) has yellow-and-rose variegation on its foliage.

CLIFTONIA monophylla

BUCKWHEAT TREE

Cyrillaceae

EVERGREEN SHRUB OR TREE

ZONES MS, LS, CS

FULL SUN OR PARTIAL SHADE

LIKES MOISTURE

Cliftonia monophylla

Outstanding multitrunked shrub or small tree native to swamps and moist forests of the Southeast. Grows upright, to 10–20 ft. Leaves are glossy, dark green, leathery, 2–3 in. long. Clusters of small pinkish white fragrant flowers appear in early spring and attract bees and butterflies. Tiny egg-shaped fruits appear in fall. Prefers acid soil with lots of organic matter.

CLIMBING HYDRANGEA. See DECUMARIA barbara, HYDRANGEA anomala

CLIMBING LILY. See GLORIOSA rothschildiana

CLIVIA miniata

KAFFIR LILY

Amaryllidaceae

TUBEROUS-ROOTED PERENNIAL

ZONE TS; OR INDOORS

PARTIAL OR FULL SHADE

REGULAR WATER

Clivia miniata

Native to South Africa. Striking member of the amaryllis family. Brilliant clusters of orange, funnel-shaped flowers rising from dense clumps of dark green, strap-shaped, 1½-ft.-long evergreen leaves. Blooming period is December–April; most bloom March–April. Ornamental red berries follow flowers. French and Belgian hybrids have very wide, dark green leaves and yellow to deep red-orange blooms on thick, rigid stalks. 'Flame' is an exceptionally hot orange red. Solomone Hybrids have pale to deep yellow flowers.

Clivias are handsome in shaded borders with ferns and azaleas. Superb in containers; grow indoors in cold-winter climates. Plant with top of tuber just above soil line. Let clumps grow undisturbed for years. Container plants bloom best with regular fertilizing, crowded roots.

CLOVE PINK. See DIANTHUS caryophyllus

CLYTOSTOMA callistegioides

VIOLET TRUMPET VINE

Bignoniaceae

EVERGREEN VINE

ZONES CS, TS

FULL SUN OR PARTIAL SHADE

REGULAR TO MODERATE WATER

Clytostoma callistegioides

Formerly *Bignonia violacea, B. speciosa*. Strong-growing vine that will clamber over anything by tendrils; needs support on walls. Leaves divided into two glossy, dark green leaflets with wavy margins. Extended terminal shoots hang down in curtain effect. Trumpet-shaped flowers in violet, lavender, or pale purple, 3 in. long and nearly as wide at the top, in sprays at end of shoots, late spring to fall. Tops hardy to 20°F, roots to 10°F. Excellent vine for areas of Florida too cold for more tender bignonia relatives such as pandorea. Remove unwanted long runners and spent flower sprays. Prune in late winter to discipline growth.

COBAEA scandens

CUP-AND-SAUCER VINE

Polemoniaceae

TENDER PERENNIAL USUALLY GROWN AS ANNUAL

ALL ZONES

FULL SUN

REGULAR WATER

Cobaea scandens

Native to Mexico. Extremely vigorous growth to 25 ft. Bell-shaped flowers are first greenish, then violet or rose purple; there is also a white-flowered form. Called cup-and-saucer vine because 2-in.-long cup of petals sits in large, green, saucerlike calyx. Leaves divided into two or three pairs of oval, 4-in. leaflets. At ends of leaves are curling tendrils that enable vine to climb rough surfaces without support.

The hard-coated seeds may rot if sown outdoors in cool weather. Start indoors in 4-in. pots; notch seeds with a knife and press edgewise into moistened potting mix, barely covering seeds. Keep moist but not wet; transplant to warm, sunny location when weather warms up. Protect from wind. Blooms first year from seed. In the Tropical South and milder parts of the Coastal South, it lives from year to year, eventually reaching more than 40 ft. in length and blooming heavily spring–fall.

COBRA LILY, SHOWY. See ARISAEMA speciosum

COBWEB HOUSELEEK. See SEMPERVIVUM arachnoideum

COCCOLOBA

SEA GRAPE

Polygonaceae

EVERGREEN SHRUBS OR SMALL TREES

ZONE TS

FULL SUN

MODERATE WATER

Coccoloba uvifera

The quintessential seaside plants: tolerant of wind, sand, and salt, though tender to frost. Useful for windbreaks. Trunk and branches thick, often picturesquely twisted. New leaves reddish or coppery, mature leaves glossy green with reddish veins. Small white flowers are followed by clusters of purple fruits that can be made into jelly. Shape plant by pruning just before new growth emerges. Small plants in containers can be used for bonsai.

C. diversifolia (C. laurifolia). PIGEON PLUM. Can reach 40 ft. high. Similar to *C. uvifera*, but with shorter flower clusters, smaller fruits, and 2–4-in. oval leaves.

C. uvifera. SEA GRAPE. Can grow to 30 ft. but is usually kept much lower. Nearly round leaves to 8 in. wide. Flowers in foot-long clusters; fruits ¾ in. wide. Will grow right on the dunes.

COCCULUS

Menispermaceae

TWINING SHRUBS AND VINES

ZONES VARY BY SPECIES

FULL SUN OR PARTIAL SHADE

PREFERS MOISTURE

Cocculus carolinus

Tropical woody vines and vinelike shrubs that grow easily in moist soil. Flowers are not prominent, but foliage is lovely glossy green.

C. carolinus. CAROLINA MOONSEED. Woody deciduous vine (evergreen in Lower South and Coastal South) native from Florida to Virginia, and west to Texas. Zones MS, LS, CS. Grows rapidly, to 10–12 ft., climbing by tendrils, so needs support. Greenish white flowers open in spring, in 3–5-in.-long clusters, but are not as showy as glossy, bright red berries vine produces in late summer to winter. Tolerates most soils, including alkaline ones.

C. laurifolius. Evergreen shrub. Native to Himalayas. Zones CS, TS. Grows slowly at first, then moderately rapidly to 25 ft. or more. Can be kept lower by pruning or may be trained as espalier. Usually multistemmed shrub with arching, spreading growth as wide as it is high. Staked, trained as a tree, it takes on an umbrella shape. Leaves shiny, leathery, oblong to 6 in., with three strongly marked veins running from base to tip. Long, willowy branches are as easily led and trained as vines; fastened to a trellis, they make an effective screen.

COCKSCOMB. See CELOSIA argentea

COCKSPUR CORAL TREE. See ERYTHRINA crista-galli

COCKSPUR THORN. See CRATAEGUS crus-galli

COCOS nucifera

COCONUT PALM

Arecaceae (Palmae)

PALM TREE

☀ ZONE TS

☼ FULL SUN

💧 MODERATE WATER

The coconut palm is both an economically valuable plant and a handsome ornamental, but it is hardy only in south Florida. Can grow to 80 ft. but is usually much shorter, with a leaning or curving trunk and a crown of feathery, 20-ft. fronds. Flowers are not notable, but the fruit is the coconut of commerce. Sprouted coconuts are seen fairly often in large pots or tubs; such plants are attractive until they grow too large. Grows best near the shore. Landscape use is limited by the risk that falling coconuts pose to passersby and by a potentially fatal plant disease, lethal yellows.

Cocos nucifera

COCOS plumosa. See SYAGRUS romanzoffianum

CODIAEUM variegatum

CROTON

Euphorbiaceae

EVERGREEN SHRUB USUALLY GROWN AS HOUSE PLANT

☀ ZONE TS; OR INDOORS

☼ ☼ ● SOME FORMS TAKE SUN, OTHERS SHADE

💧 💧 AMPLE TO REGULAR WATER

Codiaeum variegatum

Native to tropics. Can reach 6 ft. or more outdoors in Tropical South; indoors, usually seen as single-stemmed plant, 6–24 in. tall. Grown principally for coloring of large, leathery, glossy leaves, which may be green, yellow, red, purple, bronze, pink, or almost any combination of these colors. Leaves may be oval, lance shaped, or very narrow; straight edged or lobed. Dozens of named forms combine these differing features.

Outdoor exposure depends on selection. Needs bright light, regular misting indoors; does well in a warm, humid greenhouse, provided you keep an eye out for spider mites, mealybugs, and thrips. Can be brought outdoors in warm season. Some people are sensitive to croton leaves.

COFFEA arabica

COFFEE PLANT

Rubiaceae

EVERGREEN SHRUB

☀ ZONE TS; OR INDOORS

☼ ● PARTIAL OR FULL SHADE

💧 REGULAR WATER

Native to East Africa. The coffee tree of commerce can be grown as a specimen or in shrub borders in the Tropical South; elsewhere, it's a handsome container plant for patios or large, well-lit rooms. Upright shrub to 15 ft., with evenly spaced tiers of branches clothed in shiny, dark green, oval leaves to 6 in. long. Small (¾-in.), fragrant white flowers are clustered near leaf bases. These are followed by ½-in. fruits—green when they first appear, then turning purple or red. Each fruit contains two seeds—coffee beans. Use same potting mix and care as for camellias. Protect from frosts.

Coffea arabica

COFFEE PLANT. See COFFEA arabica

COLCHICUM

MEADOW SAFFRON, AUTUMN CROCUS

Liliaceae

CORMS

☀ ZONES US, MS, LS; OR INDOORS

☼ FULL SUN

💧 REGULAR WATER DURING GROWTH AND BLOOM

☠ ALL PARTS ARE HIGHLY POISONOUS IF INGESTED

Colchicum

Native to Mediterranean regions. Many species; sometimes called autumn crocus, but not true crocuses. Shining, brown-skinned, thick-scaled corms send up clusters of long-tubed, flaring, lavender-pink, rose purple, or white flowers to 4 in. across in late summer, whether corms are sitting in dish on windowsill or planted in soil. When planted out, broad, 6–12-in.-long leaves show in spring, last for a few months, and then die long before flower cluster rises from ground. Best planted where they need not be disturbed more often than every 3 years or so. Corms available during brief dormant period in July and August. Best selections are 'The Giant', single lavender, and 'Waterlily', double violet. Plant 3–4 in. deep. To plant in bowls, set upright on 1–2 in. of pebbles, or in special fiber sold for this purpose, and fill bowl with water to base of corms.

COLCHIS IVY. See HEDERA colchica

COLEUS hybridus

COLEUS

Lamiaceae (Labiatae)

ANNUAL OR TENDER PERENNIAL; OR HOUSE PLANT

☀ HARDY IN ZONE TS

☼ ☼ MOST TAKE SHADE, SOME FULL SUN

💧 AMPLE WATER

Coleus hybridus

Native to tropics. Often sold as *C. blumei*. Grown for brilliantly colored leaves; blue flower spikes are attractive but spoil shape of plant and are best pinched out in bud. Leaves may be 3–6 in. long in large-leafed strains (1½–2 ft. tall), 1–1½ in. long in dwarf (1-ft.) strains. Colors include green, chartreuse, yellow, buff, salmon, orange, red, purple, brown, often with many colors on one leaf. The more red pigment in the leaves, the more sun tolerant the plant tends to be. 'Plum Parfait' and 'Burgundy Sun' are examples of selections bred for full sun. Most coleuses perform best in strong, indirect light or filtered shade.

Giant Exhibition and Oriental Splendor are large-leafed strains. Carefree is dwarf, self-branching, with deeply lobed and ruffled, 1–1½-in. leaves. Salicifolius has crowded, long, narrow leaves; plant resembles foot-high feather duster. Named cutting-grown selections exist.

Useful for summer borders and as indoor/outdoor container and hanging basket plants. Plant in spring. Easy from seed sown indoors or, with protection, out-of-doors in warm weather. Easy from cuttings, which root in water as well as other media. Needs rich, loose, well-drained soil, warmth. Feed regularly with 20-20-20 fertilizer. Pinch stems often to encourage branching and compact habit; remove flower buds to ensure vigorous growth. To keep plants in sunny sites compact, shear by a third in midsummer. Recently renamed *Solenostemon scutellarioides*.

COLLARDS. See KALE

ᛘ COLOCASIA esculenta (Caladium esculentum)

ELEPHANT'S EAR, TARO

Araceae

TUBEROUS-ROOTED PERENNIAL

✂ ZONES LS, CS, TS; OR DIG AND STORE; OR GROW IN POTS

☼ BEST IN WARM, FILTERED SHADE

💧 AMPLE WATER; GROWS IN STANDING WATER

✦ JUICES CAN CAUSE SWELLING IN MOUTH, THROAT

Colocasia esculenta

Native to tropical Asia and Polynesia. Fast growing to 6 ft. tall. Mammoth (to 2-ft.-long), heart-shaped, gray-green leaves add lush, tropical effect to any planting within a single season. Flowers resemble giant callas but are seldom seen, except in southern Florida. The starchy roots are a staple food in Hawaii and the Pacific area in general; taro roots are increasingly available in upscale supermarkets around the South.

In zones listed above, tubers can be left in ground; tops die down at 30°F. Elsewhere, lift and store tubers or grow in containers; shelter over winter. Effective with tree ferns and other large-leafed tropical plants. Handsome in large pots, raised beds, near swimming pools. Good for massing to make a quick, if temporary, screen. Protect from wind, which tears leaves. Feed lightly once a month during growing season.

COLORADO BLUE SPRUCE. See PICEA pungens

COLUMBINE. See AQUILEGIA

COMFREY, COMMON. See SYMPHYTUM officinale

Commelinaceae. The spiderwort family is composed of herbaceous perennials. Wandering Jew (*Tradescantia albiflora, Zebrina pendula*) and spiderwort (*Tradescantia virginiana*) are examples.

Compositae. See Asteraceae

CONEFLOWER. See ECHINACEA, RUDBECKIA

CONFEDERATE JASMINE. See TRACHELOSPERMUM jasminoides

CONFEDERATE ROSE. See HIBISCUS mutabilis

CONRADINA verticillata

CUMBERLAND ROSEMARY

Lamiaceae (Labiatae)

SHRUBBY PERENNIAL

✂ ZONES MS, LS

☼ FULL SUN

💧 REGULAR WATER

Conradina verticillata

Native to sandy riverbanks of eastern Tennessee and Kentucky. Aromatic, freely branching plant that roots from trailing branches to make a small-scale ground cover. Dark green, needlelike leaves resemble those of rosemary (*Rosmarinus officinalis*) and have a minty scent. Lavender-pink flowers top the 12–15-in. plant in spring or early summer.

ᛘ CONSOLIDA ambigua (Delphinium ajacis)

LARKSPUR

Ranunculaceae

ANNUAL

✂ ALL ZONES

☼ FULL SUN

💧 REGULAR WATER

✦ ALL PARTS, ESPECIALLY SEEDS, ARE POISONOUS IF INGESTED

Consolida ambigua

Native to southern Europe. Upright, 1–5 ft. tall, with deeply cut leaves; blossom spikes densely set with flowers (most are double), 1–1½ in. wide, in white, blue and white, or shades of blue, lilac, pink, rose, salmon, or carmine, in spring and early summer. Giant Imperial strain has many 4–5-ft. vertical stalks compactly placed. Regal strain has 4–5-ft. base-branching stems, thick spikes of large flowers similar to perennial delphiniums. Super Imperial strain is base branching, has large flowers in 1½-ft. cone-shaped spikes. Steeplechase is base branching, has biggest double flowers on 4–5-ft. spikes, and is heat resistant. Sow seed onto bare soil where plants are to grow; fall planting is best except in heavy, slow-draining soils. Plant in clusters for bigger impact.

ᛘ CONVALLARIA majalis

LILY-OF-THE-VALLEY

Liliaceae

PERENNIAL GROWN FROM RHIZOME

✂ ZONES US, MS, LS; OR INDOORS

☼ PARTIAL SHADE

💧 REGULAR WATER

✦ ALL PARTS ARE POISONOUS IF INGESTED

Convallaria majalis

Graceful, creeping, 6–8-in.-high ground cover puts up one-sided, arching stems of small, nodding, delightfully sweet-scented, waxy white bells in spring. Pendent bells last only 2 to 3 weeks, but broad, bold, glossy green deciduous leaves are attractive throughout growing season. Bright red berries may appear in autumn; they, like the rest of the plant, are poisonous. Double- and pink-flowered forms are available, as well as a variegated type with cream-striped foliage. All are charming in woodland gardens; use as carpet between camellias, rhododendrons, pieris, under deciduous trees or high-branching, not-too-dense evergreen trees. Best in Upper and Middle South; does not like extended hot summers of Lower South. Where well adapted, lily-of-the-valley can become invasive.

Plant clumps or single rhizomes (commonly called pips) in fall before the soil freezes. Give rich soil with ample humus. Set clumps 1–2 ft. apart,

C

single pips 4–5 in. apart, 1½ in. deep. Cover yearly with leaf mold, peat moss, or ground bark. Large, prechilled pips available in December and January, can be potted for bloom indoors. After bloom, plunge pots in ground in cool, shaded area. When dormant, either remove plants from pots and plant in garden, or wash soil off pips and store in plastic bags in vegetable bin of refrigerator until time to repot in December or January.

Convolvulaceae. The morning glory family contains climbing or trailing plants, usually with funnel-shaped flowers. Morning glory (*Ipomoea*) is a typical example.

COONTIE. See ZAMIA pumila

COPPER BEECH. See FAGUS sylvatica 'Atropunicea'

COPPER LEAF. See ACALYPHA wilkesiana

CORAL BEAN. See ERYTHRINA herbacea

CORAL BELLS. See HEUCHERA

CORALBERRY. See SYMPHORICARPOS orbiculatus

CORAL PLANT. See JATROPHA multifida

CORAL TREE. See ERYTHRINA

CORAL VINE. See ANTIGONON leptopus

CORDYLINE

Agavaceae

EVERGREEN PALMLIKE SHRUBS OR TREES

⚡ ZONES VARY BY SPECIES

☀ ◑ ● EXPOSURE NEEDS VARY BY SPECIES

◐ ◐ ◕ WATER NEEDS VARY BY SPECIES

Cordyline australis

Woody plants with swordlike leaves, related to yuccas and agaves but with lusher foliage and needing more water. Good next to swimming pools. Often sold as *Dracaena;* for true *Dracaena*, see that entry.

C. australis (Dracaena australis). Zones CS, TS. Hardiest of cordylines, to 15°F. In youth, fountain of 3-ft.-long, swordlike leaves. Upper leaves are erect; lower leaves arch and droop. In maturity, 20–30-ft. tree, branching high on trunk, rather stiff looking. Fragrant, ¼-in. flowers in long, branching clusters in late spring. For more graceful plant, cut back when young to force multiple trunks. Grows fastest in soil deep enough for big, carrotlike root. Full sun. Tolerates some drought. Used for tropical effects, with boulders and gravel for desert look, near seashore.

'Atropurpurea'. BRONZE DRACAENA. Like species, but with bronzy red foliage. Slower growth. Combine with gray or warm yellowish green to bring out color.

C. stricta. Zone TS; or indoors. Hardy to 26°F. Slender, erect stems clustered at base or branching low. Swordlike, 2-ft.-long leaves are dark green with hint of purple. Lavender flowers in large, branched clusters, very decorative in spring. Will grow to 15 ft. but can be kept lower by cutting tall canes to ground; new canes replace them. Long cuttings stuck in ground will root quickly. Plant needs some shade. Regular water. Fine container plant indoors or out; good for tropical-looking background in narrow areas, Florida rooms, side gardens.

C. terminalis. TI. Zone TS; or indoors. Ti has many named forms with red, yellow, or variegated leaves. White, foot-long flower clusters. Plants are usually started from "logs"—sections of stem that you root. Lay short lengths in mixture of peat moss and sand, covering about one-half their diameter. Keep moist. When shoots grow out and root, cut them off and plant them. Outdoors, ti grows 6–8 ft. tall in frost-free areas where it

receives ample water and soil stays warm; accepts considerable shade. Indoors, it takes ordinary house plant care; tolerates low light.

> ### GROOMING COREOPSIS
>
> Early in the flowering season cut off spent flowers with a pair of one-hand pruning shears. But by summer the dead flowers can outnumber the new. Cut back the waves of spent blooms with hedge shears. Such wholesale removals can bring on successive bloom.

COREOPSIS

Asteraceae (Compositae)

PERENNIALS AND ANNUALS

⚡ ZONES US, MS, LS, CS, EXCEPT AS NOTED

☀ FULL SUN

◐ MODERATE WATER, EXCEPT AS NOTED

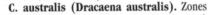
Coreopsis tinctoria

Easily grown members of sunflower family yielding profusion of yellow, orange, maroon, or reddish flowers over long bloom season. Both annual and perennial kinds are easy to propagate—annuals from seed sown in place or in pots, perennials from seed or division of root crown. Tend to self-sow; seeds attract birds.

C. auriculata 'Nana'. DWARF-EARED COREOPSIS. Perennial. Makes 5–6-in.-high mat of leaves 2–5 in. long. Under ideal conditions, it will spread by stolons to form a 2-ft.-wide clump in a year. Bright orange-yellow flower heads, 1–2½ in. wide, rise well above foliage. Long blooming season, spring to fall, if you remove faded flowers. Blooms heaviest in spring. Best used in foreground of taller plants, in border, or as edging.

C. grandiflora. BIGFLOWER COREOPSIS. Perennial. Grows 1–2 ft. high, spreading to 3 ft.; leaves narrow, dark green, with three to five lobes. Bright yellow, 2½–3-in.-wide flowers bloom all summer, carried on long slender stems high above foliage. 'Sunburst' has large, semidouble flowers; it will bloom the first year from seed sown early in spring, then spread by self-sowing. 'Early Sunrise' is similar and even earlier to bloom. Both are tough enough for roadside planting.

C. lanceolata. LANCE COREOPSIS. Perennial. Grows 1–2 ft. high. Leaves somewhat hairy, narrow, mostly in tuft near base. Flower heads 1½–2 in. across, yellow, on pale green stems, spring–summer. Some leaves on lower stem have a few lobes. When well established, will persist year after year. Excellent cut flower.

C. rosea. ROSE COREOPSIS. Perennial. Zones US, MS, LS. Finely textured plant 1½–2 ft. tall with pink, yellow-centered flowers from summer to fall. Unlike other species, prefers moist soil; also shorter lived.

C. tinctoria. CALLIOPSIS, ANNUAL COREOPSIS. Annual. All zones. Slender, upright, 1½–3 ft. tall with wiry stems; much like cosmos in growth habit. Leaves and stems are smooth. Flowers yellow, orange, maroon, bronze, or reddish, banded with contrasting colors; purple-brown centers. Dwarf and double types. Flowers spring and summer, except where hot, humid weather shortens the show. Sow seed in place in dryish soil and in full sun.

C. verticillata. THREADLEAF COREOPSIS. Perennial. Plant is 2½–3 ft. tall, half as broad. Many erect or slightly leaning stems carry many whorls of finely divided, very narrow leaves. At top are 2-in. bright yellow daisies, freely borne over long summer and autumn season. One of the most tolerant of drought, neglect. 'Moonbeam', 1½–2 ft. tall, has pale yellow flowers; 'Zagreb', 1 ft. tall, has golden yellow flowers. Divide in fall or spring every third year to maintain vigor.

CORIANDRUM sativum

CORIANDER, CHINESE PARSLEY, CILANTRO

Apiaceae (Umbelliferae)

ANNUAL HERB

⬗ ALL ZONES

☼ FULL SUN

◐ REGULAR WATER

Coriandrum sativum

Grows to 12–15 in. high. Delicate fernlike foliage; flat clusters of pinkish white flowers that look like miniature Queen Anne's lace. Aromatic seeds crushed before use as seasoning for sausage, stews, cookies, wines. Young leaves used in salads, soups, poultry recipes, and many Mexican and Chinese dishes. Grow in good, well-drained soil. Start from seed (including coriander seed sold in grocery stores); grows quickly, self-sows.

CORKSCREW WILLOW. See SALIX matsudana 'Tortuosa'

CORN

Poaceae (Gramineae)

ANNUAL

⬗ ALL ZONES

☼ FULL SUN—ALWAYS

◐ SPECIAL WATERING TIMES; SEE BELOW

Sweet Corn

Sweet corn is the one cereal grain that home gardeners are likely to grow. It requires considerable space to produce a decent crop. Once most sweet corn is picked, its sugar changes to starch very quickly; only by rushing ears from garden directly to boiling water can you capture full sweetness. Supersweet kinds of corn are actually sweeter than standard kinds and maintain their sweetness longer after harvest because of a gene that increases the quantity of sugar and slows its conversion to starch. A very few people find these types too sweet.

Among sweet hybrid corns are the all-time favorite 'Silver Queen' (resistant to southern corn leaf blight), 'Golden Queen' (tight shucks keep out earworms), 'Early Sunglow', 'Honey and Cream', and 'Merit'. For hybrid supersweets, try 'Honey 'n Pearl', 'Florida Staysweet' (resistant to southern corn leaf blight), 'Illini Gold', 'How Sweet It Is', or 'Early Xtra-Sweet'. Other good choices for sugar-enhanced hybrids are 'Breeder's Choice' and 'Kandi Korn'. For old-fashioned sweet corn, try 'Aunt Mary's', Hooker's Heirloom', 'Stowell's Evergreen', or 'Texas Honey June'.

Adaptable, but grows best in deep, rich soils; good drainage is important. Give full sun. Sow seed 2 weeks after average date of last frost, and make three or four more plantings at 2-week intervals. Or plant early, midseason, and late selections. Plant in blocks of short rows rather than single long rows; pollination is by wind, and unless good supply of pollen falls on silks, ears will be poorly filled. Don't plant popcorn near sweet corn; pollen of one kind can affect characteristics of the other. Also, some supersweet kinds have to be grown at a distance from other types. Either plant in rows 3 ft. apart and thin seedlings to 1 ft. apart, or plant in "hills" (actually clumps) 3 ft. apart each way. Place six or seven seeds in each hill and thin to three strongest plants. Give plants plenty of water and a generous feeding when stalks are 7–8 in. tall. Water deeply, thoroughly wetting entire root zone just as tassel emerges from stalk; repeat again when silk forms. Don't remove suckers that appear.

Corn earworm is a pest throughout the South. Prevent by placing dropperful of mineral oil in tip of ear when silks have withered but before they turn brown. Or plant tight-husked selections, or put a clothespin or rubber band on tip of husk. If damage occurs, just cut off damaged tips. European corn borer is a pest everywhere in the South but Florida; caterpillars tunnel into plant stalks and sometimes into ears. Dust leaf whorls on stalks

with *Bt* or carbaryl. Also watch out for southern corn leaf blight, a fungus that causes tan to red leaf spots between veins and eventually turns entire leaf brown. Plant resistant selections 'Silver Queen' and 'Florida Staysweet', or spray with Daconil 2787 when spotting first appears and then weekly during stretches of wet weather.

Ornamental Corn

Ornamental corn. Some kinds of corn are grown for the beauty of their shelled ears rather than for their eating qualities. Calico, Indian, Squaw, and rainbow corn are some names given to strains that have brightly colored kernels— red, brown, blue, gray, black, yellow, and many mixtures of these colors. Grow like sweet corn, but let ears ripen fully; silks will be withered, husks will turn straw color, and kernels will be firm. Cut ear from plant, including 1½ in. of stalk below ear; pull back husks (leave attached to ears) and dry thoroughly. Grow well away from late sweet corn; mix of pollen can affect its flavor.

Zea mays japonica includes several kinds of corn grown for ornamental foliage; one occasionally sold is 'Gracilis', a dwarf corn with bright green leaves striped white.

Popcorn. Grow and harvest popcorn just like ornamental corn described above. When ears are thoroughly dry, rub kernels off cobs and store in dry place. Strawberry popcorn, grown for either popping or ornamental value, has stubby, fat, strawberry-like ears packed with red kernels.

Popcorn

FOR THE TASTIEST EAR OF CORN

Check when corn ears are plump and silks have withered; pull back husks and try popping a kernel with your thumb. Generally, corn is ready to eat 3 weeks after silks first appear. Kernels should squirt milky juice; watery juice means immature corn. Doughy consistency means overmaturity.

Cornaceae. The dogwood family consists of trees and shrubs with clustered inconspicuous flowers (sometimes surrounded by showy bracts) and berrylike fruit. *Aucuba* and dogwood *(Cornus)* are examples.

CORNELIAN CHERRY. See CORNUS mas

CORN PLANT. See DRACAENA fragrans

CORNUS

DOGWOOD

Cornaceae

DECIDUOUS SHRUBS OR TREES

⬗ ZONES VARY BY SPECIES

☼◐ FULL SUN OR LIGHT SHADE, EXCEPT AS NOTED

◐ REGULAR WATER, EXCEPT AS NOTED

Cornus florida

All offer attractive foliage and flowers; some have spectacular fruit and winter bark. Many have bright fall foliage.

C. alba. TATARIAN DOGWOOD. Shrub. Zones US, MS. In cold-winter areas its bare, blood red twigs are colorful against snow. Upright to about 10 ft. high; wide spreading, eventually producing thicket of many stems. Branches densely clothed with 2½–5-in.-long leaves to 2½ in. wide, deep rich green above, lighter beneath; red in fall. Small, fragrant, creamy white flowers in 1–2-in.-wide, flattish clusters in spring. Whitish small fruits.

Leaves of 'Gouchaultii' have yellow borders suffused with pink. 'Argenteomarginata' (*C.* 'Elegantissima') has showy green-and-white leaves on red stems. 'Sibirica', Siberian dogwood, less rampant than species, grows to 7 ft. high with 5-ft. spread; it has coral red branches in winter. In all types, new wood is brightest; cut back in spring to force new growth.

C. alternifolia. PAGODA DOGWOOD. Shrub or small tree. Zones US, MS. Multitrunked, to 20 ft. high. Strong horizontal branching pattern makes attractive winter silhouette. Light green leaves turn red in fall. Small clusters of creamy spring flowers are not showy. Blue-black fruit.

C. drummondii. ROUGH-LEAF DOGWOOD. Shrub or small tree. Zones US, MS, LS, CS. Native from Texas to Virginia and north to Ontario. To 15–20 ft. Shrubby and rugged, quite unlike elegant *C. florida*, and likely to form a thicket, though can be trained to make a small tree. Grows quickly. Leaves are soft, furry, and hang a little limply. April flowers are true flowers, not bracts, white, in clusters 3 in. across, but flowering period is short. Planted mostly for its striking orange, red, purple fall foliage and its adaptability—rocky limestone soils, clay, wetlands, drought, full sun or full shade. A beautiful addition to a natural garden, or an understory plant in the deep shade of tall trees.

C. florida. FLOWERING DOGWOOD. Tree. Zones US, MS, LS, CS. Native to eastern U.S., from New England to central Florida. Called the most beautiful native tree of North America. Blossom is state flower of North Carolina and Virginia. Tree may reach 40 ft. high and wide, but 20–30 ft. more common. Low-branching tree has fairly horizontal branch pattern, upturned branch tips; makes beautiful winter silhouette. Old trees broadly pyramidal but rather flat topped. Small springtime flower clusters are surrounded by four roundish, 2–4-in.-wide bracts with notched tips. White is the usual color in the wild, but named selections (see below) also come in pink shades to nearly red. Only white types seem to succeed in Florida. Flowers almost cover trees in midspring before leaves expand. Oval leaves, 2–6 in. long, 2½ in. wide, are bright green above, lighter beneath; they turn glowing red and crimson before they drop. Clusters of small, oval, scarlet fruit last into winter or until birds eat them.

Flowering dogwood grows fine in full sun if planted in deep, fertile soil that retains moisture. In shallow, dry, or rocky soil, it often leaf-scorches badly in summer droughts. Safest to use it as an understory tree where it receives light shade; in heavy shade, it will not bloom.

Unfortunately, an anthracnose fungus has been infecting and destroying these trees throughout their range. Dieback symptoms show up first in lower branches and can spread to whole tree. Borers often attack trunks and limbs of stressed trees. *C. florida* has been bred with *C. kousa* to produce more disease-resistant hybrids; see *C. rutgersensis*.

'Barton'. Large white bracts, profuse even when tree is young.

'Cherokee Chief'. Deep rosy red bracts, paler at base.

'Cherokee Daybreak'. Variegated green-and-white leaves turn pink and red in fall. White bracts.

'Cherokee Princess'. Unusually heavy display of white blooms.

'Cherokee Sunset'. Variegated green-and-yellow leaves turn red purple in fall. Bracts reddish. Resistant to anthracnose.

'Cloud Nine'. Blooms young and heavily. Tolerates heat and lack of winter chill better than other selections. White bracts.

'Junior Miss'. Deep pink bracts, paler at center. Resists anthracnose.

'Pendula'. Drooping branches give it weeping look. White bracts.

'Pink Flame'. Leaves green and cream, deepening to dark green and red. Pink bracts.

'Pluribracteata'. Two sets of white bracts (some large, many tiny aborted ones) give appearance of double flowers.

'Rainbow'. Leaves strongly marked bright yellow on green. Heavy bloomer with large white bracts.

'Rubra'. Longtime favorite for its pink or rose bracts.

'Welchii'. TRICOLOR DOGWOOD. Selection best known for its variegated, 4-in.-long leaves of creamy white, pink, deep rose, and green throughout spring and summer; leaves turn deep rose to almost red in fall. Inconspicuous pinkish to white bracts are not profuse. Best with some shade.

C. kousa. KOUSA DOGWOOD. Large shrub or small tree. Zones US, MS, LS. Native to Japan and Korea. Later blooming (late spring or early summer) than other flowering dogwoods. Can be big multistemmed shrub or (with training) small tree to 20 ft. or higher. Delicate limb structure and spreading, dense horizontal growth habit. Lustrous, medium green leaves,

4 in. long, have rusty brown hairs at base of veins on undersurface. Yellow or scarlet fall color. Handsome exfoliating bark.

Flowers along tops of branches show above leaves. Creamy white, slender-pointed, narrow bracts, 2–3 in. long, surround flower cluster, turn pink along edges. In late summer–fall, red fruit hangs below branches like big strawberries. 'Milky Way' is more floriferous, has pure white bracts. 'Summer Stars' blooms later, is lavish in bloom. 'Rosabella' has pink bracts. *C. k. chinensis*, Chinese dogwood, native to China, has larger leaves and larger bracts. This species is less susceptible to diseases than *C. florida* and has been bred with the latter to produce resistant hybrids; see *C. rutgersensis*.

Cornus kousa

C. mas. CORNELIAN CHERRY. Zones US, MS, LS. Pest-free dogwood native to southern Europe and Asia. Usually an airy, twiggy shrub but can be trained as a small tree, 15–20 ft. high. Provides a progression of color throughout the year. One of earliest dogwoods to bloom, bearing clustered masses of small, soft yellow blossoms on bare twigs in late winter or early spring. Shiny green, 2–4-in.-long, oval leaves turn yellow in fall; some forms turn red. Autumn color is enhanced by clusters of bright scarlet, cherry-size fruits that hang on until birds get them. Fruits are edible and are frequently used in making preserves. In winter, flaking bark mottled gray and tan provides interest. 'Variegata' features leaves marbled creamy white.

C. rutgersensis. STELLAR DOGWOOD. Tree. Zones US, MS, LS. This hybrid between *C. florida* and *C. kousa* has greater disease resistance than *C. florida*. Single-stemmed tree to about 20 ft. Bloom time falls between the midspring bloom of *C. florida* and the late-spring or early-summer bloom of *C. kousa*; flower bracts are produced with the leaves. 'Stellar Pink' has pink bracts; 'Aurora', 'Galaxy', and 'Ruth Ellen' bear broad-bracted white flowers; 'Constellation' and 'Stardust' have narrower white bracts. 'Constellation' has the most upright growth habit; other selections are more rounded. All have brilliant red fall leaves.

C. stolonifera (C. sericea). REDTWIG DOGWOOD, RED-OSIER DOGWOOD. Shrub. Zones US, MS, LS. Native to moist places, eastern North America and Northern California to Alaska. Another dogwood with brilliant show of red fall foliage, bright red winter twigs striking against a snowy backdrop. Grows rapidly to 7–9 ft. high and wide spreading. Leaves oval, 1½–2½ in. long, fresh deep green. Blossoms throughout summer months, bearing small, creamy white flowers in 2-in.-wide clusters among the leaves; blooms are followed by white or bluish fruits.

Makes a good space filler in moist ground (good for holding banks), or plant it along property line as a screen. Spreads widely by creeping underground stems and rooting branches. To control spread, use a spade to cut off roots; also trim branches that touch ground. Shade tolerant.

C. s. coloradensis. COLORADO REDTWIG. Native from Yukon southwest to New Mexico; grows to 5–6 ft. high. Brownish red stems. Its selection 'Cheyenne' is redder.

'Flaviramea'. YELLOWTWIG DOGWOOD. Yellow twigs and branches. Susceptible to stem canker.

CORSICAN MINT. See MENTHA requienii

CORTADERIA selloana

PAMPAS GRASS

Poaceae (Gramineae)

EVERGREEN ORNAMENTAL GRASS

ZONES MS, LS, CS, TS

FULL SUN

ANY AMOUNT OF MOISTURE

Native to Argentina. Very fast growing in rich soil in mild climates; from gallon-can size to

Cortaderia selloana

8 ft. in one season. Established, may reach 20 ft. in height. Each plant is a fountain of saw-toothed, grassy leaves above which, in late summer, rise long stalks bearing 1–3-ft. white to chamois or pink flower plumes. The plant may be either male or female. Females have much showier plumes. Unfortunately, few garden centers sell pampas grass by sex. To ensure that you get a showy plant, buy it when it's in bloom or obtain a division from a known female plant.

There is a chance that, under certain conditions, this plant—like its truly worthless cousin *C. jubata*—may seed itself freely, releasing seeds into the wind to germinate and grow wherever they land. The result is a multitude of unwanted seedlings that can crowd out more desirable plants. The compact pampas grass, *C. s.* 'Pumila', is an altogether different story. It doesn't seed itself, so you can plant this one in small gardens without worry. Makes a beautiful clump 4–6 ft. tall when in flower. Leaves gray green. Creamy silky plumes produced prolifically from its first year.

CORYDALIS

Fumariaceae

PERENNIALS

✿ ZONES US, MS, LS

◑ PARTIAL SHADE

💧 MOIST, NOT SOGGY, SOIL

Corydalis lutea

Handsome clumps of dainty, divided leaves much like those of bleeding heart (to which it is closely related) or maidenhair fern. Clusters of small, spurred flowers. Plant in rich, moist soil. Effective in rock crevices, in open woodland, near pool or streamside. Combine with ferns, columbine, bleeding heart, primrose. Divide clumps or sow seed in spring or fall. Plants self-sow. Summer-flowering species may stop flowering during hottest months; keep soil moist to encourage some continued bloom.

C. cheilanthifolia. Hardy Chinese native, 8–10 in. high, with fernlike green foliage. Clusters of yellow, ½-in.-long flowers in spring.

C. flexuosa. Recently introduced from western China. Forms 1-ft. mound of blue-green, fernlike foliage. Narrow, erect clusters of sky blue flowers borne in early spring and sporadically during the growing season. Selections include 'Blue Panda', 'China Blue', and 'Pere David'.

C. heterocarpa. Native to Japan. Makes large mound, 3 ft. by 3 ft. Rich yellow flowers cover plant in late winter or early spring and continue to bloom intermittently through growing season.

C. lutea. Native to southern Europe. To 15 in. tall. Many-stemmed plant with masses of gray-green foliage. Golden yellow, ¾-in.-long, short-spurred flowers throughout summer.

C. ophiocarpa. Native to Himalayas. To 18 in. tall and wide, 3 ft. tall in flower. Evergreen foliage is gray green, feathery. Small cream-colored flowers, with dark red tips, appear in spring.

C. solida. To 10 in. high, with erect clusters of up to 20 purplish red, 1-in.-long flowers in spring. Grows from tubers that are sometimes available from bulb catalogs.

CORYLOPSIS

WINTER HAZEL

Hamamelidaceae

DECIDUOUS SHRUBS

✿ ZONES US, MS, LS

☀◑ FULL SUN OR PARTIAL SHADE

💧 REGULAR WATER

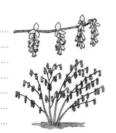
Corylopsis spicata

Valued for sweet-scented, bell-shaped, soft yellow flowers hanging in short, chainlike clusters on bare branches in spring. New foliage that follows is often tinged pink before turning bright green. Toothed, nearly round leaves somewhat resemble those of filbert (*Corylus*); fall color varies from none to poor to a good clear yellow.

Rather open structure with attractive, delicate branching pattern. Give same soil conditions as for rhododendrons. Grow in wind-sheltered location in shrub border, at edge of woodland.

C. glabrescens. FRAGRANT WINTER HAZEL. Hardiest species. Grows 8–15 ft. high and wide. Can be trained as small tree. Flower clusters 1–1½ in. long.

C. pauciflora. BUTTERCUP WINTER HAZEL. Dainty plant to 4–6 ft. high, with spreading habit. Blossoms ¾ in. long, in clusters of two or three.

C. sinensis. To 15 ft. tall, with 3-in. flower clusters. 'Spring Purple' has purplish new growth that matures to green.

C. spicata. SPIKE WINTER HAZEL. New growth purple, turning bluish green. To 8 ft. high, spreading wider; 1–2-in.-long flower clusters, 6 to 12 blossoms per cluster.

CORYLUS

FILBERT, HAZELNUT

Betulaceae

DECIDUOUS SHRUBS OR TREES

✿ ZONES VARY BY SPECIES

☀◑ FULL SUN OR PARTIAL SHADE

💧 REGULAR WATER, EXCEPT AS NOTED

Corylus avellana 'Contorta'

Although filberts and hazelnuts are usually thought of as trees grown for their edible nuts, those listed here make pleasing ornamentals. The plants have separate female and male flowers: the female blossoms are inconspicuous, while the male ones, appearing in pendent catkins on bare branches in winter or early spring, are showy. Leaves are roundish to oval, with toothed margins.

C. avellana. EUROPEAN FILBERT. Shrub. Zones US, MS, LS. Grows to 10–15 ft. high and wide. One of the species also grown for nuts. The ornamental selection that follows is more widely grown than the species.

'Contorta'. CURLY FILBERT. Rounded to 8–10 ft. tall. Grown for fantastically gnarled and twisted branches and twigs, revealed after its 2–2½-in. leaves turn yellow and drop in autumn. Branches are used in flower arrangements. Plants are almost always grafted, so suckers arising from the base below the graft should be removed; they won't have contorted form. Also known as Harry Lauder's walking stick.

C. maxima. Shrub or tree. Zones US, MS. Native to southeastern Europe. One of the species grown for nuts. Suckering shrub to 12–15 ft. high; can be trained as small tree. 'Purpurea', most widely grown ornamental form, has leaves 6 in. long in rich dark purple and heavily purple-tinted male catkins. In most areas, leaves fade to green by early summer.

COSMOS

Asteraceae (Compositae)

PERENNIALS AND ANNUALS

✿ ALL ZONES, EXCEPT AS NOTED

☀ FULL SUN

💧 MODERATE WATER

Cosmos bipinnatus

Native to tropical America, mostly Mexico. Showy summer- and fall-blooming plants, open and branching, with bright green divided leaves and daisylike flowers in many colors and forms (single, double, crested, and frilled). Heights vary from 2½ to 8 ft. Good for mass color in borders or background, or as filler among shrubs. Useful in arrangements if flowers are cut when freshly opened and placed immediately in deep, cool water. Sow seed in open ground from spring to summer, or set out transplants from flats. Plant in not-too-rich soil. Plants self-sow freely, attract birds.

C. atrosanguineus. CHOCOLATE COSMOS. Tuberous-rooted perennial. Zones MS, LS, CS. Where winters are cold, dig and store as for dahlias. To 2–2½ ft. tall, with coarsely cut foliage. Flowers are deep brownish red, nearly 2 in. wide, late summer and fall, with a strong perfume of chocolate (or vanilla). Attractive with silvery-foliaged plants. Provide well-drained soil. Winter mulching is prudent in the Middle South.

🌱 **C. bipinnatus.** COMMON COSMOS. Annual flowers in white and shades of pink, rose, lavender, purple, or crimson, with tufted yellow centers. Heights to 8 ft. Modern improved cosmos include Sensation strain, 3–6 ft. tall, earlier blooming than old-fashioned kinds. Selections include 'Dazzler' (crimson) and 'Radiance' (rose with red center); white and pink also available. 'Candystripe' has smaller (3-in.) white-and-rose flowers, blooms even earlier on smaller plants. Seashell strain has rolled, quilled ray florets like long, narrow cones.

C. sulphureus. YELLOW COSMOS. Annual. Grows to 7 ft., with yellow or golden yellow flowers with yellow centers. Tends to become weedy looking at end of season. Klondike strain grows 3–4 ft. tall and bears 2-in. semidouble flowers ranging from scarlet orange to yellow. Dwarf Klondike (Sunny) strain is 1½ ft. tall, with 1½-in. flowers.

COSTA RICAN NIGHTSHADE. See SOLANUM wendlandii

COSTUS

SPIRAL FLAG, GINGER LILY

Zingiberaceae

PERENNIALS

🌱 ZONES CS, TS

☼ LIGHT SHADE

💧 AMPLE WATER DURING ACTIVE GROWTH

Costus speciosus

Related to true gingers (*Zingiber*) and other so-called gingers (*Alpinia, Hedychium*); like them, have fleshy rhizomes and stems bearing large leaves. In *Costus*, the leaves are spirally arranged around the stem. Flowers emerge from a tight, conelike cluster of colored bracts at stem ends in summer and fall.

Plants have sprawling, mounding habit. Native to tropical forest floor, they like light shade but can stand full sun if roots are shaded. Use around foundation or near patio or pool; can be grown in large tubs. Plants are dormant in winter and need little water at that time. Provide a winter mulch.

C. speciosus. CREPE GINGER, MALAY GINGER. Clusters of stems grow to 6–8 ft. long, with 5–10-in. leaves. The flowering cone is 5 in. long, with green bracts tipped red. Crepelike white or pink flowers to 4 in. wide emerge from the cone two or three at a time.

C. spiralis. SPIRAL FLAG, SPIRAL GINGER. Stems to 4–6 ft. long; 8-in. leaves. Orange flowering cone; pink to red, 1½-in. flowers.

COTINUS coggygria (Rhus cotinus)

SMOKE TREE

Anacardiaceae

DECIDUOUS SHRUB OR SMALL TREE

🌱 ZONES US, MS, LS

☼ FULL SUN

💧 MODERATE WATER

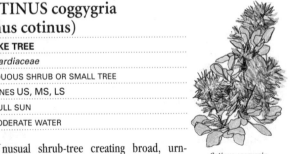
Cotinus coggygria

Unusual shrub-tree creating broad, urn-shaped mass usually as wide as it is high— typically 15 ft. tall, though it may eventually grow to 25 ft. Naturally multistemmed but can be trained to a single trunk. Common name derived from dramatic puffs of "smoke" from fading flowers: As the tiny, greenish blooms wither, they send out elongated stalks clothed in fuzzy lavender-pink hairs. In the species, the roundish, 1½–3-in. leaves are bluish green in summer. Purple-leafed types are more commonly grown. Foliage of 'Purpureus' fades to green by midsummer; 'Royal Purple' (the selection

with the deepest purple coloration) and 'Velvet Cloak' retain their purple leaves through summer. All types turn yellow or orange red in fall.

Plants are at their best under stress in poor or rocky soil. In cultivated gardens, provide fast drainage and avoid overly wet conditions.

A less widely grown native is *C. obovatus*, American smoke tree, a small, rounded tree, 20–30 ft. tall. Leaves change from blue green in summer to yellow, orange, and red in fall. Tolerates alkaline soil. Frequently found growing wild on Edwards Plateau in Texas. Deserves much wider use.

COTONEASTER

Rosaceae

EVERGREEN, SEMIEVERGREEN, DECIDUOUS SHRUBS

🌱 ZONES VARY BY SPECIES

☼ FULL SUN, EXCEPT AS NOTED

💧 MODERATE WATER

Cotoneaster apiculatus

Members of this genus range from low types used as ground covers to small, stiffly upright shrubs to tall-growing (18-ft.) shrubs of fountainlike form with graceful, arching branches. All grow vigorously and thrive with little or no maintenance, can tolerate poor soil and drought. White or pinkish springtime flowers resemble tiny single roses; though not showy, they are pretty because of their abundance. Usual color of fall and winter berries is red or orange red.

While some medium and tall growers can be sheared, they look best when allowed to maintain natural fountain shapes. Prune only to enhance graceful arch of branches. Keep medium growers looking young by pruning out portion of oldest wood each year. Prune ground covers to remove dead or awkward branches. Give flat growers room to spread. Don't plant near walk or drive where branch ends will need frequent cutting back.

Cotoneasters are useful shrubs and can be attractive in the proper setting. Some are especially attractive in form and branching pattern (*C. congestus, C. horizontalis*), while others are notable for colorful, long-lasting fruit (*C. microphyllus*). Trailing types can make excellent ground cover plants. However, ground cover plantings seldom grow dense enough to keep weeds from coming up. Branches also tend to snag blowing litter.

C. adpressus praecox. PRAECOX COTONEASTER. Deciduous. Zones US, MS. To 1½ ft. tall, 6 ft. wide, with shiny leaves turning maroon red in fall. Profuse bright red, ½-in. fruit. Bank or ground cover. Tolerates some shade. *C. adpressus* is similar, somewhat smaller.

C. apiculatus. CRANBERRY COTONEASTER. Deciduous. Zones US, MS. Best in cold-winter areas. Dense grower, 3 ft. tall, 6 ft. wide. Small round leaves turn deep red in fall. Fruit is size of large cranberry, in clusters. Can take some shade. Use as bank cover, hedge, background planting.

C. congestus (C. microphyllus glacialis). PYRENEES COTONEASTER. Evergreen. Zones US, MS, LS. Slow grower to 3 ft., with dense, downward-curving branches, tiny dark green leaves, small, bright red fruit. Use in containers, rock gardens, above walls.

C. dammeri (C. humifusus). BEARBERRY COTONEASTER. Evergreen. Zones US, MS, LS. Fast, prostrate growth to 3–6 in. tall, 10 ft. wide. Branches root along ground. Leaves bright, glossy green; fruit bright red. 'Coral Beauty' is 6 in. tall; 'Eichholz', 10–12 in. tall with a scattering of red-orange leaves in fall; 'Lowfast', 1 ft. tall; 'Skogsholmen', 1½ ft. tall. All are good ground covers in sun or partial shade and can drape over walls, cascade down slopes.

C. horizontalis. ROCK COTONEASTER. Deciduous. Zones US, MS, LS. Can be 2–3 ft. tall, 15 ft. wide, with stiff horizontal branches, many branchlets set in herringbone pattern. Leaves are small, round, bright green; turn orange and red before falling. Out of leaf very briefly. Showy fruit is red. Needs enough room to spread. Fine bank cover or low traffic barrier. 'Variegatus' has leaves edged in white. *C. h. perpusillus* is smaller, more compact than species.

Cotoneaster horizontalis

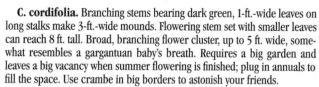

C. lacteus (C. parneyi). BRIGHTBEAD COTONEASTER. Evergreen. Zones MS, LS, CS. Graceful, arching habit to 8 ft. or more, with dark green leaves 2 in. long, clustered white flowers, and a heavy crop of long-lasting red fruit in 2–3-in. clusters. Best as informal hedge, screen, or espalier. Can be clipped as formal hedge, but form suffers.

C. microphyllus. LITTLELEAF COTONEASTER. Evergreen. Zones US, MS, LS. Its horizontal branches trail and root to 6 ft.; secondary branches grow erect to 2–3 ft. Leaves are small (⅓ in.), dark green, gray beneath. Fruit is rosy red. Thyme rockspray cotoneaster, *C. m. thymifolius*, is a smaller plant, has even tinier leaves, with edges rolled under. Both are effective in rock gardens, on banks.

Cotoneaster lacteus

C. salicifolius. WILLOWLEAF COTONEASTER. Evergreen or semievergreen. Zones US, MS, LS. Erect, spreading shrub, 15–18 ft. high, with narrow, dark green, 1–3½-in.-long leaves and bright red fruits. Graceful screening or background plant but can self-sow and become invasive.

Better known are the trailing forms used as ground cover: 'Emerald Carpet', 12–15 in. tall, to 8 ft. wide, compact habit and small leaves; 'Autumn Fire' ('Herbstfeuer'), 2–3 ft.; 'Repens' looks similar, is sometimes grafted to another cotoneaster species grown as a weeping tree.

COTTONWOOD. See POPULUS

COUNCIL TREE. See FICUS altissima

COWBERRY. See VACCINIUM vitis-idaea

COWSLIP LUNGWORT. See PULMONARIA angustifolia

CRABAPPLE

Rosaceae

DECIDUOUS FRUIT TREES

ZONES US, MS, LS

FULL SUN

REGULAR WATER DURING FRUIT DEVELOPMENT

Crabapple

Crabapple is a small, usually tart apple. Many kinds are valued more for their springtime flowers than for their fruit; these are flowering crabapples, described under *Malus*. Among the most popular crabapple selections grown for fruit (used for jelly making and pickling) are 'Transcendent', with 2-in. red-cheeked yellow apples that ripen in summer; 'Centennial', with 1½-in. scarlet-and-yellow fruit; and 'Dolgo', with 1½-in. crimson fruit. Other crabapples are prized for cider, including 'Virginia Crab' ('Hewe's Crab'), 'Geneva', and 'Giant Russian'. For information about general care, see Apple.

CRAB CACTUS. See SCHLUMBERGERA truncata

CRAMBE

Brassicaceae (Cruciferae)

PERENNIALS

ZONES US, MS, LS

FULL SUN

REGULAR WATER

Two species of these big cabbagelike perennials are occasionally seen. Both have large, smooth leaves and much-branched clusters of small, honey-scented white flowers. They appreciate rich, well-drained garden soil and require considerable space. In the Lower South, provide light afternoon shade.

C. cordifolia. Branching stems bearing dark green, 1-ft.-wide leaves on long stalks make 3-ft.-wide mounds. Flowering stem set with smaller leaves can reach 8 ft. tall. Broad, branching flower cluster, up to 5 ft. wide, somewhat resembles a gargantuan baby's breath. Requires a big garden and leaves a big vacancy when summer flowering is finished; plug in annuals to fill the space. Use crambe in big borders to astonish your friends.

C. maritima. SEA KALE. Branched, purplish stems carry blue-gray leaves up to 1 ft. wide. In early summer, sends up 1–2½-ft.-tall stem with flower clusters to 1½ ft. wide. Once widely used as a vegetable; blanch the leafstalks by placing large pots or boxes over the emerging plants.

CRANBERRY. See VACCINIUM macrocarpon

CRANBERRY BUSH. See VIBURNUM

CRANESBILL. See GERANIUM

CRASSULA

Crassulaceae

SUCCULENTS

ZONE TS; OR INDOORS

PRODUCE FLOWERS IN SUN

REGULAR WATER DURING ACTIVE GROWTH; INDOORS, LET SOIL DRY BETWEEN WATERINGS

Crassula falcata

Mostly from South Africa. All have succulent foliage; many have strange geometric forms. House plants anywhere. Need excellent drainage; be careful not to overwater.

C. arborescens. A shrubby, heavy-branched plant very like jade plant, but with gray-green, red-edged, red-dotted leaves. Summer flowers (usually seen only on old plants) are star shaped, white aging to pink. Good change of pace from jade plant; smaller and slower growing.

C. falcata. Grows to 4 ft. high. Fleshy, gray-green, sickle-shaped leaves are vertically arranged in two rows on stems. Dense clusters of scarlet flowers appear in late summer.

C. ovata (C. argentea). JADE PLANT. Top-notch house plant, large container plant, landscaping shrub in Tropical South. Sometimes sold as *C. portulacea.* Stout trunk, sturdy limbs even on small plant—and plant will stay small in small container. Can reach 9 ft. in time but is usually shorter. Leaves are thick, oblong, fleshy pads 1–2 in. long, glossy bright green, sometimes with red-tinged edges. 'Crosby's Dwarf' is a low, compact grower; variegated kinds are 'Sunset' (yellow tinged red) and 'Tricolor' (green, white, and pinkish). Clusters of pink, star-shaped flowers form in profusion, fall–spring.

Crassula ovata

Crassulaceae. This family of usually herbaceous (rarely shrubby) plants includes sedums, sempervivums, and a host of other familiar succulents. Leaves are often in rosettes, as in hen and chicks (*Echeveria imbricata*).

CRATAEGUS

HAWTHORN

Rosaceae

DECIDUOUS TREES

ZONES VARY BY SPECIES

FULL SUN, EXCEPT AS NOTED

MODERATE WATER

Crataegus laevigata

These small trees, members of the rose family, are well known for their pretty flower clusters after leaf-out in spring and for showy fruit resembling tiny apples in summer and fall, often into winter. Blossom is Missouri state flower. These multitrunked trees have thorny branches that need pruning to thin out twiggy growth. Hawthorns attract bees and birds.

Hawthorns will grow in any soil as long as it is well drained. Better grown under somewhat austere conditions, since good soil, regular water, and fertilizer all promote succulent new growth that is most susceptible to fireblight. The disease makes entire branches die back quickly; cut out blighted branches well below dead part. The rust stage of cedar-apple rust can be a problem wherever eastern red cedar (*Juniperus virginiana*) grows nearby. Aphids and scale are widespread potential pests.

C. crus-galli. COCKSPUR THORN. Zones US, MS. Wide-spreading tree to 30 ft. Stiff thorns to 3 in. long. Smooth, glossy, toothed leaves are dark green, turning orange to red in fall. Flowers are white and fruit dull orange red. Most successful hawthorn for Oklahoma. *C. c. inermis* is thornless.

C. laevigata (C. oxyacantha). ENGLISH HAWTHORN. Zones US, MS. Native to Europe and North Africa. Moderate growth to 18–25 ft. high, 15–20 ft. wide. Best known through its selections: 'Paul's Scarlet', clusters of double rose to red flowers; 'Double White'; 'Double Pink'. Double-flowered forms set little fruit. 'Crimson Cloud' ('Superba') has bright red single flowers with white centers, vivid red fruit. All have 2-in. toothed, lobed leaves lacking good fall color. Trees are prone to leaf spot, which can defoliate them and shorten their life.

C. marshallii. PARSLEY HAWTHORN. Zones MS, LS, CS. Native to southern U.S. To 10–15 ft., occasionally to 25 ft. Early spring flowers are dainty white with purple-tipped anthers. Leaves, shaped like parsley, turn red or yellow in fall. Striking cherry red fruits persist after leaves drop. Tolerates a wide range of soils. Relatively disease-free.

C. mollis. DOWNY HAWTHORN. Zone US. Big, broad tree to 30 ft.; looks like mature apple tree. Leaves to 4 in. long, lobed, toothed, covered with down. White flowers grow to 1 in. wide. Red fruit to 1 in. across, also downy; fruit doesn't last on tree as long as that of other species but has value in jelly making.

C. monogyna. SINGLESEED HAWTHORN. Zones US, MS. Native to Europe, North Africa, and western Asia. Classic hawthorn of English countryside for hedges, boundary plantings. Best known is upright selection 'Stricta', 30 ft. tall and 8 ft. wide. White flowers. Small red fruit in clusters, rather difficult to see. Very prone to fireblight, mites, and leaf diseases.

☂ **C. opaca.** MAYHAW. Zones MS, LS, CS. Native to southeastern U.S. Attractive large shrub or small tree famous for its red fruits, called mayhaws, which ripen in early summer and make good jelly. Eventually reaches 20–30 ft. Flowers white, 1 in. across. In its native range, grows in damp ground but will tolerate some dryness. For jelly, choose a heavy-yielding improved selection such as 'Super Spur'. Full sun or light shade.

C. oxyacantha. See C. laevigata

C. phaenopyrum (C. cordata). WASHINGTON HAWTHORN. Zones US, MS, LS. Native to southeastern U.S. Moderate growth to 25 ft. with 20-ft. spread. Graceful, open limb structure. Glossy leaves 2–3 in. long with three to five sharp-pointed lobes (like some maples). In Upper and Middle South, foliage turns beautiful orange, scarlet, or purplish in fall. Small white flowers in broad clusters. Shiny red fruit hangs on well into winter. Not successful in the southern Midwest but a choice hawthorn elsewhere. One of the least prone to fireblight.

C. pinnatifida. Zones US, MS. Native to northeastern Asia. To 20 ft. high, 10–12 ft. wide. Flowers white, 3/4 in. wide, in 3-in. clusters. Leaves lobed like those of *C. laevigata* but bigger, thicker; they turn red in fall. Tree more open, upright than *C. laevigata*. Fruit larger than most species listed.

C. punctata inermis. THORNLESS DOTTED HAWTHORN. Zone US. Native to eastern and midwestern U.S. Essentially thornless, 30 ft. high. White flowers followed by 3/4-in., long-lasting dark red fruits.

C. viridis. GREEN HAWTHORN. Zones US, MS. Moderate growth to 25–30 ft., with broad, spreading crown. Clustered white flowers followed by red fruit. 'Winter King' is vase shaped, with silvery stems, fruit that lasts all winter; it's among the most attractive and trouble-free hawthorns.

CREEPING BUTTERCUP. See RANUNCULUS repens 'Pleniflorus'

CREEPING FIG. See FICUS pumila

CREEPING PHLOX. See PHLOX stolonifera

CREEPING ZINNIA. See SANVITALIA procumbens

CREOSOTE BUSH. See LARREA tridentata

CREPE GINGER. See COSTUS speciosus

CREPE MYRTLE. See LAGERSTROEMIA

CRETE DITTANY. See ORIGANUM dictamnus

CRINKLED HAIR GRASS. See DESCHAMPSIA flexuosa

☂ CRINUM

Liliaceae
BULBS
🗲 ZONES VARY BY SPECIES; OR GROW IN POTS
☼ ◑ FULL SUN OR PARTIAL SHADE, OR AS NOTED
💧 💦 AMPLE WATER DURING GROWTH AND BLOOM
◊ ALL PARTS ARE POISONOUS IF INGESTED

Crinum powellii

Distinguished from their near relative amaryllis by long, slender flower tube that is longer than flower segments. Long-stalked cluster of lily-shaped, 4–6-in.-long, fragrant flowers rises in spring or summer from clump of long, strap- or sword-shaped leaves. Bulbs large, rather slender, tapering to stemlike neck; thick, fleshy roots. Bulbs available (from specialists) all year, but spring or fall planting is preferred. An old Southern favorite.

Provide soil with plenty of humus. Set bulbs 6 in. under surface; give ample space to develop. Divide infrequently. In Upper and Middle South, plant in sheltered, sunny sites and mulch heavily in winter. Move container-grown plants to frostproof location.

Excellent for tropical effect. Mail-order suppliers offer a wide selection. In the Lower South, a great many named kinds are obtainable.

C. americanum. SOUTHERN SWAMP CRINUM. Zones LS, CS, TS. Native to water edges and swamps in southeastern U.S. and Gulf Coast. Fragrant white flowers, on 2-ft. stems, appear spring–late fall. Takes deep shade.

C. asiaticum. GRAND CRINUM, ST. JOHN'S LILY. Zones MS, LS, CS, TS. Large, spidery, white flowers, 6–8 in. across, in clusters of up to 50.

C. bulbispermum (C. longifolium). HARDY CRINUM. All zones. Long, narrow, twisting gray-green leaves tend to lie on the ground. Flowers are deep pink.

C. 'Carnival'. Zones LS, CS, TS. Flowers in shades of pink and red, with white streaks.

C. 'Ellen Bosanquet'. Zones LS, CS, TS. Leaves are broad, bright green. Flowers are deep rose, nearly red.

C. 'Emma Jones'. Zones LS, CS, TS. Tall plant. Large, pink, ruffled flowers. Continuous bloomer.

C. 'Milk and Wine'. Zones LS, CS, TS. Creamy white flowers with pink stripes. Continuous bloomer. Milk and wine is also the common name for several similar-looking selections.

C. moorei. LONGNECK CRINUM. Zones MS, LS, CS, TS. Large bulbs with 6–8-in. diameter and stemlike neck 1 ft. long or more. Long, thin, wavy-edged, bright green leaves. Bell-shaped pinkish red flowers.

C. 'Peach Blow'. Zones LS, CS, TS. Long leaves. Recurving pale lavender flowers. The classic crinum of the Old South.

C. powellii. POWELL'S HYBRID CRINUM. All zones. Resembles parent *C. moorei* but has dark rose-colored flowers. 'Album' is a good pure white form, vigorous enough to serve as a tall ground cover in shade. 'Cecil Houdyshel', Zones MS, LS, CS, TS, has long, tapering leaves and deep rose red flowers.

C. 'Royal White'. Zones LS, CS, TS. Narrow semierect leaves. Very large white flowers with rose pink stripes.

CRISPED BLUE FERN. See POLYPODIUM aureum 'Mandaianum'

CROCOSMIA

Iridaceae

CORMS

ZONES US, MS, LS, CS

PART SHADE IN COASTAL SOUTH

MODERATE TO LITTLE WATER

Crocosmia crocosmiiflora

Native to tropical and southern Africa. Formerly called tritonia and related to freesia. Sword-shaped leaves in basal clumps. Small orange, red, yellow flowers in summer. Useful for splashes of garden color and for cutting.

C. crocosmiiflora (Tritonia crocosmiiflora). MONTBRETIA. A favorite for generations, montbretias can still be seen in older gardens where they have spread freely, bearing orange-crimson blooms 1½–2 in. across on 3–4-ft. stems. Sword-shaped leaves are 3 ft. long. Many once-common named forms in yellow, orange, cream, and near-scarlet are making a comeback. Good for naturalizing on slopes or in fringe areas.

C. hybrids. Sturdy plants with branching spikes of large flowers. Often called Masoniorum Hybrids. 'Jenny Bloom' and 'Jupiter' grow to 4 ft., have deep yellow flowers. 'Lucifer' is 4 ft. tall, with bright red flowers. 'Solfatare', to 2 ft., has bronze-tinted foliage and pale orange-yellow flowers.

C. masoniorum. Leaves 2½ ft. long, 2 in. wide. Flowers, 1½ in. wide, flaming orange to scarlet, borne in dense one-sided clusters on 2½–3-ft. stems. Buds open slowly from base to tip of clusters, and old flowers drop cleanly from stems. Cut flowers last about 2 weeks.

Crocosmia masoniorum

CROCUS

Iridaceae

CORMS

ZONES US, MS, LS

FULL SUN OR PARTIAL SHADE

REGULAR WATER DURING GROWTH AND BLOOM

Crocus vernus

Leaves are basal and grasslike—often with silvery midrib—and appear before, with, or after flowers, depending on species. Flowers with long stemlike tubes and flaring or cup-shaped petals are 1½–3 in. long; the short (true) stems are hidden underground.

Most crocus bloom in late winter or earliest spring, but some species bloom in fall, the flowers rising from bare earth weeks or days after planting. Mass them for best effect. Attractive in rock gardens, between stepping-stones, in containers. Set corms 2–3 in. deep in light, porous soil. Divide every 3 to 4 years. Don't bother planting crocus if your garden has chipmunks. These rodents will dig up and eat every one. Best in Upper and Middle South. Won't naturalize where winters are warm.

C. ancyrensis. Flowers golden yellow, small, very early.

C. angustifolius. CLOTH OF GOLD CROCUS. Formerly *C. susianus*. Orange-gold, starlike flowers with dark brown center stripe. Starts blooming in January in warmest areas, in March in coldest areas.

C. chrysanthus. Orange yellow, sweet scented. Hybrids and selections range from white through yellow to blue, often marked with deeper color. Spring bloom. Popular selections include 'Blue Pearl', palest blue; 'Cream Beauty', pale yellow; 'E. P. Bowles', yellow with purple featherings; 'Ladykiller', outside purple edged white, inside white feathered purple; 'Princess Beatrix', blue with yellow center; and 'Snow Bunting', pure white.

C. imperati. Bright lilac inside, buff veined purple outside, saucer shaped. Early spring.

C. kotschyanus. Formerly *C. zonatus*. Pinkish lavender or lilac flowers in early fall.

C. sativus. SAFFRON CROCUS. Lilac. Orange-red stigma is true saffron of commerce. Autumn bloom. To harvest saffron, pluck stigmas as soon as flowers open, dry them, and store them in vials. Stigmas from a dozen blooms will season a good-size paella or similar dish. For continued good yield of saffron, divide corms as soon as leaves turn brown; replant in fresh or improved soil. Mark planting site so you won't dig up dormant corms.

C. sieberi. Delicate lavender blue flowers with golden throat. One of earliest bloomers—January and February.

C. speciosus. Showy blue-violet flowers in early fall. Lavender and mauve selections available. Fast increase by seed and division. Showiest autumn-flowering crocus.

C. tomasinianus. Slender buds; star-shaped, silvery lavender blue flowers, sometimes with dark blotch at tips of segments. Very early—January or February in milder areas.

C. vernus. DUTCH CROCUS. Blooms in shades of white, yellow, lavender, purple, often penciled, streaked. February–March. Most vigorous crocus.

CROSSVINE. See BIGNONIA capreolata

CROTON. See CODIAEUM variegatum

CROWN IMPERIAL. See FRITILLARIA imperialis

CROWN OF GOLD TREE. See CASSIA excelsa

CROWN OF THORNS. See EUPHORBIA milii

Cruciferae. See Brassicaceae

CRY-BABY TREE. See ERYTHRINA crista-galli

CRYPTOMERIA japonica

JAPANESE CRYPTOMERIA, JAPANESE CEDAR

Taxodiaceae

EVERGREEN TREE

ZONES US, MS, LS

FULL SUN

REGULAR TO MODERATE WATER

Cryptomeria japonica

Graceful conifer, fast growing (3–4 ft. a year) in youth. Eventually skyline tree with straight columnar trunk, thin red-brown bark peeling in strips. Foliage is soft bright green to bluish green in growing season, brownish purple in cold weather. Branches, slightly pendulous, are clothed with ½–1-in.-long needlelike leaves. Roundish, red-brown cones ¾–1 in. wide. Trees sometimes planted in groves for Japanese garden effect. They also make a good tall screen.

'Elegans'. PLUME CEDAR, PLUME CRYPTOMERIA. Quite unlike species. Feathery, grayish green, soft-textured foliage. Turns rich coppery red or purplish in winter. Grows slowly into dense pyramid, to 20–60 ft. tall. Trunks on old trees may lean or curve. For effective display, give it space.

'Lobbii Nana' ('Lobbii'). Upright, dwarf, very slow grower to 4 ft. Foliage dark green.

'Pygmaea' ('Nana'). DWARF CRYPTOMERIA. Bushy dwarf 1½–2 ft. high, 2½ ft. wide. Dark green, needlelike leaves, twisted branches.

'Vilmoriniana'. Slow-growing dwarf to 1–2 ft. Fluffy gray-green foliage turns bronze in late fall and winter. Rock garden or container plant.

CUBAN PINK TRUMPET TREE. See TABEBUIA pallida

CUBAN ROYAL PALM. See ROYSTONEA regia

SOUTHERN HERITAGE PLANTS
IDENTIFIED BY SYMBOL

CUCUMBER

Cucurbitaceae
ANNUAL VINE
ALL ZONES
FULL SUN
MAINTAIN EVEN SOIL MOISTURE

Cucumber

Each cucumber vine needs an area of at least 25 sq. ft., but you can grow it on a fence or trellis to conserve space. Warm soil to sprout seeds and warmth for pollination are required.

There are long, smooth, green, slicing cucumbers; numerous small pickling cucumbers; and roundish, yellow, mild-flavored lemon cucumbers. Novelty types include Oriental (long, slim, very mild), Armenian cucumber (a long, curving, pale green, ribbed melon with mild cucumber flavor), and English greenhouse cucumber. This last type must be grown in greenhouse to avoid pollination by bees, which ruins form and flavor; when well grown it's the mildest of all cucumbers.

Bush cucumbers—types with compact vines—take up little garden space. Burpless kinds resemble hothouse cucumbers in shape and mild flavor but can be grown out-of-doors. Pickling cucumbers should be picked as soon as they have reached proper size—tiny for sweet pickles (gherkins), larger for dills or pickle slices. They grow too large very quickly.

'Sweet Success' has quality of greenhouse cucumber but can be grown outdoors. Flowers are all female, but plants need no pollinator. Grow on a trellis for long, straight cucumbers.

Plant seeds in sunny spot 1 or 2 weeks after average date of last frost. To grow cucumbers on trellis, plant seeds 1 in. deep and 1–3 ft. apart and permit main stem to reach top of support. Pick cucumbers while young to ensure continued production.

Row covers will protect seedlings from various insect pests, including cucumber beetles and flea beetles; remove when flowering begins so that pollination can occur. Whiteflies are potential pest late in season; hose off plants regularly or hang yellow sticky traps. Misshapen fruit is usually due to uneven watering or poor pollination. Bitter cucumbers, a common problem, result from stress brought on by drought and excessive heat.

CUCUMBER TREE. See MAGNOLIA acuminata

Cucurbitaceae. The gourd family consists of vines with yellow or white flowers and large, fleshy, typically seedy fruits—cucumbers, gourds, melons, pumpkins, and squash.

CULVER'S ROOT. See VERONICASTRUM virginicum

CUMBERLAND ROSEMARY. See CONRADINA verticillata

CUNNINGHAMIA lanceolata

CHINA FIR
Taxodiaceae
EVERGREEN TREE
ZONES MS, LS, CS
FULL SUN
REGULAR WATER

Cunninghamia lanceolata

Native to China. Picturesque conifer with heavy trunk, stout, whorled branches, and drooping branchlets. Stiff, needlelike, sharp-pointed leaves are 1½–2½ in. long, green above, whitish beneath. Brown, 1–2-in. cones are interesting but not profuse. Grows at moderate rate to 30 ft. with 20-ft. spread. Becomes less attractive as it ages. Prune out dead branchlets. Among palest

of needled evergreens in spring and summer; turns red bronze in cold winters. Protect from wind. 'Glauca', which has striking blue-gray foliage, is more widely grown and hardier than the species.

CUP-AND-SAUCER VINE. See COBAEA scandens

CUP FLOWER. See NIEREMBERGIA

CUPHEA

Lythraceae
SHRUBBY PERENNIALS OR DWARF SHRUBS
ZONES CS, TS; ANNUALS IN COLDER AREAS
POTTED PLANTS BEST IN LIGHT SHADE
REGULAR WATER

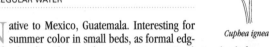

Cuphea ignea

Native to Mexico, Guatemala. Interesting for summer color in small beds, as formal edging for border, along paths, in containers. Pinch tips back for compact growth. Plants die to the ground in cold weather. Evergreen where there is little or no frost. Easy to grow from cuttings.

C. hyssopifolia. MEXICAN HEATHER, FLORIDA HEATHER. Compact shrublet 6 in.–2 ft. tall, with flexible, leafy branchlets. Leaves ½–¾ in. long, very narrow. Tiny summer flowers in pink, purple, or white are scarcely half as long as leaves.

C. ignea. CIGAR PLANT. Shrubby perennial. Leafy, compact, 1 ft. high and wide. Leaves are narrow, dark green, 1–1½ in. long. Flowers tubular, ¾ in. long, bright red with white tip and dark ring at end (hence name "cigar plant"). Blooms summer and fall.

C. micropetala. Shrub or subshrub to 3 ft., with arching stems closely set with narrow, 5-in. leaves and topped by a slender, spikelike cluster of 1½-in. bright red flowers tipped in yellow. Blooms summer and fall.

CUPID'S DART. See CATANANCHE caerulea

CUP-OF-GOLD VINE. See SOLANDRA maxima

Cupressaceae. The cypress family differs from the pine and yew families in having leaves that are usually reduced to scales and cones with few scales. Cones may even be berrylike, as in junipers (*Juniperus*).

CUPRESSOCYPARIS leylandii

LEYLAND CYPRESS
Cupressaceae
EVERGREEN TREE
ZONES US, MS, LS, CS
FULL SUN
REGULAR TO MODERATE WATER

Cupressocyparis leylandii

Hybrid of *Chamaecyparis nootkatensis* and *Cupressus macrocarpa*. Grows very fast (from cuttings to 15–20 ft. in 5 years). Usually reaches 60–70 ft. in gardens. Most often planted as a quick screen. Becoming quite popular as cut Christmas tree in Lower and Coastal South. Long, slender, upright branches of flattened, gray-green foliage sprays give youthful tree narrow pyramidal form, though it can become open and floppy. Can be pruned into tall hedge, 10–15 ft. high, but will quickly get away from you without regular maintenance. Produces small cones composed of scales. Accepts wide variety of soil and climate conditions, strong wind. In Coastal South, loses stiff, upright habit and is subject to coryneum canker fungus. Bagworms are a potential problem. Popular selections include these: 'Castlewellan' has golden new growth and narrow, erect habit; 'Emerald Isle' has bright green foliage on plant 20–25 ft. tall and 6–8 ft. wide; 'Naylor's Blue' has grayish blue foliage.

CUPRESSUS

CYPRESS

Cupressaceae

EVERGREEN TREES

⚡ ZONES VARY BY SPECIES

☀ FULL SUN

💧 MODERATE WATER

Cupressus sempervirens

These conifers have tiny scalelike leaves, closely set on cordlike branches, and interesting globular, golf ball–size cones made up of shield-shaped scales. For species well suited to the dry Southwest, choose Arizona and Italian cypresses; these species and their selections thrive in dry, rocky, alkaline soil. In high-rainfall areas, however, they are short lived; Mexican cypress is the best choice there.

C. arizonica. ARIZONA CYPRESS. Zones MS, LS, CS. Grows to 40 ft., spreading to 20 ft. Seedlings variable, with foliage from green to blue gray or silvery. Rough, furrowed bark. *C. a. glabra* (often sold as *C. glabra*) is the same, but its bark is a smooth cherry red. Other forms include 'Blue Pyramid', a dense, blue-gray pyramid to 20–25 ft.; 'Gareei', with silvery blue-green foliage; and 'Pyramidalis', a compact, symmetrical grower. Mass trees for windbreak or screen.

C. lusitanica. MEXICAN CYPRESS. Zones LS, CS. Native to northern Florida and Central America. Grows rapidly, to 50 ft., with symmetrical, spreading, pendulous branches and beautiful ferny blue-green foliage. Use as specimen tree or windbreak. Choose plants grown from cuttings of selected blue clones; these are more uniform and more blue than plants grown from seed. Likes fertile, well-drained soil.

C. sempervirens. ITALIAN CYPRESS. Zones MS, LS, CS. Native to southern Europe, western Asia. Species has horizontal branches and dark green foliage, but variants are more often sold. 'Stricta' ('Fastigiata'), columnar Italian cypress, and 'Glauca', blue Italian cypress (really blue green in color), are classic Mediterranean landscape plants; both grow into dense, narrow trees to 60 ft. high. 'Swane's Golden', another columnar form, has golden yellow new growth.

⚱ CURCUMA petiolata

HIDDEN LILY

Zingiberaceae

PERENNIAL

⚡ ZONES LS, CS, TS

☀ LIGHT SHADE OR MORNING SUN

💧 REGULAR WATER

Curcuma petiolata

Native to tropical Asia. Member of the ginger family. Grows 2–3 ft. high, with very handsome, tropical-looking, 10-in.-long, sheathlike leaves, and 6–8-in. rose purple bracts midsummer. The foliage, which largely hides the bracts, is thin and may burn in hot afternoon sun and tear in strong winds. Cut back to ground in winter; new foliage will sprout from tuberous roots in spring. Plant in soil with lots of organic matter, and keep moist. Widely grown in Lower and Coastal South.

CURLY FILBERT. See CORYLUS avellana 'Contorta'

CURRY PLANT. See HELICHRYSUM italicum

CUT-LEAF PHILODENDRON. See MONSTERA deliciosa

CYATHEA cooperi

AUSTRALIAN TREE FERN

Cyatheaceae

TREE FERN

⚡ ZONE TS; OR GROW IN CONTAINER

☀◑ FULL SUN TO PARTIAL SHADE

💧 REGULAR WATER

Cyathea cooperi

Fastest growing of the fairly hardy (to possibly 20°F, but with damage to fronds) tree ferns. To an eventual 20 ft. tall, 12 ft. wide. At first, a low wide clump (can go from 1-ft. to 6-ft. spread in a year) before growing upward. Broad fronds are finely cut, bright green. Brownish hair on leafstalks and leaf undersurfaces can irritate skin; wear long sleeves, hat, neckcloth when grooming plants. Often sold as *Alsophila australis*, *A. cooperi*, or *Sphaeropteris cooperi*.

Cycadaceae. This is the best-known family in Cycadales, an order of slow-growing evergreen plants with large, firm, palmlike or fernlike leaves and conelike fruit. Most people think of them as a kind of palm.

Most are native to tropical regions. Some are subtropical, and among these, some are hardy enough to grow out-of-doors in mild-winter climates.

Cycads include *Cycas circinalis* and *C. revoluta*, as well as *Ceratozamia mexicana* and *Zamia pumila* (members of the related family, Zamiaceae).

CYCAS

Cycadaceae

CYCADS

⚡ ZONES VARY BY SPECIES

◑ PARTIAL SHADE

💧 REGULAR WATER

Cycas revoluta

These evergreen plants are neither ferns nor palms, but rather primitive, cone-bearing relatives of conifers. A rosette of dark green, featherlike leaves grows from a central point at the top of a single trunk (sometimes several trunks). Female plants bear conspicuous, red to orange, egg-shaped seeds. Use cycads for tropical effect.

⚱ **C. circinalis.** QUEEN SAGO. Zone TS. Native to Old World tropics. Beautiful specimen plant to 20 ft. tall. Graceful, drooping leaves to 8 ft. long atop unbranching trunk. Protect from frost.

⚱ **C. revoluta.** SAGO PALM. Zones CS (protected), TS; hardy to 15°F. Native to Japan. In youth (2–3 ft. tall), has airy, lacy appearance of fern; with age (grows very slowly to 10 ft.), looks more like palm. Leaves are 2–3 ft. long (larger on very old plants), divided into many narrow, leathery segments. Tough, tolerant house or patio plant; good in foundation or entry planting. Leaf spot disease is a problem in high-rainfall areas.

CYCLAMEN

Primulaceae

TUBEROUS-ROOTED PERENNIALS

⚡ ZONES VARY BY SPECIES

☀◑ FULL SUN OR PARTIAL SHADE

💧 KEEP SOIL MOIST DURING GROWTH

Cyclamen persicum

Grown for pretty white, pink, rose, or red flowers carried atop attractive clump of basal leaves. Zones and uses for large-flowered florists' cyclamen (*C. persicum*) are given under that name. All other types are smaller flowered, hardier. They bloom as described in listings that follow; all lose their leaves during part of year. Leaves may appear before or with flowers. Use the hardier types in rock gardens, in naturalized clumps under trees, or as carpets under camellias, rhododendrons, and large noninvasive ferns. Or grow them in pots out of direct sun.

All kinds of cyclamen grow best in fairly rich, porous soil with lots of humus. Plant tubers 6–10 in. apart; cover with ½ in. soil. (Florists' cyclamen is an exception to usual planting practice; upper half of tuber should protrude above soil level.) Best planting time is dormant period, June–August—except for florists' cyclamen, which is always sold as a potted plant rather than a tuber and is available in most seasons (although most are sold during the late fall–spring blooming period). Top-dress annually with light application of potting soil with complete fertilizer added, being careful not to cover top of tuber. Do not cultivate around roots.

Cyclamen grow readily from seed; small-flowered hardy species take several years to bloom. Older strains of florists' cyclamen needed 15 to 18 months from seed to bloom; newer strains can bloom in 7 months. Grown out-of-doors in open ground, cyclamen often self-sows.

C. atkinsii. Zones US, MS. Crimson flowers are borne on 4–6-in. stems, winter–early spring. Deep green, silver-mottled leaves. Also pink, white selections.

C. cilicium. Zones US, MS. Pale pink, purple-blotched, fragrant flowers on 2–6-in. stems, fall–winter. Leaves are mottled. 'Album' is a white-flowered form.

C. coum. Zones US, MS, LS. Deep crimson rose flowers on 4–6-in. stems in winter and early spring; round, deep green leaves. Also white, pink selections.

C. europaeum. See C. purpurascens

C. hederifolium (C. neapolitanum). BABY CYCLAMEN. Zones US, MS. Large light green leaves marbled silver and white. Rose pink flowers bloom on 3–4-in. stems, late summer–fall. There is a white form. One of the most vigorous and easiest to grow; very reliable in cold-winter climates. Set tubers a foot apart.

C. persicum. FLORISTS' CYCLAMEN. Wild ancestor of florists' cyclamen. Original species has deep to pale pink or white, 2-in. fragrant flowers on 6-in. stems. Selective breeding has resulted in large-flowered florists' cyclamen (the old favorites) and, more recently, smaller strains. Fragrance has disappeared, with rare exceptions.

Florists' cyclamen blooms late fall to spring; flowers crimson, red, salmon, purple, or white, on 6–8-in. stems. Kidney-shaped dark green leaves. Mainly grown indoors, but can be bedded out in early spring for cool-season color.

Selections of dwarf or miniature florists' cyclamen are popular; they are half or three-quarter-size replicas of standards. Careful gardeners can get these to bloom in 7 to 8 months from seed. Miniature strains (profuse show of 1½-in. flowers on 6–8-in. plants) include fragrant Dwarf Fragrance and Mirabelle strains.

C. purpurascens (C. europaeum). EUROPEAN CYCLAMEN. Zones US, MS. Fragrant crimson flowers on 5–6-in. stems, late summer–fall. Bright green leaves mottled silvery white; almost evergreen.

C. repandum. Zones US, MS. Bright crimson flowers with long, narrow petals on 5–6-in. stems in spring. Rich green, ivy-shaped leaves, marbled silver, toothed on edges.

AVOID WILD BULBS

As a buyer of species cyclamen (any kind other than *C. persicum*), you should check to ascertain that the bulbs are commercially grown and not taken from the wild. Many bulb species are endangered and fast disappearing in their native habitats. Look for labels that mention "Holland" or "cultivated." In addition to cyclamen species, bulbs that have been dug in the wild for sale in the U.S. include species *Narcissus*, as well as *Eranthis*, *Galanthus*, and *Leucojum*.

CYDONIA. See CHAENOMELES

CYDONIA oblonga. See QUINCE, FRUITING

SOIL MIX FOR CYMBIDIUMS

If the store where you buy your cymbidiums doesn't offer a packaged cymbidium soil mix, here's a good one you can make: 2 parts composted bark, 2 parts peat moss, 1 part sand. Add a 4-in. pot of complete, dry fertilizer to each wheelbarrow of mix. Packaged or homemade, the medium should drain fast and still retain moisture.

CYMBIDIUM

Orchidaceae

TERRESTRIAL ORCHIDS

✄ ALL ZONES—SUBJECT TO CONDITIONS BELOW

☼ BEST WITH HALF-SHADE

💧 KEEP SOIL MOIST DURING GROWTH

Miniature Cymbidium

Native to high altitudes in southeast Asia, where rainfall is heavy and nights cool. Very popular because of their relatively easy culture. Except in frost-free areas, grow plants in containers in greenhouse or sunroom, or under overhang or high-branching tree. Excellent cut flower. Long, narrow, grasslike leaves form a sheath around short, stout, oval pseudobulbs. Long-lasting flowers grow on erect or arching spikes. Standard types usually bloom from February to early May. Bloom season for miniatures starts in September and is usually heaviest November–January.

For best bloom, give as much light as possible without burning foliage. Plants do well under shade cloth or lath. Leaf color is the guide: Plants with yellow-green leaves generally flower best; dark green foliage means too much shade. During flowering period, give plants shade to prolong bloom life, keep flowers from fading.

Plants prefer 45–55°F night temperature, rising to as high as 80° to 90°F during day. They'll stand temperatures as low as 28°F for short time only; therefore, where there's danger of harder frosts, take plants inside or protect them with covering of polyethylene film. Flower spikes are more tender than other plant tissues.

Keep potting medium moist as new growth develops and matures—usually March–September. In winter, water just enough to keep bulbs from shriveling. On hot summer days, mist foliage early in day.

Feed with a complete liquid fertilizer high in nitrogen, every 10 days to 2 weeks, January–July. Use low-nitrogen fertilizer August–December.

Transplant potted plants when bulbs fill pots. When dividing plants, keep minimum of three healthy bulbs (with foliage) in each division. Dust cuts with sulfur or charcoal to discourage rot.

Cymbidium growers typically list only the hybrids in their catalogs—large-flowered selections with white, pink, yellow, green, or bronze blooms. Most have yellow throat, dark red markings on lip. Large-flowered forms produce a dozen or more 4½–5-in. flowers per stem. Miniature selections, about a quarter the size of large-flowered forms, are popular for their size, free-blooming qualities, flower color.

CYNODON dactylon

BERMUDA GRASS, BERMUDA

Poaceae (Gramineae)

LAWN GRASS

✄ ZONES MS, LS, CS, TS

☼ FULL SUN; INTOLERANT OF SHADE

💧💧 WATER LESS THAN MOST LAWN GRASSES

Cynodon dactylon

Subtropical fine-textured grass that spreads rapidly by surface and underground runners. Tolerates heat; looks good if well maintained. It turns brown in winter; some selections stay green longer than others, and most stay green longer if well fed. Bermuda grass can be overseeded with rye grasses for winter color. Needs sun and should be cut low; ½–1½ in. is desirable. Needs thatching—removal of matted layer of old stems and stolons beneath the leaves—to look its best.

Common Bermuda is good lower-maintenance lawn for large area. Needs feeding in spring and summer, and careful and frequent mowing to remove seed spikes. Roots invade shrubbery and flower beds if not carefully confined. Can become extremely difficult to eradicate. Plant from hulled seed, plugs, or sod.

Hybrid Bermudas are finer in texture and better in color than common kind. They crowd out common Bermuda in time but are harder to overseed with rye. They also need much more maintenance, including frequent fertilizing, watering, and thatching. Grow from seed, plugs, or sod.

'Floratex'. Keeps green well into fall and greens up early in spring. Needs less water and fertilizer than most other hybrid Bermudas but produces numerous seed heads. Available only as sod or plugs.

'Tifdwarf'. Extremely low and dense; takes very close mowing. Slower to establish than others, but also slower to spread where it's not wanted.

'Tifgreen'. Fine textured, deep blue green, dense. Few seed spikes; sterile seeds. Takes close mowing; preferred for putting greens.

'Tiflawn'. Medium-fine textured, not as dense as 'Tifgreen'. More seed heads than other hybrids but extremely wear resistant.

'Tifway'. Low growth, fine texture, stiff blades, dark green, dense, wear resistant. Slow to start. Sterile (no seeds).

'Yuma'. Low, dense; tolerates heat, drought, cold.

Cyperaceae. Members of the sedge family resemble grasses, but their stems are usually three-sided and their leaves are arranged in three ranks. They generally grow in wet places; *Carex* and *Cyperus* are examples.

CYPERUS

Cyperaceae

PERENNIALS

✎ ZONES VARY BY SPECIES

☼ ◐ ● SUN OR SHADE

💧 BOG PLANTS IN NATURE

These are sedges—grasslike plants distinguished from true grasses by three-angled, solid stems and very different flowering parts. Valued for striking form, silhouette, shadow pattern.

Cyperus papyrus

Most kinds grow in rich, moist soil or with roots submerged in water, in sun or shade. Groom plants by removing dead or broken stems; divide and replant vigorous ones when clump becomes too large, saving smaller, outside divisions and discarding overgrown centers. In cold-winter climates, pot up divisions and keep them over the winter as house plants.

C. alternifolius. UMBRELLA PLANT. Zones LS, CS, TS. Narrow, firm, spreading leaves, at tops of 2–4-ft. stems, arranged like ribs of umbrella. Flowers in dry, greenish brown clusters. Grows in or out of water. Effective near pools, in pots or planters, or in dry stream beds or small rock gardens. Self-sows. Can become weedy, take over a small pool. Dwarf form is 'Gracilis' ('Nanus').

C. papyrus. PAPYRUS, BULRUSH. Zones CS, TS. Tall, graceful, dark green stems 6–10 ft. high, topped with clusters of green threadlike parts to 1½ ft. long (longer than small leaves at base of cluster). Will grow quickly in 2 in. of water in shallow pool, or can be potted and placed on bricks or inverted pot in deeper water. Protect from strong wind. Also grows well in rich, moist soil out of water. Used by flower arrangers.

CYPRESS. See *Cupressus*. True cypresses are all *Cupressus*; many plants erroneously called cypress are under *Chamaecyparis* and *Taxodium*.

CYPRESS, FALSE. See CHAMAECYPARIS

CYPRESS VINE. See IPOMOEA quamoclit

CYRILLA racemiflora

TITI, LEATHERWOOD

Cyrillaceae

SHRUB OR SMALL TREE

✎ ALL ZONES

☼ ◐ FULL SUN OR PART SHADE

💧 AMPLE TO REGULAR WATER

Cyrilla racemiflora

Beautiful native flowering shrub or small tree, 10–15 ft. tall, sometimes to 30 ft. Grows naturally at water edges and in low wet soils from Texas to Florida and Virginia. Noted for its twisted, contorted branches. Leaves narrow, glossy dark green, 1½–4 in. long; many turn orange, rust, or red in fall. Deciduous in Upper South, semievergreen in Middle South, evergreen elsewhere. Fragrant white flowers, on 4–6-in. dangling sprays in early summer, attract bees. Tan seeds form on the sprays in late summer and persist into winter. Needs moist acid soil that is high in organic matter. Tolerates seasonal standing water.

CYRTOMIUM falcatum

HOLLY FERN

Polypodiaceae

FERN

✎ ZONES LS (PROTECTED), CS, TS; OR INDOORS

☼ ● PARTIAL OR FULL SHADE

💧 REGULAR WATER

Coarse-textured but handsome evergreen fern, 2–3 ft. tall, sometimes taller. Fronds large, dark green, glossy, leathery. Hardy to 14°F. Provide good soil; take care not to plant too deeply. Protect from wind. Selection 'Rochfordianum' has fringed leaflets.

Cyrtomium falcatum

> ## THE BAD-NEWS BROOMS
>
> *Cytisus scoparius* and Spanish broom (*Spartium junceum*) escaped from landscapes starting in the early 20th century; their seedlings are now taking over areas of low-elevation wildlands. If you live near open land and want to plant a broom, use a selection with better manners.

CYTISUS

BROOM

Fabaceae (Leguminosae)

EVERGREEN, SEMIEVERGREEN, DECIDUOUS SHRUBS

✎ ZONES US, MS, LS

☼ FULL SUN

💧 MODERATE WATER

Cytisus scoparius

Deciduous, semievergreen, or evergreen shrubs (many nearly leafless, but with green or gray-green stems). Sweet pea–shaped flowers, often fragrant. Plants tolerate wind, seashore conditions, and rocky, infertile soil. Prune after bloom to keep to reasonable size and form, lessen production of unsightly seedpods.

C. praecox. WARMINSTER BROOM. Deciduous. Compact growth to 3–5 ft. high and 4–6 ft. wide, with many slender stems. Plant resembles a mounding mass of pale yellow to creamy white flowers in spring. Small leaves drop early. Effective as informal screen or hedge, along drives, paths, garden steps. 'Allgold', slightly taller, has bright yellow flowers; 'Hollandia' has pink ones. 'Moonlight', formerly considered *C. praecox,* is now thought to be a form of *C. scoparius.*

C. scoparius. SCOTCH BROOM. Evergreen. Upright-growing mass of wandlike green stems (often leafless or nearly so) may reach 10 ft. Golden yellow, ¾-in. flowers bloom in spring and early summer.

Much less aggressive than the species are its lower-growing, more colorful forms. Most of these grow 5–8 ft. tall: 'Burkwoodii', red blossoms with yellow; 'Carla', pink and crimson lined white; 'Dorothy Walpole', rose pink and crimson; 'Lena', lemon yellow and red; 'Lilac Time', compact, lilac pink; 'Lord Lambourne', scarlet and cream; 'Minstead', white flushed deep purple and lilac; 'Moonlight', compact, pale yellow; 'Pomona', orange and apricot; 'St. Mary's', white; 'San Francisco' and 'Stanford', red.

DAFFODIL. See NARCISSUS

DAHLBERG DAISY. See DYSSODIA tenuiloba

DAHLIA

Asteraceae (Compositae)

TUBEROUS-ROOTED PERENNIALS

ZONES US, MS, LS

LIGHT AFTERNOON SHADE IN LOWER SOUTH

REGULAR WATER

Native to Mexico and Guatemala. Bloom in summer, but reach their peak when weather cools in early fall. Through centuries of hybridizing and selection, dahlias have become tremendously diversified, available in numerous flower types and in all colors but true blue. Sketches illustrate types based on flower form as classified by the American Dahlia Society.

Dahlia Hybrid

Bush and bedding dahlias grow from 15 in. to over 6 ft. high. The tall bush forms are useful as summer hedges, screens, and fillers among shrubs; lower kinds give mass color in borders and containers. Modern dahlias, with their strong stems, long-lasting blooms that face outward or upward, and substantial, attractive foliage, are striking cut flowers. Leaves are generally divided into many large, deep green leaflets.

Planting. Most dahlias are started from tubers. Plant them after frost is past and soil is warm. Several weeks before planting, dig soil 1 ft. deep and work in organic matter such as ground bark or peat moss.

Dig holes 1 ft. deep and 3 ft. apart for most types; space largest kinds 4–5 ft. apart, smaller ones 1–2 ft. If you fertilize at planting, thoroughly mix ¼ cup of complete fertilizer in hole, then add 4 in. of plain soil. For tall types, drive a 5-ft. stake into hole; place tuber horizontally, 2 in. from stake, with eye (growth bud) pointing toward it. Cover tuber with 3 in. of soil. Water thoroughly. As shoots grow, gradually fill hole with soil.

Dahlias also can be started from seed. For tall types, plant seeds early indoors; transplant seedlings into garden beds after frosts are over. For dwarf dahlias, sow seed in place after soil is warm, or buy and plant

started seedlings from a garden center. Dwarf dahlias are best replaced each year, though they can be lifted and stored.

Thinning, pinching. On tall-growing types, thin to strongest shoot or two shoots (you can make cuttings of removed shoots). When shoots have three sets of leaves, pinch off tips just above top set; two side shoots develop from each pair of leaves. For large flowers, remove all but terminal flower buds on side shoots. Smaller-flowered dahlias, such as pompoms, singles, and dwarfs, need only first pinching.

Plant care. Start watering regularly after shoots are above ground, and continue throughout active growth. Dahlias planted in enriched soil don't need additional food. If soil lacks nutrients, side-dress plants with fertilizer high in phosphates and potash when first flower buds appear. Avoid high-nitrogen fertilizers: They result in soft growth, weak stems, tubers liable to rot in storage. Mulch to keep down weeds and to eliminate cultivating, which may injure feeder roots.

Cut flowers. Pick nearly mature flowers in early morning or evening. Immediately place cut stems in 2–3 in. of hot water; let stand in gradually cooling water for several hours or overnight.

Lifting, storing. After tops turn yellow or are frosted, cut stalks to 4 in. above ground. Dig around plant 1 ft. from center, carefully pry up clump with spading fork, shake off loose soil, and let clump dry in sun for several hours. From that point, follow either of two methods:

Method 1: Divide clumps immediately. This saves storage space; freshly dug tubers are easy to cut, and eyes (growth buds), easy to recognize at this time. To divide, cut stalks with a sharp knife, leaving 1 in. of stalk attached to each tuber. Each tuber must have an eye in order to produce a new plant. Dust cut surfaces with sulfur to prevent rot; bury tubers in sand, sawdust, or vermiculite; store through winter in cool (40–45°F), dry place.

Method 2: Leave clumps intact; cover them with dry sand, sawdust, peat moss, perlite, or vermiculite; store in cool, dry place. There is less danger of shrinkage with this storage method. About 2 to 4 weeks before planting in spring, separate tubers as described under method 1. Place tubers in moist sand to encourage development of sprouts.

DAHOON. See ILEX cassine

DAME'S ROCKET. See HESPERIS matronalis

DAMSON PLUM. See PRUNUS insititia

DANCING GIRL GINGER. See GLOBBA

DANCING LADY. See ONCIDIUM

DAPHNE PRUNING? IT'S SPECIAL

Correct the shape of a *Daphne odora* by cutting late-winter flower clusters to wear as corsages or for indoor display. Make cuts to outfacing buds to promote spreading, to infacing ones to promote upward growth. Cut stems of deciduous kinds for bouquets while they are in bud.

Dahlia Flower Forms

Informal Decorative

Formal Decorative

Cactus

Semicactus

Collarette

Single

Anemone

Ball

Pompom

DAPHNE

Thymelaeaceae

EVERGREEN, SEMIEVERGREEN, DECIDUOUS SHRUBS

ZONES VARY BY SPECIES

EXPOSURE NEEDS VARY BY SPECIES

REGULAR TO MODERATE WATER; OR AS NOTED

ALL PARTS, ESPECIALLY FRUITS, ARE POISONOUS IF INGESTED

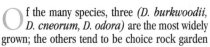

Daphne odora 'Marginata'

Of the many species, three (*D. burkwoodii, D. cneorum, D. odora*) are the most widely grown; the others tend to be choice rock garden subjects with more limited distribution in the nursery trade. Although some daphnes are easier to grow than others, all require excellent drainage, cool soil (use a mulch or noncompetitive ground cover), careful watering during dry spells, and shelter from wind and extreme sun.

D. burkwoodii. Evergreen or semievergreen to deciduous. Zones US, MS, LS. Hybrid with erect, compact growth to 3–4 ft. Densely set, narrow leaves; numerous small clusters of fragrant flowers (white aging to pink) around branch ends in late spring and again in late summer. 'Somerset' is 4–5 ft. tall, with pink flowers. 'Briggs Moonlight' has leaves of pale yellow with a narrow border of green. 'Carol Mackie' has gold-edged green leaves. Use in shrub borders, at woodland edge, as foundation planting. Full sun or light shade.

D. cneorum. GARLAND DAPHNE, ROSE DAPHNE. Evergreen. Zones US, MS. Matting and spreading; less than 1 ft. high, 3 ft. wide. Good container plant. Trailing branches covered with narrow, 1-in.-long, dark green leaves. Clusters of fragrant rosy light pink flowers appear in spring. Choice rock garden plant; give it light shade. After bloom, top-dress with mix of peat moss and sand to keep roots cool and promote rooting of trailing stems.

Selections include 'Eximia', lower growing than the species and with larger flowers; 'Pygmaea Alba', 3 in. tall, 1 ft. wide, with white flowers; 'Ruby Glow', with larger, more deeply colored flowers and with late-summer rebloom; and 'Variegata', with gold-edged leaves.

D. genkwa. LILAC DAPHNE. Deciduous. Zones US, MS, LS. Erect, open growth to 3–4 ft. high and as wide. Before leaves expand, clusters of lilac blue, scentless flowers wreathe branches, making foot-long wands of blossoms. White fruit follows flowers. Leaves are oval, 2 in. long. Use in rock garden, shrub border. Full sun or light shade.

D. mezereum. FEBRUARY DAPHNE. Deciduous. Zones US, MS, LS. Rather gawky, stiffly twigged, erect growth to 4 ft., with roundish, thin leaves 2–3 in. long. Plant in groups. Full sun or light shade. Fragrant reddish purple flowers in short stalkless clusters are carried along branches in mid- to late winter before leaf-out and continue into spring. 'Alba' is the same but is less rangy and has white flowers, yellow fruit.

D. odora. WINTER DAPHNE. Evergreen. Zones MS, LS. Prized for the pervasive fragrance of its flowers. Very neat, handsome plant usually to about 4 ft. high and spreading wider; has reached 8–10 ft. under ideal conditions. Rather narrow, 3-in.-long leaves are thick and glossy. Nosegay clusters of charming flowers—pink to deep red on outside, with creamy pink throats—appear at branch ends in winter.

Give this species good growing conditions, since it's the fussiest of the lot. Locate the plant where it will get midday shade. To avoid water mold root rot (the chief cause of failure), roots need well-aerated, neutral-pH soil. Dig planting hole twice as wide as root ball and one and a half times as deep; refill with mixture of 1 part soil, 1 part sand, and 2 parts ground bark. Top of root ball should remain higher than soil level. Feed right after bloom with complete fertilizer but not acid plant food. During dry periods, water just enough to keep plant from wilting.

'Alba'. Plain green leaves, white flowers. Terminal growth sometimes distorted by fasciation (cockscomb-like growths).

'Leucanthe'. Vigorous and relatively disease resistant, with dark green leaves and a profusion of pale pink flowers with white interiors.

'Marginata' ('Aureo-Marginata'). More widely grown than species. Leaves are edged with band of yellow. Pink flowers.

DARMERA peltata
(Peltiphyllum peltatum)

UMBRELLA PLANT, INDIAN RHUBARB

Saxifragaceae

PERENNIAL

ZONE US

PARTIAL SHADE

AMPLE WATER

Darmera peltata

Native to mountains of Northern California and southern Oregon. Large, round clusters of pink flowers on 6-ft.-tall bare stalks in spring. Shield-shaped leaves 1–2 ft. wide appear later on 2–6-ft. stalks. Stout rhizomes to 2 in. thick grow in damp ground or even into streams. A spectacular plant for pond, stream, or cool woodland site.

DASYLIRION texanum

TEXAS SOTOL

Agavaceae

EVERGREEN SHRUB OR SMALL TREE

ZONES MS, LS, CS, TS

FULL SUN

LITTLE WATER; NO WATER ONCE ESTABLISHED

Dasylirion texanum

Resembles yucca, its relative. Stiff, spiny, green leaves, with sharp edges, to 2½ ft. long, ½ in. wide, reflect light prettily as they move in a breeze. Produces small, whitish flowers on spikes to 15 feet tall. Give plenty of space in the ground, at least 4 ft., or grow in a pot. Must have fast-draining soil or roots will rot. Good for dry, rocky, alkaline soil. Rots in high-rainfall, high-humidity areas. Tolerates salt spray. Plants can be male or female. You need one of each to get seed.

DATE PALM. See PHOENIX

DATURA. See BRUGMANSIA

DAVALLIA

Polypodiaceae

FERNS

ZONE TS; OR INDOORS

PARTIAL SHADE

REGULAR WATER

Davallia trichomanoides

These ferns have long thick furry rhizomes (like animals' feet) that creep over the soil. They're epiphytes in nature, but will make a delicate ground cover in the Tropical South if the soil is fast draining. Excellent elsewhere for hanging baskets and pots; use a coarse bark or moss potting mix, and repot when the mix breaks down so the roots don't rot.

D. fejeensis. RABBIT'S FOOT FERN. Native to Fiji. Graceful, finely cut fronds 1–2½ ft. long. Makes large specimen plant with age. 'Plumosa' is exceptionally lacy and drooping.

D. trichomanoides. SQUIRREL'S FOOT FERN. Native to southeast Asia. Finely divided fronds to 1 ft. long, 6 in. wide. Rhizomes light reddish brown, very furry. Hardy to 30°F.

D

DAVIDIA involucrata

HANDKERCHIEF TREE, DOVE TREE

Nyssaceae

DECIDUOUS TREE

🗡 ZONES US, MS, LS

☼ ◑ PARTIAL SHADE IN LOWER SOUTH

💧 REGULAR WATER

Davidia involucrata

Native to China. In gardens, grows 20–40 ft. tall, with pyramidal to rounded crown and strong branching pattern. Has clean look in and out of leaf. Roundish to heart-shaped, 3–6-in.-long leaves are vivid green. Comes into bloom in spring; general effect is that of white doves resting among green leaves—or, as some say, like handkerchiefs drying on branches. Small, clustered, red-anthered flowers are carried between two large, unequal, white or creamy white bracts; one 6 in. long, the other about 4 in. long. Trees often take 10 years to come into flower, then may bloom more heavily in alternate years. No fall color. Brown fruits about the size of golf balls hang on tree well into winter.

Plant this tree by itself; it should not compete with other flowering trees. Pleasing in front of dark conifers, where vivid green and white stand out.

DAWN REDWOOD. See METASEQUOIA glyptostroboides

DAYLILY. See HEMEROCALLIS

DEAD NETTLE. See LAMIUM

DECUMARIA barbara

CLIMBING HYDRANGEA, WOOD VAMP

Saxifragaceae

DECIDUOUS VINE

🗡 ZONES MS, LS, CS

◑ ● PARTIAL OR FULL SHADE

💧 💧 AMPLE TO REGULAR WATER

Decumaria barbara

Native to wet woodlands and swamps from East Texas to Florida and Virginia. Vine grows to 30 ft. or more, attaching to walls with its aerial rootlets or running loose over the ground. Handsome glossy green oval leaves, 2–4 in. long, 1–2 in. wide. Fragrant flowers in dense clusters 2–4 in. across appear in May or June. Old vines sometimes bear showy fruit. Leaves turn yellow in fall. Likes moist shady sites and fertile soil but will also grow in fairly dry woods. Takes some direct sun if kept moist. Of the three vines known as climbing hydrangeas—*Hydrangea anomala* and *Schizophragma hydrangeoides* are the others—this is the only native, and it is the least known.

DELONIX regia

ROYAL POINCIANA, FLAMBOYANT

Fabaceae (Leguminosae)

DECIDUOUS TREE

🗡 ZONE TS

☼ FULL SUN

💧 REGULAR WATER

Delonix regia

Flamboyant is the word to describe poinciana. Its large trusses of 4-in., orange to scarlet flowers with white markings put on a spectacular display in late spring or early summer. Wide-spreading, umbrella-shaped tree of rapid growth to 30 ft. and twice as wide. Fernlike leaves, finely cut into many tiny leaflets, give filtered shade. Blooms are followed by 2-ft. black seedpods that hang on bare winter branches. Easy to grow, but sensitive to cold.

DELOSPERMA

ICE PLANT

Aizoaceae

SUCCULENT PERENNIALS

🗡 ZONES VARY BY SPECIES

☼ FULL SUN

💧 TAKE CONSIDERABLE DROUGHT

Delosperma cooperi

This huge group of succulents includes two of the hardiest ice plants, described below. These and other types thrive in full sun with good drainage and just enough water to keep them looking bright and fresh. Good plants for the Southwest. Like dry, chalky, well-drained soil.

D. cooperi. Zones MS, LS, CS. To 5 in. tall, 2 ft. wide. Brilliant, purple flowers all summer. Tolerates 0°F if protected by snow or mulch.

D. nubigenum. Zones US, MS, LS, CS. Hardiest of all ice plants, it has withstood −25°F. Barely 1 in. high, spreading to 3 ft. Fleshy, cylindrical, bright green leaves turn red in fall, then green up again in spring. Bright golden yellow flowers, 1–1½ in. wide, blanket plants in spring. Effective in rock gardens.

DELPHINIUM

Ranunculaceae

PERENNIALS, SOME TREATED AS ANNUALS

🗡 ZONES VARY BY SPECIES

☼ FULL SUN, EXCEPT AS NOTED

💧 REGULAR WATER

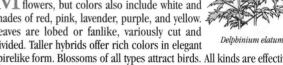

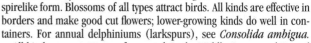

Delphinium elatum

Most people associate delphiniums with blue flowers, but colors also include white and shades of red, pink, lavender, purple, and yellow. Leaves are lobed or fanlike, variously cut and divided. Taller hybrids offer rich colors in elegant spirelike form. Blossoms of all types attract birds. All kinds are effective in borders and make good cut flowers; lower-growing kinds do well in containers. For annual delphiniums (larkspurs), see *Consolida ambigua*.

All kinds are easy to grow from seed. In the Middle, Lower, and Coastal South, sow fresh seed in flats or pots of light soil mix in July or August; set out transplants in October for bloom in late spring and early summer. (In most of the South, perennial forms are usually short lived and treated as annuals. *D. carolinianum* and *D. virescens* are exceptions. In Upper South, sow seed in March or April, set out transplants in June or July for first bloom by September (and more bloom the following summer).

Delphiniums need rich, porous soil and regular fertilizing. Improve poor or heavy soils by blending in soil conditioners. Add lime to strongly acid soils. Work small handful of superphosphate into bottom of hole before setting out plant. Be careful not to cover root crown.

D. belladonna. Sturdy, bushy perennial. Zones US, MS. To 3–4 ft. Deeply cut leaves; short-stemmed, airy flower clusters. Selections include 'Belladonna', light blue; 'Bellamosum', dark blue; 'Casa Blanca', white; 'Cliveden Beauty', deep turquoise blue. All have flowers 1½–2 in. across, are longer lived than tall hybrids listed under *D. elatum*.

D. carolinianum. CAROLINA LARKSPUR. Perennial. Zones US, MS, LS. Native to Southeast, southern Midwest, Texas. Erect spikes of blue or white flowers, 1–3 ft. tall. Blooms heavily in spring, goes dormant in summer. Reseeds readily. Tolerates just about any well-drained soil.

D. elatum. CANDLE DELPHINIUM. Perennial. Zone US. Along with *D. cheilanthum* and others, this 3–6-ft. Siberian species, with small dark or dull purple flowers, is parent of modern tall-growing delphinium strains such as the spectacular Pacific strain.

Pacific strain delphinium hybrids (also called Giant Pacific, Pacific Hybrids, and Pacific Coast Hybrids) grow to 8 ft. tall. They are available in selected color series; members of these include 'Blue Bird', medium blue; 'Blue Jay', medium to dark blue; 'Galahad', white with white center;

'Percival', white with black center; 'Summer Skies', light blue. Other purple, lavender, pink named selections also sold.

Like Pacific strain but shorter (2–2½ ft. tall) are the Blue Fountains, Blue Springs, and Magic Fountains strains. Even shorter is the Stand Up strain (15–20 in.). These shorter strains seldom require staking.

Other strains have flowers in shades of lilac pink to deep raspberry rose, clear lilac, lavender, royal purple, and darkest violet. Wrexham strain, tall growing with large spikes, was developed in England.

D. grandiflorum (D. chinense). CHINESE DELPHINIUM, BOUQUET DELPHINIUM. Short-lived perennial treated as biennial or annual. All zones. Bushy, branching, 1 ft. tall or less. Selections include 'Dwarf Blue Mirror', 1 ft., upward-facing flowers of deep blue; and 'Tom Thumb', 8 in. tall, pure gentian blue flowers.

D. virescens. WHITE LARKSPUR, PRAIRIE LARKSPUR. Perennial. Zones US, MS, LS. Native to poor rocky limestone soils from Texas north to Canada. Very slender plant, 1–2 ft. tall. Flowers white, with hint of pale blue, April–July. Plant in clusters for effect. Tolerates heat, some shade, and clay and caliche soils. Poisonous to cattle.

HOW TO GROW CLOSE-TO-PERFECT DELPHINIUMS

When new shoots develop in spring, remove all but the two or three strongest and apply a complete fertilizer alongside plants. Apply slug bait to control slugs and snails. Stake flower stalks early. After bloom, cut back flower spikes, leaving foliage at the bottom; after new shoots are several inches high, cut old stalks to ground. Fertilize to encourage good second bloom in late summer, early fall.

DENDRANTHEMA. See CHRYSANTHEMUM morifolium

DENNSTAEDTIA
punctilobula

HAY-SCENTED FERN

Dennstaedtiaceae

FERN

🗡 ZONES US, MS

☼ LIGHT SHADE

◖◖ REGULAR TO MODERATE WATER

Dennstaedtia punctilobula

Native from eastern Canada to the mid-South. Deciduous fern with finely divided fronds to 2 ft. tall arising from creeping rhizomes. Spreads quickly to make an attractive ground cover. Crushed fronds smell like freshly cut hay. If given adequate water, thrives even in poor, rocky soil. Can form mats that cover rocks. You may see it growing along the roadside or under rail fences in partly shaded areas.

DEODAR CEDAR. See CEDRUS deodara

DESCHAMPSIA

HAIR GRASS

Poaceae (Gramineae)

PERENNIAL GRASSES

🗡 ZONES US, MS

☼ ◖ FULL SUN OR PARTIAL SHADE

◖◖ REGULAR TO MODERATE WATER

Deschampsia caespitosa vivipara

Ornamental clumping grasses with narrow, rough leaves obscured by clouds of yellowish flower panicles in late spring or early summer.

Use in mass plantings. Best suited to Upper South. Evergreen in warmer part of range, semievergreen in colder part.

D. caespitosa. TUFTED HAIR GRASS. Native to much of North America, but most forms are imports from European nurseries. Dark green foliage. Purple-tinged greenish yellow panicles persist into winter. Fountainlike clumps typically 2–3 ft. high in bloom. 'Bronzeschleier' ('Bronzy Veil') has bronzy yellow blooms. Selections with golden yellow flowers include 'Goldgehaenge', 'Goldschleier', 'Goldstaub'. *D. c. vivipara* has darkest green foliage; instead of flowers, it produces plantlets that droop to the ground.

D. flexuosa. CRINKLED HAIR GRASS. Wiry, glossy green leaves in tight clumps 1–2 ft. high. Nodding, purple-tinged flowers mature to yellowish brown color.

DESERT CANDLE. See EREMURUS

DESERT CATALPA. See CHILOPSIS linearis

DESERT FAN PALM. See WASHINGTONIA filifera

DESERT HONEYSUCKLE. See ANISACANTHUS thurberi

DESERT ROSE. See ADENIUM obesum

DESERT WILLOW. See CHILOPSIS linearis

DEUTZIA

Saxifragaceae

DECIDUOUS SHRUBS

🗡 ZONES US, MS, LS

☼ ◖ FULL SUN OR LIGHT SHADE

◖◖ REGULAR TO MODERATE WATER

Deutzia scabra

They are best used among evergreens, where they can make a show when in bloom, then blend back in with other greenery during the rest of the year. Their mid- to late spring flowering coincides with that of tulips and Louisiana iris.

Prune after flowering. With low- or medium-growing kinds, cut some of oldest stems to ground every other year. Prune tall kinds by cutting back wood that has flowered. Cut to outward-facing side branches.

D. gracilis. SLENDER DEUTZIA. Native to Japan. Grows to 6 ft., sometimes less. Many slender stems arch gracefully, carry bright green, 2½-in., sharply toothed leaves and clusters of snowy white flowers. 'Nikko' (*D. g. nakaiana*) grows only 1–2 ft. tall by 5 ft. wide and has deep burgundy fall color; effective as ground cover, over walls, in rock gardens.

D. magnifica. SHOWY DEUTZIA. A leggy, multistemmed shrub. Grows 6–10 ft. tall. Very showy white flowers in late spring. Probably the showiest of the deutzias. Does best in Upper and Middle South.

🏛 **D. scabra.** FUZZY DEUTZIA. Native to Japan, China. This plant and its forms are robust shrubs 7–10 ft. tall. Leaves oval, 3 in. long, dull green, roughish to touch, with scallop-toothed edges. Flowers are white or pinkish, in narrow, upright clusters. 'Godsall' ('Godsall Pink'), 4–6 ft. tall, bears pure pink double flowers. 'Pride of Rochester' has large clusters of small, frilled double flowers, rosy purple outside.

DEVIL'S IVY. See EPIPREMNUM aureum

DEVIL'S SHOESTRING. See NOLINA lindheimeri

DEVIL'S WALKING STICK. See ARALIA spinosa

DEVILWOOD. See OSMANTHUS americanus

DIANTHUS

PINK

Caryophyllaceae

PERENNIALS, BIENNIALS, AND ANNUALS

BEST IN ZONES US, MS, LS

FULL SUN

REGULAR WATER

Dianthus caryophyllus

More than 300 species and an extremely large number of hybrids, many with high garden value. Most kinds form attractive evergreen mats or tufts of grasslike green, gray-green, blue-green, or blue-gray leaves. Single, semi-double, or double flowers in white and shades of pink, rose, red, yellow, and orange; many have rich, spicy fragrance. Main bloom period for most is spring into early summer; some rebloom later in season or keep going into fall if faded flowers are removed.

Among dianthus are appealing border favorites such as cottage pink and sweet William, highly prized cut flowers such as carnation (clove pink), and rock garden miniatures. Many excellent named selections not mentioned here are available locally.

All dianthus thrive in light, fast-draining soil. Carnations, sweet William, and cottage pinks need fairly rich soil; rock garden or alpine types require gritty growing medium, with added lime if soil is acid. Avoid overwatering. Sow seed of annual or biennial types in flats or directly in garden. Propagate perennial dianthus by cuttings made from tips of growing shoots, by division or layering, or from seed. Perennials are often short lived, especially in Lower South, where they are often treated as annuals. Carnations and sweet William are subject to rust and fusarium wilt.

D. allwoodii. Perennial. Group of modern pinks from *D. plumarius* and *D. caryophyllus*. Plants vary, but most have gray-green foliage and two blossoms on each stem; bloom over long period if deadheaded. Tend to be more compact and more vigorous than their *D. plumarius* parent. The many selections include 'Aqua', which bears very fragrant, pure white double flowers on 10–12-in. stems. Plants sold as 'Allwoodii Alpinus' are the result of crossing *D. allwoodii* with dwarf species.

D. arenarius. Perennial. Tufted plant to 1½ ft. with narrow, grass green leaves and inch-wide fringed white flowers sometimes marked with purple or green. Highly fragrant; can tolerate some shade. 'Snow Flurries' has pure white flowers.

D. barbatus. SWEET WILLIAM. Vigorous biennial often grown as annual. Sturdy stems 10–20 in. high; leaves are flat, light to dark green, 1½–3 in. long. Dense clusters of white, pink, rose, red, purplish, or bicolored flowers, about ½ in. across, set among leafy bracts; not very fragrant. Sow seed in late spring for bloom following year, or set out transplants in fall. Double-flowered and dwarf strains are obtainable from seed. Indian Carpet strain is only 6 in. tall. Roundabout and Summer Beauty strains (1 ft.) bloom the first year from seed.

D. caryophyllus. CARNATION, CLOVE PINK. Perennial. There are two distinct categories of carnations: florists' and border types. Both have double flowers, bluish green leaves, and branching, leafy stems that often become woody at base.

Border carnations are bushier and more compact than florists' type, 12–14 in. high. Flowers 2–2½ in. wide, fragrant, borne in profusion. Effective as shrub border edgings, in mixed flower border, and in containers. Hybrid carnations grown from seed are usually treated as annuals, but often live over. 'Juliet' makes compact, foot-tall clumps with long production of 2½-in. scarlet flowers; 'Luminette', 2 ft. tall, is similar. Pixie Delight strain also is similar but includes full range of carnation colors. Knight series has strong stems, blooms in 5 months from seed; Bambino strain is a little slower to bloom. There is also a strain called simply Hanging Mixed, with pink- or red-flowered plants that sprawl or hang from pot or window box.

Florists' carnations are grown commercially in greenhouses, outdoors in gardens in mild-winter areas. Greenhouse-grown plants reach 4 ft., have fragrant, 3-in.-wide flowers in many colors—white, shades of pink and red, orange, purple, yellow; some are variegated. For large flowers, leave only terminal bloom on each stem, pinching out all other buds down to fifth joint, below which new flowering stems will develop. Stake to prevent sprawling. Start with strong cuttings taken from the most vigorous plants of selected named types. Sturdy plants conceal supports, look quite tidy.

D. chinensis. CHINESE PINK, RAINBOW PINK. Biennial or short-lived perennial; most selections grown as annuals. Erect, 6–30 in. high; stems branch only at top. Stem leaves narrow, 1–3 in. long, ½ in. wide, hairy on margins. Basal leaves usually gone by flowering time. Flowers about 1 in. across, rose lilac with deeper colored eye; lack fragrance. Modern strains are compact (to 1 ft. tall or less) domes covered with bright flowers in white, pink, red, and all variations and combinations of those colors. 'Fire Carpet' is a brilliant solid red; 'Snowfire', white with a red eye. Telstar is an extra-dwarf (6–8-in.) strain. Petals are deeply fringed on some, smooth edged on others. Some flowers have intricately marked eyes. Sow directly in ground in spring, in full sun, for summer bloom. Pick off faded flowers with their bases to prolong bloom. If set out in summer, Telstar will often bloom through the winter in the Lower South.

> ### THINK PINKS FOR FRAGRANCE
> Most dianthus offer cheerful colors, striking patterns, and a strong, clovelike scent. Among those best known for fragrance are *D. arenarius*, border carnations, *D. gratianopolitanus*, and *D. plumarius*.

D. deltoides. MAIDEN PINK. Hardy perennial (even though it blooms in a few weeks from seed) forming loose mats. Flowering stems 8–12 in. high with short leaves. Flowers, about ¾ in. across with sharp-toothed petals, are borne at end of forked stems. Colors include light or dark rose to purple, spotted with lighter colors; and white. Can tolerate up to a half day of shade. Blooms in summer, sometimes again in fall. Useful, showy ground or bank cover.

Selections include 'Albus', pure white; 'Vampire', deep red; 'Zing', bright scarlet; 'Zing Rose', rose red. Microchip is a seed mixture including white, reds, and pinks, often with contrasting eyes.

D. gratianopolitanus (D. caesius). CHEDDAR PINK. Perennial. Neat, compact mound of blue-gray to green-gray foliage on weak, branching stems to 1 ft. long. Flowering stems erect, 9–12 in. high, bearing very fragrant, typically pink to rose single blooms with toothed petals. Bloom season lasts from spring to fall if flowers are deadheaded. Effective for ground cover, edging, rock gardens. Performs well in Lower South.

'Bath's Pink'. An old selection rediscovered and renamed. Blue-green mat about 4 in. high topped by 12–15-in. stems bearing fringed single blossoms of soft pink with a red eye. Blooms profusely in spring, sporadically through summer. Does not "melt" in summer heat and humidity.

'Little Boy Blue'. To 1 ft. high, 2½ ft. wide, with intensely blue-gray leaves and single white flowers dotted pink.

'Little Joe'. Forms a clump of deep blue-gray foliage 4–6 in. high and about 6 in. across. Crimson single flowers. Especially effective with rock garden campanulas.

'Rose Bowl'. Very narrow leaves form a tight mat 2–3 in. high. Cerise rose flowers 1 in. across, carried on 6-in. stems.

'Spotty'. Resembles 'Rose Bowl', but the pink flowers are heavily spotted with white.

'Tiny Rubies'. Makes a low mat of gray-green foliage to 3 in. high, spreading to 4 in. Small, double, ruby red flowers on 4-in. stems.

D. plumarius. COTTAGE PINK. Perennial. Charming, almost legendary plant, cultivated for hundreds of years, used in developing many hybrids. Typically has loosely matted gray-green foliage. Flowering stems 10–18 in. tall; flowers spicily fragrant, single or double, with petals more or less fringed, in rose, pink, or white with dark centers. Highly prized are old laced pinks, with spicy-scented white flowers in which each petal is outlined in red or pink. Blooms in late spring and summer. Indispensable edging for borders or for peony or rose beds. Perfect in small arrangements and old-fashioned bouquets.

D

'Dad's Favorite'. Centuries-old selection; double flowers on 10-in. stems. Blooms are white with ruby red edge and maroon center.

'Essex Witch'. Semidouble rose pink flowers on 5-in. stems.

'Musgrave's White'. Classic selection two centuries old. Intensely fragrant single flowers, white with a pale green eye, on 1-ft. stems.

Diapensiaceae. The diapensia family contains perennials and shrubs native to northern parts of the globe. Some, such as *Galax urceolata* and *Shortia,* are useful in shady gardens or naturalized areas.

DICENTRA

BLEEDING HEART

Fumariaceae

PERENNIALS

⚡ ZONES VARY BY SPECIES

☼ ◐ ● PARTIAL OR FULL SHADE

💧 REGULAR WATER

Dicentra spectabilis

Graceful, fernlike foliage. Dainty flowers, usually heart shaped, in pink, rose, or white on leafless stems. Combine handsomely with ferns, hostas, astilbes, epimediums, foamflowers, hellebores. In general, bleeding heart needs rich, light, moist, porous soil. Never let water stand around roots. Short lived in the Lower South.

D. canadensis. SQUIRREL CORN. Zones US, MS. Native from North Carolina to Missouri and Minnesota, and Canada. Grows to just 6–8 in. tall from small, yellow cornlike tubers. Flowers white, perfect heart shape, in early spring. Foliage dies down after flowering. Situate plants among ground cover or in other areas where shallow tubers will not be disturbed. Prefers slightly alkaline soil.

D. eximia. FRINGED BLEEDING HEART. Zones US, MS, LS. Native to northeastern U.S. Forms tidy, nonspreading clumps 1–1½ ft. high. Blue-gray, finely divided leaves at base of plant. Deep rose pink flowers with short, rounded spurs bloom midspring into summer. Cut back for second growth and occasional repeat bloom. 'Alba' has white flowers. 'Bacchanal' is nearly everblooming during the growing season, with deep red blossoms. Pink-flowered 'Bountiful' ('Zestful') is an everbloomer tolerating considerable sun. White-blossomed 'Langtrees' and deep pink 'Luxuriant' are long blooming; the latter can endure drier soil and stronger light than most. 'Snowdrift' is a long-blooming white.

🏛 **D. spectabilis.** COMMON BLEEDING HEART. Zones US, MS, LS. Native to Japan. An old garden favorite, and the showiest and largest leafed of all the bleeding hearts. Plants grow to 2–3 ft. high; stems are set with soft green leaves. In late spring, rose pink, pendulous, heart-shaped flowers, 1 in. long or longer, with protruding white petals, are borne on one side of arching stems. 'Alba' ('Pantaloons') is a lovely pure white form. Both species and selection are beautiful with maidenhair ferns and in arrangements with tulips and lilacs. Plants usually die down and become dormant by midsummer. Plant summer-maturing perennials nearby to fill the gap. Best in partial shade.

DICHORISANDRA
thyrsiflora

BLUE GINGER

Commelinaceae

PERENNIAL

⚡ ZONE TS; OR INDOORS

☼ ◐ ● PARTIAL OR FULL SHADE

💧💧 AMPLE WATER

Dichorisandra thyrsiflora

Not a true ginger but rather a robust, upright-growing relative of wandering Jew (*Tradescantia, Zebrina*). Fleshy single or sparsely branched stems to 6–8 ft. arise from a fleshy rhizome. Long (6–12-in.), oval, deep green leaves are spirally arranged around the stem. Flowers are deep violet blue, in 6-in. spikes at tops of stems in late summer and fall. Tender except in nearly tropical climates, but grown as a house plant anywhere. Will bloom at 3 ft. tall in an 8-in. pot with bright indoor light. Easy to propagate by cuttings. Provide rich soil.

DICKSONIA

Dicksoniaceae

TREE FERNS

⚡ ZONE TS; OR IN CONTAINERS

☼ ◐ ● SOME SHADE IN SUMMER

💧 REGULAR WATER

Dicksonia antarctica

Hardy, slow growing, from Southern Hemisphere. Easy to transplant and establish. See Ferns for culture.

D. antarctica. TASMANIAN TREE FERN. Native to southeastern Australia, Tasmania. Hardiest of tree ferns; well-established plants tolerate 20°F. Thick, red-brown, fuzzy trunk grows slowly to 15 ft. From top of trunk grow many arching, 3–6-ft. fronds; mature fronds are more finely cut than those of Australian tree fern (*Cyathea cooperi*).

D. squarrosa. Native to New Zealand. Slender, dark trunk grows slowly to 20 ft. tall. Flat crown of 8-ft.-long, stiff, leathery fronds. Much less frequently grown than *D. antarctica.*

Dicksoniaceae. The dicksonia family of tree ferns differs from the other tree fern family, Cyatheaceae, only in technical details. One representative is *Dicksonia.*

DIEFFENBACHIA

DUMB CANE

Araceae

PERENNIALS

⚡ ZONE TS; OR INDOORS

☼ ◐ ● SUN OR SHADE

💧 MODERATE WATER

⬦ SAP BURNS MOUTH, MAY PARALYZE VOCAL CORDS

Dieffenbachia amoena

Striking variegated evergreen foliage—colors varying from dark green to yellow green and chartreuse—with variegations in white or pale cream—is the main reason to grow dumb cane. In the Tropical South, plants will grow year-round outdoors, either in the ground as accents or in containers on the patio. In other zones, they're indoor foliage plants. Small plants generally have single stems, while older plants may develop multiple stems. Flowers resembling odd, narrow callas form on mature plants.

Outdoors, plants take sun or shade and moderate moisture. Indoors, provide ample northern light, water when soil surface feels dry, and turn pots occasionally. Give container plants well-drained potting soil, half-strength liquid fertilizer bimonthly in spring and summer. Underfed, underwatered plants show amazingly strong hold on life, recovering from severe wilting when conditions improve. Repotting is necessary when roots begin pushing plant up out of pot. Once it is repotted, plant usually sends out new basal shoots. Dumb cane will not withstand constant overwatering; sudden change from low to high light level will burn leaves. However, you can move plants into sheltered patio in summer. If plant gets leggy, air-layer it, or cut back and root the cuttings in water. If cut back to 6 in. above soil line, old, leggy plants will usually resprout with multiple stems. ▶

D

D. amoena. To 6 ft. or more. Broad, dark green, 1½-ft.-long leaves with narrow, white, slanting stripes on either side of midrib.

D. bausei. To 3 ft. or more in height. Greenish yellow, 1-ft. leaves with deep green blotches and white flecks.

D. 'Exotica'. To 3–4 ft., with small leaves featuring dull green edges and much creamy white variegation. Midrib is creamy white.

D. maculata (D. picta). Grows to 6 ft. or taller. Wide, oval green leaves, 10 in. or more in length, have greenish white dots and patches. 'Rudolph Roehrs' has leaves of pale chartreuse, blotched with ivory and edged with green. Foliage of 'Superba' is thicker and slightly more durable than that of species, with more creamy white dots and patches.

DIETES (Moraea)

MOREA IRIS, FORTNIGHT LILY

Iridaceae

PERENNIALS GROWING FROM RHIZOMES

ZONES LS (PROTECTED), CS, TS

FULL SUN OR PARTIAL SHADE

BLOOM MORE FREELY WITH REGULAR WATER

Dietes vegeta

Fan-shaped clumps of narrow, stiff, irislike, evergreen leaves. Flowers like miniature Japanese iris appear on branched stalks throughout spring, summer, and fall, sometimes well into winter in mild areas. Each flower lasts only a day but is quickly replaced by another. Bloom bursts seem to come at 2-week intervals—hence the name "fortnight lily." Break off forming seedpods to increase flower production and prevent volunteer plants. Effective near swimming pools. Plant in any fairly good soil. Divide overgrown clumps in autumn or winter.

D. bicolor. To 2 ft. Flowers light yellow, about 2 in. wide, with maroon blotches. Cut flower stems to ground after blossoms fade.

D. hybrids. 'Lemon Drops' and 'Orange Drops' are occasionally seen. These resemble *D. vegeta*, but flowers are creamy, with conspicuous yellow or orange blotches.

D. vegeta (D. iridioides, Moraea iridioides). Grows to 4 ft., with 3-in.-wide, waxy white flowers with orange-and-brown blotch, purple stippling. 'Johnsonii' is robust selection with large leaves and flowers. Break off old blossoms individually to prolong bloom and prevent self-sowing, but don't cut off long, branching flower stems (these last from year to year). Instead, cut back to lower leaf joint near plant base. Excellent in permanent landscaping with pebbles, rocks, substantial shrubs.

DIGITALIS

FOXGLOVE

Scrophulariaceae

SHORT-LIVED PERENNIALS OR BIENNIALS

ZONES US, MS, LS, CS

LIGHT SHADE

REGULAR WATER

ALL PARTS ARE POISONOUS IF INGESTED

Digitalis purpurea

Erect plants 2–8 ft. high, with basal rosette of hairy, gray-green leaves. Spires of tubular flowers shaped like fingers of glove in purple, yellow, white, pastels. Bloom spring and summer. After first flowering, cut main spike; side shoots will develop and bloom late in the season. In the Lower and Coastal South, treat as annuals. Set out new transplants in summer or fall. In the Upper and Middle South, set out plants or sow seed in spring.

Provide rich soil. Sow seed in spring for bloom following year. Plants self-sow freely. Use for vertical display. Hummingbirds like the flowers.

D. ferruginea. RUSTY FOXGLOVE. Biennial or perennial. Very leafy stems to 6 ft. Leaves deeply veined. Flowers ¾–1¼ in. long, yellowish, netted with rusty red, in long, dense spikes.

D. grandiflora (D. ambigua). YELLOW FOXGLOVE. Biennial or perennial. To 2–3 ft. high. Toothed leaves wrap around stem. Flowers are 2–3 in. long, yellowish marked with brown.

D. laevigata. Perennial. To 3 ft., with smooth, narrow dark green leaves and inch-long, creamy yellow flowers marked brownish purple.

D. lanata. GRECIAN FOXGLOVE. Perennial. To 3 ft., with dark green leaves and narrow spikelike clusters of small flowers. Blossoms are cream colored, with purplish or brownish veining and a small near-white lip.

D. mertonensis. Perennial. Spikes to 2–3 ft. high, bearing odd yet attractive coppery rose blooms. Though a hybrid between two species, it comes true from seed.

D. purpurea. COMMON FOXGLOVE. Biennial, sometimes perennial. Naturalizes in shaded places. Variable, appears in many garden forms. Bold, erect, to 4 ft. high or more. Clumps of large, rough, woolly, light green leaves. Stem leaves have short stalks and become smaller toward top of plant; these leaves are source of digitalis, a valued but highly poisonous medicinal drug. Flowers 2–3 in. long, pendulous, purple, spotted on lower, paler side; borne in one-sided, 1–2-ft.-long spikes.

There are several garden strains. Excelsior, 5 ft., has fuller spikes than species, with flowers more horizontally held, showing interior spotting. Foxy, 3 ft., performs as an annual, blooming in 5 months from seed; Gloxiniiflora, 4 ft., has flowers that are individually larger and open wider than the species. Monstrosa, 3 ft., has an unusual trait: The topmost flower of each spike is open or bowl shaped and 3 in. wide. Shirley is a tall (6-ft.), robust strain in full range of colors. Volunteer foxglove seedlings are frequently white or light colors.

FOXGLOVES—TOWERS OF FLOWERS

Flowers on spikes 3 ft. tall or more add charm and dimension to a garden. And foxgloves are perhaps the easiest of the towering flowering plants. An especially showy use for these plants is to fill a boxwood-edged flower bed with just one kind. Set plants 1 ft. apart. Or mass them at the back of perennial borders.

DILL. See ANETHUM graveolens

DIMORPHOTHECA

AFRICAN DAISY, CAPE MARIGOLD

Asteraceae (Compositae)

ANNUALS

ALL ZONES

FULL SUN

MODERATE WATER

Dimorphotheca sinuata

Cheery, free-blooming plants with daisy flowers that close when shaded, during heavy overcast, and at night. Use in broad masses as ground cover, in borders and parking strips, along rural roadsides, as filler among low shrubs. Broadcast seed in early spring (late fall or early winter in mildest climates) where plants are to grow. Does best in light soil.

D. aurantiaca. See D. sinuata

D. sinuata. Best known of annual African daisies; usually sold as *D. aurantiaca*. Plants 4–12 in. high. Leaves narrow, 2–3 in. long, with a few teeth or shallow indentations. Flower heads 1½ in. across, with orange-yellow rays, sometimes deep violet at base, and yellow center. Hybrids between this species and *D. pluvialis* come in white and shades of yellow, apricot, and salmon, often with contrasting dark centers.

SOUTHERN HERITAGE PLANTS

IDENTIFIED BY SYMBOL

DIOON

Zamiaceae

CYCADS

ZONE TS

PARTIAL SHADE

REGULAR WATER

Dioon edule

Resemble *Cycas revoluta* and take same culture but are less widely sold, more tender, and even slower growing. Male and female plants are separate.

D. edule. Very slow. Eventually forms cylindrical trunk 6–10 in. wide, 3 ft. high. Leaves spreading, slightly arching, 3–5 ft. long, made of many leaflets toothed at tips or smooth edged. Leaves dusty blue green, feathery on young plants; darker green, more rigid, shiny on mature plants.

D. spinulosum. Slow growth to 12 ft. Leaves reach about 5 ft. long, with up to 100 narrow, spine-toothed, dark green, 6–8-in.-long leaflets. Protect plants from frost.

DIOSPYROS texana

TEXAS PERSIMMON

Ebenaceae

DECIDUOUS TREE

ALL ZONES

FULL SUN OR PARTIAL SHADE

LITTLE WATER ONCE ESTABLISHED

Diospyros texana

Fruiting persimmons are described under Persimmon. This South Texas and Mexican native is grown primarily for its lovely shape and bark: Multiple slender trunks grow to 30 ft., with silvery gray bark that peels in strips; grows to 10–15 ft. wide. In early spring, bees are attracted to the fragrant greenish white, urn-shaped flowers. Leaves are thick, dark green, 1–2 in. long. Foliage is evergreen in mild-winter climates. Black fruits, on female trees, edible but small (1–2 in. across). Because fruit drop is messy, male trees are often preferred for the garden. In naturalized settings, female trees are valuable for the food they supply to birds and other wildlife. Well suited to dry, rocky, alkaline soils. Not a good choice for high-rainfall, high-humidity areas.

DIPLADENIA amoena, D. splendens. See MANDEVILLA 'Alice du Pont'

DIZYGOTHECA elegantissima. See SCHEFFLERA elegantissima

DODECATHEON meadia

SHOOTING STAR

Primulaceae

PERENNIAL

ZONES US, MS, LS

PARTIAL SHADE

AMPLE WATER DURING GROWTH AND BLOOM

Dodecatheon meadia

Native to the eastern U.S. Leaves of plant form basal rosette; flowers are carried in clusters on leafless stalks. Blossoms resemble small cyclamens, with swept-back petals and downward-thrusting stamens. Plant produces many white to occasionally pink or purple blooms with prominent yellow stamens; dies back completely at onset of hot weather. Prefers part shade and rich, porous, well-drained soil.

DOG-TOOTH VIOLET. See ERYTHRONIUM dens-canis

DOGWOOD. See CORNUS

DOLICHOS lablab
(Lablab purpureus)

HYACINTH BEAN

Fabaceae (Leguminosae)

PERENNIAL TWINING VINE ALSO GROWN AS ANNUAL

ZONES LS, CS, TS

FULL SUN

REGULAR WATER

Dolichos lablab

Perennial in the Lower, Coastal, Tropical South. Fast growing to 10 ft. Broad, oval leaflets to 3–6 in. long. Sweet pea–shaped purple or white flowers in loose clusters on long stems stand out from foliage. Flowers followed by velvety, beanlike pods to 2½ in. long. Grow plants like string beans for quick screening. Needs good drainage.

DONKEY TAIL. See SEDUM morganianum

DOUBLE BRIDAL WREATH. See SPIRAEA cantoniensis

DOUGLAS FIR. See PSEUDOTSUGA menziesii

DOVE TREE. See DAVIDIA involucrata

DOXANTHA unguis-cati. See MACFADYENA unguis-cati

DRACAENA

Agavaceae

EVERGREEN, SMALL PALMLIKE TREES

ZONE TS; OR INDOORS

FULL SUN OR PARTIAL SHADE

MODERATE WATER

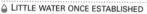
Dracaena draco

Foliage plants. Some show graceful fountain forms with broad, curved, ribbonlike leaves, occasionally striped with chartreuse or white. Some have very stiff, swordlike leaves. Outdoors, plant all but *D. draco* in a wind-protected site. Almost never flower as house plants. In containers, water only when top ½–1 in. of soil is dry.

D. australis. See Cordyline australis

D. deremensis. Native to tropical Africa. Most commonly sold selection is 'Warneckii': erect, slow growing to 15 ft., with 2-ft.-long, 2-in.-wide leaves in rich green striped white and gray. 'Bausei' is green with white center stripe; 'Janet Craig' has broad, dark green leaves; 'Longii' has broader white center stripe. Compact forms of 'Janet Craig' and 'Warneckii' exist.

D. draco. DRAGON TREE. Native to Canary Islands. Stout trunk with upward-reaching or spreading branches topped by clusters of heavy, sword-shaped leaves, 2 ft. long. Grows slowly to 20 ft. high and wide. Makes odd but interesting silhouette. Clusters of greenish white flowers form at branch ends. After blossoms drop, stemmy clusters remain. Trim them off to keep plants neat.

D. fragrans. CORN PLANT. Native to West Africa. Upright, eventually to 20 ft. high, but slow growing. Heavy, ribbonlike, blue-green leaves to 3 ft. long, 4 in. wide. (Typical plant in 8-in. pot will bear leaves about 1½ ft. long.) 'Massangeana' has broad yellow stripe in center of each leaf. Other selections with striped foliage are 'Lindenii' and 'Victoriae'.

D. marginata. MADAGASCAR DRAGON TREE. Very easy to grow, very popular. Slender, erect, smooth gray stems to an eventual 12 ft. carry chevron markings where old leaves have fallen. Stems topped by crowns of narrow, leathery leaves to 2 ft. long, ½ in. wide. Leaves are deep glossy green with narrow margin of purplish red. If

Dracaena marginata

plant grows too tall, cut off crown and reroot it. New crowns will appear on old stem. 'Tricolor' ('Candy Cane') adds a narrow gold stripe to the green and red of the species.

D. sanderana. RIBBON PLANT. Native to West Africa. Neat and upright, to a possible 6–10 ft., somewhat resembling young corn plant. Strap-shaped, 9-in.-long leaves striped with white.

DRACOPIS amplexicaulis
(Rudbeckia amplexicaulis)

CLASPING CONEFLOWER

Asteraceae (Compositae)

ANNUAL

🗡 ZONES US, MS, LS

☼ ◐ FULL SUN OR PARTIAL SHADE

◖ ◖ ◖ MUCH OR LITTLE WATER

Dracopis amplexicaulis

Closely related to coneflower *(Rudbeckia)* and Mexican hat *(Ratibida columnifera)*. Native from Kansas to Texas and Georgia. Grows 2–3 ft. tall. Late spring yellow flowers, to 2 in. across, sometimes flushed orange or brown at the petal bases, with a dark brown or purple cone at the center. Leaves clasp the stems. Tolerates wide range of soils, including poorly drained, heavy, wet soils.

DRAGON TREE. See DRACAENA draco

DRAGON'S BLOOD. See SEDUM spurium 'Coccineum'

DROPWORT. See FILIPENDULA vulgaris

DRUMSTICKS. See ALLIUM sphaerocephalum

DRYOPTERIS

WOOD FERN, SHIELD FERN, MALE FERN

Polypodiaceae

FERNS

🗡 ZONES VARY BY SPECIES

◐ ● PARTIAL OR FULL SHADE

◖ REGULAR WATER

Dryopteris dilatata

Wood, or shield, ferns number more than 100 species and are found over most of the world, though only a few are generally offered by garden centers. Use them in shade or woodland gardens, where their fronds contrast with the coarser foliage of other perennials, especially such large-leafed plants as hosta and hydrangea. They prefer rich soil with adequate organic material and moisture. However, as a rule they are rather forgiving ferns and good choices for beginning gardeners. Some species tolerate drought and less-than-ideal soil. They are seldom bothered by pests.

D. affinis. SCALY MALE FERN. Semievergreen. Zones US, MS, LS. Native to Europe and southwestern Asia. To 5 ft. high. Finely cut fronds are chartreuse green with light brown scales when they unfold, dark green later.

D. carthusiana. (D. spinulosa). SPINULOSE WOOD FERN, TOOTHED WOOD FERN, SHIELD FERN. Evergreen. Zone US. Native to Europe, Asia, and North America. Coarsely cut yellowish green fronds grow 6–18 in. tall, have shaggy black scales on frond stem and lower part of midrib.

D. dilatata. BROAD BUCKLER FERN. Evergreen. Zones US, MS. Native to many areas in Northern and Southern Hemispheres. Grows 1–2 ft. tall, possibly much more, with finely cut, widely spreading fronds.

D. erythrosora. AUTUMN FERN. Evergreen. Zones MS, LS, CS. Native to China and Japan. Erect growth to 2 ft. One of the few ferns with seasonal color variation. Expanding fronds in spring are a blend of copper, pink, and yellow; they turn green in summer, then rusty brown in fall. Bright red spore cases, produced on leaf undersides in fall, are an attractive winter feature. Takes some drought.

D. filix-mas. MALE FERN. Evergreen, sometimes becoming deciduous. Zones US, MS, LS. Native to much of Northern Hemisphere. Grows 2–5 ft. tall, with finely cut fronds to 1 ft. wide. 'Linearis Polydactyla' has narrow leaf divisions with spreading, fingerlike tips.

D. goldiana. GOLDIE'S WOOD FERN, GIANT WOOD FERN. Evergreen in milder climates, deciduous in colder-winter areas. Zones US, MS. Robust grower to 4 ft., with arching fronds to 1½ ft. wide.

D. marginalis. MARGINAL SHIELD FERN, LEATHER WOOD FERN. Evergreen. Zones US, MS, LS. Grows 2–4 ft. tall. Finely cut, dark blue-green fronds. Takes some drought.

D. wallichiana. WALLICH'S WOOD FERN. Evergreen. Zones US, MS, LS. Native to India, China. Stately fern 3–5 ft. high. Bright golden green fronds, finely cut, on scaly, brown stems, later turn dark green.

DUMB CANE. See DIEFFENBACHIA

DURANTA

Verbenaceae

EVERGREEN SHRUBS

🗡 ZONE TS

☼ FULL SUN

◖ REGULAR WATER

◖ D. REPENS BERRIES ARE POISONOUS IF INGESTED

Duranta repens

Glossy green leaves arranged in pairs or whorls along stem. Attractive blue flowers in clusters attract butterflies in summer, are followed by bunches of yellow berrylike fruit. Many plants sold as *D. stenostachya* are actually *D. repens*. Distinguishing characteristics described below. Use as quick, tall screen. Need continual thinning and pruning to stay under control.

D. repens (D. erecta, D. plumieri). GOLDEN DEWDROP, SKY FLOWER, PIGEON BERRY. Native to southern Florida, West Indies, Mexico to Brazil. Fast growing to 10–25 ft. Tends to form multistemmed clumps; branches often drooping and vinelike. Stems may or may not have sharp spines. Oval to roundish leaves are 1–2 in. long, rounded or pointed at tip. Tubular, violet blue flowers flare to less than ½ in. wide. Fruit clusters 1–6 in. long. 'Alba' has white flowers.

D. stenostachya. BRAZILIAN SKY FLOWER. Not as hardy as *D. repens*, but makes neater, more compact shrub, usually growing to 4–6 ft. (under ideal conditions, 15 ft.). Stems are spineless. Leaves are larger (3–8 in. long) than those of *D. repens* and taper to long, slender point. Lavender blue flowers are also somewhat larger; fruit clusters grow to 1 ft. long.

DUSTY MILLER. Several plants with gray foliage have this common name, including *Artemisia stellerana, Centaurea cineraria, C. gymnocarpa, Senecio cineraria,* and *S. vira-vira.*

DUTCHMAN'S PIPE. See ARISTOLOCHIA durior

DWARF BLUE ARBORVITAE. See PLATYCLADUS orientalis 'Minima Glauca'

DWARF FLOWERING ALMOND. See PRUNUS glandulosa

DWARF GOLDEN ARBORVITAE. See PLATYCLADUS orientalis 'Aureus'

DWARF PLUMBAGO. See CERATOSTIGMA plumbaginoides

DWARF RED-LEAF PLUM. See PRUNUS cistena

DWARF WHITESTRIPE BAMBOO. See PLEIOBLASTUS variegata

DWARF YAUPON. See ILEX vomitoria 'Nana'

SOUTHERN HERITAGE PLANTS
IDENTIFIED BY SYMBOL 🏛

DYSSODIA tenuiloba
(Thymophylla tenuiloba)

DAHLBERG DAISY, GOLDEN FLEECE

Asteraceae (Compositae)

ANNUAL; MAY LIVE OVER AS PERENNIAL

✂ BEST IN ZONES MS, LS

☼ FULL SUN

💧 MODERATE WATER

Dyssodia tenuiloba

Native to Southwest. To 1 ft. high. Divided, threadlike leaves make dark green background for yellow flower heads, which look much like miniature golden marguerites. Use for massed display or pockets of color. Start in flats or plant in place, preferably in sandy soil. Blooms early summer to fall, sometimes to early winter. In the Lower South, can be planted in fall for winter–spring bloom. Pull out plants that get ragged with age. Not well suited to high-rainfall, high-humidity areas.

EASTER CACTUS. See RHIPSALIDOPSIS gaertneri

EASTER LILY. See LILIUM longiflorum

EASTERN RED CEDAR. See JUNIPERUS virginiana

EBONY SPLEENWORT. See ASPLENIUM platyneuron

ECHEVERIA

Crassulaceae

SUCCULENTS

✂ ZONES LS, CS, TS; OR INDOORS

☼◐ FULL SUN OR PARTIAL SHADE

💧 MODERATE WATER, EXCEPT AS NOTED

Echeveria imbricata

All form rosettes of fleshy green or gray-green leaves, often marked or overlaid with deeper colors. Bell-shaped, nodding flowers, usually pink, red, or yellow, on long, slender, sometimes branched clusters. Good in rock gardens. Some make good house plants.

E. crenulata. House plant. Rosettes on short, thick stems. Pale green or white-powdered leaves, 1 ft. long, 6 in. wide, with crimped, purplish red edges. Flower clusters to 3 ft. high, with a few yellow-and-red flowers. Striking plant. Shelter from hottest sun; water frequently in warm weather.

E. hybrids. House plants. Generally have large, loose rosettes of big leaves on single or branched stems. Leaves are crimped, waved, wattled, or heavily shaded with red, bronze, or purple. All are splendid pot plants. 'Arlie Wright' has large, open rosettes of wavy-edged, pinkish leaves; 'Cameo', has large blue-gray leaves, each centered with a large raised lump of the same color; and 'Perle von Nürnberg' offers pearly lavender blue foliage. Smaller, with short, close-set leaves, is 'Doris Taylor'; its leaves are densely covered with short hairs. Showy, nodding flowers are red and yellow.

E. imbricata. HEN AND CHICKS. Rosettes 4–6 in. wide, saucer shaped, gray green. Clusters of bell-shaped, orange-red flowers. Makes offsets freely.

E. runyonii. Native to Mexico. Gray-green leaves, showy spikes of coral flowers. Likes dry, rocky, chalky soils of Southwest.

ECHINACEA

CONEFLOWER

Asteraceae (Compositae)

PERENNIALS

✂ ZONES VARY BY SPECIES

☼ FULL SUN

💧 LITTLE TO MODERATE WATER

Echinacea purpurea

Native to east-central U.S. Form large clumps of long-stemmed, very showy flowers with drooping, rosy purple rays and a beehivelike

central cone. Bloom over long period in mid- to late summer, may continue sporadically until frost. If left in place, bristly seed heads hang on into winter; seeds are favored by finches.

Use on outskirts of garden or in wide borders with other robust perennials such as Shasta daisies, sunflowers, Michaelmas daisies. Generally do not need staking. Perform well in summer heat. Good cut flower. Deadheading prolongs bloom. Can self-sow. Divide crowded clumps (usually after about 4 years) in spring or fall.

E. purpurea (Rudbeckia purpurea). PURPLE CONEFLOWER. Zones US, MS, LS, CS. Coarse, stiff plant with erect stems 4–5 ft. tall. Bristly, oblong leaves are 3–8 in. long. Orange-brown central cone.

'Bright Star' has 3–4-in. rosy pink rays. 'Magnus', 3 ft. tall, has horizontally spreading rays and a low, dark center cone; 'WFF Strain' is similar in appearance. 'White Lustre' and 'White Swan' have white rays around an orange-yellow cone.

E. tennesseensis. TENNESSEE CONEFLOWER. Zones US, MS, LS. Similar to *E. purpurea*, but ray petals are horizontal, rather than drooping, and cone is greenish pink. Stems to 1½ ft. tall. Forms a low, casual mound. This beautiful coneflower is rare and endangered in the wild but is being propagated under permit. Available from a few wildflower nurseries.

ECHINOCEREUS

HEDGEHOG CACTUS

Cactaceae

CACTI

✂ ZONES US, MS, LS, CS

☼ FULL SUN

💧 TAKE MUCH ARIDITY WHEN ESTABLISHED

Echinocereus triglochidiatus

Nearly 50 species of hedgehog cactus grow in various regions of the southwestern U.S., some at fairly high elevations. All have cylindrical, ribbed bodies in clumps; showy red, yellow, purple, or white flowers with many rows of petals; and fleshy fruit, edible in some species.

E. triglochidiatus. CLARET CUP. Dense mounds, sometimes with hundreds of stems to 16 in. tall, each stem to 5 in. thick. Flowers are 3½ in. wide, orange to red; inch-long fruit pink to red. Needs excellent drainage.

ECHINOPS

GLOBE THISTLE

Asteraceae (Compositae)

PERENNIALS

✂ ZONES US, MS, LS

☼ FULL SUN

💧💧 REGULAR TO MODERATE WATER

Echinops

Well-behaved, decorative thistle relatives for the perennial border. Rugged-looking, erect, rigidly branched plants 2–4 ft. tall with coarse, prickly, deeply cut gray-green leaves to 1 ft. long. Distinctive flower heads are spherical, like golf ball–size pincushions stuck full of tubular metallic blue pins. Bloom midsummer to fall.

Plants may be offered as *E. exaltatus, E. humilis, E. ritro*, or possibly *E. sphaerocephalus*. Whatever name you encounter, you're likely to get a plant closely resembling the general description above. 'Taplow Blue' is a select form 4 ft. tall. 'Veitch's Blue' has smaller, more numerous flower clusters on a somewhat shorter plant.

Grow from divisions in spring or fall, or sow seed in flats or open ground in spring. Combine with Michaelmas daisies, phlox, yellow and orange coneflowers, ornamental grasses. Given good, well-drained soil and plenty of moisture, plants may grow so vigorously that they need staking. Established plants tolerate dry periods. Flowers are excellent for dried arrangements, but they must be cut before they open, then dried upside down. Many types will rebloom if cut to the ground immediately after the flowers fade. Clumps can be left in place, undivided, for many years.

EDGEWORTHIA papyrifera

PAPER BUSH

Thymelaeaceae

DECIDUOUS SHRUB

❄ ZONES MS, LS, CS

☼ ◐ FULL SUN OR PART SHADE

💧 REGULAR WATER

Edgeworthia papyrifera

Native to China. This daphne relative produces fragrant, nodding, golden yellow flowers in late winter before it leafs out. Grows to 6 ft. Oblong leaves to 5 in. long, 2 in. wide, turn yellow in fall. Branches are a source of high-quality paper. Rarely planted; deserves wider use.

EGGPLANT

Solanaceae

ANNUAL

❄ ALL ZONES

☼ FULL SUN

💧 KEEP SOIL EVENLY MOIST

Eggplant
'Black Beauty'

Few vegetable plants are handsomer than egg-plant. Bushes resemble little trees, 2–3 ft. high and equally wide. Big leaves (usually lobed), tinged purple; drooping violet flowers are 1½ in. across. And, of course, big fruit is spectacular.
Plants are effective in large containers or raised beds; a well-spaced row of them makes distinguished border between vegetable and flower garden. Most people plant large roundish or oval types such as 'Black Beauty', 'Burpee Hybrid', or 'Early Beauty'; the Japanese, who like their eggplant small and very tender, prefer long, slender type usually sold as 'Japanese'. Specialists in imported vegetable seeds offer numerous colored selections, including the full-size 'White Beauty' and a host of smaller kinds in a range of sizes (down to ½ in.) and colors, including white as well as yellow, lavender, red, green. Some of the smaller ones genuinely resemble eggs. All are edible as well as attractive.

Eggplant can be grown from seed (sow indoors 8 to 10 weeks before date of last expected frost), but starting from nursery-grown plants is much easier. This vegetable plant needs 2 to 3 months of warm days and nights (minimum night temperatures of 65°F) to produce a crop. Set plants out in full sun in spring when frosts are over and soil is warm. Space plants 3 ft. apart in loose, fertile soil. Feed once every 6 weeks with a commercial fertilizer. Keep weeds out. Prevent too much fruit setting by pinching out some terminal growth and some blossoms; three to six large fruits per plant will result. A second crop for late summer–fall harvest can be grown in southernmost climates.

If you enjoy eating tiny whole eggplants, allow the plants to produce freely without pinching back growth or blossoms. Harvest fruits after they develop some color but never wait until they lose their glossy shine. Flea beetles are often a problem on young plants. Grow plants under row covers until big enough to tolerate leaf damage. Control aphids and whiteflies. For ornamental relatives, see *Solanum*.

EGLANTINE. See ROSA eglanteria

Elaeagnaceae. This family contains trees and shrubs with a coating of tiny silvery or brown scales on leaves (and sometimes on flowers) and with small, tart-tasting, single-seeded fruits. Flowers are not showy but can be fragrant. Most are tough plants from arid or semiarid climates.

ELAEAGNUS

Elaeagnaceae

EVERGREEN, DECIDUOUS SHRUBS OR SMALL TREES

❄ ZONES VARY BY SPECIES

☼ ◐ FULL SUN OR PARTIAL SHADE

💧 💧 REGULAR TO LITTLE WATER

Elaeagnus pungens

These useful screening plants grow fast when young, becoming dense, full, firm, and tough—and they do it with little upkeep. All tolerate seashore conditions, heat, and wind. Established plants will take considerable drought.

Foliage in evergreen forms distinguished by silvery (sometimes brown) dots on leaves, reflecting sunlight to give plants sparkle. Deciduous kinds have silvery gray leaves. Insignificant but usually fragrant flowers are followed by decorative fruit, typically red with silvery flecks. Evergreen kinds bloom in fall; in addition to their prime role as screen plants, they are useful as natural espaliers, clipped hedges, or high bank covers.

E. angustifolia. RUSSIAN OLIVE. Small deciduous tree. Zones US, MS. To 20 ft. high, but can be clipped as medium-height hedge. Angular trunk and branches (sometimes thorny) are covered by shredding dark brown bark that is picturesque in winter. Bark contrasts with narrow, willowlike, 2-in.-long silvery gray leaves. Very fragrant, small greenish yellow flowers in early summer are followed by berrylike fruit resembling miniature olives. Can take almost any kind of punishment, including hot summers, bitterly cold winters, drought, poor soil. Doesn't do as well in mild winters or very humid summers. Good background plant, barrier.

E. ebbingei (E. macrophylla 'Ebbingei'). Evergreen shrub. Zones MS, LS, CS. Hybrid derived from *E. pungens*. More upright (to 10–12 ft.) than its parent, with thornless branches. Leaves, 2–4 in. long, silvery on both sides when young, are later dark green above and silvery beneath. Tiny, fragrant, silvery flowers. Red fruit makes good jelly. 'Gilt Edge' has striking yellow margins on its leaves.

E. pungens. THORNY ELAEAGNUS, SILVERBERRY. Large evergreen shrub. Zones US, MS, LS, CS. Has rather rigid, sprawling, angular habit of growth to height of 6–15 ft.; long, naked shoots, some 5–6 ft. long, skyrocket off in all directions, creating a Medusa-like monstrosity. Fortunately, flower arrangers prize these shoots, and dutifully prune the shrub back to some semblance of neatness. Can be sheared into a nice hedge. Grayish green, 1–3-in.-long leaves have wavy edges and brown tinting from rusty dots. Branches are spiny, also covered with rusty dots. Overall color of shrub is olive drab. Oval fruit, ½ in. long, red with silver dust. Tough container plant in reflected heat, wind. Variegated forms listed below are more widespread than the species and have a brighter, lighter, and often jarring look in the landscape; they are less hardy than the species, however, and may suffer damage in the Upper South. Be sure to cut out growth that reverts to green. Effective barrier plantings: Growth is dense and twiggy, and spininess is a help, yet plants are not aggressively spiny.

'Fruitlandii'. Leaves large, silvery.
'Maculata'. GOLDEN ELAEAGNUS. Leaves have gold blotch in center.
'Marginata'. SILVER-EDGE ELAEAGNUS. Leaf margins silvery white.
'Variegata'. YELLOW-EDGE ELAEAGNUS. Yellowish white leaf margins.

ELDERBERRY. See SAMBUCUS

ELEPHANT'S EAR. See ALOCASIA, COLOCASIA esculenta

ELK'S-HORN FERN. See PLATYCERIUM hillii

ELM. See ULMUS

ELYMUS arenarius 'Glaucus'

BLUE LYME GRASS

Poaceae (Gramineae)

ORNAMENTAL GRASS

🗡 ZONES US, MS, LS, CS

☼ ◐ FULL SUN OR LIGHT SHADE

🖋 🖋 LITTLE OR LOTS OF WATER, VERY TOLERANT

*Elymus arenarius
'Glaucus'*

This Eurasian dune grass (often sold as American native, blue wild rye, *E. glaucus*) is the bluest grass of all. It's striking as a 1–3-ft.-tall specimen in a flower border or as ground cover. Give it moist fertile soil and it will spread, invasively. In dry soils and heavy clay, it's more manageable. Tolerates drought and wet soils, but not standing water or salt spray. Mow or cut back in late winter to stimulate fresh new blue growth.

EMPRESS TREE. See PAULOWNIA tomentosa

ENDYMION
(Scilla, Hyacinthoides)

Liliaceae

BULBS

🗡 ZONES VARY BY SPECIES

☼ ◐ FULL SUN OR PARTIAL SHADE

🖋 REGULAR WATER DURING GROWTH AND BLOOM

Endymion hispanicus

Spring bloomers still popularly known as *Scilla* (and sold by most dealers as such), but current botanical name is *Hyacinthoides*. They resemble hyacinths but are taller, with looser flower clusters and fewer, narrower leaves.

Area climate may determine which of the following two species is better for your garden. Spanish bluebell is the better choice for most Southern climates; the English species prefers definite winter cold and moderate summers. When grown close to each other, the two species often hybridize, producing intermediate forms. Plant bulbs in fall, 3 in. deep. A propensity for reseeding makes these plants good choices for naturalizing. Plant informal drifts among tall shrubs, under deciduous trees, among low-growing perennials. Clumps can be divided in fall. The plants also thrive in pots and are good for cutting.

🌸 **E. hispanicus (Scilla campanulata, S. hispanica).** SPANISH BLUEBELL. Zones US, MS, LS, CS. Prolific, vigorous, with sturdy, 20-in. stems bearing 12 or more nodding bells about ¾ in. long. Blue is the most popular color, 'Excelsior' (deep blue) the most popular selection. There are also white, pink, and rose forms. The inch-wide, straplike leaves can look a little ratty before they die back.

E. non-scriptus (Scilla nonscripta). ENGLISH BLUEBELL, WOOD HYACINTH. Zones US, MS. Fragrant flowers are narrower and smaller than those of Spanish bluebell, on 1-ft. stems that arch at the tip. Strap-shaped leaves are about ½ in. wide. 'Alba' is white flowered, 'Rosea' pink.

NATURALIZING A BLUEBELL PLANTING

Broadcast a handful of bulbs over an area and plant them where they fall. For a realistic effect, rearrange the bulbs before planting so they are closest together at one end of a group or toward the center—as though the colony originated at one spot and gradually increased outward. Mostly space bulbs about 6 in. apart.

ENGLISH DAISY. See BELLIS perennis

ENGLISH DOGWOOD. See PHILADELPHUS

ENGLISH FERN. See POLYSTICHUM setiferum

ENGLISH HOLLY. See ILEX aquifolium

ENGLISH IVY. See HEDERA helix

ENGLISH LAVENDER. See LAVANDULA angustifolia

ENGLISH PAINTED FERN. See ATHYRIUM otophorum

ENKIANTHUS campanulatus

REDVEIN ENKIANTHUS

Ericaceae

DECIDUOUS SHRUB

🗡 ZONES US, MS, LS

☼ ◐ FULL SUN OR PARTIAL SHADE

🖋 REGULAR WATER

*Enkianthus
campanulatus*

Native to Japan. Slow-growing, handsome shrub grows 6–8 ft. tall. Stems are upright, with tiers of nearly horizontal branches; habit is narrow in youth, broad in age, but always attractive. Bluish green leaves, 1½–3 in. long and whorled or crowded at branch ends, turn brilliant yellow to orange and red in autumn. Since color varies, choose plants in fall during color change. Blooms in spring (at approximately the time leaves are developing), producing pendulous clusters of yellow-green, red-veined, bell-shaped blossoms, ½ in. long. *E. c. palibinii* has deep red blooms, 'Albiflorus' creamy white ones. Flowers of 'Red Bells' are rosier at the tips than those of the species.

Like rhododendrons, requires moist, well-drained, acid soil to which plenty of organic matter such as peat moss or ground bark has been added. Produces flowers on previous year's growth, so prune only to remove dead or broken branches. Plant in a location where silhouette and fall color can be enjoyed close up. Best fall color occurs in Upper South.

EPIMEDIUM

Berberidaceae

PERENNIALS

🗡 ZONES US, MS, LS

◐ ● PARTIAL TO FULL SHADE

🖋 MODERATE WATER

*Epimedium
grandiflorum*

Low-growing plants with creeping underground stems and thin, wiry stems holding leathery leaves divided into heart-shaped leaflets to 3 in. long. Foliage is bronzy pink in spring, green in summer, bronzy in fall; whether it is evergreen, semievergreen, or deciduous depends on the species. Even in deciduous types, leaves last late into the year. In spring, plants produce loose spikes of small, waxy flowers like tiny columbines in pink, red, red orange, creamy yellow, or white. The flowers have four petals, which may be spurred or hooded, and eight sepals—four inner ones resembling petals and four usually small, outer ones.

Use as ground cover under trees or among rhododendrons, azaleas, camellias; good in large rock gardens. Compete well with surface-rooted trees. Prefer partial shade, but tolerate heavy shade. Foliage, flowers long lasting in arrangements. Cut back foliage of semievergreen and deciduous types in late winter before bloom. Divide large clumps in spring or fall by severing tough roots with a sharp spade. Adaptable to containers.

E. alpinum. ALPINE EPIMEDIUM. Evergreen. Rapidly spreading, to 6–9 in. high, with small flowers. Like those of *E. rubrum*, the blossoms have red inner sepals and yellow petals.

E. cantabrigiense. Semievergreen hybrid. To 8–12 in. high, with olive-tinted foliage and small yellow-and-red flowers.

E. grandiflorum. BISHOP'S HAT, LONGSPUR EPIMEDIUM. Deciduous. About 1 ft. high. Flowers 1–2 in. across, shaped like a bishop's hat; outer sepals red, inner sepals pale violet, petals white with long spurs. Selections have white, pinkish, or violet flowers. 'Rose Queen', bearing crimson flowers with white-tipped spurs, is outstanding. 'White Queen', with silvery white blooms, is another good selection.

E. perralderianum. Evergreen. To 1 ft. tall, about 6 in. wide, with shiny leaves, bright yellow flowers. A hybrid of this species and *E. pinnatum colchicum* is *E. perralchicum* 'Frohnleiten', a 1½-ft. plant with large yellow flowers and leaves marked with brown in frosty weather.

E. pinnatum. Nearly evergreen. To 12–15 in. high. Flowers are ⅔ in. across and have bright yellow inner sepals and short red spurs. *E. p. colchicum* (often sold as *E. p. elegans*) is larger, has showier flowers.

E. rubrum. RED EPIMEDIUM. Semievergreen. A hybrid of *E. alpinum* and *E. grandiflorum*. To 1 ft. high. Flowers, borne in showy clusters, have bright crimson inner sepals, white or pale yellow slipperlike petals, upward-curving spurs. Rosy 'Pink Queen' and white 'Snow Queen' are desirable selections offered by specialty nurseries.

E. versicolor. YELLOW EPIMEDIUM. Semievergreen. Several hybrids of *E. grandiflorum* and *E. pinnatum* bear this name. Best-known selection is the vigorous 'Sulphureum', 12–20 in. high with clusters of light yellow flowers and leaves marked with brownish red.

E. warleyense. Evergreen hybrid. To 1 ft. high. Light green foliage; clusters of coppery orange-red flowers. Also known as 'Ellen Wilmott'.

E. youngianum 'Niveum'. WHITE EPIMEDIUM. Deciduous. Low-growing (6–12 in.) plant with pure white blossoms.

EPIPHYLLUM

ORCHID CACTUS

Cactaceae

CACTI

✔ ZONES CS (PROTECTED), TS; OR INDOORS

☼ BEST UNDER LATH IN SUMMER OR UNDER TREES

◐ REGULAR WATER IN SUMMER, LITTLE IN WINTER

Epiphyllum Hybrid

Growers use *Epiphyllum* to cover a wide range of plants—epiphyllum itself and a number of crosses with related plants. All are tropical (not desert) cacti, and most grow on tree branches as epiphytes, like some orchids. Grow them in pots indoors; in lathhouse or shade outdoors in mild-winter climates. They need rich, quick-draining soil with plenty of sand and leaf mold, peat moss, or ground bark. Cuttings are easy to root in spring or summer. Permit the base of the cutting to dry for a day or two before potting it up. Overwatering and poor drainage cause bud drop.

In winter, epiphyllums need protection from frost. Most have arching (to 2 ft. high), trailing stems and look best in hanging pots or baskets. Stems are long, flat, smooth, quite spineless, and usually notched along edges. Spring flowers range from medium size to very large (up to 10 in. across); color range includes white, cream, yellow, pink, rose, lavender, scarlet, and orange. Many selections have blends of two or more colors. Feed with low-nitrogen fertilizer before and after bloom.

EPIPREMNUM aureum (Pothos aureus, Raphidophora aurea, Scindapsus aureus)

DEVIL'S IVY, POTHOS

Araceae

EVERGREEN CLIMBING PERENNIAL

✔ ZONE TS; OR INDOORS

☼ ◐ ● SUN OR SHADE

◐ REGULAR WATER

Epipremnum aureum

Related to philodendron. Best known as a tough house plant with 2–4-in.-long, oval, leathery, dark green leaves splashed or marbled with yellow. Commonly used as an attractive trailer for pots, window boxes, larger terrariums; requires same care as vining philodendrons, but can take more sun and regular water. Outdoors

and in greenhouses where it is given ample room, the plant becomes a big tropical vine with deeply cut leaves 2–2½ ft. long. Capable of climbing the tallest trees, the vine is sometimes used as a ground cover at the base of trees. Grows well in shade, but leaf color is better in full light.

EPISCIA

FLAME VIOLET

Gesneriaceae

PERENNIALS RELATED TO AFRICAN VIOLET

✔ ZONE TS; OR INDOORS

● FULL SHADE OUTDOORS; BRIGHT LIGHT INDOORS

◐ REGULAR WATER

Episcia cupreata

Low-growing tropical plants spread by strawberrylike runners with new plants at tips; provide an excellent display in hanging pots. Leaves 2–5 in. long, 1–3 in. wide; typically oval, velvety, beautifully colored. Flowers somewhat resembling African violets appear at scattered intervals throughout the year. Plants bloom well in high humidity of greenhouse but will also grow as house plants if given bright light but no direct sun. In south Florida, potted plants can stay outdoors most of the year if given a shady, wind-protected, warm location.

E. cupreata. Bears red flowers. *E. c. viridifolia* has green leaves with creamy veins; 'Chocolate Soldier', chocolate brown, silver-veined leaves; 'Metallica', olive green leaves with pale stripes, red edges; and 'Silver Sheen', silver leaves with darker margins.

🎋EQUISETUM hyemale

HORSETAIL

Equisetaceae

PERENNIAL

✔ ALL ZONES

☼ ◐ FULL SUN OR PARTIAL SHADE

◐◐ LOCATE IN MARSHY AREAS OR POOLS

Equisetum hyemale

Rushlike survivor of Carboniferous Age. Slender, hollow, 4-ft. stems are bright green with black-and-ash-colored ring at each joint. Spores borne in conelike spikes at end of stem. Several species, but *E. hyemale* most common. Called horsetail because many of the species have bushy look from many whorls of slender, jointed green stems that radiate out from joints of main stem.

Although horsetail is effective in some garden situations, especially near water, use it with caution: It is extremely invasive and difficult to get rid of. Best confined to containers. In open ground, root-prune unwanted shoots rigorously and constantly.

Miniature *E. scirpoides* is similar, but only 6–8 in. tall.

ERANTHIS hyemalis

WINTER ACONITE

Ranunculaceae

TUBER

✔ ZONES US, MS

☼ PARTIAL SHADE

◐ REGULAR WATER DURING GROWTH AND BLOOM

Eranthis hyemalis

Charming buttercup-like plant 2–8 in. high, blooming in early spring, even before crocuses. Single yellow flowers to 1½ in. wide, with five to nine petal-like sepals; each bloom sits on a single, deeply lobed bright green leaf that looks like a ruff. Round basal leaves divided into narrow lobes appear immediately after flowers. All traces of the plant disappear by the time summer arrives. Ideal companion for other small bulbs or bulblike plants that bloom at the same time, such as snowdrop and Siberian squill.

Plant tubers in August or early September before they shrivel. If tubers are dry, plump them up in wet sand before planting. When dividing, separate into small clumps rather than single tubers. Plant tubers 3 in. deep, 4 in. apart, in moist, porous soil. Can reseed in shady, damp conditions.

EREMOCHLOA ophiuroides

CENTIPEDE GRASS

Poaceae (Gramineae)

LAWN GRASS

✂ ZONES LS, CS

☼ ◑ FULL SUN OR VERY LIGHT SHADE

◐ ◑ REGULAR TO MODERATE WATER

*Eremochloa
ophiuroides*

Popular lawn grass in Lower South. Has finer texture than St. Augustine and is less prone to pests and diseases, but stays brown a little longer in winter and is a lighter green in summer. Good choice for poor, acid soils with a pH between 5.0 and 6.0. Relatively low maintenance. Damaged by overfertilizing (extra nitrogen will not make the grass a deeper green); apply no more than 1 lb. of actual nitrogen per 1,000 sq. ft. during entire growing season. Mow every 10 days in summer, at 1–2 in. Left unmowed, grass will reach no more than 3 in. but will look unkempt when it seeds. Fairly drought tolerant; does not take salt spray. 'Oklawn' and 'Centennial' are available as sod or plugs and are more cold-hardy than the ordinary centipede grass. 'Centennial' tolerates neutral to slightly alkaline soil.

EREMURUS

FOXTAIL LILY, DESERT CANDLE

Liliaceae

PERENNIALS

✂ ZONES US, MS

☼ FULL SUN

◐ MODERATE TO LITTLE WATER

Eremurus himalaicus

Imposing lily relatives with spirelike flowering stems 3–9 ft. tall. Unfortunately, difficult to grow well in most of the South. Bell-shaped white, pink, or yellow flowers, ½–1 in. wide, massed closely in graceful, pointed spikes on upper third to half of stem. Plants bloom in late spring, early summer. Need winter cold to bloom well. Strap-shaped basal leaves in rosettes appear in early spring, fade away after bloom in summer. Magnificent in large borders against background of dark green foliage, wall, or solid fence. Dramatic in arrangements; cut when lowest flowers on spike open. Plant in rich, fast-draining soil. Dig hole to 18 in. deep, then fill with 12 in. of excavated soil mixed with coarse sand or gravel. Set crown atop mound of this soil, mix approximately 4–6 in. below soil surface, then fill in. Handle thick, brittle roots carefully; they tend to rot when bruised or broken. When leaves die down, mark spot; don't disturb roots. Provide winter mulch in coldest areas.

E. himalaicus. To 3–8 ft. tall, with white flowers. Bright green leaves to 1½ ft. long.

E. robustus. To 6–9 ft. tall, with clear pink flowers lightly veined with brown. Dense basal rosettes of leaves to 2 ft. long.

E. Shelford hybrids. To 4–5 ft. tall; flowers in white and shades of buff, pink, yellow, and orange.

E. stenophyllus (E. bungei). To 3–5 ft. tall, with flowers in bright yellow aging to orange brown. Leaves to 1 ft. long.

ERIANTHUS ravennae

RAVENNA GRASS

Poaceae (Gramineae)

ORNAMENTAL GRASS

✂ ZONES US, MS, LS

☼ FULL SUN

◐ ◑ REGULAR OR MODERATE WATER

Erianthus ravennae

Native to southern Europe. Dense, gray-green, grassy foliage makes a 4–5-ft. fountain that erupts in late summer with giant plumes of silvery gray purple-tinted flowers. Mature plants produce as many as 40 plumes, 15 ft. high, spectacular when backlit by sun. Plumes turn into fluffy, cream-colored seed wands that last through winter, though they may become tousled and broken by storms. Very vigorous in moist, well-drained, fertile soil. Tolerates drought but not poor drainage. Similar to pampas grass, *Cortaderia selloana*, but less symmetrical in shape and much hardier. Good substitute for pampas grass in the Upper South and southern Midwest.

ERIGERON

FLEABANE

Asteraceae (Compositae)

PERENNIALS

✂ ZONES VARY BY SPECIES

☼ ◑ FULL SUN OR LIGHT SHADE

◐ MODERATE WATER

Erigeron speciosus

Free-blooming plants with daisylike flowers; similar to closely related Michaelmas daisy, except that flower heads have threadlike rays in two or more rows rather than broader rays in a single row. White, pink, lavender, or violet flowers, usually with yellow centers, early summer into fall. Sandy soil. Cut back after flowering to prolong bloom.

E. karvinskianus. MEXICAN DAISY, SANTA BARBARA DAISY. Zones CS, TS. Native to Mexico. Graceful, trailing plant 10–20 in. high. Leaves 1 in. long, often toothed at tips. Dainty flower heads ¾ in. across with numerous white or pinkish rays. Use as ground cover in garden beds or large containers, in rock gardens, in hanging baskets, on dry walls. Naturalizes easily; invasive unless controlled. 'Moerheimii' is somewhat more compact than species, with lavender-tinted flower heads.

E. pulchellus. ROBIN'S PLANTAIN. Zones US, MS, LS. Native from Maine to Minnesota, south to Georgia and East Texas. Leaves, 5 in. long and crinkled, grow in flat rosettes close to the ground. Daisy flowers blue, pink, sometimes white. Spreads slowly.

E. speciosus. Zones US, MS. Erect, leafy stemmed, 2 ft. high. Flowers 1–1½ in. across, with dark violet or lavender rays.

ERIOBOTRYA

LOQUAT

Rosaceae

EVERGREEN TREES OR LARGE SHRUBS

✂ ZONES VARY BY SPECIES

☼ ◑ FULL SUN OR PARTIAL SHADE

◐ REGULAR WATER

Eriobotrya japonica

Both kinds have large, prominently veined, sharply toothed leaves. One bears edible fruit. Attractive to birds.

E. deflexa. BRONZE LOQUAT. Zones CS, TS. Shrubby but easily trained into small tree form. New leaves have bright coppery color that they hold for a long time before turning green. Leaves aren't as leathery or as deeply veined as those of

E

E. japonica; they are shinier and more pointed. Garlands of creamy white flowers attractive in spring. No edible fruit. Good for espaliers (not on hot wall), patio planting, containers. Fast growing.

E. japonica. LOQUAT. Zones LS (protected), CS, TS. Tree is hardy to 20°F; has survived 12°F, but fruit often injured by low temperatures. Grows 15–30 ft. tall, equally broad in sun, slimmer in shade. Leathery, crisp leaves, stoutly veined and netted, 6–12 in. long, 2–4 in. wide. They are glossy deep green above and show rust-colored wool beneath. New branches woolly; small, dull white flowers, fragrant but not showy, in woolly, 3–6-in. clusters in fall. Orange to yellow, 1–2-in.-long fruit ripens in winter or spring. Sweet, aromatic, acid flesh; seeds (usually big) in center.

Plant in well-drained soil. In dry climates, it will thrive with no irrigation once established but does better with regular moisture. Mulch over root zone. Prune to shape; if you like the fruit, thin branches somewhat to let light into tree's interior. If tree sets fruit heavily, remove some while it's small to increase the size of remaining fruit and to prevent limb breakage. Fireblight is a danger; if leaves and stems blacken from top downward, prune back 1 ft. or more into healthy wood. Use as lawn tree; train as espalier on fence or trellis but not in reflected heat. Good in container for several years. Cut foliage is good for indoor decorating. Attracts bees.

Most trees sold are seedlings, good ornamental plants with unpredictable fruit quality; if you definitely want fruit, look for a grafted selection. Early-ripening 'Champagne' has yellow-skinned, white-fleshed, juicy, tart fruit. Midseason 'Gold Nugget' has sweeter orange fruit. Early 'MacBeth' has exceptionally large fruit with yellow skin, cream flesh. 'Thales' is a late yellow-fleshed selection.

SEA HOLLY FLOWERS NEED LONGER STEMS

Sea holly flowers have such dramatic form and unusual color, they call out to be used in arrangements. But their individual flower stems are too short (3–6 in.) to be seen in long-stemmed company. Cut florists' wire as needed, and fasten pieces to the stems with florists' tape. Sea hollies are everlasting; their stems don't need to be in water.

ERYNGIUM

SEA HOLLY

Apiaceae (Umbelliferae)

PERENNIALS

✿ ZONES US, MS, LS, CS

☼ FULL SUN

💧 MODERATE WATER

Eryngium amethystinum

Most are erect, stiff-branched, thistlelike plants with summer show of striking oval, steel blue or amethyst flower heads surrounded by spiny blue bracts. Upper leaves and stems are also sometimes blue. Make long-lasting cut flowers and dry well for winter arrangements. Leaves are sparse, dark green, deeply cut, spiny toothed. Use plant in borders or in fringe areas in deep, well-drained soil. Taprooted plants are difficult to divide; propagate by root cuttings or sow seed in place, thinning seedlings to 1 ft. apart. Plants often self-sow.

Another group of sea hollies has long, narrow, spine-edged leaves that resemble those of yucca. One of these plants is native to the U.S.

E. alpinum. To 2 ft., with 2-in. flower heads and large, deeply cut blue bracts. 'Blue Star' is a choice selection.

E. amethystinum. To 2½ ft. tall, with 1-in., rich blue flower heads above finely cut leaves.

E. planum. To 3 ft. high. Flowers heads small, freely borne, dark blue, with dark blue bracts.

E. variifolium. To 16 in., with small, rounded blue-gray flower heads and bluish white bracts. Thistlelike leaves are evergreen and heavily veined with white.

E. yuccifolium. RATTLESNAKE MASTER. Native to eastern and central U.S. Long (to 3-ft.), narrow, spiny-edged leaves in a basal rosette. Erect stems to 3–4 ft. branch toward top and carry small balls of white flowers without significant bracts.

ERYSIMUM

WALLFLOWER

Brassicaceae (Cruciferae)

PERENNIALS AND BIENNIALS, SOME GROWN AS ANNUALS

✿ ZONES VARY BY SPECIES

☼ ◐ FULL SUN OR LIGHT SHADE

💧 ◐ WATER NEEDS VARY BY SPECIES

Erysimum hieraciifolium

This genus swallowed up *Cheiranthus*, which included the sweetly fragrant, old-fashioned bedding wallflowers. All species have the typical clustered, four-petaled flowers that give the crucifers their name.

E. 'Bowles Mauve'. Perennial. Zones MS, LS. Massed erect stems with narrow gray-green leaves form a plant to 3 ft. tall, 6 ft. wide; each stem is topped by 1½-ft.-long, narrow, spikelike clusters of mauve flowers. Often begins blooming in midwinter, continuing until weather gets hot in May. May be short lived. Moderate to little water. 'Wenlock Beauty' is smaller, with flowers varying from buff to purple in a single spike.

E. cheiri (Cheiranthus cheiri). ENGLISH WALLFLOWER. Perennial in Zones US, MS, but usually grown as a biennial or an annual. Branching, woody-based plants 1–2½ ft. tall, with narrow bright green leaves and broad clusters of showy, delightfully sweet-scented flowers in spring. Blossoms are yellow, cream, orange, red, brown, or burgundy, sometimes shaded or veined with contrasting color. Sow seeds in spring for bloom the following year (some strains flower the first year if seeded early); or set out plants in fall or earliest spring. May self-sow. Regular water.

E. hieraciifolium (E. alpinum). SIBERIAN WALLFLOWER. Biennial or short-lived perennial (Zones US, MS, CS), frequently treated as an annual. Narrow-leafed, branching plants 1–1½ ft. tall, covered with fragrant, rich orange flowers in spring. Sow seeds or set out plants as for *E. cheiri.* Often self-sows. Regular water. 'Moonlight' has bright yellow flowers that open from red buds.

E. kotschyanum. Short-lived perennial (Zone US), often treated as an annual. Light green leaves form 6-in. mats from which rise scented, deep yellow flowers on 2-in. stems in spring. Moderate water. Use in rock garden or with other small perennials between paving stones. If plants hump up, cut out central portions, transplant them, and press original plants flat again. Divide clumps in fall.

ERYTHEA. See BRAHEA

ERYTHRINA

CORAL TREE

Fabaceae (Leguminosae)

DECIDUOUS OR NEARLY EVERGREEN TREES OR SHRUBS

✿ ZONES VARY BY SPECIES

☼ FULL SUN

💧 ◐ REGULAR TO MODERATE WATER

❖ SEEDS ARE POISONOUS IF INGESTED

Erythrina herbacea

Many species; known and used chiefly in normally frost-free areas of Florida. Only *E. crista-galli* and *E. herbacea* survive in colder areas. These trees are grown for their brilliant flowers, in colors ranging from greenish white through yellow, light orange, and light red to orange and red. The flat, beanlike pods that follow the flowers contain poisonous seeds. Leaves (divided into three leaflets) are usually shed in winter or spring. These are typically thorny plants with strong structural value, whether in or out of leaf.

E. acanthocarpa. TAMBOOKIE THORN. Deciduous shrub. Zone TS. To 3 ft. tall (rarely 6 ft.). Bluish green leaflets to 1½ in. are as broad as long. Spring flower spikes are 7 in. long, 6 in. wide, with scarlet, yellow-tipped flowers. Thorny plant grows from large, thick tuberlike root.

E. americana. Deciduous tree. Zone TS. Native to Mexico; used as street tree in Mexico City. Grows to 25 ft. tall. Resembles *E. coralloides* in both habit and flowers.

E. bidwillii. Deciduous shrub. Zones LS, CS, TS. To 8 ft., sometimes treelike to 20 ft. or more, wide spreading. Hybrid of *E. crista-galli* and *E. herbacea.* Spectacular display—2-ft.-long clusters of pure red flowers on long, willowy stalks from spring until winter; main show in summer. Cut back flowering wood when flowers are spent. Very thorny, so plant away from paths and prune with long-handled shears.

E. coralloides. NAKED CORAL TREE. Deciduous tree. Zone TS. Native to Mexico. To 30 ft. high and as wide, but easily contained by pruning. Fiery red blossoms like fat candles or pine cones bloom at the tips of naked, twisted, black-thorned branches in spring. At end of flowering season, 8–10-in. leaves develop, give shade in summer, turn yellow in late fall before dropping. Bizarre branch structure when tree is out of leaf is almost as valuable as spring flower display. Sometimes sold as *E. poianthes.*

🌿 **E. crista-galli.** CRY-BABY TREE, COCKSPUR CORAL TREE. Zones LS, CS, TS. Deciduous shrub or small tree 15–20 ft. high and wide in nearly frostless areas; perennial to 4 ft. in colder areas. Native to eastern South America. First flowers form after leaves come in spring—at each branch tip is a big, loose, spikelike cluster of velvety, birdlike blossoms in warm pink to wine red (plants vary). Teardrops of nectar that drip from the flowers give this plant the name "cry-baby tree." Depending on environment there can be as many as three distinct flowering periods, spring through fall. Cut back old flower stems and dead branch ends after each wave of bloom.

Erythrina crista-galli

E. falcata. Nearly evergreen tree. Zone TS. Native to Brazil and Peru. Grows upright to 30–40 ft. high. Must be in ground several years before it flowers (may take 10 to 12 years). Rich deep red (occasionally orange-red), sickle-shaped flowers in hanging, spikelike clusters at branch ends in late winter, early spring. Some leaves fall at flowering time.

🌿 **E. herbacea.** CORAL BEAN, CHEROKEE BEAN. Zones MS, LS, CS, TS. Native to southeastern states, Texas, northern Mexico. Perennial to 6 ft. tall in Lower South, deciduous shrub or small tree to 15 ft. tall in Coastal and Tropical South. Bright red, 2-in. blooms in 8–12-in. spikes from spring to frost. Red seeds that follow are attractive but extremely poisonous.

E. humeana. NATAL CORAL TREE. Deciduous shrub or tree (sometimes almost evergreen). Zone TS. Native to South Africa. Grows to 30 ft. but begins to bear bright orange-red flowers when 3 ft. high. Blooms continuously, late summer to late fall, with flowers in long-stalked clusters at branch ends well above foliage (unlike many other types). Dark green leaves. 'Raja' is shrubbier, has leaflets with long, pointed "tails."

E. lysistemon. Deciduous tree. Zone TS. Native to South Africa. Eventually reaches 25–40 ft. high, spreads 40–60 ft. wide. Light orange (sometimes shrimp-colored) flowers. Time of bloom varies greatly; may bloom intermittently from fall into spring, occasionally in summer. Many handsome black thorns. A magnificent tree of great landscape value. Very sensitive to wet soil. Sometimes erroneously sold as *E. princeps.*

Erythrina humeana

E. variegata. Deciduous tree. Zone TS. Native to Africa, Asia, Polynesia. To 20–30 ft. tall, with thick, prickly trunk, branches. Leaves have 3–8-in. leaflets. Profuse display of coral red flowers in late winter, early spring.

ERYTHRONIUM

Liliaceae

CORMS

ZONES VARY BY SPECIES

PARTIAL OR FULL SHADE

AMPLE TO REGULAR WATER

Erythronium americanum

S pring-blooming, dainty, nodding, lily-shaped flowers 1–1½ in. across, on stems usually 1 ft. high or less. All have two (rarely three) broad, tongue-shaped, basal leaves, mottled in many species. All need some subfreezing temperatures. Plant in groups under trees, in rock gardens, beside pools, streams. Set out corms in fall, 2–3 in. deep, 4–5 in. apart, in rich, porous soil; plant corms as soon as you receive them, and don't let them dry out. May take a few years after planting to begin blooming. Difficult to transplant once established, because corms work their way deep into the soil.

E. albidum. Zones US, MS. Native from Minnesota to Ontario south to Texas. White flowers flushed yellow at the base. Blooms later in spring than most of the other species. Leaves infrequently mottled silver green. Spreads slowly to form colonies.

E. americanum. TROUT LILY. Zones US, MS, LS, CS. Native from Minnesota to Nova Scotia south to Florida. Shiny green leaves mottled brown and purple. Blooms in late spring at about the same time as *E. albidum*, bearing pale yellow blossoms sometimes flushed with purple.

E. dens-canis. DOG-TOOTH VIOLET. Zones US, MS, LS. European species. Leaves mottled with reddish brown; 6-in. stems of purple or rose flowers. Specialists can supply named forms with white, pink, rose, and violet blossoms.

ETERNAL FLAME. See CALATHEA crocata

EUCALYPTUS

Myrtaceae

EVERGREEN TREES OR SHRUBS

ZONES VARY BY SPECIES

FULL SUN

REGULAR TO LITTLE WATER

Eucalyptus niphophila

P rized for their beautiful foliage, these fast-growing plants are drought tolerant. Most are native to Australia. Lack of cold-hardiness limits their use in the South. Sudden freezes or hard winters may kill fairly large trees to the ground, or kill them outright. For this reason, some Southerners grow them as annuals or herbaceous perennials for summer color. Still, some species are surprisingly hardy; they are listed here.

Outside of prime eucalyptus territory, you may wish to try your hand at growing the plants if you enjoy experimenting. Plants are easily started from seed; most grow very rapidly, perhaps as much as 10–15 ft. in one year. Some are large trees with great skyline value; some are medium to large shrubs or multitrunked trees. Most bear small white or cream flowers that are conspicuous only in masses, while others have colorful, showy blooms. Some have leaves of unusual form, highly valued in floral arrangements. Nearly all have foliage that is aromatic when crushed. Most have two different kinds of leaves; those on young plants or new growth differ markedly from mature foliage.

In Victorian England, some species were grown as summer annuals for bedding out. In borderline climates, such bedded-out plants function today as perennials—tops are killed, but plants resprout vigorously the next year. Sow seeds in spring or summer, in flats or pots of prepared soil or planting mix. Keep flats shaded and water sparingly. As soon as seedlings are 2–3 in. tall, separate them carefully and transplant to pots or other containers. Spray lightly and frequently with dilute liquid fertilizer. Plant in open ground or large container when 6–12 in. tall; trees seldom thrive if roots have become pot-bound. Limbs are subject to breakage on larger species, so choose planting site carefully.

The sizes listed for trees below apply to plants grown in mildest areas; plants grown elsewhere are unlikely to reach such heights. Hardiness figures are not absolute. In addition to air temperature, you must take into account the plant's age (generally, the older the hardier), its condition, and the timing of the frost (24°F following several light frosts is not as dangerous as the same low temperature following warm autumn and winter weather). Consider any eucalyptus a risk; occasional deep or prolonged freezes can kill even large trees. If you are committed to growing eucalyptus, don't hasten to remove apparently dead trees; although their appearance may be damaged, they could resprout from trunk or main branches.

EUCALYPTUS IN BOUQUETS

Though florists sell eucalyptus stems to include in arrangements, foliage you pick yourself is fresher and more fragrant. If you have an *E. cinerea*, clip young foliage regularly for its gray-green, nearly round leaves. The silvery blue young foliage of *E. gunnii* is another attractive choice.

E. cinerea. SILVER DOLLAR TREE. Zones LS (protected), CS, TS; grow as annual in Upper South. Hardy to 14–17°F. Small to medium tree, 20–50 ft. tall and nearly as wide, with irregular habit. Grown for attractive juvenile foliage of gray-green, roundish leaves in pairs, 1–2 in. long. Mature leaves are green, long, narrow. Unimportant small white flowers. Cut back frequently to maintain supply of young foliage. Recovers from freezes if base of trunk is heavily mulched.

E. gunnii. CIDER GUM. Zones MS (protected), LS, CS, TS. Hardy to 5–10°F. Medium to tall, to 40–70 ft., dense, upright tree. One of the fastest growing and hardiest of eucalypts. Young foliage silvery blue green; mature leaves 3–5 in. long, dark green. Small, creamy white flowers.

E. neglecta. OMEO GUM. Zones MS (protected), LS, CS, TS. Hardy to near 0°F. Small to medium tree, to 20 ft. or more. Handsome juvenile leaves, round, blue green, in pairs; excellent for cutting. Attractive brown, peeling bark. Unimportant white flowers. Fast-growing tree.

E. niphophila (E. pauciflora niphophila). SNOW GUM. Zones MS (protected), LS, CS, TS. Hardy to near 0°F. Small, picturesque tree, wide-spreading and open, to 20 ft. tall. Attractive foliage and trunk. Silvery blue, lance-shaped leaves, 1½–4 in. long. Smooth, peeling white bark contrasts handsomely with red branches.

E. torelliana. CADAGA. Zone TS. Hardy to about 28–30°F. Straight-trunked tree, with rounded or spreading form, fast growing to 45–60 ft. tall. Leaves 3–6 in. long, dark green. Flowers white, profuse, showy. Likes water; often grown in south Florida.

EUCOMIS

PINEAPPLE FLOWER

Liliaceae

BULBS

✂ ZONES CS, TS; OR DIG AND STORE; GROW IN POTS

☼ ☽ FULL SUN OR LIGHT SHADE

💧 REGULAR WATER DURING GROWTH AND BLOOM

Eucomis comosa

Unusual-looking plants: thick, 2–3-ft. spikes closely set with ½-in.-long flowers and topped with clusters of leaflike bracts like a pineapple top. Bloom in summer, but persistent purplish seed capsules continue the show longer. Need rich soil with plenty of humus. Dormant in winter. Plant bulbs 5 in. deep; also fairly easy to grow from spring-sown seeds. Bulbs are hardy to about 5°F; where winters are colder, dig and store bulbs or grow in pots and protect during cold weather. Divide clumps when they become crowded. Interesting potted plants for outdoor or indoor use. Good cut flower.

E. bicolor. To 2 ft.; flowers green, each petal edged with purple. Attractive leaves 1 ft. long, 3–4 in. wide, with wavy edges.

E. comosa (E. punctata). Thick spikes 2–3 ft. tall are set with greenish white flowers tinged pink or purple. Stems are spotted purple at the base. Leaves grow to 2 ft. long and are less wavy than those of *E. bicolor*.

EULALIA GRASS. See MISCANTHUS

EUONYMUS

Celastraceae

EVERGREEN, DECIDUOUS SHRUBS; EVERGREEN VINES

✂ ZONES VARY BY SPECIES

☼ ☽ ● EXPOSURE NEEDS VARY BY SPECIES

💧 💧 REGULAR TO MODERATE WATER

Euonymus alata

Deciduous and evergreen species are distinct; the characteristic squarish "hatbox" fruit provides the only hint that they're related. Deciduous types are valued for brilliant fall leaf color or prominent fruit; evergreen types, used mainly for landscape structure, include some of the most cold-tolerant broad-leafed evergreens. Most species tolerate a range of light conditions, from full sun to fairly deep shade; deciduous kinds with fall color give best display in sun. Scale can be a problem on any euonymus.

E. alata. WINGED EUONYMUS, BURNING BUSH. Deciduous shrub. Zones US, MS, LS. Though nursery tags may indicate a much smaller plant, the species can reach 15–20 ft. high and wide. Dense, twiggy, flat topped, with horizontal branching. If lower limbs are removed, makes an attractive vase-shaped, small tree. Twigs have flat, corky wings that disappear on older growth. Though fruit is smaller and less profuse than that of *E. europaea*, fall color is impressive: The dark green leaves turn flaming red in autumn. In shade, fall color is pink. Best fall color occurs in Upper and Middle South. 'Compacta', a smaller plant (to 6–10 ft. high and a little narrower) with smaller corky wings, isn't quite as hardy. Use both as screen or alone, against dark evergreens for greatest color impact. 'Compacta' also makes a good unclipped hedge or foundation plant.

E. americana. HEART'S-A-BUSTIN', STRAWBERRY BUSH. Deciduous shrub. Zones US, MS, LS, CS. Native to eastern and southern U.S. Many-stemmed, suckering shrub with green stems. To 6 ft. high. Leaves medium green, to 3 in. long, turn pale yellowish pink in fall. Showy, scarlet seed capsules, ¾ in. in diameter, open September–October to reveal purple insides and bright orange seeds. Stems stay green all winter. Plant tolerates much shade; use in native woodland plantings. Well-behaved shrub; deserves wider use.

E. europaea. SPINDLE TREE. Deciduous large shrub or small tree. Zone US. Eventually reaches a possible 30 ft. tall; narrow when young, becoming rounded with age. Leaves are dark green; fall color varies from yellowish green to yellow to red. Fruits are the ornamental feature: A profusion of four-chambered, pink to red capsules open to reveal bright orange seeds. 'Aldenham' ('Aldenhamensis') produces profuse large pink capsules on long stems; 'Red Cascade' bears rosy red capsules. Full sun or partial shade. Scale is often a serious problem.

E. fortunei. WINTERCREEPER EUONYMUS. Evergreen vine or shrub. Zones US, MS, LS, CS. One of best broad-leafed evergreens where temperatures drop below 0°F. Trails or climbs by rootlets. Use prostrate forms to control erosion. Leaves dark rich green, 1–2½ in. long, with scallop-toothed edges; flowers inconspicuous. Mature growth is shrubby and bears fruit; cuttings taken from this shrubby wood produce upright plants.

The selections of *E. fortunei*, several of which are listed here, are better known than the species itself. Many garden centers still sell them as forms of *E. radicans*, which was once thought to be the species but is now considered another variety (see *E. f. radicans*). Use restraint when considering the variegated forms; gaudy foliage can be overpowering.

'Canadale Gold'. Compact shrub with light green, yellow-edged leaves.

'Colorata'. PURPLE-LEAF WINTER CREEPER. Same sprawling growth habit as *E. f. radicans*, though makes a more even ground cover. Leaves turn dark purple in fall and winter.

'Emerald Gaiety'. Small, dense-growing, erect shrub with deep green leaves edged with white.

'Emerald 'n Gold'. Similar to above, but with gold-edged leaves.

'Golden Prince'. New growth tipped gold. Older leaves turn green. Extremely hardy; good hedge plant.

'Greenlane'. Low, spreading shrub with erect branches, deep green foliage, orange fruit in fall.

'Ivory Jade'. Resembles 'Greenlane', but has creamy white leaf margins that show pink tints in cold weather.

E. f. radicans. COMMON WINTER CREEPER. Zones US, MS, LS, CS. Tough, hardy, trailing or vining shrub with dark green, thick-textured, 1-in.-long leaves. Given no support, it sprawls; given masonry wall to cover, it does the job completely.

E. japonica. EVERGREEN EUONYMUS. Evergreen shrub. Zones MS, LS, CS. Upright, 8–10 ft. with 6-ft. spread, usually held lower by pruning or shearing. Flowers inconspicuous. Older shrubs attractive trained as trees, pruned and shaped to show their curving trunks and umbrella-shaped tops. Can be grouped as hedge or screen. Leaves very glossy, leathery, deep green, 1–2½ in. long, oval to roundish.

The species and its selections are very tolerant of heat, unfavorable soil, and seacoast conditions, but they're pest prone and susceptible to scale insects, thrips, and spider mites. Plants are notorious for powdery mildew; place in full-sun location where air circulation is good.

Variegated forms are most popular; they are among the few shrubs that maintain variegations in full sun in hot-summer climates. However, their garish foliage is difficult to work into landscaping and may quickly become an eyesore. Some confusion may exist in plant labeling of variegated types.

'Aureo-marginata'. GOLDEN EUONYMUS. Gaudy, bright golden foliage nearly glows in the dark. Extremely popular; extremely overplanted.

'Aureo-variegata'. GOLDSPOT EUONYMUS. Leaves have brilliant yellow blotches, green edges.

'Grandifolia'. Plants sold under this name have shiny dark green leaves larger than those of the species. Compact, well branched, good for shearing as pyramids, globes.

'Microphylla' *(E. j. pulchella).* BOX-LEAF EUONYMUS. Compact, small leafed, 1–2 ft. tall and half as wide. Formal looking; usually trimmed as low hedge.

'Microphylla Variegata'. Like 'Microphylla', but leaves splashed white.

'Silver King'. Green leaves with silvery white edges.

'Silver Princess'. Like 'Microphylla Variegata', but 3 ft. tall, 2 ft. wide, with larger leaves.

'Silver Queen'. Green leaves with creamy white edges.

E. kiautschovica (E. patens). Evergreen shrub. Zones US, MS, LS. To 8 ft. high and as wide or wider, with some low branches trailing on the ground and rooting. Relatively thin-textured, light green leaves and a profusion of tiny, greenish cream flowers in late summer. Bees and flies swarm the plant when it is in bloom, so it is not a good choice near porches, terraces, and walkways. Bloom followed by conspicuous pink to reddish fruits with red seeds. There are two hybrids that make good hedges: 'DuPont', 4–6-ft.-high plant with large, dark green leaves; 'Manhattan', upright grower 6–8 ft., with dark, glossy leaves. Scale is a serious problem on all forms.

EUPATORIUM

Asteraceae (Compositae)

PERENNIALS

🗡 ZONES VARY BY SPECIES

☼ ◑ FULL SUN TO LIGHT SHADE

💧 AMPLE MOISTURE, EXCEPT AS NOTED

Eupatorium purpureum

Medium-size to towering perennials with large clusters of small flower heads at the tops of leafy stems.

Except as noted, these species are native to the eastern and central U.S. and have become popular not only in wild gardens and restored meadows, but also in more ordered perennial borders. All are easy to grow. Remove faded flower heads to avoid seedlings. Divide clumps in spring or fall.

E. cannabinum. HEMP AGRIMONY. Zones US, MS, LS, CS. Native to Europe. Grows 5–6 ft. tall, with opposite pairs of deeply cut leaves and broad clusters of fluffy white, pink, or purple flower heads in summer. 'Album' bears white flowers, 'Plenum' pinkish purple blooms.

🏛 **E. coelestinum.** WILD AGERATUM, HARDY AGERATUM. All zones. Grows to 3 ft. tall, with freely branching stems set with pairs of 4-in. dark green, toothed leaves. Broad clusters of fluffy blue flowers exactly resemble those of the annual ageratum. Vigorous, freely spreading plant is invasive in fertile soil. Prefers ample moisture but will not thrive in soggy soil in winter. Late to appear in spring; blooms from late summer until frost. The 1½–2-ft.-high 'Album' bears pure white flowers; 2-ft.-high 'Cori' has exceptionally clear blue blossoms and comes into bloom later than the species; 'Wayside Form' is more compact, growing to 15 in. high.

E. maculatum. SPOTTED JOE-PYE WEED. Zones US, MS, LS, CS. Similar to *E. purpureum* but smaller (to 6 ft. at most), with green stems speckled or blotched with purple. Flat-topped clusters of pink, purple, or white flowers bloom from midsummer to early fall.

E. perfoliatum. BONESET. Zones US, MS, LS, CS. Grows 3–5 ft. tall. The long (8-in.), narrow leaves are joined at their bases, so that the stem appears to grow through the leaves. Fluffy white flowers borne in flat-topped clusters. This plant is attractive in meadow restoration, but poisonous to cattle and thus considered a nuisance by ranchers. Likes moisture but tolerates considerable drought. In the past, this plant was thought to have medicinal value for people, helping to knit broken bones—hence the common name.

E. purpureum. JOE-PYE WEED. Zones US, MS, LS, CS. Often sold as *E. fistulosum.* An imposing plant of damp meadows in the eastern U.S. Grows 3–9 ft. tall, with clumps of hollow stems and whorls of strongly toothed leaves to 1 ft. long. Leaves have a vanilla scent when bruised. Dusty rose flowers, attractive to butterflies, appear in large, dome-shaped clusters in late summer or early fall. Commonly sold is 'Gateway', a sensible 5 ft. in height, with dusky purplish rose flowers at the top of purple stems. One of autumn's showiest perennials. Deserves wider use.

EUPHORBIA

Euphorbiaceae

SHRUBS, PERENNIALS, ANNUALS, AND SUCCULENTS

🗡 ZONES VARY BY SPECIES

☼ ◑ ● EXPOSURE NEEDS VARY BY SPECIES

💧 ◑ REGULAR TO MODERATE WATER, EXCEPT AS NOTED

☙ SAP IS POISONOUS IN SOME SPECIES

Euphorbia epithymoides

On euphorbia, what are called flowers are really groups of colored bracts. True flowers, centered in the bracts, are inconspicuous. Many euphorbias are succulents; these often mimic cacti in appearance and are as diverse as cacti in form and size. Only a few of these are listed below, but specialists in succulents and cacti can supply scores of species and selections. Plant euphorbias in well-drained soil. Give winter protection in cold-winter areas.

E. amygdaloides. Perennial. Zones US, MS, LS. To nearly 3 ft., blooming late winter, early spring. 'Purpurea' has foliage heavily tinted purple, with bright green inflorescence. Best in sun, tolerates some shade. Dies back in winter.

E. biglandulosa. See E. rigida

E. epithymoides (E. polychroma). CUSHION SPURGE. Perennial. All zones. Neatly rounded hemisphere of deep green leaves symmetrically arranged on closely set stems that end in a branching, rounded cluster of tiny blossoms surrounded by bright yellow bracts. Effect is of a 1–1½-ft. gold mound suffused with green. Spring bloom. Good fall color (yellow to orange or red). Use in rock gardens, perennial borders. Give some shade in Coastal and Tropical South. Short lived, but reseeds.

E. griffithii. Perennial. Zones US, MS, LS, CS. Erect stems to 3 ft., clad in narrow, medium green leaves and topped by clusters of brick red or orange bracts. Spreads by creeping roots but is not aggressive. Sun or light shade. Dies back in winter. 'Fireglow' is the selection commonly sold.

E. lathyris. MOLE PLANT, GOPHER PLANT. Biennial. Zones US, MS, LS, CS. Legend claims that it repels gophers and moles. Stems have poisonous, caustic milky juice; keep away from skin and especially eyes, since painful burns can result. Juice could possibly bother a gopher or mole enough to make it beat a hasty retreat. Grows as tall single stem, to 5 ft. high by second summer, when it sets a cluster of unspectacular yellow flowers at the top. Flowers soon turn to seed, after which the plant dies. Long, narrow-pointed leaves grow at right angles to stem and to each other. Grow from seed. Give sun or shade, regular to little water.

E. marginata. SNOW-ON-THE-MOUNTAIN. Annual. All zones. To 2 ft. Leaves light green, oval; upper ones striped and margined white, uppermost sometimes all white. Flowers unimportant. Often used for contrast with bright-colored dahlias, scarlet sage, or zinnias, or with dark-colored plume celosia. Before using in cut arrangements, dip stems in boiling water or hold in flame for a few seconds. Sow seed in place in spring, in sun or partial shade. Thin to a few inches apart; plants are somewhat rangy.

E. milii (E. splendens). CROWN OF THORNS. Woody perennial or subshrub; evergreen but sparsely leafed. Zone TS; or indoors, greenhouse, or summer pot plant. Shrubby, climbing stems to 3–4 ft., armed with long, sharp thorns. Leaves roundish, thin, light green, 1½–2 in. long, usually found only near branch ends. Clustered pairs of bright red bracts borne nearly all year. Many selections and hybrids vary in form, size, and bract color (yellow, orange, pink). Train on small frame or trellis against sheltered wall or in container. Grow in porous soil, in full sun or light shade. Salt tolerance makes it an ideal choice for oceanfront plantings.

E. myrsinites. Evergreen perennial. Zones US, MS, LS, CS. Stems flop outward from central crown, then rise toward tip to 8–12 in. Leaves stiff, roundish, blue gray, closely set around stems. Clusters of chartreuse to yellow flowers top stem ends in late winter, early spring. Cut out old stems. Withstands cold and heat but short lived in warm-winter areas. Grow with succulents and gray-foliaged plants. Give sun.

E. pulcherrima. POINSETTIA. Evergreen, semievergreen, or deciduous shrub. Zones CS (protected), TS; or indoors. Native to Mexico. Leggy, to 10 ft. or taller. Coarse leaves grow on stiffly upright canes. Showy part of plant consists of petal-like bracts; true flowers in center are yellowish, inconspicuous. Red single form most familiar; less well known are red doubles and forms with white, yellowish, pink, or marbled bracts. Poinsettia has typical milky euphorbia juice, but it is not poisonous; it is either completely harmless or at most mildly irritating to skin or stomach.

Useful garden plant in well-drained soil and full sun. Where adapted outdoors, needs no special care. Grow as informal hedge in the Tropical South; in the Coastal South, plant against sunny walls, in sheltered corners, under south-facing eaves. Plant is still likely to die to the ground there. Thin branches in summer to produce larger bracts; prune them back at 2-month intervals for bushy growth (but often smaller bracts). To improve red color, feed every 2 weeks with high-nitrogen fertilizer, starting when color begins to show.

Euphorbia pulcherrima

To care for holiday gift plants, keep them in a sunny window and avoid sudden temperature changes. Keep soil moist; don't let water stand in pot saucer. When leaves drop in late winter or early spring, cut stems back to two buds and reduce watering to a minimum. Store in a cool place until late spring. When frosts are past, set pots in sun outdoors. Plants will prob-

ably grow too tall for indoor use the next winter, unless you cut them back in summer. Start new plants by making late-summer cuttings of stems with four or five eyes (joints).

ENCOURAGING POTTED POINSETTIAS TO BLOOM

Plants bloom only when they experience long nights. Starting in October, put them in a closet (no light at all) each night for 14 hours, then move them into light in the morning for a maximum of 10 hours. Continue this procedure for 10 weeks; you can have poinsettia blossoms by Christmas.

E. rigida (E. biglandulosa). Evergreen perennial or subshrub. Zones LS, CS. Stems angle outward, then rise up to 2 ft. Fleshy, gray-green leaves to 1½ in. long are narrow and pointed, their bases tightly set against stems. Broad, domed flower clusters in late winter or early spring are chartreuse yellow fading to pinkish. After seeds ripen, stems die back and should be removed; new stems take their place. Showy display plant in garden or container. Full sun.

E. robbiae (E. amygdaloides robbiae). MRS. ROBB'S BONNET. Evergreen perennial. Zones LS, CS. Usually under 1 ft. high. The stems are closely set with leathery dark green leaves 1½–4 in. long, over 1 in. wide. Pale lime green flower clusters in late winter, early spring. Spreads slowly but surely from underground rhizomes. It can thrive in sun (but not the hottest sun) and in deep shade. Regular to little water.

Euphorbiaceae. The euphorbia family contains annuals, perennials, shrubs, and an enormous number of succulents. Most have milky sap, and many have unshowy flowers made decorative by bracts or bractlike glands. Poinsettia (*Euphorbia pulcherrima*) is the best-known example.

EUROPEAN BIRD CHERRY. See PRUNUS padus

EUROPEAN CRANBERRY BUSH. See VIBURNUM opulus

EUROPEAN FAN PALM. See CHAMAEROPS humilis

EUROPEAN GRAPE. See VITUS vinifera

EUROPEAN HOP HORNBEAM. See OSTRYA carpinifolia

EUROPEAN PLUM. See PRUNUS domestica

EURYOPS

Asteraceae (Compositae)

SHRUBBY EVERGREEN PERENNIALS

⚡ ZONES VARY BY SPECIES

☼ FULL SUN

◌ MODERATE WATER

Native to South Africa. Leaves finely divided; flower heads daisylike. Long bloom season; keep old flowers picked off. Plants require excellent drainage. Thrive on buffeting ocean winds but are damaged by sharp frosts. Take well to container culture.

Euryops pectinatus

E. acraeus. Zone TS. Native to high South African mountains. Mounded growth to 2 ft. Leaves silvery gray, ¾ in. long. Inch-wide, bright yellow daisies cover plant in spring.

E. pectinatus. Zones CS, TS; grow as annual elsewhere. To 3–6 ft. high. Easy maintenance and extremely long flowering season make it a good filler, background plant, or low screen. Leaves are gray green, deeply divided, 2 in. long. Bright yellow, 1½–2-in.-wide daisies on 6-in. stems bloom most of the year. Cut back in late spring or early summer to maintain form and limit size. Good potted plant. 'Viridis' is identical to species but has deep green leaves. 'Munchkin' is a dwarf to 3 ft. tall, 4 ft. wide.

EUSTOMA grandiflorum (Lisianthus russellianus)

LISIANTHUS, TULIP GENTIAN, TEXAS BLUEBELL

Gentianaceae

BIENNIAL OR SHORT-LIVED PERENNIAL OFTEN GROWN AS ANNUAL

✔ ALL ZONES

☀ ☼ FULL SUN OR FILTERED LIGHT

◐ ◐ REGULAR TO MODERATE WATER

Eustoma grandiflorum

Native to U.S. High Plains, but garden forms introduced from Japan. Plants grow better and have longer stems where nights are warm. Best cut flowers are produced in greenhouses.

In summer, clumps of gray-green foliage send up 1½-ft. stems topped by tulip-shaped, 2–3-in. flowers in purplish blue, pink, or white; plants bloom all summer if old blooms are cut off. Double Eagle and Lion strains have double flowers that look similar to roses. Heidi strain of F₁ hybrids are vigorous, long stemmed, and include yellow in addition to other flower colors. 'Red Glass' has rose red flowers. Picotee types also available.

Buying started plants is easier, but lisianthus can be grown with much care from its dustlike seeds. Sprinkle seed on surface of potting soil; don't cover with soil. Soak well, then cover pot with glass or plastic until seeds germinate. At four-leaf stage (about 2 months), transplant three or four plants into each 6-in. pot. Needs good garden soil, good drainage, fertilizer. Often grown as annual. Use in pots, border, cutting garden. Excellent long-lasting cut flower. May overwinter in Lower, Coastal, and Tropical South.

EVENING PRIMROSE. See OENOTHERA

EVERGREEN CANDYTUFT. See IBERIS sempervirens

EVERGREEN RED WISTERIA. See MILLETTIA reticulata

EVERGREEN WITCH HAZEL. See LOROPETALUM chinense

EVE'S NECKLACE. See SOPHORA affinis

EVODIA daniellii (Tetradium daniellii)

KOREAN EVODIA

Rutaceae

DECIDUOUS TREE

✔ ZONES US, MS, LS

☀ FULL SUN

◐ ◐ REGULAR TO MODERATE WATER

Evodia daniellii

Native to northern China and Korea. Evodia is distantly related to citrus, but the leaves are more reminiscent of walnut. Quickly grows to 30 ft. or taller and somewhat wider. The shiny dark green leaves are 1 ft. long or a little more, with five pairs of 2–5-in. leaflets plus a single leaflet at the end. Foliage is handsome throughout summer and early fall. No fall color; leaves drop while green. Blooms in early summer, bearing small white flowers in showy, 4–6-in., rather flat clusters; they are popular with bees. Fruits are small but attractive, aging from red to black. Although the plant was introduced nearly a century ago, it remains little known, despite its attractiveness, soil tolerance, and freedom from pests.

A tree formerly known as *E. hupehensis* is now considered to be a somewhat less hardy form from southern China.

SOUTHERN HERITAGE PLANTS
IDENTIFIED BY SYMBOL 🕎

EVOLVULUS glomeratus

BLUE DAZE

Convolvulaceae

TENDER PERENNIAL OFTEN GROWN AS ANNUAL

✔ ZONE TS

☀ ☼ FULL SUN OR LIGHT SHADE

◐ ◐ REGULAR TO MODERATE WATER

Evolvulus glomeratus

Native to Brazil. Trailing stems to 20 in. are closely set with small gray-green leaves and spangled with blue morning glory flowers less than 1 in. wide. Flowers close in the evening and on darkly overcast days. Stems root where they touch the ground; cuttings root very easily in water or moist soil. Useful as a bedding plant, in summer borders, in hanging baskets. Often sold as *E. nuttallianus*.

EXOCHORDA

PEARL BUSH

Rosaceae

DECIDUOUS SHRUBS

✔ ZONES US, MS, LS

☀ FULL SUN

◐ ◐ REGULAR TO MODERATE WATER

Exochorda racemosa

Loose, spikelike clusters of 1½–2-in.-wide white flowers open from profusion of buds resembling pearls. Flowers bloom for a short time in spring, at about the same time the roundish, 1½–2-in.-long leaves expand. Foliage and arching growth suggest the related spiraea, but pearl bush's individual blossoms are considerably larger.

Showy during spring but undistinguished at other times of year, so choose your site accordingly. Prefers well-drained, acid soil but will grow in neutral or alkaline soil; will take considerable neglect. Flowers are formed on previous year's growth, so prune after bloom to control size and form.

E. giraldii. Resembles the more widely grown *E. racemosa*, but with slightly smaller flowers and red tints in leaf veins and flower stalks.

E. macrantha. Hybrid between *E. racemosa* and another species. The only selection available, 'The Bride', is a compact shrub to about 4 ft. tall and as wide. Very showy spring bloom.

🕎 **E. racemosa (E. grandiflora).** COMMON PEARL BUSH. Native to China. Loose, open, slender; grows to 10–15 ft. tall and wide, possibly larger. In small gardens, remove lower branches to make small, upright, airy, multistemmed tree. Often found in older gardens of the Middle and Lower South. Reseeds readily, and seedlings are often shared.

Fabaceae. Previously called Leguminosae, the pea family is an enormous group containing annuals, perennials, shrubs, trees, and vines. Many are useful as food (beans, peas), while others furnish timber, medicines, pesticides, and a host of other products. Many are ornamental.

The best-known kinds—sweet pea *(Lathyrus)*, for example—have flowers shaped like butterflies, with two winglike side petals, two partially united lower petals (called the keel), and one erect upper petal (the banner or standard). Others have a more regular flower shape *(Bauhinia, Cassia)*; still others have tightly clustered flowers that appear to be puffs of stamens, as in acacia and mimosa *(Albizia)*. All bear seeds in pods (legumes). The roots of many have colonies of bacteria that can extract nitrogen from the air and convert it into compounds useful as plant food.

Fagaceae. The beech family contains evergreen or deciduous trees characterized by fruit that is either a burr, as in beech *(Fagus)* and chestnut *(Castanea)*, or a nut enclosed in a cup, as in oak *(Quercus)*.

F

F

FAGUS

BEECH

Fagaceae

DECIDUOUS TREES

☇ ZONES VARY BY SPECIES

☼ ◑ FULL SUN OR LIGHT SHADE

● REGULAR WATER

Fagus grandifolia

Of the various beech types, those described here include a rarely seen Japanese species; a species native to the eastern U.S. that is widespread in nature but seldom planted in gardens; and the beautiful European beech. Though all beeches are capable of growing to 90 ft. or more, they are usually considerably smaller. With the exception of selected horticultural varieties, they have a broad cone shape, with wide, sweeping lower branches that can reach the ground unless pruned off. Smooth gray bark contrasts well with glossy dark green foliage. Leaves color yellow to red brown in fall, then turn brown; many hang on the tree well into winter. Lacy branching pattern and pointed leaf buds provide an attractive silhouette in winter. New foliage has a silky sheen. The nuts, enclosed in spiny husks, are edible but small; they will often fail to fill out, especially on solitary trees.

All beeches cast heavy shade and have a dense network of fibrous roots near soil surface, inhibiting growth of lawn or other plants under the trees. Transplant from containers or, if moving an in-ground tree, dig with a substantial ball of earth. Give any good garden soil, but beeches do best in moist, fertile, well-drained, slightly acid soil. Despite their size, they can be closely planted and trimmed as dense, impassable hedges as low as 4 ft.

F. crenata. JAPANESE BEECH. Zones US, MS. Leaves scallop edged, somewhat smaller than those of other beeches. Reddish brown fall color. Likes some shade, especially when young.

F. grandifolia. AMERICAN BEECH. Zones US, MS, LS, CS. A stately tree and a principal component of the vast hardwood forests that once covered much of the eastern U.S. Tolerates shade and makes a good understory tree when young. More tolerant of summer heat than the other two species described here; can be grown farther south. Leaves are toothed, 3–6 in. long, persist all winter, turning beautiful parchment tan; leaves golden bronze in fall. Allow plenty of room for this tree.

F. sylvatica. EUROPEAN BEECH. Zones US, MS. Lustrous green leaves to 4 in. long, turning russet and bronzy in autumn. Many selections, including the following:

'Asplenifolia'. FERNLEAF BEECH. Leaves narrow, deeply lobed or cut nearly to midrib. Delicate foliage on large, robust, spreading tree.

'Atropunicea'. COPPER BEECH, PURPLE BEECH. Leaves deep reddish or purple. Good in containers. Often sold as 'Riversii' or 'Purpurea'. Seedlings of copper beech are usually bronzy purple, then turning bronzy green in summer.

'Fastigiata'. DAWYCK BEECH. Narrow, upright tree, like Lombardy poplar in form; 8 ft. wide when 35 ft. tall. Broader in great age, but still narrower than species.

'Laciniata'. CUTLEAF BEECH. Narrow green leaves, deeply cut.

'Pendula'. WEEPING BEECH. Irregular, spreading form. Long, weeping branches reach to ground, can root where they touch. Green leaves. Without staking to establish vertical trunk, it will grow wide rather than high.

'Purpurea Pendula'. WEEPING COPPER BEECH. Purple-leafed weeping form to 10 ft. tall. Splendid container plant.

'Tricolor'. TRICOLOR BEECH. Green leaves marked white and edged pink. Slow to 24–40 ft., usually much less. Foliage burns in hot sun or dry winds. Choice container plant.

'Zlatia'. GOLDEN BEECH. Young leaves yellow, aging to yellow green. Subject to sunburn. Good container plant.

FALSE ASTER. See KALIMERIS pinnatifida

FALSE BIRD OF PARADISE. See HELICONIA brasiliensis

FALSE CYPRESS. See CHAMAECYPARIS

FALSE DRAGONHEAD. See PHYSOSTEGIA

FALSE INDIGO. See AMORPHA fruticosa

FALSE LUPINE. See THERMOPSIS

FALSE SOLOMON'S SEAL. See SMILACINA racemosa

FALSE SPIRAEA. See ASTILBE

FANFLOWER. See SCAEVOLA aemula

FARFUGIUM japonicum. See LIGULARIA tussilaginea

FARKLEBERRY. See VACCINIUM arboreum

FATSHEDERA lizei

Araliaceae

EVERGREEN VINE, SHRUB, OR GROUND COVER

☇ ZONES LS (PROTECTED), CS, TS

◑ ● PARTIAL OR FULL SHADE

● REGULAR WATER

Fatshedera lizei

Hybrid between English ivy (*Hedera helix*) and Japanese fatsia (*Fatsia japonica*), with characteristics of both parents. Highly polished, 4–10-in.-wide leaves with three to five pointed lobes resemble giant ivy leaves; plant also sends out long, trailing or climbing stems like ivy, though without aerial holdfasts. Fatshedera inherited shrubbiness from Japanese fatsia, though its habit is more irregular and sprawling than that of its parent. Several variegated forms exist.

Leaves are injured at 15°F, tender new growth at 20–25°F; seems to suffer more from late frosts than from winter cold. Give it protection from hot, drying winds. Good near swimming pools.

Fatshedera tends to grow in a straight line, but it can be shaped if you work at it. Pinch tip growth to force branching. About two or three times a year, guide and tie stems before they become brittle. If plant gets away from you, cut it back to ground; it will regrow quickly. If you use it as ground cover, cut back vertical growth every 2 to 3 weeks during growing season. Grown as vine or espalier, plants are heavy, so give them strong supports. Even a well-grown vine is leafless at base.

FATSIA japonica
(Aralia sieboldii, A. japonica)

JAPANESE FATSIA, JAPANESE ARALIA

Araliaceae

EVERGREEN SHRUB

☇ ZONES LS (PROTECTED), CS, TS

◑ ● PARTIAL OR FULL SHADE

● REGULAR WATER

Fatsia japonica

Tropical appearance with big, glossy, dark green, deeply lobed, fanlike leaves to 16 in. wide on long stalks. Moderate growth to 5–8 ft. (rarely more); sparsely branched. Many roundish clusters of small whitish flowers in fall and winter, followed by clusters of small, shiny black fruit.

Grows in nearly all soils except soggy ones. Adapted to containers. During prolonged dry spells, wash occasionally with hose to clean leaves, lessen insect attack. Established plants sucker freely; keep suckers or remove them with spade. Rejuvenate spindly plants by cutting back hard in early spring. Plants that set fruit often self-sow.

Good landscaping choice where bold pattern is wanted. Most effective when thinned to show some branch structure. Year-round good looks for shaded entryway or patio. Good near swimming pools. 'Moseri' is compact, low. 'Variegata' has leaves edged golden yellow to creamy white.

FEATHERED HYACINTH. See MUSCARI comosum 'Monstrosum'

FEATHER GRASS. See STIPA

FEATHER REED GRASS. See CALAMAGROSTIS acutifolia 'Stricta'

FEIJOA sellowiana (Acca sellowiana)

PINEAPPLE GUAVA

Myrtaceae

EVERGREEN SHRUB OR SMALL TREE

⚡ ZONES LS, CS, TS

☼ FULL SUN

💧 REGULAR WATER FOR BEST FRUITING

Feijoa sellowiana

From South America. Hardiest of so-called subtropical fruits. Normally a large multistemmed plant; if not pruned or killed back by frosts, reaches 18–25 ft., with equal spread. Can take almost any amount of pruning or training to shape as espalier, screen, hedge, or small tree. Oval leaves 2–3 in. long, glossy green above, silvery white beneath. Blooms in spring, bearing unusual inch-wide flowers with big tufts of red stamens and four fleshy white petals tinged purplish on inside. Petals are edible and can be added to fruit salads. Blossoms attract bees and birds.

Fruit ripens 4 to 5½ months after flowering in Tropical South, 5 to 7 months after bloom in Lower and Coastal South. Oval, grayish green fruit, 1–4 in. long, has soft, sweet to bland, somewhat pineapple-flavored pulp. Sometimes sold in markets under the name "feijoa" or "guava." Produces more dependably in the Southwest than in the Southeast.

Improved selections 'Beechwood', 'Coolidge', and 'Nazemetz' are self-fertile, although cross-pollination will produce a better crop. Single plants of seedlings or other named selections may need cross-pollination.

FELT PLANT. See KALANCHOE beharensis

FENNEL. See FOENICULUM vulgare

FERNLEAF YARROW. See ACHILLEA filipendulina

FERN PODOCARPUS. See PODOCARPUS gracilior

FERNS. Large group of perennial plants grown for their lovely and interesting foliage. They vary in height from a few inches to 50 ft. or more, and are found in all parts of the world; most are forest plants, but some grow in deserts, in open fields, or near the timberline in high mountains. Most have finely cut leaves (fronds). They do not flower but reproduce by spores that form directly on the fronds.

Ferns are divided into several families, according to botanical differences. Such technical differences aside, these plants fall into several groups based on general appearance.

Most spectacular are tree ferns, which display their finely cut fronds atop a treelike stem. These need rich, well-drained soil, moisture, and shade. Most tree ferns are tropical; all suffer in hot, drying winds and in extremely low humidity. Frequent watering of tops, trunks, and root area will help pull them through unusually hot or windy weather. For several types of tree ferns, see *Cibotium chamissoi, Cyathea cooperi, Dicksonia.*

Native ferns do not grow as tall as tree ferns, but their fronds are handsome and they can perform a number of landscape jobs. Naturalize them in woodland or wild gardens; or use them to fill shady beds, as ground cover, as interplantings between shrubs, or along a shady house wall. For native ferns, see *Adiantum, Asplenium, Athyrium, Dennstaedtia punc-*

tilobula, Dryopteris, Onoclea sensibilis, Osmunda, Polystichum, Thelypteris, Woodsia, Woodwardia.

Many ferns from other parts of the world grow well in the South; although some are house, greenhouse, or (in mildest climates) lathhouse subjects, many are fairly hardy. Use them as you would native ferns, unless some peculiarity of habit makes it necessary to grow them in baskets or on slabs. For exotic ferns, see *Adiantum, Asplenium, Cyrtomium, Davallia, Nephrolepis, Platycerium, Polypodium, Polystichum.*

All ferns look best if groomed. Cut off dead or injured fronds near ground or trunk—but don't cut back hardy outdoor ferns until new growth begins, since old fronds protect growing tips. Natives growing outdoors don't need it, but feed others frequently during growing season, preferably with light applications of organic-base fertilizer such as blood meal or fish emulsion. Mulch with peat moss occasionally, especially if shallow fibrous roots are exposed by rain or irrigation.

FESTUCA

FESCUE

Poaceae (Gramineae)

GRASSES

⚡ ZONES US, MS, EXCEPT AS NOTED

☼ FULL SUN, EXCEPT AS NOTED

💧 REGULAR WATER

Festuca ovina 'Glauca'

Several of these clumping grasses are used for erosion control or pasture; others have use as ornamental plants. Lawn fescues are classified as fine or coarse. All fescues need good drainage.

F. elatior. TALL FESCUE. Zones US, MS, LS (upper half). Coarse. Tall-growing (to 2½ ft.) pasture grass also used for erosion control when unmowed; or for lawns if mowed to 2–3 in. high. Takes heat better than other cool-season grasses, which makes it a good choice for gardeners in the Upper, Middle, and Lower South who like a lawn that stays green all winter. Takes full sun in the Upper and Middle South; needs afternoon shade in the Lower South. Seed heavily, at rate of 8 lb. per 1,000 sq. ft., to establish lawn. Apply 6 lb. of actual nitrogen per season, with a fertilizer formulation such as 12-4-8. To keep lawn dense, aerate in fall and overseed every 2 years at rate of 4 lb. per 1,000 sq. ft. Coarse-bladed, older selections have largely been supplanted by fine-bladed, deep green selections that resemble Kentucky bluegrass. Generally mow at 2–3 in., although dwarf types, such as 'Bonsai' and 'Twilight', can be mowed at 1–2 in. Tough blades, tolerance of compacted soils make it good play or sports turf. Selections include the following:

'Arid'. Medium green, medium coarse texture, relatively drought tolerant and resistant to pests and diseases.

'Bonanza'. Dark green, medium-fine texture.

'Bonsai'. Dark green, fine texture, slow and very low growing; can be mowed at 1 in.

'Crossfire'. Dark green, disease resistant, medium-fine texture, slow growing, especially tolerant of heat.

'Finelawn'. Medium green, medium texture.

'Houndog'. Somewhat prostrate habit; medium green, medium texture.

'Kentucky 31'. Light-medium green, coarse texture; an outdated, older selection.

'Mustang II'. Dark green, medium texture, low growing; good color in fall and spring.

'Rebel Jr.'. Medium dark green, medium-fine texture.

'Twilight'. Deep green, fine texture, low growing, drought tolerant.

F. ovina. SHEEP FESCUE. Fine. Low-growing grass (to 1 ft.) with narrow, needle-fine, soft but tough leaves. *F. o. duriuscula*, hard fescue, is sometimes used as lawn grass. 'Glauca', blue fescue, forms blue-gray tufts 4–10 in. tall. Useful ground cover for sunny or partially shaded areas, on slopes or level ground. Cannot tolerate foot traffic. Clip back near to the ground after flowering or any time it looks shabby. Not a solid cover; needs frequent weeding. Dig overgrown clumps, pull apart, and replant as small divisions. Set 6–15 in. apart, depending on desired effect. ▶

F. rubra. RED FESCUE. Fine. Principal use is in blends with bluegrass or other lawn grasses. Also used to overseed Bermuda-grass lawns in winter. Blades narrow, dark green. Not fussy about soil; takes some shade. Used alone, tends to clump; mow to 1½–2½ in. high. Type most commonly sold is sometimes called creeping red fescue; it is one of the most shade tolerant of good lawn grasses. Unmowed, all types of red fescue make attractive meadow on slopes that are too steep to mow. Does not tolerate heavy foot traffic.

FEVERFEW. See CHRYSANTHEMUM parthenium

FICUS
Moraceae
EVERGREEN OR DECIDUOUS TREES, VINES, SHRUBS
⚟ ZONES VARY BY SPECIES
☼ ◐ ● EXPOSURE NEEDS VARY BY SPECIES
💧 REGULAR WATER

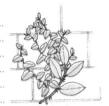

Ficus pumila

Most gardeners would never expect to find the commercial edible fig, small-leafed climbing fig, banyan tree, and potted rubber plant under one common heading—but they are classed together because they bear small or large figs (inedible in most species). Discussed below are ornamental plants; for edible figs, see Fig, Edible.

F. altissima. COUNCIL TREE, LOFTY FIG. Evergreen tree. Zone TS. Native to Asia. Once established, this tree grows quite quickly, forming multiple trunks from its numerous aerial roots, until it's 75 ft. tall and twice as broad. Not as large as the truly giant *F. benghalensis,* but far too large for home landscapes. Grows well in any soil, in full sun or light shade. Leaves thick, glossy, oval, to 8 in. long. Small, ¾-in. figs in summer.

F. benghalensis. BANYAN TREE, INDIAN BANYAN. Evergreen tree. Zone TS. Native to India, Pakistan. Giant tropical tree, to 90 ft. tall and hundreds of feet in diameter. Produces a forest of trunks from aerial roots. Oldest specimens can shelter as many as 2,000 people in the dense shade of their canopies. Sacred tree in its native habitat. Leaves dull green, leathery, rounded at the tips, to 8 in. long. Plant in full sun or partial shade.

F. benjamina. WEEPING FIG, BENJAMIN FIG. Evergreen tree. Zone TS; indoor plant anywhere. Native to India. To 30 ft. high, broadly spreading. Leathery, shining green leaves, to 5 in. long, densely clothe drooping branches. Red figs. Grow in sun or shade in frost-free, wind-protected location. Often used as small tree in entryway or patio. Good as espalier or screen. In mildest areas, can be used as clipped hedge. Undoubtedly one of most popular house plants—thrives on rich, steadily moist (not wet) soil, frequent light feeding, and abundant light.

Ficus benjamina

Plants are easy to start from semihardwood cuttings taken between May and July. 'Exotica' has wavy-edged leaves with long, twisted tips; it is often sold simply as *F. benjamina.*

F. carica. EDIBLE FIG. See Fig, Edible

F. deltoidea (F. diversifolia). MISTLETOE FIG. Evergreen shrub. Zone TS; indoor plant anywhere. Native to Malaysia. Grows very slowly to 8–10 ft. high. Interesting open, twisted branch pattern. Thick, dark green, roundish, 2-in. leaves are sparsely stippled with tan specks on upper surface and a few black dots below. Attractive, small, greenish to yellow fruit borne continuously. Most often grown in containers as patio and house plant. Grow in part shade or strong diffused light.

Ficus deltoidea

F. elastica. RUBBER PLANT. Evergreen shrub or tree. Zone TS; grow as indoor plant anywhere. Native to India and Malaysia. Familiar rubber plant found in almost every florist shop. Leaves are thick, glossy, leathery, dark green, 8–12 in. long, 4–6 in. wide. New leaves unfold from rosy pink sheaths that soon wither and drop. Grow in a shady spot outdoors. Comes

back quickly when cut to ground by frost. Can become a 40-ft. tree in south Florida. One of most foolproof indoor pot subjects; takes less light than most big house plants.

If a potted rubber plant becomes too tall and leggy, you can cut off top and select side branch to form a new main shoot, or get a new plant by air-layering the top section. When roots form, cut the branch section with attached roots and plant it in a container.

Ficus elastica

'Decora' ('Belgica'). BROAD-LEAFED INDIAN RUBBER PLANT. Considered superior to the species because of its broader, glossier leaves, bronzy when young.

'Rubra'. Reddish new leaves retain red edge as rest of leaf turns green.

'Variegata'. Leaves are long, narrow, variegated yellow and green. Variegation is interesting when viewed close up in container, but as an outdoor tree, plant has an unhealthy look.

F. lyrata (F. pandurata). FIDDLELEAF FIG. Evergreen shrub or tree. Zone TS; indoor plant anywhere. Native to tropical Africa. Strong structural form with huge, glossy, dark green, fiddle-shaped leaves to 15 in. long and 10 in. wide, prominently veined. Highly effective as indoor pot plant. In protected outdoor position (sun or light shade), can grow to 20 ft., with trunks 6 in. thick. Good near swimming pools. To increase branching, pinch back when plant is young.

Ficus lyrata

F. maclellandii. Evergreen tree. Zone TS; indoor plant anywhere. Similar to *F. benjamina,* but leaves are long, narrow, willowy, dark green, and it's easier to grow indoors, less likely to shed leaves. Let dry completely between waterings, and then water thoroughly, but don't leave plant standing in water. Feed with liquid fertilizer once in spring and once in fall, more often if plant is in very bright light. Use horticultural oil to treat scale and mealybugs, though pest problems are rare. Dust or rinse leaves with water occasionally; select a permanent position with good light and no drafts, and expect some leaf drop whenever you move it.

F. macrophylla. MORETON BAY FIG. Huge evergreen tree. Zone TS. Native to Australia. Grows to enormous dimensions. Blunt, oval, leathery leaves, 10 in. long and 4 in. wide, glossy green above, brownish beneath. Rose-colored leaf sheaths appear like candles at branch ends. Inch-long figs are purple spotted with white. Full sun. Although tender when young, acquires hardiness with size. Shows damage at 24–26°F. Plant only if you can give it plenty of room.

F. microcarpa (F. retusa). INDIAN LAUREL. Evergreen tree. Zone TS. Native to India, Malaysia. Moderate growth to 25–30 ft. Beautiful weeping form, with long branches thickly clothed with 2–4-in.-long, blunt-tipped leaves. Light rose to chartreuse new leaves, produced almost continuously, give a pleasing two-tone effect. Trim off lower trailing branches to reveal slim, light gray trunk supporting massive crown. Full sun.

F. m. nitida has dense foliage on upright-growing branches and is admirably suited to formal shearing. Leaves are clear lustrous green, similar in size to those of species. Prune any time of year to size or shape desired.

In some areas, both the species and variety are attacked by a thrips that curls new leaves, stippling them and causing them to fall. 'Green Gem' has thicker, darker green leaves and is apparently unaffected by the thrips.

🏛 **F. pumila (F. repens).** CREEPING FIG. Evergreen vine. Zones LS, CS, TS. Native to China, Japan, Australia. A most unfiglike habit; it is one of few plants that attaches itself securely to wood, masonry, or even metal in barnacle fashion. Because it is grown on walls, and thus protected, it is more often found in colder climates than any other evergreen fig. Grows in sun or shade; not for hot south or west wall.

Looks innocent enough in young stages, making a delicate tracery of tiny, heart-shaped leaves. Neat little juvenile foliage ultimately develops into large (2–4-in.-long), leathery leaves borne on stubby branches that also bear large oblong fruit. In time, stems will envelop a three- or four-story building so completely that it becomes necessary to keep them trimmed away from windows. Safe to use this fig on stone, brick, or stucco houses, but not on wood, as it will trap moisture and encourage rot. Roots are invasive, probably more so than those of most other figs. 'Minima' has shorter, narrower leaves than species. Small, lobed leaves of 'Quercifolia' are like tiny oak leaves. 'Variegata' has standard-size leaves with creamy white markings.

F. religiosa. PEEPUL, BO-TREE. Briefly deciduous tree. Zone TS. Native to India. Large, upright; less spreading than *F. macrophylla.* Foliage is open and delicate, revealing structure of tree at all times. Bark is warm, rich brown. Roundish, pale green leaves are rather crisp and thin textured, 4–7 in. long with long tail-like point. They move easily even in slightest breeze, giving foliage a fluttering effect. Foliage drops completely in spring—a frightening experience for the gardener who has bought an "evergreen" fig. Full sun.

F. retusa. See *F. microcarpa*

SUDDEN LEAF-SHEDDING ON A WEEPING FIG?

The problem is common and often results from the plant's being moved to a new location. If the shedding problem begins shortly after a move, be patient; leaves usually grow back. If the leaves that fall are green, insufficient water is another possible cause; try to keep soil evenly moist. If the plant drops yellow leaves, overwatering may be to blame. Finally, if shedding is accompanied by a sweet smell and sticky leaves, look for scale insects and control them as needed.

FIG, EDIBLE

Moraceae

DECIDUOUS TREES

✿ ZONES MS, LS, CS, TS (DEPENDING ON SELECTION); OR IN POTS

☼ FULL SUN

● REGULAR WATER

Edible Fig

For ornamental relatives, see *Ficus.* Grow fairly fast to 15–30 ft., generally low branched and spreading; where hard freezes are common, wood freezes back severely and plant behaves as a big shrub. Can be held to 10 ft. in big container, or trained as espalier.

Trunks heavy, smooth, gray barked, gnarled in really old trees, picturesque in silhouette. Leaves rough, bright green, with three to five lobes, 4–9 in. long and nearly as wide. Casts dense shade. Winter framework, tropical-looking foliage, strong trunk and branch pattern make fig a top-notch ornamental tree, especially near patio where it can be illuminated from beneath. Protect container plants in winter. Fruit drop is problem immediately above deck or paving.

Not particular about soil. In the Middle South, plant trees near south walls or train trees against them to benefit from reflected heat. Cut back tops hard at planting. As tree grows, prune lightly each winter, cutting out dead wood, crossing branches, and low-hanging branches that interfere with traffic. Pinch back runaway shoots any season. Avoid deep cultivation, which may damage surface roots. Do not use high-nitrogen fertilizers; they stimulate growth at expense of fruit. If burrowing animals are a problem, plant trees in ample wire baskets.

Home garden figs do not need pollinating, and most kinds bear two crops a year. The first comes in June–July on last year's wood; the second and more important comes in September–October from current summer's wood. Ripe figs will detach easily when lifted and bent back toward the branch. Keep fruit picked as it ripens; protect from birds if you can. In late fall, pick off any remaining ripe figs and clean up fallen fruit.

Types differ in climate adaptability; most need prolonged high temperatures to bear good fruit, while some thrive in cooler conditions. Selections are noted below.

'Alma'. Very sweet, medium-size fig with golden brown skin and amber-tan flesh.

'Brown Turkey' ('San Pedro', 'Black Spanish'). Adaptable to most fig climates; widely grown in Southeast. Good garden tree; small, cold-hardy. Fruit has purplish brown skin, pinkish amber flesh; good for fresh eating.

'Celeste' ('Blue Celeste', 'Celestial'). The most widely grown fig in the Southeast. Cold-hardy plant. Bronzy, violet-tinged skin, rosy amber flesh; good for fresh eating.

'Conadria'. Choice thin-skinned white figs blushed violet; white to red flesh, fine flavor. Takes intense heat without splitting.

'Florentine'. ITALIAN HONEY FIG. Large figs with lemon green skin and sweet amber flesh. Similar to 'Kadota'. Bears over a long season. Excellent canning quality.

'Genoa' ('White Genoa'). Greenish yellow skin, with strawberry to yellow flesh.

'Italian Everbearing'. Resembles 'Brown Turkey', but somewhat larger fruit with reddish brown skin. Good fresh or dried.

'Kadota' ('White Kadota'). Tough-skinned fruit has lemon yellow skin, light amber to yellow flesh. Commercial canning type. Strong grower; needs little pruning. If pruned severely, will bear later, with fewer, larger fruits.

'LSU Everbearing'. Medium-large figs, with yellow-green skin and sweet white to amber flesh. Produces fruit from July through fall.

'LSU Gold'. Very large bright yellow fruit with exceptionally sweet amber flesh. Vigorous tree.

'LSU Purple'. Dark purple-red figs, with excellent-flavored light amber to strawberry red flesh. Vigorous, upright tree.

'Magnolia' ('Brunswick'). Medium to large figs with reddish brown skin and amber to strawberry-colored flesh. Widely grown in Southeast.

'Mission' ('Black Mission'). Large tree bearing purple-black figs with pink flesh; good fresh or dried. Grown in areas of Southeast.

'Texas Everbearing'. Medium to large figs with brownish yellow skin, strawberry-colored flesh.

'White Adriatic'. Medium to large, sweet white figs with yellowish green skin, strawberry pink flesh. Very drought tolerant.

FILBERT. See CORYLUS

FILIPENDULA

Rosaceae

PERENNIALS

✿ ZONES US, MS, LS

☼ PARTIAL SHADE, EXCEPT AS NOTED

● ●● AMPLE TO REGULAR WATER

Filipendula rubra 'Venusta'

Like related *Astilbe,* have plumes of tiny flowers above coarsely divided leaves that look like fern fronds. Most species prefer moist to constantly damp soil. Use in borders, naturalistic landscapes, beside ponds.

F. hexapetala. See *F. vulgaris*

F. purpurea. Pink, 3–4-ft.-tall plumes rise above maplelike, 5–7-in. leaves. Selections include 'Alba', with white plumes 2 ft. tall; 'Elegans', bearing 2-ft.-tall white flowers with red stamens; and 'Nana', with salmon pink plumes 12–15 in. tall.

F. rubra. QUEEN OF THE PRAIRIE. Given plenty of moisture and rich soil, can reach 8 ft. high in bloom; bears pink plumes. 'Venusta' has purplish pink flowers and is a little shorter, to 4–6 ft. high.

F. ulmaria. MEADOW SWEET, QUEEN OF THE MEADOW. To 6 ft. high, with 10-in. creamy white plumes. 'Flore Pleno', just 3 ft. tall, has dense plumes of double white flowers; 'Variegata' is similar, but with gold-speckled leaves. 'Aurea' is grown not for flowers but for bright golden leaves; protect from sun.

F. vulgaris (F. hexapetala). DROPWORT. White plumes on 3-ft. stems rise above 10-in., fernlike leaves with 1-in. leaflets. Double-flowered 'Flore Pleno' has heavier-looking plumes. Needs less water than the other species; also prefers full sun in the Upper and Middle South.

F

FIR. See ABIES

FIRECRACKER PLANT. See RUSSELIA equisetiformis

FIRE PINK. See SILENE virginica

FIRETAIL. See ACALYPHA pendula

FIRETHORN. See PYRACANTHA

☫ FIRMIANA simplex (F. platanifolia)

CHINESE PARASOL TREE

Sterculiaceae

DECIDUOUS TREE

☫ ZONES MS, LS, CS, TS

☼ ◐ FULL SUN OR PARTIAL SHADE

● REGULAR WATER

Firmiana simplex

Native to China, Japan. To 30–45 ft. in gardens, fast growing, with unique light gray-green bark. Trunk often is unbranched for 4–5 ft. before dividing into three or more slender, upright, slightly spreading stems that carry lobed, tropical-looking, 1-ft. leaves. Each stem looks as if it could be cut off and carried away as a parasol. Large, loose, upright clusters of greenish white flowers appear at branch ends in early summer. Interesting fruit resembles two opened green pea pods with seeds on margins. Tree goes leafless for a long period in winter—an unusual trait for a tropical-looking tree.

Tolerates all soil types. Does well in courtyards protected from wind. Useful near swimming pools. Difficult to transplant large trees because of deep taproot. Prolific self-seeder; can be a pest.

FISHTAIL PALM. See CARYOTA

FIVELEAF ARALIA. See ACANTHOPANAX sieboldianus

FLAG. See IRIS

FLAMEGOLD. See KOELREUTERIA elegans

FLAME OF THE WOODS. See IXORA coccinea

FLAME VINE. See PYROSTEGIA venusta

FLAME VIOLET. See EPISCIA

FLAMING SWORD. See VRIESEA splendens

FLAX. See LINUM

FLEABANE. See ERIGERON

FLEECE FLOWER. See POLYGONUM

FLORIDA HEATHER. See CUPHEA hyssopifolia

FLORIDA LEUCOTHOE. See AGARISTA populifolia

FLOSS FLOWER. See AGERATUM houstonianum

FLOSS SILK TREE. See CHORISIA

FLOWERING ALMOND, CHERRY. See PRUNUS

FLOWERING BANANA. See MUSA ornata

FLOWERING CRABAPPLE. See MALUS

FLOWERING DOGWOOD. See CORNUS florida

FLOWERING FERN. See OSMUNDA regalis

FLOWERING NECTARINE, PEACH, PLUM. See PRUNUS

FLOWERING QUINCE. See CHAENOMELES

FLOWERING TOBACCO. See NICOTIANA alata

FLOWERY SENNA. See CASSIA corymbosa

FOAMFLOWER. See TIARELLA

FENNEL FEEDS THE GOOD GUYS

Common fennel is one of those prolific but valuable plants that provide pollen and nectar to beneficial insects when those insects aren't feeding on plant-damaging insects and mites. The good guys this plant sustains include hover flies, lacewings, ladybird beetles, paper wasps, and soldier bugs. It's also an important source of food for butterfly larvae.

FOENICULUM vulgare

COMMON FENNEL

Apiaceae (Umbelliferae)

PERENNIAL OR ANNUAL HERB

☫ ZONES VARY BY TYPE

☼ FULL SUN

● MODERATE WATER

Foeniculum vulgare

Two forms of fennel are commonly grown. One is a perennial, used for seasoning; the other is grown as an annual for its edible leaf bases.

The plain species is a perennial (Zones US, MS, LS, CS), cultivated for licorice-flavored seeds and young leaves. Grows to 3–5 ft. tall. Similar to dill, but coarser texture. Yellow-green, finely cut leaves; flat clusters of yellow flowers. Bronze fennel ('Purpurascens', 'Smokey'), 6 ft. tall, has bronzy purple foliage. Start from seed where plants are to be grown. Sow in light, well-drained soil; thin seedlings to 1 ft. apart. Use seeds to season breads; use leaves as garnish for salads, fish. Fennel often grows as a roadside or garden weed; it's attractive until tops turn brown, and even then birds like the seeds. New stems grow in spring from perennial root.

F. v. azoricum, called Florence fennel or finocchio, is grown as a summer annual in all zones. Lower growing (2 ft.) than the species, it has larger, thicker leafstalk bases that are used as a cooked or raw vegetable.

FORGET-ME-NOT. See MYOSOTIS

FORMOSA LILY. See LILIUM formosanum

FORSYTHIA

Oleaceae

DECIDUOUS SHRUBS

☫ ZONES US, MS, LS

☼ FULL SUN

●● REGULAR TO MODERATE WATER

Forsythia intermedia

From late winter to early spring, the bare branches of these fountain-shaped shrubs are covered with yellow flowers. During the rest of the growing season, medium green foliage blends well with other shrubs in the background of border plantings. Leaves are rounded, with pointed tips. Use as screen, espalier, or bank cover; or plant in shrub border. Branches can be forced for indoor bloom in winter.

Tolerate most soils; respond to fertilizer. Prune established plants after bloom: Cut a third of branches that have bloomed down to ground; remove oldest branches, weak or dead wood.

F. 'Arnold Dwarf'. Grows 1½–3 ft. high, to 6 ft. wide. Flowers are sparse and not especially attractive, but plant is a useful, fast-growing ground cover.

F. intermedia. BORDER FORSYTHIA. The most widely grown forsythias are in this hybrid group. Most grow 7–10 ft. tall and have arching branches; smaller selections are also included in the following list.

'Beatrix Farrand'. Upright to 10 ft. tall, 7 ft. wide. Branches thickly set with 2–2½-in.-wide flowers in deep yellow marked with orange.

'Fiesta'. Grows 3–4 ft. high. Deep yellow flowers followed by green-and-yellow variegated leaves that hold their color all summer long.

'Goldtide'. Compact growth to 20 in. tall by 4 ft. wide; profuse bright yellow flowers.

'Goldzauber' ('Gold Charm'). Erect to 6–8 ft. high, with large, deep yellow flowers.

'Karl Sax'. Resembles 'Beatrix Farrand' but is lower growing, neater, more graceful.

'Lynwood' ('Lynwood Gold'). Stiffly upright to 7 ft., with 4–6-ft. spread. Profuse tawny yellow blooms survive spring storms.

'Spectabilis'. Dense, upright, vigorous to 9 ft. Deep yellow flowers.

'Spring Glory'. To about 6 ft. tall, with heavy crop of pale yellow flowers.

'Tetragold'. Grows 3–5 ft. high. Deep yellow blossoms.

F. ovata. KOREAN FORSYTHIA. Shrub to 4–6 ft., spreading wider. Early bloomer, with a profusion of bright yellow flowers. Flower buds are cold-hardy to −20°F.

F. suspensa. WEEPING FORSYTHIA. Dense, upright growth habit to 8–10 ft., with 6–8-ft. spread. Drooping, vinelike branches root where they touch damp soil. Golden yellow flowers. Useful large-scale bank cover. Can be trained as vine; if you support main branches, branchlets will cascade. 'Fortunei' is somewhat more upright, more available in garden centers.

F. viridissima. GREENSTEM FORSYTHIA. Stiff-looking shrub to 10 ft. with deep green foliage, olive green stems, greenish yellow flowers. 'Bronxensis' is slow-growing dwarf form to 16 in. tall, for smaller shrub borders or ground cover. *F. v. koreana (F. koreana)*, to 8 ft., has larger, brighter yellow flowers and attractive purplish autumn foliage.

FORTNIGHT LILY. See DIETES

FOTHERGILLA

Hamamelidaceae

DECIDUOUS SHRUBS

ZONES US, MS, LS

PARTIAL SHADE IN LOWER SOUTH

REGULAR WATER

Fothergilla major

Native to southeastern U.S. Grown principally for fall foliage color, but small, honey-scented white flowers in brushlike, 1–2-in. clusters on zigzagging stems are pretty in spring. Performs best in moist, well-drained, acid soil.

F. gardenii. DWARF FOTHERGILLA, WITCH ALDER. Typically 2–3 ft. high (though it can grow considerably taller) and as wide or wider. Inch-long flower clusters appear before the 1–2½-in.-long leaves. Fall foliage intense yellow and orange red. 'Mt. Airy' is taller than the species, with larger flower clusters, deeper blue-green leaves, and better fall color. 'Blue Mist' also has bluish summer foliage.

F. major. LARGE FOTHERGILLA. Erect shrub to 9 ft. with roundish, 2–4-in.-long leaves turning yellow to orange to purplish red in autumn. Flowers appear with the leaves. Plant formerly known as *F. monticola* is now treated as this species.

FOUNTAIN GRASS. See PENNISETUM

FOUR O'CLOCK. See MIRABILIS jalapa

FOXGLOVE. See DIGITALIS

FOXTAIL LILY. See EREMURUS

FRANKLINIA alatamaha
(Gordonia alatamaha)

FRANKLIN TREE

Theaceae

DECIDUOUS TREE

ZONES US, MS, LS

FULL SUN OR LIGHT SHADE

REGULAR WATER

Franklinia alatamaha

Unusual, handsome tree once native to Georgia, but apparently extinct in the wilds before 1800. Open, airy form; may reach 30 ft., but more typically grows to 10–20 ft. high. Tree tends to be fairly slender when grown with a single trunk, broad spreading with multiple trunks. Attractive dark gray bark has faint white vertical striping. Shiny dark green, spoon-shaped leaves, 4–6 in. long, turn orange and red in fall; they hang on for a long time before dropping. Fragrant, white, 3-in.-wide, five-petaled flowers centered with clusters of yellow stamens open from round white buds July–September, sometimes coinciding with fall foliage color in the Upper South. Blossoms somewhat resemble single camellias—not surprising, since *Franklinia* and *Camellia* belong to the same family. Flowers are followed by small, woody capsules that are split into ten segments, each containing five seeds.

Provide moist, rich, light, acid soil. Good drainage is critical. Not the easiest plant to grow. Susceptible to phytophthora root rot, a fatal soil-borne disease, in heavy, wet soils during hot weather. Grows well in light shade, but has best bloom and fall color in full sun. Easy to grow from seed, blooming in 6 to 7 years. Highly decorative lawn or accent tree. Use for contrast in azalea or rhododendron plantings.

FRAXINUS

ASH

Oleaceae

DECIDUOUS TREES

ZONES VARY BY SPECIES

FULL SUN

REGULAR TO MODERATE WATER

Fraxinus americana

Trees grow fairly fast; most tolerate hot summers, cold winters, and various soils. In many areas, ashes are susceptible to a number of serious problems, including anthracnose and borers, so check before planting. They are chiefly used as street trees, shade trees, and lawn trees.

In most cases, leaves are divided into leaflets. Male and female flowers (generally inconspicuous, in clusters) grow on separate trees in some species, on same tree in others. In latter case, flowers are often followed by clusters of single-seeded, winged fruit, often in such abundance that they can be a litter problem. When flowers are on separate trees, you'll get fruit on female tree only if it grows near male tree.

F. americana. WHITE ASH. Zones US, MS, LS, CS. Native to eastern U.S. Grows to 80 ft. or more, with straight trunk and oval-shaped crown. Leaves 8–15 in. long, with five to nine oval leaflets; dark green above, paler beneath. Foliage turns purplish in fall. Male and female flowers on separate trees, but plants sold are generally seedlings, so you don't know what you're getting. If you end up with both male and female trees, you will get a heavy crop of seed; both litter and seedlings can be problems.

Seedless selections include 'Autumn Applause' and 'Autumn Purple', both with exceptionally good, long-lasting purple fall color; 'Champaign County', a dense grower with pale yellow fall color; 'Greenspire', narrow upright habit, deep orange fall color; 'Rosehill', with bronzy red fall color; 'Royal Purple', upright, with purple autumn leaves; and 'Skyline', an upright oval with brown and purple fall color. ▶

F. berlandieri. MEXICAN ASH. Zones LS, CS. Native to southern Texas and northeastern Mexico, where it's often found along stream banks. Grows very fast when young, eventually reaching 30–40 ft., with a symmetrical, dense crown that provides good shade. Leaves glossy green, three to five leaflets. 'Fan-Tex' is a seedless selection.

F. cuspidata. FRAGRANT ASH. Zones LS, CS. Native to Texas, Southwest, Mexico. Bushy shrub or small tree, often 10–15 ft. tall, sometimes 20 ft. Leaves are divided into seven leaflets, 2½ in. long, and turn yellow in fall. Long panicles of white, vanilla-scented flowers cover the tree in mid- or late spring, making a very showy display against a dark background. Tolerant of drought and alkaline soil. Grows fast if watered regularly.

F. ornus. FLOWERING ASH, MANNA ASH. Zones US, MS; best in Upper South. Native to southern Europe and Asia Minor. Grows to 30–40 ft. with rounded crown 20–30 ft. wide. Supplies luxuriant mass of foliage. Leaves 8–10 in. long, divided into seven to eleven oval, medium green, 2-in.-long leaflets with toothed edges. Foliage turns to soft shades of lavender and yellow in fall. In spring, displays quantities of fluffy, branched, 3–5-in.-long clusters of showy, fragrant white to greenish white blossoms.

F. pennsylvanica (F. lanceolata). GREEN ASH. Zones US, MS, LS, CS. Native to eastern U.S. Typically 50–60 ft. tall, forming irregular oval crown. Gray-brown bark; dense, twiggy structure. Bright green leaves 10–12 in. long, divided into five to nine rather narrow, 4–6-in.-long leaflets. Inconsistent yellow fall color. For assured fall color, plant a named selection. Takes wet soil and severe cold, but foliage burns in hot, dry winds. Male and female flowers on separate trees.

Seedless kinds include 'Emerald', round headed, glossy, deep green leaves, yellow fall color; 'Marshall's Seedless', a seedless male form with lustrous, deep green foliage and good, yellow fall color; 'Summit', upright habit, good golden yellow fall color; and 'Urbanite', pyramidal shape and bronze fall color.

F. texensis. TEXAS ASH. Zones MS, LS, CS. Native to Oklahoma and Texas. Round-headed tree to 35–50 ft., moderately fast growing. Leaves have five dark green, 3-in.-long leaflets, which turn random gold, orange, maroon in fall. Particularly suited to dry, rocky, limestone soils, but well adapted to regular garden watering and average soil. Usually long lived. Very drought tolerant.

F. velutina. ARIZONA ASH. Zones US, MS, LS, CS. Withstands hot, dry conditions and cold to about −10°F. Grows about 30 ft. (possibly to 50 ft.) tall. Pyramidal when young; spreading, more open when mature. Leaves divided into three to five narrow to oval, 3-in.-long leaflets; turn bright yellow in fall. Male and female flowers on separate trees.

'Rio Grande' is most commonly grown in Texas. Its leaflets are larger and darker green than those of the species; they resist wind.

FRECKLE FACE. See HYPOESTES phyllostachya

FREESIA

Iridaceae

CORMS

ZONES CS, TS; OR INDOORS

FULL SUN OR PARTIAL SHADE

REGULAR WATER DURING GROWTH AND BLOOM

Freesia Hybrid

Native to South Africa. Prized for rich perfume of flowers; white and yellow types tend to be more fragrant than those with blooms in other colors. Slender, branched stems grow 1–1½ ft. tall, about same height as lowest leaves; stem leaves shorter. Flowers tubular, 2 in. long, in one-sided spikes. Older selection 'Alba' has fragrant white or creamy blooms; newer, larger-flowered types with 1–1½-ft. stems are Tecolote and Dutch hybrids with white, pink, red, lavender, purple, blue, yellow, and orange flowers, mixed or in selections named for single colors. Freesias will self-sow if faded flowers are not removed; volunteers tend to revert to cream marked with purple and yellow.

Freesias are hardy to 20°F. Plant corms 2 in. deep (pointed end up) in fall in sunny, well-drained soil. Plants dry up after bloom, start growing again in fall; they increase rapidly. In Upper, Middle, and Lower South, plant 2 in. deep, 2 in. apart in pots; grow indoors in sunny window. Keep room temperature as cool as possible at night. Freesias are easily grown from seed sown in July–August; often bloom following spring. Flowering potted freesias grown from chilled and stored corms are available throughout the year.

FRENCH HOLLYHOCK. See MALVA sylvestris

FRENCH LAVENDER. See LAVANDULA dentata

FRENCH MARIGOLD. See TAGETES patula

FRENCH ROSE. See ROSA gallica

FRENCH TARRAGON. See ARTEMISIA dracunculus

FRINGE BELLS. See SHORTIA soldanelloides

FRINGED BLEEDING HEART. See DICENTRA eximia

FRINGED CAMPION. See SILENE polypetala

FRINGE HYACINTH. See MUSCARI comosum

FRINGE TREE. See CHIONANTHUS

FRITILLARIA

FRITILLARY

Liliaceae

BULBS

ZONES US, MS

FULL SUN OR LIGHT SHADE

REGULAR WATER DURING GROWTH AND BLOOM

Fritillaria imperialis

In spring, unbranched stems, 6 in.–4 ft. high, are topped by bell-like, nodding flowers, often unusually colored and mottled. Use in woodland gardens or borders. In fall, plant bulbs in porous soil with ample humus. Set *F. meleagris* 3–4 in. deep; set *F. imperialis* 4–5 in. deep. Bulbs sometimes rest a year after planting or after blooming, so put in enough for a yearly display. They also may take a year or two after planting to begin blooming. Once established, they resent disturbance.

F. imperialis. CROWN IMPERIAL. Native to Europe. Bears stout stalk 3½–4 ft. tall, clothed with broad, glossy leaves and topped by a circle of 2–3-in.-long bells in red, orange, or yellow; tuft of leaves above flowers. Bulb and plant have somewhat unpleasant odor.

F. meleagris. CHECKERED LILY, SNAKESHEAD. Native to damp meadows in Europe, Asia; tolerates occasional flooding. Showy 2-in. bells, marked with reddish brown and purple, atop 1–1½-ft. stems. Lance-shaped leaves are 3–6 in. long. There is also a white-blossomed form.

FRUITLAND ARBORVITAE. See PLATYCLADUS orientalis 'Fruitlandii'

FUCHSIA hybrida

HYBRID FUCHSIA

Onagraceae

EVERGREEN OR DECIDUOUS SHRUBS

ZONE US

PARTIAL SHADE

REGULAR WATER

Fuchsia hybrida
Double Type

Here belong nearly all garden fuchsias. Hundreds of selections are available, with many color combinations. Sepals (top parts that flare back) are always white, red, or pink. Corolla (inside part of flower) may be almost any color possible within range of white, blue violet, purple, pink, red, and shades approaching orange. Flowers may be single- or double-petaled, varying in size from as small as a shelled peanut to as large as a child's fist. Plants vary from erect-growing shrubs 3–12 ft. high to trailing types grown in hanging containers. Good hummingbird plants.

Fuchsia hybrida
Single Type

Soil mix for containers or planting beds should be porous, water retentive, and rich with organic matter. Heavy mulching helps to maintain soil moisture in beds. Plants dislike hot summers; flowers may drop off. When foliage wilts in extreme heat, mist to cool it down. Apply light doses of complete fertilizer frequently. If plant becomes leggy, pinch branch tips to force side branching. Pick off old flowers as they start to fade.

Fumariaceae. This family consists of annuals and perennials, usually with irregularly shaped flowers. *Corydalis* and bleeding heart *(Dicentra)* are examples. This family is considered by many to be included in the poppy family (Papaveraceae).

GAILLARDIA

BLANKET FLOWER

Asteraceae (Compositae)

PERENNIALS AND ANNUALS

ALL ZONES

FULL SUN

MODERATE WATER

Gaillardia grandiflora

Native to Southeast, Midwest. Low-growing summer bloomers with daisylike flowers in warm colors—yellow, bronze, scarlet. Love the heat, need good drainage. Easy to grow from seed and fine for cutting and borders; often reseed. Adapted to almost any well-drained soil. Don't need fertilizing. No serious pests.

G. aristata. Perennial. This parent of the hybrid *G. grandiflora* has been replaced to a large degree by its offspring, but the wild form is still much used in prairie restoration and wildflower mixes. Grows 2–2½ ft. tall, with flower heads up to 4 in. wide. Colors range from yellow to red; most familiar form is red with a jagged yellow border on the ray flowers.

G. grandiflora. Perennial. Developed from native species *G. aristata* and *G. pulchella*. To 2–4 ft. high. Roughish gray-green foliage; flower heads 3–4 in. across, single or double petaled. Produces much variation in flower color: warm shades of red and yellow with orange or maroon bands. Exceptionally long bloom period for a perennial—from early summer until frost. Plants flower first year from seed. Can be short lived in hottest, most humid areas.

Many strains and selections are available, including dwarf kinds and types with extra-large flowers. 'Goblin', 1 ft. tall, is a good compact kind with large, deep red flowers bordered in bright yellow. 'Goblin Yellow' is similar, but with yellow blooms. 'Baby Cole', another red-and-yellow type, grows 7–8 in. tall. The following are all 2½ ft. tall: 'Burgundy', deep red; 'Tokajer', pure orange; 'Torchlight', yellow blooms bordered with red.

G. pulchella. INDIAN BLANKET. Annual. To 1½–2 ft. high. Soft, hairy leaves. Bears 2-in.-wide flower heads in warm shades of red, yellow, gold; blossoms carried on long, whiplike stems. Easy to grow; sow seeds in warm soil after frost danger is past. Tolerates salt spray and poor, sandy soil—the best flower for planting on the beach. 'Lorenziana' has no ray flowers (petals); instead, disc flowers are enlarged into little star-tipped bells, making blooms look like balls of bright fluff. Double Gaiety strain (1½ ft. tall) has flowers that range from near white to maroon; often bicolored. Lollipop strain is similar but only 10–12 in. tall.

GALANTHUS

SNOWDROP

Amaryllidaceae

BULBS

ZONES US, MS

FULL SUN OR PARTIAL SHADE

REGULAR WATER DURING GROWTH AND BLOOM

G. NIVALIS BULB IS POISONOUS IF INGESTED

Galanthus nivalis

Closely related to *Leucojum* (snowflake) and often confused with it. White, nodding, bell-shaped blossoms are borne one per stalk. Inner flower segments have green tips; larger outer segments are pure white. Plants have two or three basal leaves. Use in rock gardens or under flowering shrubs; naturalize in woodland; or grow in pots. Plant in autumn, in moist soil with ample humus; set 3–4 in. deep, 2–3 in. apart. Do not divide often; when necessary, divide right after bloom. Best in Upper South.

G. elwesii. GIANT SNOWDROP. Globular bells to 2 in. long on 1-ft. stems; two or three strap-shaped, 1¼-in.-wide leaves, 4 in. long (elongating to as much as 1 ft. after bloom). Blooms January–February.

G. nivalis. COMMON SNOWDROP. Delicate version of *G. elwesii*; flowers 1 in. long on 6–9-in. stems, February–March; leaves very narrow.

GALAX urceolata (G. aphylla)

GALAX

Diapensiaceae

PERENNIAL

ZONES US, MS, LS

PARTIAL OR FULL SHADE

REGULAR WATER

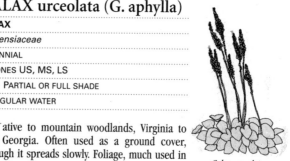

Galax urceolata

Native to mountain woodlands, Virginia to Georgia. Often used as a ground cover, although it spreads slowly. Foliage, much used in indoor arrangements, gives this plant its real distinction. Grows in basal tufts; evergreen leaves are shiny, heart shaped, 5 in. across, turn bronzy in fall unless plants are in deep shade. Foliage height is 6–9 in.; in early summer, flower stems rise to 2½ ft., bearing foxtails of small white flowers at their tips.

Grow in acid soil with much organic material—preferably mulch of leaf mold. Locate under plants that appreciate the same conditions: dogwood, rhododendron, azalea, pieris. Space 1 ft. apart.

GALEOBDOLON luteum. See LAMIUM galeobdolon

GALIUM odoratum (Asperula odorata)

SWEET WOODRUFF

Rubiaceae

PERENNIAL

ZONES US, MS, LS

PARTIAL OR FULL SHADE

REGULAR OR CONSIDERABLE WATER

Galium odoratum

Attractive, low-spreading perennial that brings to mind deep-shaded woods. Slender, square stems 6–12 in. high, encircled every inch or so by whorls of six to eight aromatic, bristle-tipped leaves. Clusters of tiny white flowers show above foliage in late spring and summer. Leaves and stems give off fragrant, haylike odor when dried; used to make May wine.

In the shade garden, sweet woodruff is best used as ground cover or edging. Will spread rapidly in rich soil with abundant moisture—can become a pest if allowed to grow unchecked. Self-sows freely. Increase by dividing in fall or spring. Give full shade in Lower South.

GALPHIMIA glauca
(Thryallis glauca)

Malpighiaceae

EVERGREEN SHRUB

🌿 ZONES CS, TS

☼ FULL SUN

💧 MODERATE WATER

Galphimia glauca

Native to Mexico and Guatemala. Tropical evergreen shrub, 4–6 ft. tall, grows outdoors only in the Coastal and Tropical South. Its 2-in., oblong, gray-green leaves are handsome, and its branched clusters of bright yellow flowers profuse and showy, summer and fall. Fertilize from spring through fall. Prune out crowded branches to keep shape open. Brittle stems break easily, so don't plant where people will repeatedly brush against the foliage. In cooler climates, grow in a pot that you can bring indoors for the winter.

GARDEN BURNET. See SANGUISORBA minor

🏛 GARDENIA

Rubiaceae

EVERGREEN SHRUBS

🌿 ZONES MS (PROTECTED), LS, CS

☼ ◑ FULL SUN OR LIGHT SHADE

💧 REGULAR WATER

Gardenia jasminoides

White, intensely fragrant flowers contrast sharply with shiny, leathery, dark green leaves. Double forms are classic corsage blooms. Gardenias do well in pots, on decks and terraces, or in greenhouses; they don't make good house plants because of susceptibility to mites, mealybugs, and whiteflies.

G. jasminoides (G. augusta). COMMON GARDENIA, CAPE JASMINE. Native to China. Glossy bright green leaves and usually double white flowers. Hardy to about 10°F without damage. Will survive 0°F, but plant is likely to die back to roots.

Soil should drain fast but retain water, too; condition it with plenty of organic matter such as peat moss or ground bark. Plant high (like azaleas and rhododendrons) and avoid crowding by other plants and competing roots. Mulch plants instead of cultivating. Feed every 3 to 4 weeks during growing season with acid plant food, fish emulsion, or blood meal. Prune to remove straggly branches, faded flowers. Control whiteflies, aphids, other sucking insects.

The many selections are useful in containers or raised beds, as hedges, espaliers, low screens, or single plants.

'August Beauty'. Grows 4–6 ft. high and blooms heavily, midspring into fall. Large double flowers.

'Chuck Hayes'. Extra-hardy type, possibly as cold-hardy as 'Klein's Hardy'. To 4 ft. high. Double flowers in summer, heavy rebloom in fall.

'First Love' ('Aimee'). Somewhat larger shrub than 'August Beauty', with larger flowers. Spring bloom.

'Golden Magic'. Reaches 3 ft. tall, 2 ft. wide in 2 to 3 years, eventually larger. Extra-full flowers open white, gradually age to deep golden yellow. Spring through summer, peaking in midspring.

'Kimura Shikazaki' ('Four Seasons'). Compact plant 2–3 ft. tall. Flowers similar to those of 'Veitchii', but slightly less fragrant. Extremely long bloom season—spring to fall.

'Klein's Hardy'. Developed for cold-winter areas; hardy to 0°F. To 2–3 ft. high. Single flowers in summer. Grow in a wind-protected site.

'Miami Supreme'. Grows to 6 ft. tall, with large double flowers (4–6 in. wide) in spring, periodic flowering through summer.

'Mystery'. Best-known selection; has 4–5-in., double white flowers, mid- to late spring or longer. Tends to be rangy and needs pruning to keep it neat. Can reach 6–8 ft.

'Radicans'. Grows 6–12 in. tall and spreads to 2–3 ft., with small dark green leaves and inch-wide double flowers in summer. Good small-scale ground cover, container plant. Not as cold-hardy as species. Not well suited to Middle South; only marginally hardy in upper half of Lower South. 'Radicans Variegata' has gray-green leaves with white markings.

'Veitchii'. Compact 3–4½-ft. plant with many 1–1½-in. fully double flowers midspring into fall, sometimes even during warm winter. Prolific bloom, reliable grower.

'White Gem'. At 1–2 ft. tall, useful for edgings, in containers, or in raised beds, where fragrance of single creamy white summer flowers can be appreciated.

GARDENIA'S DEMANDS

Like a temperamental artist, the gardenia has its own set of rules. Fuss over them and the plants give beauty. Ignore them and they yellow and die. For thriving gardenias, give acid soil, regular water and feeding, and good soil drainage. Night temperatures between 50° and 55°F are necessary for formation of flower buds.

GARLIC

Liliaceae

BULB

🌿 ALL ZONES

☼ FULL SUN

💧 REGULAR WATER

Garlic

For ornamental types, see *Allium*. Seed stores and mail-order suppliers sell mother bulbs ("sets") for planting. In Upper South, plant early in spring. In Middle, Lower, Coastal, and Tropical South, plant October–December for early summer harvest. Break bulbs up into cloves and plant base downward, 1–2 in. deep, 2–3 in. apart, in rows 1 ft. apart. Harvest when leafy tops fall over; air-dry bulbs, remove tops and roots, and store in cool place. Giant or elephant garlic has unusually large (fist-size) bulbs and mild garlic flavor. Same culture as regular garlic.

GARLIC CHIVES. See ALLIUM tuberosum

GAURA lindheimeri

GAURA

Onagraceae

PERENNIAL

🌿 ZONES US, MS, LS, CS

☼ FULL SUN

◐ 💧 REGULAR TO LITTLE WATER

Gaura lindheimeri

Native to Texas and Louisiana. Airy plant growing to 2¼–4 ft. high. Stalkless leaves, to 1½–3½ in. long, grow directly on stems. Branching flower spikes bear many 1-in.-long white blossoms that open from pink buds closely set on stems. Long bloom period (often from late spring into fall), with only a few blossoms opening at a time. Flowers age to rosy color, then drop off cleanly, but seed-bearing spikes should be cut

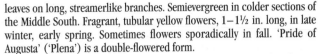

to improve appearance, prevent overly enthusiastic self-sowing, and prolong bloom. 'Whirling Butterflies' is a bit shorter and more compact than the species, with larger flowers.

Needs good drainage. Used widely in most of the South. Performs best in the Southwest, where it is a profusely blooming, long-lived perennial. Taproot makes it very drought tolerant. Clumps never need dividing; for additional plants, let some volunteer seedlings grow. Prefers lean, unfertilized soil. Planting in rich soil results in legginess and sparse bloom.

GAZANIA

GAZANIA, GAZANIA DAISY

Asteraceae (Compositae)

PERENNIALS, OFTEN TREATED AS ANNUALS

✓ ALL ZONES

☀ FULL SUN

💧 REGULAR TO MODERATE WATER

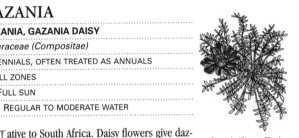

Gazania 'Copper King'

Native to South Africa. Daisy flowers give dazzling color display during peak bloom in late spring, early summer, and they continue to bloom intermittently throughout the year. Gazanias grow well in almost any well-drained soil. Feed once in spring with slow-acting fertilizer. Divide plants every 3 to 4 years. In the Upper, Middle, and Lower South, carry gazanias through winter by taking cuttings in fall as you would for annual geraniums.

The two basic types are clumping and trailing. Clumping gazanias (complex hybrids among a number of species) form a mound of evergreen leaves—dark green above, gray and woolly beneath, often lobed. Flowers 3–4 in. wide, on 6–10-in.-long stems; they open on sunny days, close at night and in cloudy weather. Available in single colors—yellow, orange, white, or rosy pink, with reddish purple petal undersides, often with dark blossom centers—or in a mixture of hybrids (as plants or seeds) in different colors. Seed-grown kinds include Carnival (many colors, silver leaves); Chansonette (early blooming, compact; medium-size round flowers); Harlequin (many colors, eyed and banded); Mini-Star (compact, floriferous plants; named selections include 'Mini-Star Tangerine', 'Mini-Star Yellow'); Sundance (5-in. flowers, striped or banded); and Sunshine (big, multicolored flowers, gray foliage).

Selections of special merit are 'Aztec Queen' (multicolored), 'Burgundy', 'Copper King', and 'Fiesta Red'; all best used in small-scale plantings, though the last is sturdy enough for large areas. 'Moonglow' is double-flowered bright yellow of unusual vigor; its blossoms, unlike most, stay open even on overcast, dull days.

Trailing gazanias (*G. rigens leucolaena*, formerly sold as *G. uniflora* or *G. leucolaena*) grow about as tall as clumping ones, but spread rapidly by long trailing stems. Foliage is clean silvery gray; flowers are yellow, white, orange, or bronze. Larger-flowered kinds are 'Sunburst' (orange, black eye) and 'Sunglow' (yellow). 'Sunrise Yellow' has large, black-eyed yellow flowers; leaves are green. Hybrids are superior to older kinds in length of bloom, resistance to dieback. Trailing gazanias are useful on banks, or grow them at top of wall and allow them to trail over. Attractive in hanging baskets.

🎋GELSEMIUM sempervirens

CAROLINA JESSAMINE, YELLOW JESSAMINE

Loganiaceae

EVERGREEN VINE

✓ ZONES MS, LS, CS

☀ ◑ ● BEST IN FULL SUN; TOLERATES SHADE

💧 REGULAR WATER

☣ ALL PARTS ARE POISONOUS IF INGESTED

Gelsemium sempervirens

Native to southeastern U.S. State flower of South Carolina. Shrubby and twining vine; moderate growth to 20 ft. Clean pairs of shiny, light green, 1–4-in.-long

leaves on long, streamerlike branches. Semievergreen in colder sections of the Middle South. Fragrant, tubular yellow flowers, 1–1½ in. long, in late winter, early spring. Sometimes flowers sporadically in fall. 'Pride of Augusta' ('Plena') is a double-flowered form.

On trellis, vine will cascade and swing in wind; when trained on house, makes delicate green curtain of branches. Often trained on fences and mailboxes. Can get top-heavy; in this case, cut back severely. Also used as ground cover, especially on banks; keep trimmed to 3 ft. high. For best bloom and densest growth, plant in full sun, though plant will tolerate shade.

GENEVA CARPET BUGLEWEED. See AJUGA genevensis

Gentianaceae. The gentian family includes annual and perennial plants from several parts of the world. Many have blue, purple, or white flowers, such as those of *Eustoma.*

Geraniaceae. The cranesbill family of annuals and perennials (the latter sometimes shrubby) includes true geranium and *Pelargonium.*

GERANIUM

CRANESBILL

Geraniaceae

PERENNIALS

✓ ZONES US, MS, LS

☀ ◑ AFTERNOON SHADE

💧 REGULAR WATER, EXCEPT AS NOTED

Geranium pratense

The common indoor/outdoor plant that most people know as geranium is, botanically, *Pelargonium.* True geraniums, considered here, are hardy plants. Many types bloom over a fairly long period, bearing flowers that are attractive though not as showy as those of pelargonium. Carried singly or in clusters of two or three, flowers have five overlapping petals that look alike. (Pelargonium blossoms also have five petals, but two point in one direction, the other three in the opposite direction.) Colors include rose, blue, and purple; a few are pure pink or white. Beaklike fruit that follows the flowers accounts for the common name "cranesbill." Leaves are roundish or kidney shaped, lobed or deeply cut; plants may be upright or trailing. Good in perennial borders; some are useful as small-scale ground covers.

Give afternoon shade. All species appreciate moist, well-drained soil. Clumps of most types can be left in place for many years before they decline due to crowding; at that point, divide clumps in early spring. Increase plantings by transplanting rooted portions from a clump's edge. Most types bloom heavily in spring and early summer, then go dormant when the weather gets hot in July and August. Longest bloom occurs in Upper South and southern Midwest.

G. cinereum. Grows to 6 in. tall, much wider, with deeply cut dark green leaves. Inch-wide pink flowers with darker veining appear in late spring–summer. 'Ballerina' has lilac-pink flowers with purple veining; blooms over a long summer season. 'Lawrence Flatman' has slightly larger flowers of a deeper color. *G. c. subcaulescens* has deep purplish red flowers with black centers.

G. dalmaticum. Dwarf (6-in.) plant with glossy, 1½-in., finely cut leaves and bright pink, 1-in. flowers in spring. Useful in rock garden.

G. endressii. Bushy, 1–1½ ft. high. Leaves 2–3 in. across, deeply cut in five lobes. Flowers rose pink, about 1 in. across. 'Wargrave Pink' is a more compact form with salmon pink flowers.

G. himalayense (G. grandiflorum). Wiry, branching stems 1–2 ft. high. Leaves roundish, five lobed, long stalked, 1¾ in. across. Flowers in

SOUTHERN HERITAGE PLANTS
IDENTIFIED BY SYMBOL 🎋

clusters, lilac with purple veins and red-purple eye, 1½–2 in. across. 'Birch Double' ('Plenum') has double flowers of somewhat lighter shade.

G. 'Johnson's Blue'. Hybrid resembling *G. himalayense* parent, but leaves are more finely divided. Blue-violet, 2-in.-wide flowers.

G. macrorrhizum. To 8–10 in. high, spreading by underground roots. Inch-wide spring flowers are deep magenta; leaves with five to seven lobes are fragrant and have attractive autumn tints. Good ground cover for small areas, though it can overwhelm delicate smaller plants. 'Bevan's Variety' has deep reddish purple flowers, 'Cambridge' pure pink blooms. Other pinks include 'Ingwersen's Variety' and 'Marjorie's'. 'Spessart' ('Album') has white flowers with pink sepals and stamens.

G. maculatum. WILD GERANIUM, WILD CRANESBILL. Native to eastern North America; the only commonly cultivated native cranesbill. To 2 ft. tall and somewhat narrower, with deeply lobed leaves and an abundance of lilac-pink, 1–1½-in. flowers in spring. 'Album' has white blooms.

G. oxonianum. Hybrid between *G. endressii* and *G. sanguineum striatum*. 'Claridge Druce' is a vigorous spreader 2–3 ft. tall, 3 ft. wide, with finely cut grayish green leaves and large pink, dark-veined flowers blooming over a long period.

G. platypetalum. Grows to 16 in. tall. Dark violet-blue flowers to nearly 2 in. wide. Late spring bloomer.

G. pratense. Common border perennial to 3 ft. Upright, branching stems; shiny green leaves, 3–6 in. across, deeply cut in seven lobes. Flowers about 1 in. wide, typically blue with reddish veins; often vary in color. Blooms late spring into summer. 'Mrs. Kendall Clark' has pale blue flowers with lighter veining.

G. sanguineum. Grows 1½ ft. high; trailing stems spread to 2 ft. Leaves roundish, 1–2½ in. across, with five to seven lobes; turn blood red in fall. Deep purple to almost crimson flowers, 1½ in. wide, bloom from late spring well into summer. 'Album' is somewhat taller than species and has white flowers. *G. s. striatum* (*G. s.* 'Prostratum', *G. lancastriense*) is a dwarf form, lower and more compact, with light pink flowers heavily veined with red (its seedlings may vary somewhat); an excellent rock garden or foreground plant. Other 1–1½-ft. selections include 'John Elsley', pink with deeper pink veins; 'Max Frei', reddish purple; 'New Hampshire', deep purple; and 'Vision', reddish purple.

G. sylvaticum. Shade-loving plant to 3 ft. tall. Late spring to early summer flowers, 1 in. wide, range in color from bluish to reddish purple.

G. wallichianum. Grows 1 ft. tall, 3 ft. wide. Lilac flowers with a white eye. 'Buxton's Variety' has pure blue flowers.

WHICH IS REALLY A GERANIUM?

Gardeners use the word "geranium" to speak of ivy geraniums, fancy-leafed geraniums, common geraniums, and scented geraniums, all of which botanically are species of *Pelargonium*. Botanists define *Geranium* by the fact that all have five identical-looking overlapping petals in their flowers. For the botanical definition of *Pelargonium*, see that entry.

GERBERA jamesonii

GERBERA DAISY, TRANSVAAL DAISY

Asteraceae (Compositae)

PERENNIAL IN COASTAL AND TROPICAL SOUTH; ANNUAL ELSEWHERE

✔ ALL ZONES

☼ ◑ FULL SUN OR PARTIAL SHADE

💧 REGULAR WATER

Gerbera jamesonii

Native to South Africa. The most elegant and sophisticated of daisies. Lobed leaves to 10 in. long spring from root crowns that spread slowly to form big clumps. Slender-rayed, 4-in. daisies (one to a stem) rise directly from crowns on 1½-ft., erect or slightly curving stems. Colors

range from cream through yellow to coral, orange, flame, and red. Flowers are first-rate for arrangements; cut them as soon as fully open and slit an inch at bottom of stem before placing in water. Blooms any time of year with peaks in early summer, late fall.

The wild Transvaal daisy was orange red. Plants sold as hybrids are merely seedlings or divisions in mixed colors. Specialists have bred duplex and double strains. Duplex flowers have two rows of rays and are often larger (to 5–6 in. across) on taller (2–2½-ft.) stems. In doubles, all flowers are rays and flowers vary widely in form—some flat, some deep, some swirled, some bicolored. Blackheart and Ebony Eyes strains have dark-centered flowers. Double Parade strain has double flowers on stems 7–10 in. long. Happipot strain has 4-in. flowers on 6-in. stems.

All types need excellent drainage; if drainage is poor, grow plants in raised beds. Plant about 2 ft. apart with the crowns at least ½ in. above surface. Feed frequently. Keep old leaves picked off. Let the plants remain until crowded; divide February–April, leaving two or three buds on each division. As a house or greenhouse plant, requires bright light and night temperature of 60°F.

Plant as seedlings from flats, as divisions or clumps, or from pots. To grow your own from seed, sow thinly in sandy, peaty soil at 70°F. Water carefully; allow 4 to 6 weeks to sprout. Takes 6 to 18 months to flower. Seed must be fresh to germinate well; seed specialists can supply fresh seed of single, double, or duplex strains. Doubles come about 60 percent true from seed.

GERMANDER. See TEUCRIUM

GERMAN STATICE. See GONIOLIMON tataricum

Gesneriaceae. The gesneriads are perennials, usually tropical or subtropical, grown for attractive flowers or foliage. Although a few are rock garden perennials, most are grown as house plants. Examples are African violet (*Saintpaulia*) and gloxinia (*Sinningia*).

GEUM chiloense

GEUM

Rosaceae

PERENNIAL

✔ ZONES US, MS, LS

☼ ◑ PARTIAL SHADE IN LOWER SOUTH

💧 REGULAR WATER

Geum chiloense

Double, semidouble, or single flowers in bright orange, yellow, and red over long season (spring to late summer) if dead blooms are removed. Foliage handsome; mounds to 15 in. Leaves divided into many leaflets. Evergreen except in coldest winters. Leafy flowering stems reach about 2 ft.; flowers are about 1½ in. wide. Good in borders and for cut flowers.

Ordinary garden soil; needs good drainage. Grow from seed sown in early spring, or divide plants in autumn or early spring. Better performer and longer lived in Upper and Middle South than in Lower South. Semidouble selections include 'Dolly North', bright orange; 'Fire Opal', orange scarlet; and 'Red Wings', scarlet with exceptionally long spring to autumn bloom season. Double types include 'Lady Stratheden', yellow; 'Mrs. Bradshaw', scarlet; and 'Princess Juliana', copper.

GIANT DAISY. See CHRYSANTHEMUM serotinum

GIANT FEATHER GRASS. See STIPA gigantea

GIANT GARLIC. See GARLIC

GIANT GROUNDSEL. See LIGULARIA wilsoniana

GIANT HYSSOP. See AGASTACHE

GIANT REED. See ARUNDO donax

GIANT TIMBER BAMBOO. See PHYLLOSTACHYS bambusoides

GINGER. See ZINGIBER officinale

GINGER LILY. See COSTUS, HEDYCHIUM

GINKGO biloba

MAIDENHAIR TREE, GINKGO

Ginkgoaceae

DECIDUOUS TREE

ZONES US, MS, LS, CS

FULL SUN

REGULAR TO MODERATE WATER

Ginkgo biloba

Graceful tree, attractive in any season, especially in fall when leathery, light green leaves of spring and summer suddenly turn gold. Fall leaves linger (they practically glow when backlit by the sun), then drop quickly and cleanly to make a golden carpet where they fall. Related to conifers but differs in having broad (1–4-in.-wide), fan-shaped leaves rather than needlelike foliage. In shape and veining, leaves resemble leaflets of maidenhair fern, hence tree's common name. Can grow to 70–80 ft., but most mature trees are 35–50 ft. May be gawky in youth, but becomes well proportioned with age—narrow to spreading or even umbrella shaped. Usually grows slowly, about 1 ft. a year, but under ideal conditions can grow up to 3 ft. a year.

Plant only male trees (grafted or grown from cuttings of male plants); female trees produce messy, fleshy, ill-smelling fruit in quantity. Named selections listed are male. Use as street tree, lawn tree. Plant in deep, loose, well-drained soil. Be sure plant is not root-bound in pot. Stake young tree to keep stem straight; young growth may be brittle, but wood becomes strong with age. In general, ginkgos are not bothered by insects or diseases, and they're very tolerant of air pollution, heat, and acid or alkaline conditions.

'Autumn Gold'. Upright, eventually rather broad and spreading.

'Fairmount'. Fast-growing, broadly pyramidal form. Straighter main stem than 'Autumn Gold', requires less staking.

'Princeton Sentry'. Fairly narrow, conical shape.

'Saratoga'. Erect, rounded, and somewhat smaller than other ginkgo selections, with narrow leaves deeply split at the ends. Pendulous leaves give tree a graceful character.

'Shangri-La'. Pyramidal shape (broader than 'Princeton Sentry', narrower than 'Autumn Gold').

GLADE FERN. See ATHYRIUM pycnocarpon

GLADIOLUS

Iridaceae

CORMS

ZONES VARY BY TYPE; OR DIG AND STORE

FULL SUN

REGULAR WATER DURING GROWTH AND BLOOM

Gladiolus callianthus

All have sword-shaped leaves and tubular flowers, often flaring or ruffled, in simple or branching, usually one-sided spikes. Extremely wide color range. Bloom from spring to fall, depending on kind and time of planting. Superb cut flowers. Good in borders or beds behind mounding plants that cover lower parts of stems, or in large containers with low annuals at base. Thrips are a pest.

Plant in rich, sandy soil. Set corms about four times deeper than their height, somewhat more shallowly in heavy soils. Space big corms 6 in. apart, smaller ones 4 in. apart. Corms can generally be left in the ground from year to year in indicated zones; in the Upper South, dig soon after first frost in autumn. Corms should be dried, then stored in single layer in flats or ventilated trays in a cool place (40–50°F). In the Tropical South, refrigerate corms for a month before planting. Dig and store when foliage withers after plant blooms.

Baby gladiolus. Zones LS, CS, TS for most; additionally, Zones US, MS for winter-hardy types. Hybrid race resulting from breeding red-flowered *G. colvillei* with other species. Flaring, 2½–3¼-in. flowers in short, loose spikes on 1½-ft. stems. Flowers white, pink, red, or lilac; solid or blotched with contrasting color. When left in the ground, will form large clumps in border or among shrubs. Plant in fall or early spring for late spring bloom.

Butterfly gladiolus. See G. primulinus

G. byzantinum (G. communis byzantinus). HARDY GLADIOLUS, BYZANTINE GLADIOLUS. Zones MS, LS, CS, TS. Mainly maroon, sometimes reddish or coppery, 1–3-in. flowers in groups of six to twelve on 2–3-ft. stems. Narrower leaves than garden gladiolus. Plant in early spring for summer bloom. An old Southern favorite.

G. callianthus (Acidanthera bicolor). ABYSSINIAN SWORD LILY. Perennial in Zones MS, LS, CS, TS, but flowering may be better if corms are dug and divided every year. Stems grow 2–3 ft. tall, bearing two to ten fragrant, creamy white flowers marked chocolate brown on lower segments. Each blossom is 2–3 in. wide and 4–5 in. long. Excellent cut flowers. Plant in spring for bloom in late summer–fall. 'Murielae' is taller, with purple-crimson blotches.

G. primulinus (G. dalenii). Zones LS, CS, TS. The 3-ft.-tall African species with hooded, primrose yellow flowers is rarely grown, but the name has been applied to its hybrids with other gladiolus. Butterfly gladiolus strain also belongs here. Frilled, medium-size flowers have a satiny sheen, vivid markings in throat. Wiry, 2-ft. stems bear as many as twenty flowers; six to eight open at a time. Colors include bright and pastel shades and pure white. Plant in spring for summer bloom.

Summer-flowering grandiflora hybrids. GARDEN GLADIOLUS. Perennial in Zones MS, LS, CS, TS, but usually lifted yearly even in those areas. Commonly grown garden gladiolus are a complex group of hybrids derived by variation and hybridization from several species. These are the best-known gladiolus, with widest color range—white, cream, buff, yellow, orange, apricot, salmon, red shades, rose, lavender, purple, smoky shades, even green shades. Individual blooms as large as 8 in. across. Stems are 4–5 ft. tall.

Gladiolus Hybrid

The newer types of garden gladiolus grow to about 5 ft. tall, have sturdier spikes bearing twelve to fourteen open flowers at a time. They are better garden plants than older types and stand upright without staking. Another group, called miniature gladiolus, grows 3 ft. tall, with spikes of fifteen to twenty flowers each reaching 2½–3 in. wide; useful in garden beds and for cutting.

High-crowned corms, 1½–2 in. wide, are more productive than older, larger corms (2 in. wide or more). After soil has warmed in spring, plant at 1- to 2-week intervals for 4 to 6 weeks for progression of bloom. Corms bloom 65 to 100 days after planting. If soil is poor, mix in complete fertilizer or superphosphate (4 lb. per 100 sq. ft.) before planting; do not place fertilizer in direct contact with corms. Be sure to treat corms with bulb dust (insecticide-fungicide) before planting. When plants have five leaves, apply complete fertilizer 6 in. from plants and water it in thoroughly. For cut flowers, cut spikes when lowest buds begin to open, leaving a minimum of four leaves on plants to build up corms. If thrips cause whitish streaking on leaves, spray foliage with diazinon according to label directions.

SOUTHERN HERITAGE PLANTS

IDENTIFIED BY SYMBOL

GLEDITSIA triacanthos

HONEY LOCUST

Fabaceae (Leguminosae)

DECIDUOUS TREE

ZONES US, MS, LS

FULL SUN

REGULAR TO MODERATE WATER

Gleditsia triacanthos

Native to South and Midwest. Fast growing, especially when young, with upright trunk and spreading, arching branches. To 35–70 ft. tall. Bright green, fernlike leaves to 10 in. long are divided into many oval, ¾–1½-in.-long leaflets. Late to leaf out; leaves turn yellow and drop early in fall. Inconspicuous flowers followed by broad, 1–1½-ft.-long pods filled with sweetish pulp and hard, roundish seeds.

Foliage casts filtered shade, allowing growth of lawn or other plants beneath. Small leaflets dry up and filter into grass, decreasing raking chores. Not good in narrow area between curb and sidewalk, since roots of old plants will heave paving. Stake tree until good basic branch pattern is established. Tolerant of acid or alkaline conditions, salt, drought, cold, heat, wind. Does best in areas with sharply defined winters, hot summers. Tree is susceptible to many pests, several of which are prevalent in humid-summer regions: mimosa webworm (chews leaves), pod gall midge (deforms foliage), honey locust borer (attacks limbs and trunks).

Trunks and branches of species are formidably thorny, and pods make a mess. Honey locusts for the garden are selections of *G. t. inermis*, thornless honey locust, with no thorns and few or no pods. Selections include:

'Halka'. Fast growing, forms sturdy trunk early, has strong horizontal branching pattern, oval shape, to 50 ft. Few seedpods.

'Imperial'. Spreading, symmetrical tree to about 35 ft. More densely foliaged than other forms; gives heavier shade.

'Moraine'. MORAINE LOCUST. Best known. Fast-growing, 50-ft., spreading tree with branches angled upward, then outward. Yellow fall color. Subject to wind breakage. Has greater resistance to webworms than do some of the newer selections.

'Rubylace'. Deep red new growth fading to bronzed green by midsummer. Subject to wind breakage, webworm attack.

'Shademaster'. More upright and faster growing than 'Moraine'—to 24 ft. tall, 16 ft. wide in 6 years. Few seedpods.

'Skyline'. Pyramidal and symmetrical; 45 ft. Bright golden fall color.

'Sunburst'. Golden yellow new leaves; showy against deep green background. Summer color best in Upper and Middle South. Defoliates early in response to temperature changes, drought. Prone to wind breakage. Very susceptible to foliage pests.

'Trueshade'. Rounded head of light green foliage; 40 ft.

GLOBBA

DANCING GIRL GINGER

Zingiberaceae

PERENNIALS

ZONES CS, TS

PARTIAL SHADE

REGULAR WATER DURING GROWING SEASON

Globba globulifera

Globbas are small, delicate-flowered members of the ginger family native to southeast Asia. Grow 1–3 ft. tall; their leaves are lustrous green sheaths and their ballerina-like flowers bloom in summer or fall among long, arching sprays of brightly colored bracts. Bulbils are often found inside the bracts, and if planted will produce new plants. Easy to grow if fertilized and kept moist during the growing season. Tolerate sun only if well watered. In areas with frost, grow indoors; mist to provide humidity if necessary, and stop watering during the winter, to give plant a period of dormancy; resume watering gradually in spring. Most make good cut flowers.

G. atrosanguinea. Produces 2½-in. panicles of deep red bracts and yellow flowers.

G. globulifera. PURPLE GLOBE GINGER. Has short panicles of purple bracts and yellow flowers.

G. schomburgkii. YELLOW DANCING GIRLS. Bears 3-in. panicles of light green-yellow bracts and yellow flowers with red spots.

G. winitii. Has 6-in. panicles of rosy purple bracts and bright yellow flowers. Particularly delicate and long blooming. 'Red Leaf' has leaves with maroon red undersides.

GLOBE AMARANTH. See GOMPHRENA

GLOBEFLOWER. See TROLLIUS

GLOBE THISTLE. See ECHINOPS

GLORIOSA DAISY. See RUDBECKIA hirta

GLORIOSA rothschildiana

GLORY LILY, CLIMBING LILY

Liliaceae

TUBEROUS-ROOTED PERENNIAL

ZONE TS; OR DIG AND STORE; OR GROW IN POTS OR GREENHOUSE

SUN OR FILTERED SHADE

REGULAR WATER DURING GROWTH AND BLOOM

ALL PARTS ARE POISONOUS IF INGESTED

Gloriosa rothschildiana

Native to tropical Africa. Climbs to 6 ft. by tendrils on leaf tips. Lance-shaped leaves 5–7 in. long. Lilylike flowers 4 in. across with six wavy-edged, curved, brilliant red segments banded with yellow. Grow on terrace, patio; train on trellis or frame.

Set tubers horizontally 4 in. deep in light, spongy soil. Start indoors or in greenhouse in February; set out after frosts. Feed with liquid fertilizer every 3 weeks. Tubers can remain in ground in Tropical South, though rotting is likely unless area is kept fairly dry. Elsewhere, dig in autumn, store over winter. Potted tubers can be stored in pots of dry soil.

GLORYBOWER. See CLERODENDRUM

GLORY LILY. See GLORIOSA rothschildiana

GLORY-OF-THE-SNOW. See CHIONODOXA

GLOXINIA. See SINNINGIA speciosa

GLOXINIA, HARDY. See INCARVILLEA delavayi

GOAT'S BEARD. See ARUNCUS

GOLD DUST PLANT. See AUCUBA japonica 'Variegata'

GOLDEN ASTER. See CHRYSOPSIS

GOLDEN BAMBOO. See PHYLLOSTACHYS aurea

GOLDEN BUTTERFLY GINGER. See HEDYCHIUM flavum

GOLDENCHAIN TREE. See LABURNUM

GOLDEN DEWDROP. See DURANTA repens

GOLDEN-EYED GRASS. See SISYRINCHIUM californicum

GOLDEN GARLIC. See ALLIUM moly

GOLDEN GLOBES. See LYSIMACHIA congestiflora

GOLDEN GROUNDSEL. See SENECIO aureus

GOLDEN MARGUERITE. See ANTHEMIS tinctoria

GOLDEN POLYPODY FERN. See POLYPODIUM aureum

GOLDENRAIN TREE. See KOELREUTERIA paniculata

GOLDEN RAY. See LIGULARIA

GOLDENROD. See SOLIDAGO

GOLDEN SEAL. See HYDRASTIS canadensis

GOLDEN STAR. See CHRYSOGONUM virginianum

GOLDEN TRUMPET. See ALLAMANDA cathartica

GOLDEN TRUMPET TREE. See TABEBUIA chrysotricha

GOLDEN WONDER SENNA. See CASSIA splendida

GOLD FLOWER. See HYPERICUM moseranum

GOLDIE'S WOOD FERN. See DRYOPTERIS goldiana

GOLD MEDALLION TREE. See CASSIA leptophylla

GOMPHRENA

GLOBE AMARANTH

Amaranthaceae

ANNUALS

ALL ZONES

FULL SUN OR PARTIAL SHADE

MODERATE WATER

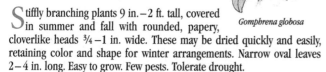

Gomphrena globosa

Stiffly branching plants 9 in.–2 ft. tall, covered in summer and fall with rounded, papery, cloverlike heads ¾–1 in. wide. These may be dried quickly and easily, retaining color and shape for winter arrangements. Narrow oval leaves 2–4 in. long. Easy to grow. Few pests. Tolerate drought.

G. globosa. White, pink, red, lavender, or purple flower heads top 1-ft. stems. Dwarf selections for use as edging or bedding plants are 9-in. 'Buddy' (purple) and 'Cissy' (white). 'Strawberry Fields' grows 2 ft. tall, has 1½-in. rose-colored heads. Planted closely in large pots—six to a shallow 10-in. pot—makes a long-lasting living bouquet.

G. haageana. To 2 ft. tall, with heads of tightly clustered, bright orange bracts that resemble inch-wide pine cones. Tiny yellow flowers peep from the bracts. Sold as 'Haageana Aurea' or simply 'Orange'.

GONIOLIMON tataricum
(Limonium tataricum)

GERMAN STATICE

Plumbaginaceae

PERENNIAL

ALL ZONES

FULL SUN

MODERATE WATER

Goniolimon tataricum

Dense clumps of dark green, narrowly oval leaves arise from a woody rootstock. Leafless flower stalks rise to 1½ ft., forking repeatedly into a broad, domed cluster to 1½ ft. wide. Tiny flowers are light purplish to white. The entire inflorescence can be dried for winter flower arrangements. Plant is heat tolerant.

Goodeniaceae. Members of this small family of perennials and shrubs—principally from the Southern Hemisphere, notably Australia—have irregularly lipped flowers. *Scaevola* is the most widely grown example.

GOOSENECK LOOSESTRIFE. See LYSIMACHIA clethroides

GOPHER PLANT. See EUPHORBIA lathyris

GORDONIA lasianthus

LOBLOLLY BAY

Theaceae

EVERGREEN TREE

ZONES LS, CS, TS

FULL SUN OR LIGHT SHADE

AMPLE TO REGULAR WATER

Gordonia lasianthus

Native to wet soils ("loblollies") of the coastal plain from Virginia to Louisiana. Narrow, erect, rather open-structured tree to 30–40 ft. tall, with shiny oval leaves 4–6 in. long. Attractive flowers up to 2½ in. wide bloom from midspring to midautumn; they look something like single white camellias and are enhanced by a big central brush of yellow stamens. Although wild trees grow in bogs, those in garden conditions seem to need good drainage. They are sometimes transplanted from the wild (with the owner's permission, of course), but these transplants are difficult to grow. Easier to grow are container-grown plants from garden centers.

G. alatamaha. See Franklinia alatamaha

⌘GOURD

Cucurbitaceae

ANNUAL VINES

ALL ZONES

FULL SUN

REGULAR DEEP WATERING

Gourd

Many plants produce gourds. One of most commonly planted is *Cucurbita pepo ovifera*, yellow-flowered gourd, that produces great majority of small ornamental gourds in many shapes and sizes. May be all one color or striped. *Luffa aegyptiaca*, dish cloth gourd or vegetable sponge gourd, also has yellow flowers. Bears cylindrical gourds 1–2 ft. long, fibrous interior of which may be used in place of sponge or cloth for scrubbing and bathing. *Lagenaria siceraria (L. vulgaris)*, white-flowered gourd, bears gourds 3 in.–3 ft. long; these may be round, bottle shaped, dumbbell shaped, crooknecked, coiled, or spoon shaped.

All grow fast and will reach 10–15 ft. Sow seeds when ground is warm. If planting for ornamental gourd harvest, give vines wire or trellis support to hold ripening individual fruits off ground. Plant seedlings 2 ft. apart or thin seedlings to same spacing. You can harvest gourds when tendrils next to their stems are dead, but it's best to leave them on the vine as long as possible—until the gourds turn yellow or brown. They can stay on the vine through frosts, but a heavy frost can discolor them. Cut some stem with each gourd so you can hang it up to dry slowly in a cool, airy spot. When thoroughly dry, preserve with coating of paste wax, lacquer, or shellac.

GOUT PLANT. See JATROPHA podagrica

GOUT WEED. See AEGOPODIUM podagraria

Gramineae. See Poaceae

GRANCY GRAYBEARD. See CHIONANTHUS virginicus

SOUTHERN HERITAGE PLANTS
IDENTIFIED BY SYMBOL ⌘

GRAPE

Vitaceae

DECIDUOUS VINES

☒ ZONES VARY BY SELECTION

☼ FULL SUN

🌢 MODERATE WATER

▶ SEE CHART, PAGE 238

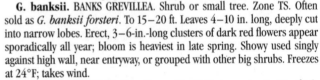
Grape

For fruit, wine, shade, and fall color. A single grapevine can produce enough new growth every year to arch over a walk, roof an arbor, form a leafy wall, or provide an umbrella of shade over deck or terrace. Grape is one of the few ornamental vines with bold, textured foliage, colorful edible fruit, and dominant trunk and branch pattern for winter interest.

For good-quality fruit, choose a type that fits your climate, train it carefully, and prune it regularly.

There are several basic types of grapes. European grapes (*Vitis vinifera*) have tight skin, a high heat requirement, and cold tolerance to about 0°F. These are the market table grapes, such as 'Thompson Seedless'. The classic wine grapes, such as 'Cabernet', 'Chardonnay', and 'Pinot Noir', are also European in origin. Production of European wine grapes is well established in Texas, Virginia, Maryland, and North Carolina.

American grapes stem from *V. labrusca*, with some influence from other American native species and also often from *V. vinifera*. These are slipskin grapes of the 'Concord' type, which have a moderate summer heat requirement and tolerate temperatures well below 0°F. American grapes are used for jelly, in unfermented grape juice, and as soft-drink flavoring; some wine, usually sweet, is also made from them. Most will not thrive in Lower and Coastal South; there, the grape of choice is the muscadine (*V. rotundifolia*), which bears large fruit in small clusters. Some muscadine selections are self-fertile, while others (called "females") require cross-pollination. (All other types of grapes are self-pollinating.)

Once established, grape vines grow rampantly. If all you want is a leafy cover for an arbor or a sitting area, you need only train a strong vine up and over its support and thin out tangled growth each year. But most people plant grapes for fruit, even if they want shade as well. For good fruit production, you'll need to follow more careful pruning procedures.

Grapes are produced on stems that develop from 1-year-old wood—stems that formed the previous season. These stems have smooth bark; older stems have rough, shaggy bark. The purpose of pruning is to limit the amount of potential fruiting wood, ensuring that the plant doesn't produce too much fruit and that the fruit it does bear is of good quality.

The two most widely used methods are spur pruning and cane pruning; see chart for recommended method for each selection. Either technique can be used for training grapes on arbors. Whichever method you choose, the initial steps—planting and creating a framework—are the same. Pruning should be done in winter or earliest spring, before the buds swell. (See illustrations on p. 237 for planting and pruning details.)

GRAPEFRUIT. See CITRUS

GRAPE HYACINTH. See MUSCARI

GRAPE IVY. See CISSUS rhombifolia

GRASSES. The grasses in this book are either lawn or ornamental plants—except for corn, the only cereal commonly grown in home gardens. They are described under entries headed by their botanical names. (All bamboos, which are grasses, are charted under Bamboo.)

Lawn grasses are *Axonopus affinis*, carpet grass; *Buchloe dactyloides*, buffalo grass; *Cynodon dactylon*, Bermuda grass; *Eremochloa ophiuroides*, centipede grass; *Festuca*, fescue; *Lolium*, ryegrass; *Paspalum notatum*, bahia grass; *Poa*, bluegrass; *Stenotaphrum secundatum*, St. Augustine grass; *Zoysia*.

Ornamental grasses in this book are *Andropogon*, bluestem; *Arundo donax*, giant reed; *Briza maxima*, rattlesnake grass; *Calamagrostis* *acutifolia* 'Stricta', feather reed grass; *Chasmanthium latifolium*, river oats; *Cortaderia selloana*, pampas grass; *Deschampsia*, hair grass; *Elymus arenarius* 'Glaucus', blue lyme grass; *Erianthus ravennae*, ravenna grass; *Festuca*, fescue; *Helictotrichon sempervirens*, blue oat grass; *Imperata cylindrica* 'Rubra', Japanese blood grass; *Miscanthus*, maiden grass; *Molinia caerulea*, moor grass; *Muhlenbergia*, bamboo muhly, Gulf muhly, Lindheimer's muhly, and purple muhly; *Panicum virgatum*, switch grass; *Pennisetum*, fountain grass; *Phalaris arundinacea*, ribbon grass; *Setaria palmifolia*, palm grass; and *Stipa*, feather grass.

GREAT BURNET. See SANGUISORBA canadensis

GREVILLEA

Proteaceae

EVERGREEN SHRUBS OR TREES

☒ ZONES VARY BY SPECIES

☼ FULL SUN

🌢 🌢🌢 MUCH TO LITTLE WATER

Grevillea robusta

Native to Australia. Many species and hybrids. Plants vary in size and appearance, but generally have fine-textured foliage and long, slender, curved flowers, usually in dense clusters. Provide good drainage. Like other members of the protea family, sensitive to high levels of phosphorus in the soil. Fertilize lightly; avoid fertilizers with high phosphorus content. Intolerant of salt.

G. banksii. BANKS GREVILLEA. Shrub or small tree. Zone TS. Often sold as *G. banksii forsteri*. To 15–20 ft. Leaves 4–10 in. long, deeply cut into narrow lobes. Erect, 3–6-in.-long clusters of dark red flowers appear sporadically all year; bloom is heaviest in late spring. Showy used singly against high wall, near entryway, or grouped with other big shrubs. Freezes at 24°F; takes wind.

G. robusta. SILK OAK. Tree. Zones CS, TS. Fast growing to 50–60 ft. (rarely to 100 ft.). Symmetrical, pyramidal when young. Old trees broad topped, picturesque against skyline, usually with a few heavy, horizontal limbs. Fernlike leaves golden green to deep green above, silvery beneath. Heavy leaf fall in spring, sporadic leaf drop through rest of year. Large clusters of bright golden orange flowers in early spring. Wood is brittle, easily damaged in high wind. Young trees damaged at 24°F; older ones hardy to 16°F. Use for quick, tall screen; or clip as tall hedge.

GROUND CHERRY. See PHYSALIS peruviana

GUAJILLO. See ACACIA berlandieri

GUAVA. See PSIDIUM

GYMNOCLADUS dioica

KENTUCKY COFFEE TREE

Fabaceae (Leguminosae)

DECIDUOUS TREE

☒ ZONES US, MS, LS

☼ FULL SUN

🌢 🌢 REGULAR TO MODERATE WATER

Native to eastern U.S. As a sapling, grows very fast, but slows down at 8–10 ft. Needs space; ultimately reaches 60–100 ft. tall and 45–50 ft. wide. Unusual tree. Provides year-round interest.

Handsome bark is dark gray to deep brown with rough, scaly ridges. The relatively few heavy, contorted branches and stout twigs make bare

Gymnocladus dioica

▶ page 239

Grape Planting and Training

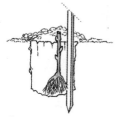

> ### DOUBLE WIRE
> To grow a grapevine on a double wire rather than a single one, stretch 2 wires—the first at the height of 2½–3 ft., the second at 5–6 ft.—between posts. When trunk tops lower wire during second summer, remove all side shoots; when it grows a foot above top wire, pinch off its tip. To develop parallel arms, choose strongest side shoot on each side of both wires and cut each to 2 buds. Remove other side shoots.

Planting: Plant bare-root grape deep in well-prepared soil, with only the top bud above soil level. Insert post or other support. Replace soil; cover exposed bud with lightweight mulch.

1st Summer: Let vine grow unchecked; don't try to train growth. The more leaves, the better the root development.

1st Winter: Select sturdiest shoot for trunk and remove all other shoots at their base. Shorten trunk to 3 or 4 lowest buds.

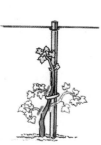

2nd Spring: Let buds grow into 6–8-in. shoots. Select a vigorous upright shoot to form the upper trunk, and tie loosely to post. Cut off all other shoots.

2nd Summer: When trunk reaches wire, cut its tip to force branching. Allow the 2 strongest developing shoots to grow, forming vine's arms; remove any others. Pinch any lateral shoots developing from arms to 10 in. long.

2nd Winter: Cut back all growth on trunk and arms; loosely tie arms to wire. Don't prune yet for fruit production; vines are too immature.

3rd Summer: Allow vine to grow. Remove any growth from trunk. Cane pruning and spur pruning differ from here on.

Cane Pruning from 3rd Winter: Cut back each arm to 12 buds; these will bear fruit the next summer. Select 2 strong lateral shoots near trunk and cut each to 2 buds; these are the renewal spurs. During next winter and every winter thereafter, remove fruiting canes at their base. Renewal spurs will have produced several new shoots from which new fruiting canes can be selected. Choose the 2 longest and strongest shoots and cut each to 12 buds; tie these shoots to wire. Select 2 next best shoots as renewal spurs and cut each to 2 buds.

Spur Pruning from 3rd Winter: Remove weak side shoots from arms. Leave strongest shoots (spurs) spaced 6–10 in. apart; cut each to 2 buds. Each spur will produce 2 fruit-bearing stems during next growing season. During next winter and every winter thereafter, remove upper stem on each spur and cut lower stem to 2 buds. Those buds will develop into stems that bear fruit the following summer.

Training on an Arbor

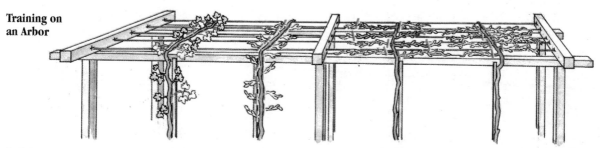

2nd Summer: When vine reaches top of arbor, bend it over and secure it as it grows across top. Remove side shoots to encourage tip to grow.

2nd Winter: Cut back main stem to point just beyond where you want the last set of branches. Cut off all side shoots. In spring, thin new shoots to 1 ft. apart.

3rd Winter, Cane Pruning: Cut back alternately to long canes (12 buds) and spurs (2 buds). Thereafter, follow cane pruning guidelines.

3rd Winter, Spur Pruning: Cut back each selected shoot (from previous summer's growth) to 2 buds. Thereafter, follow spur pruning guidelines.

GRAPE

SELECTION	ZONES	SEASON	PRUNING	COMMENTS
AMERICAN SELECTIONS				
'Canadice'	US, MS	Early	Spur	Seedless red grape. Very heavy bearing. Cane pruning often recommended, but should be spur pruned, possibly thinned, to prevent overcropping
'Concord'	US, MS, LS	Midseason	Cane	Oldest cultivated American grape and the one most commonly used for juice, jelly. Seeded dark blue fruit
'Himrod'	US, MS	Very early	Cane	Firm, seedless white grape with spicy flavor. For fresh eating, raisins. Very vigorous, suited to arbors
'Interlaken'	US, MS	Very early	Cane or spur	Like 'Himrod', but sweeter and ripens a week earlier; vines are less vigorous but more productive
'Lakemont'	US, MS	Early midseason	Cane or spur	Seedless white table grape with higher acid content than 'Himrod' or 'Interlaken'; keeps well in cold storage
'Reliance'	US, MS, LS	Early midseason	Cane or spur	Seedless red grape for fresh eating, fresh juice. May be ready to eat before it colors up. Reliable, heavy bearer. Very cold-hardy. Disease resistant
'Steuben'	US, MS	Midseason	Cane	Seeded blue grape with spicy flavor for fresh eating, juice. Very productive. Good disease resistance
'Swenson Red'	US, MS	Early	Spur	Red or reddish blue grape with excellent strawberry-like flavor, small seeds. Clusters may have distinctive dumbbell shape; vines may take a few years to develop full vigor and yield
'Valiant'	US, MS	Early	Cane or spur	Small seeded blue grape makes good cooked juice. Colors before full sweetness develops; leave on vine a while. Not very disease resistant
'Vanessa'	US, MS	Early	Cane	Seedless red grape stands up to rain. Vines tend to have excess vigor
'Venus Seedless'	US, MS, LS	Early	Cane	Large black grape, not always seedless. Flavor can be very good, aromatic. For fresh eating, juice, jelly. Good fall leaf color. Disease resistant
EUROPEAN SELECTIONS				
'Centennial'	US, MS, LS	Late midseason	Cane	Big clusters of elongated, firm white grapes for fresh eating, raisins. Among the largest of the seedless grapes. May not be widely sold
'Flame'	US, MS, LS, CS	Early	Cane or spur	Seedless red grape with excellent flavor. Tolerates heat and humidity well
'Thompson Seedless'	US, MS, LS	Late midseason	Cane or spur	Big bunches of small, sweet, mild-flavored greenish amber grapes for fresh eating, raisins, wine. The most common type sold in grocery stores
MUSCADINE SELECTIONS				
'Carlos'	MS, LS, CS	Midseason	Spur	Large clusters of seeded, small bronze fruit. Heavy producer. Best bronze muscadine for making wine. Self-fertile
'Cowart'	MS, LS, CS	Early to midseason	Spur	Large, seeded blue-black table and juice grape. Self-fertile
'Fry'	MS, LS, CS	Midseason to late	Spur	Very large clusters of seeded, big bronze fruit with excellent flavor. Female, needs pollinator. Quite vigorous and productive, but susceptible to black rot. Best for fresh eating. Developed in Georgia
'Golden Isles'	MS, LS, CS	Midseason	Spur	Seeded bronze grape for table, wine, juice. Self-fertile
'Higgins'	MS, LS, CS	Midseason to late	Spur	Medium to large clusters of seeded, huge pinkish to reddish bronze fruit. Female, needs pollinator. Cold-hardy and very productive. Good for fresh eating, but poor for wine. Great type for roadside sales. Developed by the Georgia Experiment Station

GRAPE

SELECTION	ZONES	SEASON	PRUNING	COMMENTS
MUSCADINE SELECTIONS				
'Hunt'	MS, LS, CS	Early to midseason	Spur	Large bunches of seeded, medium to large black fruit; good yield. Sweet and flavorful. Ripens uniformly. Female, needs pollinator. All purpose for wine, juice, jelly
'Jumbo'	MS, LS, CS	Midseason to late	Spur	Huge black fruit. Vigorous vines. Heavy producer. Needs pollinator
'Magnolia'	LS, CS	Midseason	Spur	Medium clusters of bronzy, medium to large, sweet fruit; seeded. Excellent quality. Self-fertile; vigorous, prolific grower. Superb for wine. Does well in Lower South
'Noble'	MS, LS, CS	Early to midseason	Spur	Large clusters of small to medium, bluish black fruits of good quality; seeded. Good disease resistance except for powdery mildew. Quite vigorous and productive. Self-fertile. Excellent for red wine, juice, and jelly. Developed in North Carolina
'Scuppernong'	MS, LS, CS	Midseason	Spur	The classic muscadine. Bronze, speckled grape with distinctive aroma and flavor. Needs pollinator. Good for fresh eating, wine
'Southland'	MS, LS, CS	Midseason	Spur	Seeded, medium to large, sweet purple-black fruit. Good quality. Self-fertile. Pest and disease resistant. Excellent fresh, or for jams, jellies. Best in Lower and Coastal South
'Triumph'	MS, LS, CS	Early midseason	Spur	Reliable heavy crop of bronze to nearly yellow grapes with pineapple flavor. For juice, fresh eating, wine. Self-fertile
'Welder'	LS, CS	Midseason	Spur	Seeded, medium-size bronze fruit; great quality. Vigorous and productive. Good for fresh eating and jelly; superb for wine. Tolerates partial shade. Good for garden and commercial plantings. Disease resistant. Self-fertile. Excellent pollinator

tree picturesque in winter. Attractive 1½–3-ft.-long leaves, divided into many 1–3-in.-long leaflets, emerge late in spring, usually in May. They are pinkish when expanding, deep bluish green in summer. Fall color is usually not effective, though leaves sometimes turn an agreeable sunny yellow. In leaf, the tree casts light shade.

Male and female plants are separate. Narrow flower panicles at ends of branches in spring are up to 1 ft. long (and fragrant) on females, to 4 in. long on males. Blossoms on female trees are followed by flat, reddish brown, 6–10-in.-long pods containing hard black seeds. Pods persist through winter. Early settlers in Kentucky and Tennessee roasted the seeds to make a coffee substitute, giving the tree its common name.

Grows best in moist, rich, deep soil, but adapts to poor soil, drought, city conditions. Established tree can take much heat and cold. Prune in winter or early spring.

GYPSOPHILA paniculata

BABY'S BREATH

Caryophyllaceae

PERENNIAL

ZONES US, MS

FULL SUN

MODERATE WATER

Gypsophila paniculata
'Bristol Fairy'

This is the classic filler in bouquets. Much branched to 3 ft. or more; leaves slender, sharp pointed, 2½–4 in. long. Single white flowers about 1/16 in. across, hundreds in a spray. 'Bristol Fairy' is an improved form, more billowy, to 4 ft. high, covered with double blossoms ¼ in. wide. Florists' favorite type is 'Perfecta', which bears larger flowers. 'Compacta Plena' is a double white dwarf 1½ ft. tall; other dwarfs

are double pink 'Pink Star' (1½ ft. tall) and 'Viette's Dwarf' (12–15 in. high). Grow all types from root grafts or stem cuttings.

Grows best in the Upper South. Dies out quickly in hot, wet weather and poor-draining soil. Add lime to strongly acid soils. For repeat bloom, cut back flowering stems before seed clusters form. Thick, deep roots of some types difficult to transplant; do not disturb often.

HABRANTHUS

RAIN LILY

Amaryllidaceae

BULBS

ZONES LS (PROTECTED), CS, TS; OR IN POTS

FULL SUN OR LIGHT SHADE

REGULAR WATER DURING GROWTH AND BLOOM

Habranthus robustus

Bulbous plants somewhat resembling miniature amaryllis (*Hippeastrum*), with narrow, grassy leaves and trumpet-shaped flowers. Native from Mexico to Argentina; widely grown in Texas and naturalized there. Where ground freezes, grow in pots. Set with bulb tops at soil level. Plants can take some drought. Use in rock gardens or naturalize.

H. andersonii (H. tubispathus). Flower stems reach 6 in., with inch-wide yellow flowers, coppery on the outside. 'Cupreus' is coppery orange.

H. brachyandrus. Lavender-pink, 3-in. flowers, with shades of black purple at petal bases, appear one per stem, just before plant leafs out. Blooms spring to fall.

H. robustus. Four-inch bright pink flowers are carried one or two to a stem. Bloom may occur any time from spring to fall. ▶

H. texanus (H. andersonii texanus). Bright yellow, 1–1½-in. flowers, with coppery shadings, similar to those of *H. andersonii,* bloom on 8–12-in. stems in late summer. Leaves, to 4 in. long, appear after flowers.

HACKBERRY. See CELTIS

HAIR GRASS. See DESCHAMPSIA

HALBERD-LEAFED ROSE-MALLOW. See HIBISCUS militaris

HALESIA

SILVER BELL

Styracaceae

DECIDUOUS TREES

ZONES US, MS, LS, EXCEPT AS NOTED

PARTIAL SHADE

REGULAR WATER

Halesia carolina

Elegant trees native to the Southeast. Grow best in acid soil, well drained and humus rich. Attractive in woodland gardens, with rhododendrons and azaleas planted beneath. Good substitute for dogwood where dogwood will not grow.

H. carolina (H. tetraptera). CAROLINA SILVER BELL, SNOWDROP TREE. Moderate rate of growth to 30–40 ft. tall, with 20–35-ft. spread. Lovely in midspring, when clusters of snow white, ½-in., bell-shaped flowers hang along length of graceful branches just as leaves begin to appear. Oval, finely toothed, 2–5-in.-long leaves turn yellow in fall. Interesting four-winged brown fruits hang on almost all winter. Train plant to a single trunk when young or it will grow as a large shrub. Flowers show off to best advantage when you can look up into tree.

H. diptera. TWO-WINGED SILVER BELL. Zones US, MS, LS, CS. Small (to 20–30 ft. tall), rounded, usually multitrunked. Flowers resemble those of *H. carolina,* but are more deeply lobed and bloom a week or two later. Fruits similar to those of *H. carolina* but have two rather than four wings. *H. d. magniflora,* probably the showiest silver bell, has larger flowers and is a more profuse bloomer.

H. monticola. MOUNTAIN SILVER BELL. Bears likeness to *H. carolina* but larger, eventually to 60–80 ft. tall. Leaves are also bigger (3–6 in. long), but tree casts only moderate shade. Flowers, fruit are also somewhat larger. 'Rosea' has light pink flowers.

Hamamelidaceae. The witch hazel family comprises deciduous (rarely evergreen) trees and shrubs. Some have showy flowers; these include *Fothergilla, Loropetalum,* witch hazel *(Hamamelis).* Many of the deciduous kinds have brilliant fall color; examples are *Parrotia* and sweet gum *(Liquidambar).*

HAMAMELIS

WITCH HAZEL

Hamamelidaceae

DECIDUOUS SHRUBS OR SMALL TREES

ZONES US, MS, LS, EXCEPT AS NOTED

FULL SUN OR PARTIAL SHADE

MODERATE WATER

Hamamelis mollis

Medium-size to large shrubs, sometimes treelike, usually with spreading habit and angular or zigzagging branches. Valued for their bright autumn foliage and interesting yellow to red blooms appearing in nodding clusters, usually in

winter. Each flower consists of many narrow, crumpled petals; depending on who is asked, blossoms are often said to resemble shredded coconut, eyelashes, or spiders. Flowers of most types are fragrant and bloom over a long period. All shrubs appreciate rich, organic soil. Prune only to guide growth, remove poorly placed branches or suckers, or obtain flowering stems for winter bouquets.

H. intermedia. HYBRID WITCH HAZEL. Group of hybrids between *H. mollis* and *H. japonica.* Big shrubs (to 15 ft. high), blooming in midwinter to early spring, depending on location. Not great performers in the Lower South. Previous year's leaves often persist until late winter there, obscuring the blooms. Often grafted; remove any growth originating from below graft. The following selections are among the best:

'Allgold'. Upright shrub bearing deep yellow flowers, reddish at base; yellow fall foliage.

'Arnold Promise'. Late bloomer. Pure yellow, very fragrant flowers nearly conceal branches at peak of bloom. Exceptionally winter cold-hardy.

'Carmine Red'. Spreading shrub with light red flowers; red-orange fall color. Vigorous.

'Diane'. Bright coppery red flowers with slight scent; a show of fine ruddy gold fall color.

'Hiltingbury'. Spreading plant with pale copper blossoms; orange, red, and scarlet autumn leaves.

'Jelena' ('Copper Beauty', 'Orange Beauty'). Spreading plant with large leaves; large yellow flowers suffused with red, and orange-red fall foliage.

'Magic Fire' ('Fire Charm', 'Feuerzauber'). Upright plant with fragrant blossoms of coppery orange blended with red.

'Moonlight'. Upright shrub with strongly perfumed blossoms of light sulfur yellow, red at base; yellow fall foliage.

'Primavera'. Late bloomer producing large quantities of sweet-scented, primrose yellow flowers. Vigorous.

'Ruby Glow'. Erect plant, with coppery red flowers and excellent rusty gold fall color.

'Sunburst'. Heavy crop of radiant yellow, unscented blooms.

H. japonica. JAPANESE WITCH HAZEL. To 10–15 ft. tall, with loose, spreading habit. Fairly small, lightly scented yellow flowers, February–March. Chief distinction is brilliant fall foliage—shades of red, purple, and yellow. *H. j. flavopurpurascens* has yellow-orange flowers, purple at the base, and reddish yellow fall foliage. *H. j. arborea,* to 20–25 ft. tall, bears a profusion of yellow blossoms and yellow autumn leaves.

H. mollis. CHINESE WITCH HAZEL. Moderately slow-growing shrub to 8–10 ft. or small tree that may eventually reach 30 ft. Roundish leaves, 3½–6 in. long, are dark green and rough above, gray and felted beneath; turn good clear yellow in fall. Sweetly fragrant, 1½-in.-wide, rich golden yellow flowers with red-brown sepals bloom February–March on bare stems. Effective against red brick or gray stone. Flowering branches excellent for arrangements. 'Coombe Wood' bears fragrant, golden yellow blooms; 'Early Bright' sports bright yellow blooms. 'Pallida' has large, pale yellow flowers.

H. vernalis. VERNAL WITCH HAZEL. Native to central and southern U.S. Slow-growing, rounded shrub to 10–15 ft., rarely taller. Leaves 2–5 in. long, medium to dark green, turning bright yellow in fall and holding for several weeks in favorable weather. Flowers are ½–¾ in. across, yellow (rarely orange or red), fragrant, and quite resistant to winter cold. Blooms January–March. 'Red Imp' has small red flowers. 'Sandra' has superior orange and red fall color.

H. virginiana. COMMON WITCH HAZEL. Zones US, MS, LS, CS. Native to eastern North America. Sometimes to 25 ft. tall but usually 10–15 ft. high; open, spreading, rather straggling habit. Moderately slow growing. Bark is the source of the liniment witch hazel. Roundish leaves similar to those of *H. mollis* but not gray and felted beneath; turn yellow to orange in fall. Fragrant, ¾-in.-wide, golden yellow blooms, October–November, tend to be lost in colored foliage.

HAMELIA patens

MEXICAN FIREBUSH, SCARLET BUSH

Rubiaceae

EVERGREEN SHRUB OR SMALL TREE

✿ ZONES CS, TS

☼ SUN

💧 AMPLE WATER

Hamelia patens

Native from southern Florida south to Central and South America. Gardenia and coffee relative growing to 9–10 ft. tall, possibly much taller, with whorls of oval, gray-green, 6-in. leaves. Leafstalks and flower stems are red. Clusters of ¾-in., tubular, orange to bright red flowers form at branch tips all summer long; thanks to shape and color of blossoms, plant is also known as firecracker shrub. Flowers are followed by small dark red, purple, or black fruits much relished by birds. Likes lots of moisture but needs good drainage. Tolerant of salt, lime.

HANDKERCHIEF TREE. See DAVIDIA involucrata

HARDY AGERATUM. See EUPATORIUM coelestinum

HARDY GLOXINIA. See INCARVILLEA delavayi

HARDY KIWI. See ACTINIDIA arguta

HARE'S FOOT FERN. See POLYPODIUM aureum

HARISON'S YELLOW ROSE. See ROSA harisonii

HARLEQUIN GLORYBOWER. See CLERODENDRUM trichotomum

HART'S TONGUE FERN. See ASPLENIUM scolopendrium

HAWAIIAN TREE FERN. See CIBOTIUM chamissoi

HAWTHORN. See CRATAEGUS

HAY-SCENTED FERN. See DENNSTAEDTIA punctilobula

HAZELNUT. See CORYLUS

HEAVENLY BAMBOO. See NANDINA domestica

HEDERA

IVY

Araliaceae

EVERGREEN WOODY VINES

✿ ZONES VARY BY SPECIES

☼ ◑ ● SHADE IN LOWER, COASTAL, AND TROPICAL SOUTH

💧 ◐ REGULAR TO MODERATE WATER

Hedera belix

Spreads horizontally over the ground; also climbs on walls, fences, trellises. Sometimes a single planting does both—wall ivy spreads to become surrounding ground cover or vice versa. Dependable, uniform, neat. Holds soil, discouraging erosion and slippage on slopes. Roots grow deep and fill soil densely. Branches root as they grow, further knitting soil.

Ivy climbs almost any vertical surface by aerial rootlets—a factor to consider in planting against walls that must be painted. Chain link fence planted with ivy soon becomes a wall of foliage. Ivy must have shade in the hottest areas, or leaves may scorch. Leaf spot can be a serious problem in wet, humid weather. To prevent its spread, pick off and dispose of infected leaves. Water only in early morning so that foliage dries thoroughly.

Thick, leathery leaves are usually lobed. Mature plants will eventually develop stiff branches toward top of vine that bear round clusters of small greenish flowers followed by black berries. These branches have unlobed leaves; cuttings from such branches will have same kind of leaves and will be shrubby, not vining. Such shrubs taken from variegated Algerian ivy are

called ghost ivy. The plain green *H. helix* 'Arborescens' is another selection of this shrubby type.

Most ivy ground covers need trimming around edges (use hedge shears or sharp spade) two or three times a year. Fence and wall plantings need shearing or trimming two or three times a year. When ground cover builds up higher than you want, mow it with rugged power rotary mower or cut it back with hedge shears. Do this in spring so ensuing growth will quickly cover bald look.

Many trees and shrubs can grow quite compatibly in ivy. But small, soft, or fragile plants won't last long with healthy ivy—it simply smothers them. Ivy can be a haven for slugs and snails; it also harbors rodents, especially when it is never cut back.

H. canariensis. ALGERIAN IVY. Zones CS, TS. Shiny, rich green leaves 5–8 in. wide with three to five shallow lobes, more widely spaced along stems than on English ivy. Luxuriant look.

'Variegata'. VARIEGATED ALGERIAN IVY. Leaves edged with yellowish white; edges sometimes suffused with reddish purple in cold weather.

H. colchica. COLCHIS IVY, PERSIAN IVY. All zones. Oval to heart-shaped leaves, 3–7 in. wide, to 10 in. long (largest leaves of all ivies). Somewhat resembles Algerian ivy in large leaf size and glossiness, but is more cold-hardy. 'Dentata' is faintly toothed; 'Dentata Variegata' is marbled with deep green, gray green, and creamy white. 'Sulphur Heart' has central gold variegation.

H. helix. ENGLISH IVY. All zones. Dull dark green leaves with paler veins are 2–4 in. wide at base and as long, with three to five lobes. Not as vigorous as Algerian ivy, better for small spaces.

'Baltica', with whitish-veined leaves half as big as those of the species, is often considered hardiest selection of English ivy. Its leaves take on purplish tone in winter. Other exceptionally hardy selections are 'Bulgarica', 'Hebron', 'Rochester', 'Thorndale', and '238th Street'.

Many small- and miniature-leafed forms of English ivy are useful for small-area ground covers, hanging baskets, and training to form intricate patterns on walls and in pots. These types are also used to create topiary shapes—globes, baskets, animals—on wire frames. Some small-leafed forms are 'Conglomerata', a slow-growing dwarf; 'Hahn's Self Branching', light green leaves, dense branching, best in part shade; and 'Minima', leaves ½–1 in. across with three to five angular lobes. Other selections include 'Buttercup', 'California', 'Fluffy Ruffles', 'Gold Dust', 'Gold Heart', 'Heart', 'Needlepoint', 'Ripple', 'Shamrock', and 'Star'; select for leaf color and shape. Some are grown as house plants, but if planted in protected sites, most are hardy.

HEDGEHOG CACTUS. See ECHINOCEREUS

HEDGE MAPLE. See ACER campestre

HEDYCHIUM

GINGER LILY

Zingiberaceae

PERENNIALS

✿ ZONES VARY BY SPECIES; OR INDOORS

☼ ◑ FULL SUN OR LIGHT SHADE

💧 AMPLE WATER

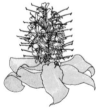

Hedychium gardneranum

Native to India and tropical Asia. An old Southern favorite. Foliage is handsome under good growing conditions. Leaves are on two sides of stems but grow in a single plane. In late summer or early fall, richly fragrant flowers in dense spikes open from cone of overlapping green bracts at ends of stalks. Southern specialist growers offer dozens of species and selections in heights from 2 to 9 ft., colors that range from white and cream through pink to red, and a host of yellows, oranges, and salmons.

Remove old stems after flowers fade for new growth. Useful in large containers, though potted specimens do not reach height of those in ground. Give soil high in organic matter. Frosts in Coastal South can kill plants to ground, but new stalks appear in early spring. Good near swimming pools, at the beach, in shade gardens and mixed borders.

H. aurantiacum. ORANGE GINGER LILY. Zones LS, CS, TS. Reaches 4–5 ft. tall. Orange flowers with red stamens.

H. coccineum. RED GINGER LILY. Zones LS, CS, TS. To 9 ft. Orange-scarlet flowers with red stamens open simultaneously on very long spikes. Particularly showy.

🏛 **H. coronarium.** COMMON GINGER LILY, WHITE GINGER LILY. Zones MS, LS, CS, TS. Grows 3–6 ft. high. Leaves 8–24 in. long, 2–5 in. across. Wonderfully fragrant white flowers in 6–12-in.-long clusters; good cut flowers.

H. flavum. GOLDEN BUTTERFLY GINGER. Zones LS, CS, TS. Old Southern favorite. To 9 ft. Spikes are dense clusters of particularly fragrant, rich yellow-orange flowers, with orange spots on their tips.

H. gardneranum. KAHILI GINGER. Zones LS, CS, TS. Grows to 8 ft. high; 8–18-in.-long leaves 4–6 in. wide. Clear yellow flowers with red stamens, in 1½-ft.-long spikes.

H. greenei. Zones MS, LS, CS, TS. Grows to 5 ft., with orange-red flowers in 5-in. spikes.

H. hasseltii. Zones LS, CS, TS. Small plant, to 2 ft., with white flowers. Seedpods split and reveal pretty red seeds.

H. pradhanii. PEARLY WHITE BUTTERFLY GINGER. Zones MS, LS, CS, TS. To 6 ft. Creamy white blooms, with peach yellow throats, pink stamens.

HEDYOTIS caerulea. See HOUSTONIA caerulea

HELENIUM autumnale

COMMON SNEEZEWEED

Asteraceae (Compositae)

PERENNIAL

🌿 ZONES US, MS, LS

☼ FULL SUN

💧 REGULAR WATER

Helenium autumnale

Species is rarely grown; plants sold as such are usually hybrids between *H. autumnale* and other species. Leaves are 2–4 in. long, toothed. Numerous branching, leafy stems to 1–6 ft. high, depending on selection. Blooms over a long period from midsummer to early fall; flowers are daisylike, with rays in yellow, orange, red, or copper shades surrounding a pompomlike, typically brown center.

Trim off faded blooms to encourage more flowers. Better looking with scant fertilizer. Taller types need staking; best suited to back of borders. Divide all types every few years. Plants can take some neglect. Drought tolerant, but look better with regular moisture. Short lived in wet, heavy soil.

The following named selections are sometimes offered. Tall types grow to 4–5 ft., compact ones to about 3 ft. high.

'Baudirektor Linne'. Tall. Velvety red petals and a brown center.

'Butterpat'. Tall. Light yellow blossoms with a deeper yellow center.

'Crimson Beauty'. Compact. Dusky deep red flowers.

'Cymbal Star' ('Zimbelstern'). Tall. Gold blooms touched with bronze.

'Dunkel Pracht'. Tall. Dark red blossoms with a brown center.

'Gold Kugel' ('Gold Ball'). Compact. Dark-centered yellow blossoms.

'Moerheim Beauty'. Compact. Coppery red petals around a brown center.

'September Gold'. Compact. Bright yellow blossoms.

'Sunball' ('Kugelsonne'). Tall. Lemon yellow rays, chartreuse centers.

'Waldtraut'. Tall. Copper-tinged rays surrounding a dark center.

'Wyndley'. Compact. Butter yellow petals around a lime yellow center.

SOUTHERN HERITAGE PLANTS
IDENTIFIED BY SYMBOL 🏛

HELIANTHEMUM nummularium

SUNROSE

Cistaceae

EVERGREEN SHRUBLETS

🌿 ZONES US, MS

☼ FULL SUN

💧 MODERATE WATER

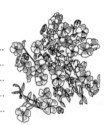
Helianthemum nummularium

Commonly sold under this name are a number of forms as well as hybrids between this species and others. They grow about 6–8 in. high and spread to about 3 ft. Leaves are ½–1 in. long and may be glossy green above and fuzzy gray beneath or gray on both sides. Plants produce a delightful late spring to early summer display of clustered, 1-in.-wide, single or double flowers in bright or pastel colors—flame red, apricot, orange, yellow, pink, rose, peach, salmon, or white. Each blossom lasts only a day, but new buds continue to open. Shear plants back after they flower to encourage repeat bloom.

Specialists offer many named selections. Especially noteworthy is one sold as *H. apenninum* 'Roseum' or as 'Wisley Pink', with comparatively large, pure pink flowers that contrast nicely with the gray, furry foliage.

Let sunroses tumble over rocks, set in niche in dry rock wall, or grow in planters on sunny terrace. Use them at the seashore (but not on the dunes) or in rock gardens; let them ramble over gentle slope. If used as ground cover, plant 2–3 ft. apart. In the Upper South, lightly cover plants with branches from evergreens in winter to keep foliage from dehydrating. Plants will be hardier if given soil that is not too rich (good drainage is essential, though) and is kept on the dry side; object is to encourage hard, nonsucculent growth.

HELIANTHUS

SUNFLOWER, NARROW-LEAFED SUNFLOWER

Asteraceae (Compositae)

ANNUALS AND PERENNIALS

🌿 ZONES VARY BY SPECIES

☼ FULL SUN

💧 REGULAR WATER, EXCEPT AS NOTED

Helianthus annuus

Coarse, sturdy plants with bold flowers. Most are tough and widely adapted. Perennial types spread rapidly, may become invasive. Tall kinds not for tidy gardens, may need staking. All bloom in late summer and fall.

H. angustifolius. SWAMP SUNFLOWER. Perennial. Zones US, MS, LS, CS. Native to eastern U.S. Grows 5–10 ft. tall, with narrow 6-in. leaves and sheaves of bright yellow, 2–3-in. daisies with dark brown centers. Likes ample moisture but adapts to ordinary garden conditions. Sometimes confused with *H. salicifolius.* Very showy in late summer and fall.

H. annuus. COMMON SUNFLOWER. Annual. All zones. From this plant with its 2–3-in.-wide flower heads have come many ornamental and useful garden selections. Best-known form is coarse, towering (to 10 ft.) plant with small rays outside and cushiony center of disk flowers, 8–10 in. across. Usually sold as 'Mammoth Russian'. 'Sunspot' carries flowers of like size on 2-ft. plants. People eat the roasted seeds; birds like them raw and visit flower heads in fall and winter. For children, annual sunflowers are easy to grow and bring a sense of great accomplishment. Sow seeds in spring where plants are to grow. Large-flowered kinds need rich soil.

H. atrorubens. DARK-EYED SUNFLOWER. Perennial. Zones US, MS, LS, CS. Native to southeastern U.S. Grows 5–6 ft. tall, with coarse, bristly foliage and 2-in. yellow flower heads centered in dark purple. 'The Monarch' has semidouble flowers somewhat resembling the quilled flowers of a cactus-form dahlia.

H. maximilianii. Perennial. Zones US, MS, LS, CS. Native to central and southwestern U.S. Clumps of 10-ft. stems clothed in narrow, 8–10-in. leaves and topped with narrow spires of 3-in. yellow flowers.

H. multiflorus (H. decapetalus). Perennial. Zones US, MS, LS, CS. Hybrid between *H. annuus* and a perennial species. To 5 ft. high, with thin, toothed, 3–8-in.-long leaves and numerous 3-in.-wide flower heads with yellow centers. Excellent for cutting. Flowers of 'Capenoch Star' are single, lemon yellow with a large central brown disk; 'Loddon Gold' ('Flore Pleno'), double-flowered form with deeper yellow blooms.

H. salicifolius (H. orgyalis). Perennial. Zones US, MS, LS, CS. Native to the central U.S. Like *H. angustifolius* (the two are sometimes confused in the nursery trade), but with narrower, more willowy, drooping leaves.

H. tuberosus. JERUSALEM ARTICHOKE. Perennial. Zones US, MS, LS, CS. Also grown as a commercial crop; tubers are edible and sold in markets as sunchokes. Grows 6–10 ft. tall, with bright yellow flower heads. Oval leaves 8 in. long. Spreads

Helianthus tuberosus

readily and can become a pest. Best to harvest tubers every year and save out two or three for replanting. If controlled, plants make a good, quick temporary screen or hedge.

SUNFLOWERS THAT MAKE THE CUT

For cut-flower bouquets, try these ten sunflower selections, all excellent for arranging: 'Autumn Beauty', 'Big Smile', 'Color Fashion Mixed', 'Double Sun Gold', 'Inca Jewels', 'Italian White', 'Music Box', 'Sunrich Lemon', 'Sunrich Orange', and 'Valentine'.

HELICHRYSUM

Asteraceae (Compositae)

ANNUALS AND PERENNIALS

✐ ZONES VARY BY SPECIES

☀ FULL SUN

💧 MODERATE WATER

Helichrysum bracteatum

Best known are the annual strawflowers used in both fresh- and dry-flower arrangements. Others, though little known, are choice plants for landscape use.

H. angustifolium. See H. italicum

H. bracteatum. STRAWFLOWER. Annual. All zones. Grows 2–3 ft. high with many flower heads; dwarf forms also available. Known as "everlasting" because pompomlike, 2½-in. summer flowers are papery and last indefinitely when dried. Also good in fresh arrangements. Flowers may be yellow, orange, red, pink, or white (seeds come in mixed colors). Straplike leaves are medium green, 2–5 in. long. Plant seed in place in late spring or early summer (same time as zinnias). 'Dargan Hill Monarch' and 'Diamond Head' are shrubby perennial forms for mild-winter areas. Both have grayish green foliage and 3-in. golden yellow flower heads; the similar 'Cockatoo' has lemon yellow heads.

H. italicum (H. angustifolium). CURRY PLANT. Woody-based perennial. Zones LS, CS, TS. Spreading, branching to 2 ft. high, about as broad, with crowded, narrow, nearly white leaves to 1½ in. long. Leaves emit a strong fragrance of curry powder when bruised or pinched; though they are not used in curry, a few can add a pleasant aroma to a salad or meat dish. Bright yellow, ½-in. flower heads grow in clusters 2 in. across, midsummer to autumn.

H. petiolare. LICORICE PLANT. Perennial in Zone TS; can be grown as annual elsewhere. Woody-based plant with trailing stems to 4 ft. with white,

woolly, inch-long leaves; insignificant flowers. Licorice aroma sometimes noticeable—in hot, still weather, for example, or when leaves are dry. 'Limelight' has luminous light chartreuse leaves; 'Variegatum' has foliage with white markings. All kinds are useful for their trailing branches, which will thread through mixed plantings or mix with other plants in large pots or hanging baskets.

H. subulifolium. Annual. All zones. Mound-shaped plant to 20 in. tall, with glossy green, 5-in. leaves and bright, shining, orange-yellow summer flowers 1½ in. wide. Excellent for fresh or dried cut flowers.

HELICONIA

Heliconiaceae

PERENNIALS

✐ ZONE TS; OR IN GREENHOUSE

☀ ◑ FULL SUN OR LIGHT SHADE

💧 AMPLE WATER

Heliconia caribaea

More than 100 species of tropical American plants with growth habit resembling that of banana or canna. Evergreen leaves are large (sometimes very large) and plants form sizable clumps. Grown for big, showy, waxy flower clusters consisting of brightly colored bracts; small true flowers peep out from bracts. Clusters may be erect or drooping, from a few inches to several feet in length; used in spectacular tropical flower arrangements.

Need rich soil, heavy feeding, and ample water. Stems that have flowered should be cut away to make room for new growth. Beyond frost-free zone, grow plants in pots, shelter from winter cold. Potted plants can bloom any time; those in the ground flower in spring and summer.

H. brasiliensis (H. farinosa). FALSE BIRD OF PARADISE. To 3–5 ft. tall, with 2½-ft. leaves and erect clusters of red bracts enfolding white or red flowers.

H. caribaea. WILD PLANTAIN. Banana-like stems 6–15 ft., with 5-ft. leaves and erect flower clusters to 1½ ft. Bracts are red or yellow, often marked with contrasting colors; flowers are white with green tips.

H. latispatha. Banana-like stem can reach 10 ft. high. Leaves to 5 ft. long; erect flower cluster up to 1½ ft. tall, with spiraling orange, red, or yellow bracts and green-tipped yellow flowers.

H. psittacorum. Highly variable species 4–8 ft. tall; leaves to 20 in. long. Bracts spread upward at 45° angle; red, sometimes shading to cream or orange, often multicolored. Flowers are yellow, orange, or red, and usually tipped dark green and white, in clusters to 7 in. long. Many named selections are available.

H. schiedeana. To 6 ft. tall, with leaves to 5 ft. long. Red or orange-red spiraling bracts enclose yellow-green flowers in a 1½-ft. cluster.

HELICTOTRICHON sempervirens (Avena sempervirens)

BLUE OAT GRASS

Poaceae (Gramineae)

PERENNIAL

✐ ZONES US, MS

☀ FULL SUN

💧 REGULAR WATER

Helictotrichon sempervirens

Evergreen, 2–3-ft. fountains of bright blue-gray, narrow leaves resemble giant clumps of blue fescue (*Festuca ovina* 'Glauca'), but are more graceful. Plants need full sun, good drainage. Combine with other grasses and broad-leafed plants. Pull out occasional withered leaves.

HELIOPSIS helianthoides (H. scabra)

OX-EYE, SUNFLOWER HELIOPSIS

Asteraceae (Compositae)

PERENNIAL

ZONES US, MS, LS, CS

FULL SUN OR LIGHT SHADE

REGULAR TO MODERATE WATER

Heliopsis helianthoides

As species name implies, resembles true sunflower, *Helianthus*. Clump-forming perennial to 5 ft. tall and half as wide, with 6-in., rough-textured, medium green leaves. Bright orange-yellow flower heads are 3 in. wide or wider. Blooms from July until frost. Plants are usually offered as *H. scabra*, a subspecies of *H. helianthoides*. Some of the best selections are 'Ballerina', an early bloomer to 3 ft., with semidouble deep yellow flowers; 'Karat', to 3½ ft., with single bright yellow flowers; and 'Summer Sun', to 3 ft., with single blossoms in rich golden yellow. Divide clumps of all types every few years.

HELLEBORUS

HELLEBORE

Ranunculaceae

PERENNIALS

ZONES VARY BY SPECIES

PARTIAL OR FULL SHADE

REGULAR TO MODERATE WATER

ALL PARTS ARE POISONOUS IF INGESTED

Helleborus orientalis

Distinctive, long-lived evergreen plants, blooming for several months in winter and spring. Basal clumps of substantial, long-stalked leaves, usually divided fanwise into leaflets. Flowers large, borne singly or in clusters, centered with many stamens. Good cut flowers; sear ends of stems or dip in boiling water, then place in deep, cold water.

Plant in good soil amended with organic material. Prefers soil pH near neutral—lime if necessary. Feed once or twice a year. Do not move often; plants reestablish slowly. Mass under high-branching trees on north or east side of walls, in beds edged in ajuga, wild ginger, primroses, violets. Use in plantings with azaleas, fatsia, pieris, rhododendrons, skimmia, ferns.

H. argutifolius (*H. lividus corsicus, H. corsicus*). CORSICAN HELLEBORE. Zones MS, LS. Leafy stems to 3 ft. high. Pale blue-green leaves divided into three leaflets with sharply toothed edges. (Not to be confused with *H. lividus*, a rare plant with pale leaf veins, leaflets with smooth edges or only a few fine teeth.) Clusters of large, firm-textured, light chartreuse flowers among upper leaves. Blooms winter and early spring. Flowers stay attractive until summer. Unlike other hellebores, this species can take some sun and is drought tolerant.

H. foetidus. BEARSFOOT HELLEBORE. Zones US, MS, LS. To 1½ ft. high. Attractive leaves—leathery, dark green, divided into seven to nine leaflets. Flowers 1 in. wide, light green with purplish margin, in large clusters at branch ends, February–April. Good with naturalized daffodils. Very handsome foliage looks good with hostas. Self-sows freely where adapted. Plant parts emit a somewhat unpleasant odor when bruised.

H. niger. CHRISTMAS ROSE. Zones US, MS. Elegant plant to 1½ ft. tall, blooming at some time between December and early spring (timing depends on severity of winter). Not easy to grow in the South. Lustrous dark green leaves divided into seven to nine leaflets with few, large teeth. White or greenish white, about 2-in.-wide flowers turn purplish with age. Named selections are sometimes available. 'White Magic' has large white flowers that take on a hint of pink as they age.

H. orientalis. LENTEN ROSE. Zones US, MS, LS. Like *H. niger* in form, but easier to grow and transplant. Basal leaves with five to eleven sharply toothed leaflets. Blooms in late winter and continues into spring. Flowering stems branched, with leaflike bracts at branching points and beneath flowers. Blossoms are white, greenish, purplish, or rose, often spotted or splashed with deep purple. Lenten rose is often mistakenly sold as "Christmas rose," but it differs from true Christmas rose in flower color and in having many small teeth on leaflets. Self-sows freely.

H. viridis. GREEN HELLEBORE. Zones US, MS, LS. Grows to 1½ ft. Graceful, bright green leaves are divided into seven to eleven leaflets. Flowers 1–2 in. wide, pure green or yellowish green, sometimes with purple markings inside. Blooms winter through late spring. *H. v. occidentalis* has smaller flowers and larger leaves.

HEMEROCALLIS

DAYLILY

Liliaceae

PERENNIALS

ALL ZONES, EXCEPT AS NOTED

FULL SUN OR LIGHT SHADE

REGULAR WATER

Hemerocallis Hybrid

Tuberous, somewhat fleshy roots give rise to large clumps of arching, sword-shaped leaves—evergreen, semievergreen, or deciduous depending on type. Lilylike flowers in open or branched clusters at ends of generally leafless stems that stand well above foliage. Older yellow, orange, and rust red daylilies have mostly been replaced by newer kinds; both tall and dwarf selections are available.

Although many species exist, only a few are offered by garden centers. Most of the daylilies available are hybrids; thanks to generations of crossing by scores of amateur and professional breeders, more than 20,000 named selections have been registered by the American Hemerocallis Society, and hundreds more appear each year.

Plant in borders with bearded iris, Michaelmas and Shasta daisies, red-hot poker, dusty miller, and lily-of-the-Nile. Mass along driveways and roadsides, in country gardens, on banks under high-branching, deciduous trees. Group among evergreen shrubs, near ponds, along streams. Plant dwarf daylilies in containers, as edgings, low ground covers. Good cut flowers. Cut stems with well-developed buds; buds open on successive days, though each flower is slightly smaller than preceding one. Arrange individual blooms in low bowls. Snap off faded flowers daily.

Few plants are tougher or more trouble-free than daylilies. They adapt to almost any kind of soil. Divide crowded plants in early spring or late fall.

H. altissima. Deciduous. A lofty plant—leaves can grow to 5 ft. long, flower stems to 6 ft. high. Fragrant, 4-in. yellow flowers appear on branching stems in late summer and autumn. 'Statuesque' has 5-ft. stems, blooms mid- to late summer.

H. fulva. ORANGE DAYLILY, TAWNY DAYLILY. Deciduous. To 6 ft. high, with leaves to 2 ft. long or longer; tawny orange-red, 3–5-in.-wide, unscented flowers in summer. Rarely sold, but commonly seen in old gardens, along roadsides; a tough, persistent plant good for holding banks. Double-flowered 'Kwanso' is sometimes seen. Both species and selection have been largely replaced by hybrids. Aggressive spreader.

H. hybrids. Deciduous, evergreen, and semievergreen. Deciduous types go completely dormant in winter. Hardier than evergreen types, they are the plants of choice in the Upper South. Evergreen hybrids keep their leaves all year long and are well adapted to the Coastal and Tropical South. Semievergreen sorts may or may not retain leaves, depending on where they are grown.

Modern hybrids are 1–6 ft. tall, have flowers 3–8 in. across. Some have broad petals, others narrow, spidery ones; many have ruffled petal edges. Colors range far beyond basic yellow, orange, and rusty red, going into pink, vermilion, buff, apricot, plum or lilac purple, creamy white, and near-white, often bicolored with contrasting eyes or midrib stripes. Many kinds are sprinkled with tiny iridescent dots known as diamond dust. Semidouble-flowered and double-flowered forms exist.

To get what you want, buy plants in bloom (either in containers or in the field), or study specialists' catalogs, many of which have fine color photographs. To prolong the bloom season, look for reblooming (remontant) types; or select early, midseason, and late bloomers. Plants listed as tetraploid (possessing twice the normal number of chromosomes) have flowers with unusually heavy textured petals. Look for daylilies with awards from the American Hemerocallis Society. The letters AM stand for Award of Merit, presented to ten selections each year. HM means Honorable Mention, awarded to any plant receiving ten or more votes from the selection committee. SM stands for Stout Medal, the highest award a daylily can receive. SM winners include the long-blooming dwarf yellow 'Stella de Oro' and the free-blooming yellow tetraploid 'Mary Todd'. An old garden type that retains its popularity amid the influx of new hybrid daylilies is 'Hyperion', a 4-ft.-tall plant with fragrant yellow flowers that bloom in midsummer.

H. lilio-asphodelus (H. flava). LEMON DAYLILY. Deciduous. Zones US, MS, LS, CS. To 3 ft.; 2-ft. leaves. Fragrant, 4-in., pure yellow flowers, late May or June. Newer hybrids may be showier, but species is still cherished for its delicious perfume and early blossom time.

HEMLOCK. See TSUGA

HEMP AGRIMONY. See EUPATORIUM cannabinum

HEN AND CHICKENS. See SEMPERVIVUM tectorum

HEN AND CHICKS. See ECHEVERIA imbricata

HEPATICA

LIVERWORT, LIVERLEAF

Ranunculaceae

PERENNIALS

ZONES US, MS, LS

PARTIAL OR FULL SHADE

REGULAR WATER

Hepatica americana

Low growers with leathery evergreen or semievergreen leaves and flowers consisting of petal-like sepals similar to those of some of the smaller anemones. (In fact, these plants were once classified as anemones.) Flowers appear early in spring, each rising on its own stalk above the clump of last year's leaves. A new crop of leaves follows bloom. Choice plants for woodland gardens or for the shaded rock garden. Little known in the South except to wildflower fanciers, they are popular among plant collectors in Japan, where many types not yet grown here are cultivated. Prefers near-neutral soil pH—lime, if necessary.

H. acutiloba. HEPATICA LIVERLEAF. Native to eastern U.S. Leathery leaves, 4 in., divided into three sharp-pointed lobes. Flowers are lilac or white, ½–1 in. across, on stems 6–9 in. tall.

H. americana (H. triloba). HEPATICA LIVERLEAF. Resembles the above, but leaves have rounded lobes; flowering stems are usually shorter, to 6 in. Flowers typically light blue, but sometimes white or pink.

HERALD'S TRUMPET. See BEAUMONTIA grandiflora

HERBS. At some time in history, plants in this category have been valued for seasoning, medicine, fragrance, or general household use.

Herbs are versatile. Some creep along the ground, making fragrant carpets. Others are shrublike. Many make attractive pot plants. However, quite a few do have a weedy look, especially next to ornamental plants. Many are hardy and adaptable. Although hot, dry, sunny conditions with poor but well-drained soil are usually considered best, some herbs thrive in shady, moist locations with light soil rich in humus.

Following are lists of herbs for specific landscape situations:

Kitchen garden. Plant these basic cooking herbs in a sunny raised bed near the kitchen door, planter box near the barbecue, or part of the vegetable garden: sweet basil *(Ocimum basilicum)*, chives, dill *(Anethum graveolens)*, sweet marjoram *(Origanum majorana)*, mint *(Mentha)*, oregano *(Origanum vulgare)*, parsley, rosemary *(Rosmarinus)*, sage *(Salvia officinalis)*, savory *(Satureja)*, Mexican mint marigold *(Tagetes lucida)*, thyme *(Thymus)*. The connoisseur may wish to plant coriander *(Coriandrum sativum)*, common fennel *(Foeniculum vulgare)*.

Ground cover for sunny areas. Prostrate rosemary, creeping thyme *(Thymus praecox arcticus)*, lemon thyme *(T. citriodorus)*, or silver thyme *(T. pseudolanuginosus)*.

Ground cover for shade. Sweet woodruff *(Galium odoratum)*.

Perennial border. Common wormwood *(Artemisia absinthium)*, garden burnet *(Sanguisorba minor)*, lavender *(Lavandula)*, monarda, rosemary, scented geraniums *(Pelargonium)*.

Hedges. Formal clipped hedge—santolina, germander *(Teucrium)*. Informal hedge—lavender, winter savory *(Satureja montana)*.

Herbs for moist areas. Mint, parsley, sweet woodruff.

Herbs for partial shade. Lemon balm *(Melissa officinalis)*, parsley, sweet woodruff.

Herbs for containers. Crete dittany *(Origanum dictamnus)*, chives, lemon verbena *(Aloysia triphylla)*, sage, pineapple sage *(Salvia elegans)*, summer savory *(Satureja hortensis)*, sweet marjoram, mint, small burnet.

> ### EDIBLE HERB BOUQUETS
> Don't worry about snipping more kitchen herbs than you need. Put the extra cuttings of basil, marjoram, mint, oregano, rosemary, sage, and thyme in a vase of water and use them to decorate the table. They remain kitchen-useful as long as they stay perky (often a week or more).

Potpourris and sachets. Lavender, lemon balm, sweet woodruff, lemon verbena, and monarda.

To dry leafy herbs for cooking, cut them early in day before sun gets too hot, but after dew has dried on foliage (oil content is highest then). Leafy herbs are ready to cut from the time flower buds begin to form until flowers are half open. (Exceptions: Parsley can be cut any time; sage may take on a strong taste unless cut early in summer.) Don't cut perennial herbs back more than a third; annual herbs may be sheared to about 4 in. from the ground. Generally you can cut two or three crops for drying during summer. Don't cut perennial herbs after September or new growth won't have chance to mature before cold weather.

Before drying, sort weeds and grass from herbs; remove dead or damaged leaves. Wash off loose dirt in cool water; shake or blot off excess moisture. Tie woody-stemmed herbs such as sweet marjoram or thyme in small bundles and hang upside down from line hung across room. Room should be dark (to preserve color), have good air circulation and warm temperature (about 70°F) for rapid drying to retain aromatic oils. If room is fairly bright, surround herb bundles with loose cylinders of paper.

For large-leafed herbs such as basil, or short tips that don't bundle easily, dry in tray with light wooden sides and window screen tacked to the bottom. On top of screen place double thickness of cheesecloth. Spread leaves out over surface. Stir leaves daily.

With good air circulation and low humidity, leafy herbs should be crumbly dry in a few days to a week. (If humidity is too high, try drying herbs in a paper bag in the refrigerator.) When herbs are dry, strip leaves from stems and store whole in airtight containers—glass is best—until ready to use. Label each container with name of herb and date dried. Check jars the first few days after filling to make sure moisture has not formed inside. If it has, pour out contents and dry for a few more days.

To gather seeds, collect seed clusters such as dill, anise, fennel, caraway when they turn brown. Seeds should begin to fall out when clusters are gently tapped. Leave a little of stem attached when you cut each cluster. Collect in box. Flail seeds from clusters and spread them out in sun to dry for several days. Separate chaff from seed and continue to dry in sun for another 1½–2 weeks. Store seed herbs the same way as leafy ones.

H

HESPERALOE parviflora

RED YUCCA

Agavaceae

PERENNIAL

✿ ZONES US, MS, LS, CS

☼ FULL SUN

◑ MODERATE TO LITTLE WATER

Hesperaloe parviflora

Native to Texas, northern Mexico. Makes dense, yucca-like clump of very narrow, swordlike, evergreen leaves 4 ft. long, about 1 in. wide. Pink to rose red, 1¼-in.-long, nodding flowers in slim, 3–4-ft.-high clusters bloom in early summer, with repeat bloom frequent. On older plants, spikes can grow as tall as 8–9 ft. Good large container plant with loose, relaxed look. *H. p. engelmannii* is similar to species, but its 1-in.-long flowers are more bell shaped. Tolerates most well-drained soils.

🪴 HESPERIS matronalis

DAME'S ROCKET, SWEET ROCKET

Brassicaceae (Cruciferae)

PERENNIAL OR BIENNIAL

✿ ALL ZONES

☼ ◑ FULL SUN OR LIGHT SHADE

◑ REGULAR WATER

Hesperis matronalis

An old-fashioned, cottage-garden plant, freely branched. Grows to 3 ft. tall and as broad, with 4-in., toothed leaves and rounded clusters of ½-in., four-petaled, lavender to purple blooms. Flowers resemble those of stock and are fragrant at night. Plant grows readily from seed and often self-sows. Old, woody plants should be replaced by young seedlings. White and double-flowered forms exist but are rare.

HEUCHERA

CORAL BELLS, ALUM ROOT

Saxifragaceae

PERENNIALS

✿ ZONES VARY BY SPECIES

☼ ◑ LIGHT SHADE IN MIDDLE AND LOWER SOUTH

◑ REGULAR WATER

Heuchera sanguinea

Compact, evergreen clumps of roundish leaves with scalloped edges. Slender, wiry stems 1–2½ ft. high bear open clusters of nodding, bell-shaped flowers ¼ in. or more across, in carmine, reddish pink, coral, crimson, red, rose, greenish, and white. Various types bloom between April and August. Flowers dainty, long lasting in cut arrangements, attractive to hummingbirds. Many recent introductions are grown more for leaf color than floral display.

Mass in borders or in front of shrubs; use as edging for beds of delphiniums, irises, lilies, peonies, roses. Grow in well-drained, humus-rich soil. Divide clumps every 3 or 4 years in spring or fall. Use young, vigorous, rooted divisions; discard older, woody rootstocks. Sow seed in spring.

H. americana. Zones US, MS. Foliage mound 1–2 ft. high. Leaves 1½–4½ in. wide, green mottled white. Flower stalks 3 ft. tall bear tiny greenish white blooms. Selections grown for their foliage include 'Garnet', deep red winter foliage, brighter red new foliage in spring; 'Lace Ruffles',

ruffled and scalloped leaves mottled silvery white; 'Pewter Moon', purple leaves with strong central silvery zone; 'Pewter Veil', shining silvery leaves, small purple flowers; 'Ring of Fire', silvery, purple-veined leaves that develop a red rim in fall; 'Ruby Veil', 8-in. silvery leaves with veins that are red at leaf bases; and 'Velvet Night', deep bluish purple leaves.

H. brizoides. Zones US, MS, LS. Hybrids between *H. sanguinea* and other species. As seed-grown plants, often called Bressingham Hybrids. Flowers come in white and shades of pink and red. 'June Bride' is a good white selection. 'Snowstorm' has deep reddish pink flowers that grow above white-variegated leaves.

H. micrantha. Zones US, MS, LS. Native to western U.S. To 1–2 ft. high. Long-stalked, roundish leaves are 1–3 in. long, hairy on both sides, toothed, lobed. Flowers are whitish or greenish, about ⅛ in. long, in loose clusters on leafy, 2–3-ft.-tall stems. Hybrid forms developed from *H. micrantha* are more widely adapted than species. 'Palace Purple' has maplelike, brownish or purplish red leaves that retain their color all year; 'Ruffles' has leaves that are deeply lobed and ruffled around edges.

H. sanguinea. CORAL BELLS. Zones US, MS, LS. Native to Mexico and Arizona. Makes neat tufts of round, 1–2-in. leaves. Wiry stems 1–2 ft. tall bear red or coral pink flowers. Forms with white, pink, or crimson flowers are also available. 'Cherry Splash' and 'Frosty' display red flowers above variegated foliage.

HEUCHERELLA tiarelloides

Saxifragaceae

PERENNIAL

✿ ZONES US, MS, LS

◑ LIGHT SHADE

◑ REGULAR WATER

Heucherella tiarelloides 'Bridget Bloom'

Hybrid of *Heuchera brizoides* and foam-flower (*Tiarella cordifolia*). Has flowering habit of *Heuchera* parent with heart-shaped leaves of foamflower, in a low, clumping, evergreen perennial. Foot-high stems bear narrow sprays of many tiny pinkish bells in late spring or early summer. Good selections include 'Bridget Bloom', which produces its shell pink flowers over a long period. 'Pink Frost', another long bloomer, has pink flowers and roundish, mottled gray-green leaves. All forms make a good ground cover for woodland or shaded rock garden. Provide humus-rich soil and good drainage.

HIBISCUS

Malvaceae

SHRUBS, PERENNIALS, AND ANNUALS

✿ ZONES VARY BY SPECIES

☼ FULL SUN, EXCEPT AS NOTED

◑ ◑ AMPLE TO REGULAR WATER

Hibiscus rosa-sinensis

Many species are grown in the South. Most are cultivated for their big showy flowers, though one is raised for colorful foliage and another is grown for food.

H. acetosella. RED-LEAF HIBISCUS. Sometimes grown from seed as an annual, but more often seen as a 5-ft.-tall evergreen shrubby perennial in the Tropical South. Foliage, lobed somewhat like a maple leaf or unlobed, may be green or deep purplish red; only the red form is commonly grown, often as a coarse hedge. Cultivated for its foliage rather than its less conspicuous dark-centered red or yellow flowers. The plant may be better known as *H. eetveldeanus.*

🪴 **H. coccineus.** TEXAS STAR. Shrubby perennial. Zones MS, LS, CS, TS. Native to coastal swamps of Florida and Georgia. Moderately fast-growing bush, to 6 ft., with handsome glossy foliage; showy scarlet flowers, 3 in. wide, June to October. Leaves palmate, with three to seven lobes, much like those of Japanese maple. Use as an accent or at the back of a perennial border. Does well in either wet or well-drained soil.

H. eetveldeanus. See *H. acetosella*

H. militaris. HALBERD-LEAFED ROSE-MALLOW. Shrubby perennial. All zones. Native of marshes and wet woods from Pennsylvania to Minnesota, south to Florida and Texas. Grows quickly to 8 ft. tall in moist soil. Leaves dagger shaped, dark green, 6 in. long; 4–6-in.-wide pinkish white flowers, May to October. Tolerates partial shade, heavy soils with poor drainage.

� **H. moscheutos.** PERENNIAL HIBISCUS, COMMON ROSE-MALLOW. Perennial. All zones. Largest flowers of all hibiscus, some to 1 ft. across, on a plant 6–8 ft. tall; bloom starts in June, continues until fall. Oval, toothed leaves deep green above, whitish beneath. Plants die down in winter. Feed at 6- to 8-week intervals during growing season. Protect from wind.

Seed-grown strains often flower the first year if sown indoors and planted out early. Southern Belle strain grows 4 ft. tall; Disco Belle, Frisbee, and Rio Carnival strains are 2–2½ ft. tall. Flowers, 8–12 in. wide, come in red, pink, rose, or white, often with a red eye. The many cutting-grown types include 'Blue River', 10-in. pure white flowers; and 'George Riegel', 10-in. ruffled pink blossoms with a red eye. Both of these selections grow about 4 ft. high, and their flowers remain open even on the hottest days. Hybrid 'Lord Baltimore', to 6 ft. tall, produces 10-in. deep red flowers over an exceptionally long bloom period.

🌸 **H. mutabilis.** CONFEDERATE ROSE. Deciduous shrub. Zones LS, CS, TS. Shrubby or treelike in the Coastal and Tropical South, it behaves more like a perennial in the Lower South, growing flowering branches from woody base or short trunk. Leaves are broad, oval, with three to five lobes. Summer flowers are 4–6 in. wide, opening white or pink and changing to deep red by evening. 'Rubrus' has red flowers. Double-flowered forms also exist. Whiteflies are a common pest.

🌸 **H. rosa-sinensis.** CHINESE HIBISCUS, TROPICAL HIBISCUS. Evergreen shrub. Zones CS, TS; provide overhead protection where winter lows frequently drop below 30°F. Where temperatures go much lower, grow in containers and shelter indoors over winter; or grow as annuals, setting out fresh plants each spring. Also makes a good house plant that can be brought outdoors during the warm season.

One of showiest flowering shrubs. Reaches 30 ft. tall in tropics, but seldom over 15 ft. tall in the U.S. Glossy foliage varies somewhat in size and texture depending on variety. Growth habit may be dense and dwarfish or loose and open. Summer flowers single or double, 4–8 in. wide. Colors range from white through pink to red, from yellow and apricot to orange. Individual flowers last only a day, but the plant blooms continuously.

Requires excellent drainage; if necessary, improve soil or set plants in raised beds or containers. Fertilize monthly (potted plants twice monthly) April to September, then let growth harden. For good branch structure, prune poorly shaped young plants when you set them out in spring. To keep a mature plant growing vigorously, prune out about a third of old wood in early spring. Pinching out tips of stems in spring and summer increases flower production. These are some of the selections available:

'Agnes Galt'. Big single pink flowers. Vigorous, hardy plant to 15 ft. Prune to prevent legginess.

'All Aglow'. Tall (10–15-ft.) plant has large single flowers with broad, gold-blotched orange petals, pink halo around a white throat.

'American Beauty'. Broad, deep rose flowers. Slow growth to 8 ft. tall. Irregular form.

'Bridal Veil'. Large pure white single flowers last 3 or 4 days. Plant 10–15 ft. tall.

'Bride'. Very large, palest blush to white flowers. Slow to moderate growth to open-branched 4 ft.

'Brilliant' ('San Diego Red'). Bright red single flowers in profusion. Tall, vigorous, compact, to 15 ft. Hardy.

'Butterfly'. Small, single bright yellow flowers. Slow, upright growth to 7 ft.

'California Gold'. Heavy yield of yellow, red-centered, single flowers. Slow or moderate growth to a compact 7 ft.

SOUTHERN HERITAGE PLANTS
....
IDENTIFIED BY SYMBOL 🌸

'Crown of Bohemia'. Double gold flowers; petals shade to carmine orange toward base. Moderate or fast growth to 5 ft. Bushy, upright. Hardy.

'Diamond Head'. Large double flowers in deepest red (nearly black red). Compact growth to 5 ft.

'Ecstasy'. Large (5–6-in.) single bright red flowers with striking white variegation. Upright growth to 4 ft.

'Fiesta'. Single bright orange flowers 6–7 in. wide; white eye zone at flower center edged red. Petal edges ruffled. Strong, erect growth to 6–7 ft.

'Fullmoon'. Double pure yellow flowers. Moderately vigorous growth to a compact 6 ft.

'Golden Dust'. Bright orange single flowers with yellow-orange centers. Compact, thick-foliaged plant 4 ft. tall.

'Hula Girl'. Large single canary yellow flowers have deep red eye. Compact growth to 6 ft. Flowers stay open several days.

'Itsy Bitsy Peach', 'Itsy Bitsy Pink', and 'Itsy Bitsy Red' are all tall (10–15-ft.) plants with small leaves and small (2–3-in.) single flowers.

'Jason Okumoto'. Semidouble scarlet-throated orange flowers surrounded by collar of large pink petals (blooms have a cup-and-saucer look). Grows 10–15 ft. tall.

'Kate Sessions'. Large red single flowers with broad petals; petal undersides tinged gold. Moderate growth to 10 ft. tall. Upright, open habit.

'Kona'. Ruffled double pink flowers. Vigorous, upright, bushy, 15–20 ft. Prune regularly. 'Kona Improved' has fuller flowers of richer pink color.

'Kona Princess'. Small double pink flowers on a 6–7-ft. shrub.

'Morning Glory'. Single blush pink flowers changing to warmer pink with white petal tips. Grows 8–10 ft. tall.

'President'. Flowers single, 6–7 in. wide, intense red shading to deep pink in throat. Upright, compact, 6–7 ft. tall.

'Red Dragon' ('Celia'). Flowers small to medium, double, dark red. Upright, compact, 6–8 ft. tall.

'Ross Estey'. Flowers heavy textured, very large, single, with broad, overlapping petals of pink shading coral orange toward tips; last 2 or 3 days on bush. Vigorous. To 8 ft. Leaves very large, ruffled, polished dark green.

'Vulcan'. Large single red flowers with yellow on back of petals open from yellow buds. Flowers often last more than a day. Compact grower, 4–6 ft. tall.

'White Wings'. Profuse, narrow-petaled, single white flowers with small red eye. Vigorous, open, upright to 20 ft.; prune to control legginess. A compact form with smaller flowers is available.

🌸 **H. syriacus.** ROSE OF SHARON, SHRUB ALTHAEA. Deciduous shrub or small tree. Zones US, MS, LS, CS. To 10–12 ft. tall, upright and compact when young, spreading and open with age. Easily trained to single trunk with treelike top or as an espalier. Leaves medium size, often with three coarsely toothed lobes. Leaves come later in spring than those of most other deciduous shrubs; drop in fall without coloring. Resembles a bush covered with hollyhock flowers in summer. Blossoms are single, semidouble, or double, 2½–3 in. across; some have a contrasting red to purple throat. Single flowers are slightly more effective, opening somewhat wider, but tend to produce many unattractive capsule-type fruits—which tend to produce many unwanted seedlings.

Easy to grow. Prefers heat, tolerates some drought. Prune to shape; for bigger flowers, cut back previous season's growth in winter, cutting down to two buds. The best selections, some of them hard to find, include:

'Albus'. Single pure white, 4-in. flowers.

'Anemoniflora' ('Paeoniflora'). Semidouble red blossoms with deeper crimson eye.

'Ardens'. Double purple flowers.

'Blue Bird'. Single blue blooms with deep red eye.

'Blushing Bride'. Double bright pink blossoms.

'Boule de Feu'. Double deep violet pink flowers.

'Coelestis'. Single violet blue flowers with reddish purple throat.

'Collie Mullens'. Double purplish lavender blossoms.

'Lucy'. Double deep rose flowers with red eye.

'Purpurea'. Semidouble purple blooms with red eye.

'Red Heart'. Single white blossoms with red eye.

'Woodbridge'. Single deep rose flowers with red eye.

Newer selections are sterile triploids, which have a long blooming season and set few or no seedpods. They include:

'Aphrodite'. Rose pink flowers with deep red eye.
'Diana'. Pure white blooms.
'Helene'. White flowers with deep red eye.
'Minerva'. Ruffled lavender-pink blossoms with reddish purple eye.

HICKORY. See CARYA

HIDDEN LILY. See CURCUMA petiolata

HIMALAYAN SWEET BOX. See SARCOCOCCA hookerana humilis

HINOKI FALSE CYPRESS. See CHAMAECYPARIS obtusa

AMARYLLIS INDOORS? IT'S EASY

A potted amaryllis bulb can bloom indoors in just a few weeks. Keep it in a warm, dark place until the roots have formed. Then move it to a warm, lightly shaded place where the air is not too dry. Increase watering as leaves form. Feed lightly every 2 weeks during the flowering period.

HIPPEASTRUM

AMARYLLIS
Amaryllidaceae
BULBS
ZONES LS, CS, TS; OR INDOORS
FULL SUN OR LIGHT SHADE
REGULAR WATER DURING GROWTH AND BLOOM

Hippeastrum Hybrid

Native to tropics and subtropics. Many species are useful in hybridizing, but only hybrids are generally available; these are usually sold as giant amaryllis or Royal Dutch amaryllis (though many are grown in South Africa or elsewhere). Named selections in reds, pinks, white, salmon, near-orange, some variously marked and striped. Two to several flowers, often 8–9 in. across, form on stout, 2-ft. stems. Where plants are grown outdoors, flowers bloom in spring; indoors, they bloom just a few weeks after planting. Broad, strap-shaped leaves usually appear after bloom, grow through summer and disappear in fall if plants are dried off; otherwise, foliage is evergreen. Many types will overwinter in ground.

Newer forms include double-flowered selections in white (some with red picotee edges), creamy yellow, or pink; miniatures, with 3–5-in. flowers topping 12–15-in. stems; and an unusual evergreen species, *H. papilio,* with 5-in. greenish white flowers heavily patterned with dark red.

H. johnsonii, Saint Joseph's lily, is an early hybrid popular in old gardens in the South. Its 5-in.-wide trumpet flowers are scarlet red with white stripes and emerge in clusters of four to six atop 2-ft. stems; mature bulbs may produce four stems and twenty-four blooms. Tough and resilient, it blooms well in sun or light shade. Hardy in Lower and Coastal South. *H. reginae,* Mexican lily, another heirloom type, has bright satiny red trumpets with white stars in the throats. Flowers appear in clusters of two, three, or four on 1-ft. stems in summer.

All types can be grown in pots. Plant November–February in rich, sandy mix with added bonemeal or superphosphate. Allow 2-in. space between bulb and edge of pot. Set upper half of bulb above soil surface. Firm soil and water it well; then keep barely moist until growth begins. Water regularly during growth and bloom. When flowers fade, cut off stem, keep up watering; feed to encourage leaf growth. When leaves start to yellow, withhold water, let plants dry out. Repot in late fall or early winter.

SOUTHERN HERITAGE PLANTS
IDENTIFIED BY SYMBOL

HIPPOPHAE rhamnoides

SEA BUCKTHORN
Elaeagnaceae
DECIDUOUS SHRUB OR SMALL TREE
ZONE US
FULL SUN
REGULAR TO MODERATE WATER

Hippophae rhamnoides

Sea buckthorn is usually seen as an open, mounding shrub 8–10 ft. tall, although it can grow much taller. Spreads by suckering from roots. Branches are thorny. Leaves are narrow (1/4 in. or less), to 3 in. long, silvery green to grayish green. Flowers are inconspicuous, but fruit on female plants is showy—bright orange, round or oval, to 1/3 in. long. Fruit lasts well through winter, apparently being too sour to appeal to birds. It can, however, be made into sauces or jam; it is high in vitamin C. To get fruit, you must have both male and female plants.

Sea buckthorn tolerates low temperatures, wind, poor soils (if they are reasonably well drained), and salt spray. A good screening plant for difficult situations, such as the beach.

HOLLY. See ILEX

HOLLY FERN. See CYRTOMIUM falcatum

HOLLYHOCK. See ALCEA rosea

HOLLYHOCK, MINIATURE. See SIDALCEA

HOLLY OLIVE. See OSMANTHUS heterophyllus

HONESTY. See LUNARIA annua

HONEY LOCUST. See GLEDITSIA triacanthos

HONEYSUCKLE. See LONICERA

HONG KONG ORCHID TREE. See BAUHINIA blakeana

HOP. See HUMULUS

HOP HORNBEAM. See OSTRYA

HORNBEAM. See CARPINUS

HORSECHESTNUT. See AESCULUS

HORSERADISH

Brassicaceae (Cruciferae)
PERENNIAL
ZONES US, MS, LS
FULL SUN
REGULAR WATER

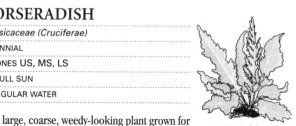

Horseradish

A large, coarse, weedy-looking plant grown for its large, white roots, which can be peeled, grated, and mixed with vinegar or cream to make a condiment. Does best in rich, moist soils in cooler areas of the Upper and Middle South. Grow horseradish in a sunny out-of-the-way corner. Start with roots planted about 1 ft. apart in late winter or early spring.

FRESH HORSERADISH

Through fall, winter, and spring, harvest pieces of horseradish roots from the outside of the root clump as you need them—that way you'll have your horseradish fresh and hot. Scrub and peel the roots, cutting away any dark parts; then grate them. Mix with vinegar, sweet cream, or sour cream—or simply sprinkle directly onto food.

HORSESUGAR. See SYMPLOCOS tinctoria

HORSETAIL. See EQUISETUM hyemale

HORSETAIL TREE. See CASUARINA equisetifolia

HOSTA

HOSTA, PLANTAIN LILY
Liliaceae

PERENNIALS

✂ ZONES US, MS, LS

◑ ● PARTIAL OR FULL SHADE

💧 REGULAR WATER

Hosta decorata

Their real glory is in their foliage. The thin spikes of blue or white, trumpet-shaped flowers that appear for several weeks in summer are an added benefit. Hostas provide a tremendous variety in leaf size, shape, and color among species and selections; to fully appreciate the diversity they offer, you'll need to consult a specialist's catalog or visit a well-stocked garden center.

Leaves may be heart shaped, lance shaped, oval, or nearly round, carried at the ends of leafstalks that rise from the ground and radiate from the center of a clump. Leaves overlap to form symmetrical, almost shingled foliage mounds ranging in size from dwarf (as small as 3–4 in.) to giant (as big as 5 ft.). Leaf texture may be smooth, quilted, or puckery; surface may be glossy or dull; edges may be smooth or wavy. Colors range from light to dark green to chartreuse, gray, and blue. There are also combinations of colors, including variegations with white, cream, or yellow.

New selections enter the scene in ever-increasing numbers. In few plants have the species undergone so many name changes; to be sure you are getting the one you want, buy the plant in full leaf or deal with an expert. The plants listed below are just a few of the many possibilities.

Generally, hostas are shade lovers, though some tolerate sun. Most grow in considerable sun in the Upper South. All forms go dormant (collapse almost to nothing) in winter. All are splendid companions for ferns and plants with fernlike foliage, such as bleeding heart. Good in containers. In ground, plants last for years; clumps expand in size, and shade out weed growth. Feeding once a year will bring on extra leafy splendor. Blanket of mulch around plants will prevent mud from splattering leaves. Where slugs or snails are a problem, use slug bait or try reportedly resistant selections (those with heavily textured or waxy leaves are best bets).

H. crispula. CURLED-LEAF HOSTA. Ovate, 7-in.-long, dark green leaves with wavy, uneven margins and drooping, curly leaf tips. Foliage mound to 1½ ft. high. Many lavender flowers early in the season. Plant is sometimes confused with *H. fortunei* 'Albo-marginata', which blooms later.

H. decorata (H. 'Thomas Hogg'). A foot-high mound of oval leaves, 6 in. long, bluntly pointed at tips, dull green with silvery white margins. Dark violet flowers bloom early.

H. fortunei. FORTUNE'S PLANTAIN LILY. May be an ancient hybrid affiliated with *H. sieboldiana*. Variable plant known for its many selections offering a wide range of foliage color. Plants grow to 1–1½ ft. high, with oval, 1-ft.-long leaves, lilac flowers. Young leaves of 'Albo-picta' are yellow with uneven green border; yellow fades by summer. Leaves of 🖼 'Albo-marginata' have an irregular yellow border that fades to white; late bloom. 'Hyacinthina' has large gray-green leaves edged with a fine white line.

H. hybrids. The following list includes some of the best, most widely grown hostas:

'Antioch'. Broad green leaves with wide, creamy white margins. Lavender flowers well above 1½-ft. foliage mound.

'August Moon'. Spade-shaped, lightly crinkled, bright chartreuse leaves in 1½-ft. mound. White flowers.

'Blue Angel'. Heavily veined blue-green leaves 16 in. long, nearly as wide, in an enormous 4-ft. mound. White flowers over long bloom period. Sun tolerant.

'Blue Wedgwood'. Slightly wavy-edged, strongly veined, heart-shaped leaves in 1½-ft. mound. Pale lavender flowers bloom early.

'Chartreuse Wiggles'. Dwarf (6 in. high), with lance-shaped, wavy-edged, chartreuse-gold leaves. Lavender flowers bloom late.

'Francee'. Broadly heart-shaped leaves to 6 in. long with striking white edges form a 1½–2-ft. mound. Lavender flowers bloom late. Sun tolerant.

'Frances Williams' ('Gold Edge', 'Gold Circle'). Mound to 2½–3 ft. high, made up of round, puckered, blue-green leaves boldly and irregularly edged in yellow. Pale lavender flowers bloom early.

'Ginko Craig'. Elongated, frosty green leaves with silver margins in a 1–1½-ft. mound. Abundant lavender flowers.

'Gold Edger'. Heart-shaped leaves, 3 in., chartreuse gold. Foliage mound to 10 in. high. Masses of lavender flowers. Among the most sun tolerant; in fact, needs some sun for best color.

'Gold Standard'. Heart-shaped, bright golden leaves with a green margin form a 2-ft. mound. Pale lavender flowers. Sun tolerant.

'Hadspen Blue'. Low (1 ft.), with slightly wavy, broadly oval blue leaves. Slug-resistant foliage. Many lavender flowers.

'Halcyon'. Heart-shaped, heavy-textured, blue-gray leaves in a 1½-ft. mound. Short spikes of rich lilac blue flowers.

'Honeybells'. Wavy-edged, yellow-green leaves in 2–2½-ft. mound. Lightly scented, pale lilac flowers.

'Krossa Regal'. Big, leathery, frosty blue leaves arch upward and outward to make a 3-ft., vase-shaped plant. Slug-resistant foliage. Late bloom of lavender flower spikes can reach 5–6 ft.

'Piedmont Gold'. Broadly heart-shaped, heavily veined, slightly wavy-edged, 7-in. leaves of glowing chartreuse gold in a 2–2½-ft. mound. White flowers. Sun tolerant.

'Royal Standard'. Glossy light green leaves, elongated and undulated, in a 2-ft. mound. Fragrant white flowers. Sun tolerant.

'Shade Fanfare'. Leaves are pointed ovals to 7 in. long, green to gold with creamy white margin. Foliage mound to 1½ ft. high. Lavender flowers. Very sun tolerant.

'Sum and Substance'. Textured, shiny yellow leaves to 20 in. long form a mound to 3 ft. high, 5 ft. wide. Slug-resistant foliage. Lavender flowers. Very sun tolerant.

H. lancifolia (H. japonica). NARROW-LEAFED PLANTAIN LILY. Leaves glossy deep green, 6 in. long, and lance shaped, the bases tapering into the long stalks. Foot-high foliage mound. Pale lavender flowers bloom late.

H. nakaiana 'Golden Tiara'. Foot-high mound of heart-shaped leaves 4 in. long, light green with gold edge. Purple flowers. Sun tolerant.

H. plantaginea (H. grandiflora, H. subcordata). FRAGRANT PLANTAIN LILY. Leaves glossy bright green, to 10 in. long, broadly oval with parallel veins and quilted surface. Foliage mound 2 ft. high. Noticeably fragrant, large white flowers bloom late. 'Aphrodite' is double flowered.

H. sieboldiana (H. glauca). SIEBOLD PLANTAIN LILY. Blue-green, broadly heart-shaped leaves, 10–15 in. long, heavily veined and puckered. Many slender, pale lilac flower spikes nestle close to 2½-ft. foliage mound early in season. Foliage dies back early. 'Elegans' has especially handsome, blue-gray leaves that are slug resistant.

H. sieboldii 'Kabitan'. Wavy, lance-shaped leaves to 5 in. long, chartreuse to yellow with thin green margins. White flowers rise above foot-high foliage mound.

H. tardiflora. Small plant (to 1 ft. high), with lance-shaped leaves to 6 in. long. Spikes of pale purple flowers, same height as foliage clump, come very late. More sun tolerant than most others.

H. tokudama. Like *H. sieboldiana*, but smaller (to 1 ft.), with a more crepelike texture. Slug-resistant foliage. White flowers. 'Flavo-circinalis', with irregular yellow margins, is more sun tolerant than the species.

H. undulata (H. media picta, H. variegata). WAVY-LEAFED PLANTAIN LILY. Wavy-edged, narrowly oval leaves, 6–8-in. long, in a 1½-ft. mound. Typical leaf is green with a creamy white center stripe. Foliage is used in arrangements. Pale lavender flowers. 'Albo-marginata' has creamy white margins on leaves. 'Erromena' is all green.

H. ventricosa (H. caerulea). BLUE PLANTAIN LILY. Named for its violet blue blooms. Leaves are glossy deep green, broadly heart shaped, prominently veined, to 8 in. long, in a 2-ft. mound. Leaves of 'Aureo-maculata'

H

are yellowish green with a green border. In 'Aureo-marginata' ('Variegata'), each leaf is green edged with creamy white; sun tolerant.

HOUSELEEK. See SEMPERVIVUM

HOUSTONIA caerulea (Hedyotis caerulea)

BLUETS, QUAKER LADIES

Rubiaceae

PERENNIAL

✿ ZONES US, MS, LS

☼ LIGHT SHADE

💧 REGULAR WATER

Houstonia caerulea

Creeping perennial making small (2–3-in.) mounds of tiny oval leaves. Flowers appear singly on 2–2½-in. stalks in late spring. The ½-in.-wide, four-lobed flowers are pale blue (sometimes white) with a yellow eye. Although small, they are profuse enough to create a charming effect. Use in woodland gardens, around stepping-stones, or as carpet for large potted shrubs like camellia or aucuba. In the wild, thrives among mosses in light shade under tall oak trees. Will also grow in sparse lawns.

HOUTTUYNIA cordata

Saururaceae

PERENNIAL

✿ ZONES US, MS, LS

☼ ☼ ● SUN OR SHADE

💧 AMPLE WATER

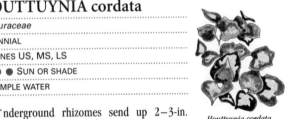

Houttuynia cordata

Underground rhizomes send up 2–3-in. leaves that look much like those of English ivy. When crushed, leaves give off a peculiar scent somewhat reminiscent of orange peel. Inconspicuous clusters of white-bracted flowers like tiny dogwood blossoms. Unusual ground cover that disappears completely in winter. 'Variegata' ('Chameleon') has showy splashes of cream, pink, yellow, and red on foliage. 'Plena' has more prominent flowers consisting of several rows of white bracts; leaves are plain green. Plants can spread aggressively in wet ground. Attractive in container or, if curbed, in shady garden. Can grow in standing water; good for pond sites.

HOWEA

Arecaceae (Palmae)

PALMS

✿ ZONE TS

☼ PARTIAL SHADE

💧 REGULAR WATER

Howea forsterana

Native to Lord Howe Island in the South Pacific. These feather palms are the kentia palms of florists and are usually sold under the name "kentia." Slow growing, to eventual 35 ft. tall; with age, leaves drop to show clean, green trunk ringed with leaf scars. When using outdoors, plant under another tree. Give indirect light indoors.

Howeas are ideal pot plants—the classic parlor palms. Keep fronds clean and dust-free to minimize spider mite problem.

H. belmoreana. SENTRY PALM. Less common than *H. forsterana*, smaller and more compact, with overarching leaves 6–7 ft. long. Withstands some watering neglect, drafts, dust.

H. forsterana. PARADISE PALM, SENTRY PALM. Larger than species *H. belmoreana*, with leaves to 9 ft. long and long, drooping leaflets.

HOYA

WAX PLANT, WAX FLOWER

Asclepiadaceae

EVERGREEN VINES

✿ ZONE TS; OR INDOORS

☼ ● PARTIAL OR FULL SHADE

💧 REGULAR WATER, EXCEPT AS NOTED

Hoya carnosa

Thick, waxy, evergreen leaves and tight clusters of small waxy flowers. Grow in sunny window. Prefer rich, loose, well-drained soil. Bloom best when pot-bound; grown in pots even outdoors. Do not prune out flowering wood; new blossom clusters appear from stumps of old ones. Specialists list dozens of species and selections.

H. bella. House or greenhouse plant. Shrubby, small leafed, to 3 ft., with slender, upright branches that droop as they grow older. Tight clusters of purple-centered, white, ½-in. flowers in summer. Best in hanging basket.

H. carnosa. WAX FLOWER, WAX PLANT. Indoor plant or outdoors in south Florida with overhead protection. Vining to 10 ft. Leaves are oval, 2–4 in. long. Fragrant summer flowers in big, round, tight clusters; each ½-in.-wide blossom is creamy white, centered with five-pointed pink star. Red young leaves give extra color. In most areas, let plant go dormant in winter, giving only enough water to keep it from shriveling. Outdoors, train on pillar or trellis in shade; indoors, train on wire in sunny window. 'Exotica' shows yellow-and-pink variegation. 'Krinkle Kurl' has crinkly leaves closely spaced on short stems; it is often sold as 'Compacta' or as Hindu-rope plant. 'Variegata' has leaves edged in white suffused with pink; it is not as vigorous or hardy as the green form.

HUMMINGBIRD BUSH. See ANISACANTHUS wrightii

HUMULUS

HOP

Cannabaceae

PERENNIAL VINES

✿ ZONES US, MS, LS, CS

☼ FULL SUN

💧 REGULAR WATER

Humulus lupulus

Extremely fast growth. Leaves are large, deeply lobed, attractive for summer screening on trellises or arbors. Plants sold in garden centers are typically female (sexes are separate). No pollinator is required.

H. japonicus. JAPANESE HOP. To 20–30 ft. Flowers do not make true hops. 'Variegatus' has foliage marked with white. Flowers in greenish clusters like pine cones. Sow seeds in spring where plants are to grow. Roots are perennial; tops die back in fall.

H. lupulus. EUROPEAN HOP. Produces the hops used to flavor beer. Grow from roots (not easy to find in garden centers) planted in rich soil in early spring. Place thick end up, just below soil surface. Furnish supports for vertical climbing. Shoots appear in midspring; by midsummer have grown to 15–25 ft. Leaves with three to five lobes, toothed. Squarish, hairy stems twine vertically; to get horizontal growth, twine stem tips by hand. Attractive light green hops (soft, flaky, 1–2-in. cones of bracts and flowers) form in late summer, have fresh, piny fragrance. Cut back stems to ground after frost. Regrowth comes the following spring. Tender hop shoots can be cooked as a vegetable. 'Aureus' has attractive chartreuse leaves in spring; needs some shade to prevent color from bleaching.

HURRICANE LILY. See LYCORIS africana

HYACINTH BEAN. See DOLICHOS lablab

HYACINTHOIDES. See ENDYMION

HYACINTHUS

HYACINTH

Liliaceae

BULBS

⬧ ZONES US, MS, LS, CS

☼ ◑ FULL SUN OR PARTIAL SHADE

⬥ REGULAR WATER DURING GROWTH AND BLOOM

⬥ BULBS CAN IRRITATE SKIN

Hyacinthus orientalis

As perennials, best adapted to the Upper and Middle South. Grow as annuals elsewhere. Bell-shaped, fragrant flowers in loose or tight spikes rise from basal bundle of narrow bright green leaves. All are spring blooming. Plant October–December. In the Lower and Coastal South, refrigerate for 10–12 weeks before planting.

H. azureus. See Muscari azureum

H. orientalis. COMMON HYACINTH. Grows to 1 ft., with fragrant, bell-shaped flowers in white, pale blue, or purple blue. Two basic forms are the Dutch and the Roman or French Roman.

Dutch hyacinth, derived from *H. orientalis* by breeding and selection, has large, dense spikes of waxy, bell-like, fragrant flowers in white, cream, buff, and shades of blue, purple, pink, red, and salmon. Size of flower spike is directly related to size of bulb. Biggest bulbs are desirable for exhibition plants or for potting; next largest size is satisfactory for bedding outside. Small bulbs give smaller, looser clusters with more widely spaced flowers. These are sometimes called miniature hyacinths.

Set the larger bulbs 6 in. deep, smaller bulbs 4 in. Hyacinth bulbs have invisible barbs on their surfaces that can cause some people's skin to itch; after handling, wash hands before touching face or eyes. Hyacinths look best when massed or grouped; rows look stiff, formal. Mass bulbs of a single color beneath flowering tree or in border. Leave bulbs in ground after bloom, continue to feed. Flowers tend to be smaller in succeeding years, but maintain same color and fragrance.

Choice container plants. Pot in porous mix with bulb tip near surface. Then cover containers with thick mulch of sawdust, wood shavings, or peat moss to keep bulbs cool, moist, shaded until roots are well formed; remove mulch, place pots in full light when plant tops show. Also grow hyacinths in water in special hyacinth glass, the bottom filled with pebbles and water. Keep in dark, cool place until rooted, give light when top growth appears; place in sunny window when leaves have turned uniformly green.

Roman or French Roman hyacinth *(H. o. albulus)* has white, pink, or light blue flowers loosely carried on slender stems; usually several stems to a bulb. Earlier to bloom than Dutch hyacinths, they are also better adapted to the Lower South and will perennialize under favorable conditions.

HYDRANGEA

Hydrangeaceae (Saxifragaceae)

DECIDUOUS SHRUBS OR VINES

⬧ ZONES VARY BY SPECIES

☼ ◑ LIGHT SHADE IN LOWER AND COASTAL SOUTH

⬥ REGULAR WATER

Hydrangea quercifolia

Big, bold leaves and large clusters of long-lasting flowers in white, pink, red, or blue. Summer, fall bloom. Flower clusters may contain sterile flowers (conspicuous, with large, petal-like sepals) or fertile flowers (small, starry petaled); or they may feature a cluster of small fertile flowers surrounded by a ring of big sterile ones (these are called lace cap hydrangeas). Sterile flowers last long, often holding up for months, gradually changing in color. Effective as single plants, massed, or in containers on paved terrace.

Easy to grow in rich, porous soil. Fast growing; prune to control size and form. Most hydrangeas bloom on previous year's wood, so prune after

flowering. (No flowering will occur if flower buds are killed in cold winters.) *H. arborescens* blooms on new growth and should be pruned in the late dormant season. To get biggest flower clusters on all types, reduce number of stems; for many medium-size clusters, keep more stems.

H. anomala. CLIMBING HYDRANGEA. Deciduous vine. Native to Japan, China. Zones US, MS, LS. Climbs high by clinging aerial rootlets. Shrubby and sprawling without support. Roundish, 2–4-in.-long, green, heart-shaped leaves. Mature plants develop short, stiff, flowering branches with flat white flower clusters, 6–10 in. wide, in lace cap effect. Old plants have peeling, cinnamon-colored bark. *H. a. petiolaris (H. petiolaris),* more common from cultivation, differs hardly at all.

H. arborescens. SMOOTH HYDRANGEA. Deciduous shrub. Native to eastern and midwestern U.S. Zones US, MS, LS, CS. Upright, dense to 10 ft. Oval, grayish green leaves, 4–8 in. In species, most flowers in a cluster are fertile; the few sterile ones are not plentiful enough for full lace cap effect. Much showier is 'Annabelle', which produces enormous (to 1-ft.) globular clusters of sterile white flowers on a plant about 4 ft. tall. 'Grandiflora', snowhill hydrangea, has 6-in. clusters on a similarly sized plant.

🌱 **H. macrophylla (H. hortensia, H. opuloides, H. otaksa).** FRENCH HYDRANGEA, BIGLEAF HYDRANGEA, GARDEN HYDRANGEA. Deciduous shrub. Native to Japan. Zones US, MS, LS, CS. Symmetrical, rounded habit; grows to 4–8 ft. or even 12 ft. high. Thick, shining, coarsely toothed leaves to 8 in. long; white, pink, red, or blue flowers in big clusters. In many selections, blue or pink is determined by soil pH—bluest color produced in acid soil, reddest in alkaline soil. Plants can be made (or kept) blue by applying aluminum sulfate to soil; plants can be kept red or made redder by liming the soil or applying superphosphate in quantity. Treatment must be started well ahead of bloom to be effective.

Hundreds of named selections exist. Plants may be sold under many names. Florists' plants are usually French hybrids, shorter (1–3 ft. tall) and

Hydrangea macrophylla

larger flowered than old garden types. Among the hardier garden selections are 'All Summer Beauty', 3–4 ft. tall, with flower heads produced on current season's growth (unlike other bigleaf hydrangeas); 'Blue Wave', 6–7 ft. tall, with lace cap flowers; 'Carmen', 4 ft. tall, with large, deep pink flower heads; 'Domotoi', with double florets in large heads; 'Forever Pink', 3 ft. tall, with 4–5-in. flower heads; 'Goliath', with 15-in. flower heads; 'Lanarth White', 3 ft. tall, with lace cap flowers composed of blue or pink fertile flowers surrounded by ring of pure white sterile ones; 'Mariesii', 4–5 ft. tall, lace cap flowers with a few sterile flowers scattered among fertile flowers in center; 'Nikko Blue', a Japanese selection, 4–6 ft. tall, with most dependably rich blue flower heads (providing soil is at least lightly acid); and 'Pia', a dwarf with tight clusters of heavy-textured carmine red florets. Several lace caps feature silver-variegated foliage: 'Quadricolor', 'Silver Variegated Mariesii', 'Tricolor', and 'Variegata'.

H. paniculata 'Grandiflora'. PEEGEE HYDRANGEA. Deciduous shrub or small tree. Native to Japan, China. Zones US, MS, LS, CS. Upright, of coarse texture. Can be trained as a 25-ft. tree, but best as a 10–15-ft. shrub. Leaves 5 in. long, turn bronzy in fall. Mainly fertile flowers in upright, 10–15-in. clusters in summer, white slowly fading to pinky bronze in fall. 'Tardiva' blooms later, has upright pyramidal clusters with a mix of sterile and fertile flowers.

H. quercifolia. OAKLEAF HYDRANGEA. Deciduous shrub. Native to Alabama, Georgia, Florida, Mississippi. Zones US, MS, LS, CS. Broad, rounded shrub to 6 ft., with handsome, deeply lobed, oaklike, 8-in.-long leaves that turn bronze or crimson in fall. Elongated clusters of fertile and sterile white flowers in late spring and early summer turn pinkish purple as they age. Improvements on the species are 'Snow Queen', with larger flower clusters; 'Snowflake', with extra petals for double-flowered effect; and 'Harmony', a low-growing shrub, 3 ft. tall, 6 ft. wide, with spectacular 12-in. cones of densely packed, sterile flowers.

H. serrata. Deciduous shrub. Native to Japan, Korea. Zones US, MS, LS, CS. Like *H. macrophylla*, but generally smaller, with smaller leaves, smaller flowers, and more slender stems. Lace cap 'Blue Billow', 3 ft. tall,

H

keeps blue color in most soils. 'Preziosa' grows to 4 ft. tall and has round pink flower clusters that age to red.

Hydrangeaceae. The hydrangea family includes several woody-stemmed plants formerly listed under Saxifragaceae. *Hydrangea* and mock orange (*Philadelphus*) are examples.

HYDRASTIS canadensis

GOLDEN SEAL

Ranunculaceae

PERENNIAL

ZONES US, MS

PARTIAL OR FULL SHADE

REGULAR WATER

Hydrastis canadensis

Native to eastern U.S. Roots are used in herbal remedies. An unusual ground cover for woodland or shade gardens. Plant grows from a thick yellow rootstock, sending up two deeply lobed, 8-in. leaves and a 1-ft. stalk topped by two smaller leaves and an inconspicuous whitish to yellowish green flower. The blossom is followed by a large, showy red berry that resembles an outsize raspberry, though it isn't edible. Plant will grow in ordinary good garden soil, but it prefers plenty of leaf mold or compost. A modestly attractive choice for native plant enthusiasts.

HYLOCEREUS undatus

NIGHT-BLOOMING CEREUS, QUEEN OF THE NIGHT

Cactaceae

CACTUS

ZONE TS; OR INDOORS

FULL SUN OR LIGHT SHADE

REGULAR OR LITTLE WATER

Hylocereus undatus

A plant that is often passed along from friend to friend, parent to child. Origin unknown, but widely cultivated and naturalized in tropical America. Deep green, three-ribbed, 2-in.-wide stems with short dark spines grow quickly to 15 ft., sometimes to 30 ft. long, attaching themselves to a tree trunk or wall or house by means of strong aerial roots. Without a support to climb on, the stems create a large, freestanding mound, with a beautiful snaking pattern. Grown primarily for its waxy, fragrant, white nocturnal flowers, which are up to 1 ft. long. Individual flowers last just one night, but plant may bloom all summer. May also produce showy, red, 4-in.-long fruits, which are edible, even deliciously sweet. Tolerates salt spray.

Easy to grow outdoors in Tropical South. Elsewhere, grow in container and bring indoors in winter; keep air moist and night temperature above 55°F. Can survive drought but does best if watered regularly until flowering starts, then sparingly through the summer, to encourage flowering.

HYMENOCALLIS

Amaryllidaceae

BULBS

ZONES VARY BY SPECIES; OR DIG AND STORE DECIDUOUS TYPES; OR GROW IN POTS

FULL SUN OR PARTIAL SHADE

REGULAR WATER DURING GROWTH AND BLOOM

BULBS ARE POISONOUS IF INGESTED

Hymenocallis caroliniana

Clumps of strap-shaped leaves like those of amaryllis. The 2-ft. stems bear several very

fragrant flowers in summer; blooms resemble daffodils in having a center cup, but cup is surrounded by six slender, spidery segments. Deciduous species maintain foliage throughout summer if watered, then die back in fall. Unusual plants for borders or containers. Plant in rich, well-drained soil—in late fall or early winter in frostless areas, after frosts in other areas. Set bulbs with tips 1 in. below surface. Deciduous sorts can be dug after foliage has yellowed (do not cut off fleshy roots), dried in an inverted position, and stored in open trays in a cool place.

H. caroliniana. SOUTHERN SPIDER LILY. Deciduous. Zones MS, LS, CS. Native to swampy woodlands of Georgia, Indiana, and Louisiana. Each bulb produces as many as 12 deep green leaves 1½ ft. long, ½ in. wide. White fragrant spidery flowers appear in spring and summer, in clusters of two to seven on 2-ft. stems. Multiplies rapidly.

H. latifolia (H. keyensis). SPIDER LILY. Evergreen. Zones CS, TS. Native to Florida, the West Indies. Clusters of six to twelve white flowers that each consist of a 3-in. cup outlined by 5-in.-long, spidery segments.

H. liriosme. Zones MS, LS, CS. Native to Texas, Mississippi. Large, white, exceedingly fragrant flowers. Likes wet soil.

H. narcissiflora (Ismene calathina). BASKET FLOWER, PERUVIAN DAFFODIL. Deciduous. Zone LS. Leaves 1½–2 ft. long, 1–2 in. wide. White, green-striped flowers in clusters of two to five. Selection 'Advance' has pure white flowers, faintly lined with green in throat.

H. 'Sulfur Queen'. Zones LS, CS, TS. Deciduous. Primrose-like yellow flowers with light yellow, green-striped throats. Leaves are much like those of *H. narcissiflora*.

HYPERICUM

ST. JOHNSWORT

Hypericaceae

SHRUBS AND PERENNIALS, MOSTLY EVERGREEN

ZONES VARY BY SPECIES

PARTIAL SHADE IN LOWER AND COASTAL SOUTH

REGULAR TO MODERATE WATER

Hypericum calycinum

Large group of shrubs and perennials bearing yellow flowers resembling single roses with prominent sunburst of stamens in center. Open, cup-shaped, five-petaled blooms range in color from creamy yellow to gold; flowers may be solitary or in clusters. Neat leaves vary in form and color. Plants are useful for summer flower color and fresh green foliage. Various kinds used for mass plantings, ground covers, informal hedges, borders. Perform especially well in mild, moist areas.

H. beanii (H. patulum henryi). Evergreen shrub or perennial; more perennial-like in Upper South. Zones US, MS. To 4 ft. tall, with light green, oblong leaves on graceful, willowy branches. Flowers brilliant golden yellow, 2 in. across, midsummer into fall. Good for low, untrimmed hedge, mass planting. Shabby winter appearance.

H. calycinum. AARON'S BEARD, CREEPING ST. JOHNSWORT. Evergreen to semievergreen shrublet; tops often killed in cold winters but come back in spring. Zones US, MS, LS. To 1 ft. high, spreads by vigorous underground stems. Short-stalked leaves to 4 in. long are medium green in sun, yellow green in shade. Flowers bright yellow, 3 in. across throughout summer. A tough, dense ground cover that competes successfully with tree roots, takes poor soil. Fast growing; will control erosion on hillsides. May be invasive unless confined. Plant from flats or as rooted stems 1½ ft. apart. Clip or mow tops every 2 or 3 years during dormant season.

H. frondosum. BLUELEAF ST. JOHNSWORT. Deciduous shrub; evergreen in mildest areas. Zones US, MS, LS. Native to southeastern U.S. Grows 1–3 ft. tall, with mounding form. Blue-green leaves set off clusters of 1½-in. bright yellow flowers that bloom from midsummer to early autumn. 'Sunburst' forms a tight mound to 3 ft. tall and wide.

H. 'Hidcote' (H. patulum 'Hidcote'). Evergreen to semievergreen shrub. Zones US, MS, LS. To 4 ft. tall. Leaves 2–3 in. long. Yellow flowers, 3 in. wide, all summer. Very prone to root rot and wilt in Lower South.

H. kouytchense. Semievergreen shrub. Zones US, MS, LS. Twiggy, rounded, to 1½–2 ft. tall, 2–3 ft. wide. Pointed oval, 2-in. leaves; golden yellow, 2–3-in.-wide flowers, bloom in summer. Often sold as *H.* 'Sungold'.

H. moseranum. GOLD FLOWER. Evergreen shrub or perennial. Zones MS, LS. Hybrid plant. Forms shrub to 1½ ft. tall. Moundlike habit with arching, reddish stems. Leaves 2 in. long, blue green beneath. Golden yellow flowers, 2½ in. across, are borne singly or in clusters of up to five. Blooms in summer, possibly into fall. Cut back in early spring. 'Tricolor' has gray-green leaves tinged with pink and edged in white.

H. patulum henryi. See H. beanii

H. 'Rowallane'. Evergreen to semievergreen shrub. Zones MS, LS. Upright, rather straggly growth to 3–6 ft. Flowers bright yellow, 2½–3 in. across, profuse in late summer and fall. Leaves 2½–3½ in. long. Remove older branches annually.

H. 'Sungold'. See H. kouytchense

HYPOESTES phyllostachya (H. sanguinolenta)

POLKA-DOT PLANT, FRECKLE FACE

Acanthaceae

PERENNIAL TREATED AS ANNUAL OR HOUSE PLANT

✿ ALL ZONES AS ANNUAL

☼ ◑ FULL SUN OR LIGHT SHADE

● REGULAR WATER

Hypoestes phyllostachya

Though this tender plant is actually a perennial, it is almost always grown as a bedding annual or house plant. Can reach 1–2 ft. tall. Slender stems bear oval, 2–3-in.-long leaves spotted irregularly with pink or white. A selected form known as 'Splash' has larger spots. Tiny, inconspicuous lavender flowers are not always produced. For indoor use, plant in loose, peaty mixture in pots or planters. Feed with liquid fertilizer. Pinch tips to make bushy.

Hypoxidaceae. The star grass family consists of a small number of perennial plants growing from corms or rhizomes. Flowers have six equal segments and resemble those of the lily and amaryllis families. Yellow star grass (*Hypoxis hirsuta*) is one of the commonly seen examples.

HYPOXIS hirsuta

YELLOW STAR GRASS

Hypoxidaceae

PERENNIAL

✿ ZONES US, MS, LS, CS

☼ ◑ FULL SUN OR LIGHT SHADE

◑ ● REGULAR TO MODERATE WATER

Hypoxis hirsuta

Native from Maine to Florida and west to Texas. Usually found in dryish woodlands, growing in sandy or stony soil in full sun or light shade. Grassy, somewhat hairy, 1-ft.-long leaves rise from a short, cormlike rhizome. In spring and early summer, a 1-ft.-tall stem carries from one to seven bright yellow, starlike, inch-wide flowers. A second bloom may follow later. Interesting primarily to native plant enthusiasts or rock gardeners.

HYSSOP, ANISE. See AGASTACHE foeniculum

IBERIS

CANDYTUFT

Brassicaceae (Cruciferae)

PERENNIALS AND ANNUALS

✿ ZONES VARY BY SPECIES

☼ FULL SUN

● REGULAR WATER

Iberis sempervirens

Free-blooming plants with clusters of white, lavender, lilac, pink, rose, purple, carmine, or crimson flowers. Perennial candytufts bloom in spring; can be used as winter annuals in Coastal South. Annual species bloom in spring and summer; they are most floriferous when nights are cool. Use all types for borders, cutting; perennials for edging, rock gardens, small-scale ground covers, containers.

All types need well-drained soil. In early spring or (in mild climates) fall, sow seed of annuals in place or in flats; set transplants 6–9 in. apart. Plant perennials in spring or fall. After they bloom, shear lightly to stimulate new growth.

I. amara. HYACINTH-FLOWERED CANDYTUFT, ROCKET CANDYTUFT. Annual. All zones. Fragrant white flowers in tight, round clusters that elongate into hyacinth-like spikes on 15-in. stems. Narrow, slightly fuzzy leaves.

I. gibraltarica. Perennial. Zones MS, LS. Resembles *I. sempervirens* but is less hardy to cold and bears flatter clusters of light pinkish or purplish flowers, sometimes white near center.

I. sempervirens. EVERGREEN CANDYTUFT. Perennial. Zones US, MS, LS. Grows 8 in. to 1 ft. or even 1½ ft. high, spreading about as wide. Narrow, shiny dark green leaves are good-looking all year. Pure white flower clusters carried on stems long enough to cut for bouquets. Lower, more compact selections include 'Alexander's White', 6 in. tall, with fine-textured foliage; 'Kingwood Compact', also 6 in. high; 'Little Gem', 4–6 in. tall; and 'Purity', 6–12 in. and wide spreading. 'Snowflake', 4–12 in., spreading to 1½–3 ft., has broader, more leathery leaves than the species; also has larger flowers in larger clusters on shorter stems. It is extremely showy in spring and continues sporadic bloom through summer and fall. 'Snowmantle' is a similar vigorous type.

I. umbellata. GLOBE CANDYTUFT. Annual. All zones. Bushy plant 12–15 in. high. Lance-shaped leaves to 3½ in. long; flowers in pink, rose, carmine, crimson, salmon, lilac, and white. Dwarf strains Dwarf Fairy and Magic Carpet, available in the same colors, grow 6 in. tall.

ICELAND POPPY. See PAPAVER nudicale

ICE PLANT. See DELOSPERMA

ILEX

HOLLY

Aquifoliaceae

EVERGREEN OR DECIDUOUS SHRUBS OR TREES

✿ ZONES VARY BY SPECIES

☼ ◑ FULL SUN OR PARTIAL SHADE

● REGULAR WATER, EXCEPT AS NOTED

Ilex aquifolium

Though English holly (*I. aquifolium*) is the most familiar in song and legend (and in Christmas wreaths), the species is not entirely satisfactory for the South. Better choices include evergreen species grown for their attractive foliage and fruit as well as deciduous types grown principally for showy autumn and winter berries. In size, hollies range from foot-high dwarfs to trees 40–50 ft. tall. More than 400 species and countless hybrids exist. Smaller hollies are attractive as foundation plantings or low hedges; larger evergreen kinds make attractive, impenetrable tall hedges or screens. ▶

All holly plants are either male or female, and as a rule both sexes must be present for the female to set fruit. Those described below are female unless otherwise noted. A few are self-fertile; these are also noted.

Most hollies prefer rich, moist, slightly acid garden soil with good drainage. (A few exceptions are noted.) All appreciate a mulch to deter weeds and keep soil cool and moist. Though hollies will grow in sun or part shade, choose a sunny spot for best berry production and most compact growth. Principal pests are scale, bud moth, and leaf miner.

I. aquifolium. ENGLISH HOLLY. Evergreen tree. Zones US, MS. The classic holly. Dislikes poor drainage, low temperatures, cold drying winds, and high humidity coupled with high temperatures. Species has succeeded in ideal locations, but chancy; *I.* 'Nellie R. Stevens' (see entry this page) is a better choice for achieving similar effect. Among the hardiest English holly selections are 'Balkans', which is the most cold tolerant and has both male and female forms; 'Boulder Creek'; and 'Zero' ('Teufel's Weeping').

I. aquipernyi. Evergreen shrub or small tree. Zones US, MS, LS. Hybrid between English holly and *I. pernyi*. May attain 20 ft. or more. The 2–4-in., spiny-edged leaves are closely set on branches. 'Aquipern' is a male selection; 'Brilliant' and 'San Jose' are female, with small red berries that set without pollination.

I. attenuata. Evergreen tree. Zones US, MS, LS, CS. Hybrid between American holly *(I. opaca)* and dahoon *(I. cassine)*. Dense, conical habit to 20–30 ft. tall; sparsely toothed foliage. 'East Palatka' and 'Foster's #2' (also known as Foster's holly) are widely planted female forms. 'Foster's #4' is a male plant. 'Nasa', a female holly, is known for its unusually narrow leaves. 'Hume #2' has almost spineless, glossy green, rounded leaves. 'Savannah', a popular old selection, female, has whitish bark, light green leaves with very small spines, and bright red berries. It tolerates limy soils well. Good as a specimen or for tall screens.

I. cassine. DAHOON. Large evergreen shrub or small tree. Zones MS, LS, CS. Native to swamps and moist lowlands from North Carolina to Florida and Louisiana. Dense, upright habit to 20–30 ft. tall; leathery medium green leaves, 2–4 in. long, toothed only at tips. Heavy crops of small berries, ranging from red to reddish orange, sometimes almost yellow. Grows naturally in wet acid soils; tolerates mild alkalinity and has some salt tolerance.

I. cornuta. CHINESE HOLLY. Evergreen shrub or small tree. Zones US, MS, LS, CS. Very tolerant of heat, drought, alkaline soil. Dense or open form to 10 ft. or more. Leaves typically glossy, leathery, nearly rectangular, with spines at four corners and at tip. Berries very large, bright red, long lasting. Selections rather than species usually grown; fruit set, leaf form, and spininess vary. The following selections set fruit without pollination.

'Berries Jubilee'. Dome-shaped plant to 6–10 ft., with large leaves and heavy crop of large, bright red berries. Leaves larger, spinier than those of 'Burfordii', on smaller plant.

'Burfordii'. BURFORD HOLLY. To 20 ft. tall and wide. Leaves nearly spineless, cupped downward. Heavy fruit set prized by mockingbirds and cedar waxwings. Useful as espalier. Discovered in Atlanta's Westview Cemetery around 1900.

'Carissa'. Dwarf to 3–4 ft. high and 4–6 ft. wide at maturity. Dense growth, small leaves. Use for low hedge. No berries. Has been known to revert to 'Rotunda', the plant from which it was developed.

'Dazzler'. Compact, upright growth. Glossy leaves have a few stout spines along wavy margins. Loaded with berries.

'D'Or'. Resembles 'Burfordii' but has bright yellow berries.

'Dwarf Burford' ('Burfordii Nana'). Resembles 'Burfordii' but is somewhat smaller, growing to about 8 ft. tall and wide. Densely covered with small (1½-in.), light green, nearly spineless leaves. Dark red berries.

'Needlepoint'. Dense, upright, a little larger than 'Dwarf Burford'. Dark green leaves, with a single spine at tip, and large crops of red berries.

'Rotunda'. DWARF CHINESE HOLLY. Compact grower to 3–4 ft. tall and 6–8 ft. wide at maturity. Usually does not produce berries. A few stout spines and rolled leaf margins between spines make the medium light green leaves nearly rectangular.

I. crenata. JAPANESE HOLLY. Evergreen shrub. Zones US, MS, LS. Looks more like a boxwood than a holly. Dense, erect, usually 3–4 ft.

high, sometimes to 10 ft. Narrow, fine-toothed leaves, ½–¾ in. long; berries are black. Extremely hardy and useful where winter cold limits choice of tender evergreens for hedges, edgings. Selections include:

'Beehive'. Dense, compact mound with leaves ½ in. long, ¼ in. wide.

'Compacta'. Rounded shrub to 6 ft. tall. Dense habit, ¾-in. leaves. Many different plants sold under this name.

'Convexa'. Compact, rounded shrub to 4–6 ft. high, spreading wider. Leaves are ½ in. long, roundish, cupped downward at the edges. Use clipped or unclipped. Many different plants sold under this name.

'Dwarf Pagoda'. Exceptionally slow growing and dense plant—to 1 ft. in 8 years. Leaves less than ½ in. long.

'Helleri'. Dwarf selection to 1 ft. high, 2 ft. wide; larger after many years, to 4 ft. tall and 5 ft. wide. Very sensitive to poor drainage.

'Jersey Pinnacle'. Compact, dense, erect. To eventual 8 ft. tall, 2 ft. wide.

'Soft Touch'. Grows 2 ft. tall, 3 ft. wide. Unlike other selections, has soft, flexible branches.

I. decidua. POSSUMHAW. Deciduous small tree. Zones US, MS, LS, CS. Native to Southeast. To 6–10 ft.; possibly to 20 ft. Pale gray stems; shiny dark green leaves to 3 in. long. Orange to red berries last into winter or spring. 'Warren's Red', eventually 15–20 ft. tall, bears a heavy crop of large red berries. 'Council Fire' is lower growing. For fruit production, need a male pollinator such as 'Red Escort' or any male selection of American holly, such as 'Jersey Knight'.

I. 'Emily Brunner'. Large evergreen shrub or small tree. Zones MS, LS, CS. Hybrid between *I. cornuta* and *I. latifolia*. Pyramidal, somewhat shrubby, to 20 ft. tall. Handsome dark green leaves, large and prominently toothed. Female plant; for fruit, use male pollinator 'James Swann'.

I. glabra. INKBERRY. Evergreen shrub. All zones. Native to eastern North America. To 10 ft. tall, with thick, dark green (olive green in winter), spineless leaves and black berries. More widely available is the dwarf form 'Compacta'; it grows to 4 ft. but can be sheared to make a 2-ft. hedge. 'Densa', 'Nordic', and 'Shamrock' are other dwarf forms. Grows in sun or shade. Prefers acid soil. Tolerates wet soil and salt spray.

I. latifolia. LUSTERLEAF HOLLY. Evergreen tree. Zones MS, LS, CS. Native to China, Japan. Slow-growing, stout-branched plant to 30 ft. tall. Leaves are 6–8 in. long (largest of all hollies), dull dark green, leathery, fine toothed. Big clusters of large, dull red berries. In youth resembles Southern magnolia *(Magnolia grandifolia)*.

I. meserveae. MESERVE HOLLY. Evergreen shrub. Zones US, MS. Most plants in this category are hybrids between English holly and a cold-tolerant species from northern Japan. Apparently the most cold-hardy of hollies that have true holly look. Dense, bushy plants 6–7 ft. tall, with purple stems and spiny, glossy blue-green leaves. Among red-fruiting female plants are 'Blue Angel', 'Blue Girl', and 'Blue Princess'; male pollinators include 'Blue Boy' and 'Blue Prince'. 'Golden Girl' has yellow berries. Red-fruited 'China Boy' and 'China Girl', both to 10 ft. tall, are crosses between Chinese holly and the northern Japanese species. They are slightly hardier and tolerate more summer heat than the Blue series.

I. 'Nellie R. Stevens'. Evergreen shrub or small tree. Zones US, MS, LS, CS. Most likely a hybrid between Chinese holly and English holly. Fast growing, densely conical to 15–25 ft. tall. Glossy, dark green, leathery, sparsely toothed leaves to 3 in. long. Sets fruit without a male holly, but forms a heavier crop if pollinated by a male selection of Chinese holly. Probably the best all-around holly for the South.

I. opaca. AMERICAN HOLLY. Evergreen tree. Zones US, MS, LS, CS. Native to eastern U.S. Slow growing to 50 ft. tall; pyramidal or round-headed

Ilex opaca

form. Leaves 2–4 in. long, spiny margined, dull or glossy green. Red berries. Hundreds of named selections exist. Among the best known are 'Dan Fenton', with large leaves glossier than those typical of the species; 'Jersey Delight' and 'Jersey Princess'; 'Jersey Knight', a male pollen source; 'Merry Christmas', with glossy, deep green leaves and bright red berries; 'Stewart's Silver Crown', with leaves edged in cream and marbled with gray green; and 'Yellow Berry', with bright yellow berries.

I. pedunculosa. LONGSTALK HOLLY. Evergreen shrub or small tree. Zones US, MS, LS. Exceptionally cold-hardy for a broad-leafed evergreen. Native to China, Japan. Grows to 15 ft. or taller; awkward shape when young. Narrow, smooth-edged leaves 1–3 in. long and half as wide. The ¼-in. bright red berries dangle on 1–1½-in.-long stalks in autumn.

I. pernyi. PERNY HOLLY. Evergreen tree. Zones US, MS, LS. Native to China. Slow growth to 20–30 ft. Glossy, 1–2-in.-long leaves, square at base, one to three spines on each side; closely packed against branchlets. Red berries set tightly against stems. 'Dr. Kassab', a hybrid between *I. pernyi* and *I. cornuta*, forms dense pyramid 15–20 ft. high, with glossy, deep green foliage and showy red berries.

I. 'Sparkleberry'. Deciduous shrub. Zones US, MS, LS, CS. Selection of hybrid between *I. verticillata* and *I. serrata*, released by the U.S. National Arboretum. Grows to 6 ft., old specimens may reach 12 ft. Sets copious amounts of large, bright red fruits that persist through winter. Probably the showiest deciduous holly of all. Tolerates wet soils. *I.* 'Carolina Cardinal', a selection made by J. C. Raulston at North Carolina State in Raleigh, is similar but more compact, growing to 5 ft. tall. Both selections are female plants. Pollinate with male selection, 'Apollo'.

I. verticillata. WINTERBERRY. Deciduous shrub. Zones US, MS, LS, CS. Native to swamps of eastern North America. Unlike most hollies, thrives in boggy soils, but will succeed in any moist, acid, organic soil. To 6–10 ft. tall, rarely taller, eventually forming clumps by suckering. Leaves are oval, to 3 in. long and 1 in. wide. Female plants bear enormous crops of bright red berries that ripen in early fall and last all winter (or until they are eaten by birds). 'Afterglow' has orange to orange-red berries on a compact plant; 'Cacapon', 'Fairfax', and 'Winter Red' are standard-size plants with dark red fruit; 'Red Sprite' is a large-berried dwarf selection. Pollinate 'Winter Red' with male winterberry 'Apollo', other female plants with 'Jim Dandy' or 'Raritan Chief'.

I. vomitoria. YAUPON. Evergreen shrub or small tree. Zones MS, LS, CS. Native to South. Grows in almost any soil—acid or alkaline, wet or dry, rich or poor. Good plant for the beach. Tolerates salt spray. Grows to 15–20 ft. tall, with narrow, inch-long, shallowly toothed dark green leaves. Can be grown as standard or sheared into columnar form; good topiary plant. Tiny scarlet berries are borne in profusion. Popular selections include the following:

'Nana'. DWARF YAUPON. Low shrub. Compact to 1½ ft. high and twice as wide. Refined, attractive. Formal when sheared. Inconspicuous berries.

'Pendula'. Weeping branches look best when plant is trained as standard.

'Pride of Houston'. Large shrub or small tree, upright, freely branching. Use as screen or hedge. Heavy fruiter.

'Stokes' ('Stokes Dwarf', 'Shillings'). Dark green, closely set leaves. Compact. Smaller growing than 'Nana'. Male.

'Will Fleming'. Narrow, upright form. Good for tight spaces. Male.

ILLICIUM

ANISE TREE

Illiciaceae

EVERGREEN SHRUBS OR SMALL TREES

ZONES VARY BY SPECIES

PARTIAL OR FULL SHADE

AMPLE TO REGULAR WATER

Illicium floridanum

Anise trees are a little-used but attractive clan of shrubs or small trees noted for their anise-scented foliage and oddly shaped and colored flowers. Thick, leathery, glossy leaves; small flowers with many petal-like segments in early spring. Fruits are small, one-seeded pods arranged in a ring; the star anise of Chinese cookery is the fruit of *I. verum*, apparently not grown in the U.S. All like shade, ample moisture, though will grow in drier soil, and soil rich with organic material. No serious pests.

I. anisatum (I. religiosum). JAPANESE ANISE. Zones LS, CS. Native to Japan. Grows 6–10 ft. (possibly 15 ft.) tall, with glossy 4-in. leaves and inch-wide creamy to yellowish green flowers.

I. floridanum. FLORIDA ANISE. Zones MS, LS, CS. Native Florida to Louisiana. To 6–15 ft. or more, with 6-in.-long leaves; inch-wide maroon flowers have a scent that most find unpleasant. 'Album' is white flowered; 'Halley's Comet' has somewhat larger, redder flowers than species.

I. parviflorum. YELLOW ANISE. Zones MS, LS, CS. Native to Southeast. Grows 10–20 ft. tall, with 4-in. olive green leaves and ½-in. yellow-green flowers. Can form small colonies by suckering. More tolerant of sun and dry soil than other anise trees, but equally at home in damp shade.

AMERICA'S NUMBER-ONE BEDDING PLANT

Impatiens wallerana does everything well and asks little. It's marvelously adaptable in shaded or semishaded landscapes; blooms prolifically from spring to late fall in beds, borders, pots, or hanging baskets. If you're willing to water almost daily, you can also grow these impatiens in full sun.

IMPATIENS

IMPATIENS, BALSAM, TOUCH-ME-NOT

Balsaminaceae

PERENNIALS AND ANNUALS

ALL ZONES

EXPOSURE NEEDS VARY BY SPECIES

REGULAR WATER

Impatiens wallerana

Of the hundreds of species, only the following are widely grown. Most of these are annuals or tender perennials treated as annuals; all are valuable for long summer bloom. Ripe seed capsules burst open when touched lightly and scatter seeds explosively.

I. balsamina. BALSAM, TOUCH-ME-NOT. Summer annual. Erect, branching, 8–30 in. tall. Leaves 1½–6 in. long, sharply pointed, deeply toothed. Flowers large, spurred, borne among leaves along main stem and branches. Blossoms are solid colored or variegated, in shades of white, pink, rose, lilac, red. Compact, bushy, double camellia-flowered forms are most frequently used. Sow seeds in early spring; set out plants after frost in full sun (light shade in Coastal and Tropical South).

I. holstii. See I. wallerana

I. New Guinea hybrids. Summer annuals most places; perennials in Tropical South. A varied group of striking plants developed from number of species native to New Guinea, especially *I. hawkeri*. Plants can be upright or spreading; they usually have large leaves, often variegated with cream or red. Flowers are usually large (though not profuse); colors include lavender, purple, pink, red, orange. Many named types, ranging from spreading, 8-in.-tall plants to erect, 2-ft. forms. 'Sweet Sue' and 'Tango', with bronzed foliage and bright orange, 2–3-in. flowers, can be grown from seed, as can Spectra hybrids. Grow in full sun or part shade. Good in pots, hanging baskets, borders.

I. sultanii. See I. wallerana

I. wallerana. IMPATIENS, SULTANA, BUSY LIZZIE. Summer annuals in most places; perennial in Tropical South. Includes plants formerly known as *I. holstii* and *I. sultanii*. Rapid, vigorous growth; tall forms reach 2 ft. tall, dwarf kinds 4–12 in. high. Dark green, glossy, narrow, 1–3-in.-long leaves on juicy pale green stems. Flowers 1–2 in. wide, in all colors but yellow and true blue.

Strains exist in bewildering variety. Single-flowered kinds are best for massing or bedding; they nearly cover themselves with flowers. Doubles have attractive blooms like little rosebuds, but they don't match singles for mass show and are better grown in pots.

All types produce months of bright color in partial or full shade. Grow from seed or cuttings; or buy plants in cell-packs or pots. Space dwarf types 6 in. apart, big ones 1 ft. apart. If plants get too tall and leggy, cut them back as close as 6 in.—it's a tonic. New growth emerges in a few days; flowers cover it in 2 weeks. Plants often reseed in moist ground.

IMPERATA cylindrica 'Rubra' ('Red Baron')

JAPANESE BLOOD GRASS

Poaceae (Gramineae)

PERENNIAL

☘ ZONES US, MS

☼ ◑ FULL SUN OR PARTIAL SHADE

💧 REGULAR WATER

Imperata cylindrica
'Rubra'

Clumping grass with erect stems 1–2 ft. tall, the top half rich blood red. Striking in borders, especially where sun can shine through blades. Completely dormant in winter. Spreads slowly by underground runners. Rarely, if ever, flowers. A good textural plant that mixes well with perennials that have yellow-green or blue-green foliage.

INCARVILLEA delavayi

HARDY GLOXINIA

Bignoniaceae

PERENNIAL

☘ ZONES US, MS

☼ ◑ SUN OR LIGHT SHADE

💧 REGULAR WATER

Incarvillea delavayi

Not related to gloxinias but rather to the many trumpet vines (*Bignonia, Campsis,* and the like). A showy perennial from high elevations in India, Tibet, and China. Carrotlike roots are available from bulb growers in autumn; set them 8 in. deep in very well drained soil. Leaves at base of plant are up to 1 ft. long. Bears 2½-in., yellow-throated, purplish pink flowers in early summer; blossoms are carried well above foliage in an elongated spikelike cluster to 2 ft. tall. A white-flowered form is available. Use in perennial borders or large rock gardens. Plant is deep rooted; needs reasonably deep soil, excellent drainage. In Upper South, mulch plants after ground has frozen to prevent heaving.

INDIAN BANYAN. See FICUS benghalensis

INDIAN BEAN. See CATALPA bignonioides

INDIAN BLANKET. See GAILLARDIA pulchella

INDIAN CURRANT. See SYMPHORICARPOS orbiculatus

INDIAN HAWTHORN. See RAPHIOLEPIS indica

INDIAN LAUREL. See FICUS microcarpa

INDIAN LOTUS. See NELUMBO nucifera

INDIAN PAINTBRUSH. See CASTILLEJA

INDIAN PINK. See SPIGELIA marilandica

INDIGO BUSH. See AMORPHA fruticosa, INDIGOFERA kirilowii

INDIGOFERA kirilowii

KIRILOW INDIGO, INDIGO BUSH

Fabaceae (Leguminosae)

SHRUBBY PERENNIAL

☘ ZONES US, MS, LS, CS

☼ ◑ FULL SUN OR LIGHT SHADE

◐ 💧 REGULAR TO MODERATE WATER

Indigofera kirilowii

Native to northern China, Korea, Japan. To 3–4 ft. high, with somewhat fernlike, bright green foliage. Small sweet pea–shaped rosy pink flowers carried in erect, 4–5-in. spikes over a long bloom period in summer. Not fussy about soil or water but requires

reasonably good drainage. Plants stay more compact and attractive if cut back hard in earliest spring. Spreads slowly by stolons. Often used in the Lower and Coastal South as a lacy ground cover atop exposed roots of old live oaks. Similar species, *I. gerardiana* and *I. incarnata,* may occasionally be seen.

INKBERRY. See ILEX glabra

INLAND SEA OATS. See CHASMANTHIUM latifolium

INTERRUPTED FERN. See OSMUNDA claytoniana

☂ IPHEION uniflorum (Brodiaea uniflora, Triteleia uniflora)

SPRING STAR FLOWER

Amaryllidaceae

BULB

☘ ZONES US, MS, LS, CS

☼ ◑ FULL SUN OR PARTIAL SHADE

💧 REGULAR WATER DURING GROWTH AND BLOOM

Ipheion uniflorum

Native to Argentina. Flattish, bluish green leaves that smell like onions when bruised. Spring flowers 1½ in. across, broadly star shaped, pale to deep blue, on 6–8-in. stems. 'Wisley Blue' is a good bright blue selection. Edging, ground cover in semiwild areas, under trees, large shrubs.

Plant 2 in. deep in any good soil in fall. Easy to grow; will persist and multiply for years. Prefers dry conditions during summer dormancy, but will accept water if drainage is good.

IPOMOEA

MORNING GLORY

Convolvulaceae

PERENNIAL OR ANNUAL VINES

☘ ZONES VARY BY SPECIES

☼ FULL SUN

◐ 💧 REGULAR TO MODERATE WATER

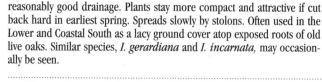

Ipomoea tricolor

This genus includes many ornamental vines and the sweet potato; it does not include the weedy plant known as wild morning glory or bindweed (*Convolvulus arvensis*). The plants described here may self-sow, but they do not spread by nearly ineradicable underground runners as does wild morning glory.

☂ **I. alba (Calonyction aculeatum).** MOONFLOWER, MOON VINE. All zones. Perennial climber in Tropical South; treat as summer annual elsewhere. Fast growing (20–30 ft. in a season), providing quick summer shade for arbor, trellis, or fence. Luxuriant leaves 3–8 in. long, heart shaped, closely spaced on stems. Flowers fragrant, white (rarely lavender pink), often banded green, 6 in. across. Flowers open in late afternoon, stay open all night, and usually close by morning, though they may remain open on dreary, overcast days. Seeds are hard; abrade them or soak them for 1 or 2 days for faster sprouting.

I. lindheimeri. Perennial. Zones LS, CS, TS. Native from Texas to New Mexico and Mexico. Flowers blue, 3½ in. long. Leaves deeply cleft. Trailing habit, but not invasive. Well suited to dry, chalky soils.

I. nil. MORNING GLORY. Summer annual. All zones. Includes rare large-flowered Imperial Japanese morning glories and a few kinds of common morning glory, including rosy red 'Scarlett O'Hara'. Early Call strain comes in a number of colors. For culture, see *I. tricolor.*

I. pes-caprae. BEACH MORNING GLORY, RAILROAD VINE. Evergreen perennial. Zones CS, TS. Sprawling vine grows to great length, rooting at leaf joints as it runs. Leaves are fleshy, 1½–4 in. long, notched at the tip, and nearly round to kidney shaped. Summer flowers pink, 2 in. wide. Florida native useful as a ground cover on sandy saltwater beaches.

I. purpurea. COMMON MORNING GLORY. All zones. Perennial in Tropical South; grow as summer annual elsewhere. Rapid growth to 30–40 ft. First flowers appear a few weeks after sowing seed; then vine quickly covers itself in 5-in.-wide purple, blue, white, and pink blooms with pale throats, especially showy because of their many colors. Water and fertilize sparingly during summer, to encourage flowers. Reseeds and returns in spring; watch that it doesn't escape and become a nuisance.

🏛 **I. quamoclit (Quamoclit pennata).** CYPRESS VINE, CARDINAL CLIMBER. Summer annual. All zones. Twines to 20 ft. Leaves 2½–4 in. long, finely divided into slender threads. Flowers are tubes 1½ in. long, flaring at mouth into five-pointed star; they are usually scarlet, rarely white. Excellent hummingbird plant.

I. tricolor. MORNING GLORY. All zones. Perennial in Tropical South; summer annual elsewhere. Showy, single or double, funnel-shaped to bell-like flowers in blue, lavender, pink, red, or white, usually with throats in contrasting colors; some bicolored or striped. Most open only in morning, fade in afternoon. However, flowers stay open in cool, overcast weather. Bloom lasts until frost. Large, heart-shaped leaves.

Among most popular selections is 'Heavenly Blue', twining to 15 ft., with 4–5-in., pure sky blue flowers with yellow throat. Dwarf strain with white markings on leaves (known as Spice Islands or simply as Variegated) is 9 in. tall, spills to 1 ft. across; blooms in red, pink, blue, and bicolors.

Sow seed in place in full sun after frost. To speed sprouting, notch seed coat with knife or file (some growers sell scarified seed); or soak seed in warm water for 2 hours. For earlier start, start seed indoors, then set out plants 6–8 in. apart.

Use on fence or trellis or as ground cover. Or grow in containers; add stakes or wire cylinder for support, or let plant cascade. For cut flowers, pick stems with buds in various stages of development, place in deep vase. Buds will open on consecutive days.

IPOMOPSIS rubra (Gilia rubra)

STANDING CYPRESS

Polemoniaceae

BIENNIAL OR SHORT-LIVED PERENNIAL

✿ ZONES MS, LS, CS

☼ ◑ FULL SUN OR PARTIAL SHADE

◐ ● REGULAR TO MODERATE WATER

Ipomopsis rubra

Native to South. To 6 ft. tall. Tubular flowers red outside, yellow marked with red inside. Erect single stems, finely divided leaves. Startling in appearance, best massed; individual plants are narrow. Sow seed in spring or early summer for bloom the following summer. Difficult to transplant once established. Adapted to almost any well-drained soil. Good hummingbird plant.

IRESINE

BLOODLEAF

Amaranthaceae

PERENNIALS

✿ ZONES CS, TS; OR INDOOR/OUTDOOR PLANTS

☼ FULL SUN

● REGULAR WATER

Iresine herbstii

Tender, upright-growing plants to 2–3 ft. tall, grown for attractive leaf color; flowers are inconspicuous. Tolerate seacoast conditions. Good in containers. North of the Coastal South, plants must be wintered indoors or treated as annuals. Pinch tips for bushiness. Easy to propagate by stem cuttings in fall or spring.

I. herbstii. Oval to round leaves, 1–2 in. long, usually notched at tip. Leaves purplish red with lighter midrib and veins; or green or bronzy, with yellowish veins. Stems are always red.

I. lindenii. Densely foliaged plant with blood red, 2½-in.-long leaves, pointed instead of notched at tip.

Iridaceae. The large iris family includes many familiar (and unfamiliar) garden bulbs, corms, and fibrous-rooted perennials. Leaves are swordlike or grasslike, often in two opposing rows. Flowers may be simply arranged with six equal segments (as in *Crocus,* for example) or highly irregular in appearance (as in *Iris*).

🏛 IRIS

Iridaceae

BULBS AND RHIZOMES

✿ ZONES VARY ACCORDING TO SPECIES OR TYPE

☼ ◑ ● EXPOSURE NEEDS VARY BY SPECIES

◐ ● ◒ WATER NEEDS VARY BY SPECIES

Tall Bearded Iris

A large and remarkably diverse group of some 200 to 300 species, varying in flower color and form, cultural needs, and blooming periods (although the majority flower in spring or early summer). Leaves swordlike or grasslike; flowers showy, complex in structure. The three inner segments (the standards) are petals; they are usually erect or arching but, in some kinds, may flare to horizontal. The three outer segments (the falls) are petal-like sepals; they are held at various angles from nearly horizontal to drooping. State flower of Tennessee.

Irises grow from bulbs or rhizomes. In floral detail, there are three categories: bearded (each fall bears a caterpillar-like adornment), beardless (each fall is smooth), and crested (each fall bears a comblike ridge instead of a full beard).

Tall bearded irises (and other bearded classes) are the most widely sold iris types; many new hybrids are cataloged every year. Specialty growers abound. A small number offer various beardless classes and some species. Retail garden centers carry bulbous irises for fall planting.

Iris borer is a potentially serious pest, but it is less problematic where winter temperatures remain above 10°F. This borer is the larval stage of a dull brown moth that appears in late summer and early fall. Eggs laid in fall in dry debris close to the soil hatch the following spring. Larvae feed on leaf margins as they work toward the rhizomes, which they consume, leaving hollow shells. Telltale signs of infestation in summer are small "sawdust" piles around plant base. Thorough cleanup of garden debris before winter is first step in control. In early spring when new iris leaves reach 6 in. high, spray plants and soil with dimethoate (Cygon) according to label directions. Repeat weekly until 2 weeks after last bloom.

BULBOUS IRISES

Irises that grow from bulbs have beardless flowers. Bulbs become dormant in summer and can be lifted and stored until planting time in fall.

Dutch and Spanish irises. Zones US, MS, LS. The species that parented this group come from Spain, Portugal, Sicily, and northern Africa. (Dutch irises acquired their name because the hybrid group was developed by Dutch bulb growers.) Flowers come atop slender stems that rise up from rushlike foliage. Standards are narrow and upright; oval to circular falls project downward. Colors include white, mauve, blue, purple, brown, orange, yellow, and bicolor combinations—usually with a yellow blotch on falls. Dutch iris flowers (the ones also sold by florists) reach 3–4 in. across, on stems 1½–2 ft. tall. Bloom in spring. Spanish irises are similar but smaller flowered and bloom about 2 weeks after Dutch irises.

Plant bulbs 4 in. deep, about 3–4 in. apart, in October–November; give full sun in Upper South, light afternoon shade in Lower South. Bulbs are hardy to about −10°F. Give regular water during growth. Bulbs can be left in the ground for several years where summers are dry; elsewhere, they should be lifted. After bloom, let foliage ripen before digging; store bulbs in cool, dry place for no more than 2 months before replanting. Dutch

Dutch Iris

and Spanish irises are good in containers; plant five bulbs in a 5–6-in. pot.

The widely sold 'Wedgwood' is a Dutch hybrid hardy only in the Middle and Lower South. Large flowers are lavender blue with yellow markings, blooming earlier than others (generally coinciding with 'King Alfred' daffodils). Bulbs are larger than those of average Dutch hybrid. Vigorous foliage is best masked by bushy annuals or perennials that will mature later in the season.

English irises. Zones US, MS. The species (*I. latifolia*) from which named selections were made is native to the Pyrenees, where it grows in moist meadows. Early botanists first noticed the iris growing in southern England, where it had been taken by traders. Flowers are similar in structure to Dutch and Spanish irises, but falls are broader and decorated with a thin yellow stripe. Colors include bluish purple, wine red, maroon, blue, mauve, white. Bloom time is early summer. Bulbs need cool, moist, acid soil; in fall, plant them 3–4 in. deep, 4 in. apart. Choose a sunny or partly shaded site. Because English irises don't need complete dryness after flowering, they can be left in ground. Or they can be lifted and replanted.

Reticulata irises. Zones US, MS, LS. Bulbs covered by a netted outer covering give the group its name. Flowers (like small Dutch irises) appear on 6–8-in. stems in early spring. Thin, four-sided blue-green leaves appear after bloom. Species include *I. reticulata*, with 2–3-in. violet-scented flowers (purple, in the usual forms), and bright yellow–flowered *I. danfordiae*, Danford iris. Pale blue–flowered *I. histrio* and large-flowered, blue-and-yellow *I. histrioides* may be carried by some specialists. More common are named hybrids such as 'Cantab' (pale blue with orange markings), 'Harmony' (sky blue marked yellow), 'J. S. Dijt' (reddish purple).

Bulbs are hardy to about −10°F and need some subfreezing winter temperatures to thrive. Plant in autumn in well-drained soil in a sunny location; set bulbs 3–4 in. deep and as far apart. Bulbs need regular moisture from fall through spring. Soil should be kept dry during summer dormant period; in rainy climates, lift bulbs in summer or grow in pots so you can control moisture. Divide only when vigor, flower quality deteriorate.

RHIZOMATOUS IRISES

Irises that grow from rhizomes (thickened, modified stems) may have bearded, beardless, or crested flowers; among this rhizomatous group are the most widely grown types. Leaves are swordlike, overlapping each other to form flat fans of foliage.

Bearded irises. Zones US, MS, LS. The most widely grown irises fall into the bearded group. Possibly the oldest is the white flag (*I. albicans*), a sterile, natural hybrid that blooms very early in spring. Originating in Yemen and traditionally cultivated in Muslim graveyards since the Middle Ages, it was brought to Europe by the Moors and eventually made its way to the New World. Today, it's often seen in cemeteries and old home sites and is shared among friends. Tough and long lived, white flag resists disease and thrives in warmer sections of the South where other bearded irises fail. Its sweet-scented, pure white flowers with yellow-tipped beards stand atop 1–2 ft. stems.

Most bearded irises aren't nearly so ancient. They are products of years of hybridizing done across the U.S., utilizing many different species. All have upright standards, flaring to pendent falls that have characteristic epaulette-like beards. Tall bearded irises are the most familiar of these, but they represent just one subdivision of the entire group.

Bearded irises need good drainage. They'll grow in soils from sandy to claylike, but in clay soils plant in raised beds or on ridges to ensure drainage, avoid rhizome rot. Plant in full sun in the Upper and Middle South; in the Lower South, they'll accept light shade during the afternoon. July–October is best planting period. Space rhizomes 1–2 ft. apart; set with tops just beneath soil surface, spreading roots well. Water to settle soil, start growth. Thereafter, water judiciously until new growth shows plants have rooted; then water regularly until fall rains or frosts arrive. If weather turns hot, shade newly planted rhizomes to prevent sunscald, possible rot. Where winters are severe, mulch new plantings to prevent heaving from alternate freezing, thawing.

DIRECTING BEARDED IRIS

Rhizomes grow outward from the end with leaves; when planting, point that end in direction you want growth to take. For quick show, plant three rhizomes 1 ft. apart, two with growing ends pointed outward, the third aimed to grow into the space between them. On slopes, set rhizomes with growing end facing uphill.

From the time growth starts in late winter or early spring, water regularly until about 6 weeks after flowers fade; increases and buds for next year's flowers form during postbloom period. During summer, plants need less water: every other week should be sufficient. For best performance, feed plants with bloom-booster fertilizer as growth begins in spring, then again after bloom has finished. If spring weather is cool and moist, leaf spot may disfigure foliage; spray with Daconil at first sign of infection. Remove old and dry leaves in fall.

Clumps become overcrowded after 3 or 4 years; quantity and quality of bloom decrease. Lift and divide crowded clumps at best planting time for your area. Save large rhizomes with healthy leaves, discard old and leafless rhizomes from clump's center. Break rhizomes apart or use a sharp knife to separate. Trim leaves, roots to about 6 in., let cut ends heal for several hours to a day before replanting. If replanting in the same soil, amend it with plenty of organic matter.

Beardless irises. Flowers in this group have smooth, "beardless" falls but otherwise differ considerably in appearance from one group or species to another. Rhizomes have fibrous roots (unlike fleshy roots of bearded types); most prefer or demand more moisture than bearded irises. Many can perform well from crowded clumps but will eventually need division. Timing varies; all should be dug and replanted quickly, keeping roots moist while plants are out of the ground.

The following four hybrid groups contain the most widely sold beardless irises. Also described are individual species (and their named selections) available from growers of specialty irises and perennials.

Japanese irises. Zones US, MS, LS. Derived solely from *I. ensata* (formerly *I. kaempferi*), these irises feature sumptuous blossoms 4–12 in. across on slender stems to 4 ft. high. Flower shape is essentially flat. "Single" types have three broad falls and much-reduced standards, giving triangular flower outline; "double" blossoms have standards marked like the falls and about the same size and shape, resulting in circular flower outline. Colors are purple, violet, pink, rose, red, white— often veined or edged in contrasting shade. Plants have graceful, narrow, upright leaves with distinct raised midribs.

Iris ensata

Plants need much moisture during growing, flowering period. Acid to neutral soil and water are required. Plant rhizomes in fall or spring, 2 in. deep and 1½ ft. apart; or plant up to three per 12-in. container. Use in moist borders, at edge of pools or streams, or even in boxes or pots plunged halfway to rim in pond or pool during growing season.

Louisiana irises. Zones US, MS, LS, CS. Approximately four species from the lower Mississippi River basin and Gulf Coast compose this group called swamp irises. Graceful, flattish blooms on stems 2–5 ft. tall, carried above and among long, narrow, unribbed leaves. The range of flower colors and patterns is extensive—nearly the equal of tall beardeds. But because they're better adapted to hot weather, heavy, wet soils, and have fewer pest problems, they're easier for most gardeners to grow.

Specialists offer a vast array of named hybrids; some may carry the basic species as well. *I. brevicaulis (I. foliosa)*, blue flag iris, has blue flowers with flaring segments carried on zigzag stems among the foliage. *I. fulva*, red flag iris, has coppery to rusty red (rarely yellow) blossoms with narrow, drooping segments. *I. giganticaerulea*, big blue iris, is indeed a "giant blue" (sometimes white) with upright standards and flaring falls; stems may reach 4 ft. or more, with foliage in proportion. *I. hexagona* also comes in blue shades with upright standards, flaring falls. *I. nelsonii*, a natural hybrid population derived from *I. fulva* and *I. giganticaerulea*, resembles *I. fulva* in its flower shape and color (but also including purple and brown tones) and approaches *I. giganticaerulea* in size.

Plants thrive in well-watered, rich garden soil as well as at pond margins; soil and water should be neutral to acid. Locate in full sun in the Upper and Middle South; choose light afternoon shade in the Lower and Coastal South. Plant in late summer; set rhizomes 1 in. deep, 1½–2 ft. apart. Mulch for winter in the Upper South.

Siberian irises. Zones US, MS, LS. The most widely sold members of this group are named hybrids derived from *I. sibirica* and *I. sanguinea* (formerly *I. orientalis*). Clumps of narrow, almost grasslike leaves (deciduous in winter) produce slender stems up to 4 ft. (depending on selection), each bearing two to five blossoms with upright standards and flaring to drooping falls. Colors include white and shades of blue, lavender, purple, wine, pink, and light yellow.

Give full sun (partial or dappled shade in Lower South), neutral to acid soil. Set rhizomes 1–2 in. deep, 1–2 ft. apart, in fall. Water liberally from onset of growth until several weeks after bloom. Divide infrequently—when clumps show hollow centers—in summer or fall.

Spuria irises. Zones US, MS, LS, CS. In flower form, the spurias resemble Dutch irises. Older members of this group had primarily yellow or white-and-yellow blossoms; *I. orientalis* (universally known as *I. ochroleuca*) has naturalized in many parts of the South, its 3–5-ft. stems bearing white flowers with yellow blotches on the falls. Dwarf *I. graminea* bears narrow-petaled, scented, blue-and-maroon blossoms on foot-high stems. Modern hybrids show a great color range: blue, lavender, gray, orchid, tan, bronze, brown, purple, earthy red, and near-black—often with a prominent yellow spot on the falls. Flowers are held closely against 3–6-ft. stems, rising above handsome clumps of narrow, dark green leaves. Flowering starts during latter part of tall bearded bloom, continues several weeks beyond.

Plant rhizomes in late summer or early fall in rich, neutral to slightly alkaline soil; choose a spot in full sun to partial light shade. Set rhizomes 1 in. deep, 1½–2 ft. apart. Plants need plenty of moisture from onset of growth through bloom period but little moisture during summer. Divide clumps infrequently (not an easy task).

I. foetidissima. GLADWIN IRIS. Zones US, MS. Native to Europe. Glossy evergreen leaves to 2 ft. make handsome foliage clumps. Stems 1½–2 ft. tall bear subtly attractive flowers in blue gray and dull tan; specialists may offer color variants in soft yellow and lavender blue, as well as a form with white-variegated leaves. Real attraction is large seed capsules that open in fall to show numerous round, orange-scarlet seeds; cut stems with seed capsules are useful in arrangements. Grow in partial shade to full shade. Very tolerant of drought.

I. laevigata. Zones US, MS, LS. Smooth, glossy leaves grow 1½–2½ ft. high, to 1 in. wide. Flower stems grow to about the same height, bearing violet blue blossoms with three upright standards and three drooping falls enlivened with yellow median stripes. Named color variants include white, magenta, and patterned purple and white. There also are selections in which standards mimic falls in shape, pattern, and carriage, producing the effect of a double blossom. 'Variegata' offers vertically striped, white-and-green leaves and cobalt blue flowers. This is a true bog plant, growing best in constantly moist, acid soil—even in shallow water.

I. pseudacorus. YELLOW FLAG. Zones US, MS, LS, CS. Impressive foliage plant; under best conditions, upright leaves may reach 5 ft. tall. Flower stems grow 4–7 ft. (depending on culture), bear bright yellow flowers 3–4 in. across. Selected forms offer ivory and lighter yellow flowers, double flowers, variegated foliage, and plants with shorter and taller leaves. Plant in sun to light shade. Needs acid soil and more than average moisture; thrives in shallow water. Native to Europe but now found worldwide in temperate regions; seeds float, aiding plant's dispersal.

Several hybrids are excellent foliage plants with distinctive blossoms. All prefer ample water (but not pond conditions), sun to light shade. 'Holden Clough' perhaps has *I. foetidissima* as the other parent. Flowers, 3–4 in. across, are soft tan heavily netted with maroon veins; stems grow to 4 ft.; leaves reach 4–5 ft. but tips arch over. Two of its seedlings are similar but larger. 'Phil Edinger' grows to 4½ ft. with arching foliage; 4–5-in. flowers are brass colored, heavily veined in brown. 'Roy Davidson' is similar, but flowers are dark yellow with fine brown veining and maroon thumbprint on falls.

I. versicolor. BLUE FLAG. Zones US, MS, LS, CS. Widely distributed North American species. Grows 1½–4 ft. tall; narrow leaves are thicker in the center but not ribbed. Shorter-growing forms have upright leaves, but foliage of taller types may recurve gracefully. The typical wild flowers are light violet blue, but lighter and darker forms exist; a wine red variant has been sold as 'Kermesina'. Selections include 'Rosea' and 'Vernal' and others with violet red flowers. Like *I. pseudacorus*, thrives in sun to light shade, in moist, acid soil or shallow water.

Specialty growers offer hybrids between *I. versicolor* and other species such as *I. ensata*, *I. laevigata*, and *I. virginica*. Violet-flowered 'Gerald Darby', a hybrid with *I. virginica*, has striking wine red stems.

I. virginica. SOUTHERN BLUE FLAG. Zones US, MS, LS, CS. In plant and flower, this species is similar to *I. versicolor*. Distinguishing floral feature is longer standards. Flower colors include light to dark blue, wine red, pink, lavender, and white. A plant sold as 'Giant Blue' is distinctly larger in all parts, approaching *I. pseudacorus* in size. Plant in moist, acid garden soil or grow in shallow water. In deep ponds, plant in large pots barely submerged beneath the surface.

Crested irises. Botanically placed with beardless irises, they represent a transition between beardless and bearded: Each fall bears a narrow, comblike crest where a beard would be in bearded sorts. Slugs, snails are especially attracted to foliage, flowers. Several tender species and hybrids form bamboolike stems carrying foliage fans aloft; flower stems 2 ft. tall are widely branched, with orchidlike sprays of fringed flowers in lavender to white with orange crests. These include *I. confusa*, *I. japonica*, *I. wattii*, and hybrids such as 'Darjeeling' and 'Nada'. Plant in organically enriched soil, in light shade. Regular water during growth. Reliable outdoors in Coastal South; elsewhere, grow in containers, move to shelter over winter.

I. cristata. DWARF CRESTED IRIS. Zones US, MS, LS; hardy to −10°F. Leaves 4–6 in. long, ½ in. wide. Slender, greenish rhizomes spread freely. Flowers white, lavender, or light blue with golden crests; specialty nurseries list named selections. Give light shade, organically enriched soil, regular water. Divide just after bloom or in fall after leaves die down.

I. tectorum. JAPANESE ROOF IRIS. Zones US, MS, LS. Its foliage fans to 1 ft. tall look like those of bearded irises, but leaves are ribbed and glossy. Flowers suggest an informal bearded iris with fringed petals and crests in place of beards. Colors are violet blue with white crests, white with yellow crests; standards are upright at first, open out to horizontal as flower matures. Give plants organically enriched soil, light shade, regular water. Handsome fans of light green foliage are decorative year-round and contrast nicely with hostas, ferns, foamflowers. Native to Japan, where it is planted on cottage roofs. Its hybrid with a bearded iris, 'Paltec', will grow with bearded irises. Height is about 1 ft., the lavender flowers suggesting a bearded iris with beards superimposed on crests.

IRISH LACE. See TAGETES filifolia

IRISH MOSS. See SAGINA subulata, SELAGINELLA kraussiana

IRISH YEW. See TAXUS baccata 'Stricta'

IRONWEED. See VERNONIA noveboracensis

IRONWOOD. See CARPINUS caroliniana

ISMENE calathina. See HYMENOCALLIS narcissiflora

ITALIAN CYPRESS. See CUPRESSUS sempervirens

ITEA

SWEETSPIRE

Grossulariaceae (Saxifragaceae)

EVERGREEN OR DECIDUOUS SHRUBS

ZONES VARY BY SPECIES

SUN OR PARTIAL SHADE

AMPLE TO REGULAR WATER

Itea virginica

Only a few of the ten or so species are cultivated in this country. Although they do not resemble one another in most details, they do have in common small, scented flowers arranged in elongated, narrow, tightly packed clusters.

I. ilicifolia. HOLLYLEAF SWEETSPIRE. Evergreen. Zones CS, LS. Native to China. Graceful, open, arching shrub 6–10 ft. tall, occasionally much taller. Leaves are oval, glossy, 4 in. long, spiny toothed; bronze red when new, maturing to dark green. Small, lightly fragrant greenish white flowers are closely set in nodding or drooping clusters to 1 ft. long. Autumn bloom; flowering is sparse where winters are mild. Needs partial shade. Not striking, but a graceful plant of distinction. Attractive near water or espaliered along a fence or wall.

I. virginica. VIRGINIA SWEETSPIRE. Deciduous. Zones US, MS, LS, CS. Native to eastern U.S. Erect shrub, 3–5 ft. tall or taller, spreading to form large patches where well adapted. Leaves oval, dark green, to 4 in. long and 1½ in. wide. In fall, they turn purplish red or bright red; they hang on plant for a long time and may persist all winter in Coastal South. Fragrant, ⅓–½-in., creamy white flowers in spring, held in erect clusters. Suckers aggressively, in rich, moist soil; can be invasive. 'Henry's Garnet' is a superior choice with 6-in. flower clusters, garnet red fall color. On 'Saturnalia', fall foliage is a mix of orange, purple, and wine red.

One selection known as 'Beppu' or 'Nana' may be in fact a form of *I. japonica*. It is lower growing (to 2½ ft.) than *I. virginica*, with somewhat smaller flowers. Spreads rapidly by suckers. Somewhat less hardy than *I. virginica*; may be injured at 0° to −10°F.

IVY. See HEDERA

IVY GERANIUM. See PELARGONIUM peltatum

IXORA

Rubiaceae

EVERGREEN SHRUBS

ZONES CS, TS; OR GREENHOUSE

FULL SUN

REGULAR WATER

Ixora coccinea

Large group of tropical evergreen shrubs with handsome foliage and showy clusters of flowers. Plants tolerate salt air. Like fertile, well-drained, acid soil. Become chlorotic in alkaline soil. Subject to a host of insects and diseases; difficult to keep healthy without constant vigilance.

I. coccinea. FLAME OF THE WOODS, JUNGLE FLAME. Native to India. Most commonly grown ixora. Long in cultivation, with many selections featuring blossoms in shades of red, orange, pink, or yellow. To 7–8 ft., but is usually kept to 4 ft. by occasional tip pinching or pruning. Whorled leaves

are glossy and leathery. Flowers are 2 in. long and appear in large, dense clusters at branch tips throughout the warm months of the year. Prefers rich, somewhat acid soil well amended with organic material. Dies back after a freeze but recovers. Favorite decorative hedge or show plant in southern Florida; greenhouse plant in most of the country.

I. duffii (I. macrothyrsa). MALAY IXORA. Native to Caroline Islands. To 3–10 ft. tall. Slender oblong leaves are somewhat leathery, 6–12 in. long, 2½ in. wide. Deep red flowers open in large clusters, sometimes as large as 10 in. across, and fade to crimson.

JACARANDA mimosifolia

JACARANDA

Bignoniaceae

DECIDUOUS OR SEMIEVERGREEN TREE

ZONES CS (PROTECTED), TS

FULL SUN

MODERATE WATER

Jacaranda mimosifolia

Native to Brazil. Often sold as *J. acutifolia*. Grows 25–40 ft. high, 15–30 ft. wide. Open, irregular, oval headed; sometimes multi-trunked or even shrubby. Finely cut, fernlike leaves, usually dropping in late winter. New leaves may grow quickly or branches may remain bare until tree comes into flower—usually in mid- to late spring, though blossoms may appear earlier or open at any time through the summer. Blossoms lavender blue, tubular, 2 in. long, in many 8-in.-long clusters. White-flowered 'Alba' is sometimes seen; it has lusher foliage, longer blooming period, and sparser flowers. All forms have roundish, flat seed capsules, quite decorative in arrangements.

Plant is fairly hardy after it attains some mature, hard wood; young plants are tender below 25°F, but often come back from freeze to make multistemmed, shrubby plants. Takes wide variety of soils but does best in sandy soil. Often fails to flower in path of ocean winds.

Stake to produce single, sturdy trunk. Prune to shape. Usually branches profusely at 6–10 ft.

JACK-IN-THE-PULPIT. See ARISAEMA triphyllum

JACKSON VINE. See SMILAX smallii

JACOBINIA carnea. See JUSTICIA carnea

JACOB'S LADDER. See POLEMONIUM caeruleum

JADE PLANT. See CRASSULA ovata

JAPANESE ANDROMEDA. See PIERIS japonica

JAPANESE ANGELICA TREE. See ARALIA elata

JAPANESE ANISE. See ILLICIUM anisatum

JAPANESE BARBERRY. See BERBERIS thunbergii

JAPANESE BLOOD GRASS. See IMPERATA cylindrica 'Rubra'

JAPANESE BUGBANE. See CIMICIFUGA japonica

JAPANESE CLETHRA. See CLETHRA barbinervis

JAPANESE CLEYERA. See TERNSTROEMIA gymnanthera

JAPANESE CLIMBING FERN. See LYGODIUM japonicum

JAPANESE FATSIA. See FATSIA japonica

JAPANESE FLOWERING APRICOT. See PRUNUS mume

JAPANESE HYDRANGEA VINE. See SCHIZOPHRAGMA hydrangeoides

JAPANESE KNOTWEED. See POLYGONUM cuspidatum

JAPANESE MAPLE. See ACER palmatum

JASMINUM

JASMINE

Oleaceae

EVERGREEN, SEMIEVERGREEN, OR DECIDUOUS VINES
OR SHRUBS

✎ ZONES VARY BY SPECIES

☼ ◐ FULL SUN OR PARTIAL SHADE

● REGULAR WATER

*Jasminum
nitidum*

W hen one thinks of fragrance, jasmine is one of the first plants that comes to mind. Yet not all jasmines are fragrant; and despite its common name, the sweet-scented Confederate or star jasmine is not a true jasmine at all, but a member of the genus *Trachelospermum*. All jasmines thrive in regular garden soil and need frequent pinching and shaping to control growth. Low-growing, shrubby kinds make good hedges.

J. angulare. SOUTH AFRICAN JASMINE. Evergreen vine. Zones CS, TS. Leaves divided into three leaflets. Blooms in summer, bearing unscented white flowers in groups of three; flowers slightly more than 1 in. wide.

J. floridum. SHOWY JASMINE. Evergreen or semievergreen, shrubby, sprawling, or half-climbing shrub. Zones LS, CS, TS. Grows to 3–4 ft. Leaves divided into three (rarely five) small leaflets, each ½–1½ in. long. Clusters of golden yellow, scentless, ½–¾-in. flowers appear April–June, sporadically until fall. Despite common name, grown more for its foliage than its mediocre flowers.

J. grandiflorum (J. officinale grandiflorum). SPANISH JASMINE. Semievergreen to deciduous vine. Zones CS, TS. Rapid growth to 10–15 ft. Glossy green leaves with five to seven leaflets, each 2 in. long. Fragrant white flowers, 1½ in. across, in loose clusters. Spent flowers stay on plant. Gives open, airy effect along fence tops or rails.

J. humile. ITALIAN JASMINE. Evergreen shrub or vine. Zones LS (protected), CS, TS. Erect, willowy shoots reach to 20 ft. and arch to make 10-ft. mound. Can be trained as shrub or, planted in a row, clipped as hedge. Light green leaves with three to seven leaflets, each 2 in. long. Clusters of fragrant, bright yellow, ½-in. flowers all summer. 'Revolutum' has larger, dull dark green leaves; flowers 1 in. across, up to twelve per cluster. Side clusters make even larger show.

Jasminum mesnyi

J. magnificum. See J. nitidum

J. mesnyi (J. primulinum). PRIMROSE JASMINE. Evergreen shrub. Zones LS, CS, TS. Long, arching branches 6–10 ft. long. Dark green leaves with three lance-shaped, 2–3-in. leaflets; square stems. Bright lemon yellow, unscented flowers to 2 in. across are semidouble or double, produced singly rather than in clusters. Main bloom in winter or spring; may flower

sporadically at other times. Needs space. Best tied up at desired height and permitted to spill down in waterfall fashion. Use to cover pergola, banks, large walls. Can be clipped as 3-ft.-high hedge. In whatever form, plants may need occasional severe pruning to avoid brush pile look.

J. multiflorum. DOWNY JASMINE. Evergreen vine often trained as shrub. Zones CS, TS. Stems and leaves have a downy coating, producing an overall gray-green effect. Leaves up to 2 in. long. Clustered flowers are white; not strongly scented. Often called star jasmine in Florida. Main bloom season comes in late winter or early spring.

J. multipartitum. AFRICAN JASMINE. Evergreen shrub. Zone TS. Sprawling form, to 2–3 ft. tall, 10 ft. wide. Pink buds at branch ends open into fragrant white summer flowers that are divided into eight to twelve narrow segments.

J. nitidum. SHINING JASMINE, ANGELWING JASMINE. Evergreen to semievergreen vine. Zones CS, TS. Not reliably hardy below 25°F. Moderate growth to 10–20 ft. Leathery, uncut, glossy medium green leaves to 2 in. long. Very fragrant flowers shaped like 1-in. pinwheels open from purplish buds in late spring and summer. Flowers white above, purplish beneath, borne in clusters of three. Responds well to drastic pruning. Good container plant. Can also be used as shrubby ground cover. Often sold as *J. magnificum.*

J. nudiflorum. WINTER JASMINE. Deciduous viny shrub. Zones US, MS, LS, CS. Unsupported, to 4 ft. high, 7 ft. wide; can grow to 15 ft. tall if trained on a trellis or wall. Slender, willowy green stems stand out in winter landscape. Unscented, bright yellow, 1-in.-wide flowers appear in winter or early spring before leaves unfold. Handsome glossy green leaves have three leaflets. Train like *J. mesnyi.* Good bank cover; spreads by rooting where stems touch soil. Attractive planted above retaining walls, with branches cascading over side. Cut back severely every few years to rejuvenate.

J. officinale. COMMON WHITE JASMINE, POET'S JASMINE. Semievergreen to deciduous twining vine. Zones LS (protected), CS, TS. Resembles *J. grandiflorum,* but covers more area (to 30 ft.) and is somewhat more tender. Very fragrant white flowers to 1 in. across; blooms all summer and into fall. Rich green leaves have five to nine leaflets, each up to 2½ in. long.

J. parkeri. DWARF JASMINE. Evergreen shrub. Zones LS (protected), CS, TS. Dwarf, twiggy, tufted habit. To 1 ft. tall, 1½–2 ft. across. Leaves bright green, ½–1 in. long, made up of three to five tiny leaflets. Small, scentless yellow flowers borne profusely in spring. Good in containers.

J. polyanthum. PINK JASMINE. Evergreen vine. Zones LS (protected), CS, TS. Fast-climbing, strong-growing vine to 20 ft. Finely divided leaflets. Dense clusters of highly fragrant flowers, white inside, rose colored outside. Blooms in late winter and spring; sporadic flowers rest of year. Prune annually to prevent tangling. Use as climber or ground cover; or grow in containers or hanging baskets.

J. sambac. ARABIAN JASMINE. Evergreen shrub. Zones CS, TS. In Asia, used in jasmine tea. To 5 ft. tall. Leaves undivided, glossy green, to 3 in. long. Blooms in summer, bearing clusters of powerfully fragrant, ¾–1-in. white flowers. Grow as small, compact shrub on trellis or in container. 'Grand Duke' has double flowers.

J. volubile. WAX JASMINE. Evergreen shrub or tall climber. Zone TS. Glossy leaves. Fragrant white flowers throughout the year.

JATROPHA

Euphorbiaceae

TREES, SHRUBS, PERENNIALS

✎ ZONE TS; OR INDOORS

◐ LIGHT SHADE

◖◗ REGULAR TO LITTLE WATER

◈ SOME SPECIES ARE EXTREMELY POISONOUS

Jatropha multifida

L arge group of tropical and subtropical plants, related to poinsettias, with milky latex or clear juice in the stems. Most commonly grown species are popular for large, deeply lobed, heart-shaped leaves and tropical effect. Not salt tolerant. ▶

J. curcas. PHYSIC NUT. Evergreen shrub or small tree, to 8–15 ft. Easy to grow; cuttings from mature stems are sometimes set out in the ground, watered, and left to make a hedge. Deep green leaves are heart shaped, to 12 in. long and 7 in. wide, on 4–6-in. stalks. Inconspicuous yellowish green flowers appear in spring. Nuts, 1½ in. long, oval, contain poisonous seeds. Leaves and stem of this species also poisonous.

J. multifida. CORAL PLANT. Evergreen shrub or small tree, or house plant. To 20 ft. Leaves 1 ft. across, almost circular but deeply divided into seven to eleven narrow lobes, white or gray on undersides. Scarlet flowers on red stems. Oval fruits to 1 in. long. All parts of plant are poisonous.

J. podagrica. GOUT PLANT. Shrub, to 1½–5 ft. tall. Most unusual feature is swollen, gouty-looking trunk. Leaves up to 10 in. across, three to five deep lobes, white undersides. Coral red flowers in branched clusters.

JAVA GLORYBOWER. See CLERODENDRUM speciosissimum

JEFFERSONIA diphylla

TWINLEAF

Berberidaceae

PERENNIAL

⚡ ZONES US, MS

◐ ● PARTIAL OR FULL SHADE

💧 MODERATE WATER

Jeffersonia diphylla

Native to Maryland and Virginia south to Georgia and Alabama. Named for Thomas Jefferson. Pretty white flower cups, 1 in. across, appear briefly in spring among new, purple-gray foliage. At bloom, plant is no taller than 8 in. high; once flowers fade, leaves develop and make a handsome, green, 1½-ft. mound. Foliage is unusual: Leaves are like shields with a 5–6 in. diameter, split into two parts.

Grows in soils rich in organic matter, in a woodland garden with ferns, primroses, trilliums, bloodroot. Cover with a humusy mulch when leaves die back. Water during dry weather. Prefers limy soils.

JERUSALEM ARTICHOKE. See HELIANTHUS tuberosus

JERUSALEM CHERRY. See SOLANUM pseudocapsicum

JERUSALEM SAGE. See PHLOMIS

JERUSALEM THORN. See PARKINSONIA aculeata

JEWEL MINT OF CORSICA. See MENTHA requienii

JICAMA. See PACHYRHIZUS erosus

JOE-PYE WEED. See EUPATORIUM maculatum, E. purpureum

JOHNNY-JUMP-UP. See VIOLA tricolor

JONQUIL. See NARCISSUS jonquilla

JOSEPH'S COAT. See AMARANTHUS tricolor

JUDAS TREE. See CERCIS siliquastrum

Juglandaceae. The walnut family consists of nut-bearing trees with leaves divided into many paired leaflets. Pecans and hickories *(Carya)* and walnuts *(Juglans)* are examples.

JUGLANS. See WALNUT

JUNEBERRY. See AMELANCHIER

JUNIPERUS

JUNIPER

Cupressaceae

EVERGREEN SHRUBS AND TREES

⚡ ZONES VARY BY SPECIES

☼ ◐ SUN; MOST TOLERATE LIGHT SHADE

💧 ● REGULAR TO LITTLE WATER

▶ SEE CHART

Large group of evergreen coniferous plants with fleshy, berrylike cones and foliage that is needlelike, scalelike, or both. Widely used woody plants; there's a form for almost every landscape use. In the chart, junipers are grouped by common use and listed by botanical name.

The ground cover group includes types ranging from a few inches to 2–3 ft. high. Space most kinds 5–6 ft. apart. In early years, mulch will help keep soil cool and weeds down.

Juniperus chinensis 'Kaizuka'

Juniperus horizontalis

Shrub types range from low to quite tall, spreading to stiffly upright and columnar. You can find a juniper in almost any height, width, shape, or foliage color. Fewer tree types are grown; they are valued for picturesque form. Many larger junipers serve well as screens or windbreaks.

Juniperus conferta

Junipers are subject to a number of pests and diseases. Among the most serious are bagworms (foliage is stripped); blight (twig and branch dieback); twig borers (browning and dying branch tips); cedar-apple rust (disease alternating between junipers and apple trees causing twig dieback); juniper scale (no new growth, yellowed foliage); juniper webworm (webbing together and browning of foliage). To confirm a problem or decide on control measures, consult your Cooperative Extension Office or local garden center.

JUSTICIA

Acanthaceae

SUBTROPICAL EVERGREEN SHRUBS

⚡ ZONES VARY BY SPECIES

◐ ● EXPOSURE NEEDS VARY BY SPECIES

💧 💧 WATER NEEDS VARY BY SPECIES

Includes plants formerly known as *Beloperone* and *Jacobinia*. Leaves are paired; flowers are tubular and tightly clustered.

Justicia brandegeana

J. brandegeana (Beloperone guttata). SHRIMP PLANT. Zones CS, TS; indoor/outdoor plant anywhere. Native to Mexico. Forms a 3-by-4-ft. mound but can be kept lower. Egg-shaped, apple green leaves to 2½ in. long often drop in cold weather or if soil is too wet or dry. Moderate water. Tubular white flowers spotted with purple are enclosed in coppery bronze, overlapping bracts to form compact, drooping spikes 3 in. long, eventually lengthening to 6–7 in. Spikes somewhat resemble large shrimp; produced mainly spring to fall, sporadically rest of year. Flowers attract birds. Plants take sun, but bracts and foliage fade there; maintain color better in partial shade. 'Chartreuse' has yellow-green spikes that sunburn more easily than do coppery bracts. To shape plant, pinch continually in early growth until compact mound of foliage is obtained; then let bloom. To encourage bushiness, cut back stems when bracts turn black. Good in containers, for close-up planting near terraces, entryways.

J. carnea (Jacobinia carnea). BRAZILIAN PLUME. Zones CS (protected), TS; anywhere as indoor/outdoor plant. Erect, soft-wooded plant with veined leaves to 10 in. long. Dense clusters of tubular pink to crimson flowers bloom on 4–5-ft. stems, midsummer to fall. Needs partial or full

▶ page 264

JUNIPER

NAME	ZONES	SIZE, HABIT	CHARACTERISTICS
GROUND COVERS			
Juniperus chinensis procumbens JAPANESE GARDEN JUNIPER	US, MS, LS, CS	To 2 ft. by 12–20 ft. Spreading	Feathery yet substantial blue-green foliage on strong branches
J. c. p. 'Nana' DWARF JAPANESE GARDEN JUNIPER	US, MS, LS, CS	To 1 ft. by 4–5 ft. Curved branches spreading in all directions	Shorter needles, slower growth than *J. c. procumbens*. Can be staked into upright, picturesque shrub
J. c. 'San Jose' SAN JOSE JUNIPER	US, MS, LS, CS	To 2 ft. by 6 ft. or more. Prostrate, dense, spreading	Dark sage green with both needle and scale foliage. Heavy trunked; slow growing
J. c. sargentii SARGENT CHINESE JUNIPER	US, MS, LS, CS	To 3 ft. by 10 ft. Ground hugging, spreading	Gray-green or green foliage. Feathery. Classic bonsai plant. Foliage of 'Glauca', blue green; 'Viridis', bright green
J. conferta SHORE JUNIPER	US, MS, LS, CS	To 1 ft. by 6–8 ft. Prostrate, creeping	Bright green, soft needles. Excellent for seashore. Takes sandy soil, salt spray. 'Blue Pacific' is denser, bluer, more heat tolerant. 'Emerald Sea' is bright green
J. davurica expansa 'Parsonii' PARSON'S JUNIPER	US, MS, LS, CS	To 1½ ft. by 8 ft. or more. Spreading	Rich sprays of dark green needles on long, slender branches. One of best junipers for the Southeast
J. horizontalis 'Bar Harbor' BAR HARBOR CREEPING JUNIPER	US, MS, LS, CS	To 1 ft. by 10 ft. Ground hugging, creeping	Fast growing. Feathery, blue-gray foliage turns plum color in winter. Tolerates salt spray
J. h. 'Plumosa' ANDORRA CREEPING JUNIPER	US, MS, LS, CS	To 1½ ft. by 10 ft. Creeping	Gray green in summer, plum color in winter. Flat branches, upright branchlets. Plumy
J. h. 'Prince of Wales'	US, MS, LS, CS	To 8 in. tall. Creeping	Medium green foliage turns purplish in fall
J. h. 'Turquoise Spreader'	US, MS, LS, CS	To 6 in. tall. Very flat, creeping	Dense turquoise green foliage
J. h. 'Wiltonii' BLUE RUG CREEPING JUNIPER	US, MS, LS, CS	To 4 in. by 8–10 ft. Very flat, creeping	Intense silver blue. Dense, short branchlets on long, trailing branches. Like *J. h.* 'Bar Harbor', but tighter, rarely shows limbs
J. h. 'Yukon Belle'	US, MS, LS	To 6 in. tall. Creeping	Silvery blue foliage. Extremely cold-hardy
J. sabina 'Broadmoor'	US, MS	To 14 in. by 10 ft. Dense, mounding, spreading	Soft, bright green foliage
J. s. 'Buffalo'	US, MS	8–12 in. by 8 ft. Very wide spreading	Soft, feathery, bright green foliage. Lower than tamarix juniper
J. s. 'Tamariscifolia' TAMARIX JUNIPER, TAM	US, MS	To 1½ ft. by 10–20 ft. Symmetrically spreading	Dense blue-green foliage. Widely used
SHRUBS			
J. chinensis 'Armstrongii' ARMSTRONG JUNIPER	US, MS, LS, CS	To 4 ft. by 4 ft. Upright	Medium green. More compact than Pfitzer juniper
J. c. 'Gold Coast' GOLD COAST JUNIPER	US, MS, LS, CS	3 ft. by 5 ft.	Soft, lacy, golden yellow foliage. Compact
J. c. 'Hetzii' HETZ CHINESE JUNIPER	US, MS, LS, CS	To 15 ft. tall and wide	Blue-gray foliage. Branches spread outward and upward at 45° angle. Fast growing
J. c. 'Kaizuka' HOLLYWOOD JUNIPER	US, MS, LS, CS	To 20 ft. by 10 ft. Irregular, upright	Rich green. Branches with outlandish, twisted appearance. Give it plenty of room. Tolerates salt spray
J. c. 'Mint Julep'	US, MS, LS, CS	4–6 ft. by 6 ft. Vase shaped	Mint green foliage, arching branches
J. c. 'Pfitzerana' PFITZER JUNIPER	US, MS, LS, CS	5–6 ft. by 15–20 ft. Arching	Feathery, gray green. Sharp-needled foliage

J

▶

JUNIPER

NAME	ZONES	SIZE, HABIT	CHARACTERISTICS
SHRUBS			
J. c. 'Pfitzerana Aurea' GOLDEN PFITZER JUNIPER	US, MS, LS, CS	3–4 ft. by 8–10 ft.	Blue-gray foliage; current season's growth golden yellow
J. c. 'Pfitzerana Glauca' BLUE PFITZER JUNIPER	US, MS, LS, CS	5–6 ft. by 10–15 ft.	Silvery blue foliage. Arching branches
J. squamata 'Blue Star' BLUE STAR JUNIPER	US, MS	To 3 ft. by 5 ft. Moundlike	Regular branching. Silver-blue foliage darkens in winter
COLUMNAR TYPES			
J. chinensis 'Blue Point'	US, MS, LS, CS	To 7–8 ft. Broadly columnar	Dense, blue-green scale and needle foliage
J. c. 'Robusta Green'	US, MS, LS, CS	To 20 ft.	Brilliant green, dense-tufted column
J. c. 'Spartan'	US, MS, LS, CS	To 20 ft.	Rich green, dense column
J. scopulorum 'Gray Gleam'	US, MS	15–20 ft. in 30–40 years	Gray-blue, symmetrical column. Slow grower
J. s. 'Pathfinder'	US, MS	To 25 ft.	Gray-blue, upright pyramid
J. s 'Skyrocket'	US, MS, LS, CS	10–15 ft. tall, 1–2 ft. wide	Narrowest blue-gray spire. Good vertical accent
J. s. 'Wichita Blue'	US, MS	To 18 ft. or taller	Broad, silver-blue pyramid
TREES			
J. ashei OZARK WHITE CEDAR, ASHE JUNIPER	US, MS, LS, CS	To 20 ft. Irregular or spherical crown	Trunk often divides near base. Gray-green foliage; shredding gray bark. Blue, ¼–½-in. berries with a waxy bloom on female plants. Native to Texas. Likes dry, chalky soil. Immune to cedar-apple rust. Pollen of male plants can trigger allergies
J. silicicola SOUTHERN RED CEDAR	LS, CS, TS	To 25 ft.	Very similar to *J. virginiana*, though often more open and wide spreading. Grows in sand; frequently planted in rows and used as windbreak
J. virginiana EASTERN RED CEDAR	US, MS, LS, CS	40–50 ft. or more. Conical	Picturesque tree with dark green foliage that turns reddish in cold weather. Tolerates drought, poor soil. Many selections sold. Aromatic foliage, wood

shade, rich soil, ample water. Cut back in early spring to encourage strong new growth. Tops freeze back at 29°F.

KAEMPFERIA

PEACOCK GINGER

Zingiberaceae

PERENNIALS

🌿 ZONES CS, TS; OR INDOORS

● FULL SHADE

◗ ◖ AMPLE WATER DURING GROWING SEASON

Kaempferia pulchra mansonii

Native to tropical Asia, these small, shade-loving plants grow outdoors only in humid, very warm climates. Flowers are like orchids or African violets, sometimes fragrant, but foliage is usually even more decorative—many species have iridescent veining and feathery zonings on the leaves that resemble a peacock's tail. The leaves of most species lie horizontally, making a low (1–6-in. tall), strikingly textured ground cover during the growing season. In winter, foliage dies back, and plant becomes dormant. Reduce watering in fall; stop watering altogether in winter; resume watering in spring. Plants grow easily in moist soil with lots of organic matter. Some spread by rhizomes. Tuberous types can be divided.

In the Upper, Middle, and Lower South, grow in containers and overwinter indoors. Keep night temperature above 60°F. During growing season, air and soil must be moist and day temperatures high; plants will thrive in temperatures over 90°F.

K. atrovirens. PEACOCK PLANT. Oval leaves, 4–6 in. long, deep green and bronze with iridescent veining, green-purple undersides. Flowers are white with violet lip, bloom spring–summer. Spreads by rhizomes.

K. galanga. Plain, rounded, shiny green leaves, to 6 in. long. Fragrant white flowers with purple spots on lip bloom in spikes of up to 12. Plant is tuberous.

K. gilbertii. VARIEGATED PEACOCK LILY. Narrow, pointed, bright green leaves, 4–7 in. long and 1–2 in. wide, with white margins and stripes, gray undersides. White flowers with violet lip bloom from late spring into summer. Spreads by rhizomes.

K. pulchra. To 6 in. tall. Broad oval leaves, to 7 in. long, dark green and bronze with silvery iridescent veining, pale green undersides. Lilac flowers with white eye bloom summer–early fall. *K. p. mansonii* is about 2 in. taller and flowers continuously from spring to fall. Its deeply veined, nearly pleated leaves are iridescent. Plant spreads by rhizomes.

K. roscoeana. PEACOCK LILY. Similar to *K. pulchra*, but leaf undersides reddish, and flowers white. Spreads by rhizomes.

K. rotunda. Narrow leaves to 12 in. are carried erect, making this a much taller plant than other species. Feathered pattern on leaves of dark and pale green above, purplish on undersides. Fragrant white flowers with purple lip bloom before leaves appear. Tuberous plant.

KAFFIR LILY. See CLIVIA miniata

KAHILI GINGER. See HEDYCHIUM gardneranum

KALANCHOE

Crassulaceae

SUCCULENTS

⚡ ZONE TS; OR INDOORS

☼ ◑ FULL SUN OR PARTIAL SHADE

◐ ◑ REGULAR TO MODERATE WATER

Kalanchoe blossfeldiana

Hardy outdoors in Tropical South. Grown principally as house plants. Plant shapes and sizes vary. Bell-shaped flowers may be erect or drooping.

K. beharensis. FELT PLANT. Often sold as *Kitchingia mandrakensis*. Stems usually unbranched, to 4–5 ft., possibly 10 ft. Thick, triangular to lance-shaped leaves—usually six to eight pairs of them—at stem tips. Each leaf 4–8 in. long or more and half as wide, covered with a dense, feltlike coating of white to brown hairs. Flowers not showy; foliage strikingly waved and crimped at edges. Hybrids between this and other species differ in leaf size, color, and degree of felting and scalloping. Striking in big rock garden, raised bed.

K. blossfeldiana. KALANCHOE. Fleshy, shiny dark green leaves edged red; smooth edged or slightly lobed, 2½ in. long, 1–1½ in. wide. Small bright red flowers in big clusters held above leaves. Hybrids and named selections come in dwarf (6-in.) and extra-sturdy (1½-ft.) sizes and in different flower colors, including yellow, orange, salmon. 'Pumila' and 'Tetra Vulcan' are choice dwarf seed-grown selections. Blooms winter, early spring. Popular house plant at Christmas.

🌿 **K. daigremontiana.** MATERNITY PLANT. Upright, single-stemmed plant 1½–3 ft. tall. Leaves fleshy, 6–8 in. long, 1¼ in. wide or wider, gray green spotted red. Leaf edges are notched; young plants sprout in notches and may root on the plant. Clusters of small, grayish purple flowers.

K. fedtschenkoi. SOUTH AMERICAN AIR PLANT. Popular ground cover in south Florida. To 1–2 ft. tall; leaves fleshy, smooth, scalloped, 1–2 in. long. Prostrate stems root. Often erroneously called gray sedum.

🌿 **K. pinnata (Bryophyllum pinnatum).** AIR PLANT. Fleshy stems eventually 2–3 ft. tall. Leaves also fleshy. First leaves to form are undivided and scallop edged; later ones divided into three to five leaflets, these also scalloped. Produces many plantlets in notches of scallops. Leaves can be removed and pinned to curtain, where they will produce plantlets until they dry up. Flowers clustered, greenish white to reddish, to 3 in. long; not particularly attractive. Likes moisture.

KALE and COLLARDS

Brassicaceae (Cruciferae)

BIENNIALS GROWN AS ANNUALS

⚡ ALL ZONES

☼ ◑ FULL SUN OR LIGHT SHADE

◐ REGULAR WATER

Kale

Vegetable crops that taste sweet once exposed to frost. The type of kale known as collards is a large, smooth-leafed plant resembling a cabbage that does not form a head. Curly-leafed kales form clusters of tightly curled dark green or blue-green leaves. Tall (to 3 ft.), heavy-yielding culinary selections include 'Red Russian', an heirloom, introduced by Russian traders, with blue-green leaves and purplish pink stems; and 'Winterbor', with particularly frilly blue-green leaves. Compact selections include 'Dwarf Blue Curled', 'Dwarf Blue Curled Scotch Vates', and 'Dwarf Siberian'. So-called flowering kale (similar to flowering cabbage) has brightly colored foliage, especially toward centers of rosettes; it is edible, though not particularly tasty.

Planted in early spring or late summer, collards and kale will yield edible leaves in fall, winter, and spring. Late summer planting is preferable for the Lower and Coastal South; plant in either season for Upper and Middle South. Crops that mature in fall have fewer pest problems. For all types of kale and collards, harvest leaves for cooking by removing them from outside of clusters; or harvest entire plant. Both kale and collards are high in vitamins A and C and in calcium. Far fewer pest and disease problems than most other cabbage-family crops.

KALIMERIS pinnatifida
(Asteromoea mongolica)

FALSE ASTER

Asteraceae (Compositae)

PERENNIAL

⚡ ZONES US, MS, LS

☼ ◑ FULL SUN OR LIGHT SHADE

◐ REGULAR WATER

Kalimeris pinnatifida

Native to east Asia. Perennial similar to *Boltonia asteroides*. Hundreds of 1-in., white chrysanthemum-like flowers are borne like a cloud on this plant all summer. Blossoms are tinged pink or blue, have creamy yellow centers. The foliage is rich green and heavily serrated. Grows to 2–4 ft., spreads slowly.

KALMIA

Ericaceae

EVERGREEN SHRUBS

⚡ ZONES VARY BY SPECIES

☼ ◑ FULL SUN OR PARTIAL SHADE

◐ REGULAR WATER

❀ FOLIAGE IS POISONOUS IF INGESTED

Kalmia latifolia

Elegant flowering shrubs related to rhododendron, with somewhat similar showy flower clusters. Notable difference is that each long flower stalk bears a small bud resembling a fluted turban; buds open to chalice-shaped blooms with five starlike points. Plants share rhododendron's need for moist air and well-drained acid soil rich in humus, but they take more sun. Tolerate full shade but bloom better with some light.

K. angustifolia. SHEEP LAUREL, LAMBKILL. Zones US, MS. Native to eastern states from Georgia to Virginia, Michigan, and Canada. Ground cover or shrub, to 1–3 ft., rarely 5 ft. Spreads by self-layering (branches root where they touch the ground). Leaves leathery, to 2½ in. long. Rose pink to purplish crimson flowers, ½ in. across, bloom in clusters, in early summer. 'Candida' has white flowers, 'Rubra' dark purple flowers.

K. latifolia. MOUNTAIN LAUREL. Zones US, MS, LS, CS. Native to eastern North America from Canada to Florida, west across the Appalachians into states drained by the Ohio and Mississippi river systems. Southern forms of plant grow better in the Lower and Coastal South; those from more northerly seed sources grow better in the Upper and Middle South. Success also depends on plant source. Named selections are unlikely to perform well in all zones listed.

Slow growing to 6–8 ft. or taller, with equal spread. Glossy, leathery, oval leaves are 3–5 in. long, dark green on top, yellowish green beneath. Blooms in late spring; typically bears 1-in.-wide light pink flowers opening ffrom darker pink buds, but blossoms often have subtly different color in their throats, may have contrasting stamens. Flowers are carried in clusters to 5 in. across.

Many named selections are available. 'Bay State' has coral flowers; 'Bullseye' bears dark purplish red blossoms with white centers; 'Olympic Fire' and 'Ostbo Red' have deep red buds opening to palest pink flowers. 'Pinwheel' produces flowers in a combination of deep red and white. 'Sarah' has pinkish red blooms opening from deep red buds. Two dwarfs, both growing to 2–2½ ft. tall and 4–5 ft. wide, are 'Elf', with nearly white blossoms, and 'Tiddlywinks', with medium pink blossoms opening from deep pink buds.

KALOPANAX septemlobus (K. pictus)

CASTOR ARALIA, TREE ARALIA

Araliaceae

DECIDUOUS TREE

🌿 ZONES US, MS

☼ FULL SUN

💧 REGULAR WATER

Kalopanax septemlobus

Unusual in being the only hardy large tree in its family. Also notable for the tropical look conferred by big (7–10-in.) leaves with five to seven lobes. On young trees, leaves may exceed 1 ft. in width. Tree is 40–60 ft. tall, with a spiny trunk and relatively few coarse, spiny branches. Spines eventually disappear from trunk and larger branches. Open and gaunt in youth but eventually develops an attractive rounded habit. Tiny white flowers in large (1–2-ft.-wide), flattish clusters at branch ends. Small black fruits follow blossoms; they are quickly consumed by birds.

KANSAS BLAZING STAR. See LIATRIS pycnostachya

KATSURA TREE. See CERCIDIPHYLLUM japonicum

KENTIA PALM. See HOWEA

KENTUCKY BLUEGRASS. See POA pratensis

KENTUCKY COFFEE TREE. See GYMNOCLADUS dioica

KENYA IVY. See SENECIO macroglossus

🏛 KERRIA japonica

JAPANESE KERRIA

Rosaceae

DECIDUOUS SHRUB

🌿 ZONES US, MS, LS

☼ ◐ FULL SUN OR LIGHT SHADE

💧 REGULAR WATER

Kerria japonica
'Pleniflora'

Native to China. Sometimes mistakenly called the yellow rose of Texas. Open, graceful, rounded shrub to 6 ft. tall. Slender stems are yellowish green to bright green in winter. Toothed, heavily veined, somewhat triangular, 2–4-in.-long, bright green leaves unfold early in spring; turn yellow in fall. Flowers come in spring, sporadically into early summer; they look like small rose blossoms. 'Kinkan' has yellow-striped stems, single yellow blooms. 'Picta' has white-edged leaves, single yellow flowers. 'Shannon' is vigorous and has large, single yellow flowers. 'Pleniflora', more commonly planted than the species, has double golden, inch-wide blossoms and taller, suckering habit.

Give kerria room to display its arching form. It blooms on previous year's wood. Spreads slowly by stolons to form a large clump, which is easily divided in fall, using a sharp spade. Prune heavily after flowering, cutting out branches that have bloomed, all dead or weak wood, and suckers. The green branches are a favorite for Japanese flower arrangements.

KING PALM. See ARCHONTOPHOENIX cunninghamiana

KING'S MANTLE. See THUNBERGIA erecta

KIRILOW INDIGO. See INDIGOFERA kirilowii

KIWI VINE, HARDY KIWI. See ACTINIDIA deliciosa, A. arguta

KLEINIA. See SENECIO

KNIPHOFIA uvaria (Tritoma uvaria)

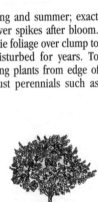

RED-HOT POKER, TORCH-LILY, POKER PLANT

Liliaceae

PERENNIAL

🌿 ZONES US, MS, LS, CS

☼ ◐ FULL SUN OR LIGHT SHADE

💧 💧 REGULAR TO MODERATE WATER

Kniphofia uvaria

Native to South Africa. Has been in cultivation long enough to give rise to a number of selections ranging in size, color. Typical plant is coarse, with large, rather dense clumps of long, grasslike leaves. Flower stalks (always taller than leaves) are about 2 ft. high in dwarf kinds, 3–6 ft. in larger kinds. The many drooping, orange-red or yellow, tubular flowers of the typical plant overlap, forming poker-like clusters 1 ft. long. Named selections, in both dwarf and taller forms, come in soft or saffron yellow, creamy white, or coral. Flowers attract hummingbirds, are good in flower arrangements.

Plants require excellent drainage. Bloom spring and summer; exact flowering time depends on selection. Cut out flower spikes after bloom. Where winter temperatures drop to 0°F or below, tie foliage over clump to protect growing points. Clumps will grow undisturbed for years. To increase plantings, carefully dig and remove young plants from edge of clump. Useful in large borders with other robust perennials such as daylilies, globe thistle.

KOELREUTERIA

Sapindaceae

DECIDUOUS TREES

🌿 ZONES VARY BY SPECIES

☼ FULL SUN

💧 REGULAR TO MODERATE WATER

Koelreuteria paniculata

Small trees native to Asia. Noted for large, loose clusters of yellow flowers followed by fat, papery fruit capsules resembling little Japanese lanterns; capsules are used in arrangements. Good courtyard, lawn, or street trees. Very adaptable to different soils as long as soil is fairly well drained. Tolerate drought. Control self-sown seedlings.

K. bipinnata (K. integrifoliola). CHINESE FLAME TREE, BOUGAIN-VILLEA GOLDENRAIN TREE. Zones MS, LS, CS. To 20–40 ft. or taller; spreading and eventually flat topped. Leaves are 1–2 ft. long, divided into many oval leaflets; turn yellow for short time before dropping. Flower clusters in late summer are similar to those of *K. paniculata*, but 2-in. fruit capsules are more colorful: orange, red, or salmon, appearing soon after flowers and persisting into fall. Stake and prune tree to develop high branching. Roots deep, not invasive; good tree to plant under. Deserves much wider use.

K. elegans (K. formosana, K. henryi). FLAMEGOLD. Zones CS, TS. To 20–30 ft. tall, round headed. Similar to other species, but not as cold-hardy, and less widely sold. Fall flowers are followed by pinkish capsules that hang on into December.

K. paniculata. GOLDENRAIN TREE, VARNISH TREE. Zones US, MS, LS, CS. To 20–35 ft., with 10–40-ft. spread. Open branching, giving light shade. Leaves to 15 in. long with seven to fifteen oval, toothed or lobed leaflets, each 1–3 in. long. New leaves are purplish, turning bright green in summer; yellow to gold fall color unreliable. Very showy flower clusters, 8–14 in. long, in early to midsummer. Fruit capsules red when young, maturing to buff and brown shades; last well into autumn. Tree takes cold, heat, drought, wind. Prune to shape; can be leggy without pruning.

🌳 KOLKWITZIA amabilis

BEAUTY BUSH

Caprifoliaceae

DECIDUOUS SHRUB

🗡 ZONES US, MS, LS

☼ ◑ FULL SUN OR PARTIAL SHADE

◗ ◗ REGULAR TO MODERATE WATER

Kolkwitzia amabilis

Native to China. Graceful, upright growth to 10–12 ft.; arching form in partial shade, denser and shorter in full sun. Gray-green leaves to 3 in. long sometimes turn reddish in fall. Blooms heavily in mid- to late spring, bearing clusters of small, yellow-throated pink flowers. Blossoms are followed by conspicuous pinkish brown, bristly fruits that prolong color display. Brown, flaky bark gradually peels from stems during winter. An old Southern favorite.

Adapts to many soils and microclimates. Flowers are borne on wood formed the previous year. Thin out oldest stems after blossoms have faded; or, to enjoy the fruit, prune lightly in early spring. Plant can be renewed by cutting to ground after bloom.

KOREAN FORSYTHIA. See FORSYTHIA ovata

KOREAN GRASS. See ZOYSIA tenuifolia

KUDZU. See PUERARIA lobata

KUMQUAT. See CITRUS

Labiatae. See Lamiaceae

LABURNUM

GOLDENCHAIN TREE

Fabaceae (Leguminosae)

DECIDUOUS LARGE SHRUBS OR SMALL TREES

🗡 ZONE US

☼ ◑ AFTERNOON SHADE

◗ REGULAR WATER

⬧ SEEDPODS ARE POISONOUS IF INGESTED

Laburnum watereri

Upright growth; usually pruned into single-stemmed tree, but can be shrubby if permitted to keep basal suckers and low branches. Green bark; bright green leaves divided into three leaflets (like clover). Handsome in bloom: In mid- to late spring, bears yellow, sweet pea–shaped flowers in hanging clusters like wisteria. Use as a single tree in lawn or border; group in front of evergreen background; or space regularly in a long border of perennials, rhododendrons, or lilacs.

Provide well-drained soil. Prune and trim regularly to keep tidy. If possible, remove seedpods; not only are they toxic, but a heavy crop drains the plant's strength.

L. anagyroides. COMMON GOLDENCHAIN. To 20–30 ft. tall; often bushy and wide spreading. Flower clusters 6–10 in. long. Has a weeping selection, 'Pendulum'.

L. watereri. Hybrid. To about 25 ft. tall. Flower clusters 10–20 in. long. 'Vossii' is the most widely grown and most graceful selection; it can be espaliered. Very showy blossoms in chains up to 2 ft. long.

LACY PINE FERN. See POLYPODIUM subauriculatum 'Knightiae'

LADY BANKS'S ROSE. See ROSA banksiae

LADYBELLS. See ADENOPHORA

LADY FERN. See ATHYRIUM filix-femina

LADY PALM. See RHAPIS

LADY'S-MANTLE. See ALCHEMILLA

LAGERSTROEMIA

CREPE MYRTLE

Lythraceae

DECIDUOUS SHRUBS OR TREES

🗡 ZONES US, MS, LS, CS, EXCEPT AS NOTED

☼ FULL SUN

◗ MODERATE WATER

▸ SEE CHART NEXT PAGE

Lagerstroemia indica

The crepe myrtles are among the most satisfactory of plants for the South: Showy summer flowers, attractive bark, and (in many cases) brilliant fall color make them year-round garden performers. Long, cool autumns yield the best leaf display. Sudden frosts following warm, humid falls often freeze leaves while they're still green, ruining the show.

Most crepe myrtles in gardens are selections of *L. indica* or hybrids of that species with *L. fauriei*. The latter species has attracted much notice for its hardiness and exceptionally showy bark. Queen's crepe myrtle, *L. speciosa*, grows only in the Tropical South.

All crepe myrtles bloom on new wood and should be pruned in winter or early spring to increase next summer's flowers. On small, shrubby forms, remove spent flower clusters and thin out small twiggy growth; to maintain compactness and eliminate leggy look, cut branches nearly to the ground in spring. On large shrubs and trees, remove basal suckers and gradually prune away side branches to 4–5 ft. tall, exposing the trunks' handsome bark. Prune larger limbs back to trunk or crotch.

L. fauriei. JAPANESE CREPE MYRTLE. Tree to 20–30 ft. with erect habit and outward-arching branches. Leaves light green, to 4 in. long and 2 in. wide, turning yellow in fall. Especially handsome bark: The smooth, gray outer bark flakes away to reveal glossy cinnamon brown bark beneath. Small white flowers are borne in 2–4-in.-long clusters; usually pauses after initial bloom, then flowers again in late summer. Resistant to mildew and best known as a parent of hardy, mildew-resistant hybrids with *L. indica*, though it is handsome in its own right. 'Fantasy', with even showier bark than the species, has a vase form—narrow below, spreading above. 'Kiowa' has outstanding cinnamon-colored bark that is uniform, not in patches.

🌳 **L. indica.** CREPE MYRTLE. The premier summer-flowering tree of the South. Tolerates heat, humidity, drought, and most well-drained soils. May be frozen to the ground in severe winters in the Upper South, but will resprout. Gardeners there should plant cold-hardy selections, such as 'Acoma', 'Centennial Spirit', and 'Hopi'. Variable in size (some forms are dwarf shrubs, others large shrubs or small trees) and habit (spreading or

▸ page 269

LAGERSTROEMIA—CREPE MYRTLE

SELECTION	FORM/HEIGHT	MILDEW RESISTANCE	FLOWERS/DAYS OF BLOOM	FALL FOLIAGE	COMMENTS
Lagerstroemia indica 'Acoma'	Spreading, arching, nearly weeping shrub; to 10 ft.	High	White; 90	Reddish purple	Light gray bark. Cold-hardy
L. i. 'Basham's Party Pink'	Broad tree; to 40 ft. tall and wide	Good	Lavender pink; 80	Orange red	Very popular in South Texas. Not recommended for Upper and Middle South. Selection not very cold-hardy
L. i. 'Biloxi'	Upright, arching, small tree; to 30 ft.	High	Light pink; 80	Yellow orange to red	Mottled dark brown bark. Fast grower; cold-hardy
L. i. 'Byers Wonderful White'	Upright, small tree; to 20 ft.	Good	Clear white; 90	Yellow	Huge flower heads larger than a basketball. Cold-hardy
L. i. 'Catawba'	Upright, small tree; to 12 ft.	Good	Dark purple; 70	Orange red	Considered the best dark purple selection. Cold-hardy
L. i. 'Centennial'	Dwarf, round shrub; to 3 ft.	Good	Bright purple; 70	Orange	Probably the best dwarf purple selection. Cold-hardy
L. i. 'Centennial Spirit'	Upright, large shrub or small tree; to 20 ft.	Good	Dark red; 110	Red orange	Extremely showy blooms. Cold-hardy
L. i. 'Comanche'	Spreading, large shrub or small tree; to 15 ft. tall and wide	High	Coral pink; 80	Orange red and purple red	Handsome tan to sandalwood bark. Cold-hardy
L. i. 'Hopi'	Spreading, semidwarf shrub; 7 ft. tall, 10 ft. wide	High	Medium pink; 100	Orange red to dark red	Attractive gray-brown bark. Exceptionally cold-hardy
L. i. 'Lipan'	Upright shrub or small tree; to 15 ft. tall and wide	High	Medium lavender; 80	Orange to red	Beautiful white to beige bark. Cold-hardy
L. i. 'Miami'	Upright, small tree; to 25 ft.	High	Medium pink; 100	Orange to dull russet	Chestnut brown bark. Very popular selection
L. i. 'Muskogee'	Broad, small tree; to 20 ft.	High	Light lavender; 120	Red	Tan and brown bark. Fast growing; cold-hardy
L. i. 'Natchez'	Small tree; 30 ft. tall and wide	High	Pure white; 110	Orange red	Considered by many to be the best all-around crepe myrtle. Spectacular cinnamon brown bark. Fast growing
L. i. 'Near East'	Spreading, small tree; to 18 ft.	Fair	Soft, light pink; 90	Yellow orange	Beautiful blooms. Not recommended for Upper or Middle South. Not very cold-hardy
L. i. 'Osage'	Arching, open-branched shrub or small tree; to 15 ft.	High	Clear light pink; 100	Red	Chestnut brown bark. Heavy bloomer
L. i. 'Potomac'	Upright shrub or small tree; to 25 ft.	Fair	Clear pink; 90	Orange	Good for narrow spaces. Fast growing
L. i. 'Prairie Lace'	Upright, semidwarf shrub; to 10 ft.	Fair	Medium pink edged in white; 90	Red to red orange	Cold-hardy; nearly seedless
L. i. 'Regal Red'	Upright, rounded, small tree; to 12 ft. tall and wide	Good	Vivid deep red; 70	Red orange	Probably the best deep red selection. Cold-hardy
L. i. 'Sioux'	Upright, large shrub or small tree; 15–20 ft.	High	Bright pink, fragrant; 100	Red	Light gray-brown bark. Showy blooms. Summer foliage dark green to burgundy green

L

LAGERSTROEMIA—CREPE MYRTLE

SELECTION	FORM/HEIGHT	MILDEW RESISTANCE	FLOWERS/DAYS OF BLOOM	FALL FOLIAGE	COMMENTS
L. i. 'Tuskegee'	Small multitrunked tree with horizontal branching; to 20 ft. tall and wide	High	Deep pink to red; 100	Bright orange red	Beautiful gray and tan bark. Cold-hardy. Fine all-around performer
L. i. 'Victor'	Dwarf, round shrub; to 3 ft.	Good	Dark red; 85	Reddish yellow	The best red dwarf. Cold-hardy
L. i. 'William Toovey'	Vase-shaped shrub or small tree; to 15 ft.	Good	Watermelon red; 90	Red orange	An old favorite. Often sold as 'Watermelon Red'
L. i. 'Yuma'	Upright, multitrunked, large shrub or small tree; to 15 ft. tall, nearly as wide	Good	Medium lavender; 90	Yellowish to brownish red	Light gray bark. Cold-hardy
L. i. 'Zuni'	Round, semidwarf shrub; 9 ft. tall, 8 ft. wide	High	Medium lavender; 100	Orange red to dark red	Light brown and gray bark; heavy bloomer. Cold-hardy

upright). Dark green leaves are 1–2½ in. long and somewhat narrower, usually tinted red on unfurling, often turning brilliant orange or red in fall. Crinkled, crepe-papery, 1–1½-in.-wide flowers in white or shades of pink, red, or purple are carried in dense clusters.

Trained as a tree, it develops an attractive trunk and branch pattern. Smooth gray or light brown bark peels off to reveal smooth, pinkish inner bark; winter trunk and branches seem polished.

Mildew can be a problem. Spray with triforine (Funginex) before plants bloom, or grow mildew-resistant hybrids of *L. indica* and *L. fauriei* (see box this page). The chart describes many choice crepe myrtle selections.

L. speciosa. QUEEN'S CREPE MYRTLE. Zone TS. Large tree (to 80 ft. tall), with leaves 8–12 in. long, 4 in. wide. White to purple flowers are borne in clusters to 16 in. long. 'Majestic Orchid', a hybrid between this tree and *L. indica*, is as hardy as the latter. It grows 20 ft. tall and 15 ft. wide, with large clusters of deep orchid purple flowers and foliage that turns yellow in fall.

MILDEW-RESISTANT CREPE MYRTLES

The most mildew-resistant crepe myrtles are the National Arboretum hybrids between *Lagerstroemia indica* and *L. fauriei* that bear the names of Indian tribes. they include 'Acoma', 'Biloxi', 'Comanche', 'Hopi', 'Lipan', 'Miami', 'Muskogee', 'Natchez', 'Osage', 'Sioux', 'Tuskegee', 'Yuma', and 'Zuni'.

LAMB'S EARS. See STACHYS byzantina

Lamiaceae. Members of the mint family of herbaceous plants and shrubs are easily recognized by their square stems, leaves in opposite pairs, and whorled flowers in spikelike, sometimes branched, clusters. Many of the group are aromatic; the family contains most of the familiar kitchen herbs, including basil *(Ocimum)*, mint *(Mentha)*, oregano *(Origanum)*, and sage *(Salvia)*. Many have attractive foliage or flowers (coleus, sage). This family was previously called Labiatae.

LAMIASTRUM galeobdolon. See LAMIUM galeobdolon

LAMIUM

DEAD NETTLE

Lamiaceae (Labiatae)

PERENNIALS

☘ ZONES US, MS, LS

◐ ● PARTIAL OR FULL SHADE

💧 REGULAR WATER

Lamium maculatum

Leaves in opposite pairs are heart shaped, toothed, marked with white. Clustered flowers are pink, white, or yellow. All are vigorous growers that thrive in shade. One species is used as a ground cover.

L. galeobdolon (Galeobdolon luteum, Lamiastrum galeobdolon). YELLOW ARCHANGEL. Upright to 2 ft., slowly spreading to form tight clumps. Yellow flowers are unimportant. Best-known selection is 'Herman's Pride', with leaves evenly streaked and spotted with white.

L. maculatum. SPOTTED DEAD NETTLE. Running or trailing perennial used as a ground cover or in hanging baskets. To 6 in. tall, spreads 2–3 ft. Grayish green leaves have silvery markings. Pink flowers bloom spring into summer. Species is vigorous, even weedy, and is planted less frequently than its choicer selections. These include 'Beacon Silver', with pink flowers and green-edged, silvery gray leaves; 'White Nancy', a 'Beacon Silver' with white blooms; 'Chequers', with pink blossoms and green leaves with a center stripe of white; and 'Pink Pewter', with abundant pink flowers above silvery leaves edged gray green. All selections nicely light up shady areas of the garden. Groom periodically to remove old, shabby growth.

LANTANA

Verbenaceae

EVERGREEN SHRUBS

☘ ZONES MS (HARDIER FORMS), LS, CS, TS

☀ FULL SUN

💧 MODERATE WATER

⚘ FRUITS ARE POISONOUS IF INGESTED

Lantana montevidensis

Fast growing, valued for profuse show of color over long season—every month of the year in frost-free areas. Light frosts merely keep plants in check. Heavier freezes may seriously damage or kill plants in some (but not all) winters. One of the top plants for attracting butterflies. Good choice for growing near the beach. ▶

Prone to mildew in shade or during prolonged overcast weather. Prune hard in spring to remove dead wood and prevent woodiness. Feed lightly. Too much water and fertilizer cuts down on bloom. Shrubby kinds used as substitutes for annuals in beds or containers, as low hedges or foundation shrubs. Spreading kinds are excellent bank covers, will control erosion. Effective spilling from raised beds, planter boxes, or hanging baskets. Crushed foliage has a pungent odor that some people find objectionable.

L. camara. COMMON LANTANA. One of two species used in hybridizing and the most popular in the South. Coarse, upright to 6 ft. Rough dark green leaves. Yellow, orange, or red flowers in 1–2-in. clusters.

The following list gives some of the named selections of lantana that are available. Some are merely forms of *L. camara*, or are hybrids between the forms. Others are hybrids between *L. camara* and *L. montevidensis*.

'Christine'. To 6 ft. tall, 5 ft. wide. Cerise pink. Can be trained into small patio tree.

'Confetti'. To 2–3 ft. by 6–8 ft. Blossoms mix yellow, pink, and purple.

'Cream Carpet'. To 2–3 ft. by 6–8 ft. Cream with bright yellow throat.

'Dwarf Pink'. To 2–4 ft. by 3–4 ft. Light pink. Rather tender.

'Dwarf White'. To 2–4 ft. by 3–4 ft.

'Dwarf Yellow'. To 2–4 ft. high and wide.

'Gold Rush'. To 1½–2 ft. by 4–6 ft. Rich golden yellow.

'Irene'. To 3 ft. by 4 ft. Compact. Magenta with lemon yellow.

'Lemon Swirl'. Slow growing to 2 ft. tall, 3 ft. wide. Yellow flowers, bright yellow band around each leaf.

'Miss Huff'. To 3 ft. by 10 ft. Very hardy once established. Has survived −3°F. Produces very little seed. Orange and pink.

'New Gold'. To 1½ ft. by 2½–3 ft. Trailing type, dwarf. Doesn't seed. Golden yellow.

'Nivea'. To 3 ft. by 6 ft. White.

'Radiation'. To 3–5 ft. high and wide. Rich orange red.

'Spreading Sunset'. To 2–3 ft. by 6–8 ft. Vivid orange red.

'Spreading Sunshine'. To 2–3 ft. by 6–8 ft. Bright yellow.

'Sunburst'. To 2–3 ft. by 6–8 ft. Bright golden yellow.

'Tangerine'. To 2–3 ft. by 6–8 ft. Burnt orange.

L. horrida. TEXAS LANTANA. Native to southern Texas and Mexico. Prickly coarse shrub, to 3 ft. tall, rarely 6 ft. Spreads by self-layering (shoots take root where they touch ground). Good ground cover on very dry sites in full sun. Flowers open yellow, age to orange.

L. montevidensis (L. sellowiana). TRAILING LANTANA. The other species used in breeding. This one is sold at garden centers. A little hardier than *L. camara*, it's a ground cover with branches trailing to 3 ft. or even 6 ft. Dark green, 1-in.-long leaves with coarsely toothed edges are sometimes tinged red or purplish, especially in winter; 1–1½-in.-wide clusters of rosy lilac flowers. 'Lavender Swirl' is a larger form that produces white, lavender, and mixed flower clusters. 'White Lightnin' is similar but has pure white flowers.

LARIX

LARCH
Pinaceae
DECIDUOUS TREES
ZONES VARY BY SPECIES
FULL SUN
REGULAR WATER

Slender pyramids with horizontal branches and drooping branchlets. Needles (½–1½ in. long) soft to touch, in fluffy tufts. Woody, roundish cones, ½–1½ in. long, are scattered all along

Larix decidua

branchlets. Notable for color in spring and fall and for winter silhouette. In spring, new needle tufts are pale green and new cones bright purple red. In fall, needles turn brilliant yellow and orange before dropping. Abundant cones create a delightful polka-dot pattern against the winter sky. Not particular about soils. Plant with dark evergreen conifers as background or near water for reflection. Larches attract birds.

L. decidua (L. europaea). EUROPEAN LARCH. Zone US. Moderate to fast growth to 30–60 ft. Summer foliage color is grass green. Branches of 'Pendula' arch out and down; branchlets hang nearly straight down.

L. kaempferi. JAPANESE LARCH. Zones US, MS. Fast growing to 60 ft. or more but can be dwarfed in containers. Summer foliage is a soft bluish green. 'Pendula' has long, weeping branches.

L. laricina. AMERICAN LARCH. Zone US. Native to northern U.S. and much of Canada. Slow to medium growth to 40–80 ft. tall. Bright blue-green summer foliage. Grows well in moist to boggy soils. Difficult to grow in the South. Dislikes long, hot summers.

LARKSPUR. See CONSOLIDA ambigua

LARREA tridentata

CREOSOTE BUSH
Zygophyllaceae
EVERGREEN SHRUB
ZONES MS, LS, CS, TS
FULL SUN
MODERATE TO LITTLE WATER

Larrea tridentata

One of the most common native shrubs in Texas and northern Mexico. Grows 4–8 ft. tall with many upright branches. Straggly and open in shallow, dry soil; attractive, dense, rounded but spreading where water accumulates. Leathery, yellow-green to dark green leaves divided into two tiny, ³⁄₈-in.-long crescents. Gummy secretion makes leaves look varnished and yields distinctive creosote odor, especially after rain. Small yellow flowers bloom off and on all year, followed by small roundish fruit covered with shiny white or rusty hairs.

Give it fertilizer along with irrigation water to produce shiny dark green leaves. Use as wind or privacy screen, foundation shrub, or small tree. Very drought tolerant because of long taproot. Established plants difficult to transplant. Needs well-drained soil. Not a good choice for high-rainfall, high-humidity areas. Sometimes sold as *L. divaricata*.

LATHYRUS

SWEET PEA
Fabaceae (Leguminosae)
ANNUAL OR PERENNIAL VINES
ZONES VARY BY SPECIES
FULL SUN
WATER NEEDS VARY BY SPECIES

Lathyrus odoratus

In this group is one of the best-known and most favorite garden flowers—the delightfully fragrant and colorful sweet pea.

Throughout this book you will find flowers described as "sweet pea shaped." The flower of the sweet pea is typical of the many members of the pea family (Fabaceae). Each flower has one large, upright, roundish petal (banner or standard), two narrow side petals (wings), and two lower petals that are somewhat united, forming a boat-shaped structure (keel).

L. latifolius. PERENNIAL SWEET PEA. Zones US, MS, LS. Vine is strong growing, to 9 ft., with blue-green foliage. Flowers usually reddish purple, often white or pink. Single colors are sometimes sold. Blooms into summer if not allowed to go to seed. Plants grow with little care, tolerate drought. May escape and become naturalized. Use as bank cover, trailing over rocks, on trellis or fence.

L. odoratus. SWEET PEA. Winter or spring annual. All zones, but performance is curtailed by heat. Bears many spikelike clusters of crisp-looking flowers with a clean, sweet fragrance, in both single colors and mixtures. Color mixtures include deep rose, blue, purple, scarlet, white, cream, amethyst on white ground, salmon, salmon pink on cream. Sweet peas make magnificent cut flowers in quantity. Bush types offer cut flowers the same as vine types and require no training.

To hasten germination, soak seeds a few hours before planting. Sow 1 in. deep and 1–2 in. apart. When seedlings are 4–5 in. high, thin to at least 6 in. apart. Pinch out tops for strong side branches. Plant peat pots 1 ft. apart, thinning each to one strong plant. This method is ideal for bush types. Never let vines lack for water; soak heavily. To prolong bloom, cut flowers at least every other day, remove all seedpods. Regular monthly feeding with commercial fertilizer keeps vines vigorous and productive.

For vining sweet peas, provide trellis, strings, or wire before planting. Seedlings need support as soon as tendrils form. Freestanding trellis running north and south is best. When planting against fence or wall, keep supports away from wall to give air circulation.

GETTING SWEET PEAS OFF TO A FINE START

In less-than-perfect soil, prepare ground for sweet peas like this: Dig trench 1–1½ ft. deep. Mix 1 part peat moss or other soil conditioner to 2 parts soil. As you mix, add in a complete commercial fertilizer according to label directions. Backfill trench with mix; plant seeds in it.

The following describes vine-type sweet peas (grouped by time of bloom) and bush types.

Early flowering. (Early Flowering Multiflora, Early Multiflora, formerly Early Spencers.) The name "Spencer" once described a type of frilled flower (with wavy petals) that is now characteristic of almost all selections. "Multiflora" indicates that the plants carry more flowers per stem than the old Spencers did. The value of early-flowering selections is that they will bloom in winter when days are short. (Spring-flowering types will not bloom until days have lengthened to 15 hours or more.) Sow seeds in October and November for blooms in late winter and spring. Use these selections for forcing in greenhouse. They are not heat resistant. Generally sold in mixed colors.

Spring flowering. (Spring-Flowering, Heat-Resistant Cuthbertson Type, Cuthbertson's Floribunda, Floribunda-Zvolanek strain.) Both mixtures and single-color named selections are available in seed packets. Wide color range: pink, lavender, purple, white, cream, rose, salmon, cerise, carmine, red, blue. Royal or Royal Family is somewhat larger flowered and more heat resistant than the others. Plant between October and early January.

Bush type. The so-called bush-type sweet peas are vines with predetermined growth, heights. Unlike vining types that reach 5 ft. and more, these stop their upward growth at 1–2½ ft. In general, don't do as well in South as early- and spring-flowering types.

Bijou. To 1 ft. Full color range in mixtures and single types. Four or five flowers on 5–7-in. stems. Useful and spectacular in borders, beds, window boxes, containers. Not as heat resistant or as long stemmed as Knee-Hi; performs better in containers.

Cupid. To 4–6 in. tall, 1½ ft. wide. Trails, or hangs from container.

Jet Set. Bushy, self-supporting, 2–3 ft. tall. All colors.

Knee-Hi. To 2½ ft. Large, long-stemmed flowers, five or six to the stem. Has all the virtues and color range of the spring-flowering types, on self-supporting, bush-type vines. Provides cutting-type flowers in mass display in beds and borders. Growth will exceed 2½ ft. where planting bed joins fence or wall. Keep in open area for uniform height. Follow same planting dates as for spring-flowering sweet peas.

Little Sweethearts. Rounded form, 8 in. tall, blooms over a long season. Full range of colors. Patio strain grows 9 in. tall. Snoopea (12–15 in.) and Supersnoop (2 ft.) need no support, come in full range of sweet pea colors.

SOUTHERN HERITAGE PLANTS
IDENTIFIED BY SYMBOL ᵀ

Lauraceae. The laurel family contains evergreen and deciduous trees and shrubs with inconspicuous flowers and (usually) aromatic foliage. Fruits are fleshy, containing a single seed. Examples are avocado, camphor tree *(Cinnamomum)*, and bay *(Laurus nobilis)*.

LAUREL. See PRUNUS

ᵀ LAURUS nobilis

BAY, SWEET BAY, GRECIAN LAUREL

Lauraceae

EVERGREEN SHRUB OR TREE

⚥ ZONES LS (PROTECTED), CS, TS; OR GROW IN POTS

☼ ◖ FULL SUN OR PARTIAL SHADE

⬦ MODERATE WATER

Laurus nobilis

Slow growth to 12–40 ft. Natural habit is compact, broad based—often that of a multi-stemmed, gradually tapering cone. Leaves are leathery, aromatic, oval, 2–4 in. long, dark green; traditional bay leaf of cookery. Clusters of small yellow flowers are followed by ½–1-in.-long, black or dark purple berries. 'Saratoga' has broader leaves, more treelike habit.

Not fussy about soil but needs good drainage. Tends to sucker heavily. Dense habit makes it a good large background shrub, screen, or small tree. Takes well to clipping into standards, hedges, or topiary shapes such as globes and cones. A classic formal container plant. In the Upper and Middle South, grow in a container so it can be moved to greenhouse or cool, well-lighted room when temperatures reach about 20°F.

LAURUSTINUS. See VIBURNUM tinus

LAVANDIN. See LAVANDULA intermedia

LAVANDULA

LAVENDER

Lamiaceae (Labiatae)

EVERGREEN SHRUBS OR SUBSHRUBS

⚥ ZONES VARY BY SPECIES

☼ FULL SUN

⬦ MODERATE WATER

Native to Mediterranean region. Prized for its fragrant lavender or purple flowers; those of some species are used for perfume, sachets. Aromatic grayish or gray-green foliage. Plant as hedge or edging, in herb gardens, or in borders with plants needing similar conditions—catmint, rosemary, santolina, verbena.

Lavandula angustifolia

Lavenders require full sun, well-drained soil, little or no fertilizer. Most will not succeed in steamy heat. Prune immediately after bloom to keep plants compact and neat. For sachets, cut flower clusters or strip flowers from stems just as color shows; dry in cool, shady place.

Since lavenders have been in cultivation for centuries and tend to interbreed, many hybrids and selections have arisen, and names are difficult to sort out. Some of the names that follow may not agree with those you see on nursery labels.

L. angustifolia (L. officinalis, L. spica, L. vera). ENGLISH LAVENDER. Zones US, MS. Hardiest species and the one most widely planted. The classic lavender used for perfume and sachets. To 3–4 ft. high and wide. Narrow, smooth-edged gray leaves to 2 in. long; lavender, ½-in.-long flowers in 1½–2-ft.-high spikes in late spring or summer. Many selections exist, among them the following: ▶

'Alba'. To 3 ft. high, pure white flower spikes, gray-green foliage.

'Compacta' ('Compacta Nana', 'Dwarf Blue'). Dark blue flowers on an 8–12-in. plant.

'Grey Lady'. To 1½ ft. tall. Silvery gray foliage, lavender blue flowers.

'Hidcote'. To 15–20 in. tall. Deep purplish blue flowers, gray foliage.

'Irene Doyle'. To 1½ ft. high. Flowers, lavender blue, in summer; reblooms in early fall.

'Jean Davis'. Pale pink flowers, gray-green foliage on a 1½-ft. plant.

'Lavender Lady'. To 10 in. tall; gray foliage, lavender flowers. Fast grower, often blooming first year from seed.

'Mitcham's Gray'. Similar to 'Hidcote', but slightly taller and with lighter blue flowers.

'Munstead'. Compact plant to 1–1½ ft. Medium blue flowers. Long blooming; good for edging.

'Rosea'. Pink flowers on a 15-in. plant.

'Twickel Purple'. Dense, compact grower to 1½ ft. high, with heavy, thick spikes of light purple flowers.

L. dentata. FRENCH LAVENDER. Zone LS. To 3 ft. tall. Narrow gray-green leaves, 1–1½ in. long, with square-toothed edges. Lavender purple flowers in short spikelike clusters, each topped with tuft of petal-like bracts. Long spring–summer flowering period. Takes summer heat better than English lavender does.

L. d. candicans, with somewhat larger leaves than the species, has dense grayish white down on young foliage.

L. intermedia. LAVANDIN. Zones US, MS, LS. Group of hybrids between *L. angustifolia* and *L. latifolia.* All are vigorous, highly fragrant, and about as hardy as English lavender parent but more tolerant of warm, humid summers. Early to midsummer bloom. 'Dutch' is a 16-in. mound of gray foliage, bears 3-ft. stems topped with dark purple flowers; 'Grappenhall' has dark violet spikes on 3½-ft. stems above 14-in. foliage mound; 'Grosso', possibly the most fragrant of all, grows in compact, 8-in.-high mound of silvery foliage with large, fat purple spikes on 2½-ft. stems; 'Provence', 2 ft. (to 3–4 ft. in bloom), bears light purple flower spikes.

L. latifolia. SPIKE LAVENDER. Zones US, MS, LS. Much like English lavender in appearance but with broader leaves and much-branched flower stalks. Bloom period same as for English lavender.

L. stoechas. SPANISH LAVENDER. Zones MS, LS. Stocky plant 1½–3 ft. tall, with narrow, gray leaves ½–1 in. long. Flowers are dark purple, grow to about ⅛ in. long, in dense, short spikes, each topped with big tuft of purple, petal-like bracts. Plant blooms in late spring or early summer. *L. s. pedunculata* is usually seen; it differs from the species in having flower stalks longer than the flower clusters themselves. 'Otto Quast', a long-stalked selection, has especially showy bracts. A good alternative to English lavender in the Lower South.

LAVATERA

TREE MALLOW

Malvaceae

ANNUAL OR PERENNIAL SHRUBS

ZONES VARY BY SPECIES

FULL SUN

REGULAR TO LITTLE WATER

Lavatera trimestris

Lavatera is named after the Lavater family of Zurich, but for many the word means "easy to grow." The flowers resemble single hollyhocks.

L. thuringiaca. Perennial shrub. Zones US, MS, LS. To 6–8 ft., with 2½-in. maplelike leaves. Flowers are purplish pink, 3 in. across, nearly everblooming. 'Barnsley' has lighter pink flowers paling to white centers. 'Rosea' has pink flowers.

L. trimestris. ANNUAL MALLOW. All zones. Reaches a height of 3–6 ft. from spring-sown seed. Satiny flowers to 4 in. across; named selections in white, pink, rosy carmine. Blooms throughout summer if spent flowers are removed to halt seed production. Colorful, fast-growing summer hedge or background planting. In the Tropical South, can also be sown in fall for winter–spring bloom. 'Loveliness' grows 3–4 ft. high, bears deep rose blooms. More compact (2–3-ft.) types include 'Mont Blanc', white; 'Mont Rose', rose pink; and 'Silver Cup', bright pink.

LAVENDER. See LAVANDULA

LAVENDER COTTON. See SANTOLINA chamaecyparissus

LEAD PLANT. See AMORPHA canescens

LEATHER LEAF SEDGE. See CAREX buchananii

LEEK

Liliaceae

BIENNIAL GROWN AS ANNUAL

ALL ZONES

FULL SUN

NEVER LET PLANTS DRY OUT

Leek

An onion relative that doesn't form distinct bulb. Plants grow 2–3 ft. tall; edible, mild-flavored bottoms resemble long, fat green onions. Leeks need very rich soil. Plant them to grow and mature in cool weather. In most areas, fall planting is best. Sow seed or set out transplants. Leeks are quite cold-hardy; can overwinter in ground. Cold temperatures improve flavor. When plants have considerable top growth, mound up soil around fat, round stems to blanch them white. Harvest when diameter of necks is 1–2½ in. Offsets may be detached and replanted. If leeks bloom, small bulbils may appear in flower clusters; plant these for later harvest. Free of many pests and diseases that attack onions.

Leguminosae. See Fabaceae

LEMON. See CITRUS

LEMON BALM. See MELISSA officinalis

LEMON BOTTLEBRUSH. See CALLISTEMON citrinus

LEMON DAYLILY. See HEMEROCALLIS lilio-asphodelus

LEMON GERANIUM. See PELARGONIUM crispum

LEMON THYME. See THYMUS citriodorus

LEMON VERBENA. See ALOYSIA triphylla

LENTEN ROSE. See HELLEBORUS orientalis

LEOPARD PLANT. See LIGULARIA tussilaginea 'Aureo-maculata'

LESPEDEZA thunbergii

SHRUB BUSH CLOVER

Fabaceae (Leguminosae)

DECIDUOUS PERENNIAL OR SHRUB

ZONES US, MS, LS

FULL SUN

MODERATE TO LITTLE WATER

Lespedeza thunbergii

Woody-based stems form a spreading, fountain-shaped plant 6 ft. tall and 10 ft. wide. Arching branches carry blue-green leaves with three leaflets 1½–2 in. long. Blooms in late summer; drooping, 6-in. clusters of rose pink, sweet pea–shaped flowers are carried in groups to form pendulous inflorescences 2–2½ ft. long. Cut plant to the ground in late fall or early spring; it will regrow rapidly and bear flowers on the new growth. Endures hot, dry sites and soil of low fertility. Needs good drainage. 'Alba' has white flowers; 'Gibraltar' is a more compact form (to 4½ ft.). Use among other shrubs or in large perennial borders.

LETTUCE

Asteraceae (Compositae)

ANNUAL

✿ ALL ZONES

☼ ◐ PARTIAL SHADE IN COASTAL AND TROPICAL SOUTH

● REGULAR WATER

A short browse through a seed catalog, seed display rack, or selection of garden center seedlings will reveal enough variety to keep your salad bowl crisp and colorful throughout the growing season. There are four principal types of lettuce: crisphead, butterhead or Boston, loose-leaf, and romaine.

Widely sold in markets, crisphead is the most exasperating for home gardeners to produce. Heads form best when monthly temperatures average around 55–60°F. Best types are strains of 'Great Lakes'.

Butterhead or Boston types have loose heads with smooth green outer leaves and yellow inner leaves. Good selections include 'Bibb' ('Limestone') and 'Buttercrunch'. 'Mignonette' ('Manoa') stands heat without bolting (going to seed).

Loose-leaf lettuce makes rosettes rather than heads. It withstands heat better than other types and is a summer mainstay in the Upper South. Choice selections: 'Black-seeded Simpson'; 'Oak Leaf'; 'Slobolt'; red-tinged 'Prizehead' and 'Ruby'; and 'Salad Bowl', with deeply cut leaves.

Romaine lettuce has erect, cylindrical heads of smooth leaves, the outer ones green, the inner ones whitish. Tolerates heat moderately well. Try 'Dark Green Cos', 'Parris Island', 'Valmaine', or 'White Paris'.

Lettuces with bronzy to pinkish red leaves add color to a salad. 'Lollo Rosso', 'Red Oak Leaf', 'Red Sails', and 'Ruby' are loose-leaf selections; 'Merveille des Quatre Saisons' and 'Perella Red' are butterheads; 'Rouge d'Hiver' is a romaine.

All types of lettuce need loose, well-drained soil. Sow in open ground at 10-day intervals for prolonged harvest. Barely cover seeds. Loose-leaf lettuce can be grown as close as 4 in. apart; thin all other types to 1 ft. apart. In Upper South, begin sowing seed after frost, as soon as soil is workable. In the Coastal and Tropical South, grow only as a winter and early spring crop. Feed plants lightly and frequently.

Lettuce

PICKING LOOSE-LEAF LETTUCE

With loose-leaf lettuce you get three opportunities to harvest over a long period. Use the thinnings for salads; clip off just the outer leaves as you need them; finally, when bloom stalks start to grow, pull up whole plants.

LEUCANTHEMUM. See CHRYSANTHEMUM

LEUCOJUM

SNOWFLAKE

Amaryllidaceae

BULBS

✿ ZONES VARY BY SPECIES

☼ ◐ FULL SUN OR LIGHT SHADE

● REGULAR WATER DURING GROWTH AND BLOOM

Strap-shaped leaves and nodding, bell-shaped, white flowers with segments tipped green. Easy to grow and permanent. Naturalize under

Leucojum aestivum

deciduous trees, in shrub borders or orchards, or on cool slopes. Plant 4 in. deep in fall. Do not disturb until really crowded; then dig, divide, and replant after foliage dies down.

L. aestivum. SUMMER SNOWFLAKE. Zones US, MS, LS, CS. One of the classic pass-along bulbs of the South, shared by gardeners for centuries. Often seen in cemeteries and on old home sites. Named "summer snowflake" by gardeners in Europe, where it blooms in summer and has been cultivated since 1594. Leaves 1–1½ ft. long. Stems 1½ ft. tall carry three to five 1-in. flowers. 'Gravetye Giant' is a bit taller and larger flowered than the species; it has as many as nine flowers per stem. Plants need little winter chill to bloom well; even bloom dependably as far south as central Florida. In the Coastal South, plants bloom November through winter; elsewhere, they bloom in late winter and early spring with early daffodils.

L. vernum. SPRING SNOWFLAKE. Zones US, MS, LS. Much less common than *L. aestivum*, less tolerant of mild winters. Leaves 9 in. long. In earliest spring, each foot-long stem bears a single large white flower (occasionally two per stem).

LEUCOPHYLLUM

TEXAS SAGE, SILVERLEAF

Scrophulariaceae

EVERGREEN SHRUBS

✿ ZONES MS, LS, CS

☼ FULL SUN

● MODERATE TO LITTLE WATER

Native to the Southwest and northern Mexico, these compact, slow-growing shrubs are highly useful and attractive in dry, chalky soils. Most have silvery foliage and a good show of open bell-shaped flowers.

Leucophyllum frutescens

They tolerate wind and heat, but often fail in high-rainfall, high-humidity areas. Flowering occurs at varying times of year, often after summer showers. Use as clipped hedges, in massed plantings, or in containers.

L. candidum. VIOLET SILVERLEAF. To 4–5 ft. tall, with small (½-in.) silvery leaves and deep purple flowers. 'Silver Cloud' blooms heavily. 'Thundercloud' is smaller (3–4 ft.) than the species.

L. frutescens. TEXAS SAGE, CENIZO, TEXAS RANGER. Grows to 6–8 ft., with silvery leaves and purple flowers. 'Compactum' is a dense grower to 3–4 ft. 'Green Cloud' has green leaves and deep violet flowers. 'White Cloud' bears white flowers, has silvery foliage. 'Rain Cloud' is an erect grower. Will grow in sandy soil on the beach.

L. laevigatum. CHIHUAHUAN SAGE. Grows 3–4 ft. tall and somewhat wider, with green leaves and blue-purple flowers.

LEUCOTHOE

Ericaceae

EVERGREEN OR DECIDUOUS SHRUBS

✿ ZONES VARY BY SPECIES

☼ ● PARTIAL OR FULL SHADE

◐ ◐ WATER NEEDS VARY BY SPECIES

☿ LEAVES AND NECTAR ARE POISONOUS IF INGESTED

Related to *Pieris*. All have leathery leaves and clusters of urn-shaped white flowers. They need acid, woodsy, deep soil; do best in woodland gardens. Best used in masses, since they are not especially attractive individually. Bronze-tinted winter foliage is a bonus.

Leucothoe fontanesiana

L. axillaris. COASTAL LEUCOTHOE. Evergreen. Zones US, MS, LS. Native to southeastern U.S. Spreading, arching growth to 2–4 ft. tall, and 3–6 ft. wide. Leathery leaves to 4 in. long are bronzy when new. Flower clusters, 1–3 in. long, droop along stems in spring. Takes regular water.

L. fontanesiana (L. catesbaei). DROOPING LEUCOTHOE. Evergreen. Zones US, MS. Native to southeastern U.S. Slow grower to 2–6 ft. high;

branches arch gracefully. Leaves are leathery, 3–6 in. long; they turn bronzy purple in fall (bronzy green in deep shade). Spreads from underground stems. Blooms in spring, bearing drooping clusters of slightly fragrant, creamy white flowers resembling lily-of-the-valley. 'Rainbow', which is 3–4 ft. high, has leaves marked yellow, green, and pink. 'Lovita' is smaller than the species (2 ft. tall, 4 ft. wide), with smaller, darker green leaves that turn mahogany red in winter. 'Scarletta' is similar in size to 'Lovita'; its leaves are brilliant red on expanding, deep green in summer, and deep red in late fall and winter.

The species and its selections take regular water. Can be controlled in height to make 1½-ft. ground cover in shade; just cut older, taller stems to ground. Blooming branches make decorative cut flowers. Where summers are hot and humid, various leaf spot diseases can cause serious disfiguration or defoliation.

L. racemosa. SWEETBELLS. Deciduous. Zones US, MS, LS, CS. Native to southeastern U.S. Grows 3–8 ft. tall, with 3-in. leaves that turn red before dropping from their red stems. White flowers in one-sided, 3-in. clusters at ends of branches in late spring or early summer. A pink-flowering form is available. Good in dry shade.

LEYLAND CYPRESS. See CUPRESSOCYPARIS leylandii

LIATRIS

BLAZING STAR

Asteraceae (Compositae)

PERENNIALS

ZONES US, MS, LS, CS

FULL SUN

REGULAR TO MODERATE WATER

Liatris spicata

Showy plants native to eastern and central U.S. Basal tufts of narrow, grassy leaves grow from thick, often tuberous rootstocks. In summer or early fall, the tufts lengthen into tall stems densely set with slender leaves and topped by a narrow plume of small, fluffy purple (sometimes white) flower heads. Flowers of most species are unusual in opening from top of spike to bottom. Choice cut flowers.

These plants endure heat, cold, drought, and poor soil. Fertilizing will give you larger flower spikes, but it also results in taller plants that need staking. Liatris is best used in mixed perennial borders, although the rosy purple color calls for careful placing to avoid color clashes.

L. callilepis. Plants grown and sold by Dutch bulb growers under this name are *L. spicata*.

L. ligulistylis. Grows 3–5 ft. tall, with reddish purple flowers that open from dark red buds.

L. microcephala. Only 12–14 in. tall, with grasslike leaves and rose purple flowers.

L. mucronata. To 3 ft. when in bloom. Rose purple spikes. Tolerates dry, limy soils, providing drainage is good.

L. pycnostachya. KANSAS BLAZING STAR. To 4 ft. tall, with purple flowers. Likes moisture, but tolerates drought.

L. scariosa. To 2½ ft. high. The reddish purple flowers differ from those of most other blazing stars in opening nearly all at once. Plant also prefers somewhat drier soil. 'September Glory' is taller, to 4–5 ft.; 'White Spire' is similar, but with white flowers.

L. spicata. SPIKE BLAZING STAR. Grows to 5 ft., with light purple flower heads tightly clustered in dense spikes. 'Alba' (3–4 ft.) is white flowered; 'Floristan White' (2–3 ft.) has a profusion of densely packed white blossom spikes that are good for cutting; 'Kobold' (2–2½ ft.) has deeper purple flowers and does not need staking; and 'Silvertips' (2½–3 ft.) has lavender flowers with a silvery finish.

L. squarrosa. To 3 ft. Branched spikes of red-purple flowers.

LICORICE PLANT. See HELICHRYSUM petiolare

LIGULARIA

GOLDEN RAY

Asteraceae (Compositae)

PERENNIALS

ZONES VARY BY SPECIES

PARTIAL OR FULL SHADE

AMPLE WATER

Ligularia stenocephala 'The Rocket'

Stately perennials with big leaves (1 ft. wide or wider in most species) and daisy flowers in yellow to orange. All need rich soil, ample moisture, and some shade; they do not tolerate drought or hot, afternoon sun. Good around pools, along stream beds, in bog gardens.

L. dentata. BIGLEAF GOLDEN RAY. Zones US, MS. Grown primarily for attractive roundish leaves, heart shaped at base. Sends up 3–5-ft. stems topped by big, branching heads of orange daisies in mid- to late summer. 'Desdemona' and 'Othello' have deep purple leafstalks, veins, and leaf undersurfaces; upper surfaces of leaves are green.

L. stenocephala. Zones US, MS, LS. Better known for flower spikes than foliage. Usually represented by selection 'The Rocket', with clumps of deeply cut leaves topped by tall (to 5-ft.), narrow spires of yellow daisies in early summer.

L. tussilaginea (L. kaempferi, Farfugium japonicum). Zones MS, LS, CS; house plant or indoor/outdoor in all zones. Choice foliage plant for shady bed or entryways. Good container plant. Top hardy to 20°F; plant dies back to roots at 0°F, puts on new growth again in spring. Leaves, typically 6–10 in. across, rise directly from rootstock on 1–2-ft. stems; flower stalks 1–2 ft. tall bear a few 1½–2-in.-wide flower heads with yellow rays. Speckled 'Aureo-maculata', leopard plant, has thick, rather leathery leaves blotched with cream or yellow; leaves are nearly kidney shaped, but with shallowly angled and toothed edges. 'Argentea' has deep green leaves irregularly mottled (particularly on edges) with gray green and ivory. 'Crispata' ('Cristata') has curled and crested leaf edges.

L. wilsoniana. GIANT GROUNDSEL. Zones US, MS. Clump of broadly triangular leaves is topped in mid- to late summer by 5–6-ft. stems carrying dense, columnar spikes of golden yellow flowers.

LIGUSTRUM

PRIVET

Oleaceae

DECIDUOUS, SEMIEVERGREEN, OR EVERGREEN SHRUBS OR SMALL TREES

ZONES VARY BY SPECIES

FULL SUN OR PARTIAL SHADE

REGULAR WATER

LEAVES, FRUITS CAUSE GASTRIC DISTRESS IF INGESTED

Ligustrum lucidum

Most widely used as hedges, though one type is a tree of small to medium size; can also be clipped into formal shapes and featured in large pots. All have abundant, showy clusters of white to creamy white flowers in late spring or early summer. Fragrance is described as pleasant to unpleasant (many describe it as cloyingly sweet). Flowers draw bees. Clipped hedges bear fewer flowers, since shearing removes most of the flower-bearing branches. Blossoms followed by small, berrylike blue-black fruits; birds eat them, thereby distributing seeds. Most privets are easily grown in any soil.

Garden centers sometimes misidentify certain privets. *L. japonicum* usually turns out to be the small tree *L. lucidum*. The true *L. japonicum* is available in two or more forms. The tall, shrubby kind is the true species; the lower-growing, more densely foliaged form is often sold as *L. texanum* and probably should be called *L. japonicum* 'Texanum'. The smaller-leafed hardy privets used for hedging are also often mislabeled: *L. amurense,*

L. ovalifolium, and *L. vulgare* look much alike; any is likely to be sold as "common privet"—a name that belongs to *L. vulgare.*

L. amurense. AMUR PRIVET. Deciduous shrub. Zone US. Much used for hedge and screen planting. Much like *L. ovalifolium* in appearance, but foliage is less glossy.

L. japonicum. JAPANESE PRIVET. Evergreen shrub. Zones MS, LS, CS, TS. Dense, compact growth habit to 10–12 ft., but can be kept lower by trimming. Roundish oval leaves 2–4 in. long, dark to medium green and glossy above, distinctly paler to almost whitish beneath; have thick, slightly spongy feel. Excellent plant for hedges or screens, or for shaping into small trees. In caliche soil, or where Texas root rot prevails, grow it in containers. Often confused with 'Texanum'.

'Howard' ('Howardii'). Two-toned shrub; leaves are yellow when new, aging to green. Both colors are usually present at once.

'Recurvifolium'. Leaves are somewhat smaller than in the species, wavy edged, and twisted at the tip. Somewhat open grower.

'Rotundifolium' ('Coriaceum'). ROUNDLEAF JAPANESE PRIVET. Grows 4–5 ft. high; has nearly round leaves to 2½ in. long. Partial shade.

'Silver Star'. Grows 6–8 ft. high. Leaves are deep green, with gray-green mottling and startling creamy white edges. Provides a good contrast to deep green foliage.

'Texanum'. Similar to the species but grows to 6–9 ft., with somewhat denser, lusher foliage. Useful as windbreak. Often sold as *L. texanum.*

'Variegatum'. Leaves have creamy white margins and blotches.

L. lucidum. GLOSSY PRIVET. Evergreen tree. Zones LS, CS, TS. Makes a round-headed tree that eventually reaches 35–40 ft. Can be kept lower as a big shrub or may form multitrunked tree. Glossy, 4–6-in.-long leaves are tapered and pointed, dark to medium green on both sides. They feel leathery but lack the slightly spongy feel of *L. japonicum's* leaves. Flowers in especially large, feathery clusters followed by profusion of fruit. Fine lawn tree. Can grow in narrow areas; good street tree if not planted near pavement or where fruit will drop on cars (see disadvantages noted below). Performs well in large containers. Or plant 10 ft. apart for tall privacy screen. Useful as windbreak.

Before planting this tree, carefully weigh the advantages against the disadvantages. Eventual fruit crop is immense; never plant where fruits will fall on cars, walks, or other paved areas (they stain). Fallen seeds (and those dropped by birds) profusely sprout in ground cover and will need pulling. Many people dislike the flowers' odor, and fruiting clusters are bare and unattractive after fruit drop.

L. ovalifolium. CALIFORNIA PRIVET. Semievergreen shrub. All zones. Native to Japan. Grows rapidly to 15 ft. but can be kept to any height. Hedges require maintenance—may need shearing every 3 weeks in hot, wet weather. Dark green, oval, 2½-in.-long leaves. Set plants 9–12 in. apart for hedge. Clip early and frequently for low, dense branching. Greedy roots. Well-fed, well-watered plants hold their leaves longest. Seedlings come up everywhere. Established plants hard to eradicate.

'Aureum'. YELLOW-EDGE CALIFORNIA PRIVET, GOLDEN PRIVET. Leaves have broad yellow edges. Sold as 'Variegatum'.

L. sinense 'Variegata'. VARIEGATED CHINESE PRIVET. Semievergreen shrub. Zones MS, LS, CS, TS. Grows quickly to 6 ft. tall and just as wide. Popular for its handsome matte green leaves with creamy white margins. Useful for brightening dull areas of the garden. One of the better-looking variegated plants.

L. vicaryi. VICARY GOLDEN PRIVET. Deciduous shrub. Zones US, MS, LS. This one has yellow leaves; color is strongest on plants in full sun. To 4–6 ft. high, possibly to 12 ft. Best planted alone; color does not develop well under hedge shearing.

L. vulgare. COMMON PRIVET. Deciduous shrub. Zones US, MS, LS. To 15 ft., unsheared. Dark green leaves less glossy and roots less greedy than those of *L. ovalifolium.* Clusters of black fruit conspicuous on unpruned or lightly pruned plants. 'Lodense' ('Nanum') is a dense dwarf form that reaches only 4 ft. with equal spread.

LILAC. See SYRINGA

Liliaceae. The lily family contains hundreds of species of ornamental plants, as well as such vegetables as asparagus and the whole onion tribe. Most grow from bulbs, corms, or rhizomes. Flowers are often showy, usually with six equal-size segments.

LILIUM

LILY

Liliaceae

BULBS

✿ ALL ZONES, EXCEPT AS NOTED, BUT MOST NEED WINTER CHILL FOR RECURRENCE

☼ ROOTS IN SHADE; TOPS IN SUN OR FILTERED SHADE

● NEVER LET ROOT ZONE DRY OUT

Lilium candidum

Most stately and varied of bulbous plants. For many years, only the species—the same plants growing wild in parts of Asia, Europe, and North America—were available, and many of these were difficult and unpredictable.

Around 1925, lily growers began a significant breeding program. They bred new hybrids from species with desirable qualities and also developed strains and selections that were healthier, hardier, and easier to grow than the original species. They produced new forms and new colors; what is more important, they developed the methods for growing healthy lilies in large quantities. Today, the new forms and new colors are the best garden lilies, but it is still possible to get some desirable species.

Lilies have three basic cultural requirements: deep, loose, well-drained soil; ample moisture year-round (plants never completely stop growing); and coolness at roots with some sun at tops where flowers form.

Plant bulbs as soon as possible after you get them. If you must wait, keep them in a cool place until you plant. If bulbs are dry, place them in moist sand or peat moss until scales get plump and new roots begin to sprout.

As noted above, lilies need deep, well-drained soil containing ample organic matter. If you want to plant in heavy clay or very sandy soil, add material such as peat moss, leaf mold, or composted ground bark. Spread a 3–4-in. layer of such material over the soil surface; broadcast complete fertilizer (follow directions for preplanting application) on top of it, then thoroughly till both into the soil to a depth of at least 1 ft.

Before planting bulbs, remove any injured portions; then dust cuts with sulfur or an antifungal seed and bulb disinfectant. For each bulb, dig a generous planting hole (6–12 in. deeper than height of the bulb). Place enough soil at bottom of hole to bring it up to proper level for bulb (see next paragraph). Set bulb with its roots spread; fill hole with soil, firming it around bulb to eliminate air pockets.

Planting depths vary according to size and rooting habit of bulb. General rule is to cover smaller bulbs with 2–3 in. of soil, medium bulbs with 3–4 in., and larger bulbs with 4–6 in. (but never cover Madonna lilies with more than 1 in. of soil). Planting depth can be quite flexible. It's better to err by planting shallowly than too deeply; lily bulbs have contractile roots that draw them down to proper depth. Ideal spacing for lily bulbs is 1 ft. apart, but you can plant as close as 6 in. for densely massed effect.

Lilies need constant moisture to about 6 in. deep. Reduce watering somewhat after tops turn yellow in fall, but never allow roots to dry out completely. Soaking is preferable to overhead watering, which may help to spread disease spores. Pull weeds by hand; hoeing may injure roots.

Viral or mosaic infection is a problem. No cure exists. To avoid it, buy healthy bulbs from reliable sources. Dig and destroy any lilies that show mottling in leaves or seriously stunted growth. Control aphids, which spread the infection. Control botrytis blight, a fungal disease, with Daconil. Gophers relish lily bulbs.

Wait until stems and leaves turn yellow before you cut plants back. If clumps become too crowded, dig up, divide, and transplant them in spring or fall. If you're careful, you can lift lily clumps at any time, even in bloom.

Lilies are fine container plants. Place one bulb in a deep, 5–7-in. pot or five in a 14–16-in. pot. First, fill pot one-third full of potting mix. Then place bulb with roots spread and pointing downward; cover with about an inch of soil. Water thoroughly and place in greenhouse just warm enough to keep out frost. During root-forming period, keep soil moderately moist. When top growth appears, add more soil mixture and gradually fill pot as stems elongate. Leave 1-in. space between soil surface and pot rim for watering. Move pots onto partially shaded terrace or patio during blooming period. Later, you can repot bulbs in late fall or early spring.

Although the official classification of lilies lists eight divisions of hybrids and a ninth division of species, the following listings describe the lilies commonly available to gardeners. Advances in breeding are producing lilies with forms, colors, and parentage hitherto considered unlikely, if not impossible. Consult specialists' catalogs to learn about these new wonders, which are reaching the market faster than books can deal with them.

ASIATIC HYBRIDS

These are the easiest and most reliable for the average garden. Some have upward-facing flowers, while others have horizontally held or drooping flowers. Stems are strong, erect, and short (1½ ft.) to moderate (4½ ft.) in height. Colors range from white through yellow and orange to pink and red. Many have dark spots or contrasting "halos." They are the earliest to bloom (early summer). Examples are 'Enchantment', orange red spotted with black; 'Impala', bright yellow; 'Pink Floyd', creamy pink banded with rose pink; and 'Sancerre', pure white and unspotted.

AURELIAN HYBRIDS

Derived from Asiatic species, excluding *L. auratum* and *L. speciosum*. They have trumpet- or bowl-shaped flowers in midsummer. Flowers range from white and cream through yellow and pink, many with green, brown, or purple shading on their outer surfaces. Plants are 3–6 ft. tall, and each stem carries 12 to 20 flowers. Examples are 'Anaconda', coppery apricot; 'Black Dragon', white with maroon petal backs; 'Golden Splendour', yellow blooms from purple buds; and 'Thunderbolt', orange-apricot blossoms.

ORIENTAL HYBRIDS

The most exotic of the hybrids. Bloom midsummer–early fall, with big (to 9-in.) fragrant flowers of white or pink, often spotted with gold and shaded or banded with red. Most are tall, with nodding flowers, but a few are dwarf and have upward-facing blooms. Examples are 'Casablanca', pure white; 'Pink Ribbons', light rose banded and spotted with deep rose; and 'Stargazer', rose red with white margins.

SPECIES AND VARIANTS

L. amabile. To 3–4 ft. tall, with 1 to 8 blooms per stem; flowers are fragrant, orange red, with dark purplish dots. Midsummer bloom.

🏛 **L. candidum.** MADONNA LILY. Zones US, MS, LS, CS. Pure white, fragrant blooms on 3–4-ft. stems in late spring, early summer. Unlike most lilies, dies down soon after bloom, makes new growth in fall. Plant while dormant in August. Does not have stem roots; set top of bulb only 1–2 in. deep in sunny location. Bulb quickly makes foliage rosette that lives over winter, lengthens to blooming stem in spring. Subject to diseases that shorten its life. Cascade strain, grown from seed, is healthier than imported bulbs. The lily of medieval romance, a sentimental choice.

L. centifolium (L. leucanthemum centifolium). Grows 7–8 ft. high. Each stem bears 15 to 20 white flowers banded brownish purple on outside of petals. Late summer bloom.

L. formosanum. FORMOSA LILY. Zones MS, LS, CS, TS. Slender, 5-ft., purple-brown stems bear one to several fragrant, outward-facing, funnel-shaped blossoms in white flushed purple. Late summer bloom. Not as showy as modern hybrids, but one of the best for reliable recurrence in the Coastal and Tropical South.

L. henryi. Slender stems to 8–9 ft., 10 to 20 bright orange flowers with sharply recurved segments. Midsummer bloom. Best in light shade.

🏛 **L. lancifolium (L. tigrinum).** TIGER LILY. To 4 ft. or taller with pendulous orange flowers spotted black. Summer bloom. An old favorite; very easy to grow. Newer tiger lilies are available in white, cream, yellow, pink, and red, all with black spots.

L. lankongense. Zones US, MS, LS, CS. Grows 4–6 ft. tall; stems bear up to 36 nodding, powerfully fragrant, pale to deep pink blossoms with purple spots. Mid- to late summer bloom.

L. longiflorum. EASTER LILY. All zones. Very fragrant, long, white, trumpet-shaped flowers on short stems. Usually purchased in bloom at Easter as forced plant. Set out in garden after flowers fade. Stems will ripen and die down. Plant may rebloom in fall; in 1 or 2 years, may flower in midsummer, its normal bloom season. Selections include 'Ace', 1½ ft. tall; 'Croft', 1 ft. tall; 'Estate', to 3 ft. tall; 'Tetraploid', 1–1½ ft. tall. Recent hybridization has yielded pink, yellow, and red offspring. Don't plant forced lilies near other lilies; they may transmit a virus.

🏛 **L. martagon.** TURK'S CAP LILY. Purplish pink, recurved, pendent flowers in early summer on 3–5-ft. stems. This lily is slow to establish but long lived and eventually forms big clumps. *L. m. album,* pure white, is one of most appealing lilies; a parent of the Paisley hybrids, a group with flowers in yellow, orange, mahogany shades, most with maroon spots.

L. regale. REGAL LILY. Superseded in quality by modern hybrid trumpet lilies but still popular and easy to grow. To 6 ft., with white, fragrant flowers in early to midsummer.

L. speciosum. SHOWY LILY. Grows 2½–5 ft. tall. Large, wide, fragrant flowers with broad, deeply recurved segments, late summer; white, heavily suffused rose pink, sprinkled with raised crimson dots. 'Album' is pure white, 'Rubrum' red; there are also other named forms. Best in light shade (or at least afternoon shade); needs rich soil with plenty of leaf mold.

L. tigrinum. See L. lancifolium

LILY OF CHINA. See ROHDEA japonica

LILY-OF-THE-NILE. See AGAPANTHUS

LILY-OF-THE-VALLEY. See CONVALLARIA majalis

LILY TURF. See LIRIOPE and OPHIOPOGON

LIME. See CITRUS

LIMONIUM (Statice)

SEA LAVENDER

Plumbaginaceae

PERENNIALS AND ANNUAL

✿ ZONES VARY BY SPECIES

☼ FULL SUN

💧 MODERATE WATER

Limonium sinuatum

Large, leathery basal leaves contrast with airy clusters of small, delicate flowers on nearly leafless, many-branched stems. Tiny flowers consist of two parts: an outer, papery envelope (the calyx) and an inner part (the corolla), which often has a different color. All tolerate heat and many soils but need good drainage. They often self-sow.

L. gmelinii. Perennial. Zones US, MS. Rosette of spoon-shaped 5-in. leaves; 2-ft., clusters of tiny blue flowers in mid- to late summer.

L. latifolium. Perennial. Zones US, MS, LS, CS. To 2½ ft. Smooth-edged leaves, 10 in. long; calyx is white, corolla bluish. Summer bloom. Vigorous; may show 3-ft.-wide haze of white or pink flowers.

L. sinuatum. Annual. All zones. To 2 ft. tall, with distinctly lobed, 6-in. basal leaves and winged stems. Calyx blue, lavender, or rose; corolla white. Widely grown as a fresh or dried cut flower.

STATICE LASTS LONG FRESH OR DRIED

Cut for fresh bouquets after most flowers in each cluster have opened. For dried arrangements, cut after opening but before sun has faded them. With a rubber band, join several bunches together by stem bases; hang upside down in a dry spot out of bright sun until flowers dry.

SOUTHERN HERITAGE PLANTS
IDENTIFIED BY SYMBOL 🏛

Linaceae. The flax family of annuals, perennials, and shrubs displays cup- or disk-shaped flowers with four or five petals. Flowers are often showy. Flax (*Linum*) is an example.

LINDEN. See TILIA

LINDERA

SPICEBUSH

Lauraceae

DECIDUOUS SHRUBS

✿ ZONES US, MS, LS

☼ ◐ ● SUN OR SHADE

● REGULAR WATER

Lindera benzoin

Large deciduous shrubs grown principally for the beauty of their bright yellow fall foliage. Fall color develops even in shade. Flowers are attractive but not showy: small, greenish yellow, clustered at the joints of leafless shoots in earliest spring. Female plants have attractive fruits, but these are seldom seen unless plants of both sexes are present. Common name refers to the foliage, which is strongly aromatic when bruised or crushed. Although too large for most gardens, spicebushes are effective at the edge of woodland. Need good drainage; tolerate some drought.

L. benzoin. SPICEBUSH. Native to woodlands of eastern U.S. Grows 6–12 ft. tall and as wide. Light green leaves are 3–5 in. long, half as wide. Fruit, noticeable after leaf fall, is bright red, 1/3–1/2 in. long. Species name describes the leaves' odor—a spicy scent reminiscent of benzoin, an aromatic gum once used in medicine and perfumery.

L. obtusiloba. JAPANESE SPICEBUSH. Native to Japan, Korea, and China. Larger than *L. benzoin* (10–20 ft. tall), somewhat narrower form, with broader leaves (to 5 in. long, 4 in. wide). The shiny dark green leaves sometimes have a mitten shape, with one lobe or two as shallow divisions from the main leaf. Small (1/4-in.) fruits turn from red to black. Fall color is an exceptionally brilliant yellow that holds for 2 weeks or more and develops even in considerable shade.

LINUM

FLAX

Linaceae

PERENNIALS AND ANNUALS

✿ ZONES VARY BY SPECIES

☼ FULL SUN

● MODERATE WATER

Linum perenne

These plants have erect, branching stems, narrow leaves, and abundant, shallow-cupped, five-petaled flowers that bloom from late spring into summer or fall. Each bloom lasts only a day, but others keep coming. The flax of commerce—*L. usitatissimum*—is grown for its fiber and seeds, which yield linseed oil.

Use in borders; some naturalize freely in uncultivated areas. Light, well-drained soil. Most perennial kinds live only 3 or 4 years and should be replaced regularly. Easy from seed; perennials also can be grown from cuttings. Difficult to divide.

L. flavum. GOLDEN FLAX. Perennial. Zones US, MS. Erect, compact, 12–15 in. tall, somewhat woody at base; grooved branches, green leaves. Flowers golden yellow, about 1 in. wide, in branched clusters. 'Compactum' is a smaller form.

L. grandiflorum 'Rubrum'. SCARLET FLAX. Annual. All zones. Bright scarlet flowers, 1–1½ in. wide, on slender, leafy, 1–1½-ft. stems. Narrow gray-green leaves. Also comes in a rose-colored form. Sow seed thickly in

place in fall (in mild areas) or early spring. Quick color for borders or bulb cover. Good with gray foliage or white-flowered plants. Reseeds but doesn't become a pest. Often included in wildflower seed mixtures.

L. narbonense. Perennial. Zones US, MS. Wiry stems to 2 ft. high. Leaves blue green, narrow. Flowers large (1¾ in. across), azure blue with white eye, in open clusters. Best selection, 'Six Hills', has rich sky blue flowers.

L. perenne. PERENNIAL BLUE FLAX. Zones US, MS, LS. Most vigorous blue-flowered flax. Stems to 2 ft., usually leafless below. Profuse bloomer, with branching clusters of light blue flowers that close in shade or late in the day. Self-sows freely.

LIPPIA citriodora. See ALOYSIA triphylla

LIQUIDAMBAR

SWEET GUM

Hamamelidaceae

DECIDUOUS TREES

✿ ZONES VARY BY SPECIES

☼ FULL SUN

◐ ● REGULAR TO MODERATE WATER

Liquidambar styraciflua

Valuable for form, foliage, fall color, and easy culture. Moderate growth rate; young and middle-aged trees are generally upright, somewhat cone shaped, spreading in age. Lobed, maplelike leaves. Flowers inconspicuous; fruits are spiny balls that ornament trees in winter, need raking in spring.

Give neutral or slightly acid soil; chlorosis in strongly alkaline soils is difficult to correct. Prune only to shape. Trees branch from ground up and look most natural that way, but they can be pruned high to expose a definite trunk.

Form surface roots that can be a nuisance in lawns or between sidewalk and curb. Good street trees with ample room, however. Effective in tall screens or groves, planted 6–10 ft. apart. Brilliant fall foliage in Upper and Middle South; fall color less effective in Lower and Coastal South.

L. formosana. CHINESE SWEET GUM. All zones. Grows to 40–60 ft. tall, 25 ft. wide. Free-form outline; sometimes pyramidal when young. Leaves with three to five lobes are 3–4½ in. across, violet red when expanding, then deep green. Yellow or red fall color.

L. orientalis. ORIENTAL SWEET GUM. Zones LS, CS, TS. Native to Turkey. To 20–30 ft., spreading or round headed. Leaves 2–3 in. wide, with five deep lobes; each again lobed to produce a lacy effect. Leafs out early after short dormant period. Fall color varies from deep gold and bright red to dull brown purple.

L. styraciflua. SWEET GUM. All zones. Native to eastern U.S. Grows to 60–75 ft. in gardens; much taller in the wild. Narrow and erect in youth, with lower limbs eventually spreading to 20–25 ft. Good all-year tree. Branching pattern, furrowed bark, corky wings on twigs, and hanging fruit provide winter interest. Leaves five to seven lobed, 3–7 in. wide; deep green in spring and summer, turning purple, yellow, or red in fall. Even seedling trees give good fall color, though color may vary somewhat from year to year. To get desired and uniform color, choose trees while they are in fall leaf or buy budded trees of a named selection, such as the following:

'Burgundy'. Leaves turn deep purple red, hang late into winter or even early spring if storms are not heavy.

'Festival'. Narrow, columnar. Light green foliage turns to yellow, peach, pink, orange, and red.

'Palo Alto'. Turns orange red to bright red in fall.

'Rotundiloba'. Lobes of leaves are rounded rather than sharp. Fall foliage is purple. Tree does not form fruit.

'Variegata'. Within a few weeks of unfurling, leaves develop streaks and blotches of yellow. They retain variegation throughout summer and early fall.

L

LIRIODENDRON tulipifera

TULIP POPLAR

Magnoliaceae

DECIDUOUS TREE

✺ ZONES US, MS, LS, CS

☼ FULL SUN

● REGULAR WATER

Native to eastern U.S. Fast rate of growth to 60–90 ft., with a spread to about 35–50 ft.; considerably larger in the wild. Straight, columnar trunk, with spreading, rising branches that form tall pyramidal crown. Its 5–6 in. leaves are variously described as lyre shaped, saddle shaped, or truncated; they're like blunt-tipped maple leaves missing the end lobe. They turn from bright yellow green to bright yellow in fall.

Liriodendron tulipifera

Tulip-shaped flowers in late spring are 2 in. wide, greenish yellow, orange at base. Handsome at close range but not showy on the tree, since they are carried high up and well concealed by leaves. Trees don't usually bloom until they are 10 to 12 years old.

Garden centers may carry two slower-growing selections that are smaller than the species. 'Arnold' ('Fastigiata') has a rigidly columnar habit useful for narrow planting areas; it will bloom 2 to 3 years after planting. 'Majestic Beauty' has yellow-edged leaves.

Tulip poplars thrive in deep, rich, well-drained neutral or slightly acid soil. Fairly weak wooded and subject to limb breakage from storms or ice; best used in wind-sheltered locations. Give them room; they make good large shade or lawn trees. Wide-spreading network of shallow, fleshy roots makes them difficult to garden under. Some sensitivity to drought in Lower and Coastal South; can cause premature leaf drop in late summer. Don't park cars under this tree: Aphids feeding on leaves drop sticky honeydew.

LIRIOPE and OPHIOPOGON

LILY TURF

Liliaceae

EVERGREEN GRASSLIKE PERENNIALS

✺ ZONES VARY BY SPECIES

◑ ● SOME SHADE, EXCEPT AS NOTED

◒ ◐ REGULAR TO MODERATE WATER

▶ SEE CHART

Liriope muscari

These two plants are similar in appearance: Both form clumps or tufts of grasslike leaves and bear white or lavender summer flowers in spikelike or branched clusters (showy in some kinds). Last well in flower arrangements. Primary use as ground cover. Also attractive as borders along paths, between stepping-stones or flower bed and lawn, among rock groupings, or in rock gardens. Grow well along streams and around garden ponds. They compete well with roots of other plants; try them in narrow planting beds, at bases of trees or shrubs in ground or in large containers. Mondo grass (*Ophiopogon japonicus*) makes an excellent shade-tolerant lawn that never needs mowing.

Provide filtered sun to full shade. Plant in well-drained soil. Foliage becomes ragged by late winter; cut back shaggy old foliage in early spring before new leaves appear. Plants don't need heavy feeding. To increase, divide in early spring before new growth starts.

Plants look best from spring until cold weather of winter. Extended frosts may cause plants to turn yellow; they take quite awhile to recover. Can show tip burn on leaves if soil contains excess salts or if plants are kept too wet where drainage is poor.

LISIANTHUS. See EUSTOMA grandiflorum

LITCHI chinensis

LITCHI TREE, LITCHI NUT

Sapindaceae

EVERGREEN TREE

✺ ZONES CS, TS

☼ FULL SUN

● REGULAR WATER

Litchi chinensis

Slow-growing, round-topped, spreading tree, 20–40 ft. tall. Leaves have three to nine leathery, 3–6-in.-long leaflets that are coppery red when young, dark green later. Inconspicuous flowers. When fruit is ripe, the brittle, warty rind surrounding it turns red. Fruit is sweet in flavor, juicy when fresh, raisinlike when dried.

Needs frost-free site, moist air, fertile acidic soil. Look for named selections if you're interested in fruit production. 'Brewster', 'Groff', 'Kwai Mi', 'Mauritius', and 'Sweet Cliff' are grown.

LITTLE BLUESTEM. See ANDROPOGON scoparius

LIVE OAK. See QUERCUS virginiana

LIVERLEAF, LIVERWORT. See HEPATICA

LIVISTONA

Arecaceae (Palmae)

PALMS

✺ ZONES CS, TS

☼ FULL SUN

● REGULAR WATER

Livistona australis

Native from China to Australia. These fan palms somewhat resemble *Washingtonia* but generally have shorter, darker, shinier leaves. All make good potted plants.

L. australis. AUSTRALIAN FAN PALM. In ground, grows slowly to 40–50 ft. Has clean, slender trunk with interesting-looking leaf scars. Dark green leaves 3–5 ft. wide.

L. chinensis. CHINESE FAN PALM, CHINESE FOUNTAIN PALM. Slow growing; 40-year-old plants are only 15 ft. tall. Self-cleaning (no pruning of old leaves needed) with leaf-scarred trunk. Roundish, bright green, 3–6-ft. leaves droop strongly at outer edges.

LOBELIA

Campanulaceae (Lobeliaceae)

PERENNIALS OR ANNUALS

✺ ZONES VARY BY SPECIES

◑ ● PARTIAL TO FULL SHADE

◐ ◖ AMPLE TO REGULAR WATER

◈ MOST CONTAIN POISONOUS ALKALOIDS

Lobelia cardinalis

Distinct differences separate the annual lobelia from the most familiar perennial kinds; the former is blue and spreading, the others red or blue and upright. On all types, the tubular, lipped flowers resemble those of honeysuckle or salvia.

L. cardinalis. CARDINAL FLOWER. Perennial. Zones US, MS, LS, CS. Native to eastern U.S. and to a few sites in mountains of the Southwest. Erect, single-stemmed, 2–4-ft.-high plant with saw-edged leaves set directly on the stems. Spikes of flame red, inch-long flowers in summer. A bog plant in nature, it needs rich soil and constant moisture through the growing season. Excellent hummingbird plant.

Crossbreeding between this species and *L. splendens (L. fulgens)*, which is closely related, has resulted in a number of hybrids. 'Queen Victoria'

▶ page 280

LIRIOPE and OPHIOPOGON

NAME	ZONES	GROWTH FORM	LEAVES	FLOWERS	COMMENTS
Liriope muscari BIG BLUE LIRIOPE, BIG BLUE LILY TURF	All zones	Forms large clumps but does not spread by underground stems. Loose growth habit, 12–15 in. high	Dark green. To 2 ft. long, ½ in. wide	Dark violet blooms in dense, 6–8-in.-long clusters (resemble grape hyacinths). Followed by round, shiny black fruits	Flowers on 5–12-in.-long stems held above leaves in young plants, partly hidden in older plants. 'Lilac Beauty' has paler violet flowers
L. m. 'Big Blue'	All zones	Stiffly arching habit, 12–15 in. high	Bright green, narrow, grasslike to 2 ft. long	Dark lavender flowers in 4–5-in.-long spikes	Good for borders or as a ground cover. Tolerates dry shade well
L. m. 'Border Gem'	All zones	Dwarf clump to 8 in.	Leaves to 8 in. long	Lilac flowers	Use as edging. 'Little Beauty' is similar
L. m. 'Evergreen Giant'	CS, TS	Tallest type, 2 ft. tall	Dark green, strappy, ⅓ in. wide, to 3 ft. long	Spikes of white flowers	Best used as edging or border. Evergreen. Not cold-hardy
L. m. 'John Burch'	All zones	Large clump, grows to 12–15 in. high	Broad, yellow green with wide green edging	Heavy flower spikes like cockscombs stand well above leaves	Performs best in full sun
L. m. 'Majestic'	All zones	Resembles *L. muscari*, but more open clumps 15–18 in. high	Similar to *L. muscari*	Dark violet flowers in clusters on stems 8–10 in. long; resemble cockscombs	Heavy flowering. Clusters held above leaves. 'Royal Purple' and 'Webster's Wideleaf' are similar
L. m. 'Monroe's White' ('Munroe's White')	All zones	Large clump, grows to 12–15 in. high	Broad, deep green	Flower spikes white, standing well above foliage	Prefers more shade than most types. 'White on White' has white leaf variegation
L. m. 'Samantha'	All zones	Dwarf clump, to 10 in. high	Dark green, narrow	Lavender-pink flowers	Colors best in a warm spot
L. m. 'Silvery Sunproof'	All zones	Open growth, strongly vertical, partly arching, 12–15 in. high	Foliage has gold stripes that turn white as leaves mature	Lilac flowers in spikelike clusters rising well above foliage	One of the best for full sun and for flowers. Leaves are whiter in sun; they become greener or yellower in part shade
L. m. 'Variegata' (may be sold as **Ophiopogon jaburan 'Variegata'**)	MS, LS, CS, TS	Like *L. muscari*, but somewhat looser, softer; 10–15 in. high	New leaves green, 1–1½ ft. long, edged with yellow; become dark green in second season	Violet flowers in spikelike clusters well above foliage. Flower stalks 1 ft. high	Does best in partial shade. Sometimes sold as *L. exiliflora* 'Vittata'
L. spicata CREEPING LIRIOPE, CREEPING LILY TURF	All zones	Dense ground cover that spreads widely by underground stems. Grows 8–9 in. high. Can be invasive	Narrow (¼-in.-wide), deep green, grasslike leaves, soft and not as upright as those of *L. muscari*. 'Silver Dragon' has white-striped leaves	Pale lilac to white flowers in spikelike clusters barely taller than leaves	For best effect, mow yearly in spring prior to new growth. Good ground cover for Upper South where *Ophiopogon japonicus* won't grow
L. s. 'Silver Dragon'	All zones	Similar to species in size but sparser habit	Leaves striped silvery white	Flowers pale purple on short spikes	Fine ground cover for shade, but slower growing than species
Ophiopogon japonicus MONDO GRASS	MS, LS, CS, TS	Forms dense clumps that spread by underground stems, many tuberlike. Slow to establish as ground cover; 6–8 in. tall	Dark green leaves ⅛ in. wide, 8–12 in. long. 'Kyoto Dwarf' and 'Nana' have half-sized leaves in tight clumps. 'Gyoku Ryu', dwarf mondo grass, has fans of erect leaves, 3 in. tall, with pale lavender flowers. Evergreen ground cover forms tight mat	Flowers light lilac in short spikes usually hidden by the leaves. Blue fruit	Can be cut back. Easy to divide; set divisions 6–8 in. apart. Roots die at 10°F. Once established, a fine-looking, low-maintenance lawn in shade
O. planiscapus 'Nigrescens' ('Nigricans') BLACK MONDO GRASS	MS, LS, CS, TS	Makes tuft 8 in. high and about 1 ft. wide	Leaves to 10 in. long. New leaves green but soon turn black	White (sometimes flushed pink) in loose spikelike clusters	Spreads slowly and does not make a solid cover. Interesting in containers. Valuable as novelty

and 'Royal Robe' have deep purple-red foliage, scarlet flowers; 'Heather Pink' has soft pink flowers.

L. erinus. Annual. All zones. Popular and dependable edging plant. Compact or trailing habit with leafy, branching stems. Flowers, ¾ in. across, are light blue to violet (sometimes pink, reddish purple, or white) with white or yellowish throats. Prefers cool temperatures. Grow it as the winter annual in Coastal and Tropical South; elsewhere, for spring and early summer flowers. Takes about 2 months for seed sown in pots to grow to planting-out size. Moist, rich soil. Self-sows where adapted. Trailing kinds make a graceful ground cover in large planters or in smaller pots; the stems, loaded with flowers, spill over the edges.

'Cambridge Blue' has clear, soft blue flowers and light green leaves on compact 4–6-in. plant. 'Crystal Palace', also compact, has rich dark blue flowers, bronze green leaves. 'Rosamond' has carmine red flowers with white eyes. 'White Lady' is pure white. Three trailing selections for hanging baskets or wall plantings are 'Hamburgia', 'Blue Cascade', and 'Sapphire'.

L. gerardii. Perennial. Zones US, MS, LS. Hybrid between *L. cardinalis* and *L. syphilitica;* needs rich soil, constant moisture, and part shade. 'Vedrariensis' grows to 4 ft., with coppery green foliage and bright royal purple flowers. 'Rosea', 2½ ft. high, has rose pink flowers. 'Ruby Slippers', 3 ft. tall, has dark red flowers.

L. syphilitica. BLUE CARDINAL FLOWER. Perennial. Zones US, MS, LS. Native to eastern U.S. Leafy plants send up 3-ft. stalks set with blue flowers. Needs ample moisture, partial shade.

Lobeliaceae. See Campanulaceae

LOBLOLLY BAY. See GORDONIA lasianthus

LOBLOLLY PINE. See PINUS taeda

LOBULARIA maritima

SWEET ALYSSUM

Brassicaceae (Cruciferae)

ANNUAL

🌿 ALL ZONES

☼ ◐ BEST IN FULL SUN, TOLERATES LIGHT SHADE

💧 REGULAR WATER

Lobularia maritima

Low, branching, trailing plant to 1 ft. tall, with narrow or lance-shaped leaves ½–2 in. long. Tiny, four-petaled white flowers crowded in clusters; honeylike fragrance. Blooms from spring until frost in the Upper South. In the Tropical South, may go dormant during hottest period but resume when weather cools. Seeds sometimes included in wildflower mixes or erosion-control mixes for bare or disturbed earth.

Easy, quick, dependable. Blooms from seed in 6 weeks; grows in almost any soil. Useful for carpeting, edging, bulb cover, temporary filler in rock garden or perennial border; between flagstones; in window boxes or containers. Attracts bees. If you shear plants halfway back 4 weeks after they come into bloom, new growth will make another crop of flowers, and plants won't become rangy.

Garden types better known than the species; these selections self-sow too, but seedlings tend to revert to taller, looser growth, less intense color, and smaller flowers. Good compact whites are 'Carpet of Snow' (2–4 in. tall), 'Little Gem' (4–6 in.), and 'Tiny Tim' (3 in.). 'Tetra Snowdrift' (1 ft.) has long stems, large white flowers. 'Pink Heather' (6 in.) and 'Rosie O'Day' (2–4 in.) are lavender pinks. 'Oriental Night' (4 in.) and 'Violet Queen' (5 in.) are rich violet purples.

LOCUST. See ROBINIA

LOLIUM

RYEGRASS

Poaceae (Gramineae)

ANNUAL OR PERENNIAL LAWN GRASSES

🌿 ZONES VARY BY SPECIES

☼ FULL SUN

💧 REGULAR WATER

Lolium perenne

Clumping grasses that are quick sprouting and useful for winter lawns, pastures, soil reclamation. Perennial ryegrass often used for year-round lawns in the Upper South.

L. multiflorum. ANNUAL RYEGRASS, WINTER RYEGRASS. All zones. Taller, coarser than perennial ryegrass. An annual in the South; sets seed, dies at onset of hot weather. Germinates rapidly. Used for temporary lawns at new homesites and for erosion control on banks and roadsides. Primary use is for overseeding warm-season grasses in fall to produce green lawn in winter. To overseed, cut existing lawn short (about 1 in.) in early fall, then sow annual rye at rate of 10 lb. per 1,000 sq. ft.

L. perenne. PERENNIAL RYEGRASS. Zone US. Finer in texture than above, deep green with high gloss. Disadvantages are clumping tendency and tough flower and seed stems that lie down under mower blades. However, improved selections do produce a uniform lawn of fine appearance. Selections include 'Derby', 'Loretta', 'Manhattan', 'Pennfine', 'Yorktown'. Sow 8–10 lb. per 1,000 sq. ft. Mow at 1½–2 in., higher in summer.

LONICERA

HONEYSUCKLE

Caprifoliaceae

EVERGREEN, SEMIEVERGREEN, OR DECIDUOUS SHRUBS OR VINES

🌿 ZONES VARY BY SPECIES

☼ ◐ FULL SUN OR LIGHT SHADE

💧 MODERATE WATER

Lonicera periclymenum

These easy-to-grow plants exist in a great many species, most of them valued for tubular, often fragrant flowers. Vining kinds need support when they are starting out. When honeysuckles become overgrown, cut them to the ground; they regrow rapidly. Prune after flowering. Blossoms attract hummingbirds. Fruit provides food for many kinds of birds. Plants are generally not bothered by serious pests or diseases. Aphids are the chief problem, distorting buds and preventing flowering.

L. brownii. Deciduous vine. Zones US, MS, LS. This hybrid between *L. sempervirens* and *L. hirsuta* is a little-grown vine from the northeastern U.S. 'Dropmore Scarlet', the only selection extensively grown, climbs to 9–10 ft. It has blue-green leaves, those on the upper stem joining at the base; clusters of tubular scarlet flowers, early summer to frost.

🐦 **L. fragrantissima.** WINTER HONEYSUCKLE. Deciduous shrub, semievergreen in Lower and Coastal South. Zones US, MS, LS, CS. Arching, rather stiff growth to 8 ft. Leaves are oval, dull dark green above, blue green beneath, 1–3 in. long. Creamy white flowers, ½ in. long, in late winter and early spring. Flowers are sweetly fragrant but not showy. Berry-like red fruit. Can be used as clipped hedge or background plant. Bring budded branches indoors for bloom.

L. heckrottii. GOLD FLAME HONEYSUCKLE. Deciduous vine or small shrub, semievergreen in Lower and Coastal South. Zones US, MS, LS, CS. Vigorous to 12–15 ft., with oval, 2-in., blue-green leaves. Free blooming from spring to frost. Clustered, 1½-in.-long flowers, bright coral pink outside and rich yellow within, open from coral pink buds. Train as espalier or on wire along eaves.

🐦 **L. japonica.** JAPANESE HONEYSUCKLE. Evergreen, semievergreen, or deciduous vine, depending on the area climate. Zones US, MS, LS, CS. Rampant—even invasive in the Southeast. Deep green, oval leaves; purple-tinged white flowers with sweet fragrance, late spring into fall.

Several selections are grown, all better known than the species itself. 'Aureo-reticulata', goldnet honeysuckle, has leaves veined yellow, especially in full sun. 'Halliana', Hall's Japanese honeysuckle, most vigorous and widely grown, climbs to 15 ft., covers 150 sq. ft.; flowers pure white changing to yellow, attractive to bees. 'Purpurea', probably the same plant as *L. j. chinensis,* has leaves tinged purple underneath and purplish red flowers that are white inside. Of these, 'Halliana' is most commonly used as bank and ground cover and for erosion control in large areas. As ground cover, set plants 2–3 ft. apart. Unless curbed, it can become a weed, smothering less vigorous plants; prune severely (cut back almost to framework) once yearly to prevent undergrowth from building up. Can be trained as a privacy or wind screen on chain-link or wire fence. Tolerates drought and poor drainage.

L. maximowiczii sachalinensis. Deciduous shrub. Zone US. An attractive, dense, rounded shrub to 6–8 ft.; dark green leaves 1½–3 in. long and half as wide. The deep red, 1½-in.-long flowers are followed by red fruit. Fall color is bright yellow.

L. morrowii. MORROW HONEYSUCKLE. Deciduous shrub. Zones US, MS. Grows in large mound 8 ft. tall and wide. Leaves bluish or grayish green, oblong, to 2 in. long. Flowers, ½ in. long, appear in late spring in pairs, creamy white at first, turning to yellow, and later followed by shiny dark red fruits. 'Xanthocarpa' has yellow fruits.

L. nitida. BOX HONEYSUCKLE. Evergreen shrub, deciduous in Upper South. Zones US, MS, LS, CS. To 4–6 ft. tall, with densely leafy branches. Tiny (½-in.), oval, dark green leaves. Attractive bronze to plum-colored winter foliage. Late spring or early summer flowers are fragrant, creamy white, ½ in. long. Translucent blue-purple berries. Rapid growth, tending toward untidiness, but easily pruned as hedge or single plant. Takes salt spray. 'Baggesen's Gold' has golden foliage in sun.

L. periclymenum. WOODBINE HONEYSUCKLE. Deciduous vine, semievergreen in Lower South. Zones US, MS, LS. Resembles *L. japonica* but is less rampant. Whorls of 2-in.-long, fragrant flowers in summer, fall. Blooms of 'Serotina' are purple outside, yellow inside. 'Berries Jubilee' has yellow flowers followed by profusion of red berries. 'Belgica' is less vining, more bushy than most, with abundant white flowers flushed purple, fading to yellow; flowers and red fruit come in large clusters. 'Graham Thomas' has white flowers that turn copper-tinted yellow.

L. pileata. PRIVET HONEYSUCKLE. Evergreen or semievergreen shrub. Zones US, MS, LS. Low, spreading plant to 3 ft. tall, with stiff horizontal branches. Dark green, 1½-in., privetlike leaves; small, fragrant white flowers in late spring; translucent violet purple berries. Good bank cover with low-growing euonymus or barberries. Does well at seashore. Give part or full shade in the Lower South.

☞ **L. sempervirens.** TRUMPET HONEYSUCKLE. Semievergreen (retains some leaves during mild winters in Lower and Coastal South) twining vine, shrubby if not given support. Zones US, MS, LS, CS. Late spring into summer, bears showy, unscented, orange-yellow to scarlet flowers—trumpet shaped, 1½–2 in. long, carried in whorls at ends of branches. Scarlet fruit. Oval, 1½–3-in.-long leaves are bluish green beneath. 'Cedar Lane' (known by the name "coral honeysuckle" in Florida) is a vigorous selection with deep red flowers. 'Sulphurea' has yellow flowers in late spring. For 'Dropmore Scarlet', see *L. brownii.*

L. tatarica. TATARIAN HONEYSUCKLE. Deciduous shrub. Zones US, MS, LS. Big, twiggy shrub to 10–12 ft. tall and wide, with bluish green foliage and white to pink flowers borne in pairs in late spring. Red berries follow. Most widely grown selection is 'Arnold Red', with dark red flowers. Too large for most gardens; use for screening, bird shelter.

L. xylosteum. Deciduous shrub. Zone US. Mounding, arching growth to 10 ft. tall, 12 ft. wide. Grayish or bluish green leaves, white or pinkish flowers in late spring. Species is seldom seen. 'Claveyi' or 'Clavey's Dwarf' is most commonly grown; selections tend to stay 3–6 ft. tall, occasionally taller. Other dwarf forms are sometimes offered. All are useful for hedges or foundation plantings.

LOOSESTRIFE. See LYSIMACHIA, LYTHRUM virgatum

LOQUAT. See ERIOBOTRYA

LOROPETALUM chinense

CHINESE FRINGE, CHINESE WITCH HAZEL, EVERGREEN WITCH HAZEL

Hamamelidaceae

EVERGREEN SHRUB

✿ ZONES MS, LS, CS

☼ ◑ FULL SUN OR PARTIAL SHADE

💧 REGULAR WATER

G enerally 10–15 ft. tall. Neat, compact habit, with arching or drooping tiered branches. Leaves roundish, light green, soft, 1–2 in. long. Throughout the year, the occasional leaf turns yellow or red, providing a nice touch of color. White to greenish white flowers in clusters of four to eight at ends of branches.

Loropetalum chinense

Each flower has four narrow, inch-long, twisted petals. Blooms most heavily in spring, but some bloom is likely at any time. 'Rubrum' ('Razzleberri') has purplish leaves and bright rosy pink flowers. *L. c. rubrum* 'Burgundy' is similar, if not identical; 'Blush' has pale purple-pink new foliage, green mature foliage, and reddish pink flowers.

Needs well-drained, nonalkaline soil. Chlorosis is a problem in high-pH soil. Subtly beautiful plant, good in corner and understory plantings, screens, mixed shrub borders, as single specimen or espalier. Prune lower limbs away for a nice small tree.

LOTUS. See NELUMBO

LOVE-IN-A-MIST. See NIGELLA damascena

LOVE-LIES-BLEEDING. See AMARANTHUS caudatus

☞ LUNARIA annua (L. biennis)

MONEY PLANT, HONESTY

Brassicaceae (Cruciferae)

BIENNIAL

✿ ZONES US, MS, LS, CS

☼ ◑ FULL SUN OR LIGHT SHADE

💧 💧 REGULAR TO MODERATE WATER

O ld-fashioned garden plant, grown for silvery, translucent circles (about 1¼ in. across) that stay on flower stalks after seeds drop. Plants are 1½–3 ft. high, with coarse, heart-shaped, toothed leaves. Spring flowers resemble wild mustard blooms but are purple or white, not yellow. There is a form with variegated leaves.

Lunaria annua

Plant in an out-of-the-way spot in poor soil or in a mixed flower bed where shining pods can be admired before they are picked for dry bouquets. Tough, persistent; can reseed and become weedy.

LUNGWORT. See PULMONARIA

LUPINE. See LUPINUS

LUPINUS

LUPINE

Fabaceae (Leguminosae)

PERENNIALS, SHRUBS, AND ANNUALS

✿ ZONES VARY BY SPECIES

☼ FULL SUN

💧 💧 WATER NEEDS VARY BY SPECIES

L eaves are divided into many leaflets (like fingers of a hand). Flowers sweet pea shaped, in dense spikes at ends of stems. Hundreds of

Lupinus texensis

species, many of them native to southwestern U.S.; occur in wide range of habitats, from beach sand to alpine rocks. Most lupines take poor conditions, but the Russell hybrids prefer rich, slightly acidic, well-drained soil.

L. hartwegii. Annual. All zones. Native to Mexico. Grows 1½–3 ft. tall; comes in shades of blue, white, and pink. Easy to grow from seed sown in place in spring for summer bloom. Moderate water.

L. havardii, L. subcarnosus, L. texensis. Annuals that reseed. Zones MS, LS, CS. All require lean conditions—thin, droughty soil—to survive; with regular flower border pampering, these Texas roadside flowers rot. For small areas, set out plants in fall to flower the following April. For meadows, scatter treated seeds (see box on this page) onto moist ground in September and lightly rake the soil surface; keep soil moist only until seeds germinate. Replant or resow each fall for several years; seed from current year's flowers do not germinate reliably to produce next spring's floral display. Adequate fall and winter rains are necessary to produce spectacular spring display.

L. havardii, Big Bend bluebonnet, is the tallest bluebonnet, 3–4 ft. high; its flowers are very deep blue. *L. subcarnosus*, the state flower of Texas, grows to 1 ft. tall, has sky blue flowers with a tinge of white. *L. texensis*, Texas bluebonnet, to 1 ft. tall, has dark blue flowers with white eyes that turn red after pollen is no longer viable, signaling bees not to visit plant.

L. perennis. WILD LUPINE. Perennial. Zones US, MS, LS, CS. Native to eastern U.S. To 2 ft. high, with purple flowers in late spring or early summer. Regular water.

L. Russell hybrids. RUSSELL LUPINES. Perennials usually treated as annuals. Zone US. Best in cool areas and higher elevations. Dislike of warm, wet weather makes them difficult to grow in most of the South. Large, spreading plants to 4–5 ft. tall, with long, dense spikes of flowers in late spring or early summer. Blooms in white, cream, yellow, pink, blue, red, orange, purple, and bicolors. Little Lulu and Minarette strains are smaller growing—to 1½ ft.

Grow from seed or buy started plants in flats or pots. Keep soil moist; give plants good air circulation to prevent mildew. Often short lived. Self-sown seedlings won't resemble parents.

HELP LUPINE SEEDS ALONG

Lupine seeds are hard coated and often slow to sprout. They will germinate faster if you soak them in hot water or scratch or nick the seed coats with a file before planting.

LYCHNIS

Caryophyllaceae

PERENNIALS

✿ ZONES US, MS, LS

☼ ◑ FULL SUN OR LIGHT SHADE

◐ ◑ WATER NEEDS VARY BY SPECIES

Hardy, old-fashioned garden flowers, all very tolerant of adverse soils. The different kinds vary in appearance but all offer eye-catching colors in summer. Plants are generally short lived and need to be replaced every few years.

Lychnis coronaria

L. arkwrightii. Complex hybrid involving several species. Remove faded flowers for repeat bloom. 'Dwarf Form' is a 10-in.-tall plant, with reddish green foliage and scarlet to orange-red flowers in few-flowered clusters. 'Vesuvius' is taller (to 2 ft.), with large orange-red flowers. Rich soil, regular water.

L. chalcedonica. MALTESE CROSS. Loose, open, growing 2–3 ft. high, with hairy leaves and stems. Scarlet flowers in dense terminal clusters, the petals deeply cut. Plants effective in large borders with white flowers, gray foliage. 'Alba' is white form. Regular water.

🌱 **L. coronaria.** ROSE CAMPION. Grows 1½–2½ ft. tall, with attractive white, silky foliage and magenta to crimson flowers a little less than an inch across. Effective massed. 'Alba' has white flowers; 'Angel's Blush' bears white blossoms with a deep pink eye. All self-sow freely if fading flowers are not removed. Moderate water.

L. haageana. Red, orange, salmon, or white flowers carried in clusters of two or three blossoms throughout summer. Stems clothed in green leaves reach 1½ ft. high. Dies down shortly after bloom ceases. Mulch to protect against extreme heat or cold. Though a hybrid, it comes fairly true from seed. Regular water.

L. viscaria. Compact, low, evergreen clumps of grasslike leaves to 5 in. long. Pinkish purple, ½-in. flowers on 1½–2-ft. stalks. 'Alba' has white blooms. Foot-high 'Splendens' has magenta blossoms; 'Splendens Flore Pleno' is similar but double flowered. Two deep red bloomers are 8-in. 'Atropurpurea' and 1½-ft. 'Zulu'. 'Alpina' is a 4-in. dwarf with rosy pink blooms. Regular to moderate water.

LYCIANTHES rantonnei (Solanum rantonnettii)

PARAGUAY NIGHTSHADE

Solanaceae

SEMIEVERGREEN SHRUB OR VINE

✿ ZONE TS

☼ FULL SUN

◐ ◑ REGULAR TO MODERATE WATER

As freestanding plant makes 6–8-ft. shrub, but can be staked into tree form or, with support, grown as a vine to 12–15 ft. or more. Can also be allowed to sprawl as a ground cover. Bright green, oval leaves to 4 in. long; flowers 1 in. wide, violet blue with yellow centers, bloom throughout the summer. Wild species has flowers only half as large. 'Royal Robe' is more compact than the species, with a longer bloom season and darker purple flowers.

Lycianthes rantonnei

Informal, fast growing, not easy to use in tailored landscape. (If you use this plant there, prune it severely to keep it neat.) In harsh cold, leaf drop is heavy and branch tips may die back.

LYCORIS

SPIDER LILY

Amaryllidaceae

BULBS

✿ ZONES VARY BY SPECIES

☼ ◑ FULL SUN OR LIGHT SHADE

◐ REGULAR WATER DURING GROWTH AND BLOOM

Lycoris radiata

Narrow, strap-shaped leaves appear in spring or winter. Foliage ripens and dies down before bloom starts. Clusters of red, pink, or yellow flowers appear on bare stems to 2 ft. tall in late summer, fall. Flowers are spidery looking, with long stamens and narrow, wavy-edged segments curved backward.

Grow in garden beds (where bulbs will survive winter) or in naturalized areas. Some kinds are tender, some half hardy. Bulbs available July–August. Set 3–4 in. deep in good soil. Don't disturb plantings for several years. When potting, set with tops exposed. Don't use too-large pots; plants with crowded roots bloom best.

L. africana (L. aurea). GOLDEN SPIDER LILY, HURRICANE LILY. Zones CS, TS; otherwise, indoor/outdoor pot plants. Bright yellow, 3-in. blooms.

🌱 **L. radiata.** SPIDER LILY. All zones. Best known and easiest to grow. Coral red flowers with gold sheen; 1½-ft. stems. 'Alba', white spider lily, has white flowers. Will take light shade. Protect in the Upper South.

L. sanguinea. Zones LS, CS. To 2 ft. tall, with 2–2½-in. bright red to orange-red flowers.

L. sprengeri. Zones US, MS, LS, CS. Similar to *L. squamigera,* but with slightly smaller purplish pink flowers.

☂ **L. squamigera (Amaryllis hallii).** MAGIC LILY, SURPRISE LILY, NAKED LADY. Zones US, MS, LS, CS. Clusters of funnel-shaped, 3-in., fragrant, pink or rosy lilac flowers on 2-ft. stems. Hardiest species.

☂ LYGODIUM japonicum

JAPANESE CLIMBING FERN

Schizaeaceae

PERENNIAL

✂ ZONES MS, LS, CS, TS; OR INDOORS

◑ PARTIAL SHADE

◐ REGULAR WATER

Lygodium japonicum

Native to eastern Asia. Lacy fern naturalized in Southeast, twines daintily to 15 ft. through shrubs or trees or up a trellis or slender posts. Fast growing in rich, moist, well-drained soil, and particularly lush if air is humid. Evergreen in the Coastal and Tropical South, dies back to roots in the Lower South. Fronds yellow green, long, triangular, 8–12 in. wide, on wiry stems. Fertile (spore-bearing) leaflets much narrower than sterile ones. In spring, prune old tangled stems to make way for new growth.

Can be grown indoors; needs bright indirect light and minimum night temperature of 40°F. Mist to raise humidity.

LYSIMACHIA

Primulaceae

PERENNIALS

✂ ZONES VARY BY SPECIES

◔◑ FULL SUN OR PARTIAL SHADE

◐ MODERATE WATER

Lysimachia nummularia

Some, notably *L. clethroides* and *L. punctata,* are notoriously aggressive spreaders, especially if water supply is plentiful while others, such as *L. congestiflora,* are well behaved. Don't let more aggressive types invade choicer plantings. Use these types for naturalizing in woodland edges or barely maintained areas. Bloom in summer, except as noted.

L. barystachys. Zones US, MS, LS. Grows to 2 ft. tall, with narrow leaves and spikes of white flowers that start out horizontal and gradually turn upright.

L. ciliata. Zones US, MS, LS, CS. Erect plant to 3 ft., with opposite or whorled oval, 5-in. leaves. Small, nodding yellow flowers appear in upper leaf joints. 'Atropurpurea' is similar, but with red leaves.

L. clethroides. GOOSENECK LOOSESTRIFE. Zones US, MS, LS. To 3 ft. high, with olive green foliage, gracefully curving spikes of white flowers.

L. congestiflora (L. procumbens). GOLDEN GLOBES. Zones MS, LS, CS. Trailing stems bend upward at tips. Leaves thick, to 2½ in. long. Branches end in clusters of bright yellow, inch-wide flowers that open from round buds. Blooms in spring, with some scattered bloom later. Use in hanging baskets or as a ground cover.

L. nummularia. MONEYWORT, CREEPING JENNY. Zones US, MS, LS. Evergreen creeping plant with long runners (to 2 ft.) that root at joints. Forms pretty light green mat of roundish leaves. Yellow flowers about 1 in. across form singly in leaf joints. Summer blooming. Best use is in corners where it need not be restrained. Will spill from wall, hanging basket. Good ground cover (plant 1–1½ ft. apart) near streams. 'Aurea' has yellow leaves, needs shade.

L. punctata. YELLOW LOOSESTRIFE. Zones US, MS, LS. To 4 ft. tall. Erect stems have narrow leaves in whorls, with whorled yellow flowers on the top third.

Lythraceae. The loosestrife family is represented in this book by *Cuphea,* crepe myrtle *(Lagerstroemia),* and wand loosestrife *(Lythrum).* Yellow loosestrife, *Lysimachia punctata,* is in the primrose family.

LYTHRUM virgatum

WAND LOOSESTRIFE

Lythraceae

PERENNIAL

✂ ZONES US, MS, LS

◯ FULL SUN

◐ REGULAR WATER; TOO MUCH MOISTURE ENCOURAGES INVASIVENESS

Lythrum virgatum

Showy plant for pond margins or moist areas (but use with caution); also valued for cut flowers. The 2-ft.-wide clumps put up 2½–5 ft.-high stems. Narrow leaves clothe lower portion of stems; the upper 8–18 in. are densely set with ¾-in. magenta flowers in late summer and fall.

L. virgatum has a bad reputation with lovers of native plants, because of the invasive nature of its cousin, purple loosestrife *(L. salicaria).* Seedlings of this latter plant often choke wetlands, crowding out native vegetation. Hybrids, including 'Dropmore Purple', 'Morden's Gleam', 'Morden's Pink', 'Pink Spires', 'Robert', 'Rose Queen', 'Roseum Superbum', and 'Rosy Spires', are said to be sterile, but they may interbreed with *L. salicaria* growing in the wild and set seed. In some states, it is illegal to plant purple loosestrife and its variants—and doing so is unwise, even if legal, wherever plants have ample moisture and may escape into unmanaged areas.

MACARTHUR PALM. See PTYCHOSPERMA macarthuri

M

MACFADYENA unguis-cati

CAT'S CLAW, YELLOW TRUMPET VINE

Bignoniaceae

PARTLY DECIDUOUS VINE

✂ ZONES LS, CS

◯◑ FULL SUN OR PARTIAL SHADE

◐ MODERATE TO LITTLE WATER

Macfadyena unguis-cati

Formerly known as *Doxantha unguis-cati* and *Bignonia tweediana.* Climbs high (to 25–40 ft.) and fast by hooked, clawlike, forked tendrils. Leaves divided into two oval, 2-in., glossy green leaflets. Blooms in early spring, bearing yellow trumpets to 2 in. long, 1¼ in. across. Vigorous; puts down roots where stems touch ground. Clings to any support—stone, wood, tree trunk. Suitable for covering chain-link fence. Tends to produce leaves and flowers at stem ends; after bloom, prune hard to stimulate new growth lower down. Loses all leaves in cold winters.

MACLEAYA (Bocconia)

PLUME POPPY

Papaveraceae

PERENNIALS

✂ ZONES US, MS, LS

◯◑ SUN OR LIGHT SHADE

◐ REGULAR WATER

Macleaya cordata

These tall perennials are often still listed as *Bocconia,* a name properly belonging to their shrubby tropical relatives. The two species described below resemble each other. Both have creeping rhizomes; tall, erect stems; large, deeply lobed leaves like those of edible fig tree; and small flowers in large, branching clusters. These plants look tropical, and their value lies in size and structure rather than flower color. Can be invasive if not controlled; plant among shrubs rather than amid delicate perennials.

M. cordata. PLUME POPPY. To 7–8 ft. tall, with 3-ft.-wide clumps of grayish green, 10-in. leaves and clouds of tiny white to beige flowers. Considered somewhat less invasive than *M. microcarpa.*

M. microcarpa. Similar to *M. cordata,* but with pinkish beige flowers. Flowers of 'Coral Plume' are more decidedly pink.

MACLURA pomifera

OSAGE ORANGE

Moraceae

DECIDUOUS TREE

ZONES US, MS, LS

FULL SUN

REGULAR TO LITTLE WATER

Native from Arkansas to Oklahoma and Texas. Fast growth to 60 ft. tall (though often less), with spreading, open habit. Young branches are thornier than mature ones. Wood is very hard and orange in color. Medium green leaves to 5 in.

Maclura pomifera

long. If there's a male plant present, female plants may bear inedible, 4-in. fruits (so-called hedge-apples) that somewhat resemble bumpy, yellow-green oranges and are prized for holiday decorations. Withstands heat, cold, wind, poor soil, moderate alkalinity, wet or dry conditions. Easily propagated by seed, stem cuttings, root cuttings; easily transplanted. 'Wichita' is nearly thornless; useful as big, tough, rough-looking hedge or background. Prune to any size from 6 ft. up. Pruned high, becomes a shade tree. Other thornless types include 'Chetopa', 'Inermis', and 'Pawhuska'. These do not produce fruits. In areas where people will be sitting or walking beneath the tree, always plant fruitless selections. A heavy, hard fruit falling from the top of a tree can knock a person silly.

MADAGASCAR DRAGON TREE. See DRACAENA marginata

MADAGASCAR JASMINE. See STEPHANOTIS floribunda

MADAGASCAR PALM. See PACHYPODIUM lamerei

MADAGASCAR PERIWINKLE. See CATHARANTHUS roseus

MADEIRA VINE. See ANREDERA cordifolia

MAGIC LILY. See LYCORIS squamigera

MAGNOLIA

Magnoliaceae

DECIDUOUS OR EVERGREEN TREES AND SHRUBS

ZONES VARY BY SPECIES

FULL SUN OR PARTIAL SHADE

REGULAR WATER

SEE CHART

Magnificent flowering plants with remarkable variety in color, leaf shape, and plant form. Magnolias are discussed here by general appearance; the chart lists them alphabetically. New selections and hybrids appear every year, but distribution is spotty in local garden centers. Mail-order specialists can supply many more kinds.

Magnolia soulangiana

EVERGREEN MAGNOLIAS

To gardeners, the word "magnolia" usually means *M. grandiflora,* the classic Southern magnolia with glossy leaves and huge, fragrant white flowers, the state flower of Louisiana and Mississippi. Few trees can touch it for year-round beauty. Sweet bay (*M. virginiana*), a hardier tree of smaller proportions, is nearly evergreen in the Lower and Coastal South. The two species are parents of the evergreen hybrids *M.* 'Freeman' and *M.* 'Maryland', which are similar to Southern magnolia but slightly more tolerant of cold.

DECIDUOUS MAGNOLIAS WITH SAUCER FLOWERS

This group includes the saucer magnolia (*M. soulangiana*) and its many selections, often erroneously called tulip trees due to the shape and bright colors of their flowers. Also included here are the yulan magnolia (*M. denudata*) and lily magnolia (*M. liliiflora*). All are hardy to cold, thriving in various climates—but all do poorly in hot, dry, windy areas; early flowers of all forms are subject to frost damage. Related to these, but more tender to cold (and heat), are the spectacular oriental magnolias from western China and the Himalayas—*M. campbellii, M. dawsoniana, M. sargentiana robusta, M. sprengeri* 'Diva'. Their early flowers are also subject to frost and storm damage.

DECIDUOUS MAGNOLIAS WITH STAR FLOWERS

This group includes Kobus magnolia (*M. kobus*); Loebner magnolia (*M. loebneri*); and star magnolia (*M. stellata*). All are cold-hardy, slow-growing, early-blooming plants with wide climatic adaptability.

OTHER MAGNOLIAS

Less widely planted is a group of magnolias generally considered foliage plants or shade trees. Among them are cucumber tree (*M. acuminata*), a big shade tree with inconspicuous flowers; and umbrella magnolia (*M. tripetala*), and bigleaf magnolia (*M. macrophylla*), both medium-size trees with huge leaves and flowers.

MAGNOLIA CULTURE

For any magnolia, pick planting site carefully. Virtually all magnolias are hard to move once established, and many grow quite large. The best soil for magnolias is fairly rich, well drained, and neutral to slightly acid; if necessary, add generous amounts of organic matter when planting. Although you can grow most magnolias in somewhat alkaline soil, the plants may develop chlorosis. Southern magnolia is good for planting at the beach, though not on dunes. Sweet bay tolerates wet soil. The species and selections listed in the chart are adapted to a wide range of growing conditions and easy for most gardeners to grow.

Magnolia grandiflora

Magnolias never look their best when crowded, and they may be severely damaged by digging around their roots. Larger deciduous magnolias are at their best standing alone against a background that will display their flowers, and their strongly patterned, usually gray limbs and big, fuzzy flower buds in winter. Small deciduous magnolias show up well in large flower or shrub borders and make choice ornaments in oriental gardens. Most magnolias are excellent lawn trees. However, dense shade and surface roots make it nearly impossible to grow grass beneath Southern or bigleaf magnolia.

Balled-and-burlapped plants are available in late winter and early spring; container plants are sold anytime. Do not set plants lower than their original soil level. Stake single-trunked or very heavy plants to prevent them from being rocked by wind, which will tear the thick, fleshy, sensitive roots. To avoid damaging the roots, set stakes in planting hole before placing tree. If you plant your magnolia in a lawn, try to provide a good-sized area free of grass around the trunk. At least in the early years, keep a cooling mulch over the root area. Prevent soil compaction around root zone by keeping foot traffic to a minimum. Prune only when absolutely necessary; best time is right after flowering, and the best technique is to remove the entire twig or limb right to the base. Magnolias seldom have serious pest or disease problems.

MAGNOLIA

NAME	ZONES	TYPE	HEIGHT	SPREAD	AGE AT BLOOM	FLOWERS	USES, CHARACTERISTICS, COMMENTS
Magnolia acuminata CUCUMBER TREE	US, MS, LS	Deciduous	60–80 ft.	25 ft.	12 yrs.	Small, greenish yellow, appear after leaves. Late spring, summer. Handsome reddish seed capsules, red seeds	Shade or lawn tree. Dense shade from glossy, 5–9-in. leaves. Hardy to cold; dislikes hot, dry winds
M. a. subcordata (M. cordata) YELLOW CUCUMBER TREE, YELLOW MAGNOLIA	US, MS, LS	Deciduous	To 35 ft.	To 35 ft.	12 yrs.	Larger (to 4 in.), chartreuse yellow outside, pure yellow within; appear as leaves start to expand. Mild lemon scent	Slow-growing lawn or border tree for large properties. Lower, shrubbier than *M. acuminata*. 'Miss Honeybee', with pale yellow flowers, is a good selection
M. ashei ASHE MAGNOLIA	US, MS, LS, CS	Deciduous	10–20 ft.	To 15 ft.	1–2 yrs.	Flowers 6–10 in. wide, with creamy white, somewhat pointed petals, sometimes spotted with red in late spring	Valuable for its tropical effect where space is limited. Multistemmed shrub with 2-ft.-long leaves. Very hardy. A shrubby version of *M. macrophylla*
M. denudata (M. conspicua, M. heptapeta) YULAN MAGNOLIA 🏛	US, MS, LS	Deciduous	To 35 ft.	To 30 ft.	6–7 yrs.	White, fragrant, may be purple at base. Somewhat tulip shaped, 3–4 in. long, to 6–7 in. wide. Early; often injured by late freezes	Somewhat irregular form; good in informal garden or at woodland edge. Plant to show off against dark background or sky. Leaves 4–7 in. long. Good cut flowers
M. 'Elizabeth'	US, MS, LS	Deciduous	To 40 ft.	To 20 ft.	2–6 yrs. from grafts	Fragrant medium yellow, 6–7 in. wide. Color is lighter in mild-winter areas	Hybrid of *M. acuminata* and *M. denudata*. Grow as single-trunk specimen or multitrunk shrub-tree
M. fraseri (M. auriculata) FRASER MAGNOLIA	US, MS, LS	Deciduous	To 50 ft.	20–30 ft.	10–12 yrs.	Creamy to yellowish white, 8–10 in. wide. Late spring. Rose red, 5-in. seed capsules showy in summer	Good lawn or woodland tree. Leaves 16–18 in. long, parchmentlike, in whorls at ends of branches. Handsome dark brown fall color
M. grandiflora SOUTHERN MAGNOLIA 🏛	US, MS, LS, CS	Evergreen	To 80 ft.	To 40 ft.	15 yrs., maybe less; 2–3 yrs. from grafts	Pure white, aging buff; large (8–10 in. across), powerfully fragrant. Carried throughout summer, fall. State flower of Louisiana and Mississippi	Street or lawn tree, big container plant, wall or espalier plant. Grafted plants need pruning to become single-trunked tree. Glossy, leathery leaves, 4–8 in. long. Tolerates salt spray, sand
M. g. 'Bracken's Brown Beauty'	US, MS, LS, CS	Evergreen	To 30 ft.	10–15 ft.	2–3 yrs. from grafts	Creamy white, lemon scented, 5–6 in. wide. Late spring	Leaves 5 in. long, with undulating edges, rust-colored felt texture beneath. Hardy. Dense, compact. Introduced by Ray Bracken, Easley, South Carolina
M. g. 'Edith Bogue'	US, MS, LS, CS	Evergreen	To 35 ft.	To 20 ft.	2–3 yrs. from grafts	As in *M. grandiflora*. In youth, slower to come into heavy bloom than some other types	Shapely, vigorous tree, one of hardiest of *M. grandiflora*. Has withstood −24°F. The one to try in Upper South. Keep it out of strong winds
M. g. 'Little Gem'	US, MS, LS, CS	Evergreen	Slow to 15–20 ft.	To 10 ft.	2 yrs. from grafts	Small (5–6 in. wide), produced continuously through summer	Good in containers, as espalier, in confined area. Half-size foliage, rusty beneath. Branches to ground
M. g. 'Majestic Beauty'	US, MS, LS, CS	Evergreen	35–50 ft.	To 20 ft.	2 yrs. from grafts	Very large, to 1 ft. across, with 9 petals	Vigorous, dense-branching street or shade tree of broadly pyramidal form. Leaves long, broad, and heavy. Most luxuriant of Southern magnolias
M. g. 'Samuel Sommer'	US, MS, LS, CS	Evergreen	Fairly fast to 30–40 ft.	To 30 ft.	Same as *M. grandiflora*	Very large and full; to 10–14 in. across, with 12 petals	Dark green leaves, large, leathery, glossy. Heavy, rusty red felting on underside

▶

MAGNOLIA

NAME	ZONES	TYPE	HEIGHT	SPREAD	AGE AT BLOOM	FLOWERS	USES, CHARACTERISTICS, COMMENTS
M. g. 'St. Mary'	US, MS, LS, CS	Evergreen	Usually 20 ft. Much larger in old age	To 20 ft.	Same as *M. grandiflora*	Heavy production of full-size flowers on small tree	Big, dense bush. Pruned and staked, it makes a small tree. Fine where magnolia of standard size is too large. Good for espalier and pots
M. g. 'Symmes Select'	US, MS, LS, CS	Evergreen	40–50 ft.	To 30 ft.	1–3 yrs. from grafts	Blooms at early age. Flowers like those of *M. grandiflora*	Dark green, lustrous leaves backed with dark brown. Introduced by Cedar Lane Farm, Madison, Georgia
M. g. 'Victoria'	US, MS, LS, CS	Evergreen	To 20 ft.	To 15 ft.	2–3 yrs. from grafts	Same as *M. grandiflora*	Withstands −10°F with little damage, but plant out of wind. Foliage exceptionally broad, heavy, dark green
M. kobus KOBUS MAGNOLIA	US, MS, LS	Deciduous	To 30 ft.	To 20 ft.	15 yrs.	White, to 4 in. across; early	Cold-hardy tree for planting singly in lawn or in informal shrub and tree groupings. Tolerates alkaline soil
M. k. stellata (see **M. stellata**)							
M. Kosar–De Vos Hybrids (the "Little Girl" series)	US, MS, LS	Deciduous	To 12 ft.	To 15 ft.	4–5 yrs.	Colors range from deep to pale purple (sometimes pink or white inside), depending on type. Bloom in spring before leaf-out; sporadic rebloom in summer	Hybrids between *M. liliiflora* 'Nigra' and *M. stellata* 'Rosea'; bred to bloom later than *M. stellata* to avoid frost damage. Erect, shrubby growers bearing girls' names: 'Ann', 'Betty', 'Jane', 'Judy', 'Pinkie', 'Randy', 'Ricki', 'Susan'
M. liliiflora **(M. quinquepeta)** LILY MAGNOLIA	US, MS, LS	Deciduous	To 12 ft.	To 15 ft.	4–5 yrs.	White inside, purplish outside; about 4 in. across. Selections 'Nigra' and 'O'Neill' are dark purple red outside, pink inside. Blooms in late spring	Good for shrub border; strong vertical effect in big flower border. Spreads slowly by suckering. Leaves 4–6 in. long. Good cut flower if buds taken before fully open
M. loebneri LOEBNER MAGNOLIA	US, MS, LS, CS	Deciduous	Slow to 12–15 ft.; can reach 30 ft.	12–15 ft.	3 yrs.	Narrow, strap-shaped petals like those of *M. stellata*, but fewer, larger. Blossoms of some selections are fragrant. Early	Hybrids between *M. kobus* and *M. stellata*. 'Ballerina' is white with faint pink blush; 'Leonard Messel' has pink flowers; 'Merrill' ('Dr. Merrill') is a free-flowering white. 'Spring Snow' has pure white flowers. Use in lawn or shrub border, at woodland edge
M. macrophylla BIGLEAF MAGNOLIA 🏛	US, MS, LS, CS	Deciduous	Slow to 50 ft.	To 30 ft.	12–15 yrs.	White, fragrant, to 1 ft. across. Late spring, early summer, after leaves are out	Show-off tree with leaves 1–2½ ft. long, 9–12 in. wide. Needs to stand alone. Needs some shade
M. soulangiana SAUCER MAGNOLIA (often erroneously called TULIP TREE) 🏛	US, MS, LS, CS	Deciduous	To 25 ft.	To 25 ft. or more	3–5 yrs.	White to pink or purplish red, variable in size and form, blooming before leaves expand. Generally about 6 in. across. Late winter into spring	Lawn tree, anchor plant in big corner plantings. Hybrid of *M. denudata* and *M. liliiflora*. Seedlings highly variable; plant named selections. Foliage good green, rather coarse. Leaves 4–6 in. long (or more)
M. s. 'Alexandrina'	US, MS, LS, CS	Deciduous	To 25 ft.	To 25 ft. or more	3–5 yrs.	Large. Color highly variable, from almost pure white to dark purple. Early	Same uses as for *M. soulangiana*. Large, rather heavy foliage. Subject to bloom damage in late freezes
M. s. 'Brozzonii'	US, MS, LS, CS	Deciduous	To 25 ft.	To 25 ft. or more	3–5 yrs.	Large (to 8 in. across). White, very slightly flushed purplish rose at base. Late	One of handsomest whites. Large, vigorous plant; often avoids bloom damage in late freezes

MAGNOLIA

NAME	ZONES	TYPE	HEIGHT	SPREAD	AGE AT BLOOM	FLOWERS	USES, CHARACTERISTICS, COMMENTS
M. s. 'Burgundy'	US, MS, LS, CS	Deciduous	To 25 ft.	To 25 ft. or more	3–5 yrs.	Large, rounded; deep purple halfway up to petal tips, then lightening to pink . Early	Earlier bloom than most makes it more susceptible to frost damage
M. s. 'Lennei'	US, MS, LS, CS	Deciduous	To 25 ft.	To 25 ft. or more	3–5 yrs.	Very large, globe shaped, deep purple outside, white inside. Late	Spreading, vigorous plant with large leaves. Late bloom helps it escape damage in late frosts
M. s. 'Lennei Alba'	US, MS, LS, CS	Deciduous	To 25 ft.	To 25 ft. or more	3–5 yrs.	Like those of *M. s.* 'Lennei', but white in color, slightly smaller, later (midseason)	Spreading, vigorous plant; often avoids bloom damage in late frosts
M. s. 'Rustica Rubra'	US, MS, LS, CS	Deciduous	To 25 ft.	To 25 ft. or more	3–5 yrs.	Large, cup shaped, deep reddish purple. Somewhat past midseason. Big (6-in.) seedpods of dark rose	Tall, vigorous grower for large areas. More treelike than many selections
M. s. 'Verbanica'	US, MS, LS, CS	Deciduous	To 20 ft.	To 15 ft.	2–3 yrs.	Late blooming; petals soft purplish rose on outside, white at tips; strap-shaped inner petals, backed with rose color	One of the hardiest and most beautiful of the saucer magnolias. Not subject to bloom damage in late frosts
M. stellata STAR MAGNOLIA	US, MS, LS, CS	Deciduous	To 10 ft.	To 20 ft.	3 yrs.	Very early, white, about 3 in. wide; 19–21 narrow, strap-shaped petals. Profuse bloom in late winter, early spring. Some types are fragrant	Slow growing, shrubby; fine for borders, entryway gardens, edge of woods. Quite hardy, but flowers often nipped by frost. Fine texture in twig and leaf. Fair yellow-and-brown fall color
M. s. 'Centennial'	US, MS, LS, CS	Deciduous	To 10 ft.	To 20 ft.	3 yrs.	White, faintly marked pink, 5 in. across	Same uses as for *M. stellata*. Like an improved *M. s.* 'Waterlily'
M. s. 'Rosea' PINK STAR MAGNOLIA	US, MS, LS, CS	Deciduous	To 10 ft.	To 20 ft.	3 yrs.	Pink buds; flowers flushed pink, fading to white. Very early	Same uses as for species. Various plants sold under this name. Plant this and other early-flowering types in a northern exposure to delay bloom, lessening frost damage
M. s. 'Royal Star'	US, MS, LS, CS	Deciduous	To 10 ft.	To 20 ft.	3 yrs.	White flowers with 25–30 petals. Bloom 2 weeks later than *M. stellata*. Fragrant	Same uses as for *M. stellata*. Faster growing
M. s. 'Waterlily'	US, MS, LS, CS	Deciduous	To 10 ft.	To 20 ft.	3 yrs.	White. Larger flowers than *M. stellata*; broader, more numerous petals. Fragrant	Faster growing than most star magnolias, but later blooming. Leaves modest in size (2–4 in. long); foliage has finer texture than other magnolias
M. tripetala UMBRELLA MAGNOLIA	US, MS, LS	Deciduous	15–35 ft.	15–20 ft.	5 yrs.	Greenish white, to 10 in. across, with purple stamens; heavily fragrant	Huge leaves cluster at ends of branches. Vigorous and unkempt, with an open and irregular crown; difficult to site in gardens. Large red seedpods
M. virginiana SWEET BAY	US, MS, LS, CS	Deciduous to semi-evergreen	10–20 ft.	To 20 ft.	8–10 yrs.	Nearly globular, 2–3 in. wide, creamy white, fragrant. June–Sept.	Prefers moist, acid soil. Grows in swamps. Deciduous in Upper South; semievergreen elsewhere; multistemmed. Leaves grayish green, whitish beneath, 2–5 in. long
M. v. australis SOUTHERN SWEET BAY	MS, LS, CS, TS	Evergreen	45–50 ft.	15–20 ft.	8–10 yrs.	White, lemon scented, 2–4 in. across	Single trunked with upright open habit; glossy green, silver-backed leaves. Gets much larger in woodland setting, sometimes to 80 ft. tall

M

Magnoliaceae. The magnolia family contains evergreen and deciduous trees and shrubs with large, showy flowers, usually with a large number of petals, sepals, and stamens. Tulip poplar (*Liriodendron tulipifera*), *Michelia*, and magnolia are examples.

MAHONIA

Berberidaceae

EVERGREEN SHRUBS

⚡ ZONES VARY BY SPECIES

☼ ◐ ● EXPOSURE NEEDS VARY BY SPECIES

◐ ● WATER NEEDS VARY BY SPECIES

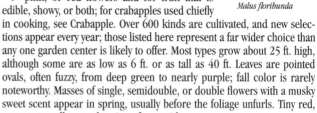

Mahonia aquifolium

Related to *Berberis* and described under that name by some botanists. Easy to grow; good looking all year. Leaves divided into leaflets, usually with spiny-toothed edges. Bright yellow flowers in dense, rounded to spikelike clusters, followed by blue-black (sometimes red), berry-like fruit. Generally disease resistant, though in some areas foliage may be disfigured by small looper caterpillars. All species attract birds.

M. aquifolium. OREGON GRAPE. Zones US, MS, LS. Native British Columbia to Northern California. Erect growth to 6 ft. tall or taller; spreads by underground stems. Leaves 4–10 in. long, with five to nine very spiny-toothed, oval, 1–2½-in. leaflets that are glossy green in some forms, dull green in others. Young growth ruddy or bronzy; scattered mature red leaves. Purplish or bronzy leaves in winter, especially in Upper South or where plants are grown in full sun. Spring flowers in 2–3-in. clusters along stems; edible powdery blue-black fruit (makes good jelly).

'Compacta' averages about 2 ft. tall and spreads freely to make broad colonies. New leaves glossy, light to coppery green; mature leaves matte medium green. 'King's Ransom', to 5–6 ft. tall, is likely a hybrid between *M. aquifolium* and *M. pinnata*; it has dark bluish green leaves that turn red purple in winter, showy yellow flowers in spring, and very dark blue fruits.'Orange Flame', 5 ft. tall, has bronzy orange new growth and glossy green mature leaves that turn wine red in winter.

Oregon grape can take any exposure, though it does best with some shade in the Lower South and wind protection in the Upper South. Plant in masses as foundation planting, in woodland garden, as low screen or garden barrier. Control height and form by pruning; if woody stems jut out, cut them down to ground (new growth fills in quickly). Regular water.

M. bealei. LEATHERLEAF MAHONIA. Zones US, MS, LS, CS. Grows to 10–12 ft., with strong pattern of vertical stems, horizontal foliage. Leaves over 1 ft. long, divided into seven to fifteen broad, leathery leaflets to 5 in. long; leaflets grayish or bluish green above, olive green below, with spiny-toothed edges. Very fragrant flowers in erect, 3–6-in.-long, spikelike clusters at branch ends in earliest spring. Powdery blue berries. Distinguished plant against stone, brick, wood, glass. Takes sun in Upper and Middle South; best in part shade elsewhere. Plant in rich soil with ample organic material. Regular water.

Mahonia bealei

M. fortunei. CHINESE MAHONIA. Zones LS, CS. Native to China. Grows to 6 ft.; stems bear 10-in., matte green leaves with seven to thirteen spiny-toothed leaflets. Undersurface of leaves is yellowish green, with heavily netted veins. Flowers in short clusters; the purple-black berries seldom develop. Plant has an unusual stiff charm and is grown for form and foliage, not fruit. Sun to light shade. Moderate water.

M. lomariifolia. BURMESE MAHONIA. Zones LS, CS. Native to China. Showy plant with erect, little-branched stems to 6–10 ft. tall. Young plants often have a single, vertical unbranched stem; with age, plants produce more, almost vertical branches from near base. Clustered near ends of these branches are horizontally held leaves to 2 ft. long. In outline, leaves look like stiff, crinkly, barbed ferns; each has as many as 47 thick, spiny, glossy green leaflets arranged symmetrically along both sides of central

stem. Flowers in winter or earliest spring grow in foot-long, erect clusters at branch tips, just above uppermost cluster of leaves. Powdery blue berries. Prune stems at varying heights to induce branching. Needs shade at least in afternoon to keep deep green color. Regular water.

M. pinnata. CLUSTER MAHONIA. Zones MS, LS. Native from southern Oregon to Southern California. Similar to *M. aquifolium,* but leaves are blue gray and more crinkly and spiny, new growth often shows lots of red and orange, and plants may grow taller (to 10 ft.) in ideal conditions. Takes heat and drought better than *M. aquifolium.* Also takes more sun, but in Lower South, plant in light shade. Little water.

MAIDEN GRASS. See MISCANTHUS sinensis 'Gracillimus'

MAIDENHAIR FERN. See ADIANTUM

MAIDENHAIR SPLEENWORT. See ASPLENIUM trichomanes

MAIDENHAIR TREE. See GINKGO biloba

MAIDEN PINK. See DIANTHUS deltoides

MAJORANA hortensis. See ORIGANUM majorana

MALE FERN. See DRYOPTERIS filix-mas

MALLOW. See MALVA

MALTESE CROSS. See LYCHNIS chalcedonica

MALUS

CRABAPPLE

Rosaceae

DECIDUOUS TREES, ONLY RARELY SHRUBS

⚡ ZONES US, MS, LS

☼ FULL SUN

◐ ● REGULAR TO MODERATE WATER

▶ SEE CHART

Malus floribunda

Valued for brief bloom of handsome white, pink, or red flowers and for fruit that is edible, showy, or both; for crabapples used chiefly in cooking, see Crabapple. Over 600 kinds are cultivated, and new selections appear every year; those listed here represent a far wider choice than any one garden center is likely to offer. Most types grow about 25 ft. high, although some are as low as 6 ft. or as tall as 40 ft. Leaves are pointed ovals, often fuzzy, from deep green to nearly purple; fall color is rarely noteworthy. Masses of single, semidouble, or double flowers with a musky sweet scent appear in spring, usually before the foliage unfurls. Tiny red, orange, or yellow apples ripen from midsummer into autumn; in some types, the fruit hangs on until late in the season, after leaves drop. Blooming and bearing may occur more heavily in alternate years. Birds are fond of small-fruited types.

Malus sargentii

Plant bare-root trees in winter or early spring; set out container plants any time. Crabapples prefer good, well-drained, deep soil, but they will grow in rocky or gravelly soils and in conditions ranging from acid to slightly alkaline. They are more tolerant of wet soil than flowering cherries or other flowering stone fruits; also hardier and longer lived than flowering stone fruits. Adapt to a variety of climates. All need some winter chill.

Crabapples may be bothered by aphids, Japanese beetles, spider mites, or tent caterpillars, but these pests are minor compared with potential disease problems: fireblight, apple scab, cedar-apple rust, and powdery mildew. In most areas where humidity is high and persistent, disease resistance of crabapples is important if you wish to avoid spraying. Where long, dry summers are the rule, diseases are less of a problem. Disease resistance (or lack of it) is noted in the chart. Avoid these disease-prone selections: 'Almey', 'Bechtel', 'Eleyi', 'Hopa', and 'Radiant'.

▶ page 290

MALUS

NAME	SIZE, HABIT	FLOWERS	FRUIT	COMMENTS
Malus 'Adams'	Dense, round headed, to 20 ft.	Red buds open to single pink	Red, over ½ in. wide, long lasting	Orange fall foliage. Good disease resistance
M. 'Adirondack'	Columnar, to 10 ft. tall and 6 ft. wide	Red buds open to large waxy white blooms with red tinge	Red to orange red	Formal in appearance. High disease resistance
M. angustifolia SOUTHERN WILD CRAB	To 25 ft. tall	Deep pink buds fade to white; 1 in., very fragrant	Aromatic, yellowish green fruit to 1½ in. across	Susceptible to fireblight, rust, and scab. Attractive in its native environment
M. 'Brandywine'	Vigorous, shapely, to 15–20 ft. tall and wide	Double rose pink, fragrant	Yellowish green	Leaves have reddish cast. Some susceptibility to disease
M. 'Callaway'	Attractive, round headed, to 25 ft.	Pink buds open to single white	Deep red, large, long lasting	Low chilling requirement for bloom. High disease resistance. Good choice for Lower South
M. 'Centurion'	Oval crowned, to 25 ft. tall and 15–20 ft. wide	Red buds open to single red	Shiny deep red, long lasting	Blooms young. High disease resistance
M. coronaria WILD SWEET CRABAPPLE	Short trunk; broad, round-headed crown. To 30 ft.	Pink buds open to single, pure white or pink-tinged white; fragrant	Yellowish green, large	Late blooming. Susceptible to rust
M. 'Dolgo'	Willowy, spreading, to 40 ft. tall and wide	Pink buds open to single white	Purple red, large. Good flavor, can be used for jelly	Moderate disease resistance
M. 'Donald Wyman'	Broad, to 20 ft. by 25 ft.	Pink to red buds open to single white	Shiny bright red, small, long lasting	Lustrous foliage. Disease resistant
M. floribunda JAPANESE FLOWERING CRABAPPLE	Broad, dense, to 15–25 ft.	Deep pink buds open to single white. Blooms fragrant, incredibly profuse	Yellow and red, small, do not last long	Moderate disease resistance
M. 'Harvest Gold'	Vigorous, narrow, to 30 ft. tall and 15 ft. wide	Pink buds open to single white. Late flowering	Yellow, showy, last until spring	High disease resistance
M. 'Hewe's Crab'	Medium, round-topped, about 20 ft. tall, 16 ft. wide	Pink buds open to 1-in. white in spring	Dull red with numerous white dots, streaked with greenish yellow; 1–1½ in.	Very popular for making cider. A good pollinator for 'Winesap' as well as other apple selections. Resistant to major diseases
M. 'Indian Magic'	Round headed, to 15–20 ft. tall and wide	Red buds open to single deep pink	Shiny red to orange, small, long lasting	Moderate susceptibility to disease
M. 'Indian Summer'	Round headed, to 18 ft. tall and wide	Single rose red	Bright red, long lasting	Good orange-red fall foliage color. High disease resistance
M. 'Jewelberry'	Dwarfish, dense, to 8 ft. by 12 ft.	Pink buds open to single white	Shiny red, ½ in. wide, long lasting	Bears young. Moderate disease resistance
M. 'Katherine'	Slow growing to 20 ft. tall and wide	Deep pink buds open to large double pink, quickly fade to white	Yellow with red cheek, very small	Fair disease resistance
M. 'Liset'	Roundish, dense, to 15–20 ft. tall and wide	Crimson buds open to single blooms of deep red to crimson	Dark red to maroon, persistent	Deep purplish green leaves. Fair disease resistance
M. 'Molten Lava'	Spreading, weeping, to 12 ft. tall and wide	Deep red buds open to single white	Red orange, small, last well on tree	Attractive yellow winter bark. Good disease resistance
M. 'Narragansett'	Broad, round headed, to 15 ft. tall and wide	Red buds open to single white with faint touch of pink	Bright red, ½ in. wide, showy	High disease resistance

M

MALUS

NAME	SIZE, HABIT	FLOWERS	FRUIT	COMMENTS
M. 'Pink Princess'	Low, broad, to 15 ft. by 12 ft.	Single rose pink	Deep red, small, lasts well on tree	Reddish green foliage. Good disease resistance
M. 'Prairifire'	Round headed, to 20 ft. tall and wide	Red buds open to single deep pinkish red blooms	Small, dark red, persistent	Leaves emerge reddish maroon, turn dark green. High disease resistance
M. 'Red Jade'	Irregular, weeping form; to 15 ft. tall and wide	Small single white	Bright red, heavy crop, holds well into fall	Moderate disease resistance
M. 'Red Jewel'	Small, rounded, to 15 ft. by 12 ft.	Large single white	Bright red, small, long lasting	Some disease resistance
M. sargentii SARGENT CRABAPPLE	Broad, dense, to 10 ft. by 20 ft.	Small single white; fragrant; profuse bloomer	Red, tiny, long lasting	Good disease resistance. 'Candymint' has red-edged pink flowers. 'Rosea', a pink form, may be more disease prone than the species
M. 'Snowdrift'	Rounded, dense, to 20–25 ft.	Red buds open to single white. Long bloom season	Orange red, small, long lasting	Good disease resistance
M. 'Strawberry Parfait'	Open, vase shaped, to 20 ft. by 25 ft.	Red buds open to single pink edged in red; profuse bloomer	Yellow with red cheek	High disease resistance ✳
M. 'Sugar Tyme'	Upright, oval, to 18 ft. by 15 ft.	Light pink buds open to single white; fragrant	Red, abundant, long lasting	High disease resistance ✳
M. 'Weeping Candied Apple'	Weeping, to 10–15 ft.	Single red	Bright red, small, persist all winter	Good disease resistance
M. zumi calocarpa (M. sieboldii zumi 'Calocarpa')	Dense, branching, rounded, to 25 ft. tall and wide	Single, open to pale pink, fade to white; fragrant	Glossy bright red, small, lasts well on tree	Susceptible to fireblight; usually resistant to scab

Crabapples are fine lawn trees. Planted near fences, they will heighten screening effect, provide blossoms and fruit, and still give planting room for primroses, spring bulbs, or shade-loving bedding plants. Prune only to build good framework, correct shape, or remove suckers. Crabapples can be trained as espaliers.

MALVA

MALLOW

Malvaceae

PERENNIALS OR BIENNIALS

✿ Zones US, MS, LS

☼ ☽ Full sun or light shade

⬤ Regular water

Malva alcea

Related to and somewhat resembling hollyhock (*Alcea*), but bushier, with smaller, roundish leaves. Easy to grow; need good drainage, average soil. Grow from seed; usually bloom first year. Use in perennial borders or for a quick tall edging. Plants not long lived.

M. alcea. Perennial. To 4 ft. by 2 ft. Saucer-shaped pink flowers, 2 in. wide, late spring to fall. Common kind is 'Fastigiata', a narrower grower that looks much like a hollyhock. Subject to root rot in hot, wet weather.

M. moschata. MUSK MALLOW. Perennial. Erect, branching, to 3 ft. tall, with finely cut leaves and inch-wide (or somewhat larger) flowers, summer to fall. Entire plant emits a mild, musky fragrance if brushed or bruised. 'Rosea' has rose pink flowers; 2-ft.-tall 'Alba' is white flowered.

🌱 **M. sylvestris.** FRENCH HOLLYHOCK. Perennial or biennial. Erect, bushy growth to 2–4 ft.; 2-in.-wide flowers appear all summer, often until frost. Common type (often sold as *M. zebrina*) has pale lavender-pink flowers with pronounced deep purple veining. 'Mauritiana' has deeper-colored flowers, often semidouble. Often seen in older gardens of the Lower South. Reseeds. Easy to grow.

Malvaceae. The mallow family contains many hundreds of species of mainly herbaceous plants and some shrubs and trees, often with lobed leaves and showy flowers. Ornamental members include *Hibiscus*, hollyhock (*Alcea*), mallow (*Malva*), and checkerbloom (*Sidalcea*). Commercially, the family is important as the source of cotton.

🌱 MALVAVISCUS arboreus drummondii

TURK'S CAP, TURK'S TURBAN

Malvaceae

PERENNIAL

✿ Zones LS, CS, TS

☼ ⬤ Partial or full shade

◐ ⬤ Little or regular water

Malvaviscus arboreus drummondii

Native to Florida, west to Texas, and Mexico. This spindly, shrubby perennial with semiwoody stems, almost evergreen in the Coastal

South, blooms from early summer right through fall, in light shade. May reach 9 ft. tall if soil is fertile and growing season long and warm, but usually 3–5 ft. Dies back to the ground in winter in the Lower and Coastal South. Yellow-green leaves are coarse textured, heart shaped, 2–3 in. wide, and borne on long petioles. Nodding, twisted, bright red flowers, 1–1½ in. long; prominent stamens are similar to hibiscus flowers before they open; they attract hummingbirds. Small, rounded, applelike fruits follow the flowers, changing from white to red as they ripen and fall. Tough, easy plant; tolerates alkaline, rocky soils, and drought.

MANDARIN ORANGE. See CITRUS, Mandarin

MANDEVILLA

Apocynaceae

EVERGREEN OR DECIDUOUS VINES

🌡 ZONES VARY BY SPECIES

☀️ ◐ FULL SUN OR PARTIAL SHADE

💧 REGULAR WATER

*Mandevilla
'Alice du Pont'*

Known for showy flowers, the genus *Mandevilla* includes plants that were formerly called *Dipladenia*. Flowers are saucer shaped, with tubular throats. Most species overwinter only in the Tropical South; elsewhere, treat as annuals or grow indoors or in greenhouse.

M. 'Alice du Pont' (M. splendens, M. amabilis, Dipladenia splendens, D. amoena). Evergreen. Zone TS; may grow as root-hardy perennial in Zone CS. To 20–30 ft., much less in containers (where it is usually grown). Twining stems; dark green, glossy, oval, 3–8-in.-long leaves. Clusters of pure pink, 2–4-in.-wide flowers appear among leaves, spring–fall. Even very small plant in 4-in. pot will bloom. Plant in rich soil and provide frame, trellis, or stake for support. Pinch young plant to induce bushiness.

M. boliviensis. Evergreen. Zone TS. Grows to 12 ft. as a vine; to 3 ft. tall, 5 ft. wide as a sprawling shrub. Glossy leaves. White flowers with yellow throats throughout the year.

M. laxa (M. suaveolens). CHILEAN JASMINE. Deciduous. Zones LS, CS, TS. Twines to 15 ft. or more. Leaves are long ovals, heart shaped at base, 2–6 in. long. Clustered summer flowers are white, 2 in. across, trumpet shaped, with powerful gardenia-like fragrance. Provide rich soil. If plant becomes badly tangled, cut to ground in winter; it will bloom on new growth. Roots hardy to about 5°F.

M. splendens (M. amabilis, M. 'Profusa', M. sanderi). Evergreen. Zone TS; may grow as root-hardy perennial in Zone CS. Similar to 'Alice du Pont', with same bloom period. 'Red Riding Hood', with deep red flowers, and white-blossomed 'Summer Snow' are lower growing and shrubbier than the species. Superb in hanging baskets.

MANGIFERA indica

MANGO

Anacardiaceae

EVERGREEN TREE

🌡 ZONE TS

☀️ FULL SUN

💧 MAINTAIN STEADY SOIL MOISTURE

⚠️ FRUIT CAN CAUSE A SKIN RASH FOR SOME PEOPLE

Mangifera indica

Large, attractive, fruit-bearing shade tree in south Florida. May remain shrubby and is likely to fruit only in most favored, frost-free locations. Yellow to reddish flowers in long clusters at branch ends. Oval fruits to 6 in. long, green to reddish or yellowish, with large flat pit and peach-flavored flesh. Some say the flavor has varnish or turpentine overtones; this quality tends to be more prevalent in seedlings. Leaves are large (8–16 in. long) and handsome; often purple or coppery

red when new, later turning dark green. Needs steady moisture but tolerates fairly poor, shallow soils.

MANILA GRASS. See ZOYSIA matrella

MAPLE. See ACER

Marantaceae. The arrowroot family consists of tropical or subtropical herbaceous plants with fleshy rhizomes or tubers. Most are grown for handsome foliage, a few for flowers. An example is *Calathea*.

MARANTA leuconeura

PRAYER PLANT

Marantaceae

PERENNIAL OR HOUSE PLANT

🌡 ZONE TS; OR INDOORS

◐ PARTIAL SHADE, INDIRECT LIGHT

💧 💧💧 AMPLE WATER DURING SUMMER

*Maranta leuconeura
erythroneura*

Native to tropical America. Dark green, satiny foliage, with light green and brown-black markings and silver or red veins, makes a striking ground cover in tropical gardens. During the day, the 5-in.-long leaves lie flat; at night, they fold toward the center; hence the common name "prayer plant." Plants spread by rhizomes, but soil must be rich and fast draining, and air very warm and humid. Indoors, place out of direct light; keep soil moist during growing season and use humidifier to keep air moist; maintain night temperature above 55°F. Indoors or outdoors, fertilize monthly during summer. Flowers insignificant. *M. l. erythroneura* has red veins; *M. l. kerchoviana*, rabbit's foot, has light green leaves with dark blotches, like animal tracks, on either side of midrib.

MARGINAL SHIELD FERN. See DRYOPTERIS marginalis

MARGUERITE. See CHRYSANTHEMUM frutescens

MARIGOLD. See TAGETES

MARJORAM. See ORIGANUM

MARLBERRY. See ARDISIA

MARSH FERN. See THELYPTERIS palustris

MARSH MARIGOLD. See CALTHA palustris

MASCAGNIA

ORCHID VINE

Malpighiaceae

DECIDUOUS VINES

🌡 ZONES VARY BY SPECIES

☀️ FULL SUN

💧 TOLERATE SOME DROUGHT

Mascagnia lilacina

Vines of Mexican origin bloom at hottest time of the year. Leaves in opposite pairs look like those of honeysuckle. Clusters of flowers are followed by oddly winged seedpods that somewhat resemble butterflies and are sometimes used in dried arrangements.

M. lilacina. LAVENDER ORCHID VINE. Zones CS, TS. To 15–20 ft., with 1½-in. leaves and lilac blue flowers followed by inch-wide "butterflies." Hardy to 15–18°F; leaves drop at 22°F.

M. macroptera. YELLOW ORCHID VINE. Zone TS. To 15 ft., with 3-in. leaves and abundant bright yellow clustered flowers followed by conspicuous, 2-in. yellow-green seedpods. Hardy to 22–24°F.

MATERNITY PLANT. See KALANCHOE daigremontiana

M

MATTEUCCIA struthiopteris

OSTRICH FERN

Polypodiaceae

FERN

🌿 ZONES US, MS

◐ LIGHT SHADE

● ◐ AMPLE TO REGULAR WATER

*Matteuccia
struthiopteris*

N ative to northern regions of North America. Best in Upper South. Clumps are narrow at base, spread out at top like a shuttlecock. Unfolding young fronds (fiddleheads) are edible. Plant can reach 6 ft. Spreads by underground rhizomes. Dormant in winter. Attractive woodland or waterside plant. Needs rich soil.

MATTHIOLA

STOCK

Brassicaceae (Cruciferae)

BIENNIALS OR PERENNIALS GROWN AS ANNUALS

🌿 ALL ZONES

◐ ◑ FULL SUN OR LIGHT SHADE

● REGULAR WATER

Matthiola incana

O ld-fashioned plants, especially well suited to the cottage garden. All have long, narrow gray-green leaves and luxuriant, scented flowers in erect, spikelike clusters.

M. incana. STOCK. Valued for fragrance, cut flowers. Oblong leaves to 4 in. long. Flowers single or double, 1 in. wide, with spicy-sweet scent. Colors include white, pink, red, purple, lavender, blue, yellow, cream. Blues and reds are purple toned; yellows tend toward cream.

Many strains are available. Earliest bloomer is Trysomic Seven Weeks (it blooms in 7 weeks), a branching plant to 12–15 in. tall. Ten Weeks, also branching, reaches 15–18 in. tall. Column stock and Double Giant Flowering are unbranched, 2–3 ft. tall; they can be planted 6–8 in. apart in rows and are ideal for cutting. Giant Imperial strain is branched, 2–2½ ft. tall, comes in solid or mixed colors.

Stock needs light, fertile soil and good drainage. In Upper South, plant in earliest spring to get flowers before hot weather; choose early bloomers. Elsewhere, plants set out in fall will bloom in winter or early spring. Take moderate frost but will not set flower buds if nights are too chilly; late planting delays bloom until spring. In areas where winter rainfall is heavy, plant in raised beds to ensure good drainage and prevent root rot.

M. longipe tala bicornis. EVENING SCENTED STOCK. Foot-tall plant with lance-shaped leaves to 3½ in. long. Small purplish flowers are not showy, but emit a powerful fragrance at night. Winter annual.

MAY APPLE. See PODOPHYLLUM peltatum

MAYHAW. See CRATAEGUS opaca

MAYPOP. See PASSIFLORA incarnata

MAZUS reptans

MAZUS

Scrophulariaceae

PERENNIAL

🌿 ZONES US, MS, LS, CS

◐ ◑ PARTIAL SHADE IN LOWER AND COASTAL SOUTH

● REGULAR WATER

Mazus reptans

S lender stems creep and root along ground, send up leafy branches 1–2 in. tall. Narrowish bright green leaves are 1 in. long, with a few

teeth along edges. Spring and early summer flowers, in clusters of two to five, are purplish blue with white and yellow markings, ¾ in. across. In shape, flowers resemble those of *Mimulus*. Use plants in rock garden or as small-scale ground cover; need rich soil. Take heavy foot traffic when planted between pavers. Evergreen in mild winters. White-flowering form of *M. reptans* often sold as *M. japonicus* 'Albiflora'.

MEADOW RUE. See THALICTRUM

MEADOW SAFFRON. See COLCHICUM

MEADOW SWEET. See ASTILBE, FILIPENDULA ulmaria

MELAMPODIUM

Asteraceae (Compositae)

ANNUALS AND PERENNIALS

🌿 ZONES VARY BY SPECIES

◯ FULL SUN

● MODERATE WATER

*Melampodium
leucanthum*

T hese tough, drought-tolerant plants produce masses of small daisies over a long period. Provide well-drained soil.

M. cinereum. BLACKFOOT DAISY. Perennial. Zones CS, TS. Native to limestone soils of Arkansas, Colorado, and Texas. Grows 4–12 in. tall. Similar to *M. leucanthum,* but not so hardy.

M. leucanthum. BLACKFOOT DAISY. Short-lived perennial. Zones US, MS, LS. To 1 ft. tall. Honey-scented white daisies with yellow centers bloom in spring, summer, and (in mild climates) sporadically during winter.

M. paludosum. MELAMPODIUM, BUTTER DAISY. Annual. All zones. To 3 ft. tall. Deep yellow daisies appear throughout summer and into fall; no deadheading required. Tolerates heat and humidity. Start seeds indoors for earliest bloom; or sow in ground after soil has warmed. Plants will also self-sow. 'Medallion' grows to 3 ft. tall and often becomes leggy by midsummer. 'Showstar' is denser and more compact, growing 1½–2 ft. tall, with showier blooms.

Melastomataceae. The melastoma family consists almost entirely of tropical shrubs and trees with strongly veined leaves and symmetrical flowers, such as princess flower (*Tibouchina*).

MELIA azedarach

CHINABERRY

Meliaceae

DECIDUOUS TREE

🌿 ZONES MS, LS, CS

◯ FULL SUN

● MODERATE WATER

◆ FRUIT IS POISONOUS IF INGESTED

Melia azedarach

T o 30–50 ft. high, with spreading, irregular habit. Leaves 1–3 ft. long, cut into many toothed, narrow or oval leaflets 1–2 in. long. In spring or early summer, bears loose clusters of lilac flowers, fragrant in evening. Blossoms are followed by hard, berrylike yellow fruits ½ in. across. Tough tree that tolerates heat, wind, poor alkaline soil, drought; valuable where others are hard to grow. Brittle wood makes it vulnerable to storm damage. Tends to self-sow and become a pest.

'Umbraculiformis', Texas umbrella tree, is less picturesque than the species. Grows to 30 ft., with dense, spreading, dome-shaped crown and drooping leaves.

M

MELISSA officinalis

LEMON BALM, SWEET BALM

Lamiaceae (Labiatae)

PERENNIAL HERB

⚡ ZONES US, MS, LS, CS

☼ ◐ SUN OR PARTIAL SHADE

💧 REGULAR WATER

Melissa officinalis

Grows to 2 ft. Light green, heavily veined leaves with lemon scent. White flowers are unimportant. Shear occasionally to keep compact. Likes rich soil. Very hardy; self-sows, spreads rapidly. Propagate from seed or root divisions. Leaves used in drinks, fruit cups, salads, fish dishes. Dried leaves help give lemon tang to sachets, potpourris.

MELON, MUSKMELON, CANTALOUPE

Cucurbitaceae

ANNUALS

⚡ ALL ZONES

☼ FULL SUN

💧 WATER MOST WHEN PLANTS ARE YOUNG

Melon

The true cantaloupe, a hard-shelled melon, is rarely grown in the U.S. Principal types cultivated here are muskmelons ("cantaloupes") and late melons. (See Watermelon for information on that fruit.)

Muskmelons are ribbed, with netted skin and usually salmon-colored flesh; they are more widely adapted than late melons. Some popular selections include 'Hale's Best', 'Honey Rock', and the hybrids 'Ambrosia', 'Mainerock', 'Samson', and 'Saticoy'. Hybrids are superior to others in disease resistance and uniformity of size and quality. (Choosing selections resistant to mildew and other diseases is particularly important.) Other muskmelons include small, highly perfumed selections from the Mediterranean region, such as white-fleshed 'Ha-Ogen' and orange-fleshed 'Chaca' and 'Charentais'.

Late melons are a varied group that includes honeydew, casaba, 'Crenshaw', 'Golden Beauty', 'Honey Ball', and 'Persian'. Because these melons need a longer growing season than muskmelons, they are less widely cultivated. They dislike high humidity and grow best in areas where summers are hot and relatively dry.

To ripen to full sweetness, melons need steady heat for 2½–4 months. Sow seed 2 weeks after average date of last frost; don't rush the season, since melons are truly tropical plants and will perish in even light frost.

You can grow melons on sun-bathed trellises, but heavy fruit must be supported in individual cloth slings. They are best grown in hills or mounded rows a few inches high at center; you will need to provide considerable space. Make hills about 3 ft. in diameter and space them 3–4 ft. apart; encircle each with a furrow for irrigation. Make rows 3 ft. wide and as long as desired, spacing them 3–4 ft. apart; make furrows for irrigation along either side. Plant seeds 1 in. deep—four or five seeds per hill, two or three seeds every 1 ft. in rows. When plants are well established, thin each hill to the best two plants; thin rows to one strong plant per foot. Fill furrows with water from time to time (furrows let you water plants without wetting foliage); do not keep soil soaked. Feed (in furrow) every 6 weeks.

To make melons taste sweeter, hold off watering a week or so before you expect to harvest the ripe fruit. To determine if a melon is ready for harvest, lift fruit and twist; if ripe, it will slip off the stem. A pleasant, perfumy fragrance also indicates ripeness.

MENTHA

MINT

Lamiaceae (Labiatae)

PERENNIAL HERBS AND GROUND COVERS

⚡ ZONES VARY BY SPECIES

☼ ◐ SUN OR PARTIAL SHADE

💧 REGULAR WATER

Mentha spicata

Spread rapidly by underground stems. Can be quite invasive. They grow almost anywhere but perform best in light, medium-rich, moist soil. Contain in pot or box to keep in bounds. Propagate from runners; replant every 3 years.

M. gentilis. GOLDEN APPLE MINT. Zones US, MS, LS, CS. To 2 ft. Smooth, deep green leaves, variegated yellow. Flowers inconspicuous. Use in flavoring foods. Foliage excellent in mixed bouquets.

M. piperita. PEPPERMINT. Zones US, MS, LS, CS. To 3 ft. Strongly scented, toothed, 3-in.-long leaves. Small purple flowers in 1–3-in. spikes. Leaves good for flavoring tea. *M. p. citrata*, called orange mint or bergamot mint, grows to 2 ft. and has broad, 2-in.-long leaves, small lavender flowers. It is used in potpourris or in flavoring foods. Crushed leaves have slight orange flavor.

M. pulegium. PENNYROYAL. Zones MS, LS, CS. Creeping plant grows a few inches tall with nearly round, 1-in. leaves. Small lavender flowers in tight, short whorls. Strong mint fragrance and flavor. Poisonous in large quantities but safe as a flavoring. Needs cool, moist site.

M. requienii. CORSICAN MINT, JEWEL MINT OF CORSICA. Zones LS, CS. Creeping, mat forming, to only ½ in. high. Tiny, round, bright green leaves give mossy effect. Tiny light purple flowers in summer. Good for planting between stepping-stones. Delightful minty or sagelike fragrance when leaves are bruised or crushed underfoot. Dislikes hot, wet weather, poor drainage, poor air circulation.

M. spicata. SPEARMINT. Zones US, MS, LS, CS. To 1½–2 ft. Dark green leaves, slightly smaller than those of peppermint; leafy spikes of purplish flowers. Use leaves fresh from garden or dried, for lamb, in cold drinks, as garnish, in apple jelly.

M. suaveolens. APPLE MINT. Zones US, MS, LS, CS. Stiff stems grow 1½–2½ ft. tall. Rounded leaves are slightly hairy, gray green, 1–4 in. long. Purplish white flowers in 2–3-in. spikes. Leaves have fragrance of apple-mint. 'Variegata', pineapple mint, has leaves with white markings, faint fragrance of pineapple. Species is usually sold as *M. rotundifolia*.

MERTENSIA virginica

VIRGINIA BLUEBELLS

Boraginaceae

PERENNIAL

⚡ ZONES US, MS, LS

◐ ● PARTIAL OR FULL SHADE

💧 REGULAR WATER

Mertensia virginica

A relative of forget-me-not (*Myosotis*); native to eastern U.S. Broadly oval, bluish green leaves form loose clumps that send up leafy, 1½–2-ft.-tall stems bearing loose clusters of nodding, 1-in. flowers. Buds are usually pink to lavender, but open to blue bells, sometimes with a pinkish cast. Appears and flowers early in spring; dies to ground soon after going to seed, usually by midsummer. Charming with naturalized daffodils or with ferns, trillium, bleeding heart in woodland garden.

Provide moist, rich soil. Use summer annuals to fill void after plants die back. Clumps can be left in place indefinitely; they will slowly spread. To get more plants, use volunteer seedlings or dig and divide clumps in early fall.

MESQUITE. See PROSOPIS

METASEQUOIA glyptostroboides

DAWN REDWOOD

Taxodiaceae

DECIDUOUS CONIFER

ZONES US, MS, LS

FULL SUN

BEST IN MOIST, WELL-DRAINED SOIL

Metasequoia glyptostroboides

Thought to have been extinct for thousands of years, but found growing in a few isolated sites in China during the 1940s. Pyramidal tree bearing small cones. Soft, light green needles turn light bronze in fall, then drop to reveal attractive winter silhouette. Branchlets tend to turn upward. Bark is reddish in youth, becomes darker and fissured in age. Trees grow moderately fast in Upper South, very fast elsewhere; can reach about 90 ft., but haven't been grown long enough in gardens to determine maximum height. Looks somewhat like bald cypress *(Taxodium distichum)*.

Grows best in good, organic, well-drained soil with regular water. Good lawn tree, though in time roots may surface. Not suited to dry areas or seacoast, since dry heat and salty ocean winds will burn foliage.

MEXICAN BUCKEYE. See UNGNADIA speciosa

MEXICAN FIREBUSH. See HAMELIA patens

MEXICAN FLAME VINE. See SENECIO confusus

MEXICAN GRASSTREE. See NOLINA longifolia

MEXICAN HAT. See RATIBIDA columnifera

MEXICAN HEATHER. See CUPHEA hyssopifolia

MEXICAN LILY. See HIPPEASTRUM reginae

MEXICAN ORANGE. See CHOISYA ternata

MEXICAN PALO VERDE. See PARKINSONIA aculeata

MEXICAN PETUNIA. See RUELLIA brittoniana

MEXICAN PLUM. See PRUNUS mexicana

MEXICAN SUNFLOWER. See TITHONIA rotundifolia

MICHAELMAS DAISY. See ASTER novi-belgii

MICHELIA

Magnoliaceae

EVERGREEN SHRUBS OR TREES

ZONES VARY BY SPECIES

SUN OR PARTIAL SHADE

REGULAR WATER

Michelia figo

Related to magnolias but bear numerous flowers among leaves rather than singly at branch ends. Plants are well known and appreciated for their fragrance. All need rich soil.

M. champaca. Tree. Zones CS, TS. To 25–30 ft. tall, with large glossy leaves to 10 in. long. Blooms off and on throughout the year, most heavily in winter and summer. Flowers many-petaled, pale orange, to 3 in. wide; national flower of Philippines. Rich, fruity fragrance is legendary.

M. doltsopa. Large shrub or tree. Zones CS, TS. To about 40 ft. tall. May be bushy in form or narrow and upright; choose plant for desired habit. Leaves thin, leathery, dark green, 3–8 in. long. Flowers open in winter from brown, furry buds that form in profusion among leaves near branch ends. Fragrant, 5–7-in.-wide, creamy or white blossoms with 12 to 16 petals; somewhat resemble flowers of saucer magnolia.

M. figo (M. fuscata). BANANA SHRUB. Zones LS, CS. Slow, dense growth to 6–8 ft., possibly to 15 ft. Glossy, 3-in.-long, medium green leaves. Heaviest bloom in spring, but scattered flowers often appear throughout summer. Flowers 1–1½ in. wide, creamy yellow shaded brownish purple, resembling small magnolia blossoms. Powerful fruity fragrance like that of ripe bananas; scent is strongest in warm, wind-free spot. Choice plant for entryway, corner plantings, or near a window. 'Port Wine' has rose to maroon flowers.

MICROBIOTA decussata

SIBERIAN CARPET CYPRESS

Cupressaceae

EVERGREEN SHRUB

ZONES US, MS

SUN OR PARTIAL SHADE

REGULAR WATER

Microbiota decussata

Native to Siberian mountains. Neat, sprawling shrub that resembles a trailing arborvitae. Shrub grows to about 1½ ft. tall and 7–8 ft. wide, with many horizontal or trailing plumelike branches closely set with scalelike leaves. Foliage is green in summer, turning purplish, reddish brown in winter. More shade tolerant than juniper. Requires excellent drainage. Good as a bank cover.

MILFOIL. See ACHILLEA millefolium

MILLETTIA reticulata

EVERGREEN RED WISTERIA

Fabaceae (Leguminosae)

SEMIEVERGREEN OR EVERGREEN VINE

ZONES CS, TS

FULL SUN

REGULAR WATER

Millettia reticulata

Vigorous, twining vine that can reach great size. Shiny, leathery leaves divided into leaflets like those of wisteria; evergreen only in the Tropical South. Tight clusters of dark purple-red flowers in fall have odor of cedar and camphor. Unlike those of true wisteria, they stand atop the foliage. An extremely fast grower when established; if permitted to climb into trees, it can overwhelm them. Best use is as cover for large arbor, pergola, or chain-link fence.

MIMOSA. See ACACIA baileyana, ALBIZIA julibrissin

MIMULUS hybridus

MONKEY FLOWER

Scrophulariaceae

ANNUAL

ALL ZONES

SUN OR LIGHT SHADE

REGULAR WATER

Mimulus hybridus

Smooth, succulent, medium green leaves form a mound to 1–1½ ft. high. Showy, velvety flowers are thought to resemble a grinning monkey face; they are funnel shaped, 2–2½ in. long, with two "lips." Colors range from cream through rose, orange, yellow, scarlet, and brown, usually with heavy brownish maroon spotting or mottling. Best suited to Upper South, where it tolerates full sun. Use in shady borders; or plant in hanging baskets or window boxes. Sow seed in spring for summer bloom, or set out plants for spring show.

MING ARALIA. See POLYSCIAS fruticosa

MINT. See MENTHA

MIRABILIS jalapa

FOUR O'CLOCK

Nyctaginaceae

TUBEROUS-ROOTED PERENNIAL

ALL ZONES; SEE BELOW

FULL SUN

MODERATE WATER

ALL PLANT PARTS ARE POISONOUS

Mirabilis jalapa

Perennial in Zones MS, LS, CS, TS; frosts kill it to ground but roots survive. In Upper South, treat as annual. Strong, bushy habit gives this plant the substance and character of a shrub: Erect, many-branched stems grow quickly to form a mounded clump 3–4 ft. high and wide. Deep green, oval, 2–6-in.-long leaves. Sweetly scented, trumpet-shaped flowers in red, yellow, or white, with variations of shades between. Blossoms open in midafternoon and stay open all night; bloom season runs midsummer through fall. Jingles strain is lower growing than old-fashioned kinds, has elaborately splashed and stained flowers in two or three colors. Four o'clock reseeds readily and has naturalized in many parts of the South. Hard, black seeds often exchanged by gardeners seeking special flower colors. Also advertised in agricultural market bulletins.

MISCANTHUS

MAIDEN GRASS, SILVER GRASS, EULALIA GRASS

Poaceae (Gramineae)

PERENNIAL GRASSES

ZONES US, MS, LS, CS

SUN OR LIGHT SHADE

REGULAR TO MODERATE WATER

Miscanthus sinensis

These are among the most popular ornamental grasses. All are large to very large clump-forming grasses; attractive flower clusters open as tassels and gradually expand into large plumes atop tall stalks in late summer or fall. Plumes are silvery to pinkish or bronze and last well into winter. Foliage is always graceful; may be broad or narrow, solid colored, striped lengthwise, or banded. In fall and winter, foliage clumps turn to shades of yellow, orange, or reddish brown, especially showy against snow or an evergreen background. Need little care. Cut back old foliage to the ground before new foliage sprouts in spring; divide clumps when vigor declines.

M. giganteus (M. floridulus). GIANT CHINESE SILVER GRASS. Can reach 10–14 ft., with leaves to 2½ ft. long, 1½ in. wide. Silvery flower plumes rise another 1–2 ft. above foliage. Leaves turn purplish green in fall, then drop off, leaving tall bare stalks over winter.

M. sinensis. JAPANESE SILVER GRASS, EULALIA GRASS. Variable in size and foliage. Flowers are held well above foliage clumps and may be cut for fresh or dry arrangements. All are attractive in borders or as focal points in a garden. Many selections available; new ones come to market every year. Here are a few of the choicest:

'Adagio'. To 2–4 ft., with gray foliage and pink flowers aging white.

'Autumn Light'. To 5–6 ft. Late bloom; red autumn foliage.

'Cabaret'. Clumps reach 6 ft. Leaves are striped with white. Reddish plumes turn creamy with age.

M. s. condensatus 'Silver Arrow'. Grows to 5–7 ft. White-striped leaves; silvery plumes.

'Cosmopolitan'. Narrow, erect, to 6 ft. or taller. Broad leaves have broad white stripes.

'Gracillimus'. MAIDEN GRASS. To 5–6 ft. Best-known selection. Reddish flowers borne late. Slender, weeping foliage with narrow white midrib turns orange or tan in the fall.

'Graziella'. To 5–6 ft., with narrow leaves and silvery plumes high above foliage. Orange fall color.

'Kirk Alexander'. Low growing (to 3 ft.); leaves horizontally banded with yellow. Tan flowers.

'Malepartus'. To 6–7 ft., with broad leaves that turn orange in fall. Rose pink plumes fade to silvery white.

'Morning Light'. To 4–5 ft. Leaves have white midrib and narrow stripes along leaf edges for overall silvery appearance. Reddish bronze flowers. One of the most elegant selections.

'Purpurascens'. Foliage clumps 3–4 ft. tall turn reddish orange in fall. Silvery plumes.

'Strictus'. PORCUPINE GRASS. Narrow, erect, to 5–6 ft., with creamy stripes that run across leaves. Copper flowers. A little more cold-hardy than the species.

'Yaku Jima'. One of the smaller growers (to 3–4 ft.). Slender green leaves and tan flowers.

'Zebrinus'. ZEBRA GRASS. Broadly arching clumps to 5–6 ft.; leaves banded with yellowish white. Coppery pink flowers age to white.

MITCHELLA repens

PARTRIDGEBERRY, TWINBERRY

Rubiaceae

EVERGREEN PERENNIAL

ZONES US, MS, LS

FULL SHADE

AMPLE TO REGULAR WATER

Mitchella repens

Attractive, small, creeping evergreen plant native to much of eastern North America. Roundish leaves less than 1 in. long, borne in pairs along trailing, rooting, somewhat woody stems. Paired small white flowers appear in late spring or early summer; these are followed by bright red berries less than ¼ in. wide. Small-scale ground cover best seen near eye level—on a shady bank or above a wall. Best in woodland garden among shade-loving native plants, such as ferns, mosses, may apple, and galax. Provide steady moisture and acid soil with plenty of leaf mold or other organic matter.

MOCK ORANGE. See CHOISYA ternata, PHILADELPHUS

MOLE PLANT. See EUPHORBIA lathyris

MOLINIA caerulea

MOOR GRASS

Poaceae (Gramineae)

PERENNIAL GRASS

ZONES US, MS

FULL SUN OR LIGHT SHADE

REGULAR WATER

Molinia caerulea
'Variegata'

Plant is long lived but slow growing, taking a few years to reach its full potential. Erect, narrow, light green leaves form a neat, dense clump 1–2 ft. tall and wide. In summer, yellowish to purplish flowers in narrow, spikelike clusters rise 1–2 ft. above clump; they turn to tan and last well into fall. Inflorescences are profuse but have a narrow structure that gives clump a see-through quality; they make good cut flowers. In late fall, both leaves and flower clusters break off and blow away. 'Skyracer' has foliage clumps to 3 ft. tall; flowers bring it to 7–8 ft. 'Windspiel' is similar. Leaves of 'Variegata' are striped lengthwise with creamy white; foliage clump is 1–1½ ft. tall, with purple flowers adding 6–12 in.

M

MOLUCCELLA laevis

BELLS-OF-IRELAND, SHELL FLOWER

Lamiaceae (Labiatae)

ANNUAL

☀ ZONES US, MS, LS

☼ FULL SUN

● REGULAR WATER

Moluccella laevis

Grows to about 2 ft. high. Flowers are carried almost from base in whorls of six. Showy part of flower is its surrounding large shell-like or bell-like, apple green calyx, very veiny and crisp textured; small white tube of united petals in center is inconspicuous. As cut flowers, spikes of little bells are attractive and quite long lasting, either fresh or dried; be sure to remove unattractive leaves.

Needs loose, well-drained soil. Doesn't perform well in the Coastal and Tropical South. Sow seed in ground in early spring for summer bloom. If weather is warm, refrigerate seed for a week before planting. For long spikes, fertilize regularly.

MONARDA

Lamiaceae (Labiatae)

PERENNIALS

☀ ZONES US, MS, LS

☼ ◑ LIGHT AFTERNOON SHADE IN LOWER SOUTH

● ● AMPLE TO REGULAR WATER

Monarda didyma

Bushy, leafy clumps spread rapidly at edges and can be invasive. Dark green leaves grow 4–6 in. long, have strong, pleasant odor like blend of mint and basil. In summer, upright square stems are topped by tight clusters of long-tubed flowers much visited by hummingbirds. Plant 10 in. apart. Divide every 3 or 4 years. Not long lived. Prone to mildew and other leaf diseases in humid weather.

🏛 **M. didyma.** BEE BALM, OSWEGO TEA. Native to eastern U.S. Basic species has scarlet flowers surrounded by reddish bracts. Garden selections and hybrids include scarlet 'Adam'; pink 'Croftway Pink' and 'Granite Pink'; 'Snow White'; and dark red 'Mahogany'. A very old selection, 'Cambridge Scarlet', is still widely grown. Mildew-resistant types include 'Violet Queen' and pink 'Marshall's Delight'. If spent flowers are removed, all selections bloom over 2 months or more. Don't let soil dry out.

M. fistulosa. BERGAMOT. Native from easternmost U.S. to Rocky Mountains. Lavender flowers to light pink encircled by whitish bracts are less showy than those of *M. didyma*. Best suited to wild garden.

M. punctata. SPOTTED HORSEMINT, DOTTED MINT. Native to eastern states. Usually reaches less than 3 ft. tall, smaller than the other species listed here. Flowers appear in midsummer, two or more whorled clusters per stem, yellow or pink, spotted with purple. Good plant for wildflower meadows, naturalized areas.

MONDO GRASS. See OPHIOPOGON japonicus, under LIRIOPE and OPHIOPOGON

MONEY PLANT. See LUNARIA annua

MONEYWORT. See LYSIMACHIA nummularia

MONKEY FLOWER. See MIMULUS hybridus

MONKEY PUZZLE TREE. See ARAUCARIA araucana

MONKSHOOD. See ACONITUM

SOUTHERN HERITAGE PLANTS
IDENTIFIED BY SYMBOL 🏛

MONSTERA

Araceae

EVERGREEN VINES

☀ ZONE TS; OR INDOORS

◑ FILTERED SHADE

● REGULAR WATER

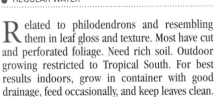

Monstera deliciosa

Related to philodendrons and resembling them in leaf gloss and texture. Most have cut and perforated foliage. Need rich soil. Outdoor growing restricted to Tropical South. For best results indoors, grow in container with good drainage, feed occasionally, and keep leaves clean. In poor light or low humidity, new leaves will be smaller. If tall plants get bare at base, replant in larger container and add younger, smaller plant to fill in; or cut plant back and let new shoots start.

M. deliciosa. SPLIT-LEAF PHILODENDRON, CUT-LEAF PHILODENDRON. Reaches great size if planted outdoors. Should be given protection from frost. Long, cordlike roots that hang from stems root into soil, help support plant on trees or moss logs. Leaves on youngest plants uncut; mature leaves heavy, leathery, dark green, deeply cut and perforated. Big plants may bear flowers similar to callas, with a thick, 10-in. spike surrounded by a boatlike white bract. Often sold as *Philodendron pertusum*.

M. friedrichsthalii. SWISS CHEESE PLANT. Leaves smaller, thinner in texture than those of *M. deliciosa*; leaf edges are wavy, not deeply cut. Common name comes from oval holes on either side of leaf midrib.

HARVESTING MONSTERA FRUIT

If heat, light, and humidity are right, monstera flower spikes may ripen a year after bloom into edible fruits with a flavor reminiscent of banana, pineapple, and apple. The green, caplike rind knocks off easily when fruit is ripe, exposing the sticky fruit kernels; before that stage, the taste can be painfully caustic.

MONTBRETIA. See CROCOSMIA crocosmiiflora, TRITONIA

MOONFLOWER, MOON VINE. See IPOMOEA alba

MOOR GRASS. See MOLINIA caerulea

Moraceae. The mulberry family includes deciduous or evergreen trees, shrubs, and vines. Individual fruits are tiny and single seeded but often aggregated into clusters. Fig *(Ficus)* and mulberry *(Morus)* are examples.

MORAEA IRIDIOIDES. See DIETES vegeta

MORAINE LOCUST. See GLEDITSIA triacanthos 'Moraine'

MOREA IRIS. See DIETES

MORNING GLORY. See IPOMOEA

MORUS

COMMON MULBERRY

Moraceae

DECIDUOUS TREES

☀ ZONES VARY BY SPECIES

☼ FULL SUN

● ● WATER NEEDS VARY BY SPECIES

Morus alba

Leaves of variable form, size, and shape—often on same tree. Yellow fall color ranges from subdued to bright. Fruits look like miniature blackberries and are favored by birds. For creating shade in home gardens, the most important kinds are fruitless forms of *M. alba.*

M. alba. WHITE MULBERRY, SILKWORM MULBERRY. Zones US, MS, LS, CS. Native to China. Fast-growing tree to 30–50 ft. high and wide, though often smaller. Leaves to 6 in. long, nearly as wide, often lobed. Fruit-bearing (female) trees have inconspicuous flowers followed by sweet but rather insipid fruit that stains decks, terraces, driveways, cars, and clothing. 'Pendula' ('Teas' Weeping') is a low-growing, strongly weeping form—but a fruit producer. Fruitless (male) forms are better for home gardens, though they produce much pollen. Males include 'Chaparral' (weeping), 'Fan-San', 'Fruitless', 'Kingan', and 'Stribling' ('Mapleleaf').

Plants tolerate heat, alkaline soil, seacoast conditions. They take some drought, but grow faster with regular water. Difficult to garden under because of heavy surface roots. Females produce multitudes of seedlings. If you have doubts about the sex of the tree, avoid white mulberry altogether.

M. australis 'Unryu' (M. bombycis 'Unryu'). CONTORTED MULBERRY. Zones US, MS, LS, CS. Grows to 25 ft. tall, with twisted, contorted branches useful in dry floral arrangements or for winter silhouette. Fast growth means that branches may be cut freely with no harm to tree. Leaves to 6 in. long. Regular water.

M. nigra. BLACK MULBERRY, PERSIAN MULBERRY. Zones US, MS, LS. To 30 ft. tall, with short trunk and dense, spreading head. Heart-shaped leaves 8 in. long. Large, juicy, dark red to black fruit. Tolerates some drought. 'Black Beauty' is smaller, 15 ft. tall. 'Illinois Everbearing' bears an early summer crop of fruit followed by a smaller autumn crop. 'Wellington' is a heavy-fruiting selection.

M. papyrifera. See Broussonetia papyrifera

M. rubra. RED MULBERRY. Zones US, MS, LS, CS. Native to eastern and central U.S. Well-behaved tree with upright, spreading habit. Somewhat resembles *M. alba,* but fruit is red in color, a bit larger, and better tasting. A much superior tree to *M. alba.* Best in rich, moist soil.

MOSES-IN-THE-CRADLE. See RHOEO spathacea

MOSS, IRISH and SCOTCH. See SAGINA subulata

MOSS ROSE. See PORTULACA

MOTHER FERN. See ASPLENIUM bulbiferum

MOTHER-IN-LAW'S TONGUE. See SANSEVIERIA trifasciata

MOTH ORCHID. See PHALAENOPSIS

MOUNTAIN ASH. See SORBUS

MOUNTAIN CAMELLIA. See STEWARTIA ovata

MOUNTAIN LAUREL. See KALMIA latifolia

MOUNTAIN ROCKCRESS. See ARABIS alpina

MOUNTAIN SILVER BELL. See HALESIA monticola

MRS. ROBB'S BONNET. See EUPHORBIA robbiae

MUGHO PINE. See PINUS mugo mugo

MUHLENBERGIA

Poaceae (Gramineae)
PERENNIAL GRASSES
✂ ZONES US, MS, LS, CS, EXCEPT AS NOTED
☼ ◐ FULL SUN OR LIGHT SHADE
◐ MODERATE TO LITTLE WATER

Mublenbergia lindheimeri

These slender-leafed, fall-flowering native grasses are showy enough to stand out in the garden. All require good drainage and resist heat and drought. Good choices for Texas and the Southwest.

M. dumosa. BAMBOO MUHLY. Zone CS. Native to Arizona, Mexico. To 3–6 ft. tall. Resembles bamboo, with narrow leaves and branching

flower clusters on slender, woody stems. Flowers barely distinguishable from foliage.

M. filipes (M. capillaris). GULF MUHLY. Native to Coastal Plains from North Carolina to Texas. Foliage clump to 2 ft. high. Reddish pink plumes increase height to 4–5 ft. Very showy in fall.

M. lindheimeri. LINDHEIMER'S MUHLY. Native to Texas and Mexico. Clump of very narrow blue-green leaves reaches 3 ft. tall. Silvery gray, 2–5-ft. plumes in fall are quite showy. Tolerates seasonally wet ground; also dry, rocky, chalky soil.

M. rigida. PURPLE MUHLY. Native to Texas, New Mexico, Mexico. Similar to *M. lindheimeri,* but plumes are dark purple in fall.

MULBERRY. See MORUS

MULLEIN. See VERBASCUM

MURRAYA paniculata (M. exotica)

ORANGE JESSAMINE
Rutaceae
EVERGREEN SHRUB
✂ ZONES CS, TS
☼ ◐ FULL SUN OR LIGHT SHADE
◐ REGULAR WATER

Murraya paniculata

Fast-growing plant to 6–15 ft. tall and wide. Good as hedge, filler, foundation plant. Sometimes grown as small, single- or multitrunked tree. Open habit; graceful, pendulous branches with glossy dark green leaves divided into three to nine oval, 1–2-in. leaflets. Flowers are white, ¾-in. bells with jasmine fragrance. Blooms in late summer and fall, sometimes in spring. Mature plants have small red fruit. Needs rich soil, frequent feeding. Slowly recovers beauty after cold, wet winters. Attracts bees.

A dwarf form is usually sold as *M. exotica.* It is slower growing, more upright and compact, reaching 6 ft. tall, 4 ft. wide. Leaves are lighter green, leaflets smaller and stiffer. Bloom is usually less profuse.

MUSA

BANANA
Musaceae
PERENNIALS, SOME TREELIKE IN SIZE
✂ ZONES VARY BY SPECIES; OR GREENHOUSE
☼ ◐ FULL SUN OR PARTIAL SHADE
◐ ◐◐ AMPLE TO REGULAR WATER

Musa paradisiaca seminifera

Bananas described here include tall, medium, and dwarf plants, all fast growing. All have soft, thickish stems and spread by suckers or underground roots to form clumps. Spectacular long, broad leaves are easily tattered by strong winds, so plant in protected sites. Fruiting requires a very long growing season, so fruits seldom appear outside the Tropical South. In areas where plants aren't winter-hardy, store them for winter. Cut off top of plant in fall, lift heavy corm, and store it in a garage or basement that doesn't freeze. No water or fertilizer needed until planted out after last spring frost. Give rich soil; feed heavily.

M. acuminata 'Dwarf Cavendish' (M. cavendishii, M. nana). Zones CS, TS. To 6–8 ft. tall, with leaves 5 ft. long, 2 ft. wide. Large, heavy flower clusters with reddish to dark purple bracts, yellow flowers. In warmest gardens, can bear sweet, edible, 6-in. bananas. 'Enano Gigante' is similar, but its young leaves have red markings. Some authorities place these fruiting types under *M. paradisiaca.*

M. coccinea. RED BANANA. Zone TS. Ornamental species to 4½ ft. tall, with leaves 3½ ft. long, 1½ ft. wide. Flowers, on upright stalks, are bright scarlet red with yellow tips, very showy and long lasting as cut flowers. Fruits just 2 in. long, not prized for eating.

M. ornata. FLOWERING BANANA. Zone TS. Grows to 9 ft. tall, with leaves 4–6 ft. long and 1–1½ ft. wide and red-purple midribs on undersides. Erect flower stalks with pale pink or pale purple bracts tipped with yellow. Used as cut flowers. Fruits small, to 3 in. long, not for eating.

M. paradisiaca (M. sapientum). Zones CS, TS. Many ornamental and edible forms. Most common type is often called *M. p. seminifera.* Large clump to 20 ft. tall, with leaves to 9 ft. Drooping flower stalk with powdery purple bracts; fruit (usually seedy and inedible) sometimes follows. Many selections are available.

Musaceae. The banana family consists of giant herbaceous plants that resemble palm trees; the bases of the enormous leaves form a false trunk. *Musa* is only one member of the family.

MUSCARI

GRAPE HYACINTH

Liliaceae

BULBS

❀ ZONES US, MS, LS, EXCEPT AS NOTED

☼◑ FULL SUN OR LIGHT SHADE

💧 REGULAR WATER DURING GROWTH AND BLOOM

Muscari armeniacum

Clumps of grassy, fleshy leaves appear in fall and live through cold and snow. Small, urn-shaped, blue or white flowers in tight spikes appear in early spring. Plant 2 in. deep in fall, setting bulbs in masses or drifts under flowering fruit trees or shrubs, in edgings and rock gardens, or in containers. Very long lived. Lift and divide when bulbs become crowded. Plants self-sow under favorable conditions.

M. armeniacum. Bright blue flowers on 4–8-in. stems above heavy cluster of floppy foliage. 'Cantab' is lower growing, has neater foliage, and produces clear light blue flowers later than species. 'Blue Spike' has double blue flowers in a tight cluster at top of spike.

M. azureum (Hyacinthella azurea, Hyacinthus azureus). Between hyacinth and grape hyacinth in appearance. Stalks 4–8 in. high have tight clusters of fragrant, bell-shaped (not urn-shaped) sky blue flowers.

🌱 **M. botryoides.** COMMON GRAPE HYACINTH. Most cold-hardy of the commonly grown grape hyacinths. Medium blue flowers on 6–12-in. stems. 'Album' has white flowers.

M. comosum. FRINGE HYACINTH, TASSEL HYACINTH. Unusual, rather loose clusters of shredded-looking flowers borne on 1–1½-ft. stems. In the species, blossoms are greenish brown on lower part of spike, bluish purple at top. 'Monstrosum' ('Plumosum'), feathered or plume hyacinth, bears violet blue to reddish purple flowers like shredded coconut.

M. latifolium. Zones US, MS. Largest and possibly the showiest of the grape hyacinths. Bears deep indigo blue flowers on 1-ft. stems. Plants have a single large leaf.

M. tubergenianum. Stems to 8 in. tall. Flowers at top of spike are dark blue; those lower down are light blue.

MUSTARD

Brassicaceae (Cruciferae)

ANNUAL

❀ ALL ZONES

☼ FULL SUN

💧 REGULAR WATER

Mustard

Curly-leaf mustard somewhat resembles curly-leaf kale in appearance. It is usually cooked like spinach or cabbage; young leaves are sometimes eaten raw in salads or used as garnishes. Tendergreen mustard has

smooth dark green leaves. It ripens earlier than curly mustard and is more tolerant of hot, dry weather. 'Red Giant' ('Chinese Red'), with large, crinkled leaves with strong red shadings, is handsome enough for a border. Use tendergreen mustard when young as a salad green; older leaves are useful as boiled greens.

Mustard is fast and easy to grow; it will be ready for the table 35 to 60 days after planting. Sow in early spring and make successive sowings when young plants are established. Thrives in cool weather but quickly goes to seed in summer heat. Sow in late summer for fall use. In the Coastal and Tropical South, plant again in fall and winter. Thin seedlings to stand 6 in. apart in rows. Harvest outer leaves as needed.

MYOSOTIS

FORGET-ME-NOT

Boraginaceae

PERENNIALS, BIENNIALS, AND ANNUALS

❀ ZONES US, MS, LS

◑ PARTIAL SHADE

💧💧 AMPLE TO REGULAR WATER

Myosotis sylvatica

Both forget-me-not species feature exquisite, typically blue springtime flowers, tiny but profuse. They grow easily and thickly as ground covers.

M. scorpioides. Perennial. Similar in most respects to *M. sylvatica*, but grows lower and blooms over an even longer season, and roots live over from year to year. Flowers, about ¼ in. wide, are blue with yellow centers, pink, or white. Bright green, shiny, oblong leaves. Plant spreads by creeping roots. Does well in moist soil or average garden soil.

M. sylvatica. Annual or biennial. To 6–12 in. Soft, hairy leaves, ½–2 in. long, set closely along stem. Clear blue, white-eyed flowers to ⅓ in. wide loosely cover upper stems. Flowers and seeds profusely for a long season, beginning in late winter or early spring. With habit of reseeding, plant will persist in garden for years unless weeded out. Often sold as *M. alpestris*. Improved selections are available, best of which are 'Blue Ball' and 'Royal Blue Improved'. Performs best in cool, moist growing conditions—in woodland gardens, along stream beds, around pond edges.

MYRICA

WAX MYRTLE, BAYBERRY

Myricaceae

EVERGREEN OR DECIDUOUS SHRUBS OR TREES

❀ ZONES VARY BY SPECIES

☼◑ FULL SUN OR PARTIAL SHADE

💧💧💧 WATER NEEDS VARY BY SPECIES

Myrica pensylvanica

Several species are useful as screen plants, informal hedges, or roadside plantings. Foliage is pleasantly aromatic. Although none is showy in flower, female plants bear attractive though inconspicuous fruits favored by birds. Generally tough, adaptable plants with no serious pests.

M. cerifera. WAX MYRTLE. Evergreen shrub or tree. Zones MS, LS, CS, TS. Native to southeastern U.S. Grows quickly to 15–20 ft., possibly taller. Leaves glossy dark green, to 3½ in. long. Grayish white fruits are heavily coated with a wax valued in candle making. Good specimen tree, hedge, screen, corner plant. Good plant for beach; tolerates drought, sand, salt air.

M. gale. SWEET FERN, SWEET GALE. Deciduous shrub. Zone US. Native to much of the Northern Hemisphere. Dense, erect growth to as tall as 6 ft., more typically 2–4 ft. Grown for fragrant leaves, to 2½ in. long. Takes regular moisture or boggy conditions.

M. pensylvanica. BAYBERRY. Deciduous to semievergreen shrub. Zones US, MS. Native to eastern U.S. Dense, compact to 9 ft. Leaves about 4 in. long, glossy green, dotted with resin glands. Roundish fruit is covered with white wax—bayberry wax used for candles. Tolerates seashore conditions—poor sandy or salty soil, wind. Regular water.

MYROBALAN. See PRUNUS cerasifera

Myrsinaceae. This family consists of evergreen shrubs and trees with (usually) inconspicuous flowers, attractive foliage and habit, and sometimes showy fruits. Marlberry *(Ardisia)* is a representative of the group.

Myrtaceae. The immense myrtle family of trees and shrubs is largely tropical and subtropical. Leaves are evergreen and often aromatic. Flowers are often showy, thanks to large tufts of stamens. Fruits may be fleshy *(Feijoa)* or dry and capsular *(Eucalyptus)*. Other family members include myrtle *(Myrtus),* bottlebrush *(Callistemon),* and guava *(Psidium).*

MYRTLE. See MYRTUS communis, VINCA

MYRTUS communis

MYRTLE

Myrtaceae

EVERGREEN SHRUB

ZONE CS

FULL SUN OR PARTIAL SHADE

MODERATE WATER

Myrtus communis

R ounded form to 5–6 ft. high, 4–5 ft. wide. Old plants can reach treelike proportions, to 15 ft. tall and 20 ft. across. Glossy bright green leaves are pointed, 2 in. long, pleasantly aromatic when brushed or bruised. White, sweet-scented, ¾-in. flowers with many stamens bloom in summer; these are followed by bluish black, ½-in. berries. Any soil, but good drainage is essential. Good formal or informal hedge or screen. Can also be trained to reveal attractive branches.

Named selections vary in foliage character and overall size. 'Variegata' fits basic species description but has white-edged leaves. 'Boetica' is especially upright, with thick, twisted branches and larger, darker leaves, while 'Buxifolia' has small leaves like a boxwood. Dwarf forms include 'Compacta', a small-leafed selection popular for edgings and low formal hedges; 'Compacta Variegata', similar but with white-margined foliage; and 'Microphylla', with tiny, closely set leaves.

☗ NANDINA domestica

NANDINA, HEAVENLY BAMBOO

Berberidaceae

EVERGREEN OR SEMIDECIDUOUS SHRUB

ZONES US, MS, LS, CS

SUN OR SHADE; COLORS BETTER IN SUN

REGULAR TO MODERATE WATER

Nandina domestica

A true survivor. Old plants often seen growing in cemeteries, overgrown gardens, on abandoned homesites, where they fruit and flower for decades with absolutely no care. Nandina takes sun or shade and tolerates drought, though well-drained soil is essential. No serious pests. Hardy shrub everywhere, though semievergreen or deciduous in the Upper South. Loses leaves at 10°F; stems are damaged at 5°F, but plant usually recovers fast.

Belongs to the barberry family but is reminiscent of bamboo in its lightly branched, canelike stems and delicate, fine-textured foliage. Slow to moderate growth to 6–8 ft. Spreads slowly by stolons to form large clumps. Can be divided in spring, winter, or fall. Leaves intricately divided into

many 1–2-in., pointed, oval leaflets, creating lacy pattern. Foliage expands pinkish and bronzy red, then turns to soft light green. Picks up purple and bronze tints in fall; often turns fiery crimson in winter, especially in sun and with some frost. Pinkish white or creamy white blossoms in loose, erect, 6–12-in. clusters at branch ends, late spring or early summer. If plants are grouped, shiny red berries follow the flowers; single plants seldom fruit as heavily. Berries supply winter food for birds; clusters cut for holiday decorations last a long time.

Best in rich soil with regular water, but its roots can even compete with tree roots in dry shade. Foliage may become chlorotic in alkaline soil. To reduce height, use hand pruners, never hedge shears. Maintain natural look by pruning each stalk to a different height, cutting back to a tuft of foliage. Renew neglected clumps by cutting one-third of the main stalks to the ground each year for 3 years. Good for screen, containers. Selections include the following:

'Alba' *(N. d. leucocarpa).* Standard-size plant with creamy white berries and yellowish green foliage that turns yellow in fall. More subject to cold damage than the species.

'Compacta'. DWARF NANDINA. Lower growing than species (4–5 ft.), with narrower, more numerous leaflets; has very lacy look.

'Fire Power'. Compact plant to 2 ft. tall and wide. Red-tinged summer foliage turns bright red in winter.

'Gulf Stream' ('Compacta Nana'). Slow-growing, dense mound, 3–4 ft. tall. Dark blue-green summer foliage; good red foliage in winter. Does not sucker. No berries.

'Harbour Dwarf'. HARBOUR DWARF NANDINA. Freely spreading, low-growing (1½–2-ft.) plant. Underground rhizomes send up stems several inches from parent plant. Winter color ranges from orange red to bronzy red. Good ground cover.

'Moyers Red'. Standard-size plant with broad leaflets. Brilliant red winter color in areas that get frost.

'Nana' ('Nana Purpurea', 'Atropurpurea Nana'). To 1–2 ft. tall. Coarse foliage, mottled green, purplish red, and yellow green, with somewhat cupped or crinkled leaflets. Out of place in most gardens. Much overused.

'Woods Dwarf'. Rounded form to 3–4 ft. tall, densely foliaged, crimson orange to scarlet in winter.

'Yellow Berries'. Similar to species in habit but its light green foliage lacks typical reddish bronze tinge; berries are creamy yellow, not red.

NANKING CHERRY. See PRUNUS tomentosa

NANNYBERRY. See VIBURNUM lentago

☗ NARCISSUS

DAFFODIL

Amaryllidaceae

BULBS

ZONES US, MS, LS, CS, EXCEPT AS NOTED

SUN; LATE KINDS LAST WELL IN LIGHT SHADE

REGULAR WATER DURING GROWTH AND BLOOM

Narcissus—Daffodil

T hese spring-flowering bulbous plants are valuable in many ways. They are permanent, increasing from year to year; they stand up to cold and heat; they are useful in many garden situations; and they provide fascinating variety in flower form and color. Most offer early, midseason, and late selections for extended bloom season, starting in winter in the Lower and Coastal South. Most types are hardy to −30°F (exceptions are noted). Finally, rodents and deer won't eat them—good news for gardeners in areas where those creatures are common.

Leaves are straight and flat (strap shaped) or narrow and rushlike. Flowers are composed of ring of segments (usually called petals) that are at right angles to the corona or crown (also called trumpet or cup, depending on its length) in center. Flowers may be single or clustered. Colors are basically yellow and white, but there are many variations— orange, red, apricot, pink, cream.

▶

Narcissus Divisions (Groups)

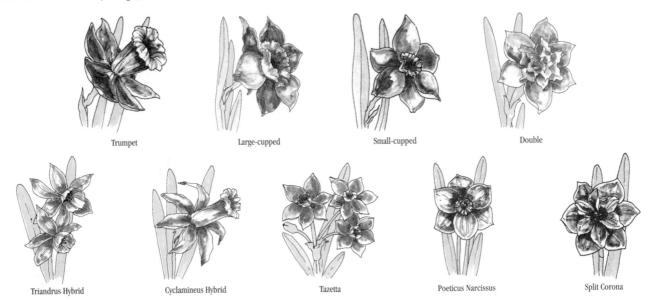

Trumpet   Large-cupped   Small-cupped   Double

Triandrus Hybrid   Cyclamineus Hybrid   Tazetta   Poeticus Narcissus   Split Corona

Flowers usually face sun; keep that in mind when planting. Use under trees and flowering shrubs, among ground cover plantings, near water, in woodland gardens, or in borders. Naturalize in sweeping drifts where space is available. Good in containers; fine cut flowers.

Plant bulbs as early in fall as you can get them. Look for solid, heavy bulbs. Plant with about 5–6 in. of soil over tops of bulbs (3–4 in. for smaller bulbs). Set bulbs about 8 in. apart and you won't have to divide them for a number of years.

Let foliage mature and yellow naturally after bloom. Lift and divide clumps of daffodils when flowers get smaller and fewer in number; wait until foliage has died down. Don't forcibly break away any bulbs that are tightly joined to mother bulb; remove only those that come away easily. Replant at once, or store for only a short time—not more than 3 weeks.

Following are the generally recognized divisions of daffodils and representative selections in each division.

Trumpet daffodils. Trumpet is as long as or longer than surrounding flower segments. Yellows are the most popular; old selection 'King Alfred' best known, top seller, although newer 'Unsurpassable' and 'William the Silent' are superior. White selections include 'Cantatrice', 'Empress of Ireland', 'Mount Hood'. Bicolors with white segments, yellow cup, include 'Spring Glory', 'Trousseau'. Reverse bicolors like 'Spellbinder' have white cup and yellow segments.

Large-cupped daffodils. Cups are more than one-third the length of flower segments, but not as long as segments. Selections include 'Carlton' and 'Carbineer', yellow; 'Ice Follies', white; 'Binkie' and 'Mrs. R. O. Backhouse', bicolors.

Small-cupped daffodils. Cups less than one-third the length of segments. Less widely available; for specialists.

DAFFODILS IN CONTAINERS

For maximum show, set bulbs close together, the tips level with soil surface. Place pots in well-drained trench or cold frame and cover with 6–8 in. of moist peat moss, wood shavings, or sand. Look for roots in 8 to 10 weeks (carefully tip soil mass from pot), then move pots to greenhouse, cool room, or sheltered garden spot to bloom. Keep well watered until foliage yellows; then plant in garden. Sink pots in borders when flowers are almost ready to bloom, then lift pots when flowers fade.

Double daffodils. 'Golden Ducat'; 'Mary Copeland', white and bright red; 'Texas', yellow and orange scarlet; 'White Lion', creamy white and yellow; 'Windblown', white and pale lemon.

Triandrus hybrids. Cups at least two-thirds the length of flower segments. Clusters of medium-size, slender-cupped, often nodding flowers. 'Hawera', just 8 in. tall, has four to six lemon yellow flowers with recurved segments per stem. Good for naturalizing; will spread by seed. 'Silver Chimes' has six or more yellow-cupped white flowers per stem. 'Thalia' is a favorite white with two or three beautifully proportioned flowers per stem.

Cyclamineus hybrids. Early medium-size flowers with recurved segments. Gold, bright to creamy pale yellow, and white with yellow or orange cup. Selections include 'February Gold', 'February Silver', 'Jack Snipe', 'Jetfire', 'Peeping Tom', and 'Tête à Tête'.

Jonquilla hybrids. Clusters of two to four rather small, very fragrant flowers. Yellow (like 'Suzy' and 'Trevithian'), soft yellow (like miniature 'Baby Moon'), orange, ivory.

Tazetta and Tazetta hybrids. Hardy to about 10°F. These are polyanthus or bunch-flowered daffodils with small-cupped white and yellow flowers in clusters. Good double selections are 'Cheerfulness' (white) and 'Golden Cheerfulness'. 'Minnow' (white, yellow cup) is a pretty dwarf, 6–8 in. tall. Division also includes 'Geranium', paper white narcissus, and *N. tazetta* 'Orientalis'. These last two, along with 'Cragford' (white, scarlet cup) and 'Grand Soleil d'Or' (golden yellow), can be grown indoors in bowls of pebbles and water. Keep dark and cool until growth is well along, then slowly bring into light.

Narcissus tazetta 'Orientalis'

Poeticus narcissus. POET'S NARCISSUS. Late white flowers with shallow, broad yellow cups edged red. 'Actaea' is largest.

Heirloom species. These old favorites often can be seen today blooming at old homesites, graveyards, and along roadsides throughout the South.

Narcissus bulbocodium

N. bulbocodium. HOOP PETTICOAT DAFFODIL. Hardy to −10°F. To 6 in. tall, with little, upward-facing flowers that are mostly trumpet, with very narrow, pointed segments. Deep and pale yellow selections.

N. 'Butter and Eggs' ('Golden Phoenix', 'Aurantius Plenus'). An old Southern favorite similar to *N. pseudonarcissus* 'Telemoneus Plenus', but flowers open dependably throughout climate range and are softer colored, without streaks.

N. cyclamineus. Hardy to −10°F. Backward-curved lemon yellow segments and narrow, tubular golden cup; 6 in. high.

N. jonquilla. JONQUIL. Cylindrical, rushlike leaves. Clusters of early, very fragrant, golden yellow flowers with short cups.

N. medioluteus. TWIN SISTERS. To 14 in. tall. Two flowers per stem; white petals, small yellow cup. Very late. Last daffodil of season.

N. odorus. CAMPERNELLE JONQUIL. A sweet-scented, old-fashioned favorite. Often found in older gardens and cemeteries in Texas, Louisiana, and Arkansas. To 12 in. tall. Golden yellow bell cups with recurved round petals, two to four flowers per stem. Leaves rushlike. Tolerates heavy clay and limy soils. *N. odorus* 'Plenus' has double flowers.

N. recurvus (N. poeticus recurvus). PHEASANT'S EYE. Old favorite. To 12 in. tall. Small yellow cup with green center "eye" and red rim, and pure white, reflexed petals.

N. pseudonarcissus 'Telemoneus Plenus'. To 12–14 in. tall. Double flowers. Many consider it synonymous with 'Van Sion'. Flowers often fail to open properly in warm, humid springs of the Lower and Coastal South.

N. triandrus. ANGEL'S TEARS. Clusters of small white or pale yellow flowers on stems to 10 in. Rushlike foliage.

Miscellaneous. This group serves as a catchall for a variety of new flower forms. Typical are 'Baccarat', light yellow with deeper yellow corona cut into six equal lobes; and 'Cassata', white with ivory split corona, the segments of which lie flat along the petals.

SUREFIRE DAFFODILS FOR THE SOUTH

These daffodils bloom dependably in most areas and increase with little care: 'Carlton', 'Ice Follies', 'Thalia', 'Tête à Tête', 'Hawera', 'Geranium', 'Trevithian', 'February Gold', campernelle, and hoop petticoat.

NASTURTIUM. See TROPAEOLUM

NATAL IVY. See SENECIO macroglossus

NATAL PLUM. See CARISSA macrocarpa

NECTARINE. See PEACH and NECTARINE

NEEDLE GRASS. See STIPA

NEEDLE PALM. See RHAPIDOPHYLLUM hystrix

NELUMBO (Nelumbium)

LOTUS

Nymphaeaceae

AQUATIC PLANTS

☀ ALL ZONES

☀ ◗ FULL SUN OR PARTIAL SHADE

💧 LOCATE IN PONDS, WATER GARDENS

These are water plants. If you acquire started plants in containers, put them in pond with 8–12 in. of water over soil surface. If you get roots, plant in spring, horizontally, 4 in. deep, in 1–1½-ft.-deep container of fairly rich soil. Place soil surface 8–12 in. under water. Huge round leaves attached at center to leafstalks grow above water level. Large, fragrant flowers form in summer. Ornamental woody fruit, perforated with holes like a salt shaker, good

Nelumbo nucifera

SOUTHERN HERITAGE PLANTS
IDENTIFIED BY SYMBOL 🏛

for dried arrangements. Roots should not freeze; where freezing is possible, cover pond or fill it deeper with water.

N. lutea (Nelumbium luteum). AMERICAN LOTUS. Similar to following but somewhat smaller in leaf and flower. Flowers are pale yellow.

N. nucifera (Nelumbium nelumbo). INDIAN or CHINESE LOTUS. Round leaves, 2 ft. or wider, carried 3–6 ft. above water surface. Pink, 4–10-in.-wide flowers carried singly on stems. Both tubers and seeds are esteemed in Chinese cookery, and the entire plant holds great religious significance for Buddhists. White, rose, and double selections exist; dwarf forms suitable for pot culture are becoming available.

🏛 NEOMARICA gracilis

WALKING IRIS

Iridaceae

PERENNIAL

☀ ZONES CS, TS; OR INDOORS

☀ ◗ FULL SUN OR PARTIAL SHADE

💧 REGULAR WATER

Neomarica gracilis

Native from southern Mexico to Brazil. Tropical iris that grows outdoors in the Coastal and Tropical South. Heavy mulching will help to protect roots through an occasional frost, but plant is badly damaged by prolonged cold. Leaves to 2½ ft. long, 1 in. wide, in fanlike, 2-ft.-tall clumps. In late spring and summer, white flowers with blue markings bloom toward the ends of 2-ft.-long stalks, which look like leaves. In loose, moist, fertile soil, plant "walks" by producing roots where stalks touch soil. Grow in containers or as ground cover. Fertilize regularly through summer.

NEOREGELIA

Bromeliaceae

BROMELIADS

☀ ZONE TS; OR INDOORS

◐ ● PARTIAL OR FULL SHADE

💧 KEEP WATER IN CUP AT BASE OF ROSETTE

Neoregelia carolinae

Bromeliads with rosettes of leathery leaves, often strikingly colored or marked; short spikes of usually inconspicuous flowers buried in hearts of rosettes. Need light, open, fast-draining planting mix that holds moisture but does not exclude air. Feed lightly. Grow outdoors in sheltered, frost-free location in a mixed herbaceous border; can also be grown on tree branch with sphagnum moss around roots. In cold-winter areas, lift in fall, pot up, and bring inside. Indoors, give strong indirect light.

N. carolinae. Many narrow, shiny leaves 1 ft. long, 1½ in. wide. Medium green leaves turn rich red at base as plant approaches bloom. 'Tricolor' has leaves striped lengthwise with white. Center turns bright red.

N. spectabilis. PAINTED FINGERNAIL PLANT. Leaves are olive green with bright red tips, 1 ft. long and 2 in. wide. Plant takes on bronzy color in strong light.

NEPETA

Lamiaceae (Labiatae)

PERENNIALS

☀ ZONES US, MS, LS

☀ ◗ AFTERNOON SHADE IN LOWER SOUTH

💧 MODERATE WATER

Nepeta cataria

Vigorous, spreading, aromatic-leafed plants of the mint family. Produce flowers in shades of blue or white. Will tolerate regular moisture if soil is well drained. ▶

N

N. cataria. CATNIP. To 2–3 ft. high, with downy gray-green leaves and clustered lavender or white flowers at branch tips in late spring, early summer. Easy grower in light soil; reseeds readily. Attractive to cats; some fall into a rapturous frenzy, rolling wildly on the plants. Sprinkle dried leaves over cats' food or sew some into toy cloth mouse. Some people use catnip to flavor tea.

N. faassenii. CATMINT. Makes soft, gray-green, undulating mounds to 1½ ft. high in bloom. The small leaves (like those of catnip) are attractive to cats, who enjoy nibbling foliage and rolling in plantings. Loose spikes of lavender blue flowers are produced in late spring and early summer. If dead spikes prove unsightly, shear them back; this may bring on another bloom cycle. Set plants 1–1½ ft. apart for ground cover. Often sold as *N. mussinii.* 'Dropmore Hybrid' is taller than the species (to 2 ft.); 'Six Hills Giant' is taller still (2–3 ft.).

N. sibirica. Dark green clump to 2–3 ft. high, topped by 10-in. spikes of bright blue flowers in early summer. 'Souvenir d'Andre Chaudron' ('Blue Beauty'), larger flowered than the species, is a compact grower to 1½ ft. high.

NEPHROLEPIS

SWORD FERN

Polypodiaceae

FERNS

🌿 ZONE TS; OR INDOORS

◐ ● PARTIAL OR FULL SHADE

● REGULAR WATER

Nephrolepis exaltata 'Bostoniensis'

Tough, and easy to grow, these are the most widely used of all ferns. (For native western sword fern, see *Polystichum munitum*.) For house plants, provide well-drained fibrous soil, monthly applications of dilute liquid fertilizer, and strong indirect light. Sometimes used as a ground cover in frost-free areas.

N. cordifolia. SOUTHERN SWORD FERN. Plant will not take hard frosts. Bright green, narrow, upright fronds grow in tufts to 2–3 ft. tall. Fronds have closely spaced, finely toothed leaflets. Roots often have small roundish tubers. Plant spreads by thin, fuzzy runners and can be invasive if not watched. Tolerates poor soil and erratic watering. Good in narrow, shaded beds; can thrive in full sun with adequate water. Effective ground cover if kept watered. Also used in pots and hanging baskets. Often sold as *N. exaltata.*

N. exaltata. SWORD FERN. Taller than *N. cordifolia* (to 5 ft.), with broader fronds (to 6 in. wide). Most common are named selections grown as house plants. Best known is 'Bostoniensis', Boston fern; this is the classic parlor fern, with a spreading, arching habit and graceful, eventually drooping fronds broader than those of the species. Many more finely cut and feathery forms exist, including 'Fluffy Ruffles', 'Rooseveltii', and 'Whitmanii', Whitman fern.

NERIUM oleander

COMMON OLEANDER

Apocynaceae

EVERGREEN SHRUB

🌿 ZONES LS, CS, TS

☀ FULL SUN

◐ ● REGULAR TO LITTLE WATER

◊ ALL PARTS ARE POISONOUS IF INGESTED

Nerium oleander

Moderate to fast growth; most selections grow 10–15 ft. tall and wide. Ordinarily broad and bulky but easily trained into single- or multi-trunked tree. Excellent screen, windbreak, border for road or driveway, container plant. Narrow, 4–12-in.-long leaves are dark green, leathery, and glossy, attractive in all seasons. Plants are surprisingly hardy and survive brief periods of 0–5°F, but may be killed to the ground. They'll quickly resprout the next spring. In the Upper and Middle South, grow in container and bring indoors for winter.

Flowers 2–3 in. across, clustered at twig or branch ends, from mid- to late spring continuing into autumn. Many selections are fragrant. Forms with double and single flowers are sold; colors range from white to shades of yellow, pink, salmon, and red. 'Sister Agnes', single white, is most vigorous grower, often reaching 20 ft. tall; 'Mrs. Roeding', double salmon pink, grows only 6 ft. tall and has proportionally smaller, finer-textured foliage than big oleanders; 'Cherry Ripe' has bright rose red, single flowers. Flowers of all double types hang on after bloom and turn brown. For the same luscious salmon pink as 'Mrs. Roeding' in blossoms that drop clean, try single-flowered 'Hawaii'.

'Petite Pink' and 'Petite Salmon' can easily be kept to 3–4 ft. with moderate pruning and make excellent informal flowering hedges, though they are not as cold-hardy as regular oleanders. 'Little Red', bright red, is completely hardy—as are the following, intermediate-size (between dwarf and full size) plants: 'Algiers', deep red; 'Casablanca', white; 'Ruby Lace', bright red with 3-in., wavy-edged individual flowers; and 'Tangier', soft pink. Even smaller (5–7 ft.) are red 'Marrakesh' and white 'Morocco'.

Oleanders need little water once established but can take more. They are not at all particular about soil, even tolerating soil with relatively high salt content. Excellent plants for the beach.

Prune in early spring to control size and form. Cut out old wood that has flowered. Cut some branches nearly to ground. To restrict height, pinch remaining tips or prune them back lightly. To prevent bushiness at base, pull (don't cut) unwanted suckers. Removing spent flowers before they form seed extends bloom period. Oleander caterpillar sometimes defoliates plants in the Coastal and Tropical South.

Caution children against eating leaves or flowers; keep prunings, dead leaves away from hay or other animal feed; don't use wood for barbecue fires or skewers. Smoke from burning prunings can cause severe irritation.

For a plant called yellow oleander, see *Thevetia peruviana*.

NEVIUSIA alabamensis

ALABAMA SNOW-WREATH

Rosaceae

DECIDUOUS SHRUB

🌿 ZONES US, MS, LS

☀ ☀ FULL SUN OR PARTIAL SHADE

● REGULAR WATER

Neviusia alabamensis

Native to Alabama. Ornamental multistemmed shrub 3–6 ft. tall, with arching delicate branches and a cloud of feathery white flowers in spring. Grows rather slowly. Leaves oval, to 3 in. long. Flowers unusual and showy: 1-in.-wide spreading bunches of white stamens, without petals. Easy to grow if soil is well drained and ample water is provided during summer.

NEW YORK FERN. See THELYPTERIS noveboracensis

NICOTIANA

FLOWERING TOBACCO

Solanaceae

TENDER PERENNIALS GROWN AS ANNUALS

🌿 ALL ZONES

☀ ☀ FULL SUN OR PARTIAL SHADE

● REGULAR WATER

◊ ALL PARTS ARE POISONOUS IF INGESTED

Nicotiana alata

Upright-growing plants with slightly sticky leaves and stems. Usually grown for their fragrant flowers, which often open at night or on cloudy days; some kinds open during daytime. Flowers tubular, usually flaring at ends into five pointed lobes; grow near top of branched stems in summer. Large, soft, oval leaves. Some kinds reseed readily.

N. alata (N. affinis). FLOWERING TOBACCO. Wild species is a 2–3-ft. plant with large, very fragrant white flowers that open toward evening. Seed is available. Selection and hybridization with other species have produced garden strains that stay open day and night and come in colors ranging from white through pink to red (including lime green); scent is not as strong as in the "unimproved" species.

Domino strain grows to about 12–15 in. and has upward-facing flowers that can take heat and sun better than taller kinds. Nicki strain is taller (to about 15–18 in.). The older Sensation strain is taller still (to 4 ft.), looks best in informal mixed borders. If scent (especially during evening) is important, plant 'Grandiflora'.

Nicotiana alata

N. langsdorffii. Grows to 3–6 ft. tall. The branching stems are hung with drooping, inch-long, tubular light green flowers. No noticeable scent. Excellent for cutting.

🎋 **N. sylvestris.** OLD-FASHIONED FLOWERING TOBACCO. To 5 ft. Intensely fragrant, long, tubular white flowers grow in tiers atop a statu-esque plant. Striking in a night garden.

NIEREMBERGIA

CUP FLOWER
Solanaceae
PERENNIALS TREATED AS ANNUALS
⚡ ALL ZONES
☼ FULL SUN
💧 REGULAR WATER

Nierembergia repens

Flowers are tubular but flare into saucerlike or bell-like cups. The first species listed here grows as a spreading mound; the other is a ground-covering mat. Both are covered with blooms during summer. Can be grown as perennials in the Lower South, cool-weather annuals in the Coastal and Tropical South, summer annuals elsewhere.

N. hippomanica violacea (N. h. caerulea). DWARF CUP FLOWER. To 6–12 in. high. Much-branched mounded plant, with very small, stiff leaves. Flowers are blue to violet. Trimming back plant after bloom to induce new growth seems to lengthen its life. 'Purple Robe' is a common selection. 'Mont Blanc' bears white flowers.

N. repens (N. rivularis). WHITE CUP. Prostrate, 4–6-in. mat of bright green leaves. Blooms are white. For best performance, don't crowd it with more aggressive plants. Not as heat tolerant as dwarf cup flower.

NIGELLA damascena

LOVE-IN-A-MIST
Ranunculaceae
ANNUAL
⚡ ALL ZONES
☼ ◑ FULL SUN OR PARTIAL SHADE
💧 REGULAR WATER

Nigella damascena

Branching to 1–1½ ft. high. All leaves, even those that form under collar beneath each flower, are finely cut into threadlike divisions. Blue, white, or rose flowers, 1–1½ in. across, are borne singly at ends of branches in spring. Curious papery-textured, horned seed capsules lend airiness to bouquets or mixed borders, are very decorative in dried bouquets. 'Miss Jekyll', with semidouble cornflower blue blossoms, is an outstanding selection; Persian Jewels is a superior strain in mixed colors.

Plants come into bloom quickly in spring and dry up in summer heat. Sow seed in fall on open ground where plants are to grow; long taproot makes transplanting unsatisfactory. Self-sows freely.

NIGHT-BLOOMING CEREUS. See HYLOCEREUS undatus

NIGHT-BLOOMING JASMINE. See CESTRUM nocturnum

NIPPON DAISY. See CHRYSANTHEMUM nipponicum

NOLANA paradoxa

Nolanaceae
ANNUAL
⚡ ALL ZONES
☼ ◑ SUN OR LIGHT SHADE
💧 BEST IN FAIRLY DRY SOIL

Nolana paradoxa

Unusual plant from Chile that looks like a trailing sky blue petunia. Trailing stems bear 2-in.-long, ¾-in.-wide leaves and bright blue, 2-in. flowers with white throats. A selection is sold as 'Blue Bird' or *N. napiformis* 'Blue Bird'. Use as edging or in hanging basket. Withstands wide range of temperatures; needs good drainage.

NOLINA

Agavaceae
EVERGREEN SHRUBS
⚡ ZONES VARY BY SPECIES
☼ FULL SUN
💧 TOLERATE MUCH DROUGHT ONCE ESTABLISHED

Nolina longifolia

Yucca and century plant relatives with narrow, tough, grassy leaves. Good for dry areas. Tiny flowers are borne on showy, tall stalks. Plants tolerate poor, alkaline soil. Not good in high-rainfall, high-humidity areas.

N. erumpens. BEAR GRASS. Zones LS, CS, TS. Native to Mexico and western Texas. Sharp-edged, thick, 3-ft.-long leaves form a mound 3–4 ft. tall. Spikes of showy, creamy white flowers with rose blush tower several feet above foliage.

N. lindheimeri. DEVIL'S SHOESTRING. Zone LS. Native to Central Texas. Wiry narrow leaves, 2–3 ft. long. Tall, 3–4 ft., wands of white flowers in late spring.

N. longifolia. MEXICAN GRASSTREE. Zones CS, TS. Native to central Mexico. In youth, forms fountain of 3-ft.-long, 1-in.-wide grasslike leaves. In time, fountains top thick trunks 6–10 ft. tall, sometimes with a few branches. Tiny flowers are borne on showy, tall stalks.

N. texana. SACAHUISTA, BASKET GRASS. Zones MS, LS, CS, TS. Native to Texas, the Southwest, and Mexico. Very grasslike foliage, in 1½–2 ft. mound. Stalks of creamy white flowers are 1–1½ ft. tall and do not emerge above the leaves. Especially hardy.

NORFOLK ISLAND PINE. See ARAUCARIA heterophylla

Nyctaginaceae. The four o'clock family includes annuals, perennials, shrubs, and vines with showy flowers or bracts. Two familiar examples are bougainvillea and four o'clock (*Mirabilis jalapa*).

NYMPHAEA

WATER LILY
Nymphaeaceae
AQUATIC PLANTS
⚡ ALL ZONES
☼ PRODUCE FLOWERS IN SUN
💧 LOCATE IN PONDS, WATER GARDENS

Nymphaea

Leaves float and are rounded, with deep notch at one side where leaf stalk is attached. Showy flowers either float on surface or stand above it on stiff stalks. Cultivated water lilies, composed of hardy and tropical types, are largely hybrids that cannot be traced back to exact parentage. The hardy types bear flowers in white, yellow, copper, pink, or red. Tropical types add blue and purple; recent introductions include an unusual greenish blue. Some tropicals in the white-pink-red color range are night bloomers; all others close at night. Many are fragrant.

When you buy water lilies, choose selections suitable for the depth of your pond; consult your supplier.

Hardy kinds are easiest for beginners. Plant them in fall or spring. Set 6-in.-long pieces of rhizome on soil at pool bottom or in boxes, placing rhizome in nearly horizontal position with bud end up. In either case, top of soil should be 8–12 in. below surface of water. Enrich soil with 1 lb. of complete dry fertilizer (3–5 percent nitrogen) for each lily. Groom plants by removing spent leaves and blooms. They usually bloom throughout warm weather and go dormant in fall, then reappear in spring.

Tropical kinds begin to grow and bloom later in summer but last longer, often up to first frost. Buy started tropical plants and set at same depth as hardy rhizomes. Plants go dormant but do not survive really low winter temperatures. Best long-term survival in the Tropical South. Elsewhere, store dormant tubers in damp sand over winter or buy new plants each year.

Nymphaeaceae. The water lily family consists of aquatic plants, usually with floating leaves and flowers. Two examples are lotus *(Nelumbo)* and water lily *(Nymphaea)*.

Nyssaceae. Deciduous trees from Asia and North America. Examples include black gum *(Nyssa sylvatica)* and handkerchief tree *(Davidia)*.

NYSSA sylvatica

BLACK GUM, SOUR GUM, TUPELO, PEPPERIDGE

Nyssaceae

DECIDUOUS TREE

✂ ZONES US, MS, LS, CS

☼ ◐ FULL SUN OR PARTIAL SHADE

◖ ● REGULAR TO MODERATE WATER

Nyssa sylvatica

Native to eastern U.S. Slow to moderate growth to 30–50 ft. or more, spreading to 20–30 ft. Pyramidal when young; spreading, irregular, and rugged in age. Crooked branches and dark bark make dramatic picture against winter sky. Dark green, glossy, 2–5-in.-long leaves emerge rather late in spring. Plants have separate sexes. Both male and female trees bear inconspicuous flowers; females will bear fruit if a male is growing nearby (though males sometimes set some fruit as well). Fruits are bluish black and shaped like small olives; birds like them. In fall, leaves turn yellow and orange, then bright red before dropping. One of the best native trees for consistent, blazing fall color, even in the Lower South.

Prefers moist, deep, well-drained, acid soil, but tolerates poor drainage, some drought. Does not thrive in polluted air. Excellent specimen or shade tree; very attractive in naturalized landscapes. Select a permanent location, since this tree's taproot makes it difficult to move later on.

N. aquatica, water tupelo, is similar, but has larger leaves and fruits. It grows in areas subject to flooding. *N. ogeche,* Ogeechee tupelo, native to South Carolina, Georgia, and Florida, has edible, ¾-in. red fruits that are pickled to make Ogeechee "limes."

OAK. See QUERCUS

OAT GRASS, BLUE. See HELICTOTRICHON sempervirens

OBEDIENT PLANT. See PHYSOSTEGIA virginiana

SOUTHERN HERITAGE PLANTS
IDENTIFIED BY SYMBOL ⌗

OCIMUM basilicum

SWEET BASIL

Lamiaceae (Labiatae)

ANNUAL HERB

✂ ALL ZONES

☼ FULL SUN

● REGULAR WATER

Ocimum basilicum

Somewhat bushy plant to 2 ft. tall, with green, shiny, 1–2-in.-long leaves and spikes of white flowers. Forms with purple or variegated leaves have purple flowers. Most popular basil for cooking. Used fresh or dry, it gives a pleasant, sweet, mild flavor to tomatoes, cheese, eggs, seafood, salads. Several small-leafed, dwarf kinds, such as 'Dwarf Bush Fineleaf', 'Minnette', and 'Spicy Bush', thrive in containers and can also be used for edging. Top culinary basils include 'Genovese', an intensely aromatic, spicy basil favored for pesto, and 'Siam Queen', a large-leafed Thai basil good for Thai and Vietnamese dishes.

'Dark Opal', with large, dark, purple-bronze leaves and small lavender pink flowers, is attractive in borders and mass plantings. Grows 1–1½ ft. high, about 1 ft. wide. Other good purple-leafed selections include 'Purple Ruffles', deeply fringed and ruffled leaf edges; and 'Red Rubin', uniform dark color.

Sow seeds of any basil in early spring; make successive sowings 2 weeks apart to have replacements for the short-lived older plants. Or set transplants out after last frost. Space plants about 10–12 in. apart. Fertilize once during growing season with complete fertilizer. Keeping flower spikes pinched out will prevent seeding and subsequent death of plant.

OCONEE BELLS. See SHORTIA galacifolia

OCTOPUS TREE. See SCHEFFLERA actinophylla

OENOTHERA

EVENING PRIMROSE

Onagraceae

PERENNIALS, EXCEPT AS NOTED

✂ ZONES VARY BY SPECIES

☼ ◐ FULL SUN OR LIGHT SHADE

● MODERATE WATER

Oenothera fruticosa

Valued for showy, four-petaled, silky flowers in bright yellow, pink, or white. Some types display their blossoms during the day, but others open in late afternoon and close the following morning. Carefree plants that grow in tough places. Can withstand light shade.

O. biennis. EVENING PRIMROSE. Annual or biennial. Zones US, MS, LS, CS. Growth variable, from 1–4 ft., sometimes to 6 ft. Best grown in meadows because it's usually weedy, reseeds, and can be invasive. Flowers yellow, aging to gold, fragrant, and open in the evening. Japanese beetles particularly attracted to this species.

⌗ **O. fruticosa (O. tetragona).** SUNDROPS. Zones US, MS, LS. Grows to 2 ft. high, spreading vigorously. Reddish stems and bright green foliage. Daytime display of 1½-in. bright yellow flowers all summer. Plant thrives in full sun or light shade. 'Fireworks', 1½ ft. high, has red stems, red flower buds, and brownish-tinted leaves. Leaves of 'Summer Solstice' turn purplish red in autumn.

O. hookeri. Zones MS, LS. Biennial western native. To 2–6 ft. high. Bright yellow, 3½-in. flowers open late afternoon to sunrise. Leaves are hairy, elliptical.

O. macrocarpa (O. missouriensis). Zones US, MS, LS. Prostrate, sprawling stems to 10 in. long. Soft, velvety leaves, 5-in. Blooms in late spring and summer. Flowers bright yellow, 3–5 in. wide, open in the afternoon. Large winged seedpods follow the flowers. Best in full sun.

🏛 **O. speciosa.** MEXICAN EVENING PRIMROSE. Zones MS, LS. Often sold as *O. berlandieri* or *O. s. childsii*. Grows 10–12 in. high, with profuse showing of 1½-in. rose pink blooms in summer; flowers open in daytime, despite plant's common name. Stems die back after bloom. Spreads rapidly by underground stems and can invade other plantings. Full sun. 'Alba' is a white-flowered form; 'Siskiyou' is an especially vigorous, long-blooming selection with 2-in. light pink blossoms; 'Woodside White' opens white but ages to pale pink.

OHIO BUCKEYE. See AESCULUS glabra

🏛 OKRA

Malvaceae

ANNUAL

🗡 ALL ZONES

☼ FULL SUN

💧 REGULAR WATER

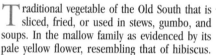

Okra

Traditional vegetable of the Old South that is sliced, fried, or used in stews, gumbo, and soups. In the mallow family as evidenced by its pale yellow flower, resembling that of hibiscus.

Sow in late spring (May, for most of South) when soil has warmed to 75°F; seeds won't germinate in cool soil. To speed germination, soak seeds in water overnight; then sow ½ in. deep and 2 in. apart in rows 3 ft. apart. When seedlings are 2 in. tall, thin to 6–12 in. apart. Sprinkle 10-10-10 or 10-14-10 fertilizer around bases of plants, about ¼ cup per 10 ft. of row.

Allow 48 to 60 days from planting to harvest. Developing pods grow quickly, as much as 1 in. a day in hot weather. Harvest regularly, as pods allowed to mature cause the plant to stop producing, and pods longer than 4 in. are usually too tough to eat. Use a knife or pruners to cut pods, and wear gloves to protect hands from tiny prickles on pods.

For small gardens, choose a dwarf selection (to 3 ft. tall) such as 'Annie Oakley' or 'Lee'. Standard selections, to about 6 ft. tall, include 'Burgundy', with 8-in.-long red pods popular for arrangements (they turn green when cooked and are tender even at 8 in. long); and 'Clemson Spineless', the old standby, without the ridges typical of most okra pods.

OLD-FASHIONED FLOWERING TOBACCO. See NICOTIANA sylvestris

Oleaceae. The olive family includes about 900 species of trees and shrubs with opposite leaves and flower parts usually in fours. Typical members include privet *(Ligustrum)* and lilac *(Syringa)*.

OLEANDER, COMMON. See NERIUM oleander

Onagraceae. Most members of the evening primrose family have flower parts in fours, but otherwise are diverse in appearance and structure. They include *Fuchsia, Gaura,* and evening primrose *(Oenothera)*.

ONCIDIUM

Orchidaceae

EPIPHYTIC ORCHIDS

🗡 ZONE TS; OR GREENHOUSE OR INDOOR PLANTS

◐ FILTERED SHADE

💧 REGULAR WATER

Oncidium

Native from Florida to Brazil, and from sea level to high mountains. Hundreds of species and hybrids available. Most produce long spikes of yellow flowers spotted or striped with brown; a few have white or rose-colored blooms. Some have compressed pseudobulbs topped by one or two fleshy leaves; others are almost without bulbs; and still others have pencil-like leaves. Blossoms may be small or large. Excellent cut flowers. Sometimes called dancing lady.

Outdoor plants in Tropical South: grow in pots or on slabs of bark attached to tree trunks, and bring indoors only when a freeze is imminent. Indoors, grow on a bright windowsill or in a greenhouse. Treat as you would *Cattleya*. Also see Orchidaceae.

ONION

Amaryllidaceae

BIENNIAL GROWN AS ANNUAL

🗡 ALL ZONES

☼ FULL SUN

💧 REGULAR WATER

Onion

Grow onions from seed or sets (small bulbs). Sets are easiest for beginners, though seed offers more choices among selections. In the Lower, Coastal, and Tropical South, plant onion sets late fall–winter; elsewhere, plant in early spring, as soon as soil is workable. Soil should be loose, rich, and well drained. Push sets just under soil surface so that point of bulb is visible; space a little wider than bulb size at maturity (closer if you want to harvest some as green onions). Sow seed ¼ in. deep, in rows 15–18 in. apart. In the Lower, Coastal, and Tropical South, sow in fall and winter for winter–spring crop; in the Upper and Middle South, sow in early spring. When seedlings are pencil size, thin to same spacing as for sets, transplanting thinnings to extend planting. Trim back tops of transplants about halfway. In some areas, onion plants (field-grown, nearly pencil-size transplants or seedlings growing in pots) are available.

Onions are shallow rooted and need moisture fairly near the surface. Feed plants, especially early in season: the larger and stronger the plants grow, the larger the bulbs they form. Carefully eliminate weeds that compete for light, food, and water. When most of the tops have begun to yellow and fall over, dig bulbs and let them cure and dry on top of ground for several days. Then pull off tops, clean, and store in dark, cool, airy place.

Selections differ in bulb size, shape, color, flavor, and storage life. Also keep in mind that onions form bulbs in response to day length. If you choose a type inappropriate for your area, it may make small premature bulbs or not bulb up at all. Long-day types that need 14 to 16 hours of daylight are best for the Upper and Middle South. They tend to be pungent and store well; examples are 'Early Yellow Globe', 'Ebenezer', 'Ruby', 'Southport White Globe', 'Sweet Spanish'. Short-day types that require 10 to 12 hours of daylight are recommended for the Coastal and Tropical South. They start making bulbs early in the year, tend to be sweet, and are poor keepers; examples are 'Bermuda', 'California Red', 'Granex', 'Super Sweet', 'Texas 1015', and 'Vidalia', the last three being the very sweetest. Gardeners in the Lower South can plant long- or short-day onions or intermediate types. Examples of intermediate-day types, requiring 12 to 14 hours of daylight, are 'Autumn Spice', 'Red Torpedo', 'Ringmaker'.

For ornamental relatives, see *Allium*.

ONOCLEA sensibilis

SENSITIVE FERN

Polypodiaceae

FERN

🗡 ZONES US, MS, LS

☼ FULL SUN

💧💧 MOIST TO WET SOIL

Onoclea sensibilis

Native to eastern U.S. Coarse-textured fern with 2–4-ft. sterile fronds divided nearly to midrib; fertile fronds

O

smaller, with clusters of almost beadlike leaflets. Fronds come from underground creeping rhizome that can be invasive. Dies to the ground in winter. Fronds seem coarse to many gardeners, but fern is useful for planting along streams and ponds. Takes regular moisture, but won't be as big as in wetter conditions. Called sensitive fern because it is among the first plants to show frost damage in fall.

OPHIOPOGON. See LIRIOPE and OPHIOPOGON

OPIUM POPPY. See PAPAVER somniferum

OPUNTIA

PRICKLY PEAR CACTUS

Cactaceae

CACTI

ZONES VARY BY SPECIES

FULL SUN

MODERATE TO LITTLE WATER

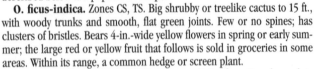

Opuntia humifusa

Several species are native to the South. Some are entirely hardy even in the coldest winters, though they all need perfect drainage, so are best grown in raised beds or on mounds. One of the more tender species described below is a popular house plant.

O. ficus-indica. Zones CS, TS. Big shrubby or treelike cactus to 15 ft., with woody trunks and smooth, flat green joints. Few or no spines; has clusters of bristles. Bears 4-in.-wide yellow flowers in spring or early summer; the large red or yellow fruit that follows is sold in groceries in some areas. Within its range, a common hedge or screen plant.

O. humifusa. PRICKLY PEAR. All zones. Native from Canada south to Florida and eastern Texas. Spreading clump, 2–3 ft. tall. Not many spines on 3–6-in.-long pads. Yellow flowers, 3–4 in. across, in early summer. Fruits purple when ripe, to 2 in. long. Tolerates more soil moisture than most cacti. Very cold-hardy. Good plant for the beach.

O. imbricata. CHAIN-LINK CACTUS, WALKING-STICK CHOLLA. All zones. Native from Colorado to Mexico. Treelike cactus, with short trunk and branching cylindrical stems, 3–6 ft., sometimes 10 ft., but very slow growing. Many 1-in. sharp spines, and small hairline spines that are more painful and harder to remove. Never plant near walkways or in gardens where children play. Magenta flowers, 2–3 in. across, in early summer. Yellow fruit, 1½ in. long. Very cold-hardy.

O. lindheimeri. TEXAS PRICKLY PEAR. Zones LS, CS, TS. Native to southern Texas. Large, clumping cactus, with pads to 1 ft. long; often 2–5 ft. tall, but it can reach 12 ft. and spread even wider. Spines 1–2 in. long. Yellow flowers, 3–4 in. across, in summer. Red-purple fruits, 2–3 in. long.

O. microdasys. BUNNY EARS. Zone TS; or house plant. Fast growth to 2 ft. high, 4–5 ft. wide (much smaller in pots). Pads flat, thin, nearly round, to 6 in. across, velvety soft green with neatly spaced tufts of short golden bristles in polka-dot effect. 'Albispina' has white bristles. Small, round new pads atop larger old ones give plant silhouette of animal's head. A favorite with children.

O. phaeacantha. Zones MS, LS, CS, TS. Native from northern Texas to California. Low spreading clump, with 4–6-in. pads and thick, 2-in. spines. Yellow flowers, 2–3 in. across, in spring. Red fruit, 1-in. long.

ORANGE. See CITRUS

ORANGE CLOCK VINE. See THUNBERGIA gregorii

ORANGE-EYE BUTTERFLY BUSH. See BUDDLEIA davidii

ORANGE JESSAMINE. See MURRAYA paniculata

Orchidaceae. The orchid family is probably the largest in the plant kingdom, with nearly 800 genera and over 17,000 species. Flowers have an unusual shape: one or more petals united to form a lip, and the stamens,

style, and stigma united into a single organ, the column. Best-known are *Bletilla, Cattleya, Cymbidium, Oncidium,* and *Phalaenopsis.*

Orchid growers' terms. Here are definitions of the orchid growers' terms you will encounter in this book.

Epiphytic. In nature epiphytic orchids cling to high branches of trees in tropical or subtropical jungles, deriving their nourishment from air, rain, and whatever decaying vegetable matter they can trap in their root systems.

Pseudobulb. Epiphytic orchids have thickened stems called pseudobulbs that store food and water and allow the plants to survive drought. These may be short and fat (like bulbs) or erect and slender. They vary from green to brown in color. Leaves may grow along pseudobulbs or from their tips.

Terrestrial. Some orchids (including most native orchids) are terrestrial and must grow in loose, moist soil rich in humus. They often occur in wooded areas but sometimes in open meadows as well. These orchids require constant moisture and food.

Sepals, petals, lip, and pouch. Segments of an orchid flower include three sepals and three petals; one of the petals, usually the lowest one, is called the lip. The lip is usually larger and more brightly colored than other segments. Sometimes it is fantastically shaped, with various appendages and markings. It may be folded into a slipperlike "pouch."

Rafts, bark. Nearly all orchids, terrestrial or epiphytic, are grown in pots. A few are grown on "rafts" (slabs of bark or wood), or in baskets of wood slats; a few natives are grown in open ground.

Potting and growing. Potting materials for cattleyas (the most commonly grown orchids) will work for most epiphytic orchids: osmunda fiber, hapuu (tree fern stem), or ground bark. Most popular is bark; it's readily available, easy to handle, fairly inexpensive. Use fine grade for pots 3 in. or smaller, medium grade for pots 4 in. or larger. You can use ready-made mixes, blended for proper texture and acidity and sold by orchid growers.

Water plants once a week, or when mix dries out and becomes lightweight. Feed with a commercial water-soluble orchid fertilizer once every 2 weeks during growing season. To provide humidity for house plants, fill a metal or plastic tray with gravel and just enough water to reach almost to top of gravel. Stretch hardware cloth over tray, with 1 in. between gravel and wire for air circulation. Set pots on top. Maintain water level.

Temperature requirements. This list classifies orchids according to temperature requirements. Some cool-growing orchids are hardy enough to grow outdoors in most places.

Temperate-climate orchids can be grown in pots on a windowsill with other house plants, but will perform best if given additional humidity. An excellent method of supplying humidity is described in "Potting and growing," above. Most temperate-climate orchids can be moved outdoors in summer; put in the shade of high-branching trees, on patio, or in lathhouse.

Warm-climate orchids need greenhouse conditions to provide the uniform warm temperatures and high humidity they require.

Cool-climate orchids: *Bletilla* and *Cymbidium.* Take colder temperatures than other types. Chinese ground orchid (*Bletilla striata*) is hardy as far north as the Middle South.

Temperate-climate orchids: *Cattleya* and *Oncidium.*

Warm-climate orchid: *Phalaenopsis.*

ORCHID CACTUS. See EPIPHYLLUM

ORCHID TREE. See BAUHINIA

ORCHID VINE. See MASCAGNIA, STIGMAPHYLLON

OREGANO. See ORIGANUM vulgare

OREGON GRAPE. See MAHONIA aquifolium

ORIENTAL ARBORVITAE. See PLATYCLADUS orientalis

ORIENTAL POPPY. See PAPAVER orientale

O

ORIGANUM

Lamiaceae (Labiatae)

PERENNIALS

🗲 ZONES VARY BY SPECIES

☼ FULL SUN

💧 MODERATE TO LITTLE WATER, EXCEPT AS NOTED

Origanum majorana

Mint relatives that have tight clusters of small flowers and foliage with a strong, pleasant scent. Bracts in the flower clusters overlap, giving the effect of small pinecones. Soil must be well drained.

O. dictamnus (Amaracus dictamnus). CRETE DITTANY. Zone LS. Native to Mediterranean area. Aromatic herb with slender, arching stems to 1 ft. long. Thick, roundish, somewhat mottled, woolly white leaves to ¾ in. long. Flowers pink to purplish, ½ in. long; rose purple fruit in conelike heads. Blooms summer to fall. Shows up best when planted individually in rock garden, container, or hanging basket. Short lived in most places. Dislikes heat, humidity, heavy soil.

O. laevigatum. Zones US, MS, LS. Sprawling, arching plant, with stems rooting at joints; branching clusters of purple flowers. 'Herrenhausen' has lilac-pink blooms, purplish leaves in cool seasons; 'Hopley's' has large heads of deep purplish pink flowers. Useful as bank or ground cover.

O. majorana (Majorana hortensis). SWEET MARJORAM. Perennial in Zones LS, CS, but often treated as annual. To 1–2 ft. Tiny, oval gray-green leaves; spikes of white flowers in loose clusters at top of plant. Grow in fairly moist soil. Keep blossoms cut off and plant trimmed to prevent woody growth. Propagate from seeds, cuttings, or root divisions. It's a favorite herb for seasoning meats, salads, vinegars. Use leaves fresh or dried. Often grown in container indoors on windowsill.

O. onites. POT MARJORAM. Zone LS. To 2 ft. tall and as broad, with bright green aromatic leaves and flattish heads of tiny white or purplish flowers. Sometimes called Cretan oregano.

O. vulgare. OREGANO, WILD MARJORAM. Zones US, MS, LS. Upright growth to 2½ ft. Spreads by underground stems. Medium-size oval leaves; purplish pink blooms. Grow in medium-rich soil; needs good drainage. Keep trimmed to prevent flowering. Replant every 3 years. Fresh or dried leaves of culinary selections are used in many dishes, especially Italian and Spanish ones. 'Compactum' is a few inches tall, spreads widely, and seldom flowers. It can be used as a ground cover. Greek oregano (*O. v. hirtum*) has the finest flavor.

ORNITHOGALUM

Liliaceae

BULBS

🗲 ZONES VARY BY SPECIES; OR DIG AND STORE; OR GROW IN POTS INDOORS

☼ FULL SUN

💧 WATER NEEDS VARY BY SPECIES

☘ ALL PARTS, ESPECIALLY BULB, ARE POISONOUS IF INGESTED

Ornithogalum umbellatum

Leaves vary from narrow to broad and tend to be floppy. Flowers mostly star shaped, in tall or rounded clusters, appearing in late spring or early summer. Use in borders. In areas beyond their hardiness, lift and store bulbs during winter; or grow in pots, protected.

O. arabicum. STAR OF BETHLEHEM. Zones CS, TS. Handsome clusters of 2-in., white, waxy flowers with beady black pistils in centers. Stems 2 ft. tall. Floppy bluish green leaves to 2 ft. long, 1 in. wide. Excellent cut flower. Moderate water.

O. caudatum. PREGNANT ONION. Zone TS. Grown for bulb and foliage rather than for tall wands of small green-and-white flowers. Strap-shaped leaves hang downward and grow to 5 ft. long. Big, gray-green, smooth-skinned bulb (3–4 in. thick) grows on, not in, the ground. Bulblets form just beneath bulb skin, grow quite large before bulb splits open

and they drop out and root. Hardy to 25° F; will lose leaves without occasional watering. Often grown as house plant and conversation piece.

O. thyrsoides. CHINCHERINCHEE. Zone TS. Tapering, compact clusters of white, 2-in. flowers with brownish green centers. Flower stems 2 ft. high. Leaves bright green, upright, to 1 ft. long, 2 in. wide. May survive colder winters along Gulf Coast if given sheltered southern or southwestern location and protected with mulch. Long-lasting cut flower. Moderate water.

O. umbellatum. STAR OF BETHLEHEM. Zones US, MS, LS, CS. May naturalize and become a pest. Clusters of 1-in.-wide flowers, striped green on outside, atop 1-ft. stems. Grasslike leaves about as long as flower stems. Cut flowers last well but close at night. Regular water.

OSAGE ORANGE. See MACLURA pomifera

OSMANTHUS

Oleaceae

EVERGREEN SHRUBS, SMALL TREES

🗲 ZONES VARY BY SPECIES

☼ ◐ FULL SUN OR PARTIAL SHADE

💧 REGULAR TO MODERATE WATER

Osmanthus fragrans

All have clean, leathery, attractive foliage and inconspicuous but fragrant flowers. Plants aren't particular about soil; once established, they are fairly drought tolerant.

O. americanus. DEVILWOOD. Zones US, MS, LS, CS. Native from North Carolina to Florida and Mississippi, and Mexico. Large shrub or small, neat, upright, oval tree, eventually to 25–30 ft., or even 45 ft. Moderately slow growing. Foliage is handsome, leathery, shiny green with smooth margins. Leaves to 7 in. long, 2½ in. wide. Creamy, fragrant flowers in spring. Dark blue fruit, ½ in. long, in early fall. Very cold-hardy. Tolerates wet soil.

O. delavayi (Siphonosmanthus delavayi). DELAVAY OSMANTHUS. Zones CS, TS. Slow growing, graceful, to 4–6 ft., with arching branches spreading wider. Leaves dark green, oval, to 1 in. long, with toothed edges. Profuse clusters of four to eight white, fragrant flowers (largest of any osmanthus) in spring. Attractive all year. Easily controlled by pruning. Good choice for foundations, massing. Handsome on retaining wall where branches hang down. Does best in partial shade.

O. fortunei. FORTUNES OSMANTHUS. Zones MS, LS, CS. Hybrid between *O. heterophyllus* and *O. fragrans*. Slow, dense growth to an eventual 20 ft. tall. Leaves are oval, hollylike, to 4 in. long. Small, fragrant white flowers bloom during fall. 'San Jose' is similar but has cream to orange blooms.

O. fragrans. SWEET OLIVE, TEA OLIVE. Zones LS (protected), CS, TS. Moderate growth to 10 ft. and more with age. Broad, dense, compact. Can be pruned to upright growth where space is limited. Can be trained as small tree, hedge, screen, background, espalier, container plant. Pinch out growing tips of young plants to induce bushiness.

Leaves glossy, medium green, oval, to 4 in. long, toothed or smooth edged. Tiny white flowers have sweet fragrance of apricots. Bloom is heaviest in spring, early summer, but plants flower sporadically through the year. Give afternoon shade. *O. f. aurantiacus* has less glossy, narrower leaves than species; its fragrant orange flowers bloom in early fall.

O. heterophyllus (O. aquifolium, O. ilicifolius). HOLLY OSMANTHUS. Zones US, MS, LS, CS. Grows 8–10 ft. tall (possibly to 20 ft.), with 2½-in., spiny-edged leaves. Resembles English holly, but leaves appear opposite one another on stems. Fragrant white flowers in late fall and winter are followed by berrylike blue-black fruit.

'Goshiki'. Erect, 3½ ft. tall, 5 ft. wide. Pinkish orange markings on new leaves mature to yellow variegations on dark green. Few flowers.

'Gulftide'. Dense, upright, to 10–15 ft. More cold-hardy than species. Probably the most popular selection. Very glossy, deep green foliage.

'Ilicifolius'. Dense, symmetrical upright growth to 6–8 ft., eventually to 20 ft. Leaves dark green, strongly toothed, hollylike, to 2½ in. long. Fragrant white flowers in fall, winter, early spring. Good for screen, background. ▶

'Purpureus' ('Purpurascens'). Same habit as species. Dark purple new growth, with purple tints through summer.

'Rotundifolius'. Slow growing to 5 ft. Roundish small leaves are lightly spined along edges.

'Variegatus'. Slow growing to 4–5 ft., with densely set leaves edged creamy white. Useful for brightening shady areas. A bit less cold tolerant than the species.

OSMUNDA

Osmundaceae

FERNS

☒ ZONES VARY BY SPECIES

☼ ☽ ● EXPOSURE NEEDS VARY BY SPECIES

● ◑ DAMP TO WET SOIL

Osmunda regalis

Three species of coarse, imposing deciduous ferns useful in naturalistic plantings. All like plenty of moisture but can survive with less, responding with smaller, less vigorous growth. Rhizomes have heavy growth of matted brown roots—the source of the osmunda fiber used for potting orchids.

O. cinnamomea. CINNAMON FERN. Zones US, MS, LS. Plant has erect sterile fronds to 5 ft., arching out toward top. Spores are borne on different fronds—narrow, erect, much shorter, turning cinnamon brown as spores ripen. Unfolding young fronds (fiddleheads) are harvested for food. Fronds turn showy yellow to orange in fall. Full or light shade.

O. claytoniana. INTERRUPTED FERN. Zones US, MS, LS. If given ample water, grows as tall as 5 ft., more typically to 3 ft. Shorter in dryish soils. Each frond is "interrupted" in the middle by several short brown spore-bearing segments. Full or light shade.

O. regalis. ROYAL FERN, FLOWERING FERN. Zones US, MS, LS, CS. Large fern (to 6 ft.) with twice-cut fronds, each leaflet quite large. Coarser in texture than most ferns. Tips of fronds have modified segments that somewhat resemble flower buds; these produce the spores. One of the better ferns for fall color. Fronds may turn bright yellow. 'Cristata' has crested fronds; 'Purpurascens' has purplish red new growth and stems that remain purple throughout the season. Light shade, but will thrive in sun in wet soil, even in mud. Especially attractive beside streams or ponds.

OSTRICH FERN. See MATTEUCCIA struthiopteris

OSTRYA

HOP HORNBEAM

Betulaceae

DECIDUOUS TREES

☒ ZONES VARY BY SPECIES

☼ ☽ FULL SUN OR LIGHT SHADE

● ◑ REGULAR TO MODERATE WATER

Ostrya virginiana

Hop hornbeams are so named because female flowers and fruit are enclosed in bractlike husks forming 1½–2½-in. clusters that resemble hops. Trees are small to medium size (seldom exceeding 40 ft.), slow growing, and produce inch-long male catkins that are attractive in winter. Foliage is dark green, turning yellow in fall. Attractive, but little used because of their slow growth—a fault to nurserymen, but a possible advantage to the gardener. Wood is hard, heavy, and dense.

O. carpinifolia. EUROPEAN HOP HORNBEAM. Zones US, MS, LS. Scarcely differs from the more common American species, *O. virginiana*.

O. virginiana. AMERICAN HOP HORNBEAM, IRONWOOD. Zones US, MS, LS, CS. Native to eastern North America, where it is an understory tree.

OXALIS

Oxalidaceae

PERENNIALS; SOME GROW FROM BULBS OR RHIZOMES

☒ ZONES VARY BY SPECIES

☼ ☽ FULL SUN OR LIGHT SHADE, EXCEPT AS NOTED

● REGULAR WATER

Oxalis rubra

Leaves usually divided into three leaflets like clover leaves. Flowers pink, white, rose, or yellow. Some selections tolerate cold winters; those that don't you can use as container plants.

O. acetosella. WOOD SORREL, SHAMROCK. One of several plants known as shamrock. See Shamrocks.

O. adenophylla. Zones US, MS, LS. Dense, low (4-in.-high), compact tuft of leaves, each leaf with 12 to 22 crinkly, gray-green leaflets. Flowers are 1 in. wide, on 4–6-in. stalks, bell shaped, lilac pink with deeper veins, in late spring. Plant roots in fall. Needs good drainage. Good rock garden plant or companion to bulbs such as species tulips or the smaller kinds of narcissus, in pots or in the ground.

O. purpurea (O. variabilis). Zones LS, CS. Low growing (4–5 in. tall), with large leaves and rose red flowers an inch across. Spreads by bulbs and rhizomelike roots, but is not aggressive or weedy. Plant bulbs in early fall for late fall and winter bloom. Improved kinds sold under the name Grand Duchess have larger flowers of rose pink, white, or lavender.

O. rubra. OXALIS, WOOD SORREL. All zones. Native of Brazil and Argentina. Forms low mounds, 6–12 in. tall and wide. Cloverlike leaves, with three notched leaflets. Showy flowers in pink, rose, or lavender, with darker veins, late winter or early spring. Pretty as ground cover or in rock garden or front of border. In fertile, moist soil, it may spread and become hard to eradicate. ☜ *O. crassipes,* Zones MS, LS, CS, is similar, though slightly less hardy. It often invades lawns in the Lower and Coastal South. Highly susceptible to rust; foliage usually melts away by midsummer.

O. versicolor. Zones CS, TS. Bulbs give rise to erect or spreading stems up to 6 in. tall. Leaves bear three deeply notched leaflets less than ½ in. wide. Flowers are white, over 1 in. wide, with yellow throat and purplish edges. 'Candy Cane' is commonly seen; has white flowers striped red. Striped buds especially colorful. Plant in fall for spring bloom.

OXBLOOD LILY. See RHODOPHIALA bifida

OX-EYE. See HELIOPSIS helianthoides

OX-EYE DAISY. See CHRYSANTHEMUM leucanthemum

OXYDENDRUM arboreum

SOURWOOD, SORREL TREE

Ericaceae

DECIDUOUS TREE

☒ ZONES US, MS, LS, CS

☼ ☽ FULL OR PARTIAL SUN; TOLERATES LIGHT SHADE

● REGULAR WATER

Oxydendrum arboreum

Native from Pennsylvania and Ohio south to Florida, Mississippi, and Louisiana. Not the best choice for the Coastal South, though it grows there. Beautiful flowering tree with year-round interest. Very slow growth (often less than 1 ft. a year), to 25–30 ft. tall and across, though 50 ft. is possible. Pyramidal shape with slender trunk, rounded top, slightly pendulous branches; handsome winter silhouette. Narrow, 5–8-in.-long leaves somewhat resemble peach leaves; they are bronze tinted in early spring, rich green in summer, orange and scarlet to blackish purple in autumn. Bark of new stems is bright red. Blooms in summer, with fragrant, bell-shaped, creamy white flowers in 10-in.-long, drooping clusters at branch tips. In fall, when foliage is brilliantly colored, branching clusters of greenish seed capsules extend outward and downward like fingers; capsules turn light silver gray, hang on late into winter.

Grow in moist, well-drained acid soil. Tolerates some drought, but not urban pollution. Will grow in partial shade, but best flowering and fall color in full sun. Among earliest and best trees for colorful autumn foliage. Also grows well in containers.

OZARK WHITE CEDAR. See JUNIPERUS ashei

PACHYPODIUM lamerei

MADAGASCAR PALM

Apocynaceae

SUCCULENT SHRUB

ZONE TS; OR HOUSE PLANT

FULL SUN; BRIGHT LIGHT INDOORS

WATER ONLY WHEN SOIL IS DRY

Pachypodium lamerei

Not a palm, though somewhat palmlike in appearance. Easy-to-grow plant with impressive silhouette: spiny, succulent, unbranched trunk 2–4 ft. high (as tall as 18 ft. under ideal conditions) is topped with a circle of strap-shaped leaves to 1 ft. long and 1–4 in. wide. Saucer-shaped white flowers to 4 in. wide are seldom seen; they usually appear only on large, old plants. Plant can be grown outdoors year-round only in south Florida; elsewhere, it can be raised in a pot and summered outside or kept exclusively indoors as a house plant. Leaves usually drop in winter (specimens in south Florida and house plants may hold their foliage); plant needs no water until growth resumes. Indoors, give it the brightest window, and check foliage regularly for spider mites.

PACHYRHIZUS erosus

JICAMA

Fabaceae (Leguminosae)

ANNUAL VINE

ZONES LS, CS, TS

FULL SUN

DO NOT LET ROOT ZONE DRY OUT

Pachyrhizus erosus

Grown for its edible root, which looks similar to a large brown turnip and tastes something like a water chestnut. Twining or scrambling vines are attractive, with luxuriant deep green foliage and pretty purple or violet flower clusters. Leaves have three leaflets, each the size of a hand; upright spikes of sweet pea–shaped flowers appear in late summer. Flowers should be pinched out for maximum root production, but you can allow seed for next year's crop to form on one or two plants. Needs long, warm growing season and rich garden soil. Sow seeds after danger of frost is past, 1–1½ in. deep, 6–12 in. apart in rows. Feed once or twice in early or midsummer. The roots or tubers will form as days begin to grow shorter; harvest them before first frost.

PACHYSANDRA

PACHYSANDRA, SPURGE

Buxaceae

PERENNIAL GROUND COVERS

ZONES VARY BY SPECIES

LIGHT TO HEAVY SHADE

REGULAR WATER

Pachysandra terminalis

Low-growing evergreen perennials used for ground cover in shady places. These are slow but sure spreaders from underground runners and invaluable landscape plants. Hardy to cold; well able to compete with

tree roots. Compact growth and clean, attractive foliage are their chief virtues. Flowers are not showy when viewed casually, but look attractive at close range. Provide moist, preferably somewhat acid soil, well amended with organic material. Too much sun causes yellowing foliage.

P. procumbens. ALLEGHENY PACHYSANDRA, ALLEGHENY SPURGE. Zones US, MS. Not as widely available or as fast spreading as Japanese species. Grows 6–12 in. high; grayish green leaves are 2–4 in. long and 2–3 in. wide, clustered near top of stem. Leaves often mottled with gray or brownish markings. Small white or pinkish flowers are fragrant.

P. terminalis. JAPANESE PACHYSANDRA, JAPANESE SPURGE. Zones US, MS, LS. Grows 8–12 in. high. Shiny dark green leaves are 2–4 in. long and ½–1½ in. wide; upper half of leaf has shallowly toothed edges. Small white flowers are borne in 1–2-in. spikes. 'Green Carpet' is shorter and denser in growth than the species, with shinier, deeper green leaves. 'Green Sheen' has especially glossy leaves; 'Silver Edge' ('Variegata') has creamy-edged foliage; fast-spreading 'Cut Leaf' has deeply dissected leaves. Luxuriant look; top ground cover for shade in the Upper and Middle South. But in the Lower South, it sulks during long, dry summers.

Japanese pachysandra can stand very heavy shade and is widely used as a ground cover under trees. Plant 6 in. apart for reasonably quick cover; apply a mulch and keep moist until established. Seldom bothered by pests, but a leaf blight can cause serious damage if it gets out of hand; control with fungicides and, if possible, by limiting overhead watering.

PACHYSTACHYS

Acanthaceae

TROPICAL EVERGREEN SHRUBS

ZONES CS, TS

EXPOSURE NEEDS VARY BY SPECIES

WATER NEEDS VARY BY SPECIES

Pachystachys lutea

Large-leafed plants with showy terminal flower spikes. Stems are soft-wooded, more herbaceous than shrubby. Similar to *Justicia*.

P. coccinea. CARDINAL'S-GUARD. Native to West Indies and South America. Produces lanky growth to 5 ft. or taller; for a tidier look, cut back established plants in late winter. Leaves oval, to 8 in. long, prominent veins. Flower spikes, to 6 in. long, have green bracts and blazing scarlet, 2-in., tubular flowers. Summer flowering. Prefers light shade and moist, well-drained soil. Good plant for hummingbirds.

P. lutea. YELLOW SHRIMP PLANT, LOLLIPOPS PLANT. Native to Peru. Grows to 3–6 ft. tall. Narrow, dark green leaves, to 5 in. long. Spikes, 3–6 in. long, of neatly overlapping golden yellow bracts. Flowers are slender white tubes that emerge between the bracts. Blooms constantly in warm weather. Flowers attract hummingbirds. Good plant for massing or for mixed borders. Pinch tips during growing season and cut back in winter to reduce lankiness. Full sun or light shade. Moderate water.

PAEONIA

PEONY

Paeoniaceae

PERENNIALS AND DECIDUOUS SHRUBS

ZONES VARY BY TYPE

AFTERNOON SHADE

REGULAR WATER

Paeonia
Single Type

Most garden peonies are hybrids. The two basic types are herbaceous and tree peonies. Herbaceous types die to the ground in late fall; they are mostly descendants of *P. lactiflora*. Tree (actually shrub) peonies flower from permanent woody branches; they are chiefly descendants of *P. suffruticosa*. All peonies are extremely long-lived plants of significant size, demanding more than ordinary care in site preparation. In return, they can provide outstanding garden beauty for as long as you live. ▶

P

Herbaceous peonies are planted in fall (preferably) or earliest spring as bare-root plants: compact rhizomes with several "eyes" (growth buds) and thick, tuberous roots. Tree peonies, practically all of them grafted onto herbaceous peony roots, may be planted in the same way. Many growers now offer tree peonies as container plants from spring to fall. These cost more than bare-root plants; they take more time and labor to produce.

Ideally, the planting site for peonies should be deeply dug several days before planting. Work in plenty of thoroughly decayed manure or compost and superphosphate; allow the soil to settle before planting. Herbaceous peony roots should be set with eyes 1 in. deep; deeper planting will prevent flowering. Set tree peonies so that the graft line is 3–4 in. below the soil surface (the object is to get the shrubby top to root on its own). In Upper South, mulch the first year after the ground has frozen. Plants are unlikely to bloom the first year, but should bloom every year after that if fertilized after the flowering period and again in fall (the American Peony Society recommends 8-8-8 and bonemeal).

In humid weather, the fungus disease botrytis is sometimes a problem: buds blacken and fail to develop, stems wilt and collapse. Prevent the problem by sanitation: in autumn, dispose of all leaves (also all stems on herbaceous peonies). As new growth emerges in spring, spray with copper fungicide or zineb.

Paeonia
Double Type

Herbaceous peonies. Perennials. Zones US, MS, LS. Bloom well only where they have a period of pronounced winter chill. Grow to 3–4 ft. tall. Large blossoms borne in late spring or early summer are 4–6 in. (even up to 10 in.) across; many selections have a refreshing old-rose scent. Flowers are in three basic groups: single or semidouble, with one or two rows of petals; Japanese, with one single row of petals and a central mass of narrow petal-like segments called staminodes; and double, with full flowers composed of many petals. In the South, single, early-flowering types tend to do best, and all profit from light afternoon shade. In warm wet weather, the doubles often fail to open; however, some doubles bloom reliably every year. Choosing the right selection is the key to success. If you have room for only one peony, choose ❦ 'Festiva Maxima' (double white flowers with red flecks), a Southern heirloom that has bloomed dependably for generations. Other double types include 'Edulis Superba', 'Martha Bulloch', 'Mons. Jules Elie', 'Sarah Bernhardt', 'Therese', 'Walter Faxon', all with pink flowers; 'Elsa Sass', 'Florence Nicholls', 'Gardenia', 'Kelway's Glorious', with white flowers; and 'Big Bend', 'Felix Crousse', 'Karl Rosenfield', and 'Philippe Rivoire', red flowers. Among single selections, consider 'Imperial Red'; 'Le Jour', white flowers; 'Seashell', pink flowers; and 'Sparkling Star', dark pink. Recommended Japanese types include 'Ama-No-Sode', dark pink; 'Do Tell' and 'Largo', pink; 'Isani-Gidui' and 'Shaylor's Sunburst', white; 'Comanche', 'Dignity', 'Mikado', and 'Nippon Brilliant', red. 'Primevere' is a good white "anemone" type; 'Minnie Shaylor' (pink fading to white) or 'Phyllis Kelway' (pink) are good semidouble selections.

Provide support for the heavy flowers. All types are choice cut flowers; cut just as buds begin to open. Leave at least three leaves on every cut stem, and do not remove more than half the blooms from any clump. The object is to preserve leaf growth to nourish the plant for next year. Remove faded flowers from plants to prevent seed formation. The only reason to divide a peony plant is to increase your stock. Dig in early fall, hose off soil, and divide rhizome into sections, making sure that each has at least three eyes; these appear at top of root cluster, at or near bases of past season's stems. Plant at once to establish before freezing weather.

Tree peonies. Deciduous shrubs. Zones US, MS, LS. Slow growth rate to 3–5 ft. tall, with handsome divided leaves and large (to 10–12-in.) single to double flowers in early spring. Take several years to reveal their true potential, but the spectacular results are worth the wait. Imported small grafted plants are sometimes available, usually sold only by color (red, pink, white, yellow, purple); these are a good buy if you can wait for them to attain good size. Catalogs offer named selections of Japanese origin in white, pink, red, and purple. More recent and considerably more expensive (but worth it) are yellow and orange hybrids from crosses of *P. suffruticosa* with *P. delavayi* and *P. lutea*.

Tree peonies require less winter chill than herbaceous peonies. The flowers are fragile and should be sheltered from strong wind. Prune only to remove faded blooms and any dead wood.

PAGODA FLOWER. See CLERODENDRUM paniculatum

PAINTED DAISY. See CHRYSANTHEMUM coccineum

PAINTED DROP-TONGUE. See AGLAONEMA crispum

PAINTED FINGERNAIL PLANT. See NEOREGELIA spectabilis

Palmae. See Arecaceae

PALMETTO. See SABAL

PALM GRASS. See SETARIA palmifolia

PALMS. Most palms are tropical or subtropical; a few are surprisingly hardy (specimens are seen in Edinburgh, London, and southern Russia). Palms offer great opportunity for imaginative planting. In nature they grow not only in solid stands but also with other plants, notably broad-leafed evergreen trees and shrubs. They are effective near swimming pools.

Most young palms prefer shade, and all palms tolerate it; this fact makes them good house or patio plants when they are small. As they grow, they can be moved into sun or partial shade, depending on the species and the area. Growth rates vary, but keeping plants in pots usually slows growth of faster-growing kinds. Fertilize potted palms often; also wash them off frequently to provide some humidity in drier environments and clean the foliage. Washing also dislodges insects, which (indoors, at any rate) are protected from their natural enemies and can increase with alarming speed.

To pot a palm, supply good potting soil, adequate drainage, and not too big a container. As with all potted plants, pot or repot a palm in a container just slightly larger than the one it's in.

Some shade-tolerant palms, such as *Rhapis, Chamaedorea, Howea*, can spend decades in pots indoors. Others that later can reach great size —*Phoenix, Washingtonia, Chamaerops*—make charming temporary indoor plants but must eventually be moved outdoors.

Planting holes for palms should generally be the same depth as and 1–2 ft. wider than root ball. Amend the backfill with organic matter; water faithfully until established. From then on, palms need little maintenance; they thrive with reasonably fertile soil and adequate water. All tropical palms do their growing during warm times of year. Washing with a hose is beneficial, especially for palms exposed to dust and beyond reach of rain or dew; it helps keep down spider mites and sucking insects that find refuge in the long leaf stems.

Feather palms and many fan palms look neater when old leaves are removed after they have turned brown. Make neat cuts close to trunk, leaving leaf bases. Some palms shed old leaf bases on their own. Others, including *Syagrus* and *Chamaedorea*, may hold old bases. You can remove them by slicing them off at the very bottom of base (be careful not to cut into trunk).

Several palms can take frost and some even tolerate freezing temperatures. Frost becomes more damaging to palms as it extends its stay and is repeated. Simplest damage is burned leaf edges, but frost may affect whole leaf, parts of trunk, or crown. Damage in crown is usually fatal (though some have recovered). Hardiness is also a matter of size; larger plants may pass through severe frosts unharmed while smaller ones perish.

P

Here are nine roles that the right kinds of palms can fill. Palms named in each listing are described under their own names elsewhere in this book.

Sturdy palms for street trees and vertical effects in large gardens. Alexander palm (*Ptychosperma elegans*), *Archontophoenix*, *Brahea*, cabbage palm *(Sabal palmetto)*, Canary Island date palm (*Phoenix canariensis*), cliff date palm (*Phoenix rupicola*), coconut palm (*Cocos nucifera*), date palm (*Phoenix dactylifera*), *Livistona*, *Phoenix loureiri*, queen palm (*Syagrus romanzoffianum*), royal palm (*Roystonea*), and *Washingtonia*.

Small to medium-size palms for frost-free gardens. *Archontophoenix*, areca palm (*Chrysalidocarpus lutescens*), *Chamaedorea*, European fan palm (*Chamaerops humilis*), *Howea*, and fishtail palm (*Caryota*).

Small to medium-size palms that tolerate light, brief frost. *Acoelorrhaphe wrightii*, blue fan palm (*Brahea armata*), Canary Island date palm, *Chamaedorea*, date palm, European fan palm, *Livistona*, Macarthur palm (*Ptychosperma macarthuri*), *Phoenix loureiri*, pindo palm (*Butia capitata*), pygmy date palm (*Phoenix roebelenii*).

Hardiest palms that tolerate temperatures below freezing. Blue fan palm, cabbage palm, dwarf palmetto (*Sabal minor*), European fan palm, lady palm (*Rhapis*), *Livistona*, needle palm (*Rhapidophyllum histrix*), Texas palmetto (*Sabal mexicana*), *Washingtonia*, windmill palm (*Trachycarpus fortunei*).

Salt-tolerant palms for seaside planting. Cabbage palm, Canary Island date palm, coconut palm (*Cocos nucifera*), date palm, European fan palm, Hispaniolan palmetto *(Sabal blackburniana)*, pindo palm, royal palm (*Roystonea*), Senegal date palm (*Phoenix reclinata*), thread palm (*Washingtonia robusta*).

Palms for hot, dry climates. Blue fan palm, Canary Island date palm, Chinese fan palm (*Livistona chinensis*), date palm, dwarf palmetto, European fan palm, *Phoenix loureiri*, pindo palm, silver date palm (*Phoenix sylvestris*), Texas palmetto, *Washingtonia*.

Palms to grow under overhangs, or indoors. *Archontophoenix*, Burmese fishtail palm (*Caryota mitis*), Canton fishtail palm (*Caryota ochlandra*), *Chamaedorea*, *Howea*, lady palm, young *Livistona*, pygmy date palm, Senegal date palm (when young), wine palm (*Caryota urens*). Indoor palms should occasionally be brought outdoors into mild light.

Palms as underplantings. Young palms, especially slow growers such as Chinese fan palm and European fan palm, stay low for 5 to 10 years; can be used effectively as plantings under tall trees. Or choose dwarf palmetto or needle palm. These shrubby palms rarely exceed 6 ft. tall.

Palms for night lighting. Thanks to their stateliness and spectacular leaves, all palms are good subjects for this. Backlight them, light them from below, or direct light to silhouette them against light-colored wall.

PAMPAS GRASS. See CORTADERIA selloana

PANDANUS utilis

SCREW PINE

Pandanaceae

TROPICAL TREE

ZONE TS; OR INDOORS

FULL SUN

REGULAR WATER

Pandanus utilis

Striking tree with aerial brace roots, and spirals of stiff, spiny, 3-ft.-long, yucca-like leaves at the ends of stubby branches. Grows outdoors only in southern Florida. Can reach 25–30 ft. tall. Old specimens may produce flowers on stringlike stems and then round, thick-skinned fruits.

Makes a picturesque container plant elsewhere in the South; bring indoors during winter and maintain night temperature above 55°F. Needs high humidity, direct or bright filtered light, and ample water in summer, less water in winter. Fertilize frequently during growing season.

PANDOREA

Bignoniaceae

EVERGREEN VINES

ZONE CS, TS

PARTIAL SHADE

REGULAR TO MODERATE WATER

Leaves divided into glossy oval leaflets; clusters of trumpet-shaped flowers. Climb by twining. They are attractive even out of bloom.

Pandorea jasminoides

P. jasminoides (Bignonia jasminoides, Tecoma jasminoides). BOWER VINE. Fast growing to 20–30 ft. Slender stems, distinguished glossy medium to dark green foliage. Leaves have five to nine egg-shaped leaflets 1–2 in. long. Flowers white with pink throats, 1½–2 in., drop cleanly after June–October bloom. 'Alba' and more vigorous 'Lady D.' have pure white flowers. 'Rosea' has pink flowers with rose pink throats. One form has variegated leaves. Plant in lee of prevailing wind. Prolonged freezes will kill it.

P. pandorana (Bignonia australis, Tecoma australis). WONGA-WONGA VINE. More vigorous than *P. jasminoides*; needs room to grow. Glossy foliage handsome in all seasons. Small (to ¾-in.-long) spring flowers are yellowish or pinkish white, usually with brownish purple spots in throat. Prune ends of branches heavily after bloom.

PANICUM virgatum

SWITCH GRASS

Poaceae (Gramineae)

PERENNIAL GRASS

ZONES US, MS, LS

FULL SUN OR LIGHT SHADE

MUCH TO LITTLE WATER

Native to the tall-grass prairie of the Midwest. Upright clump of narrow, deep green or gray-green leaves is topped by slender flower clusters; clump grows 4–7 ft. high in bloom. Clusters open into loose, airy clouds of pinkish blossoms that fade to white, then brown. Foliage turns yellow in fall, gradually fades to beige. Both foliage and flowers persist all winter. 'Haense Herms' is grown for red fall foliage, 'Heavy Metal' for stiffly upright silvery blue leaves that turn bright yellow in autumn; both reach 4–5 ft. high.

Panicum virgatum

Plant tolerates many soils, moisture levels, and exposures, even salt winds. Attractive silhouette in winter. Use as accent in large informal flower border or as screening.

PANSY. See VIOLA

PAPAVER

POPPY

Papaveraceae

PERENNIALS AND ANNUALS

ZONES VARY BY SPECIES

FULL SUN

REGULAR TO MODERATE WATER

Papaver orientale

Poppies provide bright spring and summer color for borders and cutting. Give plants ordinary soil and good

P

311

drainage; feed lightly until established. Perennials tend to be short lived. When using poppies as cut flowers, sear the ends of clipped stems in flame before placing in water.

P. alpinum (P. burseri). ALPINE POPPY. Perennial. Zones US, MS; best adapted to Upper South. Rock garden plant with basal foliage rosette and 5–8-in.-high flower stalk. Blue-green, nearly hairless, divided leaves. Spring flowers are 1–1½ in. across, come in white, orange, yellow, salmon. Blooms first year from seed sown in fall or early spring.

P. atlanticum. Perennial. Zones US, MS. To 1½ ft. high, with jagged-edged, softly hairy leaves to 6 in. long. Orange, 3-in. flowers in summer.

P. nudicaule. ICELAND POPPY. Short-lived perennial in Zones US, MS; grown as an annual in most places. Divided leaves with coarse hairs. Slender, hairy stems 1–2 ft. high. Cup-shaped, slightly fragrant flowers to 3 in. across, in yellow, orange, salmon, rose, pink, cream, white. For winter or spring bloom, sow seed onto bare soil, or set out transplants in fall. Gardeners in colder parts of Upper South should set out transplants in spring. To prolong bloom, pick flowers frequently. Champagne Bubbles is most widely grown strain. Low-growing Wonderland strain (to 10 in.) comes in mixed or single colors. Oregon Rainbows strain has larger flowers than species, but many buds fail to open; wider color range includes bicolors and picotees. Misato Carnival strain has 6-in. flowers on 2–3-ft. stems.

P. orientale. ORIENTAL POPPY. Perennial. Zones US, MS. Needs winter chill for best performance. Height variable; some types 16 in. tall, others reach 4 ft. Hairy, coarsely cut leaves. Single or double flowers are large to very large (to 11 in. across in some types); colors include white, pink, orange yellow, orange, scarlet, and dark red, usually with a dark blotch at base of each petal. A great many named selections are sold; they bloom in late spring and early summer, then die back in midsummer. The sterile Minicap Hybrids were bred for greater heat tolerance and for profuse bloom over a longer period (2 to 4 months). In all types, new leafy growth appears in fall, lasts over winter, and develops rapidly in spring. Set sprawling plants such as baby's breath nearby to cover bare areas after poppies die down. Plant dormant roots in fall with tops 3 in. deep. Set container-grown plants flush with soil line. Provide good drainage and air circulation. Divide crowded clumps in August, after foliage has died down.

P. rhoeas. SHIRLEY POPPY, FLANDERS FIELD POPPY. Annual. All zones. Slender, branching, hairy-stemmed plant 2–5 ft. high. Short, irregularly divided leaves; single or double flowers 2 in. or wider, in red, pink, white, orange, scarlet, salmon, bicolors. Selections bearing single scarlet flowers with a black base are sold as 'American Legion' or 'Flanders Field'. Angels' Choir strain offers double flowers in a wide range of colors on 2–2½-ft. stems. Broadcast seed mixed with fine sand onto bare soil in late fall. Take cut flowers when buds first show color. Remove seed capsules (old flower bases) weekly to prolong bloom season. Notorious self-sower.

☞ **P. somniferum.** OPIUM POPPY. Annual. All zones. To 4 ft. tall, with virtually hairless gray-green leaves and usually double, sometimes single, 4–5-in. flowers in white or rosy shades (pink and red to purple). Late spring bloom. Large, decorative seed capsules. Opium is derived from sap of the green seed capsules; ripe ones yield large quantities of the poppy seed used in baking. Because of its narcotic properties, this species is not as widely offered as many other types. However, because the flowers are exceedingly beautiful, the seed is often shared among gardeners.

Papaveraceae. The poppy family of annuals, perennials, and shrubs displays showy flowers usually borne singly. *Papaver* is a significant member.

PAPAYA. See CARICA papaya

PAPER BUSH. See EDGEWORTHIA papyrifera

PAPER MULBERRY. See BROUSSONETIA papyrifera

PAPYRUS. See CYPERUS papyrus

PARADISE PALM. See HOWEA forsterana

PARAGUAY NIGHTSHADE. See LYCIANTHES rantonnei

PARIS DAISY. See CHRYSANTHEMUM frutescens

PARKINSONIA aculeata

JERUSALEM THORN, MEXICAN PALO VERDE

Fabaceae (Leguminosae)

⚊ DECIDUOUS TREE

✂ ZONES CS, TS

☼ FULL SUN

💧 💧 REGULAR TO LITTLE WATER

Parkinsonia aculeata

Rapid growth at first, then slowing; eventually grows to 15–30 ft. high and wide. Yellow-green bark, spiny twigs, picturesque form. Sparse foliage; leaves 6–9 in. long, with many tiny leaflets that quickly fall in drought or cold. Numerous yellow flowers in loose, 3–7-in.-long clusters. Long bloom season in spring; intermittent bloom throughout year.

A tree for water-conserving gardens, since it grows in dry soil; also performs well in moist soil as long as it's well drained. Tolerates alkaline soil. Stake young trees and train for high or low branching. Requires minimal attention once established. As shade tree, it filters sun rather than blocking it. Litter drop is a problem on hard surfaces. Thorns and sparse foliage rule it out of tailored gardens. Use flowering branches in arrangements.

PARLOR PALM. See CHAMAEDOREA elegans

PARROTIA persica

PERSIAN PARROTIA

Hamamelidaceae

⚊ DECIDUOUS SHRUB OR SMALL TREE

✂ ZONES US, MS, LS

☼ FULL SUN

💧 💧 REGULAR TO MODERATE WATER

Parrotia persica

Native to Iran. Slow growing to 30 ft. or more, but most often seen as a 15-ft. shrub or multitrunked tree. Young trees are fairly upright; older ones are wide-spreading, rounded. Choice and colorful; attractive all year. Most dramatic display comes in autumn: Leaves usually turn golden yellow, then orange or rosy pink, and finally scarlet. Attractive smooth, gray bark; in mature trees, it flakes off to reveal white, tan, and green patches beneath. Blooms in late winter or early spring before leaves open. Flowers have dense heads of red stamens surrounded by woolly brown bracts; blooming plants have an overall reddish haze. New foliage unfurls reddish purple, matures to lustrous dark green. Leaves are ¾ in. long, oval, shallowly toothed along upper half.

Prefers slightly acid soil but tolerates alkaline and chalky soils. Will also withstand light shade. Pest resistant.

PARROT LILY. See ALSTROEMERIA psittacina

PARSLEY

Apiaceae (Umbelliferae)

⚊ BIENNIAL HERB TREATED AS ANNUAL

✂ ALL ZONES

☼ ☽ AFTERNOON SHADE

💧 REGULAR WATER

Parsley

Attractive edging for herb, vegetable, or flower garden; also looks good in boxes, pots. Its foliage is a favorite food of swallowtail butterfly caterpillars. Plants are 6–12 in. high, with tufted, finely cut, dark green leaves. Use leaves fresh or dried as seasoning, fresh as garnish. Plants die after flowering in their second year of life. Replace with new plants. Buy plants at garden centers or sow seed in place (in spring in the Upper South; in fall or early spring elsewhere). Soak seed in warm water for 24 hours before planting. Even after soaking, seed may not sprout for weeks: According to an old story, parsley seeds must go to the devil and come back before sprouting. Thin seedlings 6–8 in. apart.

> ### THE SHOWY PARSLEY OR THE COOKING PARSLEY?
> The Italian, flat-leafed parsley is the tastiest kind for cooking. The curly types make the most attractive garnish and are appealing as a low border in a flower bed.

PARSLEY PANAX. See POLYSCIAS fruticosa

PARSNIP

Apiaceae (Umbelliferae)

BIENNIAL GROWN AS AN ANNUAL

ZONES US, MS, LS

FULL SUN

MAINTAIN EVEN SOIL MOISTURE

Parsnip

Needs deep, well-prepared, loose soil for long roots; roots of some varieties are 15 in. long. In the Upper and Middle South, plant seeds in late spring and harvest in fall; leave surplus in ground to be dug as needed in winter. Cold makes the roots sweeter. In the Lower South, sow in late summer or fall and harvest in spring; in these areas, mature roots will continue to grow if they are left in ground, becoming tough and woody. Soak seeds in water 24 hours before planting to improve germination. Sow ½ in. deep in rows spaced 2 ft. apart; thin seedlings to 3 in. apart.

PARTHENOCISSUS (Ampelopsis)

Vitaceae

DECIDUOUS VINES

ZONES VARY BY SPECIES

SUN OR SHADE

REGULAR WATER

Cling to walls by sucker discs at ends of tendrils. Superb, dependable orange to scarlet fall leaf color. Flowers are insignificant. Attractive to birds. Think twice before planting vines against wood or shingle siding; they can creep under it, and their clinging tendrils are hard to remove at repainting time.

P. quinquefolia. VIRGINIA CREEPER, WOODBINE. Zones US, MS, LS, CS. Native to eastern U.S. Vigorous vine to 30–50 ft. or more; clings or runs over ground, fence, trellis, trees. Looser growth than *P. tricuspidata;* will drape trailing branches over trellis. Leaves divided into five separate 6-in. leaflets with saw-toothed edges; foliage turns bright to dull red in fall. Good ground cover on slopes; can control erosion. 'Engelmannii' has smaller leaves, denser growth.

P. tricuspidata. BOSTON IVY. Zones US, MS, LS. Native to China, Japan. Even more vigorous than *P. quinquefolia.* Glossy leaves to 8 in. wide are variable in shape, usually three lobed or divided into three leaflets; fall color varies from orange to burgundy. Vine clings tightly and grows quickly to make dense, even wall cover. This is the ivy of the Ivy League; covers brick or stone in

Parthenocissus tricuspidata

Parthenocissus quinquefolia

areas where English ivy freezes. Leaves of 'Beverly Brooks' and 'Green Showers' are larger than those of the species; leaves of 'Lowii' and 'Veitchii' are considerably smaller.

PARTRIDGEBERRY. See MITCHELLA repens

PASPALUM

Poaceae (Gramineae)

LAWN AND PASTURE GRASSES

ZONES VARY BY SPECIES

FULL SUN

REGULAR OR LITTLE WATER

Paspalum notatum

Large genus of grasses including several species that are used for pasture or hay. One species is a lawn grass.

P. notatum. BAHIA GRASS. Zones CS, TS. Tough, rather coarse grass used for lawns in Florida. Needs little fertilizer and can endure periodic drought, but seed heads need frequent mowing to prevent unkempt look. Takes heavy foot traffic. Selections include 'Argentine', generally recognized as best selection for lawns, and 'Pensacola'.

P. vaginatum. SEASHORE PASPALUM. Zones MS, LS, CS, TS. Native to sandy soils near seashore, North Carolina to Texas. Finer textured than bahia grass and deeper green; tolerates salty soil better than most grasses.

PASSIFLORA

PASSION VINE

Passifloraceae

EVERGREEN, SEMIEVERGREEN, OR DECIDUOUS VINES

ZONES VARY BY SPECIES

FULL SUN

REGULAR TO MODERATE WATER

Passiflora alatocaerulea

Climb by tendrils to 20–30 ft.; bloom during warm weather. Flower parts can be seen to symbolize elements of the passion of Christ, hence plant's common name. The lacy crown represents a halo or crown of thorns; the five stamens, the five wounds; the ten petal-like parts, the ten faithful apostles.

Vigorous, likely to overgrow and tangle; to keep plant open and prevent buildup of dead inner tangle, prune annually after second year, cutting excess branches back to base or juncture with another branch. Tolerant of many soils. Favorite food of caterpillars of gulf fritillary butterfly.

Use vines on trellises, arbors, or walls for their vigor and bright, showy flowers; or use as soil-holding bank cover. In areas where they aren't hardy, use as greenhouse or house plants. Or train them on a trellis in a pot that you take outside in spring and bring indoors in fall.

P. alatocaerulea (P. pfordtii). PURPLE PASSION FLOWER. Evergreen or semievergreen. Zone TS. Hybrid between *P. caerulea* and *P. alata,* a species not described here. Best known, most widely planted, probably least subject to damage from caterpillars. Three-lobed leaves 3 in. long. Fragrant, 3½–4-in. flowers, white shaded pink and lavender; deep blue or purple crown. Forms no fruit. Excellent windowsill bloomer.

P. caerulea. BLUE PASSION FLOWER. Evergreen or semievergreen. Zones CS, TS; dies to ground in Lower South, but will come back if roots are mulched in late fall. Leaves are five lobed, smaller than those of *P. alatocaerulea.* Flowers also smaller, in greenish white with white-and-purple crown. Edible small, oval fruit with orange rind and red seeds.

P. coccinea. RED PASSION FLOWER. Evergreen or semievergreen. Zones CS, TS. Native to South America. Not as vigorous as *P. incarnata.* Leaves oblong, to 5 in. by 2½ in. Flowers, 3–5 in. across, brilliant scarlet with white, pink, and purple crowns. Mottled orange or yellow fruits, 2 in., are edible and have good flavor. Grown for its fruit in countries of origin.

P. edulis. PASSION FRUIT. Semievergreen. Zone TS. Leaves three lobed, deeply toothed, light yellow green. Flowers white with white-and-purple crown, 2 in. across. Fruit produced in spring and fall: deep purple, fragrant, 3 in. long, delicious used in beverages, fruit salads, sherbets. 'Nancy Garrison' is a hardier version. There is also a yellow-fruited variety.

🎍 **P. incarnata.** MAYPOP, WILD PASSION VINE. Deciduous. All zones. Native to Southeast. Hardiest of the passion flowers, surviving temperatures at least as low as −10°F and possibly even lower. Dies to ground in most areas. Three-lobed leaves are 4–6 in. wide; freely produced flowers are 2–3 in. wide, white or pale lavender, with filaments banded in purple or pink. Yellow, 2-in. fruits are edible. Spreads vigorously from seeds and underground roots and can become an attractive pest. Although this plant is seldom sold in garden centers, it is easily grown from seed.

P. 'Incense'. Deciduous. Zones LS, CS, TS. Hardy to 0°F; holds its leaves through short cold spells, dies to ground when weather turns colder. Hybrid between *P. incarnata* and an Argentinian species. Flowers are 5 in. wide, violet with lighter crown, with sweet pea–like fragrance. Egg-shaped, 2-in. fruit has fragrant, tasty pulp; when ripe, it turns from olive to yellow green, then drops.

P. jamesonii. Evergreen. Zones CS, TS. Glossy, three-lobed leaves. Profusion of long-tubed (to 4-in.) salmon to coral flowers. Fast bank or fence cover. This and similar plants are sold as 'Coral Seas'.

P. 'Lavender Lady'. Evergreen. Zones CS (protected), TS. Profuse show of 4-in. lavender purple flowers with deep violet crown.

P. mollissima. BANANA PASSION VINE. Evergreen. Zone TS. Soft green foliage; leaves three lobed, deeply toothed. Long-tubed pink to rose flowers 3 in. across. Yellow, 4–6-in.-long fruit. May be better as indoor plant; prefers cooler temperatures and lower humidity than others.

P. vitifolia. GRAPE LEAF PASSION FLOWER. Evergreen. Zone TS. Grapelike, 6-in. deep green leaves set off bright red flowers 3½ in. long. Quite similar in appearance to *P. coccinea*.

PASSION FLOWER, PASSION VINE. See PASSIFLORA

PASSION FRUIT. See PASSIFLORA edulis

PATRINIA

Valerianaceae

PERENNIALS

🌡 ZONES US, MS, LS

☼ ◐ EXPOSURE NEEDS VARY BY SPECIES

● REGULAR WATER

Patrinia triloba

Perennials with mounds of deeply cut or lobed leaves that produce stems bearing few or no leaves and flat-topped clusters of tiny yellow or white flowers. Summer bloom. They are useful for blending with other border perennials. Long-lasting cut flowers. All appreciate rich, well-drained soil.

P. scabiosifolia. Grows to 5–6 ft. and may require staking, but thinly foliaged flower stalks and open showers of yellow flower clusters give plant a see-through quality that makes it appropriate for either front or rear of border. Finely divided leaves to 6 in. 'Compact Selection' and 'Nagoya' grow only 1½–3 ft. tall. Cut flowers last several weeks and mix well with other kinds in arrangements. Full sun.

P. triloba. Grows 1 ft. tall and spreads slowly to make a small-scale ground cover. Glossy deep green, three- to five-lobed leaves are 2 in. long, finely divided. Yellow flowers. Grows best in light shade.

P. villosa. Leaves to 6 in. long, either divided or uncut. Sprawling flower stems to 1½ ft. hold showers of white blossoms. Full sun.

🎍 # PAULOWNIA tomentosa
(P. imperialis)
EMPRESS TREE, PRINCESS TREE

Bignoniaceae

DECIDUOUS TREE

🌡 ZONES US, MS, LS

☼ ◐ FULL SUN OR PARTIAL SHADE

● ● REGULAR OR MODERATE WATER

Paulownia tomentosa

Native to China. Somewhat similar to catalpa in growth habit, leaves. Fast growth to 40–50 ft., with nearly equal spread. Can grow 8–10 ft. a year in youth. Often advertised as "miracle shade tree" in weekly garden tabloids. Heavy trunk and heavy, nearly horizontal branches. Foliage gives tropical effect; light green, heart-shaped leaves are 5–12 in. long, 4–7 in. wide. No significant fall color. Brown flower buds the size of small olives form in fall, persist through winter; they open before the leaves in early spring, forming 6–12-in.-long clusters of trumpet-shaped, 2-in.-long, fragrant flowers of lilac blue with darker spotting and yellow stripes on inside. Flowers followed by 1½–2-in. seed capsules shaped like tops; these remain on tree with flower buds. Does not bloom well where winters are very cold (buds freeze) or very mild (buds may drop off).

Performs best in deep, moist, well-drained soil, though it will grow in many soils. Will grow in cracks in the pavement and in mine spoil. Tolerates air pollution. Protect from strong winds. Plant where falling flowers and leaves are not objectionable. Not a tree to garden under because of dense shade, surface roots. If tree is cut back annually or every other year, it will grow as billowy foliage mass with giant-size leaves up to 2 ft. long; however, such pruning will reduce or eliminate flower production. Light wood is highly prized in Japan for making bowls, pots, spoons, furniture, and sandals. A mature tree commands a high market price. Unfortunately, this is the most likely cause of "tree rustling" in the South. A happy tree owner retires at night, only to discover a stump the next morning.

PAUROTIS wrightii. See ACOELORRHAPHE wrightii

PAVONIA lasiopetala
PAVONIA, ROCK ROSE

Malvaceae

PERENNIAL

🌡 ZONES MS, LS, CS, TS

☼ ◐ FULL SUN OR PARTIAL SHADE

● LITTLE WATER

Pavonia lasiopetala

Grows in rugged, dry, limestone soils of Texas; nearly evergreen except in coldest parts of range, where it dies back to roots each winter. Bears numerous, showy, 2-in., rose pink flowers all summer, from June to first frost. Leaves are slightly lobed, coarsely toothed, to 1½ in. long and wide. Makes a spindly open bush, to 5 ft. tall, but can be cut back in winter for a neater appearance. Useful for dry, shady areas of garden.

PAWPAW. See ASIMINA triloba

PAXISTIMA canbyi

Celastraceae

EVERGREEN SHRUB

🌡 ZONES US, MS

☼ ◐ FULL SUN OR PARTIAL SHADE

● REGULAR WATER

Paxistima canbyi

Native to mountains of Virginia and West Virginia. Slowly forms a mat 9–12 in. by 3–5 ft. Leathery leaves, ¼–1 in. long, ¼ in. wide, are shiny dark green, turning bronzy in fall and winter. Good as edging and ground cover. Best in well-drained soil. Tolerates alkaline soil.

PEA

Fabaceae (Leguminosae)

ANNUAL

✔ ALL ZONES

☀ FULL SUN

● REGULAR WATER

Sometimes called garden or English pea to distinguish it from Southern pea (a category including black-eyed pea, cowpea, and crowder pea); for the latter, see Southern Pea.

Pea

Easy crop to grow when conditions are right, and delicious when freshly picked. Peas need coolness and humidity and must be planted at just the right time. If you don't mind the bother and have space, grow tall (vining) peas on trellises, strings, or screen; they reach 6 ft. or more and bear heavily. Two good tall selections are 'Alderman' and 'Multistar'. Bush types are more commonly grown in gardens; they don't require support. Fine bush selections are 'Blue Bantam', 'Freezonian', 'Green Arrow', 'Little Marvel', 'Maestro', and 'Morse's Progress No. 9'. Two unusually good peas, popular in Asian cooking, are edible-pod snow pea (thin, crispy pod) and sugar snap pea (thicker, edible pod with full-size peas). They grow in both spring and fall. As a fall crop, they may be more successful than English pea because the plants tolerate heat better. Snow pea selections include 'Mammoth Melting Sugar', a tall vining type; 'Norli'; 'Oregon Giant'. Dwarf forms include 'Dwarf Gray Sugar', a bushy one, and 'Snowbird', a type that is good for fall. Sugar snap selections include 'Sugar Ann'; 'Sugar Bon', an early-maturing dwarf sugar snap; 'Sugar Daddy', compact and stringless; 'Sugar Pod II'; and 'Sugar Snap', which is good for shelling.

Peas need soil that is slightly acid to slightly alkaline, water retentive but fast draining. In the Upper South, plant as soon as soil can be worked in spring. In the Middle and Lower South, plant in late summer for fall crop, in late winter for spring crop. In the Coastal and Tropical South, plant around Christmas time. Sow 2 in. deep in light soil, ½–1 in. deep in heavy soil or in winter. Moisten ground thoroughly before planting; do not irrigate until seedlings have broken through surface. Leave 2 ft. between rows; thin seedlings to stand 2 in. apart. Successive plantings several days apart will lengthen bearing season, but don't plant so late that summer heat will overtake ripening peas; most ready to harvest in 60 to 70 days.

Plants need little fertilizer, but if soil is very light, give them one application of complete fertilizer. If weather turns warm and dry, supply water in furrows; overhead watering encourages mildew. Provide support for vining peas as soon as tendrils form. When peas begin to mature, pick all pods that are ready; if seeds ripen, plant will stop producing. Vines are brittle; steady them with one hand while picking with the other. Above all, shell and cook (or freeze) peas right after picking.

PEACE LILY. See SPATHIPHYLLUM

PEACH and NECTARINE

Rosaceae

DECIDUOUS FRUIT TREES

✔ ZONES VARY BY SELECTION

☀ FULL SUN

● REGULAR WATER

▶ SEE CHART NEXT PAGE

Peach

Trees of both peach (*Prunus persica*) and nectarine (*P. p. nucipersica*) look much alike and have the same cultural needs. Where fruit is concerned, nectarines differ from peaches in several respects: they have smooth skins; in some selections, flavor is slightly different; and many are more susceptible to brown rot of stone fruit (see below for controls). Here we consider fruiting peaches and nectarines; for strictly flowering types, see *Prunus*.

Peaches and nectarines of one type or another can be grown throughout the South. Extra-hardy types extend peach and nectarine growing into the Upper South. Selections tend to be regionally adapted; for the best choices for your area, see the chart and also consult local garden centers and your Cooperative Extension Office.

In most areas, crops ripen between June and September, depending on selection. For good harvests, trees need some winter chilling; most peach and nectarine selections require 600 to 900 hours of 45°F or lower temperatures during the dormant season. Only selections with a low winter-chill requirement do well in the Coastal and Tropical South. An insufficient number of winter-chill hours means delayed leaf-out, a scanty crop, and eventual death of tree.

In areas of late frosts, early-blooming selections are very risky. Plants also need clear, hot weather during the growing season; where spring is cool and rainy, peach and nectarine trees set few flowers, pollinate poorly, and get peach leaf curl.

A standard-size fruiting peach or nectarine grows rapidly to 25 ft. high and wide; properly pruned trees are usually kept at a height of 10–12 ft. They start bearing large crops when 3 or 4 years old and reach peak production at 8 to 12 years. Natural or genetic dwarf trees, most of which grow 5–6 ft. tall and produce medium-size fruit, are useful in tubs and confined planting areas. With a few exceptions (see comments in chart), peaches and nectarines are self-fertile.

Peach and nectarine trees are not low-maintenance plants; they require good drainage, a regular fertilizing program, and heavier pruning than other fruit trees. When planting a bare-root tree that is an unbranched "whip," cut it back to 2–3½ ft. above ground (the thicker the trunk, the less severe the cutting back). New branches will form below the cut. After first year's growth, select three well-placed branches for scaffold limbs. Remove all other branches. On mature trees, in each dormant season, cut off two-thirds of previous year's growth by removing two of every three branches formed that year; or head back each branch to one-third its length; or head back some branches and cut out others. Trees can be trained as espaliers.

Peaches and nectarines tend to set too much fruit even with good pruning. When fruits are about 1 in. wide, remove (thin) some of the excess; remaining fruits should be 8–10 in. apart. If growth becomes weak and leaves yellowish, feed with nitrogen fertilizer.

Peaches and nectarines are plagued by a host of diseases and insects. If you're philosophically opposed to spraying, you may want to reconsider growing them. Among the most serious ailments are peach leaf curl and brown rot of stone fruit. To control both diseases, practice sanitation (get rid of diseased plant parts) and give two dormant-season sprayings of Daconil (chlorothalonil), captan, Bordeaux mixture, or lime sulfur—the first after autumn leaf drop, the second in spring before buds swell. To control the diseases as well as scale insects, use sprays combining oil with lime sulfur. Peach tree borer is the most serious insect pest; it tends to attack trees stressed by poor growing conditions or wounds, causing defoliation, branch dieback, and possibly death. Jellylike material exuding from base of tree is the first indication of the pest's presence. The insect holes will be evident at or just below ground level. Prevention through good growing conditions is the best control; if tree is attacked, spray with either lindane or endosulfan.

PEACH-LEAFED BLUEBELL. See CAMPANULA persicifolia

PEACOCK GINGER. See KAEMPFERIA

PEACOCK LILY. See KAEMPFERIA roscoeana

PEACOCK MOSS. See SELAGINELLA uncinata

PEACOCK PLANT. See CALATHEA makoyana, KAEMPFERIA atrovirens

PEACH and NECTARINE

SELECTION	ZONES	FRUIT	COMMENTS
PEACHES			
'Belle of Georgia'	US, MS, LS	Large. Freestone. Skin is creamy white blushed red; flesh is white. Fine flavor. Midseason	Vigorous tree; heavy bearer. Old favorite. Originated in Georgia around 1810. Bruises easily
'Contender'	US, MS	Freestone with good-quality yellow flesh. Resists browning. Blooms late, fruit often survives late freezes; ripens about 9 days before 'Elberta'	Consistent cropper. Needs 1,050 hours of winter chill. Introduced by North Carolina State University
'Dixiland'	US, MS, LS	Large. Freestone. Yellow skin blushed red; little fuzz. Firm yellow flesh. Good quality. Late midseason	From Georgia. Vigorous, productive. Showy flowers
'Dixired'	US, MS	Yellow-fleshed clingstone. Round, deep red fruit, sweet and juicy. Early, 21 days before 'Elberta'. Thin fruit; tends to overbear	Good quality. Requires 900 or more hours of winter chill. Bears young. Self-fertile. Holds well on the tree
'Early Elberta' ('Improved Elberta')	US, MS, LS	Better color and flavor than 'Elberta'; also ripens about 1 week earlier	Needs somewhat less heat and less winter chill than 'Elberta'; less subject to fruit drop. Thin heavily for good-size fruit
'Elberta'	US, MS, LS (northern half)	Medium to large. Freestone. Yellow skin blushed red; yellow flesh. Good quality. Midseason	From Georgia. The classic peach by which all others are measured
'Flordaking'	LS, CS	Medium to large. Semiclingstone. Firm yellow fruit. Early	Very vigorous. Good fruit if thinned well. Low winter-chill requirement (350 hours)
'Flordaprince'	CS	Small. Early-ripening, semiclingstone. Yellow skin speckled with red. Good flavor	Good peach for central Florida. Needs only 150 hours of chill. Susceptible to bacterial spot
'Gold Prince'	US, MS, LS, CS	Yellow-fleshed clingstone. Attractive, firm, round-ovate fruit of fair to good quality. Early, ripens 47 days before 'Elberta'	Requires 650 hours of winter chill. Introduced by the USDA. Good disease resistance
'Halehaven'	US, MS	Medium to large. Freestone. Highly colored yellow fruit is firm, very sweet. Midseason	Flower and leaf buds are very winter-hardy. Use fruit fresh or canned
'Harvester'	US, MS, LS	Medium-size. Freestone. Yellow fruit of excellent quality. Early	Needs 4–5 years to produce heavy crops
'Indian Cling'	US, MS, LS	Large. Clingstone. Dark crimson skin and flesh. Midseason	Old-fashioned, disease-resistant peach. Heavy yielder, dependable. Needs 800 chilling hours
'J. H. Hale'	US, MS, LS	Very large. Freestone. Highly colored, fairly smooth-skinned yellow fruit of good quality. Fine keeper. Late midseason	Needs cross-pollination by another selection
'La Feliciana'	LS, CS	Medium-size. Freestone. Yellow fruit of high quality. Early midseason	Originated in Louisiana. Needs only 450 hours of winter chill. Disease resistant
'Loring'	US, MS, LS	Large. Freestone. Attractive yellow skin imbued with red, little fuzz. Moderately juicy yellow flesh. Good quality. Midseason	Vigorous. Showy flowers appear early; susceptible to frost. Needs 750 hours of winter chill
'Madison'	US, MS	Medium-size. Freestone. Golden yellow skin blushed bright red. Firm golden flesh. Very good flavor. Midseason	Seedling of 'Redhaven' from Virginia. Good frost tolerance during bloom period. Heavy bearer
'Ranger'	US, MS	Freestone. Medium to large, red blushed fruit; firm, yellow, well-flavored flesh. Ripens 3 weeks before 'Elberta'	Vigorous, productive tree; requires 900 winter-chill hours. Good for areas with late spring frosts. Can or freeze
'Redhaven'	US, MS	Medium-size. Freestone. Yellow skin blushed bright red. Firm yellow flesh. Good flavor. Early	Among best of early peaches. Productive. Thin out fruit. Colors up early, so test for ripeness. Good fresh; freezes well

P

PEACH and NECTARINE

SELECTION	ZONES	FRUIT	COMMENTS
PEACHES			
'Redskin'	US, MS, LS	Large. Freestone. Yellow skin with good red coloring; yellow flesh. High quality. Midseason	'Elberta' seedling from Maryland. Showy flowers. Fruit good for eating fresh, canning, or freezing
'Reliance'	US, MS	Medium to large. Freestone. Yellow skin blushed dull medium red; yellow flesh can be fairly soft. Fair flavor. Midseason	Very hardy; has produced crops after temperatures of −25°F. Showy flowers. Needs heavy thinning
'Rio Grande'	LS, CS	Medium to large. Freestone. Red-blushed yellow skin. Firm yellow flesh. Mild flavor. Early	Low-chill selection from Florida. Productive. Showy flowers. Fruit has irregular surface and varies in size
'Rio Oso Gem'	US, MS, LS	Large. Freestone. Red-blushed yellow skin. Firm yellow flesh. Excellent flavor. Late midseason	Small tree. Large, showy flowers. Fruit freezes well
'Surecrop'	US, MS	Semifreestone, with yellow flesh. Ripens 6 weeks before 'Elberta'. Late bloomer, fruit often survives spring freezes	Cold-hardy. Needs good amount of winter chill (950 hours). Resists bacterial spot
'Suwanee'	MS, LS, CS	Freestone, with large, yellow fruit flushed with red; yellow flesh of good quality. Ripens 3 weeks before 'Elberta'	Grows well in Lower and Coastal South. Needs 650 hours of winter chill
'TropicSweet'	CS	Large. Semiclingstone. Red-blushed skin. Very sweet and tasty. Midseason	Excellent choice for central Florida. Needs only 175 hours of winter chill
NECTARINES			
'Fantasia'	US, MS, LS, CS	Large. Freestone. Bright yellow-and-red skin. Firm yellow flesh. Midseason	Vigorous. Showy flowers. Relatively low winter-chill requirement (600 hours)
'Karla Rose'	US, MS, LS, CS	Freestone with white flesh. Ripens 5 weeks before 'Elberta'	Requires 650 hours of winter chill. Good in cooler parts of the Gulf Coast region and farther north
'Mayfire'	US, MS, LS, CS	Clingstone, with small to medium fruit, yellow flesh. Fruit is firm and flavorful. Ripens 9 weeks before 'Elberta'	Very productive. Requires 650 hours of winter chill
'Redgold'	US, MS, LS	Large. Freestone. Deep red skin; golden yellow flesh. Good flavor. Midseason	Vigorous, productive. Excellent flavor. Fair disease resistance
'Rose Princess'	US, MS, LS	Attractive, round to elongate, ivory flushed with rose; freestone white flesh. Slightly tart but of good quality. Ripens 3 weeks before 'Elberta'	Requires 850 hours of chilling. Good fruit set. Introduced by USDA
'Sunglo'	US, MS, LS	Semicling, large red and yellow fruit of high quality; firm, sweet, deep yellow flesh. Ripens 24 days before 'Elberta'	Developed in California. Requires 850 hours of winter chill. Very sweet
'Sunraycer'	CS	Large. Semiclingstone. Beautiful red-and-yellow fruit of good flavor. Midseason	Needs only 250 hours of winter chill. Good choice for central Florida

PEANUT

Fabaceae (Leguminosae)

ANNUAL

ALL ZONES

FULL SUN

REGULAR WATER

Peanut

Best production where summers are long. Tender to frost but worth growing even in the Upper South. Peanut plants resemble small sweet pea bushes 10–20 in. high. After bright yellow flowers fade, a so-called peg (shootlike structure) develops at each flower's base, grows down into the soil, and develops peanuts underground. For best performance, give fertile, well-drained soil; sandy or other light-textured soil is ideal for penetration by pegs.

The four basic classes of peanuts are Virginia and Runner types, with two large seeds per pod; Spanish, with two or three small seeds per pod; and Valencia, with three to six small seeds per pod. Buy seeds (unroasted peanuts) from mail-order seed firms. Plant as soon as soil warms up, setting nuts 1½–2 in. deep. Sow seeds of Virginia and Runner peanuts 6–8 in. apart; sow Spanish and Valencia peanuts 4–6 in. apart. Fertilize at planting time. In 110 to 120 days after planting, foliage yellows and plants are ready to dig; loosen soil, then pull up plants. Cure peanuts on vines in warm, airy place out of sunlight for 2 to 3 weeks, then strip from plants.

SOUTHERN HERITAGE PLANTS
IDENTIFIED BY SYMBOL 𝍄

PEAR (Pyrus communis)

Rosaceae

DECIDUOUS FRUIT TREES

✂ ZONES VARY BY SELECTION

☀ FULL SUN

◖ REGULAR WATER

▶ SEE CHART NEXT PAGE

Pear

Most pears sold in markets and grown in gardens are selections of this European species. Trees are long lived, pyramidal in form with vertical branching, and grow 30–40 ft. tall, sometimes more. Pears on dwarfing understock make good small garden trees and excellent espaliers. Leaves of all types are leathery, glossy, bright green. Clustered white flowers are handsome in early spring. For ornamental relatives, see *Pyrus calleryana.*

To produce good crops, most European pears need at least 600 hours of winter chill (45°F temperatures or lower); most do better with 900 hours. Still, there are a number of low-chill pears that do quite well in the Coastal South, including 'Ayers', 'Baldwin', 'Kieffer', and 'Warren'.

Pears do best in well-drained loam, but they tolerate damp, heavy soil better than other fruit trees. They normally need cross-pollination for good fruit set; plant two or more kinds. Train trees early to good framework of main branches; then prune lightly to keep good form, eliminate crowding branches. Harvest season is July to late October, depending on selection. Thinning the fruit is not usually necessary. Fruit should be picked when full size but unripe (green and firm), then put in a cool, dark place to ripen. If a pear is ready to harvest, the stem will snap free when you lift the fruit so that it is horizontal. If the stem stays intact, try again in a few days.

Pears are highly subject to fireblight in warm, humid areas. In areas that are problem-prone, fireblight-resistant selections offer the best chance of success. Fireblight can cause entire branches to die back quickly; as soon as you see blackened growth, cut it back to a growth bud or stem with green, healthy tissue, disinfecting pruning tools between cuts. To avoid heavy new growth, with resultant risk of fireblight, do not prune heavily in any one dormant season; also fertilize sparingly. Dormant oil sprays will control pear psylla and various other pests that may bother pear trees. Codling moth can ruin fruit; pheromone traps may be an effective control for one or two trees in a home garden.

PEAR, ASIAN or ORIENTAL

Rosaceae

DECIDUOUS FRUIT TREES

✂ ZONES VARY BY SELECTION

☀ FULL SUN

◖ REGULAR WATER

Asian Pear

Descendants of two Asiatic species: *Pyrus pyrifolia (P. serotina)* and *P. ussuriensis.* Fruit differs from European pears in being generally round in shape, with flesh that is gritty, crisp, and firm to hard. Asian pears are often called apple pears because of their roundness and crispness, but they are not hybrids of those two fruits. All benefit from pollination by a second selection or by a European pear that flowers at the same time, such as 'Bartlett'. Unlike European selections, they should be thinned to one pear per fruiting spur and should be picked ripe.

Because of their unpearlike texture and taste, fresh Asian pears should not be compared with European types, but they can be mixed with other fruits and vegetables in salads. They require the same culture as European pears, but need fewer hours of winter chill (as few as 400) and are more resistant to fireblight. 'Orient' and 'Pineapple' are two of the best selections to grow in the South.

PEARL BUSH. See EXOCHORDA

PEARLY WHITE BUTTERFLY GINGER. See HEDYCHIUM pradhanii

PECAN. See CARYA illinoensis

PEEPUL. See FICUS religiosa

PELARGONIUM

GERANIUM

Geraniaceae

TENDER PERENNIALS GROWN AS ANNUALS

✂ ZONES CS, TS; OR GROW AS ANNUAL; OR INDOORS

☀ ◑ FULL SUN TO LIGHT SHADE

◖◖ REGULAR TO MODERATE WATER

Pelargonium domesticum

Those bedding and hanging basket plants most of us call geraniums are really forms of *Pelargonium*—tender perennials that endure light frosts but not hard freezes and have slightly asymmetrical flowers. Most are native to South Africa. True geraniums, on the other hand, are annual or perennial plants. Most have symmetrical flowers and are native to the Northern Hemisphere. While some plants of the latter genus are weeds, many are valued for woodland gardens, perennial borders, or rock gardens.

Most garden geraniums are one of three species of *Pelargonium: P. domesticum,* Lady Washington geranium; *P. hortorum,* common geranium (this group also includes variegated forms usually referred to as fancy-leafed or color-leafed geraniums); and *P. peltatum,* ivy geranium. In addition, many other species have scented leaves.

These plants are popular annual bedding plants or house plants. In the Upper, Middle, and Lower South, move geraniums indoors before the first frost or take cuttings for the next year.

Pelargonium graveolens

All geraniums do well in pots. Common geraniums grow well in garden beds; Lady Washington geraniums are also planted in beds but tend to get rangy. Some forms of Lady Washington are used in hanging baskets. Ivy geraniums are good in hanging containers, in raised beds, and as a bank or ground cover. Use scented geraniums in close-up situations—in pots or in ground. For good bloom on a potted geranium indoors, place it in a sunny window or in the brightest light possible.

Pelargonium tomentosum

Plant in any good, fast-draining soil. Remove faded flowers to encourage new bloom. Pinch tips while plants are small to force side branches. Geraniums in pots bloom best when somewhat pot bound. Aphids, whiteflies, and spider mites are common pests. Tobacco budworm may be a problem in some areas; suspect this pest if flowers are tattered or fail to open.

P. domesticum. LADY WASHINGTON GERANIUM, MARTHA WASHINGTON GERANIUM, REGAL GERANIUM. Erect or somewhat spreading, to 3 ft. More rangy than common geranium. Leaves heart shaped to kidney shaped, dark green, 2–4 in. wide, with crinkled margins, unequal sharp teeth. Large, showy flowers 2 in. or more across in loose, rounded clusters, in white and many shades of pink, red, lavender, purple, with brilliant blotches and markings of darker colors.

P. hortorum. COMMON GERANIUM, GARDEN GERANIUM. Most popular, widely grown. Shrubby, succulent stemmed, to 3 ft. or more; older plants grown in the open (in Coastal and Tropical South) become woody. Round or kidney-shaped leaves are velvety and hairy, soft to the touch, aromatic, with edges indistinctly lobed and scallop toothed; most selections show zone of deeper color just inside leaf margin, though some are plain green. Fancy-leafed or color-leafed selections have zones, borders, or splashes of

Pelargonium hortorum

▶ page 320

Handwritten note (overlay):

MONDAY — control pane — display
8–11 studio
✓ get design down
10 minute break outside
11:15 – 12:30 Danny Divine
Type up presentation for Thursday send shortened power point Firefly
lunch break — 12:30–1:15
2-mail
  Baldasare Brooks
  Susan Wentz
  Sawhill Dale Hall
register for portfolio — drop studio
Type up Blueberry story
:30–3:45 Spooner proj.
4–6 Engineering

Selection	Regions	Description	COMMENTS
		...ge, round or short necked, yellow to russeted ...vor. Late	Tree upright and vigorous. Tie down limbs for more consistent bearing. Moderately susceptible to fireblight. 'Red d'Anjou' is red-skinned selection
		...m size, yellow flushed with red. Ripens ...ccellent for fresh eating	Requires pollinator. Resists fireblight. One of the best for Lower and Coastal South
		...e oblong fruits, light green and russeted. ...nned. Ripens mid-October	Moderately resistant to fireblight and leaf spot. Requires little winter chill. Good selection for Lower and Coastal South
		...e, with short but definite neck. Thin skinned, ...ly blushed, very sweet and tender. Midseason	Standard summer pear of fruit markets. Use any selection listed here except 'Seckel' to pollinate. Tree does not have the best form, is susceptible to fireblight. Nevertheless a good home selection. 'Sensation Red Bartlett' is bright red over most of skin, less vigorous than 'Bartlett'
		...e, quite long necked, interesting and ...m. Heavy russeting on green or yellow skin. ...ough flesh is firm, fruit is juicy eaten fresh. ...en cooked. Midseason	Large, upright, vigorous tree. Needs pruning in youth. Highly susceptible to fireblight
		...lett'. Soft, sweet flesh. Early	Productive, shapely tree; good foliage. Highly susceptible to fireblight
		...yellow skin and juicy, spicy white flesh. Late	Self-fertile. Slow growing, but bears fruits when young. Susceptible to fireblight
		...yellow flushed with red, similar to its parent 'Bartlett', but a week earlier. Good for fresh eating, preserves, and canning	Pollen-compatible with most selections except 'Bartlett'. Resists fireblight. Hardy
'Kieffer'	US, MS, LS, CS	Medium to large, oval; greenish yellow skin blushed dark red. Gritty in texture, fair in flavor. Late. Good for canning, baking	Selection quite resistant to fireblight. Most widely grown pear in the South
'Louisiana Beauty'	MS, LS, CS	Yellow-green skin; sweet, crisp, tender flesh. Great for fresh eating. Ripens late summer	Consistent bearer. Very resistant to fireblight. Low winter-chill requirement. An excellent selection for Louisiana and the Gulf Coast
'Maxine'	US, MS, LS, CS	Large, yellow, smooth-textured fruit. Good for eating fresh and canning. Midseason	Highly resistant to fireblight
'Moonglow'	US, MS, LS	Somewhat like 'Bartlett' in looks. Juicy, soft fruit of good flavor. Ripens 2 weeks before 'Bartlett'	Upright, vigorous tree. Very heavy bearer. Highly resistant to fireblight
'Orient'	US, MS, LS, CS	Large, bell-shaped fruit with russeted yellow skin. Firm, juicy, slightly sweet; good for canning, baking. Late	Asian pear hybrid. Heavy producer. Highly resistant to fireblight. A good selection for Lower and Coastal South
'Pineapple'	LS, CS	Yellow fruit with red blush and pineapple flavor. Good for preserves. Coarse texture	Asian pear hybrid. Self-pollinating. Good resistance to fireblight. Needs only 150 hours of winter chill. Good choice for central Florida
'Seckel' ('Sugar')	US, MS, LS	Very small, very sweet, aromatic. Roundish to pear shaped; yellow-brown skin, granular flesh. Early midseason. A favorite for home gardens, preserving	Good resistance to fireblight. Any selection listed here except 'Bartlett' and its strains will do as a pollinator
'Tyson'	US, MS, LS, CS	Medium-size yellow fruit with spicy-sweet flavor. Great for fresh eating. Early–midseason	Resists fireblight
'Warren'	US, MS, LS, CS	Medium to large, green fruits sometimes flushed with red. Smooth, juicy flesh, excellent quality and flavor	Heavy producer. Self-pollinating selection. Hardy. Resistant to fireblight. Has a low winter-chill requirement. Discovered in Mississippi

P

brown, gold, red, white, or green in various combinations. Some also have highly attractive flowers. Single or double flowers are flatter and smaller than those of Lady Washington geranium, but clusters bear many more blossoms. Flowers are usually in solid colors. Many selections in white and shades of pink, rose, red, orange, and violet.

Pelargonium peltatum

There are also dwarf-growing, cactus-flowered, and other novelty kinds. Tough, attractive geraniums for outdoor bedding can be grown from seed, flowering the first summer. Widely available strains are Diamond and Elite (quick to reach bloom stage, compact, need no pinching); Orbit (distinct leaf zoning and broad, rounded clusters of flowers); and Sprinter (slow growing, very free flowering). Common geraniums often fall victim to "heat check"—they simply stop blooming in summer heat. To avoid this condition, give geraniums light afternoon shade, or grow heat-tolerant types such as Freckles or those of Orbit, Pinto, or Americana series.

P. peltatum. IVY GERANIUM. Trailing plants to 2–3 ft. or longer. Leaves rather succulent, glossy bright green, 2–3 in. across, ivylike, with pointed lobes. Inch-wide single or double flowers in rounded clusters of five to ten; colors include white, pink, rose, red, and lavender. Upper petals may be blotched or striped. Many named selections. 'L'Elegante' has white-edged foliage; other selections have white or yellow veins in leaves. Summer Showers strain can be grown from seed; it comes as a mixture of white, pink, red, lavender, and magenta. Intolerance of heat makes ivy geraniums a poor summer annual outside the Upper South, though they make good winter annuals in the Coastal and Tropical South.

Scented geraniums. Many aromatic species are available; all fall into the 1–3-ft.-high range and bear clusters of small blossoms in white or rosy colors (flowers are secondary to the foliage in appeal). The common name of each refers to the plant's fragrance. Types include apple (*P. odoratissimum*), lemon (*P. crispum*), lime (*P. nervosum*), peppermint (*P. tomentosum*), and rose (*P. capitatum, P. graveolens*). All such

Pelargonium crispum

scented kinds are more tolerant of hot, humid summers than other types. Good for herb garden, edgings, the front of borders, window boxes, hanging baskets. Peppermint geranium makes a good ground cover in frost-free gardens. Use fresh leaves of all types for flavoring jelly and iced drinks; use dried leaves in potpourri and sachets.

PELTIPHYLLUM peltatum. See DARMERA peltata

PENNISETUM

FOUNTAIN GRASS

Poaceae (Gramineae)

PERENNIAL GRASSES

⚡ ZONES VARY BY SPECIES

☼ ◑ EXPOSURE NEEDS VARY BY SPECIES

◖ ◕ WATER NEEDS VARY BY SPECIES

Pennisetum alopecuroides

Fountain grasses are generally clump forming, with arching stems tipped with fat, furry flower plumes in summer. They are among the most graceful of ornamental grasses. Use them in containers, in perennial or shrub borders, as bank cover.

P. alopecuroides. CHINESE PENNISETUM. Zones US, MS, LS, CS. Bright green, 3–4-ft. foliage clumps are topped by pinkish plumes in early summer. Leaves turn yellow in fall, brown in winter. In dwarf 'Hameln', white plumes double the height of a 1–1½-ft. clump. In late summer, 'Moudry' has black plumes rising a foot or more above a 1½–2-ft. clump. 'Cassian' is a dwarf (2-ft.) selection with cream-colored flowers and yellow-tinted foliage that turns to orange and dark red in fall. Sun or light shade. Regular to moderate water. Can self-sow.

P. 'Burgundy Giant'. Zones CS, TS. Almost tropical-looking tower, 4–5-ft. tall, of burgundy foliage. Leaves broad, to 1 in. wide and 12 in. long, on strong, tall, burgundy stems. Red-purple plumes, 8–12 in. long, resemble foxtails, appear on nodding stems above foliage in midsummer, fade to cream in fall. Vigorous, beautiful, but tender plant; grow as annual in the Upper, Middle, and Lower South. Regular water. Full sun.

P. orientale. ORIENTAL FOUNTAIN GRASS. Zones US, MS, LS, CS. The 1–1½-ft. clumps of leaves are topped by pinkish plumes that stand a foot or more above the foliage. Plumes mature to light brown and foliage turns straw color in winter. Growing conditions are the same as for *P. alopecuroides*.

P. setaceum. FOUNTAIN GRASS. Perennial in Zones CS, TS; treated as an annual elsewhere. Dense, rounded clump to 4 ft. high. Coppery pink or purplish flowers, borne on 3–4-ft. stems, are held within the foliage clump or just above it. Dies back in winter. Full sun. Can take regular water, but is extremely drought tolerant when established. Seeds itself freely and threatens to crowd out native vegetation when planted near open country. To prevent seeding, cut plumes before seeds mature. 'Rubrum' ('Cupreum'), purple-leafed fountain grass, with reddish brown leaves and dark plumes, does not set seed.

PENNYROYAL. See MENTHA pulegium

PENSTEMON

BEARD TONGUE

Scrophulariaceae

PERENNIALS, EVERGREEN SHRUBS AND SHRUBLETS

⚡ ZONES VARY BY SPECIES

☼ ◑ AFTERNOON SHADE

◖ ● REGULAR TO MODERATE WATER

Penstemon digitalis

A few are widely grown; most are sold only by specialists. All have tubular flowers. Bright reds and blues are the most common colors, but there are penstemons in white and soft pinks through salmon and peach to deep rose, lilac, deep purple, and, rarely, yellow. Hummingbirds are attracted to the flowers. Of some 250 species, most are native to the western U.S. Need excellent drainage. Usually short lived (3 to 4 years). Hybrids and selections tend to be easier than wild species to grow alongside regular garden plants.

P. australis. Perennial. Zones MS, LS, CS. Native from southeastern Virginia to Florida and west to Mississippi. Grows to 3 ft. Flowers reddish purple and white. Summer bloom.

P. baccharifolius. ROCK PENSTEMON. Low-growing shrubby perennial. Zones LS, CS, TS. Native to Texas. To 1½ ft. Scarlet flowers all summer long. Grows on limestone; prefers dry conditions.

P. barbatus. BEARDLIP PENSTEMON. Perennial. Zones US, MS, LS. Needs some winter chill for best performance. Open, somewhat sprawling habit to 3 ft. tall. Bright green, 2–6-in.-long leaves. Red flowers 1 in. across in tall, loose spikes in midsummer to early fall. Selections include 'Elfin Pink', bright pink flowers on 1-ft. spikes; 'Pink Beauty', pink flowers on 2–2½-ft. spikes; 'Prairie Dusk', deep purple flowers on 2-ft. spikes; 'Prairie Fire', scarlet blooms, 2–2½-ft. spikes; 'Rose Elf', coral pink, 2-ft. spikes, some rebloom; and 'Schooley's Yellow', lemon yellow, 2-ft. spikes.

P. cardinalis. CARDINAL PENSTEMON. Perennial. Zones LS, CS. Native to New Mexico. Good for border; takes irrigation well and also some drought. To 2–3 ft. tall. Spikes of brilliant red, 1-in. flowers in summer.

P. cobaea. WILD FOXGLOVE. Perennial. Zones US, MS, LS, CS. Native from Nebraska to Texas. Bears showy clusters of large, foxglove-like flowers, in white or lavender, with deeper-colored throat markings, in mid- or late spring. Leathery, glossy green leaves form basal rosette. Well adapted to regular or little water, and tolerates limy soil and black clay.

P. digitalis. SMOOTH PENSTEMON. Perennial. Zones US, MS, LS. Native to much of the East and Midwest. Perennial to 5 ft. tall. Leaves to 7 in. long; flowers to 1½ in. long in white or pink shades, often with faint purple

P

lines. Spring to early summer bloom. 'Husker Red', 2½–3 ft. tall, has maroon leaves and white flowers.

P. havardii. HAVARD PENSTEMON. Perennial. Zones MS, LS, CS, TS. Native to Texas. In spring, plant produces several upright stems 2–4 ft. high from winter foliage rosette. Leaves on stems are rounded, light green, interesting. Flowers scarlet, to 2 in. long, late spring to June. Plant tolerates wide range of soils including limestone and clay. Needs good drainage. Cut back after bloom.

P. smallii. SMALL'S PENSTEMON. Perennial. Zones US, MS, LS. Native to North Carolina and Tennessee. Grows 1–3 ft. tall. Pink-purple or lavender flowers, 1 in. long, in late spring. Tolerates moist woodland soils well and also dry soils.

P. tenuis. GULF COAST PENSTEMON. Perennial. Zones MS, LS, CS. This native to the wet prairies of Louisiana, Texas, and Arkansas bears numerous, ¾-in. pink or purple flowers through spring. Tolerates wet soils well and partially shaded areas. Self-sows to produce plenty of new plants.

PENTAS lanceolata

PENTAS, STAR CLUSTERS
Rubiaceae
PERENNIAL USUALLY TREATED AS ANNUAL
🌿 ALL ZONES
☼ ☼ FULL SUN OR PARTIAL SHADE
💧💧 AMPLE TO REGULAR WATER

Pentas lanceolata

Grown as a perennial in the Coastal and Tropical South, where it is an easy source of nearly year-round color for semishady locations. Elsewhere, it is a summer annual. Likes moist, fertile, well-drained soil. Excellent butterfly and hummingbird plant. Spreading, multistemmed, to 2–3 ft. tall. Leaves are long, somewhat hairy ovals; stems are topped by tight, 4-in.-wide clusters of small, star-shaped flowers in white, pink, lilac, or red. Remove dead flowers for a long bloom season. Feed monthly in summer. If growing as a house plant, give it as much sunlight as possible by setting in a bright west or south window. Cut flowers have a long vase life.

PEONY. See PAEONIA

PEPPER

Solanaceae
TENDER PERENNIALS GROWN AS ANNUALS
🌿 ALL ZONES
☼ FULL SUN
💧 REGULAR WATER

Bell Pepper

Peppers grow on attractive, bushy plants ranging from less than a foot high to 4 ft. tall, depending on variety. Use plants as temporary low informal hedge; or grow and display them in containers. The two basic kinds of peppers are sweet and hot.

Sweet peppers always remain mild, even when flesh ripens to red. This group includes big stuffing and salad peppers commonly known as bell peppers; best known of these are 'California Wonder' and 'Yolo Wonder'. Hybrid types have been bred for early bearing, high yield, or disease resistance. Big peppers are also available in bright yellow and purple (purple types turn green when cooked). Other sweet types are thick-walled, very sweet pimientos used in salads or for cooking or canning; sweet cherry peppers for pickling; and long, slender Italian frying peppers and Hungarian sweet yellow peppers, both used for cooking.

Hot peppers range from tiny (pea-size) types to narrow, 6–7-in.-long forms, but all are pungent, their flavor ranging from the mild heat of Italian peperoncini to the near-incandescence of 'Habañero'. 'Anaheim' is a mildly spicy pepper used for making canned green chiles. 'Long Red Cayenne' is used for drying; 'Hungarian Yellow Wax (Hot)', 'Jalapeño', and 'Fresno Chile Grande' are used for pickling. Mexican cooking utilizes an entire palette of peppers, among them 'Ancho', 'Mulato', and 'Pasilla'.

Peppers need a long, warm growing season, and in most areas must be set outdoors as seedlings if they are to produce fruit. Buy nursery plants, or sow seed indoors 8 to 10 weeks before average date of last frost. When weather warms up and night temperatures remain consistently above 55°F, set transplants outdoors, spacing them 1½–2 ft. apart. Fertilize once or twice after plants become established, before blossoms set. Sweet peppers are ready to pick when they have reached good size, but they keep their flavor until red-ripe. Pimientos should be picked only when red-ripe. Pick hot peppers when they are fully ripe. Possible pests include aphids, whiteflies, cutworms, pepper maggots, and Colorado potato beetles.

PEPPERMINT. See MENTHA piperita

PERENNIAL RYEGRASS. See LOLIUM perenne

PERICALLIS cruenta. See SENECIO hybridus

🏛 PERILLA frutescens

PERILLA, WILD BASIL
Lamiaceae (Labiatae)
ANNUAL
🌿 ALL ZONES
☼ ☼ FULL SUN OR LIGHT SHADE
💧 REGULAR TO MODERATE WATER

Perilla frutescens

Sturdy, leafy warm-weather plant to 2–3 ft. tall. Deeply toothed, egg-shaped leaves to 5 in. long. Kind most commonly seen has bronzy or purple leaves that look much like those of purple basil or coleus. Seed heads of dead plants are prominent in winter. Leaves of Fancy Fringe strain are deeply cut and fringed, deep bronzy purple in color. Use leaves as vegetable or flavoring (they taste something like mint, something like cinnamon); fry long, thin clusters of flower buds as a vegetable in tempura batter. Extremely fast and easy to grow; self-sow freely. In Asia, seeds are pressed for edible oil. An old Southern favorite.

PERIWINKLE. See VINCA

PEROVSKIA

RUSSIAN SAGE
Lamiaceae (Labiatae)
SHRUBBY PERENNIAL
🌿 ZONES US, MS, LS, CS
☼ FULL SUN
💧 MODERATE WATER; TOLERATES DROUGHT

Perovskia 'Blue Spire'

Woody-based clump with many upright, gray-white stems clothed in gray-green foliage. Leaves are 2–3 in. long and deeply cut on lower part of stem, become smaller and merely toothed toward top of stem. Each stem is topped with a widely branched spray of small lavender blue flowers; when plants are in full bloom in late spring and summer, flowers form a haze above the foliage. To extend flowering period, trim off spent blossoms. Mature clumps may reach 3–4 ft. high, with equal spread.

Often sold as *P. atriplicifolia*, but plants in circulation are probably hybrids between that species and *P. abrotanoides*. Widely grown 'Blue Spire', with deep violet blue blooms, is sometimes sold as *P. atriplicifolia* 'Superba' or *P.* 'Longin'. 'Blue Mist' (earliest-flowering selection) and 'Blue Haze' bear lighter blue blossoms. 'Filagran' has silvery, very finely cut leaves. Mass plants or use them individually in borders. Plants take any soil, as long as it is well drained. Extremely resistant to heat and drought. Best in warm summers, even where weather is humid. Cut nearly to ground each spring before new growth starts.

PERSEA borbonia

RED BAY

Lauraceae

EVERGREEN TREE

ZONES US (PROTECTED), MS, LS, CS, TS

FULL SUN OR PARTIAL SHADE

REGULAR OR AMPLE WATER

Ornamental native to swamps from Delaware to Florida. For *P. americana,* see Avocado. Grows 20–40 ft. tall, with dense crown of handsome, thick, shiny, dark green, aromatic leaves, to 6 in. long, 2 in. wide. Often multitrunked and shrubby. Creamy flowers in May or June are inconspicuous. Fruit small, to ½ in. long, dark blue to black, on red stalks. Tolerates very wet situations and salt spray. Medium growth rate.

Persea borbonia

PERSIAN LILAC. See SYRINGA persica

PERSIAN SHIELD. See STROBILANTHES dyeranus

PERSIMMON (Diospyros)

Ebenaceae

DECIDUOUS FRUIT TREES

ZONES VARY BY SPECIES

FULL SUN

REGULAR TO MODERATE WATER

Of the two types of fruiting persimmons, the native species is a bigger, more cold-tolerant tree than the Asian species; however, the Asian type bears larger fruit that is sold in markets. Neither species is fussy about soil. For the ornamental Texas persimmon, see *Diospyros texana.*

Persimmon

American persimmon (*Diospyros virginiana*) is native from Connecticut to Kansas and southward to Texas and Florida. Grows well in Zones US, MS, LS, CS. As a landscape tree, it is not as ornamental as Asian species and probably best suited to woodland gardens, where its tendency to form thickets from root suckers can be tolerated. Reaches 35–60 ft. tall, 20–35 ft. wide, with a broad, oval crown and attractive gray-brown bark fissured into a deep checkered pattern. Glossy, broad, oval leaves, 6 in. long, turn yellow, pink, or reddish purple in fall. Fruit is round, yellow to orange (or blushed red), 1½–2 in. across; puckering until soft-ripe, then very sweet. Fruit of wild species ripens in early fall after frost; some do not require chill. Both male and female trees are usually needed to get fruit. Fruit of self-fertile 'Meader' is seedless if not pollinated.

Japanese or oriental persimmon (*Diospyros kaki*) grows and fruits in Zones US (protected), MS, LS, CS. To 30 ft. or more, with handsome, wide-spreading branch pattern. One of the best landscape fruit trees; good small shade tree, espalier. Oval leaves, 6–7 in. long and 2–3½ in. wide, turn from glossy dark green to vivid yellow, orange, or red in fall, even in the Lower and Coastal South. Brilliant orange, 3–4-in. fruits appear in fall, persist until winter unless harvested. They look like ripe tomatoes hanging on the tree. Species sets fruit without pollination, though crops are often tastier and more abundant when pollinated. Selections include:

'Chocolate'. Brown-flecked, very sweet flesh.

'Fuyu'. Nonpuckering even when underripe; firm fleshed (like an apple), reddish yellow, about size of baseball but flattened like tomato. Similar but larger is 'Gosho', widely sold as 'Giant Fuyu'.

'Hachiya'. Shapeliest tree. Yields big (4-in.-long, 2½–3-in.-broad), slightly pointed fruit. Pick before fully ripe to save from birds; bring to soft-ripe before eating—puckering unless mushy.

'Tamopan'. Very large, turban shaped, puckering until fully ripe.

PETREA volubilis

QUEEN'S WREATH

Verbenaceae

EVERGREEN VINE

ZONE TS

FULL SUN OR LIGHT SHADE

REGULAR WATER

Petrea volubilis

Twines to 40 ft., but can be kept much smaller. Deep green leaves with sandpapery surface. Stunning display of purplish blue (occasionally white), star-shaped flowers in long, slender clusters, several times a year during warm weather. Although individually small, flowers are profusely borne. Sensitive to frost.

PETUNIA hybrida

PETUNIA

Solanaceae

TENDER PERENNIAL GROWN AS ANNUAL

ALL ZONES

FULL SUN

REGULAR TO MODERATE WATER

Petunia hybrida

Not the evening-fragrant, pastel, reseeding petunias you see blooming in meadows and around old homesites. These are low-growing, multicolored hybrids, bushy to spreading, with thick, broad leaves that are slightly sticky to the touch. Flower form varies from single and funnel shaped to very double and heavily ruffled (like carnations); the many colors include cream, yellow, pure white, and the whole range from soft pink to deepest red, light blue to deepest purple. Bicolors and picotees are available, as are types with contrasting veins on the petals and those with fluted or fringed edges. In the Upper, Middle, and Lower South, these hybrid plants bloom throughout summer until frost. In the Lower South, you can also set out transplants in late summer or early fall for bright color all the way to a hard freeze. In the Coastal and Tropical South, they are done in by summer heat and humidity; grow them for winter and spring color.

Plant in good garden soil. Single-flowered kinds tolerate alkalinity, will grow in poor soil if it's well drained. Plant 8–18 in. apart, depending on size of plant. Once established, pinch back halfway for compact growth. Feed monthly with complete fertilizer. In late summer (except in Coastal and Tropical South), cut back rangy plants by about half to force new growth. Botrytis disease can damage blossoms and foliage of most petunias; Multifloras are somewhat resistant. Smog damage (spotting on seedling leaves), tobacco budworm (flowers look tattered or fail to open) may be problems in some areas.

Described below are the three classes of petunias (the long-standing Grandiflora and Multiflora classes and the new Milliflora) and the new ground cover selections. Petunias are generally labeled F_1 or F_2 hybrids.

P

F_1 refers to first-generation hybrids, which are more vigorous and more uniform in color, height, and growth habit than their offspring, F_2 hybrids.

Hybrid Grandiflora. Of the three classes, these bear the largest flowers but bloom the least profusely and are most troubled by hot, wet weather. Sturdy plants to 15–27 in. high, 2–3 ft. wide. Flowers usually single, ruffled or fringed, to 4½ in. across, in pink, rose, salmon, red, scarlet, blue, white, pale yellow, or striped combinations. Fluffy Ruffles strain has the largest blossoms, to 6 in. across. Cascade, Countdown, and Supercascade series' cascading habit makes them good for hanging baskets. Magic and Supermagic strains give heavy bloom on compact plants: large (4–5-in.) single flowers in white, pink, red, blue. Heavily ruffled flowers of Double Hybrid Grandifloras come in all petunia colors except yellow.

Hybrid Multiflora. (Also called Hybrid Floribunda.) About same size as Grandifloras; blooms are generally smooth edged and smaller (to 2 in. across), single or double. Neat, compact growth for bedding, massed planting. Named selections in pink, rose, salmon, yellow, white, blue. Joy and Plum strains have single, satiny flowers in white, cream, pink, coral, red, blue. Celebrity and Madness series take summer heat especially well.

Hybrid Milliflora. Newest class of petunias, with smaller flowers and more dwarf habit than Multiflora. Fantasy strain makes neat, compact mound to 10 in. high, with plentiful 1–1½-in. blooms in pink, red, blue, ivory. Good for pots, hanging baskets, window boxes.

'Purple Wave'. First-ever ground cover petunia, growing 4–6 in. high, with 4-ft. spread. Bounty of vivid purple, 2–3-in. blooms for banks, borders, pots, hanging baskets. 'Pink Wave' has bright pink flowers and spreads about 3 ft. Both take summer heat, need good drainage.

PHACELIA

Hydrophyllaceae

ANNUAL, BIENNIAL

ZONES VARY BY SPECIES

EXPOSURE NEEDS VARY BY SPECIES

REGULAR WATER

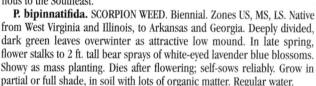

Phacelia bipinnatifida

Large genus of flowering plants native mostly to western U.S. and Mexico. One of the species listed here is native to the Texas prairie; the other is a shade- and moisture-loving wildflower indigenous to the Southeast.

P. bipinnatifida. SCORPION WEED. Biennial. Zones US, MS, LS. Native from West Virginia and Illinois, to Arkansas and Georgia. Deeply divided, dark green leaves overwinter as attractive low mound. In late spring, flower stalks to 2 ft. tall bear sprays of white-eyed lavender blue blossoms. Showy as mass planting. Dies after flowering; self-sows reliably. Grow in partial or full shade, in soil with lots of organic matter. Regular water.

P. congesta. BLUE CURLS. Annual or biennial. All zones. Native to Texas and New Mexico. Grows to 3 ft. tall. Deeply cut, soft leaves, to 4 in. long, 1½ in. wide. Buds form on curled spike, which uncurls as buds develop into blue-purple flowers. Blooms throughout spring. Easy to grow from seed. For a long bloom period, water during dry periods. Full sun.

PHALAENOPSIS

MOTH ORCHID

Orchidaceae

EPIPHYTIC ORCHIDS

ZONE TS; OR INDOOR AND GREENHOUSE PLANTS

FILTERED LIGHT

KEEP SOIL MOIST AT ALL TIMES

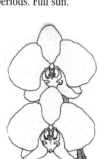

Phalaenopsis

Epiphytic orchids with thick, broad, leathery leaves and no pseudobulbs. Long sprays of 3–6-in.-wide flowers in white, cream, pale yellow, or light lavender pink, spring–fall; some are spotted, barred, or have contrasting lip color. Leaves are rather flat, spreading to 1 ft. long. Flower sprays may reach 3 ft. long. Cut faded sprays back to a node; secondary sprays may form.

If you've never grown orchids before, moth orchids are good ones to start with. They require warmer growing conditions than most orchids (minimum of 60–70°F, night, 70–85°F, day) and fairly high humidity. Place near bathroom or kitchen window with gauzelike curtain that filters light (foliage burns easily in direct sun). Give them same potting medium as for cattleyas (see Orchidaceae). When cutting flowers, leave part of main stem so another set of flowers can develop from dormant buds. Many lovely, large-flowered hybrids. Some smaller-flowered new hybrids may be easier to grow, take somewhat lower nighttime temperatures.

PHALARIS arundinacea

RIBBON GRASS

Poaceae (Gramineae)

ORNAMENTAL PERENNIAL GRASS

ZONES US, MS, LS, CS

FULL SUN OR PARTIAL SHADE

MUCH TO MODERATE WATER

Phalaris arundinacea

Tough, tenacious, bamboolike grass that spreads aggressively by underground runners to form spreading, 2–3-ft.-high clumps. Deep green leaves turn buff in fall. Airy flower clusters are white, aging to pale brown. 'Picta' has green leaves with longitudinal white stripes. The following selections are less invasive: 'Dwarf Garters', a slow spreader half as tall as the species; and 1½–2-ft.-high 'Mervyn Feesey' ('Feesey's Form'), with white variegation strongly blushed with pink.

PHEASANT'S EYE. See NARCISSUS recurvus

PHILADELPHUS

MOCK ORANGE

Hydrangeaceae (Saxifragaceae)

DECIDUOUS SHRUBS, EXCEPT AS NOTED

ZONES VARY BY SPECIES

FULL SUN TO PARTIAL SHADE

REGULAR TO MODERATE WATER

Philadelphus lemoinei

Grown for typically white, usually fragrant flowers that bloom in late spring or early summer. Four-petaled, 1–2-in. blossoms range from single through semidouble to double. Generally large, vigorous plants of fountainlike form with medium green foliage. Prune every year just after bloom, cutting out oldest wood and surplus shoots at base. To rejuvenate, cut to ground. Taller types are striking in lawns or as background and corner plantings; smaller kinds can be planted near foundations or used as low screens or informal hedges. Buy in bloom to ensure plant is fragrant. These plants are not fussy about soil, as long as drainage is good.

P. coronarius. SWEET MOCK ORANGE, ENGLISH DOGWOOD. Zones US, MS, LS, CS. Old Southern favorite. Strong growing, 10–12 ft. tall and wide. Leaves are oval, 1½–4 in. long. Clusters of fragrant, 1½-in. flowers. Selection 'Aureus' has bright golden leaves that turn yellow green in summer; does not grow as tall as species.

P. coulteri. Zones LS, CS, TS. Native to Mexico. Grows 4–10 ft. tall. Small leaves, 1–2 in. long, are soft white on undersides. White, 1-in. flowers appear singly, not in clusters. 'Bull's Eye' has red spots at base of petals.

P. lemoinei. Zones US, MS, LS. This hybrid includes many garden selections; most grow 5–6 ft. tall, and all have clusters of very fragrant flowers. Oval leaves to 2 in. long. Double-flowered 'Avalanche', 'Enchantment', and 'Mont Blanc' are well-known selections. ▶

P

P. mexicanus. EVERGREEN MOCK ORANGE. Zones CS, TS. Best used as vine or bank cover; long, supple stems with 3-in. evergreen leaves will reach 15–20 ft. if given support. Fragrant creamy flowers in small clusters.

P. purpureomaculatus. Zones US, MS, LS. Hybrids including medium-size shrubs with purple-centered flowers. 'Belle Etoile' is upright, to 5 ft. tall; fragrant, fringed, single flowers to 2½ in. Oval leaves 2 in. long.

P. texensis. TEXAS MOCK ORANGE. Zones MS, LS, CS. To 3 ft. tall. Leaves small, shiny, dark green, semievergreen. Fragrant spring flowers, 1–3 in. across. Grows in limestone, clay, sand, loam, if well drained.

P. virginalis. VIRGINAL MOCK ORANGE. Zones US, MS, LS. Another hybrid that has produced several excellent mock oranges, usually with double flowers. Selections 'Minnesota Snowflake' (reputedly hardy to −30°F) and 'Virginal' (6–8 ft. tall) are both double. Lower growing are double 'Glacier' (3–4 ft.) and 'Dwarf Minnesota Snowflake' (2–3 ft.). Selection 'Natchez' (8–10 ft.) is the showiest of all. Its single white blooms are to 2 in. across, though not fragrant.

PHILODENDRON

Araceae

EVERGREEN VINES AND SHRUBS

ZONE TS, EXCEPT AS NOTED; OR INDOORS

EXPOSURE NEEDS VARY BY TYPE

MOIST, NOT SOGGY, SOIL

Philodendron domesticum

Philodendrons are tough, fast-growing, and durable plants grown for their attractive, leathery, usually glossy leaves. These plants fall into two main classes. The class of each species is indicated in the list that follows.

Arborescent (treelike) and relatively hardy. These plants become big, reaching 6–8 ft. high (sometimes higher) and as wide, with large leaves and sturdy, self-supporting trunks. They will grow indoors but need much more space than most house plants. They grow outdoors in Zones CS, TS. As landscape plants, they do best in sun (some shade at midday where light is intense) but can survive considerable shade. Use them for tropical jungle effects or as massive silhouettes against walls or glass. Excellent in large containers; effective near swimming pools.

Vining or self-heading and tender. These forms can grow outdoors only in the Tropical South, where they require partial or full shade. Elsewhere, they are house plants. Many kinds, with many different leaf shapes and sizes. Vining types do not really climb and must be tied to or leaned against a support until they eventually shape themselves to it. The support can be almost anything, but certain water-absorbent columns (sections of tree fern stems, wire and sphagnum "totem poles," slabs of bark) serve especially well, since they can be kept moist. Self-heading types form short, broad plants with sets of leaves radiating out from central point.

Whether in containers or open ground, a philodendron needs rich, loose, well-drained soil. House plant philodendrons grow best in good light (but not direct sun) coming through a window. Feed lightly and frequently for good growth and color. Dust leaves of indoor plants once a month.

Most philodendrons—especially when grown in containers—will drop the lower leaves, leaving a bare stem. To fix a leggy philodendron, you can air-layer the leafy top and, when it develops roots, sever it and replant it. Or cut the plant back to short stub and let it start over again. Often the best answer is to throw out an overgrown, leggy plant and replace it with a new one. Aerial roots form on stems of some kinds; push them into soil or cut them off—it won't hurt the plant.

Flowers may appear on old plants if heat, light, and humidity are high; they resemble callas, with a boat-shaped bract surrounding a club-shaped, spikelike structure. Bracts are usually greenish, white, or reddish.

Here are the kinds. Note that one great favorite—the so-called split-leaf philodendron—is not a philodendron at all, but a *Monstera*.

P. bipinnatifidum. Arborescent. Deeply cut 3-ft. leaves on upright trunks (leaning with age). Old plants may develop greenish cream inflorescences like giant (to 1-ft.-long) callas.

P. cordatum. See P. scandens oxycardium

P. domesticum. SPADE-LEAF PHILODENDRON. Vining. Usually sold as *P.* 'Hastatum'. Fairly fast, open growth. Leaves 1 ft. long, arrow shaped, deep green. Subject to leaf spot if kept too warm and moist. A number of selections and hybrids have become available; these are more resistant to leaf spot and tend to be more compact and upright. Some, possibly hybrids with *P. erubescens,* have much red in new foliage and in leafstalks. 'Emerald Queen' is a choice deep green, 'Royal Queen' a good deep red.

P. 'Lynette'. Self-heading. Makes tight cluster of foot-long, broadish, bright green leaves with strong patterning formed by deeply sunken veins. Good tabletop plant.

P. martianum (P. cannifolium). Vining. Leathery, lance-shaped leaves to 18 in. long, 6–8 in. wide, with broad midrib and swollen, spongy, deeply channeled, 15-in.-long leafstalks.

P. melanochrysum (P. andreanum). BLACK-GOLD PHILODENDRON. Vining. Velvety, green-black, lance-shaped leaves to 3 ft. by 1 ft.; pale green midrib, lateral veins. New leaves heart shaped and tinged copper.

P. melinonii. Self-heading. Slightly arrow-shaped or oval leaves, to 3 ft. long, 1½ ft. wide, with pale green concave midrib. Juvenile leaves rose purple on undersides. Fibrous stems.

P. oxycardium. See P. scandens oxycardium

P. pertusum. See *Monstera deliciosa.* This is commonly sold as split-leaf philodendron.

P. scandens oxycardium. HEART-LEAF PHILODENDRON. Vining. The most common philodendron, usually sold as *P. oxycardium* or *P. cordatum.* Heart-shaped, deep green leaves, usually 5 in. or less in length on juvenile plants, up to 1 ft. long on mature plants in greenhouses or outdoors. Easily grown (cut stems will grow for some time in vases of water). Thin stems will trail gracefully or climb fast and high. Train on strings or wires to frame window or hang from rafter, or grow on moisture-retentive columns.

P. selloum. SADDLE-LEAF PHILODENDRON. Arborescent. Hardiest big-leafed philodendron used outdoors. Deeply cut leaves to 3 ft. long. 'Lundii' is more compact.

P. wendlandii. Self-heading. Compact clusters of 12 or more deep green, foot-long, broadly lance-shaped leaves on short, broad stalks. Useful as tough, compact foliage plant for tabletop. *P.* 'Lynette' is similar.

P. williamsii. Arborescent. Large, arrow-shaped, glossy, deep green leaves to 2½ ft. long and 1 ft. wide. Leafstalks almost as long as leaves.

Philodendron scandens oxycardium

PHLOMIS

JERUSALEM SAGE

Lamiaceae (Labiatae)

PERENNIALS OR SHRUBBY PERENNIALS

ZONES US, MS, LS

FULL SUN, EXCEPT AS NOTED

MODERATE WATER

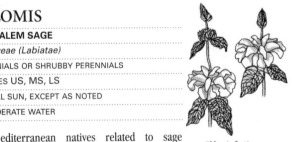

Phlomis fruticosa

Mediterranean natives related to sage (*Salvia*). Erect stems are set with whorls of tubular flowers in yellow, purple, or lavender; late spring and early summer bloom. Tolerate poor soil as long as drainage is good. Withstand considerable drought, but do better with moderate water.

P. fruticosa. Shrubby growth to 4 ft., woolly, gray-green, 6–8-in. leaves. Yellow, 1-in. flowers are ball-shaped whorls along upper half of stems. Several waves of bloom if cut back after each flowering. Evergreen in mild winters. Cut back by half in fall for compact plant. Takes light shade.

P. russelliana. Spreads by runners, making clumps of large (to 8-in.), heart-shaped, furry leaves. Mats can be an effective weed-suppressing ground cover. Spikes with whorls of yellow flowers grow to 3 ft.

P. samia. Similar to *P. russelliana,* but with purplish pink flowers.

PHLOX

Polemoniaceae

PERENNIALS AND ANNUALS

🌡 ZONES VARY BY SPECIES

☼ ◑ FULL SUN OR LIGHT SHADE, EXCEPT AS NOTED

💧 REGULAR WATER, EXCEPT AS NOTED

Phlox paniculata

Most are natives of North America. With the exception of *P. drummondii*, which is an annual, the species described here are perennial. The many types of phlox show wide variation in growth form, but all have showy flower clusters. Tall kinds are excellent border plants; dwarf forms are mainstays in the rock garden. Unless otherwise noted, plants perform well in average garden soil with regular moisture. Two major problems affect phlox: red spider mites (which attack almost all species) and powdery mildew (*P. paniculata* is especially susceptible).

P. arendsii. Zones US, MS, LS, CS. Hybrid between *P. divaricata* and *P. paniculata*. To 1½ ft. high, with 1-in.-wide blossoms in clusters to 6 in. across, early summer. Cut off faded flowers for later rebloom. 'Anja' has reddish purple blooms, 'Hilda' lavender, 'Suzanne' white with red eye.

P. bifida. SAND PHLOX. Zones US, MS, LS. Clumps to 8–10 in. tall, with narrow light green leaves. Blooms spring–early summer, bearing profuse ½-in. lavender to white flowers with deeply notched petals. Likes full sun, excellent drainage. Drought tolerant.

P. carolina. See P. maculata

P. 'Chattahoochee'. See P. pilosa

🌿 **P. divaricata.** BLUE PHLOX, WILD SWEET WILLIAM. Zones US, MS, LS, CS. To 1 ft. high, with slender, leafy stems and creeping underground shoots. Oval leaves 1–2 in. long. Blooms in spring, bearing open clusters of ¾–1½-in.-wide, somewhat fragrant blossoms in pale blue (sometimes with pinkish tones) varying to white. Use in woodland gardens, in combination with spring bulbs, and at front of mixed borders. Give light shade and good, deep soil. Selections include 'Arrowhead', with light lavender blue blossoms; 'Dirgo Ice', with palest blue; 'Fuller's White'; *P. d. laphamii*, bright blue; *P. d. laphamii* 'Louisiana Purple', intense blue purple; and the compact 'London Grove', deep blue.

P. drummondii. DRUMMOND PHLOX. All zones. Grows 6–18 in. tall, with erect, leafy stems more or less covered with rather sticky hairs. Flowers numerous, showy, in tight clusters at tops of stems. Bright and pastel colors (no blue or orange), some with contrasting eye. Tall strains in mixed colors include Finest and Fordhook Finest. Dwarf strains include Beauty and Globe, both with rounded flowers, and starry-petaled Petticoat and Twinkle. Bloom lasts from early summer until frost if faded flowers are removed. Plant in spring in Upper South, in fall elsewhere. Give full sun and light, rich loam.

P. glaberrima triflora. SMOOTH PHLOX. Zones US, MS, LS. Grows to 1½–2 ft. tall, with smooth, narrow, 3-in.-long leaves. Lavender pink flowers in late spring. This species is mildew-free.

P. maculata (P. carolina, P. suffruticosa). CAROLINA PHLOX. Zones US, MS, LS. To 3–4 ft. Early summer flowers ¾ in. wide, in 15-in.-long clusters, in colors ranging from white with pale pink eye to magenta. Shiny, mildew-resistant foliage. Selections include 'Alpha', rose pink; 'Delta', white, pink eye; 'Miss Lingard' (white; best-known selection); 'Rosalinde', deep rose pink; and 'Omega', white, purplish pink eye.

P. nivalis. TRAILING PHLOX. Zones US, MS, LS. Trailing plants form loose, 4–6-in.-high mats of narrow leaves. Pink or white, 1-in.-wide flowers in fairly large clusters, late spring–early summer. Excellent in rock gardens; needs good drainage. 'Camla' is a good salmon pink selection.

P. ovata. MOUNTAIN PHLOX. Zones US, MS, LS. To 15–20 in. tall, with smooth green, oval, mildew-free leaves to 6 in. long. Deep pink flowers in late spring.

🌿 **P. paniculata.** PERENNIAL PHLOX, SUMMER PHLOX. Zones US, MS, LS, CS. To 3–5 ft. tall. Long, narrow, 2–5-in.-long leaves taper to a slender point. Fragrant, 1-in.-wide flowers in large, dome-shaped clusters throughout summer. Colors include white and shades of lavender, pink, rose, and red; blooms of some selections have a contrasting eye. Plants do not come true from seed; seedlings often revert in color to common magenta purple kind, which is the easiest one to grow. Thrives in full sun, but flower colors may bleach where conditions are intensely hot. Mulch to keep roots cool. Divide every few years, replanting young shoots from outside of clump.

Very susceptible to mildew at end of bloom season. To minimize problem, provide good air circulation: don't crowd plants and keep only six to eight stems on a mature plant. Spray with fungicide if necessary. Among mildew-resistant selections are white-flowered 'David' and 'Mt. Fuji'; 'Eva Cullum', pink with red eye; and lilac-pink 'Franz Schubert'.

P. pilosa. DOWNY PHLOX. Zones US, MS, LS, CS. Semievergreen. Grows 15 in. tall; mildew-free. Spreads rapidly by stolons and might be considered invasive if it weren't so pretty. Blue to pink or white blossoms in spring. 'Chattahoochee', now properly known as 'Moody Blue', has blue flowers with a red eye; 'Eco Happy Traveler' bears deep pink flowers; and 'Ozarkana' has fragrant, light pink blooms with a white eye.

P. procumbens. Zones US, MS, LS. Hybrid between *P. stolonifera* and *P. subulata*, but less widely creeping than either. Forms a 6–12-in.-tall mound of semievergreen foliage, with purplish pink flowers in spring. 'Millstream Hybrid' has lavender pink flowers; 'O.G.K.' has rose pink blooms; 'Variegata' has pink blossoms and leaves edged in creamy white.

🌿 **P. stolonifera.** CREEPING PHLOX. Zones US, MS, LS. Creeping, mounding plant to 6–8 in. high, with narrow evergreen leaves to 1½ in. long. Does well in dry shade. Profusion of 1-in. lavender flowers arrives in spring. Selections include 'Blue Ridge', lavender blue; 'Bruce's White'; 'Sherwood Purple', deep lavender; and pink forms 'Home Fires', 'Melrose', and 'Pink Ridge'. Provide light shade.

🌿 **P. subulata.** THRIFT, CREEPING PHLOX, MOSS PINK. Zones US, MS, LS, CS. Stiffish, ½-in., needlelike, evergreen to semievergreen leaves on creeping stems; forms mat to 6 in. high. Blooms in spring, with ¾-in.-wide flowers that range in color from white through pink to rose and lavender blue. Makes sheets of brilliant color in rock gardens, on banks, and along drainage ditches. Provide loose, not-too-rich soil, moderate water. Specialists offer two dozen or more selections; many of these are actually selections of other low-growing species or hybrids between such species and *P. subulata*. 'Laurel Beth' has variegated green-and-white foliage.

P. suffruticosa. See P. maculata

PHOENIX

DATE PALM

Arecaceae (Palmae)

PALMS

🌡 ZONES CS (MILDER PARTS), TS

☼ FULL SUN, EXCEPT AS NOTED

💧 REGULAR WATER

Phoenix canariensis

Mostly large feather palms, but one is a dwarf. Trunks patterned with bases of old leafstalks. Small yellowish flowers in large, hanging sprays. On female trees, blossoms are followed by clusters of dates—but only if the tree has been in the ground 3 to 6 years and if a male tree is nearby. Fruit does not always mature in Florida. Dates of two species are used commercially; those of other species don't have as much edible flesh. Date palms hybridize freely, so buy from a reliable garden center that knows seed or plant source.

P. canariensis. CANARY ISLAND DATE PALM. Hardy to 20°F; slow to develop new head of foliage after damage from hard frosts. Big, heavy-trunked plant to 60 ft. tall, with a great many gracefully arching fronds that form a crown 50 ft. wide. Grows slowly until it forms trunk, then speeds up a little. Young plants do well in pots for many years, looking something like pineapples. Best planted on slopes, in big spaces, along wide streets; not for small city lots. Takes seacoast conditions.

P. dactylifera. DATE PALM. Leaves killed at 20°F, but plants have survived 4–10°F. Native to Middle East. Classic palm of movie desert oases. Very tall (to 80 ft.), with slender trunk and gray-green, waxy leaves; stiff, sharp-pointed leaflets. Suckers from base; natural habit is clump of several trunks. Bears dates of commerce; principal selection is 'Deglet Noor'. Too stiff and large for most home gardens. Does well at seaside, in dry areas.

P. loureiri (P. humilis). Hardy to 20°F. Resembles the smaller, more slender and refined *P. canariensis.* Slow grower to 10–18 ft. tall. Leaves are dark green, flexible, to 10 ft. long. Does well in containers.

P. reclinata. SENEGAL DATE PALM. Expect trouble below 28°F. Native to tropical Africa. Makes picturesque clumps from offshoots, with several curving trunks 20–30 ft. high. If you want a single-trunked tree, remove offshoots. Fertilize for fast growth. Good seaside palm.

P. roebelenii. PYGMY DATE PALM. Native to Laos. Fine-leafed, small-scale, single-trunked palm; grows slowly to about 6 ft. Curved leaves form dense crown. Good container plant. Does best in partial or full shade, but will not succeed in dark indoor corners.

P. rupicola. CLIFF DATE PALM. Hardy to 26°F. From India. As stately as *P. canariensis,* but much smaller, reaching only 25 ft. tall. Slender trunk; lower leaves droop gracefully.

P. sylvestris. SILVER DATE PALM. Hardy to 22°F. Native to India. Beautiful palm with single trunk to 30 ft., tapering from wide base to narrow top. Thick, round crown of gray-green leaves. Fruit is used commercially for making date sugar.

Phoenix dactylifera

Phoenix roebelenii

PALMS FOR MANY USES

The various species of *Phoenix* can fill a number of roles. Some are good as stately sentinels along an avenue. Several are quite cold-hardy, taking temperatures well below freezing. Some are salt-tolerant plants for seashore gardens; others flourish in hot, dry climates. See Palms.

PHOTINIA

Rosaceae

EVERGREEN OR DECIDUOUS SHRUBS OR SMALL TREES

ZONES VARY BY SPECIES

FULL SUN

REGULAR TO MODERATE WATER

Related to hawthorn (*Crataegus*), pyracantha. Densely foliaged plants, most with large, elliptical to oval leaves and bright-colored new growth. In early spring, all bear flattish clusters of small white flowers. Most types have red or black berries during fall and into winter. Evergreen species may suffer considerable damage if temperatures remain below 10°F for prolonged periods. Good screens, background. Prune to shape; never allow new growth to get away and make long, bare switches. Attractive to birds. All are susceptible to fireblight; all but *P. fraseri* are subject to powdery mildew.

P. fraseri. FRASER PHOTINIA, REDTIP. Evergreen shrub or small tree. Zones US (protected), MS, LS, CS. Moderate to fast growth to 10–15 ft., spreading wider. Oval leaves to 5 in. long are bright, showy bronzy red when new, maturing to dark green. The flower clusters resemble those of *P. glabra* but are not followed by berries. Good as espalier or small single-stemmed tree, or hedge or tall screen. Cut branches excellent in arrangements. Resists mildew. A fungus-induced leaf spot can be a serious problem; control by spraying new, healthy foliage with chlorothalonil.

Photinia fraseri

Aphids may be a problem. The original Fraser photinia, officially named 'Birmingham' (a name that is hardly ever used), was born at Fraser Nursery in Birmingham, Alabama, around 1940. Because of the shrub's fast growth and appealing red-tipped evergreen foliage, it quickly became overplanted in the South; susceptibility to disease hasn't dimmed its popularity. Superior selections now exist, including 'Indian Princess', which has smaller leaves than those of species, and 'Red Robin', a compact grower resistant to leaf spot. Japanese cleyera (*Ternstroemia gymnanthera*) is a good substitute where leaf spot is a problem.

P. glabra. JAPANESE PHOTINIA. Evergreen shrub. Zones LS, CS. Broad, dense growth to 6–10 ft. or more. Leaves oval, broadest toward tip, to 3 in. long. Coppery new growth; scattered leaves of bright red give touch of color through fall and winter. Summer pruning will restrict size of plant to neat 5 ft. and give continuing show of new foliage. Flowers with hawthorn fragrance in 4-in.-wide clusters. Berries red, turning black.

P. serrulata. CHINESE PHOTINIA. Evergreen shrub or small tree. Zones US, MS, LS, CS. Broad, dense growth to 35 ft., but easily held to 10 ft. high and wide. Stiff, crisp, deep green leaves to 8 in. long, prickly along edges. Bright copper new growth; scattered crimson leaves in fall, winter. Foul-smelling flower clusters to 6 in. across. Bright red berries often last until winter. Birds eat them and spread seedlings far and wide. 'Aculeata' (often sold as 'Nova' or 'Nova Lineata') is more compact, has midrib and main leaf veins of ivory yellow.

P. villosa. ORIENTAL PHOTINIA. Deciduous shrub or small tree. Zones US, MS, LS. Usually multistemmed, to 15 ft. tall and 10 ft. wide. Leaves are 1½–3-in. long, pale gold with rosy tints when expanding, dark green at maturity, and bright red or yellow in fall. Flower clusters 1–2 in. across. Bright red fruit. Susceptibility to fireblight limits its use in the Lower South. Do not feed with high-nitrogen fertilizer in spring.

PHYGELIUS

CAPE FUCHSIA

Scrophulariaceae

PERENNIALS

ZONES US, MS, LS, CS

FULL SUN OR LIGHT SHADE

REGULAR WATER

Woody-based perennials that die back to the ground in winter in the Upper and Middle South, remain shrubby elsewhere. Related to snapdragon and penstemon, but drooping flowers also suggest fuchsia. Plants grow 3–4 ft. tall and spread by underground stems or rooting prostrate branches. Tubular, curved flowers borne in loosely branched clusters at branch ends, summer–fall. Prune to keep plants neat; mulch in Upper South. Species can be started from seed, but named selections should be grown from cuttings or by layering branches.

Phygelius capensis

P. aequalis. Flowers dusty rose, in pyramidal clusters. 'Yellow Trumpet' has showy pale yellow flowers.

P. capensis. More open and sprawling than *P. aequalis,* with open clusters of orange to red flowers.

P. rectus. Hybrid between the previous two species. 'African Queen' has deep salmon orange flowers; 'Devil's Tears', dark red buds, opening to red-pink flowers with yellow throats; 'Moonraker' bears pale yellow blooms; 'Salmon Leap', orange flowers; 'Winchester Fanfare' has deep rose flowers with yellow throats.

PHYLLITIS scolopendrium. See ASPLENIUM scolopendrium

PHYLLOSTACHYS. See BAMBOO

PHYSALIS

Solanaceae

PERENNIALS AND ANNUALS

ALL ZONES, EXCEPT AS NOTED

FULL SUN OR LIGHT SHADE

REGULAR WATER

Physalis alkekengi

Fruit is surrounded by loose, papery husk (enlarged calyx of flower). First species below is ornamental; other two are edible.

P. alkekengi (P. franchetii). CHINESE LANTERN PLANT. Perennial often grown as annual. Zones US, MS, LS. Plant is 1–2 ft. high, angularly branched. Long, creeping, whitish, underground stems; may become invasive without control. Long-stalked, light green leaves are 2–3 in. long. Often riddled with insects by end of summer. Flowers white, rather inconspicuous, appearing in leaf joints. Ornamental part of plant is calyx, which forms around ripened berry as loose, papery, orange-red, 2-in.-long, inflated envelope shaped like lantern. Fruit brightens garden in late summer and fall; dry, leafless stalks hung with merry lanterns make choice winter arrangements. Sow seed in spring in light soil. Increase by root division in fall or winter. 'Pygmy', 8-in. dwarf selection, makes a good container plant.

P. ixocarpa. TOMATILLO. Annual of bushy, sprawling growth to 4 ft. Fruit about 2 in. wide, swelling to fill—or sometimes split—the baggy calyx. Fruit yellow to purple and very sweet when ripe, but usually picked green and tart and used (cooked) in Mexican cuisine.

P. peruviana. GROUND CHERRY, POHA. Tender perennial grown as annual. Bushy, 1½ ft. high. Leaves 2–4 in. long. Flowers bell shaped, ⅜ in. long, whitish yellow marked with five brown spots. Seedy yellow fruit is sweet, rather insipid; can be used for pies or preserves (remove papery husks before using in cooking). Grow in same way as tomatoes. Plants sprawl quite a bit and are slow to start bearing but eventually productive. Several species, including *P. pruinosa* and *P. pubescens,* are similar.

PHYSIC NUT. See JATROPHA curcas

PHYSOSTEGIA

Lamiaceae (Labiatae)

PERENNIALS

ZONES US, MS, LS, CS

FULL SUN OR PARTIAL SHADE

REGULAR WATER

Physostegia virginiana

Slender, upright, leafy stems to 4 ft. Oblong leaves 3–5 in. long, with toothed edges and pointed tips. Funnel-shaped, 1-in.-long flowers in glistening white, rose pink, or lavender rose, carried in dense spikes. Blossoms resemble snapdragons and will remain in place if twisted or pushed out of position (hence the name "obedient plant").

Plant has a spiky form that makes it useful in borders, cut arrangements. Combine with taller fleabanes, pincushion flower, Michaelmas daisy. Stake taller stems to keep upright. Cut to ground after bloom. Vigorous and notoriously invasive; divide every 2 years to keep in bounds.

P. angustifolia. Native to Texas, Illinois, Mississippi. Grows 2–6 ft. tall; tallest in swampy conditions, where plant forms thick colonies. Pink-purple flowers on 4–6-in. spikes in spring and summer.

P. pulchella. Native to eastern Texas. Grows to 2 ft., taller if kept moist. Bears rose-purple flower spikes in spring and summer.

P. virginiana. OBEDIENT PLANT. Native to eastern U.S. To 4 ft. or taller. Flowers are borne on 10-in. spikes from mid- to late summer into fall. The 3-ft. 'Bouquet Rose' has rose pink blossoms. The following selections grow 2 ft. high: white 'Summer Snow'; 'Variegata', with bluish pink flowers and white-edged leaves; and rose pink 'Vivid'.

PICEA

SPRUCE

Pinaceae

EVERGREEN TREES OR SHRUBS

ZONES US, MS

FULL SUN OR LIGHT SHADE

REGULAR TO MODERATE WATER

Picea pungens 'Glauca'

Like firs, spruces are pyramidal and stiff needled, with branches arranged in neat tiers. But unlike firs, they have pendent cones, and their needles are attached to branches by small pegs that remain after needles drop. Most spruces are tall timber trees that lose their lower branches fairly early in life as they head upward; their canopies thin out noticeably as they age. Many species have dwarf forms useful as foundation plantings, for rock gardens, in containers. Spruces grow best in the Upper South.

Check spruces for aphids in late winter; if the pests are present, take prompt control measures to avoid spring defoliation. Other common pests are bagworms, spruce budworms, pine needle scale, and spider mites.

Prune only to shape. If a branch grows too long, cut it back to a well-placed side branch. For slower growth and denser form, trim part of each year's growth to force side branches. When planting larger spruces, don't place them too close to buildings, fences, or walks; they need space.

P. abies (P. excelsa). NORWAY SPRUCE. Native to northern Europe. Fast growth to 100–150 ft. Stiff, deep green, attractive pyramid in youth; ragged in age, as branchlets droop and oldest branchlets (those nearest trunk) die back. Extremely hardy and wind resistant; valued for windbreaks. Tolerates heat and humidity better than most. 'Sherwoodii' is a rugged, picturesque shrub with compact but irregular habit; it was developed from a tree that at age 60 was only 5 ft. tall and 10 ft. across at base.

P. glauca. WHITE SPRUCE. Native to Canada and northern U.S. Cone-shaped tree grows 60–70 ft., dense when young, with pendulous twigs and silver-green foliage. Crushed needles have an unpleasant odor. The following two selections are widely grown:

'Conica'. DWARF ALBERTA SPRUCE, DWARF WHITE SPRUCE. Compact, pyramidal tree, slowly reaching 7 ft. in 35 years. Short, soft needles are bright grass green when new, gray green when mature. Needs shelter from drying winds (whether hot or cold) and from strong reflected sunlight. Popular container plant. Often sold as *P. albertiana.*

P. g. densata. BLACK HILLS SPRUCE. Slow-growing, dense pyramid; can reach 20 ft. in 35 years.

P. omorika. SERBIAN SPRUCE. Native to southeastern Europe. Narrow, conical, slow-growing tree to 50–60 ft. tall. Shiny dark green needles with silvery undersides. Retains branches to the ground for many years. Considered by some to be the most attractive spruce; one of the best for hot, humid climates. 'Nana' is a dwarf to 3–4 ft. tall (possibly to 10 ft. high), with short, closely packed needles.

P. orientalis. ORIENTAL SPRUCE. Native to Caucasus, Asia Minor. Dense, compact, cone-shaped tree with very short needles; grows slowly to 50–60 ft. high. Can tolerate poor soils if they are well drained, but may suffer leaf burn in very cold, dry winds.

P. pungens. COLORADO BLUE SPRUCE. The only spruce that will succeed in the Southwest and southern Midwest. Slow to moderate growth rate. In gardens, reaches 30–60 ft. tall, 10–20 ft. wide; in the wild, grows to a possible 100 ft. tall, 25–35 ft. across. Very stiff, regular, horizontal branches form a broad pyramid. Foliage of seedlings varies in color from dark green through all shades of blue green to steely blue. The following selections have consistent color:

'Fat Albert'. Compact, erect, broad, formal-looking blue cone. Slow growth (to 10 ft. in 10 years) makes it a good living Christmas tree.

'Foxtail'. Vigorous, heat tolerant. Well suited to the Lower South. Does quite well in Texas. Upright, symmetrical habit. Bluish new growth bushy, needles slightly twisted. Much faster growing than species.

'Glauca'. COLORADO BLUE SPRUCE. Distinctive gray-blue color.   ▶

P

'Hoopsii'. Beautiful, striking silvery blue color. Fast growing; train early to ensure erect, cone shape. Many consider this the finest selection.

'Koster'. KOSTER BLUE SPRUCE. Bluer than 'Glauca'; growth habit sometimes irregular.

'Moerheimii'. Same blue as 'Koster', but shape is more compact and symmetrical.

'Montgomery'. Dwarf, slow-growing plant that becomes a broad cone shape to 2 ft. high, with strikingly blue foliage.

'Pendula'. WEEPING BLUE SPRUCE. Gray blue, with weeping branchlets. Stake main trunk while plant is young.

'Thomsen'. Similar in color to 'Hoopsii'. Vigorous, symmetrical habit.

PICKEREL WEED. See PONTEDERIA cordata

PIERIS

Ericaceae

EVERGREEN SHRUBS

ZONES VARY BY SPECIES

SOME SHADE, ESPECIALLY IN AFTERNOON

REGULAR WATER

LEAVES AND NECTAR ARE POISONOUS IF INGESTED

*Pieris
japonica*

Elegant in foliage and form all year, these plants make good companions for rhododendron and azalea, to which they are related. Whorls of leathery, narrowly oval leaves; clusters of small, typically white, urnshaped flowers. Most plants form flower buds by autumn, so potential flower clusters are a subtle decorative feature over winter. Resembling strings of tiny greenish pink beads, the buds open late winter–midspring. New spring growth is often bright colored (pink to red or bronze), but matures to glossy dark green.

Same cultural needs as rhododendron and azalea. Need well-drained but moisture-retentive acid soil; do not thrive in hot, dry conditions. Choose a planting location sheltered from wind, where plants will get high shade or dappled sunlight at least during the warmest afternoon hours. Prune by removing spent flowers. Splendid in containers, in oriental and woodland gardens, in entryways for year-round good looks.

P. floribunda (Andromeda floribunda). MOUNTAIN PIERIS. Zones US, MS. Compact, rounded shrub 3–6 ft. tall. New growth is pale green; mature leaves are dull dark green, 1½–3 in. long. Blossoms in upright clusters. Very cold-hardy. Tolerates sun and low humidity better than the others, but does not thrive in hot, humid regions.

P. japonica (Andromeda japonica). JAPANESE ANDROMEDA, LILY-OF-THE-VALLEY SHRUB. Zones US, MS, LS. Upright, dense, tiered growth to 9–10 ft. New growth is bronzy pink to red; mature leaves are glossy green, 3 in. long. Drooping clusters of white, pink, or nearly red flowers. Buds are often dark red. Many selections, some rare. The following are grown for unusual habit or foliage:

'Bert Chandler'. New foliage turns from salmon pink through cream to white, then pale green.

'Compacta'. Grows 4–6 ft. tall; compact. Heavy bloomer.

'Crispa'. Grows to 6–7 ft., with handsome, wavy-edged leaves.

'Karenoma'. Compact growth to 3–6 ft., with upright flower clusters.

'Mountain Fire'. Fiery red new growth.

'Pygmaea'. Tiny dwarf less than 1 ft. tall, with very few flowers and narrow leaves to 1 in. long.

'Spring Snow'. Similar to 'Karenoma'.

'Variegata'. Slow grower with leaves marked with creamy white, tinged pink in spring. Prune out any green-leafed shoots.

The following selections are grown principally for their flowers:

'Christmas Cheer'. Early-blooming bicolor with flowers in white and deep rose red; flower stalks are rose red.

'Coleman'. Pink flowers opening from red buds.

'Daisen'. Compact plant. Flowers are similar to those of 'Christmas Cheer', but leaves are broader.

'Dorothy Wyckoff'. Tall growing, with white flowers opening from deep red buds. Leaves turn purplish in winter.

'Pink'. Shell pink flowers fading to white.

'Purity'. To 3–4 ft. Late blooming; unusually large white flowers.

'Temple Bells'. Compact, tiered habit; a bit less cold tolerant than the species. Ivory flowers.

'Valley Rose'. Pink-and-white flowers; open habit.

'Valley Valentine'. Deep red buds and flowers.

'White Cascade'. Extremely heavy show of pure white blooms.

P. taiwanensis. Zones US, MS. Similar to *P. japonica*, but flower clusters are somewhat larger and more erect. 'Snowdrift', a hybrid between this species and *P. japonica*, has unusually profuse pure white blooms.

PIGEON PLUM. See COCCOLOBA diversifolia

PIGGYBACK PLANT. See TOLMIEA menziesii

Pinaceae. Members of the pine family are evergreen trees with narrow, usually needlelike leaves and seeds borne on the scales of woody cones. Pine (*Pinus*), spruce (*Picea*), true cedar (*Cedrus*), larch (*Larix*), Douglas fir (*Pseudotsuga menziesii*), and hemlock (*Tsuga*) are examples.

PINCUSHION FLOWER. See SCABIOSA

PINDO PALM. See BUTIA capitata

PINE. See PINUS

PINEAPPLE

Bromeliaceae

BROMELIAD; CAN BEAR FRUIT

ZONE TS; OR GREENHOUSE, HOUSE PLANT

FULL SUN FOR FRUIT

REGULAR WATER

Pineapple

Plant is rosette of long, narrow leaves with sawtoothed edges. To grow it, cut leafy top from a market pineapple. Root base of top in water or fast-draining but moisture-retentive potting mix. When the roots have formed, move pineapple to 7–8-in. pot of rich soil. Will overwinter only in Tropical South; elsewhere, grow it as a full-time house plant, or in a pot you can take indoors in winter. Water when soil is dry. Feed every 3 or 4 weeks with liquid fertilizer. Fruit forms (if you're lucky) in 2 years, on top of sturdy stalk in center of clump. A selection with foliage variegated in pink, white, and olive green is sometimes available as a house plant. Plants grown for foliage rather than fruit will take reduced light.

PINEAPPLE FLOWER. See EUCOMIS

PINEAPPLE GUAVA. See FEIJOA sellowiana

PINK. See DIANTHUS

PINK POWDER PUFF. See CALLIANDRA haematocephala

PINK TRUMPET TREE. TABEBUIA heterophylla, T. impetiginosa

PINK TRUMPET VINE. See PODRANEA ricasoliana

SPRING PRUNING TO SHAPE A PINE TREE

To fatten up a rangy pine or to keep a young one teddy-bear chubby, cut back the candles of new growth by half (or even more) when the new growth begins to emerge in spring. Leave a few clusters untrimmed if you want growth to continue along a branch.

P

PINUS

PINE

Pinaceae

EVERGREEN TREES, RARELY SHRUBS

🌡 ZONES VARY BY SPECIES

☼ FULL SUN

💧 REGULAR TO LITTLE WATER

▶ SEE CHART NEXT PAGE

Pinus palustris

Pines are the great individualists of the garden, each species differing not only in its characteristics but also in way it responds to wind, heat, and other growing conditions. Cone size and shape are an identifying feature of pines; another is the number of long, slender needles in a bundle. Most species have needles in groups of two, three, or five. Those with two needles tend to be more tolerant of unfavorable soil and climate than three-needle species, and three-needle pines more so than five-needle ones. As a group, pines are much more adaptable to Southern growing conditions than spruces or firs. The chart describes pines best adapted to Southern climate zones.

Pines tend to be pyramidal in youth, becoming more open or round topped with age. They grow best in full sun and will thrive in most soils that are reasonably well drained. Too much water results in yellow needles (with the yellowing appearing first in the older needles) and a generally unhealthy appearance—and can even cause sudden death. Most pines are fairly drought tolerant; exceptions are typically among the five-needle species. Pines rarely need fertilizer, and trees that receive it generally produce undesirable, rank growth.

A healthy tree usually can cope with the pests and diseases that afflict pines. Trees most at risk are those weakened by drought or air pollution. Aphids, spider mites, scale, and bark beetles are possible wherever pines are grown. Most five-needle species are susceptible to white pine blister rust (a bark disease that can kill the tree). Aphids usually show their presence by sticky secretions, sooty mildew, and yellowing needles. Birds are attracted to seeds in pinecones.

All pines can be shaped, and usually improved, by pruning. The best time to prune is in spring, when needles start to emerge from the spires of new growth (the so-called candles). Cutting back partway into these candles will promote bushiness and allow some overall increase in tree size; cutting out candles entirely will limit size. Don't cut the tree's leading shoot unless you want to limit its height. Careful pruning will allow you to maintain some pines as informal hedges or screens.

PISTACIA

Anacardiaceae

DECIDUOUS TREES, SEMIEVERGREEN LARGE SHRUB

🌡 ZONES VARY BY SPECIES

☼ EXPOSURE NEEDS VARY BY SPECIES

💧 MODERATE WATER

Pistacia chinensis

Divided leaves on all species. Flowers are not showy. Female trees will bear fruit after several years if male trees are nearby. Of species described, only *P. vera* bears edible fruits (nuts). Others are ornamental trees.

P. chinensis. CHINESE PISTACHE. Deciduous tree. Zones US, MS, LS, CS. Native to China. Slow to moderate growth to 30–60 ft. tall, with nearly equal spread. Young trees often gawky, lopsided; older ones become dense, shapely with reasonable care. Foot-long leaves consist of 10–16 paired dark green leaflets, each 2–4 in. long, ¾ in. wide. Good fall color even in mild climates: Foliage turns luminous orange to red (sometimes yellow). Trees are either male or female; if the two

sexes are near each other, the female will bear clusters of small red fruits that ripen to blue black.

Tolerant of many soils, including alkaline types. Where verticillium wilt is present, minimize risk by providing good drainage and by watering as little as possible during dry periods. Very drought tolerant. Stake young tree and prune for the first few years to develop a head high enough to walk under. Good tree for street, lawn, or courtyard. Full sun.

P. texana. TEXAS PISTACHIO. Large, semievergreen shrub or small multitrunked tree. Zones LS, CS, TS. Native to Texas. Grows to 20–30 ft. tall, rarely 40 ft. Makes a feathery screen, with attractive red fall berries on female plants, or, if cut back every year when young to promote a dense habit, a fine-textured hedge. New foliage has reddish cast; mature leaves glossy, dark green and persist late into winter; partly evergreen if temperature stays above 15°F. Given regular water, grows quickly. Thrives in fertile garden soils, but well adapted to a range of conditions, including limestone and caliche, providing drainage is good. Partial shade or full sun.

P. vera. PISTACHIO, PISTACHIO NUT. Deciduous tree. Zones CS, TS. Native to Iran, central Asia. Broad, bushy tree to 30 ft. high, with one or several trunks. Leaves have three to five roundish, 2–4 in.-long leaflets. Fruit reddish, wrinkled, borne in heavy clusters. Inside husks are hard-shelled pistachio nuts. Include male tree in your planting. 'Peters' is the male selection most planted; 'Kerman' is principal fruiting (female) type. When planting, avoid rough handling; budded tops are easily broken away from understock. Pistachios are inclined to spread and droop; stake them and train branches to good framework of four or five limbs beginning at 4 ft. above ground. Established trees need little watering. Full sun.

Pittosporaceae. The pittosporum family consists of evergreen shrubs, trees, and vines from Australia, New Zealand, and eastern Asia. Many have attractive flowers, foliage, or fruit. *Pittosporum* is representative.

PITTOSPORUM

Pittosporaceae

EVERGREEN SHRUBS

🌡 ZONES VARY BY SPECIES

☼ ◑ FULL SUN OR PARTIAL SHADE

💧 REGULAR TO MODERATE WATER

Pittosporum tobira

Pittosporums are valued most for their foliage and form, though they also bear clusters of small, often sweetly fragrant flowers followed by fairly conspicuous fruits the size of large peas. All are basic, dependable shrubs. Some make good clipped hedges; all have pleasing outlines when left unclipped. Excellent screens, windbreaks, foundation or container plants. Susceptible to aphids and scale insects; sooty black covering on leaves is a sure sign of infestation. Ripe fruits (usually orange) split open to reveal sticky seeds; fallen fruit can be a nuisance on lawns, paving.

P. tobira. JAPANESE PITTOSPORUM. Zones LS (protected), CS, TS. Dense, rounded shrub, eventually reaching 10–15 ft. if not restricted by pruning. Lower limbs can be removed from older plants to make small trees. Whorls of leathery, narrowly elliptical, shiny dark green leaves to 5 in. long. Creamy white flowers, borne at branch tips in early spring, smell like orange blossoms. Very tolerant of seacoast conditions. One of the few plants to plant on dunes. 'Wheeler's Dwarf', dwarf pittosporum, grows 3–4 ft. high; it's not as hardy as species (may die at 10°F), but makes a good house plant where winters are cold. 'Variegata', whitespot Japanese pittosporum, 5–10 ft., has gray-green leaves edged white. 'Turner's Dwarf' is a low plant with same foliage color as 'Variegata'.

P. undulatum. VICTORIAN BOX. Zone TS. Moderately fast to 15 ft., then slow to 30–40 ft. high and wide. Planted 5–8 ft. apart, can be kept to dense, 10–15-ft. screen by pruning (not shearing). Glossy green, lance-shaped, wavy-edged leaves to 6 in. long. Very fragrant creamy white flowers in early spring. Strong roots become invasive with age. Susceptible to insects and disease in Florida.

PINE

NAME, NATIVE HABITAT	ZONES	GROWTH RATE, SIZE	GROWTH HABIT	NEEDLES AND CONES	COMMENTS
P. bungeana LACEBARK PINE Northern and central China	US, MS, LS. Hardy to −20°F	Slow, to 75 ft.	Often multitrunked, spreading. Sometimes shrubby. Picturesque	Needles: in 3s, 3 in., bright green. Cones: 2–2½ in., yellowish brown	Smooth, dull gray bark flakes off like sycamore bark to show smooth, creamy white branches and trunk. Brittle limbs can break under heavy snow loads
P. cembroides MEXICAN PIÑON PINE Arizona to Baja California and northern Mexico	US, MS, LS, CS	Slow, to 10–25 ft.	Stout, spreading branches form round-topped head. In youth rather rangy	Needles: in 3s or 2s, dark green, 1–2 in. Cones: 1–2 in., yellowish or reddish brown	Most treelike of piñons. Very drought tolerant; adapted to poor, rocky, limy soils. Good choice for drier areas of Texas and Oklahoma
P. clausa SAND PINE Gulf Coast and coastal areas of Florida	CS, TS	To 30 ft.	Irregular crown	Slender dark green needles 2–3½ in. long, in bundles of 2; ovoid-conic cones 2–3 in. long	Good in sandy soils along the coasts
P. echinata SHORTLEAF PINE Dry uplands soils of Georgia, Oklahoma, and Texas	US, MS, LS, CS	Fast, to 50–80 ft.	An open pyramidal habit when mature, with sinuous branches	Slender dark bluish green needles, 3–5-in.-long, in bundles of 2 or 3; pale brown, ovoid-oblong cones 1½–2½ in.	Important timber species. Adaptable, but deep rooted and difficult to move once established. Good lawn tree. Resistant to most diseases and insects that affect most other pines
P. edulis (**P. cembroides edulis**) PIÑON, NUT PINE California's desert mountains; east to Arizona, New Mexico, and Texas; north to Wyoming	US, MS, LS	Slow, to 10–20 ft.	Horizontal-branching tree; picturesque form; gnarled trunks. Symmetrical and bushy in youth; low, round or flat crowned in maturity	Needles: usually in 2s, dark green, ¾–1½ in., dense, stiff. Cones: 2 in., roundish, light brown	Beautiful small pine for containers, rock gardens, courtyard. Cones contain edible seeds (pine nuts). Well adapted to dry, rocky soils of Southwest
P. eldarica AFGHAN PINE Southwestern Asia	US, MS, LS	Rapid, to 30–80 ft.	Denser, more erect than *P. halepensis*, more classic pine tree shape	Needles in 2s, dark green, 5–6½ in. Cones: like those of *P. halepensis*, but not stalked or bent back	Tolerates drought, alkaline soil. Well adapted to Southwest. Often grown there for Christmas trees
P. elliottii SLASH PINE Coastal plains, South Carolina to Louisiana	MS, LS, CS	Fast, to possible 100 ft.	Dense, rounded crown	Needles: in 2s or 3s, to 1 ft., dark green, stiff. Cones: 3½–6 in., shiny brown	Usually planted for quick shade, erosion control. Adapted to acid-soil areas of East Texas. *P. e. densa* thrives in southern Florida
P. glabra SPRUCE PINE From South Carolina to Louisiana	LS, CS	To 50–90 ft.	Horizontal branching at top of trunk; rounded crown. Branches low; casts heavy shade; difficult to grow grass under	Dark green, twisted, 2–3½-in. needles in bundles of 2; buff ovoid cones 2–2½ in. long	Likes fertile, moist, acid soil; tolerates heavy clay. Widely planted in Lower South gardens east of Mississippi River
P. halepensis ALEPPO PINE Mediterranean region	LS, CS	Moderate to rapid, to 30–60 ft.	Attractive as 2-year-old; rugged character at 5 years; in age, has open, irregular crown of many short, ascending branches	Needles: usually in 2s, 2½–4 in., light green. Cones: 3 in., oval to oblong, reddish to yellow brown	Can grow in poor soils under trying conditions: in desert heat, on seacoast, with little or no water. Better-looking trees can be found for less harsh climates
P. mugo mugo MUGHO PINE Eastern Alps and Balkans	US, MS	Slow, to 4 ft.	From the start, a shrubby, symmetrical little pine. May spread in age	Needles: in 2s, 2 in., dark green. Cones: 1–2 in., oval, dark brown	Widely used in rock gardens, containers. Pick plants with dense, pleasing form
P. nigra (formerly **P. austriaca**) AUSTRIAN PINE, AUSTRIAN BLACK PINE Europe, western Asia	US, MS	Slow to moderate, usually not more than 40 ft. in gardens	Dense, stout pyramid with uniform crown. Branches in regular whorls. In age, broad and flat topped	Needles: in 2s, 3–6½ in., very dark green, stiff. Cones: 2–3½ in., oval, brown	Tolerant of urban and seacoast conditions. Problem of tip blight has caused severe dieback in Upper South

P

PINE

NAME, NATIVE HABITAT	ZONES	GROWTH RATE, SIZE	GROWTH HABIT	NEEDLES AND CONES	COMMENTS
P. palustris LONGLEAF PINE Virginia to Florida and west to Mississippi, southeastern coast	MS, LS, CS, TS	Slow for 5–10 years, then fast, to 55–80 ft.	Gaunt, sparse branches ascend to form open, oblong head	Needles: in 3s, dark green; 1½ ft. in youth (called grass stage) replaced by 9-in. needles when mature. Cones: 6–10 in., dull brown	Young plants look like fountains of grass. Prefers deep soils (grows on sandy ridges in its native range). The classic, graceful pine of the South
P. parviflora JAPANESE WHITE PINE Japan and Taiwan	US, MS. Will survive −20°F	Slow to moderate, to 20–50 ft.	In open ground, a broad pyramid, nearly as wide as high	Needles: in 5s, 1½–2½ in., bluish to green. Cones: 2–3 in., reddish brown	Widely used as bonsai or container plant. There are blue-gray ('Glauca') and dwarf forms
P. resinosa RED PINE Newfoundland to Manitoba, south to mountains of Pennsylvania, west to Michigan	US, MS	Moderate, to 50–80 ft.	Short trunked, densely branched, eventually a dense oval	Needles: in 2s, 5–6 in., dark green. Cones: 3–6 in., light brown	Orange-red bark in youth, reddish brown plates in maturity. Attractive tree for difficult situations, poor soils. Use for windbreak, shelter belt, erosion control
P. strobus WHITE PINE, EASTERN WHITE PINE Newfoundland to Manitoba, south to Georgia, west to Illinois and Iowa	US, MS	Fast, to 100 ft. or more	Symmetrical cone shape with horizontal branches in regular whorls. In age, broad, open, irregular. Fine textured, handsome	Needles: in 5s, 2–4 in., blue green, soft. Cones: 3–8 in., slender, often curved, light brown	Intolerant of strong winds, pollution, salts. Subject to white pine blister rust, white pine weevil. Popular Christmas tree. Selections include 'Fastigiata', among most beautiful of upright pines; 'Pendula', with weeping, trailing branches; 'Prostrata', a low, trailing form; 'Nana', good in containers for many years
P. sylvestris SCOTCH PINE Northern Europe, western Asia, northeastern Siberia	US, MS	Fast, then moderate, usually to 70–100 ft.	In youth, a straight, well-branched pyramid. In age, irregular, open, and picturesque, with drooping branches	Needles: in 2s, blue green, 1½–3 in., stiff. Cones: 2 in., gray to reddish brown	Popular as Christmas tree. Showy red bark in maturity; sparse foliage. Pick young trees for good green winter color. Wind resistant. Garden forms include dwarfs 'Nana' and 'Watereri', weeping 'Pendula', columnar 'Fastigiata'
P. taeda LOBLOLLY PINE Southern New Jersey to Florida, East Texas, and Oklahoma	US, MS, LS, CS	Fast, to 50–90 ft.	Loose cone shape in youth; as it matures, loses lower branches to become a rather open-crowned tree	Needles: in 3s (rarely 2s), 6–10 in., dark yellowish green. Cones: 3–6 in., oval to narrowly conical, rust brown, in clusters of 2–5	Tough tree, withstands poor soils. Useful in Lower South for quick screening and shade. Adapted to acid-soil areas of East Texas. Widely planted for pulp, lumber. Provides light shade; good to garden under
P. thunbergiana (**P. thunbergii**) JAPANESE BLACK PINE Japan	US, MS, LS, CS	To 20–40 ft.	Spreading branches form broad, conical tree, irregular and spreading in age, often with leaning trunk	Needles: in 2s, 3–4½ in., bright green, stiff. Cones: 3 in., oval, brown	Handsome tree in youth. Takes well to pruning, even shearing. Excellent for bonsai or pots. Very salt tolerant. 'Majestic Beauty' stands up to smog. 'Thunderhead' is a dwarf (6 ft. at 10 years) with showy white winter buds and spring candles. Subject to nematodes
P. virginiana VIRGINIA PINE, SCRUB PINE Poor, dry, or clayey soils from New York to Georgia and Alabama	US, MS, LS, CS	Slow, to 45–55 ft. or more	Broad, open habit with sparse branching; wide, stiff top	Twisted needles 1¼–4 in. long, 2 per bundle; persistent conical-ovoid cones to 3 in. long, in 2s, 3s, or 4s	Seldom used as an ornamental, but valuable in clay or impoverished soils. Popular cut Christmas tree in Lower and Coastal South. Adapts to most well-drained soils
P. wallichiana (**P. griffithii**, **P. excelsa**) HIMALAYAN WHITE PINE Himalayas	US	Slow to moderate; reaches 40 ft. in gardens, 150 ft. in wild	Broad, conical, open. Often retains branches to the ground in age	Needles: in 5s, 6–8 in., blue green, drooping, soft. Cones: 6–10 in., light brown	Eventually large, but good form and color make it a good choice for featured pine in big lawn or garden. Resistant to white pine blister rust

P

PLANTAIN LILY. See HOSTA

PLATANUS

SYCAMORE, PLANE TREE

Platanaceae

DECIDUOUS TREES

ZONES VARY BY SPECIES

FULL SUN OR LIGHT SHADE

REGULAR WATER

Platanus occidentalis

A ll grow large, with heavy trunks and sculptural branch pattern. Older bark sheds in patches to reveal pale, smooth, new bark beneath. Big leaves (to 10 in. across) are rough surfaced and maplelike with three to five lobes; disappointing yellowish to brown autumn color. Ball-shaped brown seed clusters hang on threadlike stalks from bare branches through winter; these are prized for winter arrangements. Best in rich, deep, moist, well-drained soil. All are subject to anthracnose, which causes early leaf drop and twig dieback. Rake up and dispose of dead leaves, since fungus spores can overwinter on them.

P. acerifolia. LONDON PLANE TREE. Zones US, MS, LS. Hybrid between *P. occidentalis* and *P. orientalis,* and often sold under the latter name. Grows 30–40 ft. tall in 20 years; may reach 70–100 ft. tall, 65–80 ft. wide in gardens. Smooth, cream-colored upper trunk and limbs. Handsome in winter. Tolerates many soils, city smog, soot, dust, reflected heat. Good avenue, street tree. Can fit smaller spaces when pollarded to create a low, dense canopy. 'Columbia' and 'Liberty' are resistant to both anthracnose and powdery mildew (can cause premature leaf drop) and somewhat resistant to cankerstain disease, which can kill branches or the entire tree. 'Bloodgood' resists anthracnose; 'Yarwood' is mildew resistant.

P. mexicana. MEXICAN SYCAMORE. Zones MS, LS, CS, TS. Native to northeastern Mexico. To 60 ft. tall. Leaves 8 in. wide, five lobed, smooth edged, and felty white on undersides. Well adapted to dry, rocky, alkaline soils of the Southwest.

P. occidentalis. SYCAMORE, AMERICAN PLANE TREE. Zones US, MS, LS, CS. Very hardy. Native to the South and north to Maine and Minnesota. Similar to *P. acerifolia,* but has whiter new bark and a longer leafless period. Irregular habit, contorted branches. Occasionally grows with multiple or leaning trunks. Good climbing tree. Old trees near streams sometimes reach 100 ft. or more in height and spread. Because of its size and habit of dropping bark, seedballs, and leaves year-round, it's not a good choice for small properties.

P. orientalis. See P. acerifolia

PLATYCERIUM

STAGHORN FERN

Polypodiaceae

FERNS

ZONE TS, EXCEPT AS NOTED

PARTIAL SHADE

REGULAR TO MODERATE WATER

*Platycerium
bifurcatum*

N ative to tropical regions, where they grow on trees; gardeners grow them on slabs of bark or tree fern stem, sometimes in hanging baskets or attached to trees. In the absence of rainfall, water only when slab or moss to which plant is attached is actually dry to the touch. Plant has two kinds of fronds. Sterile ones are flat, pale green, aging to tan and brown; they support plant and accumulate organic matter to help feed it. Fertile fronds are forked, resembling deer antlers.

P. bifurcatum. STAGHORN FERN. Zones CS (protected), TS. From Australia and New Guinea. Surprisingly hardy; survives 20–22°F with only lath

structures for shelter. Fertile fronds clustered, gray green, to 3 ft. long. Its numerous offsets can be used in propagation. Often sold as *P. alcicorne.*

P. coronarium. From southeast Asia. Sterile fronds are thick and deeply lobed at top. Deeply forked fertile fronds droop in a mass, some 3 ft. long, some 6 or even 9 ft. long. Particularly cold sensitive; needs night temperatures above 60°F.

P. grande. From Australia. Sterile fronds erect, fan shaped. Fertile fronds pendulous, forked, to 6 ft. long. Very similar to *P. superbum,* but more cold sensitive; needs minimum temperature of 50°F.

P. hillii. ELK'S-HORN FERN. From Australia. Similar to *P. bifurcatum.* Kidney-shaped sterile fronds grow like plaques behind the fertile fronds, which fan out almost horizontally, like deep green, wide fingers, to 3 ft. long and forked at tips.

P. superbum. From Australia. Fertile and sterile fronds both forked, the former broad but divided somewhat like moose antlers. To 6 ft. long. Protect from frosts.

PLATYCLADUS orientalis
(Thuja orientalis)

ORIENTAL ARBORVITAE

Cupressaceae

EVERGREEN SHRUB

ALL ZONES

FULL SUN OR LIGHT SHADE

REGULAR WATER

*Platycladus
orientalis*

F oliage is carried in flattened sprays that are held vertically, forming a conical to pyramidal plant. Juvenile leaves are tiny and needlelike; mature leaves are minute, overlapping scales. Oval, ¾-in. cones are waxy blue green before ripening. Species (to 25 ft. high, 15 ft. wide) is rarely grown; garden centers offer more attractive, shrubbier selections 3–10 ft. high (see below). Widely used around foundations, by doorways or gates, in formal rows.

Less cold-hardy than American arborvitae *(Thuja occidentalis),* but tolerates heat and low humidity better. Takes the place of American arborvitae in the Lower, Coastal, and Tropical South. Tolerates many soils, but will not take boggy ones. Protect from strong winds. Bagworms and red spider mites are potential pests.

'Aureus' ('Aureus Nana', 'Berckmanii'). DWARF GOLDEN ARBORVITAE, BERCKMAN DWARF ARBORVITAE. Dwarf, compact, golden, globe shaped, usually 3 ft. tall, 2 ft. wide. Can reach 5 ft. Widely planted.

'Bakeri'. Compact, cone shaped, with bright green foliage. Reaches 5–8 ft. high in 10 years.

'Blue Cone'. Dense, upright, conical; blue-green color. To 8 ft. tall by 4 ft.

'Bonita' ('Bonita Upright', 'Bonita Erecta'). Rounded, full, dense cone to 3 ft. tall. Dark green with slight golden tinting at branch tips.

'Fruitlandii'. FRUITLAND ARBORVITAE. Compact, upright, cone shaped, with deep green foliage.

'Minima Glauca'. DWARF BLUE ARBORVITAE. Grows 3–4 ft. tall and as wide. Blue-green foliage.

PLATYCODON grandiflorus

BALLOON FLOWER

Campanulaceae (Lobeliaceae)

PERENNIAL

ZONES US, MS, LS, CS

AFTERNOON SHADE

REGULAR WATER

Platycodon grandiflorus

A ttractive, easy-to-grow, and pest-free plant. Inflated, balloonlike buds are carried on slender stalks at the ends of upright stems clad in broadly oval, 3-in. leaves. Buds open into 2-in.,

P

star-shaped blue-violet flowers with purple veins. Bloom begins in early summer and will continue for 2 months or more if spent blossoms (but not entire stems) are removed. Double-flowered types are available, as well as pink- and white-flowered types. *P. g. mariesii* (sometimes sold as *P. g.* 'Mariesii') is rich blue dwarf form 1–1½ ft. high; 'Misato Purple' has deep purple flowers, grows to just 8 in. tall. 'Album' has white flowers, often blue veined, on tall, 3-ft., plant; 'Double Blue' bears intense blue double flowers, on 2-ft. plant. 'Shell Pink' and 'Mother of Pearl' flowers are soft pink; 'Komachi' flowers are clear blue and maintain their balloon shape, never opening fully.

Plant is deep rooted and takes 2 or 3 years to get well established. Dies back completely in fall, and new growth appears quite late in spring; mark position to avoid digging up fleshy roots. If you do unearth a root, replant it—or the pieces—right away.

BALLOON FLOWER IN BORDERS

With its round buds, graceful star-shaped blossoms, and several-month-long bloom season, balloon flower is a nice choice for a summer border. Companion plants in shades of pink, yellow, deep to light blue, and white make for a lovely color combination; try astilbe, various kinds of yarrow (*Achillea*), phlox, coral bells (*Heuchera*), and mallow (*Malva*). Lush foliage plants such as hosta are good partners, too.

PLECTRANTHUS

SWEDISH IVY

Lamiaceae (Labiatae)

PERENNIALS

🌿 ZONE TS; OR INDOORS

🔆 ● SHADE OUTDOORS; BRIGHT LIGHT INDOORS

💧 REGULAR WATER

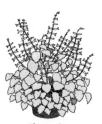

Plectranthus oertendahlii

Leaves somewhat thick, with scalloped edges and prominent veins. Small white or bluish flowers in spikes. In Tropical South, can be grown as ground cover or as trailing plants that drape over walls or planter edges. As greenhouse or house plants, grow in hanging pots or wall containers. Among easiest plants to grow. Will root in water or soil. Many people remove flower buds before bloom to keep plants compact; others allow plants to bloom, then cut them back afterward. The following are the best known of many species and selections:

P. australis. To 6 in. high; wide spreading. Shiny dark green leaves. Some forms have white-variegated foliage.

P. coleoides 'Marginatus'. To 2 ft. high; less trailing in habit than the others. Leaves green and gray green, edged in cream.

P. oertendahlii. To 6 in. high; wide spreading. Leaf veins are silvery above, purplish beneath. Leaf margins are purplish, scalloped.

PLUM, FLOWERING. See PRUNUS

PLUM and PRUNE

Rosaceae

DECIDUOUS FRUIT TREES

🌿 ZONES VARY BY SELECTIONS

🔆 FULL SUN

💧 PERIODIC DEEP SOAKINGS

▶ SEE CHART NEXT PAGE

Plum

Like their cherry, peach, and apricot relatives, these are stone fruits belonging to the genus *Prunus;* for flowering plums, see pages 342–344. Three categories of edible plums and prunes are grown in the diverse climates of North America: European, Japanese, and native species. They tolerate many soil types but do best in fertile, well-drained soil. Plants bloom in late winter or early spring. Harvest season is from June into September, depending on type and selection.

The two most widely grown groups in the South are European (*P. domestica*) and Japanese (*P. salicina*). Damson plum is often considered a type of European plum; it freely intercrosses with European plums. Prunes are types of European plum with a high sugar content, a trait that allows them to be sun-dried without fermenting at the pit.

In general, Japanese types are the best plums for the South. Compared with European plums, they need less winter chill, better tolerate heat and humidity, and have fewer disease and insect problems. Just about the only choices for the Lower and Coastal South, they also grow well in the Upper and Middle South. European plums are more cold-hardy and bloom a little later (and so are less subject to frost damage) but need much more care to remain healthy. Most European selections perform poorly outside the Upper and Middle South.

Native species include wild plum, Chickasaw plum, and Mexican plum. These tough, hardy trees are easy to grow; their fruits are used to make jelly and preserves.

Most plum types are grafted onto another rootstock. Standard trees grow about 15 ft. high, dwarf trees about half that size. There is also an intermediate semidwarf category.

Plums come in many colors. The skin may be yellow, red, purple, green, blue, or almost black; the flesh may be yellow, red, or green. Japanese plums are the largest and juiciest of the lot, with a pleasant blend of acid and sugar; they are typically eaten fresh. European kinds are firmer fleshed, can be cooked or eaten fresh; prune types are used for drying or canning but can also be eaten out of hand if you like the very sweet flavor.

Train young trees to a vase shape. After selecting framework branches, cut back to lateral branches. If tree tends to grow upright, cut to outside branches; if it is spreading, cut to inside branches. Prune to avoid formation of V-shaped crotches. On types that produce excessive upright growth (mainly Japanese plums), shorten shoots to outside branchlets. Mature European plum trees require limited pruning, mainly to thin out annual shoot growth.

Most European plums don't require a pollinator, though they set fruit better when grown near other European selections. Japanese plums produce better crops when cross-pollinated; plant two Japanese selections.

Certain insects and disease plague most plums. Black knot (black, warty growths caused by a fungus) is a common problem. To control the disease, prune off infected branches, cutting at least 4 in. below signs of disease. Or plant black knot–resistant selections 'Damson', 'Methley', 'Santa Rosa', 'Shiro', and 'Stanley'. Peach tree borer may cause trouble. The more humid the climate, the more troublesome are plum curculio (which infests the fruit) and the diseases bacterial canker (which causes open wounds on trunk and branches) and brown rot of stone fruit. If you only have a few fruit trees, you may be able to control the curculio with traps. Dormant-season applications of sprays combining horticultural oil with lime sulfur will control brown rot and various insect pests such as scale; also prune trees to provide good air circulation. To reduce risk of bacterial canker, prevalent in the South, don't leave stubs when pruning, and remove dead or broken branches right away.

SOME PLUMS NEED TO BE THINNED

Heavy bearing of Japanese varieties results in much small fruit and, possibly, damage to the tree. Thin fruit drastically as soon as it is big enough to be seen, spacing the plums 4–6 in. apart. Other plums do not require as much thinning as Japanese types.

Plumbaginaceae. The leadwort family consists of shrubs and perennials with clustered, funnel-shaped flowers, such as thrift (*Armeria*), *Ceratostigma*, and *Plumbago*.

PLUM and PRUNE

NAME, GROUP	ZONES	FRUIT	COMMENTS
EUROPEAN SELECTIONS			
'Damson' 🏛	US, MS, LS	Small. Purple or blue-black skin, green flesh. Very tart flavor. Late	Fruit makes fine jam and jelly. Strains of this selection are sold as 'French Damson', 'Shropshire'
'Earliblue'	US, MS	Medium. Blue skin; tender green-yellow flesh. Early	Light to moderate producer. Slow to begin bearing
'Explorer'	US, MS, LS	Large. Reddish black fruit, sweet and juicy. Midseason	Developed at the Georgia Agricultural Experiment Station
'Green Gage' (**P. domestica italica**) 🏛	US, MS, LS	Small to medium. Greenish yellow skin, amber flesh. Good flavor. Midseason	Very old selection; still a favorite for eating fresh, cooking, canning, or jam. Selected strain sold as 'Jefferson'
'Stanley' 🏛	US, MS, LS	Large. Purplish black skin, yellow flesh. Sweet and juicy. Midseason	Good canning selection. Resembles larger 'Italian Prune'. Tends to overbear; best if fruit is thinned
'Sugar'	US, MS, LS	Medium to large. Dark blue. Very sweet, highly flavored. Early midseason	Good fresh, for home drying and canning. Tends to bear heavily in alternate years
JAPANESE SELECTIONS			
'AU-Amber'	US, MS, LS, CS	Medium. Red-purple skin, yellow flesh. Very sweet. Early	Released by Auburn University, Alabama. Very disease resistant. Early bloom often results in reduced yields
'AU-Producer'	US, MS, LS, CS	Small to medium. Dark red skin, red flesh. Good quality. Midseason	Released by Auburn University, Alabama. Very disease resistant. Good yields
'AU Rosa'	US, MS, LS, CS	Small to medium. Dark red skin with yellow flesh of excellent quality. Midseason, a few days after 'Santa Rosa'	Released by Auburn University, Alabama. Very disease resistant.
'Beauty'	US, MS, LS	Medium. Bright red skin, amber flesh with scarlet streaks. Good flavor. Very early	Consistent heavy bearer. Fruit softens quickly
'Crimson'	US, MS, LS	Small. Crimson red fruit. Excellent flavor and texture. Early June to mid-July	Productive; excellent fruit set. Good for eating fresh or for jams, jellies. Disease resistant
'Elephant Heart'	US, MS, LS, CS	Very large. Dark red skin, rich red flesh, highly flavored. Midseason to late	Tart skin; some prefer to peel fruit. Long harvest season. Pollinate with 'Santa Rosa'
'Homeside'	US, MS, LS, CS	Medium to large. Orange to light red skin with orange flesh. Very good texture; excellent flavor. Mid- to late June	Tree is quite vigorous and spreading
'Howard Miracle'	US, MS, LS, CS	Medium. Yellow skin with red blush; yellow flesh with distinctive spicy, pineapple flavor; sweet and juicy. Midseason	Very vigorous. Fruit more acid than most Japanese plums, but truly distinctive in flavor
'Methley'	US, MS, LS, CS	Medium. Reddish purple skin, dark red flesh. Sweet, mild flavor. Early	Bud-hardy, with early bloom. Good pollinator for other Japanese plum selections
'Ozark Premier'	US, MS, LS, CS	Very large. Red to purple skin, juicy yellow flesh. Very good flavor. Late midseason	Vigorous, productive. Fruit good for eating fresh, canning, cooking, jelly
'Red Heart'	US, MS, LS, CS	Medium to large. Dark red fruit of good quality, but rather tough skin. Early to mid-August	One of best pollinators for other Japanese selections; not self-fertile. Vigorous, productive. Fruit holds well
'Santa Rosa'	US, MS, LS, CS	Medium to large. Purplish red skin with heavy blue bloom, flesh yellow to dark red near skin. Rich, pleasing, tart flavor. Early	Important commercial type for fresh eating. Good canned if skin is removed. Very prone to disease in Southeast; best in drier climates. 'Late Santa Rosa' follows by a month

PLUM and PRUNE

NAME, GROUP	ZONES	FRUIT	COMMENTS
JAPANESE SELECTIONS			
'Satsuma'	US, MS, LS	Small to medium. Dull deep red skin; dark red, solid, meaty flesh. Mild, sweet flavor. Small pit. Early midseason	Preferred for jams and jellies. Sometimes called blood plum because of red juice. Tends to overbear; thin fruit for best size
'Shiro'	US, MS	Medium to large. Flavorful fruit with yellow skin and flesh. Early midseason	Heavy producer. Fruit good for eating fresh or cooking
'Wade'	MS, LS, CS	Large. Dark red skin, yellow flesh streaked red; juicy, sweet. Flattish shape. Late May to mid-June	Not self-fertile. Low winter-chill requirement. Good choice for Florida, Coastal South

⛬ PLUMBAGO auriculata (P. capensis)

CAPE PLUMBAGO, LEADWORT

Plumbaginaceae

EVERGREEN TO SEMIEVERGREEN SHRUB OR VINE

⚊ ZONES CS, TS

☼ FULL SUN

⬤ MODERATE TO LITTLE WATER

Plumbago auriculata

If grown without a support, forms a sprawling, mounding bush to 6 ft. tall, 8–10 ft. wide; with support, can reach 12 ft. or more. Fresh-looking, light to medium green leaves, 1–2 in. long. Inch-wide flowers in phloxlike clusters, varying (in seedling plants) from white to clear light blue. Select plants in bloom to get color you want. Typically blooms spring–fall, but may flower throughout year in frost-free areas. 'Alba' is white flowered; 'Royal Cape' has sky blue blooms.

Needs good drainage. Young growth blackens and leaves drop in heavy frosts, but recovery is good. Prune out damaged growth after frost danger is past. Plant is slow to start, but tough. Good cover for bank, fence, hot wall; good background and filler plant. Widely used as a hedge in central Florida. Withstands light salt drift from ocean. For dwarf plumbago, see *Ceratostigma*.

PLUMBAGO larpentae. See CERATOSTIGMA plumbaginoides

PLUME CEDAR. See CRYPTOMERIA japonica 'Elegans'

PLUME HYACINTH. See MUSCARI comosum 'Monstrosum'

PLUME POPPY. See MACLEAYA

PLUMERIA

Apocynaceae

DECIDUOUS SHRUBS OR SMALL TREES

⚊ ZONE TS

☼ ◑ FULL SUN OR HIGH SHADE

⬤ MODERATE WATER

Plumeria rubra

Handsome, useful plants with an open, gaunt character; grow to 18 ft. tall, with leathery, pointed leaves clustered near tips of thick branches. Bloom during warm weather, bearing clusters of large, showy, waxy, fragrant flowers. These are the flowers used in making Hawaiian leis. All are easy to grow

from cuttings. Tender to frost; won't take cold, wet soil. Feeding late in year will result in soft growth that will be nipped by lightest frosts. In frost-prone regions, grow in containers; when cold weather is expected, move to bright window for continued bloom or to a frost-free garage or shed. In insufficient light, foliage will yellow and drop. Leafless plants can be stored over winter in a dark room, without any watering.

P. alba. WHITE FRANGIPANI. Narrow, lance-shaped, puckered leaves to 1 ft. long. Flowers 2½ in. wide, yellow with white center.

P. obtusa. SINGAPORE PLUMERIA. Leaves dark green, 6 in. long, 2 in. wide, very glossy. White, 2-in. flowers.

P. rubra. PLUMERIA, FRANGIPANI. Thick leaves 8–16 in. long. Clusters of 2–2½-in.-wide red flowers. There are varieties with pink, red, yellow, or white blossoms. Classic examples include 'Aztec Gold', 4-in. flowers, buttercup yellow shading to white at the petal edges; 'Sherman', 4½-in. flowers, white with deep yellow centers; and 'Samoan Fluff', 3½-in. flowers, with round, overlapping white petals and canary yellow centers. Recent introductions include vibrant red hybrids with strong scents and delicate rose, cream, and pink selections from Key West.

PLUM YEW. See CEPHALOTAXUS

POA

BLUEGRASS

Poaceae (Gramineae)

PERENNIAL AND ANNUAL GRASSES

⚊ ZONES VARY BY SPECIES

☼ FULL SUN (EXCEPT FOR P. TRIVIALIS)

⬤ REGULAR WATER

Poa pratensis

One is the best-known cool-season lawn grass; the other two sometimes turn up in lawns, either intentionally or as an annual weed. Leaves of all have characteristic boat-prow tip.

P. annua. ANNUAL BLUEGRASS. All zones. Cool-season weed of lawns. Bright green, soft textured. Germinates in fall; goes to seed and dies when weather warms in spring. Discourage it by maintaining thick turf of good grasses, or apply pre-emergence herbicide to lawn in fall.

P. pratensis. KENTUCKY BLUEGRASS. Zone US. Rich blue-green perennial lawn grass best adapted to Upper South and southern Midwest. High-maintenance grass, requiring regular watering and fertilizing. Susceptible to disease during warm, humid weather. Mow at 2 in. high in spring and fall, at 3 in. in summer. Use alone or in mixture with other grasses. Many selections are available as seed or sod, including the following:

'Adelphi'. Darkest green, medium texture, good disease resistance.

'Bonnieblue'. Medium dark green, medium texture, establishes quickly.

'Glade'. Dark green, fine texture, dense, tolerates shade better than most.

'Majestic'. Dark green, medium texture, establishes fast. ▶

'Parade'. Medium green, fine texture, good disease resistance.

'Touchdown'. Medium dark green, fine texture, tolerates shade well.

'Victa'. Dark green, medium texture, establishes fast.

P. trivialis. ROUGH-STALKED BLUEGRASS. Zone US. Fine-textured, bright green perennial meadow and pasture grass. Occasionally used in shady lawn mixtures for its tolerance of shade and damp soil.

Poaceae. The grass family is undoubtedly the most significant plant group in terms of usefulness to humans. All the world's important grain crops are grasses; the bamboos (giant grasses) are useful in building and crafts. Many grasses are used in lawns or as ornamental annual or perennial plants. Some botanists still use Gramineae as the family name for grasses.

PODOCARPUS

Podocarpaceae

EVERGREEN TREES OR SHRUBS

ZONES VARY BY SPECIES

FULL SUN OR PARTIAL SHADE

REGULAR TO MODERATE WATER

Podocarpus gracilior

Versatile plants grown for their good-looking foliage, interesting form; adaptable to many area climates, many garden uses. Good screen or background plants. Foliage generally resembles that of yews *(Taxus)*, to which these plants are related, though leaves of the better-known species are longer, broader, and lighter in color than those of yews. If a male plant is growing nearby, female plants bear fruit after many years, producing small fleshy fruits rather than cones. Grow well in most soils, but may develop chlorosis where soil is alkaline or heavy and damp. Some botanists divide these plants into three genera *(Afrocarpus, Nageia, Podocarpus)*; in the following listings, new names are in parentheses.

P. gracilior (Afrocarpus gracilior, P. elongatus). FERN PODOCARPUS. Tree, often grown as espaliered vine or even as hanging basket plant. Zone TS. To 20–60 ft. tall (70 ft. in its native East Africa). Among the cleanest, most pest-free trees for street, lawn, courtyard, garden; good hedge, container plant.

Method of propagation determines growth habit. Plants grown from seed are upright when young, with 2–4-in.-long, ½-in.-wide, glossy dark green leaves somewhat sparsely set on branches. With age, they produce soft grayish to bluish green, 1–2-in.-long leaves that are more closely spaced on branches. Plants grown from cuttings or grafts of a mature tree retain the small, closely set leaves, but they have very limber branches and are often reluctant to produce strong vertical growth. These more willowy plants, suitable for espalier or growing as vines along fences, are often sold as *P. elongatus;* the larger-leafed, more upright kinds are sold as *P. gracilior.* The *P. elongatus* types eventually become upright trees, though their foliage mass persists in drooping for some time.

P. macrophyllus. SOUTHERN YEW. Shrub or tree. Zones LS, CS, TS. Native to China, Japan. To 50 ft. tall, but usually much shorter, generally narrow and upright. Bright green leaves 4 in. long, ½ in. wide. Grow indoors or out, in tubs or open ground. Large shrub, screen, street or lawn tree (with staking and thinning). Limber enough to espalier. Easily pruned as clipped hedge, topiary. Very heat tolerant.

P. m. maki. SHRUBBY YEW PINE. Smaller, slower growing than species; reaches 6–8 ft. in 10 years. Dense, upright form. Leaves to 3 in. long, ¼ in. wide. One of the best container plants for outdoor or indoor use, and a choice shrub generally.

P. nagi (Nageia nagi). BROADLEAF PODOCARPUS. Tree. Zones CS, TS. Slow growth to 15–20 ft. (to 80–90 ft. in its native Japan). Branchlets drooping, sometimes to a considerable length. Leaves 1–3 in. long, ½–1½ in. wide, leathery, smooth, sharp pointed. More treelike in youth than other species. Makes decorative foliage pattern against natural wood or masonry. Plant in groves. Excellent container plant.

PODOPHYLLUM

Berberidaceae

PERENNIALS

ZONES VARY BY SPECIES

PARTIAL OR FULL SHADE

REGULAR WATER

RHIZOMES, LEAVES, STEMS, SEEDS POISONOUS IF INGESTED

Podophyllum peltatum

Odd herbaceous relatives of barberry, with thick, spreading underground rhizomes that send up stalks crowned with large, shield-shaped, deeply lobed leaves. Shoots with a single leaf are barren; those with two leaves bear a single 2-in.-wide flower (set between the leaves) followed by a juicy, 2-in.-long berry. Berries are edible but can have a powerful laxative effect. Attractive, slow-spreading deciduous ground cover plants for shady areas with rich, moist, woodsy soil.

P. hexandrum (P. emodii). Zones US, MS, LS. Native to Himalayas and China. Grows 1–1½ ft. high, with 10-in. umbrellalike leaves mottled brown. Leaves divided into three or five lobes, with each lobe further divided. White or pink flower; red berry.

P. peltatum. MAY APPLE, WILD MANDRAKE. Zones US, MS, LS, CS. Native to the East. To 1½ ft. high. Leaves 1 ft. across, divided into five to nine lobes. White flower; yellow berry. Leaves pushing up through the forest leaf litter are one of the earliest signs of spring in woodlands.

PODRANEA ricasoliana

PINK TRUMPET VINE, PANDOREA

Bignoniaceae

EVERGREEN VINE

ZONES CS (PROTECTED), TS

FULL SUN OR LIGHT SHADE

REGULAR TO MODERATE WATER

Podranea ricasoliana

Native to South Africa. Twining vine to 20 ft. Dark green leaves divided featherwise into three or four pairs of 2-in. leaflets. In spring or summer, loose clusters of flowers shaped like open trumpets appear at ends of new growth. Blooms are 2–3 in. wide, pink with red veins. Slow grower when young but speeds up as it matures. Likes heat, good drainage. Planting in sterilized, fertile soil is recommended in Florida, since plant is very subject to nematode damage there. May drop leaves in frost but can recover from roots even if top growth is frozen. Looks good draped on arbors, fences, pergolas, or scrambling up a palm trunk.

POINCIANA. See CAESALPINIA, DELONIX regia

POINSETTIA. See EUPHORBIA pulcherrima

Polemoniaceae. The phlox family consists mostly of annuals and perennials, including many wildflowers; examples are *Ipomopsis* and *Phlox*. Cup-and-saucer vine *(Cobaea scandens)* is another member.

POLEMONIUM

Polemoniaceae

PERENNIALS

ZONES US, MS, LS

PARTIAL OR FULL SHADE

REGULAR WATER

Rosettes of finely divided fernlike foliage; clusters of bell-shaped flowers, spring–summer. Combine nicely with bellflower, bleeding heart, ferns, hellebore, hosta, and lilies. Plants need good drainage. Grow from

Polemonium caeruleum

P

seed or from divisions made after bloom or in spring. Listed below are the types most commonly available in garden centers. All are good under trees.

P. caeruleum. JACOB'S LADDER. Clusters of lavender blue, pendulous, 1-in.-long flowers on leafy, 1½–2-ft.-high stems.

P. 'Firmament'. Hybrid between *P. caeruleum* and *P. reptans*. Grows to 20 in. high, with bright blue flowers.

P. foliosissimum. To 2½ ft. high, with leafy stems and lavender blue flowers enhanced by bright orange stamens. Native to western U.S.; short lived where summer heat is accompanied by high humidity.

P. reptans. Wildflower in eastern woodlands and midwestern plains. Species best known through its selection 'Blue Pearl', a profusely blooming blue-flowered dwarf with spreading growth to 9 in. high, 1½ ft. wide. Good in shaded, dampish rock garden.

⚱ POLIANTHES tuberosa

TUBEROSE

Agavaceae

TUBEROUS-ROOTED PERENNIAL

✂ ALL ZONES

☼ ◐ FULL SUN OR PARTIAL SHADE

💧 REGULAR WATER DURING GROWTH AND BLOOM

Polianthes tuberosa

Native to Mexico. Noted for powerful, heady fragrance. Glistening white, tubular flowers are loosely arranged in spikelike clusters on stems to 3 ft. tall, late summer–fall. Long, narrow, grasslike basal leaves. Double-flowered selection 'The Pearl' is most widely available; it's a good garden plant but not as long lasting a cut flower as the single type. 'Mexican Single' is a more dependable bloomer in the Lower, Coastal, and Tropical South.

To bloom year after year, tuberose requires a warm season of at least 4 months before flowering. Start indoors or plant outside after soil is warm. Set rhizomes 2 in. deep, 4–6 in. apart. If soil or water is alkaline, apply acid fertilizer when growth begins. Where winter temperatures remain above 20°F, rhizomes may stay in ground all year, but many gardeners (and all those living in cold-winter areas) dig rhizomes and store them over winter. Dig plants in fall after leaves have yellowed; cut off dead foliage. Allow rhizomes to dry for 2 weeks, then store them in a cool (40–50°F), dry place. Tuberose can be grown in pots and moved to a protected area during cold weather. Divide clumps every 4 years.

P. howardii, a Mexican native, grows in alkaline soil, has red-and-green blooms that attract hummingbirds. Hybrids between it and other species are good choices for the Southwest.

POLYANTHUS PRIMROSES. See PRIMULA polyantha

Polygonaceae. The buckwheat family consists of annuals, perennials, shrubs, trees, and vines. Flowers lack petals, but sepals are often showy. Stems are jointed. Fruit is small, dry, single seeded. Representatives include rhubarb, fleece flower (*Polygonum*), and coral vine (*Antigonon*). True buckwheat—the pancake flour kind—is *Fagopyrum,* a crop plant of no ornamental value.

POLYGONATUM

SOLOMON'S SEAL

Liliaceae

PERENNIALS

✂ ZONES US, MS, LS, CS

◐ ● WOODSY SHADE

💧 REGULAR WATER

Polygonatum biflorum

Slowly spreading underground rhizomes send up stems that grow upright for a distance, then bend outward. On either side of arching

stems are broadly oval, bright green leaves arranged in nearly horizontal planes. Where leaves join stems, pairs or clusters of small, bell-shaped greenish white blossoms hang beneath the stems on threadlike stalks in spring. Small blue-black berries sometimes follow the flowers. Leaves and stems turn bright yellow in autumn before plant dies to the ground.

Attractive for form and flowers in woodland garden; good with astilbe, ferns, hellebore, hosta, wild ginger. Need loose, woodsy soil. Don't need dividing; to get more plants, remove rhizomes from a clump's edge in early spring. Attractive in containers. For false Solomon's seal, see *Smilacina*.

P. biflorum. SOLOMON'S SEAL. Native to eastern North America. Bears 4-in. leaves on stems to 3 ft. tall. Flowers usually in pairs or threes.

P. commutatum. GIANT SOLOMON'S SEAL. Carries 7-in. leaves on stems normally reaching 4–5 ft. high, possibly 7 ft. tall. Flowers in groups of two to ten. This species is considered a vigorous form of *P. biflorum*. It is sometimes sold as *P. canaliculatum.*

P. humile. DWARF SOLOMON'S SEAL. Native to China, Japan. A dwarf species. Stems 4–6 in. tall, topped with small, dark green leaves, and, in spring, pairs of tiny white bell flowers.

P. odoratum (P. japonicum). FRAGRANT SOLOMON'S SEAL. Native to Europe, Asia. To 3½ ft. tall, with 4–6-in. leaves. Scented flowers usually borne in pairs, sometimes singly. 'Variegatum' has white-edged leaves carried on stems that are dark red until fully grown.

POLYGONUM

FLEECE FLOWER, KNOTWEED

Polygonaceae

EVERGREEN OR DECIDUOUS PERENNIALS AND VINES

✂ ZONES VARY BY SPECIES

☼ FULL SUN, EXCEPT AS NOTED

💧 REGULAR WATER, EXCEPT AS NOTED

Polygonum cuspidatum compactum

Sturdy, sun-loving plants with jointed stems and small white or pink flowers in open sprays. Some kinds tend to get out of hand and need to be controlled.

P. affine. Evergreen perennial. Zones US, MS, LS. Tufted plant 1–1½ ft. tall. Leaves mostly basal, 2–4½ in. long, finely toothed, deep green turning to bronze in winter. Rose red blooms in dense, 2–3-in. spikes, summer into fall. Informal border or ground cover. Tolerates some shade. 'Darjeeling Red' forms 3-in.-high mats with 10-in. flower spikes, deep pink aging to red; foliage turns red in fall. 'Dimity' has fatter, paler flower spikes. 'Superbum' is larger-leafed than species, has taller pale pink spikes.

P. aubertii. SILVER LACE VINE. Deciduous. Zones US, MS, LS. Fast growing: can cover 100 sq. ft. in a season. Heart-shaped, glossy, wavy-edged leaves 1½–2½ in. long. Small, creamy white flowers appear in a frothy mass from late spring until fall. Use as quick screen on fences or arbors, on hillsides, at seashore. You can prune severely (to ground) each year; bloom will be delayed until well into summer. Drought tolerant.

P. bistorta 'Superbum'. Deciduous perennial. Zones US, MS. Forms a mound to 2½ ft. high, with leaves to 8 in. long. Flowers are pink aging to deep red, in dense, 4–6-in.-long, bottlebrush spikes held well above the foliage. Blooms in early summer, with sporadic repeat bloom until frost. Leaves turn bright red in autumn. Likes rich, moist soil and light shade.

P. cuspidatum (P. japonicum). JAPANESE KNOTWEED. Deciduous perennial. Zones US, MS, LS. Tough, vigorous plant forming large clumps of red-brown, wiry, 4–8-ft. stems. Leaves nearly heart shaped, to 5 in. long. Greenish white flowers in late summer and fall. Extremely invasive, so keep it away from choice plants. Useful in untamed parts of garden. Cut to ground in late fall or winter. Often called bamboo or Mexican bamboo because of jointed stalks. Grows in full sun or partial shade. 'Crimson Beauty' bears fiery red flowers on 7–8-ft. stems in late summer through fall. Unlike the species, it is clump forming and not invasive. ▶

P. c. compactum (P. reynoutria) is a lower-growing, less rampant form than species, 10–24 in. high and spreading by creeping roots. In late summer, showy clusters of small, pale pink flowers open from red buds. Red-veined foliage turns red in fall before plant dies to the ground.

P. virginianum (Tovara virginiana). Deciduous perennial. Zones US, MS, LS. Native to the eastern U.S. Rhizome produces upright, leafy stems to 2–3 ft. high; spreads aggressively. Late to leaf out in spring. Species is green leafed; it is less often grown than forms with variegated foliage. 'Variegata' has green leaves marbled with creamy white. 'Painter's Palette' is similar, but with a V-shaped reddish mark in center of each leaf; new leaves are creamy white splashed with light green and pink. Give part shade; protect from wind.

Polypodiaceae. The polypody family contains the vast majority of ferns. They differ from other ferns only in technical details concerning spore-bearing bodies (sporangia).

POLYPODIUM

POLYPODY FERN

Polypodiaceae

FERNS

🗲 ZONES VARY BY SPECIES; OR INDOORS

◐ ● PARTIAL OR FULL SHADE

● ◑ AMPLE TO REGULAR WATER

Polypodium aureum 'Mandaianum'

Widespread and quite variable group. Types described here are tropical plants most commonly used in hanging baskets, often in the house or greenhouse. As with many ferns, reclassification has added new names, which are given below in parentheses.

P. aureum (Phlebodium aureum). GOLDEN POLYPODY FERN, HARE'S FOOT FERN. Zone TS. Native to tropical America, including Florida. Heavy, brown, creeping rhizomes. Coarse, 3–5-ft.-long, blue-green fronds drop if hit by frost, but plants recover fast. 'Mandaianum', sometimes called crisped blue fern or lettuce fern, has frilled and wavy frond edges. Both it and the species are showy.

🗇 **P. polypodioides.** RESURRECTION FERN. All zones. Native from Delaware to southern Illinois, south to Florida, Texas, and Central and South America. Slender creeping rhizomes. Deeply cut, leathery fronds, to 7 in. long, 2 in. wide, with scaly undersides. Tolerates dryness; tips curl, but extend again when it rains or humidity rises, hence its common name.

P. subauriculatum 'Knightiae' (Goniophlebium subauriculatum 'Knightiae'). LACY PINE FERN, KNIGHT'S POLYPODY. Zone TS. Native to tropical Asia. Gracefully drooping fronds to 3 ft. or longer, with fringed edges. Spectacular when well grown. Outdoor plants shed old fronds in spring, then quickly produce new ones.

POLYSCIAS

Araliaceae

EVERGREEN SHRUBS

🗲 ZONE TS; OR INDOORS

◐ ◑ FULL SUN OR PARTIAL SHADE

◖ ● REGULAR TO MODERATE WATER

Polyscias fruticosa 'Elegans'

Like many other aralia relatives, they are grown for their handsomely divided leaves; flowers are unimportant and seldom produced outside the tropics. Plants appreciate warmth, humidity. Outdoors, they need adequate water and protection from frost and mites. Often grown as hedges in south Florida. As house plants, they are considered fussy: They need fresh, fairly still air (they cannot tolerate drafts), good light but no direct sun, and enough water but not too much. Overwatering and mite damage are the two main causes of failure. Misting is useful, along with light feeding. If plants are doing well, don't move them. They will grow slowly, maintaining their shapeliness for years.

P. balfouriana (P. scutellaria 'Balfourii'). To 25 ft. tall. Species has green foliage. More commonly sold 'Marginata' bears white-edged leaflets. 'Pennockii' has white to pale green leaflets with irregular green spots.

P. fruticosa. MING ARALIA, PARSLEY PANAX. Grows 6–8 ft. tall. Leaves finely divided and redivided into multitude of narrow, toothed segments. 'Elegans' is a small, extremely dense foliaged selection.

P. guilfoylei 'Victoriae'. Grows to 15 ft. tall. Has white-edged leaflets that are deeply slashed and cut.

POLYSTICHUM

Polypodiaceae

FERNS

🗲 ZONES VARY BY SPECIES

◐ ● PARTIAL OR FULL SHADE

● REGULAR WATER, EXCEPT AS NOTED

Polystichum acrostichoides

Hardy symmetrical plants with medium-size, evergreen (except on *P. braunii*) fronds. Among most useful and widely planted ferns, they combine well with other plants and are easy to grow. Do best in rich, organic, well-drained soil. Use in shady beds, along house walls, in mixed woodland plantings.

P. acrostichoides. CHRISTMAS FERN. Zones US, MS, LS, CS. Native to eastern North America. Grows to 1–1½ ft., with dark green leaves that make a fine contrast to snow or to the brown of dead leaves at Christmas time. Stiff fronds upright until pushed over by heavy snow or hard frost.

P. aculeatum. PRICKLY SHIELD FERN, HARD SHIELD FERN. Zones US, MS, LS. Native to Europe. Grows 2–4 ft. tall. Glossy, firm, fairly upright, once- or twice-cut fronds; final segments are tipped by soft prickles. Pale young fronds make an attractive show against the dark green mature ones.

P. braunii. BRAUN'S HOLLY FERN. Zones US, MS. Semievergreen to deciduous. Native to northern latitudes. Grows 1–3 ft. tall, with twice-divided fronds. Silvery green new growth.

P. munitum. SWORD FERN. Zone US. Native to western North America. Leathery, shiny dark green fronds are 2–4 ft. long. Plant has erect form, spreading habit. Old plants may have 75 to 100 fronds. Once established, plants need little water.

P. polyblepharum. TASSEL FERN, JAPANESE LACE FERN. Zones US, MS, LS. Native to Asia. Handsome, dense, lacy. Resembles *P. setiferum* but is taller, darker green, and somewhat coarser; fronds are a little more upright (to 2 ft. high). Usually sold as *P. setosum*.

P. setiferum. SOFT SHIELD FERN. Zones US, MS, LS. Native to Europe. Finely cut fronds give effect of dark green lace, spread out in flattened vase shape. Many forms, 2–4½ ft. tall. 'Proliferum' makes plantlets on midribs of older fronds; these can be used for propagation. Other fancy selections are sometimes sold under the name "English fern."

P. setosum. See P. polyblepharum

POMEGRANATE. See PUNICA granatum

POND CYPRESS. See TAXODIUM ascendens

Pontederiaceae. The pickerel weed family contains aquatic or marsh plants with showy, often blue flowers, such as *Pontederia*.

PONTEDERIA cordata

PICKEREL WEED

Pontederiaceae

AQUATIC PLANT

✔ ALL ZONES

☼ ◐ FULL SUN OR LIGHT SHADE

💧 LOCATE IN PONDS, WATER GARDENS

Pontederia cordata

Grown as companion to water lilies; best planted in pots of rich soil placed in 1 ft. of water. Long-stalked leaves stand well above surface of water; these are heart shaped, to 10 in. long and 6 in. wide. Short spikes of bright blue or white flowers top 4-ft. (or shorter) stems. Gives wild-pond look to informal garden pool. Plant roots underwater in shallow shelf (6–12 in. under water surface) at edge of pond. Foliage will emerge above water. Dormant in winter.

PONYTAIL. See BEAUCARNEA recurvata

POPCORN. See CORN

POPLAR. See POPULUS

POPPY. See PAPAVER

POPPY MALLOW. See CALLIRHOE

POPULUS

POPLAR, COTTONWOOD, ASPEN

Salicaceae

DECIDUOUS TREES

✔ ZONES VARY BY SPECIES

☼ FULL SUN

💧💧 REGULAR TO LITTLE WATER

Populus alba

Fast-growing, tough trees, best suited to rural areas and fringes of large properties. They are almost signature trees in semiarid plains regions and westward into desert and intermountain territory. If they are planted in smaller gardens, their network of aggressive surface roots crowds out other plants, heaves pavement, and clogs sewer and drainage lines. Most poplars will sucker profusely if their roots are cut or disturbed. These trees are also subject to many pest and disease problems. Nonetheless, some poplars are quite beautiful or distinctive enough to be widely sold despite their liabilities; several have good fall color. Leaves of most poplars are roughly triangular, sometimes toothed or lobed. Pendulous catkins appear before spring leaf-out; those on male trees are denser textured. Female trees later bear masses of cottony seeds that blow about and become a nuisance; for that reason, male (seedless) selections are offered in garden centers.

STAY OUT OF ROOT TROUBLE

Do not plant any kind of *Populus* near pavement, sewer lines, septic tanks, or their leach lines. Also keep them out of lawns and small gardens. Their roots are invasive, and they form suckers.

P. alba. WHITE POPLAR. Zones US, MS, LS. Native to Europe, Asia. Broad, wide-spreading tree to 40–60 ft. tall. Leaves are dark green above, white and woolly beneath, 2–5 in. long, usually with three to five lobes. A "lively" tree even in light breezes, with flickering white-and-green highlights. Poor fall color. Tolerates a wide range of soils. Suckers profusely.

A seedless selection, 'Pyramidalis', the Bolleana poplar (often sold as *P. bolleana*), forms a narrow column and has a birchlike white trunk.

P. balsamifera (P. candicans). BALM-OF-GILEAD. Zone US. Native to northern climates. To 30–60 ft., broad topped. Leaves 4½–6 in. long. Two male selections, 'Idahoensis' ('Idaho Hybrid') and 'Mojave Hybrid' (nearly white bark), are large, fast-growing trees.

P. deltoides. EASTERN COTTONWOOD. Zones US, MS, LS, CS. Native from Quebec to Florida and Texas. Very fast growing in moist soils, quickly reaching 30 ft., eventually 75–100 ft. Provides fast shade and tolerates wet sites, drought, salt spray, acid and alkaline soils, and winter cold, but not good in gardens because it's huge, short lived, and breaks up in storms.

P. fremontii. WESTERN COTTONWOOD, FREMONT COTTONWOOD. Zones US, MS, LS. The cottonwood of desert waterholes and watercourses. To 40–60 ft. or taller, with 2–4-in.-wide, thick, coarsely toothed, glossy yellow-green leaves that turn bright lemon yellow in fall. Does well in West Texas. 'Nevada' is a male selection.

P. nigra 'Italica'. LOMBARDY POPLAR. Zones US, MS, LS. Male selection of European native. Beautiful columnar tree to 40–100 ft., with upward-reaching branches. Bright green, 4-in. leaves turn beautiful golden yellow in fall. Few problems in cold-winter, dry climates. In other regions, however, tree is subject to a canker disease that will soon kill it; in these areas, best as a quick, temporary screen. Upright English oak (*Quercus robur* 'Fastigiata'), a columnar, more permanent tree, is a good substitute.

P. tremula. EUROPEAN ASPEN. Zone US. Similar to *P. tremuloides* but has somewhat darker bark and leaves that are more coarsely toothed. Seedless 'Erecta', sometimes called Swedish columnar aspen, is narrow like Lombardy poplar, but it has red fall color and is less prone to canker.

P. tremuloides. QUAKING ASPEN. Zones US, MS. Widely distributed in North America; native to northern latitudes and mountains. Tolerates poor soil; generally performs poorly or grows slowly at low elevations. To 40–50 ft. tall, 20–30 ft. wide; often grows with several trunks or in a clump. Smooth, pale gray-green to whitish bark. Dainty, round light green leaves flutter and quake with the slightest movement of air. Brilliant golden yellow fall foliage. Apt to suffer from sudden dieback or borers.

P. wislizenii. TEXAS COTTONWOOD. Zones US, MS, LS. Native from Colorado to northern Mexico. Like *P. fremontii*, a good choice for arid West Texas.

PORCELAIN BERRY. See AMPELOPSIS brevipedunculata

PORCUPINE GRASS. See MISCANTHUS sinensis 'Strictus'

PORTUGAL LAUREL. See PRUNUS lusitanica

PORTULACA

MOSS ROSE, PORTULACA

Portulacaceae

ANNUALS

✔ ALL ZONES

☼ ◐ FULL SUN OR VERY LIGHT SHADE

💧💧 REGULAR TO LITTLE WATER

Portulaca grandiflora

Low-growing plants with fleshy leaves and stems. Brilliant flowers usually open fully only in bright light and close by midafternoon in hot weather. Plants bloom from late spring until frost, though quality may decline in late summer. Thrive in high temperatures, intense sunlight. Drought tolerant; ideal for sunbaked places. Not fussy about soil; don't require deadheading. Good in rock gardens, dry banks, edgings, hanging baskets.

P. grandiflora. MOSS ROSE, PORTULACA. To 6 in. high, 1½ ft. across. Leaves cylindrical, pointed, 1 in. long. Trailing, branched reddish stems. Lustrous, roselike, 1-in.-wide flowers in red, cerise, rose pink, orange, yellow, white, pastel shades. Single colors or mixes available, in single- or double-flowered strains. Prize Strain, Magic Carpet, Sunglo, Sunkiss are popular. Afternoon Delight and Sundance strains stay open longer in afternoon. Plants self-sow, though hybrid types don't come true from seed. ▶

P. oleracea. PURSLANE. Unimproved form is a weed with tiny yellow flowers and edible stems and leaves. Warm weather and moisture encourage its growth. Control by hoeing or pulling before it goes to seed; don't let pulled plants lie about, since they can reroot or ripen seed.

A strain called Wildfire (sometimes offered as *P. oleracea* and sometimes as *P. grandiflora*, but actually a strain of *P. umbraticola*) is popular in the Lower South and Texas. Plants have the broad, plump leaves of *P. oleracea*, but the 1–1½-in. single flowers come in white, bright shades of red, pink, magenta, lavender, yellow, orange, and peach, and bicolors. Each flower lasts only a day, but new flowers keep coming. Plants are a few inches tall and spread to 2 ft. Good temporary ground cover.

PURSLANE FOR DINNER?

The French call it *pourpier*, the Mexicans call it *verdolaga*, and both cultures use it in cooking. You can use purslane in salad, soup, pork stew, tomato sauce, and scrambled eggs.

Portulacaceae. The portulaca family contains annuals, perennials, and a few shrubs, usually with succulent foliage and frequently with showy flowers. An example is moss rose, *Portulaca*.

POSSUMHAW. See ILEX decidua

POTATO

Solanaceae

TUBEROUS-ROOTED PERENNIAL TREATED AS ANNUAL

✿ ALL ZONES

☼ FULL SUN

🌢 EVENLY MOIST SOIL

☠ GREEN SKIN AND RAW SHOOTS ARE TOXIC

For ornamental relatives, see *Solanum*. Although not the most widely grown home garden vegetables, potatoes can be very satisfying: 2 lb. of seed potatoes can yield 50 lb. of potatoes

Potato

for eating. The many pests and diseases that beleaguer commercial growers are not likely to plague home gardeners. One of the most damaging insect pests is Colorado potato beetle, found mainly in eastern U.S. To avoid disease problems, the best tactic is to start with certified disease-free starter potatoes or disease-resistant selections.

Can be grown from minitubers (these are planted whole) or from seed potatoes that you cut into 1½-in.-sq. pieces, each with at least two eyes. Since minitubers are uncut, they are less likely to rot in the ground. Home gardeners have access to an increasing number of potato types, including those with red, yellow, or bluish purple skins, sorts with yellow flesh, and even all-blue kinds. Shapes vary from round to fingerlike. Some types mature faster than others, but most take about 3 months. Heat-tolerant selections perform better in the South. They include 'Anoka', 'Caribe', 'Irish Cobbler', 'Kennebec', 'Red La Soda', 'Red Pontiac', and 'Yukon Gold'.

Potatoes need sandy, fast-draining, fertile soil; tubers become deformed in heavy, poorly drained soil. Most types dislike the South's summer heat, preferring instead temperatures that are cool to moderate. In the Upper, Middle, and Lower South, plant in early spring, as soon as soil can be worked. Elsewhere, plant in fall or winter. Set minitubers or seed potato pieces 2 in. deep, 1–1½ ft. apart. Add loose soil as plant grows, taking care not to cover stems completely. The aboveground potato plant is sprawling and bushy, with much-divided dark green leaves somewhat like those of a tomato plant. Clustered inch-wide flowers are pale blue. Round yellow or greenish fruit is rarely seen.

Dig early potatoes (so-called new potatoes) when tops begin to flower; dig mature potatoes when tops die down. Dig carefully to avoid bruising or cutting tubers. Well-matured potatoes free of defects are the best keepers. Store in cool (40°F), dark place. Where ground doesn't freeze, late potatoes can remain in ground until needed. Dig before mild temperatures start them into growth again.

Another method of growing potatoes is to prepare soil so surface is loose, plant ½–2 in. deep, water well, and cover with a 1–1½-ft. layer of straw, hay, or dead leaves; surround with fence of chicken wire to keep loose material from blowing away. Potatoes will form on surface of soil or just beneath, requiring little digging. You can probe with your fingers and harvest potatoes as needed.

POTATO VINE. See SOLANUM jasminoides

POTENTILLA

CINQUEFOIL

Rosaceae

EVERGREEN PERENNIALS AND DECIDUOUS SHRUBS

✿ ZONES VARY BY SPECIES

◐ SOME SHADE

🌢 MODERATE WATER

Potentilla fruticosa

Hardy plants useful for ground covers and borders. Leaves are bright green or gray green, divided into small leaflets. Small, roselike, typically single flowers are cream to bright yellow; white; or pink to red. Plants generally prefer cool nights and cool soils.

EVERGREEN PERENNIALS

These include creeping plants used as ground covers and sturdy clumping plants for use in rock gardens or perennial borders. Leaves are divided fanwise into leaflets and are reminiscent of strawberry foliage.

P. alba. WHITE CINQUEFOIL. Zone US. To 4 in. high and spreading, with 2½-in. bright green leaves with five leaflets. White, 1-in.-wide flowers in early spring; occasionally reblooms.

P. atrosanguinea. RUBY CINQUEFOIL. Zones US, MS, LS. Sprawling, mounding plant to 1½ ft. high, 2 ft. wide, with furry, three-leafleted leaves and 1-in. red blossoms in summer. A parent of superior hybrids, including 1½-ft. 'Gibson's Scarlet'; 1-ft. 'Vulcan', deep red flowers; and 15-in. 'William Rollisson', semidouble bright orange blooms with yellow center.

P. nepalensis. NEPAL CINQUEFOIL. Zones US, MS. To 1–2 ft. high. Leaves divided into five roundish leaflets; branching clusters of 1-in. purplish red blossoms in summer. Selections are superior to the species for borders, cut flowers. 'Willmottiae' ('Miss Willmott'), 10–12 in. high, has salmon pink flowers. 'Melton Fire', 12–15 in. high, bears bright red flowers with yellow blending to a deep red center.

P. recta 'Warrenii'. WARREN'S SULFUR CINQUEFOIL. Zones US, MS, LS. To 15 in. tall, with leaves divided into five to seven leaflets. Profuse show of bright yellow, 1-in. flowers in late spring. Longer blooming and less weedy than the species. Tolerates a wide range of soils. Sometimes sold as *P. warrenii*. 'Macrantha' (which may be listed as *P. warrenii* 'Macrantha') is the same or a very similar plant.

P. tonguei. STAGHORN CINQUEFOIL. Zones US, MS. Hybrid between *P. nepalensis* and another species. Creeping plant with 1-ft.-long stems, leaves with three to five leaflets, and ½-in., red-centered apricot flowers.

P. tridentata 'Minima'. MINIMA WINELEAF CINQUEFOIL. Zones US, MS. Creeping ground cover with shiny, 1-in. leaves divided into three leaflets. Foliage turns red in fall. Small white flowers in spring and summer resemble those of strawberry.

P. verna 'Nana'. DWARF SPRING CINQUEFOIL. Zones US, MS, LS. Botanists keep running with the name of this plant and nurseries never seem to catch up. Also known as *P. crantzii* and *P. tabernaemontanii*. The first may be *P. villosa*; the second is now called *P. neumanniana*, which is likely the correct name for this dainty-looking yet tough and persistent creeper. Grows 2–6 in. high. Bright green leaves divided into five leaflets; butter yellow, ¼-in. flowers in spring and summer. Stands more water than most cinquefoils, but also takes heat and drought. May turn brown in cold winters. Fast-growing ground cover, bulb cover. Good lawn substitute for no-traffic areas. Subject to a disfiguring rust in some areas.

P. warrenii. See P. recta 'Warrenii'

DECIDUOUS SHRUBS

The shrubby potentillas, most often sold as named forms of bush cinquefoil *P. fruticosa*, are native to northern latitudes everywhere. They perform well in Zones US, MS. All have leaves divided into three to seven leaflets; some are distinctly green on top, gray beneath, while others look more gray green all over. All bloom cheerfully from late spring to early fall.

Fairly trouble-free. Best in well-drained soil with moderate water, but tolerate poor soils, limestone, drought, heat. Selections with red or orange tinting should be lightly shaded, since they tend to fade quickly in hot sun. After bloom period ends, cut out older stems from time to time to make room for new growth. Some selections found in garden centers:

'Abbotswood'. To 3 ft., with dark blue-green leaves, 2-in. white flowers.

'Goldfinger'. Dense, dark green, grows to 3 ft. tall, with golden yellow, 1½-in. blooms.

'Goldstar'. Low mound to 2 ft., with 2-in. bright yellow flowers.

'Jackman's Variety'. To 4 ft. tall and somewhat wider, with 1½-in. bright yellow blossoms.

'Katherine Dykes'. Can reach 5 ft. but usually stays much lower; spreads at least as wide as high. Pale yellow, 1-in. flowers.

'Klondike'. Dense grower to 2 ft. high, 1½–2-in. yellow blooms.

'Mount Everest'. Bushy, upright to 4½ ft.; 1½-in. pure white blossoms.

'Pixie Gold'. To 1–1½ ft. high, with ¾-in. yellow flowers.

'Primrose Beauty'. Silvery gray-green foliage on a 2–3-ft. plant. Pale yellow, 1½-in. flowers.

'Red Ace'. To 2 ft. high, 3–4 ft. wide. Flowers are 1½ in. wide, bright red with yellow center and yellow reverse. Blooms fade to yellow as they age (fading is rapid in hot summer weather or poor growing conditions).

'Sunset'. To 2–2½ ft., with bright green foliage, 1½-in. yellow flowers shaded orange.

'Sutter's Gold'. To 1 ft. high, spreading to 3 ft. Clear yellow flowers about 1 in. across.

'Tangerine'. To 2½ ft. high, with 1½-in. bright yellow-orange blooms.

POTERIUM. See SANGUISORBA

POTHOS aureus. See EPIPREMNUM aureum

POT MARIGOLD. See CALENDULA officinalis

POT MARJORAM. See ORIGANUM onites

PRAIRIE CONEFLOWER. See RATIBIDA pinnata

PRAIRIE LARKSPUR. See DELPHINIUM virescens

PRAYER PLANT. See MARANTA leuconeura

PREGNANT ONION. See ORNITHOGALUM caudatum

PRICKLY PEAR CACTUS. See OPUNTIA

PRICKLY SHIELD FERN. See POLYSTICHUM aculeatum

PRIMULA

PRIMROSE

Primulaceae

PERENNIALS USUALLY TREATED AS ANNUALS

✿ ZONES VARY BY SPECIES OR TYPE

◐ LIGHT SHADE

◐ ◑ WATER NEEDS VARY BY TYPE

Primula polyantha

Primroses form a foliage rosette, above which rise circular, five-petaled flowers, each petal indented at the apex. Blossoms may be borne on individual stems, in clusters at stem ends, or in tiered clusters like candelabra up the stem. Most are spring blooming, but some start flowering in late winter, and a few bloom in early summer.

Specialists have organized the hundreds of species, selections, named hybrids, and hybrid strains into 34 sections, but primroses that are fairly easy to grow in home gardens are few. Primroses thrive with a combination of moist, rich soil and cool, humid air. Few areas in the South supply these conditions. Most kinds that winter over do so only in the Upper South; a few tolerate warmer climates. *P. auricula, P. japonica,* and *P. veris* can be grown as perennials, but most should be treated as annuals.

Specialty nurseries offer seeds and plants of many kinds of primroses. Fanciers exchange seeds and plants through primrose societies.

P. acaulis. See P. vulgaris

P. auricula. AURICULA. Zones US, MS. Evergreen rosettes of broad, leathery, gray-green leaves. Clusters of fragrant flowers on 6–8-in. stems in white, cream, orange, pink, rose, red, purple, blue, or brownish, with a yellow or white eye, early spring. Usually grown in pots. Regular water.

P. elatior. OXLIP. Zones US, MS. Leaves to 8 in. long, with hairy undersides. Sulfur yellow blooms in many-flowered clusters on 8–12-in. stems in spring. Regular water.

P. japonica. JAPANESE PRIMROSE. Zone US. Stout 2½-ft. stems bear whorls of up to five yellow-eyed purple flowers. Leaves 6–9 in. long, 3 in. wide. 'Miller's Crimson' is choice red selection. White and pink forms are available. Bloom late spring–early summer. Ample water. Can grow in shallow water.

P. malacoides. FAIRY PRIMROSE, BABY PRIMROSE. Annual or potted plant. Evergreen rosettes of soft, pale green, long-stalked leaves, oval with lobed and cut edges, 1½–3 in. long. White, pink, rose, red, and lavender blooms in lacy whorls along upright, 8–15-in. stems. Regular water. Available from greenhouses late winter–early spring.

P. obconica. Annual, seasonal plant, or house plant. White, pink, salmon, lavender, reddish purple flowers, 1½–2 in. wide, in broad clusters on 1-ft. stems. Evergreen, roundish, hairy leaves, long stems. Hairs on stems (except those of Freedom strain) may irritate skin. Regular water. Available from greenhouses late winter–early spring.

P. polyantha. POLYANTHUS PRIMROSES. Zone US; treat as annual elsewhere. Often called English primroses. Clumps of 8-in.-long green leaves resemble romaine lettuce. Brilliant flowers in many colors, 1–2 in. across, in large, full clusters on 1-ft.-tall stems. Bloom winter–early or midspring. Miniature Polyanthus have smaller flowers on shorter stalks. Fine large-flowered strains include Barnhaven, Clarke's, Concorde, Pacific, Santa Barbara. Novelties include Gold Laced, with gold-edged mahogany petals. All good for massing, bulb companions, or pots. Regular water.

Primula malacoides

P. veris. COWSLIP. Zones US, MS. Leaves to 8 in. long, slightly hairy undersides. Fragrant, bright yellow blossoms, sometimes red or apricot, in large clusters on 8–12 in. stems. Blooms in spring. Regular water.

P. vulgaris (P. acaulis). ENGLISH PRIMROSE, PRIMROSE. Zones US, MS. Leaves tufted; much like those of polyanthus primroses. Flowers in white, yellow, red, blue, and bronze, brown, and wine borne singly on stalk; some garden strains have two or three on a stalk. Double type available. Nosegay and Biedermeier strains are very heavy blooming. All bloom in spring. Use as edging, in woodland garden. Regular water.

Primulaceae. The primrose family of annuals and perennials has single or variously clustered flowers with five-lobed calyxes and corollas. Examples are *Cyclamen* and primrose (*Primula*).

PRINCE'S FEATHER. See AMARANTHUS hybridus erythrostachys

PRINCESS FLOWER. See TIBOUCHINA

PRINCESS TREE. See PAULOWNIA tomentosa

PRIVET. See LIGUSTRUM

ꗂ PROSOPIS glandulosa

MESQUITE, HONEY MESQUITE

Fabaceae (Leguminosae)

DECIDUOUS TREE

🗡 ZONES MS, LS, CS, TS (DRY AREAS)

☼ FULL SUN

🌢 LITTLE TO NO WATER

Prosopis glandulosa

Native to Mexico and a common sight on dry grasslands and hills of West, Southwest, and Central Texas. Seeds believed to have entered Texas in the stomachs of cattle driven across the Rio Grande. Plant quickly spread and is now considered a nuisance by ranchers, because its greedy, wide-spreading roots compete with pasture grasses for water.

Mesquite's gnarled, sculptural trunks and wispy, light green foliage make it a picturesque lawn tree. Its light shade allows grass to grow right up to the trunk. Reaches 30 ft. tall. Nearly impossible to transplant, because of its deep taproots. Does not need watering. Will tolerate lawn irrigation if soil is sandy, but quickly declines in clay or caliche if given additional water.

Many prize mesquite for its wood, which is used in flavoring smoked and grilled meats. But its long bean pods, which change from red to mottled purple and tan as they dry, do just as good a job.

PRUNE. See PLUM and PRUNE

PRUNUS

Rosaceae

EVERGREEN OR DECIDUOUS SHRUBS OR TREES

🗡 ZONES VARY BY SPECIES

☼ FULL SUN, EXCEPT AS NOTED

🌢🌢🌢 REGULAR TO MODERATE WATER

▷ SEE CHARTS, PAGES 343 AND 344

Fruit trees that belong to *Prunus*, the "stone fruits," are described under their common names; see entries under Cherry; Peach and Nectarine; Plum and Prune.

Ornamentals are divided into two classes: evergreen and deciduous. Evergreens are used chiefly as structure plants: shade trees, street trees, hedges, screens. Deciduous flowering trees and shrubs, closely related to the fruit trees mentioned above, are valued for their mostly springtime floral display as well as for attractive form and texture of foliage. Many of these bear edible fruit.

Prunus cerasifera

EVERGREEN FORMS

The following evergreen species are all large shrubs or small trees.

P. caroliniana. CAROLINA CHERRY LAUREL. Zones US, MS, LS, CS. Native from North Carolina to Texas. As an upright shrub, it can be well branched from the base and used as clipped hedge or tall screen to 20 ft. high. Can be sheared into formal shapes. Trained as a tree, it is a broad-topped plant reaching 35–40 ft.; attractive with multiple trunks. Densely foliaged; leaves are glossy green, smooth edged, 2–4 in. long. Small, creamy white flowers in 1-in. spikes appear in late winter or spring, followed by black fruit to ½ in. wide. Flower and fruit litter can be a problem in paved areas. Very tolerant of heat, wind, drought. 'Bright 'n Tight' and 'Compacta' are denser than the species and reach only about 10 ft.

P. laurocerasus. CHERRY LAUREL. Zones US, MS, LS. Hardy to 5°F; selections listed below are hardier. Native from southeastern Europe to

Iran. To 20 ft. tall, though generally seen as a lower clipped hedge. Leathery, glossy dark green leaves are 3–7 in. long, 1½–2 in. wide. Blooms in summer, bearing 3–5-in. spikes of creamy white flowers that are often hidden by leaves. Small black fruit appears in late summer and fall.

Where adapted, a fast-growing, greedy plant that's difficult to garden under or around. However, compact selections (see list that follows) are good garden plants. Regular water and nutrients will speed growth and keep top dense. Needs reasonably good drainage. Give partial shade in hot-summer areas. Tolerates salt spray. Stands heavy shearing but with considerable mutilation of leaves; best pruned by one cut at a time, using hand pruners, to remove overlong twigs just above a leaf.

'Otto Luyken'. Zones US, MS, LS. To 4 ft. tall, twice as broad. Leaves 2–4 in. long. Deep green, glossy foliage.

'Schipkaensis'. SCHIPKA LAUREL. Zones US, MS, LS. Usually 4–5 ft. high (possibly 10 ft. tall), wide spreading. Narrow leaves 2–4½ in. long.

'Zabeliana'. ZABEL LAUREL. Zones US, MS, LS. Narrow-leafed selection with branches angling upward and outward from plant base. Eventually reaches 6 ft., with equal or greater spread. More tolerant of full sun than species. Versatile plant; good for low screen, big foundation plant, bank cover (with branches pegged down), espalier.

Prunus laurocerasus
'Zabeliana'

P. lusitanica. PORTUGAL LAUREL. Zones MS, LS, CS. Native to Spain, Portugal. Densely branched shrub 10–20 ft. high; or multitrunked spreading tree to 30 ft. or more. Trained to a single trunk, it is used as formal street tree. Glossy dark green leaves to 5 in. by 2 in. Small, creamy white flowers in 5–10-in. spikes in spring and early summer, followed by clusters of tiny, bright red to dark purple fruit. Slower growing than *P. laurocerasus,* more tolerant of heat, sun, and wind. Drought tolerant.

DECIDUOUS FLOWERING FRUIT TREES

Flowering cherry. Zones vary by type; see chart. Cultural needs of all are identical. They require full sun and fast-draining, well-aerated soil; if your soil is substandard, plant in raised beds. Prune only to remove awkward or crossing branches; pinch back the occasional overly ambitious shoot to force branching. You can cut during bloom time and use branches in arrangements. Early to midspring bloom, depending on type.

All are good trees to garden under. Use them as their growth habit indicates: large, spreading kinds make good shade trees, while smaller ones are indispensable in oriental gardens. Foliage may sustain damage from insect pests. Plants growing in heavy soil are sometimes subject to root rot (for which there is no cure); an afflicted tree will usually bloom, then send out new leaves that suddenly collapse.

Flowering peach. Identical to fruiting peach in size, growth habit, cultural needs, and potential problems, but more widely adapted. Flowering peach can be grown in Zones US, MS, LS, CS. Place trees where they will be striking when in bloom yet fairly unobtrusive out of bloom. Bloom period is late winter–early spring.

The following selections are strictly "flowering" in that blooms are showy and fruit is either absent or inferior. In areas with late frosts, choose late bloomers; early bloomers are best in areas with hot, early springs.

'Early Double Pink'. Very early.

'Early Double Red'. Deep purplish red or rose red. Very early and brilliant, but color likely to clash with other pinks and reds.

'Early Double White'. Blooms with 'Early Double Pink'.

'Helen Borchers'. Semidouble clear pink, 2½-in.-wide flowers. Late.

'Icicle'. Double white flowers. Late.

'Late Double Red'. Later than 'Early Double Red' by 3 to 4 weeks.

'Peppermint Stick'. Double flowers striped red and white; may also bear all-white and all-red flowers on same branch. Midseason.

'Weeping Double Pink'. Smaller than other flowering peaches, with weeping branches. Requires careful staking and tying to develop main stem of suitable height. Midseason.

'Weeping Double Red'. Similar to above, but with deep rose red flowers. Midseason.

'Weeping Double White'. White version of weeping forms listed above.

PRUNUS—FLOWERING CHERRY

NAME	ZONES	GROWTH HABIT, FOLIAGE	HEIGHT, SPREAD	FLOWERS, SEASON, COMMENTS
P. campanulata TAIWAN FLOWERING CHERRY	US, MS, LS, CS	Graceful, densely branched, bushy, upright, slender small tree	To 20–25 ft.; not as wide as high	Single, bell shaped, drooping, in clusters of 2–5. Striking color—electric rose, almost neon purple pink. Blooms early. Good choice for Coastal South
P. 'Okame'	US, MS, LS, CS	Upright, oval, fast growing. Dark green, finely textured foliage. Yellow-orange to orange-red fall color	To 25 ft. tall, 20 ft. wide	Single pink. Very early bloomer. Hybrid between *P. campanulata* and another species. Blooms well even in Coastal South
P. serrulata 'Amanogawa' (Species **P. serrulata**, JAPANESE FLOWERING CHERRY)	US, MS	Columnar tree. Use as you would small Lombardy poplar	To 20–25 ft. tall, 8 ft. wide	Semidouble light pink, with deep pink margins. Early midseason
P. s. 'Kwanzan' ('Kanzan', 'Sekiyama')	US, MS, LS	Branches stiffly upright, forming inverted cone. Orange fall foliage	To 30 ft. high, 20 ft. wide	Large, double, deep rosy pink, in pendent clusters displayed before or with red young leaves. Midseason. Tolerates heat and humidity well
P. s. 'Shirofugen'	US, MS	Wide horizontal branching	To 25 ft. and as wide	Double, long stalked, pink, fading to white. Latest to bloom; flowers appear with coppery red new leaves
P. s. 'Shirotae' ('Mt. Fuji')	US, MS, LS	Strong horizontal branching	To 20 ft.; wider than high	Semidouble. Pink in bud; white when fully open, turning to purplish pink. Early
P. s. 'Shogetsu' ('Shimidsu Sakura')	US, MS, LS	Spreading growth, arching branches	To 15 ft.; wider than high	Semidouble and very double pale pink, often with white centers. Late
P. subhirtella 'Autumnalis'	US, MS, LS	Loose branching, bushy, with flattened crown, slender twigs	To 25–30 ft. and as wide	Double white or pinkish white. Often blooms during mild autumn or winter weather as well as in early spring
P. s. 'Pendula' WEEPING HIGAN CHERRY	US, MS, LS	Usually sold grafted at 5–6 ft. high on upright-growing understock. Graceful branches hang down, often to ground	To 15–25 ft. and as wide	Single small pale pink, in profusion. Early. Trees grown on own roots are rare but more graceful than those grown from grafts on straight trunk
P. yedoensis YOSHINO FLOWERING CHERRY	US, MS, LS	Horizontal branches; graceful, open pattern	Fast to 40 ft., with 30-ft. spread	Single light pink to nearly white, fragrant. Early. Famous planting exists around the Tidal Basin in Washington, D.C. Tolerates heat and humidity
P. y. 'Akebono' (sometimes called 'Daybreak')	US, MS, LS	Same as *P. yedoensis*	To 25 ft. and as wide	Flowers pinker than those of *P. yedoensis*. Early

P

FLOWERING PLUM FOR INDOOR BLOOM

Branches of flowering plum (or flowering cherry, peach, or nectarine) are beautiful for indoor decoration. For the longest-lasting bloom, cut branches when buds first begin to show color or when they have just opened. Follow proper pruning procedures when you cut branches: prune to thin or shape; always cut back to a side branch; and never leave stubs. Place branches in a deep container of water, not in florist's foam; strip off any buds or flowers that will be below water level.

Flowering plum. Zones vary by type; see chart. Flowers appear before leaves, from late winter to early spring. Less particular about soil than flowering cherries, nectarines, and peaches, but will fail if soil is waterlogged for long periods. If soil is boggy, plant in raised beds, 6–12 in. above grade. Little pruning is needed. Potential pests include aphids, borers, scale, tent caterpillars. Possible diseases include canker and leaf spot. The most ornamental flowering plums, including purple-foliaged ones, are described in chart; for more flowering plums, see listings for *P. americana, P. angustifolia, P. cistena, P. maritima,* and *P. mexicana.*

ADDITIONAL DECIDUOUS SPECIES

P. americana. WILD PLUM, GOOSE PLUM. Shrub or small tree. Zones US, MS, LS. To 15–20 ft. high, forming thickets. Profusion of clustered white, 1-in. flowers appears before the dark green leaves emerge. Fruit yellow to red, to 1 in. wide, sour but good for jelly. Tough and hardy.

P. angustifolia. CHICKASAW PLUM. Large shrub. Zones US, MS, LS, CS. Native from New Jersey to Missouri, south to Florida and Texas. Grows to 12–16 ft., forming somewhat thorny, shiny, dark green thicket; spreads by root suckers. Cloud of white blossom in early spring; ¾-in. red or yellow fruits prized by wildlife. Likes sandy soils; takes sun or partial shade.

P. besseyi. WESTERN SAND CHERRY. Shrub. Zone US. Native from Manitoba to Wyoming, south to Kansas and Colorado. To 3–6 ft. tall. Good show of white flowers in spring, followed by sweet black cherries used for pies, jams, jellies. Withstands heat, cold, wind, drought.

P. cistena. PURPLE-LEAF SAND CHERRY, DWARF RED-LEAF PLUM. Shrub. Zones US, MS, LS. Dainty, multibranched hybrid to 6–10 ft. high. Can be trained as single-stemmed tree; good for small patios. Bears white to light pink flowers as leaves emerge, then covers itself in red-purple foliage. May offer a summer crop of small blackish purple fruit.

P. fruticosa. Similar to *P. besseyi,* but 2–3 ft. tall, with smaller red-purple fruit. ▶

PRUNUS—FLOWERING PLUM

NAME	ZONES	GROWTH HABIT	FOLIAGE, FLOWERS, FRUIT
P. blireiana (hybrid between **P. cerasifera** 'Atropurpurea' and **P. mume**)	US, MS, LS	Graceful, to 25 ft. high, 20 ft. wide. Long, slender branches	Leaves reddish purple, turning greenish bronze in summer. Flowers double, fragrant, pink to rose. Very little or no fruit
P. cerasifera MYROBALAN PLUM, CHERRY PLUM	US, MS, LS	Used as rootstock for various stone fruits. Grows to 30 ft. Species not widely grown; its purple- and red-leafed selections are more popular	Leaves dark green. Flowers pure white. Small red plums, 1–1¼ in. across, are sweet but bland. Self-sows freely; some seedlings bear yellow fruit
P. c. 'Allred'	US, MS, LS	Upright, slightly spreading, 20 ft. tall, 12–15 ft. wide	Red leaves, white flowers. Red, 1¼-in.-wide, tart fruit is good for preserves, jelly
P. c. 'Atropurpurea' (**P. 'Pissardii'**) PURPLE-LEAF PLUM	US, MS, LS	Fast growing to 25–30 ft. high, rounded in form	New leaves copper red, deepening to dark purple, gradually becoming greenish bronze in late summer. White flowers. Sets heavy crop of small red plums
P. c. 'Krauter Vesuvius'	US, MS, LS	To 18 ft. high, 12 ft. wide; upright, branching	Darkest foliage of all flowering plums. Light pink flowers, purple-black leaves. Little or no fruit
P. c. 'Mt. St. Helens'	US, MS, LS	Upright, spreading, with rounded crown. Fast growth to 20 ft. high and wide	A sport of 'Newport', it grows faster and leafs out earlier; it has richer leaf color and holds it later in summer
P. c. 'Newport'	US, MS, LS	To 25 ft. high, 20 ft. wide	Purplish red leaves. Single pink flowers. Will bear a little fruit
P. c. 'Thundercloud'	US, MS, LS	Rounded form to 20 ft. high and as wide	Dark coppery leaves. Flowers light pink to white. Sometimes sets good crop of red fruit. Most popular purple-leafed plum

P. glandulosa. DWARF FLOWERING ALMOND. Shrub. Zones US, MS, LS. Native to China, Japan. In early spring, before leaves appear, the many slender stems are transformed into wands of blossoms. Typically sold are the double-flowered selections 'Alboplena' (white) and 'Sinensis' (pink), both with 1–1¼-in. blooms like fluffy pompom chrysanthemums. Rare, single-flowering type known in some areas as Easter cherry is the only one that fruits. Plants grow 4–6 ft. high, with clumps of upright, spreading branches and light green, 4-in., willowlike leaves. Prune heavily during or after flowering to promote new growth for next year's bloom. Can be flowering hedge. Suckers freely. Fireblight can be a problem.

P. maackii. AMUR CHOKECHERRY. Tree. Zone US. Native to Manchuria and Siberia; extremely hardy to cold and wind. To 25–30 ft. tall. Main feature is handsome trunk bark, which is yellowish and peeling, like birch bark. Leaves strongly veined, rather narrow and pointed, to 4 in. long. Small white flowers in narrow clusters 2–3 in. long. Fruit is black, ¼ in.

P. maritima. BEACH PLUM. Zones US, MS. Native to Atlantic coast from Maine to Virginia. Suckering shrub to 6 ft. tall or taller, forming colonies. Dull green leaves are 1½–3 in. long, half as wide. White flowers are followed by ½–2-in., dark red to dark purple fruits that are cherished for preserves. Tolerates strong winds, salt spray.

P. mexicana. MEXICAN PLUM. Small tree. Zones US, MS, LS, CS. Native from Kentucky to Texas and northeast Mexico. Beautiful native plum, with delicate, spreading form, usually single-trunked, 15–25 ft. tall, occasionally 35 ft. Not a suckering species. Very fragrant, white, fading to pink, flowers in early spring. Purplish red fruit in late summer. Good for making jelly and preserves. Tolerant of drought (grows fast with regular water) and many soils, including limestone and sand, but not poorly drained, wet soils. Handsome peeling bark. Full sun or partial shade.

P. mume. JAPANESE FLOWERING APRICOT. Tree. Zones US, MS, LS, CS. Not a true apricot. Longer-lived, tougher, more trouble-free plant than many other flowering fruit trees. Eventually develops into gnarled, picturesque 20-ft. tree. Leaves to 4½ in. long, broadly oval. Winter blossoms are small and profuse, with clean, spicy fragrance. Sudden freezes following warm spells in the Lower and Coastal South will kill just-opened blossoms. Fruit is small, inedible. Selections include:

'Bonita'. Semidouble rose red.

'Dawn'. Large ruffled double pink.

'Peggy Clarke'. Double deep rose flowers with extremely long stamens and red calyxes. Most widely planted selection.

'Rosemary Clarke'. Double white flowers with red calyxes. Very early.

'W. B. Clarke'. Double pink flowers on weeping plant. Effective large bonsai or container plant, focus of attention in winter garden.

P. padus. EUROPEAN BIRD CHERRY, MAYDAY TREE, MAYBUSH. Tree. Zone US. Very cold-hardy. Moderate growth to 15–20 ft., occasionally taller. Rather thin and open in habit while young. Dull dark green, oval leaves, 3–5 in. long, are among the first to unfold in spring. Big midspring show of small white flowers in slender, drooping, 3–6-in. clusters that nearly hide foliage. Small black fruit, bitter but loved by birds, follows.

P. serotina. BLACK CHERRY, WILD CHERRY. Large tree. Zones US, MS, LS, CS. Native from Canada to Florida and Texas. Fast growing, eventually to 80 ft., sometimes 100 ft. Fragrant, white spring flowers in drooping clusters; red to purple-black bittersweet cherries, used in jellies and wines. Wood is prized for furniture. Tolerates many soils, but not extremely wet or very dry sites. Yellow to red fall foliage. Not a good tree for planting close to the house; dropping fruits are messy, and large nests of eastern tent caterpillars in branches are unsightly in spring. Also reseeds with abandon.

P. tomentosa. NANKING CHERRY. Shrub. Zones US, MS. Like *P. besseyi*, extremely tough and cold-hardy. To 6–8 ft. tall. Small, fragrant white flowers open from pinkish buds in spring; ½-in. scarlet fruit follows.

P. triloba. DOUBLE FLOWERING PLUM, FLOWERING ALMOND. Small tree or treelike large shrub. Zone US. Slow to 8–10 ft. (possibly 15 ft.) tall, with equal spread. Rather broad, 1–2½-in.-long leaves. Double pink flowers about 1 in. wide appear in early spring before leaf-out. A white form is sometimes available.

P. virginiana. CHOKECHERRY. Shrub or small tree. Zones US, MS. Native Newfoundland to Saskatchewan, south to Kansas, east to North Carolina. To 20–30 ft. high, with suckering habit; 2–4-in. leaves. After leaf-out, tiny white flowers appear in slender, 3–6-in. clusters; these are followed by astringent, dark red to black fruit to ½ in. wide. 'Canada Red' ('Shubert') has leaves that open green, turn red as they mature.

PSEUDOCYDONIA sinensis

CHINESE QUINCE

Rosaceae

DECIDUOUS SHRUB OR SMALL TREE

☘ ZONES US, MS, LS

☼ FULL SUN

💧 REGULAR WATER

Pseudocydonia sinensis

Seldom seen, curious tree, usually 15–20 ft. high (sometimes taller) and half as wide. Trunk is attractive, with bark that flakes off to reveal shades of brown, green, and gray. Trunks on old trees are often fluted. Roundish oval, dark green leaves to 4½ in. long turn yellow and red in fall. Spring bloom produces a scattering of flowers rather than a show—the pale pink, 1–1½-in. flowers are borne singly at ends of year-old twigs. Blossoms are followed by extraordinary fruits: fragrant yellow quinces to 7 in. long, weighing over a pound apiece. The fruits can be made into jam. Very susceptible to fireblight in warm, humid areas; control by pruning out damaged wood.

PSEUDOSASA. See BAMBOO

PSEUDOTSUGA menziesii (P. taxifolia)

DOUGLAS FIR

Pinaceae

EVERGREEN TREE

☘ ZONES US, MS

☼◑ FULL SUN; TAKES PART SHADE IN YOUTH

💧💧 REGULAR TO LITTLE WATER

Pseudotsuga menziesii

Of the five (possibly eight) species of *Pseudotsuga*, only this one grows over a wide territory and is much cultivated. Also a popular Christmas tree. Reaches 70–200 ft. tall in western forests. Trees are cone shaped and foliaged to the ground when young, lose lower limbs as they age. Soft, densely set, green or blue-green needles to 1½ in. long radiate in all directions from the branches. Needles are lemon scented when crushed. Pointed wine red buds form at branch tips in winter, open to apple green new growth in spring. Reddish brown, oval cones are about 3 in. long with three-pronged bracts. Unlike upright cones of true firs *(Abies)*, these hang down.

Native from Alaska through Northern California, eastward into the Rocky Mountains, and southward into northern Mexico. In the Upper South, tree is fast growing, dark green, with slightly drooping branchlets. Rocky Mountain form, *P. m. glauca*, is blue green and slower growing, more cold tolerant, more compact, and stiffer than the species. Compact, weeping, and other forms are grown mostly in arboretums and botanical gardens. All forms tolerate wind, will grow in most soils except boggy ones.

PSIDIUM

GUAVA

Myrtaceae

EVERGREEN SHRUBS OR SMALL TREES

☘ ZONE TS

☼◑ FULL SUN OR HIGH SHADE

💧 MODERATE WATER

Psidium cattleianum

White flowers are composed principally of brush of stamens. Berrylike fruit usually matures during the warm months; it is excellent eaten fresh or used in jellies, purées, and juice

drinks. Guava does best in rich soil. Plants are self-fertile, but may produce more fruit with a pollinator.

P. cattleianum (P. littorale). STRAWBERRY GUAVA. Moderate, open growth to 8–10 ft. as shrub; can be trained as multitrunked, 10–15-ft. tree. Especially beautiful bark and trunk—greenish gray to golden brown. Leaves glossy green, to 3 in. long; new growth bronze. Fruit is dark red (nearly black when fully ripe), 1½ in. wide, with white flesh and a sweet-tart, slightly resinous flavor. 'Lucidum', yellow strawberry guava or lemon guava, has yellow fruit, fairly dense growth.

P. guajava. GUAVA. To 25 ft. tall, with strongly veined leaves to 6 in. long. May lose some of its leaves briefly in spring; new growth is an attractive salmon color. Fruit 1–3 in. across, with white, pink, or yellow flesh and a musky, mildly acid flavor. Most selections of this species ripen in summer, but the old selection 'Redland' ripens in winter.

PTYCHOSPERMA (Actinophloeus)

Arecaceae (Palmae)

PALMS

☘ ZONE TS

◑ PARTIAL SHADE

💧 REGULAR WATER

Ptychosperma macarthuri

Small-scale, attractive, erect palms with slender, ringed trunks and feathery fronds toothed at apex. Often produce red fruits in warmest frost-free areas.

P. elegans. ALEXANDER PALM, SEAFORTHIA PALM, SOLITAIRE PALM. Native to Australia. To 25 ft. tall, with a single trunk. Fronds to 8 ft. long.

P. macarthuri. MACARTHUR PALM. Native to New Guinea. Clustered trunks, 10–15 ft. high. Fronds to 6½ ft. long. Often grown in containers.

🏛 PUERARIA lobata

KUDZU

Fabaceae (Leguminosae)

DECIDUOUS VINE OR GROUND COVER

☘ ZONES MS, LS, CS, TS

☼ FULL SUN

💧 REGULAR WATER

Pueraria lobata

Native to Japan. The Vine That Ate the South; has covered millions of acres since it was introduced in 1876. Smothers arbors, telephone poles, houses, and fields—and any plant in its path—at the rate of up to 1 ft. per day. Thrives under almost any condition. Leaves 3–6 in. long, broadly oval, with three leaflets. Leaves and stems somewhat hairy, coarse. Fragrant, red-purple flowers in clusters 8–12 in. long, July–September. Too invasive for garden use unless you're hiding from the government and need something to cover your tracks. Its good points: Tubers and leaves are edible, and you can make a tasty jelly from the flowers.

PULMONARIA

LUNGWORT

Boraginaceae

PERENNIALS

☘ ZONES US, MS, LS

◑● PARTIAL OR FULL SHADE

💧 REGULAR WATER

Pulmonaria saccharata

Low-growing shade lovers with quiet charm. Many kinds have foliage attractively dappled with gray or silver. The long-stalked leaves are mostly in basal clumps, though there are a few on the flower stalks. Bear drooping clusters of funnel-shaped blue or purplish flowers in spring, just before leaves emerge or at the same time. After flowering finishes, more leaves emerge from the base. If you keep plants well watered, foliage will remain ornamental throughout the growing season.

All have creeping roots and can be used as small-scale ground covers in shaded areas. They associate well with ferns, azaleas, rhododendrons, blue scillas, pink tulips under spring-flowering trees. Divide every 4 or 5 years, either after flowering or in autumn.

P. angustifolia. COWSLIP LUNGWORT. Tufts of narrowish, unspotted, dark green leaves. Clustered pink buds open to dark blue flowers on 6–12-in. stems. 'Azurea' has sky blue flowers.

P. longifolia. Slender, silver-spotted deep green leaves to 20 in. long. Blooms a bit later than the other species. 'Bertram Anderson' has deep blue flowers; leaves remain attractive throughout season.

P. montana (P. rubra). MOUNTAIN LUNGWORT. Hairy, unspotted light green leaves to 20 in. long, 5 in. wide. Blooms very early in spring. Flowering stems can reach 16 in. Blossoms may be white, blue, or red, the last most commonly seen. Blooms of 1-ft. 'Redstart' are an odd shade between salmon and brick red.

P. 'Roy Davidson'. Hybrid between *P. saccharata* and *P. longifolia*. Resembles *P. l.* 'Bertram Anderson' but has slightly wider leaves and flowers that open pink and deepen to blue.

P. saccharata. BETHLEHEM LUNGWORT. To 1½ ft. high and spreading to 2 ft. wide, with blue flowers and silvery-spotted leaves. Specialists usually offer named selections; the following are compact, foot-high plants. Flowers of 'Mrs. Moon' open pink and turn blue; 'Pierre's Pure Pink' has pink flowers; 'Sissinghurst White' has white blooms. 'Janet Fisk', a selection with blooms that turn from pink to blue, has silvery leaves.

PUMPKIN

Pumpkin

Cucurbitaceae

ANNUAL VINE

ALL ZONES

FULL SUN

WATER AT FIRST SIGNS OF WILTING

Related to gourds, melons, and squash. Wide range of fruit size, depending on selection. One of the best for a jumbo-size Halloween pumpkin is 'Atlantic Giant'. 'Small Sugar' is a smaller pumpkin with finer-grained, sweeter flesh. 'Sweetie Pie' and 'Jack Be Little' are 3-in.-wide miniatures useful as decorations. 'Lumina' is a novelty white pumpkin with orange flesh; it weighs 10–12 lbs. Seeds of all kinds are edible, but the easiest to eat are those of hull-less types like 'Trick or Treat'.

Pumpkin vines need lots of room: one vine can cover 500 sq. ft., and even bush types can spread over 20 sq. ft. Where the growing season is short, start plants indoors. In most areas, sow seeds outdoors in late spring after soil has warmed. For vining pumpkins, sow five or six seeds 1 in. deep in hills 6–8 ft. apart; thin seedlings to two per hill. For bush pumpkins, sow a cluster of three or four seeds 1 in. deep, 2 ft. apart, in rows spaced 3 ft. apart; thin seedlings to one or two plants per cluster. Water regularly during dry periods, but keep foliage dry to prevent leaf diseases. Some types are ready to harvest 90 to 120 days after sowing, when shell has hardened. They're usually picked after first frost kills the plant.

Pumpkins need rich soil, periodic fertilizer. They do not perform well in high heat and humidity. Subject to same pests and diseases as squash.

GROW A GIANT PUMPKIN

Plant 'Atlantic Giant' seeds in spring as soon as soil warms. Grow one plant per hill, spacing hills 40 ft. apart, and one pumpkin per plant. Feed every few weeks with a balanced, water-soluble fertilizer. Keep soil moist, but don't overdo it—too much water causes pumpkins to split. To avoid damaging the stem, don't move pumpkins until harvest. Good luck!

PUNICA granatum

POMEGRANATE

Punicaceae

DECIDUOUS SHRUB OR SMALL TREE

ZONES MS, LS, CS, TS

FULL SUN

REGULAR WATER FOR FRUIT PRODUCTION

Punica granatum

Bears showy summer flowers with ruffled petals surrounding central clump of stamens. Some selections yield fruit in fall. Narrow leaves open bronzy, then turn glossy bright green to golden green; brilliant yellow fall color except in the Coastal and Tropical South. All selections tolerate great heat and a wide range of soils, including alkaline soil that would kill most plants. Grows in Tropical South, but does not flower or fruit well there. In the Middle South, plant against south or west wall. Prune late in dormant season, since plant blooms on new wood. Non-fruiting selections need little water once established.

'Chico'. DWARF CARNATION-FLOWERED POMEGRANATE. Compact bush can be kept to 1½ ft. if pruned occasionally. Double orange-red flowers over long season. No fruit. Use under windows, in containers, as edging.

'Legrellei' ('Madame Legrelle', 'California Sunset'). Dense 6–8-ft. shrub with double creamy flowers heavily striped coral red. No fruit.

'Nana'. DWARF POMEGRANATE. Dense shrub to 3 ft. Blooms when a foot tall or less. Orange-red single flowers followed by small, dry red fruit. Excellent garden or container plant; effective bonsai.

'Nochi Shibari'. To 8–10 ft. tall, with double dark red flowers.

'Tayosho'. To 8–10 ft. tall, with double light apricot flowers.

'Wonderful'. Best-known fruiting pomegranate. Grow as 10-ft. fountain-shaped shrub, tree, or espalier. Single orange-red flowers to 4 in. wide are followed by fruit with burnished red skin and red pulp. Water deeply and regularly if fruit is important. Other fruiting selections, only rarely seen, include yellow-blooming 'Sweet' and pink-blooming 'Fleshman', 'King', and 'Phil Arena's'; all have sweet pink pulp.

PURPLE GLOBE GINGER. See GLOBBA globulifera

PURPLE GLORY TREE. See TIBOUCHINA granulosa

PURPLE HEART. See SETCREASEA pallida 'Purple Heart'

PURPLE-LEAF PLUM. See PRUNUS cerasifera 'Atropurpurea'

PURPLE-LEAF SAND CHERRY. See PRUNUS cistena

PURPLE-LEAF WINTER CREEPER. See EUONYMUS fortunei 'Colorata'

PURPLE ORCHID TREE. See BAUHINIA variegata

PURPLE PAINTBRUSH. See CASTILLEJA purpurea

PURSLANE. See PORTULACA oleracea

PUSCHKINIA scilloides

Liliaceae

BULB

ZONE US

FULL SUN OR LIGHT SHADE

REGULAR WATER DURING GROWTH AND BLOOM

Puschkinia scilloides

Late winter or early spring bloomer closely related to squill (*Scilla*) and glory-of-the-snow (*Chionodoxa*). Performs best where ground freezes in winter. Bell-like flowers are pale blue or whitish with darker, greenish blue stripe on each segment, in spikelike clusters on 3–6-in. stems. Strap-shaped bright green leaves are broad, upright, a little shorter than flower stems. 'Alba' has white flowers. The most commonly sold selection is *P. s. libanotica*, a vigorous plant with pale blue, striped flowers like those of the species.

Plant in autumn, placing 3–4 in. deep. If not disturbed, will grow for years. Needs very little water during summer dormant period. Most effective in masses; good choice for naturalizing.

PUSSY TOES. See ANTENNARIA

PUSSY WILLOW. See SALIX discolor

PYRACANTHA

FIRETHORN

Rosaceae

EVERGREEN SHRUBS

🌿 ZONES VARY BY SPECIES

☼ FULL SUN

💧 MODERATE WATER

Pyracantha coccinea

Grown for bright fruit, evergreen foliage (may be semievergreen in Upper South), variety of landscape uses, and ease of culture. All grow fast and vigorously, with habit from upright to sprawling; nearly all have needlelike thorns. All have glossy green leaves, usually oval or rounded at ends, ½–1 in. wide, 1–4 in. long. All bear flowers and fruit on spurs along wood of last year's growth. Spring flowers are small, malodorous, dull creamy white, carried in flattish clusters; they're effective thanks to their profusion.

The real glory of firethorns is in the thick clusters of pea-size orange-red berries that light up the garden for months. Selections with red, orange, and yellow fruit are also available; if berry color is important, buy plants when in fruit. Depending on selection, berries color up from late summer to midautumn; some types hang on until late winter, when they're cleared out by birds, storms, or decay. Dislodge old withered or rotted berries with a jet of water or an old broom.

As shrubs and ground covers, firethorns look better and fruit more heavily if allowed to follow their natural growth habit. Prune only occasionally to check wayward branches. Plants can be espaliered; they can also be sheared as hedges, though at the expense of much fruit. Tolerate most soils but should not be overwatered. Potential pests include aphids and scale insects. Two serious problems are fireblight (which can kill the plant) and scab (which causes defoliation and turns fruit sooty); for best success, choose disease-resistant selections.

P. coccinea. SCARLET FIRETHORN. Zones US, MS, LS, CS. Cold-hardy. Rounded growth to 8–10 ft. high (20 ft. trained against wall). Red-orange fruit. Best known for its selections, which include the following:

'Kasan'. Long-lasting orange-red berries. Spreading growth habit. Susceptible to scab.

'Lalandei' and 'Lalandei Monrovia'. Similar selections with orange berries. Susceptible to scab.

'Wyattii'. Orange-red berries that color early. Very prone to fireblight and scab.

P. fortuneana (P. crenatoserrata, P. yunnanensis). Zones MS, LS, CS. Vase-shaped plant to 15 ft. tall, 10 ft. wide. Limber branches make it a good choice for espalier. Orange to coral berries last through winter. 'Cherri Berri', to 10 ft. tall and 8 ft. wide, has deep red berries. 'Graberi', more upright than species, has huge clusters of dark red fruit.

P. hybrids. This category includes some of the most desirable firethorns. Plants vary in size, habit, and cold-hardiness.

'Apache'. Zones US, MS, LS, CS. To 5 ft. high and 6 ft. wide. Large bright red berries last well into winter. Resistant to fireblight and scab.

'Fiery Cascade'. Zones US, MS, LS, CS. To 8 ft. tall, 9 ft. wide; berries orange turning to red. Good disease resistance.

'Gnome'. Zones US, MS, LS. Very cold-hardy. Densely branched, 6 ft. high, 8 ft. wide. Orange berries. Highly susceptible to scab.

'Lowboy'. Zones US, MS, LS, CS. Spreading plant to 2–3 ft. high. Orange fruit. Very prone to scab.

'Mohave'. MOHAVE PYRACANTHA. Zones US, MS, LS, CS. To 12 ft. tall and wide. Heavy producer of big orange-red fruit that colors in late summer and lasts well into winter. Resistant to fireblight and scab.

'Red Elf'. Zones MS, LS, CS. Densely branched, to 2 ft. high and wide, small enough for container culture. Long-lasting bright red fruit. Some disease resistance. Apparently the same as the plant sold as 'Leprechaun'.

'Ruby Mound'. Zones MS, LS, CS. Among the most graceful of ground cover firethorns. Long, arching, drooping branches make broad mounds 2½ ft. high, spreading to about 10 ft. Bright red fruit.

'Teton'. TETON PYRACANTHA. Zones US, MS, LS, CS. Very cold-hardy. Columnar growth to 12 ft. tall, 4 ft. wide. Golden yellow fruit. Resistant to fireblight and scab.

'Tiny Tim'. Zones MS, LS, CS. Compact plant to 3 ft. high. Small leaves, few or no thorns. Red berries. Informal low hedge, barrier, tub plant.

'Watereri'. Zones US, MS, LS, CS. To 8 ft. tall and wide. Very heavy producer of long-lasting bright red fruit.

'Yukon Belle'. Zones US, MS, LS, CS. Cold-hardiest orange-fruited firethorn. Dense growth, to 6–10 ft. high and wide.

P. koidzumii. FORMOSA FIRETHORN. Zones LS, CS. Unruly grower to 8–12 ft. tall and wide. Best known for its selections, including these:

'Santa Cruz' ('Santa Cruz Prostrata'). Low growing, branching from base, spreading. Easily kept below 3 ft. by pinching out the occasional upright branch. Red fruit. Plant 4–5 ft. apart for a ground cover or bank cover. Very resistant to scab.

'Victory'. Vigorous growth to 10 ft. tall, 8 ft. wide. Dark red berries color late in the year but hold on well. Resistant to scab.

'Walderi' ('Walderi Prostrata'). Wide-spreading, low-growing ground cover (to 1½ ft. high, with a few upright shoots that should be cut out). Red berries. Plant 4–5 ft. apart for fast cover.

PYRETHRUM marginatum. See CHRYSANTHEMUM pacificum

PYRETHRUM roseum. See CHRYSANTHEMUM coccineum

PYROSTEGIA venusta
(P. ignea, Bignonia venusta)

FLAME VINE

Bignoniaceae

EVERGREEN VINE

🌿 ZONES CS (MILDER PARTS), TS

☼◐ FULL SUN OR PARTIAL SHADE

💧 MODERATE WATER

Pyrostegia venusta

Native to South America. Fast growth to 20 ft. or more, climbing by tendrils; where well adapted, grows rampantly. Leaves consist of 2–3-in. oval leaflets. Impressive show of tubular, 3-in. orange flowers in clusters of 15 to 20 at branch ends; main bloom in winter. Plants growing in Florida sometimes form slender, 1-ft.-long fruit capsules. Tolerates many soils. In central Florida, most popular vine for covering fences and other structures. Prune right after bloom to restrain growth.

PYRUS calleryana

CALLERY PEAR

Rosaceae

DECIDUOUS TREE

🌿 ZONES US, MS, LS, CS

☼ FULL SUN

💧💧 REGULAR OR MODERATE WATER

Pyrus calleryana 'Bradford'

Fruiting pear is described under Pear. The following ornamental pears are grown for their profuse white flowers in late winter or early spring and for glossy, attractive leaves that turn color in fall. These trees grow 25–50 ft. tall with strong, horizontal branching pattern and generally pyramidal shape. Limbs are savagely thorny, but improved selections listed below are thornless. Leaves are broadly oval, scalloped, glossy dark green, and leathery, 1½–3 in. long; they turn yellow, orange, scarlet, and burgundy in late fall. Pure white flowers appear before leaves; late spring freezes sometimes ruin floral display. Fruits are very small, inedible.

Callery pear tolerates pollution, drought, and most well-drained soils. Makes a good city, street, or lawn tree. A row also makes a handsome tall screen. Most selections are subject to fireblight (see Fireblight, page 433) that varies in intensity from year to year, though the disease is usually more an aesthetic problem than a life-threatening one. Selections include:

'Aristocrat'. ARISTOCRAT PEAR. Grows to 40 ft. tall, 20 ft. wide. Pyramidal, with well-spaced branches that are more horizontal than those of 'Bradford' and less prone to storm damage. Fall color ranges from yellow to red. Somewhat subject to fireblight.

'Bradford'. BRADFORD PEAR. Fast growing, easy to transplant, easy to grow, with showy spring flowers and spectacular red fall foliage. These attributes have led it to become one of the South's most overplanted trees. Lacks a central leader; main branches emerge from a common point on trunk, often causing tree to split in storms. Bradford pear grows much bigger than people usually envision. In 20 years, trees can reach 50 ft. high, 40 ft. wide. Newer pears, such as 'Chanticleer' and 'Trinity', are better choices for most gardens.

Pyrus calleryana
'Bradford'

'Capital'. Narrowly columnar; 35–40 ft. tall. Coppery fall color.

'Chanticleer' ('Cleveland Select', 'Stone Hill'). Narrow but not columnar; about 40 ft. tall, 15 ft. wide. Fall color varies from orange to reddish purple. Resistant to fireblight.

'Redspire'. Shorter, narrower pyramid than 'Aristocrat', 40 ft. tall. Large blossom clusters; yellow to red fall color. Quite prone to fireblight.

'Trinity'. Round-headed form to 30 ft. tall. Orange-red fall color.

'Whitehouse'. Narrowly columnar; 35–40 ft. tall. Red to reddish purple fall color. Often gets a disfiguring leaf spot.

QUAKING GRASS. See BRIZA maxima

QUAMOCLIT pennata. See IPOMOEA quamoclit

QUEEN OF THE NIGHT. See HYLOCEREUS undatus

QUEEN OF THE PRAIRIE. See FILIPENDULA rubra

QUEEN PALM. See SYAGRUS romanzoffianum

QUEEN SAGO. See CYCAS circinalis

QUEENSLAND UMBRELLA TREE. See SCHEFFLERA actinophylla

QUEEN'S WREATH. See ANTIGONON leptopus, PETREA volubilis

QUERCUS

OAK

Fagaceae

DECIDUOUS OR EVERGREEN TREES

🗡 ZONES VARY BY SPECIES

☼ FULL SUN

💧 REGULAR WATER, EXCEPT AS NOTED

Quercus coccinea

The oaks comprise 600 or so species of widely varying appearance and hardiness. Their common feature is the production of acorns— single nuts more or less enclosed in a cup. Some oaks are widely planted, while others have a limited range.

Homeowners acquire oaks either by planting them or by inheriting trees that were present before the land was developed. Oaks that have been planted usually thrive without difficulty; inherited types often require special attention; they are very sensitive to any disturbance of the soil. Protect

trunks from earth-moving machinery with cribs of 2-by-4s or heavier timbers. Avoid piling excavated soil around trunks or above root systems (which extend somewhat beyond the branch spread); or provide drains for aeration and removal of excess water. Do not excavate or pave above the root zone without consulting a tree expert. Do not cut roots. Avoid compacting soil. Do not park vehicles underneath these trees.

Caterpillars are the most serious potential pest of oaks. Gypsy moth caterpillars are most common in the Upper South. Heavy infestation can cause defoliation; serious attacks for 2 or more years in a row can weaken or even kill a tree. However, these pests tend to be cyclical problems, striking perhaps every 7 to 10 years. If control becomes necessary, consult a professional arborist or tree service; oak trees are too large for the limited spray equipment available to the home gardener.

Oak wilt, a fungus disease, has killed millions of oaks, especially in Texas. It is spread by oak bark beetles and by contact between healthy and infected roots; starting from the treetop down, leaves wilt, turn dull, curl, dry, and drop. Avoid pruning in spring, when bark beetles are most active. Don't plant a new oak within the root zone of a tree that has died.

When choosing an oak for your yard, it is essential to consider your soil. While some oaks adapt to many soils, others require specific conditions. A common mistake is to plant acid-loving oaks, such as pin oak (*Q. palustris*) and red oak (*Q. rubra*) in alkaline soil. Trees quickly become chlorotic (leaves turn yellow between the veins) and eventually die. Good oaks for alkaline soil include chinkapin oak (*Q. muehlenbergii*), Chisos red oak (*Q. gravesii*), live oak (*Q. virginiana*), Shumard red oak (*Q. shumardii*), and Texas red oak (*Q. texana*).

Q. acutissima. SAWTOOTH OAK. Deciduous. Zones US, MS, LS, CS. Native to China, Korea, Japan. Moderate to fast growth to 35–45 ft. tall, usually with open, spreading habit. Deeply furrowed bark. Bristle-toothed, shiny dark green leaves are 3½–7½ in. long, a third as wide; they look like chestnut leaves. Foliage is yellowish on expanding, yellow to yellowish brown in fall; it may hang on late into winter. Fairly tolerant of various soils, though it prefers well-drained acid soil. Stands up well to heat and humidity. No serious problems. Good shade, lawn, or street tree.

Q. alba. WHITE OAK. Deciduous. Zones US, MS, LS, CS. Native from Maine to Florida, west to Minnesota and Texas. Slow to moderate to 50–80 ft., taller in the wild. Pyramidal when young; in maturity, a majestic round-headed tree with massive limbs, often broader than tall. Leaves are 4–8 in. long, dark green above, lighter beneath, with deep, rounded lobes. Folklore has it that when the emerging leaves are as big as a mouse's ear, it is time to plant corn. Fall color varies from brown to wine red. Light gray bark is beautiful in early morning or late afternoon sun. Best in rich, deep, moist, preferably acid soil. One of the handsomest oaks, useful for timber, flooring, and barrel making, but not widely planted because of its ultimate size and slow growth. Where it occurs naturally, however, it is among the most cherished of trees; it is the oak associated with treaty signings and other historic events.

Q. bicolor. SWAMP WHITE OAK. Deciduous. Zones US, MS, LS. Native from Quebec to Georgia, west to Michigan and Arkansas. Slow to moderate growth to 50–60 ft., rarely taller, with equal or greater spread. Shallowly lobed or scalloped leaves are 3–7 in. long, a little more than half as wide, shiny dark green above, silvery white beneath. Fall color usually yellow, sometimes reddish purple. Bark of trunk and branches flakes off in scales. Tolerates wet soil; also thrives where soil is well drained. Drought tolerant. Needs acid soil.

Q. coccinea. SCARLET OAK. Deciduous. Zones US, MS, LS, CS. Native from Maine to Florida, west to Minnesota and Missouri. Moderate to rapid growth in deep, rich soil. Can reach 60–80 ft. tall. High, light, open-branching habit. Bright green leaves are 3–6 in. long, a little more than half as wide, with deeply cut, pointed lobes. Foliage turns scarlet where fall nights are cold. Deep roots. Good street or lawn tree. Fine to garden under.

Q. emoryi. EMORY OAK. Evergreen. Zones MS, LS, CS, TS. Native to Arizona, New Mexico, Texas, northern Mexico. Handsome tree to 40 ft., in gardens usually smaller. Leathery, oval, 2–3-in. leaves can turn golden just before new growth starts in late spring. Tolerates a variety of soils.

Q. falcata. SOUTHERN RED OAK, SPANISH OAK. Deciduous. Zones US, MS, LS, CS. Native from Virginia to Florida, westward to southern Illinois and Arkansas. Moderate growth to 70–80 ft., eventually with rounded crown. Leaves 5–9 in. long, sometimes longer, with sharp-pointed lobes varying in number from three to nine. Fall color not significant. Tolerates relatively poor and dry soils as well as occasionally flooded soils.

Q. glauca. BLUE JAPANESE OAK, EVERGREEN OAK. Evergreen. Zones LS, CS. Native to Japan, China, Taiwan. Moderately slow growth rate to 20–30 ft., rarely 45 ft. Shape is upright and oval, with spread approximately half of height. Makes an excellent screen, because foliage grows in dense mass. Leaves leathery, dark green, to 5½ in. long and 2½ in. wide, with wavy margins; undersides are silky gray. New leaves particularly handsome, often bronze green or purple green. Prefers well-drained, fertile, slightly acid soil, but tolerates heavy clay.

Q. gravesii. CHISOS RED OAK. Deciduous. Zones US, MS, LS, CS. Native to Texas. Grows to 40 ft. Leaves lobed, but smaller and not as deeply indented as those of *Q. texana*. Dark, blackish bark. Foliage often turns bright yellow and red in fall. Tolerates limy soils and drought.

Q. hemisphaerica. See Q. laurifolia

Q. ilex. HOLLY OAK. Evergreen. Zones LS, CS, TS. Native to Mediterranean region. Moderate growth to 40–70 ft. high, with equal spread. Though variable, leaves are generally 1½–3 in. long and a third as wide, either toothed or smooth edged, rich dark green above, yellowish or silvery beneath. Tolerates wind and salt air; will grow in areas with constant sea winds, but tends to be shrubby there. Good street or lawn tree. Can take clipping into formal shapes or hedges.

Q. imbricaria. SHINGLE OAK. Deciduous. Zones US, MS, LS. Native from Pennsylvania to Georgia, west to Nebraska and Arkansas. Slow growing and pyramidal in youth, eventually growing at a moderate rate into a rounded tree. Typical height is 50–60 ft., though tree sometimes reaches 100 ft. Shallowly ridged brown-gray bark. Oval, smooth-edged leaves are 2½–6 in. long, half as wide. Foliage is reddish on unfolding, dark glossy green in summer, yellowish brown to brownish red in autumn; often hangs on through winter. Thrives with pruning and can be trimmed into a hedge. Best in rich, deep, moist, well-drained, acid soil; tolerates some drought.

Q. laurifolia. LAUREL OAK. All zones. Evergreen in Coastal and Tropical South. Native to Coastal Plains and piedmont from southern New Jersey to Florida, eastward to East Texas and southeast Arkansas. To 40 ft. or more in height, somewhat less in spread. Narrowly oval, smooth-edged, leathery leaves are shiny dark green, 1–4 in. long, ½–1¼ in. wide. *Q. hemisphaerica*, also called laurel oak, is similar. Both are useful street trees, being smaller and less spreading than *Q. virginiana*.

Q. macrocarpa. BUR OAK, MOSSY CUP OAK. Deciduous. Zones US, MS, LS. Native from Nova Scotia to Pennsylvania, westward to Manitoba and Texas. Rugged-looking tree growing slowly to 60–80 ft. high and at least as wide. Deeply furrowed dark gray bark. Leaves are glossy green above, whitish beneath, 4–10 in. long and half as wide, broad at tip, tapered at base. Yellowish fall color. Large acorns form in mossy cups. Similar to *Q. bicolor* but faster growing, more tolerant of adverse conditions. Needs lots of room. Acid or alkaline soil.

Q. muehlenbergii. CHINKAPIN OAK. Deciduous. Zones US, MS, LS, CS. Native from New England, west to Minnesota and Texas. Moderate growth during early years, slowing with age. Reaches 80 ft. or more in wild, with an even greater spread; usually smaller in cultivation, and slender until middle-aged. Dark, glossy green

Quercus macrocarpa

leaves, to 6½ in. long and 3 in. wide, have coarse, saw-edged margins, are silvery beneath. Fall color varies from yellow brown to rust brown. Grows in wide range of soils, including clay and dry, rocky limestone.

Q. myrsinifolia. JAPANESE LIVE OAK. Evergreen. Zones MS, LS, CS. Native to Japan, China. To 20–30 ft. tall and nearly as wide, usually round headed in age. Narrow, glossy dark green leaves 2½–4 in. long, toothed toward tip. Purplish new foliage. Grows well in almost all soils. Unlike most oaks, it is graceful rather than sturdy; typically identified as an oak by its acorns. No serious problems. Most cold-hardy evergreen oak.

Q. nigra. WATER OAK. Deciduous. Zones US, MS, LS, CS. Native to lowland stream banks throughout southeastern U.S. Moderate to fast growth to 50–80 ft. tall, with conical or rounded canopy. Fairly narrow leaves,

1½–4 in. long, vary in shape from obovate to lobed; turn yellow to brown in fall, hang on late. Limbs subject to breakage by wind, snow, ice. Tolerates many soils, but not alkaline ones. Provide moist to wet conditions. Used as shade and street tree. A favorite host for mistletoe.

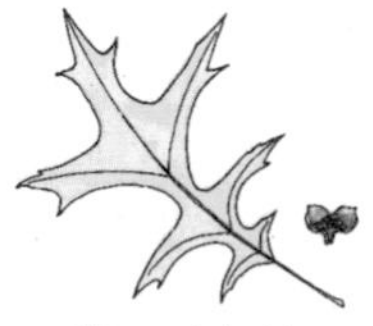

Q. palustris. PIN OAK. Deciduous. Zones US, MS, LS, CS. Native from Massachusetts to Delaware, westward to Wisconsin and Arkansas. Moderate to fairly rapid growth to 50–80 ft. Slender and pyramidal when young, open and round headed at maturity. Smooth brownish gray bark becomes shallowly ridged with age. Lower branches tend to droop almost to ground; if lowest whorl is cut away, branches above will adopt same habit. Only when fairly tall will it

Quercus palustris

have good clearance beneath lowest branches. Glossy dark green leaves, 3–6 in. long and nearly as wide, are deeply cut into bristle-pointed lobes. In fall weather, leaves turn yellow, red, and then russet brown; may hang on in winter. Needs plenty of water; tolerates poorly drained soils. Wide use as lawn and street tree. Needs acid soil.

Q. phellos. WILLOW OAK. Deciduous. Zones US, MS, LS, CS. Native from New York to Florida, westward to Missouri and Texas. Fast to moderate growth to 50–90 ft. tall. Superior lawn or street tree. Somewhat like *Q. palustris* in growth habit and spreading form. Smooth gray bark becomes shallowly ridged in age. Leaves resemble those of

Quercus phellos

willows rather than oaks, 2½–5 in. long, ⅓–1 in. wide, and smooth edged. Foliage turns yellowish or russet red before falling. Most delicate foliage pattern of all oaks. No serious problems. Tolerates poor drainage. Needs acid soil.

Q. prinus. CHESTNUT OAK, BASKET OAK. Deciduous. Zones US, MS, LS. Native from southern parts of Maine and Ontario southward to South Carolina and Alabama. Moderate growth to an eventual dense, rounded, 60–70 ft. Large, edible acorns are prized by wildlife. Bark often quite dark, even nearly black, becoming deeply furrowed with age. Unlobed leaves with coarse, rounded teeth are 4–6 in. long, 1½–3½ in. wide; in fall, their deep yellowish green color changes to yellow or orange. This tree tolerates poor, dry, rocky soil but looks better and grows faster with adequate water, good soil. Does not tolerate poor drainage. Needs acid soil.

Q. robur. ENGLISH OAK. Deciduous. Zones US, MS, LS. Native to Europe, northern Africa, western Asia. Moderate growth to 40–60 ft. in gardens (to 90 ft. in wild), with rather short trunk and very wide, open head in maturity. Leaves 3–4½ in. long, half as wide, with three to seven pairs of rounded lobes. Leaves hold until late in fall and drop without much color change. 'Fastigiata', upright English oak, is narrow and upright (like Lombardy poplar) when young, branches out to broad, pyramidal shape when mature. Both this selection and the species are prone to mildew. Other selections include 'Skymaster', a broad pyramid to 50 ft. tall and half as wide (narrower in youth); and 'Westminster Globe', a round-headed tree to 45 ft. tall and wide. Acid or alkaline soil.

Q. rubra (Q. r. maxima, Q. borealis). RED OAK, NORTHERN RED OAK. Deciduous. Zones US, MS, LS. Native from Nova Scotia to Pennsylvania, westward to Minnesota and Iowa. Fast growth to 60–75 ft. in gardens (over 100 ft. in wild). Broad, spreading branches and round-topped crown. With age, bark becomes quite dark and fissured. Leaves 5–8 in. long, 3–5 in. wide, with three to seven pairs of sharp-pointed lobes. New leaves and leafstalks are red in spring, turning dark red, ruddy brown, or orange in fall. Needs fertile soil and plenty of water. Stake young plants. High-branching habit and reasonably open shade make it a good tree for big lawns, parks, broad avenues. Deep roots make it good to garden under. Usually fairly trouble-free. Needs acid soil.

Q. shumardii. SHUMARD RED OAK. Deciduous. Zones US, MS, LS, CS. Native from Kansas to southern Michigan, southward to North Carolina and Florida, westward to Texas. Similar to *Q. coccinea*, slightly less hardy. Yellow to red fall color. Tolerates drought, wide range of soils, acid or alkaline.

Q. stellata. POST OAK. Deciduous. Zones US, MS, LS, CS. Native from Florida to Massachusetts, west to Kansas and Texas. Slow growing, to 40–50 ft., rarely 100 ft. Forms dense, round canopy and stout, picturesque

Q

branches. Leaves are large, to 8 in. long, dark green, leathery, and have straplike lobes that give them a cruciform appearance. Fall color is not usually bright, varies from yellow to brown, but leaves hang from branches through winter. Distinctive bark: scales, ridges, furrows, cracks. Tolerates dry, rocky, and sandy soils. Acid or alkaline soil.

Q. texana. TEXAS RED OAK. Deciduous. Zones US, MS, LS, CS. Native to Texas. To 15–30 ft. with nearly equal spread, either a low-branching, multitrunked small tree or a multistemmed shrubby clump. Yellow-green leaves, to 4 in. long, are deeply cut into five to seven sharp-pointed lobes, similar to those of *Q. shumardii;* maroon and scarlet in fall. Grows on limestone; tolerates drought.

Q. virginiana. LIVE OAK. Evergreen. Zones LS, CS, TS. Native from Virginia to Florida, westward to Texas. Signature tree of the South. Moderate growth to 40–80 ft. tall, with spreading, heavy-limbed crown up to twice as wide. Very long lived; with age, bark becomes very dark and checked. Smooth-edged, quite narrow leaves, 1½–5 in. long, shiny dark green above, whitish beneath. Old leaves are all shed in spring before new growth emerges. Tree is often draped with Spanish moss. Thrives on moisture and does best in deep, rich soil, though it tolerates most soils. Also tolerates salt spray, and is an excellent tree for the beach when planted in groups back from the dunes. Widely used as street tree in native range. Needs lots of space. A gall insect causes unsightly damage to leaves. Loss of trees to oak wilt has been severe in Central Texas. Termites have killed many live oaks in New Orleans.

QUINCE, FRUITING
(Cydonia oblonga)

Rosaceae

DECIDUOUS SHRUB OR SMALL TREE

ZONES US, MS, LS

FULL SUN

MODERATE WATER

Fruiting Quince

Slow growing to 10–25 ft. Unlike flowering quince (*Chaenomeles*), fruiting quince has thornless branches. Generally overlooked by planters of flowering fruit trees and home orchard trees, yet its virtues make fruiting quince worth considering as an ornamental. Its winter form can be dramatic in pattern of gnarled and twisted branches. In spring, it bears white or pale pink, 2-in.-wide flowers at tips of leafed-out branches. Attractive, oval, 2–4-in. leaves are dark green above and whitish beneath, turn yellow in fall. Large, yellow, wonderfully fragrant fruit ripens in early fall.

Best in heavy, well-drained soil but tolerates wet soil. Avoid deep cultivation, which damages shallow roots and causes suckers. Prune only to form trunk and shape frame; thin out and cut back only enough to stimulate new growth. Do not use high-nitrogen fertilizer, as this results in growth that is susceptible to fireblight. Remove suckers that sprout freely around the base of the tree; they rarely fruit and tend to weaken the tree.

Fruit is inedible when raw but useful in making jams and jellies. Fruit is also made into candy and blended with other fruits in pies. Some popular selections follow:

'Apple' ('Orange'). Old favorite. Round, golden-skinned fruit. Tender orange-yellow flesh.

'Cooke's Jumbo'. Large yellowish green fruit with white flesh. Can be nearly twice the size of other quinces.

'Pineapple'. Roundish, light golden fruit. Tender white flesh; pineapple-like flavor.

'Smyrna'. Round to oblong fruit with lemon yellow skin. Strong quince fragrance.

RABBIT'S FOOT. See MARANTA leuconeura kerchoviana

RABBIT'S FOOT FERN. See DAVALLIA fejeenisis

RADICCHIO. See CHICORY

RADISH

Brassicaceae (Cruciferae)

ANNUAL

ALL ZONES

FULL SUN OR LIGHT SHADE

MAINTAIN EVEN SOIL MOISTURE

Radish

You can pull radishes for the table as early as 3 weeks after you sow the seed (the slowest kinds take 2 months). To grow well, they need moist soil and some added nutrients. Supply nutrients by blending rotted manure into soil before planting, or—about 10 days after planting—feed beside row as for carrots, or apply liquid fertilizer. Sow seeds as soon as ground can be worked in spring and at weekly intervals until warm weather approaches (heat causes plants to go to seed, with roots becoming bitter in the process). In the Coastal and Tropical South, radishes make a fall and winter crop. Sow seeds ½ in. deep and thin to 1 in. apart when tops are up; space rows 1 ft. apart. Row covers will help protect against flea beetles, which attack foliage; will also deter root maggots by preventing adult flies from laying eggs.

Most familiar radishes are short, round, red or red-and-white types like 'Cherry Belle', 'Crimson Giant', and 'Scarlet White-tipped'. These should be used just as soon as they reach full size. Slightly slower to reach edible size are long white radishes, of which 'Icicle' is best known. Late radishes 'Long Black Spanish' and 'White Chinese' grow 6–10 in. long, can be stored in moist sand in a frost-free place for winter use. The last named, along with 'Alpine Cross' and similar very large, mild radishes, are sold as daikon (pronounced "dye-con").

RAIN LILY. See HABRANTHUS, ZEPHYRANTHES

RANGPUR LIME. See CITRUS, Sour-Acid Mandarin

Ranunculaceae. The immense buttercup family numbers nearly 2,000 species, among them numerous ornamental annuals and perennials. Members include *Anemone*, columbine (*Aquilegia*), *Clematis*, *Delphinium*, hellebore (*Helleborus*), and *Ranunculus.* Many are poisonous if eaten.

RANUNCULUS

Ranunculaceae

PERENNIALS WITH TUBEROUS OR FIBROUS ROOTS

ZONES VARY BY SPECIES

EXPOSURE NEEDS VARY BY SPECIES

REGULAR WATER

Ranunculus asiaticus

A very large group (up to 250 species of widely different habit and appearance), but the two listed are the only ones grown to any extent.

R. asiaticus. PERSIAN RANUNCULUS, TURBAN RANUNCULUS. All zones (see below). A tuber produces many stalks 1½ ft. or taller; in spring, each stalk bears one to four flowers, for a profuse bloom. Semidouble to fully double flowers, 3–5 in. wide, in white and shades of yellow, orange, red, pink, cream. Leaves bright green. Popular strain Tecolote Giants available in single colors, mixed colors, and picotees. Bloomingdale is a dwarf (8–10-in.) strain.

Tubers are hardy to 10°F. In Zones LS, CS, TS, plant in fall for bloom in winter, early spring; elsewhere, as soon as ground is workable in spring. Needs full sun, perfect drainage (if necessary, plant in raised beds). Set tubers with prongs down, 2 in. deep (½–1 in. deep in heavy soil), 6–8 in. apart. Tubers rot if overwatered before roots form; you can start them in flats of moist sand, then plant after sprouts appear. Cover young sprouts with netting to protect from birds. Where hardy, tubers can be left in ground, but they tend to rot if they get moisture during summer dormancy.

R

Most gardeners in all regions lift tubers when foliage yellows, cut off tops, and store in cool, dry place. Nursery-grown seedlings are sold in some areas. Good pot plant.

R. repens 'Pleniflorus' (R. r. 'Flore Pleno'). CREEPING BUTTER-CUP. Zones US, MS, LS, CS. Vigorous plant with thick, fibrous roots and runners growing several feet in a season, rooting at joints. Leaves are glossy, roundish, deeply cut, toothed. Blooms in spring, bearing fully double, 1-in., button-shaped bright yellow flowers on 1–2-ft. stems. Ground cover in full sun to deep shade. Can be invasive. Basic species is single flowered and as aggressive as the selection (or more so).

RAPHIDOPHORA aurea. See EPIPREMNUM aureum

RAPHIOLEPIS

Rosaceae

EVERGREEN SHRUBS

ZONES LS (PROTECTED), CS

FULL SUN OR LIGHT SHADE

REGULAR TO MODERATE WATER

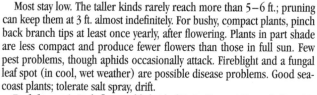

Raphiolepis indica

Where temperatures never (or very rarely) fall to 0°F, these are among the most widely planted shrubs, and for good reason: Their glossy, leathery leaves and compact form make them attractive, dense background plants or informal hedges. They bloom profusely from late fall or midwinter to late spring, with flowers ranging from white to near red. Berrylike dark blue fruit (not especially showy) follows flowers. New leaves in tones of bronze and red often add more touches of color.

Most stay low. The taller kinds rarely reach more than 5–6 ft.; pruning can keep them at 3 ft. almost indefinitely. For bushy, compact plants, pinch back branch tips at least once yearly, after flowering. Plants in part shade are less compact and produce fewer flowers than those in full sun. Few pest problems, though aphids occasionally attack. Fireblight and a fungal leaf spot (in cool, wet weather) are possible disease problems. Good seacoast plants; tolerate salt spray, drift.

R. delacouri. Pink-flowered hybrid of *R. indica* and *R. umbellata*. To 6 ft. tall. Small pink flowers in upright clusters. Leaves smaller than most.

R. indica. INDIAN HAWTHORN. To 4–5 ft. high, with 1½–3-in.-long, pointed leaves and ½-in. white flowers tinged pink. Its selections are widely grown and sold, although the species is not. Selections differ mainly in color of bloom and in size and form of plant. Flower color is especially inconsistent. In the Coastal South, blossoms are usually lighter; in general, bloom is paler in fall than spring. Selections include the following:

'Ballerina'. Deep rosy pink flowers. Stays low (not much taller than 2 ft.) and compact (no wider than 4 ft.). Reddish tinged leaves in winter.

'Clara'. White flowers on compact plants 3–5 ft. high, about as wide. Red new growth.

'Dancer'. Clear pink flowers. Dense. To about 4 ft. tall.

'Enchantress'. Rose pink flowers. Grows 3 ft. tall, 5 ft. wide. A white form is called 'White Enchantress'.

'Indian Princess'. Light pink flowers. To 3 ft. high.

'Jack Evans'. Bright pink flowers. To about 4 ft. tall, with wider spread. Compact and spreading. Leaves sometimes have purplish tinge.

'Spring Rapture'. Compact 4-ft.-tall plant with rose red single flowers.

'Springtime'. Deep pink flowers. Vigorous, upright to 4–6 ft. high.

R. 'Majestic Beauty'. Fragrant light pink blooms in clusters 10 in. wide. Leaves 4 in. long. Plant larger than others; can reach 15 ft. Thought by some to be a hybrid from *Raphiolepis* and loquat (*Eriobotrya*). Use as background shrub or small tree with single or multiple trunk. Stake tree form carefully until sturdy trunk has formed. Thin branches to reduce wind resistance and minimize wind damage.

R. umbellata (R. u. ovata, R. ovata). YEDDO HAWTHORN. Easily distinguished from *R. indica* by its roundish, leathery, dark green leaves, 1–3 in. long. White flowers about ¾ in. wide. Vigorous plants 4–6 ft. tall,

sometimes to 10 ft. Thick and bushy in full sun. This plant is sometimes called Yedda hawthorn. 'Minor' is a dwarf, slow-growing form.

RASPBERRY

Rosaceae

DECIDUOUS SHRUBS WITH BIENNIAL STEMS

ZONE US, EXCEPT AS NOTED

FULL SUN

REGULAR WATER

Raspberry

Most popular, heaviest bearing raspberries are red. Two types exist: summer-bearing raspberries, which bear annually in summer on 2-year-old canes; and everbearing (also called fall-bearing) raspberries, which bear twice on each cane—in autumn of first year, then in summer of second year. In both types, fruit follows loose clusters of white flowers.

Raspberries aren't well adapted to much of the South. They need winter chill or cold and a slowly warming, lingering springtime to reach perfection. However, 'Dorman Red' is a good producer in the Lower and Coastal South; 'Bababerry' also performs well in the Coastal South. In Florida, the tropical mysore raspberry (*Rubus niveus*) bears black raspberry crops in winter and spring. Good drainage is essential; if your soil is heavy clay, consider planting in raised beds. Slightly acid soil (pH 6 to 6.5) is ideal. Water need is greatest during flowering and fruiting. Feed at bloom time.

Plants are erect; they can be grown as free-standing shrubs and staked, but they are most easily handled if tied to wires fastened between two stout posts. The lower wire should be at 2½ ft., the upper one at 4–5 ft. The best time to plant is late winter or early spring. Set plants an inch deeper than they grew originally; space them 2½–3 ft. apart, in rows 7–9 ft. apart. Cut back the cane that rises from the roots, leaving only enough (about 6 in.) to serve as a marker.

Summer-bearing selections should produce three to five canes the first year; these will bear the next year and should be cut out at ground level after fruiting. Second-year canes will appear all around parent plant and even between hills and rows. Remove all except five to twelve closely spaced, vigorous canes that come up near the crown. Tie these to top wire. In spring, before growth begins, cut them back to 4½–5½ ft. Fruit-bearing laterals will appear from these canes.

Everbearing raspberries differ slightly in pruning needs; they fruit in their first autumn on top third of cane and in their second summer on lower two-thirds of cane. Cut off upper portion that has borne fruit and leave lower portion to bear next spring. Cut out cane after it has fruited along its whole length.

You can follow the example of growers who cut everbearing canes to the ground yearly in fall after fruiting is finished; wait until late winter in colder areas. You'll sacrifice one crop in return for easy maintenance and prolonged crop in summer. In a large patch, use a powerful rotary mower.

To control anthracnose and other fungus diseases, spray with lime sulfur during the dormant season and again when bloom time begins; this will also help control many insect pests. Cane borer may attack canes; prune out and destroy any damaged canes below entry points (pinhead-size holes in canes at or near ground level).

The following selections are summer bearing unless indicated:

'Bababerry'. Everbearing. Needs little winter chill; stands heat well.

'Canby'. Large, bright red berries. Thornless.

'Cuthbert'. Medium-size berries of good quality.

'Fallgold'. Everbearing. Large, very sweet, yellow berries. High yielding, very cold-hardy.

'Heritage'. Everbearing. Tasty, medium-size berries. Easy to grow. Good selection for the Upper, Middle, and Lower South.

'Indian Summer'. Everbearing. Small crops of large, tasty red berries. Fall crop often larger.

'Latham'. Older, hardy selection. Late ripening. Berries often crumbly.

'Newburgh'. Late-ripening selection. Large, light red berries. Takes heavy soil fairly well.

▶

'September'. Everbearing. Medium to small berries of good flavor. Fall crop the heavier one.

'Summit'. Everbearing. Can bear the first year. Heavy producer.

'Sumner'. Early selection with some resistance to root rot in heavy soils. Fine fruit.

RASPBERRY, BLACK or BLACKCAP

Rosaceae

DECIDUOUS SHRUBS WITH BIENNIAL STEMS

ZONE US, EXCEPT AS NOTED

FULL SUN OR LIGHT SHADE

REGULAR WATER

Black Raspberry

For ornamental relatives, see *Rubus*. Resemble regular red raspberry in many ways, but even less tolerant of Southern climates. Blue-black fruit is firmer and seedier, with a more distinct flavor. Plants do not sucker from roots; new plants form when arching cane tips root in soil. No trellis needed. Head back new canes at 1½–2 ft. to force laterals. At end of growing season, cut out all weak canes and remove canes that fruited during current season. In late winter or early spring, cut back laterals to 10–15 in. on strong canes, 3–4 in. on weak ones. Fruit is produced on side shoots from these laterals. If you prefer trellising, head new canes at 2–3 ft. Subject to same pests and diseases as red raspberry.

Selections usually sold are 'Cumberland', an old selection; 'Morrison', large berry on productive vine; and 'Black Hawk', a heat-tolerant selection that does well in the southern Midwest. 'Jewel', a recent introduction, is disease resistant and vigorous; it's the only black raspberry suited to the Middle and Lower South.

RATIBIDA

Asteraceae (Compositae)

PERENNIALS

ZONES US, MS, LS, CS

FULL SUN

REGULAR WATER

Ratibida columnifera

Native to prairie and western states. Plants are stiffly erect, branched, roughly hairy, with deeply cut leaves. Flower heads resemble black-eyed Susan *(Rudbeckia hirta)* but have fewer ray flowers and a round or cylindrical (rather than flat) central disk. Use in casual, natural-looking borders with grasses and other minimum-care perennials.

R. columnifera. MEXICAN HAT. To 2 ft. tall. Flower heads have drooping ray flowers of yellow or brownish purple, and a tall, columnar brown disk. Effect is that of a sombrero with drooping brim.

R. pinnata. PRAIRIE or YELLOW CONEFLOWER. To 4 ft. tall, with yellow ray flowers and a nearly globular brown disk.

RATTLE BOX. See SESBANIA punicea

RATTLESNAKE GRASS. See BRIZA maxima

RATTLESNAKE MASTER. See ERYNGIUM yuccifolium

RATTLESNAKE PLANT. See CALATHEA insignis

RAVENNA GRASS. See ERIANTHUS ravennae

RED BAY. See PERSEA borbonia

REDBUD. See CERCIS

RED GINGER. See ALPINIA purpurata

RED-HOT POKER. See KNIPHOFIA uvaria

RED YUCCA. See HESPERALOE parviflora

REHMANNIA elata

CHINESE FOXGLOVE

Gesneriaceae

PERENNIAL

ZONES MS (PROTECTED), LS, CS

SUN OR SHADE; BEST WITH SOME SHADE

REGULAR WATER

Rehmannia elata

Spreads by underground roots to form big clump of coarse, deeply toothed leaves. Stalks to 2–3 ft. tall are loosely set with 3-in.-long, tubular flowers that look something like big, gaping foxgloves. Common form is rose purple with yellow, red-dotted throat; there is a fine white-and-cream form that must be grown from cuttings or divisions. Blooms in spring and summer. Long lasting as a cut flower. Spreads quickly in fertile, moist soil. Can be invasive.

RESURRECTION FERN. See POLYPODIUM polypodioides

Rhamnaceae. The buckthorn family of shrubs and trees has small, usually clustered flowers and fruits that are drupes (single seeded, juicy) or capsules. Family members include *Rhamnus* and Chinese jujube *(Ziziphus)*.

RHAMNUS caroliniana

CAROLINA BUCKTHORN, INDIAN CHERRY

Rhamnaceae

DECIDUOUS SHRUB OR SMALL TREE

ZONES US, MS, LS, CS

FULL SUN OR PARTIAL SHADE

MODERATE WATER

Rhamnus caroliniana

Native from New York to Florida and Texas. Grows moderately fast to 15–20 ft., sometimes reaches 30 ft. Small clustered flowers rather inconspicuous. Grown for its form, foliage and color. Coarse, dark green leaves, to 6 in. long, turn yellow in fall. Bears clusters of showy, sweet berries, which ripen from red to black in fall (often both colors on shrub at same time). Good as an understory tree.

RHAPHIOLEPIS. See RAPHIOLEPIS

RHAPIDOPHYLLUM hystrix

NEEDLE PALM

Arecaceae (Palmae)

HARDY PALM

ALL ZONES

SUN OR SHADE

MUCH OR LITTLE WATER

Rhapidophyllum hystrix

May be the hardiest palm in the world. Takes temperatures well below 0°F. Has reportedly survived winter as far north as Massachusetts. A very slow-growing, shrubby palm, native to the Coastal Plains from South Carolina to Florida and Mississippi. Eventually reaches 6–8 ft. tall and wide. Does not have a distinct trunk. Needle palm gets its name from the sharp, black needles that protect its crown and seeds. Leaf fans at ends of smooth stems are dramatic; fans are lustrous dark green, 3 ft. across, deeply cut into six to twelve segments. Plant tolerates a wide range of soils. Makes a good accent or understory plant. Hard to find in garden centers; available by mail order. Buy only nursery-propagated plants, not those collected from the wild.

R

RHAPIS

LADY PALM

Arecaceae (Palmae)

PALMS

✂ ZONES VARY BY SPECIES; OR INDOORS

◐ ● PARTIAL OR FULL SHADE

💧 REGULAR WATER

Rhapis excelsa

Fan palms that form bamboolike clumps with lush, deep green foliage. Trunks covered with net of dark, fibrous leaf sheaths. Choice, slow growing, and expensive. Several variegated forms exist. Good indoor plants; give indirect light.

R. excelsa. BROADLEAF LADY PALM. Zones CS, TS. Hardy to 20°F. Slow growing to 5–12 ft. tall, usually less. One of the finest container plants; takes poor light and neglect but responds quickly to good light, fertilizer.

R. humilis. SLENDER LADY PALM, RATTAN PALM. Zone TS. Hardy to 22°F. Tall, bamboolike stems (to 18 ft.) give charming, graceful, tropical air. Larger, longer-leafed palm than *R. excelsa.*

RHIPSALIDOPSIS gaertneri (Schlumbergera gaertneri)

EASTER CACTUS

Cactaceae

CACTUS

✂ ZONE TS; OR INDOORS

◐ PARTIAL SHADE

💧● REGULAR OR MODERATE WATER

Rhipsalidopsis gaertneri

For culture and general description, see *Schlumbergera.* Much like *S. bridgesii,* but more upright or horizontal rather than completely drooping. Blooms in spring, often again in late summer or early fall. There are many selections, with flowers in shades of pink and red. In marginal climates, protect under lathhouse or covered terrace. Good house plant; give bright light indoors and carry outdoors in warm season, if desired. Recently renamed *Hatiora gaertneri,* but not generally offered under that name.

RHODODENDRON (includes Azalea)

Ericaceae

EVERGREEN OR DECIDUOUS SHRUBS

✂ SEE BELOW

◐ GENERALLY BEST IN FILTERED SHADE

💧 💧💧 CONSTANTLY MOIST SOIL AND HUMID AIR

☣ LEAVES ARE POISONOUS IF INGESTED

Rhododendron 'Trude Webster'

Many think of azaleas and rhododendrons as different plants, but they all are in the genus *Rhododendron,* which comprises more than 800 species and 2,000 plant selections. Both azaleas and rhododendrons rank among the South's favorite shrubs.

With careful selection, gardeners in almost all areas of the South can grow some of these plants, even if that means growing them in containers. Rhododendrons generally do better in the Upper and Middle South, though a number of selections thrive in the Lower South. Azaleas, however, are much more accommodating. With careful attention to soil, light, and selection, they can be grown throughout the South.

Rhododendrons and azaleas have much the same basic soil and water requirements. They require acid soil. They need more air in the root zone

than most other garden plants but, at the same time, they need a constant moisture supply. In other words, they need soil that is both fast draining and moisture retentive. Yellowing, wilting, and collapse of plants indicate root rot caused by poor drainage. Soils rich in organic matter often have the desired qualities; improve your soil with liberal quantities of organic matter. Plant azaleas and rhododendrons with top of root ball slightly above soil level. Never allow soil to wash in and bury stems. Plants are surface rooters and benefit from a mulch such as pine needles and ground bark. Never cultivate around these plants.

Sun tolerance of azaleas and rhododendrons differs by species and selection. Too much sun causes bleaching or burning in leaf centers, though most can take full sun in the Upper South. Ideal location is in filtered shade beneath tall trees; east and north sides of house or fence are next best. Too-dense shade results in lanky plants that bloom sparsely. Any fertilizing should be done immediately after bloom.

Both rhododendrons and azaleas require acid soil. In limy, alkaline soils, they quickly develop chlorosis (yellow leaves with green veins), due to a lack of iron. However, alkaline soil hasn't kept azalea lovers in Texas and Oklahoma from planting them. The standard practice there is to excavate shrub beds to a depth of 2 ft., discard the original soil, and backfill with a mixture of sphagnum peat moss and ground bark before planting. Even so, the soil begins reverting to its original pH after several years, requiring periodic applications of garden sulfur and chelated iron.

> ### RHODODENDRONS IN CLAY OR ALKALINE SOIL?
> They don't like it. Planting in raised beds that are 1–2 ft. above the original soil level is the simplest way to give these plants the conditions they need. Liberally mix organic material into top foot of native soil, then fill bed above it with a mixture that's 50 percent organic material, 30 percent soil, 20 percent sand. This mixture will hold air and moisture while allowing excess water to drain.

Though both are subject to many pests and diseases, well-tended plants are not usually beset by problems. Damage by root weevil adults, which notch leaves, is usually minor, but their larvae can girdle roots. Prevent new generations by controlling adults with a systemic insecticide, such as Orthene (acephate). Lacebugs, which suck sap from leaf undersides, can be a severe problem in warm weather; spray with insecticidal soap or summer oil to control wingless nymphs. Or use a systemic or contact insecticide to combat winged adults as well. Azalea petal blight fungus quickly ruins open blossoms of both azaleas and rhododendrons during warm, humid weather, turning flowers brown and mushy. Because spores form from resting bodies in petal debris from previous year, thorough cleanup of infected blossoms reduces infection later. To control an infection, spray with Daconil (chlorothalonil) according to label.

Wind and soil salts burn leaf edges; windburn shows up most often on new foliage, salt burn on older leaves. Late frosts often cause deformed leaves. In extremely cold weather, sun and wind can severely damage plants; protect them by erecting a windbreak of burlap fastened to stakes. Protect roots against damage from alternate freezing and thawing by placing a mulch over the root system after the soil has frozen.

Prune evergreen azaleas by frequent pinching of tip growth from after flowering until July or August if you wish to have a compact plant with maximum flower production.

Prune large-flowered rhododendrons early in spring at bloom time if needed. Pruning in early spring will sacrifice some flower buds, but that is the best time for extensive pruning. Plant's energies will be diverted to dormant growth buds, which will then be ready to open early in the growing season. Tip-pinch young plants to make them bushy; prune older, leggy plants to restore shape by cutting back to side branch, leaf whorl, or cluster of dormant buds. (Some selections will not initiate new growth from dormant buds.) Clip or break off faded flower heads or spent clusters, taking care not to injure new buds and growth just beneath them. ▶

R

KINDS OF RHODODENDRONS

Most people know rhododendrons as big, leathery-leafed shrubs with rounded clusters ("trusses") of stunning white, pink, red, or purple blossoms. But there are also dwarfs a few inches tall, giants that reach 40 ft. or even 80 ft. in their native southeast Asia, and a host of species and hybrids in every intermediate size, in a color range including scarlet, yellow, near-blue, and a constellation of blends of orange, apricot, and salmon.

The following sections list named selections by categories, to give you some idea of their adaptability to different climates and garden roles. Many of them are described later. These are the generally available kinds, only a portion of the best rhododendrons grown throughout the country.

Ironclad hybrids for cold winters. These can take −25°F: 'America', 'Boule de Neige', 'English Roseum', 'Ignatius Sargent', 'Nova Zembla', 'Parsons Gloriosum', 'PJM', 'President Lincoln', 'Roseum Elegans'.

Ironclad hybrids that tolerate heat. 'Album Elegans', 'Anah Kruschke', 'Anna Rose Whitney', 'Belle Heller', 'Caroline', 'Cheer', 'County of York', 'Cynthia', 'English Roseum', 'Fastuosum Flore Pleno', 'Holden', 'Nova Zembla', 'PJM', 'Roseum Elegans', 'Scintillation', 'Trude Webster', and Vulcan'.

RHODODENDRON RATINGS AND HARDINESS

Each plant in the list that follows includes a two-number rating (3/3, for example) assigned by the American Rhododendron Society. Flower quality is shown first and shrub quality second; 5 is superior, 4 above average, 3 average, 2 below average, 1 poor.

The list also gives each plant a cold-hardiness rating, which indicates minimum temperatures a mature plant can tolerate without serious injury. Heights given are for plants 10 years old; older plants may be taller, and crowded or heavily shaded plants may reach up faster. Bloom time given is approximate and varies with weather and location.

'A. Bedford'. 4/3. −5°F. To 6 ft. Lavender blue with darker flare. Large trusses. Late midseason.

'Album Elegans'. 2/3. −20°F. To 6 ft. White flowers tinged with fading pale mauve. Vigorous, somewhat open form. Late.

'America'. 3/3. −25°F. To 5 ft. tall and wide. Dark red. Late.

'Anah Kruschke'. 2/3. −10°F. To 5 ft. Lavender purple. Color mediocre, but plant has good foliage; tolerates heat, not fussy about soil. Midseason.

'Anna Rose Whitney'. 4/3. 5°F. Compact grower to 5 ft., with excellent foliage. Big trusses in rich, deep pink. Midseason. Heat tolerant.

'Antoon Van Welie'. 3/3. −5°F. Grows to 6 ft. Big trusses of 'Pink Pearl'–type, carmine pink flowers. Late midseason.

'Belle Heller'. 4/3. −10°F. To 5 ft. Pure white with gold blotch. Midseason. Sun, heat tolerant.

Rhododendron
'Anna Rose Whitney'

'Blue Diamond'. 5/4. 0°F. Compact, erect to 3 ft. Small leaves. Lavender blue blooms cover plant early to midseason. Takes sun in cooler areas.

'Blue Ensign'. 4/3. −15°F. Compact, well-branched, rounded plant grows to 4 ft. Leaves tend to spot. Lilac blue flowers have a striking dark spot in the upper petal. Midseason.

'Blue Peter'. 4/3. −10°F. Broad and sprawling to 4 ft.; needs pruning. Big trusses of purple-spotted lavender blue flowers. Midseason.

'Boule de Neige'. 3/3. −25°F. To 5 ft. Rounded plant with bright green leaves and snowball-like clusters of white flowers. Midseason.

'Bow Bells'. 3/4. 0°F. Compact, rounded to 4 ft. Round leaves; bronzy new growth. Bright pink, loose clusters of bell-like flowers. Midseason.

'Caroline'. 3/4. −15°F. To 6 ft. Lightly fragrant, orchid pink flowers. Midseason to late. Light green, twisted leaves. Heat tolerant.

R. carolinianum. CAROLINA RHODODENDRON. 3/3. −25°F. Native to mountains of the Carolinas and Tennessee. To 3–6 ft. tall and as broad or broader. Leaves turn purplish in cold winters. Tight clusters of pink flowers in midseason. 'Album' is similar but bears white flowers.

R. catawbiense. CATAWBA RHODODENDRON. 3/3. −25°F. Native to mountains from West Virginia to Alabama. To 5 ft., eventually much larger. Lavender purple flowers. Midseason. Ancestor of many heat-tolerant selections. 'Album' has pink buds opening to white with greenish yellow blotch.

R. chapmanii. CHAPMAN'S RHODODENDRON. 3/3. −5°F. Native to pine woods in northwest Florida. To 4 ft. tall, eventually to 6 ft., very upright. Rose pink, spotted or flecked flowers, with distinctive dark anthers, borne in round clusters up to 4 in. across. Leaves small, to 3 in. long, shiny, oblong. On list of federally endangered plants; be careful to buy only nursery-propagated plants. Heat tolerant. Midseason.

'Cheer'. 3/3. −10°F. Mound-shaped, glossy-leafed plant to 4 ft. Pink flowers. Early. Heat tolerant.

'Cunningham's White'. 2/3. −15°F. An old-timer. To 4 ft. tall; white blooms with greenish yellow blotch. Late midseason.

'Cynthia'. 4/3. −15°F. To 6 ft. Rosy crimson with blackish markings. Midseason. Old favorite for background. Heat tolerant.

'Dora Amateis'. 4/4. −15°F. To 3 ft. tall. Compact, small-foliaged plant; spreading, good for foreground. Profuse bloomer with green-spotted white flowers. Early midseason.

'Elizabeth'. 4/4. 0°F. Broad grower to 3 ft. tall, with medium-size leaves. Blooms very young. Bright red, waxy, trumpet-shaped flowers in clusters of three to six at branch ends and in upper leaf joints. Main show early; often reblooms in autumn. Very susceptible to fertilizer burn, salts in water.

'English Roseum'. 3/4. −25°F. Erect shrub to 6 ft. Lavender blooms with yellowish green petal blotches. Midseason. Hardy to both cold and heat.

'Fastuosum Flore Pleno'. 3/3. −10°F. To 5 ft. Double mauve flowers in midseason. Dependable old-timer. Heat tolerant.

R. fortunei. FORTUNE'S RHODODENDRON. 4/4. −15°F. To 6 ft., eventually 12 ft., open and treelike. Very fragrant, waxy, blush pink to rosy lilac flowers, to 4 in. across. Attractive large, oblong leaves, to 8 in. long. Late.

'Furnival's Daughter'. 5/4. −5°F. To 5 ft. Bright pink flowers with deep red blotch. Midseason.

'Ginny Gee'. 5/5. −5°F. Striking 2-ft. plant with small leaves, dense growth. Covered with small flowers in early midseason. Blooms range from pink to white, with striped and dappled patterns.

'Gomer Waterer'. 3/4. −15°F. To 5 ft. White flushed lilac. Late midseason. Old-timer.

'Holden'. 3/3. −15°F. Compact grower to 4 ft. Rose red flowers marked with deeper red. Midseason. Heat tolerant.

'Janet Blair'. 4/3. −15°F. Vigorous plant to 6 ft. tall and spreading. Large, ruffled pastel flowers blend pink, cream, white, and gold; rounded trusses. Midseason to late.

'Jean Marie de Montague'. 3/4. 0°F. To 5 ft., with good foliage. Brightest scarlet red. Midseason.

'Johnny Bender'. 5/5. −5°F. To 4 ft. Glossy dark green leaves set off blood red flowers. Midseason.

'Lem's Stormcloud'. 4/4. −15°F. To 5 ft. Bright red flowers on large, erect trusses. Midseason.

'Leo'. 5/3. −5°F. To 5 ft., well clothed in large dark green leaves. Rounded to dome-shaped trusses packed with rich cranberry red blooms. Midseason.

'Loder's White'. 5/5. 0°F. Shapely form to 5 ft. Big trusses of blooms are white tinged pink when they open, turn pure white as they age. Midseason. Blooms freely even when young. Best white for most areas.

'Lodestar'. 4/4. −20°F. To 5 ft. Large white or palest lilac flowers marked deep greenish yellow. Midseason to late.

'Lord Roberts'. 3/3. −10°F. To 5 ft. Handsome dark green foliage and rounded trusses of black-spotted red flowers. Midseason to late. Plants grown in sun have more compact growth, bloom more profusely.

'Mars'. 4/3. −10°F. To 4 ft. Dark red. Late midseason. Handsome form, foliage, flowers.

R. maximum. ROSEBAY. 2/4. −25°F. Native from New England to Georgia, Alabama. Blossom is the state flower of West Virginia. Large, striking, densely foliaged, shrub or small tree with open habit, usually 10–15 ft. tall, but may reach 30 ft. Striking satiny, dark green leaves, 4–10 in. long. Small clusters of many rose or purplish pink, 1½-in. flowers; white centers, green freckles. Tolerates full shade. Late to very late.

'Molly Ann'. 4/5. −10°F. Compact grower to 2 ft. Rose-colored, upright trusses are set against round leaves. Midseason.

'Mrs. Furnival'. 5/5. −10°F. Compact, to 4 ft. Tight, round trusses of clear pink flowers; light brown blotch in upper petals. Late midseason.

R

R. mucronulatum. KOREAN RHODODENDRON. 4/3. −25°F. Deciduous azalea-like rhododendron with open growth to 5 ft. Makes up for bare branches by very early bloom. Flowers are generally bright purple. There is a pink form, 'Cornell Pink'.

'Nova Zembla'. 3/3. −25°F. To 5 ft. Profuse red flowers come late in the season. Hardy to both cold and heat.

'Parsons Gloriosum'. 2/2. −25°F. To 5 ft., upright but fairly compact. Pinkish lavender flowers. Midseason to late.

'Patty Bee'. 5/5. −10°F. Dense, moundlike growth to 1½ ft. Leaves are small, giving plant a finely textured look. Trumpet-shaped yellow flowers cover plant in midseason.

'Pink Pearl'. 3/3. −5°F. To 6 ft. or more; open, rangy growth without pruning. Rose pink, tall trusses in midseason.

'PJM'. 4/4. −25°F. To 4 ft. Lavender-pink blooms come early. Foliage turns mahogany in winter. Takes heat as well as cold.

'President Lincoln'. 2/3. −25°F. To 6 ft. Lilac-toned lavender pink with bronze blotch. Midseason to late.

'Purple Splendour'. 4/3. −10°F. Informal growth to 4 ft. Ruffled, deep purple blooms blotched black purple. Midseason. Easy to grow.

'Ramapo'. 3/4. −20°F. Dense, spreading, to 2 ft. in sun, taller in shade. Dusty blue-green new growth. Violet blue flowers cover plant midseason.

'Roseum Elegans'. 2/3. −25°F. Vigorous plant to 6 ft., with small trusses of pinkish lilac flowers. Midseason to late. Hardy to cold and heat.

'Sapphire'. 4/4. 0°F. Twiggy, rounded, dense shrublet to 1½ ft., with tiny gray-green leaves. Small, bright blue, azalea-like flowers. Early.

'Sappho'. 3/2. −5°F. To 6 ft. White with dark purple spot in throat. Midseason. Easy to grow; gangly without pruning. Use at back of border.

'Scarlet Wonder'. 5/5. −10°F. Outstanding dwarf (to 2 ft. tall) of compact growth. Shiny, quilted foliage forms backdrop for many bright red blossoms. Midseason.

'Scintillation'. 4/5. −15°F. Compact, 5-ft. plant covered in lustrous, dark green leaves. Rounded trusses carry gold-throated pink flowers. Midseason. Heat tolerant.

'Sumatra'. 4/4. −15°F. Dwarf to 2 ft. tall, with deep pure red flowers. Midseason.

'Trude Webster'. 5/4. −10°F. Strong, 5-ft. plant, with large leaves. Huge trusses of clear pink flowers, midseason. One of best pinks. Heat tolerant.

'Unique'. 3/5. 5°F. To 4 ft.; outstanding neat, rounded, compact habit. Apricot buds open to tight, rounded trusses in deep cream fading to light yellow. Early midseason.

'Van Nes Sensation'. 3/4. 0°F. To 5 ft. Pale lilac flowers in large trusses. Midseason. Strong grower.

'Vulcan'. 3/4. −5°F. To 4 ft. Bright brick red flowers. Midseason to late. New leaves can grow past flower buds, partly hiding blooms. Heat tolerant.

R. yakushimanum. 4/4. −20°F. Dense, spreading growth to 3 ft. Gray-felted new foliage; older leaves have heavy tan or white felt beneath. Clear pink bells changing to white. Late midseason. Selections range from 'Ken Janeck', a large (and large-leafed) form with very pink flowers, to 'Yaku Angel', with pink-tinged buds opening to pure white.

KINDS OF EVERGREEN AZALEAS

The evergreen azaleas fall into more than a dozen groups and species, though an increasing number of hybrids have such mixed parentage that they don't conveniently fit into any group. The following includes some of the most popular groups. Unless noted, bloom is in spring. In greenhouses, plants can be forced for winter bloom. Sizes vary within groups.

Belgian Indica Hybrids. Indoor plants. This group of hybrids was developed for greenhouse forcing. They have lush, full foliage and large, profuse blossoms. Most widely sold include 'Albert and Elizabeth', white and pink; 'California Sunset', salmon pink with white border; 'Chimes', dark red; 'Mardi Gras', salmon with white border; 'Mission Bells', red semidouble; 'Mme Alfred Sanders', cherry red; 'Orange Sanders', salmon orange; 'Orchidiflora', orchid pink; 'Paul Schame', salmon; and 'Red Poppy'.

Beltsville Hybrids. Zones US, MS, LS. Hardy to 0°F. Similar to the Glenn Dale Hybrids. 'Casablanca Improved' is a large white single; 'Eureka' and 'Guy Yerkes', pink flowers; 'Polar Bear' is an exceptionally hardy white.

Carla Hybrids. Zones MS, LS. Hardy to 5–15°F. Bred at North Carolina State University. Single to double flowers in pink, red, or white. Midseason.

Gable Hybrids. Zones US, MS, LS. Bred to produce azaleas of Kurume type that take 0°F temperatures. In the Upper South, they may lose some leaves. Bloom heavily in midseason. Frequently sold are 'Caroline Gable', bright pink; 'Herbert', purple; 'Louise Gable', pink; 'Pioneer', pink; 'Purple Splendor'; 'Purple Splendor Compacta' (not as rangy as 'Purple Splendor'); 'Rosebud', pink; and 'Rose Greeley', white.

Girard Hybrids. Zones US, MS, LS. Hardy to −5°F or somewhat colder. These originated from Gable crosses. Examples are 'Girard's Fuchsia', reddish purple; 'Girard's Hot Shot', orange red with orange-red fall and winter foliage; 'Girard's Roberta', with 3-in. double pink flowers.

Glenn Dale Hybrids. Zones US, MS, LS. Hardy to 0°F. Developed primarily for hardiness, but drop some leaves in cold winters. Some are tall and rangy, others low and compact. Growth rate from slow to rapid. Some have small leaves like Kurume Hybrids; others have large leaves. Familiar selections are 'Anchorite', orange; 'Aphrodite', pale pink; 'Buccaneer', orange red; 'Copperman', orange red; 'Everest', white; 'Fashion', orange red; 'Geisha', white with red stripes; 'Glacier', white; 'Martha Hitchcock', white edged with magenta; and 'Treasure', white edged with pale pink.

Kaempferi Hybrids. Zones US, MS, LS. Based on *R. kaempferi*, the torch azalea, a cold-hardy plant with orange-red flowers. These are somewhat hardier than Kurume Hybrids, to −15°F, taller and more open in growth, nearly leafless in coldest winters. Profuse bloom. Among those sold are 'Fedora', salmon rose; 'Holland', late, large red; 'John Cairns', orange red; and 'Palestrina', white.

Kurume Hybrids. Zones US, MS, LS, CS. Hardy to 5–10°F. Compact, twiggy plants, densely foliaged with small, glossy leaves. Small flowers are borne in incredible profusion. Plants mounded or tiered, handsome even out of bloom. Widely used in foundation plantings, to point of cliché. Many selections available; the most widespread are 'Coral Bells', pink; 'Hershey's Red', bright red; 'Hexe', crimson; 'H. H. Hume', white; 'Hino-crimson', bright red; 'Hinodegiri', cerise red; 'Sherwood Orchid', red violet; 'Sherwood Red', orange red; and 'Snow'.

Kurume Evergreen Azalea

North Tisbury Hybrids. Zones US, MS, LS. Hardy to about 0°F. Low, spreading habit; naturals for ground covers. Some of the best include 'Alexander', very hardy, bronze fall foliage, red-orange flowers; 'Pink Cascade; and 'Red Fountain', with dark red-orange blooms.

Robin Hill Hybrids. Zones US, MS, LS. Hardy to 5–10°F. A large group that got its start more than 50 years ago. These medium-size plants bloom late; large flowers somewhat resemble those of Satsuki Hybrids. There are so many good ones—several with "Robin Hill" in their names—that it's hard to single out a few. Try 'Betty Ann Voss', pink; 'Conversation Piece', pink with light center; 'Hilda Niblett', light and deep pink and white; 'Nancy of Robin Hill', pink with red blotch; and 'Robin Hill Gillie', red orange.

Rutherfordiana Hybrids. Zone CS. Greenhouse plants, good in garden to 20°F; need midday shade. Bushy 2–4-ft. plants with handsome foliage. Flowers intermediate between those of Kurumes and Belgian Indicas. Selections include 'Alaska', white; 'Constance', light orchid pink; 'Dorothy Gish', brick red; 'Firelight', rose red; 'L. J. Bobbink', orchid pink; 'Purity', white; 'Rose Queen', deep pink; 'White Gish', pure white.

Satsuki Hybrids. Zones US, MS, LS, CS. Includes azaleas referred to as Gumpo and Macrantha Hybrids. Hardy to 5°F. Plants low growing, some make nice ground covers. Large flowers come late. Popular selections: 'Bunkwa', blush pink; 'Flame Creeper', orange red; 'Gumpo', white; 'Gumpo Pink', rose pink; 'Hi Gasa', bright pink; 'Macrantha Pink', bright pink; 'Macrantha Red', salmon red; 'Rosaeflora', rose pink; 'Shinnyo-No-Tsuki', violet red with white center; and 'Wakebisu', salmon pink.

Southern Indica Hybrids. Zones MS, LS, CS. Azaleas selected from Belgian Indica Hybrids for their vigor and hardiness. Most take temperatures of 10–20°F, but some are damaged at even the upper end of that range. They generally grow faster, more vigorously, and taller than other kinds of evergreen azaleas. Popular choices sold include 'Brilliant', carmine red; 'Duc de Rohan', salmon pink; 'Fielder's White'; 'Formosa' (also sold as 'Coccinea', 'Phoenicia', 'Vanessa'), brilliant rose purple; 'George Lindley Taber', light pink; 'Imperial Countess', deep salmon pink; 'Imperial Princess', rich pink; 'Imperial Queen', pink; 'Iveryana', white with orchid streaks; 'Little John', a dense bush to 6 ft. (despite its name), with burgundy foliage and

'Fielder's White'
Southern Indica
Evergreen Azalea

a few deep red flowers; 'Mrs. G. G. Gerbing', white; 'Orange Pride', bright orange; 'President Claeys', orange red; 'Pride of Dorking', brilliant red; 'Pride of Mobile', deep rose pink; 'Southern Charm' (may be sold as 'Judge Solomon'), watermelon pink; and 'White April'.

R. mucronatum ('Indica Alba', 'Ledifolia Alba'). Zones US, MS, LS, CS. Spreading growth to 6 ft. (but usually 3 ft.); large, hairy leaves. White or greenish flowers 2½–3 in. across; early. 'Indica Rosea' ('Ledifolia Rosea') has white flowers flushed and blotched with rose; it blooms very early (about a month before the species). 'Sekidera' is white flushed reddish purple. 'Delaware Valley White' is slightly more cold tolerant.

KINDS OF DECIDUOUS AZALEAS

Few deciduous shrubs equal deciduous azaleas in show and range of color. Flowers of their evergreen relatives can't match these in the yellow, orange, and flame red range or in bicolor contrasts. Fall foliage is often brilliant orange red to maroon. Deciduous azaleas tend to be less particular about soil and watering than most evergreen types. Many deciduous species are native to the East and South. These plants are becoming increasingly popular. In high-rainfall, high-humidity areas, powdery mildew can be a serious problem for many Ghent, Knap Hill, and Mollis Hybrids.

Aromi Hybrids. Zones US, MS, LS, CS. Bred for hardiness from native heat-tolerant species and Exbury Hybrids by Dr. Eugene Aromi of Mobile, Alabama, these azaleas have striking incandescent blooms and large flower trusses; all are very tolerant of summer heat. Upright form to 12–15 ft. tall, but in some areas may reach only half that size. Popular selections include 'Aromi Sunny Side Up', golden yellow with egg-yolk blotch; 'Aromi Sunrise', orange red buds opening to light orange with dark orange center; 'Carousel', pale pink with bright, contrasting golden blotch; 'Centerpiece', white with yellow spot; 'Sunstruck', pale yellow buds open to lemon yellow with darker patch. Midseason.

Ghent Hybrids. Zones US, MS. Many are hardy to −25°F. Upright growth variable in height. Flowers generally smaller than those of Mollis Hybrids. Colors include shades of yellow, orange, umber, pink, and red. Midseason.

Knap Hill–Exbury Hybrids. Zones US, MS, LS. Hardy to −25°F. Spreading to upright form, 4 to 6 ft. tall. Flowers large (3–5 in.), in clusters of seven to eighteen, can be ruffled or fragrant, white through pink and yellow to orange and red, often with contrasting blotches.

Knap Hill–Exbury
Deciduous Azalea

Both Knap Hill and Exbury azaleas come from same original crosses; first crosses were made at Knap Hill (in England), and subsequent improvements were made at both Exbury (also in England) and Knap Hill. The "Rothschild" azaleas are Exbury plants.

Midseason to late bloom. Choose from named selections to be sure of color and flower size. Some of the best are 'Cannon's Double', pink;

'Gibraltar', orange; 'Homebush', double deep pink; 'Klondyke', golden tangerine; 'Oxydol', white with yellow markings. Don't consider all seedlings inferior plants, however—but do select them in bloom.

Mollis Hybrids. Zones US, MS. Hardy to −25°F. Hybrids of *R. molle* and *R. japonicum*. Upright to 4–5 ft.; 2½–4-in.-wide flowers carried in clusters of seven to thirteen. Blossom color ranges from chrome yellow through poppy red. New growth has a light skunky fragrance, but foliage turns a lovely yellow to orange in fall. Very heavy bloom in midseason.

Viscosum Hybrids. Zones US, MS. Hardy to −15°F. Hybrids between Mollis azaleas and *R. viscosum*. Deciduous shrubs with flower colors of Mollis Hybrids but fragrance of *R. viscosum*. Late.

NATIVE WILD HONEYSUCKLES

The South is home to almost all of the deciduous azaleas indigenous to North America. Many are intensely fragrant (hence their name, wild honeysuckle); their leaves may turn brilliant fall colors. Purchase only nursery-propagated plants, and plant them in small groves or drifts in filtered light below native trees. Native wild honeysuckles include *Rhododendron alabamense, R. arborescens, R. atlanticum, R. austrinum, R. bakeri, R. calendulaceum, R. canescens, R. flammeum, R. oblongifolium, R. periclymenoides, R. prinophyllum, R. prunifolium, R. serrulatum, R. vaseyi,* and *R. viscosum.*

R. alabamense. ALABAMA AZALEA. Zones MS, LS. Hardy to −5°F. Native to Alabama, Georgia. Grows 5–6 ft. tall and spreads by suckering to form colonies. Highly fragrant white flowers usually blotched with yellow. Early.

R. arborescens. SWEET AZALEA. Zones US, MS, LS. Hardy to −10°F. Native to mountains from Pennsylvania to Alabama. Erect, open shrub grows to 8 ft. (possibly 20 ft.) tall. Fragrant white to pale pink flowers appear late, after leaves have expanded.

R. atlanticum. COAST AZALEA. Zones US, MS, LS, CS. Hardy to −15°F. Native from Delaware to South Carolina. Suckering shrub to 3–6 ft. tall, with white to pink fragrant, somewhat sticky flowers early, before or as leaves expand. Hybrids between this species and *R. periclymenoides* were discovered along the Choptank River in Maryland, and named Choptank River Hybrids. Available by mail order, they're noted for fragrant spring blooms in rose, yellow, cream, orange, and white.

R. austrinum. FLORIDA FLAME AZALEA. Zones US, MS, LS, CS. Hardy to 5°F. Native to northern and western Florida and southern parts of Georgia, Alabama, Mississippi. To 8–10 ft. tall, with fragrant flowers that may be pale yellow, cream, pink, orange, or red in color. One of the easiest native azaleas to grow. Tolerates heat, humidity, drought. Early.

R. bakeri. CUMBERLAND AZALEA. Zones US, MS. Hardy to −15°F. Native to mountains of Kentucky, Virginia, Tennessee, Georgia, Alabama. Grows 3–8 ft. tall. Flowers range from yellow and orange to (usually) red. Late midseason. Does not like long, hot summers.

R. calendulaceum. FLAME AZALEA. Zones US, MS, LS. Hardy to −25°F. Native to mountain regions from southern Pennsylvania to Georgia. Grows to 4–8 ft. or taller. Clusters of 2-in.-wide yellow, red, orange, or scarlet flowers. Late. A very important parent of many hybrid deciduous azaleas. Dislikes extended summer heat and drought.

R. canescens. PIEDMONT AZALEA. Zones US, MS, LS, CS. Hardy to −5°F. Native from North Carolina to Texas. Large (to 10-ft.), suckering shrub with fragrant white to pink or rose flowers. Early. Sun or shade.

R. flammeum. OCONEE AZALEA. Zones US, MS, LS, CS. Hardy to −15°F. Native to South Carolina, Georgia. Fairly compact to 6 ft., with clusters of 1¾-in. flowers, midseason. Color from red and pink to yellow or orange. Resembles *R. calendulaceum*, but more heat and drought tolerant.

R. oblongifolium. TEXAS AZALEA. Zones US, MS, LS, CS. Hardy to −5°F. Native to East Texas, Oklahoma, and Arkansas. To 6 ft. tall. Slightly fragrant white flowers to 1 in. long appear in midseason, after leaves emerge.

R. periclymenoides (R. nudiflorum). PINXTERBLOOM AZALEA. Zones US, MS, LS. Hardy to −15°F. Native from Massachusetts to Ohio and North Carolina. Suckering shrub grows 2–3 ft. high, sometimes much taller. Pale pink to deep pink, fragrant, 1½-in. flowers appear in midseason, as leaves expand. 'Paxton's Blue' has showy, lavender blue flowers.

R. prinophyllum (P. roseum). ROSESHELL AZALEA. Zones US, MS, LS. Hardy to −25°F. Native from southern Quebec to Virginia, west to Missouri and Oklahoma. To 4–8 ft. tall, occasionally much taller; bright pink (sometimes white), 1½-in. flowers with strong clove fragrance. Blooms in midseason, before or with leaves.

R. prunifolium. PLUMLEAF AZALEA. Zones US, MS, LS, CS. Hardy to −15°F. Native to Georgia and Alabama. To 10 ft., with orange-red to bright red flowers. This is the signature plant of Callaway Gardens in Pine Mountain, Georgia. One of the latest azaleas, blooming in July and August.

Rhododendron prunifolium

R. serrulatum. SWEET AZALEA, SOUTHERN SWAMP AZALEA. Zones US, MS, LS, CS. Hardy to −5°F. Native from Georgia and Florida to Louisiana. Tall shrub, to 12–20 ft., with reddish branches. Extremely fragrant white flowers, sometimes tinged cream, pale pink, or pale violet, bloom among new foliage. Leaves small, to 3 in. long, distinctly toothed. Blooms very late, July into September.

R. vaseyi. PINKSHELL AZALEA. Zones US, MS. Hardy to −20°F. Native to mountains of North Carolina. Upright, irregular habit; spreads to 15 ft. wide. Light pink flowers in clusters of five to eight in midseason.

R. viscosum. SWAMP AZALEA. Zones US, MS, LS, CS. Hardy to −25°F. Native to damp or wet ground, Maine to Alabama. To 5–8 ft. tall. Flowers are white (sometimes pink), 2 in. long, sticky on the outside, with a powerful clove scent. Blooms late, often in June.

ﾠ RHODOPHIALA bifida

OXBLOOD LILY

Amaryllidaceae

BULB

✂ ZONES MS, LS, CS

☼ SUN

◖◗ REGULAR OR MODERATE WATER

Rhodophiala bifida

South American bulb resembling a small amaryllis (*Hippeastrum*), with a few footlong leaves and a 1-ft. flower stalk bearing two to six bright red, 2-in.-long flowers with narrow petals. Plants spread willingly and put on a fine show in fall. It is considered by some to be *Hippeastrum advenum*. Very dependable; tolerates heavy clay soils, heat, drought. Often found in old cemeteries in Texas.

ﾠ RHODOTYPOS scandens

BLACK JETBEAD

Rosaceae

DECIDUOUS SHRUB

✂ ZONES US, MS, LS

☼ ◖ ● SUN OR SHADE

◖ REGULAR WATER

Rhodotypos scandens

Trouble-free shrub for light shade or tough soil conditions, with interesting, showy flowers and fruits. Native to Japan and China. Shrub grows moderately fast to 6 ft., often much more in the wild, with widespreading branches that leaf out early in spring. Single flowers, 2 in. across, appear in late spring and early summer, followed by pea-size, jet black, shiny berries, four per cluster, in fall and persisting through winter. Leaves are opposite, bright green, oval, prominently veined and toothed, to about 4 in. long and 2 in. wide.

Thin out overcrowded mature plants by cutting back old branches to base, after flowering.

ﾠ RHOEO spathacea (R. discolor)

MOSES-IN-THE-CRADLE

Commelinaceae

PERENNIAL

✂ ZONES CS, TS; OR INDOORS

☼ ◖ ● SUN OR SHADE

◖ REGULAR WATER

Rhoeo spathacea

Stems to 8 in. high. Leaf tufts grow to 6–12 in. wide, with a dozen or so broad, sword-shaped, rather erect leaves that are dark green above and deep purple underneath. Flowers are interesting rather than beautiful; the small, white, three-petaled blooms are crowded into boat-shaped bracts borne down among leaves. Selection 'Variegata' has leaves striped red and yellowish green.

Avoid overwatering; try to keep water out of leaf axils. Tough plant that takes high or low light intensity, casual watering, low humidity, and heat. Plant most often grown in pots or in hanging baskets; grown as ground cover and edging in Florida.

RHUBARB

Polygonaceae

PERENNIAL GROWN FROM RHIZOME

✂ ZONES US, MS, LS, CS

☼ ◖ SOME SHADE IN LOWER AND COASTAL SOUTH

◖ WATER FREELY DURING ACTIVE GROWTH

◊ LEAVES ARE POISONOUS IF INGESTED; USE STEMS ONLY

Rhubarb

Big, elongated, heart-shaped, crinkled leaves and red-tinted leafstalks are showy enough to qualify for display spot in garden. Delicious leafstalks are used like fruit in sauces and pies. Flowers are insignificant, in spikelike clusters. Preferred selections are 'Cherry' ('Crimson Cherry'), 'MacDonald', and 'Strawberry', all of which have red stalks; and 'Victoria', with greenish stalks.

Grows best in Upper South; needs some winter chill for thick stems, good red color. Plant divisions (containing at least one bud) in late winter or early spring. Set tops of divisions at soil line; space 3–4 ft. apart.

Permit plants to grow for two full seasons before you begin harvesting leafstalks. During the next spring, you can pull off leafstalks for 4 or 5 weeks; older, huskier plants will provide up to 8 weeks of pulling. Harvest leafstalks by grasping each near base of plant and pulling sideways and then outward; do not cut leafstalks, since cutting with a knife leaves a stub that will decay. Never remove all leaves from a single plant. Stop harvesting when slender leafstalks appear on plant. After final harvest, feed and water freely; cut out any blossom stalks that appear.

In the Lower South, best started from seed and harvested twice: pull outer stalks in spring, remaining center stalks in fall. In the Coastal South, set out divisions in the fall for winter–spring harvest (plants tend to rot in heat of late spring, summer).

SOUTHERN HERITAGE PLANTS
IDENTIFIED BY SYMBOL ﾠ

R

RHUS

SUMAC

Anacardiaceae

EVERGREEN OR DECIDUOUS SHRUBS OR TREES

ZONES VARY BY SPECIES

FULL SUN, EXCEPT AS NOTED

REGULAR TO LITTLE WATER

Rhus typhina

Of the ornamental sumacs, deciduous kinds are extremely hardy; they are noted for brilliant fall color and, on female plants, showy clusters of (usually) red fruits. Tend to produce suckers, especially if roots are disturbed by cultivation. Evergreen species less hardy. All species thrive in most soils, if well drained; soggy soils can kill them.

R. aromatica. FRAGRANT SUMAC. Deciduous shrub. Zones US, MS, LS, CS. Native to eastern North America. Fast growing to 3–5 ft. tall, sprawling much wider. Leaves to 3 in. long, with three leaflets; fragrant when brushed against or crushed. Foliage turns red in fall. Tiny yellowish flowers in spring, small red fruit in late summer. Coarse bank cover, ground cover for poor or dry soils. Two available selections are 'Green Mound' (to 4 ft.) and 'Gro-low' (to about 2 ft.).

R. copallina. SHINING SUMAC. Deciduous shrub, small tree. Zones US, MS, LS, CS. Native to eastern U.S. Grows quite fast to 10–25 ft. tall, becoming very broad as it matures, with a picturesque flat top. A particularly ornamental sumac, but produces suckers and self-seeds freely into large colonies, so unsuitable for a small garden. Leaves are shiny, dark green, with 9 to 21 leaflets. Fall color varies from plant to plant, so purchase in fall for a reliably rich crimson, red-purple, or scarlet display. Showy chartreuse flower spikes in summer, on females, followed by fuzzy clusters of crimson fruits that persist into winter. Grows on dry, poor, rocky soils.

R. cotinus. See Cotinus coggygria

R. glabra. SMOOTH SUMAC. Deciduous shrub or small tree. Zones US, MS, LS, CS. Native to much of North America. Upright to 10 ft., sometimes treelike to 20 ft. In the wild, spreads by underground roots to form large patches. Looks much like *R. typhina*, but usually grows lower and does not have velvety branches. Leaves divided into 11 to 23 toothed, rather narrow, 2–5-in.-long leaflets, deep green above and whitish beneath; turn scarlet in fall. Inconspicuous flowers are followed by showy, erect clusters of scarlet fruit that remain on bare branches from fall well into winter. Garden use same as for *R. typhina*. 'Laciniata' has deeply cut, slashed leaflets, giving it a fernlike appearance.

R. trilobata. SQUAWBUSH, SKUNKBUSH. Deciduous shrub. Zones US, MS, LS. Native from Illinois southwest to Texas. Similar to *R. aromatica*, but scent of bruised leaves considered unpleasant by most people. Clumping habit makes it a natural low hedge. Brilliant yellow to red fall color.

R. typhina. STAGHORN SUMAC. Deciduous shrub or small tree. Zones US, MS, LS. Upright to 15 ft. (sometimes 30 ft.) tall, spreading wider. Very similar to *R. glabra*, but branches are covered with short, velvety brown hairs and resemble a deer's antler "in velvet." Leaves divided into 11 to 31 toothed, 5-in.-long leaflets; foliage is deep green above, grayish beneath, turns rich red in fall. Tiny greenish blossoms in 4–8-in.-long clusters appear in early summer; these are followed by clusters of fuzzy crimson fruit that lasts all winter, gradually turning brown. 'Laciniata', cutleaf staghorn sumac, with deeply cut leaflets, does not grow quite as large as the species and develops outstanding fall color.

Both *R. typhina* and *R. glabra* take extreme heat and cold. Big divided leaves give tropical effect; fall show is brilliant (for best effect, plant among evergreens). Bare branches make fine winter silhouette; fruit is decorative. Both species will grow in large containers. Their aggressive colonization by root suckers can be a problem, especially in small gardens.

R. virens. EVERGREEN SUMAC. Evergreen shrub. Zones LS, CS. Native to Texas and Southwest. Generally makes a mounding clump about 6 ft. tall and wide, with lowest branches close to or touching ground, but can reach 12 ft. high. Relatively slow growing. New leaves often reddish; mature leaves (to 6 in. long, 5 to 9 leaflets) glistening dark green, with purple winter tints. Honey-scented white flowers in late summer attract bees and butterflies and are followed by plump, fuzzy clusters of red fruits. Tolerates dry, rocky, or chalky soils. Sun or light shade.

RIBBON GRASS. See PHALARIS arundinacea

RIBBON PLANT. See DRACAENA sanderana

RICE PAPER PLANT. See TETRAPANAX papyriferus

RICINUS communis

CASTOR BEAN

Euphorbiaceae

TENDER SHRUB USUALLY TREATED AS ANNUAL

ZONES CS, TS

FULL SUN

REGULAR WATER

SEEDS (OR BEANS) ARE HIGHLY POISONOUS

Ricinus communis

Bold and striking plant. Can provide tall screen or leafy background in a hurry; grows to 6–15 ft. in a season. In the Tropical South, will live over winter and become quite woody and treelike. Should not be planted in areas where small children play—the poisonous seeds are attractive. Foliage or seeds occasionally cause severe contact allergies as well. To prevent seed formation, pinch off the burrlike seed capsules while they are small.

Large-lobed leaves are 1–3 ft. across on vigorous young plants, smaller on older plants. Unimpressive small, white flowers are borne in clusters on foot-high stalks in summer, followed by attractive prickly husks that contain seeds. Grown commercially for castor oil extracted from seeds. Many selections available: 'Dwarf Red Spire' is lower-growing plant (6 ft.) with red leaves and seedpods; 'Sanguineus' has blood red foliage and stems; 'Zanzibarensis' has very large green leaves.

RIVER OATS. See CHASMANTHIUM latifolium

ROBINIA

LOCUST

Fabaceae (Leguminosae)

DECIDUOUS SHRUBS OR TREES

ZONES US, MS, LS, CS

FULL SUN

MODERATE TO LITTLE WATER

BARK, LEAVES, AND SEEDS ARE POISONOUS IF INGESTED

Leaves are divided much like feathers into many roundish leaflets; clusters of sweet pea–shaped, white or pink flowers midspring to early summer. Fairly fast growing and well adapted to dry, hot areas. Will take poor soil.

Robinia pseudoacacia

Drawbacks: brittle wood, aggressive roots; plants often spread by suckers.

R. ambigua. Name given to hybrids between *R. pseudoacacia* and *R. viscosa,* a seldom-grown pink-flowering locust. The following are best-known selections:

'Decaisneana'. To 40–50 ft. tall, 20 ft. wide. Flowers like those of *R. pseudoacacia* but pale pink.

'Idahoensis'. IDAHO LOCUST. Tree of moderately fast growth to shapely 40 ft. Bright magenta rose flowers in 8-in. clusters; one of showiest of locusts in bloom.

'Purple Robe'. Resembles 'Idahoensis' but has reddish bronze new growth and darker, purple-pink flowers; also blooms longer and starts 2 weeks earlier.

R. hispida. ROSE ACACIA, BRISTLY LOCUST. Shrub. Native from Virginia and Kentucky to Georgia and Alabama. Small, showy shrub that will form colonies from root suckers. Extremely invasive in good soil. Grows to 7 ft., sometimes 10 ft. Stems bristly. Leaves blue green, to 10 in. long, with 7 to 15 leaflets. Rose or pale purplish pink flowers in 4 in. dangling clusters in late spring. Tolerates dry, poor soils. Use on dry banks, in naturalized settings. Available selections include the following:

'Casque Rouge'. Purplish pink flowers, and pinkish new growth.

'Flowering Globe'. Taller than species, to 18 ft., with long, 8–10-in clusters of dark pink flowers.

'Monument'. Narrow, conical form, to 13 ft., with flowers like species. Sometimes listed as a hybrid of *R. fertilis.*

R. pseudoacacia. BLACK LOCUST. Tree. Native to eastern and mid-western U.S. Fast growth to 75 ft., with rather open and sparse-branching habit. Deeply furrowed brown bark. Thorny branchlets. Leaves divided into 7 to 19 leaflets 1–2 in. long. Flowers white, fragrant, ½–¾ in. long, in dense, hanging clusters 4–8 in. long. Beanlike, 4-in.-long pods turn brown and hang on tree all winter.

Little valued in its native territory, but a favorite tree in Europe. Rot-resistant wood is sought after for fence posts. Bees make delicious honey from the nectar of its flowers. Black locust manufactures its own fertilizer through nitrogen-fixing root nodule bacteria and can colonize the poorest soil. Given some pruning and training in its early years, it can be a truly handsome flowering tree, but locust borer limits its usefulness in many areas; locust leaf miner is also a damaging pest, especially in Upper South.

Often used as street tree, but not good in narrow parking strips or under power lines. Wood is extremely hard; suckers are difficult to prune out where not wanted. Selections include the following:

'Frisia'. New growth nearly orange; mature leaves yellow, turning greener in summer heat. Thorns and new wood are red.

'Pyramidalis' ('Fastigiata'). Very narrow, columnar tree.

'Tortuosa'. Slow growing, with twisted branches. Few flowers in blossom clusters.

'Umbraculifera'. Dense, round headed. Usually grafted 6–8 ft. high on another locust to create a living green lollipop. Very few flowers.

ROBIN'S PLANTAIN. See ERIGERON pulchellus

ROCKROSE. See CISTUS

RODGERSIA

Saxifragaceae

PERENNIALS

ZONE US

PARTIAL SHADE

AMPLE WATER

Rodgersia aesculifolia

Native to China, Japan. Large plants with imposing leaves and clustered tiny flowers in plumes somewhat like those of astilbe. Primary feature is handsome foliage, which often takes on bronze tones in late summer. Plants spread by thick rhizomes, need rich soil. The different species hybridize freely. Showy in moist woodland or bog gardens.

R. aesculifolia. To 6 ft. Leaves are divided like fingers of hand into five to seven toothed, 10-in. leaflets; they resemble those of horsechestnut (*Aesculus*). Shaggy brown hairs on flower stalks, leaf stems, major leaf veins. White flowers.

R. henricii. Resembles *R. aesculifolia,* but leaves taper to a long point and flowers are purplish red.

R. pinnata. To 4 ft. Leaves have five to nine 8-in. leaflets. Red flowers.

R. podophylla. To 5 ft. Coppery green leaves divided into five 10-in. leaflets. Creamy flowers.

R. sambucifolia. To 3 ft. Leaves have up to eleven leaflets. Flat-topped flower clusters are white or pink.

R. tabularis (Astilboides tabularis). To 3 ft. Shield-shaped round leaves are 2 ft. wide. White flowers.

ROHDEA japonica

LILY OF CHINA, SACRED LILY

Liliaceae

PERENNIAL

ZONES MS, LS, CS

PARTIAL TO LIGHT SHADE

REGULAR OR LITTLE WATER

Rohdea japonica

Native to Japan and China. Useful, low-maintenance plant for massing in a shade garden. Evergreen, leathery leaves grow in thick, arching or erect tufts, each leaf to 2 ft. long, 2–3 in. wide. Pale yellow flowers bloom on small spikes low in the foliage in early spring; they're barely noticeable but are followed by showy red berries. Grows slowly; stands neglect; not fussy about soils. Several selections are available with white or creamy yellow stripes and variegations on the leaves. Combines well with plantings of fern, hosta, hellebore.

ROSA

ROSE

Rosaceae

DECIDUOUS OR EVERGREEN SHRUBS

ALL ZONES, EXCEPT AS NOTED

FULL SUN OR LIGHT SHADE

REGULAR WATER, EXCEPT AS NOTED

Hybrid Tea Rose
'Seashell'

The rose is undoubtedly the best-loved flower and most widely planted shrub in temperate parts of the world. Although mostly deciduous, can be evergreen in mild climates. Centuries of hybridizing have brought us the widest possible range of form and color. There are foot-high miniatures, tree-smothering climbers, flowers the size of a thumbnail or a salad plate, and all possible variations in between. Red, pink, and white are traditional rose colors, but you also find cream, yellow, orange, and blended and bicolored flowers, as well as magenta, purple, lavender, and even green.

Growing roses is not difficult, provided you choose types and selections suited to your climate, buy healthy plants, locate and plant them properly, and attend to their basic needs—water, nutrients, any necessary pest and disease control, and pruning. Despite the delicate appearance of their blooms, roses are often quite resilient plants. However, most require a good bit of maintenance.

CLIMATE

Every year, the American Rose Society rates modern roses (and an increasing number of old roses) on a scale of 1 to 10. The higher the rating, based on a national average of scores, the better the rose. The highest-rated roses are likely to perform well in most climates and so are good choices for novice growers. But a rating does not tell the entire story: A rose with a low rating may do especially well in certain areas but fail in others. The following general tips will help guide your selection. ▶

In areas with cool, wet springs, avoid types with a great number of petals. Many of these tend to "ball," opening poorly or not at all. The warm, humid summers in much of the South encourage foliar diseases—primarily mildew, rust, black spot. Choose disease-resistant roses; be sure to plant them in open areas where air circulation is good.

In the South, rose plants grow vigorously, but flowers also open rapidly. Selections with few (under 30) petals may go from bud to flat-open blossom in several hours. Flowers with more petals take longer to open and stay attractive longer. Some colors fade readily, and dark reds may sunburn. Therefore, roses are more satisfactory in most places if they receive light midday or afternoon shade. Avoid planting roses where they will receive reflected heat from light-colored walls or fences—especially in southern or western exposures. Best flowering is always in spring and fall (and in winter, in the Coastal and Tropical South); summer flower production may drop as plants approach dormancy during intensely hot weather.

In any area, the best place to see roses suitable for your climate is a municipal or private rose garden. The types and selections that are performing well are obviously good choices for your garden.

BUYING PLANTS

All roses are available as bare-root plants from late fall through early spring. In the Lower, Coastal, and Tropical South, you may plant bare-root roses throughout winter. Where the soil freezes, either plant in fall before ground freezes (then protect plants over winter), or plant in early spring after soil has thawed.

The majority of modern roses sold are budded plants: growth eyes of desired selections budded onto understock plants that furnish the root systems. The understocks are carefully selected to promote rapid top growth of the desired roses and make root systems capable of thriving in a wide range of soils and climates. For example, in Florida, hybrid roses should be budded onto nematode-resistant rootstocks of *Rosa fortuneana* or Dr. Huey. However, many old roses, species and their hybrids, and virtually all miniatures are "own-root" plants raised from cuttings. Usually, it makes no difference whether the plant is budded or own-root; either can grow well and produce fine flowers. Both kinds should be husky within a year or two. But own-root roses have one advantage: If an own-root plant is killed to the ground by cold (or mowed down by accident), it will regrow from the roots as the rose you want, not as understock.

Grandiflora Rose 'Camelot'

Bare-root plants are the best buy, and they are graded 1, 1½, or 2 according to strict standards. Plants graded 1 and 1½ are the most satisfactory, number 1 being the best. Number 2 plants may take longer to develop into decent bushes than the huskier numbers 1 and 1½. Retail nurseries and mail-order suppliers of modern roses usually offer only number 1 plants, and they will often replace plants that fail to grow. Old roses, shrub roses, and species roses (most commonly available by mail order) may be offered as budded plants that conform to the numbered grading standards, but some growers offer own-root (not budded) plants that may or may not be up to number 1 size. Catalogs usually state what size plant to expect.

During bare-root planting time, garden centers also may offer a selection of "boxed" roses with root systems encased in cartons. Markets, discount stores, and some garden centers sell dormant roses that have roots encased in moist material and enclosed in long, narrow bags. These packaged roses may be a good value, but buy them as soon as they appear for sale. Those displayed indoors on store shelves may be dried out or encouraged into premature growth by the indoor heating. Be prepared, too, for a number of these bargain roses to be mislabeled.

If you wish to plant roses during their growing season, you can buy roses growing in containers. This way, you can see and evaluate unfamiliar selections before purchase and quickly fill in gaps in your garden. But container roses are more expensive than bare-root plants. The best time to buy container-grown roses is mid- to late spring—when plants are fairly well rooted and can be set out before summer heat arrives. For standard bush and climbing roses, look for robust plants that are growing in large

containers (preferably 5-gal.): The root systems will have received little or no pruning to fit the container. Avoid plants that have been growing in containers for more than a year or those showing a fair amount of dead or twiggy growth. Miniature roses usually are sold in containers that range from 4-in. pots to 2-gal. cans. Healthy new growth and foliage are signs of a good miniature plant, regardless of container size.

LOCATION AND PLANTING

Generally, for best results, plant roses where they will receive full sun (exceptions noted under "Climate," page 359). Avoid planting where roots of trees or shrubs will take all the water and nutrients. To minimize any problem with foliar diseases, plant roses where air circulates freely (but not in path of regular, strong winds). Generous spacing between plants will also aid air circulation. How far apart to plant varies according to the climate and the growth habit of the roses. The colder the winter and shorter the growing season, the smaller the bushes will be; where growing season is long and winters are mild, bushes can attain greater size. In the Upper South, you might plant most vigorous sorts 3 ft. apart, whereas the same roses could require 6-ft. spacing in the Coastal South.

Soil for roses should drain reasonably well; if it does not, the best alternative is to plant in raised beds. Dig soil deeply, incorporating organic matter such as ground bark, peat moss, or compost; this preparation will help aerate dense clay soils and will improve moisture retention of sandy soils. Add complete fertilizer to soil at the same time, and dig supplemental phosphorus and potash into planting holes; this gets nutrients down at the level where roots can use them.

Healthy, ready-to-plant bare-root roses should have plump, fresh-looking canes (branches) and roots. Plants that have dried out slightly in shipping or in nursery can be revived by burying them, tops and all, for a few days in moist soil, sand, or sawdust. Just before planting any bare-root rose, it is a good idea to immerse entire plant in water for several hours to be certain all canes and roots are plumped up. Plant according to directions for bare-root planting (see page 449), making sure that holes are large enough that you can spread out roots without bending or cutting them back. Just before planting, cut back broken canes to below breaks, and broken roots to just above breaks. Set plant in hole so that bud union ("knob" from which canes grow) is just above soil level. After you have planted a rose and watered it well, mound soil over bud union and around canes to conserve moisture. Gradually (and carefully) remove soil or other material when leaves begin to expand.

If you plan to plant new roses in ground where rose bushes have been growing for 5 or more years, dig large (1½-ft.-wide, 1½-ft.-deep minimum) planting holes and replace old soil with fresh soil from another part of the garden. A condition known as "specific replant disease" inhibits growth of new roses planted directly in soil of established rose gardens.

ROUTINE CARE

All roses require water, nutrients, some pruning, and, at some point in their lifetimes, pest and disease control. (Exceptions are some antique and species roses that thrive on little water once established.)

Water. For best performance, the most popular garden roses need watering at all times during the growing season. Inadequate water slows or halts growth and bloom. Water deeply so that entire root system is moistened. How often to water depends on soil type and weather. Big, well-established plants need more water than newly set plants, but you will need to water new plants more frequently to get them established.

Mulch spread 2–3 in. deep will save water, prevent soil surface from baking hard, keep soil cool in summer, deter weed growth, and contribute to healthy soil structure (aerated, permeable by water and roots).

Nutrients. Regular applications of fertilizer will produce the most gratifying results. In the Lower, Coastal, and Tropical South, begin feeding established plants with complete commercial fertilizer in February. Elsewhere, give first feeding just as growth begins. Time fertilizer application in relation to bloom period. Ideal time to make subsequent feedings is when a blooming period has ended and new growth is just beginning for next cycle of bloom. Depending on expected arrival of freezing temperatures, stop feeding in late summer or fall, about 6 weeks before earliest normal hard frost. In areas that experience little or no subfreezing temperatures, fertilizing may continue until mid-October for crop of late fall flowers.

Dry commercial fertilizer, applied to soil, is most frequently used. A variation on that type is slow-release fertilizer that provides nutrients over prolonged period; follow directions on package for amount and frequency of applications. Liquid fertilizers are useful in smaller gardens utilizing basin watering. Most liquid fertilizers can also be sprayed on rose leaves, which absorb some nutrients immediately.

Pest and disease control. Roses require certain controls during the growing season. Principal rose pests are aphids, spider mites, and (in some areas) Japanese beetles, rose midges, and thrips. If you don't want to rely on natural predators, start controlling aphids and spider mites when they first appear in spring, and repeat as needed until they are gone or their numbers severely reduced. Spray with insecticidal soap, horticultural oil, or contact insecticide. To control Japanese beetles, apply carbaryl. Rose midge larvae in the soil are susceptible to applications of diazinon in granular or liquid drench form. Thrips do their damage inside flower buds, discoloring petals or disfiguring them so that buds may not open. Contact insecticide sprays can't reach most thrips hidden in petals; systemic insecticides are more successful.

LAZY ROSES

The following roses flourish with little or no spraying: China roses 'Louis Philippe' and 'Old Blush'; climbing Noisette rose 'Lamarque'; tea roses 'Duchesse de Brabant', 'Marie van Houtte', and 'Mrs. B. R. Cant'. Also try Lady Banks's rose *(R. banksiae)*; polyanthas 'Perle d'Or' and 'The Fairy'; David Austin English roses 'Abraham Darby' and 'Mary Rose'; and Bourbon roses 'Souvenir de la Malmaison' and 'Zépherine Drouhin'.

Powdery mildew, rust, and black spot are the Big Three of foliar diseases. First line of defense for all three is thorough cleanup of all dead leaves and other debris during the dormant season; this is simplest right after you have pruned plants. Then, before new growth begins, spray plants and soil with dormant-season spray of horticultural oil or lime sulfur (calcium polysulfide). This will destroy many disease organisms (as well as insect eggs) that might live over winter to reinfect plants in spring. During the growing season, apply Funginex (triforine) or Daconil (chlorothalonil) to control these diseases. Preventive measures usually are recommended for disease control; unchecked infections can weaken plants, especially if defoliation occurs from rust or black spot.

Chlorosis—evidenced by leaves turning light green to yellow while veins remain dark green—is not a disease but a symptom, usually of iron deficiency. This occurs in strongly alkaline soil. Iron chelate corrects chlorosis most quickly; iron sulfate also is effective but slower to act.

Leaves that show irregular patterning in yellow or cream indicate that the plant is infected with a mosaic virus. Some plants show the virus consistently; others display symptoms just occasionally. Although plants may appear to grow with vigor, virus infection does impair overall strength and productivity—and it can make foliage unsightly. Fortunately, it does not transfer from plant to plant by insects or pruning; it is transmitted in propagation—from infected rootstock or budwood. If you have a virused plant that is growing poorly or is unattractive, remove it from the garden.

Pruning. Done properly each year, pruning will contribute to the health and longevity of your rose plants. Sensible pruning is based on several facts about the growth of roses. First, blooms are produced on new growth. Unless pruning promotes strong new growth, flowers will come on spindly outer twigs and be of poor quality. Second, the more healthy wood you retain, the bigger the plant will be; and the bigger the plant, the more flowers it can produce. Nutrients are stored in woody canes, so a larger plant is a stronger plant. Therefore, prune conservatively; never chop down a vigorous, 6-ft. bush to 1½-ft. stubs unless you want only a few huge blooms for exhibition. Third, the best pruning time for most roses (certain

climbers and shrub types excepted) is at the end of dormant season when growth buds begin to swell. Exact time will vary according to locality.

General pruning guidelines. The following pruning practices apply to all roses except certain shrub and species roses. Special instructions for pruning those roses are included later in this section.

Use sharp pruning shears; make all cuts as shown in the Practical Gardening Dictionary under "Pruning" (see page 453). Remove obviously dead wood and wood with no healthy growth coming from it; branches that cross through the plant's center and any that rub against larger canes; branches that make bush appear lopsided; and any old and unproductive canes that strong new ones have replaced during past season. Cut back growth produced during previous year, making cuts above outward-facing buds (except for spreading types: Some cuts to inside buds will promote more height without producing many crossing branches). In general, remove one-third to no more than one-half the length of previous season's growth. Ideal result is a V-shaped bush with relatively open center.

Floribunda Rose 'Cathedral'

If any suckers (growth produced from understock, not the rose selection growing on it) are present, completely remove them. Dig down to where suckers grow from understock and pull them off with downward motion; that removes basal growth buds that would have produced additional suckers in subsequent years. Let wound air-dry before you replace soil around it.

Be certain you are removing a sucker rather than a new cane growing from the bud union of the budded selection. Usually you can note a distinct difference in foliage size and shape, as well as in size of thorns, on sucker growth. If in doubt, let the presumed sucker grow until you can establish its difference from cane. A sucker's blooms will be different; a flowerless, climbing cane from a bush rose is almost certainly a sucker.

Consider cutting flowers as a form of pruning. Cut off enough stem to support flower in vase, but don't deprive plant of too much foliage. Leave on plant a stem with at least two sets of five-leaflet leaves. Prune to outward-growing bud or to five-leaflet leaf.

The most widely planted modern roses—hybrid teas and grandifloras—can be pruned successfully according to these guidelines. A few additional tips apply to other popular types:

Floribunda, polyantha, and many shrub roses are grown for quantities of flowers, so amount of bloom rather than quality of individual flower is the objective. Cut back previous season's growth by only one-fourth, and leave as many strong new canes and stems as plant produced. Most produce more canes per bush than do hybrid teas and grandifloras. If you have a hedge of one selection, cut back all plants to uniform height.

Climbing roses may be divided into two general types: those that bloom in spring only (including a large category known as natural climbers, discussed in "Climbing roses," page 363), and those that bloom off and on in other seasons as well as in spring (including the very popular climbing sports of hybrid tea roses). All climbers should be left unpruned for the first 2 or 3 years after planting; remove only dead, weak, twiggy wood, allowing plants to get established and produce long, flexible canes. Most bloom comes from lateral branches that grow from long canes; most of those flowering branches develop when long canes are spread out horizontally (as along a fence). Types that bloom only in spring produce strong new growth after they flower; that new growth bears flowers the following spring. Prune these climbers just after they bloom, removing oldest canes with no signs of strong new growth. Repeat-flowering climbers (many are climbing sports of bush selections) are pruned at the same time you'd prune bush roses in your area. Remove oldest, unproductive canes and any weak, twiggy growth; cut back lateral branches on remaining canes to within two or three buds from canes.

Pillar roses are not quite bush or climber. They produce tall, somewhat flexible canes that bloom profusely without having to be trained horizontally. Prune pillar roses according to general guidelines for bush roses.

Tree roses, more properly called "standards," are an artificial creation: a bush rose budded onto a 2–3-ft.-high understock stem. Be sure to stake trunk securely to prevent its breaking from weight of bush it supports. A ½-in. metal pipe makes good permanent stake; use cross tie between stake and trunk to hold them secure. General pruning guidelines apply, with particular attention to maintaining symmetrical plant.

Miniature roses should be pruned back to at least half the height they attained during the previous year, removing all weak and twiggy stems. Some growers prune miniatures severely—back to the lowest outward-facing growth buds on the previous year's new stems.

Winter protection. Where winter low temperatures regularly reach 10°F and lower, winter protection is needed for nearly all modern roses. Low temperatures can kill exposed canes; repeated freezing and thawing will kill them by rupturing cells; and winter winds can fatally desiccate exposed canes because plants are unable to replace moisture from frozen soil.

A healthy, well hardened off plant withstands harsh winters better than a weak and actively growing one. Prepare plants for winter by timing your last fertilizer application so that bushes will have ceased putting on new growth by expected date of first sharp frost. Leave the last crop of blooms on plants to form hips (fruits), which will aid the ripening process by stopping growth. Keep plants well watered until soil freezes.

After a couple of hard freezes have occurred and night temperatures seem to remain consistently below freezing, mound soil over base of each bush to height of 1 ft. Get soil from another part of garden; do not scoop soil from around roses, exposing surface roots. Cut excessively long canes back to 2–4 ft. (the lower figure applies in colder regions); then, with soft twine, tie canes together to keep them from whipping around in wind. When mound has frozen, cover it with evergreen boughs, straw, or other fairly lightweight material that will act as insulation to keep mounds frozen. Your objective is to prevent alternate freezing and thawing of mound.

Remove protection in early spring when you are reasonably certain hard frosts will not recur. Gradually remove soil mounds as they thaw; do it carefully to avoid breaking new growth that may have begun sprouting under the soil.

Standards (tree roses) may be insulated in the same manner as for climbers, but they still may not survive, since the head of the tree is the most exposed. Some rosarians wrap with straw and burlap, then construct a plywood box to cover the insulated plant. Others dig their standards each year and pack the roots loosely in soil or other medium in a cool garage, basement, or shed, then replant in spring. A simpler technique is to grow standards in large containers and move them in fall to cool shed or garage where temperatures won't drop below 10°F.

TYPES OF ROSES

A renewed interest in old roses, continued developments of new hybrids, and breeding programs directed toward producing landscape shrubs have led to a greatly expanded offering of roses to the gardening public. For convenience, the following sections describe three broad categories: modern roses, old roses, and species and species hybrids.

Modern roses. Types described below constitute the majority of roses offered for sale and planted by hundreds of thousands each year. Those that have been All-America Rose Selections, recognized on the basis of their performance in nationwide test gardens, are indicated by "AARS"; those with an asterisk (*) before their names have been rated 8.0 or higher by the American Rose Society.

Hybrid teas. This, the most popular class of rose, outsells all other types combined. Flowers are large and shapely, generally produced one to a stem on plants that range from 2 ft. to 6 ft. or more, depending on the selection and climate zone. Thousands of selections have been produced since the first rose in the class, 'La France', appeared in 1867; hundreds are cataloged, and new ones appear each year. The most popular ones are listed in the following color groups:

Red: 'Chrysler Imperial' (AARS), *'Mr. Lincoln' (AARS), *'Olympiad' (AARS).

Pink: 'Bewitched' (AARS), 'Brigadoon' (AARS), *'Century Two', *'Color Magic' (AARS), *'Dainty Bess' (single), 'Duet' (AARS), *'First Prize' (AARS), *'Miss All-American Beauty' (AARS), 'Perfume Delight' (AARS), *'Royal Highness' (AARS), 'Secret' (AARS), 'Sheer Bliss' (AARS), *'Tiffany' (AARS), *'Touch of Class' (AARS).

Multicolors, blends: 'Broadway' (AARS), 'Chicago Peace', *'Double Delight' (AARS), *'Granada' (AARS), 'Just Joey', 'Medallion' (AARS), 'Rio Samba' (AARS), 'Seashell' (AARS), 'Voodoo' (AARS).

Orange, orange tones: 'Brandy' (AARS), *'Folklore', *'Fragrant Cloud', 'Tropicana' (AARS).

Yellow: *'Elina', 'Graceland', 'King's Ransom' (AARS), 'Oregold' (AARS), 'Midas Touch' (AARS), *'Peace' (AARS), 'Summer Sunshine', 'Sunbright'.

White: *'Garden Party' (AARS), 'Honor' (AARS), 'John F. Kennedy', *'Pascali' (AARS), *'Pristine'.

Lavender: 'Blue Girl', 'Blue Ribbon', 'Heirloom', *'Lady X', *'Paradise' (AARS).

Grandifloras. Vigorous plants, sometimes 8–10 ft. tall, with hybrid tea–type flowers borne singly or in long-stemmed clusters. Some are derived from crosses between hybrid teas and floribundas; others are just extra-vigorous, cluster-flowering plants with hybrid tea ancestry. They're good for mass color effect, for number of cuttable flowers produced per plant, and as background or barrier plants.

Red: 'Love' (AARS), 'Olé'.

Pink, blends: *'Aquarius' (AARS), 'Camelot' (AARS), *'Earth Song', *'Pink Parfait' (AARS), *'Queen Elizabeth' (AARS), *'Sonia', *'Tournament of Roses' (AARS).

Orange, blends: 'Arizona' (AARS), 'Montezuma', 'Solitude' (AARS).

Yellow: *'Gold Medal'.

White: 'White Lightnin' (AARS).

Lavender: 'Lagerfeld'.

Floribundas. Originally developed from hybrid teas and polyanthas (see below), these produce quantities of flowers in clusters on vigorous and bushy plants. Plant and flower sizes are smaller than those of most hybrid teas. Some have flowers of elegant hybrid tea shape; others are more informal. Use for informal hedges, low borders, barriers, as container plants.

Red: *'Europeana' (AARS), 'Impatient', *'Sarabande' (AARS), *'Showbiz' (AARS), *'Trumpeter'.

Pink: *'Betty Prior', *'Bridal Pink', 'Cherish' (AARS), 'Gene Boerner' (AARS), 'Pleasure' (AARS), *'Sexy Rexy', 'Sweet Inspiration' (AARS), *'Sweet Vivien'.

Orange, blends: *'Apricot Nectar' (AARS), 'Cathedral', *'First Edition' (AARS), 'Gingersnap', 'Marina', *'Orangeade', 'Redgold' (AARS), *'Summer Fashion'.

Yellow: *'Sun Flare' (AARS), *'Sunsprite'.

White: *'Evening Star', *'French Lace' (AARS), *'Iceberg', *'Ivory Fashion' (AARS).

Lavender: *'Angel Face' (AARS), 'Intrigue' (AARS).

Polyanthas. Original members of this class appeared in the late 19th century, the result of crosses with *R. multiflora*. Small flowers (under 2 in.) come in large sprays; plants are vigorous, usually low growing, nearly everblooming, and quite disease resistant. 'Margo Koster' has coral orange, double flowers that resemble ranunculus; it has sported to produce color variants in white, pink, orange scarlet, and red. 'The Fairy' has huge clusters of light pink flowers on a plant that can reach 4 ft. high. 'China Doll' is a knee-high plant with larger, deeper pink flowers in smaller clusters. With light pruning two 19th-century classics make sizable bushes that resemble bushy Noisettes (see under "Old roses," page 363). 'Cécile Brunner' (often called the 'Sweetheart Rose') has light pink flowers of perfect hybrid tea form; 'Perle d'Or' (sometimes called 'Yellow Cécile Brunner') is similar except for its apricot orange flower color.

Miniature roses. These plants are perfect replicas of modern hybrid teas and floribundas but plant size is reduced to about 1–1½ ft. tall (grown in the ground) with flowers and foliage in the same reduced proportion.

Polyantha Rose 'Margo Koster'

R

Derived in part from *R. chinensis minima,* they come in all colors of modern hybrid teas. Plants are everblooming. Grow them outdoors in containers, window boxes, or as border and bedding plants. You can grow them indoors: Pot in rich soil in 6-in. (or larger) containers, and locate in a cool, bright window. Miniatures are hardier than hybrid teas but may still need winter protection in the Upper South. They also demand a good amount of care. Shallow roots demand regular water and fertilizer, mulch. Also, powdery mildew and spider mites are common problems. On the plus side, nearly all are own-root, cutting-grown plants.

Many new miniature selections are introduced on the market each year. Among the best available are the following, all rated 8.5 or higher:

Red, orange: 'Orange Sunblaze', 'Peggy', 'Starina'.

Pink: 'Coral Sprite', 'Cupcake', 'Millie Walters', 'Pierrine', 'Pink Meillandina'.

Blends: 'Dreamglo', 'Earthquake', 'Jean Kenneally', 'Little Artist', 'Little Jackie', 'Loving Touch', 'Magic Carrousel', 'Minnie Pearl', 'Party Girl', 'Rainbow's End', 'Shortcake', 'Wow'.

Yellow: 'Morain', 'My Sunshine', 'Rise 'n' Shine'.

White: 'Pacesetter', 'Snowbride'.

Lavender, purple: 'Ruby Pendant', 'Winsome'.

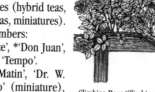

Miniature Rose

Climbing roses. Modern climbing roses may be divided into two general categories: natural climbers (large flowered, except for miniatures) and climbing versions of bush roses (hybrid teas, grandifloras, floribundas, polyanthas, miniatures). Here are some popular natural climbers:

Red: *'Altissimo' (single), 'Blaze', *'Don Juan', *'Dortmund', *'Dublin Bay', 'Solo', 'Tempo'.

Pink: 'Blossomtime', *'Clair Matin', 'Dr. W. van Fleet', *'Galway Bay', *'Hi Ho' (miniature), *'Jeanne Lajoie' (miniature), 'New Dawn', *'Pink Perpétue', *'Rhonda'.

Climbing Rose 'Climbing Mrs. Sam McGredy'

Orange, blends: *'America' (AARS), *'Compassion', *'Handel', 'Joseph's Coat', *'Royal Sunset', 'Spectra'.

Yellow: 'Golden Showers' (AARS), 'Royal Gold'.

White: *'City of York', 'Lace Cascade', 'White Dawn'.

Here are popular selections of climbing bush roses:

Red: 'Cl. Chrysler Imperial', 'Cl. Crimson Glory'.

Pink: 'Cl. Cécile Brunner' (polyantha), 'Cl. China Doll' (polyantha), 'Cl. Dainty Bess', 'Cl. First Prize', 'Cl. Queen Elizabeth'.

Orange, blends: 'Cl. Double Delight', 'Cl. Granada', 'Cl. Mrs. Sam McGredy', 'Cl. Peace'.

White: *'Cl. Iceberg'.

Shrub roses. Significant breeding is under way to develop roses for general landscape use. These are collectively known as shrub roses. The goal is a combination of showy flowers, disease-resistant foliage, and increased cold-hardiness. Mail-order rose specialists lead the way in offering these plants, but retail nurseries are offering them more and more. Here is an overview of types available.

Hybrid musk roses. The hybrid musks are large (6–8-ft.) shrubs or small climbers that perform well in dappled or partial shade or in sun. Most are nearly everblooming, with fragrant, clustered flowers in white, yellow, buff, pink shades, red. Popular selections include 'Buff Beauty', buff apricot; 'Cornelia', coral; 'Felicia', pink; 'Kathleen', single pink, like apple blossoms; 'Penelope', salmon; 'Will Scarlet', red.

English roses. England's David Austin has crossed various old roses (albas, centifolias, gallicas) with modern roses in order to combine the forms and fragrances of old roses with the colors and repeat-flowering of modern hybrids. The group is extremely varied and includes low shrubs as well as plants that are determined to be climbers regardless of pruning. Popular selections include 'Abraham Darby', pink-yellow-apricot blend, upright to climbing plant; 'Charles Austin', apricot, bushy plant; 'Fair Bianca', creamy white, spreading bush; 'Gertrude Jekyll', deep pink, tall and upright; 'Graham Thomas', rich yellow, tall plant; 'Mary Rose', rose pink, tall and upright; 'Othello', dusky dark red, tall bush or climber.

Ground cover roses. European and American breeders are producing roses that spread widely but grow to no more than 2 ft. tall—perfect for covering slopes, cascading over walls, or for container culture. Vigor, disease resistance, profusion of bloom are the hallmarks of these roses. Examples are 'Essex', 'Flower Carpet', 'Nozomi', 'Pink Bells', 'Rosy Carpet'.

Other shrub roses. Many modern shrub roses of complex ancestry can't be pigeonholed into categories according to species affiliation or specific characteristic. The plants may be spreading or upright; they are usually 3 ft. or greater in height, and their flowers come in small to large clusters. These include such gems as 'Alchymist'; 'Ballerina' (classed as hybrid musk but more like a giant polyantha); 'Carefree Beauty' and 'Carefree Wonder' (like large floribundas); 'Erfurt'; the various Meidiland roses ('Bonica', 'Pink Meidiland', 'Red Meidiland', 'White Meidiland'); 'Pearl Drift'; 'Sally Holmes'; and 'Sea Foam'. Check individual descriptions of catalog offerings to find appealing candidates that meet your specific landscape needs and conditions.

HOW TO BE HAPPY WITH ROSES

Recognize that roses take more care than most other plants, and don't plant more than you can easily maintain. Choose roses that do well in your area, and select the right rose for the right spot. (Don't plant a vigorous rambler where you have to prune it constantly.) Give your roses good soil, regular feedings, and plenty of water and sun. Favor plants that are disease resistant or need little spraying (see "Lazy Roses", page 361; Carefree Plants, page 88).

Old roses. Old roses belong to the various rose classes that existed prior to 1867 (even though some in these classes were introduced as late as the early 20th century). Old roses may be divided into two categories. The old European roses comprise the albas, centifolias, damasks, gallicas, and moss roses—the oldest hybrid groups derived from species native to Europe and western Asia. Most flower only in spring; many are hardy throughout the South with little or no winter protection. The second group contains classes derived entirely or in part from east Asian roses: Chinas, Bourbons, damask perpetuals, hybrid perpetuals, Noisettes, and teas. The original China and tea roses were brought to Europe from eastern Asia; 19th-century hybridizers greatly increased their numbers and also developed the other classes from crosses with European roses. Repeat flowering is a characteristic of these classes; hardiness varies, but nearly all need winter protection in cold-winter areas.

Alba roses. Developed from *R. alba,* the White Rose of York; associated with England's War of the Roses. Spring flowers range from single to very double, white to delicate pink. Upright plants, vigorous and long lived, with green wood, handsome, disease-resistant, gray-green foliage. Garden forms include white 'Alba Semiplena' and these in shades of pink: 'Celestial', 'Great Maiden's Blush', 'Félicité Parmentier', 'Königin von Dänemark'.

Centifolia roses. The roses often portrayed by Dutch painters; developed from *R. centifolia,* the cabbage rose. Plants are open growing with prickly stems; stems reach 6 ft. tall but arch with weight of blossoms. Intensely fragrant spring flowers typically are packed with petals, often with large outer petals that cradle a multitude of smaller petals within. Colors include white, pink shades. 'Paul Ricault' produces silken, deep pink flowers on an upright plant; 'Rose des Peintres' is a typical rich pink cabbage rose; 'Tour de Malakoff' is a tall, rangy plant with peony-like blossoms of pink fading to grayish mauve. Dwarf forms (3 ft. or less) are 'Petite de Hollande', 'Pompon de Bourgogne', and 'Rose de Meaux'.

Damask roses. Originating with *R. damascena.* Plants reach 6 ft. or more, typically with long, arching, thorny canes and light or grayish green, downy leaves. The summer damasks flower only in spring; forms of these are cultivated to make attar of roses (used in the perfume industry). Available selections include 'Celsiana', blush pink; 'Leda', white with crimson markings; 'Mme Hardy', white; and 'Versicolor' ('York and Lancaster'), with

R

petals that may be pink, white, or blend of pink and white. The autumn damask rose, *R. d.* 'Semperflorens' *(R. d. bifera),* flowers more than once in a year; slender buds open to loosely double, clear pink blossoms. This is the "Rose of Castile" of the Spanish missions.

Gallica roses. Cultivated forms of *R. gallica,* the French rose. Fragrant spring flowers run from pink through red to maroon and purple shades. Plants reach 3–4 ft. tall with upright to arching canes bearing prickles but few thorns and dark green, often rough-textured leaves. Grown on their own roots, these plants will spread into clumps from creeping rootstocks. Historic 'Officinalis', known as the Apothecary rose, is presumed to be the "Red Rose of Lancaster" from the War of the Roses; flowers are semidouble, cherry red, on a dense, medium-height plant. A mutation, 'Versicolor'—generally known as 'Rosa Mundi'—has pink petals boldly striped and stippled red. Other gallicas include 'Belle de Crécy', pink aging to violet; 'Cardinal de Richelieu', slate purple; 'Charles de Mills', crimson to purple; and 'Tuscany', dark crimson with gold stamens.

Moss roses. Two old rose classes—centifolia and damask—include variant types that feature mosslike, balsam-scented glands that cover unopened buds, flower stems, and sometimes even leaflets. The moss of centifolias is soft to the touch; that of damask mosses is more stiff and prickly. Flowers are white, pink, red, often intensely fragrant. 'Centifolia Muscosa' ('Muscosa') and 'Communis' are typical pink centifolias with moss added; 'White Bath' is 'Centifolia Muscosa' done in white. Other available selections are 'Comtesse de Murinais', pale pink to white; 'Gloire des Mousseux', deep pink; 'Mme Louis Lévêque', salmon pink; 'Nuits de Young', dark red; 'William Lobb', dark red to purple. Repeat-flowering mosses include 'Alfred de Dalmas', creamy pink; 'Gabriel Noyelle', apricot; 'Henri Martin', red; and 'Salet', bright pink.

China roses. The first two China roses to reach Europe (around 1800) were cultivated forms of ⚱ *R. chinensis* that had been selected and maintained by Chinese horticulturists. Flowers were pink or red, less than 3 in. across, in small clusters, on 2–4-ft.-high plants. 'Old Blush' ('Parson's Pink China'), one of the original two, is still sold. Others available include red 'Cramoisi Supérieur' ('Agrippina'); white 'Ducher'; pink changing to crimson 'Archduke Charles'; the bizarre-looking green rose *(R. chinensis viridiflora);* yellow changing to pink and crimson 'Mutabilis'; and crimson 'Louis Philippe'. China rose ancestry was the primary source of repeat-flowering habit in later 19th– and early 20th–century roses.

Bourbon roses. The original Bourbon rose was a hybrid between *R. chinensis* and the autumn damask rose. Later developments were shrubs, semiclimbers, and climbers with flowers in white, pink shades, and red, mostly quite fragrant. Best known today are 'La Reine Victoria', 'Madame Ernst Calvat', 'Madame Pierre Oger', 'Souvenir de la Malmaison' (all pink); 'Zéphirine Drouhin' and the supremely fragrant 'Madame Isaac Pereire' (magenta red). A famous Bourbon-China hybrid, 'Gloire des Rosomanes', gained widespread distribution as an understock (called Ragged Robin) in commercial rose production. Occasionally it is offered as a hedge plant; growth is upright to fountainlike, with coarse foliage and semidouble, cherry red flowers throughout the growing season.

Damask perpetuals. This was the first distinct hybrid group to emerge, beginning around 1800, combining the China roses with old European rose types. Ancestries vary, but all appear to include China roses and the autumn damask rose; generally they were known as Portland roses after the first representative, 'Duchess of Portland'. All are fairly short, bushy, repeat-flowering plants with centifolia- and gallica-like flowers. Among those sold are 'Comte de Chambord', cool pink; 'Duchess of Portland', crimson; 'Jacques Cartier', bright pink; and 'Rose du Roi', crimson purple.

Hybrid perpetuals. In the 19th and early 20th centuries, before hybrid teas dominated the catalogs, these were *the* garden roses. They are big, vigorous, and hardy to about −30°F with minimal winter protection. Plants need more water and fertilizer than hybrid teas to produce repeated bursts of bloom. Prune high, thin out oldest canes, arch over remaining canes to encourage many blooms. Watch for rust. Flowers often large (to 6–7 in.), full, and strongly fragrant; buds usually are shorter, plumper than those of

hybrid tea. Colors range from white through pink shades to red and maroon. Selections still sold include 'Frau Karl Druschki', white; 'Général Jacqueminot', cherry red; 'Mrs. John Laing', rose pink; 'Paul Neyron', deep pink, peony-like; 'Ulrich Brünner Fils', carmine red.

Noisette roses. The union of a China rose and the musk rose *(R. moschata)* produced the first Noisette rose, 'Champneys' Pink Cluster', a shrubby, repeat-flowering climber with small pink flowers in medium-size clusters. Crossed with itself and China roses, it led to a race of similar roses in white, pink shades, and red; crossed with tea roses, it yielded tea-Noisettes that are large-flowered and climbing. Noisettes aren't reliably hardy in the Upper and Middle South. Small-flowered Noisettes include 'Aimée Vibert Scandens', white; 'Blush Noisette', light pink; and 'Fellenberg', cherry red. Larger-flowered tea-Noisettes are 'Alister Stella Gray', yellow; 'Crepuscule', orange; 'Lamarque', white; 'Madame Alfred Carrière', white; 'Maréchal Niel', yellow; and 'Rêve d'Or', buff apricot.

Tea roses. A race of elegant, virtually everblooming, relatively tender roses best in the Lower, Coastal, and Tropical South. Plants are long lived, building on old wood and disliking heavy pruning. Flowers are in pastel shades—white, soft cream, light yellow, apricot, buff, pink, and rosy red; flower character varies, but many resemble hybrid teas in flower quality. In crosses with hybrid perpetuals, tea roses were parents of the first hybrid teas. Available selections include 'Duchesse de Brabant', warm pink, tulip-like; 'Lady Hillingdon', saffron; 'Maman Cochet', creamy rose pink; 'Marie van Houtte', soft yellow and pink; 'Mlle Franziska Krüger', pink and cream to orange; 'Monsieur Tillier', dark pink and brick red; 'Mrs. B. R. Cant', silvery pink; 'Sombreuil', creamy white; and 'White Maman Cochet', creamy white shaded pink. The cross of a tea and the tea ancestor *R. gigantea* produced 'Belle Portugaise' ('Belle of Portugal'), a rampant climber bearing large pale pink blossoms in spring.

TEN SWEET ROSES

For those who love fragrant roses most of all, here are a few of our favorites: 'Blanc Double de Coubert', white rugosa; 'Blush Noisette', light pink noisette; 'Chrysler Imperial', deep red hybrid tea; 'Double Delight', creamy white and dark pink hybrid tea; 'Fragrant Cloud', coral red hybrid tea; 'Mme Hardy', white damask; 'Madame Isaac Pereire', deep rose Bourbon; 'Mr. Lincoln', dark red hybrid tea; 'Sombreuil', creamy white tea.

Species and species hybrids. Among this diverse assemblage of wild species and their hybrids are excellent shrub and climbing roses, useful for mass floral effect and for attractiveness of plant and foliage.

⚱ **R. banksiae.** LADY BANKS'S ROSE. Evergreen climber. Zones LS, CS, TS. Vigorous grower to 20 feet or more. Aphid resistant, almost immune to disease. Stems have almost no prickles; glossy and leathery leaves have three to five leaflets to 2½ in. long. Large clusters of small yellow or white flowers bloom in spring. Good for covering banks, ground, fence, or arbor. The two forms sold are 'Lutea', with scentless, double yellow flowers; and *R. b. banksiae* ('Alba Plena' or 'White Banksia'), with violet-scented, double white flowers. The fragrant 'Fortuniana' *(R. fortuniana)* sometimes is sold as the double white banksia; it differs in having thorny canes, larger leaves, and larger flowers that come individually rather than in clusters.

R. bracteata. MACARTNEY ROSE. Evergreen climbing shrub with large, creamy white single blossoms. Zones LS, CS, TS. Naturalized in Southeast. Its celebrated offspring is 'Mermaid', an evergreen or semievergreen climber hardy in the Coastal and Tropical South. Vigorous (to 30 ft.), thorny, with glossy, leathery, dark green leaves and many single, creamy yellow, lightly fragrant flowers, 5 in. across, in spring, summer, fall, and intermittently through winter. Tough, disease resistant, thrives in sun or partial shade. Plant 8 ft. apart for quick ground cover; or use to climb wall (will need tying), run along fence, or climb tree.

R. eglanteria (R. rubiginosa). SWEET BRIAR ROSE, EGLANTINE. Deciduous shrub or climber. Zones US, MS, LS. Vigorous to 8–12 ft. Prickly stems. Dark green leaves have the fragrance of green apples, especially after rain. Single flowers, pink, 1½ in. across, appearing singly or in clusters in late spring. Red-orange fruit. Can be hedge, barrier, screen; plant 3–4 ft. apart and prune once a year in early spring. Can be held to 3–4 ft. Good hybrid forms are 'Lady Penzance', 'Lord Penzance'.

R. foetida (R. lutea). AUSTRIAN BRIER. Deciduous shrub. Zones US, MS, LS. Slender, prickly stems 5–10 ft. long, erect or arching. Leaves dark green, smooth or slightly hairy, especially susceptible to black spot; may drop early in fall. Flowers (mid- to late spring) are single, bright yellow, 2–3 in. across, with odd scent. This species and its well-known selection 'Bicolor', Austrian copper rose, are the source of orange and yellow in modern roses. 'Bicolor' is a 4–5-ft.-tall shrub with brilliant coppery red flowers, their petals backed with yellow. Its form 'Persiana', Persian yellow rose, has fully double, yellow blossoms.

All forms perform best in warm, fairly dry, well-drained soil and in full sun. Prune only to remove dead wood.

R. glauca (R. rubrifolia). REDLEAF ROSE. Deciduous shrub. Zones US, MS, LS. Foliage, not flower, is the main feature of this species: The 6-ft. plant is covered in leaves that combine gray green and coppery purple. Small, single spring flowers are pink, forming small, oval hips that color red in fall.

🏛 **R. harisonii.** HARISON'S YELLOW ROSE. Deciduous shrub. Zones US, MS, LS. Thickets of thorny stems to 6–8 ft.; finely textured foliage; flowers (in late spring) profuse, semidouble, bright yellow, fragrant. Occasionally reblooms in fall. Showy fruit. Hybrid between *R. foetida* and *R. spinosissima*. Very old rose that was taken westward to Texas by pioneers from New York. Vigorous growing, disease free, cold-hardy, and drought tolerant. Useful deciduous landscaping shrub. Also called the yellow rose of Texas.

R. hugonis. FATHER HUGO'S ROSE, GOLDEN ROSE OF CHINA. Deciduous shrub. Zones US, MS, LS. Dense growth to 8 ft. Stems arching or straight, with bristles near base. Handsome foliage; leaves are deep green, 1–4 in. long, with five to eleven tiny leaflets. Blooms profusely in mid- to late spring. Branches become garlands of 2-in.-wide, bright yellow, faintly scented flowers. Good in borders, for screen or barrier plantings, against fence, trained as fan on trellis. Takes high, filtered afternoon shade. Prune out oldest wood to ground each year to shape plant, get maximum bloom.

🏛 **R. laevigata.** CHEROKEE ROSE. Evergreen climber. Zones LS, CS, TS. Native to southeast Asia but widely naturalized in southern U.S., from which it gained its common name. Green stems with sharp, hooked thorns bear lacquered, dark green leaves, each with three leaflets. Single white flowers to 3½ in. wide appear only in spring. It is the state flower of Georgia. Crossed with a tea rose, it produced 'Anemone', a mostly spring-flowering climber bearing soft, silvery pink, single flowers that resemble blooms of Japanese anemone. 'Ramona' is magenta pink variation.

🏛 **R. moschata.** MUSK ROSE. Deciduous shrub. All zones. Vigorous, arching plant is densely covered with matte-finish, mid-green foliage that turns butter yellow in late fall. Clustered, ivory white, single flowers appear in late spring, continue through summer; scent is delicious, somewhat like honey. *R. m. plena* has double blossoms, though their effect is lessened because inner petals wither before outer ones.

R. moyesii. Deciduous shrub. Zones US, MS, LS. Large, loose shrub is best as background plant or featured shrub-tree specimen. Spring bloom is a glorious display of bright red single flowers to 2½ in. across, carried singly or in groups of two. A second display comes in fall, when the large, bottle-shaped hips ripen to brilliant scarlet. 'Geranium' is a selection with somewhat shorter, more compact growth and red flowers in clusters of up to five. The hybrid 'Sealing Wax' offers pink flowers, also on a smaller and more compact bush.

R. multiflora. JAPANESE ROSE. Deciduous shrub. Zones US, MS, LS. Arching growth on dense, vigorous plant 8–10 ft. tall and as wide. Susceptible to mildew, spider mites. Many clustered, small white flowers (like blackberry blossoms) in mid- to late spring; sweet fragrance akin to that of honeysuckle. Profusion of ¼-in. red fruit, much loved by birds, in fall. (Fruit display has a downside: Profuse volunteer seedlings can put this rose in the "weed" category. The plant has become so invasive in some areas that it has been declared a noxious weed, and people have been forbidden to sell or plant it.) Promoted as hedge but truly useful for this purpose only on largest acreage—far too large and vigorous for most gardens. One of the most widely used understocks in commercial rose production.

A number of distinctive climbing roses, known as multiflora ramblers, are hybrids of this species, and not invasive. Best known are several "blue ramblers": 'Bleu Magenta', crimson purple fading to gray violet; 'Rose-Marie Viaud', crimson purple to violet and lilac; 'Veilchenblau', maroon purple to gray lilac; and 'Violette', maroon purple to grayish plum.

🏛 *R. multiflora platyphylla*, 'Seven Sisters', is an heirloom rose often seen in old Southern gardens. Not invasive like the species.

R. roxburghii. CHESTNUT ROSE. Deciduous shrub. Zones US, MS, LS, CS. Spreading plant with prickly stems 8–10 ft. long. Gray, peeling bark. Light green, very finely textured, ferny foliage; new growth bronze and gold tipped. Immune to mildew. Buds and fruit are spiny, like chestnut burrs. Flowers—generally double, soft rose pink, very fragrant—appear in mid- to late spring. Normally a big shrub for screen or border, but if stems are pegged down it makes good bank cover, useful in preventing erosion.

R. rugosa. RUGOSA ROSE. Deciduous shrub. Zones US, MS, LS. Vigorous, hardy shrub with prickly stems. To 3–8 ft. tall. Leaves bright glossy green, with distinctive heavy veining that gives them crinkled look. Flowers are 3–4 in. across and range from single to double and from pure white and creamy yellow through pink to deep purplish red, all wonderfully fragrant. Blooms spring, summer, early fall. Bright red, tomato-shaped fruit, an inch across or more, is seedy but edible, sometimes used in preserves.

All rugosas are extremely tough, withstanding hard freezes, wind, aridity, salt spray. They make fine hedges; plants grown on their own roots make sizable colonies and help prevent erosion. Foliage remains quite free of diseases and insects, except possibly aphids. Among most widely sold rugosas and rugosa hybrids are 'Blanc Double de Coubert', double white; 'Frau Dagmar Hartopp', single pink; 'Hansa', double purplish red; 'Will Alderman', double pink. Three unusual rugosa hybrids are 'F. J. Grootendorst'; 'Grootendorst Supreme', crimson red; and 'Pink Grootendorst'; their double flowers with deeply fringed petals resemble carnations more than roses.

R. spinosissima (R. pimpinellifolia). SCOTCH ROSE, BURNET ROSE. Deciduous shrub. Zones US, MS, LS. Suckering, spreading shrub 3–4 ft. tall. Stems upright, spiny, bristly, closely set with small, ferny leaves. Handsome bank cover on good soil; helps prevent erosion. Spring flowers white to pink, 1½–2 in. across; fruit dark brown to blackish. Its form 'Altaica' can reach 6 ft. tall, with larger leaves and garlands of 3-in. white flowers on branches. Several hybrids are noteworthy. 'Stanwell Perpetual' produces blush pink, double blossoms from spring to fall on a mounding, twiggy plant with small gray-green leaves. 'Frühlingsmorgen' is best known of several German hybrids; tall, arching bush bears large, single yellow flowers edged cherry pink and centered with maroon stamens. 'Golden Wings' makes a 6-ft. bush that flowers throughout the growing season; 4-in. blossoms are single, light yellow with red stamens.

R. wichuraiana. MEMORIAL ROSE. Vine. Evergreen or partially evergreen. Zones US, MS, LS, CS. Trailing stems grow 10–12 ft. long in one season, root in contact with moist soil. Leaves 2–4 in. long, with five to nine smooth, shiny, ¼–1-in. leaflets. Midsummer flowers are white, to 2 in. across, in clusters of six to ten. Good ground cover, even in relatively poor soil. Wichuraiana ramblers, produced in the first 20 years of this century, are group of hybrids between the species and various garden roses. Pink 'Dorothy Perkins' and red 'Excelsa' produce smothering spring displays of small, formless blooms that obscure the often-mildewed leaves. Larger, better-shaped flowers and glossy, healthier leaves are found in 'Albéric Barbier', creamy white; 'François Juranville', coral pink; 'Gardenia', light yellow; 'Paul Transon', coppery salmon; and 'Sander's White Rambler', white.

SOUTHERN HERITAGE PLANTS
IDENTIFIED BY SYMBOL 🏛

Rosaceae. The rose family contains an immense number of horticulturally important plants. Besides roses, family members include strawberry, bramble fruits (blackberry, raspberry), many flowering and fruiting trees (apple, crabapple, pear, plum), *Photinia*, firethorn *(Pyracantha)*, and *Spiraea*, as well as other ornamental trees, shrubs, and perennials.

ROSE ACACIA. See ROBINIA hispida

ROSEBAY. See RHODODENDRON maximum

ROSE CAMPION. See LYCHNIS coronaria

ROSE-MALLOW, COMMON. See HIBISCUS moscheutos

ROSE OF SHARON. See HIBISCUS syriacus

ROSMARINUS officinalis

ROSEMARY

Lamiaceae (Labiatae)

EVERGREEN SHRUB OR HERB

ZONES MS (PROTECTED), LS, CS

FULL SUN

MODERATE TO LITTLE WATER

Rosmarinus officinalis

Basic species is 3–4 ft. high, rounded and a bit spreading, but generally with upward-sweeping branches. Narrow, almost needlelike, inch-long leaves usually glossy green above, grayish white beneath, aromatic when brushed or bruised. Bears small clusters of small, typically lavender blue flowers over long winter–spring bloom period. Plants must have well-drained soil. Prune as needed, making all cuts to side branches or into leafy stems.

Selections include the following. Foliage of all types has culinary use.

'Alba'. Resembles basic species but bears white flowers.

'Arp'. The hardiest rosemary; takes temperatures to −10°F. Found in Arp, Texas. Open grower to 4 ft. Bright blue flowers.

'Collingwood Ingram' *(R. ingramii)*. To 2–2½ ft. high, spreading to 4 ft. or more. Branches curve gracefully. Flowers in rich, bright shade of blue violet. Tallish bank or ground cover with high color value.

'Huntington Carpet' ('Huntington Blue'). To 1½ ft. high; spreads quickly yet maintains dense center. Pale blue flowers.

'Ken Taylor'. Resembles 'Collingwood Ingram' but is lower growing and has a greater tendency to trail.

'Lockwood de Forest' *(R. lockwoodii, R. forestii)*. Resembles 'Prostratus', but with lighter, brighter foliage and bluer flowers.

'Majorca Pink'. Erect shrub to 2–5 ft. Lavender-pink flowers.

'Miss Jessup's Upright'. Very upright form to 4 ft.; pale blue flowers. Suitable for formal herb gardens.

'Old Salem'. Dense, erect growth to 3 ft.; pale blue flowers. Fairly cold-hardy under snow cover.

'Prostratus'. CREEPING ROSEMARY. To 2 ft. high with 4–8-ft. spread. Will trail over wall or edge of raised bed to make curtain of bright to dark green. Pale lavender blue flowers. Slightly less cold-hardy than most other types of rosemary.

'Tuscan Blue'. Rigid, upright branches to 6 ft. or taller grow directly from base of plant. Rich green leaves, blue-violet flowers. Makes an attractive tall, narrow screen.

ROYAL FERN. See OSMUNDA regalis

ROYAL PALM. See ROYSTONEA

ROYAL POINCIANA. See DELONIX regia

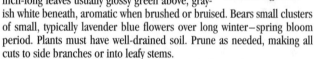

ROYSTONEA

ROYAL PALM

Arecaceae (Palmae)

PALMS

ZONE TS

FULL SUN

AMPLE TO REGULAR WATER

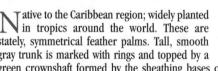

Roystonea regia

Native to the Caribbean region; widely planted in tropics around the world. These are stately, symmetrical feather palms. Tall, smooth gray trunk is marked with rings and topped by a green crownshaft formed by the sheathing bases of the feathery fronds. Rapid growers; tolerate wind, even salt-laden ocean wind. Especially majestic planted in rows.

R. elata. FLORIDA ROYAL PALM. Native to southern Florida. Similar to *R. regia* except in minor details. Considered by some to be a taller palm than *R. regia*.

R. regia. CUBAN ROYAL PALM. To 75 ft., with erect trunk swollen at base, tapering toward top, sometimes swollen toward middle. Arched fronds, 9–20 ft. long, with leaflets that stand out from the midrib at many angles.

RUBBER PLANT. See FICUS elastica

Rubiaceae. The widespread and varied madder family contains herbs, shrubs, and trees with opposite or whorled leaves and (usually) clustered flowers. Among the family members are coffee plant *(Coffea)*, *Gardenia*, and sweet woodruff *(Galium)*.

RUDBECKIA

CONEFLOWER

Asteraceae (Compositae)

PERENNIALS AND BIENNIALS

ZONES VARY BY SPECIES

FULL SUN OR LIGHT SHADE

REGULAR TO MODERATE WATER

Rudbeckia hirta

Garden rudbeckias are descendants of wild plants native to North America. All are tough, and easy to grow, thriving in any except soggy soils. Showy yellow or orange daisy flowers brighten summer and fall borders. Good cut flowers. Cutting also encourages rebloom late in season. Divide perennials when they become crowded, usually every few years.

R. amplexicaulis. See Dracopis amplexicaulis

R. fulgida. ORANGE CONEFLOWER. Perennial. Zones US, MS, LS, CS. To 3 ft. with branching stems. Leaves 5 in. long. Yellow, 2–2½-in.-wide summer flowers with black to brown center. Spreads by rhizomes, forming large clumps. Selections more often grown than species. Among most popular is *R. f. sullivantii* 'Goldsturm', bearing 3-in. black-eyed Susan flowers on 2–2½-ft. stems. Some garden centers offer the taller, more variable seed-grown Goldsturm strain.

R. hirta. BLACK-EYED SUSAN, GLORIOSA DAISY. All zones. Biennial or short-lived perennial; often grown as annual: It blooms first summer from seed sown in early spring. To 3–4 ft. tall, upright branching habit and rough, hairy stems and leaves. Daisylike single flowers 2–4 in. wide, with orange-yellow rays and purplish black center. State flower of Maryland.

Gloriosa Daisy strain has 5–7-in.-wide single daisies in yellow, orange, russet, or mahogany, often zoned or banded. 'Irish Eyes' has golden yellow blooms with light green center that ages to brown. 'Pinwheel' has mahogany-and-gold flowers. 'Marmalade' (2 ft.), 'Goldilocks' (8–10 in.) are lower growing, can be used at front of border or as ground cover. Gloriosa Double Daisy strain has somewhat smaller (4½-in.) double flower heads, nearly all in lighter yellow and orange shades.

R

R. laciniata. CUTLEAF CONEFLOWER. Perennial. Zones US, MS, LS, CS. To 3 ft. tall, with deeply lobed, light green leaves. Blooms summer–fall, bearing 2–3½-in.-wide flowers with drooping yellow rays around a green central disk. Very heat tolerant. The following two selections are more widely grown in gardens: 🏛 'Hortensia', golden glow, to 6–7 ft. tall with double bright yellow flowers, makes a good summer screen or tall border plant. Aphids seem to like it. Does not seed but spreads rapidly (sometimes aggressively) by underground stems and is easily divided. Less aggressive is 'Goldquelle', a 2½-ft.-tall plant with double yellow blooms.

R. maxima. Perennial. Zones US, MS, LS, CS. Large (to 5-in.) bluish gray leaves form a mound to 2–3 ft. tall and wide. In midsummer, 5–6-ft. stems bear flower heads that have a 2-in. brown center cone and drooping yellow rays.

R. nitida. Perennial. Zones US, MS, LS, CS. Similar to *R. laciniata* but shorter. More widely grown than the species is 'Herbstsonne' ('Autumn Sun'), a 4–6-ft. plant bearing single yellow flower heads with a bright green central disk.

R. purpurea. See Echinacea purpurea

R. triloba. BROWN-EYED SUSAN. Biennial or perennial. Zones US, MS, LS. To 4 ft., sometimes taller, with 5-in.-long leaves, some deeply lobed. Yellow-orange flowers, to 3 in. across, with dark brown-purple centers. Stems stiff and much branched. Can be weedy looking.

RUE ANENOME. See ANEMONELLA thalictroides

RUELLIA

RUELLIA	
Acanthaceae	
EVERGREEN SHRUBS AND PERENNIALS	
☀ ZONES MS, LS, CS	
☼ ◑ FULL SUN OR LIGHT SHADE	
◐ ◐ REGULAR TO MODERATE WATER	

Ruellia brittoniana

Ruellias have opposite leaves and flaring bell-shaped flowers with five shallow lobes. They are carefree, easy-to-grow plants.

R. 'Blue Shade'. Perennial. Low-growing plant (usually 10 in. high) popular in Central Texas as a ground cover for light shade. Narrow, pointed-oval, olive green leaves; lavender blue flowers. Spreads fairly slowly.

🏛 **R. brittoniana.** MEXICAN PETUNIA. Shrubby perennial. Mexican native naturalized in parts of the U.S. To 3 ft. high, with narrow leaves and 2-in. blue flowers. Should be contained (by an edging, for example), since it can be invasive. 'Katie' is a well-behaved dwarf (10–12 in.).

R. caroliniensis. Perennial. Native to eastern U.S. To 2½ ft. tall. Oval to lance-shaped leaves, 1½–4 in. long. Lilac to lavender blue, 2-in. flowers in summer and early fall.

R. malacosperma. Shrubby perennial. Native to Mexico. Very similar to *R. brittoniana*. Tough plant that tolerates dry or wet soils.

RUGOSA ROSE. See ROSA rugosa

🏛 RUSCUS

BUTCHER'S BROOM	
Liliaceae	
EVERGREEN SHRUBLETS	
☀ ZONES MS, LS, CS	
◑ ● BEST IN SHADE; TOLERATE SOME SUN	
◐ ◐ REGULAR TO LITTLE WATER	

Ruscus hypoglossum

Unusual leafless plants with some value as small-scale ground cover, curiosity, or source of dry arrangement material and Christmas greens. Not usually sold by garden centers, but rather passed around by gardeners. Flattened leaflike branches do work of leaves and bear tiny greenish white flowers in center of upper surfaces. If male and female plants are present, or if you have plant with male and female flowers, bright red (sometimes yellow), marble-size fruit follows the flowers. Plants spread by underground stems. Subject to chlorosis in alkaline soil.

R. aculeatus. To 1–4 ft. tall, with branched stems. Spine-tipped "leaves" are 1–3 in. long, a third as wide, leathery, dull dark green. Fruit ½ in. across, red or yellow.

R. hypoglossum. To 1½ ft.; unbranched stems. "Leaves" to 4 in. long, 1½ in. wide, glossy green, not spine tipped. Fruit ¼–½ in. across. Spreads faster than *R. aculeatus*. A good small-scale ground cover.

RUSSELIA equisetiformis

FIRECRACKER PLANT, CORAL FOUNTAIN	
Scrophulariaceae	
PERENNIAL	
☀ ZONES CS (MILDER PARTS), TS; OR INDOORS	
☼ ◑ FULL SUN OR PARTIAL SHADE	
◐ KEEP SOIL MOIST	

Russelia equisetiformis

Shrubby plant, 4–5 ft. tall, with trailing, bright green, practically leafless stems that look attractive spilling from a wall or hanging basket; stems can also be fastened to a trellis or wall. Many side branches bear a profusion of bright red, narrowly tubular flowers that look like little firecrackers; bloom lasts all spring and summer outdoors, goes on continuously in house or greenhouse. Give filtered light indoors. Needs regular fertilizing. Easy to propagate with pencil-size cuttings taken in spring.

RUSSELL LUPINES. See LUPINUS

RUSSIAN OLIVE. See ELAEAGNUS angustifolia

RUSSIAN SAGE. See PEROVSKIA

RUTABAGA. See TURNIP and RUTABAGA

Rutaceae. Besides rue (*Ruta*), the rue family includes many perennials, shrubs, and trees, most important of which are the citrus clan. Most members have oil glands in leaves or other parts and are aromatic. Mexican orange (*Choisya*) and *Skimmia* are other notable members.

RUTA graveolens

BLUE-LEAFED RUE, HERB-OF-GRACE	
Rutaceae	
PERENNIAL HERB	
☀ ZONES US, MS, LS	
☼ FULL SUN	
◐ ◐ REGULAR TO MODERATE WATER	

Ruta graveolens

To 2–3 ft., with aromatic, fernlike blue-green leaves. Small, greenish yellow flowers are followed by decorative brown seed capsules. Sow seeds in flats; transplant to 1 ft. apart. Needs good garden soil; add lime to strongly acid soil. Cut back in early spring to encourage bushiness. Seed clusters can be dried for use in wreaths or swags. 'Blue Beauty' and 'Jackman's Blue' are dense, compact selections with fine blue-gray color. 'Blue Mound' and 'Curly Girl' are even more compact.

Rue owes its status as an herb to history and legend rather than to any medicinal or culinary use. It was once thought to ward off disease, guard against poisons, and aid eyesight. It was also used to make brushes for sprinkling holy water. Sap causes dermatitis in some people.

RYEGRASS. See LOLIUM

SABAL

PALMETTO

Arecaceae (Palmae)

PALMS

🌡 ZONES VARY BY SPECIES

☀ ◐ FULL SUN OR PARTIAL SHADE

💧 MODERATE WATER

Sabal palmetto

Large, slow-growing, cold-hardy fan palms, some with trunks, some without. When plants are mature, large clusters of tiny flowers appear among leaves. Tolerate salt spray.

S. blackburniana (S. domingensis, S. umbraculifera). HISPANIOLAN PALMETTO. Zones LS, CS, TS. Native to the Caribbean. Ultimately reaches 80 ft. or taller, with immense green fans 9 ft. across.

S. mexicana (S. texana). TEXAS PALMETTO, OAXACA PALMETTO. Zones LS, CS, TS. Native from Texas to Guatemala. Leaf stems hang on trunk in early life, then drop to show attractive, slender trunk. Grows 30–50 ft. high. Established trees hard to transplant.

S. minor. DWARF PALMETTO. Zones MS, LS, CS, TS. Shrubby palm native to the forest understory, scrublands, and alluvial floodplains of the Southeast. Slow growing to 6 ft. tall. Usually trunkless; older specimens have short, thick trunk. Old leaves fold at base, hang down like closed umbrellas. Tolerates wet or dry soils and salt spray. One of the hardiest palms. Some plants reportedly have survived −24°F.

🌵 **S. palmetto.** CABBAGE PALM. Zones LS (milder parts), CS, TS. Native to the hammocks, marshes, and Coastal Plains of the Southeast from North Carolina to Florida. Grows slowly to 90 ft., with a dense, globular head formed by leaves 5–8 ft. across. Together with live oak, cabbage palm helps define the urban character of Charleston, Savannah, and other coastal cities of the Old South. Excellent street or lawn tree; best tree for the beach. Tolerates wind, salt spray, and sand; can be planted right on dunes. Very easy to transplant. Huge, dormant specimens are often stacked up like cordwood, then trucked to new locations and plopped like telephone poles into deep, narrow holes.

SACAHUISTA. See NOLINA texana

SAGE. See SALVIA

SAGE, RUSSIAN. See PEROVSKIA

SAGINA subulata

IRISH MOSS, SCOTCH MOSS

Caryophyllaceae

PERENNIAL

🌡 ZONES US, MS, LS

☀ ◐ FULL SUN OR PARTIAL SHADE

💧 REGULAR WATER

Sagina subulata

Of two different plants of similar appearance, *Sagina subulata* is the more common. The other is *Arenaria verna*, usually called *A. v. caespitosa*. Both make dense, compact, mosslike masses of slender leaves on slender stems. But *A. verna* has tiny white flowers in few-flowered clusters, while *S. subulata* bears flowers singly and differs in other technical details. In common usage, however, green forms of the two are called Irish moss, while golden green forms (*A. v.* 'Aurea' and *S. s.* 'Aurea') are called Scotch moss. Both *Sagina* and *Arenaria* are grown primarily as ground covers for small areas. They're useful for filling gaps between paving blocks.

These plants look like moss, but they won't grow well under conditions that suit true mosses. Need good soil, good drainage, occasional feeding with slow-acting, nonburning fertilizer. Take some foot traffic and tend to hump up in time; control humping by occasionally cutting out narrow

strips, then pressing or rolling lightly. Control slugs, snails, cutworms. Cut squares from flats and set 6 in. apart for fast cover. To avoid lumpiness, plant so that soil line of squares is at or slightly below the surface.

SAGO PALM. See CYCAS revoluta

ST. AUGUSTINE GRASS. See STENOTAPHRUM secundatum

ST. JOHNSWORT. See HYPERICUM

SAINT JOSEPH'S LILY. See HIPPEASTRUM johnsonii

🌵 SAINTPAULIA ionantha

AFRICAN VIOLET

Gesneriaceae

EVERGREEN PERENNIAL HOUSE PLANT

◐ ● FILTERED EARLY SUN, BRIGHT INDIRECT LIGHT

💧 WATERING IS AN ART; SEE BELOW

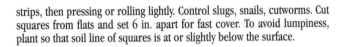

Saintpaulia ionantha

Extremely popular house plant. Fuzzy, heart-shaped leaves with smooth edges grow in rosettes to 1 ft. wide. Pale lavender flowers grow in clusters of three or more. Hybrids and named selections have leaves that are plain or scalloped, green or variegated; flowers are purple, violet, pink, white, or bicolored. Keep where temperatures average 60–70°F. Humidity should be high; if house air is quite dry, increase humidity around plants by setting each plant on a saucer filled with wet gravel.

African violets need a moisture-retentive yet fast-draining potting mix. You can purchase packaged mixes composed specifically for African violets; if you prefer to concoct your own, use 3 parts peat moss to 1 part perlite and 1 part compost or sterilized loam. Don't use too large a pot; plants bloom best when roots are crowded.

Water plants from top or below; avoid watering crown or leaves. Wick-irrigated pots work well. Use room-temperature water or slightly warmer, wet soil thoroughly, let potting mixture become dry to the touch before watering again. Don't let water stand in pot saucers for more than 2 hours after watering plants. If plant is well established, feed—only when soil is moist—with slightly acid fertilizer once every 2 to 4 weeks. Propagate from seeds, leaf cuttings, or divisions. Common pests are aphids, cyclamen mites, thrips, mealybugs. Pluck off spent leaves and flowers.

Salicaceae. The willow family consists of deciduous trees or shrubs with flowers in catkins and (generally) with silk-tufted seeds that blow about. Besides willow *(Salix)*, examples are cottonwood and poplar *(Populus)*.

SALIX

WILLOW

Salicaceae

DECIDUOUS SHRUBS OR TREES

🌡 ZONES US, MS, LS, EXCEPT AS NOTED

☀ FULL SUN

💧 LOTS OF WATER

Salix babylonica

Fast-growing, somewhat weak-wooded trees. Take any soil; most even tolerate poor drainage. All have shallow, invasive roots and are hard to garden under. Most are subject to borers, blights, cankers, and other problems. Weeping willows are best used as single trees near a stream or lake, though they can, with training, become satisfactory shade trees for patio or terrace. They leaf out very early in spring and hold leaves late. Shrubby willows are grown mainly for catkins ("pussy willows") or colored twigs, as screen plants, or for erosion control on banks of streams and rivers. For this last purpose, types native to the area are best. The many willow species hybridize readily; as a result, names are much confused in the nursery trade.

S. alba. WHITE WILLOW. Tree. Upright, to 75–100 ft. Yellowish brown bark. Narrow, 1½–4-in.-long leaves are bright green above, silvery beneath; may turn golden yellow in fall. These are valued for colorful twigs.

'Britzensis' ('Chermesina'). Young twigs turn radiant orange red in winter. For best display, cut back clump to about a foot high just before spring growth begins. Stems will grow as much as 8 ft. in a single season.

S. a. tristis (S. babylonica aurea, S. 'Niobe'). GOLDEN WEEPING WILLOW. Pendulous habit. To 80 ft. high; wider than tall. Young stems are bright yellow. Among the most attractive weeping willows.

S. a. vitellina. Brilliant yellow winter twigs. Cut back heavily, as for 'Britzensis'.

S. babylonica. WEEPING WILLOW. Tree. Zones US, MS, LS, CS. To 30–50 ft., with equal or greater spread. Smaller than *S. alba tristis,* with longer (3–6-in.) leaves and even more pronounced weeping habit. Greenish or brown branchlets. 'Crispa' ('Annularis'), ringleaf willow, has leaves twisted and curled into rings or circles; it is a somewhat narrower tree than the species.

S. caprea. GOAT WILLOW, FLORIST WILLOW. Shrub or small tree. To 25 ft. tall. Broad leaves 3–6 in. long, dark green above, gray and hairy beneath. Male plants produce fat, woolly pinkish gray catkins about 1 in. long in early spring before leaf-out. Can be kept to shrub size by cutting to ground every few years. 'Pendula', Kilmarnock willow, forms a trailing mound suitable for ground cover; it can also be grafted onto an upright trunk and used as a small weeping tree. 'Weeping Sally' is the female form.

🌱 **S. discolor.** PUSSY WILLOW. Shrub or small tree. To 20 ft. tall. Slender stems are red brown; 2–4-in. leaves are bright green above, bluish beneath. Catkins of male plants (usually only kind sold) are the feature attraction—soft, silky, pearl gray, to 1½ in. long.

S. gracilistyla. ROSE-GOLD PUSSY WILLOW. Upright, spreading shrub. To 6–10 ft. tall. Narrowly ovate, 2–4-in.-long leaves are gray green above, bluish green beneath. Male plants produce plump, 1½-in.-long, furry gray catkins with numerous stamens with rose-and-gold anthers. Every 3 or 4 years, cut back plant to short stubs; you'll be rewarded by especially vigorous shoots with large catkins. *S. g. melanostachys* has black catkins with red anthers.

S. matsudana. HANKOW WILLOW. Tree. Upright, pyramidal growth to 40–50 ft. Narrow, bright green, 2–4-in.-long leaves. Can thrive on less water than most willows. 'Navajo', globe Navajo willow, is a large, spreading, round-topped tree to 70 ft. tall. 'Tortuosa', corkscrew willow, grows to 30 ft. tall and 20 ft. wide, has branches fantastically twisted into upright, spiraling patterns; it is valued for winter silhouette and for cut branches for arrangements. 'Umbraculifera', globe willow, reaches 35 ft. high and has an umbrella-shaped top with upright branches, drooping branchlets.

SALVIA

SAGE
Lamiaceae (Labiatae)
ANNUALS, BIENNIALS, PERENNIALS, SHRUBS
🗡 ZONES VARY BY SPECIES
☼ FULL SUN, EXCEPT AS NOTED
💧 REGULAR WATER, EXCEPT AS NOTED
▷ SEE CHART NEXT PAGE

Salvia officinalis

The sages, along with the ornamental grasses, became horticultural stars in the 1980s and 1990s. Botanical gardens and collectors have introduced scores of new species and selections from Mexico, South America, Eurasia, and Africa, along with superior forms of our native species. Some are annual bedding plants, others are border perennials, and still others serve as shrubs or ground covers. Where available at garden centers, many of the tender perennials and shrubs are sometimes grown as annuals in the Upper South.

Flowers range from white and yellow through pink to scarlet, and from pale lavender to true blue and dark purple; all are arranged in whorls of two-lipped flowers either distinctly spaced along the flower stalks or so tightly crowded they look like one dense spike. Inflorescences in some species are branched. Many salvias are aromatic, some strongly. Some are sweet scented; others, such as common sage (*S. officinalis*), have a more savory fragrance.

At least 60 species and an additional 40 to 50 selections are grown. The chart on pages 370–371 lists some of the best.

SAMBUCUS canadensis

AMERICAN ELDERBERRY
Caprifoliaceae
DECIDUOUS SHRUB
🗡 ZONES US, MS, LS, CS
☼ ◑ FULL SUN OR LIGHT SHADE
💧 REGULAR WATER

Sambucus canadensis

Native to central and eastern North America. Spreading, suckering shrub to 6–8 ft. high. Foliage is almost tropical looking; each leaf has seven 2–6-in.-long leaflets. Flat, creamy white flower clusters to 10 in. wide in early summer, followed by tasty purple-black fruit. Fruit used for pies; both flowers and fruit used for wine. Strictly fruiting selections include 'Adams', 'Johns', and many more; plant any two for pollination. Ornamental selections include 'Aurea', with golden green foliage (golden in full sun) and red berries; and 'Laciniata', cutleaf or fernleaf elder, with finely cut foliage and dark berries.

SANGUINARIA canadensis

BLOODROOT
Papaveraceae
PERENNIAL
🗡 ZONES US, MS, LS
☼ ● PARTIAL OR FULL SHADE
💧 💧 AMPLE TO REGULAR WATER

Sanguinaria canadensis

A North American native, this member of the poppy family gets its common name from the orange-red juice that seeps from cut roots and stems. Big, deeply lobed grayish leaves. Blooms in spring, bearing lovely (but ephemeral) white or pink-tinged, 1½-in. flowers carried singly on 8-in. stalks. Plant dies back in mid- to late summer. For damp, shaded rock or woodland garden where it can spread. 'Multiplex' has double flowers.

SANGUISORBA

BURNET
Rosaceae
PERENNIALS
🗡 ZONES US, MS, LS, UNLESS NOTED
☼ ◑ LIGHT SHADE IN LOWER AND COASTAL SOUTH
💧 REGULAR WATER

Sanguisorba canadensis

Perennials that grow from creeping rhizomes. Leaves are divided featherwise into toothed roundish or oval leaflets. Flowers are small, carried in dense, feathery spikes resembling small bottlebrushes. Often sold as *Poterium*.

S. canadensis. GREAT BURNET, CANADIAN BURNET. Grows in bright green clumps, 3–6 ft. tall; 8-in. spikes of white flowers in late autumn. Dies to ground in winter.

S. minor. GARDEN BURNET, SALAD BURNET. Zones US, MS, LS, CS. Can grow to 1½ ft. tall, with roundish red flower heads 1 in. long, but is usually kept clipped to a few inches to maintain a supply of fresh new leaves for culinary use. Leaves have a light cucumber flavor and are used in salads,

▶ page 371

S

SALVIA

NAME, TYPE	ZONES	GROWTH HABIT	FLOWERS	COMMENTS
Salvia argentea SILVER SAGE Biennial	US, MS, LS, CS	Flat 1-ft. rosette of white, furry, 6–8-in.-long leaves	Branched flowering stems to 4 ft.; white summer flowers, tinged pink or yellow	Use at front of border for striking foliage
S. azurea grandiflora (S. pitcheri) BLUE SAGE, PITCHER SAGE Perennial	US, MS, LS, CS	To 5 ft., with smooth or hairy, 2–4-in. leaves	Gentian blue, 1/2-in.-long blooms; mass of color, summer to frost	Tolerant of heat, humidity. Not always permanent in wet winters
S. blepharophylla Shrubby perennial	LS, CS, TS	Mounding, spreading by underground stems, to 11/2 ft. tall	Brilliant red to rose pink, nearly everblooming. Very showy	Provides midheight mass of color over a long period; blooms well in part shade
S. coccinea TEXAS SAGE Perennial, but usually a self-seeding annual	CS, TS	Bushy, to 2–3 ft., with dark green furry leaves	Red, in 4-in. spikes, spring–fall	'Brenthurst' is pink. 'Lady in Red' is a shorter selection; use in foreground planting
S. elegans PINEAPPLE SAGE Perennial	CS, TS	To 2–3 ft.; light green leaves have fruity scent and taste	Red flowers in short spikes, autumn. Attract hummingbirds	Use leaves in cool drinks, fruit salads
S. farinacea MEALY-CUP SAGE Perennial grown as annual	MS, LS, CS, TS	Fast growth to 2–3 ft., grayish green leaves	Spikes of small blue flowers rise above foliage mound in summer	Plants are perennial where winter temperature remains above 10°F. 'Mina' (1 ft.) and 'Victoria' (11/2 ft.) are dwarfs
S. greggii AUTUMN SAGE Shrub	MS, LS, CS	Erect, bushy, to 3–4 ft., with small, medium green leaves	Forms with flowers in yellow, red, peach, purple; spring–fall	Needs excellent drainage; drought tolerant. Best in Southwest
S. guaranitica BRAZILIAN SAGE Shrubby perennial	MS, LS, CS, TS	Bushy, spreading, to 5 ft., with dark green, 5-in. leaves	Dark blue, 2-in. flowers in 10-in. spikes, summer–fall	Lush plant, likes some shade. 'Argentina Skies' has pale blue flowers. Costa Rica form has much larger flowers
S. 'Indigo Spires' Tender shrub	LS (protected), CS, TS	Rounded, to 4 ft. tall and wide. Medium green, oval leaves with serrated edges	Two-lipped, violet blooms, 1/2 in. long; deep purple calyxes similar in length, in clusters on 12-in.-long spikes	Long blooming in full sun and good-draining, humus-enriched soil. Pinch back, prune to shape. Propagate by cuttings. Excellent background for perennial, mixed borders
S. koyamae JAPANESE YELLOW SAGE Perennial	All zones	Loose ground cover; branches to 1 ft. tall. Yellow-green, heart-shaped leaves on 6-in.-long stems	Whorls of pale yellow flowers on 6–12-in. spikes, summer and fall	Best in rich, moisture-retentive soil with good drainage. Good plant to weave among other shade-loving plants
S. leucantha MEXICAN BUSH SAGE Shrub	LS (protected), CS, TS	To 3–4 ft., with graceful arching stems, grayish green foliage	Long velvety purple spikes set with small white flowers arch outward in summer, fall; attract hummingbirds	Takes some drought. May be hardier if old stems are not cut back until spring. All-purple and pink forms exist. Often treated as annual. Sun or light shade
S. madrensis FORSYTHIA SAGE Perennial	MS, LS, CS, TS	Spreading colonies, 4–7 ft. tall, with bright green, heart-shaped leaves; squarish, 2-in.-thick stems	Spikes of butter yellow blooms, early fall to frost. Good cut flower	Plant in sun or light shade in well-drained, moist soil. Propagate by division or cuttings. Cold-hardy selection 'Dunham', from the garden of Rachel Dunham in Cary, North Carolina, has survived −9°F
S. nemorosa VIOLET SAGE Perennial	US, MS, LS	Narrow, erect, to 3 ft., with narrow, 4-in., roughish leaves	Violet blue, in narrow spikes above foliage, summer–fall	Species rarely seen. 'East Friesland', 21/2 ft., is widely sold. Pink 'Rose Queen' is lower, not so vigorous. See also *S. superba*
S. officinalis COMMON SAGE Perennial	US, MS, LS, CS	To 21/2 ft., with aromatic, wrinkled gray-green leaves	Lavender blue, in short spikes above the foliage, summer	All selections good for seasoning. 'Berggarten' has biggest leaves, is longest lived. Colored types: 'Icterina', yellow and green leaves; 'Purpurascens', purplish tints; 'Tricolor', gray, white, and purplish pink. 'Nana' is a dwarf

S

SALVIA

NAME, TYPE	ZONES	GROWTH HABIT	FLOWERS	COMMENTS
S. pratensis MEADOW SAGE Perennial	US, MS, LS	To 3 ft., with large (6-in.), coarse basal leaves	Spikes of lavender blue blooms on branching stems, spring	'Haematodes', most commonly grown form. Makes a great show, but bloom period short. Reseeds. Needs warm, well-drained site
S. regla ROYAL SAGE Shrub	LS, CS	To 5 ft., possibly more, with bright green leaves	Downy, 2 in. long, bright red or orange red, with persistent orange calyx, spring through fall	'Huntington' grows 4–5 ft. tall, 'Royal' 6–8 ft. tall
S. sclarea CLARY Perennial or biennial	US, MS, LS, CS	Rough, gray-green, highly aromatic leaves to 8 in. long	White to lilac in big branching clusters to 3 ft., spring–summer	'Turkestanica' has pink flower stalks, white-and-pink flowers. Species and selection can be grown as annuals in all zones
S. splendens SCARLET SAGE Perennial grown as annual	All zones	Branched plant 1–3 ft. tall, depending on selection, with bright green foliage	Scarlet flowers, in tall, dense clusters; also in pink, purple, white, in tall or dwarf strains. Summer	Grow from seed or buy young plants from a garden center. Effective with gray-foliaged plants
S. superba Perennial	US, MS, LS	Erect, branched, 2–3-ft., with narrow leaves; narrow, erect flower spikes top each stalk	Violet blue or purple, summer–fall	Closely related to *S. nemorosa*. Plants often sold under either name are 'Blue Hill', dark blue, tall, nearly everblooming; 'Lubeca', tall, early flowering, deep violet; 'May Night', low growing, with deep blue flowers
S. texana BLUE TEXAS SAGE Perennial	MS, LS, CS, TS	Well-branched bush to 18 in., densely covered with hairs. Tapering leaves, 2 in. long, hairy; margins may be toothed	Spikes of 1-in. purplish blue flowers	In nature, grows in dry limestone soil in hills of Central and West Texas
S. uliginosa BOG SAGE Perennial	US, MS, LS, CS	Clumping plant with erect stems 6–7 ft. tall, with narrow, bright green, highly aromatic leaves	Pale blue and white blooms in erect, branched clusters to 5 in. long, summer–fall	Spreads by rhizomes. Can be invasive. Divide from time to time. Much or little water

soups, cool drinks. Can be used as an edging for border planting or herb garden. Evergreen in all but the Upper South.

S. obtusa. To 4 ft. tall, with grayish green leaves and 4-in. pink flower spikes in summer. Evergreen in all but the coldest winters.

SAN JOSE HESPER PALM. See BRAHEA brandegeei

SANSEVIERIA trifasciata

SNAKE PLANT, MOTHER-IN-LAW'S TONGUE

Agavaceae

EVERGREEN PERENNIAL

ZONE TS; OR INDOORS

SUN OR LIGHT SHADE

MODERATE OR LITTLE WATER

Grown outdoors all year in the Tropical South; indoor/outdoor or house plant elsewhere. Often sold as *S. zeylandica*. Appreciated for its patterned leaves that grow in rosettes from thick rhizomes. Leaves to 4 ft. tall, 2 in. wide, rigidly upright or spreading slightly at top, dark green banded with gray green. 'Laurentii' is identical but has broad, creamy yellow stripes on leaf edges. Dwarf 'Hahnii' has rosettes of 6-in.-long, broad, triangular, dark green leaves with silvery banding; rosettes pile up to make a 1-ft. mass. It's a good small potted plant or focus for dish garden.

First common name comes from leaf banding or mottling, which resembles some snakeskins; second probably comes from toughness of leaves and plant's persistence under neglect. The plant's tough leaf fibers are used as bowstrings. Occasionally bears erect, narrow clusters of greenish white,

Sansevieria trifasciata 'Laurentii'

fragrant flowers. Indoors, plants will grow in much or little light, seldom need repotting, and withstand considerable neglect—dry air, uneven temperatures, and light, capricious watering.

Other *Sansevieria* selections and species are collectors' items; scores can be found in catalogs of succulent plant dealers.

SANTOLINA

Asteraceae (Compositae)

EVERGREEN PERENNIALS

ZONES US, MS, LS

FULL SUN

REGULAR TO LITTLE WATER

Santolina chamaecyparissus

These have attractive foliage, a profusion of small, round, buttonlike flower heads in summer, and stout constitutions. Good as ground covers, bank covers, or low clipped hedges. Grow in any well-drained soil but prefer gritty soils of low fertility. All plants are aromatic if bruised and look best if kept low by pruning. Clip off spent flowers. Cut back to a few inches tall in early spring.

S. chamaecyparissus (C. incana). LAVENDER COTTON. Reaches 2 ft., but looks best clipped to 1 ft. or less. Brittle, woody stems are densely clothed with rough, finely divided, whitish gray leaves. Unclipped plants produce bright yellow flower heads. Set 3 ft. apart as ground cover, closer as edging for walks, borders, foreground plantings. Replace if woodiness takes over. 'Lemon Queen', 2 ft. tall and wide, has lemon yellow button flowers. 'Nana' is smaller than the species, to 1 ft. tall and 2–3 ft. wide.

S. rosmarinifolia (S. virens). GREEN SANTOLINA. To 2 ft., with narrow, green-and-silvery leaves like those of rosemary. Leaves may have tiny teeth or none at all. Bright yellow flowers.

SANVITALIA procumbens

CREEPING ZINNIA

Asteraceae (Compositae)

ANNUAL

✿ ALL ZONES

☼ FULL SUN

◐ REGULAR TO MODERATE WATER

*Sanvitalia
procumbens*

Not really a zinnia, but it looks enough like one to fool most people. Grows only 4–6 in. high but spreads or trails to 1 ft. or more. Leaves are like miniature (to 2-in.-long) zinnia leaves. Flower heads nearly 1 in. wide, with dark purple-brown center and bright yellow or orange rays. Bloom lasts from midsummer until frost. Selections are 'Mandarin Orange' and double-flowered 'Gold Braid'.

Needs good drainage. Resents transplanting; in spring, sow seeds where plants will grow. Heat resistant. Plant in hanging baskets or pots, or use as temporary filler in border, edging, or cover for slope or bank.

Sapindaceae. Members of the soapberry family are trees and shrubs with (usually) divided leaves, clustered small flowers (sometimes showy), and fruit that is berrylike, often showy. Some have edible fruit. Examples are *Koelreuteria, Litchi,* and western soapberry (*Sapindus drummondii*).

SAPINDUS drummondii

WESTERN SOAPBERRY

Sapindaceae

DECIDUOUS TREE

✿ ZONES US, MS, LS, CS

☼ FULL SUN

◐ MODERATE TO LITTLE WATER

Sapindus drummondii

Native to south-central U.S. Attractive round-headed, spreading tree to 25–30 ft. tall, with 10–15-in. leaves divided into many 3-in. leaflets. Tiny yellowish white flowers in clusters 8–10 in., early summer; these are followed by round, beadlike, ½-in. orange-yellow fruits that turn black in winter. More common in Texas and Oklahoma than elsewhere in the South. Makes a good shade or street tree because of its tolerance of adverse conditions—poor, dry, alkaline, rocky soil, low-quality air, wind, occasional drought. Fruit drop and self-sown seedlings can be problems.

⚘SAPIUM sebiferum

CHINESE TALLOW, POPCORN TREE

Euphorbiaceae

DECIDUOUS TREE

✿ ZONES LS, CS, TS

☼ FULL SUN

◐ REGULAR WATER

☘ SAP IS POISONOUS

Sapium sebiferum

Native to China and Japan. Fast-growing tree to 40 ft. tall, with a rounded or conical crown. Its names come from its unusual seeds: The Chinese once extracted wax from the seed capsules to make soap and candles, and the ripened, whitish seeds resemble popcorn. Decorating wreaths with this "popcorn" is a popular tradition in Charleston and other southeastern cities. The tree is prized for its spectacular scarlet, orange, burgundy, and yellow fall color, November and December, which is more intense in the Coastal rather than Lower South. In the northern end of the Lower South, young trees may be killed to the ground and branches of established trees may be frozen back several feet.

Leaves are rounded, top shaped, and medium green. They flutter in the slightest breeze. Tree has an airy look and casts moderate shade, making it a good choice for lawns and terraces. In summer, flowers appear as yellowish green stringlike catkins. The seed capsules that follow open by October, revealing the white, waxy seeds.

Chinese tallow tolerates almost any soil. Seedlings can easily grow 5 ft. tall the first year. Unfortunately, almost every seed produced germinates somewhere. The tree has spread so prolifically in Florida and along the South Atlantic coast that in those areas it is considered a noxious weed. Japanese tallow, *Sapium japonicum,* is similar except that the seeds are borne singly instead of in clusters.

> ### TRY CHINESE TALLOW FOR FLAMING COLORS
> If a Chinese tallow grows in full sun and gets moderate autumn chill, its foliage can turn to brilliant, translucent neon red, plum purple, yellow orange, or mixed colors. Select your tree while it is in fall color; some plants may color only in an uninteresting purplish or yellow.

SAPONARIA

Caryophyllaceae

PERENNIALS

✿ ZONES VARY BY SPECIES

☼ FULL SUN

◐ REGULAR TO MODERATE WATER

Saponaria officinalis
'Rosea Plena'

Generally low growing; closely related to *Lychnis* and *Silene.* Easy to grow in well-drained soil. Useful as border or in rock garden.

S. lembergii 'Max Frei'. Zones US, MS. Hybrid between two Mediterranean species. Compact, trailing plant 6–15 in. tall, with blue-green foliage and a midsummer show of inch-wide, bright reddish pink flowers.

S. ocymoides. ROCK SOAPWORT. Zone US. Trailing habit to 1 ft. high and 3 ft. across. Oval dark green leaves. In spring, plants are covered with small pink flowers in loose bunches shaped much like those of phlox. Useful for covering walls and as ground cover. 'Alba' is a white form; 'Rubra Compacta' has deep pink flowers.

⚘ **S. officinalis.** SOAPWORT, BOUNCING BET. Zones US, MS, LS, CS. To 2 ft. tall, spreading by underground runners. Can be invasive in rich, moist soil. Dark green leaves. Loose clusters of 1-in. red, pink, or white flowers in midsummer. If vigorously rubbed with water, plant produces suds. This is a tough plant; before the days of herbicides, it could be seen growing in the cinders along railroad rights-of-way. 'Rosea Plena', with double light pink flowers, is the common garden form. Selection 'Rubra Plena' has crimson blooms that turn paler as they age.

SAPPHIREBERRY. See SYMPLOCOS paniculata

SARCOCOCCA

SWEET BOX

Buxaceae

EVERGREEN SHRUBS

✿ ZONE LS, EXCEPT AS NOTED

◑ PARTIAL OR FULL SHADE

◐ REGULAR TO MODERATE WATER

*Sarcococca bookerana
bumilis*

Native to Himalayas, China. Grown for handsome, dark green, waxy foliage and for tiny, fragrant white flowers hidden in foliage in late winter or early spring. Small berrylike fruit. Useful in landscaping shaded areas—under overhangs, in entryways, beneath low-branching evergreen trees. They maintain slow, orderly growth and polished appearance in deepest shade. Grow best in soil rich in organic matter; add peat moss, ground bark, or the like to planting bed. Scale insects are the only pests.

S. confusa. Similar to (and generally sold as) *S. ruscifolia*. However, latter has red fruit, while that of *S. confusa* is black.

S. hookerana humilis (S. humilis). HIMALAYAN SWEET BOX. Zones US, MS, LS. Low growing, seldom more than 1½ ft. high; spreads by underground runners to 8 ft. or more. Oval, pointed leaves (1–3 in. long, ½–¾ in. wide) are closely set on branches. Flowers are followed by glossy blue-black fruit. Good ground cover.

S. ruscifolia. FRAGRANT SARCOCOCCA. Slow growth to 4–6 ft. high, 3–7 ft. wide. Will form natural espalier against wall, branches fanning out to create patterns. Leaves to 2 in. long, densely set on branches. Red fruit follows the flowers.

SASA. See BAMBOO

SASKATOON. See AMELANCHIER alnifolia

SASSAFRAS albidum

SASSAFRAS

Lauraceae

DECIDUOUS TREE

ZONES US, MS, LS, CS

FULL SUN

REGULAR WATER

Sassafras albidum

Native to eastern U.S. Fast grower to 20–25 ft. high, then more slowly to reach an eventual 50–60 ft. Often shrubby in youth; with age, becomes dense and pyramidal, with heavy trunk and rather short branches. Dark reddish brown, furrowed bark. Interesting winter silhouette. Leaves 3–7 in. long, 2–4 in. wide; they may be oval, mitten shaped, or lobed on both sides. Excellent fall color—shades of yellow, orange, scarlet, and purple. Yellow flowers aren't showy, but clusters outline the bare branches in early spring. Male and female flowers on separate trees; when the two sexes are grown near each other, the female tree bears dark blue, ½-in. berries on bright red stalks.

Pleasantly aromatic tree; bark of roots sometimes used for making tea, which has a flavor reminiscent of root beer. The tree's volatile oil, which contains safrole, is carcinogenic in animals; the bark is safrole-free. Extracts sold in markets for making sassafras tea are safrole-free as well.

Performs best in well-drained, nonalkaline soil; won't take prolonged drought. Hard to transplant. Tends to produce suckers, especially if roots are cut during cultivation. No noteworthy diseases. Japanese beetles can be a serious problem in the Upper South.

SATUREJA

Lamiaceae (Labiatae)

ANNUALS AND PERENNIALS

ZONES VARY BY SPECIES

FULL OR PARTIAL SUN

REGULAR TO MODERATE WATER

Satureja montana

These aromatic plants serve many culinary purposes. They're used to flavor sauces, vinegars, stews, soups, meat stuffings, and green beans. Summer savory has a mild, delicate flavor. Winter savory has a strong, pungent taste and retains this degree of flavor when dried.

S. hortensis. SUMMER SAVORY. Annual. All zones. Upright to 1½ ft.; loose, open habit. Rather narrow, aromatic leaves to 1½ in. long; use fresh or dried as mild seasoning for meats, fish, eggs, soups, beans, vegetables.

Whorls of tiny, delicate pinkish white to rose flowers appear in summer. Light, rich soil. Good pot plant.

S. montana. WINTER SAVORY. Shrubby perennial. Zones US, MS, LS, CS. Low, spreading, 6–15 in. high. Stiff, narrow to roundish leaves to 1 in. long; not as delicate in flavor as summer savory. Use leaves fresh or dried; clip at start of bloom season for drying. Profuse summer bloom; whorls of small white to lilac flowers, attractive to bees. Needs light, well-drained soil. Short-lived plant needs replacing after 2 to 3 years.

SAVORY. See SATUREJA

Saxifragaceae. The saxifrage family once included a number of shrubs, but these now occupy their own families—Hydrangeaceae and Grossulariaceae (currants and gooseberries). Remaining in Saxifragaceae are a number of herbaceous plants, including *Astilbe*, *Bergenia*, coral bells (*Heuchera*), and strawberry geranium (*Saxifraga*).

SAXIFRAGA stolonifera

STRAWBERRY GERANIUM, STRAWBERRY BEGONIA

Saxifragaceae

EVERGREEN PERENNIAL OR HOUSE PLANT

ZONES MS, LS, CS; OR INDOORS

PART OR FULL SHADE

REGULAR WATER

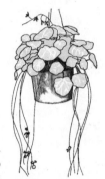
Saxifraga stolonifera

Creeping plant that makes runners like strawberry. Nearly round, white-veined leaves to 4 in. across, pink underneath; blend well with pink azaleas. White flowers to 1 in. across, in loose, open clusters to 2 ft. tall, late summer–fall. Can be used as house plant in hanging baskets or pots; good ground cover in the Lower and Coastal South where hard freezes are infrequent. Give bright indirect light indoors, shade outdoors.

SCABIOSA

PINCUSHION FLOWER

Dipsacaceae

ANNUALS AND PERENNIALS

ZONES US, MS, EXCEPT AS NOTED

FULL SUN TO PARTIAL SHADE

REGULAR TO MODERATE WATER

Scabiosa caucasica

Stamens protrude beyond curved surface of flower head, giving illusion of pins stuck into a cushion. Bloom begins in midsummer, continues until frost if flowers are cut. Most species dislike the South's hot, humid summers, but selection 'Butterfly Blue' takes heat fairly well. Good in mixed or mass plantings. Excellent for arrangements.

S. atropurpurea. PINCUSHION FLOWER, MOURNING BRIDE. Annual. Usually sold as *S. grandiflora*. To 2½–3 ft. tall. Oblong, coarsely toothed leaves. Many long, wiry stems carry flowers to 2 in. wide or more, in colors ranging from blackish purple to salmon pink, rose, and white.

S. caucasica. PINCUSHION FLOWER. Perennial. To 1½–2½ ft. high. Leaves vary from finely cut to uncut. Flowers 2½–3 in. across; depending on selection, color may be blue to bluish lavender or white. Excellent cut flowers. Give part shade in hot-summer areas. Fama strain has light blue, 3-in. flowers with large rays around the edge. House Hybrids strain is a mix of white and blue shades. 'Alba' is white flowered; 'Blue Perfection' has lavender blue blooms with fringed petals.

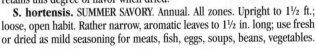
SOUTHERN HERITAGE PLANTS
IDENTIFIED BY SYMBOL

SCAEVOLA aemula

FANFLOWER

Goodeniaceae

SHRUBBY PERENNIAL

ZONE TS; OR GROW AS ANNUAL

FULL SUN

REGULAR TO MODERATE WATER

Scaevola

Australian native with fan-shaped flowers (all petals on one side) in blue shades. Evergreen perennial in Tropical South, nearly everblooming; annual elsewhere, blooms late spring–frost. Fleshy-stemmed, sprawling plants used for hanging baskets, as ground covers, or spilling over walls. Excellent drainage is essential. Lavender blue, 1½-in. flowers produced along branches. Available mainly through selections 'Blue Wonder', 'New Wonder', and 'Purple Fanfare' ('Diamond Head').

SCALY MALE FERN. See DRYOPTERIS affinis

SCARLET WISTARIA TREE. See SESBANIA grandiflora

SCHEFFLERA

Araliaceae

EVERGREEN SHRUBS OR SMALL TREES

ZONE TS, EXCEPT AS NOTED; OR INDOORS

FULL SUN OR LIGHT AFTERNOON SHADE

REGULAR WATER

Schefflera actinophylla

Fast-growing, tropical-looking plants; long-stalked leaves divided into leaflets that spread like fingers of a hand. Summer bloom, showy in some species. All need rich, moisture-retentive, well-drained soil. Useful near swimming pools. Good container plants.

Give house plants standard potting mix, occasional feeding, bright light but not direct sunlight. Let mix dry between waterings. Wash leaves occasionally; mist plants to discourage mites. Unlikely to bloom indoors.

S. actinophylla (Brassaia actinophylla). QUEENSLAND UMBRELLA TREE, OCTOPUS TREE, SCHEFFLERA. Zones CS (milder parts), TS. As garden plant, grows fast to 20 ft. or more. "Umbrella" name comes from horizontal tiers of leaves divided into 7 to 16 large (to 1-ft.-long) leaflets that radiate outward like ribs of umbrella. "Octopus" refers to arrangement of flowers in narrow, spreading clusters to 3 ft. long. Flowers age from greenish yellow to pink to dark red. Tiny dark purple fruit. Use for striking tropical effects, for silhouette, and for foliage contrast with ferns. Cut out tips occasionally to keep plant from becoming leggy. Cut overgrown plant nearly to ground; it will branch into better form.

S. arboricola (Heptapleurum arboricolum). DWARF SCHEFFLERA, HAWAIIAN ELF SCHEFFLERA. Outdoor plant can reach 20 ft. or more, with equal or greater spread, but can be easily pruned to smaller dimensions. Leaves dark green, much smaller than those of *S. actinophylla,* with 3-in. leaflets that broaden toward rounded tips. If stems are planted at angle, they continue to grow at that angle, which can give attractive multistemmed effects. Flowers yellowish aging to bronze, clustered in flattened spheres 1 ft. wide. Overall, gives a denser, darker, less treelike effect than *S. actinophylla.* Loves humidity.

Schefflera arboricola

S. elegantissima (Aralia elegantissima). House plant in youth, evergreen garden shrub in age. Leaves on young plants lacy looking, divided into ½-in. leaflets with notched edges; shiny dark green above, reddish beneath. Leaflets on mature plants grow to 1 ft. long, 3 in. wide.

SCHIZACHYRIUM scoparium. See ANDROPOGON scoparius

SCHIZOPHRAGMA hydrangeoides

JAPANESE HYDRANGEA VINE

Hydrangeaceae

DECIDUOUS VINE

ZONES US, MS, LS

PARTIAL SHADE

REGULAR WATER

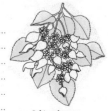

Schizophragma hydrangeoides

Resembles *Hydrangea anomala,* the climbing hydrangea. Climbs by holdfasts to 30 ft. Leaves are dark green, 3–5 in. long, oval, pointed, toothed. Broad clusters of flowers appear summer–fall; they resemble lace cap hydrangeas, but the showy white parts are the enlarged (to 1½-in.) sepals of the outermost flowers. In contrast to hydrangea, in which sterile flowers contain several showy sepals, sterile flowers of this plant have one sepal each. 'Moonlight' has blue-green foliage with a silvery cast. Use species or selection in shaded areas to climb masonry walls or trees.

SCHLUMBERGERA

Cactaceae

CACTI

ZONE TS; OR INDOORS

PARTIAL SHADE

REGULAR WATER

Schlumbergera bridgesii

In nature, these cacti live on trees like certain orchids. Plants are often confused in the nursery trade; many hybrids, selections differ principally in color. Remember, they come from the jungle—so give them rich, porous soil with plenty of leaf mold and sand. Feed frequently with liquid fertilizer, as often as every 7 to 10 days during growth and flowering. Give bright light indoors; if desired, set outdoors in partly shaded area in warm season.

S. bridgesii. CHRISTMAS CACTUS. Often sold as species *Zygocactus truncatus* (which is actually an alternate name for *S. truncata*). Old favorite. Arching, drooping branches made up of flattened, scallop-edged, smooth, bright green, spineless, 1½-in. joints. Plants may reach 3 ft. across and have hundreds of many-petaled, long-tubed, 3-in.-long, rosy purplish red flowers at Christmas time. To ensure late December bloom, keep plant where it will receive cool night temperatures (50–55°F) and 12 to 14 hours of darkness per day during November.

S. gaertneri. See Rhipsalidopsis gaertneri

S. truncata (Zygocactus truncatus). CRAB CACTUS. Joints 1–2 in. long, sharply toothed, with two large teeth at end of last joint on each branch. Short-tubed scarlet flowers with spreading, pointed petals, fall and winter. Many selections in white, pink, salmon, orange.

Schlumbergera truncata

SCIADOPITYS verticillata

UMBRELLA PINE

Taxodiaceae

EVERGREEN TREE

ZONES US, MS

AFTERNOON SHADE

REGULAR WATER

Sciadopitys verticillata

Grows to 100–120 ft. in its native Japan, but not likely to exceed 25–40 ft. in gardens here. Very slow grower. Young plant is symmetrical, dense, rather narrow; older plant opens up

S

and branches tend to droop. Small, scalelike leaves grow scattered along branches and bunch at branch ends. At branch and twig ends grow whorls of 20 to 30 long (3–6-in.), narrow, flattened, firm, fleshy needles of glossy dark green (they radiate out like spokes of umbrella). In time, woody cones, 3–5 in. long, may appear.

Choice decorative tree for open ground or container use. Plant in rich, well-drained, neutral or slightly acid soil. Leave unpruned, or thin to create oriental effect. Good bonsai subject. Boughs are beautiful and long lasting in arrangements. These are trees for connoisseurs, scarce because of their extremely slow growth.

SCILLA

SQUILL, BLUEBELL
Liliaceae
BULBS
ZONES US, MS, LS, EXCEPT AS NOTED
FULL SUN OR LIGHT SHADE
REGULAR WATER DURING GROWTH AND BLOOM
ALL PARTS ARE POISONOUS IF INGESTED

Scilla siberica

All have basal, strap-shaped leaves and clusters of bell-shaped or star-like flowers in winter or spring. Best planted in informal drifts among shrubs, under deciduous trees, among low-growing spring perennials. Good in pots, for cutting. All but *S. peruviana* need some winter chill. Plant cold-hardy species 2–3 in. deep, about 4 in. apart. All types are dormant in summer.

S. hispanica. See Endymion hispanicus

S. nonscripta. See Endymion non-scriptus

S. peruviana. PERUVIAN SCILLA. Zones LS, CS. Despite the name, this is a Mediterranean native. In late spring, clump of floppy leaves puts up foot-tall stems, each topped by a domed cluster of 50 or more purplish blue, starlike flowers. Bulbs go dormant only for a short time after leaves wither; replant then if necessary. Plant about 4 in. deep, 6 in. apart.

S. siberica. SIBERIAN SQUILL. Blooms very early, with loose spikes of intense blue flowers on 3–6-in. stems. 'Spring Beauty', with darker blue stripes, is choice. Also white, purplish pink, and violet blue selections.

S. tubergeniana (S. mischtschenkoana). Blooms in winter, at about same time as snowdrops and winter aconite. Flowers are pale blue with a darker blue stripe down center of each flower segment. Four or more flowers to each 4-in. stalk; three or more stalks to each bulb.

SCORPION WEED. See PHACELIA bipinnatifida

SCOTCH BROOM. See CYTISUS scoparius

SCOTCH MOSS. See SAGINA subulata, SELAGINELLA kraussiana

SCREW PINE. See PANDANUS utilis

Scrophulariaceae. The figwort family consists mainly of annuals and perennials. Most have irregular flowers, with four or five lobes. Examples are snapdragon *(Antirrhinum)*, foxglove *(Digitalis)*, beard tongue *(Penstemon)*, and wishbone flower *(Torenia fournieri)*.

SEA BUCKTHORN. See HIPPOPHAE rhamnoides

SEAFORTHIA elegans. See ARCHONTOPHOENIX cunninghamiana

SEA GRAPE. See COCCOLOBA

SEA HOLLY. See ERYNGIUM

SEA KALE. See CRAMBE maritima

SEA LAVENDER. See LIMONIUM

SEA PINK. See ARMERIA

SEASHORE PASPALUM. See PASPALUM vaginatum

SEDGE. See CAREX

SEDUM

STONECROP
Crassulaceae
SUCCULENT PERENNIALS
ZONES US, MS, LS, EXCEPT AS NOTED
FULL SUN OR LIGHT SHADE, EXCEPT AS NOTED
MODERATE TO LITTLE WATER, EXCEPT AS NOTED

Sedum kamtschaticum 'Variegatum'

They come from many parts of the world and vary in hardiness, cultural needs; some are among hardiest succulent plants. Some are tiny and trailing, others upright. Leaves fleshy, highly variable in size, shape, and color; evergreen unless otherwise noted. In the Upper South, leaves of evergreen types may turn red when weather cools. Flowers usually small, starlike, in fairly large clusters, sometimes brightly colored.

Smaller sedums are useful in rock gardens, as ground or bank cover, in small areas where unusual texture, color are needed. Some smaller types are prized by collectors of succulents, who grow them as potted or dish garden plants. Larger types good in borders or pots. Most propagate easily by stem cuttings—even detached leaves will root and form new plants. Soft and easily crushed, they will not take foot traffic; otherwise they are tough, low-maintenance plants. Set ground cover kinds 10–12 in. apart.

The botanically precise will note that several plants sold as *Sedum* have been reassigned to the genus *Hylotelephium;* changes are indicated below.

S. acre. GOLDMOSS SEDUM. Zones US, MS, LS, CS. To 2–5 in. tall, with upright branchlets from trailing, rooting stems. Tiny light green leaves; clustered yellow flowers in spring. Extremely hardy but can get out of bounds, become a weed. Use as ground cover, between stepping-stones, or on dry walls.

S. album. Often sold as *S. brevifolium.* Creeping plant 2–6 in. high. Leaves to ½ in. long, light to medium green, sometimes red tinted. White or pinkish summer flowers. Ground cover. Roots from smallest fragment, so beware of placing it near choice, delicate rock garden plants. 'Coral Carpet' has orange new growth, turns reddish bronze in winter.

S. cauticolum (Hylotelephium cauticolum). Arching stems to 8 in. long are set with blue-gray, slightly toothed leaves. Clusters of small rose red flowers top stems in late summer or early fall. Dies to ground in winter.

S. dasyphyllum. LEAFY SEDUM. Low, spreading mat with tiny, closely packed gray-green leaves and small white flowers with pink streaks. Selection 'Riffense' has plump, succulent, blue-gray leaves. Partial shade.

S. ellacombianum. Occasionally offered as a selection of species *S. kamtschaticum,* but is a shorter plant (6 in.) with more compact growth, unbranched stems, and scalloped rather than toothed leaves.

S. kamtschaticum. ORANGE SEDUM. Trailing stems to 1 ft. long are set with thick, somewhat triangular, 1–1½-in., slightly toothed leaves. Summer flowers age from yellow to red. Useful as small-scale ground cover, rock garden plant. 'Variegatum' has cream-edged leaves. *S. k. floriferum* is a more profuse bloomer than the species, with smaller, lighter yellow flowers. Its selection 'Weihenstephaner Gold' bears abundant bright yellow blossoms opening from red buds in late spring.

S. mexicanum. Zones MS, LS. Forms mat of sprawling stems, 4–8 in. tall. Leaves, to ¾ in. long, in whorls of three or five. Clusters of golden yellow flowers in late spring.

S. morganianum. BURRO TAIL, DONKEY TAIL. Safely outdoors in the Tropical South; house plant anywhere. Long, trailing stems grow to 3–4 ft. in 6 to 8 years. Thick, light gray-green leaves overlap each other along stems to give braided or ropelike effect. Pink to deep red flowers (rarely

Sedum morganianum

S

seen) may appear from spring to summer. Because of long stems, most practical place to grow this plant is in hanging basket or wall pot. Provide rich, fast-draining soil. Protect from wind and give half shade; water freely and feed two or three times during summer with liquid fertilizer.

Sedum sieboldii

S. sieboldii (Hylotelephium sieboldii). SIEBOLD SEDUM. Spreading, trailing, unbranched stems to 8–9 in. long. Leaves in threes, nearly round, stalkless, toothed in upper half, blue gray edged red. Plant turns coppery red in fall, dies to ground in winter. Each stem shows broad, dense, flat cluster of dusty pink flowers in fall. Use in rock garden or hanging basket. Light shade. Leaves of 'Variegatum' marked yellowish white.

S. spectabile (Hylotelephium spectabile). SHOWY SEDUM. Zones US, MS, LS, CS. Upright or slightly spreading stems to 1½ ft. tall, well set with blue-green, roundish, 3-in. leaves. Pink flowers in dense, dome-shaped clusters, to 6 in. wide, atop stems in late summer, autumn. If stems are not cut after bloom, flower clusters age into brownish maroon seed clusters atop bare stems. Dies to ground in winter. 'Brilliant' has deep rose red flowers, 'Carmen' is soft rose, 'Meteor' is carmine red, and 'Ruby Jewel' is deep maroon. Full sun. Regular to moderate water. Species resembles *S. telephium* in foliage and flowers, and in the developing seed heads that put on a long-lasting show.

Sedum spectabile 'Brilliant'

S. spurium. TWO-ROW SEDUM. Zones US, MS, LS, CS. Low grower with trailing stems. Leaves thick, an inch or so long, nearly as wide, dark green or bronze tinted. Pink summer flowers in dense clusters at ends of 4–5-in. stems. Good for rock garden, pattern planting, ground cover. 'Coccineum', often known by the name "dragon's blood," has bronzy leaves, rosy red flowers.

S. telephium (Hylotelephium telephium). LIVE-FOREVER SEDUM. Zones US, MS, LS, CS. To 2 ft. high. Resembles *S. spectabile*, but leaves are narrower. Like *S. spectabile*, it is showy over a long season, dies down in winter. 'Indian Chief' blooms are deep pink. Hybrid 'Autumn Joy' has blossoms of bright salmon pink turning to russet; hybrid 'Mohrchen' has rosy pink flowers and purple new growth. 'Atropurpureum' (often listed as a variety of *S. maximum*, a species no longer considered distinct from *S. telephium*) has burgundy leaves all season and dusty pink flowers. Full sun. Regular to moderate water.

S. ternatum. MOUNTAIN SEDUM. Native to moist, open woodlands in eastern U.S. Creeping stems form large mats of pretty foliage 3–6 in. tall. Small, roundish leaves, ½–1 in. long, grow in whorls of three, pale green when new, aging to dark dull green. Numerous ½-in. white flowers, with purple-red stamens, open along the stems in late spring, early summer. Thrives in moist soil with lots of organic matter. Full or partial shade.

S. 'Vera Jameson'. Hybrid with the habit and flowers of *S. sieboldii*, but with purple leaves.

SELAGINELLA

Selaginellaceae

MOSSLIKE GROUND COVERS

ZONES MS, LS, CS, TS

PARTIAL OR FULL SHADE

REGULAR WATER

Selaginella kraussiana

Mosslike, evergreen or semievergreen ground covers that are beautiful and easy to grow in humid, moist shade and slightly acid soils with lots of organic matter. Some of the many species are erect tufts of green often mistaken for ferns, but most spread very low to the ground, the sprawling stems rooting as they grow. One has electric blue leaves.

S. involvens. Grows 6–12 in. tall. Erect, tufty habit. Stems much branched and crowded with bright green leaves.

S. kraussiana. IRISH MOSS, SCOTCH MOSS, CLUB MOSS. Creeping, trailing habit, with stems to 12 in. long that root rapidly. Bright green leaves. Useful for hanging baskets. 'Aurea' has bright golden green foliage. 'Brownii' is especially dwarf, forms a cushion on the soil.

S. uncinata. PEACOCK MOSS. Creeping, trailing habit, with stems to 2 ft. long. In filtered light, leaves are bright metallic blue green.

SEMPERVIVUM

HOUSELEEK

Crassulaceae

SUCCULENT PERENNIALS

ZONES US, MS, LS, CS

FULL SUN

REGULAR TO LITTLE WATER

Sempervivum tectorum

Evergreen perennial plants with tightly packed rosettes of leaves. Little offsets cluster around parent rosette. Flowers star shaped, in tight or loose clusters, white, yellowish, pink, red, or greenish, pretty in detail but not especially showy. Summer bloom. Blooming rosettes die after setting seed, but easily planted offsets carry on. Many species, all good in rock gardens, containers, even in pockets on boulders or pieces of porous rock. Need good drainage.

S. arachnoideum. COBWEB HOUSELEEK. Tiny (¾-in.-across) gray-green rosettes of many leaves joined by fine hairs give a cobweb-covered look to plant. Spreads slowly to make dense mats. Bright red flowers borne on 4-in. stems; seldom blooms.

S. tectorum. HEN AND CHICKENS. Rosettes gray green, 4–6 in. across, spreading quickly by offsets. Leaves tipped red brown, bristle pointed. Flowers red or reddish in clusters on stems to 2 ft. tall. Easy to grow in rock gardens, borders, pattern planting.

SENECIO

Asteraceae (Compositae)

ANNUALS, PERENNIALS, SHRUBS, VINES

ZONES VARY BY SPECIES

EXPOSURE NEEDS VARY BY SPECIES

WATER NEEDS VARY BY SPECIES

Senecio cineraria

Daisy relatives that range from garden cineraria and dusty miller to vines, shrubs, perennials, succulents, even a few weeds. Succulents are often sold as *Kleinia*, an earlier name.

S. aureus. GOLDEN GROUNDSEL. Perennial. Zones US, MS, LS. Native to eastern North America. To 2 ft. high. Clump of bright green, toothed leaves is topped in spring by flat clusters of deep yellow, ½–1-in.-wide daisies. Full sun or part shade. Good bog garden plant.

S. cineraria. DUSTY MILLER. Shrubby perennial in Zones MS, LS, CS; annual in the Upper South. To 2–2½ ft. tall and spreading. Woolly white leaves cut into many blunt-tipped lobes. Clustered heads of yellow or creamy yellow flowers in summer. Gets leggy unless sheared occasionally. Full sun. Needs good drainage, moderate water. Striking in night garden.

WILL THE REAL DUSTY MILLER PLEASE STAND UP?

Many plants answer to the name; all have whitish, silvery, or grayish foliage, grow in full sun, and tolerate some drought. A number of plants are sold by this common name; the best known is *Senecio cineraria*. Others include species *S. vira-vira, Artemisia stellerana,* and *Centaurea cineraria*.

S. confusus. MEXICAN FLAME VINE. Zones CS, TS; dies to ground in mild frost but comes back fast from roots. Twines to 8–10 ft. Light green,

S

rather fleshy leaves are 1–4 in. long, ½–1 in. wide, coarsely toothed. Large clusters of ¾–1-in., startling orange-red blooms with golden centers appear at branch ends; 'São Paulo' is deeper orange, almost brick red. Plants bloom all year where winters are mild. Provide light soil, regular water. Full sun or light shade. Use on trellis or column, let cascade over bank, wall, or plant in hanging basket.

S. glabellus. BUTTER-WEED. Annual. All zones. Native to southeastern U.S. Fast-growing, prolifically self-seeding plant that makes a bright, easy swath of yellow in wet soils from very early spring to the beginning of summer. Leaves in basal rosette, broadly toothed. Daisy-like flowers in clusters, each flower 1 in. across. Full sun or partial shade.

S. hybridus (S. cruentus, Pericallis cruenta). CINERARIA. Annual grown for seasonal color. All zones. Most common are large-flowered dwarf kinds usually sold as Multiflora Nana or Hybrida Grandiflora. These are compact, 12–15-in.-high plants with broad clusters of 3–5-in. daisies. Colors range from white through pink and purplish red to blue and purple, often with contrasting eyes or bands. Plants usually for sale in greenhouses between Valentine's Day and Easter. All types need cool, moist, loose, rich soil. Once they finish blooming, throw them away.

Senecio hybridus

S. leucostachys. See S. vira-vira

S. macroglossus. KENYA IVY, NATAL IVY, WAX VINE. Evergreen vine in the Tropical South; house plant anywhere. Twining or trailing vine to 6½ ft., with thin, succulent stems and thick, 2–3-in.-wide, waxy or rubbery leaves. Leaves shaped like ivy leaves, with three, five, or seven shallow lobes. Tiny yellow daisies in summer. Leaves of 'Variegatum' boldly splashed with creamy white. Give part shade and moderate water. As house plant, grow in sunny window and water only when soil is dry.

S. vira-vira (S. leucostachys, S. cineraria 'Candissimus'). DUSTY MILLER. Subshrub. Zones MS, LS. To 4 ft. tall, with broad, sprawling habit. Leaves like those of *S. cineraria* but more strikingly white, more finely cut into much narrower, pointed segments. Creamy white summer flowers are not showy. In full sun, it is brilliantly white and densely leafy; in part shade, it is looser and more sparsely foliaged, with larger, greener leaves. Tip-pinch young plants to keep them compact. Moderate water.

SENEGAL DATE PALM. See PHOENIX reclinata

SENNA. See CASSIA

SENSITIVE FERN. See ONOCLEA sensibilis

SENTRY PALM. See HOWEA

SERISSA foetida

SERISSA

Rubiaceae

EVERGREEN SHRUB

✚ ZONES CS, TS

◐ PARTIAL SHADE

◔◑ BEST WITH REGULAR WATER

Serissa foetida 'Variegata'

Coffee relative, native to southeast Asia. Small, rounded shrub, 2–4 ft. tall, with ½-in.-long, oval, dark green leaves. Tiny white flowers in late spring and intermittently in other seasons. Tolerates most soils, except constantly wet ones. Many dwarf, pink-flowering, and variegated selections available, including 'Flore-pleno', to 2 ft. tall, with double white flowers; 'Pink Swan', pink flowers, leaves edged with cream; and 'Variegata', to 2 ft. tall, white flowers, leaves edged with white. Popular bonsai plants. Leaves and stems smell fetid when bruised.

SERVICEBERRY. See AMELANCHIER

SESBANIA

Fabaceae (Leguminosae)

DECIDUOUS SHRUBS, TREES

✚ ZONES CS, TS

◐ FULL SUN

◔ REGULAR WATER

◇ POISONOUS PODS

Sesbania punicea

Fast-growing but short-lived plants with broad, open canopies of feathery foliage and pretty, hanging clusters in summer of flowers reminiscent of wisteria, followed by beanlike seedpods that dry and then rattle in the wind. Need well-drained soils. Some drought tolerance.

S. grandiflora. SCARLET WISTARIA TREE. Deciduous tree native to tropical Asia, almost evergreen in warmest parts of South. To 30–40 ft. tall. Leaves to 12 in. long, with many pairs of 1–2-in. leaflets. Pealike rusty red, pink, and white flowers dangle in clusters. Pods can be over 1 ft. long.

S. punicea. RATTLE BOX. Deciduous shrub native to South America, naturalized in Coastal South. Sometimes sold as *Daubentonia, Ditripettii.* Usually grows to 6 ft. tall, though it can reach up to 10 ft. Self-seeds and forms sometimes rangy-looking colonies with broad flat tops of delicate foliage. Leaves are variable in length, with 6 to 20 pairs of ½–1-in. leaflets. Vermilion flowers in 4-in. clusters appear from early summer into early fall.

SETARIA palmifolia

PALM GRASS

Poaceae (Gramineae)

PERENNIAL

✚ ZONES CS, TS

◐ FULL SUN OR LIGHT SHADE

◔ REGULAR WATER

Setaria palmifolia

This tropical-looking grass has long (1–3-ft.), wide (2–3-in.), pleated, deep green leaves in clumps 3–6 ft. tall. Evergreen, but top freezes at 28°F, resprouting if roots do not freeze. Use for tropical look along walks or in woodland plantings. Where adapted, it can seed itself and become a pest; remove flowers before seeds ripen.

ꔢ SETCREASEA pallida 'Purple Heart' (Tradescantia pallida 'Purpurea')

PURPLE HEART

Commelinaceae

PERENNIAL

✚ ZONES MS, LS, CS, TS; OR INDOORS

◐ FULL SUN

◔ MODERATE WATER

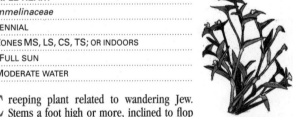
Setcreasea pallida 'Purple Heart'

Creeping plant related to wandering Jew. Stems a foot high or more, inclined to flop over. Deep purple leaves rather narrowly oval and pointed. Pale or deep purple flowers not showy. Use discretion in planting, since the vivid foliage can create a harsh effect. Pinch back after bloom. Generally unattractive in winter. Frost may kill tops, but recovery is fast in warm weather. Outdoors, use as ground cover, bedding plant, or pot plant. In the Upper South, give house plants strong indirect light.

SHADBLOW. See AMELANCHIER

SOUTHERN HERITAGE PLANTS
IDENTIFIED BY SYMBOL ꔢ

S

SHAMROCKS. Around St. Patrick's Day, garden centers and florists sell "shamrocks." These are small potted plants of *Medicago lupulina* (hop clover, yellow trefoil, black medic), an annual plant; *Oxalis acetosella* (wood sorrel), a perennial; or *Trifolium repens* (white clover), a perennial and the most common. All have leaves of three leaflets, symbolic of the Trinity. They can be kept on a sunny windowsill or planted out, but they have little ornamental value and some can become weeds.

SHASTA DAISY. See CHRYSANTHEMUM maximum

SHEEP LAUREL. See KALMIA angustifolia

SHELL GINGER. See ALPINIA zerumbet

SHIELD FERN. See DRYOPTERIS, POLYSTICHUM

SHOOTING STAR. See DODECATHEON meadia

SHORTIA

Diapensiaceae

PERENNIALS

☀ ZONES US, MS

◐ ● WOODSY SHADE

◐ ◐ AMPLE TO REGULAR WATER

Shortia galacifolia

Beautiful, small spring-blooming evergreen plants that spread slowly by underground stems. *S. galacifolia* is native to the U.S.; the other two species are native to Japan. Intolerant of heat. Need acid, leafy, or peaty soil. Grow with azaleas or rhododendrons.

S. galacifolia. OCONEE BELLS. Native to mountains of North and South Carolina. Forms clump of glossy green, round or oval leaves 1–3 in. long, with scallop-toothed edges. Each of the species many 4–6-in.-high stems is topped with a single, nodding, 1-in.-wide white bell with toothed edges.

S. soldanelloides. FRINGE BELLS. Round, coarsely toothed leaves form clumps similar to those of *S. galacifolia*, but flowers are pink to rose in color, with deeply fringed edges.

S. uniflora 'Grandiflora'. Like *S. galacifolia* but with indented and wavy-edged leaves, and flowers that are large fringed bells of clear soft pink.

SHOWER OF GOLD. See CASSIA fistula

SHOWY COBRA LILY. See ARISAEMA speciosum

SHRIMP PLANT. See JUSTICIA brandegeana

SHRUB BUSH CLOVER. See LESPEDEZA thunbergii

SHRUBBY YEW PINE. See PODOCARPUS macrophyllus maki

SIBERIAN BUGLOSS. See BRUNNERA macrophylla

SIBERIAN CARPET CYPRESS. See MICROBIOTA decussata

SIDALCEA

CHECKERBLOOM, MINIATURE HOLLYHOCK

Malvaceae

PERENNIALS

☀ ZONES US, MS

☀ FULL SUN

◐ REGULAR WATER

Sidalcea malviflora

Most commonly grown forms are hybrids, typically 2–3 ft. high, with rounded, lobed leaves and silky-petaled, 1–2-in. flowers like little hollyhocks. They include 'Brilliant', with carmine red flowers; 'Elsie Heugh', bright pink blossoms with fringed petals; and 'Loveliness', shell pink flowers. 'Party Girl', with deep pink blooms, is a little taller (to 3½ ft.). Plants bloom all summer if faded flowers are removed. These and other improved garden plants were developed mainly from *S. malviflora*, with lavender-pink or bright pink flowers, and *S. candida*, a white-flowered High Plains native. Best in cool, fairly dry climates. Provide good drainage. Divide clumps every few years.

SILENE

Caryophyllaceae

PERENNIALS

☀ ZONES VARY BY SPECIES

☀ ◐ FULL SUN OR PARTIAL SHADE

◐ ◐ WATER NEEDS VARY BY SPECIES

Silene virginica

Many species, some with erect growth habit, others cushionlike. Provide well-drained soil. For front of border or rock garden.

S. caroliniana. WILD PINK. Zones US, MS, LS, CS. Native from Florida to New Hampshire, west to Missouri. Low-growing mound, 4–8 in. tall and 12 in. across. Bluish green leaves 5 in. long, 1 in. wide; clusters of up-facing, white to deep pink flowers with notched petals in late spring, early summer. Tolerates dry, thin soils.

S. laciniata. INDIAN PINK, MEXICAN CAMPION. Zones LS, CS. Native to mountains of Mexico, New Mexico, and California. Leaves 1–5 in. long; stems 2–3 ft. long, somewhat sprawling. Showy bright red flowers, with deeply fringed petals, one (or a few) per stem. Likes dryish soil, full sun.

S. polypetala. FRINGED CAMPION. Zones US, MS, LS. Native to southern Appalachians, rare and endangered; be careful to buy only nursery-propagated plants. Makes a dark green mat, to 1½ ft. across and 4–6 in. high. Large, soft pink, fringed flowers in late spring. Leaves spoon shaped. Beautiful woodland garden plant: needs partial shade and moist, well-drained soil with lots of organic matter.

S. virginica (Melandrium virginicum). FIRE PINK. Zones US, MS, LS. Native to eastern and central U.S. Narrow, lance-shaped leaves in a clump to 2–3 ft. high. Clusters of crimson flowers with notched petals in late spring or early summer. 'Longwood', a hybrid between *S. virginica* and *S. polypetala*, has fringed, deep pink flowers and forms an evergreen mound to 8 in. high. Regular water. Unlike *S. polypetala*, is easily obtained through mail-order nurseries.

SILK FLOWER. See ABELMOSCHUS moschatus

SILK OAK. See GREVILLEA robusta

SILVER BELL. See HALESIA

SILVER DATE PALM. See PHOENIX sylvestris

SILVER GRASS. See MISCANTHUS

SILVER LACE VINE. See POLYGONUM aubertii

SILVER SPREADER. See ARTEMISIA caucasica

SILVER TRUMPET TREE. See TABEBUIA argentea

SINARUNDINARIA. See BAMBOO, FARGESIA

SINNINGIA speciosa (Gloxinia speciosa)

GLOXINIA

Gesneriaceae

TUBER

☀ INDOOR/OUTDOOR OR HOUSE PLANT

● SHADE OUTDOORS; BRIGHT LIGHT INDOORS

◐ SEE INSTRUCTIONS BELOW

Sinningia speciosa

Leaves oblong, dark green, toothed, fuzzy, 6 in. or longer. Flowers are spectacular—large, velvety, bell shaped, ruffled edges, in blue, red, purple, violet, pink, or white. Some blooms have dark dots or blotches, others contrasting bands at flower rims. Leaves occasionally white veined. Tubers usually available December–March. Plant 1 in. deep in rich, loose mix. Water sparingly until first leaves appear; increase watering after roots form. Apply water around base of plant, not on top of leaves. When roots fill pot, move plant to larger pot. Feed regularly during growth period.

After bloom has finished, gradually dry off plants. Dig tubers and store in cool, dark place with just enough moisture to keep them from shriveling; or store tubers, soil and all, in pots until new growth starts. Repot in January–February. Tubers can be set in garden beds in spring for early summer bloom; lift and store before first frost.

SISYRINCHIUM

BLUE-EYED GRASS

Iridaceae

PERENNIALS

✍ ZONES VARY BY SPECIES

☼ ◑ FULL SUN OR LIGHT SHADE

◐ ● REGULAR TO MODERATE WATER

Sisyrinchium angustifolium

R elated to iris. Narrow, rather grasslike leaves. Small flowers, made up of six segments, open in sunshine. Pretty but not showy, best suited for informal gardens or naturalizing.

S. angustifolium. Zones US, MS, LS. Native to the East. To 6–18 in.; narrow dark green leaves and clusters of ½-in. blue flowers in summer.

S. atlanticum. Zones US, MS, LS. Native to eastern U.S. Violet blue flowers with yellow centers on slender, wiry, branched stems 4–30 in. tall. Pale glaucous green leaves. Blooms late spring–early summer.

S. bellum. Zones MS, LS. Native to coast of California. To 4–16 in. tall. Narrow green or bluish green leaves. Flowers purple to bluish purple, ½ in. across, early to midspring. Several named forms, many dwarf.

S. bermudiana. Zones US, MS, LS. Native to Bermuda. Branched, flattened, stout stems to 2 ft. tall, with violet blue flowers, yellow eye. Flowers spring–early summer.

S. californicum. GOLDEN-EYED GRASS. Zones MS, LS. Native to Oregon, California. Low clump of dull green leaves. Flower stems unbranched, broad, 6–24 in. tall; bright yellow, 1-in. star flowers, late spring and early summer. Self seeds but not invasive. Likes moisture, even wet places.

SKIMMIA

Rutaceae

EVERGREEN SHRUBS

✍ ZONE US

☼ ◑ PARTIAL OR FULL SHADE

● REGULAR WATER

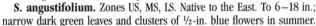

Skimmia japonica

S low growing and compact, with glossy, rich green leaves neatly arranged along the branches. In spring, tiny white flowers open from clusters of pinkish buds held well above foliage. Red fruit resembling holly berries appears in fall and winter if pollination requirements are met. Individual plants are dense mounds; when massed, they form a solid foliage cover. Good under windows, beside shaded walks, flanking entryways, in containers. Blend well with all shade plants.

Prefer moist, highly organic, acid soils. Excellent drainage a must. Mites are the main pests; they give foliage a sunburned look. Thrips may also attack. Water mold can be a problem. Shield from cold, sweeping winds.

S. foremanii. Hybrid between *S. japonica* and *S. reevesiana*. Resembles *S. japonica*, but is more compact, with broader, heavier, darker green leaves. Plants may be male, female, or self-fertile.

S. japonica. JAPANESE SKIMMIA. Size variable. Slow growth to 2–5 ft. or taller, 3–6 ft. wide. Oval, blunt-ended leaves to 3–4 in. long and 1 in. wide, most often clustered near the twig ends. Flowers are borne in clusters

2–3-in. across; they are larger and more fragrant on male plants. If a male plant is present, female plants produce bright red berries—attractive enough to make planting both sexes worth the effort. A form with ivory white berries is available. Male selection 'Macrophylla' is a rounded, spreading shrub to 5–6 ft. tall, with large leaves and flowers.

S. reevesiana (S. fortunei). Dwarf, dense-growing shrub 2 ft. tall. Self-fertile, with dull crimson fruit. Fragrant flowers.

SKY FLOWER. See DURANTA repens, THUNBERGIA grandiflora

SMILACINA

Liliaceae

PERENNIALS

✍ ZONES US, MS, LS

◑ LIGHT SHADE

● REGULAR WATER

Smilacina racemosa

S pread by creeping rhizomes to form dense colonies. Need rich, loose, moist, slightly acid soil. Good for naturalizing in wild garden. Fruit favored by wildlife.

S. racemosa. FALSE SOLOMON'S SEAL, FALSE SPIKENARD. Native to woods throughout much of North America. Grows 1–3 ft. tall. Each arching stalk has several 3–6-in.-long leaves with hairy undersides; foliage turns golden yellow in autumn. Stalks are topped by fluffy, conical clusters of small, fragrant, creamy white flowers in spring. Red autumn berries with purple spots. Resembles true solomon's seal *(Polygonatum)*.

S. stellata. STARFLOWER. Native to Virginia, north to Newfoundland and west to Kansas and California. Grows to 1 ft. tall usually, sometimes to 2½ ft. Stems erect or somewhat spreading. Light green, 6-in. leaves are folded lengthwise, or channeled, and clasp the stem. Creamy white, spring flowers smaller than those of *S. racemosa*. Red-black berries.

SMILAX

Liliaceae

WOODY VINES

✍ ZONES MS, LS, CS

☼ ◑ FULL SUN OR PARTIAL SHADE

◐ ● REGULAR TO LITTLE WATER

Smilax lanceolata

N ative to eastern U.S. Tough, moderately fast growing, tidy vines that grow from rhizomes or large underground tubers (the roots of some species are used to make sarsaparilla). Vines climb by tendrils. Not related to florists' smilax, which is *Asparagus asparagoides*.

S. lanceolata. GREENBRIER SMILAX. Evergreen. To 30–40 ft. A popular vine for framing doorways in the Lower South. Young stems are very thorny. Difficult to find in garden centers. Plants usually started from enormous tubers dug from the wild. Main attraction is the leaves: dark, glossy green, pointed and lance or oval shaped, to 3½ in. long, 2 in. wide. Foliage often used in holiday wreaths. Small, dull reddish brown berries.

S. smallii. JACKSON VINE. Evergreen. Vining stems to 10 ft. Only bases of stems have spines. Dark green, glossy, thin leaves, 6 in. long, 3 in. wide, prominently five veined. Inconspicuous green flowers followed by black berries. Leaves and stems retain color long after cutting; used in Christmas decorations. Good for trellis, training over doorway, arbor.

S. walteri. Deciduous. Leaves similar to those of *S. lanceolata*. Showy red berries, occasionally white. Older stems often spiny.

SMOKE TREE. See COTINUS coggygria

SMOOTH WITHE-ROD. See VIBURNUM nudum

SNAKE PLANT. See SANSEVIERIA trifasciata

SNAPDRAGON. See ANTIRRHINUM majus

SNEEZEWEED, COMMON. See HELENIUM autumnale

SNOWBALL, FRAGRANT. See VIBURNUM carlcephalum

SNOWBELL. See STYRAX

SNOWBERRY. See SYMPHORICARPOS

SNOWDROP. See GALANTHUS

SNOWDROP TREE. See HALESIA carolina

SNOWDROP TREE, JAPANESE. See STYRAX japonicus

SNOWFLAKE. See LEUCOJUM

SNOW-IN-SUMMER. See CERASTIUM tomentosum

SNOW-ON-THE-MOUNTAIN. See EUPHORBIA marginata

SOAPWEED. See YUCCA glauca

SOAPWORT. See SAPONARIA officinalis

SOCIETY GARLIC. See TULBAGHIA violacea

SOFT SHIELD FERN. See POLYSTICHUM setiferum

Solanaceae. Members of the potato family bear flowers that are nearly always star or saucer shaped and five petaled; fruits are berries or capsules. Plants are frequently rank smelling or even poisonous, but many are important food crops—eggplant, pepper, potato, tomato. Others are garden annuals, perennials, shrubs, or vines—including amethyst flower (*Browallia*), *Cestrum*, *Nicotiana*, and *Petunia*.

SOLANDRA maxima

CUP-OF-GOLD VINE, CHALICE VINE

Solanaceae

EVERGREEN VINE

✿ ZONE TS

☀ FULL SUN; SHADE ROOTS

◗ REGULAR, DEEP WATERING

Solandra maxima

Usually sold as *Solandra guttata*, a similar plant. Fast, sprawling, rampant vine to 40 ft.; fasten it to a support. Large, broad, glossy leaves 4–6 in. long. Blooms midwinter–early spring, intermittently at other times. Bowl-shaped flowers are 6–8 in. wide, golden yellow striped brownish purple.

Prune to induce branching and more flowers. Can be cut back to make rough hedge. Takes salt spray directly above tide line; stands wind, fog. Use on big walls and pergolas, along eaves, or as bank cover. For easy viewing inside the big flowers, encourage growth low on plant by tip-pinching. This vine is spectacular trained along swimming pool fence.

SOLANUM

Solanaceae

EVERGREEN OR DECIDUOUS SHRUBS, VINES, PERENNIALS

✿ ZONES VARY BY SPECIES

☀ ◗ FULL SUN OR PARTIAL SHADE

◗ ◗ REGULAR TO MODERATE WATER

✦ MANY SPECIES ARE POISONOUS IF INGESTED; MOST ARE SUSPECT

Solanum pseudocapsicum

In addition to eggplant and potato (described under those names), *Solanum* includes several ornamental plants, all with small, five-petaled, blue or white blooms; a few have decorative fruit.

S. jasminoides. POTATO VINE. Evergreen vine. Zones CS, TS. Twining habit; fast growth to 30 ft. Leaves purplish-tinged, 1½–3 in. long; 1-in.-wide flowers in pure white or in white tinged with blue, in clusters of 8 to 12. Nearly perpetual bloom, heaviest in spring. Grown for flowers or for light overhead shade. Cut back severely at any time to prevent tangling, promote vigorous new growth. Control rampant runners that grow along ground.

S. pseudocapsicum. JERUSALEM CHERRY. Evergreen shrub. Zones CS, TS; annual or indoor/outdoor plant anywhere. To 3–4 ft. high (shorter if grown as an annual). Deep green, smooth, shiny leaves to 4 in. long. White flowers followed in autumn by fine show of scarlet (rarely yellow), ½-in. fruits that look similar to miniature tomatoes but are poisonous. Plant blooms, fruits, seeds itself year-round. The many dwarf strains (1 ft. high) are more popular than taller kinds and bear larger fruit (to 1 in.).

S. rantonnetii. See Lycianthes rantonnei

S. seaforthianum. BRAZILIAN NIGHTSHADE. Evergreen vine. Zone TS. Leaves to 8 in. long, some undivided, others divided featherwise into leaflets. Clusters of violet blue, inch-wide flowers in summer; small red fruits edible only to birds.

S. wendlandii. COSTA RICAN NIGHTSHADE. Deciduous vine. Zone TS. Tall, twining vine with prickly stems. Leaves larger than those of other species (4–10 in. long), lower ones divided into leaflets. Loses leaves in low temperatures even without frost; slow to leaf out in spring. Big clusters of 2½-in., lilac blue flowers in summer. Use to clamber into tall trees, cover a pergola, decorate eaves of large house.

SOLENOSTEMON scutellarioides. See COLEUS hybridus

SOLIDAGO and SOLIDASTER

GOLDENROD

Asteraceae (Compositae)

PERENNIALS

✿ ZONES US, MS, LS, CS

☀ ◗ FULL SUN OR LIGHT SHADE

◗ MODERATE WATER

Solidago

Goldenrods are not as widely grown as they deserve, largely due to the mistaken belief that their pollen causes hay fever (in fact, other plants are responsible). Although a few of the hundred-plus species are weeds in many regions, many are choice garden plants. All have leafy stems rising from tough, woody, spreading rootstocks; all bear small yellow flowers in large, branching clusters from mid- or late summer into fall. All are tough plants that thrive in not-too-rich soil. Use in borders with black-eyed Susan or Michaelmas daisy, or naturalize in meadows. For a similar plant, try the goldenrod relative *Solidaster luteus,* also described below.

Solidago altissima. TALL GOLDENROD. Every part of 3–7-ft.-tall plant is bristly. Stems are erect, stiff, and much branched. Large, branched, pyramidal flower heads. Blossom is state flower of Kentucky.

S. canadensis. CANADA GOLDENROD. Stands 3–5 ft. tall. Large, dense, showy, one-sided flower panicles. Starts blooming in late summer, continues into fall. Robust, vigorous, spreads by underground runners, can be invasive. 'Golden Baby' is neat, well-behaved, 2-ft.-tall dwarf. Tolerates very wet conditions.

S. nemoralis. GRAY GOLDENROD. Neat small plant, 6 in. to 3 ft. tall, with soft gray-green basal leaves and rich yellow, one-sided, curved flower plumes. Blooms open July–fall, last longer than most. Likes dryish soil. Short lived, so treat as biennial.

S. odora. SWEET GOLDENROD. Tall species, can reach 6½ ft. Anise-scented leaves. Stems unbranched. Large, long-lasting flower heads bloom July–September. Particularly tolerant of dry, poor soils.

S. rigida. STIFF GOLDENROD. Stems 2–5 ft. tall. Dense golden blooms August–October. Very adaptable to garden conditions: average or rich soil, moist or dry.

S

S. rugosa. ROUGH-LEAFED GOLDENROD. Hairy-stemmed plant to 5 ft. tall, with flowers on widely branching, arching stems. 'Fireworks' makes a more compact, 4-ft. clump.

S. sempervirens. SEASIDE GOLDENROD. Stately species, to 8 ft. tall. Tolerates dry soil, heat, salt, wind. May topple in rich soil. Spoon-shaped basal leaves. One-sided flower plumes open August–November.

S. sphacelata 'Golden Fleece'. Stands just 1½–2 ft. high when in bloom. Low foliage mound makes it a good ground cover. Set 15 in. apart, plants will form a solid mat in a year.

S. virgaurea. To 3 ft. tall. Flower clusters in a tight spikelike inflorescence or a looser cluster with upright branches. Not as well known as its selections or hybrids. 'Cloth of Gold', to 18–20 in. tall, has a long bloom season beginning in midsummer. 'Goldenmosa', probably the best known, grows 2½–3 ft. tall, has very large flower clusters reminiscent of florists' mimosa. 'Strahlenkrone' ('Crown of Rays') is a stiff, erect 2-footer with wide, flat, branched flower clusters.

Solidaster luteus. Hybrid of goldenrod and a perennial aster. To 2 ft. tall. Plant resembles goldenrod but has larger, softer yellow flowers like small asters. Unlike most goldenrods, needs staking to remain upright.

SOLOMON'S SEAL. See POLYGONATUM

SOPHORA

Fabaceae (Leguminosae)

DECIDUOUS OR EVERGREEN TREES OR SHRUBS

⚡ ZONES VARY BY SPECIES

☼ ◐ FULL SUN OR PARTIAL SHADE

💧 MODERATE WATER

☣ SEEDS OF S. AFFINIS AND S. SECUNDIFLORA ARE POISONOUS IF INGESTED

Sophora japonica

Attractive flowering plants with showy, drooping clusters of sweet pea–shaped blossoms that are followed by seedpods. Leaves are divided into numerous leaflets.

S. affinis. EVE'S NECKLACE. Small deciduous tree. Zones MS, LS, CS. Native to Southwest. Grows fast, to 15–20 ft. tall, rarely 30 ft., with round canopy. Dark green leaves, to 3–10 in. long, with numerous 1½-in.-long leaflets. Pink to white, lightly fragrant flowers in 4–6-in. dangling clusters, late spring (choose tree when it's in flower, because flower color varies and can be disappointing). Flowers followed by lovely, slender, black, twisted pods, like necklaces, which persist through fall and winter. Tolerates limy, thin, or dry soils.

S. japonica. JAPANESE PAGODA TREE, CHINESE SCHOLAR TREE. Deciduous tree. Zones US, MS, LS. To 50–75 ft. Young wood smooth, dark gray green. Old branches and trunk gradually take on rugged look of oak. Dark green, 6–10-in. leaves divided into 7 to 17 oval leaflets; no fall color. Small, yellowish white flowers carried in branched, foot-long sprays in summer. Pods 2–3½ in. long, narrowed between big seeds for a bead necklace effect. Give well-drained soil. Takes heat, drought, city conditions. 'Regent' is an exceptionally vigorous, uniform grower. 'Pendula', to 25 ft., has weeping branches. 'Princeton Upright' is similar to 'Regent' but more erect. Spreading forms are good shade trees, though stains from flowers and pods may be a problem on paved surfaces and parked cars.

🌱 **S. secundiflora.** TEXAS MOUNTAIN LAUREL, MESCAL BEAN. Evergreen shrub or tree. Zones LS, CS. Shrubby, but can be trained into 25-ft. tree with short, slender trunk or multiple trunks, narrow crown, upright branches. Leaves 4–6 in. long, divided into 7 to 9 oval, glossy dark green leaflets. Sweet-scented violet blue flowers in drooping, 4–8-in. clusters reminiscent of wisteria; midwinter to early spring bloom. Silvery gray, woody, 1–8-in.-long seedpods open when ripe to show poisonous, bright red, ½-in. seeds. If possible, remove pods before they mature. Thrives in heat and alkaline soil, but needs good drainage. Choice small tree for street, lawn, courtyard.

SORBUS

MOUNTAIN ASH

Rosaceae

DECIDUOUS TREES OR SHRUBS

⚡ ZONES VARY BY SPECIES

☼ ◐ FULL SUN OR LIGHT SHADE

💧 REGULAR TO MODERATE WATER

Sorbus aucuparia

Valued for showy flowers and showier fruit. Blossoms are grouped in broad, flat clusters scattered over foliage canopy in spring; they develop into hanging clusters of small, berrylike fruit that colors up in late summer or early fall. Typically fruit is red or orange red, but white, pink, and golden forms are occasionally available. Birds eat the fruit, but usually not until after leaves have fallen. Foliage is typically finely cut and somewhat fernlike, although some less widely planted species have undivided leaves. Some have good fall color; these are noted below.

Mountain ashes need some winter chill. Dislike of summer heat makes them poor for most of the South. Provide good, well-drained soil. Like other members of the rose family, subject to fireblight. Borers and cankers are problems for trees under stress. Where adapted, they are good small garden or street trees, though fruit can be messy over paving.

S. alnifolia. KOREAN MOUNTAIN ASH. Tree. Zones US, MS. Broad, dense, to 40–50 ft. tall. The name *alnifolia* refers to the leaves, which are undivided (like those of alder); they are 2–4 in. long, toothed, dark green, turning yellow to orange in fall. Red-and-yellow fruit. Tolerates heat and humidity better than other mountain ashes.

S. americana. AMERICAN MOUNTAIN ASH. Tree, sometimes large shrub. Zone US. Native to mountains of eastern North America. To 30 ft. tall. Leaves to 10 in. long, divided into 11 to 17 leaflets; dark green above, paler beneath, turning yellow in fall. Orange-red fruit. Attractive in native environment, but not considered a choice or long-lived tree elsewhere.

S. aucuparia. EUROPEAN MOUNTAIN ASH, ROWAN. Tree. Zone US. Naturalized in North America. To 20–40 ft. or taller. Sharply rising branches form a dense, oval to round crown. Leaves are 5–9 in. long, with 9 to 15 leaflets; they are dull green above, gray green below, turning tawny yellow to reddish in autumn. Orange-red fruit. 'Cardinal Royal' has especially large, bright red berries. 'Fastigiata' is a narrow, erect form; 'Blackhawk', another columnar form, is resistant to fireblight.

S. tianshanica. TURKESTAN MOUNTAIN ASH. Shrub or small tree. Zone US. To 16 ft. tall. Leaves 5–6 in. long, with 9 to 15 leaflets. Bright red fruit. Neat form, slow growth; excellent plant for small garden. 'Red Cascade' is compact, oval crowned.

SORREL, WOOD. See OXALIS acetosella

SORREL TREE. See OXYDENDRUM arboreum

SOTOL, TEXAS. See DASYLIRION texanum

SOUR GUM. See NYSSA sylvatica

SOURWOOD. See OXYDENDRUM arboreum

SOUTHERN BLACK HAW. See VIBURNUM rufidulum

🌱 SOUTHERN PEA

Fabaceae (Leguminosae)

ANNUAL

⚡ ALL ZONES (SEE BELOW)

☼ FULL SUN

💧 REGULAR WATER

Southern Pea

The name "Southern pea" describes various hot-weather shelled beans, including cream peas, black-eyed peas, cowpeas, and crowder peas. A long-time staple of Southern cuisine, Southern peas grow somewhat like ordinary green peas ("garden" or "English" peas), but their pods look more like lumpy string beans. They grow best in the long, hot summers of the Lower South, where they are ready for harvest about 65 days after sowing.

Wait until early summer nights are warm before sowing seeds; make successive sowings for a long harvest. Better to grow in poor soil than in rich, fertile soil. Sow 1 in. deep; plants will support each other if grown close together (2 in. apart, 3–4 ft. between rows). A space-saving trick is to intersperse peas with corn; the cornstalks provide a natural trellis for vining kinds of Southern peas to climb. Harvest for fresh peas when pods are plump, firm, and still green. Harvest for dry peas when pods turn yellow, tan, or purple; pods should rattle when shaken. Subject to attack by Mexican bean beetles; see Bean, Snap for control methods.

SOUTHERN RED CEDAR. See JUNIPERUS silicicola

SOUTHERN SHIELD FERN. See THELYPTERIS kunthii

SOUTHERN SPIDER LILY. See HYMENOCALLIS caroliniana

SOUTHERN SWORD FERN. See NEPHROLEPIS cordifolia

SOUTHERNWOOD. See ARTEMISIA abrotanum

SOUTHERN YEW. See PODOCARPUS macrophyllus

SPANISH BAYONET. See YUCCA aloifolia

SPANISH BLUEBELL. See ENDYMION hispanicus

SPANISH DAGGER. See YUCCA treculeana

SPANISH MOSS. See TILLANDSIA usneoides

SPATHIPHYLLUM

PEACE LILY

Araceae

EVERGREEN PERENNIALS

ZONE TS; OR INDOORS

PARTIAL OR FULL SHADE

AMPLE TO REGULAR WATER

Spathiphyllum

Large, dark green leaves—carried erect on slender stalks that rise directly from soil—are oval or elliptical, narrowed to a point. Flowers resemble those of calla lily or anthurium, consisting of a central column of tiny, closely set flowers surrounded by a leaflike white bract. Among the many selections are 6-ft. 'St. Mary'; 1½-ft. 'Silver Streak', with matte green leaves with a silvery midrib and insignificant flowers; and 2-ft. 'Tasson', considered by some to be the surest bloomer.

Outdoors, use as pot plant or textural plant for shady areas. Among the few flowering plants that grow and bloom readily indoors. Place in good light but not a hot window. Provide loose, fibrous potting mix; feed weekly with dilute liquid fertilizer.

SPEARMINT. See MENTHA spicata

SPEEDWELL. See VERONICA

SPHAEROPTERIS cooperi. See CYATHEA cooperi

SPICE BUSH. See CALYCANTHUS occidentalis, LINDERA

SPIDER FLOWER. See CLEOME hasslerana

SPIDER LILY. See HYMENOCALLIS latifolia, LYCORIS

SPIDER PLANT. See CHLOROPHYTUM comosum

SPIDERWORT. See TRADESCANTIA virginiana

SPIGELIA marilandica

INDIAN PINK, PINKROOT

Loganiaceae

PERENNIAL

ZONES US, MS, LS, CS

LIGHT SHADE

REGULAR WATER

ALL PARTS ARE POISONOUS IF INGESTED

Spigelia marilandica

Native to Southeast. Woodland plant 1–2 ft. high, with stiff, erect stems set with pairs of glossy green, 4-in. leaves. Clusters of 2-in., trumpet-shaped flowers; blossoms are red on the outside and yellow inside, facing upward to show a yellow five-pointed star at the mouth. Early summer bloom. Easy to grow if given light shade and moist, acid soil. With enough moisture, will tolerate full sun. Although once used medicinally, the plant is actually poisonous.

SPINACH

Chenopodiaceae

ANNUAL

ALL ZONES

FULL SUN

KEEP SOIL EVENLY MOIST

Spinach

Leafy cool-season vegetable. Matures slowly during fall, winter, and spring; long daylight of late spring and heat of summer make it go to seed quickly. Requires rich, fast-draining soil.

For fall and winter harvests, plant seeds 4 to 8 weeks before first frost. Be sure to plant enough to last through the winter; although growth stops when cold weather arrives, plants will survive freezing temperatures and you can harvest them through the winter. Look for selections with disease resistance and cold-hardiness, such as 'Bloomsdale Long Standing', 'Chesapeake', 'Dixie Market', 'Early Hybrid No. 7', 'Melody Hybrid', or 'Winter Bloomsdale', .

For a spring planting, choose selections that are heat tolerant and slow to bolt, such as 'Avon', 'Bloomsdale Long Standing', 'Estivato', 'Italian Summer', or 'Tyee Hybrid'. Make small sowings at weekly intervals to get successive harvests.

Space rows 1½ ft. apart. After seedlings start growing, thin the plants to 6 in. apart. One feeding will encourage lush foliage. When plants have reached full size, harvest by cutting off entire clump at ground level. Leaf miner is often a pest.

SPINACH, NEW ZEALAND

Tetragoniaceae

PERENNIAL USUALLY GROWN AS ANNUAL

ALL ZONES

FULL SUN

REGULAR WATER

New Zealand Spinach

Warm-season vegetable used as substitute for true spinach, which needs cool weather to succeed. Harvest greens from plants by plucking off top 3 in. of tender stems and attached leaves. A month later, new shoots grow up for another harvest. Plant is spreading, 6–8 in. high. Evergreen perennial in the Coastal and Tropical South, but goes dormant in heavy frosts. Sow seed in early spring after frost danger is past. Feed once or twice yearly with complete fertilizer. Though heat and drought tolerant, also thrives in cool, damp conditions and even grows wild in some areas.

S

SPINDLE TREE. See EUONYMUS europaea

SPIRAEA

Rosaceae

DECIDUOUS SHRUBS

⚥ ZONES VARY BY SPECIES

☼ ☼ FULL SUN OR LIGHT SHADE

◑ ◑ REGULAR TO MODERATE WATER, EXCEPT AS NOTED

Spiraea bumalda 'Anthony Waterer'

Very widely planted shrubs varying in size, form, and flowering season. There are two distinct kinds of spiraeas: the bridal wreath type, with clusters of white flowers cascading down arched branches in spring or early summer; and the shrubby type, typically growing knee-high and bearing pink, red, or white flowers clustered at ends of upright branches in summer to fall.

Like other members of the rose family, these are subject to various pests and diseases, but tend not to be seriously bothered. Tough, easy to grow. With few exceptions, not fussy about soil. After flowers have finished, prune the mostly spring-blooming, bridal wreath spiraeas; cut to the ground the wood that has bloomed. Prune the summer-blooming, shrubby spiraeas in winter or earliest spring; they generally need less severe pruning than bridal wreaths. If you remove spent flower clusters, plants will produce a second (but less lavish) bloom.

S. albiflora. See S. japonica 'Albiflora'

S. bumalda. BUMALDA SPIRAEA. Zones US, MS, LS. Name given to a group of hybrids between selections of *S. japonica*. All are low, shrubby spiraeas that bloom summer–fall. Selections include:

'Anthony Waterer'. Several forms; the best grows 3–4 ft. tall and slightly wider. All have flat-topped, carmine pink flower clusters and maroon-tinged foliage.

'Coccinea'. Like 'Anthony Waterer', but grows 2–3 ft. tall and bears brighter flowers.

'Dolchica'. To 1½–2½ ft. tall, with deeply cut leaves and bright pink flowers. Purplish new growth.

'Froebelii'. Resembles 'Anthony Waterer', but grows slightly taller.

'Goldflame'. Resembles 'Froebelii', but leaves are bronzy on unfolding, then yellow to chartreuse in summer and reddish orange before falling. Pink flowers. Prune out any green-leafed stems.

'Goldmound'. Compact, 1–3-ft. shrub with yellow to chartreuse foliage, pink flowers. Sometimes considered a variety of *S. japonica*.

'Limemound'. Resembles 'Goldmound', but is somewhat hardier. Pink flowers; lime green foliage that turns orange red in fall.

S. cantoniensis (S. reevesiana). REEVES SPIRAEA, DOUBLE BRIDAL WREATH. Zones US, MS, LS, CS. Upright grower to 5–6 ft., with arching branches. White flowers wreathe leafy branches, late spring–early summer. In the Upper South, the small dark green leaves may turn red in fall; elsewhere, they remain on the plant without changing color. 'Lanceata' is the form commonly grown.

S. japonica. Zones US, MS, LS. Upright shrubby spiraea to 4–6 ft. tall, with flat clusters of pink flowers carried above sharply toothed, oval green leaves. Best known through its selections, which are typically lower growing than the species and bloom in summer. These include:

'Albiflora' (*S. albiflora*). Rounded, compact shrub 1–1½ ft. tall, with white flowers.

'Alpina'. DAPHNE SPIRAEA. Low (1-ft.) mound with pink flowers. Foliage turns red and orange in fall.

'Fortunei'. Unusually tall (to 5 ft.), with pink flowers.

'Little Princess'. Resembles 'Alpina', but is larger (to 2½ ft. tall).

'Magic Carpet'. To 1½–2 ft. tall. Reddish bronze new growth contrasts with chartreuse to yellow older foliage. Pink flowers.

'Neon Flash'. To 3–4 ft. tall, 4–5 ft. wide. Purplish-tinted foliage, bright rosy pink flowers.

'Norman'. Grows to 1½–2 ft. tall, with deep pink flowers and dark purple autumn foliage.

'Shirobana' ('Shibori'). To 2–3 ft. tall, with flowers of white, light pink, and deep rose pink on the same plant.

S. nipponica tosaensis 'Snowmound'. Zones US, MS, LS. Compact, spreading plant to 2–3 ft. tall. Profusion of white flowers in late spring or early summer. Narrow dark green leaves have little autumn color.

🏛 **S. prunifolia 'Plena'.** BRIDAL WREATH. Zones US, MS, LS. Graceful, arching branches on a suckering, clump-forming plant to 6 ft. tall and wide. In early to midspring, bare branches are lined with small double white flowers resembling tiny roses. Small dark green leaves turn bright shades of red, orange, and yellow in autumn.

🏛 **S. thunbergii.** BABY'S BREATH SPIRAEA, THUNBERG SPIRAEA. Zones US, MS, LS, CS. Showy, billowy, graceful shrub 3–5 ft. tall, with many slender, arching branches. Round clusters of small single white flowers appear all along bare branches in early spring. Blue-green, extremely narrow leaves turn yellow or soft reddish brown in fall.

S. trilobata 'Swan Lake'. Zones US, MS. Like a small version of *S. prunifolia* 'Plena'. To 3–4 ft. tall, with a massive show of tiny white flowers in mid- to late spring. Small leaves often have three lobes. 'Fairy Queen' is more compact, seldom exceeding 3 ft., and blooms well in shade.

🏛 **S. vanhouttei.** VAN HOUTTE SPIRAEA. Zones US, MS, LS, CS. Widely planted hybrid between *S. cantoniensis* and *S. trilobata*. The classic bridal wreath spiraea. Arching branches form a fountain to about 6 ft. high by 8 ft. or wider. Leafy branches are covered with circular, flattened clusters of single white blossoms in mid- to late spring. Dark green foliage may turn yellow in fall.

SPIRAL FLAG. See COSTUS

SPIRAL GINGER. See COSTUS spiralis

SPLEENWORT. See ASPLENIUM

SPLIT-LEAF PHILODENDRON. See MONSTERA deliciosa

SPOTTED DEAD NETTLE. See LAMIUM maculatum

SPOTTED HORSEMINT. See MONARDA punctata

SPREKELIA formosissima

AZTEC LILY, JACOBEAN LILY, ST. JAMES LILY

Amaryllidaceae

BULB

⚥ ZONES LS (PROTECTED), CS, TS; OR DIG AND STORE; OR GROW IN POTS

☼ FULL SUN

◑ REGULAR WATER DURING GROWTH AND BLOOM

Sprekelia formosissima

Often sold as *Amaryllis formosissima*. Native to Mexico. Foliage looks like that of daffodil. Stems 1 ft. tall, topped with dark crimson blooms resembling orchids: three erect upper segments and three lower ones rolled together into tube at base, then separating again into drooping segments. Plant in fall, setting bulbs 3–4 in. deep and 8 in. apart. Blooms 6 to 8 weeks after planting. Most effective in groups. In mild climates, may flower several times a year under conditions of alternating moisture and drying out. Where winters are cold, plant outdoors in spring; lift plants in fall when foliage yellows, and store over winter (leave dry tops on). Or grow plant in pots like amaryllis (*Hippeastrum*); repot every 3 to 4 years.

SPRING SNOWFLAKE. See LEUCOJUM vernum

SOUTHERN HERITAGE PLANTS
IDENTIFIED BY SYMBOL 🏛

SPRING STAR FLOWER. See IPHEION uniflorum

SPRUCE. See PICEA

SPRUCE PINE. See PINUS glabra

SQUASH

Cucurbitaceae

ANNUAL

🌿 ALL ZONES

☼ FULL SUN

💧 REGULAR WATER

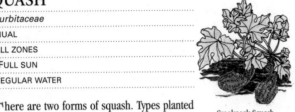

Crookneck Squash

There are two forms of squash. Types planted for a warm-weather harvest and eaten in the immature state are called summer squash; this group includes scalloped white squash (pattypan squash), yellow crookneck and straightneck types, and cylindrical, green or gray zucchini or Italian squash. The other form is winter squash, grown for harvest in late summer or fall; it stores very well and is used for baking and pies. Selections come in many sizes, colors, textures, and shapes (turban, acorn, and banana are a few); all kinds of winter squash have hard rinds and firm, close-grained, good-tasting flesh. In both forms of squash, blossoms and tiny, developing fruit at base of female flowers can be picked as delicacies.

Summer squash yields prodigious crops from just a few plants (within 50 to 65 days after sowing) and continues to bear for weeks. Vines are large (2½–4 ft. across at maturity) and need plenty of room; if space is limited, look for bush types. 'Early Prolific Straightneck' and 'Early Summer Crookneck' are good yellow summer squash. 'Early White Bush' (white) and 'Scallopini Hybrid' (green) are choice scalloped selections. 'Ambassador Hybrid', 'Aristocrat Hybrid', and 'Burpee Hybrid' are productive zucchini selections. Zucchini and scalloped squash also come in golden yellow variants. Novelties include 'Gourmet Globe', a round, striped zucchini, and 'Kuta', a whitish squash that can be eaten like summer squash at 6 in. or allowed to ripen into a 1-ft. winter squash.

Winter squash is planted and grown on vines like pumpkins, and typically needs more space than summer squash. Most are ready to harvest 60 to 110 days after sowing. Types for storing include the small 'Acorn', 'Buttercup', 'Butternut', 'Table Queen', and the large 'Hubbard', 'Blue Hubbard', and 'Jumbo Pink Banana'. Spaghetti squash looks like any other winter squash, but when you open it after cooking, you find that the nutty-tasting flesh is made up of long strands like spaghetti. Winter squash doesn't grow well in the Coastal and Tropical South.

Bush selections of summer squash can be planted 2 ft. apart in rows. If planted in circles (hills), they need more room; allow a 4-ft. diameter for each plant. Runner-type winter squash needs 5-ft. spacing in rows, with 8-ft.-diameter hills. The few bush selections of winter squash can be spaced as for bush types of summer squash. Provide rich soil, periodic fertilizer. Roots need regular moisture, but leaves and stems should be kept as dry as possible to prevent leaf diseases such as powdery mildew. Late squash should stay on vines until thoroughly hardened; harvest these with an inch of stem and store in a cool place (about 55°F).

Pests include squash bug (set out boards or burlap as their hiding places and destroy your catch each morning) and squash vine borer (dust stems with rotenone or plant early or late to avoid peak midsummer damage). Control cucumber beetles, which can spread incurable bacterial wilt disease as they chew holes in leaves and flowers.

SQUAWBUSH. See RHUS trilobata

SQUILL. See SCILLA

SQUIRREL CORN. See DICENTRA canadensis

SQUIRREL'S FOOT FERN. See DAVALLIA trichomanoides

STACHYS

LAMB'S EARS, BETONY

Lamiaceae (Labiatae)

PERENNIALS

🌿 ZONES US, MS, LS

☼ FULL SUN

💧 MODERATE WATER

Stachys byzantina

All have paired, typically rough or hairy leaves and spikelike clusters of small, usually two-lipped flowers. All are tough, tolerant plants. Of the 300-odd species, only a few are commonly grown. Provide well-drained soil. Plants often die out in center; divide and replant outer sections.

S. byzantina (S. lanata, S. olympica). LAMB'S EARS. Dense, ground-hugging rosettes of soft, thick, rather tongue-shaped, woolly white leaves to 4 in. long, 1 in. wide; clumps spread by surface runners. Some (not all) rosettes send up 1–1½-ft. flowering stems with small leaves and whorls of small purple flowers in late spring–early summer; these are attractive but become dowdy when they fade. Plant is more useful for foliage effect, so many people cut off or simply pull out flowering stems. Continued rain can smash the plants down and make them mushy, and frost can damage leaves, but recovery is strong.

'Silver Carpet' does not produce flower spikes and is somewhat less vigorous than the species. 'Countess Helene von Stein', commonly called 'Big Ears' (the plant, not the countess), has longer, broader leaves than the species and produces fewer flowering stems. There are also harder-to-find lime green and variegated forms.

Use all forms for contrast with dark green foliage and with leaves of different shapes, such as those of strawberry or some sedums. Good edging plants for paths, flower beds; highly effective edgings for bearded iris. Excellent ground covers in high, open shade.

S. coccinea. Native to Southwest. Plant forms neat carpet of softly hairy, oval to triangular, dark green leaves. Bright, scarlet tubular flowers open on 1–2 ft. stems. Blooms over a long season, from spring until late fall. Attracts hummingbirds.

S. macrantha (S. grandiflora). BIG BETONY. Dense, foot-high clump of long-stalked, heart-shaped, wrinkled, roughly hairy, scallop-edged green leaves 3 in. across. Showy purplish pink flowers, carried two or three whorls to a spike, held 8 in. above leaves. Spreads rapidly in rich, moist soil. Most common form is 'Robusta', to 2 ft. high; its blossom spikes bear four or five whorls of flowers. 'Superba' has deep violet blossoms. 'Alba' is a white-flowered form.

S. officinalis. BETONY. Similar to *S. macrantha*, but leaves are elongated (to 5 in. long) and may be hairy or nearly smooth. The purplish or dark red flowers are densely packed into short spikes atop leafy stems. Little grown except by herb fanciers, but white-blooming 'Grandiflora Alba' and pink-blooming 'Grandiflora Rosea' are attractive 2-ft. plants for perennial border or woodland edge.

STAGHORN FERN. See PLATYCERIUM

STANDING CYPRESS. See IPOMOPSIS rubra

STAPELIA

STARFISH FLOWER, CARRION FLOWER

Asclepiadaceae

SUCCULENT PERENNIALS

🌿 ZONES CS (WARMER PARTS), TS

☼ FULL SUN

💧 MODERATE WATER

Stapelia variegata

Plants resemble cacti, with clumps of four-sided, spineless stems. Summer flowers are large, fleshy, shaped like five-pointed stars; they usually have elaborate circular fleshy disk in center. Most smell like carrion, but odor is not usually pervasive enough to be offensive. They need cool, dry rest period in winter. Best managed in pots. Tolerate extreme heat. Protect plants where frosts can occur.

S. gigantea. Grow this plant as a remarkable novelty. Stems 9 in. tall. Brown-purple flowers marked in yellow are 10–16 in. wide, fringy edged.

S. variegata. Most common. Stems to 6 in. Flowers to 3 in. across, yellow spotted and barred in dark purple brown, not strongly scented. There are many hybrids and color variants. Plant can take light frost.

STAR ANISE. See ILLICIUM verum

STAR CLUSTERS. See PENTAS lanceolata

STARFISH FLOWER. See STAPELIA

STARFLOWER. See SMILACINA stellata

STAR JASMINE. See TRACHELOSPERMUM

STAR OF BETHLEHEM. See ORNITHOGALUM

STAR OF PERSIA. See ALLIUM christophii

STATICE. See LIMONIUM

STELLARIA pubera

CHICKWEED

Caryophyllaceae

PERENNIAL

☀ ZONES US, MS, LS

☼ ◐ FULL SUN OR PARTIAL SHADE

💧 REGULAR WATER

Stellaria pubera

Native to eastern U.S. and related to common annual chickweed *(S. media)*, but this one is a pretty plant for a wild garden, not a pest. Grows 6–24 in. tall. Leaves 1–4 in. long, elliptical. White, early spring flowers, with four or five petals, bloom at the ends of slender stems, in loose, forking clusters.

STENOLOBIUM stans. See TECOMA stans

STENOTAPHRUM secundatum

ST. AUGUSTINE GRASS

Poaceae (Gramineae)

PERENNIAL LAWN GRASS

☀ ZONES LS, CS, TS

☼ ◐ FULL SUN OR LIGHT SHADE

💧 REGULAR WATER

Stenotaphrum secundatum

Coarse-textured, subtropical grass native to the Southeast. Spreads rapidly by surface runners that root at the joints. In warm, rainy weather, runners can completely hide a front sidewalk in a few weeks. Turns brown in winter, but never goes completely dormant; greens up early in spring. Tough to mow, especially when tall and wet; only slightly drought tolerant. On the plus side, St. Augustine grass establishes quickly, takes a good amount of wear, and tolerates more shade than most other lawn grasses; it also grows on almost any soil and accepts salt spray, making it the best choice for beach areas.

St. Augustine grass is very popular in Florida, South Texas, and along the Gulf and South Atlantic coasts. Start from sod or plugs. Mow established lawn at 2–4 in. Recommended selections include 'Floralawn', 'Floratam', 'FX-10', 'Jade', 'Palmetto', 'Raleigh', and 'Seville'. Where chinch bugs are a problem, choose resistant selection 'FX-10' or tolerant selections 'Floralawn' and 'Floratam'.

STEPHANOTIS floribunda

MADAGASCAR JASMINE

Asclepiadaceae

EVERGREEN VINE

☀ ZONE TS; OR INDOORS

☼ ROOTS IN SHADE, TOPS IN FILTERED SUN

💧 REGULAR WATER

Stephanotis floribunda

Moderate growth to 10–15 ft. (taller if grown in open ground); can be kept small in pots. Needs warmth, support of frame or trellis. Waxy, glossy green leaves to 4 in. long. Funnel-shaped, waxy white flowers are very fragrant, 1–2 in. long, blooming in open clusters from June through the end of summer. A favorite flower for bridal bouquets.

As house plant, will bloom almost all year if given enough bright light but not direct sun; better suited to greenhouse. Allow indoor plants to rest by letting them dry out in winter; they will flower 6 weeks after resuming growth. Can be brought outdoors during warm season. Feed liberally; watch for scale, mealybugs.

Sterculiaceae. The sterculia family of shrubs and trees has flowers in which the calyx (the collective sepals), usually bowl shaped and five lobed, replaces the corolla (the collective petals) as the conspicuous element. A familiar example is Chinese parasol tree *(Firmiana)*.

STERNBERGIA lutea

STERNBERGIA

Amaryllidaceae

BULB

☀ ZONES US, MS, LS

☼ FULL SUN

💧 REGULAR WATER DURING GROWTH AND BLOOM

Sternbergia lutea

Narrow, 6–12-in. leaves appear in fall simultaneously with flowers and remain green for several months after blooms have gone. Golden yellow, 1½-in. flowers resemble large crocuses on 6–9-in. stems and provide a pleasant autumn surprise in borders or rock gardens, near ponds. Good cut flowers. Dies to the ground in spring. Plant bulbs as soon as they become available (in August or September). Set 4 in. deep, 6 in. apart. Clumps bloom well only after 2 or 3 years; wait at least 6 to 8 years before dividing. Don't worry if they fail to bloom one year. They are temperamental bulbs and sensitive to yearly fluctuations in the weather. There is nothing the gardener can do about this but sigh.

STEWARTIA

STEWARTIA

Theaceae

DECIDUOUS SHRUBS OR TREES

☀ ZONES VARY BY SPECIES

☼ LIGHT SHADE

💧 REGULAR WATER

Stewartia koreana

These are all-season performers. They show off fresh green leaves in spring, white flowers like single camellias in summer, and colorful foliage in fall; winter reveals a distinctive pattern of bare branches and smooth bark that flakes off in varying degrees, depending on species. *S. koreana* and *S. pseudocamellia* have the showiest bark; it flakes off to show a patchwork of green, gray, brown, rust, terra-cotta, and cream. ▶

S

Best in well-drained, acid soil with high content of organic matter. Good in woodland garden and as foreground specimens against backdrop of larger, darker-leafed trees.

S. koreana. KOREAN STEWARTIA. Tree. Zones US, MS. Pyramidal growth to 20–25 ft.; may eventually reach 50 ft. Leaves are 1–4 in. long, turn orange to red orange in fall. Flowers, carried on short stalks among leaves, reach 3 in. wide and have yellow-orange stamens. Very similar to *S. pseudocamellia.*

S. malacodendron. SILKY STEWARTIA. Shrub or small tree. Zones MS, LS, CS. Native to Southeast. To 10–15 ft. tall and wide. Shoots and undersides of 2–4-in. leaves are downy. Blooms 3½ in. wide, purple stamens with blue anthers. Bark not as showy as that of other species. Heat tolerant.

S. monadelpha. TALL STEWARTIA. Tree. Zones US, MS, LS. To 25 ft. tall, with slender, upward-angled branches. Leaves are 1½–3 in. long, turn brilliant red in fall. Flowers to 1½ in. wide. Older limbs and trunk have smooth, cinnamon brown bark. Heat tolerant.

S. ovata. MOUNTAIN CAMELLIA. Shrub or small tree. Zones US, MS, LS. Native to Southeast. To 10–15 ft. tall and wide. Leaves grow 2–5 in. long, turn orange to scarlet in fall. Flowers, 3 in. wide, have frilled petals. Bark not as handsome as on other species. *S. o. grandiflora* has 4-in. flowers with lavender anthers; it will bloom even as a young plant.

S. pseudocamellia. JAPANESE STEWARTIA. Tree. Zones US, MS. Forms a pyramid that may reach 30–40 ft. after many years. Leaves to 2½–3 in. long; fall color bronze to purple. Flowers are more cup shaped than those of *S. koreana;* they reach 2½ in. wide, have orange anthers. Needs afternoon shade and cool, moist soil. Suffers badly from leaf scorch if planted in hot, dry areas.

STIGMAPHYLLON

AMAZON VINE, ORCHID VINE

Malpighiaceae

EVERGREEN OR PARTIALLY DECIDUOUS VINES

✔ ZONES VARY BY SPECIES

☼ FULL SUN

● REGULAR WATER

Stigmaphyllon ciliatum

Tall twiners of fairly fast growth to 20–30 ft. Leaves borne in pairs. Bright yellow, irregularly shaped flowers that somewhat resemble oncidium orchids arise in long-stalked clusters from upper portions of stems. Plants bloom most heavily in summer, but they may produce some flowers all year in the Tropical South. Do best in rich soil. Provide support and prune out dead or straggling growth.

S. ciliatum. FRINGED AMAZON VINE. Zones CS, TS; or house or greenhouse plant. Foliage open and delicate; plants easily kept small. Leaves heart shaped, 1–3 in. long, with a few long, bristly teeth on edges. Clusters of three to seven flowers 1½ in. across.

S. littorale. BRAZILIAN GOLDEN VINE. Zone TS. Larger, coarser vine than *S. ciliatum,* with larger (to 5-in.-long) oval leaves and larger clusters (ten to twenty) of smaller flowers (1 in. across). Extremely vigorous; can climb to tops of tall trees.

STIPA

FEATHER GRASS, NEEDLE GRASS

Poaceae (Gramineae)

PERENNIAL GRASSES

✔ ZONES US, MS, LS

☼ ◐ FULL SUN OR LIGHT SHADE

◖ ● WATER NEEDS VARY BY SPECIES

Stipa gigantea

Feather or needle grasses have large, open, airy inflorescences that can impart lightness and motion to the garden. Of the 150 or so species, a few have special merit.

S. gigantea. GIANT FEATHER GRASS. Clumps of narrow, arching leaves grow 2–3 ft. tall. Open, airy sheaves of yellowish flowers shimmer in a broad cloud reaching to 6 ft. in height and breadth. Regular water; established plants endure some drought.

S. tenuissima. MEXICAN FEATHER GRASS, TEXAS NEEDLE GRASS. Very thin bright green leaves form erect clumps arching out toward the top. Many thin flowering stems divide and redivide into almost hairlike fineness, green, then golden. Single or scattered clumps are effective among ground cover or boulders, on slopes. Larger plantings can create effective erosion control. Tolerates drought, limy soil. Good grass for Southwest.

STOCK. See MATTHIOLA

STOKESIA laevis

STOKESIA, STOKES' ASTER

Asteraceae (Compositae)

PERENNIAL

✔ ALL ZONES

☼ FULL SUN

● REGULAR WATER

Stokesia laevis

Native to Southeast. A rugged and most adaptable plant. One of the best perennials for Florida. Much branched, with stiff, erect stems 1½–2 ft. high. Smooth, firm-textured, medium green leaves, 2–8 in. long, sometimes toothed at base, evergreen (to semievergreen in Upper South). Leafy, curved, finely toothed bracts surround tight flower buds; from May to September, these open to 3–4-in.-wide, asterlike flower heads in blue, purplish blue, or white. Each blossom has a central button of small flowers surrounded by a ring of larger ones. Long-lasting cut flower. Grows best in well-drained soil. Easy to divide. This should be done every 3 years.

Choices include these favorite selections: 10-in.-high 'Bluestone', medium blue flowers; 1½-ft.-tall 'Blue Danube', lavender blue blossoms and long bloom season; 'Klaus Jelitto', light blue; 'Silver Moon', white; and 'Wyoming', deep purple.

STONECROP. See SEDUM

STRAWBERRY

Rosaceae

PERENNIAL

✔ ALL ZONES

☼ FULL SUN

● REGULAR WATER

▸ SEE CHART

Strawberry

Plants have toothed, roundish, medium green leaves and white flowers. They grow 6–8 in. tall, spreading by long runners to about 1 ft. across.

June-bearing types produce one crop per year in late spring or early summer; generally, they are the highest-quality strawberries you can grow. Everbearing or day-neutral kinds put out fewer runners than June bearers, and flower and set fruit over a longer season. Their harvest tends to peak in early summer, then typically continues (often unevenly) through fall; the exact fruiting pattern depends on the selection. Everbearers don't do well in Florida.

Check the accompanying chart for some of the best selections, and look for other good choices in local garden centers.

To bring in a big crop of berries, plant in rows—on flat ground if soil drains well, or on a raised mound (5–6 in. high) if soil is heavy or poorly

▸ page 388

S

STRAWBERRY

SELECTIONS	ZONES	DESCRIPTION	RESISTANCE
JUNE-BEARING TYPES			
'Allstar'	US, MS, LS, CS	Large, light red fruit of good flavor. Consistent producer. Best all-around selection	Resistant to red stele, verticillium wilt, leaf diseases
'Annapolis'	US, MS	Early, consistent production of medium-large fruit	Resistant to red stele
'Apollo'	US, MS, LS, CS	Good-size, firm, flavorful fruit. Fairly late	Tolerant of leaf diseases
'Atlas'	US, MS, LS, CS	Firm berries with good aroma	Tolerant of leaf scorch and leaf spot
'Cardinal'	US, MS, LS	Large, firm fruit of good flavor, color. Can be acidic	Susceptible to anthracnose
'Chandler'	All zones	Very large, bright red berries of good flavor. Produces over long period. Does well in Florida	Resists leaf spot
'Delmarvel'	US, MS, LS	Early berry with excellent flavor. Moderate yields	Some resistance to anthracnose. Resistant to red stele
'Earliglow'	US, MS, LS, CS	Early crop of medium-size berries of excellent flavor and quality. Moderate yields	Resistant to red stele. Tolerates fruit rot better than many other selections
'Florida 90'	CS, TS	Heavy yields of sweet fruit over long period	
'Midway'	US, MS, LS	Medium to large, firm, dark red fruit, juicy, slightly tart; tough skin. Excellent for freezing, preserves. Vigorous, productive over long period	Suffers in high heat, drought, especially in sandy soil. Best in heavier soil. Resistant to verticillium wilt, one race of red stele. Susceptible to leaf spot, leaf scorch
'Sunrise'	US, MS, LS	Medium to large, light red berries of good flavor and aroma. Excellent for desserts, but poor for freezing. Vigorous; above-average yields	Drought tolerant. Resistant to verticillium wilt, leaf scorch and mildew, three types of red stele. Susceptible to leaf spot
'Surecrop'	US, MS, LS	Medium to large fruit with glossy skin. Primary berries irregular, wedge shaped; later berries uniform, conical. Excellent flavor; ideal for desserts, freezing. Vigorous; above average yields	Resists red stele, verticillium wilt, leaf spot, leaf scorch. Tolerates drought and poor, dry soils
'Sweet Charlie'	CS, TS	Large, dark red berries, very tasty. Does well in Florida	Resistant to anthracnose
'Tennessee Beauty'	US, MS, LS	Late crop of medium to large, dark red berries with slightly tart flavor. Good for fresh eating; excellent for freezing, processing. Vigorous; heavy yields	Resistant to leaf spot, leaf scorch. Needs good drainage. Susceptible to red stele
EVERBEARING TYPES			
'Ozark Beauty'	US, MS, LS, CS	Large, long-necked fruit with mild, sweet flavor, high sugar content; freezes well. Plant produces many runners. Tolerates much cold	
'Quinault'	US, MS	Large, attractive fruit with very good flavor	Resistant to viruses and red stele. Susceptible to botrytis
'Selva'	US, MS, LS, CS	Sweet fruit is large for everbearer	Appears to have some resistance to red stele
'Tribute'	US, MS, LS	Medium to large fruit with excellent flavor	Resistant to red stele, verticillium wilt
'Tristar'	US, MS, LS	Medium-size berries with excellent flavor	Resistant to red stele and mildew. Moderately susceptible to viruses

S

drained. Set plants 14–18 in. apart in rows spaced 2–2½ ft. apart. For a small harvest, grow a dozen or so plants in a sunny patch in a flower or vegetable garden, or put them in boxes or containers on the terrace.

Planting season is usually determined by availability of plants at local garden centers. In the Coastal and Tropical South, set out June bearers in fall for a crop the next spring; elsewhere, plant in early spring for harvest the following year. Set out everbearing plants in spring for summer–fall berries (in milder areas, they may be available for fall planting); pinch off the earliest blossoms to increase plant vigor.

Plant carefully. The crown should be above soil level (a buried crown will rot), the topmost roots ¼ in. beneath soil level (exposed roots will dry out). Mulch to deter weeds, conserve moisture, and keep berries clean.

Strawberry plants need about 1 in. of water per week throughout the growing season, even more moisture when bearing fruit. Drip irrigation is ideal to help reduce disease problems, but overhead irrigation is satisfactory. Feed June bearers twice a year—very lightly when growth begins and again, more heavily, after fruiting. Everbearing types prefer consistent light fertilization. Heavy feeding of either type in spring leads to excessive plant growth, soft fruit, and fruit rot.

Most selections reproduce by runner plants; some make few or no offsets. Pinch off all runners to get large plants with smaller yields of big berries; allow runner plants to grow 7–10 in. apart for heavy yields of smaller berries. When plants have made enough offsets, pinch off additional runners. Do not let the planting become too dense, since that leads to much lower yields, diseases, and poor-quality fruit.

Harvest strawberries when they are fully red. They'll continue to ripen and soften for several days afterward. If you aren't going to eat, freeze, or preserve fruit right away, leave the calyxes (caps) on the berries when you harvest them. The fruit will last longer.

Most perennially grown June bearers benefit greatly from renovation. After the harvest is over, cut off the foliage; you can use a lawn mower set high so it won't injure the crowns. If diseases were a problem, dispose of the leaves. Water and fertilize to encourage new growth. This is also a good time to reduce a dense planting by removing the old "mother" plants and leaving the younger, more productive "daughter" plants.

Some home gardeners are following the example of commercial growers who treat strawberries as annuals. Plants are installed in summer or early fall, usually with a plastic mulch; they are not allowed to make offsets. After harvest, the plants are removed and a new planting made. Benefits are healthier plants, fewer weeds, and bigger fruit.

Strawberries benefit from a winter mulch in the Upper South. Cover the planting with a 4–6-in. layer of straw or other light, weed-free organic material. When it gets warm in spring, rake the mulch between the plants.

Plants are subject to many diseases: fruit rots (botrytis, anthracnose, leather rot), leaf diseases (leaf spot, leaf scorch, leaf blight), crown diseases (anthracnose), root diseases (verticillium wilt, red stele, black root rot), and viruses. Anthracnose is the biggest disease problem in Florida. Root weevils, aphids, mites, and slugs and snails are among potential pests. To help reduce problems, install only certified disease-free plants; also remove diseased foliage and ripe or rotten fruit. Replace plants with new ones as they begin to decline, usually after 3 years.

See selection chart for choices in standard strawberries. Ornamental types suitable for full sun or light shade include selections with white-and-green leaves grown mainly as ground covers, since they do not fruit well. 'Pink Panda', a hybrid between a strawberry and a potentilla, has typical strawberry foliage and an occasional tasty berry, but it is grown chiefly for the inch-wide pink flowers it bears from spring through fall.

**STRAWBERRY BEGONIA, STRAWBERRY GERANIUM.
See SAXIFRAGA stolonifera**

STRAWBERRY BUSH. See EUONYMUS americana

STRAWBERRY GUAVA. See PSIDIUM cattleianum

STRAWBERRY TREE. See ARBUTUS unedo

STRAWFLOWER. See HELICHRYSUM bracteatum

STRELITZIA

BIRD OF PARADISE

Strelitziaceae

EVERGREEN PERENNIALS

✺ ZONES VARY BY SPECIES

☼ ☽ LIGHT AFTERNOON SHADE IN SUMMER

● REGULAR WATER

Strelitzia reginae

Tropical plants of extremely individual character. Both species are good to use by pools; they make no litter and tolerate some splashing. Endure temperatures to about 28°F.

S. nicolai. WHITE BIRD OF PARADISE, GIANT BIRD OF PARADISE. Zone TS. This one is grown for its dramatic display of leaves (similar to those of banana plants); flowers are incidental. Treelike and clumping, with many stalks to 30 ft. Gray-green, leathery, 5–10-ft. leaves are arranged fanwise on erect or curving trunks. Floral envelope is purplish gray, flower is white with dark blue tongue. Feed young plants frequently to push to full dramatic size, then give little or no feeding. Goal is to acquire and maintain size without lush growth and need for dividing. Cut off dead leaves and thin out any surplus growth.

S. reginae. BIRD OF PARADISE. Zones CS (protected), TS. Grown for its spectacular flowers, which bear a startling resemblance to tropical birds. Flowers combine orange, blue, and white, are borne on long, stiff stems; they appear intermittently throughout year, but flowering is best in cool season. Long lasting on plant and as cut flower. Trunkless plant grows 5 ft. high, with leathery, long-stalked, blue-green leaves to 1½ ft. long, 4–6 in. wide. Benefits greatly from frequent and heavy feedings. Divide infrequently, since large, crowded clumps bloom best. Good in containers. Recovers slowly from frost damage.

STREPTOCARPUS

CAPE PRIMROSE

Gesneriaceae

EVERGREEN PERENNIALS

✺ ZONE TS; OR HOUSE OR GREENHOUSE PLANTS

☽ ● PARTIAL OR FULL SHADE

◗◗ AMPLE WATER

Streptocarpus Hybrid

Related to gloxinias and African violets and look something like a cross between the two. Leaves are fleshy, sometimes velvety. Flowers are trumpet shaped, with long tube and spreading mouth. Long bloom season; some flower intermittently all year. Indoors, handle like African violets. Many species and hybrids of interest to fanciers; most widely available kinds are hybrids.

Large-flowered hybrids (Giant Hybrids). Clumps of long, narrow leaves and 1-ft.-high stems with long-tubed, 1½–2-in.-wide flowers in white, blue, pink, rose, red; often show contrasting blotches. Usually bloom after 1 year from seed. Wiesmoor hybrids are similar but grow taller (stems to 2 ft. high).

S. saxorum (Streptocarpella saxorum). Unlike other types; shrubby, much-branched perennial that makes a spreading mound of furry, gray-green, 1½-in.-long, fleshy leaves. Bloom comes in waves over much of year; the two-tone flowers are pale blue and white, 1½ in. wide, carried on 3–4-in. stems. Makes a splendid hanging container plant. Among hybrids developed from it, 'Concord Blue', with large flowers, blooms continuously.

S

STROBILANTHES dyeranus

PERSIAN SHIELD

Acanthaceae

TENDER PERENNIAL OR SHRUB

ZONES LS (PROTECTED), CS, TS

PARTIAL SHADE

REGULAR WATER

Strobilanthes dyeranus

Native to Burma. Beautiful foliage plant for warm, humid gardens. Grows to 4 ft. tall; soft stemmed and more like a perennial than a shrub. Leaves are 6–8 in. long, somewhat puckered, dark green but richly variegated with purple and iridescent silver-blue tints. Leaf undersides are bright purple. Pale violet tubular flowers in summer on 1½-in. spikes; less showy than foliage. Needs rich soil and regular watering. Becomes straggly with age; replace or start over from cuttings. May survive freezing in Lower South if mulched heavily in late fall; or grow in container, move to shelter over winter. Can grow indoors in sunny window.

STYLOPHORUM diphyllum

CELANDINE POPPY, WOOD POPPY

Papaveraceae

PERENNIAL

ZONES US, MS, LS

PARTIAL SHADE TO FULL SHADE

REGULAR WATER

Stylophorum diphyllum

Native to eastern U.S. Basal rosette of downy, gray-green leaves, deeply lobed into five or seven segments. Golden yellow, 2-in. flowers, quite showy, solitary or a few together in a loose cluster on branched stems, to 2 ft. tall. Resembles greater celandine *(Chelidonium majus)*, but shorter and blooms in spring rather than summer. Easy to grow, in acid or alkaline soil; reseeds and forms colonies if soil is rich and moist. Stems leak yellow sap when cut. Excellent companion in woodland garden to blue phlox, foamflower, Virginia bluebells, trillium, and may apple.

Styracaceae. The storax family includes trees and shrubs with bell-shaped, usually white flowers. Members include *Halesia* and *Styrax*.

STYRAX

SNOWBELL

Styracaceae

DECIDUOUS TREES

ZONES VARY BY SPECIES

FULL SUN OR PARTIAL SHADE

REGULAR WATER

Styrax japonicus

Neat, well-behaved flowering trees of modest size for patios or lawns; make a nice contrast in front of larger, darker-leafed trees. Those species described below put on a spring or early summer show of white, bell-shaped flowers in hanging clusters. Easy to garden under, since roots are deep and nonaggressive. Provide good, well-drained, acid soil, except as noted.

S. americanus. AMERICAN SNOWBELL. Zones US, MS, LS, CS. Native from Florida to Virginia, west to Missouri, Arkansas, Louisiana. Round-topped shrub, 6–9 ft. tall, with bright green leaves, to 3½ in. long, on zigzagging stems. Fragrant flowers, solitary or in clusters of four. Some tolerance of poor drainage. Performs better in light shade.

S. grandifolius. BIGLEAF SNOWBELL. Zones US, MS, LS, CS. Native from Virginia to Florida. To 12 ft. tall, but often smaller. Dark green leaves, up to 7 in. long. Fragrant flowers, as many as twelve together in 8-in.-long, drooping clusters. Does better in light shade and cool, moist soil.

S. japonicus. JAPANESE SNOWBELL, JAPANESE SNOWDROP TREE. Zones US, MS, LS. To 30 ft. tall, with slender, graceful trunk; branches often strongly horizontal, giving tree a broad, flat top. Oval, scallop-edged leaves to 3 in. long; turn from dark green to red or yellow in fall. Faintly fragrant, white, ¾-in. flowers hang in small clusters on short side branches. Leaves angle upward from branches while flowers hang down, giving the effect of parallel green and white tiers. Prune to control shape; tends to be shrubby unless lower side branches are suppressed. Splendid tree to look up into; plant it in raised beds near outdoor entertaining areas, or on a high bank above a path. 'Pendula' ('Carillon') is a shrubby selection with weeping branches; 'Pink Chimes', also shrubby, has more upright form with pink flowers.

S. obassia. FRAGRANT SNOWBELL. Zones US, MS, LS. To 20–30 ft. tall, rather narrow. Oval to round, deep green, 3–8-in.-long leaves. Where frosts come very late, leaves may color yellow in autumn. Foliage may partly obscure fragrant, 1-in. flowers carried in drooping, 6–8-in. clusters at branch ends. Blooms earlier in spring than *S. japonicus*. Newly planted trees often take a few years to start blooming. Good against background of evergreens, or for height and contrast above border of rhododendrons and azaleas.

SUCCULENTS. Strictly speaking, a succulent is any plant that stores water in juicy leaves, stems, or roots to withstand periodic drought. Practically speaking, fanciers of succulents exclude such fleshy plants as epiphytic orchids and include in their collections many desert plants such as yuccas that are not fleshy. Although cacti are succulents, common consent sets them up as a separate category (see Cactaceae).

Most succulents come from desert or semidesert areas in warmer parts of the world. Mexico and South Africa are two very important sources. Some (notably sedums and sempervivums) come from colder climates, where they grow on sunny, rocky slopes and ledges.

Succulents are grown everywhere as house plants; many are useful and decorative as landscaping plants, either in open ground or in containers. When well grown and well groomed, they look good all year, in bloom or out. Although considered low-maintenance plants, they look shabby if neglected; they may live through extended drought but will drop leaves, shrivel, or lose color. The amount of irrigation needed depends on summer heat, humidity, rainfall level. Give plants just enough water to keep them healthy, plump of leaf, and attractive.

One light feeding at the start of the growing season should be enough for plants in open ground. Larger-growing and later-blooming kinds may require additional feeding.

Some succulents make good ground covers. Some are sturdy and quick growing enough for erosion control on large banks. Other smaller kinds are useful among stepping-stones or for creating patterns in small gardens. Most of these come easily from stem or leaf cuttings, and a stock can quickly be grown from a few plants. See *Echeveria*, ice plant, *Sedum*, *Senecio*.

Many large succulents have decorative value. See *Agave*, *Aloe*, *Crassula*, *Echeveria*, *Kalanchoe*, *Yucca*.

Many succulents have showy flowers. For some of the best, see *Aloe*, some species of *Crassula*, *Hoya*, *Kalanchoe*.

Some smaller succulents are primarily collectors' items, grown for odd form or flowers. See the smaller species of *Aloe*, *Crassula*, *Echeveria*, *Euphorbia*, *Stapelia*.

The variety of forms, colors, and textures offers many possibilities for handsome combinations, but there's a fine line between successful grouping and jumbled medley. Beware of using too many kinds in one planting. Mass a few species instead of putting in one of each.

You can combine succulents with other types of plants, but plan combinations carefully. Not all plants look right with succulents. Consider also their different cultural requirements.

S

SUGARBERRY. See CELTIS laevigata

SUMAC. See RHUS

SUMMER SAVORY. See SATUREJA hortensis

SUMMER SNOWFLAKE. See LEUCOJUM aestivum

SUMMERSWEET. See CLETHRA alnifolia

SUNDROPS. See OENOTHERA fruticosa

SUNFLOWER. See HELIANTHUS

SUNROSE. See HELIANTHEMUM nummularium

SWAMP MILKWEED. See ASCLEPIAS incarnata

SWEDISH IVY. See PLECTRANTHUS

SWEET ALYSSUM. See LOBULARIA maritima

SWEET BASIL. See OCIMUM basilicum

SWEET BAY. See LAURUS nobilis, MAGNOLIA virginiana

SWEETBELLS. See LEUCOTHOE racemosa

SWEET BOX. See SARCOCOCCA

SWEET BRIAR ROSE. See ROSA eglanteria

SWEET FERN, SWEET GALE. See MYRICA gale

SWEET FLAG. See ACORUS gramineus

SWEET GUM. See LIQUIDAMBAR

SWEET OLIVE. See OSMANTHUS fragrans

SWEET PEA. See LATHYRUS

SWEET POTATO

Convolvulaceae

PERENNIAL GROWN AS ANNUAL

☒ ZONES US, MS, LS

☼ BEST IN FULL SUN

💧 REGULAR WATER

Sweet Potato

Not a potato, but the thickened root of a trailing tropical vine closely related to morning glory *(Ipomoea)*. Bush and short vine selections also available. Thrives in long, hot growing season of the South. Also requires well-drained soil (preferably sandy loam) and plenty of room. Start with certified disease-free slips (rooted cuttings) from a garden center or mail-order supplier. Look for disease-resistant types. To avoid buildup of disease organisms in the soil, don't grow sweet potatoes in the same location 2 years in a row.

There are two classes of sweet potatoes. One has soft, sugary yellow-orange flesh (examples are 'Centennial', 'Gold Rush', 'Vineless Puerto Rico'); the other has firm, dry whitish flesh (members of this group include 'Nemagold' and 'Yellow Jersey'). The sweet yellow-orange type is sometimes incorrectly labeled "yam" when sold in grocery stores. Most types are ready to harvest 110 to 120 days after planting.

Plant in late spring when soil temperature has warmed to 70°F. Work in a low-nitrogen fertilizer before planting; too much nitrogen produces leafy growth at the expense of roots. Set slips so that only stem tips and leaves are exposed; space 1 ft. apart, in rows 3 ft. apart. To ensure good drainage, mark off rows and dig ditch between them to form planting ridges. Row covers provide added heat and keep out many pests. Harvest before first frost; if tops are killed by sudden frost, harvest immediately. Dig carefully to avoid cutting or bruising roots. Flavor improves in storage (starch is converted to sugar). Dry roots in sun, then cure by storing for 10 to 14 days in warm (about 85°F), humid place. Store in cooler environment (but not below 55°F) until ready to use.

Sweet potatoes are sometimes grown for decorative foliage—leaves are heart shaped in some types, cut or lobed in others. Ornamental selection 'Blackie' has deep purple leaves on purple stems; it is handsome in hanging baskets and as edging. 'Margarita' and 'Sulfur' are similar, but with bright yellow to chartreuse foliage.

SWEETSHRUB, COMMON. See CALYCANTHUS floridus

SWEETSPIRE. See ITEA

SWEET SULTAN. See CENTAUREA moschata

SWEET WILLIAM. See DIANTHUS barbatus

SWEET WOODRUFF. See GALIUM odoratum

SWISS CHARD

Chenopodiaceae

BIENNIAL GROWN AS ANNUAL

☒ ALL ZONES

☼ FULL SUN

💧 REGULAR WATER

Swiss Chard

A form of beet grown for leaves and stalks instead of roots. One of the easiest and most practical of vegetables for home gardens. Sow big, crinkly, tan seeds ½–¾ in. deep in spaded soil, any time from early spring to early summer. Thin seedlings to 1 ft. apart. About 2 months after sowing (plants are generally 1–1½ ft. tall) you can begin to cut outside leaves from plants as needed for meals. New leaves grow up in center of plants; continues yield all summer and plants seldom bolt to seed (if one does, pull it up and throw it away). Plants can be grown as fall–spring crop. Selections include 'Fordhook Giant', which produces heavy yields of dark green leaves even in hot weather; 'Joseph's Coat', an heirloom selection with bright green leaves and stalks in many colors: orange, red, pink, yellow, white; 'Lucullus', vigorous and tall like 'Fordhook Giant' but with light green leaves; and 'Swiss Chard of Geneva', with large white stalks and ribs; more winter-hardy than most selections.

Regular green-and-white chard looks presentable in flower garden. 'Rhubarb' chard has red stems and reddish green leaves; it looks attractive in garden beds or containers. Its leaves are valuable in floral arrangements and tasty when cooked, too—sweeter and stronger flavored than green chard. Cook leaves and leafstalks separately, since stalks take longer.

SWISS CHEESE PLANT. See MONSTERA friedrichsthalii

SWITCH GRASS. See PANICUM virgatum

SWORD FERN. See NEPHROLEPIS, POLYSTICHUM munitum

SYAGRUS romanzoffianum (Arecastrum romanzoffianum)

QUEEN PALM

Arecaceae (Palmae)

PALM

☒ ZONES CS (PROTECTED), TS

☼ FULL SUN

💧 REGULAR WATER

Syagrus romanzoffianum

South American palm with exceptionally straight trunk to 50 ft. Arching, bright glossy green leaves 10–15 ft. long; leaves break in high winds. Grows quickly with fertilizer. May produce decorative orange dates. Subject to mites; wash young plants frequently. Damaged at 25°F but has recovered from 16°F freeze. A good substitute for the more tender royal palm *(Roystonea)*. Sometimes sold as *Cocos plumosa*.

SYMPHORICARPOS

SNOWBERRY, CORALBERRY

Caprifoliaceae

DECIDUOUS SHRUBS

✂ ZONES VARY BY SPECIES

☼ ◐ ● EXPOSURE NEEDS VARY BY SPECIES

◐ MODERATE WATER

Symphoricarpos albus

North American natives. Low growing, often spreading by root suckers. Small, pink-tinged or white flowers in clusters or spikes. Attractive round, berrylike fruit remains on stems after leaves drop in autumn; nice in winter arrangements, attracts birds. Use as informal hedge or to control erosion on slopes.

S. albus (S. racemosus). COMMON SNOWBERRY. Zones US, MS. Upright or spreading shrub. Grows 2–6 ft. tall. Leaves roundish, dull green, ¾–2 in. long (to 4 in. and often lobed on sucker shoots). Pink flowers in spring, followed by white fruit from late summer to winter. Best fruit production in full sun. Not a first-rate shrub, but useful in its tolerance of poor soil, urban air, and shade. Withstands neglect.

S. chenaultii. Zones US, MS. Hybrid. Resembles parent *S. orbiculatus*, but red fruit is lightly spotted white and leaves are larger. Selection 'Hancock' is a 1-ft.-high dwarf that is valued as woodland ground or bank cover. Provide high shade.

S. orbiculatus (S. vulgaris). CORALBERRY, INDIAN CURRANT. Zones US, MS, LS. Resembles *S. albus*, but bears a profusion of small purplish red fruit in clusters. These are bright enough and plentiful enough to provide a good fall–winter show. Full sun.

SYMPHYTUM officinale

COMMON COMFREY

Boraginaceae

PERENNIAL HERB

✂ ZONES US, MS, LS, CS

☼ ◐ FULL SUN OR PARTIAL SHADE

● REGULAR WATER

◇ LEAVES ARE POISONOUS IF INGESTED

Symphytum officinale

Deep-rooted, clumping plant to 3 ft. high. Furry leaves with stiff hairs; basal leaves to 8 in. long or more, upper leaves smaller. Flowers not showy, ½ in., usually dull rose in color, occasionally white, cream, or purple. Leaves can be dried and brewed to make a medicinal tea, but this use is no longer recommended. To keep leaf production high, cut out flowering stalks and mulch each spring with compost. Grow from root cuttings.

Although comfrey has a long history as a folk remedy, think hard before establishing it in your garden. Plant spreads freely from roots and is difficult to eradicate. Herb enthusiasts claim that comfrey accumulates minerals, enriches compost.

SYMPLOCOS

Symplocaceae

DECIDUOUS OR SEMIEVERGREEN SHRUBS, SMALL TREES

✂ ZONES VARY BY SPECIES

☼ FULL SUN

● REGULAR WATER

Symplocos paniculata

Handsome, large shrubs with fragrant flowers, and berries in early fall. The native species is semievergreen; a few red leaves hang among the glossy green leaves in winter. The more commonly grown deciduous species listed here bears extremely showy sapphire blue berries.

S. paniculata. SAPPHIREBERRY. Zones US, MS, LS. Native to China and Japan. Deciduous shrub. To 10–20 ft. tall; wider than tall in maturity. Can be trained as a low-branching or multitrunked small tree. Dark green leaves to 3½ in. long and half as wide. In late spring or early summer, 2–3-in. clusters of small, fragrant white flowers bloom on previous year's wood. Main draw is the autumn show of sapphire blue, ⅓-in. fruits that garland the branches. Berries are much appreciated by birds. Single plants set little or no fruit, so it's best to plant groups of seedlings; cutting-grown plants from a single parent are not self-fertile. Some growers sell groups of three seedlings as a single plant to ensure fruiting. Use for screening or as a feature in a large shrub border.

S. tinctoria. HORSESUGAR, SWEETLEAF. Zones US, MS, LS, CS. Native from Delaware to Florida and Louisiana. Semievergreen shrub or small tree, to 20 ft., sometimes 30 ft. Dark green lustrous leaves, to 6 in. long, 2–3 in. wide. Fragrant, yellowish green flowers in dense, 2½-in.-wide clusters in early spring. Orange-brown berries in late summer. Sweet foliage is a favorite food for horses and cattle.

SYNGONIUM

ARROWHEAD VINE

Araceae

EVERGREEN VINES, HOUSE PLANTS

✂ ZONE TS; OR INDOORS

☼ PARTIAL SHADE, INDIRECT LIGHT

● REGULAR WATER

Syngonium podophyllum

Outdoors in the Tropical South, these vines trail over the ground or loop around palm trees, their stems wrist thick and their leaves huge, green, and multifingered. These plants are hardly recognizable against the juvenile forms, which are common house plants. Young leaves are arrowhead shapes that range from solid green to shades of green with white, pink, or yellow markings that usually fade on adult leaves. Grow fast in moderately moist soil with lots of organic matter. Indoors, maintain a minimum temperature of 60°F, place in bright light, and mist to keep leaves looking lush. For a compact clumping plant that keeps producing young leaves, pinch stem tips and cut back runaway vining stems.

S. podophyllum. Native from Mexico to Panama. Dark green, glossy, arrowhead leaves, 6–12 in. long, on slender, 1–2-ft.-long leafstalks. Many selections are available, including 'Emerald Gem', quilted green leaves with a varnished luster; 'Maya Red', pink young leaves; and 'White Butterfly', green-and-white marbled leaves on stout stems.

S. wendlandii. Native to Costa Rica. Velvety, thin, green arrowhead leaves, 4–8 in. long, with silver-gray veins.

SYRINGA

LILAC

Oleaceae

DECIDUOUS SHRUBS, RARELY SMALL TREES

✂ ZONES VARY BY SPECIES

☼ ◐ FULL SUN OR LIGHT SHADE

● REGULAR WATER

Syringa vulgaris

Cherished for big, flamboyant, usually fragrant flower clusters at branch tips. Best known are common lilac *(S. vulgaris)* and its many selections, but there are other species of great usefulness. All are medium-size to large shrubs with no special appeal when out of bloom. Individual flowers are tubular, flaring into four petal-like lobes (in single types) or into a clutch of "petals" (in double kinds). Floral show comes from number of small flowers packed into dense pyramidal to conical clusters. Depending on climate, bloom

S

occurs from early spring (in the earliest kinds) to early summer, always after leaves have formed. Some forms bloom well with only light winter chill. *S. laciniata* and some selections described here bloom well in the Lower South. Most lilacs won't bloom in the Coastal South and certainly not in the Tropical South.

Provide well-drained, neutral to slightly alkaline soil; if soil is strongly acid, dig lime into it before planting. Most lilacs bloom on wood formed the previous year, so prune just after flowering ends. Remove spent flower clusters, cutting back to a pair of leaves; growth buds at that point will make flowering stems for next year. Renovate old, overgrown plants by cutting a few of the oldest stems to the ground each year. For the few types that bloom on new growth, prune in late dormant season. Stem borer, scale, and leaf miner are the major pests; powdery mildew, leaf spot, and bacterial blight may be problems.

S. chinensis (S. rothomagensis). CHINESE LILAC. Zones US, MS. Hybrid between common lilac and *S. persica*. To 15 ft. high, usually much less. More graceful than common lilac, with finer-textured foliage and twigs. Profusion of airy, open clusters of fragrant rose purple flowers. 'Alba' has white flowers.

S. hyacinthiflora. Zone US. Group of fragrant hybrids between common lilac and *S. oblata,* a Chinese species. Resemble common lilac, but generally bloom 7 to 10 days earlier. 'Assessippi' (single lavender), 'Excel' (single lilac blue), 'Grace McKenzie' (single lilac blue), 'Mt. Baker' (single white) are very early blooming. Other types include 'Alice Eastwood' (double magenta), 'Blue Hyacinth' (single lavender), 'Clarke's Giant' (single lavender, larger flowers), 'Esther Staley' (single magenta), 'Gertrude Leslie' (double white), 'Pocahontas' (single purple), 'Purple Heart' (single purple), and 'White Hyacinth' (single white).

S. laciniata (S. persica laciniata). CUT-LEAF LILAC. Zones US, MS, LS, CS. To 8 ft. tall, with open habit and good rich green foliage color. Leaves to 2½ in. long, divided nearly to midrib into three to nine segments. Many small clusters of fragrant lilac-colored flowers. Blooms well in Lower and Coastal South.

S. meyeri 'Paliban'. Zones US, MS, LS. Dense, neat habit to 4–5 ft. high, somewhat wider. Fine-textured, mildew-resistant foliage. Blooms when only 1 ft. high. Profusion of reddish purple buds open to softly fragrant light pink flowers. Sometimes sold as *S. palibiniana* or *S. velutina*.

S. microphylla 'Superba'. Zones US, MS, LS. Compact grower to 7 ft. tall. Mildew-resistant leaves. Deep red buds open to fragrant, single bright pink flowers. May rebloom in early fall. Bronze fall color. Heat tolerant.

S. patula 'Miss Kim'. Zones US, MS, LS. Dense, twiggy, rounded habit; eventually to 8–9 ft., but stays small for many years. Sometimes grafted high to make standard tree. Purple buds open to very fragrant icy blue flowers. Leaves may turn burgundy in fall. Heat tolerant.

S. persica. PERSIAN LILAC. Zones US, MS. Graceful, loose form to 6 ft. high, with arching branches and 2½-in.-long leaves. Many clusters of fragrant pale violet flowers appear all along branches.

S. prestoniae. Zone US. Group of extra-hardy hybrids developed in Canada. Flowers come on new growth at the end of the lilac season, after common lilac has bloomed. Bulky, dense plants resemble common lilac, but they are shorter (to 6–10 ft.) and individual flowers are smaller and not particularly fragrant. Good selections include 'Donald Wyman' (dark rosy purple), 'Isabella' (lilac), 'Jessica' (violet), 'Minuet' (pale lilac), 'Miss Canada' (true bright pink), 'Nocturne' (bluish lilac), and 'Royalty' (purple to violet).

S. reticulata (S. japonica, S. amurensis japonica). JAPANESE TREE LILAC. Zone US. Can be grown as large shrub to 30 ft. tall or easily trained as single-trunked tree. Smooth bark, something like cherry bark in glossiness. Leaves to 5 in. long. White flower clusters, to 1 ft. long, produced on new growth late in lilac season. Flowers showy, but scent is like that of privet flowers.

S. vulgaris. COMMON LILAC. Zones US, MS, some in LS. Can eventually reach 20 ft. tall, with nearly equal spread. Suckers strongly. Prune out suckers on grafted plants (no need to do so on own-root plants). Leaves roundish oval, pointed, dark green, to 5 in. long. Blooms in midspring, bearing pinkish or bluish lavender flowers in clusters to 10 in. long or more ('Alba' has pure white flowers). Fragrance is legendary; lilac fanciers

swear that the species and its older selections are more fragrant than newer types. Excellent cut flowers.

Selections, often called French hybrids, number in the hundreds. They generally flower a little later than the species and have larger clusters of single or double flowers in a wide range of colors. Singles are often as showy as doubles, sometimes more so. All lilacs require 2 to 5 years to settle down and produce flowers of full size and true color. Here are just a few of the many choice selections:

'Charles Joly' (double dark purplish red), 'Ludwig Spaeth' (single reddish purple to dark purple), 'Miss Ellen Willmott' (double pure white), 'President Lincoln' (single Wedgwood blue), 'President Poincaré' (double two-tone purple), 'Sensation' (single wine red with white picotee edge), and 'William Robinson' (double pink).

Newer hybrids include 'Krasavitsa Moskvy' ('Beauty of Moscow'), with large clusters of pink buds opening into white double flowers; 'Nadezhda' ('Hope'), with deep purple buds opening into lilac blue double flowers; and 'Primrose', with pale yellow blooms.

The Descanso Hybrids, developed to accept mild winters, perform exceptionally well in the Lower South. Best known is 'Lavender Lady'; others include 'Blue Boy', 'Blue Skies', 'Chiffon' (lavender), 'Forrest K. Smith' (light lavender), 'Sylvan Beauty' (rose lavender), and 'White Angel' ('Angel White').

TABEBUIA

TRUMPET TREE

Bignoniaceae

BRIEFLY DECIDUOUS, SOMETIMES EVERGREEN TREES

ZONE TS

FULL SUN OR LIGHT SHADE

REGULAR WATER

Tabebuia chrysotricha

Fast growth to 25–30 ft.; tend to have a gangly or irregular habit, especially in youth. Showy trumpet-shaped flowers grow in rounded clusters that become larger (up to 23 flowers) and more profuse as trees mature. Leaves dark olive green (except as noted), usually divided into three to seven leaflets arranged like fingers of hand.

Useful as patio trees or as stand-alone flowering trees for display. Tolerate many soils and degrees of maintenance, but respond well to feeding. Good drainage essential. Stake while young and keep plants to single leading shoot until 6–8 ft. tall, then allow to develop freely. Hardy to about 24°F.

T. argentea. SILVER TRUMPET TREE. Leaves silvery gray above and on undersides. Yellow flowers, to 2½ in. long, followed by gray fruit with black streaks.

T. chrysotricha. GOLDEN TRUMPET TREE. This species sometimes sold as *T. pulcherrima.* Young twigs, undersides of leaves covered with tawny fuzz. Flowers are 3–4 in. long, golden yellow, often with maroon stripes in throat. Bloom heaviest in spring, when tree loses leaves briefly. May bloom lightly at other times with leaves present.

T. heterophylla. PINK TRUMPET TREE. Sometimes grown as a large shrub. Summer blossoms are 2–3 in. long; color ranges from white to mauve, but dark pink is typical.

T. impetiginosa (T. ipe). PINK TRUMPET TREE. Lavender-pink, 2–3-in.-long flowers have white throats banded with yellow. Blooms late winter, sometimes again late summer to fall. Does not bloom as a young tree.

T. pallida. CUBAN PINK TRUMPET TREE. Leaves with one to three leaflets. Lilac-white, yellow-throated, 2-in. flowers sometimes appear singly, sometimes in small clusters.

MAKE A TALL MARIGOLD PLANT STAND STRAIGHT

To help tall marigold plants stand firm (perhaps stoutly enough not to need staking), dig planting holes extra deep, strip any leaves off lower 1–3 in. of stem, and plant with stripped portion below soil line.

TAGETES

MARIGOLD

Asteraceae (Compositae)

ANNUALS AND PERENNIALS

⚡ ZONES VARY BY SPECIES

☼ FULL SUN

💧 REGULAR WATER, EXCEPT AS NOTED

Tagetes erecta

Robust, free-branching, nearly trouble-free plants ranging from 6 in. to 4 ft. tall, with flowers from pale yellow through gold to orange and brown maroon. Leaves finely divided, ferny, usually strongly scented. Annuals will bloom from early summer to frost if old flowers are picked off. Handsome, long-lasting cut flowers; strong aroma from leaves, stems, and flowers permeates a room, but some odorless selections are available. Easy to grow from seed, which sprouts in a few days in warm soil; to get earlier bloom, start seeds in flats or buy flat-grown plants.

T. erecta. AFRICAN MARIGOLD. Annual. All zones. Original strains were 3–4-ft.-tall plants with single flowers. Modern strains more varied; most have fully double flowers. They range from dwarf Guys and Dolls and Inca series (12–14 in.) through Galore, Lady, and Perfection (16–20 in.) to Climax (2½–3 ft.). Novelty tall strains are Odorless and First Whites (28–30 in.). 'Snowbird' (1½ ft.) is a white form with uniform habit and color. Triploid hybrids, crosses between African and French marigolds, have exceptional vigor, bear profusion of 2-in. flowers over a long bloom season. Shorter than other *T. erecta* strains, they range from Nugget (10 in.) to Fireworks, H-G, Solar, and Sundance (12–14 in.).

T. filifolia. IRISH LACE. Annual. All zones. Mounds of bright green, finely divided foliage, 6 in. tall and as wide, resemble fluffy, round ferns. Tiny white flowers are attractive. Used primarily as edging plant.

T. lemmonii. LEMON MARIGOLD. Shrubby perennial. Zones LS, CS. Native from southeastern Arizona, where it can reach 3 ft., to southern Mexico and Central America, where it is a shrub to 6 ft. or taller and as wide. Finely divided, 4-in. leaves are aromatic when brushed against or rubbed—a strongly fragrant blend of marigold, mint, and lemon. Golden orange flower heads at branch ends; bloom is sporadic all year, heaviest winter–spring. Damaged by frost in open situations; cut back to remove damaged growth or to correct shape and limit size. Takes drought.

T. lucida. MEXICAN MINT MARIGOLD. Perennial in Zones MS, LS, CS, TS, but often grown as an annual. Single, usually unbranched stems grow to 2–2½ ft. Narrow, uncut, smooth dark green leaves have strong scent and flavor of tarragon. Yellow flowers appear in late summer.

T. patula. FRENCH MARIGOLD. Annual. All zones. Selections from 6–18 in. tall, in flower colors from yellow to rich maroon brown; flowers may be fully double or single, and many are strongly bicolored. Best series for edging are the dwarf, very double Janie (8 in.), Bonanza (10 in.), and Hero (10–12 in.), in a range of colors from yellow through orange to red and brownish red. The Aurora and Sophia series have flowers that are larger (2½ in. wide) but not as double.

T. tenuifolia (T. signata). SIGNET MARIGOLD. Annual. All zones. Infrequently planted. Smaller flower heads than French marigold, but incredibly profuse in bloom. Finely cut foliage. Golden orange 'Golden Gem' ('Ursula') and bright yellow 'Lemon Gem' both form 8-in. mounds.

TAMARIX

TAMARISK

Tamaricaceae

DECIDUOUS SHRUBS OR TREES

⚡ ZONES VARY BY SPECIES

☼ FULL SUN

💧 MODERATE TO VERY LITTLE WATER

Tamarix ramosissima

These large shrubs or small trees are useful in areas where wind, salt, and poor soil are challenges, as in coastal gardens. Only demands are sun and good drainage. Tiny, scalelike, light green or bluish foliage on airy, arching, reddish branches; in spring or summer, narrow plumes of small pink or rose blossoms appear at branch ends. Prune regularly to maintain graceful effect. Locate where plant won't be prominent while out of leaf. There is much confusion in labeling of tamarisks in nurseries and among botanists.

T. gallica. FRENCH TAMARISK, SALT CEDAR. Zones US, MS, LS, CS. Variable height, from 12–30 ft. Reddish brown to dark purple bark and fine, blue-green foliage. Blooms in summer, mostly on new season's growth, so prune in late winter; flowers are white to pink, in 2-in.-long clusters. Thrives in sandy, alkaline soil. Tolerates drought and salt spray. Good plant for beach areas. Excellent drainage essential. Dislikes heavy soil.

T. parviflora. Zones US, MS, LS. To 12–15 ft., not as wide. Light pink blossoms in late spring. Blooms on old wood; prune right after bloom.

T. ramosissima (T. pentandra). Zones US, MS, LS. Grows 10–15 ft. tall, usually not as wide. Bears rosy pink flowers in spring or early summer. Blooms on new wood; prune in late dormant season. Selection 'Cheyenne Red' has deeper pink blooms than the species; 'Rosea' bears rich pink flowers later in summer; 'Summer Glow' has bright pink flowers and blue-tinged foliage.

TAMARIX JUNIPER. See JUNIPERUS sabina 'Tamariscifolia'

TAMBOOKIE THORN. See ERYTHRINA acanthocarpa

TANACETUM

Asteraceae (Compositae)

PERENNIAL HERBS

⚡ ZONES VARY BY SPECIES

☼ FULL SUN

💧💧 REGULAR TO MODERATE WATER

Tanacetum vulgare

Most kinds of *Tanacetum* have finely divided leaves (often highly aromatic) and clusters of daisylike flower heads. Some have gray to nearly white foliage.

T. coccineum. See Chrysanthemum coccineum

T. parthenium. See Chrysanthemum parthenium

T. ptarmiciflorum. See Chrysanthemum ptarmiciflorum

T. vulgare. TANSY. Zones US, MS, LS, CS. Coarse garden plant to 3 ft. with finely divided, bright green, aromatic (some say smelly) leaves, and yellow button flowers. Thin clumps yearly to keep in bounds. No longer used medicinally but still grown in herb gardens.

T. v. crispum, fern-leaf tansy, grows to 2½ ft., has finely cut foliage, and is more decorative than the species.

TANGELO, TANGERINE, TANGOR. See CITRUS, Mandarin Hybrids and Mandarin

TANSY. See TANACETUM vulgare

TARO. See COLOCASIA esculenta

TARRAGON, FRENCH. See ARTEMISIA dracunculus

TASMANIAN TREE FERN. See DICKSONIA antarctica

TASSEL FERN. See POLYSTICHUM polyblepharum

TASSEL FLOWER. See AMARANTHUS caudatus

TASSEL HYACINTH. See MUSCARI comosum

TATARIAN ASTER. See ASTER tataricus

Taxaceae. The yew family contains needle-leafed evergreens with single-seeded fruit. Yew *(Taxus)* is the most notable example.

T

Taxodiaceae. The taxodium family includes evergreen (and some deciduous) coniferous trees, usually with small cones containing two to six seeds on each scale. Family members include *Cryptomeria*, dawn redwood *(Metasequoia)*, umbrella pine *(Sciadopitys)*, and *Taxodium*.

TAXODIUM

Taxodiaceae

DECIDUOUS TREES

☘ ZONES US, MS, LS, CS

☼ FULL SUN

◐ ◑ ◑ MUCH OR LITTLE WATER

Conifers of great size with shaggy, cinnamon-colored bark and graceful sprays of short, narrow, flat, needlelike leaves. Female flowers produce round, fragrant, 1-in. cones. All are very tough, tolerant trees. Need acid soil. The following species are native to the southeastern U.S.:

Taxodium distichum

T. ascendens. POND CYPRESS. Somewhat narrower, more erect than bald cypress; trunk not as strongly buttressed. Awl-shaped leaves stand erect on branchlets; those of bald cypress are spirally arranged. Can grow 70–80 ft. tall. Leafs out late in spring. In the wild, found on higher ground around ponds, but will grow in standing water, as bald cypress does. 'Nutans' is the main form grown. 'Prairie Sentinel' is very narrow.

T. distichum. BALD CYPRESS. Can grow into 100-ft.-tall, broad-topped tree in the wild, but young and middle-aged garden trees are pyramidal to 50–70 ft. high. Foliage sprays delicate and feathery, with narrow, about ½-in.-long leaves of a pale, delicate, yellow-toned green. Foliage turns orange brown before dropping. Interesting winter silhouette.

Any soil except strongly alkaline. Takes extremely wet conditions (even grows in swamps) but also tolerates rather dry soil. Trunk is buttressed near base. Develops knobby growths called "knees" when growing in waterlogged soil. Bagworms may be troublesome in some years. Requires only corrective pruning to remove deadwood and unwanted branches. Outstanding tree for stream bank or edge of lake or pond.

TAXUS

YEW

Taxaceae

EVERGREEN SHRUBS OR TREES

☘ ZONES US, MS

☼ ◑ ● SUN OR SHADE

◐ ● REGULAR TO MODERATE WATER

✤ FRUIT (SEEDS) AND FOLIAGE ARE POISONOUS IF INGESTED

Yews are conifers—but they do not bear cones. Instead, they produce fleshy, scarlet (rarely yellow), cup-shaped, single-seeded fruit.

Taxus baccata 'Stricta'

In general, yews are more formal, darker green, and more tolerant of shade than most cultivated conifers. Long lived; tolerant of much shearing and pruning, since they sprout from bare wood. Excellent for hedges, screens, foundation plantings, bank covers.

Easily moved even when large, but since plants grow at a slow to medium rate, big ones are luxury items. They take many soils, but do not thrive in strongly alkaline or strongly acid ones. Excellent drainage is essential. Yews planted in heavy, wet soil soon yellow and die. They do not like extreme heat. Reflected heat from hot south or west wall will burn foliage. Only female plants produce berries, but many do so without male plants nearby; types described are female, except as noted. As a rule, yews are rather pest-free.

T. baccata. ENGLISH YEW. To 25–40 ft., sometimes taller, with wide-spreading branches forming broad, low crown. Needles ½–1½ in. long,

dark green and glossy above, pale beneath; spirally arranged. Garden selections are far more common than the species. These include:

'Adpressa'. Usually sold as *T. brevifolia*. Wide-spreading, dense shrub to 4–5 ft. high.

'Aurea'. Broad pyramid to 25 ft. tall after many years. New foliage is golden yellow from spring to fall, then turns green.

'Repandens'. SPREADING ENGLISH YEW. Long, horizontal, spreading branches make 2–4-ft.-high ground cover, spreading to 8–10 ft. after many years. Useful low foundation plant. Will arch over wall.

'Stricta' ('Fastigiata'). IRISH YEW. Dark green column to 20 ft. or taller. Has larger needles and more crowded, upright branches than does English yew. Branches tend to spread near top, especially in snowy regions or where water is ample. Branches can be tied together with wire. Plants that outgrow their space can be reduced by heading back and thinning; old wood sprouts freely. There is a form with yellowish white variegation on leaves.

T. cuspidata. JAPANESE YEW. To 50 ft. in Japan; usually grown as compact, spreading shrub in U.S. Needles ½–1 in. long, dark green above, tinged yellowish beneath; usually arranged in two rows along twigs, making flat or V-shaped spray. The two commonly grown types are:

'Capitata'. PYRAMIDAL YEW. Upright, pyramidal form. Dense growth to 10–25 ft., possibly taller. Can be held lower by pinching new growth. Fruits heavily.

'Nana'. Often sold as *T. brevifolia*. Slow-growing male selection to 3 ft. tall, 6 ft. wide in 20 years, eventually to a possible 20 ft. tall. Makes a good low barrier or foundation plant for many years.

T. media. A group of hybrids between Japanese yew and English yew. Intermediate between the two in color and texture. Of the dozens of selections, these are among the most widely offered:

'Brownii'. Compact, rounded plant to 4–8 ft. tall, possibly larger. Male selection. Good low, dense hedge.

'Densiformis'. Dense, flat-topped shrub grows 2–3 ft. tall, 4–6 ft. wide.

'Hatfieldii'. Broad column or pyramid to 10 ft. or taller; good dark green color. Male selection.

'Hicksii'. Narrow, upright, to 10–12 ft. or taller; slightly broader at center than at top or bottom, widening with age. Good hedge, foundation plant.

'Wardii'. Wide-spreading, flat-topped shrub to 6 ft. tall, 15 ft. wide.

TEA PLANT. See CAMELLIA sinensis

TECOMA

Bignoniaceae

EVERGREEN SHRUB OR SMALL TREE

☘ ZONES CS, TS

☼ FULL SUN

◐ ● REGULAR TO MODERATE WATER

Various trumpet vines once lumped together as *Tecoma* now have different names. What remains is a showy large shrub or small tree.

T. australis. See Pandorea pandorana

T. capensis. See Tecomaria capensis

T. jasminoides. See Pandorea jasminoides

Tecoma stans

T. stans (Stenolobium stans). YELLOW BELLS, YELLOW TRUMPET FLOWER, YELLOW ELDER. In Tropical South, can be trained as tree. Usually a large shrub in the Coastal South. Much of wood may die back in winter, but recovery is quick in warm weather: rapid, bushy growth to 20 ft. Leaves divided into five to thirteen toothed, 1½–4-in.-long leaflets. Flowers bright yellow, bell shaped, 2 in. across, in large clusters, late spring–winter. Needs heat, deep soil, fairly heavy feeding. Cut faded flowers to prolong bloom; prune to remove dead and bushy growth. Showy mass in large garden. Boundary plantings, big shrub borders, screening.

T. s. angustata is a hardier form, better adapted to Texas and Southwest. Has narrow leaflets; late spring–fall flowers.

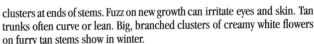

TECOMARIA capensis
(Tecoma capensis)

CAPE HONEYSUCKLE

Bignoniaceae

EVERGREEN VINE OR SHRUB

🌡 ZONES CS (WARMER PARTS), TS

☀ ◑ FULL SUN OR LIGHT SHADE

💧 REGULAR TO MODERATE WATER

Tecomaria capensis

Native to South Africa. Can scramble 15–25 ft. if tied to support. With hard pruning, an upright shrub to 6–8 ft. Leaves divided into many glistening dark green leaflets. Blooms fall–winter, bearing compact clusters of tubular, 2-in., brilliant orange-red blossoms. 'Aurea' bears yellow flowers; it has lighter green foliage than the species, is smaller growing and less showy, and requires more heat to perform well.

Both species and selection need good drainage. Take wind, light salt drift, sandy soil, drought. Use as espalier, bank cover (especially good on hot, steep slopes), coarse barrier hedge.

TERNSTROEMIA gymnanthera (T. japonica)

JAPANESE CLEYERA

Theaceae

EVERGREEN SHRUB

🌡 ZONES MS, LS, CS, TS

☀ ◑ ● SUN OR SHADE

💧 REGULAR WATER

Ternstroemia gymnanthera

A good substitute for the overly popular but disease-prone Fraser photinia (*Photinia fraseri*). Large, slow-growing, carefree evergreen to 10 ft. tall, 6 ft. wide, but is easy to keep smaller through yearly pruning. Glossy, leathery foliage. Red-stalked, rounded oval to narrow oval leaves are 1½–3 in. long, bronzy red when new; when mature, they turn deep green to bronzy green to purplish red, depending on season, exposure, and plant itself. Red tints are deeper in cold weather.

Summer flowers are ½ in. wide, creamy yellow, fragrant but not showy. Fruit (uncommon on small plants) resembles little yellow to red-orange holly berries or cherries, splits open to reveal shiny black seeds.

Grow in moist, well-drained acid soil. Tip-pinch to encourage compact growth. Use as basic landscaping shrub, informal hedge, foundation plant, poolside plant. Good companion for camellias (to which it is related), azaleas, nandina, pieris, ferns. Cut foliage keeps well.

In the Southeast, plants often sold as species *Cleyera japonica* are usually *Ternstroemia gymnanthera*.

TETRADIUM daniellii. See EVODIA daniellii

TETRAPANAX papyriferus
(Aralia papyrifera)

RICE PAPER PLANT

Araliaceae

EVERGREEN SHRUB

🌡 ZONES LS (PROTECTED), CS, TS

☀ ◑ SUN OR LIGHT SHADE

💧 REGULAR WATER

Tetrapanax papyriferus

Fast growing to 10–15 ft., often multitrunked. Big, bold, long-stalked leaves are 1–2 ft. wide, deeply lobed, gray green above, white-felted beneath, carried in clusters at ends of stems. Fuzz on new growth can irritate eyes and skin. Tan trunks often curve or lean. Big, branched clusters of creamy white flowers on furry tan stems show in winter.

Plants seem to suffer only from high winds (which break or tatter leaves) and cold (may freeze to ground in the Lower South but will quickly recover, sprouting from suckers to form thickets). Digging around roots stimulates sucker formation; suckers may arise 20 ft. from parent plant. Use for silhouette against walls, on patios; combine with other sturdy, bold-leafed plants for tropical effect. Name comes from the thick pith of the stems, used to make rice paper.

TEUCRIUM chamaedrys

GERMANDER

Lamiaceae (Labiatae)

EVERGREEN SHRUB

🌡 ZONES US, MS, LS, CS

☀ FULL SUN

💧 MODERATE WATER

Teucrium chamaedrys

Tough plant, enduring poor, rocky soil, often used for edging or as a low, clipped hedge in formal, parterre gardens. Needs good drainage.

Grows to 1 ft. high, spreading to 2 ft.; many upright, woody-based stems densely set with toothed, ¾-in.-long, dark green leaves. Red-purple or white flowers in loose spikes (white-flowered form is looser). Shear back once or twice a year to force side branching. 'Prostratum' is 4–6 in. high, spreading to 3 ft. or more.

TEXAS BLUEBONNET. See LUPINUS texensis

TEXAS MADRONE. See ARBUTUS xalapensis

TEXAS MOUNTAIN LAUREL. See SOPHORA secundiflora

TEXAS PERSIMMON. See DIOSPYROS texana

TEXAS PISTACHIO. See PISTACIA texana

TEXAS RANGER. See LEUCOPHYLLUM

TEXAS SAGE. See LEUCOPHYLLUM, SALVIA coccinea

TEXAS SOTOL. See DASYLIRION texanum

TEXAS STAR. See HIBISCUS coccineus

THALICTRUM

MEADOW RUE

Ranunculaceae

PERENNIALS

🌡 ZONES VARY BY SPECIES

◑ LIGHT SHADE

💧 REGULAR WATER

Thalictrum aquilegifolium

Foliage clumps, often blue green in color, resemble those of columbine. In late spring or summer, plants send up sparsely leafed stems topped by puffs of small flowers, each consisting of four sepals and a prominent cluster of stamens. Superb for airy effect; delicate tracery of leaves and flowers is particularly effective against dark green background. Pleasing contrast to sturdier perennials. Foliage good in flower arrangements.

Most meadow rues need some winter chill. All thrive in dappled sunlight at woodland edges. Grow in moist, humus-rich soil. Protect from wind. Divide clumps every 4 or 5 years.

T. aquilegifolium. COLUMBINE MEADOW RUE. Zones US, MS. Grows to 2–3 ft. tall, with bluish green foliage. Earliest of the meadow rues to bloom. Clouds of fluffy stamens (the white or greenish sepals drop off) appear for a couple of weeks in mid- to late spring. Rosy lilac is the usual color; white and purple selections are available. If left in place, spent flowers are followed by attractive, long-lasting seed heads. Heat tolerant.

T. delavayi (T. dipterocarpum). CHINESE MEADOW RUE. Zones US, MS, LS. To 3–4 ft. (even 6 ft.) tall, with thin, dark purple stems that need support. Green foliage. Lavender to violet sepals, yellow stamens. 'Hewitt's Double' has double lilac-colored flowers; bloom lasts 2 months or longer. Heat tolerant.

T. flavum glaucum (T. speciosissimum). Zones US, MS, LS. Grows to 3–5 ft. tall; stems need staking. Blue-green foliage; summer flowers like those of *T. aquilegifolium,* but color is lemon yellow. Heat tolerant.

Theaceae. The tea family consists of evergreen or deciduous trees and shrubs with leathery leaves and five-petaled flowers that have many stamens. *Camellia, Franklinia,* and *Stewartia* are important members.

THEA sinensis. See CAMELLIA sinensis

THELYPTERIS

Thelypteridaceae (Polypodiaceae)
FERNS
✂ ZONES VARY BY SPECIES
◐ ● PARTIAL OR FULL SHADE, EXCEPT AS NOTED
● ◓ AMPLE TO REGULAR WATER

Thelypteris palustris

The plants commonly sold under this name have undergone more name changes than is usual even for ferns. Botanically current names are noted in parentheses below; garden centers may not have caught up. Species grown in the South are deciduous and commonly thrive in shade, though some tolerate sun if moisture is plentiful. All have their place in fern collections or wild gardens.

T. hexagonoptera (Phegopteris hexagonoptera). BROAD BEECH FERN. Zones US, MS, LS. Medium green, triangular fronds to 1½–2 ft. long and wide. Fronds are once divided, each division deeply toothed.

 **T. kunthii.** SOUTHERN SHIELD FERN, WOOD FERN. Zones MS, LS, CS. Light green, triangular fronds, 3 ft., sometimes 5 ft. long, contrast well with dark green–leafed plants; leaflets widely spaced along frond stem. Fern spreads quickly by rhizomes to form a soft, tall, pretty mass. Tolerates limy and moderately dry soils. Also takes more sun than most ferns. Brown winter foliage quite attractive, but cut back before new growth starts in spring. One of the easiest ferns to grow.

T. noveboracensis (Parathelypteris noveboracensis). NEW YORK FERN. Zones US, MS. Pale green, 1–2-ft.-long fronds are once divided, with the segments deeply lobed. A vigorous colonizer, it can be used as a ground cover in shade—or even in full sun if kept moist.

T. palustris. MARSH FERN. Zones US, MS, LS. Spreads rapidly by rhizomes. Fronds, which occur singly or in tufts, are of two kinds: sterile and fertile. Sterile fronds are 6–24 in. long and half as wide, tapered at both ends, once divided, with segments deeply lobed. Fertile fronds are 1–3 ft. long, sturdier and stiffer than the sterile ones.

THERMOPSIS

BUSH PEA, FALSE LUPINE
Fabaceae (Leguminosae)
PERENNIALS
✂ ZONES VARY BY SPECIES
◌ ◑ FULL SUN OR LIGHT SHADE
● REGULAR WATER

Thermopsis caroliniana

These easy-to-grow perennials resemble lupines. Silvery leaves are divided into leaflets that spread like fingers on a hand; erect, spikelike clusters of sweet

pea–shaped yellow flowers appear in spring. Because of their tendency to spread by underground rhizomes, they are best in informal or wild gardens. Need little care. Somewhat drought tolerant.

T. caroliniana. CAROLINA BUSH PEA. Zones US, MS, LS. Native to the Carolinas and Georgia. To 3–4 ft. tall, with 10-in. flower clusters. More heat tolerant than the other species.

T. montana. MOUNTAIN BUSH PEA. Zone US. Native to western North America. To 2–4 ft. tall, with 8-in. flower clusters.

THEVETIA

Apocynaceae
EVERGREEN SHRUBS OR SMALL TREES
✂ ZONES VARY BY SPECIES
◌ FULL SUN
● REGULAR WATER
☠ ALL PARTS ARE POISONOUS IF INGESTED

Thevetia peruviana

Fast-growing plants with narrow, glossy, deep green leaves and clusters of showy funnel-shaped flowers at branch ends. Thrive in heat; take very little frost.

T. peruviana (T. neriifolia). YELLOW OLEANDER, LUCKY NUT. Zones CS (protected), TS. Can be trained as 20-ft. tree or pruned into 6–8-ft. hedge, screen, or background planting. Leaves 3–6 in. long, with edges rolled under. Fragrant, 2–3-in., yellow to apricot flowers bloom almost any time (mostly summer–fall). Provide good drainage, wind protection. In colder part of range, mound dry sand 6–12 in. deep around base of stem; if top is then frozen, plant will recover quickly and new growth will bloom same year.

T. thevetioides. GIANT THEVETIA. Zone TS. Open habit, to 12 ft. tall and as wide. Leaves are darker green than those of *T. peruviana;* they resemble oleander leaves but are corrugated, heavily veined beneath. Large clusters of 4-in., brilliant yellow flowers from summer to winter.

THREAD PALM. See WASHINGTONIA robusta

THRIFT. See ARMERIA, PHLOX subulata

THUJA

ARBORVITAE
Cupressaceae
EVERGREEN SHRUBS OR TREES
✂ ZONES VARY BY SPECIES
◌ ◑ FULL SUN OR PARTIAL SHADE
● ◓ REGULAR TO MODERATE WATER

Thuja occidentalis

Grow in neat, symmetrical, geometrical plants in stages of globes, cones, cylinders. Juvenile foliage is feathery, with small, needlelike leaves; mature foliage is scalelike, carried in flat sprays. Foliage in better-known selections is often yellow green or bright golden yellow. Urn-shaped cones with overlapping scales are ½ in. long, green turning brownish.

Although arborvitaes will take both damp and fairly dry soils, they grow best in well-drained soil. Need humidity and suffer in areas where summers are dry. They are subject to some problems, including bagworms and heart rot.

T. occidentalis. AMERICAN ARBORVITAE, EASTERN ARBORVITAE. Zones US, MS. Native to eastern U.S. Upright, open growth to 40–60 ft., with branches that tend to turn up at ends. Leaf sprays bright green to yellowish green. Foliage turns bronze in severe cold. The species itself is seldom seen, but smaller garden types are common. Among these, the taller ones make good informal or clipped screens, while shorter kinds are often used around foundations, along walks or walls, as hedges. Some good selections are:

'Douglasii Pyramidalis'. Vigorous-growing pyramid to 15 ft. or taller.

'Emerald' ('Emerald Green', 'Smaragd'). Neat, dense-growing, narrow cone to 10–15 ft. tall, 3–4 ft. wide. Holds its color throughout winter.

'Fastigiata' ('Pyramidalis', 'Columnaris'). Tall, narrow, dense, columnar plant to 25 ft. high, 5 ft. wide; can be kept lower by pruning. Good plant for tall hedges and screens (6 ft. or more), especially in cold-winter areas and damp soils. Set 4 ft. apart for neat, low-maintenance screen.

'Globosa' ('Little Gem', 'Little Giant', and 'Nana' are similar). GLOBE ARBORVITAE, TOM THUMB ARBORVITAE. Dense, rounded, with bright green foliage. Usually 2–3 ft. tall with equal spread; eventually larger.

'Nigra'. Tall, dense, dark green cone to 20–30 ft. tall, 4–5 ft. wide.

'Rheingold' ('Improved Ellwangeriana Aurea'). Cone-shaped, slow-growing, bright golden plant with a mixture of scalelike and needlelike leaves. Even very old plants seldom exceed 6 ft.

'Woodwardii'. Widely grown dense, globular shrub of rich green color. May attain considerable size with age, but remains a small plant over long period. If you can wait 72 years, it may reach 8 ft. high by 18 ft. wide.

T. orientalis. See Platycladus orientalis

THUNBERGIA

Acanthaceae

VINES OR SHRUBS

✺ ZONE TS, EXCEPT AS NOTED

☼ ◑ FULL SUN OR PARTIAL SHADE

💧 REGULAR WATER

Tropical plants noted for showy flowers. Some grow fast enough to bloom the first season and can thus be treated as annuals. Those grown

Thunbergia alata

as perennials are evergreen in the Tropical South. Provide rich, well-drained soil. Good greenhouse plants.

T. alata. BLACK-EYED SUSAN VINE. Perennial vine grown as summer annual. May live over in Zones CS, TS. Small, trailing or twining plant with triangular, 3-in. leaves. Flowers are flaring tubes to 1 in. wide in orange, yellow, or white, all with purple-black throat. Start seed indoors; set plants out in good soil in sunny spot as soon as weather warms. Use in hanging baskets or window boxes or as ground cover; or train on strings or low trellis.

T. erecta. KING'S MANTLE. Evergreen shrub. To 6 ft. tall, erect, sometimes twining, with dark green leaves. Velvety dark blue flowers with orange or cream throats (like gloxinia blossoms) in joints of upper leaves through summer and fall. 'Alba' is white-flowering form.

T. grandiflora. SKY FLOWER, SKY VINE. Perennial vine. Vigorous twiner to 20 ft. or more; 8-in., heart-shaped leaves. Slightly drooping clusters of tubular, flaring, 2½–3-in., pure blue flowers. Blooms summer, fall. Takes a year to get started, then grows rapidly. Comes back to bloom in a year if frozen. Use to cover arbor, fence; makes dense shade. There is also a white form. *T. laurifolia* looks much like *T. grandiflora* and has same needs.

T. gregorii (T. gibsonii). ORANGE CLOCK VINE. Perennial vine; grow as summer annual outside Tropical South. Twines to 6 ft. tall or sprawls over ground to cover 6-ft. circle. Leaves 3 in. long, toothed. Flowers tubular, flaring, bright orange, borne singly on 4-in. stems. Plant 3–4 ft. apart to cover a wire fence, 6 ft. apart as a ground cover. Can cascade over a wall, or grow in a hanging basket. Showy and easy to grow.

T. mysorensis. MYSORE CLOCK VINE. Perennial vine. Tall climber with spectacular hanging clusters of gaping flowers that are red on the outside, yellow within; summer bloom. Clusters can reach several feet in length. Vine should be trained to overhead pergola or other support to permit flowers to hang unimpeded.

THYMOPHYLLA tenuiloba. See DYSSODIA tenuiloba

THYMUS

THYME

Lamiaceae (Labiatae)

EVERGREEN SHRUBBY PERENNIALS

✺ ZONES VARY BY SPECIES

☼ ◑ FULL SUN OR PARTIAL SHADE

💧 MODERATE WATER

Thymus vulgaris

Members of the mint family with tiny, usually heavily scented leaves and masses of colorful little flowers in late spring or summer. Diminutive plants well suited to herb garden, rock garden; prostrate, mat-forming types make good ground covers for small spaces. Attractive to bees. Provide warm, light, well-drained soil; restrain plants as needed by clipping back growing tips.

T. citriodorus. LEMON THYME. Zones US, MS, LS, CS. Hybrid grows to 4–12 in. high; erect or spreading. Lemon-scented foliage; summer flowers of palest purple. Leaves of 'Argenteus' are splashed with silver, those of 'Aureus' marked with gold.

T. lanuginosus. See T. pseudolanuginosus

T. praecox arcticus (T. serpyllum, T. drucei). CREEPING THYME, MOTHER-OF-THYME. Zones US, MS, LS. Main stems form a flat mat, with branches rising 2–6 in. high. Roundish dark green leaves; clusters of small, purplish white flowers in summer. Good for small areas or filler between stepping-stones where foot traffic is light. Soft and fragrant underfoot. Leaves can be used for seasoning and in potpourri. Among the many garden forms are the following:

'Album'. Pure white flowers.

'Coccineum'. Deep pink flowers.

'Linear Leaf Lilac'. Needlelike leaves, red stems, lilac flowers.

'Longwood'. Strong grower, furry gray leaves, 4-in. spikes of lilac blooms.

'Minus'. Tiny, dense, compact, slow-growing plant with pink flowers; 'Elfin' even tinier.

'Pink Ripple'. Larger than species; aromatic, lemon-scented foliage, salmon pink flowers.

'Reiter's'. Profuse rose red blooms.

T. pseudolanuginosus (T. lanuginosus). SILVER THYME, WOOLLY THYME. Zones US, MS, LS. Forms flat to undulating mat 2–3 in. high. Stems densely clothed with small, woolly gray leaves. Sparse, seldom-seen midsummer bloom of pinkish flowers in leaf joints. Becomes slightly rangy in winter. Use in rock crevices, between stepping-stones, to spill over bank or raised bed, to cover small patches of ground. 'Hall's Woolly' is not as furry but blooms more heavily.

T. vulgaris. COMMON THYME. Zones US, MS, LS, CS. To 6–12 in. high. Narrow to oval, gray-green leaves. Tiny lilac flowers in dense whorls in late spring or summer. Low edging for flower, vegetable, or herb garden. Good container plant. Use leaves fresh or dried for seasoning fish, shellfish, poultry stuffing, soups, vegetables.

TI. See CORDYLINE terminalis

TIARELLA

FOAMFLOWER

Saxifragaceae

PERENNIALS

✺ ZONES US, MS, LS

◑ ● PARTIAL OR FULL SHADE

💧 REGULAR WATER

Tiarella wherryi

Clump-forming perennials spread by rhizomes (and by stolons, in the case of *T. cordifolia*). Leaves arise directly from rhizomes; foliage is evergreen, though it may change color in autumn. Selections with year-round colorful foliage are becoming popular; look for new introductions in addition to ones described below. Narrow, erect flower stems carry many small white (sometimes pinkish) flowers. Useful in shady rock gardens; make pretty ground covers but will not bear foot traffic.

T. cordifolia. FOAMFLOWER. Rapid spreader. Forms foot-wide clumps of light green, lobed, 4-in. leaves that show red-and-yellow fall color. Flower stalks 1 ft. tall. Leaves of 'Dunvegan' are deeply cut, veined with maroon; 'Slickrock' is a compact grower with 8-in. flower stalks.

T. wherryi (T. cordifolia collina). Resembles *T. cordifolia*, but has no stolons and spreads more slowly. Flower clusters are somewhat more slender; flowers can be pink tinted. Leaves of 'Eco Red Heart' have dark red centers and veins. 'Oakleaf' has deeply lobed leaves, pink flowers.

TIBOUCHINA

PRINCESS FLOWER, GLORYBUSH, GLORY TREE

Melastomataceae

EVERGREEN SHRUBS OR TREES

ZONE TS

FULL SUN OR PARTIAL SHADE

REGULAR WATER

Tibouchina urvilleana

Tropical trees and shrubs, most of Brazilian origin, with large, deeply veined, usually hairy leaves and big, showy, five-petaled purple flowers. Bloom is intermittent over a long period. Prefer rich, well-drained, slightly acid soil. The shrubs have a tendency to legginess and should be pruned lightly after every bloom cycle, somewhat more heavily in spring. They resprout quickly after heavy pruning. Pinch tips of young plants to encourage bushiness.

T. elegans. Shrub. To 6 ft. tall, with glossy green, 2-in. leaves and purple flowers 1½–2½ in. across.

T. grandifolia. Shrub. To 10 ft. tall, with 5–9-in.-long leaves and inch-wide violet flowers in 8–16-in.-long clusters.

T. granulosa. PURPLE GLORY TREE. To 40 ft., with broad, spreading habit. Leaves are 5–8 in. long. Purple, 2-in.-wide flowers come in clusters up to 1 ft. long.

T. urvilleana (T. semidecandra). PRINCESS FLOWER. Shrub. Open growth to 5–18 ft. high. Branch tips, buds, and new growth shaded with velvety hairs in orange and bronze red. Velvety, 3–6-in.-long leaves are often edged red; older leaves add spots of red, orange, or yellow, especially in winter. Clusters of brilliant royal purple, 3–5-in.-wide flowers. Protect from strong winds.

TIGER LILY. See LILIUM lancifolium

TILIA

LINDEN

Tiliaceae

DECIDUOUS TREES

ZONES VARY BY SPECIES

FULL SUN

REGULAR WATER

Tilia cordata

Large, dense trees, usually taller than wide. All have irregularly heart-shaped leaves and small, fragrant, yellowish white flowers in drooping clusters, late spring–early summer. Flowers develop into nutlets, each with an attached papery bract. Stately good looks, moderate growth rate have made lindens favorite park and street trees in Europe.

Best growth in deep, rich, moist soil. Fall color varies from negligible to lively yellow. Young trees need staking, shaping; older trees need only corrective pruning. Aphids can cause honeydew drip and sooty mold.

T. americana. AMERICAN LINDEN, BASSWOOD. Zones US, MS, LS. Native to eastern and central North America. To 60–80 ft. tall, 30–50 ft. wide. Straight-trunked tree with a narrow crown. Dull dark green leaves to 4–6 in. long, nearly as wide. 'Redmond' is a pyramidal form with glossy foliage. Bees make excellent honey from the blossoms.

T. cordata. LITTLELEAF LINDEN. Zones US, MS. Native to Europe. Dense pyramid to 60–70 ft. or taller. Leaves 1½–3 in. long and as wide (or wider), dark green above, silvery beneath. Excellent medium-size lawn or street tree. Given space to develop its symmetrical crown, it can be a fine patio shade tree (but expect bees in flowering season). Can be sheared into hedges. Very tolerant of city conditions. Japanese beetle may be a problem in some areas. Selected forms include 'Chancellor', 'Glenleven', 'Greenspire', 'June Bride' (especially heavy bloomer), and 'Olympic'.

T. heterophylla. See T. americana

TILLANDSIA

Bromeliaceae

PERENNIALS

ZONE TS, EXCEPT AS NOTED; OR INDOORS

EXPOSURE NEEDS VARY BY SPECIES

WATER NEEDS VARY BY SPECIES

Tillandsia usneoides

These are bromeliads grown in pots of fast-draining, loose soil mix or as epiphytes on tree branches or slabs of bark. The best known is *T. usneoides*, the "Spanish moss" of the Deep South. In some, leaf rosettes are bright green; in others, they are gray and scaly or scurfy. Bright green ones need regular water and filtered light. Gray types need less water and are more sun tolerant. They are often mounted on plaques of wood or bark and used as wall ornaments indoors or outside (where hardy). Let potting mix dry out between waterings.

T. cyanea. Rosette of bright green, arching, 1-ft. leaves produces showy flower cluster: a flattened plume of deep pink or red bracts, from which violet blue flowers emerge one or two at a time for a long period.

T. ionantha. Miniature rosettes of 2-in.-long leaves covered with a silvery gray fuzz. Small, tubular flowers are violet; at bloom time, center of rosette turns red. Tough and undemanding plant.

T. lindenii (Vriesea lindenii). Like *T. cyanea*, but plume of bracts is green or green marked rose. As with other bromeliads, each rosette produces just one long-lasting inflorescence. Offsets replace original plant.

T. usneoides. SPANISH MOSS. Zones LS, CS, TS. Festoons itself on live oaks, cypresses, and telephone lines, hanging as long as 15 ft. Greenish gray stems and leaves are wiry, threadlike. Has no roots. Inconspicuous green flowers in late spring. Thrives in shade and high humidity; very sensitive to air pollution. A live oak draped with Spanish moss is a classic image of the South.

TITHONIA rotundifolia (T. speciosa)

MEXICAN SUNFLOWER

Asteraceae (Compositae)

PERENNIAL GROWN AS ANNUAL

ALL ZONES

FULL SUN

REGULAR OR MODERATE WATER

Tithonia rotundifolia

Husky, gaudy, rather coarse plant with spectacular flowers, velvety green leaves. Grows rapidly to 6 ft. tall. Blooms from summer to frost, bearing 3–4-in.-wide flower heads with orange-scarlet rays and tufted yellow centers. Use as a temporary screen. 'Torch', to 4 ft., makes a bushy summer hedge. 'Goldfinger' and 'Sundance' are 3-footers for smaller gardens. All have inflated hollow stems; cut with care for bouquets to avoid bending stalks. Sow seed in place in spring, in well-drained soil that is not too rich. Tolerant of drought, humidity, intense heat. Attractive to butterflies, hummingbirds. Will self-sow.

TITI. See CYRILLA racemiflora

TOAD LILY. See TRICYRTIS

TOLMIEA menziesii

PIGGYBACK PLANT

Saxifragaceae

PERENNIAL

⚡ ZONE TS; OR INDOORS

◐ ● PARTIAL OR FULL SHADE

💧 💧 TOLERATES WET SOIL

Tolmiea menziesii

Native to Coast Ranges from Northern California northward to Alaska. Chief asset is abundant production of attractive, 5-in.-wide basal leaves—shallowly lobed and toothed, rather hairy. Leaves can produce new plantlets at junction of leafstalk and blade. Tiny, rather inconspicuous reddish brown flowers top 1–2-ft.-high stems. Good ground cover for shade. As house plant, needs filtered light, cool temperatures, frequent watering. Mealybugs, spider mites are occasional pests. Makes handsome hanging basket plant. Start new plants any time of year: Take leaf with plantlet and insert in moist potting mix so base of plantlet contacts soil.

TOMATILLO. See PHYSALIS ixocarpa

TOMATO

Solanaceae

PERENNIAL GROWN AS ANNUAL

⚡ ALL ZONES

☼ FULL SUN

💧 REGULAR WATER

Tomato

Easy to grow and prolific, tomatoes are just about the most widely grown of all garden plants, edible or otherwise. Amateur and commercial growers have varying ideas about how best to grow tomatoes; if your own particular scheme works, continue to follow it. But if you're a novice or you're dissatisfied with previous attempts, you may find the following useful.

First, choose types suited to your area that will yield the kinds of tomatoes you like on the plants that you can handle. Some plants are determinate, others indeterminate. Determinate types are bushier and not as suitable for staking or trellising. Indeterminate plants are more vinelike, need more training, and generally have a longer bearing period. (Though the tomato plant is really a sprawling plant incapable of climbing, you'll often see it referred to as a "vine.") Plant a few each of early, midseason, and late selections for a long period of production. Six plants can supply enough fruit for a family of four.

Set out tomato plants in spring after frost danger is past and the soil has warmed. To grow your own plants from seed, sow seeds 5 to 7 weeks before you intend to set out plants. Sow in pots of light soil mix or in a ready-made seed starter (sold at garden supply stores). Cover seeds with ½ in. of fine soil. Firm soil over seeds. Keep soil surface damp. Place seed container in cold frame or sunny window—a temperature of 65–70°F is ideal, although a range of 50°F at night to 85°F in the day will give acceptable results. When seedlings are 2 in. tall, transplant them into 3- or 4-in. pots. Keep in sunny area until seedlings reach transplant size. When buying tomato plants, look for compact ones with sturdy stems; avoid plants that are tall for their pots or that already have flowers or fruit.

Plant in a sunny site in well-drained soil. Tomato plants prefer neutral to slightly acid soil; plan to add lime to very acid soil or sulfur to alkaline soil

the autumn before setting out plants. Space plants 1½–3 ft. apart (staked or trained) or 3–4 ft. apart (untrained). Make planting hole extra deep. Set seedlings in hole so lowest leaves are just above soil level. Additional roots will form on buried stem and provide a stronger root system.

Tomato management and harvest will be most satisfying if you train plants to keep them mostly off the ground (left alone, they will sprawl and some fruit will lie on soil, often causing rot, pest damage, and discoloration). Most common training method for indeterminate types is to drive a 6-ft.-long stake (at least 1 by 1 in.) into ground a foot from each plant. Use a soft tie to hold the plants to these stakes as they grow.

Slightly easier in the long run, but more work at planting time, is to grow each plant in wire cylinder made of concrete reinforcing screen (6-in. mesh). Screen is manufactured 7 ft. wide, which is just right for cylinder height; most indeterminate vines can grow to top of such a cylinder. Put stakes at opposite sides of cylinder and tie cylinder firmly to them. As vine grows, poke protruding branches back inside cylinder every week. Reach through screen to pick fruit.

Tomato plants need regular moisture at the root level. Since they are deep rooted, water heavily when you do water. If soil is fairly rich, you won't need to fertilize at all. But in ordinary soils, give light application of fertilizer every 2 weeks from the time first blossoms set until end of harvest; or give a single application of slow-release fertilizer.

Tomato plant pests include Colorado potato beetles and whiteflies. If you see large green caterpillars with diagonal white stripes feeding upside down on leaf undersides, your plant has hornworms; handpick them or spray young caterpillars with *Bacillus thuringiensis*. Tomatoes are prone to several diseases. Early blight (also called alternaria blight) shows up on leaves as dark spots with concentric rings inside, and on fruit as sunken lesions with same ring pattern. Sprays of liquid copper fungicide will control early blight and several other diseases; consult a local garden center or your Cooperative Extension Office for spray schedule. If plants are growing strongly, then suddenly wilt and die, the cause is probably verticillium wilt, fusarium wilt, or both. Pull and dispose of such plants. Diseases live over in soil, so plant in a different location every year and try selections resistant to these and other diseases (see "Tomato selections").

Some tomato problems—leaf roll, blossom-end rot, cracked fruit—are physiological; these can usually be corrected (or prevented) by maintaining uniform soil moisture. A mulch will help conserve moisture in very hot or dry climates.

If you have done everything right and your tomatoes have failed to set fruit in the spring, use hormone spray on blossoms. Tomatoes often fail to set fruit when night temperatures drop below 55°F. Fruit-setting hormone often speeds up bearing in the earlier part of the season. Tomatoes can also fail to set fruit when temperatures rise above 90°F, but hormones are not effective under those conditions. Heat-tolerant selections, such as 'Heatwave', set fruit despite high temperatures.

Keep ripe fruit picked to extend season. When frost is predicted, harvest all fruit, both green and partly ripe. Store in a dry place out of direct sunlight at 60–70°F; check often for ripening.

HEAT-TOLERANT TOMATOES

Once daytime temperatures rise above 90°F or nighttime temperatures exceed 75°F, most tomato plants stop setting fruit. Those that can best take the heat and go on producing through the swelter of Southern summers include standards 'Atkinson', 'Creole', 'Heatwave', 'Hotset', 'Ozark Pink', 'Solar Set', and 'Sunmaster'; paste tomato 'Viva Italia'; cherry tomato 'Sungold'; and heirloom 'Arkansas Traveler'.

TOMATO SELECTIONS

Following are types of tomatoes you can buy as seeds or started plants. The number of selections is enormous and increases every year. There are tomatoes for every taste and every part of the South. Consult a knowledgeable garden center, your Cooperative Extension Office, and other gardeners to find out which types will flourish in your local climate and soil. ▶

If certain diseases or nematodes cause trouble locally, you may be able to grow selections that resist one or more problems. Keys to resistance you may see on plant labels or in catalog descriptions include V (verticillium wilt), F (fusarium wilt), FF (Race 1 and Race 2 fusarium), T (tobacco mosaic virus), N (nematodes), A (alternaria blight), and L (septoria leaf spot). For example, a plant labeled VFFNT resists verticillium wilt, two races of fusarium wilt, nematodes, and tobacco mosaic virus.

Main crop or standard tomatoes. 'Atkinson', 'Better Boy', 'Big Boy', 'Celebrity', 'Creole', 'Heatwave', 'Hotset', 'Ozark Pink', 'Solar Set', and 'Sunmaster' are widely grown. 'Heatwave' is popular in the Coastal and Tropical South. 'Ace' and 'Pearson' are also popular, as well as old selections 'Marglobe' and 'Rutgers'.

Early tomatoes. These selections set fruit at lower night temperatures than other tomatoes do. 'Burpee's Early Pick', 'Dona', 'Early Girl', 'First Lady', and 'Pilgrim' are good selections for early summer and late fall crops.

Novelty tomatoes. Among these are yellow and orange selections such as 'Husky Gold', 'Lemon Boy', 'Mountain Gold', and 'Orange Queen'. 'Caro Rich' is very high in vitamin A and beta carotene. Those who have a special taste for novelties can grow tomatoes with deep reddish brown flesh ('Black Prince'), white tomatoes ('New Snowball', 'White Beauty'), tomatoes with striped fruit ('Green Zebra', 'Tigerella'), and even one with fruit that is green when fully ripe ('Evergreen'). 'Long Keeper' will stay fresh in storage for 3 months, and 'Stuffer' and 'Yellow Stuffer' yield large, nearly hollow fruits that resemble bell peppers.

Large-fruited tomatoes. These grow to full size in areas where both days and nights are warm. Fruits can weigh a pound or even more. 'Beefmaster', 'Beefsteak', and 'Big Beef' are typical. 'Burpee's Supersteak Hybrid' can produce 2-lb. fruits, and 'Delicious' has produced a tomato weighing 7 lb. 12 oz. for Gordon Graham of Edmond, Oklahoma.

Paste tomatoes. These bear prodigious quantities of small oval fruits with thick meat and small seed cavities. Sometimes called plum tomatoes, they are favorites for canning, sauces, and tomato paste. They are also good for drying. 'Roma', 'San Marzano', 'Viva Italia', and the yellow 'Italian Gold' are examples.

Small-fruited tomatoes. Fruits range from the size of currants to that of large marbles. Shapes and colors are indicated by names: 'Red Cherry', 'Red Pear', 'Yellow Cherry', 'Yellow Pear'. Those with very small fruits include 'Gardener's Delight', 'Sungold', 'Supersweet 100', 'Sweet 100', and 'Sweet Million'. Small-fruiting types that grow on small plants suitable for pots or hanging baskets include 'Patio', 'Small Fry', and 'Tiny Tim'.

Heirloom tomatoes. Varying in size, appearance, and plant habit, these represent old types that have been maintained by enthusiasts in different parts of the country. Most are grown for excellent flavor. 'Arkansas Traveler' produces well in hot weather; 'Brandywine' is a popular selection.

TONKIN CANE. See ARUNDINARIA amabilis under BAMBOO

TORENIA fournieri

WISHBONE FLOWER

Scrophulariaceae

ANNUAL

ALL ZONES

PARTIAL SHADE

REGULAR WATER

Torenia fournieri

Compact, bushy plant grows to 1 ft. high. Blooms summer–fall; light blue flowers with deeper blue markings and bright yellow throats look like miniature gloxinias. Stamens arranged in wishbone shape. A white-flowered form is also available. Sow seed in pots; transplant to garden after frosts. Prefers cool, moist soil and some shade. Use in borders, pots, window boxes. Plants in the ground can be lifted for winter bloom indoors.

TORREYA taxifolia

FLORIDA TORREYA, STINKING CEDAR

Taxaceae

EVERGREEN TREE

ZONE CS

FULL SUN OR PARTIAL SHADE

MODERATE WATER

Torreya taxifolia

Conifer native to Florida, best adapted to the Panhandle. Grows to 40 ft. tall, with a broad conical form. Slender horizontal branches droop at the tips. Leaves are glossy and deep green, with two whitish bands underneath, sharp-pointed, to 1½ in. long and ⅛ in. wide; produce a fetid odor when bruised. Purple plum-shaped fruits in late summer. Rare tree. Needs slightly acid, fertile, well-drained soil.

TOUCH-ME-NOT. See IMPATIENS

TOVARA virginiana. See POLYGONUM virginianum

TRACHELOSPERMUM

STAR JASMINE

Apocynaceae

EVERGREEN VINES OR SPRAWLING SHRUBS

ZONES LS, CS, TS

SUN OR SHADE

REGULAR TO MODERATE WATER

Trachelospermum jasminoides

Ground covers, spillers, or climbers with delightfully fragrant, pinwheel-shaped blossoms in spring or early summer. They are among the most versatile and useful of shrubby plants. Cut stems exude a milky sap.

T. asiaticum. ASIAN STAR JASMINE. An excellent, tough, fast-growing ground cover. Has smaller, darker, duller green leaves than those of *T. jasminoides;* flowers are also smaller, in creamy yellow or yellowish white. Hardier than *T. jasminoides.*

T. jasminoides. CONFEDERATE JASMINE. Given support, a twining vine to 20 ft.; without support and with some tip-pinching, a spreading shrub or ground cover 1½ – 2 ft. tall, 4 – 5 ft. wide. New foliage is glossy light green; mature leaves are lustrous dark green, to 3 in. long. Profusion of 1-in. white flowers in small clusters on short side branches. Attractive to bees. 'Variegatum' has leaves bordered and blotched with white. Good to train on a wall, pergola, trellis, or over a doorway.

TRACHYCARPUS

Arecaceae (Palmae)

PALMS

ZONES VARY BY SPECIES; OR INDOORS

FULL SUN OR PART SHADE

REGULAR WATER

Trachycarpus fortunei

Fan-leafed palms of moderate size and surprising hardiness. Characteristic dense, blackish fiber grows on trunks; as trunks elongate, fiber falls off their lower portions. Can be grown as indoor potted plants.

T. fortunei. WINDMILL PALM. Zones LS, CS, TS. Hardy to 10°F or even lower temperatures. Native to China. Moderate to fast growth to 30 ft. in the Tropical South. Trunk is dark, usually thicker at top than at bottom. Leaves 3 ft. across, carried on toothed, 1½-ft. stalks. May become untidy and ruffled in high winds. Sometimes sold as *Chamaerops excelsa.*

T. martianus. Zones CS, TS. Hardy to 22°F. Native to Himalayas. Slower growing (to an eventual 45 ft. tall) and more slender than *T. fortunei.* Trunk is ringed with leaf scars.

TRADESCANTIA

Commelinaceae
PERENNIALS
☀ ZONES VARY BY SPECIES; OR INDOORS
◑ ● PARTIAL OR FULL SHADE, EXCEPT AS NOTED
◐ ◑ ◖ WATER NEEDS VARY BY SPECIES

Tradescantia fluminensis

Most are long-trailing, indestructible plants, typically grown indoors in strong light (but not direct sun) or outdoors in shady sites. Usually seen in pots or hanging baskets, but can be used as ground covers; however, the most vigorous, rambling types are likely to be invasive. Long-stemmed ramblers are often called wandering Jew; the name is also applied to the related *Zebrina pendula.*

T. albiflora. WANDERING JEW. Zones CS, TS; or house plant. Trailing, or sprawling and rooting at joints. Oblong, 2–3-in.-long leaves; small white flowers. 'Albovittata' has leaves finely and evenly streaked with white; 'Aurea' ('Gold Leaf') has chartreuse yellow foliage; 'Laekenensis' ('Rainbow') has bandings of white and pale lavender. Variegated forms are unstable and tend to revert to green, so keep solid green growth pinched out. Does best in well-drained soil with ample water. Trailing stems will live a long time in water, rooting quickly and easily. Renovate overgrown plants by cutting back severely or by starting new plants with fresh tip growth.

T. andersoniana. See T. virginiana

T. blossfeldiana. Zones CS, TS; or house plant. Fleshy, furry stems spread and lean, but do not really hang. Leaves are shiny dark green above, furry and purple beneath, to 4 in. long. Flowers showier than those of most trailing or semitrailing tradescantias: Clusters of furry purplish buds open into ½-in. pink flowers with white centers. Moderate water.

T. fluminensis. WANDERING JEW. Zones CS, TS; or house plant. Rapid grower with prostrate or trailing habit. Succulent stems have swollen joints where 2½-in.-long, dark green, oval or oblong leaves are attached. Leaves of 'Variegata' are striped yellow or white. Tiny white flowers are not showy. Easy to grow; excellent for window boxes and dish gardens. Give ample water. A few stems will live for a long time and even grow in a glass of water.

T. pallida 'Purpurea'. See Setcreasea pallida 'Purple Heart'

🏛 **T. virginiana.** SPIDERWORT. Zones US, MS, LS, CS. Border perennial for sun or shade. Grows in 1½–3-ft.-tall clumps, with long, deep green, erect or arching grasslike foliage. Three-petaled flowers open for only a day, but buds come in large clusters and plants are seldom out of bloom during late spring, summer. Named selections available in white, shades of blue, lavender, purple, gradations of pink from pale pink to near red. Ample water. May self-sow and become somewhat invasive. Divide clumps when crowded. Usually sold as *T. andersoniana.*

T. zebrina. See Zebrina pendula

TRANSVAAL DAISY. See GERBERA jamesonii

TREE ARALIA. See KALOPANAX septemlobus

TREE MALLOW. See LAVATERA

SOUTHERN HERITAGE PLANTS
IDENTIFIED BY SYMBOL 🏛

TRICYRTIS

TOAD LILY
Liliaceae
PERENNIALS
☀ ZONES US, MS, LS
◑ ● PARTIAL OR FULL SHADE
◐ ◑ AMPLE TO REGULAR WATER

Tricyrtis hirta

These are woodland plants that resemble false Solomon's seal (*Smilacina racemosa*) in foliage. Though not especially showy, the late summer–fall flowers are interesting—complex, heavily spotted, somewhat like orchids. Each 1-in. flower has three petals and three sepals with a column of decorative stamens and styles rising from the center. Flowers appear at leaf bases and in terminal clusters. Need woodsy soil.

T. formosana. FORMOSA TOAD LILY. To 2½ ft. tall; spreads by stoloniferous roots but is not invasive. Stems are more upright than those of *T. hirta,* and flowers are mostly in terminal clusters. Green leaves mottled with deeper green. Clusters of brown or maroon buds open to flowers in white to pale lilac densely specked with purple. Begins blooming a little earlier than *T. hirta.* Blossoms of 'Amethystina' are typically lavender blue spotted in dark red, with a white throat. This and the species below are easy to root from cuttings.

T. hirta. HAIRY TOAD LILY. To 3 ft. tall, with arching stems. Flowers, appearing in leaf joints all along the stems, are white to pale lilac, densely peppered with purple. 'Miyazaki' and 'Miyazaki Gold' are improved forms that bloom more profusely; the latter has yellow-edged leaves.

TRILLIUM

WAKE ROBIN
Liliaceae
PERENNIALS
☀ ZONES US, MS, LS
◑ ● PARTIAL OR FULL SHADE
◐ REGULAR WATER

Trillium grandiflorum

Bloom in early spring; need some winter chill. Each stem is topped with a whorl of three leaves; from center of these rises a single flower with three maroon or white petals. Plant the thick, deep-growing, fleshy rhizomes in shady, woodsy site. Left undisturbed, they will gradually increase. Plants die to the ground in mid- to late summer. In addition to species listed below, many others are offered by native plant specialists.

T. catesbaei (T. stylosum). CATESBY TRILLIUM. But for its pink flowers, resembles *T. grandiflorum.*

T. decipiens. Native to Alabama, Georgia, and Florida. Stems 6–18 in. high. Mottled green leaves with pale centers, to 7 in. long. Flowers greenish, sometimes with purplish tints. Grows in limestone soils.

T. erectum. PURPLE TRILLIUM. Grows to 2 ft. high, with 7-in. leaves and 2-in., erect, brownish purple flowers. Sometimes known by the name "stinking Benjamin" due to the odd odor of its flowers.

T. grandiflorum. WHITE TRILLIUM. Stout stems 8–18 in. high. Leaves 2½–6 in. long. Flowers are nodding, to 3 in. across, white aging to rose. 'Flore Pleno' has double flowers. The showiest trillium.

T. recurvatum. PRAIRIE TRILLIUM, BLOODY BUTCHER. To 15 in. high. Leaves spotted in reddish purple; purple-brown flowers.

T. sessile. TOADSHADE. To 1 ft. high, with purple-spotted leaves and dark purplish red flowers. *T. s. luteum (T. luteum)* bears yellow flowers with a faint lemon scent.

T. undulatum. PAINTED TRILLIUM. To 20 in. high, with upright or somewhat nodding, 1½-in. white flowers marked reddish purple within. Considered difficult; needs cool conditions, acid soil.

TRINIDAD FLAME BUSH. See CALLIANDRA tweedii

TRITOMA uvaria. See KNIPHOFIA uvaria

TROLLIUS

GLOBEFLOWER

Ranunculaceae

PERENNIALS

✄ ZONES US, MS

☀ ◐ FULL SUN OR PARTIAL SHADE

💧 💧 AMPLE TO REGULAR WATER

Trollius ledebouri

Clumps of finely cut, shiny dark green leaves put up 2–3-ft.-tall stems terminating in yellow to orange, roundly cupped to globe-shaped flowers. Some types begin blooming in spring, others in summer; remove faded flowers to prolong bloom. Excellent cut flowers.

Intolerant of drought, extreme heat. Continually damp ground near a pond or stream is ideal planting site. If growing in a standard garden bed, generously amend soil with organic matter and keep well watered. Divide clumps when they thin out in the middle.

T. cultorum. Name given to a group of hybrids between *T. europaeus* and two Asiatic species. Hybrids grow to 2–3 ft., resemble *T. europaeus* in most details. Bloom comes sometime from spring into summer, depending on hybrid. Choices include 2-ft. 'Earliest of All', with pale orange-yellow blooms; 2-ft. 'Golden Queen', deep orange; and 2½-ft. 'Lemon Queen', soft yellow.

T. europaeus. COMMON GLOBEFLOWER. To 1½–2 ft. tall. Globular, lemon yellow flowers, 1–2 in. across, in spring. Some selections have orange blooms. Somewhat more tolerant of dry soil than other species.

T. ledebouri. Plant sold under this name grows 3 ft. tall, bears 2-in., golden orange, cup-shaped flowers in summer. 'Golden Queen' reaches 4 ft., has 4-in. blossoms.

TROPAEOLUM majus

GARDEN NASTURTIUM

Tropaeolaceae

ANNUAL

✄ ALL ZONES

☀ ◐ FULL SUN OR LIGHT SHADE

💧 REGULAR WATER

Tropaeolum majus

Distinctive appearance, rapid growth, and easy culture are three of garden nasturtium's many strong points. There are two main kinds. Climbing types trail over the ground or climb to 6 ft. by coiling leaf stalks; dwarf kinds are compact, to 15 in. tall. Both have round, shield-shaped, bright green leaves on long stalks. Broad, long-spurred flowers, to 2½ in. across, have a refreshing fragrance, come in colors ranging through maroon, red brown, orange, yellow, and red to creamy white. Good cut flowers. Young leaves, flowers, and unripe seedpods have peppery flavor like watercress and may be used in salads.

Dwarf forms are most widely sold. You can get seeds of mixed colors in several strains, or a few separate colors, including cherry rose, mahogany, and gold. Both single- and double-flowered forms are available. All types are easy to grow in most well-drained soils; they do best in sandy soil. Use nitrogen fertilizer sparingly, or you will get all leaves and no flowers. Sow in early spring; plants grow and bloom quickly and will often reseed unless stopped by heat or humidity. Sow in fall for winter–spring bloom. Somewhat drought tolerant. Aphids can be a problem.

TROUT LILY. See ERYTHRONIUM americanum

TRUMPET CREEPER, TRUMPET VINE. See CAMPSIS

TSUGA

HEMLOCK

Pinaceae

EVERGREEN TREES

✄ ZONES VARY BY SPECIES

☀ ◐ FULL SUN OR PARTIAL SHADE; AFTERNOON SHADE IN LOWER SOUTH

💧 REGULAR WATER

Tsuga canadensis

These are mostly big trees with unusually graceful appearance. Branches horizontal to drooping. Needlelike leaves are banded with white beneath, flattened and narrowed at the base to form distinct, short stalks. Small, oval, medium brown cones hang down from branches. Bark is deeply furrowed, cinnamon colored to brown.

All hemlocks need some winter chill; all are shallow rooted. Best in acid soil and high summer humidity, with protection from hot sun and wind. Take well to heavy pruning; make excellent clipped hedges, screens. Easily damaged by salt and drought. Subject to various pests and diseases, but damage is not always serious if plants are well grown. Recently, a woolly adelgid (an aphid) has caused the decline and even death of many hemlocks stressed by drought and improper cultural practices.

T. canadensis. CANADIAN HEMLOCK. Zones US, MS, LS (cooler parts). Native from Nova Scotia to Minnesota, southward along mountain ranges to Alabama and Georgia. Dense, pyramidal tree to 40–70 ft. or taller, half as wide. Tends to grow two or more trunks. Outer branchlets droop gracefully. Dark green needles, about ½ in. long, are mostly arranged in opposite rows on branchlets. Fine specimen tree, tall screen, or clipped hedge. 'Pendula', Sargent weeping hemlock, grows slowly to 10–20 ft. tall and twice as wide, with pendulous branches; with careful pruning, can easily be kept to handsome, 2–3-ft., cascading mound suitable for a large rock garden. Many dwarf, weeping, and variegated selections are sold.

T. caroliniana. CAROLINA HEMLOCK. Zones US, MS. Native to mountains in the southeast U.S. Resembles *T. canadensis,* but is somewhat slower growing, a little stiffer in habit, and darker green in color. Longer needles are arranged all around the twigs instead of in opposite rows. More tolerant of polluted air and city conditions than *T. canadensis,* but not as well adapted to lowlands of the eastern seaboard.

TUBEROSE. See POLIANTHES tuberosa

TUFTED HAIR GRASS. See DESCHAMPSIA caespitosa

TULBAGHIA

Amaryllidaceae

PERENNIALS

✄ ZONES LS (PROTECTED), CS, TS

☀ FULL SUN

💧 REGULAR WATER

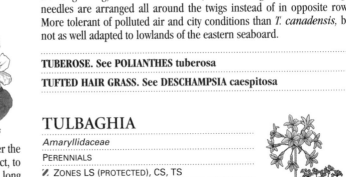

Tulbaghia violacea

Many narrow leaves grow from central point to make broad clumps. Long stems bear clusters of star-shaped flowers. Evergreen in the Tropical South. Suffer frost damage at 20–25°F, but recover quickly.

T. fragrans. Gray-green, 1-in.-wide leaves to 12–14 in. long or longer. Fragrant, lavender-pink flowers, 20 to 30 on 1½–2-ft. stalk. Blooms midwinter–spring. Good cut flower.

⚘ **T. violacea.** SOCIETY GARLIC. Bluish green, narrow leaves to 1 ft. long. Rosy lavender flowers, 8 to 20 in cluster on each 1–2-ft. stem. Some bloom most of year, with peak in spring and summer. Leaves and blossom stems have onion or garlic odor if cut or crushed. Unsatisfactory cut flower for this reason (but can be used as seasoning). 'Silver Lace' has white-margined leaves. 'Tricolor' foliage suffused with pink in spring, leaves edged in white. 'Variegata' has creamy stripe down the center of each leaf.

T

TULIPA

TULIP

Liliaceae

BULBS

ZONES US, MS; TREAT MOST AS ANNUALS IN LOWER AND COASTAL SOUTH

FULL SUN

REGULAR WATER DURING GROWTH AND BLOOM

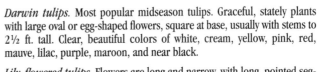

Darwin Hybrid Tulip

Tulips vary considerably in color, form, height, and general character. Some look stately and formal, others dainty and whimsical; a few are bizarre. Bloom comes at some time from March to May, depending on type.

Use larger tulips in colonies or masses with low, spring-blooming perennials such as candytuft or pinks, or with annuals such as forget-me-not, sweet alyssum, pansy, or viola. Plant smaller, lower-growing species in rock gardens, near paths, in raised beds, or in patio or terrace insets for close-up viewing. Tulips are superb container plants, especially the more unusual kinds, such as Double Early, Parrot, and Rembrandt strains.

Nearly all hybrid tulips and most species (wild) tulips need an extended period of winter chill for best performance. But even with sufficient winter chill, there's no guarantee of a good performance after the first year. Tulip bulbs form offsets that need several years to get to blooming size, but as the offsets mature, they draw energy from the mother bulb. The result is a decline in flowering. For this reason, most tulips are best treated as annuals or short-lived perennials. You can encourage repeat flowering by fertilizing with nitrogen before bloom and by allowing foliage to yellow and wither before removing it after bloom. In the Coastal South and much of the Lower South, prechill tulip bulbs in the refrigerator for 10 weeks before planting. In areas with warm, wet summer soil, bulbs are prone to rot and shouldn't be expected to bloom for more than a year or two.

Bulbs can be planted under deciduous trees that leaf out after tulip flowers fade. Light shade helps prolong bloom of late-flowering kinds. Good light should come from overhead; otherwise, stems will lean toward light source. Rich, sandy soil is ideal, although tulips will grow in any good soil with fast drainage. They do not like soil where tulips were recently growing—choose an entirely different site, or put in fresh soil to the requisite planting depth. Set bulbs three times as deep as they are wide (a little shallower in heavy soils), from 4 to 8 in. apart depending on ultimate size of plant. Plant bulbs as early as mid-October in Upper South, as late as December or January in the Coastal South.

To protect tulips from burrowing animals, plant in baskets of ¼-in. wire mesh. Thwart ground squirrels and other animals that like to dig up bulbs by securing chicken wire over new plantings.

Tulips have been classified into many divisions; the most important of these are listed below, in approximate order of bloom.

Single Early tulips. Large single flowers of red, yellow, or white grow on 10–16-in. stems. Much used for forcing indoors in pots.

Double Early tulips. Double peony-like flowers to 4 in. across bloom on 6–12-in. stems. Same colors and bloom season as Single Early tulips. In rainy areas, mulch around plants or surround with ground cover to keep mud from splashing short-stemmed blooms. Effective massed in borders.

Darwin hybrids. Spectacular group bred from Darwin tulips and huge, brilliant species *T. fosterana.* Bloom before Darwins; have enormous, brightly colored flowers on 24–28-in. stems. Most are in scarlet-orange to red range; some have contrasting eyes or penciling; some measure 7 in. across. Pink, yellow, and white selections exist.

Mendel tulips. Single flowers grow on stems to 20 in. tall. Bloom after Single Early and Double Early kinds, before Darwin tulips. Shades of white, rose, red, orange, yellow.

Triumph tulips. Single flowers on medium-tall (20-in.), sturdy stems. Bloom earlier than Darwin tulips and (like Mendel tulips) are valuable in providing continuity of bloom.

Darwin tulips. Most popular midseason tulips. Graceful, stately plants with large oval or egg-shaped flowers, square at base, usually with stems to 2½ ft. tall. Clear, beautiful colors of white, cream, yellow, pink, red, mauve, lilac, purple, maroon, and near black.

Lily-flowered tulips. Flowers are long and narrow, with long, pointed segments. Graceful, slender stemmed, fine in garden (where they blend well with other flowers) or for cutting. Stems 20–26 in. tall. Late blooming. Full range of tulip colors.

Cottage tulips. Often called May-flowering tulips. About same size and height as Darwins. Flower form variable, long oval to egg shaped to vase shaped, often with pointed segments.

Double Late tulips (often called Peony-flowered). Large, heavy blooms like peonies. They range from 18 to 22 in. tall; flowers may be damaged by rain or wind in exposed locations. Not very reliable in the South.

Parrot tulips. Late-flowering, with large, long, deeply fringed and ruffled blooms striped and feathered in various colors. Many have descriptive names, e.g., 'Blue Parrot', 'Red Parrot'. Good in pots, unusual cut flowers.

TULIPS IN MILD-WINTER AREAS

Refrigerate bulbs in paper bags (away from ripening fruit) 10 weeks before planting. Plant between Christmas and mid-January. Mix low-nitrogen granular fertilizer into soil, then set bulbs 4–6 in. deep. Water sparingly until leaves emerge, then generously.

In addition to divisions and groups described above, there are many classes covering species and species hybrids. Most important are:

Hybrids and selections of *T. fosterana,* including huge, fiery red variety 'Red Emperor' ('Mme. Lefeber'), 16 in. tall.

Selections and hybrids of *T. greigii* resemble those of *T. kaufmanniana,* with leaves usually heavily spotted and streaked with brown.

Selections and hybrids of *T. kaufmanniana,* 5–10 in. tall, very early blooming, in white, pink, orange, and red, often with markings, some with leaves patterned brown.

Most species tulips—wild tulips—are low growing and early blooming with shorter, narrower leaves than garden hybrids, but there are exceptions. In general, they take the South's heat better than their cousins and are true perennials, blooming reliably for years.

Outstanding species and selections for the South include the following:

T. bakeri. Similar to *T. saxatilis.* 'Lilac Wonder' has lovely, open, pastel mauve flowers with buttercup yellow centers and yellow anthers.

T. clusiana. LADY or CANDY TULIP. Slender, medium-size flowers on 9-in. stems. Rosy red on outside, white inside. Grows well in mild-winter areas. Give sheltered position in colder areas. Midseason.

T. c. chrysantha (T. stellata chrysantha). To 6 in. tall. Outer segments rose carmine, shading to buff at base; inner segments are bright yellow. Midseason.

T. greigii. GREIG TULIP. Scarlet flowers 6 in. across, on 10-in. stems. Foliage mottled or striped with brown. Early.

T. kaufmanniana. WATERLILY TULIP. Medium-large creamy yellow flowers marked red on outside and yellow at center. Stems are 6 in. tall. Produces very early bloom. Permanent in gardens. Many choice named selections.

Tulipa kaufmanniana

T. praestans. Cup-shaped, orange-scarlet flowers, two to four blooms to a 10–12-in. stem, in midseason. 'Fusilier' is shorter than the species, has four to six flowers to a stem.

T. saxatilis. Fragrant, yellow-based pale lilac flowers open nearly flat, one to three to each 1-ft. stem. Early bloom.

T. stellata chrysantha. See T. clusiana chrysantha

T. tarda (T. dasystemon). On each 3-in. stem, three to six star-shaped flowers, facing up, with gold centers and white-tipped segments. Early. ▶

T. turkestanica. TURKESTAN TULIP. Vigorous, with up to eight flowers on each 1-ft. stem. Flowers slender in bud, star shaped when open, gray green on outside, off-white with yellow base inside. Very early bloom.

TULIP POPLAR. See LIRIODENDRON tulipifera

TURKEYFOOT. See ANDROPOGON gerardii

TURK'S CAP. See MALVAVISCUS arboreus drummondii

TURK'S CAP LILY. See LILIUM martagon

TURNIP and RUTABAGA

Brassicaceae (Cruciferae)

BIENNIALS GROWN AS ANNUALS

⚊ ALL ZONES

☼ FULL SUN

● REGULAR WATER

Turnip

Both are cool-season crops. Although turnips are best known in other parts of the country for their roots, here their leaves are also enjoyed as a green vegetable. Some selections are grown for leaves only. Turnip roots come in various colors (white, white topped with purple, creamy yellow) and shapes (globe, flattened globe). Rutabaga is a tasty turnip relative with large yellowish roots; its leaves are palatable only when very young (turn coarse as they mature). Turnip roots are quick growing and should be harvested and used as soon as big enough to eat; rutabaga is a late-maturing crop that stores well in the ground. Flavor of rutabaga improves with light frost.

Grow both in rich, loose, well-drained soil. In the Upper South, plant in early spring for early summer harvest, or in summer for fall harvest. Elsewhere, treat as fall–spring crops. Sow seeds ½ in. deep, 1 in. apart. Thin turnips to 2–6 in. apart for roots, 1–4 in. apart for greens. Thin rutabagas to 5–8 in. apart; to reach full weight of 3–5 lb., they need room for roots.

Roots of both turnip and rutabaga are milder flavored if soil is kept moist, become more pungent under drier conditions. Turnip roots are ready to harvest about 75 days after sowing, rutabaga in 90 to 120 days. Cabbage root maggot is a pest of turnip (it is less likely to infest rutabaga); see Cabbage for control.

TURTLEHEAD. See CHELONE

TWINBERRY. See MITCHELLA repens

TWIN SISTERS. See NARCISSUS medioluteus

Ulmaceae. The elm family contains trees and shrubs, usually deciduous, with inconspicuous flowers, and fruit that may be nutlike, single seeded and fleshy, or winged. Elm (*Ulmus*), hackberry (*Celtis*), and *Zelkova* are representative.

ULMUS

ELM

Ulmaceae

DECIDUOUS OR SEMIEVERGREEN TREES

⚊ ZONES VARY BY SPECIES

☼ FULL SUN

● REGULAR WATER, EXCEPT AS NOTED

Ulmus americana

Once much-prized shade trees, elms have fallen on hard times. Dutch elm disease (spread by a bark beetle) has killed millions of American elms throughout North America and can attack most other elm species. Many larger elms are attractive fare for various beetles, leafhoppers, aphids, and scale, making them either time-consuming to care for or messy (or both). Beyond their pest problems, elms have other drawbacks. Their root systems are aggressive and near the surface, making it difficult to grow any other plants beneath. Many types produce suckers. Branch crotches are often narrow, splitting easily in storms. Despite their flaws, elms are widely planted, valued for their fast growth, moderate shade, and environmental toughness. Research continues for disease-resistant types. All elms are fairly soil tolerant, and all have handsome oval leaves. Poor yellow fall color, except as noted.

U. alata. WINGED ELM. Deciduous. Zones US, MS, LS, CS. Native to Southeast. To 20–40 ft. tall, not quite as wide. Open, airy canopy. Leaves 1–2½ in. long, finely toothed, dark green turning pale yellow in fall. Common name derives from corky outgrowths ("wings") on twigs and young branches. Degree of winging varies among seedlings—the wings stand out on some, while on others they're almost nonexistent. Your best bet is to get a cutting-grown tree from a parent with good bark characteristics. Clusters of small reddish seeds in spring. 'Lace Parasol' is a weeping form (to 8 ft. tall, 12 ft. wide after 45 years) being introduced in the nursery trade.

U. americana. AMERICAN ELM. Deciduous. Zones US, MS, LS, CS. Native to eastern North America. This majestic, arching tree once graced lawns and streets throughout its range, but it has been decimated by Dutch elm disease. Fast growth to 100 ft. or taller with nearly equal—sometimes greater—spread. Main branches upright, outer ones pendulous. Rough-surfaced, 3–6-in.-long, toothed dark green leaves; great variation in shade of yellow fall color. Leafs out very late where winters are mild. Papery, pale green seeds in spring are messy.

Long search for disease-resistant selections with classic vase shape seems to have been fruitful. 'American Liberty' elms, a series of six selections recently released by the Elm Research Institute, appear to be resistant to Dutch elm disease; they are hardy, vigorous trees that turn golden yellow in fall. Four other resistant selections, from different sources, should be available to the public soon: 'Delaware #2', 'New Harmony', 'Valley Forge', and 'Washington'.

U. crassifolia. CEDAR ELM. Deciduous, or semievergreen in extreme south Texas. All zones. Native from Texas to Mississippi and northern Mexico. Moderately fast growth to 50–70 ft. tall, 40–60 ft. wide. Shiny, dark green leaves, to 2 in. long, stiff and rough to the touch. Like *U. alata*, twigs and branches have corky wings. Turns burnt yellow or gold in fall. Flowers in late summer. Well adapted to alkaline soils, very drought tolerant.

U. parvifolia. CHINESE ELM, LACEBARK ELM. Semievergreen or deciduous, depending on winter temperatures and particular selection. Zones US, MS, LS, CS. The best elm for home gardens and an excellent shade or lawn tree. Fast growth to 40–60 ft. tall. Extremely variable in form, but generally spreading, with long, arching, eventually weeping branchlets. On trunks of older trees, bark sheds in patches (somewhat as bark of sycamore does), creating beautiful mottling in many specimens. Leathery dark green leaves are ¾–2½ in. long, evenly toothed; mediocre display of yellow to reddish orange in fall. Good resistance to Dutch elm disease, elm leaf beetle, and Japanese beetle.

Reliably semievergreen to nearly evergreen selections such as 'Drake', 'Sempervirens', and 'True Green' are widely sold in the Coastal South. They are not as cold-hardy as other selections and are not recommended for the Upper and Middle South.

A word of caution: A less desirable species, *U. pumila*, Siberian elm, is sometimes sold as Chinese elm.

UMBRELLA MAGNOLIA. See MAGNOLIA tripetala

UMBRELLA PINE. See SCIADOPITYS verticillata

UMBRELLA PLANT. See CYPERUS alternifolius, DARMERA peltata

UMBRELLA TREE, QUEENSLAND. See SCHEFFLERA actinophylla

SOUTHERN HERITAGE PLANTS

IDENTIFIED BY SYMBOL 🛆

UNGNADIA speciosa

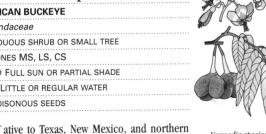

MEXICAN BUCKEYE

Sapindaceae

DECIDUOUS SHRUB OR SMALL TREE

✄ ZONES MS, LS, CS

☼ ◑ FULL SUN OR PARTIAL SHADE

◔ ◕ LITTLE OR REGULAR WATER

◈ POISONOUS SEEDS

Ungnadia speciosa

Native to Texas, New Mexico, and northern Mexico. Easy, small, multitrunked tree, usually 12–15 ft. tall, occasionally 30 ft., with fragrant flowers, lush green foliage, interesting seed capsules, fall color. Tolerance of a wide range of soils, including dry, limy soils. Clusters of showy flowers, with crenellated, purplish pink petals and red anthers, appear in early spring, before or with the new leaves. In fall, dark green leaves, 5–12 in. long, with three to seven leaflets, turn golden yellow; leathery, dark brown, buckeye-like seed capsules split and drop shiny, black, ½-in. seeds.

VACCINIUM

Ericaceae

EVERGREEN OR DECIDUOUS SHRUBS

✄ ZONES VARY BY SPECIES

☼ ◑ ● EXPOSURE NEEDS VARY BY SPECIES

◔ ◕ ◖◗ WATER NEEDS VARY BY SPECIES

Vaccinium arboreum

Excellent ornamental shrubs with clusters of bell-shaped flowers and colorful, edible fruit that attracts birds. Species described here are shrubs—ranging from ground covers to the height of a small tree—that are grown for decorative, landscaping use; see Blueberry for relatives grown primarily for their edible fruits. All require rich, organic, acid soil. Good for woodland gardens.

V. arboreum. FARKLEBERRY. Zones MS, LS, CS. Native to the South and Southeast and East Texas. Evergreen or deciduous, depending on winter cold. Spreading form, 10–25 ft. tall, with shiny, dark green leaves, to 2 in. long, that turn rich red and crimson in fall and persist through most of winter. White, fragrant, bell-like flowers in spring. Black, unpalatable berries. Older shrubs have beautiful, exfoliating, cinnamon brown to gray-orange bark. Full sun or partial shade. Needs only moderate water.

V. ashei. See Blueberry

V. corymbosum. See Blueberry

V. crassifolium. CREEPING BLUEBERRY. Zones MS, LS. Native from southeast Virginia to South Carolina. Sprawling evergreen ground cover, to 6 in. tall and 6 ft. across. Rosy red flowers in late spring. Sweet black berries. 'Bloodstone' has reddish new and mature leaves and red stems in winter; 'Wells Delight' is particularly broad spreading and disease tolerant. Provide regular water, and full sun or partial shade.

V. darrowii. Zones LS, CS. Native to Florida, Georgia, Alabama. Evergreen shrub that grows to 2 ft. tall in wild, but can reach 5 ft. tall and 3 ft. wide in garden conditions. Very small blue-green leaves; new growth pinkish. White flowers in spring, followed by small, sweet black berries with blue bloom. Two named selections: 'John Blue' and 'Sebring'. Full sun, little or regular water.

V. elliottii. ELLIOTT'S BLUEBERRY. Zones US, MS, LS, CS. Native from Florida to Virginia, west to Arkansas and Louisiana. Deciduous, clump-forming, straggly shrub of variable size, 6–13 ft. tall. Shiny green, thin leaves, to 1½ in. long. Pink to white flowers appear in spring, often before the leaves. Dark purple-blue or black berries. Accepts moderate or regular water, full sun or partial shade.

V. macrocarpon. CRANBERRY. Zone US. Native from Newfoundland to Minnesota, south to North Carolina. Creeping plant 2–6 in. high, spreading and rooting from stems. Narrow, ¾-in.-long leaves are dark green in summer, turning coppery or purplish red in winter. Tiny pinkish spring flowers are followed by tart red fruits in autumn. Commercial producers

grow cranberries in bogs—beds that can be flooded to control weeds and pests, provide winter protection, and make harvesting easier. Gardeners can use cranberry as an attractive small-scale ground cover in damp soil and full sun.

V. myrsinites. GROUND BLUEBERRY. Zones MS, LS, CS. Native from Virginia to Florida and Louisiana. Evergreen shrub, to 2 ft. tall, more sprawling than erect. White to pink flowers in spring. Blue-black or black berries. Full sun, dry to very moist soil.

V. vitis-idaea. COWBERRY, FOXBERRY. Zone US. Native to Europe. Slow growth to 1 ft. high, spreading to 3 ft. wide by underground stems. Glossy dark green leaves to 1 in. long; new growth often tinged bright red or orange. Clustered white or pinkish spring flowers are followed by sour red berries similar to tiny cranberries and valued for preserves, syrups. Handsome little plant for small-scale ground cover, informal edging for larger plantings. Needs moist or damp soil. Prefers part or full shade.

VALERIAN. See CENTRANTHUS ruber

Valerianaceae. The valerian family of perennial herbs (rarely shrubs), has clustered small flowers. Members include red valerian (*Centranthus*) and *Patrinia*.

VARIEGATED CHINESE PRIVET. See LIGUSTRUM sinense 'Variegatum'

VARIEGATED GINGER. See ALPINIA sanderae

VARIEGATED PEACOCK LILY. See KAEMPFERIA gilbertii

VARNISH TREE. See KOELREUTERIA paniculata

VELVET-LEAF SENNA. See CASSIA lindheimeriana

VERBASCUM

MULLEIN

Scrophulariaceae

BIENNIALS AND PERENNIALS

✄ ZONES US, MS, LS, EXCEPT AS NOTED

☼ FULL SUN

◔ MODERATE WATER

Verbascum chaixii

Large group of rosette-forming, summer-blooming plants that send up 1–6-ft. stems closely set with nearly flat, five-petaled, circular flowers about an inch across. Both foliage and stems are often covered in woolly hairs. Taller mulleins make striking vertical accents. Grow all in well-drained soil. Cut off spent flowers of perennial kinds to encourage a second round of blooming. Leave spikes of biennial species in place for reseeding. Mulleins self-sow freely—and some are downright weedy, such as the attractive roadside weed *V. thapsus*, common mullein. Perennial species are short lived in hot, humid climates.

V. blattaria. MOTH MULLEIN. Biennial. Low clumps of smooth, dark green, cut or toothed leaves. Purple-centered, pale yellow or white flowers on stems 1½–2½ ft. high.

V. chaixii. CHAIX MULLEIN. Perennial. Leaves to 6 in. long. Red-eyed, pale yellow flowers in narrow, often branched spikes to 3 ft. high. 'Album' has white flowers with purple centers.

V. hybrids. Perennials. Zones US, MS. These include the Cotswold and Benary hybrids. Flower spikes in white, cream, and shades of pink or purple are carried on 3–4-ft. stems. Named selections in separate colors exist, such as the popular 'Pink Domino'.

V. olympicum. OLYMPIC MULLEIN. Perennial. Large white leaves with soft, downy hairs form a rosette to 3 ft. across. Many stems to 5 ft. high carry bright yellow flower spikes.

V. phoeniceum. PURPLE MULLEIN. Perennial. Leaves are smooth on top, hairy underneath. Slender spikes of purple flowers on 2–4-ft. stems.

V

VERBENA

Verbenaceae

PERENNIALS, SOME GROWN AS ANNUALS

⚡ ZONES VARY BY SPECIES

☀ FULL SUN

💧 MODERATE WATER

Verbena peruviana

Most produce their clusters of small, five-petaled, tubular blossoms in summer. Perennial species usually have purple flowers and are often treated as annuals. Low verbenas make good ground covers, hanging basket plants; taller sorts are good in borders. Most thrive in heat, tolerate drought. They dislike continually wet conditions, so provide good air circulation and well-drained soil. Most are susceptible to mildew and spider mites.

V. bipinnatifida. DAKOTA VERBENA. Perennial. All zones. Native from Great Plains to Mexico. Grows 8–15 in. high, with finely divided leaves and blue flowers. Spreads by self-sowing in most areas.

V. bonariensis. Perennial in Zones MS, LS, CS; annual in Upper South. Native to South America, but naturalized in the Southeast. Airy, branching stems to 3–6 ft. carry purple flowers. Leaves mostly in 1½-ft.-high basal clump. Plant's see-through quality makes it suited for foreground or back of border. Self-sows freely.

V. canadensis. ROSE VERBENA. Perennial in Zones US, MS, LS, CS, but usually treated as annual. Native from Virginia to Florida west to Colorado and Mexico. To 1½ ft. high, with rosy purple flowers. There is a compact (6-in.-high) form suitable for rock gardens; white- and pink-flowering forms are also sold. 'Homestead Purple', to 6–10 in. high and spreading to 2 ft., has dark green leaves and deep purple flowers; it thrives in the South. When growing the species or its selections as perennials, provide good winter drainage; in the Upper South, cover with light winter mulch.

V. gooddingii. Short-lived perennial. Zones LS, CS. Native to Southwest. Grows to 1½ ft. high, spreading. Oval, deeply cut leaves. Heads of flowers, usually pinkish lavender, at ends of short spikes. Will bloom first summer from seed sown in spring. Can reseed where moisture is adequate. Tolerates dry heat.

V. hybrida (V. hortensis). GARDEN VERBENA. Annual. All zones. Many-branched plant 6–12 in. high, spreading to 1½–3 ft. Oblong, bright green or gray-green leaves, 2–4 in., with toothed margins. Flowers in flat, compact clusters to 3 in. wide. Colors include white, pink, bright red, purple, blue, and combinations. Superior strains include Romance (6 in.) and Showtime (10 in.). Colorful but prone to insect damage.

V. peruviana (V. chamaedryfolia). Perennial in Zone CS, but usually treated as annual in all zones. Spreads rapidly, forming flat mat. Leaves small, closely set. Flat-topped clusters of scarlet-and-white flowers on slender stems cover foliage. Hybrids—with flowers in white, pinks, or reds—spread more slowly, have slightly larger leaves, stouter stems.

V. rigida (V. venosa). Perennial in Zones MS, LS, CS, or grow as annual. Native to South America, but naturalized in Southeast. To 10–20 in. high, spreading. Rough, strongly toothed, dark green leaves to 2–4 in. long. Lilac to purple-blue flowers in cylindrical clusters on tall, stiff stems. Blooms in 4 months from seed. 'Flame', to 4 in. high, is a cutting-grown selection with bright scarlet flowers.

V. tenuisecta (V. erinoides). MOSS VERBENA. Perennial. Zones MS, LS, CS; annual in Upper South. Native to South America, but naturalized in Lower South. To 8–12 in. high, with finely cut leaves. Rose violet to pink flowers. 'Alba' is a white-flowered form. Short lived.

VERBENA, LEMON. See ALOYSIA triphylla

Verbenaceae. The immense verbena family contains annuals, perennials, shrubs, and a few trees and vines. Leaves are usually opposite or in whorls, flowers in spikes or spikelike clusters. Fruit may be berries or nutlets. Glorybower (*Clerodendrum*), *Lantana*, *Verbena*, and chaste tree (*Vitex*) are examples.

VERNONIA noveboracensis

IRONWEED

Asteraceae (Compositae)

PERENNIAL

⚡ ZONES US, MS, LS

☀◐ FULL SUN OR LIGHT SHADE

💧💧💧 MUCH TO LITTLE WATER

Vernonia noveboracensis

Seldom considered for gardens, this meadow plant is a handsome choice for the back of a border or for a contrasting color scheme with goldenrod and black-eyed Susan. Clumps of leafy stems to 6–8 ft. tall are topped in late summer by broad, flat clusters of fluffy, brilliant purple flower heads. These should be clipped off before they develop into the rust-colored seed clusters that give the plant its name (unless you want plant to naturalize from volunteer seedlings). Grows in wet or dry soils and needs no coddling.

V. altissima is a similar species, somewhat taller and with longer leaves. Selection 'Purple Pillar' produces 10-ft. tall stalks topped, in midsummer, with large clusters of clear purple flowers.

VERONICA

SPEEDWELL

Scrophulariaceae

PERENNIALS

⚡ ZONES VARY BY SPECIES

☀ FULL SUN, EXCEPT AS NOTED

💧💧 WATER NEEDS VARY BY SPECIES

Veronica prostrata

Handsome plants ranging from 4 in. to 2½ ft. in height. Small flowers (¼–½ in. across) in white, rose, pink, or pale to deep blue are massed for an effective color display. Use in sunny borders and rock gardens. Prostrate, mat-forming kinds are generally less tolerant of damp conditions than bushy kinds and should be watered less often. Named selections are not easily assigned to a species; authorities differ.

V. alpina. ALPINE SPEEDWELL. Zones US, MS, LS. Creeping rootstock forms low rosette of foliage that sends up spikelike clusters of flowers in spring or early summer; often reblooms in fall. Selections include 10-in. 'Alba', with white flowers; 10-in. 'Barcarolle', rose pink; and 1-ft. 'Corymbosa', deep blue. Hybrid 'Goodness Grows', 1–2 ft. tall, has an extra-long bloom period, producing violet blue blossoms from late spring to frost if old flowers are removed. Regular water.

V. grandis holophylla. Zones US, MS, LS. Many stems to 2 ft. tall are densely clothed with waxy, glossy dark green leaves ending in spikelike clusters of blue flowers. These appear all summer if old clusters are deadheaded. 'Lavender Charm' ('Blue Charm') grows 1½–2 ft. tall. 'Icicle', to 1½ ft., has white flowers. Regular water.

V. incana. SILVER SPEEDWELL. Zones US, MS. Furry, silvery white, mat-forming foliage clumps. Deep blue flowers on 10-in. stems in summer. Selections include 10-in. 'Pavane', with rose pink flowers; 15-in. 'Minuet', pink, 'Red Fox', deep rose pink, and 'Romilley Purple', deep violet purple; and 1½-ft. 'Saraband', deep blue. Moderate to little water. Plants don't do well in extreme heat or in high-rainfall areas.

V. longifolia subsessilis (V. subsessilis). Zones US, MS, LS. Clumps of upright stems to 2 ft. tall are topped in midsummer by spikes of deep blue flowers about ½ in. wide; deadhead to prolong bloom. Stems are leafy and rather closely set with narrow, pointed leaves. Regular water.

V. prostrata (V. rupestris). Zones US, MS, LS. Small leaves to ¾ in. long. Tufted, hairy stems; some are prostrate and form mats of hairy foliage, while others grow upward to 8 in. tall and are topped by short clusters of pale blue flowers in late spring or early summer. 'Alba' bears white blooms, 'Mrs. Holt' pale pink ones. 'Trehane' has golden yellow leaves, bright blue flowers. Moderate to little water.

V

V. spicata (V. austriaca, V. austriaca teucrium). SPIKE SPEEDWELL. Zones US, MS, LS, CS. Rounded green clumps send up spikelike flower clusters to 2 ft. tall. Long summer bloom period if plants are deadheaded. 'Crater Lake', the old standby, grows to 15 in. tall, bears bright blue flowers. Other selections include 'Blue Fox', to 20 in. high, and rosy pink 'Heidekind', to 10 in. high. All take regular water. Need good drainage.

V. 'Sunny Border Blue'. Zones US, MS, LS. Compact plant with crinkled foliage. Dark violet blue flowers in spires to 2 ft. tall over an exceptionally long bloom season, beginning in late spring or early summer. Remove faded blooms to prolong the floral display until frost. Regular water.

Veronica spicata

VERONICASTRUM virginicum (Veronica virginica)

CULVER'S ROOT
Scrophulariaceae

PERENNIAL

☀️◑ ZONES US, MS

☀️◑ FULL SUN OR LIGHT SHADE

💧 REGULAR WATER

Veronicastrum virginicum

Native to eastern U.S. Resembles a very tall *Veronica*. Stems to 5–7 ft. high, clothed with whorls of toothed, 6-in., lance-shaped leaves. Stems branch in the upper portions and are topped by slender spikelike clusters (to 9 in. long) of tiny pale blue or white flowers. Pink selections exist. Useful plant for background in large borders. Makes a striking pattern against dark background, such as tall hedge or woodland edge, but too much shade makes it floppy. Likes fertile, well-drained, slightly acid soil.

VIBURNUM
Caprifoliaceae

DECIDUOUS OR EVERGREEN SHRUBS, SMALL TREES

☀️◑ ZONES VARY BY SPECIES

☀️◑ FULL SUN OR PART SHADE, EXCEPT AS NOTED

💧 REGULAR WATER, EXCEPT AS NOTED

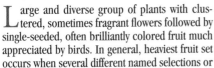

Viburnum opulus 'Roseum'

Large and diverse group of plants with clustered, sometimes fragrant flowers followed by single-seeded, often brilliantly colored fruit much appreciated by birds. In general, heaviest fruit set occurs when several different named selections or seedlings that bloom at the same time are planted together. Some viburnums are valuable for winter flowers. Some evergreen types are used principally as foliage plants. A few species, as noted, can be grown as small trees.

Viburnums prefer slightly acid soil but are very tolerant, even accepting heavy soils. Many have a wide range of climate adaptability. Where summers are long and hot, most evergreen kinds look better with some shade. Prune to prevent legginess; some evergreen kinds can be sheared. Nematodes can be a problem; aphids, thrips, spider mites, scale, and root weevils are potential pests in many areas. However, plants are not usually seriously troubled.

V. acerifolium. MAPLE-LEAF VIBURNUM. Deciduous. Zones US, MS, LS. Native from North Carolina and Georgia, north to Minnesota, New Brunswick. Suckering shrub forms clumps of stems; erect, sparsely branched, to 6 ft. tall, 4 ft. wide. Dark or bright green leaves, to 5 in. long, have three lobes, like maple leaves, and turn pink or reddish purple in fall.

Late-spring flowers, in creamy white, flat-topped clusters, to 3 in. across. Purple- or blue-black berries in late summer. Tolerates deep shade and rather dry soil.

V. bodnantense. BODNANT VIBURNUM. Deciduous. Zones MS, LS. To 10 ft. or more. Oval leaves 1½–4 in. long are deeply veined, turn dark scarlet in fall. Loose clusters of very fragrant flowers, deep pink fading paler, bloom in winter. More often than not they are killed by the cold. Red fruit is not showy. This plant is a hybrid; there are several selections. Best known is 'Dawn' ('Pink Dawn').

V. burkwoodii. BURKWOOD VIBURNUM. Deciduous or semievergreen. Zones US, MS, LS. Hybrid to 6–12 ft. tall, 4–8 ft. wide. Leaves to 3½ in. long, glossy dark green with white, hairy undersides; turn purplish red in cold weather. Fragrant white flowers open in late winter or early spring from dense, 4-in. clusters of pink buds. Blue-black fruit. Early growth is straggly; mature plants are dense. Can be trained as espalier.

'Chenault' *(V. chenaultii)*. Denser, more compact, slightly later blooming, more deciduous than the species.

'Mohawk'. To 7 ft. tall. Red buds are showy long before they expand into white flowers. Bright orange-red fall color. Resistant to bacterial leaf spot.

V. carlcephalum. FRAGRANT SNOWBALL. Deciduous. Zones US, MS, LS. Hybrid to 6–10 ft. tall and wide. Leaves 2–3½ in. long, dull grayish green, downy beneath; reddish purple in autumn. Long-lasting, waxy white, perfumed flowers in showy, dense, 4–5-in. clusters in spring.

🎍 **V. carlesii.** KOREAN SPICE VIBURNUM. Deciduous. Zones US, MS, LS. To 4–8 ft. tall and wide. Leaves are like those of *V. carlcephalum*; inconsistent reddish fall color. Sweetly fragrant, clove-scented, 2–3-in. clusters of white flowers open from pink buds in spring. Blue-black summer fruit is not showy. Best in part shade during summer, in sun during spring, winter. The hardy hybrid 'Cayuga' grows 5 ft. tall and has white flowers opening from pink buds.

V. cassinoides. WITHE-ROD. Deciduous. Zones US, MS, LS. Native to eastern and central North America. Attractive dense, rounded plant 5–6 ft. (possibly 10 ft.) tall, with dull dark green leaves; red-orange to red-purple fall color. Flat clusters of white flowers bloom in late spring or early summer; these are followed by showy, mixed-color clusters of green, pink, red, and blue fruits that eventually turn black. Plant can tolerate damp soil, wind, and coastal conditions.

V. dentatum. ARROWWOOD. Deciduous. Zones US, MS, LS. Native from New Brunswick to Minnesota, south to Georgia. To 6–10 ft. tall (or taller) and as wide. Cream-colored flowers in late spring are followed by blue-black, ¼-in. fruit. Dark green, 4-in. leaves turn yellow, orange, or deep red in autumn. Plants tolerate heat, cold, and alkaline soil. Use as screen or tall hedge.

V. dilatatum. LINDEN VIBURNUM. Deciduous. Zones US, MS. Grows to 8–10 ft. tall and not quite as wide. Nearly round, 2–5-in. gray-green leaves; inconsistent rusty red fall color. Tiny, creamy white, somewhat unpleasant-smelling flowers in 5-in. clusters, late spring or early summer. Showy bright red fruits ripen in early fall, hang on into winter. Outstanding named selections include the following:

'Catskill'. Compact growth to 5–8 ft. tall, 8–10 ft. wide, with smaller leaves than species. Dark red fruit. Fall color is a combination of yellow, orange, and red.

'Erie'. Rounded habit to 6 ft. tall, 10 ft. wide. Coral fruit. Leaves turn yellow, orange, and red in autumn. Highly disease resistant.

'Iroquois'. To 9 ft. tall, 12 ft. wide. Selected for heavy production of larger, darker red fruit. Orange-red to maroon fall foliage.

V. farreri (V. fragrans). FRAGRANT VIBURNUM. Deciduous. Zones US, MS, LS. Loose habit, to 8–12 ft. tall and as wide. Smooth green leaves are oval, heavily veined, 1½–3 in. long; turn soft russet red to reddish purple in fall. Fragrant white to pink flowers in 2-in. clusters appear before leaves open, in winter or early spring. Blossoms survive to 20–22°F but are often browned by winter cold. Bright red fruit. Prune to prevent leggy growth. 'Album' has white flowers. Pink-flowered 'Nanum' is lower growing (to 2 ft.) form.

V. hybrids. This group includes plants of complex ancestry. The following, all spring bloomers, are widely offered: ▶

V

'Chesapeake'. Semievergreen. Zones US, MS, LS. To 6 ft. tall, 10 ft. wide, with wavy-edged, glossy dark green leaves. Small, fragrant white flowers open from pink buds; dull red to black fruit follows.

'Conoy'. Evergreen. Zones US, MS, LS. Dense, rounded plant to 5 ft. tall, 8 ft. wide. Lustrous dark green leaves, whitish beneath. Creamy white, slightly fragrant flowers; long-lasting red berries. Tolerates shearing.

'Eskimo'. Semievergreen. Zones US, MS, LS. Dense, compact habit to 5 ft. tall and wide. Shiny dark green foliage; unscented white flowers in 3–4-in., snowball-like clusters.

V. japonicum. JAPANESE VIBURNUM. Evergreen. Zones CS, TS. To 10–20 ft. tall; can be trained as small tree. Leathery, glossy dark green leaves 6 in. long. Sparse spring show of fragrant white flowers in 4-in. clusters. Red fruit is likewise sparse, but very attractive. Give some shade. Hybrids 'Chippewa' and 'Huron' hardier to cold; have semievergreen to deciduous, glossy green leaves that turn maroon and red in fall.

V. juddii. JUDD VIBURNUM. Deciduous. Zones US, MS, LS. Hybrid plant to 4–8 ft. tall. Bushier and more spreading than *V. carlesii*, but similar to it in other respects, including fragrance.

V. lantana. WAYFARING TREE. Deciduous. Zone US. Large (10–20-ft.), rounded, multistemmed shrub with 2–5-in. dark green leaves that turn an inconsistent purplish red in autumn. Flat, 3–5-in. clusters of creamy flowers in midspring develop into yellow fruits that gradually age to red, then black; all colors are sometimes present at one time. Berries of 'Mohican' hold their red color longest. This species tolerates drought and lime soils better than most other viburnums.

V. lentago. NANNYBERRY. Deciduous. Zones US, MS. Native to eastern and central North America. Will grow as single-trunked tree to 30 ft. tall or as massive shrub to lesser height. Creamy white flowers in flat, 4–6-in. clusters in spring. Edible fruit is red, then turns to blue black. Glossy dark green, 2–4-in.-long leaves turn an inconsistent purplish red in fall. Good in dappled shade of taller trees, at woodland edge. Moist or dry soils.

V. macrocephalum macrocephalum (V. m. 'Sterile'). CHINESE SNOWBALL. Deciduous. Zones US, MS, LS. To 12–20 ft. tall, with broad, rounded habit. Leaves oval to oblong, 2–4 in. long, dull green. Spectacular big, rounded, 6–8-in. flower clusters in spring (or anytime during warm weather) are composed of sterile blossoms that are lime green at first, changing to white. No fruit. Can be trained as espalier.

V. nudum. SMOOTH WITHE-ROD. Deciduous. Zones US, MS, LS, CS. Native from Louisiana and Florida, north to Connecticut. Resembles *V. cassinoides*, but with shiny leaves, and sometimes to 15 ft. tall. 'Winterthur' is an improved, compact form, with heavy crop of berries from pink, ripening to red, and black. Tolerates constantly wet soils.

V. odoratissimum. SWEET VIBURNUM. Evergreen. Zones CS, TS. To 10–20 ft. tall; becomes treelike with age. Leaves bright green, 3–8 in. long, with glossy, varnished-looking surface. Conical, 3–6-in. clusters of white, lightly fragrant flowers in spring. Red fruit ripens to black. Good screen. 'Emerald Lustre' has larger leaves.

V. opulus. EUROPEAN CRANBERRY BUSH. Deciduous. Zones US, MS, LS. To 8–15 ft. tall and wide, with arching branches. Lobed, maple-like dark green leaves to 2–4 in. long and wider than long; fall color may be yellow, bright red, or reddish purple. Creamy white spring flowers consist of 2–4-in. clusters of small fertile blossoms ringed with larger sterile blossoms for a lace cap effect. Large, showy red fruit, fall–winter. Takes moist to boggy soils. Control aphids. Selections include:

'Aureum'. To 10 ft. tall. Golden yellow foliage needs some shade to prevent sunburn.

'Compactum'. Same as *V. opulus* but smaller: 4–5 ft. high and wide.

'Nanum'. To 2 ft. tall, 2 ft. wide. Needs no trimming as low hedge. Cannot take poorly drained, wet soils. No flowers, fruit.

'Roseum' ('Sterile'). COMMON SNOWBALL. To 10–15 ft. Resembles *V. opulus*, but flower clusters are like snowballs, to 2–2½ in. across, composed entirely of sterile flowers (so no fruit). Aphids are especially troublesome on this form.

V. plicatum plicatum (V. tomentosum 'Sterile'). JAPANESE SNOWBALL. Deciduous. Zones US, MS, LS. Grows to 8–15 ft. tall and wide. Oval, 3–6-in. long, strongly veined, dull dark green leaves turn purplish red in fall. Showy, 3-in. snowball-like clusters of white sterile flowers in mid-

spring look like those of *V. opulus* 'Roseum', but this plant is less bothered by aphids. Horizontal branching pattern gives plant a tiered look, especially when in bloom: Flower clusters are held above the branches, while leaves hang down. No fruit. Tolerates occasionally wet soils.

V. plicatum tomentosum. DOUBLEFILE VIBURNUM. Deciduous. Zones US, MS, LS. A truly beautiful viburnum. Resembles Japanese snowball, but midspring flower display consists of small fertile flowers in flat, 2–4-in. clusters edged with 1–1½-in. sterile flowers in lace cap effect. Fruit is red aging to black, showy, not always profuse. Needs good drainage and moist soil. Excessive summer heat and drought often result in leaf scorch. Selections include the following:

'Cascade'. To 10 ft. Wide-spreading branches, large sterile flowers.

'Mariesii'. Grows to 10 ft. tall, 12 ft. wide. Has larger flower clusters, larger sterile flowers than the species.

'Newport'. To 5–6 ft. tall and wide.

'Pink Beauty'. To 8–10 ft. tall, with light pink flowers that fade to white in warm season.

'Shasta'. More horizontal habit than the species (to 10 ft. tall, 15 ft. wide), with large sterile flowers.

'Shoshoni'. To 5 ft. tall, 8 ft. wide.

'Summer Snowflake'. To 5–8 ft. tall. Blooms from spring to fall.

V. prunifolium. BLACK HAW. Deciduous. Zones US, MS, LS. Native to the East. Upright to 15 ft., spreading as wide. Can be trained as small tree. Common name comes from dark fruit and plant's resemblance to hawthorn (*Crataegus*). Oval, finely toothed leaves to 3 in. long turn purplish to reddish purple in fall. Many clusters of creamy white flowers in spring; edible blue-black fruit in fall and winter. Use as dense screen or barrier, attractive specimen shrub. Best in full sun. Tolerates drought.

Viburnum rhytidophyllum

V. rhytidophyllum. LEATHERLEAF VIBURNUM. Evergreen. Zones US, MS, LS. Narrow, upright, to 6–15 ft. tall. Leaves narrowish, to 4–10 in. long, deep green and wrinkled above, densely fuzzy underneath. Yellowish white spring flowers in 4–8-in. clusters. Fruit is scarlet, aging to black. Tattered-looking plant where cold winds blow. Leaves droop in cold weather. Tolerates deep shade. Some find this plant striking; others consider it coarse. 'Alleghany' and 'Willowwood' are hybrids similar to the parent. Hybrid 'Pragense' has a finer texture than the parent.

V. rufidulum. SOUTHERN BLACK HAW. Deciduous. Zones US, MS, LS, CS. Native from Texas to Florida and north to Virginia. Large shrub or small tree, 12–30 ft. tall. White flower clusters 5 in. across, late spring. Young shoots, leafstalks, leaf undersides covered with rust-colored hairs. Surfaces of oval, 2–4-in. leaves are glossy dark green. Fall color ranges through orange, yellow, red, and purple. Berries handsome dark blue.

V. setigerum. TEA VIBURNUM. Deciduous. Zones US, MS, LS. Grows to 8–12 ft. tall, rather erect, multistemmed, often bare at the base. (Plant lower shrubs around it for concealment.) Leaves, once used for making tea, are 3–6 in. long, dark green or blue green, turning purplish in fall. White spring flowers in 1–2-in. clusters are not striking, but heavy production of scarlet fruit makes this the showiest of fruiting viburnums.

V. tinus. LAURUSTINUS. Evergreen. Zone CS. To 6–12 ft. tall, half as wide. Leathery, dark green, oval leaves to 2–3 in. long, with edges slightly rolled under. New stems wine red. Tight clusters of pink buds open to lightly fragrant white flowers in winter. Bright metallic blue fruits last through summer. Dense foliage right to ground makes it good plant for screens, hedges, clipped topiary shapes. Susceptible to mildew, mites.

V. trilobum. AMERICAN CRANBERRY BUSH. Deciduous. Zones US, MS. Native to Canada, northern U.S. To 10–15 ft. tall. Leaves look much like those of *V. opulus*; they emerge reddish tinged, mature to dark green, turn yellow to red purple in fall. White lace cap flowers in midspring, followed by edible fruit that looks like that of *V. opulus*. 'Compactum' grows 6 ft. tall; 'Wentworth' berries are larger than those of species.

V. wrightii. WRIGHT VIBURNUM. Deciduous. Zones US, MS. Similar to *V. dilatatum* except for its larger leaves, which may turn a good red in fall. Useful tall hedge.

VICTORIAN BOX. See PITTOSPORUM undulatum

VINCA

PERIWINKLE, MYRTLE

Apocynaceae

PERENNIALS

☀ ZONES VARY BY SPECIES

◐ ● PARTIAL OR FULL SHADE

◗ MODERATE WATER

*Vinca
minor*

Trailing, arching stems that root where they touch the soil make these evergreen plants useful as ground and bank covers. Shiny dark green leaves are oval to oblong. Lavender blue, five-petaled, pinwheel-shaped flowers appear in leaf joints in spring. Tolerate sun if well watered.

V. major. GREATER PERIWINKLE. Zones LS, CS. The larger, more aggressive species. Leaves to 3 in. long, flowers to 2 in. across. Spreads rapidly; can be extremely invasive in areas that are sheltered and forested. Will mound up 1–2 ft. high. Shear close to ground occasionally to bring on new growth. A form with creamy leaf variegation exists.

V. minor. COMMON PERIWINKLE, DWARF PERIWINKLE. Zones US, MS, LS, CS. Miniature version of *V. major,* with smaller leaves and flowers and a height of just 6 in. More restrained, less likely to invade adjacent plantings. Among the many selections are 'Alba', with white flowers; 'Atropurpurea', deep purple flowers and small leaves; 'Aureola', light blue flowers, yellow veins in leaf centers; 'Bowles' Variety', larger leaves, deeper blue flowers; 'Miss Jekyll', small grower with white flowers; 'Ralph Shugert', white-edged leaves, blue flowers, autumn rebloom. 'Sterling Silver' is a blue-flowered form with green leaves that are specked with pale green and edged in cream. 'La Grave' is similar to (if not the same plant as) 'Bowles' Variety'.

V. rosea. See Catharanthus roseus

VIOLA

VIOLA, VIOLET, PANSY

Violaceae

PERENNIALS, SOME TREATED AS ANNUALS

☀ ZONES VARY BY SPECIES

☀ ◐ ● EXPOSURE NEEDS VARY BY SPECIES

● REGULAR WATER

Viola wittrockiana

Botanically speaking, violas, pansies, and violets are all perennials belonging to the genus *Viola*. However, pansies and violas are treated as annuals; they are invaluable for winter and spring color. Pansies and violas provide mass color in borders and edgings, as ground covers for spring-flowering bulbs, and in containers. Violets are more often used as woodland or rock garden plants. Pansies and violas take sun or shade, while violets thrive in part or full shade.

V. affinis. LECONTE VIOLET. Zones US, MS, LS, CS. Native from New England, south to Georgia, Alabama, and west to Wisconsin. Small, triangular, wavy-toothed leaves. Lavender-violet flowers, dark-veined, white at base of petals, and with a lighter eye, open above the leaves in spring.

V. blanda. SWEET WHITE VIOLET. Zones US, MS, LS. Native to eastern North America. To 2–3 in., spreads by runners. Fragrant early spring flowers are white veined purple, with reflexed petals. Likes humus-rich soil.

V. cornuta. VIOLA. Annuals in most zones. To 6–8 in. high, with smooth, wavy-toothed, somewhat oval leaves. Purple, pansylike flowers, 1½ in. across, have slender spur. Modern strains have larger flowers with shorter spurs, in solid colors of purple, blue, yellow, apricot, ruby red, and white. Crystal strain has especially large flowers in clear colors. Set out plants or sow seed as for pansy.

Some garden centers offer English violas—named selections are propagated by cuttings or division. These form clumps to 2 ft. wide and are reliably perennial in the Upper South. They include 'Better Times', 2-in. yellow flowers; 'Columbine', creamy white flowers liberally splashed with purple; 'Etain', pale yellow flowers with purple borders; 'Mt. Spokane', white flowers with a shading of palest blue; and 'Whiskers', cream-colored flowers marked with thin purple lines.

V. cucullata (V. obliqua). MARSH BLUE VIOLET. Zones US, MS, LS. Native to eastern and central North America. Leaves to 4 in. wide. Early spring flowers are blue, ¾ in. wide. Good ground cover, but self-sows and can become a nuisance. One of most intractable lawn weeds. 'Freckles' has white flowers liberally dotted with purple; comes true from seed.

V. odorata. SWEET VIOLET. Zones US, MS, LS. The violet of song and story. Spreads by long runners at moderate rate. Dark green, heart-shaped leaves, toothed on margins. Fragrant, short-spurred flowers in deep violet, bluish rose, or white. Deep purple 'Royal Robe', a large plant with long stems (to 6 in.), is widely grown. 'Royal Elk' has single, fragrant, violet-colored, long-stemmed flowers. 'Rosina' is pink flowered. 'Charm' grows in clumps, has small white blooms. Plant size varies from 2 in. for smallest types to 8–10 in. for largest.

Remove runners and shear rank growth in late fall for better spring flower display. For heavy bloom, apply a complete fertilizer in very early spring, before flowering. Like many other violets, these can become genuine pests if allowed to spread into other perennial plantings or lawns.

V. pedata. BIRD'S-FOOT VIOLET. Zones US, MS, LS. Native to eastern North America. So named because its finely divided leaves resemble a bird's foot. Blooms early spring to early summer; 1-in. flowers on 4-in. stems are usually two-toned violet blue with darker veins. Forms clumps; does not spread by runners. Not as easy to grow as other violets; likes excellent drainage, filtered sun or high shade, acid conditions.

V. priceana. See V. sororia

V. sororia (V. priceana). CONFEDERATE VIOLET. Zones US, MS, LS. Leaves are somewhat heart shaped, to 5 in. wide. Blooms spring–early summer; flowers are ½–¾ in. across, white, heavily veined with violet blue, flat faced like pansies. No runners. Self-sows readily; best in woodland garden. Good ground cover among rhododendrons.

V. tricolor. JOHNNY-JUMP-UP. All zones as annual. To 6–12 in. tall, with oval, deeply lobed leaves. Purple-and-yellow spring flowers resemble miniature pansies. Flowers of 'Molly Sanderson' are so deep a purple that they appear black. Self-sows profusely. Like pansy, takes sun or shade.

V. tricolor hortensis. See V. wittrockiana

V. walteri. WALTER'S VIOLET. Zones US, MS, LS, CS. Native from South Carolina to Florida and west to Texas, Ohio. To 6–8 in. tall, with evergreen, mottled, dark green foliage, often tinged purple beneath. Stems root where they touch the ground, producing new plants. In spring, bears blue-violet flowers with dark veins, and white petal bases, paler eye.

V. wittrockiana (V. tricolor hortensis). PANSY. All zones as annual. Many strains with flowers 2–4 in. across, in white, blue, mahogany red, rose, yellow, apricot, purple; also bicolors. Petals often striped or blotched; Crown and Crystal Bowl strains have unblotched flowers. Plants grow to about 8 in. high. F_1 and F_2 hybrids more free flowering, heat tolerant. To prolong bloom of pansies, pick flowers (with some foliage) regularly, remove faded blooms before they seed. Plants get ragged by midsummer and should be removed.

Set out plants in spring in the Upper South; in fall for winter–spring bloom elsewhere. Or start plants from seed.

VIOLET. See VIOLA

VIOLET SILVERLEAF. See LEUCOPHYLLUM candidum

VIOLET TRUMPET VINE. See CLYTOSTOMA callistegioides

VIRGINIA BLUEBELLS. See MERTENSIA virginica

VIRGINIA CREEPER. See PARTHENOCISSUS quinquefolia

Vitaceae. The grape family contains vines that climb by tendrils and produce berries. In addition to grape, best-known representatives are Boston ivy and Virginia creeper (both species of *Parthenocissus*).

VITEX

CHASTE TREE

Verbenaceae

DECIDUOUS OR EVERGREEN SHRUBS OR TREES

✂ ZONES VARY BY SPECIES

☼ FULL SUN

💧 💧 REGULAR OR MODERATE WATER

Vitex agnus-castus

Large group of mostly tropical and subtropical trees, only a few of which are grown in the U.S. They have handsome, divided leaves and clustered flowers. Prized for their showy, blue summer blossoms. All tolerate coastal conditions and drought.

V. agnus-castus. CHASTE TREE. Deciduous shrub or small tree. All zones. Native to southern Europe, western Asia. In most areas, grows fast to make a 25-ft., usually multitrunked tree with a broad, spreading habit. In the Upper South, growth is slower and mature size is lower—to 8–10 ft.

Aromatic leaves divided fanwise into five to seven narrow, 2–6-in.-long leaflets that are grayish green above, gray beneath. No real fall color. Small, fragrant blue flowers in 6–12-in. spikes at branch ends and in leaf joints, summer–fall. Selections include 'Alba' and 'Silver Spire', white flowers; 'Latifolia' (sometimes sold as *V. macrophylla*), a sturdy plant with large leaflets; 'Abbeville Blue', deep blue flowers; and 'Rosea', pinkish flowers.

Thrives in heat. No serious pests. Tolerant of various soils, but prefers well-drained soil. Good in shrub border. Remove lower limbs to form good, small shade tree.

V. negundo. Deciduous shrub or small tree. All zones. Native to southeast Africa, eastern Asia. Similar to *V. agnus-castus,* but a little larger and more cold-hardy; 5–8-in. flower spikes aren't as showy. 'Heterophylla' has delicate-looking, finely lobed leaflets.

V. trifolia. Evergreen shrub or small shrubby tree. Zones CS, TS. Native to Asia and Australia. Fast growth, to 12–20 ft. Leaves sometimes simple but usually divided into three leaflets, each 4 in. long, felty gray on undersides. Lavender blue flowers, with white spot on lip, open in summer on 4–10-in.-long spikes. Makes fine-textured hedge; clip regularly. 'Variegata' has white-variegated foliage; cut out shoots that revert to plain green.

VITIS. See GRAPE

VRIESEA

Bromeliaceae

PERENNIALS

✂ ZONE TS; OR INDOORS

☼ STRONG LIGHT BUT NOT DIRECT SUN

💧 WATER LEAF BASES, DAMPEN MOSS

Vriesea hieroglyphica

Bromeliads with rosettes of long, leathery leaves and oddly shaped flower clusters. Grow as epiphytes in pockets of sphagnum moss on tree branches or in pots of loose, highly organic mix. Mist if grown in hot, dry rooms. Feed lightly and often.

V. hieroglyphica. Rosettes of 30 to 40 leaves, each 3 ft. long, 3 in. wide, dark green with pronounced cross-banding of blackish purple. Greenish flower spike with dull yellow flowers.

V. lindenii. See Tillandsia lindenii

V. splendens. FLAMING SWORD. Rosettes of up to 20 dark green, 1½-ft. leaves barred transversely with blackish purple. Flower stalk resembles a 1½–2-ft.-wide feather of bright red bracts from which small yellow flowers emerge. 'Chantrierei' is a brightly colored selection.

WAKE ROBIN. See TRILLIUM

WALKING FERN. See ASPLENIUM rhizophyllum

WALKING IRIS. See NEOMARICA gracilis

WALLFLOWER. See ERYSIMUM

WALNUT (Juglans)

Juglandaceae

DECIDUOUS TREES

✂ ZONES VARY BY SPECIES

☼ FULL SUN

💧 REGULAR WATER

Walnut

Large, spreading trees suitable for big properties. All produce oval or round, edible nuts in fleshy husks; those of native species have a wild flavor, those of English walnut are the ones sold commercially. Among the drawbacks of these trees are their large size; shallow, competitive roots (roots of black walnut even inhibit growth of some other plants); and windborne pollen, which causes an allergic reaction in many people. Moreover, trees tend to be out of leaf for a long time—and they are often messy when in leaf (drip and sooty mildew from aphid exudations) and in fruit (husks from nuts can stain).

J. cinerea. BUTTERNUT. Zones US, MS. Native from New Brunswick to Georgia, west to Arkansas and North Dakota. To 50–60 ft. (or to 100 ft.) tall, with broad, spreading canopy. Resembles black walnut—but tree is smaller, leaves have fewer leaflets (11 to 19), and nuts are oval or elongated rather than round. Flavor is good, but shells are thick and hard to crack. Tolerates alkaline soil.

J. microcarpa. RIVER WALNUT. All zones. Native to Oklahoma, Texas, New Mexico, and northwest Mexico. Grows to about 20 ft. tall, rarely 30 ft., and often multistemmed and more shrubby than treelike. Leaves have 15 to 23 leaflets, to 3 in. long. Tree produces small, ¾-in nuts. Thrives in dry, rocky, limy soil.

J. nigra. BLACK WALNUT. Zones US, MS, LS, CS. Native from Massachusetts to Florida, west to Texas and Minnesota. Can reach 150 ft. tall (though often attains only half that height in gardens), with high-branched, oval- to round-headed habit. Furrowed blackish brown bark. Leaves have 15 to 23 leaflets, each 2½–5 in. long. Richly flavored nuts, 1–1½ in. across, are thick shelled and very hard. Some types, however, are easier to crack. Wood is highly prized for furniture, cabinets.

J. regia. ENGLISH WALNUT. Zones US, MS, LS. Native to southwest Asia, southeast Europe. To 60 ft. high, with equal spread. Fast growing, especially when young. Trunk and heavy, horizontal or upward-angled branches covered with smooth gray bark. Leaves have 5 to 7 (occasionally more) 3–6-in.-long leaflets.

WANDERING JEW. See TRADESCANTIA, ZEBRINA pendula

WAND LOOSESTRIFE. See LYTHRUM virgatum

WARMINSTER BROOM. See CYTISUS praecox

WASHINGTON HAWTHORN. See CRATAEGUS phaenopyrum

WASHINGTONIA

Arecaceae (Palmae)

PALMS

✂ ZONES CS, TS

☼ FULL SUN

💧 💧 REGULAR TO LITTLE WATER

Washingtonia robusta

Native to California, Arizona, northern Mexico. Fast-growing palms that quickly become too tall for most gardens. Best suited for planting on large properties, along avenues, on parkways. A common sight throughout Florida.

W. filifera. DESERT FAN PALM. To 60 ft., with thicker trunk than that of its Mexican cousin. Long-stalked, 3–6-ft. leaves stand well apart in open crown. As leaves mature, they bend down to form a petticoat of thatch. Hardy to 18°F.

W. robusta. THREAD PALM, MEXICAN FAN PALM. Taller (to 100 ft.) than desert fan palm, with slimmer, slightly curved or bent trunk. Head of foliage is more compact; leafstalks are shorter, with a red streak on the underside. Hardy to 20°F. Good plant for the beach.

WATER LILY. See NYMPHAEA

🏛 WATERMELON

Cucurbitaceae

ANNUAL

🗓 ALL ZONES

☼ FULL SUN

💧 WATER MOST HEAVILY WHEN PLANTS ARE YOUNG

Watermelon

One of the South's favorite late-summer treats. World records for size of melons have been held by families in Arkansas and Tennessee. Needs a long growing season, more heat than most other melons, and more space than other vine crops—about 8 ft. by 8 ft. for each hill (circle of seed). Other than that, culture is as described under Melon. Large selections such as 'Charleston Gray', 'Congo', and 'Crimson Sweet' may need as many as 85 to 95 days of hot, sunny weather to mature. If your summers are shorter, choose a smaller, earlier-ripening "icebox" type, such as 'Minilee' and 'Sugar Baby', that will produce in 70 to 75 days. Seed companies also offer yellow-fleshed kinds ('Golden Honey', 'Yellow Doll'), seedless types ('Honey Red Seedless Hybrid', 'Redball Seedless'), and heirlooms ('Amish Moon and Stars', 'Sugar Lump White'). Dwarf-fruited types are also available. Unlike other melons, watermelon does not grow sweeter after harvest—it must be picked ripe. Three tests for ripeness: thumping the melon produces a "thunk"; underside has turned from white to pale yellow; tendril opposite stem has withered.

WATER TUPELO. See NYSSA aquatica

WAVY-LEAFED PLANTAIN LILY. See HOSTA undulata

WAX MYRTLE. See MYRICA

WAX PLANT. See HOYA

WAYFARING TREE. See VIBURNUM lantana

WEDELIA trilobata

WEDELIA

Asteraceae (Compositae)

PERENNIAL GROUND COVER

🗓 ZONES CS (WARMER PARTS), TS

☼◑ FULL SUN OR LIGHT SHADE

💧 REGULAR WATER

Wedelia trilobata

Trailing plant to 1½ ft. high that roots wherever stems touch damp earth. Fleshy evergreen leaves are dark glossy green, to 4 in. long and half as wide, with a few coarse teeth or shallow lobes toward tips. Inch-wide flower heads resemble tiny yellow zinnias or marigolds. Blooms almost year-round. Spreads fast; easily propagated by lifting rooted pieces or by placing tip cuttings in moist soil. Best in sandy, fast-draining soils but will take heavier

SOUTHERN HERITAGE PLANTS
IDENTIFIED BY SYMBOL 🏛

soils if drainage is acceptable. If killed to ground by frost, it makes fast comeback. Tolerates high heat, seaside conditions. Plant 1½ ft. apart, feed lightly. Cut back hard if plantings mound up or become stemmy.

WEEPING WILLOW. See SALIX babylonica

🏛 WEIGELA florida

WEIGELA

Caprifoliaceae

DECIDUOUS SHRUB

🗓 ZONES US, MS, LS

☼◑ FULL SUN OR LIGHT SHADE

💧 REGULAR WATER

Weigela florida

Valuable for lavish, attractive springtime display of funnel-shaped, 1-in.-long flowers. Fast-growing shrub to 6–10 ft. tall, 9–12 ft. wide, with branches often arching to the ground. Leaves 2–4½ in. long, half as wide. Pink to rose red flowers are borne singly or in short clusters all along previous season's shoots. After flowering, cut back branches that have bloomed. Thin new suckers to a few of the most vigorous. A simpler method is to cut back entire plant about halfway every other year, just after blooms fade. New growth that follows will provide plenty of flowers the next spring. Use for flower or mixed shrub borders, as summer screen. Selections include:

'Bristol Ruby'. To 6–7 ft. tall and nearly as wide, with ruby red flowers. Some repeat bloom in midsummer and fall.

'Candida' ('Alba'). To 5 ft. tall, with white flowers tinged green.

'Java Red'. Compact growth to 2½–4 ft. Deep red flowers and red-tinted deep green foliage.

'Minuet'. Dwarf (to 2–3 ft. high), with purplish leaves and flowers that blend red, purple, and yellow.

'Newport Red' ('Vanicekii', 'Cardinal', 'Rhode Island Red'). To 6 ft. tall, with brilliant red flowers. Young stems are bright green in winter.

'Pink Delight'. Compact growth to 3–4 ft. tall. Deep pink flowers.

'Pink Princess'. Loose, open habit to 6 ft. tall. Lilac pink blossoms.

'Red Prince'. To 6 ft. tall, with nonfading red flowers; some rebloom in late summer.

'Variegata'. Compact growth to 4–6 ft. tall. Deep rosy red flowers; bright green leaves edged pale yellow to creamy white. Popular and showy.

WESTERN REDBUD. See CERCIS occidentalis

WESTERN SAND CHERRY. See PRUNUS besseyi

WESTERN SOAPBERRY. See SAPINDUS drummondii

WHITE CEDAR. See CHAMAECYPARIS thyoides

WHITE CUP. See NIEREMBERGIA repens

WHITE FRANGIPANI. See PLUMERIA alba

WHITE LARKSPUR. See DELPHINIUM virescens

WHITE MUGWORT. See ARTEMISIA lactiflora

WHITE RAIN LILY. See ZEPHYRANTHES candida

WILD AGERATUM. See EUPATORIUM coelestinum

WILD FOXGLOVE. See PENSTEMON cobaea

WILD GINGER. See ASARUM

WILD HYACINTH. See CAMASSIA scilloides

WILD PINK. See SILENE caroliniana

WILD PLANTAIN. See HELICONIA caribaea

WILD PLUM. See PRUNUS americana

WILLOW. See SALIX

W

WISTERIA

Fabaceae (Leguminosae)

DECIDUOUS VINES

✿ ZONES US, MS, LS, CS

☼ FULL SUN

◐ ◑ WATER YOUNG ONES WELL, OLDER ONES LESS

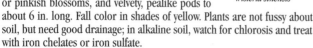
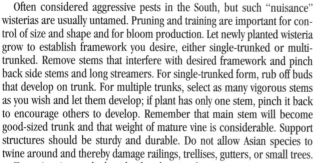

Wisteria sinensis

Twining, woody vines of great size, long life, and exceptional beauty in flower. So adaptable they can be grown as trees, shrubs, or vines. All have large bright green leaves divided into many leaflets, spectacular clusters of blue, white, or pinkish blossoms, and velvety, pealike pods to about 6 in. long. Fall color in shades of yellow. Plants are not fussy about soil, but need good drainage; in alkaline soil, watch for chlorosis and treat with iron chelates or iron sulfate.

Often considered aggressive pests in the South, but such "nuisance" wisterias are usually untamed. Pruning and training are important for control of size and shape and for bloom production. Let newly planted wisteria grow to establish framework you desire, either single-trunked or multitrunked. Remove stems that interfere with desired framework and pinch back side stems and long streamers. For single-trunked form, rub off buds that develop on trunk. For multiple trunks, select as many vigorous stems as you wish and let them develop; if plant has only one stem, pinch it back to encourage others to develop. Remember that main stem will become good-sized trunk and that weight of mature vine is considerable. Support structures should be sturdy and durable. Do not allow Asian species to twine around and thereby damage railings, trellises, gutters, or small trees.

Tree wisterias can be bought already trained; or you can train your own. Remove all but one main stem and stake this one securely. Tie stem to stake at frequent intervals, using plastic tape to prevent girdling. When plant has reached height at which you wish head to form, pinch or prune out tip to force branching. Shorten branches to beef them up. Pinch back long streamers and rub off all buds that form below head.

In general, wisterias do not need fertilizer. Prune blooming plants every winter: Cut back or thin out side shoots from main or structural stems, and shorten back to two or three buds the flower-producing spurs that grow from these shoots. It's easy to recognize fat flower buds on these spurs.

In summer, cut back long streamers before they tangle up in main body of vine; save those you want to use to extend height or length of vine and tie them to support—eaves, wall, trellis, arbor. If old plants grow rampantly but fail to bloom, withhold all nitrogen fertilizers for an entire growing season (buds for the next season's bloom are started in early summer). If that fails to produce bloom the next year, you can try pruning roots in spring—after you're sure no flowers will be produced—by cutting vertically with spade into plant's root zone. Using an herbicide is the most effective way to eradicate an unwanted wisteria. First, fill a large bucket with glyphosate solution mixed to the strength specified on the label. Then push as much of the vine's leaves and green stems into the bucket as you can (choose young, flexible shoots). Leave the stems there for several days; leaves and stems will absorb the chemical and carry it down to the roots.

W. floribunda. JAPANESE WISTERIA. Leaves are 12–16 in. long, divided into 15 to 19 leaflets. Fragrant, 1½-ft. clusters of violet or violet blue flowers appear during leaf-out. Clusters open gradually, starting from the base; this prolongs bloom season but makes for a less spectacular burst of color than that provided by Chinese wisteria. Many selections are sold in white, pink, and shades of blue, purple, and lavender, usually marked with yellow and white. 'Longissima' ('Macrobotrys') has long (1½–3-ft.) clusters of violet flowers. 'Longissima Alba' has white flowers in 2-ft. clusters; 'Ivory Tower' is similar. 'Rosea' is lavender pink. 'Plena' has very full clusters of double flowers in deep blue violet. 'Texas Purple' blooms at an early age.

W. frutescens. AMERICAN WISTERIA. Native from Virginia to Florida and Texas. Leaves 7–12 in. long, divided into 9 to 15 leaflets. Less vigorous, thinner stems, later bloom, not as potentially destructive as the Asian species. Fragrant, pale lilac flowers with yellow blotch appear in dense clusters, 4–6 in. long, in late spring after leaf-out; blossoms are followed by 2–4-in. pods. White-flowered 'Nivea' blooms earlier than species.

W. macrostachya. KENTUCKY WISTERIA. Native from Illinois to Texas. A good choice for smaller gardens. Like *W. frutescens*, blooms among new leaves in late spring, after the Asian species bloom. Flowers are light blue to violet or blue purple, in 8–12-in.-long, fragrant, pendulous clusters. Shiny leaves divided usually into 9 leaflets, each to 3 in. long. The 4-in. pods are smooth, sometimes twisted. Less vigorous and better behaved than Asian species. 'Clara Mack' has white flowers.

🕊 **W. sinensis.** CHINESE WISTERIA. Leaves are 10–12 in. long, divided into 7 to 13 leaflets. Plants bloom before leaves expand in spring. Clusters of violet blue, slightly fragrant flowers are shorter (to 1 ft.) than those of Japanese wisteria but make quite a show by opening all at once nearly all along the cluster. Has escaped cultivation and smothers entire woods and hillsides in Lower South with blue blossoms in spring. 'Alba' is white-flowered form; 'Caroline' and 'Cooke's Special', grafted forms.

WOODSIA obtusa

BLUNT-LOBED WOODSIA, COMMON WOODSIA

Thelypteridaceae (Polypodiaceae)

FERN

✿ ZONES US, MS, LS

☼ ◑ FULL SUN OR LIGHT SHADE

◑ REGULAR WATER

Woodsia obtusa

Small deciduous fern. Fronds 12–15 in. long, 4 in. wide, bright green in shade, gray green in sun. May be once cut into deeply lobed segments or twice cut. Fronds produced throughout growing season. Likes well-drained soil that is neutral or even slightly alkaline. Use in woodland or rock garden.

WOOD SORREL. See OXALIS acetosella

WOODWARDIA

CHAIN FERN

Blechnaceae (Polypodiaceae)

FERNS

⚡ ZONES US, MS, LS, CS

☼ PART SHADE, EXCEPT AS NOTED

💧 AMPLE WATER

Woodwardia virginica

Medium to large, usually coarse-textured ferns with rich green fronds. Name comes from chainlike pattern of spore cases beneath frond segments. Most like shade beneath canopy of tall trees, but some will withstand full sun if roots are kept wet.

W. areolata. NETTED CHAIN FERN. Deciduous. Native to eastern, southeastern U.S. To 2½ ft. high, with deeply lobed fronds, the lobes finely toothed. Spore-bearing fronds are narrower. Can take considerable sun.

W. virginica. Deciduous. Native to eastern, southern U.S. To 1–2 ft. tall, with twice-cut fronds that are bronzy green when they emerge. Likes wet soil and can even grow with roots submerged.

WORMWOOD, COMMON. See ARTEMISIA absinthium

XANTHORHIZA
simplicissima

YELLOWROOT

Ranunculaceae

DECIDUOUS SHRUB

⚡ ZONES US, MS, LS, CS

☼ ☼ 🌑 SUN OR SHADE

💧 💧 💧 AMPLE TO MODERATE WATER

Xanthorhiza simplicissima

Native to eastern U.S. Thicket-forming ground cover to 2–3 ft. high. Lacy leaves like those of celery, usually divided into five toothed leaflets to 2½ in. long. Foliage is shiny bright green in summer, golden yellow and orange in fall; drops fairly late. Roots and inner bark are yellow. Nodding clusters of tiny, star-shaped purplish flowers before spring leaf-out are attractive though not showy.

Extremely cold-hardy. Prefers moist, well-drained, slightly acid soil, but tolerates heavy soils and dry sandy soils. Spreads fastest in damp, shady places; thrives along stream banks. Rejuvenate an overgrown planting by cutting it to the ground in spring. Plant root divisions in spring or fall. No serious pests or diseases.

YARROW. See ACHILLEA

YAUPON. See ILEX vomitoria

YEDDO HAWTHORN. See RAPHIOLEPIS umbellata

YELLOW ARCHANGEL. See LAMIUM galeobdolon

YELLOW BELLS, YELLOW ELDER, YELLOW TRUMPET FLOWER. See TECOMA stans

YELLOW DANCING GIRLS. See GLOBBA schomburgkii

YELLOW OLEANDER. See THEVETIA peruviana

YELLOWROOT. See XANTHORHIZA simplicissima

YELLOW SHRIMP PLANT. See PACHYSTACHYS lutea

YELLOW STAR GRASS. See HYPOXIS hirsuta

YELLOW TRUMPET VINE. See MACFADYENA unguis-cati

YELLOW WOOD. See CLADRASTIS lutea

YESTERDAY-TODAY-AND-TOMORROW. See BRUNFELSIA pauciflora 'Floribunda'

YEW. See TAXUS

YUCCA

Agavaceae

EVERGREEN PERENNIALS, SHRUBS, TREES

⚡ ZONES VARY BY SPECIES; OR INDOORS

☼ FULL SUN

💧 💧 WATER NEEDS VARY BY SPECIES

Yucca aloifolia

Yuccas grow over much of North America, and hardiness depends on species. All have tough, sword-shaped leaves and large clusters of white or whitish, rounded to bell-shaped flowers. Some are stemless, while others reach tree size. Best in well-drained soil.

Taller kinds make striking silhouettes, and even stemless species provide important vertical effects when in bloom. Some have stiff, sharp-pointed leaves; keep these away from walks, terraces, and other well-traveled areas.

Young plants of some species can be used as indoor plants. They withstand dry indoor atmosphere and will grow well in hot, sunny windows. Buy 1-gallon size or smaller; set out in ground when plants become too large for indoors. Successful indoors are *Y. aloifolia* (but beware of sharp-pointed leaves), *Y. elephantipes*, *Y. filamentosa*, *Y. gloriosa*, *Y. recurvifolia*.

🏵 **Y. aloifolia.** SPANISH BAYONET. Zones MS, LS, CS, TS. Native to South. Slow growth to 10 ft. or more; trunk may be single or branched, sometimes sprawling in picturesque effect. Stems densely clothed in sharp-pointed leaves to 2½ ft. long and 2 in. wide (spiny leaf tips present a hazard if plant is near walkway). Leaves are dark green; in 'Variegata', marked with yellowish white. White flowers (sometimes tinged purple) to 4 in. across, in dense, erect clusters to 2 ft. tall in summer. Moderate water.

Y. baccata. DACTIL YUCCA. Zones US, MS, LS, CS. Native to southwestern U.S. Foliage clump may have no stem or a short, prostrate one. Leaves to 2 ft. long, 2 in. wide, with fibers along the edges. Large, fleshy flowers in late spring are red brown outside, white inside, in dense, 2-ft.-long clusters. Fleshy fruit was eaten by Native Americans. Little water.

Y. elata. SOAPTREE YUCCA. Zones LS, CS, TS. Native to Southwest, northern Mexico. Slow growth to 6–20 ft. tall, with single or branched trunk. Leaves to 4 ft. long, ½ in. wide. Tall spikes of white flowers in summer. Little water.

Y. elephantipes (Y. gigantea). GIANT YUCCA. Zones CS, TS. Native to Mexico. Fast growing (to 2 ft. per year), eventually 15–30 ft. tall, usually with several trunks. Leaves 4 ft. long, 3 in. wide, dark rich green. Striking silhouette alone or combined with other big-scale foliage plants; out of scale in smaller gardens. Large spikes of creamy white flowers in spring. Does best in good, well-drained soil with regular water.

Y. filamentosa. ADAM'S NEEDLE. Zones US, MS, LS, CS. Native to Southeast. Stemless. Stiff leaves 2½ ft. long, 1 in. wide, with long, loose fibers at edges. Blooms late spring–summer with , lightly fragrant, yellowish white flowers, 2–3 in. wide, carried in tall, narrow clusters 4–7 ft. or taller. Looks similar to *Y. flaccida* and *Y. smalliana*. One of the most cold-hardy and widely planted yuccas. 'Bright Edge' has leaves edged in yellow; 'Concava Variegata', with cream-edged leaves tinted pink in cold weather; 'Garland Gold' leaves with gold center stripe; 'Ivory Tower', with out-facing rather than drooping flowers. Moderate water.

Y. flaccida. Zones US, MS, LS, CS. Native to Southeast. Stemless. Differs from *Y. filamentosa* in having less rigid leaves, straight fibers on leaf edges, and somewhat shorter flower clusters. Moderate water.

Y. glauca. SOAPWEED. Zones US, MS, LS. Native to central and southwestern U.S. Stiff, narrow, 1–2½-ft.-long leaves form a clump 3–4 ft. wide. Stem is low or prostrate. Leaves are grayish green, edged with a hairline of white and a few thin threads. White summer flowers bloom on a spike 4–5 ft. tall. Moderate water. ▶

Y

Y. gloriosa. MOUND-LILY YUCCA, SPANISH DAGGER, SOFT-TIP YUCCA. Zones US, MS, LS, CS. Native to Southeast. Much like *Y. aloifolia;* generally multitrunked to 10 ft. tall. Plant is usually stemless. Leaf points are soft and will not penetrate skin. Summer bloom. Good green color blends well with tropical-looking, lush plants. Needs moderate water; too much moisture may produce black areas on leaf margins.

Y. pallida. PALE-LEAF YUCCA. All zones. Native to Texas. Low-growing, small rosettes of 1–2-ft.-long, pale blue-green leaves with yellow margins and spine at tip. Foliage clump is usually no more than 1 ft. tall, but branched flower spike can be 6–7 ft. high. Moderate to little water.

Y. recurvifolia (Y. pendula). CURVE-LEAF YUCCA. Zones US, MS, LS, CS. Native to Southeast. Single, unbranched trunk to 6–10 ft. tall; may be lightly branched in age. Can be cut back to stay single trunked. Spreads by offsets into large groups. Beautiful blue-gray-green leaves are 2–3 ft. long, 2 in. wide, sharply bent downward. Leaf tips spined but bend to touch; they are not dangerous. Less stiff and metallic looking than most yuccas. Large white flowers in late spring or early summer are borne in loose, open clusters 3–5 ft. tall. Easy to grow in all garden conditions. Moderate water.

Y. rostrata. Zones CS, TS. Native to Mexico, extreme southwestern Texas. Notable feature is the trunk: 6–12 ft. tall, 5–8 in. thick, covered with soft gray fuzz (fibers remaining from old leaf bases). Needle-pointed leaves to 2 ft. long, ½ in. wide. Blooms in autumn, bearing 2-ft. clusters of white flowers on a 2-ft. stalk. Moderate to little water.

Y. rupicola. TWISTED-LEAF YUCCA. All zones. Native to Texas. Clump-forming yucca, to 3 ft. high and wide, with sharp-pointed, green leaves, to 2 ft. long, that are straight when young but that twist with age. Creamy white, tinged yellow-green, bell-shaped flowers open on 3–8-ft.-tall spikes. Moderate to little water.

Y. smalliana. ADAM'S NEEDLE, BEAR'S GRASS. Zones US, MS, LS, CS. Native to southeastern and south-central U.S. Like *Y. filamentosa,* but has narrower, flatter leaves and smaller individual flowers. Moderate water.

Y. thompsoniana. THOMPSON'S YUCCA. All zones. Native to Texas. Tree, 6–10 ft. tall, with asymmetrical rosette of thin, blue-green, 1-ft.-long leaves at top and old brown leaves hanging from trunk. Trunk may be branched. White to cream flowers are tinged green at base of petals, carried on 4–5 ft. spike. Moderate water.

Y. treculeana. SPANISH DAGGER. All zones. Native to Texas and Mexico. Simple or branched tree, 10–15 ft. tall, topped with symmetrical rosettes of sharp-pointed, stiff, thick leaves, 2½–4 ft. long. Flowers are white or purple tinged. They open on 3-ft. spikes. Moderate to little water.

ZABEL LAUREL. See PRUNUS laurocerasus 'Zabeliana'

🏛 ZAMIA

Zamiaceae

CYCADS

🗡 ZONES CS, TS; OR INDOORS

◑ FILTERED SHADE

◖◗ REGULAR TO MODERATE WATER

Zamia pumila

Of the 100 or so species, only the following two are often seen. They have short trunks usually marked with scars from old leaf bases; trunks may be completely or partially buried. Circular crowns of leaves resemble stiff fern fronds or small palm fronds. Grow in fast-draining soil amply enriched with organic material. Outdoor plants need filtered shade; house plants need strong light. Slow growing and costly, but plants will last many years with good care.

Z. furfuracea. CARDBOARD PALM. Native to Mexico. Short, sometimes subterranean trunk. Fronds to 3 ft. long (usually less) with up to 12 pairs (usually fewer) of extremely stiff, leathery, dark green leaflets to 4½ in. long, 1½ in. wide. Leaflets may have a few teeth toward the tip.

Z. pumila (Z. floridana). COONTIE, FLORIDA ARROWROOT. Native to Florida, Cuba, and West Indies. Short trunk is largely below soil level. Fronds to 3 ft. long, with as many as 30 pairs of dark green leaflets.

Leaflets can grow to 5 in. long, are narrower than those of *Z. furfuracea.* Good seaside plant. Tolerates salt spray.

Zamiaceae. This family is closely related to the Cycadaceae, differing only in technical details; both families are generally considered to be cycads. *Ceratozamia, Dioon,* and *Zamia* are representatives.

ZANTEDESCHIA

CALLA

Araceae

RHIZOMES

🗡 ZONES CS, TS; OR DIG AND STORE; OR GROW IN POTS

☼ ◑ FULL SUN OR PARTIAL SHADE

● REGULAR WATER DURING GROWTH AND BLOOM

Zantedeschia aethiopica

Native to South Africa. Basal clumps of long-stalked, shiny, rich green, arrow- or lance-shaped leaves, sometimes spotted white. Flower bract (spathe) surrounds central spike (spadix) that is tightly covered with tiny true flowers.

Common calla (*Z. aethiopica*) is basically evergreen, but goes partly dormant even in the Tropical South. It is soil tolerant and will thrive in moist, even boggy, soil all year. It cannot withstand storage and so should be grown as a container plant where winter temperatures fall below 10°F.

The other species described here die to the ground yearly. They need slightly acid soil and regular water during growth and bloom, followed by a resting period in which, ideally, water is withheld. In rainy climates, rhizomes will tolerate moisture if soil is well drained. Store potted rhizomes dry in their containers. Beyond their hardiness range, rhizomes of deciduous species can be dug and stored over winter, then replanted in spring.

Where callas are hardy, plant all types in fall, setting rhizomes of common calla 4–6 in. deep, those of other species 2 in. deep. Leave undisturbed until overcrowding causes a decline in vigor and bloom quality. Elsewhere, plant in spring. Lift rhizomes in fall in cold-winter areas.

Z. aethiopica. COMMON CALLA. Forms large clump of unspotted deep green leaves that are 1½ ft. long, 10 in. wide. Pure white or creamy white, 8-in.-long spathes on 3-ft. stems appear mostly in spring and early summer. 'Green Goddess' is a robust selection with large spathes that are white at the base, green toward the tip. 'Hercules', larger than species, has big spathes that open flat, curve backward. 'Childsiana', baby common calla, is 1 ft. tall. 'Minor' grows 1½ ft. tall, with 4-in. spathes.

Z. albomaculata. SPOTTED CALLA. Grows to 2 ft. high, with bright green, white-spotted leaves 1–1½ ft. long, 10 in. wide. Creamy yellow or white, 4–5-in.-long spathes have purplish crimson blotch at base. Spring–summer bloom.

Z. elliottiana. GOLDEN CALLA. To 1½–2 ft., with bright green, white-spotted leaves 10 in. long, 6 in. wide. Spathes 4–5 in. long, changing from greenish yellow to rich golden yellow, late spring or early summer. Tolerates full sun.

Z. pentlandii. Resembles *Z. albomaculata,* but leaves unspotted and spathes (5 in. long) deep golden yellow with a purple blotch at the base.

Z. rehmannii. RED or PINK CALLA. To 1–1½ ft., with narrow, lance-shaped, unspotted green leaves 1 ft. long. Pink or rosy pink spathes to 4 in. long in spring. 'Superba', a deeper pink, improved selection, is generally sold rather than species. Hybrids of this and other callas are available; flowers range through pinks and yellows to orange and buff tones, with some purplish and lavender tones on yellow grounds.

ZEBRA GRASS. See MISCANTHUS sinensis 'Zebrinus'

ZEBRA PLANT. See APHELANDRA squarrosa, CALATHEA zebrina

SOUTHERN HERITAGE PLANTS

IDENTIFIED BY SYMBOL 🏛

ZEBRINA pendula
(Tradescantia zebrina)

WANDERING JEW

Commelinaceae

PERENNIAL

✈ ZONE TS; OR INDOORS

◐ ● PARTIAL OR FULL SHADE

💧 REGULAR WATER

Zebrina pendula

Has much the same growth habit and leaf shape as *Tradescantia fluminensis* but is not as hardy. Small clusters of flowers are purplish rose and white. Known mostly in its variegated forms. 'Purpusii' has leaves of dark red or greenish red; 'Quadricolor' has purplish green leaves with longitudinal bands of white, pink, and carmine red. Other selections add white, pink, and cream to prevailing colors.

Use as ground cover in shady, frost-free sites. Good container plants for patio or house. When selecting a location indoors, remember that variegated plants need more light than all-green ones.

ZELKOVA serrata

JAPANESE ZELKOVA, SAWLEAF ZELKOVA

Ulmaceae

DECIDUOUS TREE

✈ ZONES US, MS, LS

☼ FULL SUN

💧💧 REGULAR TO MODERATE WATER

Zelkova serrata

Closely related to elms and sometimes used as a substitute for the ill-fated American elm, which has fallen victim to Dutch elm disease. (Zelkova, too, can get the disease, but the infection is rarely fatal.) A good shade tree, it grows at a moderate to fast rate, eventually reaching a height and spread of 60 ft. or more. Silhouette ranges from urn shaped to quite spreading. Has smooth gray bark; on old trees, bark often flakes off to show orange patches. Leaves 2–3½ in. long, 1½ in. wide; similar to those of elm but rougher in texture, with sawtooth margins. Fall foliage color varies from yellow to dark red to dull reddish brown. Garden centers offer several selections that approach the vase shape of American elm; of these, 'Halka' is the fastest growing and best elm look-alike. 'Green Vase' has a narrower vase shape than the vigorous 'Village Green'.

Takes wide range of soils. Water deeply to encourage deep rooting; established trees are fairly tolerant of drought, wind. You will need to train and prune young trees to establish a good framework; thin out crowded ascending branches. Foliage may be visited by Japanese beetles and by elm leaf beetles if local elms have died.

ZENOBIA pulverulenta

DUSTY ZENOBIA

Ericaceae

SEMIEVERGREEN TO DECIDUOUS SHRUB

✈ ZONES US, MS, LS, CS

◑ PARTIAL SHADE

💧 💧💧 AMPLE TO REGULAR WATER

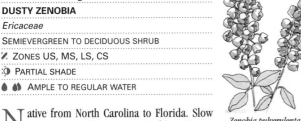

Zenobia pulverulenta

Native from North Carolina to Florida. Slow growth to 2–4 ft. or possibly 6 ft. tall, with open, loose, arching habit. Pale green leaves are 1–2 in. long, half as wide; new growth heavily dusted with bluish white powder for a pearly gray effect. Fall foliage is yellowish with a red tinge. White, bell-shaped, anise-scented flowers, ½ in. wide, in loose clusters, late spring–early summer. Sometimes spreads by underground stems. Needs well-drained, acid soil.

☂ ZEPHYRANTHES

RAIN LILY, ZEPHYR FLOWER, FAIRY LILY

Amaryllidaceae

BULBS

✈ ZONES VARY BY SPECIES; OR GROW IN POTS

☼ FULL SUN

💧 REGULAR WATER DURING GROWTH AND BLOOM

Zephyranthes candida

Clumps of grassy leaves give rise to slender, hollow stems, each bearing a single funnel-shaped flower with six segments. Flowers of some kinds resemble lilies; those of other types look like crocuses. In the wild, flowers bloom after a rain (hence the common name, "rain lily"), and they may appear in the garden after a good soaking.

Need little care. Pretty in rock garden or foreground of border. Excellent pot plant for patio or greenhouse. Plant in late summer or early fall; set bulbs 1–2 in. deep. In the Upper South, mulch hardier species heavily over winter. Container plants bloom better when somewhat pot-bound.

Z. atamasco. ATAMASCO LILY. Zones US (milder parts), MS, LS, CS, TS. Native to Southeast. Semievergreen leaves to 1½ ft. by ¼ in. Pink-striped buds open to fragrant, crocus-like, pure white blossoms in midspring.

Z. candida. WHITE RAIN LILY. Zones US (milder parts), MS, LS, CS, TS. Large clumps of glossy evergreen leaves to 1 ft. long. Glossy-textured, crocus-like flowers are 2 in. long, pure white outside, tinged rose inside, borne singly on stems as long as leaves. Blooms in late summer, early fall.

Z. citrina. YELLOW RAIN LILY. Zones LS, CS, TS. About the same size as *Z. candida* and blooms at the same time but bears fragrant yellow flowers.

Z. grandiflora. PINK RAIN LILY. Zones LS, CS, TS. Lily-like, 4-in.-wide, rose pink flowers on 8-in. stems in summer. Blossoms are flat at midday, close in afternoon. Leaves to 1 ft. long.

Z. hybrids. Zones LS, CS, TS. Most widely offered is *Z. ajax* (a cross between *Z. candida* and *Z. citrina*), a free-flowering plant with light yellow blossoms. Other hybrids available from mail-order specialists include 'Alamo', with deep rose pink flowers flushed yellow; 'Apricot Queen', yellow flowers stained pink; 'Prairie Sunset', large light yellow flowers suffused with pink; and 'Ruth Page', rich pink blooms.

Z. treatiae. Zones CS, TS. Native to Florida. Pure white, crocus-like flowers open from red buds. Blooms 2 to 4 weeks before *Z. atamasco.* Gray-green leaves are extremely slender, reach 1 ft. long.

ZEPHYR FLOWER. See ZEPHYRANTHES

ZINGIBER

COMMON GINGER, GINGER

Zingiberaceae

PERENNIALS WITH THICK RHIZOMES

✈ ZONES CS, TS

◑ PARTIAL SHADE

💧💧 WATER HEAVILY AFTER GROWTH STARTS

Zingiber officinale

Rhizomes are aromatic, knobby; one species, *Z. officinale*, is the source of ginger used in cooking. Both culinary and ornamental gingers need heat and humidity. Plant in rich, moist soil, placing rhizome just below soil surface. Pot culture is common. Water cautiously until top and root growth are active. Feed once a month. Plants are dormant in winter; rhizomes may rot in cold, wet soil. Plant with tree ferns, camellias, fuchsias, and begonias.

Z. officinale. COMMON GINGER. Native to southeast Asia. This is the ginger used in cooking. Stems 2–4 ft. tall. Narrow, glossy bright green leaves to 1 ft. long. Summer flowers (rarely seen) are yellowish green, with purple lip marked yellow; not especially showy. Buy roots (fresh, not dried) at grocery store in early spring; cut into 1–2-in.-long sections with

Z

well-developed growth buds. Let cut ends dry before planting. Allow several months for roots to reach some size, then harvest at any time.

Z. spectabile. BEEHIVE GINGER. Native to Malaysia. To 6 ft. tall. Deep green, slender-pointed leaves, 1–1½ ft. long. Showy inflorescence, to 1 ft. long, on 3-ft. stem, with overlapping yellow bracts that turn scarlet and yellowish flowers with black tips. Good cut flower.

Z. zerumbet. PINE CONE GINGER, SHAMPOO GINGER. Native to India and Malaysia. To 6 ft. tall. Dark green leaves, to 1 ft. long and 3 in. wide, broader than those of *Z. officinale*. Inflorescence is a 3–5-in. green cone that appears on a separate, short stalk in late summer, then turns brilliant red for 2 to 3 weeks. Small yellow flowers open between the bracts. 'Darcyi' (*Z. darceyi*) has cream-striped leaves. Good cut flower.

Zingiber zerumbet

Zingiberaceae. The ginger family contains tropical or subtropical perennials with fleshy rhizomes and canelike stems clothed with sheathing leafstalks; usually bear large leaves. Flowers are irregular in form, in spikes or heads, often showy or with showy bracts. Many are aromatic or have fragrant flowers. Includes *Alpinia*, ginger lily (*Costus, Hedychium*), and common ginger (*Zingiber*).

ZINNIA

Asteraceae (Compositae)

ANNUALS AND A PERENNIAL

☘ ALL ZONES

☼ FULL SUN

💧 REGULAR WATER, EXCEPT AS NOTED

Zinnia elegans

Longtime garden favorites for colorful, round flower heads in summer and early fall. Hot-weather plants, they do not gain from being planted early, but merely stand still until weather warms up. Subject to mildew if leaves are habitually wet at night. Sow seeds where plants are to grow (or set out plants) May–July. Give good garden soil; feed generously.

Z. angustifolia (Z. linearis). NARROW-LEAF ZINNIA. Annual. Compact, mounding plants to 16 in. tall. Leaves very narrow. Inch-wide flower heads are orange; each ray has a paler stripe. Blooms in 6 weeks from seed, continues late into fall. 'Classic' grows 8–12 in. tall, to 2 ft. wide. There are also white and yellow forms. Can be perennial in Tropical South. Good in hanging baskets. One of the best, longest-blooming, most carefree annuals. Does not need deadheading. Mildew not a problem, but this species may get spider mites in hot, dry weather.

🏵 **Z. elegans.** COMMON ZINNIA. Annual. Grows to 1–3 ft., leaves to 5 in., flower head size from less than 1 in. to as much as 5–7 in. Forms include full doubles, cactus flowered (with quilled rays), and crested (cushion center surrounded by rows of broad rays); colors include white, pink, salmon, rose, red, yellow, orange, lavender, purple, and green.

Many strains are available, from dwarf plants with small flowers to 3-ft. sorts with large blooms. The Mini series and Thumbelina strain are extra-dwarf types (to 6 in. tall). Other small-flowered kinds on larger (1-ft.) but still compact plants are Cupid and Buttons; still taller (to 2 ft.) but small flowered are the Lilliputs. Dreamland and Peter Pan strains have 3-in. blooms on bushy dwarf plants to 1 ft.; Whirligig has large bicolored flowers on 1½-ft. plants. Large-flowered strains with 2–3-ft. plants include Border Beauty, Burpeeana California Giants, Dahlia-flowered, Giant Cactus–flowered, Ruffles, State Fair, and Zenith. 'Rose Pinwheel', with single, daisy-type, rose pink flowers, is a 1½–2-ft.-tall hybrid between *Z. elegans* and *Z. angustifolia*. All are great for attracting butterflies, cutting, drying.

Z. grandiflora. ROCKY MOUNTAIN ZINNIA. Perennial in Zones CS, TS; annual elsewhere. Native to High Plains, the Southwest, Mexico. To 10 in.

tall, spreading by seeds or runners. Leaves to 1 in. long, ⅛ in. wide. Flower heads are 1½ in. wide, bright yellow with orange eye. In its native range, it will bloom spring–fall if watered during dry season. Very drought tolerant once established.

Z. haageana. ORANGE ZINNIA. Annual. Plants compact, 1–1½ ft. tall; narrow, 3-in. leaves. Double strains Persian Carpet (1 ft. tall) and Old Mexico (16 in. tall) have flowers in mahogany red, yellow, and orange, usually mixed in the same flower head. Colorful, long blooming.

ZIZIPHUS jujuba

CHINESE JUJUBE

Rhamnaceae

DECIDUOUS SMALL TREE

☘ ZONES US, MS, LS, CS

☼ FULL SUN

💧 MODERATE WATER

Ziziphus jujuba

Slow to moderate growth to eventual 20–30 ft. tall, with rounded habit. Usually grown as tree, but sometimes seen as large shrub. Spiny, gnarled, somewhat pendulous branches. Glossy bright green, 1–2-in.-long leaves with three prominent veins. Foliage may turn a good yellow in autumn. Clusters of small yellowish flowers bloom in late spring; these are followed in fall by shiny, reddish brown, ½–2-in.-long fruits with a sweet, apple-like flavor. Candied and dried, fruits resemble dates. Two thornless, grafted selections are 'Lang' (1½–2-in. fruits, bears young) and 'Li' (2-in. fruits).

Very decorative, but also tough—withstands drought, heat, saline and alkaline soils. Grows better in good garden soil. Thrives in lawns. Prune in winter to shape, encourage weeping habit, or reduce size.

ZOYSIA

Poaceae (Gramineae)

PERENNIAL LAWN GRASSES

☘ ZONES VARY BY SPECIES

☼ ◑ THRIVE IN SUN, TOLERATE SOME SHADE

💧💧 REGULAR TO MODERATE WATER

Zoysia japonica 'Meyer'

Among the South's best and most popular lawn grasses. These grasses are tough, pest resistant, drought tolerant, and withstand much wear. Green in summer, straw colored in winter. Started from sod or plugs. Spread more slowly and are more expensive than other warm-season grasses. Form dense carpet of turf that chokes out weeds. Mow at 1–2 in. Susceptibility to nematodes limits use in Florida.

Z. 'Cashmere'. Dark green, fine, dense turf, similar to 'Emerald', but softer. Most suitable for the Lower South, not cold-hardy.

Z. 'Emerald'. EMERALD ZOYSIA. Zones MS, LS, CS, TS. Hybrid between *Z. japonica, Z. tenuifolia*. Dense, fine-textured, medium green; beautiful beige in winter. Somewhat prickly to bare feet. Not hardy in Upper South.

Z. japonica. All zones. Several selections: 'Meyer' ('Z-52') is coarser than *Z.* 'Emerald', and even tougher. 'Meyer' is the preferred selection for the Upper South. Turns brown earliest in winter, turns green latest in spring. 'Belaire' is medium green, particularly cold-hardy, coarser textured than 'Meyer', and faster to establish. 'El Toro' resembles 'Meyer' but has a faster establishment rate, better color in cool season, and less thatch buildup.

Z. matrella. MANILA GRASS. Like Bermuda grass in color, texture. Holds color a little better than Meyer zoysia, but not as cold-hardy. Good in Lower, Coastal, and Tropical South. Susceptible to nematodes.

Z. tenuifolia. KOREAN GRASS. The finest-textured zoysia grass, but also the least cold-hardy. Recommended only for the Coastal and Tropical South. Can develop excessive thatch.

ZUCCHINI. See SQUASH

Z

Practical Gardening
DICTIONARY

On the following pages, you'll find a wealth of gardening knowledge—definitions of common gardening terms and techniques, information about plant growth, step-by-step techniques, and plenty of problem-solving tips and advice.

Each entry in the dictionary is listed alphabetically; to help you locate the more detailed entries—including advice on controlling specific pests, weeds, and diseases—page numbers are given below.

GARDENING TECHNIQUES

PEST CONTROL

WEED CONTROL

DISEASE CONTROL

VISUAL GUIDES

Acid Soil

An acid soil is one with a pH below 7. See Soil pH (p. 462).

Actual

In such phrases as "actual nitrogen," "actual" refers to the amount (by weight) of the specified nutrient in a fertilizer. For example, we sometimes recommend applying a certain amount of actual nitrogen. To find out how to calculate "actual" nutrient contents from fertilizer labels, see the illustration below.

Aeration

Loosening or puncturing the soil by mechanical means to increase water penetration and air permeability is called aeration. It can be as simple as cultivating around newly planted seedlings with a trowel or, in the case of lawns, can involve the use of a gas-powered machine that removes small cores of soil. Aeration usually improves plant growth.

Alkaline Soil

An alkaline soil is one with a pH above 7. See Soil pH (p. 462).

Annual

A plant that completes its life cycle in a year or less is called an annual. Seed germinates and the plant grows, blooms, sets seed, and dies—all in one growing season. Examples are most marigolds (*Tagetes*) and zinnias. The phrase "grow as an annual" means to sow seed or set out plants in spring after the last frost, enjoy their flowers or foliage from spring through autumn, and then pull them out or let the frosts kill them at the end of the year. Some plants that Coastal and Tropical South gardeners treat as annuals are planted in fall, grow and bloom during winter and spring, and then are killed by summer heat.

Think of annuals as the real workhorses of the garden. Their lives are short but extremely productive. Annuals can bloom for months, from the moment the plants bear flowers until they are cut down by frost. In areas of no or mild frosts, certain annuals can brighten a winter garden with blossoms.

Good soil, the foundation on which a successful annual planting is built, requires some advance preparation. See Planting Techniques: Seeds (p. 448).

Planting and timing. You may prefer to sow annual seeds or buy popular types already started at garden centers—sold in small individual containers, in packs of four or six, or in flats. See Planting Techniques: Annuals and Perennials (p. 449).

In the South, there are two principal times of year for planting annuals: early spring, for those that bloom in late spring, summer, and autumn (warm-season annuals); and late summer or autumn, for winter and early-spring bloomers (cool-season annuals). Both are periods of moderately cool temperatures preceding the sort of weather that favors development of annuals. Gardeners in cold-winter zones generally can plant only in spring to early summer.

To hasten growth and bloom warm-season annuals need to establish roots before really warm days come along. Set out cool-season annuals while days are still warm enough for good plant growth but nights are lengthening. If you set them out while days are longer than nights, they may perish or rush to maturity as stunted, poorly established plants. The Plant Selection Guide on page 45 lists annuals according to their season of bloom.

The secret to success with annuals is to keep the plants growing steadily by watering, fertilizing, and deadheading them.

Watering. Sprinkling is the easiest way to irrigate annuals, but not the best. It wastes a lot of water and can topple tall or weak-stemmed plants. Also, wetting the foliage can promote leaf diseases. A better method is to hold the hose end or nozzle down near the bases of the plants and gently, but thoroughly, soak the soil. More water will get to the roots, and you won't wet the foliage. Drip irrigation, using any of the various sorts of emitters available, is another option (see p. 470). And don't forget to mulch; this technique conserves soil moisture and keeps down weeds.

Fertilizing. Mixing a slow-release complete fertilizer into the soil before planting annuals generally supplies enough nutrients to last several months. If you can't dig up your bed, broadcast the fertilizer over the soil surface after planting. Repeat in about 6 weeks. For a spectacular show, supplement this with applications of water-soluble fertilizers at least every month. Use a bloom-booster fertilizer, such as 15-30-15 or 15-40-15, that contains 2 or 3 times as much phosphorus (the middle number) as nitrogen or potassium.

Deadheading. To keep blooms coming all season long, remove spent blossoms before the plant can begin seed formation (see p. 428).

WATER JUNKIES. *Many annuals sold at garden centers are water junkies. Because they receive all the water and fertilizer they can handle, they expect this care to continue. So they grow more leaves, stems, and flowers than their roots can normally support. When you plant them at home, however, they wilt and die unless you water them every day. Help water junkies break their thirsty habit by trimming them back by a third before planting. It gives them time to adjust to their new home and soon they'll be blooming profusely.*

Anthracnose. See Leaf Spot   p. 441

Ants

By themselves, ants are not serious garden pests, although some types may damage young seedlings, and nests of others may disturb lawns and planting beds. However, they are closely associated with honeydew (p. 436) produced by sucking insect pests and are often the most visible clue that the pest is present. Ants can also interfere with the effectiveness of biological controls. See Aphids (above, right) for control measures.

Fire ants, common in most of the South, do not directly damage plants but can be a serious

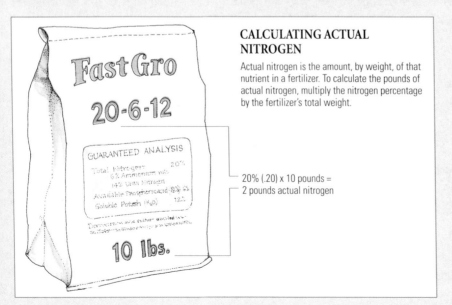

CALCULATING ACTUAL NITROGEN

Actual nitrogen is the amount, by weight, of that nutrient in a fertilizer. To calculate the pounds of actual nitrogen, multiply the nitrogen percentage by the fertilizer's total weight.

FastGro

20-6-12

GUARANTEED ANALYSIS
Total Nitrogen   20%

20% (.20) x 10 pounds =
2 pounds actual nitrogen

10 lbs.

nuisance because of their painful sting. Their raised mounds also disrupt lawns and planting beds. Try various techniques to make fire ants relocate their mounds, including drenching them with boiling or soapy water. Drenches containing pyrethrins (p. 445) or boric acid may also be effective. Some baits labeled for fire ants work, but they take time. The most effective control of fire ants is drenching or dusting the mound with an appropriately labeled pesticide, such as Dursban or diazinon (p. 445). Repeat applications may be necessary.

ANTS IN YOUR PANTS? *Except for fire ants, ants are most beneficial. These relentless predators dispatch a host of harmful insects. But when ants invade your home, how do you give them the heave-ho without using chemical insecticides? One way is to mix boric acid, a natural insecticide, with sugar, then place small amounts in ant trails and problem areas. The ants will carry the mixture back to their nest, share it with others, and eventually decimate the colony.*

Aphids

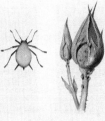

Aphids are soft, oval, pinhead- to match-head-size insects that cluster together on young shoots, buds, and leaves. They come in various colors, including green, pink, red, and black, with and without wings (see photograph, p. 454).

Numerous creatures keep aphid populations in check; often the best tactic is to let natural controls go to work. Lacewings, ladybird beetles, syrphid flies, predatory midges, parasitic wasps, and even lizards and some small birds are among the many natural aphid controls that may live in your garden. If you spray with a toxic insecticide, you risk killing the insect predators along with the aphids.

Controls. Fortunately, you can get rid of most aphids with a blast of water from the hose. For greater effectiveness, spray them with an insecticidal soap (p. 445).

The most troublesome aphids curl leaves around themselves or stay in protected places (inside a head of cabbage, for example). The best control for these aphids is anticipation: If you had them last year, expect them this year; hose or wash them off when the aphid colony is young and leaves are still open. You can also prevent aphids from reaching vegetables by planting under floating row covers (p. 459).

A dormant oil spray is effective in killing overwintering eggs of many species of aphids on trees and shrubs. On herbaceous plants, clean up old plant debris before growth starts in spring. If an aphid infestation is severe, spray with insecti-

dal soap, pyrethrin, rotenone, diazinon, malathion, or (on nonedible plants) Orthene.

Ants often maintain aphid colonies, fighting off parasites and predators to feed on the sticky honeydew aphids produce. Getting rid of the ants often permits natural aphid controls to reestablish themselves. To keep ants out of plants, encircle trunks with bands of a sticky ant barrier, put out diazinon or Dursban granules (p. 445), or use poisonous ant baits.

Armadillos

These unusual looking mammals can become pests when they dig through lawn and garden hunting for grubs. The best way to solve an armadillo problem is to eliminate the grubs—larvae of beetles like the Japanese beetle (p. 436), and rose chafer (p. 459).

Another method of control is to enclose the yard or garden with a fence or wire screen, at least 2 feet aboveground, and buried at least a foot underground.

Backfill

This is soil returned to a planting hole after a plant's roots are in position. In very sandy or heavy clay soils, mix the backfill with peat moss, compost, or ground bark to loosen it and improve its texture.

Bacterial Wilt

A common disease of cucumbers, bacterial wilt can also damage muskmelons, squash, and pumpkins. Prevalent during cool, moist weather, it is usually spread by cucumber beetles feeding on plant foliage. Symptoms include rapid wilting and death of young seedlings. Older plants may wilt and die all at once, or more slowly.

Check for the disease by cutting a stem near the base. If thin strands of milky ooze form as you pull apart the end of the stem, it's probably bacterial wilt.

Once a plant gets infected, it will not recover. However, you can lessen the chance of infection by reducing the cucumber-beetle population (see p. 426) and by removing and destroying infected plants. Some vegetable selections have varying degrees of resistance to bacterial wilt.

Bagworms

Bagworms, which are really moth larvae, or caterpillars, feed on the foliage of many trees and shrubs, particularly junipers. They usually start from the top and work their way down, leaving devastation in their wake. See photograph, p. 454.

The individual caterpillars are not as noticeable as the dangling silken bags they create and drag along as they feed. During winter, the bags are filled with as many as 1,000 eggs. In spring,

the small brown caterpillars hatch and disperse to feed, often blowing from tree to tree on thin threads. In summer, each caterpillar tethers its bag to a twig and enters to pupate. In a few days the moths emerge. The wingless females remain in the bag, where the black-winged males join them. After mating and laying eggs, the females die.

Spraying trees with *Bacillus thuringiensis (Bt,* see p. 420) is the preferred control for bagworms; however, it is effective only when the young caterpillars are feeding in spring. On smaller plants, hand-pick the bags in winter and burn them; be thorough to get adequate control. Malathion, diazinon, Sevin, and Orthene (on nonedibles) are also effective (p. 445).

Balled-and-Burlapped

Garden centers sell balled-and-burlapped (B-and-B) trees from late autumn to early spring. The name comes from the large ball of soil around the roots, which is wrapped in burlap. See Planting Techniques: Trees and Shrubs (p. 449) for planting instructions.

Bare-Root

In winter and early spring, garden centers offer many deciduous shrubs and trees, and some perennials, with all soil removed from their roots. For planting instructions, see Planting Techniques: Trees and Shrubs (p. 449).

Bedding Plants

Plants (mainly annuals) suitable for massing in beds for their colorful flowers or foliage are called bedding plants.

Beneficial Insects. See Visual Guide to Identifying Biological Controls   p. 420

Biennial

These plants complete their life cycle in 2 years. Two familiar biennials are foxglove *(Digitalis)* and hollyhock *(Alcea).* Typically, you plant seeds in spring or set out seedling plants in summer or autumn. They flower the following spring, then set seed and die.

Biological Pest Control. See Visual Guide to Identifying Biological Controls; and Pest Management   pp. 420, 445

Bird Protection

Most gardeners see birds as friends rather than enemies, but certain birds (crows in particular) at certain times can be nuisances, eating newly planted seeds, tender seedlings, transplants, fruits, nuts, or berries.

▶ page 421

Visual Guide to Identifying
BIOLOGICAL
CONTROLS

The use of living organisms such as beneficial insects to destroy garden pests is called biological control. It is an effective way to reduce plant damage without using strong chemicals or sprays. Here are beneficial insects that either naturally occur in gardens or that you can release to reduce pest populations. Also described are organisms that kill insect pests and a natural hormone product that hopelessly confuses them. For more information, see Pest Management (p. 445).

Scale Parasites
One tiny parasitic wasp *(Aphytis melinus)* attacks and kills red scale and other types of hard scale. *Metaphycus helvolus* attacks black scale and other hemispherical scales.

Cryptolaemus Beetle
The larvae and adults of the cryptolaemus beetle, a ladybird-beetle relative, feed on mealybugs.

Lacewings
Commonly found in gardens, both lacewing larvae and adults feed on a variety of insects and mites.

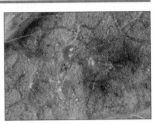

Predator Mites
Various species of mites feed on spider mites and sometimes thrips, but do no damage to plants.

Fly Parasites
Tiny wasps (many species) that lay their eggs in the pupae of several types of flies, including houseflies, are very effective and most useful in controlling flies on ranches or farms.

Ladybird Beetle
The ladybird beetle (or ladybug, as most people know it) occurs naturally in gardens. Larvae (left) and adults (right) feed on aphids, mealybugs, small worms, spider mites, and similar soft-bodied insects. Releasing ladybird beetles in your garden is often not effective because they fly away. They also migrate annually. Release them in the evening, as daylight encourages them to fly away.

Whitefly Parasite
Several species of small wasps attack immature stages of whiteflies. The wasps are most effective in greenhouses. Control of the greenhouse whitefly using *Encarsia formosa* requires average temperatures above 75°F.

Trichogramma Wasps
Larvae of the tiny trichogramma wasp develop within the eggs of caterpillars and eat their way out, destroying the eggs. Adult wasps then fly off to find new eggs to parasitize. Repeated releases are usually necessary to reduce a caterpillar infestation.

Chemical messengers
Insects emit special chemicals to communicate. Two general groups are available as pest-control devices known as semiochemicals: pheromones, which affect communications between insects, and kairomones, which affect feeding behavior. Both attract insects: sometimes to trap or confuse pests; at other times, to lure beneficial insects into the garden. Semiochemicals are very target specific and are available for several common pests.

Parasitic Nematodes
Parasitic nematodes include several species of microscopic worms that seek out and eat their way into more than 250 soil-dwelling pests, such as grubs, weevils, sod webworms, and carpenter worms. Read directions carefully. Soil conditions and release techniques must be just right for the nematodes to be effective.

Bacillus thuringiensis (Bt)
The bacterium *Bt* controls caterpillars (including wormlike budworms). After eating *Bt*-treated leaves, caterpillars die within 2 to 3 days. You can use *Bt* on all food crops up to harvest. Mixing it in alkaline water (pH 8 or higher) reduces its effectiveness. Apply it when caterpillars are small; reapply in 3 to 14 days. The strain for most caterpillars is *B. t. kurstaki.* Other available strains include *B. t. israeliensis* for mosquitoes and *B. t. tenebrionis* for Colorado potato beetle and elm-leaf beetle. *Bt* is sold under several trade names (p. 445).

Reflective tape, fluttering objects, and scarecrows may reduce damage briefly, but birds soon become accustomed to them and resume their activities. The only surefire solution is to use screen or nylon or plastic netting material.

Broad-mesh netting (¾ inch) is popular for trees because it easily lets in air, water, and sunlight. Enclose fruit trees with nets 2 or 3 weeks before fruit ripens; tie nets off where the lowest branches spring from the trunk. Remove netting to harvest the fruit.

For protecting sprouting seedlings and maturing vegetables, floating row covers (p. 459) are the easiest to use because they need no supports. Other options—which need to be held up with stakes and string, in tent fashion—are fine-mesh screen and nylon netting. If crows are the problem, fold chicken wire into a tent shape over the rows.

Several species of sapsuckers, a type of woodpecker, peck holes in the trunks of trees with sugary sap, such as apples and maples. These birds can create so many holes that the abundance of flowing sap and damaged bark weaken the tree, and it can die or be attacked by other pests.

The size of most trees makes them difficult to protect from sapsuckers. If you can get up high enough, you can wrap the trunk with burlap or smear a sticky ant barrier, such as Tanglefoot, around the holes.

In most areas it is illegal to shoot or poison nuisance birds. Check with your Cooperative Extension Office for alternative control measures for local bird species.

Black Spot. See Leaf Spot; and Visual Guide to Identifying Plant Problems   pp. 441, 456

Blanching

Tying outer leaves over the inner head or leaves of a plant to produce a lighter color or a milder flavor is termed blanching. It is most often done to keep heads of cauliflower white. See p. 139 for information on how to blanch asparagus spears.

Bolt

Annual flowers and vegetables that produce an elongated flower stalk are said to bolt. This happens most often when you plant cool-season annuals and vegetables too late in the year or when hot weather hastens growth.

Bonsai

Bonsai (the word is Japanese) is one of the fine arts of gardening: growing carefully trained, dwarfed plants in containers selected to harmonize with them. The objective is to create in miniature scale a tree or landscape; often the dwarfed trees take on the appearance of very old, gnarled specimens. To get the desired effect, branches must be wired and pruned, and the roots must be trimmed.

Borers and Bark Beetles

In their larval stage, numerous types of beetles and some types of clearwing moth tunnel beneath or bore into the bark of many trees and shrubs. There they feed, girdling the trunk, cutting off the flow of water and nutrients, and weakening the plant structurally.

Borers and bark beetles tend to attack trees stressed by drought, poor growing conditions, or wounds. The first signs of infestation are usually wilting, yellowing foliage on a single branch or limb. With borers you can also see small holes bordered by sawdust, excrement, or sap. The bark around the hole may feel spongy. Eventually the whole plant dies. Some species of borers and bark beetles attack below the soil line; then the evidence may be at the base of the plant. Many tree species are susceptible to borer attack, particularly mountain ash, European birch, lilac, dogwood, pine, and fruits, nuts, and cane berries.

Prevention is the best way to control borers and bark beetles. Keep plants healthy. Avoid wounding tree trunks with string trimmers.

If borers or beetles are present, prune out infested branches, making sure to cut well into healthy wood. Cutting out individual borers with a knife may do more damage than good. Remove and destroy borer-infested pines immediately.

If timed properly to coincide with laying of eggs by adults, chemicals can help prevent infestations of bark beetles and borers. Use Dursban, lindane (if available), and Thiodan (p. 445).

Botrytis

Botrytis, also known as gray mold, is a fungus common in cool, moist weather. It usually starts out on plant debris and weakened or overcrowded plants and quickly spreads to other plants by splashing water or rain. Small brown lesions gradually grow larger, turning mushy and coating the plant with fuzzy gray mold. Fruit, foliage, stems, and flowers may be infected. Many plants are susceptible, especially strawberries, onions, tomatoes, peonies, camellias, tulips, lilies, and begonias.

To prevent botrytis, make sure plants have adequate room to grow and good air circulation. Rotate vegetable crops often. Water in the morning so plants dry quickly. Remove diseased plants or plant parts as soon as you see them. Keep the garden clean. Prevent strawberries from touching the ground by planting through a plastic or thick organic mulch. Buy certified, disease-free onion sets.

Daconil (p. 429) is an effective fungicide for treating botrytis. Use only for the plants listed on the label.

Bracts

Modified leaves called bracts may grow just below a flower or flower cluster. These are usually green, but in some cases they are conspicuous and colorful, constituting what people regard as "flowers"; examples are bougainvillea, dogwood, and poinsettia.

Broadcast

To scatter seed or fertilizer over the soil. See Planting Techniques: Seeds (p. 448).

Broad-Leafed

The phrase "broad-leafed evergreen" refers to a plant that has green foliage all year but is not an evergreen conifer (such as a juniper) with needlelike or scalelike foliage. A broad-leafed weed is any weed that is not a grass.

Brown Patch

This fungal lawn disease is common during hot, humid weather. Lawns that have been overwatered, excessively fertilized, or have a thick layer of thatch are most susceptible. It is most serious on centipede and St. Augustine lawns, but can infect other grasses.

Like the name suggests, the symptoms of brown patch are large, irregular, circular brownish to gray dead spots up to several feet in diameter. The grass blades along edges of the patches appear water soaked, turn purplish green then brown. Grass in the center of the patch may actually recover, turn green, and give the patches a halo or smoke-ring appearance.

The best way to cure brown patch is to water deeply but infrequently, aerate the lawn to improve drainage, and avoid overuse of nitrogen fertilizers. Reducing the amount of shade by pruning trees overhead will also help. Several fungicides, including Daconil (p. 429), can control brown patch.

Bud

The word "bud" has several definitions. A flower bud is one that develops into a blossom. A growth bud may be at the tip of a stem (terminal) or along its sides (lateral); these buds will produce new leafy growth.

Bulbs

Bulbs are a specialized group of perennial plants. Following popular usage, we use this term for a number of plants that are not true bulbs—corms, rhizomes, tubers, and tuberous roots. They all have a thickened underground storage organ, which almost guarantees that the bulb you purchase in summer or autumn will bloom the following spring: all the nutrients the plant needs to complete its

B

THE FIVE BULB TYPES

True bulb and bulblet. A true bulb is a short underground stem (on solid basal plate) surrounded by modified fleshy leaves (scales) that protect and store food for use by the embryonic plant. Outer scales are dry and form papery covering (tunic).

The new bulb (often called an offset) forms from a lateral bud on the basal plate; the old bulb may die or, like daffodils, keep coming back each year. Separate the bulblets from the mother bulb and replant to increase stock of the original plant.

So-called bulbils are small bulbs that form in the axils of leaves, in flowers, or on the stems of certain bulbous plants.

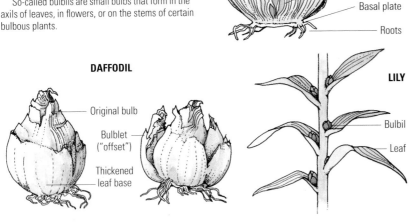

ONION
- Tunic
- Fleshy leaves (scales)
- Embryonic plant
- Basal plate
- Roots

DAFFODIL
- Original bulb
- Bulblet ("offset")
- Thickened leaf base

LILY
- Bulbil
- Leaf

Corm and cormel. A corm is a swollen, underground stem base—solid tissue (in contrast to bulb scales) but with a basal plate from which roots grow. Growth point is on the corm's top; many corms have tunics that consist of dried bases of previous season's leaves. An individual corm lasts just one year. New corms form from axillary buds on the top of an old corm as it completes its growth cycle. Fingernail-size cormels take 2 to 3 years to flower; larger corms should bloom the following year.

GLADIOLUS
- Dead leaf bases
- Basal plate
- Roots
- Cormels
- New corms
- Old corm
- Roots

Rhizome. A rhizome is a thickened stem that grows partially or entirely beneath the ground. Roots generally develop from the underside; the principal growing point is at the tip, although additional growing points will form along the rhizome's length. To divide, cut into sections that have these visible points.

CALLA
- Growth bud ("eye")

IRIS
- Leaves
- Scalelike leaves
- Roots
- Growth bud ("eye")

Tuber. A tuber is a swollen, underground stem base, like a corm, but it lacks the corm's distinct organization. There is no basal plate, so roots can grow from all sides; there are multiple growth points over the upper surface—each is a scalelike leaf with a growth bud in its axil. An individual tuber can last for many years. Some (*Cyclamen*, for example) continually enlarge, but never produce offsets; others (such as *Caladium*) form protuberances that you can remove and plant separately. Divide tubers by cutting into sections that have growth buds.

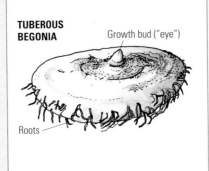

TUBEROUS BEGONIA
- Growth bud ("eye")
- Roots

Tuberous roots. Tuberous roots are actual roots (rather than stems) that store nutrients. In a full-grown dahlia, daylily, or other tuberous-rooted plant, the roots grow in a cluster, with the swollen tuberous portions radiating out from a central point. Growth buds are at the bases of old stems rather than on the tuberous roots. To divide, cut apart so that each division contains both roots and part of the stem's base with one or more growth buds.

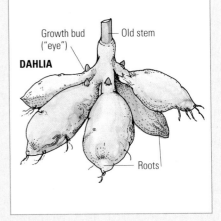

DAHLIA
- Growth bud ("eye")
- Old stem
- Roots

life cycle are in this organ, waiting for the right combination of moisture and soil temperature to trigger the cycle.

Planting. Although the bulb you purchase from a garden center or mail-order supplier is likely to flourish its first year, performance in subsequent years will depend on the care you give it. Most bulbs prefer soil that drains well yet retains a certain amount of water. See Soil Texture (p. 461).

When planting true bulbs and most corms, the rule of thumb is to dig a hole about three times as deep as the bulb's greatest diameter.

(To determine planting depths for specific bulbs and other bulblike plants, see the individual plant entries in the Plant Encyclopedia.) If you will be planting many bulbs in one bed, it may be easier to dig a trench or to excavate the entire bed to the desired depth than to dig individual holes for each bulb.

Fertilizer. At planting time, add a complete bulb fertilizer. Ones with controlled-release nitrogen are very effective. See Fertilizers (p. 431). If you plant bulbs in individual holes, put up to a tablespoonful of fertilizer at the bottom of each hole, then cover with about 2 inches of soil and plant the bulb. Otherwise, dig fertilizer into the bottom of the trench or excavated bed.

Water. Once you set all the bulbs in place and cover them with soil, soak the area thoroughly. In some regions this initial watering, along with subsequent rain, will supply all the moisture bulbs will need until their leaves poke above the soil surface. But if you live in an arid climate or have an unusually dry winter, you must soak the bulbs periodically throughout the winter and into the blooming season. Water summer-flowering bulbs at least until they have finished blooming.

Water deeply and mulch to retain moisture.

Care. Bulb plantings established for a year or more may benefit from application of bulb fertilizer at the start of the growing season (see Perennial, p. 444). However, it is even more important to apply fertilizer after the blooms have faded.

When a bulb has finished flowering, much of its stored nutrients are depleted. It must replenish those nutrients if it is to perform well the next year. For this reason, it is essential to leave the foliage on the plant, even if it begins to look unsightly, until it turns yellow and you can pull it easily off. The leaves continue to manufacture food for the plant. Cutting them off prematurely amounts to removing or reducing the next year's blossoms.

Furthermore, fertilizer application at this time helps bulbs form not only next year's flowers but also create new bulbs that will increase the planting. Phosphorus and potassium—the nutrients emphasized in "bulb food"—are most useful now, although they must reach the root zone to be fully effective (see Nutrients, Basic, p. 443). In an established planting, you may be able only to scatter fertilizer over the soil surface, scratch it in, and hope that some phosphorus and potassium will reach the roots. Where bulbs are far enough apart or in rows, you may be able to get fertilizer deep into the soil by digging narrow trenches or holes, 8 inches deep, placing fertilizer at the bottom, and filling them with soil.

FOILING LITTLE ALVIN. *If chipmunks and other small rodents keep eating your crocus and other small bulbs and corms, start saving those plastic mesh strawberry or blueberry cartons when you buy berries at the supermarket. When you plant, put the bulbs in the bottom of the hole, then place the carton upside down on top of them and fill in the hole. The flowers and foliage will come through the holes in the mesh, but rodents can't find their way in.*

Caliche

A soil condition found in some areas of the arid Southwest, caliche is a deposit of calcium carbonate (lime) beneath the soil surface. See also Hardpan (p. 435).

Cambium. See Plant Anatomy and Growth p. 447

Canker. See Gummosis and Cankers p. 435

Caterpillars

Caterpillars are larvae of moths or butterflies. There are many types that feed on the foliage and fruit of a variety of plants. The most serious pests—including tomato hornworm (p. 399), bagworms (p. 419), borers (p. 421), tent caterpillar (p. 464), and cabbage loopers (p. 158)—are described in other parts of the Dictionary and Plant Encyclopedia.

In general, treat caterpillars with the biological agent *Bacillus thuringiensis* (see p. 420). However, tall trees that are infested require high-pressure spray equipment for adequate coverage. This is true of the notorious gypsy moth (see p. 455), whose larvae (about 2 inches long, blackish with rows of blue and red spots, and tufts of fine hair on the sides) periodically defoliate a variety of trees and shrubs. Consult a local arborist or spray company.

Trichogramma wasps (p. 420) can also reduce caterpillar populations. For nonedibles, use appropriately labeled chemical controls, such as Sevin and Orthene (p. 445). You can keep gypsy moth caterpillars out of trees by placing a band of burlap around the trunk. Leave the bottom of the burlap loosely attached so caterpillars can get underneath. During the day, they'll hide there where you can easily collect them. Helping trees to grow vigorously, with proper water and fertilizer, will help them recover from gypsy moth damage.

Catkin

A catkin is a slender, spikelike, and often drooping flower cluster.

Chelate

A chelate (pronounced key-late) is a complex organic substance that holds micronutrients, usually iron, in a form that plants can absorb. Iron chelates, for example, help cure the mineral deficiency known as chlorosis.

Chilling Requirement

Many deciduous shrubs and trees (fruit trees in particular), bulbs, and perennials need a certain amount of cold weather in winter to grow and bloom well the following year. (Chilling requirement is measured in hours needed at temperatures below 45°F.) Where winters are mild and these plants don't get the necessary winter chill, they may leaf out late, fail to flower or fruit well, and often decline in health and vigor, even to the point of dying. Gardeners in the Coastal and Tropical South should choose selections with low chilling requirements.

Chinch Bugs

Chinch bugs are a serious pest of lawn grasses, particularly St. Augustine. The small (¼-inch) gray brown insects congregate on grass leaves and stems and suck plant juices. The grass finally dies, creating brown irregular patches. The symptoms usually show up in sunny, dry areas of the lawn or next to walks or driveways where heat radiates from the paved surfaces.

Chinch bug damage resembles drought stress. To confirm the presence of chinch bugs, press a bottomless can into the grass where it is just starting to turn yellow. Fill the can with warm water and the chinch bugs will float to the surface. Control with insecticidal soap or pyrethrins, or stronger insecticides such as diazinon or Dursban (p. 445).

Chlorosis

A systemic condition in which a plant's newer leaves turn yellow, chlorosis is usually caused by a deficiency of iron. (It sometimes results from lack of another mineral, such as zinc.) If the deficiency is mild, areas of yellow show up between the veins of the leaves, which remain a dark green (see photograph, p. 456). In severe cases, the entire leaf turns yellow. Iron deficiency is sometimes the result of a lack of iron in the soil; but often it is the result of some other substance (usually lime) making the iron unavailable to the plant.

To correct chlorosis, treat the soil with sulfur, iron sulfate, or iron chelate. You can also apply foliar sprays containing iron.

Clone

A plant propagated vegetatively (cuttings, layers, budding, tissue culture) and genetically identical to its parent plant.

Clover

Although useful as a green manure in pastures and grazing land, this low-growing perennial can be troublesome in lawns throughout the South because its flowers are so attractive to bees. These round, white, flower heads bloom from late winter through autumn. Not only does the plant self-sow, but it has creeping stems that form roots, allowing it to spread quickly, shading out nearby turf grass. ▶

C

COMPOSTING: SIMPLE TO SOPHISTICATED

This simple compost receptacle is a cylinder of welded wire. To turn compost, lift up cylinder, move it to one side, fork material to aerate, then return it to cylinder.

Classic composting setup includes three sections. One holds new material (left), another holds partly decomposed material (center), and the third holds finished compost (right). Fork the material from bin to bin as composting progresses. Sideboards allow air penetration and slide out for easy turning and removal of compost.

4 by 4 post

1 by 1

4'

2 by 6

2 by 2 spacer on bottom

Mow regularly enough to prevent clover-seed formation, especially in the spring. Keep grass well fed; clover fixes nitrogen in the soil and is able to thrive in lawns that are nitrogen-deficient. For chemical control, apply a herbicide such as Weed-B-Gon (p. 474).

COLD PROTECTION

Constructing a burlap screen on the windward side of recent plantings will buffer drying winds and reduce cold damage.

Cold Frame

A cold frame is a shallow box, usually made of wood, with a slanting transparent lid that's easy to open. Use cold frames to harden off young plants and early spring seedlings.

Cole Crops

A group of vegetables belonging to the cabbage family, cole crops include broccoli, brussels sprouts, cabbage, and cauliflower. They perform best in cool growing conditions; plant in late summer or early spring.

Colorado Potato Beetles

Colorado potato beetles (see photograph, p. 455) occur almost everywhere in the South. The 3/8-inch adult beetle is easy to spot; the showy polka-dot vest and striped pants are a dead giveaway. The larvae are humped, yellow to orange red, with a black head, and about 1/2 inch long. They hatch from clusters of bright yellow eggs laid on the undersides of leaves.

Both adult beetles and larvae feed voraciously on the leaves of vegetables and flowers. They prefer potato plants but will also eat peppers, tomatoes, eggplant, and flowering tobacco.

Sanitation helps keep the beetles at bay. Discard plants after harvest and till the soil to expose overwintering adults. Hand-picking of adults, larvae, and egg clusters will also reduce pest numbers. Heavy mulching may stop overwintering adults from reaching plants in spring.

Bacillus thuringiensis tenebrionis is an effective biological control for Colorado potato beetle larvae. Ladybird beetles, lacewings, spined soldier beetles, as well as many other beneficial insects, prey on the Colorado potato beetle (p. 420). Try the botanical insecticides rotenone, neem, or pyrethrin (p. 445) against the adult insects. Several traditional chemicals are also labeled for control of this beetle, but the pest has become resistant to some. See Pest Management (p. 445).

Complete Fertilizer

Any fertilizer that contains all three primary nutrient elements—nitrogen, phosphorus, and potassium—is called "complete."

Compost

Well-made compost is a soft, crumbly, brownish or blackish substance resulting from decomposition of organic material. It has limited value as a nutrient source but great value as an organic soil amendment (p. 461). Composting takes time, effort, and space but is worth considering, especially if you have a ready supply of plant waste. Remember, though, that a poorly maintained compost pile will be slow to yield its reward, can breed flies and give off an obnoxious odor.

In its simplest form, composting consists of piling up grass clippings, leaves, and other garden debris—plus vegetable kitchen refuse—and letting them decompose. In 6 weeks to 6 months, depending on temperature, moisture, frequency of turning, and size of materials, the compost will be ready.

Composters. For the average garden, a better system is to stack the material for composting to a height of 4 to 6 feet inside an enclosure that has side vents. A slatted bin or a wire-mesh cylinder will do the trick. Turn the piled-up material at least once a week to aerate the mass and to relocate pieces in various stages of decomposition. (Compost decomposes more rapidly in the heat and moisture of the pile's interior than on the outside.) Thoroughly moisten the pile as needed; it should be about as wet as a squeezed-out sponge. Adding a few handfuls of complete fertilizer with every sizable load of raw material hastens decomposition. Compost additives—or boosters, as they are sometimes called—are of little benefit.

A more sophisticated composting operation uses three receptacles (left). Commercial pre-fabricated composters are also available for purchase.

Because large, coarse pieces decompose slowly, chop them up before adding them to the pile. A good mixture consists of green and dried materials in about equal proportions.

If you live beyond the service area of garbage collectors—or are prevented by ordinance from burning debris—consider a compost grinder. These machines chop everything from leaves to thumb-thick branches into uniformly small fragments.

Conifer

Conifer is a more precise word for the plants that bear seeds in cones or modified conelike structures, such as cedars, cypresses, junipers, and pines. Leaves on most are narrow and needlelike or tiny and scalelike. Not all conifers are evergreen. A few, such as bald cypress and dawn redwood, are deciduous.

Container Gardening

Container plants generally require more attention than plants growing in the ground, but their potential advantages may make the extra care worthwhile. If you have just a balcony or a paved patio, planting in containers is the only way to have a garden. And even those with garden space can use container plants to bring seasonal flowers onstage when they are colorful and remove them when they have passed their prime. Other plants have such handsome foliage that they deserve to be grown in containers so they can be appreciated at close range throughout the year.

Container culture also lets you enjoy plants that are not well suited to your garden conditions. You can grow acid-soil plants where native soil is alkaline or plants that demand fast drainage even if your garden soil is clay. Plants too tender for your climate can be moved to

shelter when cold weather comes, and those sensitive to winter cold or summer heat can become house plants.

The routine extra attention container plants need falls into three categories: soil preparation, watering, and fertilizing. These plants also require periodic transplanting and replanting.

Soil mixes for containers. Container plants need a soil mix that is porous and well drained but that retains moisture. The soil must allow roots to grow easily, and it must drain fast enough that roots don't suffocate in soggy soil. Yet the soil should retain enough moisture so that continuous watering isn't necessary.

Even the best garden soil fails to satisfy container soil requirements: it inevitably forms a dense mass that roots can't penetrate easily, and it remains soggy for too long after watering.

Bagged soil mixes. You can purchase packaged potting mixes that are ready to use directly out of the bag. Formulations (listed on the bags) vary somewhat from brand to brand, but none contain actual soil. Look for a mix high in bark, or sphagnum peat plus vermiculite or perlite. A 2-cubic-foot bag of potting mix will fill a planter box 36 by 8 by 10 inches; it will also be enough to transplant 8 to 10 plants from 1-gallon nursery containers to separate 10- or 12-inch pots. Some mixes contain nutrients. Most do not.

Homemade soil mixes. If you prefer to mix your own potting soil—or if you are planning a large-scale operation that would be too costly using packaged mixes—you can purchase the basic component materials and combine them yourself. There are countless possible formulations, but they all combine organic material (bark, peat moss, leaf mold, compost) and mineral matter (soil, sand, perlite, vermiculite) in proportions that produce the desired porosity, drainage, and moisture retention.

One time-honored basic container mixture consists of 1 part good garden soil (not clay), 1 part sand (river or builder's sand) or perlite, and 1 part peat moss or nitrogen-stabilized bark. For plants that prefer acid soil (such as rhododendrons and azaleas), alter the above mix to 2 parts peat moss or nitrogen-stabilized bark.

The use of soil-less mixes lessens the danger from soilborne diseases. But these mixes dry faster than those containing soil, and they will need more fertilizer applications due to leaching from frequent watering. For a large quantity of soil-less mix, combine 2/3 cubic yard of nitrogen-stabilized bark (or peat moss) and 1/3 cubic yard washed coarse sand; add to this 6 pounds of 0-10-10 dry fertilizer and 10 pounds of dolomitic limestone. For ways to increase the water retention of a potting soil, see Soil Polymers (p. 462).

Watering. In hot, dry, windy weather, you may need to water actively growing plants more than once a day; when the weather is cool, still, and overcast or if plants are semidormant, weekly (or

even less frequent) watering may suffice. It's time to water if the soil feels dry beneath the surface.

To water thoroughly, apply water over the entire soil surface until it flows out the pot's drainage holes. This guarantees moistening the entire soil mass and also prevents mineral salts from accumulating in the soil mix.

Note: If water comes out the drainage holes too fast, check to see if it is just running down the inside surface of the container and not through the soil. A root ball that has become too dry can shrink away from the sides of the container; when that happens, water will run around the root ball without penetrating it. To correct the problem, set the container in a tub of water and soak the plant until bubbles stop rising. If that isn't practical, cork the container's drainage holes and then water the plant. Remove corks after soaking the soil. ▶

TRANSPLANTING CONTAINER-GROWN PLANTS

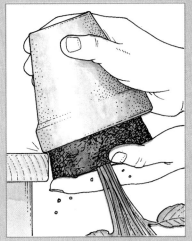

1 Tap pot gently against edge of workbench to free root ball. Pull apart coiled roots.

2 Set root ball into new pot partially filled with soil; top of root ball should be about an inch below pot's rim. Add soil around edges, firming lightly. Water thoroughly.

C

Fertilizing. Heavy and thorough watering leaches out plant nutrients from container soils, calling for regular fertilizer applications. Apply either liquid or dry fertilizer according to label directions. The slow-release dry fertilizers, which release nutrients steadily over a period of time, don't need to be applied as often as other fertilizers. With other types, give light and frequent applications for best results.

Transplanting. When you notice roots protruding from the drainage holes of a pot, move the plant to a slightly larger container, rather than a much larger one, to keep the soil mass fairly well filled with roots (unused soil in a container can stagnate and become a haven for potentially harmful organisms). With fast-growing plants, it's safe to shift to a larger container. And you can always put a number of small plants in a large container—their combined root will occupy the total soil mass.

When moving a plant to a larger container, select one that will allow you to fill in an inch or two of fresh soil on all sides of the root mass. If the plant's root ball appears compacted, cut it vertically with a sharp knife to encourage roots to move out into the new soil in the larger container. Make at least four equally spaced cuts about ¼ to 1 inch into the mass of compacted roots, depending on the size of the root ball.

To keep an older plant in the same large container indefinitely, you can periodically root-prune the plant. During the plant's dormant period, gently turn it out of the container. Shave off an inch or two of the outer root mass on all sides and on the bottom with a sharp knife; then replant in the same container with fresh soil mix around and underneath the roots.

GONE TO POTS. *When selecting trees to grow in containers, choose those that either stay small or grow slowly. That way, you'll be able to enjoy them a long time in the container you have chosen. The best candidate for most gardeners is laceleaf Japanese maple. Other good choices include dogwood, sourwood, dwarf crepe myrtle, Sargent crabapple, weeping yaupon, edible fig, Sasanqua camellia, calamondin, star magnolia, sweet bay, and loblolly bay. In the Upper and Middle South, you can also grow many different dwarf and slow-growing conifers, such as dwarf Alberta spruce and Japanese white pine.*

Cool-Season Plants

These are plants that thrive in cool weather, including some vegetables (cole crops, lettuce, spinach, peas), annual flowers (pansies, violas, calendula), and lawn grasses (bluegrass, tall fescue).

Corm

Technically, a corm is a thickened underground stem capable of producing roots, leaves, and flowers during the growing season. See Bulbs (p. 421).

Cover Crops

You dig or fill a cover crop, sometimes referred to as "green manure," into the soil in early spring to add organic matter and nitrogen to it. Legumes such as clover, cowpeas, and vetch are the most common cover crops.

Crabgrass

An infamous summer annual, crabgrass grows well in hot, damp areas. This shallow-rooted weed thrives in lawns and flower beds that receive frequent surface watering, in underfed lawns, and in poorly drained fields. See photograph, p. 475.

Seeds germinate in early spring. As the plant grows, it branches out at the base; stems can root where they touch the soil. Seed heads form in mid- to late summer. As crabgrass declines in autumn, it turns purplish, becoming especially noticeable in lawns.

In flower beds, pull crabgrass before it makes seeds. Keep lawns well fertilized and vigorous to provide tough competition for weeds; crabgrass seed needs light to germinate and quickly sprouts in bare spots. In late winter or early spring, apply a granular pre-emergent herbicide—such as Dacthal (p. 474), Balan, or pendimethalin (Halts)—with a fertilizer spreader. Cut the lawn at 2 inches or higher; tall grass reduces crabgrass germination.

Crown

The crown of a tree is its entire branch structure, including foliage. In another usage, "crown" refers to the point at which a plant's roots and top structure join (usually at or near the soil line).

Cucumber Beetles

Two types of cucumber beetles are common garden pests. Both are about ¼ inch long and yellowish green, but one species has black spots on its shell, the other black stripes. They are appropriately named spotted and striped cucumber beetles.

Adult cucumber beetles feed on the foliage, flowers, fruit, and stems of a variety of plants, particularly members of the cucurbit family of vegetables. Young seedlings are particularly vulnerable. Cucumber beetles also attack other vegetables and flowers like asters, dahlias, and roses. To make matters worse, they spread bacterial wilt to vine crops (see p. 419) as they feed. The small, ⅓-inch larvae feed on plant roots (especially corn roots) and stems.

Controlling cucumber beetles starts with good sanitation and prevention. Clean up and discard plant debris that might serve as overwintering sites. Planting as early as possible in spring may help seedlings get established before the pest emerges. Some vegetable varieties are resistant to cucumber beetles. Use floating row covers to prevent adult beetles from reaching plants (see p. 459). These covers are most effective when supported by hoops. Make sure to remove them when plants are blooming so bees can reach the flowers for pollination.

Apply parasitic nematodes (p. 420) to reduce larvae populations. Pyrethrin, rotenone, and sabadilla are useful botanical sprays for controlling cucumber beetles. For chemical control, use Sevin (p. 445).

Cultivate

Cultivating is the process of breaking up the soil surface. It aerates the soil, allowing it to warm earlier in spring and dry faster in wet weather, improves plant growth, and often removes weeds.

Cuttings

Most gardeners who propagate new plants start cuttings from plant stems, roots, or leaves. Stem cuttings are of three types—softwood, semihardwood, and hardwood—depending on the maturity of the plant.

Softwood and semihardwood stem cuttings. You can propagate many deciduous and evergreen shrubs and trees, as well as perennials, from softwood or semihardwood cuttings.

Softwood stem cuttings, taken from spring until late summer, are the easiest stem cuttings and the quickest to root. Take them during the active growing season from soft, succulent, flexible new growth (see right). Take semihardwood cuttings after the active growing season or after a growth flush, usually in summer or early autumn. Growth is then firm enough that a sharply bent twig snaps (if it just bends, the stem is too mature for satisfactory rooting).

Choices of rooting medium are several, but all allow for easy water penetration and good drainage. Pure sand (builder's sand or river sand) is the simplest but requires the most frequent watering. Better are half-and-half mixtures of sand and peat moss or of perlite and peat moss, or of perlite or vermiculite alone.

Loss of water through the leaves that remain

SOFTWOOD STEM CUTTINGS

Take softwood and semihardwood stem cuttings during the growing season. Cut below a leaf, remove lower leaves, dip cut in rooting hormone, then plant. Maintain high humidity around cutting.

HARDWOOD STEM CUTTINGS

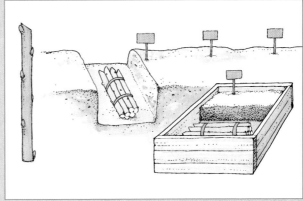

Take hardwood stem cuttings at onset of dormant season. Make cut below a leaf bud, dip cut in rooting hormone. Refrigerate over winter in areas where the ground freezes; bury in a trench or soil-filled box outdoors in warmer climates.

LEAF CUTTINGS

Leaf cuttings will increase many succulents, African violets, snake plant, begonia, and other plants. With some, cut veins and lay leaf flat on soil; others will grow from part of leaf inserted in soil.

ROOT CUTTINGS

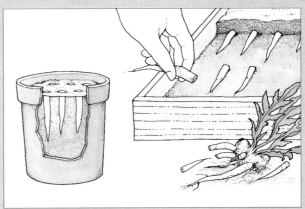

To make root cuttings, cut pencil- to finger-thick sections of roots; place them on their sides and cover with soil, or insert upright in soil with tops just at soil surface. Moisten, cover with plastic, and place in shade.

on the cuttings is the greatest threat to softwood and semihardwood cuttings. To minimize this water loss, provide a greenhouse atmosphere —high humidity—for the cuttings while they are striking roots. The easiest way is to place a plastic bag over the cuttings and container, then tie it around the container to confine humid air within the bag. Ventilate any of these improvised greenhouses for a few minutes every day or two by removing or loosening the bag.

When new growth forms on the cuttings, you can be fairly sure that they have rooted and are ready for transplanting.

Hardwood stem cuttings. Make hardwood cuttings during the autumn-to-spring dormant season from wood of the previous season's growth. You can increase many deciduous shrubs and trees from cuttings taken during the dormant season. See the illustration above.

Hardwood cuttings may take longer to root and start growth than softwood cuttings, so put your hardwood cuttings in an area where they can remain undisturbed. In areas where the ground freezes in winter, bundle the cuttings together and bury them outside in a shallow trench. Elsewhere, seal the cuttings inside a plastic bag and refrigerate.

During the winter, the lower ends of the cuttings will begin to form calluses from which roots will grow. When weather starts to warm as spring approaches, take out the cuttings and plant them in the open ground or in containers. Plant the cuttings top side up; to be sure which end is which, make the top cut slanted, the bottom cut square.

Leaf cuttings. Some plants will root successfully from a leaf or portion of a leaf. New plants will sprout from the base of each leaf section or from the cut veins (above).

Root cuttings. Any plant that produces sprouts from its roots will grow from root cuttings. Check cuttings every week for moisture and for sprouts; remove the covering when growth shows.

Cutworms

Cutworms are the hairless larvae of a large number of night-flying moths. They feed at night and on overcast days, and most can cut off young plants just at ground level—hence their name. In the daytime, they hide in the ground, curled up. Early in spring, the moths tend to lay eggs on garden weeds. The larvae begin feeding on the weeds, then move to garden plants once they destroy the weeds. See photograph, p. 454.

Barriers. Protect susceptible seedlings from cutworms by putting a physical barrier around each seedling. One simple barrier is a sleeve made from a cutoff milk carton: Sink it 1 inch

D

below soil level, allow 2 inches above, and provide at least an inch of space between the sleeve and the plant. As an extra precaution, put petroleum jelly or a sticky ant barrier, such as Tanglefoot, on the sleeve's upper edge.

Some cutworms crawl up into plants and eat buds, leaves, and fruit. One way to keep them out is to spread a sticky ant barrier around the base of each susceptible plant.

If you have too many plants to employ barriers, try hand-picking cutworms at night. Or trap them by placing cardboard, plywood, wide boards, or heavy paper sacks in garden paths. During daylight, lift the traps and destroy the worms beneath.

Cutworms in lawns. These are more difficult to eradicate. Your clue to infestation is small bare patches that grow rapidly in size day by day. If you're not sure the damage is from cutworms, drench a square yard with 1 tablespoon of dishwashing soap diluted in a gallon of water. That should bring the cutworms to the surface. Sometimes you can also see them with a flashlight at night.

Biological and chemical controls. Parasitic nematodes (p. 420) are the first line of defense against cutworms. *Bacillus thuringiensis* has limited effectiveness. Control seedling-eating cutworms by dusting the ground where they feed with Sevin or use Sevin baits; for lawns, apply diazinon, Dursban, or Sevin (p. 445).

Damping Off

This is the most common killer of new seedlings. In most cases, weblike fungi cause the stem of a seedling to collapse at or near the soil surface. In some woody seedlings, infected plants remain alive for a while. Another type rots the seedling before it emerges from the soil or causes the seed to decay before sprouting. See photograph, p. 454.

You can prevent damping off by taking the following steps:

- Buy fungicide-treated seeds, or dust them with fungicide powder before planting.

- Provide good air circulation and ventilation (especially if growing seedlings indoors) to keep tops of seedlings dry and standing moisture to a minimum.

- Sow seeds or root cuttings in an inert (sterile) material rather than in garden soil. Vermiculite, perlite, pumice, sand, sphagnum moss, and soil-less commercial mixes are all safe—at least the first time they are used.

You can reduce problems by not planting too deeply or too close together and by avoiding overwatering.

A number of chemical fungicides help control damping off. Look for products that contain captan (p. 429), or other properly labeled fungicides. But one product may not be effective against all damping-off organisms. If one product doesn't work, switch to another.

Dandelion

This familiar lawn weed grows from a deep, taproot that may break (and can regrow) when the weed is pulled out. It often spreads by windborne seeds and by sprouting root crowns (see photograph, p. 475). Flowering begins in spring and often continues until frost; in mild weather, seeds can germinate year-round.

Pull out young plants before the taproot has a chance to grow deep into the soil. On lawns, apply Weed-B-Gon in spring and fall. Spray isolated plants with Roundup or Finale (p. 474).

Deadheading

Removing individual flowers after they fade but before they set seed is called deadheading. This channels the plants' energy into making more flowers instead of producing seed. Deadheading can greatly prolong the bloom of many annuals and perennials, as well as repeating flowering shrubs such as roses. In most cases, cut or pinch back to the next shoot or bud below the spent flower. With roses, cut back to the first leaf with five leaflets.

Deciduous

A plant that sheds all its leaves once each year (usually in autumn) is deciduous.

Deer Protection

With their soulful eyes and graceful gait, deer may be pleasant to watch, but they can make a garden ragged by nipping off flower heads and nibbling tender leaves and new shoots. As more and more of their native habitat disappears, deer look for food in gardens on the fringes of suburbia. They develop browsing patterns, visiting tasty gardens regularly—most often in the evening. Fond of a wide array of flowering plants, especially roses, deer will eat foliage or fruit of nearly anything you grow.

Planning a deer-proof garden is additionally challenging because the animal's diet differs from place to place. What they snub at one garden they may devour a few miles away.

Physical controls. For the best protection, build a fence. On level ground, a 7-foot woven-wire fence will usually keep deer out, although some determined deer will jump over even an 8-foot fence. A horizontal "outrigger" extension on a fence makes it harder for a deer to jump it. On a slope, you may need to erect a 10- to 11-foot fence to guard against deer jumping from higher ground. Because deer can jump high or jump wide—but not simultaneously—some gardeners have had success with a pair of parallel 5-foot fences, with a 5-foot-wide "no-deer's-land" between.

If you don't fancy a fortress garden, focus on individual plants (or areas). Put chicken-wire cages around young plants and cylinders of wire fencing around larger specimens. Cover raised beds with mesh, and use floating row covers (p. 459) on vegetables. It sometimes helps to keep a zealous (and vocal) watchdog in the yard, particularly during evening and nighttime hours.

Chemical controls. Commercial repellents can work if sprayed often enough to keep new growth covered and to replace what rain and watering wash away (though some repellents may make sticky, unsightly spots on flowers and foliage). Do not apply repellents to edible portions of plants unless the label advises you to do so; some are not safe to eat. Some gardeners repel deer by hanging small cloth bags filled with blood meal among their plants; disadvantages are that blood meal attracts dogs and smells unpleasant, especially when wet.

KEEP BAMBI AT BAY. *Hungry deer will eat almost anything. But one way to decrease their destruction is using plants they normally don't like. These include cedar, oak, Southern magnolia, redbud, ginkgo, persimmon, barberry, boxwood, daphne, flowering quince, forsythia, juniper, mahonia, oleander, thorny elaeagnus, wax myrtle, yaupon, Asian star jasmine, English ivy, chrysanthemum, columbine, daffodil, Lenten rose, petunia, pink, tulip, yarrow, yucca, and zinnia.*

Defoliation

The unnatural loss of a plant's leaves, usually to the detriment of the plant's health, is called defoliation. It may result from high winds that strip foliage away; intense heat (especially if accompanied by wind) that critically wilts leaves; drought; unusually early or late frosts that strike a plant still in active growth or just beginning growth; or severe damage by chemicals, insects, or diseases.

Dethatch

The process of removing dead stems (thatch) that build up beneath certain ground covers and lawn grasses is known as dethatching. You can do this by hand using a thatching rake or, in the case of lawns, with the aid of a gas-powered electric dethatcher, also known as a vertical mower. Dethatch in autumn or early spring on cool-season lawns and in late spring for warm-season grasses. Follow up with fertilizer, for healthier, more vigorous growth.

Dieback

When a plant's stems die, beginning at the tips, for a part of their length, the causes may be too little water, nutrient deficiency, a plant's inability to adapt to the climate, or severe insect, mite, cold, or disease injury.

Diseases

Different kinds of organisms cause plant diseases. Most leaf, stem, and flower diseases result from bacteria, fungi, or viruses. Most soilborne diseases are caused by fungi.

Sometimes disease results from plants interacting with unfavorable environmental factors, such as air pollution, a deficiency or excess of nutrients or of sunlight, or the wrong climate (too hot, cold, dry, or wet). Read the exposure and climate preferences for each plant listed in the Plant Encyclopedia. This discussion focuses on the various plant diseases that are caused by harmful organisms.

Bacterial diseases. Bacteria are single-celled microorganisms that are unable to manufacture their own food (as green plants do); those bacteria that cause plant diseases must obtain their nutrients from the host plants.

Fungal diseases. Certain multicellular branching, threadlike organisms called fungi obtain their food parasitically from green plants, causing diseases in the process. Many fungi produce great numbers of tiny reproductive bodies, or spores, which can be carried by wind or water from leaf to leaf and from plant to plant. Each spore, under the right conditions, will germinate and grow—producing new infections. Fungus diseases are among the most widespread of plant maladies, but you can control many with good sanitation, the choice of resistant selections, use of fungicides, and cultural practices.

Viral diseases. Ultramicroscopic viruses are capable of invading plant tissue and reproducing in it, usually at the expense of the host plant. Viruses may produce varied symptoms such as abnormalities in growth, color variegation of foliage, or "breaking" (color distortion) of blossoms.

There is no home cure at this time for a virus-infected plant, but you can reduce chances of a virus spreading to other plants in two ways.

DISEASE CONTROL

Numerous packaged products are available for control of diseases: preventatives (products that prevent diseases from occurring but are ineffective in controlling them once they are established), eradicants (materials that help control diseases—many simply protect new growth—once established), and systemics (materials that move inside the plant and act as preventatives, eradicants, or both). The controls described here are the ones most useful and commonly available. Other products—generally less widely sold—are mentioned in the entries for the specific diseases they control.

Some products will control a disease on one plant but not on another; moreover, certain products can do damage if applied to inappropriate plants. Read product labels carefully to be sure your plant is listed.

- **Bayleton (triadimefon):** Wettable powder; systemic for prevention or eradication of powdery mildew, rust, and some lawn diseases; also effective against azalea petal blight.
- **Captan:** Dust or wettable powder for prevention or eradication of damping off, leaf spots, and many other fungal diseases. Future registration limitations are possible.
- **Copper compounds:** A group of general-purpose fungicides and bactericides, most often used to prevent fireblight, peach leaf curl, and shot hole diseases.
- **Daconil (chlorothalonil):** Multipurpose liquid fungicide for prevention of diseases on lawns, fruits, vegetables, and ornamentals.
- **Funginex (triforine):** Liquid systemic for prevention and eradication of powdery mildew, rust, black spot, and other diseases. Wear goggles and a face mask when using it.
- **Lime sulfur (calcium polysulfide):** Liquid preventative for various leaf spots, peach leaf curl, and powdery mildew. Can be used as a dormant spray. Also controls some mites, scale insects, and thrips.
- **Maneb:** Wide-spectrum, manganese-based fungicide that controls leaf spot, blight, gray mold, downy mildew, and rust on vegetables and ornamentals.
- **Sulfur:** Dust or wettable powder; one of the oldest fungicides. Prevents powdery mildew, scab, and rust.
- **Thiomyl (thiophanate-methyl):** Systemic, wettable powder effective against many plant diseases, including powdery mildew and black spot, of roses.
- **Zineb:** Wide-spectrum, zinc-based fungicide controls leaf spot, rust, gray mold, downy mildew, and scab on ornamentals and fruits.

Controls are listed by trade name. The active ingredient then appears in parentheses. Some controls are known by their active ingredient.

First, remove any plants that are severely stunted or mottled. Second, try to control the insects that carry viruses. Aphids are most efficient in spreading different kinds of viruses; leafhoppers and thrips can be vectors, too. And humans may spread viruses by vegetatively propagating virus-infected plants or by handling tobacco while working around plants (thereby spreading tobacco mosaic virus, which affects many plants in addition to tobacco).

Dividing

The easiest way to propagate perennials, bulbs, and shrubs that form clumps of stems with rooted bases is by dividing. In fact, to keep these plants healthy and strong, it's necessary to divide them periodically. Each rooted segment or division is actually a plant in itself or is capable of becoming a new plant. For perennials that form a taproot and grow from a compact crown, make stem cuttings (p. 427), or sow seeds.

Divide plants in autumn or early spring, when they are dormant. In most areas, autumn is the best time to divide perennials that bloom in spring or early summer, whereas early spring is better for those that blossom in late summer and autumn. But in the Upper South divide spring-blooming perennials in early autumn. If you plant them out in fall, the roots will have a chance to grow before the onset of cold weather.

To divide deciduous and semideciduous perennials, prune the foliage back to about 4 inches from the ground. With evergreen perennials, leave all young, healthy foliage, but remove all dead leaves.

When decline in flower quantity and quality signals overcrowding of bulbs and bulblike plants, let their foliage start to turn brown and lose vigor before digging and separating the bulbs. Replant the bulbs or offset (p. 442) in well-prepared soil or store until the appropriate planting time.

DIVIDING

Daylily

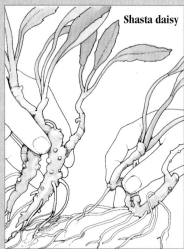

Shasta daisy

Iris

Dividing is an easy way to increase stock of many perennials and bulblike plants. Pull apart individual plants of clump-forming perennials (such as daylilies and Shasta daisies); break or cut apart separate plants of rhizomes (such as iris), some bulbs, and tuberous-rooted plants.

DIVIDE AND MULTIPLY. *A single pot of lily turf or mondo grass bought at a garden center can easily yield a half-dozen or more plants. Just slip the root ball out of the pot and use a knife, trowel, or pruning shears to divide the ball into smaller pieces. Ensure that each piece of root has a tuft of leaves. Then plant the new plants about 6 inches apart in a grid pattern. The ground cover completely fills in within a few years.*

Dollar Weed

Also called pennywort, dollar weed is particularly troublesome in the Coastal and Tropical South, where it thrives in moist sites, shady, damp lawns, and uncultivated spaces. It resembles dichondra, with scallop-edge leaves held erect on long stems, and spreads by seeds, rhizomes, and tubers, forming thick mats that crowd out other plants. (See photograph, p. 476.)

To control dollar weed, dig it out with a hand weeder, removing all stems to prevent them from sprouting again. Avoid overwatering and improve drainage, if necessary. For chemical control, apply a postemergent herbicide such as Weed-B-Gon or Mecoprop (p. 474) between late spring and autumn, when the weeds are actively growing.

Dormancy

The period when a plant's growth greatly slows down is called dormancy. In many plants it starts with the coming of winter, as days grow shorter and temperatures drop. Dormancy can also occur during dry periods.

Dormant Spray

An insecticide or a fungicide applied to a plant during the season it is not putting on new growth is a dormant spray. Usually including, or composed only of, a dormant oil, this type of spray kills overwintering insects and disease organisms and reduces the necessity for multiple sprays during the growing season (see the illustration at right).

Double Flower

A double flower has a large number of petals that give the blossom an unusually full appearance. Many fruit trees with double flowers, including selections of pomegranate, plum, and cherry, do not produce fruit and are commonly grown as ornamentals.

Drainage

Drainage refers to the movement of water through the soil in a plant's root area. When this happens quickly, the drainage is "good" or "fast," and the soil is "well drained"; when it happens slowly, the drainage is "slow" or "bad," and the soil is "poorly drained." For plants to grow, water must pass through the soil. Plant roots need oxygen as well as water, and soil that remains saturated deprives roots of necessary oxygen. Good drainage (water disappears from a planting hole in 10 minutes or less) is typical of sandy soils; poor drainage (water still remains in planting hole after several hours) is found in clay soils and where hardpan exists. Refer to Soils (p. 462) for more information on soil types and drainage.

Drip Line

The imaginary circle on the soil under the tips of a tree's outermost branches is called a drip line. Rainwater tends to drip from the tree at this point. The term is used in connection with feeding, watering, and grading around existing trees and shrubs.

USING DORMANT SPRAY

If diseases and insects have troubled your fruit or shade trees in the past, spray them while leafless (dormant). Use horticultural oil mixed with either lime sulfur or copper. For complete coverage, spray branches (A), crotches (B), trunk (C), and ground within drip line (D).

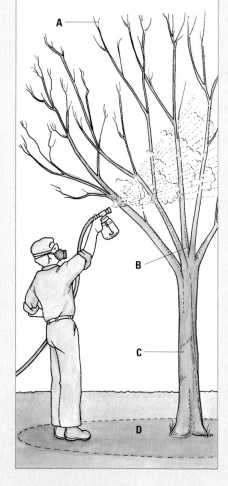

Drought Tolerant

Plants that can withstand long periods with little or no water, plants that have relatively low water requirements, or plants that are well adapted to arid conditions are drought tolerant or drought resistant. However, because water requirements vary greatly from plant to plant and from region to region, the phrase is often ambiguous. A plant that needs little water in the Blue Ridge Mountains may need a lot more in Central Texas. Soil conditions, exposure, degree of establishment, length of time without water, and other factors also affect a plant's water needs, its appearance, and its survival.

Dust

Dust is a finely ground type of insecticide or fungicide as well as its method of application. Apply in early morning when the air is still, so that the dust makes a large cloud, and the particles slowly settle as a thin, even coating over everything. The advantage of dusting over spraying is convenience: no mixing, fast application, and easy cleanup. The disadvantage is that dust can be difficult to apply to the undersides of all the foliage.

Epiphyte

Epiphytes grow on host plants for support but receive no nourishment from them. Familiar examples of these plants are Spanish moss and staghorn ferns. Epiphytes are not parasites; true parasites steal nourishment from the host plant.

Espalier

This is a method of training a tree or shrub so that its branches grow in a flat pattern against a wall or fence, on a trellis along wires. The illustration below shows several forms.

POPULAR ESPALIER PATTERNS

Espalier training can take a number of different forms. Here are some common ones.

Evergreen

An evergreen plant never loses all its leaves at one time. See also Broad-Leafed (p. 421).

Eye

An undeveloped growth bud, an eye will ultimately produce a new plant or new growth. The eyes on a potato will, when planted, develop into new potato plants. "Eye" is synonymous with one definition of Bud (p. 421).

Family. See Plant Classification   p. 447

Female Plant

A plant that produces fruit or seed but does not produce pollen is female.

Fertilize

In popular usage, this term has two definitions. To fertilize a flower is to apply pollen (the male element) to the flower's pistil (the female element) for the purpose of setting seed. To fertilize a plant is to feed it.

Fertilizers

A visit to a garden center may reveal a bewildering selection of fertilizers. An understanding of the basic fertilizer types will help you select the right product.

Dry fertilizers. The majority of fertilizers are dry. You spread them onto a lawn; sprinkle them onto the soil around plants; or scratch, rake, or dig them in. Dissolving when they contact water, the dry granules begin their fertilizing action quickly. Slow-release fertilizers can last for several months.

Liquid fertilizers have several advantages:

- They are easy to use, especially on container-grown plants.

- There is little risk of burning a plant as long as you follow label directions for dilution.

- The nutrients in the fertilizer are available to the roots immediately.

Liquids are less practical than solids for large-scale use because they cost more and must be reapplied more often (their nutrients in solution leach through the root zone more rapidly).

Available in a variety of different formulations, liquid fertilizers include complete formulas and special types that offer just one or two of the major nutrients. All need to be diluted with water; some are concentrated liquids; others are powder or pellets. You can also buy liquid fertilizers in ready-to-use, hose-end sprayers. Formulations for lawns may also include herbicides for weed control.

Growers of container plants often use liquid fertilizers at half the strength and twice the frequency recommended so that plants receive a steadier supply of nutrients.

Foliar fertilizers. Some nutrients, particularly nitrogen in urea form and micronutrients, can be absorbed quickly through plant leaves. Many liquid or water-soluble fertilizers include rates for foliar feeding on their labels. In general, actively growing plants show the best response. But remember, foliar feeding is a quick fix and not a substitute for soil feeding. To avoid burning plant leaves, first water the plants well; don't apply foliar fertilizers if temperatures will soon rise above 85°F.

Complete fertilizers contain all three of the primary nutrient elements—nitrogen (N), phosphorus (P), and potassium (K). Many fertilizer manufacturers put their product's N, P, and K percentages on the label, right under the product name, in big numbers—for example, 20-6-12. Without looking at the fine print under Guaranteed Analysis (on every fertilizer label), you know that the fertilizer contains 20 percent total nitrogen, 6 percent phosphate (P_2O_5), and 12 percent potash (K_2O). See illustration. p. 433.

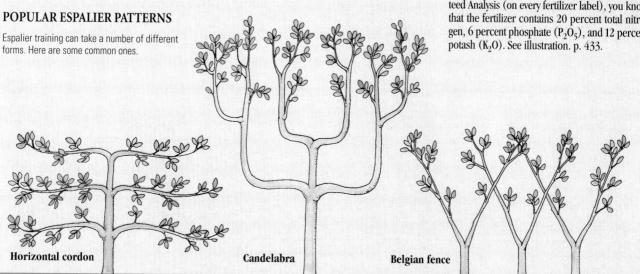

Horizontal cordon   **Candelabra**   **Belgian fence**

THREE WAYS TO FERTILIZE TREES

Surface feeding. In sandy soil or wet climates, broadcast granular fertilizer on the surface, by hand or using a spreader. Soak it in thoroughly with a sprinkler.

Root plug. With a soil-sampling tube or pipe, make 6- to 12-inch-deep holes 2 to 3 feet apart. Pour granular fertilizer into holes, fill with soil, and water well.

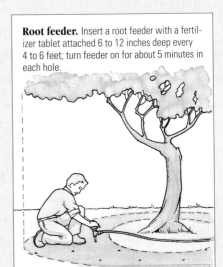

Root feeder. Insert a root feeder with a fertilizer tablet attached 6 to 12 inches deep every 4 to 6 feet; turn feeder on for about 5 minutes in each hole.

There are fertilizers with many different nutrient ratios. (See Nutrients, Basic, p. 443.) The higher the numbers in the analysis, the stronger or more concentrated the fertilizer is (a 22-6-4 formula contains twice as much nitrogen as does an 11-6-4 formula). And the higher the concentration (of N especially), the less you apply at one time.

Complete fertilizers are most useful when you work them into the soil where active roots can take up the phosphorus and potassium. If you want only the benefits of nitrogen, choose a nitrogen-only simple fertilizer.

Simple fertilizers. Simple fertilizers contain just one of the three major nutrients. Most familiar are the nitrogen-only types, such as ammonium sulfate (21-0-0), but you can find phosphorus-only and potassium-only fertilizers as well. Falling between the two extremes are "incomplete" types that contain just two of the three major elements: N and P, N and K, or P and K.

Special-purpose fertilizers. Some packaged fertilizers are formulated for specific plants— "camellia food," "rhododendron and azalea food," and "rose food," for example. The camellia and rhododendron-azalea fertilizers belong to an old, established group, the acid fertilizers. Some fertilizers packaged for specific plants are done so for marketing purposes alone, rather than to meet the needs of that plant (compare, for example, the NPK ratios of three different brands of "tomato food").

All chemical fertilizers except calcium nitrate lower the pH of soil by producing acids as they decompose. Those that are especially acid producing are labeled "acid fertilizers" and are useful on acid-loving plants. They also are good for general-purpose fertilizing in alkaline-soil regions, to reduce alkalinity.

Organic fertilizers. The word "organic" simply means that the nutrients contained in the product are derived solely from the remains, part of the remains, or a by-product of a once-living organism. Cottonseed meal, blood meal, bonemeal, fish emulsion, and manures are examples of organic fertilizers. (Urea is a synthetic organic fertilizer—an organic-like substance manufactured from inorganic materials.) Most of these products packaged as fertilizers will have their NPK ratios stated on the package labels. Usually, an organic fertilizer is high in just one of the three major nutrients and low in the other two, although some are chemically fortified with the missing nutrients. In general, the organics release their nutrients over a fairly long period. The potential drawback is that they may not release enough of their principal nutrient at a time to give the plant what it needs for best growth. Because they depend on soil organisms to release the nutrients, most organic fertilizers are effective only when the soil is moist and warm enough for the soil organisms to be active.

Although manure is a complete organic fertilizer, it is low in N, P, and K and is best used as a soil conditioner. Nutrient content varies according to the animal species and its diet, but an

THREE WAYS TO FERTILIZE VEGETABLE TRANSPLANTS

Work dry fertilizer into soil with spading fork before planting.

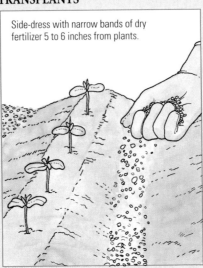

Side-dress with narrow bands of dry fertilizer 5 to 6 inches from plants.

Liquid-feed in watering basins. (This is the most precise way to apply.)

NPK ratio of 1-1-1 is typical. Use only aged or composted manure. Some fresh manures have a high salt content, which will burn plants.

Controlled-release fertilizers. The beadlike granules of controlled-release fertilizers are balls of complete fertilizer coated with resin, sulfur, or another permeable substance. When you wet the granules, as in normal watering, some of the fertilizer diffuses through its coating into the surrounding soil—a little bit with each watering—until the encapsulated fertilizer is used up. Some products are effective for 3 to 4 months; others, for 8 or more months. Scratch or dig the pellets into the soil so that you cover them. These are particularly useful for fertilizing container plants, which need frequent nutrient replenishment.

Sticks, stakes, and tablets. Some fertilizers are compressed into hard cylinders or tablets; you push or hammer the sticks or stakes into the soil or drop the tablets into holes. Dissolving slowly in the presence of water, they yield nutrients gradually, sometimes for a year or more. These products are convenient (but expensive) for getting phosphorus and potassium to the regions of active root growth of established shrubs and trees.

Combination products. You can buy fertilizers combined with insecticides (chiefly for roses) or with weed killers, fungicides, or moss killers (all for lawns). These products are appropriate if you need the extra ingredient every time you fertilize; if not, it is more economical to buy it separately. The herbicides included in some products can damage plants whose roots are growing into areas where you apply the product. Read labels carefully.

Fire Ants. See Ants   p. 418

BROADCASTING FERTILIZER BY HAND

Fill a bucket with the amount of granular fertilizer recommended on the package. Wearing gloves, distribute this in even bands as you walk slowly forward, using an underhand, sweeping toss; minimize overlap (too much fertilizer can burn).

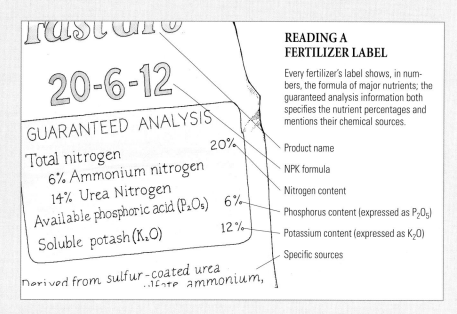

20-6-12

GUARANTEED ANALYSIS

Total nitrogen   20%
  6% Ammonium nitrogen
  14% Urea Nitrogen
Available phosphoric acid (P_2O_5)   6%
Soluble potash (K_2O)   12%

Derived from sulfur-coated urea
...lfate ammonium,

Fireblight

Troublesome in all parts of the South, fireblight affects only the plants in the rose family. When a flowering shoot of apple, cotoneaster, crabapple, hawthorn, pear, pyracantha, or quince dies suddenly and looks as though it has been scorched by fire (see photograph, p. 456), fireblight has probably caused the damage.

The bacteria that cause fireblight survive in blighted twigs and cankers. In early spring—especially during moist weather, when temperatures are above 65°F—the bacteria are spread to open blossoms by rain and insects. Once in the blossoms, bees spread them to other flowers. Infection progresses from the blossoms down the shoots into the larger limbs, where dark, sunken cankers form. Bacteria are also able to enter a plant through fresh cuts or tears in the foliage.

Controls. Wherever fireblight is a persistent problem, avoid growing susceptible plants, or plant resistant selections. If you grow susceptible plants, take preventative measures. Spray the tree just before the blossoms open with copper sulfate (p. 429) or streptomycin. Repeat twice at intervals of 7 days.

Control the bacteria by pruning out and burning the diseased twigs and branches as soon as you see them. Make cuts at least 10–12 inches below blighted tissue. Disinfect pruning shears between cuts with bleach or denatured alcohol. Avoid excess fertilizing with high amounts of nitrogen.

Flat

A shallow box or tray used to start cuttings or seedlings is called a flat.

Fleas

Most pet owners fight infestations of fleas at one time or another. Not only do these sucking insects infest cats and dogs, but they are happy to feed off rodents such as squirrels and rats—and one type can spread disease to its human prey, too. Because they jump on and off their host to feed, they can quickly spread through the house and garden. Fleas are able to extend their life cycle until they find a suitable host, so long-term vigilance is often required to truly control them.

It's important to control fleas on your pets, inside the home, and in the garden—otherwise you are treating only part of the problem. Sprays, dusts, or dips for treating pets are readily available; consult a vet for more advice. For indoor control, thoroughly clean linens, upholstery, and carpets, followed by commercial fogging bomb or spray. Try diatomaceous earth and pyrethrins (p. 445).

For the garden, use an insecticide such as Dursban, diazinon, or malathion (p. 445). If treating a lawn, first wet the area thoroughly to drive the fleas up into grass. To prevent the fleas from developing resistance, it can be helpful to apply a second treatment in 45 days with a different insecticide.

Flea Beetles

These tiny, oval jumping insects vary in color with the species, but most types are black, shiny bronze, or dark blue (see photograph, p. 455). Except for a species with a particular fondness for corn, all have an appetite for a broad range of edible plants, particularly tender young seedlings.

Adult flea beetles riddle leaves with small holes, leaving the foliage dried and desiccated. Leaves drop. Seedlings are most susceptible. The small white grubs feed on roots, leaving brown streaks in root crops such as potatoes.

Flea beetles are attracted to the color white; you can check for their presence by putting a white card or piece of paper among the plants or on the lawn. If they're nearby, they'll jump onto the white surface.

To control flea beetles, keep the garden clean and free of plant debris that might serve as overwintering sites. Till the soil in fall to expose grubs. Plant vigorous seedlings and cover vegetables with floating row covers to exclude adults. Treat grubs with parasitic nematodes (p. 420), or with pyrethrin, rotenone, or sabadilla. For chemical control, use diazinon or Dursban (p. 445).

Foliar Fertilizer

Apply foliar fertilizer in liquid form to a plant's foliage. The nutrients it contains are absorbed through the plant's leaves. See Fertilizers (p. 431).

Forcing

Forcing is the process of growing a plant to the flowering or fruiting stage out of its normal season. This usually takes place in a greenhouse, where you are able to control temperature, humidity, and light.

Frond

In the strictest sense, fronds are the foliage of ferns. Often, however, the word also applies to the leaves of palms and even to designate any foliage that looks fernlike.

Frost and Freeze Protection

Virtually no place in the country is completely free from the threat of frost. From the dip below freezing that may hit Miami once or twice in a decade to the occasional Big Freeze that sweeps down on the Deep South, these sudden deviations from the norm can wreak havoc on a landscape. Even established plants may die. Fortunately, there are ways to prepare for the occasional big chill. For information on protecting vegetables, see p. 468.

Know your plants. Select trees, screen and hedge plants, and shrubs that are hardy enough for the extremes of your climate zone. Use the chancy or tender plants as fillers, as summertime display plants, or put them in sheltered sites or containers that can be brought indoors.

Know your garden. Learn your garden's microclimates: discover which areas are warm and which are cool. Most dangerous for marginally hardy plants (and all tender vegetation) are stretches of open ground exposed to the air on all sides, particularly to the north. Hollows and low, enclosed areas that catch cold air as it sinks also are poor choices. The safest sites are under overhanging eaves (the best protection), lath structures, or branches of evergreen trees. The warmest location of all is a south-facing wall with an overhang.

Condition plants and soil for frosts. Feed and water while plants are growing fastest, in late spring and early summer. To discourage production of new growth that would not have time to mature before cold weather hits, decrease feeding in late summer. Reducing water helps harden growth, but keep the soil around plants moist at the onset of the frost season; moist soil holds and releases more heat than dry soil does.

Some hardy plants have early blossoms that are damaged by spring frosts. Try to delay bloom of deciduous magnolias, quince, and winter daphne beyond the time of heavy frosts by planting them with a north exposure or in the shade of high-branching deciduous trees.

Be especially watchful for frosts early in autumn or in spring after growth is under way. These are much more damaging than frosts that occur while plants are semidormant or dormant. The warning signs are still air; low humidity; and low temperature (45°F or less at 10 P.M.). If you notice these danger signs at bedtime, move any at-risk container plants under a porch roof or eaves or into a garage. Shelter any such plants that are in the ground: Use burlap or plastic secured over frames or stakes so that the covering material does not touch the plant. (Freezing is likely where the material touches foliage.) Remove coverings during the daytime.

After a frost. When frost damages plants, don't hurry to prune them. Such trimming is premature and may stimulate new, tender growth that later frosts will nip. And you may mistake still-alive growth for dead. Wait until new growth begins in spring; then remove only clearly dead wood.

Fungicide

Any product used to control fungus diseases is called a fungicide (p. 429).

Galls

Galls are growths on plant leaves and stems (see photograph, p. 454). The cause is usually abnormal cell growth stimulated by sucking insects like aphids or reactions to fungal, bacterial, or viral infections. Most leaf galls are harmless, although they may be unsightly. Prune off galls on smaller branches. It may be better to leave large galls in place; pruning them out may harm the plant.

Genus. See Plant Classification   p. 447

Girdling

Girdling occurs most often in woody plants tightly tied to a stake or support. As the tied limb or trunk increases in girth, the tie cuts off supplies of nutrients and water to the part of the plant above the tie. If girdling goes unnoticed, the part of the plant above the constriction will die. The word "girdling" also applies to pest damage or to an encircling cut made through the bark of a trunk or branch to improve fruiting.

Grasshoppers

There are many different kinds, shapes, and sizes of grasshoppers. During their periodic outbreaks, grasshoppers can do devastating damage, especially in hot-summer areas. By preference, they lay their eggs in dry, undisturbed areas, such as in empty lots, but they also will lay eggs in gardens.

Eggs begin hatching from March to early June, depending on temperature and climate. Newly hatched nymphs resemble adults but are

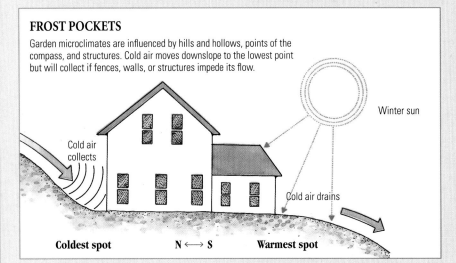

FROST POCKETS

Garden microclimates are influenced by hills and hollows, points of the compass, and structures. Cold air moves downslope to the lowest point but will collect if fences, walls, or structures impede its flow.

Winter sun

Cold air collects

Cold air drains

Coldest spot   N ⟷ S   **Warmest spot**

smaller and lack wings; these nymphs feed voraciously, sometimes stripping entire areas bare. When they mature and develop wings, they fly out and find new feeding areas.

Controls. When you are cultivating in autumn, winter, and early spring, watch for and destroy egg clusters, which contain up to 75 cream or yellow rice-shaped eggs. In spring and early summer, while grasshoppers are still young and wingless, they are most vulnerable to chemicals and baits. Use malathion, diazinon, Dursban, Orthene, or Sevin (p. 445). Grasshoppers roost at night in hedges, tall weeds, and shrubs. Observe their evening behavior to locate roosting sites, then spray in these areas after dark.

Your best defense against large numbers of grasshoppers may be to protect desirable plants with floating row covers (p. 459) or netting.

In summer, when grasshoppers are mature and less vulnerable to chemicals, hand-pick them in early morning.

The disease-producing organism *Nosema locustae* causes grasshoppers to produce fewer eggs. Over large areas—on a ranch, for example—applying this commercially packaged material can help reduce grasshopper problems in later years.

Greenhouse

The ultimate in climate modification is a greenhouse. In such a structure, of glass or plastic, you can control temperature, humidity, and day length. Use a greenhouse to:

- Overwinter plants that are too tender for the normal outdoor winter low temperatures

- Start seeds of annuals and vegetables early so that you can set out in the garden as soon as weather permits

- Start cuttings and seeds that require the growth stimuli a greenhouse can provide

- Raise vegetables and flowers out of season (particularly when outside conditions are too cold), or mature them earlier than would be normal if they were outdoors

- Grow specialty plants (orchids and tropical plants, for example) that will not grow outdoors because temperature or humidity or both are unfavorable

A greenhouse may be a simple lean-to constructed of plastic, a small bay window attached to a house window, or a more elaborate separate structure with precise controls for regulation of heat, humidity, ventilation, and water.

Ground Covers

Gardeners select ground covers to blanket a prescribed area of soil and create a uniform appearance. The area may be just a small patch beneath a tree or it may run to an acre or more. The best-known ground cover is, of course, grass; you'll find information on lawn grasses beginning on page 440. Other ground covers include perennials, shrubs, and vines—particular types that produce a relatively even surface (which may be as low as turf or as tall as 3 feet). You can walk on some matlike plants, although none will take the amount of foot traffic a lawn will tolerate.

Choosing a ground cover. Is the ground you want to cover level or sloping, sunny or shady, small or large in extent? Do you want a cover that will act as a barrier, or do you want to be able to walk across it? Will the ground cover have the space all to itself, or will it flow around shrubs, landscape boulders, or trees? And what about appearance: Do you prefer foliage only or green punctuated by colorful flowers or fruits? Answers to these questions will help you select the ground cover you need. Also consider the relationships that will exist between the ground cover and the adjacent landscape; take into account foliage textures and colors. Use the lists beginning on page 94 as a guide to more than 100 of the most popular ground covers.

MOW NO MORE. *Steep slopes planted with turf can be difficult and dangerous to mow. Instead, kill the grass with a herbicide and then plant a ground cover. To prevent erosion from washing away the growing plants, first lay 3 to 4 inches of pine straw. Next, cover the straw with a biodegradable jute netting, available at some garden centers or home supply stores. Cut holes in the jute and plant the young ground-cover starts through the holes. By the time the jute rots away, the plants will have covered the slope.*

Growing Season

Specifically, this is the number of days between the average date of the last killing frost in spring and the average date of the first killing frost in autumn. In general terms, the phrase also describes the period of time a plant is actively growing and not dormant.

Gummosis and Cankers

Gummosis (see photograph, p. 454) and canker describe various bacterial or fungal diseases that usually cause oozing, sunken, woundlike lesions on the trunks or limbs of trees and shrubs, usually fruit trees. If the disease is serious enough, limbs above the lesions grow poorly, wilt, and may die.

Gummosis and cankers often start in wounds or mechanical injuries (including pruning cuts) to the plant. In some cases, they can also be caused by overwatering. Using protective tree wraps or painting trunks of young trees white to prevent sunburn (see p. 465) will help prevent the diseases. So will good watering practices and keeping the plant as healthy as possible.

Vigorous plants will naturally seal off cankers, preventing them from spreading. In smaller limbs, prune out the limb well below the canker. Sterilize pruning shears with a 5 percent bleach solution between cuts. Cut out larger cankers, but if they are too large, you may kill the plant. If you suspect that borers are present, take appropriate measures to control them (see p. 421).

Gypsum. See Soil Amendments, Inorganic p. 461

Harden Off

Hardening off is the process of adapting a plant grown in a greenhouse, indoors, or under protective shelter to full outdoor exposure. Over a week or more, you expose the plant to increasing intervals of time outdoors. "Hardened off" also refers to a plant's ability to withstand cold temperatures.

Hardpan

A tight, impervious layer of soil, hardpan can cause trouble if it lies at or near the surface. Such a layer can be a natural formation—in the Southwest, the most common natural hardpan layer is called caliche—or it can develop when builders spread excavated subsoil on the surface and then drive heavy equipment over it. If the subsoil is clay and is damp while construction is going on, it can dry to a bricklike hardness. A thin layer of topsoil may conceal hardpan, but roots cannot penetrate the hard layer and water cannot drain through it. Planting holes may become bath tubs: Plants will fail to grow, be stunted, or die. ▸

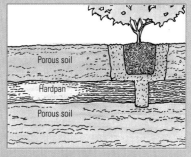

PLANTING IN HARDPAN

Porous soil

Hardpan

Porous soil

For thin hardpan under shallow soil, dig down from planting hole to hardpan. Drill or chip to porous soil below. Backfill with porous soil.

Planting in hardpan. If the hardpan layer is thin, you may be able to improve the soil by plowing it to a depth of 12 inches or more. If this is impractical, you can drill through it with a soil auger when planting (see illustration, p. 435). If the layer is too thick, a landscape architect can help you with a drainage system, which might involve drain tiles. To improve the soil over large planting areas, dig up the area to a depth of 18 inches or so with heavy equipment, then add organic matter and thoroughly mix it in. As a beneficial extra step, you can then grow a crop of some heavy-rooting grass, and after it grows, rototill it into the soil as additional organic material.

If drainage problems prove especially difficult or costly to surmount, consider installing raised beds for most of your garden plantings. Fill them with good, well-aerated soil, and make them deep enough to allow for root growth.

Hardy

A plant's hardiness is its resistance to, or tolerance of, frost or freezing temperatures (as in "hardy to −20°F"). A half-hardy plant is frost-resistant in a given situation in normal years but may freeze in coldest winters.

Heading Back

Cutting a 1-year-old shoot back to a bud or cutting an older branch or stem back to a stub or tiny twig is called heading back.

Heavy Soil

A rather imprecise term, "heavy soil" refers to dense soil made up of extremely fine particles packed closely together. The term is synonymous with "clay." Such soils tend to be poorly aerated, slow to dry out, and easily compacted. You may improve them by adding organic matter. See Soil Texture (p. 461).

Heeling In

Heeling in is a means of preventing the roots of a bare-root plant from drying out before you can set it out in the garden. The simplest approach is to dig a shallow trench in the shade, lay the plant on its side so that its roots are in the trench, and then cover the roots with moist, good-quality soil.

Henbit

Also known as dead nettle or bee nettle, henbit is a weakly upright annual weed with lobed leaves and pink to purple flowers atop the stems in spring. It is common in the South, particularly east of the Mississippi River, and can be especially troublesome in newly seeded or sodded lawns (see photograph, p. 475).

Seeds of henbit usually germinate in fall. Plants grow slowly over winter and become most obvious in spring. They are relatively easy to pull by hand, and you can reduce late-winter or early-spring cultivation. Roundup (p. 474) is an effective herbicide for use outside lawn areas, where the weed can be treated alone. In lawns, keeping the grass thick and healthy will reduce the germination of henbit.

Herb

The general term "herb" applies to a variety of herbaceous plants valued for their flavor, fragrance, or medicinal purposes.

Herbaceous

Herbaceous, the opposite of woody, describes a plant with soft (nonwoody) tissues. In the strictest sense, it refers to plants that die to the ground each year and regrow stems the following growing season. In the broadest sense, it means any nonwoody plant—annual, perennial, or bulb.

Herbicide

A herbicide destroys undesirable plants. See Weed Control (p. 472).

Honeydew

Aphids, scales, and whiteflies, and some other sucking insects, secrete a sticky substance called honeydew; ants (p. 418) and fungi (see Sooty Mold, p. 462) can feed on it, adding to the mess. Often honeydew from a tree will drip onto whatever is below: car, deck, or other plants. See the entries for individual pests for control measures.

APHID R.I.P. *Here's an easy way to rid your plants of aphids and other soft-bodied insects without using chemical pesticides. Just add 4 or 5 drops of liquid detergent to a quart of water and pour the mixture into a spray bottle. Thoroughly spray the foliage and stems in early morning while the day is still cool. Bye-bye, aphids!*

Horticultural Oil

A horticultural oil is a refined oil you spray on plants to help control insects. See Pest Management (p. 445).

Humus

The soft brown or black substance formed in the last stages of decomposition of animal or vegetable matter is called humus.

Hybrid

Any plant resulting from a cross between two unlike plants.

Insecticide

An insecticide kills or repels insects. See Pest Management (p. 445).

| **Iron Chelate.** See Chelate | p. 423 |
| **Irrigation.** See Watering | p. 468 |

Japanese Beetles

These coppery-colored beetles with metallic green heads attack a variety of plants, skeletonizing leaves and devouring flowers (see photograph, p. 455). Favorite foods include members of the rose family, zinnias, marigolds, and most vegetables. The small grayish white grubs feed on the roots of plants and are particularly troublesome in lawns. Japanese beetles are most common east of the Mississippi River.

Controlling Japanese beetles can require multiple approaches. Install floating row covers (p. 459) to exclude adults from vegetable plants. Floral-scented, sticky traps will attract Japanese beetles, but they can make matters worse by bringing in more pests than you had before. If you try these traps, keep them at least 100 feet away from plants you want to protect.

Milky spore, a form of *Bacillus thuringiensis*, is effective against grubs but tends not to reduce populations of adults, which will continue to move in from other areas. For adults, you must use milky spore over entire neighborhoods, not single gardens. Parasitic nematodes (p. 420) also kill grubs, but, as with milky spore, may not reduce numbers of adult beetles.

For adult beetles, try insecticidal soaps, rotenone, or pyrethrin. For chemical control try diazinon, Dursban, carbaryl, and Orthene (on nonedibles). See p. 445 for details.

Kudzu

Kudzu spreads very rapidly, growing as much as 60 feet each year. This deep-rooted, perennial climbing vine has engulfed much of the Southeast. Once welcomed for erosion control and as protein-rich animal fodder, it has since become a weedy, aggressive, out-of-control nuisance.

Heavy, hairy, brown stems send the vine twining over shrubs and trees, which it can kill by shading them from needed sunlight. The woody stems carry large leaves with three leaflets, 3 to 6 inches long. Small red and purple flowers bloom in summer and produce long, hairy, flat pods containing seeds that are dispersed by birds (see photograph, p. 475).

Controlling kudzu is difficult; chemicals may be the best option. In late summer when the leaves are fully expanded, apply a herbicide such as Roundup or Brush-B-Gon (p. 474). If the weed resprouts, repeat the treatment. Where kudzu vine overruns shrubs and trees, cut off any runners and remove them before spraying. Or cut back climbing vines and paint undiluted Roundup or Brush-B-Gon on freshly cut stumps.

Landscape Fabrics

Roll various fibrous or plastic materials called landscape fabrics over the ground before planting to reduce weed growth and soil erosion. Use an old knife to make small holes in the fabric for planting. Cover fabrics with an attractive organic mulch.

Lath

In gardening, lath is an overhead structure (originally a roof of spaced laths) that reduces the amount of sunlight that reaches plants beneath or protects them from frost.

Lawns

It's a nice summer morning and your spouse is out inspecting the lawn. Oblivious to the lovely roses, heedless of the jewel-like flowers, indifferent to the meticulously sculpted shrubs, your better half marches back up the walk and inquires, "When are you going to do something about this scraggly lawn?"

It doesn't matter that you're the only Southerner to master Himalayan poppies. It doesn't matter that *The Victory Garden* filmed a segment at your house. In the South, if your lawn doesn't put the neighbors to shame, you could be considered a slacker.

To win back the respect you sorely deserve, you first must choose the right grass. If you live in the Upper South and cooler parts of the Middle South, you'll probably want a cool-season grass that stays green all winter—Kentucky bluegrass, perennial ryegrass, or tall fescue. (Tall fescue also grows well in the upper half of the Lower South but needs plenty of wear and filtered shade there.) Elsewhere, select a warm-season grass—Bahia, Bermuda, buffalo grass, carpet grass, centipede, St. Augustine, or zoysia. (Bahia and carpet grass are common in Florida and buffalo grass in Texas.) Specific information on all of these grasses appears on p. 440 and in the Plant Encyclopedia.

Before selecting a particular grass, ask yourself these questions:

- Do you hate watering? If so, don't plant carpet grass, bluegrass, or perennial ryegrass. They drink like sailors on shore leave. But Bahia, Bermuda, and zoysia are near teetotalers. Buffalo grass is the least thirsty of all common turf grasses.

- Will football teams be scrimmaging on your lawn? Then you'll need a resilient, wear-resistant grass such as Bahia or common Bermuda. Zoysia is tough, too, but once you wear it down to the dirt, it's gone.

- Are you trying to grow grass in the shade? St. Augustine and tall fescue are able to tolerate shade fairly well.

- Do you enjoy feeling your temples pound as you strain to push the lawn mower uphill? Then plant St. Augustine and let it go a week without mowing in hot, rainy weather. Mowing zoysia or Bahia is highly aerobic, too. But bluegrass, fescue, and perennial ryegrass are easy to mow. And buffalo grass looks great when you let it grow tall. You have to mow it only three times a year—in early spring, mid-June, and early autumn.

WATER LAWNS AT SUNRISE. *Early morning is the best time to water the lawn. The air is cool, so most of the water will get to the roots before evaporating. Plus, the grass blades can dry quickly before fungus strikes. If possible, avoid watering in the heat of the day. Most of the water will simply evaporate. And don't water at night unless that's the only time your community allows. Grass that stays wet all night often falls victim to disease.*

Lawns, Planting

A good lawn begins with a good environment for roots: It needs loose, permeable soil at least 8 to 12 inches deep, rich in nutrients, and neither highly acid nor overly alkaline.

If you're replacing an existing lawn, first make sure the old lawn, and any weeds it contains, are dead. The easiest way to do this is to get the old lawn growing vigorously (it may take several weeks of watering for a brown lawn), then spray it with a broad spectrum herbicide like Roundup or Finale (p. 474). Then rent a sod cutter and remove the old sod. You can also rent a power rake, tear up the old turf, and rake it up. If you remove the sod, you may have to add topsoil to raise the grade. Buy the best you can and till it into the existing soil.

Test soil. See Soil pH (p. 462) for information on how to determine your soil's acidity or alkalinity. If tests indicate that your soil is highly acid (pH below 6.0), add lime.

If the soil is highly alkaline (pH above 8.0), add iron sulfate or elemental sulfur. Iron sulfate is fast acting and will supply the iron that is lacking in alkaline soils.

Mix nutrients into rooting area. Till your first application of lawn fertilizer into the soil along with any necessary lime, sulfur, or iron sulfate.

SECRETS OF A GREAT-LOOKING LAWN

Here are some tips for keeping a lawn healthy.

- **Think small.** A small lawn means less work, and it takes less time and money to care for than a big one. It also demands less water. Keep it a simple geometric shape so you can irrigate without overspray, and make it fairly level to minimize runoff.

- **Choose the right grass.** Select a lawn grass that is well-adapted to your area.

- **Water efficiently.** To encourage deep rooting and to conserve water, irrigate lawns as deeply and infrequently as possible. Where summer rainfall is plentiful, irrigate to supplement rainfall (most lawns need between 1 and 2 inches of water a week). In dry climates, twice-a-week watering should be adequate.

  Step on the grass. If the blades don't spring back from your footprint, it's time to water. You can also poke the soil with a screwdriver; if it doesn't penetrate easily, the lawn probably needs water (or the soil is compacted).

Many sprinklers apply water faster than soil can absorb it. To prevent runoff, water in cycles. Let the sprinklers run until just before runoff or puddling occurs (often in 10 or 15 minutes); repeat the cycle in an hour. Also, make sure that you adjust your sprinklers properly so they don't overshoot onto paving.

To improve water penetration and reduce runoff, aerate and dethatch your lawn once a year.

- **Fertilize regularly.** Lawns are heavy feeders and require periodic applications of slow-release, balanced fertilizer. In acid soils, applying lime is also beneficial. Feed cool-season lawns throughout autumn and spring. Feed warm-season lawns in the warm months of late spring and summer. If you cut back on watering for any reason, hold back on fertilizing, too.

- **Mow often.** To keep a lawn healthy, mow the grass when it's about a third taller than the recommended height. Grass is weakened if you let it grow too long before mowing. Also, leave shorter clippings on the lawn to decompose and add nitrogen to the soil. Mow at ½ to 1 inch higher than your grass's recommended height (see chart, p. 440) during hot, dry weather.

HOW TO LAY SOD

1 Till the soil with a power tiller, loosening it to a depth of 12 inches. Then incorporate fertilizer and any necessary amendments, such as topsoil, organic matter, sand, lime, or sulfur.

2 Rake the sod bed, discarding sticks, stones, and other debris. Use a drag leveler to level the area. Slope the bed slightly away from the house to facilitate drainage and to avoid a wet basement.

3 Begin laying sod along a straight edge, such as the sidewalk or driveway. If your yard lacks a straight side, stretch a line across the area where the lawn will be and lay sod along either side.

4 Roll out the strips of sod, tightly pressing the edges against strips already laid. Stagger the joints so that they don't line up. If possible, walk or kneel on a board to avoid leaving depressions in the sod or soft soil.

Use a complete fertilizer, containing nitrogen, phosphorus, and potassium.

Smooth the bed. Usually you'll have to match the level of the surrounding paving, but if you have a choice, try to have a slight pitch away from the house—a fall of 3 inches per 10 feet will provide good drainage. After raking, level the bed with a drag leveler, making passes in two directions. Relevel if necessary.

Seed sowing. Sow cool-season grasses in autumn and spring. Autumn seeding saves water, since fall and winter rains help germinate the seed and establish the roots. It also reduces danger of heat injury. Sow warm-season grasses in spring and summer.

Pick a windless day for sowing, and sow seed as evenly as possible; a spreader or mechanical seeder will help. After sowing, rake in seed very lightly to ensure contact with seedbed. If you expect hot, dry weather or drying winds, put down a thin, moisture-holding mulch, such as clean wheat straw, and cover 50 percent of soil surfaces. After mulching, roll with an empty roller to press seed into contact with soil.

Water thoroughly, taking care not to wash out seed, and then keep seedbed moist until all the grass sprouts. This may mean watering 5 to 10 minutes each day (sometimes two or three times a day, depending on the weather) for up to 3 weeks if your seed mixture contains slow-germinating kinds. Although a well-designed

underground system may do the job, hand sprinkling is best.

Mow most grasses for the first time when blades are about a third higher than their recommended mowing height. Keep mower blades sharp, and let sod dry out enough so that mower wheels will not skid or tear the turf.

Sod and plugs. Compared with the cost of seeds, sod is expensive, but the saving in time and labor is considerable. Prepare the soil as for seeds, but make the surface about ¾ inch lower than any surrounding paving. Spread a layer of complete fertilizer (the amount the label suggests for new lawns), and then unroll sod on the prepared seedbed. Lay strips parallel, with strips pressed against each other, and

5 Fill any gaps between the strips of sod with clean sand. Grass from the surrounding sod will quickly spread into the sand, closing the gap.

6 When you come to a curved edge, use a shape spade, edging tool, or knife to cut the sod to fit.

7 Use a water-filled roller to press the new sod into contact with the soil and to level the area. Roll across the strips, not along them.

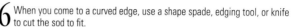
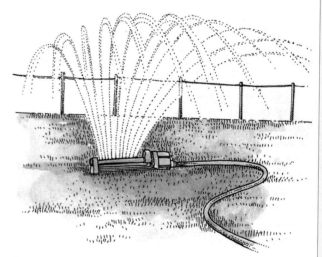

8 Water thoroughly, leaving a sprinkler on for several hours. Water every other day until the sod "knits" with the soil. Erect a barrier to keep children, pets, and other traffic off the new lawn for several weeks.

stagger the joints. Roll with a half-filled roller, and then water carefully until roots have penetrated deeply into the seedbed (see above).

To plant plugs of grass from flats, first prepare the soil as previously described. Then space the plugs evenly in all directions, about 12 to 15 inches apart.

Layering

A method of propagating plants from a branch that is still attached to a plant. The two layering methods—ground layering and air layering—tend to be slow, but with some hard-to-root plants layering is more likely to be successful than is propagating from cuttings. Because

you don't remove the branch from the parent plant until it forms roots, the original plant continues to keep the layer alive. See the illustrations on the next page.

Ground layering. Keep the soil around the layer moist. When you are sure roots have formed (it may take more than a year; gently dig around the cut to check), cut the new plant free from the parent plant, dig it up, and move it to its intended location.

Air layering. The principle of air layering is the same as that of ground layering; the difference is that air layering is used for branches higher on a plant. It is especially useful with some large house plants.

If the rooting is successful, you'll see roots appearing in the sphagnum moss after several months. Then you can sever the newly rooted stem from the parent plant and pot it or plant it out on its own. At that time it is usually wise to halve the number of leaves—to prevent excessive loss of moisture through transpiration while the newly independent plant establishes itself. If no roots form, new bark will eventually grow over the cut area.

Leaching

To understand leaching, think of brewing tea or coffee. When you pour hot water through tea leaves or ground coffee, you are

SOUTHERN LAWN GRASSES AT A GLANCE

Bahia ZONES CS, TS
Drought-tolerant, durable turf grass that thrives in sun but does poorly in shade. Good for dry, sandy, acid soil; requires only light feeding. Numerous seedheads. Establish by seed or sod; mow to 3 or 4 inches.

Bermuda (common) ZONES MS, LS, CS, TS
Tolerant of drought and most soil types, Bermuda spreads rapidly and is highly resistant to wear. Requires full sun, moderate feeding. Establish by seed, sod, or plugs. Mow from ½ to 1½ inches.

Bermuda (hybrid) ZONES MS, LS, CS, TS
Less drought tolerant than common Bermuda, the improved type is just as wear resistant but has a finer texture and requires more maintenance including heavy fertilizing. Does not thrive in shade. Establish by seed, sod, or plugs. Mow to ½ to 1½ inches.

Buffalo Grass ZONES US, MS, LS
Low-maintenance, drought-tolerant grass with good wear resistance. Requires little feeding; will not thrive in shade. Establish by seed, sod, or plugs; mow from 1 to 6 inches depending on season and preference.

Carpet Grass ZONES CS, TS
Moisture-loving and fragile, this is the lawn grass of last resort even though it requires little feeding and is fairly shade-tolerant. Does best on wet, acid soil. Establish by seed or sod; mow from 1 to 2 inches.

Centipede ZONES LS, CS
Although fairly shade-tolerant, centipede grass cannot tolerate much wear. It prefers poor, acid soil, and needs little fertilizer. Establish by seed, sod, or plugs; mow from 1 to 2 inches.

Kentucky Bluegrass ZONE US
Beautiful, but high-maintenance turf; requires average feeding and plenty of water. Will tolerate some traffic and some shade but not too much of either. Establish by seed or sod; mow from 2 to 3 inches.

Perennial Ryegrass ZONE US
Fair to good wear resistance; moderate drought and shade tolerance. Average feeder. Establish by seed; good for overseeding dormant grass in Lower South and Coastal South. Mow from 1½ to 2½ inches.

St. Augustine ZONES LS, CS, TS
Shade tolerant, and able to withstand salt spray by the coast; also moderately drought-resistant. Requires average fertilizer. Establish by sod or plugs; spreads quickly. Mow from 2 to 4 inches.

Tall Fescue ZONES US, MS, LS (upper half)
Can grow in shade; fairly drought-tolerant and able to resist wear. Medium feeder. Good alternative to bluegrass or ryegrass. Establish by seed only; mow from 2 to 3 inches.

Zoysia ZONES MS, LS, CS, TS
Extremely drought-tolerant and tough, this dense, slow-spreading turf can be established by sod or plugs. Tolerates light shade and a great deal of wear; chokes out weeds. Mow from 1 to 2 inches.

---

essentially leaching substances out of the tea or coffee. You leach soil with water to remove excess salts. In high-rainfall areas, rainwater unfortunately leaches good nutrients as well as bad substances from the soil, sometimes leaving these soils deficient in essential minerals.

Leader

In a single-trunked shrub or tree, the leader is the central, upward-growing stem.

Leaflet

Completely separated divisions of a leaf are called leaflets. They look like the fingers of a hand (palmate, fanwise) or like the divisions of a feather (pinnate, featherwise).

Leaf Miners

Certain moth, beetle, and fly larvae tunnel within plant leaves, leaving twisting trails on the surface (see photograph, p. 456). You rarely see adult leaf miners. American holly, boxwood, and columbine are frequent victims. Fortunately, the damage from leaf miners is mostly cosmetic. In severe infestations, leaves may turn brown and drop.

Chemical control is difficult once the leaf miner has tunneled inside a leaf. Pick off affected leaves. Use Cygon or Orthene on ornamentals (p. 445). Protect vegetables under floating row covers (p. 459).

GROUND LAYERING

1 Select a low, flexible branch that can be bent into shallow hole. Cut halfway through it, put pebble in cut, and stake tip upright.

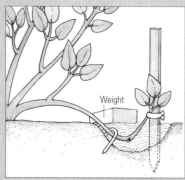

2 Secure prepared branch in shallow hole, using wire pin if needed. Brick or rock on soil also helps hold branch in place.

AIR LAYERING

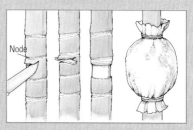

Begin air layering below a node. Make a slanting cut (inserting matchstick to keep it open) or remove ring of bark. Dust cut with rooting hormone, encase in damp moss, and wrap with polyethylene to keep moss moist.

Leaf Scorch

Leaf scorch results from excessive evaporation of moisture from the leaves, usually during hot, dry weather. Leaves turn brown on the edges (see photograph, p. 454). In severe cases, entire leaves brown, curl, and drop. Dogwood, horse chestnut, and Japanese maple are especially susceptible.

Leaf Spot

Occasionally red, brown, yellow, or black spots on leaves and stems appear on a number of different plants. On some *Prunus*, the spots drop out, leaving a "shot hole" appearance. Spots enlarge and coalesce, and then infected leaves drop; severe infections can defoliate plants.

These symptoms represent several different diseases, including anthracnose, black spot (familiar to rose growers), and scab, which affects some fruits. The fungus spores that cause these diseases are airborne or waterborne. Because the spores need free moisture to germinate, these diseases are far less serious in low-rainfall areas. Some types of leaf-spot fungi, activated by moisture during the winter rainy period, affect evergreen plants.

The source of these diseases is mainly live infected plants, although some disease-producing organisms can overwinter in plant refuse. Thorough garden cleanup each winter is important to lessen or eradicate infection. Use a spray to control infections: captan, Daconil, Funginex, or Thiomyl (p. 429).

Three particular leaf-spot diseases are troublesome enough to warrant further explanation.

Anthracnose. Anthracnose fungi infect leaves and tender shoots as they emerge in spring; these fungi also infect older leaves, on which they produce large, irregular brown blotches and cause premature dropping of leaves (see photograph, p. 456). The fungi also cause twig dieback and canker on small branches; these blighted twigs and cankers will be a source of infection the following spring. Rain and sprinkling spreads spores; hence, the disease is most severe in wet springs and is checked when dry weather arrives.

Control by eliminating sources of future infection: Prune out all infected twigs and branches, if feasible. To prevent infection in spring, use Daconil (p. 429). Spray when leaves unfold, then two or three more times at 2-week intervals. Consult a commercial sprayer for help.

Some anthracnoses are very difficult to control, and you may need to tolerate them—especially if the disease affects a large tree. But the best approach is to grow plants that can resist disease. Among susceptible trees such as ash, Chinese elm, and sycamore, resistant selections are available. Ask at your local Cooperative Extension Service for types that grow well in your area.

Black spot. Black spot thrives where humidity runs high and summer rainfall is common. It is especially troublesome on roses east of the Mississippi River. The

fungus appears on leaves and stems as roughly circular spots of black with fringed edges, usually circled with a yellow halo (see photograph, p. 456). In severe cases, the plant will defoliate; unchecked infections, with repeated defoliation, can seriously weaken the host plant.

The black-spot fungus lives through winter in lesions on canes and on old leaves on the ground. In spring, the fungus again becomes active and produces spores, which are then spread by splashing water to new leaves. Preventive control consists of planting resistant selections and sanitation: Clean up and destroy old leaves in winter; burn or discard this refuse; don't put it in the compost as the fungus can survive to reinfect plants when the compost is applied. Rose growers often have good luck controlling black spot with weekly applications of a solution of 2 teaspoons baking soda and 2 teaspoons summer oil in a gallon of water. Otherwise, in spring, spray new foliage with Funginex (which is the favorite of most rose growers) or Daconil (p. 429). Repeat sprayings as long as weather conditions favor the fungus's development.

Scab. Scab produces disfiguring lesions on apple and crabapple fruits and, when severe, can cause defoliation. Other types of scab affect peach, pyracantha, citrus, pecan, and willow. Scab is most prevalent in high-rainfall regions. The scab fungus (as well as the fungus that causes black spot on roses) differs from other leaf-infesting fungi in that the dark spots on leaves represent fungus growth on the foliage rather than dead tissue.

Try to avoid the problem by planting scab-resistant selections of apple, pyracantha, pecan, and crabapple. For control on fruit trees, spray just before flower buds open with captan or Thiomyl (p. 429). Spray again when blossoms show color and again when three-quarters of the blossom petals have fallen.

Light Soil

The opposite of "heavy soil," the imprecise term "light soil" refers to soil composed of relatively large particles loosely packed together. The term is often synonymous with "sandy soil." See Soil Texture (p. 461).

Loam

Gardeners call loam the ideal soil. It is rich in organic material, does not compact easily, and drains well after watering. See Soil Texture (p. 461).

Macronutrients

These are the basic nutrients required by plants in relatively large amounts—nitrogen, phosphorus, potassium, calcium, magnesium, and sulfur.

Male Plant

A male plant that produces pollen but not fruit or seed.

Mealybugs

Closely related to scale insects, mealybugs have an oval body with overlapping soft plates and a white, cottony covering (see photograph, p. 456).

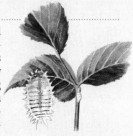

Unlike most scale insects, mealybugs can move around—slowly. These pests suck plant juices, causing stunting or death. Often a black, sooty mold grows on the honeydew they excrete.

Mealybugs are prime house-plant pests everywhere; outdoors, they are particularly troublesome in areas with mild winters. For any infestation indoors or for a minor infestation outdoors, daub them with a cotton swab dipped in rubbing alcohol. Outdoors, hose plants with jets of water (or insecticidal soap) every 2 to 4 weeks to remove adult mealybugs, their eggs and young, and the black mold. Ants have the same symbiotic relationship to mealybugs as to aphids and scale insects; see Aphids (p. 419) for control.

Natural predators, such as ladybird beetles, can help control mealybugs—as can some commercially available predators such as cryptolaemus beetles and lacewings. Cryptolaemus beetle larvae are "sheep in wolves' clothing": they look like mealybugs but have chewing mouth parts and a ropy wax covering (p. 420).

For heavy infestations, spray with horticultural oil (p. 436), or apply malathion, diazinon, or Orthene (p. 445).

Microclimate

The climate of a small area or locality (such as a backyard or portion of it) is called a microclimate. The ability to recognize microclimates around your garden—or, if necessary, to create them—will influence which plants you choose and how well they grow in a particular area. Hills and hollows, points of the compass, and structures all affect microclimates.

To get a true picture of your garden's microclimates, observe your garden during different seasons and at different times during the day. You may discover areas where wind, frost, or structures change the growing conditions.

M

N

Micronutrients

Plants require these mineral elements in small amounts.

Mites

To the naked eye, mites look like tiny specks of red, yellow, or green; in reality, they are tiny spider relatives (each has eight legs). Spider mites are especially troublesome. The first (and sometimes only) sign of spider mite damage is yellow-stippled leaves (see photograph, p. 456). But there are many reasons for leaf yellowing. To confirm that mites are the problem, hold a piece of white paper beneath the stippled leaves and sharply rap the stem from which they are growing. If mites are present, the blow will knock some onto the paper—where they look like moving specks. Some mites also make fine webbing across leaves (especially on the undersides) and around stems.

Spider mite controls. If the plant is small, spray it thoroughly with water to wash off the mites; add insecticidal soap to a water spray to increase the spray's effectiveness. Dust that settles on leaves encourages mites, so continual hosing helps keep mite populations down. Increased humidity also helps. Drought-stressed plants are more prone to mites.

Control mites with natural predators, including lacewing larvae and five different species of predator mites (p. 420).

If you can't wash the plant or if washing is not effective, try spraying. Summer horticultural oils are especially effective or apply sulfur but not in combination with oil sprays (it can be toxic to plants). If infestation is severe, try Kelthane (p. 445).

Mole Crickets

Several species of mole crickets are pests of lawns in the Lower and Coastal South. They prefer Bahia and Bermuda grasses, but also attack St. Augustine, zoysia, and centipede. The greenish gray, 1½-inch long insects have small front legs with shovel-like feet. They burrow through the top few inches of soil at night, feeding on organic matter and grass roots. As mole crickets tunnel along, they dislodge grass plants and push small mounds of soil to the surface. The result is a spongy, rough-looking lawn that dries out quickly, is easy to scalp with a lawn mower, and has irregular dead areas. If you pull on dead sections of turf, the grass comes up easily.

To test for mole crickets, soak a 3-foot square area of turf with soapy water (a tablespoon of dish washing soap in 2 gallons of water). They'll come to the surface in 2 to 3 minutes.

Control with parasitic nematodes (p. 420) or a chemical such as diazinon or Dursban (p. 445).

Moles

Notorious pests in good soils throughout North America, moles have short forelegs pointing outward; large, flattened hands; and claws for digging tunnels.

Moles are primarily insectivorous, eating earthworms, bugs, and larvae (controlling Japanese beetle and other beetle grubs may reduce mole problems in lawns), and only occasionally nibbling greens and roots. Irrigation and rain keep them near the soil surface, where they do the most damage as they tunnel: heaving plants from the ground, severing tender roots, and disfiguring lawns. A mole's main runways, which it uses repeatedly, are usually from 6 to 10 inches underground and are frequently punctuated with volcano-shaped mounds of excavated soil. Shallower burrows, created while feeding, are used for short periods and then abandoned.

Controls. Trapping is the most efficient way to control moles. The spear- or harpoon-type trap is the easiest to set because you simply position the trap above the soil. Carefully set a scissor-jaw trap into the main runway (probe with a sharp stick to find it); a wily mole will spring, heave out, or walk around a faultily set trap.

Due to their feeding habits, moles are very difficult to control with poison baits. And moles, like gophers, are hard to control with toxic gas. To be successful, place gas "mole bombs" directly in the main runways and block all holes. Be persistent with follow-up treatments.

You can dispatch a mole with a shovel blade, but you may wait a long time for a mole to appear. Your chances are best at dawn. If you see a mole scuttling along below ground (you'll notice the ground surface heaving), try the two-shovel method: Block the runway in front of the mole with one shovel blade and try to dig out the creature with the other.

MOLES OR VOLES? *Moles are often blamed when plants are chewed off at the ground, but voles are the likely culprits. These mouselike rodents burrow under leaf litter or just below the soil surface, eating roots and stems as they go. And they're very difficult to discourage. One useful strategy is to pull away all mulch and leaf litter from around their favorite plants, such as hostas. It also helps to place a few shovelfuls of sharp gravel in the hole around the roots when you plant.*

Mosquitoes

For gardeners and homeowners in regions where summers are warm and humid—which includes most of the South—these sucking insects can make outdoor living miserable. There are dozens of different mosquitoes that infest the South; most of them prefer standing water, including swimming pools, birdbaths, ponds, children's wading pools, gutters, water barrels, discarded tires, and anywhere else they can find a wet spot. Only the females bite, and most of them do so in the evening. Smell attracts them to humans.

You can't kill all the mosquitoes in your garden, but you can reduce their numbers and make yourself less attractive to them. Remove still and stagnant water, when practical, or cover it with fine screen. In hollow tree trunks and other spots where water collects, add some vegetable oil, which coats the surface and kills the larvae. Clear underbrush and low foliage, which provide hiding places for mosquitoes during the day. Don't linger close to standing water in the evening, when most mosquitoes are active. Burn citronella-scented candles or run a strong fan to blow them away. Keeping your skin clean removes compounds they like—especially for women—and light-colored clothing is said to be less attractive to them than dark.

Repellents containing DEET are effective, but can be toxic for children; choose less concentrated products for them. Floating "wafers" containing a strain of Bt (see p. 420) can be placed in standing water to reduce larvae populations. Don't rely on bug zappers for adults; they fry lots of moths but kill few mosquitoes.

Mulch

Any loose, usually organic material placed over the soil—such as ground bark, sawdust, straw, or leaves—is a mulch. The process of applying such materials is called mulching. A mulch may reduce evaporation of moisture from soil, stall weed growth, insulate soil from extreme or rapid changes of temperature, prevent mud from splashing onto foliage and other surfaces, protect falling fruit from injury, or make a garden bed look tidy.

Naturalize

To plant out randomly, without a precise pattern, and leave place to spread the plants at will is called naturalizing. Some plants naturalize readily, meaning that they can spread or reseed themselves, growing as wildflowers do.

Nematodes

Nematodes are microscopic worms that live in the soil. Some types are beneficial (see p. 420), feeding on pests or aiding in nitrogen fixation. Other nematodes feed on plant roots or foliage (see photograph, p. 456).

Without a soil test, the presence of nematodes is hard to detect. And pest types are even harder to control. Infested plants (usually flowers and vegetables, but also woody plants) slowly deteriorate, grow poorly and become stunted, turn yellow, wilt, and often succumb. The symptoms are very similar to moisture stress. Roots will often have small bumps or nodules where the nematodes feed and inject toxins. But the nodules are not a sure sign of their presence.

Nematodes are most common in sandy, moist soils in warm-summer climates, especially in Florida. If you think they may be present, contact your local Cooperative Extension Office about testing procedures available in your area. Other than fumigating the soil, a difficult and dangerous procedure, there are few surefire control measures. The best answer is to choose plants that aren't susceptible.

Nitrogen. See Nutrients, Basic   p. 443

Node

T he joint in a stem where a leaf starts to grow is a node. The area of stem between joints is the internode.

Nutgrass, Yellow

A n upright perennial weed that thrives in moist areas, yellow nutgrass has bright green, ¼-inch-wide leaves with a conspicuous midvein. Its flower head is golden brown (see photograph, p. 475). Small, roughly round tubers, or nutlets, may be found at the root tips. Nutgrass spreads by tubers or seed. Control can be difficult. Try Roundup (p. 474).

Nutrients, Basic

G rowing plants need a steady supply of nutrients—elements necessary to carry out their life processes. Six nutrients, called macronutrients, are needed in relatively large amounts. The most commonly deficient macronutrient for all plants is nitrogen (chemical symbol N). Two others, phosphorus (P) and potassium (K), are often needed for annual plants, bulbs, and shallow-rooted perennials, including grass, but seldom needed for trees and deep-rooted shrubs and vines. These three nutrients are the basis for commercial fertilizers.

Micronutrients, so called because plants require them only in very small quantities, are present in adequate amounts in most soils.

Nitrogen. The most commonly deficient nutrient, nitrogen, is not a mineral and hence is not present in the soil. All nitrogen must come from other sources: organic matter, air, water, or fertilizers. In nature, nitrogen comes primarily from decomposing organic material, which is generally in very short supply in some soils—especially in drier regions. Rainfall carries

nitrogen from the atmosphere into the soil. Some groundwater may also contain nitrogen. In addition, specialized nitrogen-fixing bacteria that live on the roots of certain plants (legumes in particular) extract nitrogen from air between soil particles.

Plants use nitrogen to form proteins, chlorophyll, and enzymes needed for plant cells to live and reproduce. When nitrogen is deficient, leaves yellow from their tips toward the stem, the plant yellows from the bottom upward, and growth is stunted (see photograph, p. 456).

Nitrogen can be absorbed by plant roots as nitrate, ammonium, or urea. Nitrate is soluble and can be easily leached through the soil. The ammonium ion, in contrast to nitrate, does not move through the soil with water. If you apply it to the soil surface, it must be converted to nitrate by soil organisms before it will move into the root zone. Urea is unique in that it moves with water, is converted to ammonium ion, and stays in the root zone until converted to nitrate. At that point it can be leached from the soil. Soil organisms also need nitrogen to thrive, and they, too, place demands on the available supply. For these reasons, many plants need supplemental nitrogen.

Nitrogen fertilizers. The first of the three numbers on a fertilizer label indicates the percentage of nitrogen. If the label says that all or most of the nitrogen is in either nitrate or nitric form, nitrogen will be released quickly. But if it is in the ammonium form (ammonium sulfate, for example), nitrogen release will be slower—anywhere from 2 weeks to 3 months—but more sustained.

Ammonium nitrate consists of half ammonium nitrogen and half nitric nitrogen; it therefore yields some of its nitrogen quickly and some more slowly. Organic nitrogen—as in blood meal and IBDU (isobutylidene diurea)—first must go through a conversion to ammoniac nitrogen, which then is converted to nitrogen in the nitrate form. These are the slowest acting of nitrogen sources. As a nitrogen source, organic matter is no more beneficial than inorganic sources because, ultimately, plants absorb it in the nitrate form. Organic fertilizers do, however, contribute organic matter to the soil, which can improve soil texture. See Soil Amendments, Organic (p. 461).

Phosphorus. The second percentage of the three on a fertilizer label indicates the amount of phosphorus (expressed as phosphate, P_2O_5, and listed as available phosphoric acid). It promotes healthy roots and flower and fruit production. Phosphorus does not move readily through the soil for roots to absorb. Soil particles that contain phosphorus ions release them reluctantly.

Phosphoric acid ionizes in the soil to form phosphate compounds. Some of these compounds are useful to plants; others are so insoluble that plants cannot use them. When you simply spread phosphate fertilizer on the soil and water in, the phosphoric acid binds chemically to the mineral particles in only the top

inch or two of soil. This means that surface applications of phosphorus fertilizers are largely ineffective, because they reach only surface roots. Symptoms of phosphorus deficiency include stunted plants, few flowers or fruits, and a purplish tinge to the leaves.

The most effective way to apply phosphorus is to concentrate it where roots can get at it. When you plant a lawn, annuals, or perennials (including bulbs), dig in superphosphate or a complete fertilizer that contains phosphorus as well as nitrogen and potash. Thoroughly mix the amount suggested in the label directions into what you estimate will be the root area for a few years to come.

Potassium. The third percentage on a fertilizer label represents potassium (expressed as potash, K_2O). Described as "available or soluble potash" or "water-soluble potash." Plants remove more potassium from the soil than any other nutrient except nitrogen and calcium.

Potassium exists naturally in the soil in several forms, but only about 1 percent of it is available to the plant.

Annuals, perennials, and lawns often need extra potassium, but in most soils trees and shrubs seldom respond to its addition. Potassium deficiencies occur in soils that are acid, sandy, low in organic matter, and low in nutrient-holding capacity. Symptoms include slow growth, leaf scorch, and mottled leaves.

Like phosphorus, potassium is effective only if placed in roots in the growth path.

Calcium, magnesium, sulfur. These elements are usually present in the soil in adequate supply.

Calcium and sulfur often enter the soil in other kinds of garden products: lime (calcium), lime-sulfur fungicide and soil conditioner (calcium and sulfur), gypsum (calcium and sulfur), superphosphate (sulfur), and soil sulfur used for acidifying alkaline soils.

Calcium plays a fundamental part in cell growth—most roots must have some calcium right at the growing tips. Magnesium forms the core of every chlorophyll molecule in the cells of green leaves. And sulfur acts with nitrogen in making new protoplasm for plant cells; it is just as essential as nitrogen, but its deficiency is not so widespread.

Iron, zinc, manganese. If soil is highly alkaline, as some soils in low-rainfall areas are, plants may not be able to absorb enough of these micronutrients. Gardeners can buy products to put on soil or spray on leaves to correct the deficiency.

Iron is essential to chlorophyll formation. Zinc and manganese seem to function as "triggers" in the utilization of other nutrients.

Offset

S ome mature perennials may send out from their base a short stem, at the end of which a small new plant develops. The new plant is

O

an offset. Some familiar examples are hen and chicks *(Echeveria)* and strawberry.

Organic Gardening

In simplest terms, organic gardening means using only materials derived from living things to grow plants. Such materials include organic fertilizers, soil amendments, and pest controls. The goals of organic gardening are to minimize impact on the environment, to reduce risks to people enjoying the garden, and to produce the healthiest food possible. However, "organic" is often considered a synonym for "safe," which is not always the case. Some organic pesticides, such as nicotine sulfate and rotenone, are toxic. Others, like pyrethrins, can cause allergic reactions in humans. Still others kill beneficial insects as well as plant pests.

Organic Matter

Any material originating from a living organism—peat moss, compost, or manure, for example—that can be dug into soil to improve its condition is referred to as organic matter. See Soil Amendments, Organic (p. 461).

Peat Moss

A highly water-retentive, spongy organic soil amendment, peat moss is the partially decomposed remains of any of several mosses. It is somewhat acid in reaction, adding to soil acidity. Sphagnum peat moss is generally highest in quality. There is a sedge peat, not composed of mosses, which is not necessarily acid.

Perennial

A perennial is a nonwoody plant that lives for more than 2 years. The word frequently refers to a plant whose top growth dies each winter and regrows the next spring, although some perennials keep their leaves all year.

Perennials are as diverse an assortment of plants as you'll find under one collective heading. Typically, a perennial has one blooming season each year, from only a week to more than a month long. After blooming, the plant may put on new growth for the next year; it may die down and virtually disappear until the time is right, some months later, for growth to resume; or it may retain much the same appearance throughout the year.

Garden uses. Like annuals, perennials provide color masses, but unlike annuals, they will bloom several years in a row without your having to dig up and replant them. Perennials are thus more permanent than annuals but less permanent than flowering shrubs. In fact, their semipermanence is a definite selling point. You can leave perennials in place for several years with little maintenance beyond annual cleanup, some fertilizing, and routine watering; but if you want to change the landscape, perennials are easy to dig up and replant.

PLANTING A BARE-ROOT, MAIL-ORDERED PERENNIAL

1 Gingerly unwrap packaged plant, being careful not to damage roots. Look in packing material for a label and growing advice.

2 Gently pull moist packing material from roots, untangling them carefully. Many gardeners soak roots overnight in water.

3 Spread roots over cone of soil in the center of a generous planting hole. Refill hole, burying roots just to where new foliage emerges (crown).

Planting. For instructions on planting most perennials, see Planting Techniques: Annuals and Perennials (p. 449). Garden centers and mail-order suppliers sell a number of popular perennials (irises, daylilies, peonies, Oriental poppies) and perennial fruits and vegetables (asparagus,

rhubarb, and strawberries) during their dormant periods as bare-root plants. Keep the roots moist before planting. They also benefit from a several hours' soak in water before planting. For handling mail-order perennials, see illustration.

Before planting dormant, bare-root perennials, prepare the soil well, as recommended under Planting Techniques: Seeds (p. 448), and be sure to set out each plant at its proper depth; refer to individual entries in the Plant Encyclopedia for specific planting information. Be sure to spread roots out well in the soil, gently firm soil around them, and then water thoroughly to establish good contact between roots and soil.

Care of established perennials. Feed perennials with a complete fertilizer just prior to the normal growth cycle—in late winter to early spring. Repeat after bloom.

Routine watering during the growth and bloom periods will satisfy most perennials. Refer to the Plant Encyclopedia for exceptions.

After a perennial stops blooming, remove the old blossoms to prevent the plant's energy from going into seed production.

Later in the season (usually in autumn), remove dead growth to minimize overwintering diseases and eliminate hiding and breeding places for insects, snails, and slugs.

Where the ground freezes in winter, many gardeners routinely mulch their perennials to protect them from alternate freezing and thawing. After the ground first freezes, apply a lightweight mulch that won't pack down into a sodden mass. Straw is one popular choice; evergreen boughs are good where available.

Digging, dividing, and replanting. Over time many perennials grow into such a thick clump that performance declines because the plants are crowded. When this happens, dig up the clump during its dormant period and divide it. See instructions under Dividing (p. 429).

MORE FLOWERS IN A PINCH. *There's a simple way to get two or three times as many flowers from perennials—pinching. As the plant grows, pinch out the top of each stem back to a node (the point at which the leaves and stem meet). Two stems will then grow from this spot. After they grow a while, pinch them too. You'll then have four stems. Each stem should have as many flowers as the original if you hadn't pinched it. This technique works on perennial phlox, fall asters, ironweed, purple coneflower, Joe-Pye weed, salvia, speedwell, balloon flower, butterfly weed, and toad lily.*

Perlite

Perlite is a mineral expanded by heating to form very lightweight, porous white granules useful in container soil mixes to enhance moisture and air retention.

Pest Management

The notion of pest control—where control implies eradication—has been superseded by the concept of pest management. This concept acknowledges that many perceived "problems" are natural components of gardens; the presence of pests doesn't necessarily spell trouble. In a diversified garden, natural forces (such as predators and weather) keep insect pests in check. If pests reach damaging levels, however, you may need to restore a balance.

Because of this natural system of checks and balances in a garden, it makes sense to determine which form of intervention will return the

CONTROLLING PESTS WITH INSECTICIDES

Insecticides carry one or more active ingredients in a liquid, powder, or granular form. On the label of each product is a list of plants and pests on which you can use the control. It is illegal to apply the control to a plant or pest not listed on the label, so always read the label.

- **Azadirachtin (neem).** A botanical insecticide from the African neem tree *(Azadirachta indica)*, this liquid spray is nontoxic to mammals; it stops feeding of many insects and prevents normal growth of immature insects. It's also effective against some fungal diseases, including black spot and powdery mildew. Neem has limited registration in some states.

- **Baygon (propoxur).** Common in earwig baits and wasp and hornet sprays. Do not use propoxur on edible crops.

- ***Bacillus thuringiensis (Bt).*** A biological control sold under the names Javelin, Dipel, and Thuricide, among others, *Bt* paralyzes and destroys the stomach cells of the insects that consume it. Its various strains are toxic to caterpillars, mosquitoes, and some beetles. It works best on young larvae (see p. 420 for more information.).

- **Contact dusts.** Differing from insecticidal dusts, these powdered materials cling to, scratch, and destroy the waxy exterior of some pests. Diatomaceous earth, boric acid, and silica aerogels are among the most useful, but they can be hazardous to humans if inhaled.

  Use natural-grade, properly labeled diatomaceous earth to discourage ants, slugs, and snails. Boric acid, usually a dust or powder, is also available as a spray or paste and in baited traps. Silica aerogels dehydrate an insect's body, killing it. In the garden, apply as a dust for ants, fleas, and ticks.

- **Diazinon.** A broad-spectrum insecticide also widely used to control various lawn pests, diazinon is the only chemical control for soil pests in vegetable gardens. It is toxic to bees and birds.

- **Dursban (chlorpyrifos).** A control for certain borers in shade trees, lawn insects, termites, and many pests of ornamental plants. Do not use it on vegetables.

- **Kelthane (dicofol).** Designed to control spider mites. Dicofol may also be found in multipurpose insecticides.

- **Lindane.** Kills many insects, including aphids, thrips, leaf miners, pine bark beetles, and borers in peach trees, dogwood, rhododendron, lilac, and iris.

- **Malathion.** A broad-spectrum insecticide for use on both edible and ornamental crops, malathion is toxic to honeybees.

- **Mesurol (methiocarb).** An effective control for slugs and snails, methiocarb will also kill earthworms. Do not use on edible crops.

- **Metaldehyde.** The most common slug and snail control, metaldehyde is usually the active ingredient in baits and some liquids. It may be used around vegetable and fruit crops, but it loses effectiveness in moist weather and after waterings. It can be toxic to pets.

- **Oil sprays.** Special, highly refined oils smother insects and their eggs. "Dormant oils" are used during winter or early spring for control of insects that overwinter on deciduous plants. "Summer oils" can be used after leaves have emerged and on woody evergreen plants such as citrus. Use in summer to control aphids, pear psylla, scale insects, mites, and eggs of some insects. Oils can burn sensitive leaves; test-spray on a small area of plant first. Two common brands are SunSpray and Ultra-Fine Spray Oil.

- **Pyrethrin.** Pyrethrin is a natural insecticide derived from *Pyrethrum* daisies. It is effective against many insects (especially quick knockdown of flying ones) but will break down within a few hours after exposure to sunlight. Pyrethroids are synthetic versions, which are more toxic and last longer in the environment.

- **Rotenone.** A botanical insecticide derived from South American plants, rotenone dust controls chewing insects on vegetables. It is fairly toxic to mammals and extremely toxic to fish.

- **Ryania.** A botanical insecticide derived from the powdered stem of a tropical shrub, ryania acts as a stomach poison, controlling codling moth, citrus thrips, corn earworm, and asparagus beetle. It is gentle on beneficials.

- **Sabadilla.** Made by grinding seeds of the sabadilla lily, this control acts as a stomach and contact poison against caterpillars, leafhoppers, and thrips. It has low toxicity to people but is highly toxic to birds.

- **Sevin (carbaryl).** This insecticide, commonly used in vegetable gardens, is effective against most chewing insects but ineffective against sucking insects. It often increases problems with the latter pests by destroying their natural predators. Sevin is highly toxic to honeybees and earthworms.

- **Soaps.** These mixtures of special fatty acids are of low toxicity to humans but will control most small insects and mites. They are safe for use on edible plants and fast acting, but have no residual effectiveness. Soaps injure some plants. They are most effective in soft water. Once dry, soaps will not kill beneficials. Safer insecticidal soap is a common brand.

- **Sulfur.** You can dust finely ground sulfur mixed with clay, talc, and gypsum over plants to control mites, psyllids, and certain mildews. Or, you may dilute with water and spray. Never use when temperature will exceed 90°F.

- **Systemics.** These are absorbed by a plant's foliage or roots; insects such as scales and leafminers that pierce the plant's tissues are killed. Sprayed on the foliage, some systemics also kill insects on contact. Widely available are Cygon (dimethoate) and Orthene (acephate). Do not use on edible crops.

- **Thiodan (endosulfan).** This broad-spectrum insecticide is particularly effective against thrips, aphids, borers, fuchsia mites, and whiteflies. Some areas restrict its use.

Pesticides are listed by trade name. The active ingredient appears in parentheses. Some pesticides are commonly known by their active ingredient.

P

situation to a normal balance with the least risk of destroying helpful (as well as harmless) organisms that maintain the equilibrium. Choices range from doing nothing (giving nature a chance to correct the imbalance), using restraints (washing plants, or repelling or physically destroying the damagers), biological controls (improving the helpful side of nature's own system), or applying chemical controls.

More and more gardeners are turning to physical restraints and biological controls (see Visual Guide to Identifying Biological Controls, p. 420) as a first line of defense against garden pests because they want natural gardens that are safer for children, pets, and wildlife. Yet almost all horticulturists acknowledge the need for at least occasional treatment with chemical controls. This approach—the preferred use of natural and mechanical controls, plus chemicals as a discretionary second choice—is called integrated pest management (IPM).

The IPM approach. The following points explain how to implement IPM in your own garden.

- **Select well-adapted plants.** Choose plants that are suitable to your area and that are resistant to your region's particular pest and disease problems.

- **Adjust planting time.** If by planting early you can avoid an inevitable pest, do so. Keep records of planting dates and temperatures so you can make adjustments from one season to another.

- **Try mechanical controls.** Hand-picking, traps, barriers, floating row covers, or a strong jet of water can reduce or thwart many pests, especially in the early stages of a

potential problem. Cleanup of plant debris can remove the environment in which certain pests and diseases breed or overwinter.

- **Accept minor damage.** A totally pest-free garden is impossible. Allow natural control methods to play the major role in maintaining a healthy balance between pests and the beneficial (plus the harmless) insects and creatures that are normal garden components.

- **Solarize the soil.** Using the sun to heat the soil before planting is an effective way to reduce or eliminate soil-inhabiting pests. Just before the hottest time of the year (usually mid-July) and well before fall planting, till soil and remove weeds. Water soil, then lay 1½- to 2-mil clear plastic over it; anchor edges with soil. Leave in place for 4 to 6 weeks.

- **Use less toxic alternatives.** Release or encourage beneficial insects; use soaps, horticultural oils, botanical insecticides such as natural pyrethrins (p. 445), and one of several packaged forms of *Bacillus thuringiensis* (p. 420). Realize that beneficial insects may take a while to reduce the pests they prey upon, and that you may have to use nonchemical controls at more frequent intervals than you would chemical controls. And although many natural insecticides have a relatively low impact on the environment, they can be harmful to humans if you use them carelessly. Follow label instructions exactly.

- **Use chemical preparations prudently.** Occasionally, you will need to use a chemical control—especially for management of diseases (p. 429). Before you purchase a chemical control and begin applying it, be sure you

have correctly identified the problem. Only use a pesticide to solve a problem if both the pest and the target plant are listed on the pesticide's label. If you are at all uncertain, ask at a local garden center or contact the nearest Cooperative Extension Office. Follow label directions exactly. For help identifying specific plant problems, see p. 454.

Biological controls. A number of living organisms can provide some measure of pest control. Many occur naturally in gardens (and unwise pesticide use may kill them). For information on beneficial insects—insects that prey on garden insect pests—and other biological controls, see p. 420.

Petals. See Plant Anatomy and Growth
p. 446, 447

Phosphorus. See Nutrients, Basic   p. 443

Pillbug, Sowbug

These familiar creatures have sectioned shells and seven pairs of legs. Pillbugs roll up into black balls about the size of a large pea; sowbugs are gray and cannot roll up as tightly. Their principal food is decaying vegetation, but they also will eat very young seedling plants and the skins of melons, cucumbers, squash, and berries—

ANATOMY OF A FLOWER

Among flowering plants, blossom form varies enormously. But this diversity obscures the fact that all flowers share a basic structural plan and that the structural elements always appear in the same order. The illustration shows a schematic flower and its parts.

- **Receptacle** is the point where floral parts attach to the specialized stem that bears the flower.

- **Sepals** make up the outer circle, or ring, of floral parts. Collectively, the sepals are the *calyx*.

- **Petals** form the next circle of flower parts, just inward from the sepals. In showy flowers, it is usually the petals that make the display. Petals may be separate, as in camellias and roses, or united into tubular, cupped, or bell-like shapes, as in rhododendrons and petunias. Collectively, the petals are called the *corolla* (the calyx and corolla together are known as the *perianth*).

- **Stamens,** positioned inward from the petals, contain the male reproductive elements. Typically a stamen consists of a slender stalk (the filament) topped by an anther (most often a yellow color). The latter contains grains of pollen, which is the male element needed to fertilize the flower for it to produce seeds. See Pollination (p. 452).

- **Pistils,** found in the center of a flower, bear the female reproductive parts. Each pistil typically consists of an ovary at the base (in which seeds will form following pollination) and a stalklike tube called the style that rises from the ovary. The style is topped by a stigma, the part that receives the pollen.

A complete flower —a term that describes most of the flowers we grow— comprises all the parts described above. An incomplete flower lacks one or more of the floral parts, but those it does contain appear in the order listed. For more information on flowers and flower parts, see Single Flower (p. 460) and Double Flower (p. 430).

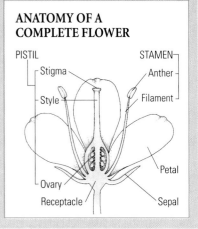

ANATOMY OF A COMPLETE FLOWER

PISTIL

Stigma

Style

Ovary

Receptacle

STAMEN

Anther

Filament

Petal

Sepal

particularly if the fruits are overripe and have a break in the skin.

Mulching and composting encourage pillbugs and sowbugs. If you sprout seeds near a compost pile or in heavily composted soil, you may get some pillbug and sowbug damage. You can apply Sevin (p. 445) to the seedlings or to the ground where the pests are active. Or lift fruit off the ground onto the top of small saucers or boards, plastic mulch, or landscape fabric, out of the pests' reach.

Pinching

Using thumb and forefinger to nip off the tips of branches is called pinching back. This basic pruning technique (p. 457) forces side growth, making the plant more compact and dense. It can also result in more flowers.

Plant Anatomy and Growth

Knowledge about how plants grow is an important key to becoming a successful gardener. The box (below, left) explains the anatomy of a flower; the box below illustrates plant growth.

Plant Classification

Botanists classify the world's plants into an orderly, ranked system reflecting similarities among them. They divide the plant kingdom into groups that are less and less inclusive: division, class, order, and then the groups defined here, which are the ones of most significance to home gardeners.

Family. Each plant belongs to a family, members of which share certain broad characteristics that are not always immediately evident. The rose family, for instance, includes such diverse plants as the rose, the apple tree, and the familiar perennial geum. Most family names end in *-aceae* (Orchidaceae, Asteraceae, Liliaceae).

Genus. A plant family is divided into groups of more closely related plants; each group is called a genus (the plural is "genera"). Sometimes a family contains only one genus: for example, Ginkgoaceae contains only the genus *Ginkgo*. At the other extreme, the daisy family (Asteraceae) contains around 950 genera. The first word in a

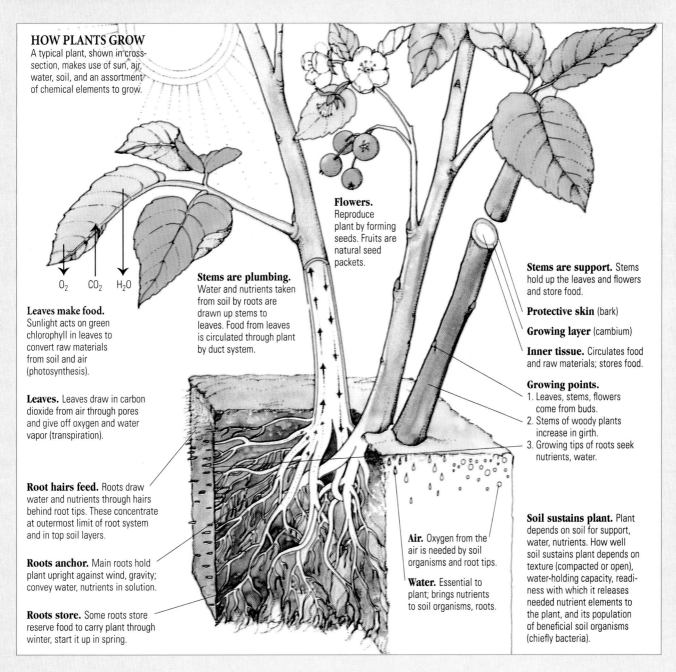

HOW PLANTS GROW
A typical plant, shown in cross-section, makes use of sun, air, water, soil, and an assortment of chemical elements to grow.

O_2 CO_2 H_2O

Leaves make food. Sunlight acts on green chlorophyll in leaves to convert raw materials from soil and air (photosynthesis).

Leaves. Leaves draw in carbon dioxide from air through pores and give off oxygen and water vapor (transpiration).

Root hairs feed. Roots draw water and nutrients through hairs behind root tips. These concentrate at outermost limit of root system and in top soil layers.

Roots anchor. Main roots hold plant upright against wind, gravity; convey water, nutrients in solution.

Roots store. Some roots store reserve food to carry plant through winter, start it up in spring.

Flowers. Reproduce plant by forming seeds. Fruits are natural seed packets.

Stems are plumbing. Water and nutrients taken from soil by roots are drawn up stems to leaves. Food from leaves is circulated through plant by duct system.

Air. Oxygen from the air is needed by soil organisms and root tips.

Water. Essential to plant; brings nutrients to soil organisms, roots.

Stems are support. Stems hold up the leaves and flowers and store food.

Protective skin (bark)

Growing layer (cambium)

Inner tissue. Circulates food and raw materials; stores food.

Growing points.
1. Leaves, stems, flowers come from buds.
2. Stems of woody plants increase in girth.
3. Growing tips of roots seek nutrients, water.

Soil sustains plant. Plant depends on soil for support, water, nutrients. How well soil sustains plant depends on texture (compacted or open), water-holding capacity, readiness with which it releases needed nutrient elements to the plant, and its population of beneficial soil organisms (chiefly bacteria).

P

plant's botanical name is the name of the genus to which it belongs: for example, *Ginkgo, Liquidambar, Primula*.

Species. Within each genus are groups of individuals called species; the second word in a plant's botanical name designates the species. Each species is a generally distinct entity, reproducing from seed with only a small amount of variation. Species in a genus share many common features. When a third word occurs in a plant name, it indicates a variety, either botanical or horticultural. The botanical variety denotes a natural geographical or other variant of a given species. This name is represented in italic *(Juniperus chinensis sargentii)*. The botanical variety is sometimes called a subspecies. The horticultural variety is a plant of garden origin that results from hybridization or selection. It is also called a selection or cultivar and is represented in Roman type and set off by single quotation marks, thus: *Rosa* 'Chrysler Imperial'.

Planting Techniques: Seeds

In nature, seeds are scattered randomly. And scattering, or broadcasting, seeds is a common method for planting lawn grasses and wildflowers. To plant seeds of most garden plants, though, the gardener sows seeds more carefully in the open ground or in some sort of container.

You can buy seeds of most ornamental plants in three different forms. The traditional packaging is the seed packet, with a picture of the flower, fruit, or plant on the outside, the loose seeds within. You also can buy packets or packages of pelletized seeds: each seed is coated, like a small pill, to make handling and proper spacing easier. The third form is seed tapes—strips of biodegradable plastic in which seeds are embedded, properly spaced. You just unroll the tape in a prepared furrow and cover it with soil. In all three cases, you will find planting instructions on the package.

Direct sowing. One advantage of sowing seeds directly in the earth is that you usually avoid the need to transplant. The seeds germinate and grow into mature plants in one place. You may need to thin seedlings to prevent overcrowding, filling in a few sparse spots with thinned plants. But most of the seedling plants will need no handling once they break ground.

You can choose between broadcasting and row planting, depending on the results you want.

Broadcasting. Some flower seeds will make a reasonably good show if you simply scatter them—in time to catch autumn rains—where they are to grow. But they will do even better if you first clear the ground of weeds and grasses; then till it, and add organic amendments. If you plan to broadcast seeds in drifts or patterned plantings, or if you wish to sow a broad area with tough, easy-to-grow plants, you can achieve a more even distribution by mixing the seed with several times its bulk of fine sand.

You can also sow most garden annuals and vegetables in place, but they will benefit from a bit more attention than simple broadcasting. With a fork, spade, or rototiller, prepare the seedbed, working in plenty of soil amendments and a complete fertilizer (p. 431). Smooth the prepared soil with a rake and moisten it well a few days before you intend to plant (if rains don't do the watering for you). Then follow the sowing and covering directions outlined for broadcasting.

GOING TO SEED. *Many flower gardeners want instant color, so they opt to buy transplants. But if you like an informal look and want to save a little money, try this method. In late autumn or early spring, mix seeds of annuals with fine sand, sprinkle the mixture over bare soil, rake lightly, and water. When the weather warms, you'll enjoy drifts of beautiful flowers. Annuals recommended for direct sowing include cosmos, zinnias, bachelor's buttons, spider flower (cleome), poppies, and marigolds.*

Row planting. If you intend to grow vegetables or annuals in rows, prepare the soil as described previously. But you can omit the fertilizer and apply it, instead, at seeding time in furrows 1 inch deeper than the seeds and 2 inches on either side of the seed row (again, consult label recommendations for the proper amount of fertilizer per foot of row). Follow the seed packet instructions for optimum planting depth and

TWO WAYS TO PLANT STRAIGHT

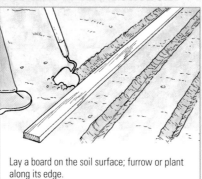

Lay a board on the soil surface; furrow or plant along its edge.

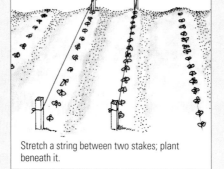

Stretch a string between two stakes; plant beneath it.

spacing of the rows, and lay them out in a north-south direction so that both sides will receive equal sunlight . Use a hoe, rake, or stick to form the furrow; for perfectly straight rows, use a board or a taut string as a guideline.

Thinning. When seedlings appear, thin excess plants (if necessary) so that those remaining are spaced as directed on the seed packet. Bare seeds scattered in furrows almost always come up too thickly; pelletized seeds are easier to sow at the proper spacing, and seed tapes do the spacing for you. If you wait too long to thin seedlings, plants will develop poorly, and it will be more difficult to remove one without disturbing those around it.

Sowing in flats and containers. Many plants get off to a better start if you sow them in containers and later transplant them into place in the garden.You can start your own seedlings indoors or in a greenhouse—or in any location that is warmer than the out-of-doors and has adequate light.

Choosing a container. Almost anything that will hold soil and has provision for drainage will do. Plastic or wooden nursery flats will accommodate the largest number of seeds; other choices are clay or plastic pots, peat pots, aluminum foil pans (the sort sold for kitchen use), Styrofoam or plastic cups, cut-down milk cartons, or shallow wooden boxes that you can make yourself.

Remember to punch holes for drainage in the bottom of any container that holds water; if you make your own wooden flats or boxes, leave about a ¼-inch space for drainage between the boards that form the container's bottom.

If you use containers that have held plants before, give them a thorough cleaning to avoid the possibility of infection by damping-off fungi, which destroy seedlings. A vigorous scrubbing followed by a few days of drying in the sun usually suffices.

Choosing a planting mix. Buy a prepared planting mixture for starting seeds. Garden centers carry a variety of such mediums—look for labels that say "potting soil." See Container Gardening (p. 425). Gently firm the mixture into the container and level it off about ¾ to 1 inch from the top of the container. If the mixture is powdery dry, water it thoroughly and wait a day or two to plant.

How to sow. You can broadcast very fine seeds over the surface and cover with sand; plant larger seeds in shallow furrows scratched into the surface or in individual holes. Always remember that seeds should be planted no deeper than recommended on packet labels; a good general rule is to cover seeds to a depth equal to twice their diameter. Cover seeds, press down gently but firmly, and then water. Direct watering of the soil surface can sometimes dislodge the seeds. Instead, place the container in a tub, sink, or bucket containing a few inches of water. The planting mix in the container will absorb enough water within a few hours. From

P

SOWING SEEDS IN CONTAINERS

For small seeds like lettuce, first mix ¼ package with 2 tablespoons sand. Scatter over moist potting mix in flat or aluminum pan with holes punched in bottom. Sprinkle with soil, firm, and water lightly. Set in protected area with bright light. Keep moist.

For large seeds like Swiss chard, sow in furrows made with a small stake. Sow according to label directions and water lightly. Set in protected area with bright light. Keep moist.

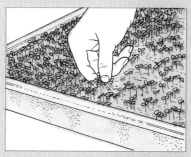

Thin seedlings of small, scatter-sown seeds (top drawing) to about 1 to 2 inches apart by snipping with scissors or pinching off with fingers.

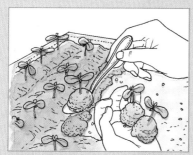

Transplant when seedlings have at least their second set of leaves. Scoop out with a kitchen spoon. Water regularly. If it's hot, shade plants.

then on, keep the seeding mixture moist but not soaking wet.

For slow-sprouting seeds or for plants whose seedlings develop slowly, sow seeds in a pot, and then tie a clear plastic bag around it. Place the pot where it receives good light but not direct sunlight. Air can get through the plastic, but water vapor cannot get out; seedlings will have enough moisture to complete germination without further watering. If you use this technique, be sure that your planting mixture is sterile and that the container is clean.

Transplanting seedlings. When the new seedlings develop their second set of true leaves, it's time to transplant or thin them. If you don't need many plants, you can thin them in place. Give them enough "elbowroom" (1½ to 2 inches between them) to grow larger before you plant them out in the garden. But if you want to save most of the germinated plants, you will need to transplant them to larger containers for growth to planting-out size. Preferably, transplant them into individual pots or cups; then when you plant out in the garden, they'll suffer a minimum of root disturbance.

First transplanting. Fill a new container with moist planting mix. Loosen the soil around the seedling plants (a kitchen fork or spoon is handy for this) and carefully lift out a seedling. Or lift a clump of seedlings and gently tease individual plants apart from the tangled mass of roots. Handle a seedling by its leaves to avoid bruising or crushing its tender stem. With a pencil, poke a hole in the new container's planting mix, place the seedling in the hole, and firm the soil around it. Water the transplant right away. Do this for each seedling plant. Keep them out of direct sunlight for a few days, until they have adjusted.

Final transplanting. A few weeks to a month after the initial transplant, the seedlings should be ready to plant in the garden. During that month, you can help their development by watering once with a half-strength liquid fertilizer solution or by sprinkling lightly with a slow-acting fertilizer.

Planting Techniques: Annuals and Perennials

Busy gardeners often forgo the pleasures of seed planting and buy seedlings of annuals, vegetables, and perennials at garden centers. These plants—as well as some ground covers and hedge plants—are sold in plastic cellpacks, individual plastic pots, peat pots, or flats.

You'll get the best results from small bare-root plants in pots and flats if you prepare the soil as for sowing seeds (see p. 448). Be sure not to let these plants dry out while they're waiting to be planted. For all small plants, plant so that the tops of their root balls are even with the soil surface.

From cell-packs. Plants in plastic cell-packs, with each plant in an individual cube of soil, are

easy to remove. Push down with your thumb on the bottom of a soil cube, and remove the root ball with the other hand. If there is a mat of interwoven roots at the bottom of the root ball, tear it off—the plant will benefit from its removal. Otherwise, loosen the roots by pulling apart the bottom third of the root ball.

From pots. Dislodge plants in individual pots by placing one hand over the top of the container, with the plant stem between index and middle fingers, and then turning the container upside down. The plant and its root ball should slip out of the container into your hand.

From peat pots. If the plant is in a peat pot, plant it pot and all; the roots will grow through the pot. But make sure that the peat pot is moist before you plant it. A dry peat pot takes up moisture slowly from the soil, so roots may be slow in breaking through it. This can stunt the plant's growth or cause roots within the peat pot to dry out completely. Several minutes before transplanting, set the peat pot in a shallow container of water. Also, be sure to cover the top of a peat pot with soil because exposed peat acts as a wick to draw moisture out of the soil. If covering the peat would bury the plant too deeply, break off the top of the pot to slightly below the plant's soil level.

From flats. For plants in flats, a putty knife or spatula is a handy transplanting tool: Separate the plants in the flat by cutting straight down around each one. Many gardeners prefer to separate individual plants out of flats gently with their fingers; they lose some soil this way, but keep more roots on the plant. If you work quickly, there will be little transplant shock.

Planting Techniques: Trees and Shrubs

At all times of the year, you can purchase trees and shrubs for immediate planting: bare-root in the dormant season, balled-and-burlapped generally in the cooler months, and those planted year-round.

Bare-root plants. In winter and early spring, you can buy bare-root plants at many garden centers or from mail-order suppliers. Many deciduous plants are available bare-root: fruit and shade trees, deciduous flowering shrubs, roses, grapes, and cane fruits.

Why go out in the cold and wet of winter to buy and set out bare-root plants when you can wait until the warmth of spring, summer, or autumn and plant the same plants from containers? There are two reasons:

- You can save money. Typically, a bare-root plant costs only 40 to 70 percent of the price of the same plant purchased in a container later in the year.

- How you plant a bare-root tree or shrub makes it establish itself faster and often better than if you set it out later from a container.

P

▶

PLANTING FROM CELL-PACKS

1 Poke plants out of cell-pack by pushing on bottom of individual cell; let gravity help. If tight, run a knife between side of container and soil.

2 Lightly separate matted roots. If there's a pad of coiled-up white roots at the bottom, cut it off so roots will grow outward into soil.

3 Without squeezing roots, position plant in generous planting hole. Form a watering basin around each plant. Water each one separately, with a gentle flow that won't disturb soil or roots.

The advantage of bare-root planting is that, when you set out the plant, you can refill the planting hole with the backfill soil that you dug from the hole: The roots will grow in only one kind of soil. In contrast, when you plant from a container or balled-and-burlapped, you put two soils, usually with different textures, in contact with each other. The two different kinds of soil can make it difficult to get uniform water penetration into the rooting area.

Planting techniques. For successful bare-root planting, the roots should be fresh and plump. Even if roots look fine, soak the root system overnight in a bucket of water.

Dig the planting hole broad and deep enough to accommodate roots easily without cramping, bending, or cutting them to fit. Cut back any broken roots to healthy tissue. In areas with shallow or problem soils, a wider hole will speed establishment. Follow the illustrations at right to dig the planting hole and set out the bare-root plant.

After the initial soaking, water bare-root plantings conservatively. Dormant plants need less water than actively growing ones, and if you keep the soil too wet, new feeder roots may not form. Check soil periodically for moisture and water accordingly.

When weather turns warm and growth becomes active, water more frequently. Do not overwater: Check soil for moisture before watering. If hot, dry weather follows planting, shade the new plant at least until it begins to grow. And be patient—some bare-root plants are slow to leaf out.

Plants in containers. Plants grown in containers are popular for many reasons. Most broadleafed evergreen shrubs and trees are only offered in containers, and you can buy them in all seasons. Available in a variety of sizes and prices, they are easy to transport and you don't need to plant them immediately. Furthermore, you can buy a container plant in bloom or fruit and see exactly what you are getting.

When shopping for container-grown plants, look for ones with a generally healthy, vigorous appearance and good foliage. The root system should be unencumbered—that is, not badly tangled or constricted by the plant's own roots. Two signs of a seriously rootbound plant are roots protruding above the soil level and good-sized roots growing through the container's drainage holes. When selecting young trees, feel for circling roots around the trunk in the top two inches of soil. Additional indicators of crowded roots: plants that are large for the size of their containers, leggy plants, and dead twigs or branches. If you find any of these signs, buy another plant.

Planting techniques. Follow the steps shown in the illustration at right to set out plants from containers. Set plant in hole, spread roots, and fill in around roots with unamended backfill, firming with your fingers until hole is about half full and air pockets are eliminated. After planting, pump the plant up and down slightly to settle wet soil around the roots, and check that the top of the root ball remains about 2 inches above soil grade.

Balled-and-burlapped plants. Certain plants such as deciduous shrubs and trees, such evergreen shrubs as rhododendrons and azaleas, and various conifers, have roots that won't survive bare-root transplanting. Instead, garden centers or growers dig them up with a ball of soil around the roots which they usually wrap in burlap and tie with twine. These are called balled-and-burlapped (or B-and-B) plants.

Treat B-and-B plants carefully: don't use the trunk as a handle; and don't drop them, because the root ball could shatter. Cradle the root ball well by supporting the bottom with one or both hands. If it is too heavy for one person to carry, get a friend to help you transport it in a sling of canvas or stout burlap.

THE PLANTING HOLE

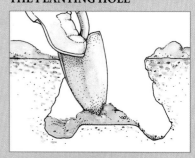

All tree and shrub planting begins with digging a hole. Dig it so that sides taper outward into the soil and are roughened, not smoothly sculpted (use a spading fork to dig, or to roughen shovel-dug sides); this lets roots penetrate more easily into surrounding soil. To prevent or minimize settling of the plant after planting and watering, make the hole a bit shallower than the root ball or root system of the plant it will receive, then dig deeper around edges of the hole's bottom. This leaves a firm plateau of undug soil to support plant at proper depth.

P

PLANTING BARE-ROOT...

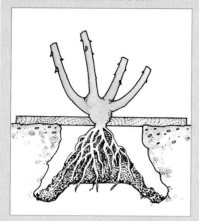

1 Make a firm cone of soil in hole. Spread roots over cone, positioning plant at same depth as (or slightly higher than) it was in growing field; use stick to check depth.

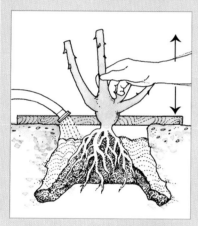

2 Fill in backfill soil nearly to top, firming it with your fingers as you fill. Then add water. If plant settles, pump it up and down, while water saturates soil. Then raise plant to the proper level.

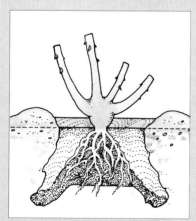

3 After plant is watered in and at the correct level, fill in any remaining soil. When growing season begins, make ridge of soil around hole to form a watering basin.

...FROM A CONTAINER

1 If roots are matted, spray soil off outer few inches of root ball and loosen. Cut off any roots that are permanently kinked.

2 Spread roots out over firm plateau of soil, then add unamended backfill soil. Ensure that top of root ball is about 2 inches above surrounding soil.

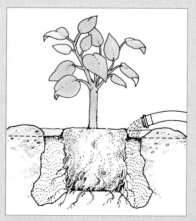

3 Make berm of soil to form watering moat. Irrigate gently—water should remain in moat rather than flood basin; objective is to keep base of trunk dry.

...OR BALLED-AND-BURLAPPED

1 Set balled-and-burlapped plant into planting hole, placing root ball on firm plateau of undug soil; top of root ball should be about 2 inches above surrounding soil.

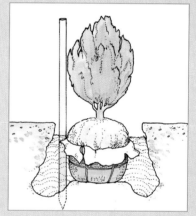

2 Untie burlap and spread it out to uncover about half of root ball. Drive stake into soil alongside root ball before filling hole with backfill soil.

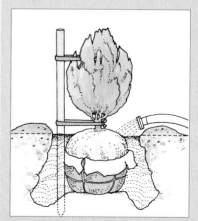

3 After firming in backfill soil, make berm of soil to form watering moat. Gently water in plant; then loosely tie plant to stake. Burlap will slowly decay.

P

Planting techniques. Dig a hole twice as wide as the root ball and follow the instructions in the illustration on p. 451. You can leave burlap or another biodegradable fabric in place, but if a synthetic material was used to wrap the root ball, carefully remove it so that the roots can grow into the surrounding soil. Then fill the hole half full with backfill soil, firming it with your fingers or a stick.

If your soil is light to medium (and your B-and-B soil is heavier), mix one shovelful of organic amendment to each three shovelfuls of backfill soil. This will improve the water retention of the backfill soil, creating a transition zone between root ball and garden soil. Use peat moss, ground bark, or similar organic amendments—but not animal manures.

If you are setting out a B-and-B plant in a windy location, drive a stake firmly into the soil beside the planting hole on the side of the plant that faces the prevailing winds.

During the first couple of years after planting, pay close attention to watering—especially if the root-ball soil is heavier than your garden soil. Keep the surrounding garden soil moist (but never continuously soggy) so that the roots will grow out of the root ball into the surrounding soil as fast as possible.

Note: If a root ball becomes dry, it will shrink, harden, and fail to absorb water. Where there's a great difference between garden soil and root-ball soil, you can achieve better water penetration if you carefully punch holes in the root ball with a pointed instrument, ¼ to ½ inch wide. Or use a root irrigator (see Watering Devices, p. 470). After several years, when roots have grown out and become established in your garden soil, the difference between soil types won't matter.

Plant Problems. See Visual Guide to Identifying Plant Problems   p. 454

Pleaching

Pleaching is a method of training plant growth where branches are interwoven and plaited together to form a hedge or an arbor. Subsequent pruning merely maintains a neat, rather formal pattern. Trees that are commonly pleached include beech, hornbeam, apple, peach, and pear.

Poison Ivy and Poison Oak

Poison ivy *(Toxicodendron radicans),* is common in shady areas and along the edges of woodlands (see photograph, p. 476). It will grow as a sprawling plant until it finds something to climb on; then it becomes a clinging vine. Established poison ivy plants bear clusters of pale green flowers in spring followed by small white berries.

Poison oak *(T. diversilobum)* grows in open or in filtered sun as a dense, leafy shrub (see photograph, p. 476). Where shaded, it becomes a tall, climbing vine. Its leaves are divided into three leaflets, edges of which are scalloped, toothed, or lobed.

The new growth of both poison oak and poison ivy is tinged red. Foliage turns bright orange to scarlet in fall—beautiful but to be avoided. It's hardest to identify the bare branches in winter and early spring; even brushing against these can cause the typical rash.

Control poison oak and poison ivy with an appropriately labeled herbicide such as Brush-B-Gon or Roundup (p. 474).

DIE, IVY, DIE! *Here's an easy way to kill established poison ivy, roots and all. First, pull a long stem of poison ivy from a tree (wear gloves), making sure the stem remains attached to the ground. Then fill a bucket with water and add the amount of Roundup recommended on the label. Place as much of the poison-ivy stem as you can into the solution and leave it there for several days. The stem will gradually take the chemical down to the roots, This technique also works for wisteria and other hard-to-kill vines.*

Pollarding

In pollarding, a style of pruning, the main limbs of a young tree are cut back to short lengths. Each dormant season following, the growth from these branch stubs is cut back to one or two buds. In time, branch ends become large and knobby. The result is a compact, leafy dome during the growing season and a somewhat grotesque branch structure during the dormant months. The London plane tree *(Platanus acerifolia)* often endures this treatment.

Pollination

The transfer of pollen from stamens to pistil accomplishes pollination—which leads to seed formation and thus to a new generation of plants. Usually pollination happens by natural means—insects, birds, self-pollination, wind—although gardeners can transfer pollen from one flower to another to ensure fruit or to attempt a hybrid cross. An insect or animal that carries pollen from one part of a flower to another, or from one plant to another, is a pollinator.

Some plants produce separate male flowers (with stamens only) and female flowers (with pistils only). These may appear on the same plant (in pecans and walnuts, for example) or on separate plants (as in hollies). In the latter case, you need a male plant nearby to produce fruits on the female plant. To get a crop from some fruit and nut trees, you must plant two selections—either because a selection will not set fruit using its own pollen or because its own pollen will not be ripe at the time its pistils are receptive. A plant used to provide pollen for another plant is called a pollinator or pollenizer.

Potassium. See Nutrients, Basic   p. 443

Pot-Bound. See Root-Bound   p. 458

Potting Soil

A potting soil is a soil mix designed especially for plants growing in containers.

Powdery and Downy Mildews

Powdery mildew and downy mildew are two diseases that gardeners often confuse. Powdery mildew first appears as small gray or white circular patches on plant tissue, spreading rapidly to form powdery areas of fungus filaments and spores (see photograph, p. 456). It can infect leaves, buds, flowers, and stems, depending on the exact kind of mildew and the host plant. Powdery mildew attacks young growth of some woody plants, such as roses and sycamores, and mature leaves of non-woody plants such as dahlias, chrysanthemums, peas, beans, and squash. Infected leaves may become crumpled and distorted.

Powdery mildew spores are unique in that they can cause infection in the absence of moisture. Most powdery mildews (there are many kinds) thrive in humid air, but spores need dry leaves on which to become established. You're likely to find powdery mildew when days are warm and nights are cool; it also resurges when days shorten and cool, humid nights lengthen.

Some plants are notoriously mildew-prone (phlox, bee balm, crepe myrtle, and roses). Where powdery mildew is especially troublesome, it is best to exclude such plants from your garden or plant disease-resistant selections.

Downy mildew differs from powdery mildew in several ways. It is common in cool, moist conditions and spreads fastest on wet foliage. It can pop up almost anywhere but becomes less serious where summers eventually warm up. The white fuzzy fungus appears on the undersides of the leaves and yellow spots develop on top. The leaves often dry, become brittle, and drop. Grapes (a common host) may also be infected and fail to ripen properly. Downy mildew infects many vegetables, including peas and cucurbits, and flowers such as roses and pansies.

Controls. Several fungicides are effective at controlling powdery mildew. Rose growers consider Bayleton the most effective at both preventing and eradicating powdery mildew, although it has a tendency to shorten growth and can be difficult to find. Or try the chemicals

Funginex or Thiomyl (p. 429). Also try spraying with antitranspirant products or the baking soda/oil spray described for Black Spot, under Leaf Spot (p. 441). Overhead watering can also reduce problems with powdery mildew.

To control downy mildew, avoid overhead watering and irrigate early in the morning so foliage dries out quickly. Prune plants to keep them open and allow room for air to circulate freely. Clean up plant debris to prevent reinfection. Some plant species are available in varieties that resist downy mildew.

Controlling downy mildew with fungicides is difficult. Although several are labeled for control of downy mildew, not all are effective. Prevention through good cultural practices is the best method of control.

Propagation

In gardening usage, propagation refers to the many ways of starting new plants. These methods range from planting seeds to the more complicated arts of budding and grafting.

With the exception of seed sowing, all methods of starting new plants are known as vegetative propagation: the new plants that result will be identical to the parent plant. Vegetative propagation therefore maintains uniformity—ensuring, for example, that each plant propagated from the rose 'Queen Elizabeth' will be identical to every other.

Pruning

Pruning is both a skill and an art. The skill is in making cuts that callus (form a thickened tissue that seals off wounds) properly and minimize the chance for decay. The art is in making cuts in the right places so that the plant takes on a handsome form and is prolific if grown for flowers or fruit.

No matter how much or how little pruning you do on an established plant, the objective is to modify the plant's growth for any of the following reasons, singly or in combination:

- To maintain plant health by removing dead, diseased, or injured wood

- To control or direct growth

- To increase quality or yield of flowers or fruit

- To train young plants to position their main branches or to ensure strong structure

It shouldn't be necessary to cut back a plant continually to keep it in bounds. A plant that seems to require such treatment may have been the wrong choice for its garden location; the repeated cutting back only destroys the plant's natural beauty.

Exceptions to this rule are when you are pruning formal hedges, espaliering fruit trees, shaping topiary, and pollarding.

▶ page 457

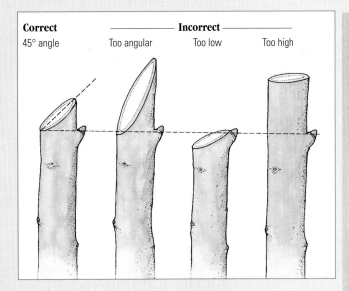

Correct — **Incorrect** —
45° angle | Too angular | Too low | Too high

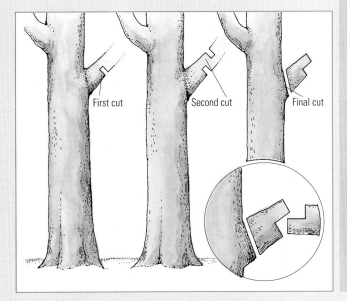

Correct
Blade
Cutting edge
Hook

Incorrect
Hook
Cutting edge
Blade

First cut | Second cut | Final cut

HOW TO MAKE A PRUNING CUT

A correct pruning cut has its lower point even with the top of a growth bud and slants upward at about a 45° angle.

HOW TO POSITION SHEARS

To make a proper close pruning cut, hold pruning shears with the blade closest to the growth that will remain on the plant. A stub results when you reverse the position and place the hook closest to the plant.

P

HOW TO REMOVE A LARGE LIMB

First, cut beneath branch, one-third to one-half through; then cut off limb beyond first cut. Finally, remove limb stub, cutting just outside bark ridges at limb's base as shown in circled inset illustration (or on a line bisecting top and bottom angles branch makes to trunk).

Visual Guide to Identifying
PLANT
PROBLEMS

Problems on plant leaves are often difficult to diagnose—there are so many possible causes, including insects, disease organisms, nutrient deficiencies, and improper cultural practices. Yet identifying the cause is the most important step in finding a solution. These pages will help you identify common pests and maladies, so that you can refer to the entry for the pest to determine effective control measures. Also be sure to read Pest Management (p. 445).

DISTORTED LEAVES, STEMS, AND FRUIT

Cutworms
Chewed, toppled stems; bare patches in lawn   p. 427

Galls
Unusual growths   p. 434

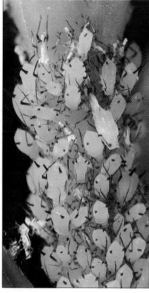

Aphids
Wilted or malformed new leaves
                                        p. 419

Bagworm
Small, baglike nests, eaten foliage
                                        p. 419

Gummosis
Oozing liquid from lesions on branches and trunk   p. 435

Leaf scorch
Brown, curled, or fallen leaves   p. 441

Thrips
Twisted, discolored, distorted leaves, flowers   p. 464

Damping Off
Collapsed or decayed seedlings p. 428

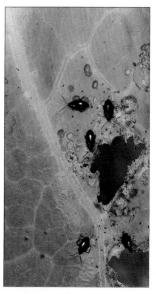

Flea Beetles
Small holes in leaves, foliage dried
p. 433

Gypsy Moth
Eaten leaves, plant defoliated
p. 423

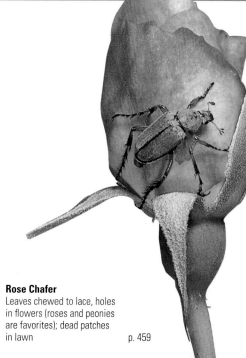

Rose Chafer
Leaves chewed to lace, holes in flowers (roses and peonies are favorites); dead patches in lawn
p. 459

Tent Caterpillars
Eaten leaves, weblike nest
p. 464

Colorado Potato Beetle
Chewed leaves and flowers
p. 424

Slugs, Snails
Eaten leaves
p. 460

Japanese Beetle
Skeletonized leaves, eaten flowers
p. 436

Root Weevil
Notches in leaf edges
p. 459

Squash Bug
Eaten, wilted leaves
p. 463

Mealybugs
White cottony masses
p. 441

Bacterial Wilt
Wilted leaves, especially on cucumbers; prevalent in cold weather   p. 419

Whiteflies
Whitish specks on leaf undersides
p. 473

Nitrogen Deficiency
Yellow leaves   p. 443

Leaf Miner
Tunnel-like trails in leaves   p. 440

Southern Blight
Wilted foliage, turns yellow, dies
p. 462

Nematodes
Wilted foliage, nodules on roots
p. 442

Spider Mites
Yellow stippling   p. 442

Chlorosis (Iron Deficiency)
Yellow leaves, green veins
p. 423

Anthracnose
Irregular blotches of dead tissue,
dropping leaves   p. 441

Scale
Bumps on stems, leaves   p. 459

Black Spot
Black spots with fringed edges   p. 441

Rust
Yellow-to-orange pustules on leaf
undersides   p. 459

Sooty Mold
Black sticky mold that grows on
leaves and twigs   p. 462

Fireblight
Dry, scorched leaves   p. 433

Verticillium Wilt
Leaf dieback   p. 467

Powdery Mildew
Small gray or white patches, distorted leaves coated with white powder   p. 452

A word of caution: Leave pruning large trees to professional arborists or tree trimmers. They are properly trained and have the right equipment to do the job safely. To make sure you'll get the job done right, review pruning guidelines published by the International Society of Arboriculture. Your pruner should have a copy.

Pruning and growth. To understand how to approach the pruning of any plant, you should know how growth occurs. Because all growth originates in buds, they are the first plant parts to consider.

The terminal growth bud develops at the end of a stem or branch. This bud causes the stem to grow in length.

Lateral buds grow along the sides of stems. These buds produce the side, or lateral, growth that makes a plant bushy.

Some plants may have latent buds—those that lie dormant beneath the bark. Some of these buds may grow after pruning or injury removes the actively growing part of the stem.

Terminal buds produce hormones, called auxins, that stimulate their growth and, in many species, prevent lateral buds below them from growing during the current season. If you remove the terminal bud, either while the plant is growing or dormant, subsequent growth occurs from the uppermost lateral buds. You can use these growth patterns when pruning to encourage structural strength or shape the plant into different forms.

Make all pruning cuts, including pinching, just above some growth—a bud, stem, or branch.

Types of pruning. Prune with a specific goal in mind. Common approaches are explained in the illustration.

■ **Thinning.** Thinning is the removal of a lateral branch at its point of origin or the shortening of a branch to a smaller lateral branch. Thin a plant to open it up to sunlight and reduce its size, while accentuating its natural form. In most cases thinning cuts are preferable to heading cuts.

■ **Heading back.** In this sort of pruning—also called cutting back—you cut a currently growing shoot to a bud, or cut an older branch back to a stub or a tiny twig. Pinching and shearing are forms of heading. With a few exceptions, including pruning fruit trees to establish main framework branches, shearing hedges to keep them compact, and pruning roses for flower production, heading is a less desirable type of pruning because it results in vigorous growth below the cut, usually from several to many buds, depending on the severity of the heading. While a plant that has been headed does become more compact, its natural shape is ruined and will be difficult to repair. In addition, new growth is often weakly attached and prone to breaking. Every year, scores of beautiful trees are ruined when they are headed back ("topped") instead of thinned.

■ **Pinching.** The first opportunity you have to control or direct plant growth is to remove—to pinch out—new growth before it elongates into stems. This is especially useful with young plants that you want to make bushier. For example, you can pinch all the terminal buds on every branch of a young oleander. This will force growth from buds that are at the leaf bases along the stems, creating perhaps two, three, or four new side branches instead of just one lengthening branch. When this happens, you get all-over growth. Conversely, if you want a plant to gain height, keep side growth pinched back so that the terminal bud on the main stem continues to elongate.

■ **Shearing.** In this indiscriminate form of pruning, you clip the surface of densely foliaged plants. Shearing maintains the even surfaces of formal hedges and topiary. Because the plants that normally are used for these purposes have buds and branches that are close together on their stems, every cut is close to a growing point.

Pruning cuts. It is important to know how to make good cuts. The first lesson: Never leave a stub. Or to put it another way, always cut just above some sort of growth (a bud or a stem). To understand why, think of a stem or branch as a conveying tube for water and plant nutrients. If you cut a branch some distance above its uppermost bud, you leave nothing in the stub itself to maintain growth. The stub withers and dies, although still attached to the plant. In time it decays and drops off, leaving an open patch of dead tissue where it was attached. In contrast, when you cut just above a growing point, callus tissue begins to grow inward from the cut edges and the cut surface heals.

There is a right way to make pruning cuts—and there are several wrong ways. The best cuts place the lowest part of the cut directly opposite and slightly above the upper side of the bud or branch to which you are cutting back.

Using pruning shears. When you cut with shears, be sure that the cuts are sharp: clean cuts heal faster than cuts with ragged edges. Use shears that are strong enough for the job. If you can't get them to cut easily through a branch, the shears are too small, too dull, or both. Switch to a stronger pair of shears or use a pruning saw instead. With hook-and-blade pruning shears, remember to place the blade, not the hook, closer to the branch or stem that will remain on the plant. As illustrated on p. 453, if you reverse the position of the shears, you will leave a small stub.

P

FOUR WAYS TO PRUNE

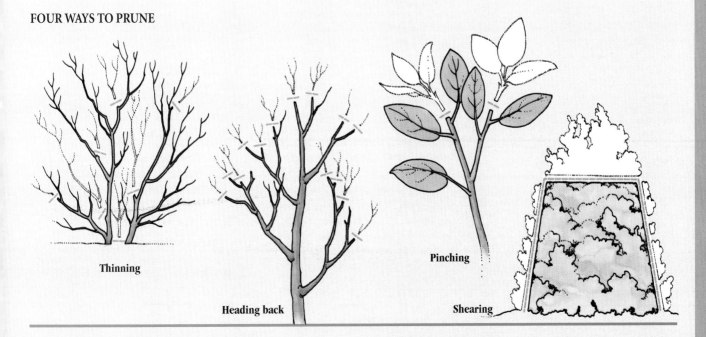

Thinning

Heading back

Pinching

Shearing

Using pruning saws. A saw comes in handy when you need to cut limbs that are too thick for shears or loppers, or when a plant's growth won't allow your hand and the shears to get into position to make a good cut.

Larger limbs—from wrist size upward—are heavy and need special attention. If you try to cut through one with a single cut, the branch is likely to fracture before you finish the cut. The limb may fall, tearing wood and bark with it and leaving a large, ugly wound. To cut a larger limb safely, do it in three steps, as illustrated. Make the final cut very carefully. For years, the recommended approach was to cut the branch flush to the trunk. That has changed slightly. To avoid decay, make the final cut slightly outside the branch bark ridge (compressed bark in the branch crotch) and branch collar (the natural circles or ridges where the branch meets the trunk), as shown in the illustration on p. 453.

Pruning to shape. Every plant has a natural shape; its growth tends to conform to a certain pattern, whether round, gumdrop-shaped, wide-spreading, vase-shaped, or arching. It's usually a good idea to observe a plant's natural shape, and then prune the plant in a manner that will allow this form to continue to develop as the plant grows. Remove any excess growth that obscures the basic pattern or any errant growth that departs from the natural form. Use thinning cuts.

When pruning to shape, make your cuts above a bud or side branch that points in the direction you want the new growth to take. If you have no preference, remember that generally it is better for a new branch to grow toward an open space than toward another branch and toward the outside of the plant than toward its interior. Try to eliminate branches that cross and touch one another. Crossing branches may rub together, suffering injury, and usually contribute to a less attractive overall form, especially in deciduous plants when they are out of leaf.

Pruning for flower production. Flowering shrubs bloom either from new growth or from old wood, depending on the plant species. Before you prune, determine which sort of growth bears flowers. In this way, you can avoid inadvertently cutting out flower-bearing stems.

Most spring-flowering shrubs bloom from wood formed during the previous year. Wait until these plants have finished flowering before pruning them (or do some pruning by cutting flowers while they are in bud or bloom). Growth that the shrubs make after flowering will provide blooms for the next year.

Most summer-flowering shrubs bloom on growth from the spring of the same year. These are the shrubs you can prune during the winter dormant season without sacrificing the next crop of blooms.

A few shrubs bloom twice or throughout the growing season (many roses, for example). Spring flowers grow from old wood; later blooms come both from recent growth and from

wood of previous years. During the dormant season, remove weak and unproductive stems and, if necessary, lightly head back remaining growth. During the growing season, prune as necessary to shape while you remove spent blossoms.

Pruning conifers. These evergreens fall into two broad classes: those with branches radiating out from the trunk in whorls and those that sprout branches in a random fashion. Spruce, fir, and most pines are examples of the whorl type; arborvitae, hemlock, juniper, and yew are examples of random-branching conifers. Pruning guidelines differ for the two groups.

On whorl-branching types, buds appear at the tips of new growth, along the lengthening new growth, and at the bases of new growth. You can cut back the new growth "candles" about halfway to induce more branching, or you can cut them out entirely to force branching from buds at their bases. The point to remember is that you must make cuts above potential growth buds or back to existing branches. Cutting back into an old stem—even one that still bears foliage—won't force branching unless you're cutting back to latent buds.

Prune the random-branching conifers selectively, head them back, or shear them; new growth will emerge from stems or branches below the cuts. But when you shorten a branch, don't cut into bare wood below green growth. Most kinds (yew is an exception) won't develop new growth from bare wood.

Controlling height. You can keep some conifers—chiefly the random-branching kinds, plus deodar cedar and hemlock—at a controlled size, either as dense specimens or as hedges. When growth reaches within a foot or so of the size you desire, cut back all but about 1 inch of the new growth. This will produce enough small side branchlets to make full, dense foliage. Once this bushy growth forms at the ends of the branches, you can hold the plant to a small size year after year by shortening new growth that develops and cutting out any wild shoots.

Repairing damaged trees. When a conifer has been damaged by cold or breakage, you may have to remove entire limbs. It's almost impossible to restore the natural shape, but you can often make the most of the situation by trimming or training the damaged plant into an unusual sculptural form. If the central leader has been damaged, stake one of the next lower branches vertically and train it as a new leader.

NO TREE PAINT. *Painting tree wounds and the cut ends of branches may make you feel better and it used to be commonly advised by specialists. However, it doesn't promote faster healing and, in some instances, can actually encourage disease. So if you truly care about your tree, do the most important thing—prune it correctly.*

Pseudobulb

A thickened, aboveground modified stem is called a pseudobulb. Found in some orchids such as *Cymbidium*, it serves as a storage organ for nutrients.

Ragweed

Ragweed is particularly irritating because it produces copious amounts of pollen. This results in hay fever for millions of people in late summer and autumn.

There are two troublesome species of ragweed: common ragweed, *Ambrosia artemisiifolia,* and giant ragweed, *A. trifida.* Common ragweed has ferny foliage on hairy stems, ranging from 1 to 6 feet high. Greenish male flowers grow at the end of the stems, producing huge amounts of pollen.

Giant ragweed grows taller—to 10 feet high—and has three-lobed leaves.

Ragweeds are most prevalent in the Southeast, where summer rains are common. They are common on the edge of fields or vacant lots.

Young ragweed plants can easily be controlled by pulling, hoeing, or rototilling. Once the plants are older, they are harder to remove. Control with Roundup (p. 474).

Rhizome

A thickened modified stem, a rhizome grows horizontally along or under the soil surface (see illustration, p. 422). It may be long and slender, as in some lawn grasses, or it may be thick and fleshy, as in many irises.

Root Ball

The network of roots and the soil clinging to them when a plant is lifted from the soil or removed from a container is called its root ball.

Root-Bound

When a plant grows for too long in its container, it generally becomes root-bound. With no room for additional growth, roots become tangled, matted, and grow in circles. Root-bound plants placed in the ground without having their roots untangled often fail to overcome their choked condition and don't grow well—or don't grow at all.

Rooting Hormone

A rooting hormone is a powder or liquid, containing growth hormones (auxins), that stimulates root formation on a cutting.

Roots. See Plant Anatomy and Growth p. 447

Rootstock

The rootstock is the part of a budded or grafted plant that furnishes the root system and sometimes part of the branch structure. "Understock" has the same meaning.

Root Weevils

Many species of root weevils are found throughout the South. From the time they emerge in spring through autumn, flightless gray or black adults eat notches from leaf edges of many plants—especially azaleas and rhododendrons, roses, and viburnums (see photograph, p. 455). In late summer, the weevils lay eggs on the soil or in folds of leaves. Eggs hatch into legless larvae with pinkish or whitish bodies and tan heads; these burrow into the soil and eat roots, particularly of strawberry plants. Controlling root weevils isn't easy. Floating row covers below can exclude adults from vegetable plants. For adults, spray the botanical insecticide rotenone at dusk. Use Orthene to control adults (which feed only at night) on nonedible plants (p. 445). For larvae, apply parasitic nematodes (p. 420).

Rose Chafers

Rose chafers are slender, ½-inch-long beetles with long legs and light tan bodies (see photograph, p. 455). The adults feed in swarms, attacking flowering plants first (roses and peonies are favorites), then moving on to other plants. They eat holes in blossoms and chew leaves to lace. The slim, ¾-inch-long, white grubs attack lawns like other beetle grubs, but they prefer sandy soils. Dead patches of lawn are severed at the roots and easy to pull up.

Controlling rose chafers is similar to controlling Japanese beetles; however, milky spore is not effective against rose chafers. Row covers will protect flowers and vegetables. Try rotenone, pyrethrin, or insecticidal soap to control adults. Regularly till the soil to expose grubs to birds, or apply parasitic nematodes (p. 420).

For chemical control, apply diazinon to lawns, Sevin on vegetables, and Orthene on ornamentals (p. 445).

Rosette

Plants are said to grow in rosettes if their leaves are closely set around a crown or center—as in the case of hen and chicks (*Echeveria*) or coral bells (*Heuchera*).

Row Covers

These semitransparent materials are used to cover plants (see illustration). They trap heat, enhancing growth or providing frost protection, and exclude pests.

USING ROW COVERS

Row covers let you get the jump on the vegetable season or prolong it into fall. Covers trap heat, warming soil; light and water penetrate it, but insect pests and birds are excluded.

BEAT THE FROST. *When a sudden frost threatens tender plants, here's an easy way to save them. Fill plastic milk jugs with water and place them in between your plants. Then drape a sheet of spunbonded polyester row cover (you can get this at garden centers) over your plants. As the water freezes, it gives off heat. The row cover holds the heat inside, protecting the plants.*

Runner

A runner is a slender stem—sent out from the bases of certain perennials—at the end of which an offset develops. In common usage, however, the term "runner" refers to either offsets or stolons.

Rust

Rust are fungi that attack the leaves, stems, and fruits of many plants, including apples, crabapples, hawthorns, roses, cedars, figs, and hollyhocks. Each rust is specific to a certain plant—rose rust will not infect hollyhocks, for example, and hollyhock rust will not infect roses. On roses, the fungus usually appears in late spring as yellow-to-orange pustules on undersides of older leaves. (Other rusts may be brownish or even purple.) As the infection progresses, powdery masses of spores cover the undersides of the leaves (see photograph, p. 456), and upper surfaces display a yellow mottling. In advanced stages on some plants, entire leaves may turn yellow and drop.

Warm days, cool nights, and moisture (even heavy dew) encourage rust development; rain, sprinkling, and wind spread the fungus from plant to plant. Leaf surfaces must be wet for a minimum of 4 to 5 hours for spores to germinate and infect the plant. Prolonged hot, dry weather will usually halt rust development. However, the fungus can survive over winter on both live and dead leaves.

Controls. Choose rust-resistant selections, if possible. Thoroughly clean up fallen leaves and debris; remove any rust-infected leaves that remain on plants. During the rust season, choose from a number of fungicide sprays that kill the fungus. Funginex is favored by rose growers; Bayleton also is effective (although it has a tendency to shorten growth), as are Daconil and wettable sulfur (p. 429). If you water by overhead sprinkling, do it in early morning on sunny days so that leaves will dry quickly. For information on cedar-apple rust, see the encyclopedia entry for Apple (p. 130).

Scab. See Leaf Spot   p. 441

Scale

Scale insects are closely related to mealybugs and aphids. They differ in having a waxy shell-like covering that camouflages them and protects them from many natural enemies (and insecticides). Most scales are either "armored" (hard) or "soft"; the latter produce a sticky honeydew (see photograph, p. 456).

An adult scale insect lives under its stationary waxy shell, which sticks to a plant. Running from the underside of the insect into the plant tissue is a tiny filamentous mouth part, through which the scale sucks plant juices. Scale eggs hatch beneath the stationary shell; then, sometime in spring or summer, the young crawl out from under the protective cover and seek their own feeding sites.

Controls. If scale infestation is light, you may control it by picking scales off the plant or scraping them off with a plastic scouring pad. On deciduous plants, you can kill some adult scales in winter with a dormant oil spray. Insecticides are effective against scales only during the juvenile "crawler" stage, before waxy shells develop. Apply summer oil spray, malathion, diazinon, Orthene, or Sevin (p. 445). (To check for "crawlers," wrap a sticky ant barrier, such as Tanglefoot, around infested branch.)

Many naturally occurring parasites and predators control or limit scale insect populations. Unless a valuable plant is in jeopardy from scale infestation, don't spray with an insecticide,

S

because it can also kill the scale's natural enemies. *Aphytis* wasps, a parasite of some kinds of scale, are sometimes sold for release in the home garden (see p. 420).

Ants tend and protect scale insects on plants as they do aphids.

Scion

A scion is a bud or a short length of stem of one plant budded or grafted onto a rootstock of another.

Seeds. See Plant Anatomy and Growth; and Planting Techniques: Seeds

pp. 447, 448

Selection

A selection is a naturally occurring variant of a species chosen and propagated for some desirable trait, such as flower or leaf color, growth habit, disease resistance, etc. "Selection" is synonymous with "cultivar."

Self-Branching

Certain annuals that produce numerous side growths and have naturally compact growth are self-branching.

Sepals. See Plant Anatomy and Growth p. 447

Shot Hole. See Leaf Spot p. 441

Shrub

A shrub is a woody plant that usually increases in size by growing new wood from older wood, as well as new stems from the plant's base. Unless specially trained, a shrub will have many stems that rise from ground level or close to it (in contrast to most trees, which grow a single trunk and branch higher up). Shrubs range from ankle-height dwarfs to multi-stemmed giants you can walk under; forms run from spreading to upright, from stiff to vinelike.

Single Flower

The single-flower type has the minimum number of petals for its kind, usually four, five, or six. (The basic number of petals for roses, for example, is five.)

Slugs and Snails

In many parts of the South, slugs and snails are the most troublesome garden pests. These similar creatures (a slug is simply a snail without a shell) feed on various plants by biting tissue with rasping mouths underneath their bodies (see photograph, p. 455). Both hide by day and feed at night, although they may be active during daytime hours on gray, damp days.

Nobody ever gets rid of slugs or snails for good. They always return—from neighbors' lots, on new plants, or even in new soil (often in container-grown plants) as eggs. The eggs resemble clusters of $1/8$-inch pearls; look for them under rocks, boards, and pots, and destroy those you find.

Chemical controls. The most popular controls are packaged baits containing metaldehyde or methiocarb in pellets, meal, or emulsion form. Metaldehyde is the most widely used, but its effectiveness is limited during periods of high humidity. Do not put methiocarb, commonly used in slug bait, around fruits and vegetables. If you put out pellets, scatter them so there is space between them rather than making piles. And be careful using baits where dogs live or visit, because the bait can poison dogs, too. Never apply it when dogs are present; it may look as though you're putting out dry dog food.

Physical controls. Hand-picking is an easy way to control snails: Simply grab them by their shells and dispose of them however you wish. (Slugs are harder to pick up because they have no shell to grab. Some gardeners kill them with a 5 percent ammonia solution in a hand sprayer or sprinkle salt on them.) The best hunting time for slugs and snails is after 10 P.M.

You can also trap slugs and snails. One easy-to-set trap is a wide plank or piece of plywood elevated about an inch off the ground. Placed in an infested area, it offers a daytime hiding place—from which you can collect and dispatch the pests. Empty halves of grapefruit rinds placed upside-down in the garden accomplish the same thing. Beer or a solution of sugar water and yeast appeals to slugs' fondness for fermented foods. Put the liquid in a saucer or other shallow container and set it in the garden so the rim is even with the soil. Slugs will crawl into the dish and drown. Refill the container daily with fresh liquid.

You can prevent snails from damaging such plants as citrus by wrapping copper bands around the tree trunks. Snails and slugs will not cross this barrier. They also don't like crossing the contact dust diatomaceous earth (p. 445), which cuts their soft skin. Sprinkling it around

---

SHRUBS IN DESIGN

In times past, homeowners sought out bulky shrubs for "foundation plantings," to provide transition from house to garden by hiding the unattractive house foundation. But with the disappearance of high foundations in many modern homes, shrubs have taken on new roles. Because they encompass such a diversity of sizes, shapes, and appearances, shrubs naturally can perform a great range of landscape functions in the garden.

In choosing shrubs for your garden, don't be guided solely by flashy color or sentimental attachment. Keep in mind the following points:

- **Adaptability.** No shrub will satisfy you unless it is suited to your climate, your soil, and your garden environment. Check specific descriptions in the Plant Encyclopedia.

- **Plant size.** If you have a space for a 4-by-4-foot shrub but plant one that will reach 12 feet in all directions, you're bound to be unhappy in time. Remember that the most attractive shrubs (except those intended for sheared hedges) are those that are allowed to reach their natural size without severe restriction.

- **Growth rate.** Hand in hand with knowledge of a plant's ultimate size should go the realization of how fast it will get there. Slow

growth is the price you will have to pay for some of the most desirable shrubs, so place those plants where their slowness will not be detrimental to your plans.

- **Texture.** The texture of individual leaves, as well as the texture of many leaves in mass, varies almost as much as do shrubs themselves. Shiny, dull, hairy or fuzzy, smooth, quilted—these qualities, combined with the size and shape of the leaf, give a plant its character. You can do much to highlight a shrub's inherent beauty if you consider how its foliage texture will complement that of neighboring plants and how it will relate to any nearby structure. If you capitalize on differences in texture—whether large leaves against small (or vice versa) or fine-textured against broad and stiff—the individual plants will have a chance to show off.

- **Color.** Though many shrubs are planted for the floral display they will make, foliage colors can be just as important in the landscape picture, as can bark and berries.

  Much of the advice about plant texture also applies to choosing and combining foliage colors. Visualize the combinations and juxtapositions, remembering that too much of a good thing—color, in this case—produces not an artistic statement but a jumble.

SOIL TEXTURE AND SOIL STRUCTURE

Clay particles are the smallest mineral component of a soil, sand particles are the largest, and silt are intermediate. Clay and sand give their names to two soil types. A combination of the three particle sizes forms the basis for the soil called loam.

Clay soils. Also called adobe, gumbo, or just "heavy" soils, clay soils consist of microscopically small mineral particles, flattened and fit closely together. The pore spaces between particles (for air and water) also are small. But because small clay particles offer the greatest surface area per volume of all soil types, clay soils can contain the greatest volume of nutrients in soluble or exchangeable form (see Nutrients, Basic, p. 443). When clay soils get wet, drainage—the downward movement of water—is slow. This means that loss of soluble nutrients by leaching also is slow. And because of its high density, clay soil is the slowest to warm in spring.

Sandy soils. These soils have comparatively large particles that are cube-shaped. The particle size and shape allow for large pore spaces between particles; consequently, sandy soils contain a lot of air, drain well, and warm quickly. In a given volume of sandy soil, the surface area of particles is less than that in the same volume of clay. The volume of soluble and exchangeable nutrients in sandy soil is therefore correspondingly less. And because sandy soil drains quickly, plants in sand need watering and fertilizing often.

Loam. A gardener's term for soil intermediate between clay and sand, loam contains a mixture of clay, silt, and sand particles. In addition, it is well supplied with organic matter. Thus loam—a compromise between the extremes of clay and sand—is the ideal gardening soil: draining well (but not drying too fast), leaching only moderately, and containing enough air for healthy root growth.

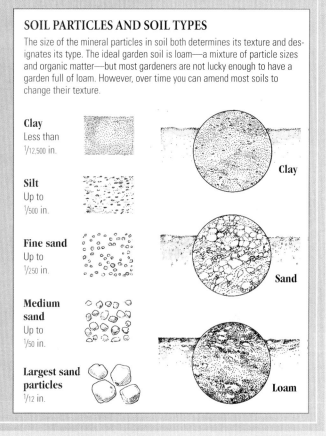

SOIL PARTICLES AND SOIL TYPES

The size of the mineral particles in soil both determines its texture and designates its type. The ideal garden soil is loam—a mixture of particle sizes and organic matter—but most gardeners are not lucky enough to have a garden full of loam. However, over time you can amend most soils to change their texture.

Clay
Less than 1/12,500 in.

Silt
Up to 1/500 in.

Fine sand
Up to 1/250 in.

Medium sand
Up to 1/50 in.

Largest sand particles
1/12 in.

Clay

Sand

Loam

---

small plants will protect them, until a hard rain or a good watering. Then you'll have to reapply it.

Soil Amendments, Inorganic

Inorganic soil amendments may be useful in special situations. But because they provide no nourishment for microorganisms in the soil, they are no substitute for organic amendments. Use inorganic materials only to supplement organic amendments when a need arises.

Physical amendments. This group of mineral amendments includes perlite and vermiculite. These materials improve the texture of clay soils and increase the capacity of sandy soils to hold water and dissolved nutrients. But their relatively high cost limits use to small-scale projects: amending soil in containers or in small planting beds.

Perlite is a hard, spongelike material that is inert (as sand is), but its porosity makes it water absorbent. Soft-textured vermiculite (expanded mica) can absorb nutrients as well as water and will contribute some potassium and magnesium, which are essential to plant growth. Vermiculite breaks down after several years; perlite lasts considerably longer.

Chemical amendments. Included among the chemical amendments are lime and gypsum, both sold as fine powder or granules to be scattered over the soil surface and dug or tilled in. Although lime is the traditional remedy for raising the pH of overly acid soils, both lime and gypsum may improve some clay soils by causing the tiny clay particles to group together into larger ones. This produces larger spaces between the particles, with a corresponding improvement in aeration and drainage.

Which material to use depends on the pH of your soil. Where soil is alkaline and high in sodium—the "black alkali" soils of the low-rainfall Southwest—gypsum (calcium sulfate) reacts with the sodium and clay to produce larger particles. If your soil is too acid—generally in regions of plentiful rainfall—lime is the material to use. Lime adds calcium to soil; gypsum furnishes both calcium and sulfur. Use either material as a supplement in areas where these minerals are deficient.

Soil Amendments, Organic

Vital to the fertility of all soils—and particularly needed in sand and clay—is organic matter, the decaying remains of once-living plants and animals. Gardeners therefore incorporate organic soil amendments into their soil to improve or maintain the soil's texture and thus encourage healthy root growth.

Advantages. Organic soil amendments immediately improve aeration and drainage of clay soils by acting as wedges between particles and particle aggregates. In sandy soils, organic amendments help hold water and dissolved nutrients in the pore spaces, so the soils will stay moist and retain dissolved nutrients for a longer time.

As organic matter decomposes, it releases nutrients, which add to soil fertility. But the nitrogen released by decaying organic matter isn't immediately available to plants. First it must be converted by soil microorganisms (bacteria, fungi, molds) into ammonia, then into nitrites, and finally into nitrates, which can then be absorbed by plant roots. See Nutrients, Basic (p. 443).

The microorganisms that do this converting are living entities themselves and need a certain amount of warmth, air, water, and nitrogen to live and carry on their functions. Soil amendments, by improving aeration and water penetration, also improve the efficiency of these organisms in making nitrogen available.

The final product of the action by soil bacteria and other organisms on organic materials is known as humus.

Types of amendments. Because all organic materials are continuously decomposed, even the best soil benefits from periodic applications

S

of organic amendments. Included among common organic amendments are ground bark, peat moss, leaf mold, manure, compost (see p. 424), and other plant remains.

When you add organic amendments to your soil, be generous. Add a volume equal to 25 to 50 percent of the total soil volume in the cultivated area. Mix in thoroughly, either by spading or rototilling. The mixing will add air to the soil, and amendments will help keep it there.

In the Upper South, use gypsum to remove sodium from soils poisoned by road salt applied to icy streets.

Note: Organisms that break down organic materials need nitrogen to sustain their own lives. If they cannot get all the nitrogen they require from the organic material itself, they will draw upon any available nitrogen in the soil. This, in effect, "steals" the nitrogen that is vital to plants' roots; the result can be a temporary nitrogen depletion and reduced plant growth.

To raw wood shavings, ground bark, straw, or manure containing much litter (such as straw or sawdust), you will need to add nitrogen. After application, use 1 pound of ammonium sulfate for each 1-inch-deep layer of raw organic material spread over 100 square feet. A year later, apply half as much ammonium sulfate, and in the third and fourth years, use one-fourth as much.

Liberal and prolonged use of organic matter can significantly lower soil pH—that is, increase its acidity. Where soil already is neutral or acid, this can result, over a period of time, in an overly acid soil. A simple soil test (see entry on this page) will reveal your soil's pH.

Soil pH

Soil pH is a measurement of one aspect of the soil's chemical composition: the concentration of hydrogen ions (an ion is an electrically charged atom or molecule). The symbol pH, followed by a number, represents the relative concentration of hydrogen ions. A pH of 7 means that the soil is neutral, neither acid nor alkaline. A pH below 7 indicates acidity; one above 7 indicates alkalinity. The surest way to determine your soil's pH is to test it.

Acid soil. Most common in regions where rainfall is heavy, acid soil is often associated with sandy soils and soils high in organic matter. Most plants grow well in mildly acid soil, but highly acid soil is inhospitable.

East of the Mississippi River, most soils are on the acid side. Add lime to such soils if a soil test indicates that it is needed.

Alkaline soil. Common in regions with light rainfall, alkaline soil is high in calcium carbonate (lime) or certain other minerals, such as sodium. Many plants grow well in moderately alkaline soil; others, notably camellias, rhododendrons, and azaleas, will not thrive there because the alkalinity reduces the availability of particular elements necessary for their growth.

Large-scale chemical treatment of highly alkaline soil is expensive and complex. A better bet is to plant in raised beds or containers, using a good prepared soil mix. Or choose native plants that accept such soil.

Soils that are only slightly alkaline will support many garden plants. To grow acid-loving plants give them liberal additions of peat moss or ground bark; fertilize with acid-type fertilizers; and periodically apply sulfur and chelates (see Chlorosis, p. 423).

Deep watering can help lessen alkalinity but is advisable only if the soil drains quickly.

Soil Polymers

Superabsorbent polymers can increase water retention of soils. Particularly useful in potting mixes, these gel-like polymers absorb hundreds of times their weight in water; in potting soil, the gel holds both water and dissolved nutrients for plant roots to use. Because the gel retains water that normally drains from the soil, plants still have a source of moisture when their potting soil becomes dry. This lets you stretch intervals between waterings. And plants grow better because the gel eliminates the wide fluctuations of moisture that can occur between waterings. Polyacrylamide gel is the longest-lasting kind.

Soils

An understanding of your soil is perhaps the most important aspect of gardening. It will guide you in watering and fertilizing your plants—in other words, in caring for them.

Soil is a mass of mineral particles mixed with air, water, and living and dead organic matter. The size (texture) and arrangement (structure) of the mineral particles greatly influence a soil's water- and nutrient-holding capacity, aeration, and ease of workability. The basic structure and texture of soil—together with its pH and its content of organic matter, air, and nutrients—determine the soil's quality. For a discussion of soil texture and structure, see p. 461.

Soil Test

A soil analysis will disclose your soil's pH (acidity or alkalinity) and also can reveal nutrient deficiencies. In some states, the Cooperative Extension Office can test your soil; if not, try a commercial soil laboratory that can make such analyses. Many nurseries sell soil-test kits that can indicate definite problems.

Sooty Mold

A common black mold (see photograph, p. 456) that grows on leaves and twigs of trees and shrubs, sooty mold occurs when a fungus grows on honeydew secreted by sap-sucking insects such as aphids and scale. You'll often see it on crepe myrtles. Wash or wipe the mold from leaves. Control the insects.

Southern Blight

A soilborne fungal disease that rots plant stems, Southern blight thrives in the warm soils and wet weather of the Southeast (see photograph, p. 456). It is also known as Southern wilt, sclerotium root rot, and mustard seed fungus; the last names refer to the organism's small yellow resting bodies.

Southern blight infects many flowers and vegetables, some shrubs, and occasionally lawns. White cottony growth appears on the plants' stems near the soil level and often spreads to the surrounding soil. The fungus gradually cuts off the flow of water through the stems. Plants rot at the base, wilt, turn yellow, and die.

Control is difficult. The fungus can survive in the soil for years without a host. Crop rotation and good sanitation are very important. Clean up all plant debris and discard infected plants, root ball and all. Avoid adding abundant organic matter to the soil, and till the soil in winter to bury overwintering resting bodies (sclerotium). Soil solarization may also help. PCNB (terriclor) is effective on ornamentals.

Sowbug. See Pillbug, Sowbug	p. 446
Species. See Plant Classification	p. 447

Specimen

The term "specimen" refers to a tree or shrub large enough to make an immediate, significant contribution to a planting. "Specimen" may also describe a single large plant in a conspicuous location.

Sphagnum

Various mosses native to bogs are called sphagnum. Much of the peat moss sold in garden centers is composed partly or entirely of decomposed sphagnum. These mosses also are collected live and packaged in whole pieces, fresh or dried. Use them for lining hanging baskets and for air layering.

Spike

A flowering stem with flowers directly attached (without any short flower stems) along its upper portion is a spike. The flowers open in sequence, typically beginning at the bottom of the spike. Familiar examples are *Gladiolus* and red-hot poker (*Kniphofia*). The term applies loosely to flower clusters that resemble spikes—especially to racemes, which differ in that each individual flower on a raceme has its own short stem.

S

Spore

A spore is a simple type of reproductive cell capable of producing a new plant or fungus. Certain kinds of organisms (such as algae, fungi, mosses, and ferns) reproduce by spores.

Spur

Some fruit trees, particularly apples and cherries, bear their blossoms on a specialized short twig called a spur. Spurs are also short and saclike or long and tubular projections from a flower. The columbine *(Aquilegia)* is a familiar flower with pronounced spurs. Spurs can arise from either sepals or petals.

Squash Bugs

About ⁵⁄₈ inch in length, squash bugs are a problem on many plants of the squash family. Damage is usually greatest on winter squash and pumpkin plants. The bugs can cause leaves to wilt completely and also will damage the fruit (see photograph, p. 455). Summer squash, melons, and cucumbers are seldom affected.

In spring, adult bugs lay their eggs on squash leaves. If you find a mass of hard brown eggs crowded together on a leaf underside, destroy them. Squash bugs spend nights under flat objects, so put out boards in the evening; in early morning, turn over the boards and kill the bugs (they can emit an unpleasant odor).

Sevin (p. 445) is an effective chemical control, but getting it applied to all the leaves is a problem—particularly on older plants with plenty of foliage. For best results, start control when plants are small or as soon as you see eggs. Sabadilla may also work.

Squirrels and Chipmunks

Both ground and tree squirrels can be troublesome in gardens. Chipmunks (right) are capable of climbing trees, but they live in underground burrows where they store food, raise their young, and hide from predators. If a burrow is active, you'll see freshly excavated soil around the entrance (a hole about 4 inches wide). The animals wall themselves off when hibernating, but the plug isn't visible. Chipmunks feed above ground during the day, nibbling through tomato patches, digging up bulbs, gnawing roots and bark, and climbing trees after fruits and nuts.

Tree squirrels spend most of their life in trees; they build nests in branch crotches or take up residence in convenient holes in tree trunks. Active all year, these agile animals can easily jump a distance of 6 feet from limb to limb. They live largely on seeds, nuts, fruits, and bark; they also gnaw into buildings and invade attics.

Controls. To control chipmunks, place a live animal cage trap designed for small creatures (Havahart is one brand), baited with walnuts, almonds, sunflower seeds, or pieces of orange. Control tree squirrels with squirrel traps. Always release the animals into the wild.

Staking

Technically, staking is the practice of driving a stake or rod into the ground close to a plant to provide support for its stems. Whenever you stake a plant, make sure ties are loose enough so they don't restrict growth or girdle plant stems. See also Tree (p. 465).

Staking also refers to supporting tall flowers that may fall over without support (see right). For staking vegetables, see page 467.

Stamens. See Plant Anatomy and Growth
p. 447

Standard

You can train a plant that does not naturally grow as a tree into a standard—a small treelike form with a single, upright trunk topped by a rounded crown of foliage. The "tree rose" is the most familiar example of a standard.

Stolon

A stolon is a stem that creeps along the surface of the ground, taking root at intervals and forming new plants where it roots—as opposed to offsets (p. 443), which may form at the ends of runners. Bermuda and St. Augustine grasses spread by stolons.

Stone Fruit

Fruits containing a single seed in the center—such as peaches, plums, and apricots—are stone fruits.

Strain

A variant of a selection that differs from its parent in color, size, or growth pattern is called a strain.

Stress

Stress refers to a condition or conditions that endanger the health of a growing plant. It may stem from lack of water; too much heat, wind, or moisture; or low temperatures. What is stressful varies according to the particular plant

STAKING FLOWERS

Wire fencing cylinder
Good for bushy sprawlers

Bamboo stake and tie
Inexpensive and easy support for stems such as those of delphinium

Metal hoop support
Widths range from 12 to 18 inches; plants grow through crossbars. Good for peonies

S

and its needs. Stress shows up as wilting, loss or dulling of color in foliage, or browning of leaf edges. Causes of stress may not be immediately obvious; for instance, wilting may result not from lack of water but from destruction of roots caused by too much water—a common condition in house plants.

Sucker

In a grafted or budded plant, sucker growth originates from the rootstock rather than from the desired grafted or budded part of the plant. In trees, any strong vertical shoot growing from the main framework of trunk and branches is sometimes called a sucker, although the proper term is "watersprout."

Summer Oil

Spray this highly refined horticultural oil (see p. 436) on plants to control insect pests during the growing season.

Sunburn

Sunburn—damage to leaves, fruit, or bark from sunlight—may result from high temperatures, exposure of previously shaded bark to sun, or improper hardening off (p. 435) of transplants. Symptoms are most common on plant parts facing south, southwest, or west. They include cracked or split bark, wilting, bleached-out or yellowing foliage, and/or dead portions of leaves.

Protect newly set-out plants from strong sun and wind with temporary shelters. These can be as simple as a shingle lean-to on the sunny side of the plant or a small newspaper pup tent held down at the edges by a few handfuls of soil. Or they can be as elaborate as lath or burlap panels supported above the plants on low stakes. Whichever type you choose, the object is to keep strong sun and wind from the young plants until the roots are able to do an efficient job of taking water from the soil to meet the growing plants' needs.

To protect newly planted trees, paint the exposed trunk with a white latex (water-based) paint or wrap it with a commercial tree wrap sold in garden centers. Paint tree branches and limbs newly exposed to sunlight following heavy pruning with white latex paint.

Surface Roots, Feeder Roots

A plant's surface, or feeder, roots are the network of roots near the soil surface through which it absorbs most nutrients and water. Most are in the top 12 to 18 inches of the soil.

Systemic

A systemic chemical is absorbed into a plant's system, either to kill the plants or pests that feed on it. There are systemic insecticides, fungicides, and weed killers.

Taproot

This main root grows straight down, like the root of a carrot or dandelion. In dry areas, some plants have very deep taproots to reach a deep water table.

Tender

Tender is the opposite of hardy (p. 436). It denotes a low tolerance for freezing temperatures. Tender can also refer to seedlings not properly hardened off to outdoor conditions.

Tent Caterpillars

Tent caterpillars form huge, weblike nests in many trees and shrubs (see photograph, p. 455). At night the caterpillars hide in the nest; during the day they venture out to feed on foliage, often defoliating entire plants.

One way to control tent caterpillars is to cut out the nest and destroy it. If that will seriously deform the plant, break up the nest with a stick and spray with an appropriately labeled insecticide. Use *Bacillus thuringiensis* (p. 420) for young caterpillars. For adults, treat with Sevin or malathion (p. 445).

Texas Root Rot

Texas root rot is a damaging and widespread disease in the dry Southwest. Caused by a fungus *(Phymatotrichum omnivorum)*, it destroys the outer portion of roots, thus cutting off the water supply to the upper parts of the plant.

The first symptom of the disease is a sudden wilting of leaves in summer, with the wilted leaves remaining attached to the plant. When this occurs, at least half the root system has already been damaged.

The fungus is favored by high temperatures and a highly alkaline soil low in organic matter. Fortunately, the fungus does not compete well with other soil-inhabiting organisms. Therefore, you can control it by lessening alkalinity (by adding soil sulfur) and increasing the population of organisms that "crowd out" the fungus (by adding organic matter that decomposes rapidly).

Thatch

This layer of dead stems builds up beneath certain grasses and ground covers, reducing water and nutrient penetration. See Dethatch (p. 429).

Thinning

A pruning term, thinning means to remove entire branches—large or small—back to the main trunk, a side branch, or the ground. The object is to give the plant a more open structure. See Pruning (p. 453).

When growing plants from seed, thinning out means removing excess seedlings so that those remaining have enough space to develop well. See Planting Techniques: Seeds (p. 448).

Thrips

Almost-microscopic pests (see photograph, p. 454), thrips feed by rasping soft flower and leaf tissue and then drinking the plant juices. In heavy infestations, both flowers and leaves fail to open normally, appearing twisted or stuck together and discolored. Look closely and you'll see stippled puckerings in flower or leaf tissue and the small black fecal pellets that thrips deposit while feeding. Leaves may take on a silvery or tan cast, distinguished from spider mite damage by the black, varnishlike fecal pellets on leaf undersides.

Thrips can be a problem starting in early to mid-spring, and they can breed rapidly, increasing in numbers as the season goes on. They are notoriously fond of white and light pink rose blossoms and of gladiolus leaves and flowers. Thrips also attack strawberries, onions, cabbage, and tomatoes.

Thrips natural enemies include ladybird beetles and larvae, green lacewing larvae, and predaceous thrips and mites (p. 420).

For serious thrips infestations on ornamental plants, try malathion, diazinon, Dursban, or Orthene. On edible plants, use malathion or insecticidal soap. See p. 445 for details.

Topdress

To topdress means to apply on the surface—usually referring to the spreading of an organic material, such as ground bark or manure, on the soil as a mulch.

Topiary

Topiary is the technique of pruning and training shrubs and trees into shapes resembling animals or geometrical figures.

Topsoil

Topsoil is the top layer of native soil, which is usually better for plant growth than what is beneath it. The term is often also used to describe good soil (see Soils, p. 462) sold at nurseries and garden supply stores.

Native topsoil can be nonexistent, only a few inches thick, or deeper. It is often removed to level ground during home construction or lost through erosion.

If you must bring additional soil into the garden to fill in low spots or raise the level of your soil, don't add it as a single layer on top of existing soil. Instead, put down a portion of the new soil (up to half, depending on projected depth) and mix it thoroughly with the existing soil by spading or rototilling. Then add the remaining new soil up to the desired height and mix it thoroughly into the previously tilled soil. This extra work prevents formation of an interface—a barrier between the two dissimilar soils—that can slow or stop the free upward and downward movement of water.

If you purchase topsoil to add to your garden, try to find material that closely approximates your existing soil. Look for crumbly texture and avoid very fine-textured clays and silts.

Transpiration

The release of moisture (absorbed largely by plant roots) through the plant's leaves is transpiration. Temperature and humidity affect the rate of transpiration.

Transplanting

The process of digging up a plant and planting it in another location is transplanting. The term is also sometimes used to describe moving plants from containers into garden soil or into larger pots.

Tree

No distinct line separates plants known as trees from those called shrubs. There are trees that reach 15 feet at maturity, but some shrubs reach up to 20 feet. Some of those will serve as small trees, particularly if you prune the lower branches.

Think of a tree as having a trunk topped by a foliage canopy. Some trees assume that aspect readily; others go through a prolonged, shrubby youth during which they maintain branches down to ground level. In time, though, most develop a canopy high enough to walk under and have a single trunk.

Planting young trees. You can buy some trees with roots bare (no soil) during the dormant season, from late autumn through early spring. Many of these trees, and others as well, are sold in containers or as balled-and-burlapped plants all year. Refer to Planting Techniques: Trees and Shrubs (p. 449) for planting instructions.

Caring for young trees. Whether a tree flourishes or languishes can depend on the care you give it when it is young. Keep the following six guidelines in mind:

Water when young. For all trees, follow a regular watering schedule during the first several years. Even a drought-tolerant tree needs routine watering for the first year or two after it is planted so the roots can grow enough to carry the tree through dry periods. See Watering (p. 468) for advice on frequency, based upon your climate and soil type.

Wrap the trunk. A newly planted tree's trunk benefits from protection during the first year after planting. Drying winds; scorching sun; freezes; and physical damage by chewing dogs, scratching cats, gnawing wild animals (rabbits, deer, rodents), and careless lawn mowers can injure tender bark, resulting in anything from slowed growth to death. As a precaution, loosely wrap the trunk with burlap or a manufactured trunk wrapping. If animals are likely to be a problem, you can also encircle the lower portion of the trunk with a cylinder of woven wire.

Stake only if necessary. If possible, it is better to leave a newly planted tree unstaked; the trunk will strengthen and thicken faster without additional support. But if a new tree is top-heavy enough to topple in a strong wind, stake it by the method shown in the illustration (proven best in university experiments). This technique strengthens the trunk by permitting some flexibility in the wind—but not so much that the tree will fall or tilt.

Whenever you encircle a trunk or limb with a nonexpandable tie (for staking or protection), check the tie several times each growing season. A tree can grow enough for the tie to constrict and damage the trunk. Remove the stakes as soon as possible—no longer than a year.

Don't prune lower branches. Young trees increase in trunk girth faster if you allow lower branches to remain on the trunk for several years. Cut back low branches only if they show signs of growing at the expense of higher branches that you intend for the tree's permanent framework. Then, in 3 to 5 years, remove the unwanted lower branches from the trunk.

Fertilize for the first few years. You may want to include young trees in a regular, annual fertilizer program for several years after you plant them. Ensuring a nitrogen supply for the springtime growth surge encourages young trees to establish themselves as quickly as possible.

After a tree is established, it may grow satisfactorily with no further nutrient assistance. If it continues to put out healthy, vigorous new growth, fertilizer applications may be a waste of time, effort, and materials. (Exceptions are fruit and nut trees that are fertilized to ensure or enhance productivity; for specific guidelines, check your Cooperative Extension Office.) But if new growth appears weak, sparse, or unusually pale, or if the tree has much dieback (and you know that soil and watering practices are appropriate), supplemental nutrients may be in order. Other times of need are following periods of stress: a severe insect or disease attack (especially one that partially or entirely defoliates the tree) or tree damage that requires heavy pruning.

Most trees will continue to absorb nutrients and moisture after going dormant, so autumn applications of nitrogen fertilizers can be effective. However, if applied too early or to plants that are borderline hardiness, autumn fertilizer could promote cold-tender growth. In these cases, it's better to apply fertilizer about a month before the expected flush of late-winter or spring growth.

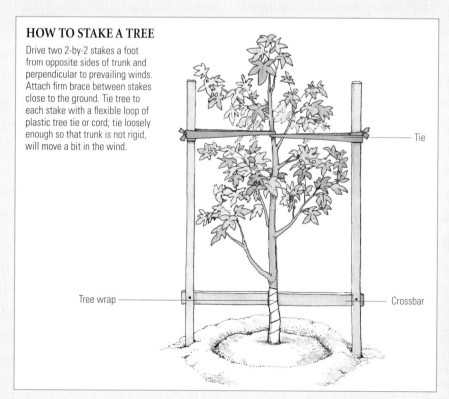

HOW TO STAKE A TREE

Drive two 2-by-2 stakes a foot from opposite sides of trunk and perpendicular to prevailing winds. Attach firm brace between stakes close to the ground. Tie tree to each stake with a flexible loop of plastic tree tie or cord; tie loosely enough so that trunk is not rigid, will move a bit in the wind.

Tie

Tree wrap

Crossbar

T

SELECTING A TREE

Because trees are the largest plants in the landscape, it is no surprise that they require more years to reach mature height, or even to begin to fulfill your expectations, than other garden plants do. That fact underscores the importance of selecting just the right trees for your needs and desires. Consider these seven points:

- **Climate adaptability.** First be sure that any tree you consider will grow in your climate zone.

- **Garden adaptability.** If a tree will grow in your climate zone, read its cultural requirements in the Encyclopedia and decide how well your garden can satisfy them.

- **Growth rate.** Different trees grow at different rates. Their speed— or lack of it—can be a crucial factor when you are choosing a tree to solve some garden problems. If, for example, you need a tree to screen hot sun from south-facing windows or to block an objectionable view, you may want one that will grow fast to do the job in a hurry. On the other hand, if you are choosing a tree only for the beauty of its flowers, you may be willing to wait a number of years before the plant assumes mature proportions.

- **Root system.** A tree with a network of greedy surface roots is a poor candidate for a lawn or garden area; the tree will take most of the water and nutrients. But the same tree planted at the garden's edge or along a country drive may be outstanding. Some trees grow surface roots that can lift and crack nearby pavement, a point to check out if you're planting a tree near a sidewalk, driveway, or pool.

- **Maintenance.** Notice words like "messy" or "litter" in a tree's description. Those words may refer to foliage, flower, or fruit drop; they may spell work if the litter gathers in a place that you want to keep neat, such as a lawn or a patio. But the same tree may pose no problem if you plant it toward the back of the garden or in a naturalistic setting so that litter can remain where it falls. Avoid trees described as having weak or brittle wood or weak crotches. Such trees can be hazardous to people and property. And removing broken limbs can ruin the beauty of the tree as well as be costly.

- **Pest and disease problems.** Some trees may be plagued by particular insects or diseases. Often damage may be trivial. But if the action of a particular pest or disease will spoil your enjoyment of a tree (or compel you to wage eternal battle), you would be wise to plant a less troublesome one.

- **Longevity.** There are trees you can plant for your grandchildren to enjoy, and others that will grow quickly but slide into unattractive old age while the rest of your garden is still maturing. The short-lived trees are not necessarily less desirable, but plant them only where their removal won't be difficult or seriously compromise your overall garden design. Many attractive flowering trees will run their course in about 20 years but you can replace them with another of the same kind to fill the gap again within a few years. If you want to screen out the neighboring high-rise for a long time, look for a tree that's likely to last as long as you will.

Watch for nitrogen deficiency. A tree that displays the poor growth symptoms mentioned above should benefit from the application of nitrogen. One application may suffice, or you may need to extend treatment over several years; the tree's growth will be your guide. For a moderate application, measure the trunk diameter at 4 feet above ground, then multiply that number by 0.1; this gives you the pounds of actual nitrogen to apply. For methods of applying fertilizer to trees, see the illustration Three Ways to Fertilize Trees (p. 432).

YOU CAN'T TOP THIS. *It's ironic. One of the worst things you can do to a tree is top it. Yet this is the practice that many tree services push the hardest. Topping doesn't make a tree healthier or less prone to storm damage. In fact, it does just the opposite. It leaves large, ugly stubs that slowly rot. The weak, whiplike branches that sprout near the end of each stub often break in storms. What's more, topping permanently ruins the appearance of a tree. So the next time someone offers to top your tree, tell them thanks, but no thanks.*

Tuber

A tuber is a fat underground stem from which a plant grows, similar to a rhizome, but usually shorter and thicker and doesn't lengthen greatly as it grows (p. 422). The world's most famous tuber is the potato.

Tuberous Root

A tuberous root—a thickened underground food-storage structure—is an actual root (not a modified stem, as in the case of true tubers). Growth buds are in the old stems at the upper end of the root.

Underplanting

Planting beneath another plant, such as under a tree, is called underplanting.

Variegated

These are leaves that are striped, edged, or otherwise marked with a color different from the primary leaf color.

Vegetable Gardening

Raising your own vegetables can be fun, fulfilling, and economical. But you will need to invest some effort in planning and, later, in maintenance. It's worth taking the time to plan your vegetable garden properly.

Before you take a shovel to the soil, evaluate your needs. How many people do you hope to feed from your vegetable plot? It is all too easy to overplant.

Make a list of vegetables you really like, and choose your plants from that list. If your garden area is limited, raise only those plants that will give you a satisfactory return from the space they occupy. Melons, some squashes, and corn, for example, require large land areas relative to their edible yield. Beans, tomatoes, and zucchini, on the other hand, can overwhelm you with their bounty from a postage-stamp-size plot.

Location. Success with vegetables begins with choosing the right location for your garden. Vegetables demand plenty of sunshine for steady growth, so be sure to plant them where they will receive at least 6 hours of sunlight each day. To avoid not only shade but also possible root competition, locate your vegetable patch at a distance from trees and large shrubs. If possible, choose a spot that is sheltered from regular high winds, which can dehydrate plants and therefore increase watering frequency. And don't plant vegetables in low-lying areas that can become winter "frost pockets"—you want to aim for the longest possible growing season for the greatest productivity.

Level ground makes vegetable growing easier. You can run rows in north-south alignment so that plants receive an even amount of sunlight during the day. Level ground also gives you the greatest choice of watering options—soaking, sprinkling, drip irrigation—with the least risk of runoff.

If you have to plant on sloping land, try to select a slope that faces south or southeast for maximum sunlight; plant the tallest vegetables on the north side of the plot to avoid shading shorter ones. Lay out rows along the slope's contours to minimize water runoff and erosion.

Planting. Most of the commonly grown vegetables are annual plants. Prepare your vegetable garden soil as described for seeds (p. 448).

In planting vegetables, you usually have two options: planting seeds or setting out young plants sold by a garden center. Seed planting is far more economical, but for a small garden, the purchase of young plants will not represent any great outlay. The earliest crops usually will come on plants set out as early as possible in the growing season. Garden centers often have young plants available at the earliest moment it is advisable to plant outdoors.

If you prefer to start from scratch, remember that seeds started indoors just before garden soil warms up enough to plant outdoors will be ready to set out at the very beginning of the growing season.

Care. For the best possible crop, bear in mind this one tip: keep plants growing. Be sure vegetable plants receive steady amounts of both water and nutrients; any check in growth detracts from productivity, quality, or both.

The basic advice for care after planting provided under Annual (p. 418) covers vegetables as well. The one difference is that, whereas you groom annuals to prolong bloom, you harvest vegetables to prolong crop production.

Part of the care for some vegetables is providing support for the vining or sprawling plants. Pole beans and peas, tomatoes, cucumbers, and melons, for example, benefit from support that raises them off the ground. Plants will produce larger crops, and the fruit won't rot due to contact with the soil. Four ideas for supporting vegetable plants are shown in the illustrations (right).

Warm-season vs. cool-season vegetables. A distinct difference in the heat requirements for growth separates warm-season from cool-season vegetables and determines which of each adapts best to your climate.

Warm-season vegetables, the summer crops, need warmth both to germinate and to form and ripen fruit. With nearly all of these vegetables, the fruit (rather than the leaves, roots, or stems) is the object of the harvest. The basic need of warm-weather vegetables is for enough growing heat—without significant cooling at night—both to keep plants growing steadily and to ripen the edible portions of the plants. Cool-season vegetables grow steadily at average temperatures 10 to 15 degrees below those needed by warm-season crops. Many of them will endure some frost. But the most important difference is that you do not grow cool-season vegetables for their fruit or seeds: most of them are leaf or root crops. The exceptions are peas and broad beans (grown for edible seeds) and broccoli and cauliflower (grown for their edible flowers).

VEGETABLE SUPPORTS

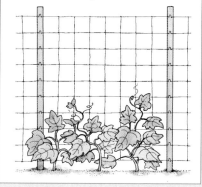

To support cucumbers, squash, pole beans, and peas, drive in a row of metal fencing stakes 4 to 6 feet apart. Attach broad-mesh plastic netting to hooks in the fence posts.

To support a single tomato plant, tie plant to a wood stake—or surround it with a cylinder of welded wire fencing to minimize tying.

For a row of plants, use crossed pairs of bamboo poles tied together at the crosspole.

In general, you plant in very early spring so that the crop will mature before summer heat settles in, or in late summer so that the crop matures during fall or even winter. In the Coastal and Tropical South many cool-season vegetables can be planted in autumn to harvest either in winter or in early spring.

TOMATOES TILL CHRISTMAS. *You can enjoy ripe tomatoes well after a killing frost destroys your plants. How? First, pick all the tomatoes (green ones, too) from the vine before the first frost. Leave a piece of stem attached to each fruit. Dip each green tomato in a solution of 4 tablespoons of bleach to a gallon of water. This kills rot-causing fungi. Dry the fruit, then wrap it in newspaper. Place all wrapped tomatoes in a basket—greenest ones on the bottom—and put the basket in a cool, dark place. Check them occasionally for ripeness or rot.*

Vermiculite

Derived from heated and puffed-up mica, vermiculite is lightweight, spongelike granules useful in conditioning container soils. Vermiculite granules hold both water and air.

Verticillium Wilt

Verticillium wilt is one of the most widespread and destructive plant diseases. The verticillium fungus invades and plugs the water-conducting tissues in the roots and stems of plants. A common symptom is wilting of one side of the plant. Leaves yellow, starting at their margins and progressing inward, and then turn brown and die. The dieback progresses upward or outward from the base of the plant or branch (see photograph, p. 456). Affected branches die. If you cut one of these branches, you may find that the sapwood (the outer layer of tissue just under the bark) is discolored—it frequently is streaked olive green, dark brown, or black. Development of the fungus is favored by cool, moist soil, but wilting of foliage may not show until days are sunny and warm and the plant is under water stress (the leaves transpire water faster than the diseased roots and stems can supply it).

The fungus can survive in the soil for years in the absence of susceptible plants. Even rotation (the growing of nonsusceptible plants in the infested soil) will not rid the soil of the fungus. Highly susceptible crops—such as tomatoes, potatoes, cotton, strawberries, and various melons—frequently leave the soil infested.

Controls. Mildly affected plants may recover. You can aid recovery by deep but infrequent irrigation. Apply fertilizer to neglected plants to stimulate new root growth. However, shrubs and

EXTENDING THE SEASON FOR HARVEST

Traditionally, gardeners wanting to extend nature's vegetable season have used glass or plastic covers to shelter young transplants from late frosts and, in the process, warm the soil. By planting earlier than their climate normally allowed, then protecting and warming the young plants, they brought vegetables to bearing size earlier.

Now gardeners can use row covers —made of polyethylene, polyester, or polypropylene—both to get a jump on the growing season and to extend it into the chill of autumn. Lay these rolls of fabric over vegetables at planting time or over bearing plants toward the season's end, where they can serve as miniature greenhouses—trapping heat, warming soil, and boosting growth (p. 459). The various materials are extremely lightweight, transmit 80 to 95 percent of sunlight, and let both water and air pass through. Burying the cover's edges in soil or holding them securely against it also seals off plants from outside pests (although any insect pests already present on the plants will proliferate).

Laying row covers. To use row covers, just lay the material over rows of plants 1 to 3 feet wide, and secure the edges by burying them in the soil or holding them in place with 2-by-4s. Covers float on top of the plants without restricting or distorting growth.

Most gardeners who use row covers put them up for 4 to 6 weeks in early spring. As the weather turns warm, the covers come off: when the air temperature climbs to 80°F, for example, it may be 110°F under the covers. But row covers can also extend the fall harvest. For example, at the end of a growing season, row covers can ripen the last crop of tomatoes that otherwise would remain green.

Watering covered crops. Because row covers are permeable to water, you can water covered plants by sprinkling— and rainfall gets through too. Young plants will be somewhat weighted down after a sprinkling but will pop back up once the material dries.

a plant dies of verticillium, don't plant another of the same plant in the same hole.

Vine

A vine is a flexible plant that doesn't stop growing in height or length (depending on whether you grow it vertically or horizontally). Most need some sort of support if they are to be anything more than a sprawling mass or a ground cover. But therein lies their usefulness—with their ability to wander and their willingness to be guided, they can be decorative garden frosting; as emphasizers (or maskers) of architectural lines; or as screens.

Choosing a vine. You've heard of "a clinging vine," but not all vines cling in the same manner—and some don't cling at all. Vines fall into four general climbing types (see illustration right). When you select a vine for a particular location or purpose, be sure to choose one whose mode of climbing suits the situation.

Violets

A spreading habit and propensity for reseeding can make several species of violets (see photograph, p. 476) troublesome weeds in shady flower beds and lawns. The surest solution is hand-digging; naturally, this is also the slowest and most laborious. Some gardeners report good control by first cutting the violet foliage with the lawn mower, then spraying with Weed-B-Gon. This works better on young violets than mature ones. Brush-B-Gon (p. 474) kills violets, but it also kills most other plants it touches. In a lawn, you'll have to spot-treat each violet or apply the chemical solely and carefully to the violet leaves.

Warm-Season Plants

The term "warm-season plants" describes plants that grow best in warm weather. These plants include summer vegetables, such as tomatoes, melons, and peppers; annual flowers like marigolds, petunias, and zinnias; and turf such as Bermuda grass.

Wasps

Although wasps serve some useful purposes in the garden—pollinating plants and eating larvae and caterpillars—most gardeners would rather not have them buzzing around the picnic table. Of the various species of wasps, some are solitary (such as the white grub parasites), while others are social, living in colonies. Of this latter type, hornets are particularly aggressive and will defend their football-shaped nests in swarms. For those people who suffer from wasp allergies, a sting can cause severe illness or even death. Wasps also inflict damage on soft-skinned fruits such as plums and grapes.

Control wasps in the garden by keeping garbage and compost piles securely covered. Enclose ripening fruit in bags, and pick fruit as soon as it is ripe. Yellowjacket traps (placed downwind) or sprays containing resmethrin can temporarily eliminate insects, but for complete control find and destroy the wasps' hives. Some species build their hives in trees or in house eaves; others construct underground nests, which can be identified by a raised mound of dirt and the presence of pests themselves as they come and go.

Take extreme caution when destroying a wasp nest; clear the area of pets and children first, and wear long pants, long sleeves, and a hat. The best time to spray is in the evening or night, while the wasps are less active. Spray from several feet away. Use a jet wasp-killer that boasts a quick "knockdown." Repeat the treatment until the wasps are all dead; then remove and destroy the nest. Ingredients commonly found in wasp sprays are malathion, carbaryl, or methycarbamate.

Watering Basin

A ridge of soil several inches high that you make around a plant at its drip line is a watering basin. Water applied within the basin will thoroughly moisten the plant's root zone without runoff.

Watering

How often should I water? is perhaps the question most frequently asked by the novice gardener. No other question is quite so difficult to answer. "Give a plant as much water as it needs for healthy growth"—although accurate—is not really a helpful reply. The variable factors involved are many and complex: the needs of the particular plant, its age, the season, the weather (temperature, humidity, rainfall, and amount of wind), the nature of the soil, and the method of application. To ignore these factors and water by calendar or by clock may subject your garden to drought or drowning. But frequent light sprinkling and frequent heavy soaking alike are bad. Water thoroughly—and infrequently.

To understand this advice, it helps to know how water and soil interact, and what roots need for good health.

Watering depth and root growth. Roots develop and grow in the presence of water, air, and nutrients. Except for naturally shallow-rooted plants (rhododendrons and azaleas, for example), plants will root where these essentials are found. If you keep only the top foot of soil well watered, roots develop primarily in the top foot. But under ideal conditions, roots of some plants can reach much deeper than that. Even lawn grasses, frequently thought of as shallow rooted, can run roots from 10 to 24 inches deep. When shallow watering keeps a

trees showing lush growth should not be fertilized after the disease appears.

No measures will kill the fungus once it has invaded a plant. The most certain solution to verticillium wilt is to grow wilt-resistant selections, if available. (In tomatoes, for example, look for the letter V after the selection name.) If

FOUR TYPES OF VINES

Vines climb by various means. How a vine climbs will influence your choice of supports and training.

- **Twining vines.** New growth twists or spirals as it grows. It will twist around other growth, new or old, or around itself (and around nearby plants as well), requiring some thinning and guidance. Most twining vines have too small a turn circumference to encircle a large post; the best support is a cord or wire.

- **Vines with twining tendrils.** Specialized growths along the stems or at the ends of leaves reach out and wrap around whatever is handy—wire or rope, another stem of the vine, or another plant. Tendrils grow out straight until they make contact; then they contract into a spiral.

- **Clinging vines.** Special growths along the stems attach to a flat surface. Some clingers have tendrils with holdfast discs at the ends; others have hooklike claws or tips on tendrils that hook into small irregularities or crevices of a flat surface. Still others possess small roots along the stems; these roots cling fast even to vertical surfaces.

- **Vines that require tying.** These vines have no means of attachment and you must tie them to a support. Some of these plants—climbing roses, for example—can anchor or stabilize themselves in adjacent shrubs or trees by means of their thorns. Others, such as *Fatshedera lizei*, are naturally sprawling and somewhat shrubby but will grow reasonably flat as long as you tie and train them.

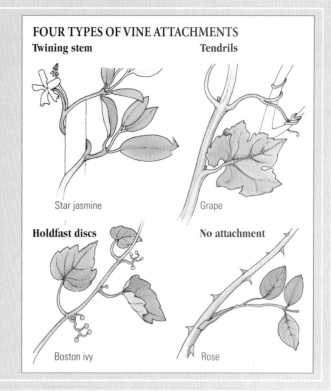

FOUR TYPES OF VINE ATTACHMENTS

Twining stem — Star jasmine

Tendrils — Grape

Holdfast discs — Boston ivy

No attachment — Rose

---

plant's roots near the surface, it can suffer severe damage if you go away for a long weekend and the weather turns hot, drying the top inches of soil. The plant will have no deep reserves of water to tap—and few roots with which to tap them.

Water penetration. A little water wets only a little soil, so you can't dampen soil to any depth by watering it lightly. Water moves down through the soil by progressively wetting soil particles. Once a particle acquires its clinging film of water, every additional drop becomes "free" water—free to move and wet other particles. Although water moves primarily downward, it also moves laterally (to a much lesser extent), particularly in claylike soils. Water penetrates sand the quickest and clay the slowest. See illustration, p. 470.

Watering frequency. To maintain a healthy air-to-water ratio for plant roots, don't keep your soil constantly saturated. Water deeply but not too often (depending, of course, upon the various factors mentioned below that influence rate of soil drying). If damp soil remains low in oxygen for any length of time, both root development and nutrient absorption are reduced, slowing plant growth; at the same time, organisms harmful to the roots proliferate. Plants vary in their ability to tolerate such unfavorable conditions, but all plants (except water plants) need air in the soil.

If temperature, humidity, wind, and day length never varied, you could water your garden by the calendar. Weather conditions, however, will upset such a schedule at least part of the time. Under the influence of a hot, dry wind, plants use water so rapidly that shallow-rooted ones sometimes cannot absorb water from the soil fast enough to prevent wilting. In such weather, you need to water more frequently than a fixed schedule would call for. Conversely, when coolness or humidity prevails, you should water less frequently. The one watering rule that applies to all types of soils and climates is this: test the soil. If the top layer (3 to 4 inches) is dry—especially during the growing season—you probably need to water.

In winter, when the days are short and the sun is low on the horizon (diminishing light intensity and lowering plant water use), plants in leaf can exist for days or weeks on much less water than they demand in summer.

Watering Devices

A variety of sprinklers, soaker hoses, root irrigators, and drip irrigation systems can simplify watering.

Sprinklers. Familiar types sold in garden centers are the oscillating fan spray, the fountain of water (or fan of water in those manufactured to cover less than a full circle), the single- or multistream rotor sprinklers, and the "machine gun" impact types. Information about delivery rates, which can vary greatly, should be available from the retailer or the manufacturer. Common to all sprinklers is an uneven distribution pattern, although the exact pattern varies from model to model.

Avoiding runoff. Runoff may occur when a sprinkler delivers water faster than some soils can absorb it. Inadequate water penetration results, even after extended watering. In a clay soil—especially on slopes—penetration can be so slow that more than 50 percent of the water is lost as runoff. In other words, you could easily sprinkle on 6 inches of water and have only 3 inches enter the soil.

The best way to avoid runoff is to alter your sprinkling procedure or change sprinkler heads—or possibly both. Slow the delivery rate so that the soil can absorb more of the water delivered to it. Or water at intervals, each time just to the runoff point, with a period between waterings so that the water will have a chance to soak in. Water as many times as necessary to get the penetration you want. An electronic controller simplifies this operation.

You also can buy low-volume sprinkler heads that significantly cut the volume of water delivered; the decreased delivery rate more nearly matches the slower penetration rate of heavy soils. For the most even coverage, look for matched-precipitation sprinkler heads. These guarantee, for example, that a half-circle head will deliver just half as much water as a full-circle head, rather than deliver the same amount of water over a smaller area.

Another solution to the runoff problem—especially on steeply sloping ground—is drip irrigation. The low-volume delivery of emitters and tubing can eliminate runoff without sacrificing thorough penetration. Or, you can enhance water penetration for a particular plant by forming an irrigation basin around it. ▸

HOW DEEP DO ROOTS GROW?

Under ideal conditions, roots can reach the depths shown here. In most gardens, roots that reach two-thirds to three-quarters this depth are doing well. Most are concentrated in the upper third of this zone.

Fruit   **Vegetables**   **Flowers, shrubs**

0'

1'

2'   Beets   Sweet
            Lettuce   alyssum
            Onions Broccoli   Daffodil
3'   Carrots   Tulip   Azalea
            Cauliflower
4'   Celery Chard
            Spinach Peppers
5'   Pole beans
            Potatoes Cucumbers   Camellia
6'   Summer squash   Melons   Rhododendron
     Fig
     Citrus   Sweet corn
7'
     Apple
     Cherry
8'   Peach
     Pear   Grape
9'   Persimmon
     Plum
10'   Tomatoes
11'

Soil soaker hoses. Soaker hoses were the forerunners of drip irrigation—and still are quite useful for watering plants in rows. Attached to a hose nozzle, a long tube of canvas (or of perforated or porous plastic) seeps or sprinkles water along its entire length. You also can water trees and shrubs with a soaker by placing it in a circle around the plant's drip line.

WATERING TO ENCOURAGE DEEP ROOTS

To wet a 4-by-5-foot flower bed to a depth of 2 feet*

Clay   Sprinkle for a total of 30 minutes. (If there is runoff, pause occasionally to let water soak in.)

Loam   Sprinkle bed evenly for 20 minutes.

Sand   Sprinkle for 10 minutes. Be sure to water the bed evenly from one side to the other.

with hose delivering about 2 to 3 gpm (check your hose delivery with a watch and bucket of known volume)

Simply position the soaker, attach the hose, and turn on the water for slow and steady water delivery. You will need to leave soakers on longer than you would a sprinkler.

Updated versions of soaker hoses are available for use with drip irrigation systems. They include several kinds of porous tubing: drip tubing with laser-drilled holes, soaker that oozes water through its walls, and double-walled tubing.

Root irrigators. Some special hose-end attachments can soak the soil beneath the surface. They are particularly useful for getting water deep into the soil on sloping land, where deep penetration without runoff can be a problem. They also can help trees root more deeply than they would with shallow watering. This may minimize pavement damage and uneven lawn surfaces caused by surface roots. In appearance and in effect, a root irrigator is like a giant hypodermic needle. You attach it to a hose, insert it into the root zone of a tree or shrub, and then turn on the valve: water flows through holes near the irrigator's tip, 12 to 18 inches below ground.

Drip irrigation. The term "drip irrigation" describes application of water not only by controlled-drip emitters but also by soaker tubing and miniature sprayers and sprinklers. What all these have in common is that they operate at low pressure and deliver a low volume of water compared with standard sprinklers. Because the water emits slowly and near or on the ground, there should be no waste from runoff and little or no loss to evaporation. You place emitters so that water is delivered just where the plants

need it, and you control penetration by varying either the time the system runs or the delivery capacity (in gallons per hour: gph) of the emitters you use. And you can regulate the volume of water to each plant by selecting the type and number of emitters for each one.

The chief advantage of drip irrigation systems is their flexibility. You can tailor them to water each plant with its own emitter(s), or you can distribute water over larger areas with microsprayers, minisprinklers, and porous tubing. A standard layout might include hookups to two or more valves, and could include many kinds of parts (see illustrations, right). Because lines are aboveground (they can be concealed by mulch) and are limber plastic, you can easily change line position and system layout, adding or subtracting emitters at will. About the only task drip irrigation isn't suited for is watering lawns.

You can set up a drip system to connect to a hose end, or you can make a permanent connection to your main water source, as you would for an underground, rigid-pipe setup. Such a permanent connection can be operated by an electronic controller.

Emitters for drip systems. A number of different emitters are available—varying in shape, size, and internal mechanism—but all operate on the principle of dispensing water slowly to the soil. You can choose various flow rates, ranging from $1/2$ to about 4 gph. Non-pressure-compensating emitters (the standard kind) work well on flat and relatively level ground, and with lines not exceeding 200 feet in length. But when either gravity or friction (on hillsides or with long lines) will lower water pressure, choose pressure-compensating emitters. These

W

A SAMPLE DRIP SYSTEM

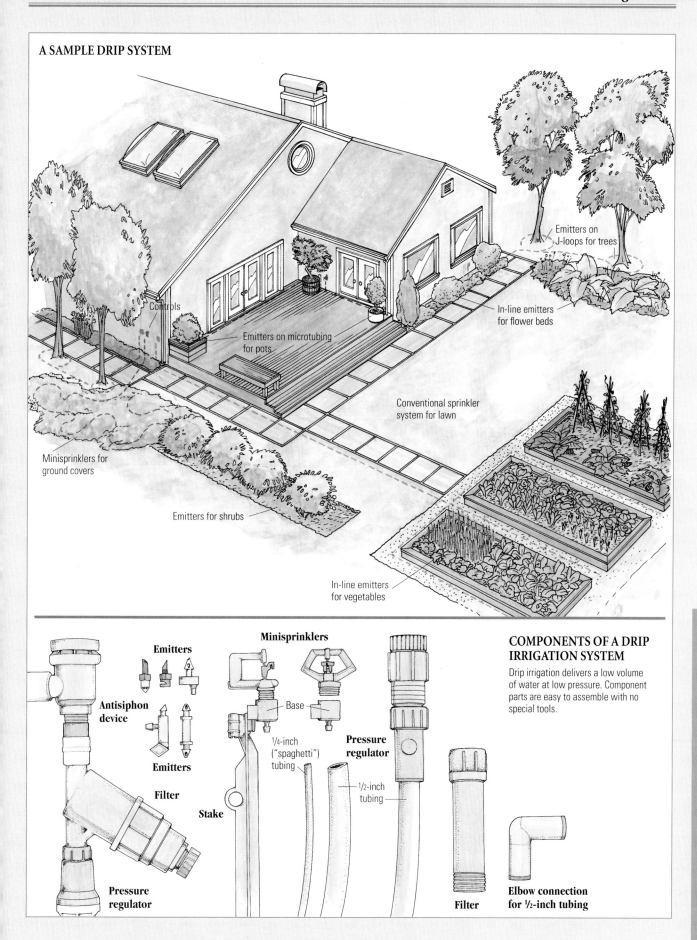

Emitters on J-loops for trees

In-line emitters for flower beds

Controls

Emitters on microtubing for pots

Minisprinklers for ground covers

Emitters for shrubs

Conventional sprinkler system for lawn

In-line emitters for vegetables

COMPONENTS OF A DRIP IRRIGATION SYSTEM

Drip irrigation delivers a low volume of water at low pressure. Component parts are easy to assemble with no special tools.

Emitters

Minisprinklers

Antisiphon device

Base

Emitters

¼-inch ("spaghetti") tubing

Pressure regulator

Filter

Stake

½-inch tubing

Pressure regulator

Pressure regulator

Filter

Elbow connection for ½-inch tubing

W

will deliver the same amount of water throughout the system.

In addition to standard emitters that simply drip, you can buy a variety of other specialized emitters. There are special setups for container plants. Microspray and minisprinkler heads offer low-volume equivalents of standard sprinkler-irrigation fixtures, delivering sprays of water over full- and partial-circle areas. These are useful for watering entire beds (where plants don't obstruct their flow and prevent even coverage). Just like regular sprinkler heads, however, they deliver water unevenly over the areas they cover. For even distribution, overlap their coverages by half. Flow rates are greater than those of drip emitters; you can find ones that deliver as little as 3 gph—and others that emit as much as 40 gph. Some operate at the water pressure used for drip emitters, but others require higher pressure. If you want to combine these specialized emitters with standard drip emitters, be sure to check manufacturers' specifications for operating pressure.

Watering Techniques

Other than drip irrigation, there are really only two ways to apply water: by sprinkling or by soaking the ground. Many different sprinklers and soakers are available for use. Here are the basics of sprinkling and soaking.

Sprinkling. The simplest way to apply water evenly over a large surface is by sprinkling—essentially, producing artificial rainfall. Many plants, particularly those that like a cool, humid atmosphere, thrive with overhead sprinkling. Plants benefit from having dust rinsed off their leaves; sprinkling also discourages certain pests, especially spider mites.

But sprinkling has a negative side. It wastes water. Wind can carry off some water before it reaches the ground, and water sprinkled on, or running off onto, pavement is water lost. In areas where humidity is high, sprinkling encourages some foliage diseases (black spot

and rust, for example), although you can minimize the risk by sprinkling early in the morning so that leaves dry quickly as the day warms. Another potential drawback of sprinkling is that some plants with weak stems or heavy flowers bend and can break under a heavy load of water. For information on types of sprinklers, see page 469.

Application rates. To sprinkle effectively, you need to know the speed at which water penetrates in your soil and the water delivery rate of your sprinklers. Assume that 1 inch of rainfall (or sprinkling) will penetrate about 12 inches in sandy soil, 7 inches in loam, and 4 to 5 inches in clay. Therefore, if you want to water to a depth of 12 inches, you will need about an inch of sprinkling if your soil is sandy, or 2½ to 3 inches if your soil is clay.

To determine a sprinkler's delivery rate, place a number of equal-size containers (such as coffee cans) at regular intervals outward from the sprinkler, and turn on the water. Note the length of time it takes to fill a container with an inch of water. In this process, you'll also learn the sprinkler's delivery pattern. That is, you'll notice that containers fill at an unequal rate. See illustration, below.

To achieve fairly even coverage, you'll have to overlap sprinkler coverage so that all areas watered receive approximately equal amounts.

Soaking. This involves putting the water right at the base of the plant at soil level, thereby avoiding wetting the foliage. You can reduce run off by constructing basins around trees, shrubs, and even large vegetables. To water, simply fill the basin slowly. From the depth of water in a full basin, the length of time it takes to fill it, and knowledge of your soil type and absorption rate, you can calculate the time it will take to achieve the water penetration depth you desire.

If you grow vegetables in rows, you can also make furrows between rows (see illustration, p. 473). Broad, shallow furrows are generally better than deep, narrow ones; there is less danger to roots in scooping out shallow furrows,

and less likelihood that roots will be exposed by a strong flow of water. And a wide furrow will ensure soaking of a wide root area (remember that water in all except clay soils moves primarily downward). Make furrows before root systems have developed and spread; if you wait, you may damage roots when you form even a shallow furrow.

From a water-conservation standpoint, furrow irrigation is much less efficient than drip irrigation. It also does not work well in sandy soils.

Watersprout. See Sucker   p. 464

Weed

A plant that grows out of place and competes with desired plants for water, nutrients, and space is a weed. See the Visual Guide to Identifying Weeds (pp. 475 and 476) for help in recognizing these problem plants.

Weed Control

Weed control is more than mere garden housekeeping. A weed-free garden is not only more attractive than a weed-filled one but also healthier. Weeds compete with garden plants for water, nutrients, light, and space. In some instances, they harbor insect and disease populations you'd rather live without.

You can control weeds several ways: physically (by pulling, hoeing, digging, mulching, or mowing) or chemically (with herbicides). The old slogan "Keep weeds from going to seed" goes far toward holding weed populations in check. In fact, you can prevent weeds from germinating in the first place with mulches (p. 442), landscape fabrics (p. 437), or the more extreme practice of soil solarization.

Physical control. Pulling annual weeds by hand is sometimes necessary, especially when weeds grow among choice, shallow-rooted plants such as rhododendrons and azaleas. Where damage to

MEASURING SPRINKLER DELIVERY RATE AND DISPERSION

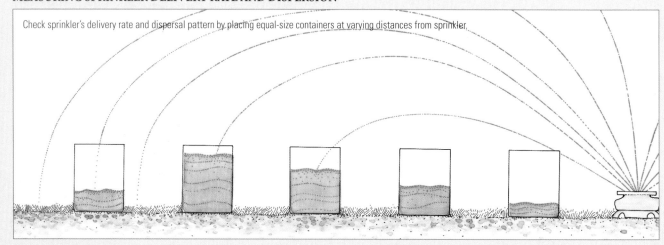

Check sprinkler's delivery rate and dispersal pattern by placing equal-size containers at varying distances from sprinkler.

IRRIGATING VEGETABLES AND FLOWERS

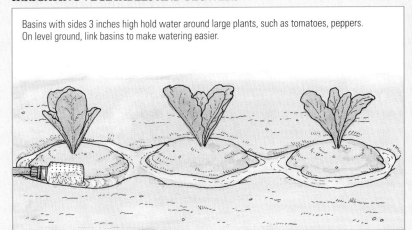

Basins with sides 3 inches high hold water around large plants, such as tomatoes, peppers. On level ground, link basins to make watering easier.

Furrows 3 to 8 inches deep help irrigate straight rows. Bubbler on hose softens flow of water.

surface roots is not a risk, hoe and cultivate to control weeds. In roughing up the soil surface and breaking the crust, you may temporarily improve water penetration.

Many tools are available for weeding and cultivating. Common garden hoes and cultivating forks in a variety of sizes are useful for working among row crops, small garden plants, and shrubs. Scuffle hoes (flat-bladed, disk type, or U-shaped) are easier to use in close quarters or under spreading plants. As you push and pull them, they cut weeds without digging into roots of desirable plants.

For larger areas, rototilling will do the job. This method will not only knock down weeds but also incorporate them into the soil, where they will decay to form humus. String-trimmers knock down weed growth but leave severed tops on the ground; rotary mowers cut weeds and grind up the refuse in one operation.

Chemical control. Herbicides, or chemical weed killers, were conceived as agricultural aids but years ago were welcomed into home gardens. These chemicals offer several approaches to weed control. Preplant herbicides are for use before you set out vegetables, bedding plants, or ornamentals. Pre-emergence herbicides applied to the soil kill weed seeds as they germinate. Contact herbicides kill weeds onto which they are sprayed or sprinkled. Translocated herbicides contain an active ingredient that, when absorbed by a weed, moves to another part of the plant and interferes with its metabolism, killing the weed.

Chemical weed killers can, in certain situations, save the home gardener a great amount of time—especially if there is a severe weed problem or if the weeds are in difficult-to-work areas. Chemical controls are more effective in established plantings (shrubs, ground covers, turf grasses) than among bedding plants. No herbicide should be used in a small vegetable garden after planting, although you can safely use a preplant herbicide, if it is labeled for that purpose, to prepare the area for vegetables.

Herbicide safety. Use chemical herbicides with extreme care so that you run no risk of damaging other plants. Begin by identifying the weeds that are present. See the Visual Guide to Identifying Weeds (p. 475) for help. (Check with a local garden center or your Cooperative Extension Office for those you cannot identify.) Then choose the right product, labeled for your specific weed situation. Thoroughly read product labels for directions and cautions, and always follow directions to the letter. Some of these chemicals are so persistent that traces will remain in a sprayer even after rinsing. Play it safe and keep a separate sprayer just for applying weed killers. And always apply herbicides when there is no wind that could blow the spray onto ornamental or crop plants. Label all herbicides clearly and keep them in a safe place. Many communities have specific rules about the disposal of chemicals such as herbicides; find out what these rules are in your area instead of throwing bottles in the trash or pouring leftover herbicide down the drain.

The herbicides listed on page 474 are the most widely available and useful in home gardens. Other chemicals are most common in "weed and feed" fertilizer-herbicide combinations or in products for use on lawns.

Weed Prevention

There are several effective ways to prevent weed seeds from germinating or weed plants from growing. You can plant annuals and vegetables close together so that their growth will shade out weeds. Ground-cover plantings—and ground-hugging plants beneath taller ones in a mixed planting—can blanket the soil so that even when weed seeds sprout, they'll have trouble getting the sunlight necessary to become established. Any sort of mulch (p. 442) cuts down on annual weeds; any weeds that do appear will be quite easy to remove. Landscape fabrics (p. 437) will prevent weeds in ornamental plantings. Weeds can also be prevented with pre-emergent herbicides.

THREE STEPS TO FEWER WEEDS. Lawn weeds are opportunists. They grow wherever grass doesn't. You can have far fewer weeds by doing the following. First, don't park your car on the lawn. Weeds like compacted soil; grass doesn't. Second, don't scalp your lawn. This weakens grass more than weeds. Mow your grass no lower than two inches. Taller grass shades the soil surface and keeps weed seeds from sprouting. Finally, water and fertilize regularly. Thick, healthy grass allows fewer openings for weeds.

Wettable Powder

Mix this finely ground pesticide with water and spray it onto plants. You can apply some powders as dust (p. 431).

Whiteflies

Aptly named, whiteflies are annoying winged insects about 1/8 inch long that fly up from a plant when you brush or touch it. Turn over an infested plant's leaf and you'll see winged adults, stationary pupae, and nymphs that suck plant juices and exude a sticky substance. With a sharp eye or lens, you may see tiny eggs and freshly hatched, mobile young (see photograph, p. 456).

Standard controls. Nature keeps whitefly populations in check most of the time: tiny wasp species (p. 420) are parasites of the nymphs and pupae, and some predatory creatures feed on them. When you spray with a chemical insecticide, you may also kill those parasites and predators—resulting in an increase of whiteflies. So before you decide to use a chemical control, consider these options:

W

- Eliminate plants to which whiteflies are especially attracted.

- Hose off infested plants, hitting both sides of all leaves to wash off adults and crawlers (newly hatched nymphs); repeat every few days. Insecticidal soap (p. 445) can be more effective than water, and it is less harmful than insecticides to natural enemies.

- Place yellow cards or stakes covered with sticky material among infested plants. The color attracts adult whiteflies.

- Buy and release in your garden a commercially reared natural parasite: *Encarsia formosa* wasps. They are parasites of the greenhouse whitefly (common species) and will kill them in a greenhouse or outdoors.

- On plants like squash, get rid of old, nonproductive yellow leaves in the center of the plant. These leaves carry many whitefly nymphs.

On edible plants, use pyrethrins or malathion. For nonedible plants, use systemics, neem, Dursban, or summer oils (p. 445). Spray at night, while whiteflies are resting.

Cool-climate controls. Except in the Coastal and Tropical South, whiteflies don't overwinter outdoors; all garden infestations originate from indoor plants or are imported as transplants. Inspect greenhouse and indoor plants and eliminate any whiteflies you find. When you buy plants for your garden—particularly bedding plants, which may have started their lives in a greenhouse—carefully examine the undersides of leaves for the nymphs.

Whorl

An arrangement of three or more leaves, branches, or flowers growing in a circle from a joint (node) on a stem or trunk.

Wild Onions and Wild Garlic

These common perennial weeds, *Allium canadense* and *A. vineale,* grow from bulbs. Their leaves, which smell of onion or garlic when crushed, stand 10 to 14 inches tall. The dark-green foliage usually appears in late fall and winter and is especially objectionable protruding above the beige carpets of dormant, warm-season lawns. These weeds spread rapidly by seed, bulbs, and bulblets and are difficult to control. If you have just a few clumps, dig the bulbs before they spread. For serious infestations, spray as needed with Weed-B-Gon (see below).

Xeriscape

Derived from *xeros,* Greek for "dry," Xeriscape is a patented name that stands for water-conserving landscapes.

WEED CONTROL WITH HERBICIDES

Caution is the byword in using any chemical herbicide. First identify your weed (the following pages will help you do that). Then read (and follow) label directions to ensure that you kill only those plants you want to get rid of. If you cause any damage to your neighbor's plants, you can be held responsible, especially if the damage is due to a use that was not specified on the product label.

PRE-EMERGENCE. These herbicides work by inhibiting growth of germinating weed seeds and very young seedlings. Apply them to weed-free soil. Common pre-emergents include:

- **Balan (benefin).** Used to control weedy grasses in lawns, including annual bluegrass and crabgrass.

- **Dacthal (DCPA).** Controls annual grasses and some broad-leafed weeds. Can be used on a wide variety of ornamental plantings, including turf.

- **Halts (pendimethalin).** Inhibits the growth of many lawn weeds, especially crabgrass. Often added to lawn fertilizer.

- **Purge (atrazine).** Prevents weed seeds from germinating. Can also be used as a postemergent. Leaches readily; avoid use near desirable plantings, streams, and ponds.

- **Treflan (trifluralin).** Controls many grasses and annual broad-leafed weeds in ornamental plantings.

POSTEMERGENCE. Two types of weed killer act on growing weeds and other unwanted vegetation. The contact herbicides are effective when they touch the plant. Translocated herbicides must be absorbed by the plant, which they kill by interfering with plant metabolism; these are slower to show effectiveness than the contact kinds. Common postemergents include:

- **Brush-B-Gon (triclopyr).** Translocated. Used on hard-to-kill brush and weeds, such as poison oak and poison ivy.

- **Finale (glufosinate-ammonium).** Fast-acting herbicide that controls a variety of grassy and broad-leafed weeds, including poison oak and poison ivy.

- **Fusilade, Grass-B-Gon (fluazifop-p-butyl).** Translocated. Controls annual and perennial grassy weeds.

- **Mecoprop (MCPP).** Translocated. Controls many broad-leafed weeds in lawns. Often mixed in with lawn weed killers. Safer than 2,4-D on St. Augustine and centipede grasses.

- **Purge (atrazine).** Controls both broad-leafed and grassy weeds in lawns; also used as a pre-emergent. Leaches readily; do not use near desirable plantings, Bermuda grass, streams, or ponds.

- **Roundup (glyphosate).** Translocated. Controls a wide variety of actively growing vegetation: grasses, perennial weeds, woody plants (including poison ivy). Repeat applications sometimes needed on perennial and woody plants. Effectiveness may be enhanced by use of a surfacant (spreader-sticker).

- **Superfast (herbicidal soap).** Contact. Made from selected fatty acids, like insecticidal soap, and degrades quickly. Provides quick top kill. Works best on annual weeds.

- **Weed-B-Gon (2,4-D and MCPP).** Translocated. Controls many broad-leafed weeds.

Soil Sterilants. Chemicals for total soil cleanup (prometon is the most common) have a broad-spectrum toxicity and/or a significant longevity in the soil. They are often misused with disastrous results. Follow the special procedures on the product label. Use only with caution as a last resort.

Controls are listed by trade name. The active ingredient appears in parentheses. Some controls are known by their active ingredient.

Visual Guide to Identifying
WEEDS

Uninvited and usually unattractive, weeds poke their scruffy leaves up into flower beds and lawns, ramble freely around the garden stealing moisture and nutrients from ornamental plants, and make a garden look unkempt. Some of them even jump fences to invade native plant habitats. Use this visual guide to help you identify common weeds. For controls, see the guidelines here, where provided, the individual weed entry, or Weed Control (p. 472).

Crabgrass
Well-known grassy weed common in lawns and flower beds; thrives in warm, wet soil   p. 426

Spotted Spurge
Low-growing, rapidly spreading broad-leafed weed that reproduces prolifically by seed. Control with Mecoprop, Weed-B-Gon, Purge

Henbit
Annual weed particularly troublesome in Southeastern lawns   p. 436

Dandelion
Edible, broad-leafed weed common to beds and lawns   p. 428

Black Medic, Burclover
Two similar, low, spreading, broad-leafed weeds with small yellow flowers, usually annual, that are common in under-fertilized lawns and gardens; pull young weeds, increase nitrogen fertilizer in lawns, or control with Mecoprop, Weed-B-Gon, Purge

Quack Grass
Aggressive perennial weed in gardens and lawns; Roundup, Grass-B-Gon are the most effective controls

Nutgrass (Nutsedge)
Grasslike perennial common to wet areas; yellow or purple flowering forms   p. 443

Kudzu
Aggressive, vining plant common in parts of the South   p. 436

Annual Bluegrass (Poa annua)
Common annual weed in lawns; control with pre-emergent herbicide, such as Balan or Halts

Common Groundsel
Upright, broad-leafed perennial with small yellow flowers and puffball seed heads; hoe or pull young plants

Violets
Invasive ornamental in shady beds and lawns   p. 468

Common Mallow
Deep-rooted, broad-leafed weed; mature plants hard to pull, so hoe or pull when young, or use Weed-B-Gon or Roundup

Poison Oak
Vining, deciduous shrub that causes skin irritation; use the same control as poison ivy   p. 452

Poison Ivy
Sprawling, climbing plant. Can cause skin rash   p. 452

Pigweeds
Two species, upright and prostrate, of troublesome summer weeds. Control with Weed-B-Gon, Purge

Bermuda Grass
Warm-season grass that spreads by seed or underground runners. Control with Roundup or Grass-B-Gon

Dollar Weed
Spreads by seeds, rhizomes, and tubers, especially in moist areas   p. 430

Bindweed
Vining, broad-leafed weed with white flowers; tough to control because of its long-lived seeds and deep taproots. Control with Brush-B-Gon

Yellow Oxalis
Broad-leafed weed that thrives in sun or shade; deep taproot makes it hard to control. Use Mecoprop, Weed-B-Gon, Purge

Chickweed
Fast growing, prostrate, winter weed common in beds and lawns. Control similar to henbit (p. 436)

Ground Ivy
Aggressive, spreading perennial, often a weed in lawns. Hand-pulling and "Weed and Feed" products provide the best control

Wild Onion
Perennial weed that grows from bulb   p. 474

476

RESOURCE DIRECTORY

N o one knows everything. Fortunately, however, the South is blessed with many fine
botanical gardens, display gardens, and nurseries
that can provide the answers to your gardening questions—and some inspiration as well. Public gardens
feature native and exotic plants in garden settings, giving you
ideas on how to use them in your own garden. Nurseries from Florida to Maryland to
Texas showcase a vast array of beautiful selections—everything from azaleas to roses, hostas, gingers,
and heirloom daffodils. Because the world of horticulture is always expanding, there are scores of new annuals,
perennials, bulbs, trees, and shrubs to try each year.

Botanical Gardens and Display Gardens

The outstanding public gardens described on pages 478–485 range in scale from backyard-size to estates that cover hundreds of acres. Some were designed by acclaimed landscape architects who shared a belief in conserving the natural landscape. One such designer was Robert Marvin of Walterbob, South Carolina, who was so inspired by the orange blossoms of the rare, summer-flowering plumleaf azalea found at Pine Mountain, Georgia, that he restored native vegetation to played-out cotton fields and created Callaway Gardens.

Just as some public gardens emulate nature, others present a carefully tailored, or even formal design. But the best gardens share one thing—they can teach you about new plants. How to grow them, how to use them, and, most of all, how to appreciate them. Whether you're planting your very first garden or adding to an existing one, you'll benefit by visiting public gardens and exploring what they have to offer.

Mail-Order Suppliers

Local nurseries, far too numerous to list in this directory, offer a good range of plants and seeds throughout the year. But as you expand your gardening horizons, you might want to try something new and strange, such as blue potatoes or walking iris. These plants might not be so easy to find at the corner garden center. That's when it's time to turn to mail-order catalogs. Many specialize in a particular type of plant, or in unusual, hard-to-find selections.

Catalogs can be tantalizing, but before you blow a mortgage payment on your next order, keep in mind a few things. First, always check the company's guarantee policy. Some catalogs guarantee their plants for a full year. Others only promise that the plants will arrive alive. If a catalog won't guarantee that its dormant plants will leaf out in spring, don't order.

Check shipping dates, too. Mail-order nurseries in the North often can't ship plants between December and March, because the plants are under snow. Most Southern nurseries have no such constraints. The best nurseries in any region will ship plants at the best time for planting in your area, and they should be able to offer you advice. If you feel confident in your ability to judge the best planting time, some will let you specify the delivery date.

Don't order blindly based on price. You don't get something for nothing. If someone offers a 5-foot tree for $1.29, it probably means that roots are extra. And shy away from catalogs that mislabel plants, or that have offers that sound too good to be true ("Monet's Garden—In a Can!"). And although all catalogs show plants in better condition than can be achieved in most home gardens, the only true blue roses in the world are the phony ones air-brushed on a catalog's cover.

Most worthwhile catalogs include cultural information with the plants, giving you the plants' preferences for sun or shade, wet or dry soil, hardiness, and so on. Unfortunately, many catalogs from suppliers in the North and Northeast will tell you how cold-hardy a plant is, but not how much heat it can tolerate. For instance, you may read that delphiniums are perennial, even though our Southern heat and humidity usually kills them within a year. Check the Plant Encyclopedia for more detailed information on the cultural needs of individual plants, and talk to experienced local gardeners before ordering some exotic plant you've never grown before.

Many nurseries and garden suppliers now sell or advertise their products over the World Wide Web, and the Internet can be a great resource to locate obscure plants, browse electronic catalogs, pose questions by e-mail, or communicate with gardeners in other areas. Although the Internet can also provide a convenient way to order plants and supplies, never give a credit card number on-line unless you are sure that the company has a secure system for processing orders.

Botanical Names

It's inevitable. No matter where you look, in public gardens, nurseries, books, or catalogs, you'll find Latin plant names. To learn more about what they mean and why you need them, see pages 492 and 493.

477

Birmingham Botanical Gardens, Alabama

BOTANICAL GARDENS, DISPLAY GARDENS,
and Other Gardens of Note

B otanical gardens, estate gardens, and arboretums display plants from around the world as well as local native species, often in landscape settings. Some have demonstration gardens filled with flowers, fruits, and vegetables; others include displays featuring irrigation devices, mulches, fencing, or paving. Many offer classes in gardening techniques, operate horticultural libraries, and sell hard-to-find plants. Some are living laboratories, overseeing the propagation and preservation of endangered plants. The gardens described below, listed alphabetically by region, are the major establishments (and a few lesser-known ones) that we have visited across the South. Hours are subject to change.

ALABAMA

Bellingrath Gardens and Home
12401 Bellingrath Garden Road
Theodore, AL 36582-9704
(334) 973-2217
Sixty-five landscaped acres including an Oriental-American garden in a 906-acre wooded setting.

Birmingham Botanical Gardens
2612 Lane Park Road
Birmingham, AL 35223
(205) 879-1227
Herb garden, bog garden, natural woodlands garden. All-America Selections display garden. Also vegetable, rose, daylily, wildflower, rhododendron, camellia, iris, and magnolia gardens, as well as a Japanese garden, a *Southern Living* garden, a fern glade, and tropical plants in the conservatory.

Dothan Area Botanical Gardens
P.O. Box 5971
Dothan, AL 36302
(334) 793-3224
Rose, herb, camellia and demonstration gardens, pond and greenhouse. Gardens expanding to include butterfly garden, Oriental garden, and amphitheater.

Huntsville–Madison County Botanical Garden
4747 Bob Wallace Avenue
Huntsville, AL 35805
(205) 830-4447
Annual, butterfly, daylily, herb, perennial and vegetable gardens as well as a fern glade, new aquatic garden, wildflower walk, and dogwood trail.

Jasmine Hill Gardens and Outdoor Museum
3001 Jasmine Hill Road
Wetumpka, AL 36093-1718
(334) 567-6463; fax (334) 567-6466
Twenty acres reminiscent of ancient Greece with jasmines, azaleas, flowering cherry trees, Japanese magnolias, water plants, and Greek statuary.

Bellingrath Gardens and Home, Alabama

Minamac Wildflower Bog

13199 MacCartee Lane

Silverhill, AL 36576

(334) 945-6157

Hillside meadow alongside 5-acre lake smothered in unusual wildflowers that like wet soil, including pitcher plants, rare orchids and lilies, and blazing star. Blooms April through September. Tours by reservation only.

Mobile Botanical Gardens

Pat Ryan Drive

P.O. Box 8382

Mobile, AL 36608

(334) 342-0555

Native azaleas, camellias, ferns, magnolias, hollies, perennial displays, an herb garden, and a fragrance and texture garden accessible to the physically challenged.

ARKANSAS

Arkansas State Capitol Rose Garden

Office of Secretary of State

Information Services Division

State Capitol

Little Rock, AR 72201-1094

(501) 682-1010

All-America Rose Selections trial garden with over 1,200 roses.

Eureka Springs Gardens

Route 6

Eureka Springs, AR 72632

(501) 253-9244

Thirty-three acres of developed grounds with daffodils, tulips, anemones, dogwoods, redbuds, crabapples, azaleas, annuals, perennials, and wildflowers.

DELAWARE

Mount Cuba Center for the Study of Piedmont Flora

P.O. Box 3570

Greenville, DE 19807

(302) 239-4244

Native trees, shrubs, ferns, perennials, and wildflowers. Prearranged tours for horticultural groups only; not open to the general public.

Winterthur Museum, Garden, and Library

Route 52

Winterthur, DE 19735

(800) 448-3883

Mansion of Henry Francis du Pont with acres of mature and rare azaleas, rhododendrons, daffodils, primroses, and irises. Also features a mature pinetum, quarry and sundial gardens, and ponds. Gardens designed to have a succession of blooms for color throughout the year.

DISTRICT OF COLUMBIA

Dumbarton Oaks

1703 32nd Street, NW

Washington, DC 20007

(202) 339-6401

Beautiful garden designed by Beatrix Farrand. Majestic trees, perennial borders, orangery, green garden, beech and urn terraces, fountain and arbor terraces, rose garden, and pebble and star gardens.

Hillwood Museum and Gardens

4155 Linnean Avenue, NW

Washington, DC 20008

(202) 686-8500

Former mansion of Marjorie Merriweather Post. Twenty-five acres of rose, parterre, cutting, and Japanese gardens. A greenhouse with an orchid collection.

U.S. Botanic Garden and Bartholdi Park

245 First Street, SW

Washington, DC 20024

(202) 225-8333

Medicinal plants, orchids, carnivorous plants, cacti and succulents, bromeliads, epiphytes, cycads, ferns, and landscaped display gardens. Bartholdi Park is part of the U.S. Botanic Garden and a place where people come to get landscape ideas.

U.S. National Arboretum

3501 New York Avenue, NE

Washington, DC 20002

(202) 245-2726

Outstanding collections of bonsai, flowering trees, azaleas, dwarf conifers, hollies, roses, native plants, an Asian collection, and the largest designed herb garden in the United States.

FLORIDA

Bok Tower Gardens

1151 Tower Boulevard

Lake Wales, FL 33853-3412

(941) 676-1408

One hundred and fifty-seven acres surrounding a stunningly beautiful bell tower. Azaleas, camellias, magnolias, ferns, palms, tropical plants, oaks, and pines.

Bok Tower Gardens, Florida

Callaway Gardens, Georgia

Cypress Gardens

2641 South Lake Summit Drive

Winter Haven Cypress Gardens, FL 33884

(800) 282-2123

Over 8,000 kinds of plants, 11 theme gardens including Oriental gardens, Biblical gardens, and a butterfly conservatory. Collections of tropical and subtropical plants.

Fairchild Tropical Garden

10901 Old Cutler Road

Miami, FL 33156

(305) 667-1651

http://www.ftg.org

Designed by William Lyman Phillips and opened in 1938, this tropical garden displays flowering trees, palms, shrubs, vines, bromeliads, orchids, and other epiphytes on 83 acres.

H.P. Leu Botanical Gardens

1920 North Forest Avenue

Orlando, FL 32803-1537

(407) 246-2620; fax: (407) 246-2849

Over 2,000 different kinds of plants including camellias, roses, azaleas, and lilies.

Alfred B. Maclay State Gardens

3540 Thomasville Road

Tallahassee, Fl 32308

(904) 487-4115

Pines, oaks, flowering shrubs, including dogwoods, redbuds, camellias, and azaleas, in addition to other kinds of native plants and exotic flora.

Marie Selby Botanical Gardens

811 South Palm Avenue

Sarasota, FL 34236-7726

(941) 366-5730

http://www.selby.org

World-renowned orchid and bromeliad center. Cacti, succulent, and cycad collections, fernery, hibiscus garden, palm grove, tropical food garden, butterfly garden, perennial wildflower garden, flower walk, orchid center, conservatory, and rain-forest canopy research center. Shoreline restoration in progress.

GEORGIA

Atlanta Botanical Garden

1345 Piedmont Avenue

Atlanta, GA 30309

(404) 876-5859

Fifteen acres of woodland gardens and a variety of demonstration gardens, including Japanese, rose, herb, vegetable, and seasonal plant gardens and a fragrance garden for the visually impaired. Seven thousand specimens of tropical and desert plants in the Fuqua conservatory.

Callaway Gardens

Highway 27

Pine Mountain, GA 31822

(706) 663-2281

Features the world's largest public display of hollies and over 700 varieties of native and exotic azaleas. Six walking trails—the Wildflower, Rhododendron, Azalea, Holly, Laurel Springs, and Mountain Creek trails—as well as a 7.5-mile bicycle trail wandering through a woodland garden. The Cecil B. Day Butterfly Center is home to more than 50 species of tropical butterflies, and its outdoor gardens are planted to attract native butterflies. More than 400 vegetables, fruits, and herbs are grown in Mr. Cason's Vegetable Garden. The John A. Sibley Horticultural Center features temperate and tropical plants.

Lockerly Arboretum

1534 Irwinton Road

Milledgeville, GA 31061

(912) 452-2112

Perennial, herb, iris, and daylily beds; rhododendron collection, butterfly garden, vineyard; tropical and desert greenhouses.

The State Botanical Garden of Georgia

2450 South Milledge Avenue

Athens, GA 30605

(706) 542-1244

International garden; collection of beneficial tropical and semitropical plants in the conservatory; 313-acre outdoor garden with collections of roses, wildflowers, spring bulbs, azaleas, camellias, laurels, dogwoods, and boxwood.

KENTUCKY

Ashland, The Henry Clay Estate

120 Sycamore Road

Lexington, KY 40502

(606) 266-8581

Nineteenth-century home of Henry Clay with gardens designed by Henry Fletcher Kenney. Parterre and herb gardens, herbaceous borders, boxwoods, hollies, hornbeams, peonies, roses, and a wide variety of perennials. Maintained by the Garden Club of Lexington.

Bernheim Arboretum and Research Forest

Highway 245
Clermont, KY 40110
(502) 955-8512

Largest collection of American hollies in the United States—over 250 selections. Also collections of Japanese and deciduous hollies, maples, crabapples, dwarf conifers, dogwoods, beeches, and buckeyes. Fourteen thousand acres with 35 miles of nature hiking trails.

LOUISIANA

American Rose Society

P.O. Box 30000
8877 Jefferson Paige Road
Shreveport, LA 71130-0030
(318) 938-5402

This 118-acre park is home to the nation's largest private rose garden.

Briarwood

Foundation for the Preservation of the Caroline Dormon Nature Preserve
P.O. Box 226
Natchitoches, LA 71458
(318) 576-3379

Native shrubs, trees, perennials, and wildflowers in a largely untouched setting. Large collection of Louisiana irises.

Briarwood, Louisiana

Hodges Gardens

P.O. Box 900
Many, LA 71449
(318) 586-3523

Old roses, herb garden, native annuals and perennials.

Longue Vue House and Gardens

7 Bamboo Road
New Orleans, LA 70124-1065
(504) 488-5488; fax (504) 486-7015
http://www.longuevue.com

Listed on the National Register of Historic Places. Classically beautiful Greek revival mansion, surrounded by 8 acres of gardens with fountains. Designed by William and Geoffrey Platt; landscape architect was Ellen Biddle Shipman. Theme gardens include the magnificent Spanish Court, the Oak Alley, the Walled Garden (featuring roses), and the Wild Garden with natural forest walks.

Rip Van Winkle Gardens

505 Rip Van Winkle Road
New Iberia, LA 70560
(318) 365-3332; (800) 375-3332

Semitropical garden and nature preserve on 20 acres next to Lake Peigneur. Azaleas, camellias, hibiscus, magnolias, gingers, crinums, palms, and spring bulbs. Rose garden, rock garden, and daylily garden.

Rosedown Plantation and Historic Gardens

12501 Highway 10
St. Francisville, LA 70775
(504) 635-3332

Nineteenth-century mansion and 2,000-acre estate. Formal French garden with magnolias, azaleas, camellias, hydrangeas, cryptomerias, gardenias, crepe myrtles, and deutzias. Also kitchen, herb, and flower gardens.

MARYLAND

Brookside Gardens

1500 Glenallen Avenue
Wheaton, MD 20902
(301) 949-8231

Thirty-five acres featuring collections of flowering trees and shrubs. Two conservatories; displays changed five times a year.

Cylburn Arboretum

4915 Greenspring Avenue
Baltimore, MD 21209
(410) 367-2217

All-America Selections display garden, perennial and herb gardens, sensory garden, and collections of magnolias, tree peonies, and Japanese maples, as well as a large collection of wildflowers.

Hampton National Historic Site

535 Hampton Lane
Towson, MD 21286
(410) 823-1309

Georgian mansion with formal gardens, exotic trees, herb garden, and 18th-century English-style landscape.

Ladew Topiary Gardens

3535 Jarrettesville Pike
Monkton, MD 21111
(410) 557-9466

Twenty-two acres of formal topiary and flower gardens on the late Harvey Ladew's 250-acre estate.

Lilypons Water Gardens

6800 Lilypons Road
Buckeystown, MD 21717
(800) 999-5459

Display garden on 300-acre aquatic farm, featuring water lilies, lotus, other water plants, and goldfish. Ponds in bloom from Memorial Day to Labor Day.

London Town House and Gardens

839 Londontown Road
Edgewater, MD 21037
(410) 222-1919

Eighteenth-century inn and tavern with 8 acres of gardens. Native plants and exotics including magnolias, tree peonies, narcissus, irises, daylilies, wildflowers, and camellias.

William Paca Garden

1 Martin Street
Annapolis, MD 21401
(410) 263-5553

Restored 18th-century pleasure garden with terraces and formal parterres.

MISSISSIPPI

Crosby Arboretum

370 Ridge Road

P.O. Box 1639

Picayune, MS 39466-1639

(601) 799-2311

Pitcher plant bog, grass savanna, wetland and woodland areas with swamp sunflowers, asters, gum and cypress trees, gallberry, azaleas, and pines.

Mynelle Gardens

4736 Clinton Boulevard

Jackson, MS 39209-2402

(601) 960-1894

Azalea and camellia trails, white garden, Oriental island, naturalized bulbs, daylilies, perennials, and annuals.

MISSOURI

Missouri Botanical Garden

4344 Shaw Boulevard

St. Louis, MO 63110

(314) 577-9400; (800) 642-8842

Arguably the finest botanical garden in the United States. English woodland, Chinese, Victorian, Japanese, scented, rock, and succulent gardens. Also features azaleas, rhododendrons, roses, irises, and daylilies. Home to the Kemper Center for Home Gardening, as well as the Climatron®, the world's first geodesic dome conservatory.

Missouri Botanical Garden, Missouri

Tryon Palace Historic Sites and Gardens, North Carolina

NORTH CAROLINA

Botanical Gardens at Asheville

151 W. T. Weaver Boulevard

Asheville, NC 28804

(704) 252-5190

Native flora of the southern Appalachian Mountains including over 800 species of wildflowers, a heath cove, an azalea garden, and a sensory garden.

Sarah P. Duke Gardens

Duke University

Durham, NC 27708

(919) 684-3698

Native plants, roses, cherries, crabapples, magnolias, and perennials. Iris garden, formal and terraced gardens, and an Asian collection.

North Carolina Botanical Garden

CB 3375 Totten Center

University of North Carolina at Chapel Hill

Chapel Hill, NC 27599-3375

(919) 962-0522

Southeastern native species, carnivorous plant collection, economic plant collection, ferns, Piedmont forest flora, traditional herbs. Shade and wildflower gardens.

Orton Plantation Gardens

9149 Orton Road SE

Winnabow, NC 28479

(910) 371-6851

Twenty acres of gardens including camellias, azaleas, oleanders, hydrangeas, crepe myrtles, and magnolias.

Reynolda Gardens of Wake Forest University

100 Reynolda Village

Winston-Salem, NC 27106

(910) 759-5593

Restoration of original 1917 formal gardens with English, Italian, and Japanese influences. Field and woodland nature trails on 125 acres.

J. C. Raulston Arboretum at North Carolina State University

Department of Horticultural Science

Raleigh, NC 27695-7609

(919) 515-3132

Six thousand species of plants including collections of dwarf loblolly pine, junipers, redbuds, and magnolias. Also an extensive mixed herbaceous border, an All-America Selections display garden, a Japanese garden, and a collection of shade plants.

Sandhills Horticultural Garden

Sandhills Community College

2200 Airport Road

Pinehurst, NC 28374

(910) 695-3882

Rose, conifer, hillside, holly, fruit, vegetable, rhododendron, azalea, camellia, and succulent gardens, as well as the Desmond Native Wetland Trail garden and the Sir Walter Raleigh English garden.

Daniel Stowe Botanical Garden
6500 South New Hope Road
Belmont, NC 28012
(704) 825-4490
Perennial borders and a daylily collection. Cottage, vegetable, and children's gardens.

Tryon Palace Historic Sites and Gardens
P.O. Box 1007
610 Pollock Street
New Bern, NC 28563
(919) 514-4900; (800) 767-1560
Eighteenth-century-style ornamental gardens with pre-1770 native and imported plants.

University of North Carolina at Charlotte Botanical Gardens
Biology Department, UNCC
9201 University City Boulevard
Charlotte, NC 28223-0007
(704) 547-2364
Native plants of the Carolinas, hybrid rhododendrons, bromeliads, ferns, pitcher plants, and orchids, in addition to rain-forest and desert plants.

Myriad Botanical Gardens, Oklahoma

Brookgreen Gardens, South Carolina

OKLAHOMA

Myriad Botanical Gardens
100 Myriad Gardens
Oklahoma City, OK 73102
(405) 297-3995
Seventeen-acre botanical garden featuring the Crystal Bridge Tropical Conservatory with collections of exotic plants.

Oklahoma Botanical Garden and Arboretum
Oklahoma State University
Department of Horticulture and Landscape Architecture
360 Agriculture Hall
Stillwater, OK 74078-6027
(405) 744-6460
Display gardens and over 100 species and selections of trees that are adapted to central Oklahoma.

SOUTH CAROLINA

Brookgreen Gardens
Highway 17 South
Murrells Inlet, SC 29576
(803) 237-4218
Over 2,000 kinds of plants including oaks, azaleas, magnolias, hollies, and wildflowers. Magnificent sculptures located throughout the gardens.

Cypress Gardens
3030 Cypress Gardens Road
Moncks Corner, SC 29461
(803) 553-0515
Azaleas, camellias, wisteria, woodland garden, thousands of bulbs; butterfly habitat and freshwater aquarium.

Magnolia Plantation and Its Gardens
Route 4, Highway 61
Charleston, SC 29414
(803) 571-1266
Wide range of displays including Biblical, Barbados tropical, topiary, herb, blackwater swamp, and wildflower gardens.

Middleton Place
Highway 61
Charleston, SC 29407
(803) 556-6020
Oldest landscaped garden in the United States, with over 65 acres of floral terracing, river vistas, and ornamental lakes. Featured plants include camellias, azaleas, crepe myrtles, hydrangeas, and magnolias.

The South Carolina Botanical Garden
Clemson University Box 340375
Clemson, SC 29634-0375
(864) 656-3405
Camellia, conifer, hosta, rhododendron, wildflower, butterfly, and turf displays. Also wildlife habitat and low-water use gardens. Bob Gamble geology and natural history museum and *Southern Living* center.

Tyler Rose Garden, Texas

TENNESSEE

Cheekwood, Nashville's Home of Art and Gardens

1200 Forrest Park Drive
Nashville, TN 37205

(615) 356-8000

A former 1920s estate, Cheekwood's 55 acres include a botanical garden, a museum of art, and facilities for workshops and classes.

The Hermitage

4580 Rachel's Lane
Hermitage, TN 37076-1344

(615) 889-2941

The former home of Andrew Jackson features a 1-acre historical formal garden with old roses, irises, peonies, pinks, jonquils, herbs, crepe myrtles, and old trees, including red cedars planted by Jackson himself.

Memphis Botanic Garden

750 Cherry Road
Memphis, TN 38117

(901) 685-1566

Home of Goldsmith Civic Garden Center. World-class Japanese garden. Twenty different plant collections including the Tennessee Bicentennial iris garden, wildflower and sensory gardens, azalea and dogwood trails, magnolia grove, daffodil hill, and All-America Rose Selections test garden.

TEXAS

Bayou Bend Collection and Gardens

1 Westcott Street
Houston, TX 77007

(713) 639-7750

Eight specialized gardens on the estate of a 1927 mansion, including a 17th-century parterre garden, an English garden, a topiary garden, and a butterfly garden.

The Dallas Arboretum

8525 Garland Road
Dallas, TX 75218

(214) 327-8263

English-style perennial garden, 200 types of trees and shrubs, 2,000 different selections of azaleas, and seasonal color.

Fort Worth Botanic Garden

3220 Botanic Garden Boulevard
Fort Worth, TX 76107

(817) 871-7686

Rose, fragrance, and Japanese gardens. Also a conservatory and an exposition greenhouse.

Mercer Arboretum and Botanic Gardens

22306 Aldine Westfield Road
Humble, TX 77338

(281) 443-8731

Herb, fern, perennial, and tropical gardens; iris bog and azalea walk.

National Wildflower Research Center

4801 La Crosse Avenue
Austin, TX 78739

(512) 292-4200

Founded by Lady Bird Johnson, this 42-acre center showcases native plants of the Texas Hill Country. Theme gardens, wildflower meadow, nature trails, and North America's largest rooftop rain water collection system.

San Antonio Botanical Gardens

555 Funston Place
San Antonio, TX 78209

(210) 821-5115

Native Texas plants; rose, old-fashioned, sacred, and herb gardens; a garden for the visually impaired; a low-water use demonstration garden; and a conservatory with tropical and desert plants.

Agecroft Hall Museum and Gardens, Virginia

Colonial Williamsburg, Virginia

Tyler Rose Garden

Tyler Parks Department
P.O. Box 7039
420 South Rose Park Drive
Tyler, TX 75710
(903) 531-1213
One of the largest rose gardens in North America with 30,000 bushes, including modern and heritage roses.

VIRGINIA

Agecroft Hall Museum and Gardens

The Agecroft Association
4305 Sulgrave Road
Richmond, VA 23221
(804) 353-4241
Thematic gardens reflecting the style of early 17th-century England, including crepe myrtle walk, woodland walk, and fragrance, sunken, knot, herb, and terraced gardens.

Colonial Williamsburg

P.O. Box 1776
Williamsburg, VA 23187
(800) 447-8679
Extensive 18th-century restoration with 500 buildings and 100 gardens spread over more than 90 acres. Kitchen, herb, formal, fruit, and parterre gardens of the Colonial period; European and Asian species imported by the colonists; and native flora cultivated by plantsmen.

Lewis Ginter Botanical Garden

1800 Lakeside Avenue
Richmond, VA 23228-4700
(804) 262-9887
Thousands of species including seasonally changing floral displays; cottage, perennial, conifer, and children's gardens; wildflower meadow, and wetlands garden.

Gunston Hall

10709 Gunston Road
Mason Neck, VA 22079
(703) 550-9220
Formal boxwood garden and allée planted by the 18th-century American patriot, George Mason.

Maymont

1700 Hampton Street
Richmond, VA 23220
(804) 358-7166
One-hundred-acre Victorian estate and arboretum with formal Italian, Japanese, English, herb, and daylily gardens.

Monticello

Thomas Jefferson Memorial Foundation
P.O. Box 316
Charlottesville, VA 22902
(804) 984-9822
Thomas Jefferson's renowned 1770–1826 home with restored flower and vegetable gardens, orchards, vineyards, and ornamental grove.

Norfolk Botanical Gardens

6700 Azalea Garden Road
Norfolk, VA 23518-5337
(757) 441-5830
Bicentennial rose garden with over 4,000 rose bushes. Also California redwood trees, 200,000 azaleas, tropical pavilion with equatorial plants, Japanese garden, wildflower meadow, healing garden of medicinal plants, Renaissance garden, colonial herb garden. Award-winning camellia collection.

George Washington's Mount Vernon: Estate and Gardens

Mount Vernon Ladies Association
P.O. Box 110
George Washington Memorial Parkway
Mount Vernon, VA 22121
(703) 780-2000
Five-hundred-acre estate of George Washington contains a kitchen garden, a botanical garden, a vegetable garden, the George Washington fruit garden and nursery, and a pleasure garden.

Woodlawn Plantation

P.O. Box 37
Mount Vernon, VA 22121
(703) 780-4000
Federal-style estate—originally part of George Washington's Mount Vernon property—with 19th-century-style gardens, parterres, and a heritage rose garden.

WEST VIRGINIA

Core Arboretum

Department of Biology
P.O. Box 6057
West Virginia University
Morgantown, WV 26506-6057
(304) 293-5201, ext. 2547
http://www.as.wvu.edu/biology
Fifty acres of old-growth forest and 3 acres of lawn. Over 300 kinds of woody plants and over 300 species of herbaceous plants. Birding and wildflowers in spring.

Antique roses

MAIL-ORDER SUPPLIERS

When you just have to have a blue potato, green rose, black bamboo, or hosta named 'Red Neck Heaven', who can you call? Probably not your local garden center. Fortunately, mail-order suppliers abound, offering strange, quirky plants and hard-to-find heirlooms as well as mainstream plants. You'll find specialists in seeds, roses, bulbs, fruits, perennials, trees, shrubs, herbs, house plants, native plants, and tropical plants.

The following pages list reputable firms that ship good plants. We're sorry if we've left somebody out, but we only have space for so many. A number of these nurseries reside in the South. Regardless of geographic location, however, all ship far and wide. Call or write the companies to request a catalog. Many charge a modest price, but some credit the payment when you place your first order. Keep in mind that addresses and phone numbers are subject to change.

FLOWERS AND VEGETABLES: SEEDS

W. Atlee Burpee Company
300 Park Avenue
Warminster, PA 18974
(800) 888-1447
Seeds of flowers and vegetables; also herbs and bulbs.

The Cook's Garden
P.O. Box 535
Londonderry, VT 05148
(800) 457-9703; fax (800) 457-9705
Herb and vegetable seeds for the serious kitchen garden. Peppers, lettuces, and broccoli. Selections from France and Italy. Also seeds of flowers for cutting gardens.

Ferry-Morse Seeds
P.O. Box 488
Fulton, KY 42041-0488
(800) 283-3400
Good selection of seeds, ranging from annuals to vegetables to herbs. Informative catalog with good plant descriptions.

J. L. Hudson, Seedsman
Star Route 2, Box 337
La Honda, CA 94020
no telephone service
Large variety of flowers, vegetables, shrubs, trees, perennials, and herbs. Includes Zapotec Collection of seeds from the Sierra Madre del Sur in southern Oaxaca, Mexico. Best source for hard-to-find seeds.

Johnny's Selected Seeds
310 Foss Hill Road
Albion, ME 04910
(207) 437-4301; fax (800) 437-4290
Flowers and vegetables, including unusual

Sweet peas

corn, bean, and squash varieties, heirloom tomatoes, and herbs.

Geo. W. Park Seed Co., Inc.
1 Parkton Avenue
Greenwood, SC 29647-0001
(800) 845-3369; (864) 223-7333
Seeds, plants, bulbs; nearly 2,000 varieties of flowers and vegetables.

Ronniger Seed Potatoes
P.O. Box 307
Ellensburg, WA 98926
(800) 846-6178
Large selection of seed potatoes, garlic, shallots, and onions. Each described by color, flavor, disease resistance, and keeping qualities.

Seeds of Change
P.O. Box 15700
Santa Fe, NM 87506-5700
(888) 762-7333; fax (505) 438-7052
http://www.seedsofchange.com
Many rare heirloom and traditional native vegetables, as well as a unique selection of flowers and medicinal and culinary herbs. Sizable collections of beans, corn, sunflowers, and tomatoes. Seeds are organic.

Radishes and carrots

Select Seeds Antique Flowers

180 Stickney Road
Union, CT 06076-4617

(860) 684-9310; fax (860) 684-9224

Main focus is fragrant old-fashioned flowers. Beautifully illustrated catalog; includes flowers that attract hummingbirds and butterflies. Seeds and plants available.

Shepherd's Garden Seeds

30 Irene Street
Torrington, CT 06790

(860) 482-3638

Vegetables, herbs such as scented basils, greens like arugula and French dandelion. Also flowers for fragrance, drying, or attracting beneficial insects; chilies; and sunflowers. Catalog includes recipes.

Southern Exposure Seed Exchange

P.O. Box 170
Earlysville, VA 22936

(804) 973-4703

Flowers, herbs, sunflowers, peppers, spinach, and tomatoes. Many heirloom selections. New medicinal herbs and vegetable varieties. All seeds are free of any chemical treatment and safe for children.

Paste tomatoes

Thompson & Morgan, Inc.

P.O. Box 1308
Jackson, NJ 08527-0308

(800) 274-7333

Rare and unusual varieties of annuals, bulbs, perennials, vegetables, and grasses.

Tomato Growers Supply Company

P.O. Box 2237
Fort Myers, FL 33902

(941) 768-1119

More than 310 selections of tomato seed, from beefsteaks to cherry tomatoes.

Vermont Bean Seed Company

Garden Lane
Fair Haven, VT 05743-0250

(802) 273-3400

Numerous selections of beans, cabbage, melons, corn, gourds, greens, and tomatoes, as well as other vegetables; also herbs and some flowers.

Wildseed Farms

P.O. Box 308
Eagle Lake, TX 77434

(800) 848-0078

Free wildflower reference guide and seed catalog; gives the success rate for each plant. Diagrams indicate the diameter of mature plant. Wildflower seed mixes designed for specific regions.

ROSES

Antique Rose Emporium

9300 Lueckemeyer Road
Brenham, TX 77833

(800) 441-0002

Old garden roses on their own roots selected for Southern climate. Also have perennials.

Carroll Gardens

444 East Main Street
Westminster, MD 21157

(800) 638-6334

Large selection of plants. Catalog provides good descriptions and information on plant culture.

Heirloom Old Garden Roses

24062 Riverside Drive NE
St. Paul, OR 97137

(503) 538-1576; fax (503) 538-5902

Catalog includes albas, Bourbons, damasks, hybrid musks, Noisettes; substantial collection of David Austin English roses.

Jackson & Perkins

P.O. Box 1028
Medford, OR 97501

(800) 292-4769; (503) 776-2000

Roses of every kind and color, plus perennials, garden accessories, and gifts.

Nor'East Miniature Roses, Inc.

P.O. Box 307
Rowley, MA 01969

(800) 426-6485

Large selection of miniature roses and ministandards.

'Iceberg' rose

Wayside Gardens

1 Garden Lane
Hodges, SC 29695

(800) 845-1124; fax (800) 457-9712

Varied collection of roses, including antique types and David Austin English roses.

Witherspoon Rose Culture

P.O. Box 52489
Durham, NC 27717

(800) 643-0315

Selections include hybrid teas, grandifloras, floribundas, tree roses, miniatures, climbers, and Ol' country garden, as well as a collection of David Austin English roses.

'Casablanca' lily

BULBS, CORMS, AND TUBERS

Big Tree Daylily Garden
777 General Hutchison Parkway
Longwood, FL 32750
(407) 831-5430 (no telephone orders)
Large selection of daylilies; listed alphabetically in catalog.

Daffodil Mart
85 Broad Street
Torrington, CT 06790
(800) 255-2852; fax (800) 420-2852
Enormous selection of bulbs, including novelty, miniature, and species daffodils.

Dutch Gardens
P.O. Box 200
Adelphia, NJ 07710
(800) 775-2852
Bulbs of all kinds for spring or summer bloom: anemones, crocus, irises, daffodils, dahlias, fritillaries, hyacinths, lilies, tulips.

Louisiana Nursery
5853 Highway 182
Opelousas, LA 70570
(318) 948-3696
Huge selection of daylilies, crinums and other rare bulbs, and Louisiana and other irises. Seven separate catalogs offering selection of magnolias and other trees, shrubs, and vines; bamboo and other ornamental grasses; fruiting trees, shrubs, and vines; clivia in different colors.

McClure & Zimmerman
P.O. Box 368
Friesland, WI 53935
(414) 326-4220
Extensive list of bulbs, including many rare and hard-to-find selections.

Old House Gardens
536 Third Street
Ann Arbor, MI 48103
Specialty catalog for antique bulbs such as narcissus, crocus, hyacinths, and tulips. Historical facts provided for each selection. Many bulbs from United States, including the South; Southern heirloom bulbs are a specialty. Catalog also offers a great selection of reference books.

Geo W. Park Seed Co., Inc.
1 Parkton Avenue
Greenwood, SC 29647-0001
(800) 845-3369; fax (864) 223-7333
Wide variety of bulbs for indoor and outdoor use. Also includes perennials suited for underplanting while bulbs are dormant.

John Scheepers, Inc.
23 Tulip Drive
Bantam, CT 06750
(860) 567-0838 or (860) 567-7022
Spring- and summer-blooming bulbs of species narcissus, allium, amaryllis, hybrid lilies, crocus, and others. Catalog has fine illustrations. Majority of bulbs are from Holland for autumn planting.

Swan Island Dahlias
P.O. Box 700
Canby, OR 97013
(503) 266-7711; fax (503) 266-8768
Dahlias of all types, colors, flower forms, and sizes.

Tulip and hyacinth bulbs

Van Bourgondien Brothers
P.O. Box 1000
245 Farmingdale Road, Route 109
Babylon, NY 11702-0598
(800) 622-9997
Bulbs of many kinds, including amaryllis, daffodils, tuberous begonias, peonies, tulips, dahlias, Asiatic and Oriental hybrid lilies; also a large selection of perennials.

FRUITS AND NUTS

Bass Pecan Company
P.O. Box 42
Lumberton, MS 39455-0042
(800) 732-2671; fax (601) 796-3630
Sell trees, and in-shell or shelled pecans. Woodgrain buckets and gift tins available.

Calhoun's Nursery
295 Blacktwig Road
Pittsboro, NC 27312
(919) 542-4480
Specializes in old Southern apple varieties. Will custom graft for specific needs or from existing trees.

Chestnut Hill Nursery
15105 NW 94th Avenue
Alachua, FL 32615
(800) 669-2067
Specialty is blight-resistant chestnuts; also offers Oriental persimmons, hardy citrus, and figs.

Classical Fruits
8831 Highway 157
Moulton, AL 35650
(205) 974-8813; fax (205) 974-4060
Unique selection of fruit varieties; heirloom apples (including disease-resistant types), pears, peaches, nectarines, cherries, plums, figs, grapes, raspberries, blackberries, and muscadines.

Edible Landscaping
P.O. Box 77
Afton, VA 22920
(800) 524-4156; fax (804) 361-1916
http://www.eatit.com
Fruit for mid-Atlantic gardeners, from hardy kiwi to black currants and pawpaw. Catalog has good plant descriptions.

Hidden Springs Nursery

170 Hidden Springs Lane
Cookeville, TN 38501

(615) 268-2592

Trees and bushes include apple, blueberry, chestnut, grape, kiwi, pawpaw, pear, quince, and raspberry.

Ison's Nursery and Vineyards

Brooks, GA 30205

(770) 599-6970; (800) 733-0324 (Sept.–May); fax (770) 599-1727

Large nursery offers muscadines, blackberries, blueberries, raspberries, and strawberries.

Johnson Nursery

Route 5, Box 29-J
Ellijay, GA 30540

(888) 276-3187; fax (706) 276-3186

Heirloom and modern apples. Also blueberries, pears, peaches, plums, cherries, raspberries, and grapes. Supplies, tools, books, and other accessories available.

Louisiana Nursery

5853 Highway 182
Opelousas, LA 70570

(318) 948-3696

Numerous selections of fruiting trees (apricots, plums, figs), shrubs, and vines. See description under *Bulbs, Corms, and Tubers*.

Stark Brothers' Nurseries & Orchards Co.

P.O. Box 10
Louisiana, MO 63353

(573) 754-5511; (800) 325-4180; fax (573) 754-5290

Berries, fruit trees of all kinds; specializes in 'Delicious' apples. All plants shipped bare root.

PERENNIALS

Kurt Bluemel, Inc.

2740 Greene Lane
Baldwin, MD 21013-9523

http://www.bluemel.com/kbi/

Numerous ornamental grasses, bamboos, ferns, and aquatic plants.

Bluestone Perennials

7211 Middle Ridge Road
Madison, OH 44057

(800) 852-5243; fax (216) 428-7198

Perennials, grasses, ground covers. Small plants, good prices.

Carroll Gardens

444 East Main Street
Westminster, MD 21157

(800) 638-6334; fax (410) 857-4112

Large selection of plants. Catalog provides good descriptions and information on plant culture.

Crownsville Nursery

P.O. Box 797
Crownsville, MD 21032

(410) 849-3143; fax (410) 849-3427

Offers more than 250 selections of hostas. Ornamental grasses, perennials, shrubs, and vines are also available.

ForestFarm

990 Tetherow Road
Williams, OR 97544-9599

(541) 846-7269; fax (541) 846-6963

Native plants, ferns, grasses, common and uncommon perennials, shrubs, and trees. Extensive listings.

Goodness Grows, Inc.

P.O. Box 311
Highway 77 North
Lexington, GA 30648

(706) 743-5055; fax (706) 743-5112

Perennials, annuals, roses, and shrubs. Excellent descriptions.

Japanese blood grass

Klehm Nursery

4210 North Duncan Road
Champaign, IL 61821

(800) 553-3715

Hostas, daylilies, irises, herbaceous and tree peonies, ferns, and ornamental grasses.

Nature's Nook

1578 Marion-Russell Road
Meridian, MS 39301

(601) 485-5161

Catalog offers perennial and native plants to the enthusiastic gardener. Plant descriptions make for enjoyable reading.

Niche Gardens

1111 Dawson Road
Chapel Hill, NC 27516

(919) 967-0078; fax (919) 967-4026

Southeastern wildflowers and native plants; ornamental grasses and perennials.

Plant Delights Nursery, Inc.

9241 Sauls Road
Raleigh, NC 27603

(919) 772-4794; fax (919) 662-0370

Extensive hosta breeding program includes Hosta 'Soft Shoulders', Hosta 'Sweet Tater Pie', and Hosta 'Elvis Lives'. Traditional hostas also included. Impressive selection of perennials and native and exotic plants. Price of catalog: 10 stamps or a box of chocolates.

Hosta

Weigela

Shooting Star Nursery

444 Bates Road

Frankfort, KY 40601

(502) 223-1679

Assortment of plants and seeds native to U.S. forests, prairies, and wetlands; includes perennials, seeds, and seed mixes.

Sunlight Gardens

174 Golden Lane

Andersonville, TN 37705

(800) 272-7396

Wildflowers, ferns, perennials, vines, trees, and shrubs of eastern North America. Catalog addresses common questions and provides excellent background material.

Andre Viette Quality Perennials

P.O. Box 1109

Fishersville, VA 22939

(540) 943-2315; fax (540) 943-0782

Includes a perennial handbook and landscaping kit. Over 3,000 selections of poppies, irises, peonies, daylilies, and flowering shrubs suitable for sun, shade, or rock gardens.

Wayside Gardens

1 Garden Lane

Hodges, SC 29695

(800) 845-1124; fax (800) 457-9712

Unusual and hard-to-find perennials, bulbs (including tulips, daffodils, lilies), grasses, ornamentals, shrubs, trees, and vines.

White Flower Farm

P.O. Box 50

Litchfield, CT 06759-0050

(800) 503-9624; fax (860) 496-1418

Full-color catalog of perennials, annuals, bulbs, and shrubs. Unique selection of garden tools and water garden accessories.

TREES AND SHRUBS

Camellia Forest Nursery

125 Carolina Forest Road

Chapel Hill, NC 27516

(919) 967-5529

Cold-hardy and heirloom camellias; large selection of hard-to-find exotic and native trees and shrubs.

Carroll Gardens

444 East Main Street

Westminster, MD 21157

(800) 638-6334; fax (410) 857-4112

Large selection of plants. Catalog provides good descriptions, information on plant culture.

Fairweather Gardens

P.O. Box 330

Greenwich, NJ 08323

(609) 451-6261

Ornamental trees and shrubs, viburnums, perennials, camellias, hollies; very informative catalog.

Girard Nurseries

P.O. Box 428

Geneva, OH 44041

(216) 466-2881; fax (216) 466-3999

Full-color catalog with lengthy descriptions of flowering trees and shrubs, ground covers, perennials, seeds, ornamental grasses, conifers, and fruits.

Camellia

Greer Gardens

1280 Goodpasture Island Road

Eugene, OR 97401

(541) 686-8266; (800) 548-0111; fax (514) 686-0910

Rhododendrons, Japanese maples, magnolias, and rare plants. Perennials, bonsai, conifers, ornamental grasses, horticulture books.

Louisiana Nursery

5853 Highway 182

Opelousas, LA 70570

(318) 948-3696

See description under *Bulbs, Corms, and Tubers.*

Roslyn Nursery

211 Burrs Lane

Dix Hills, NY 11746

(516) 643-9347; fax (516) 427-0894

Azaleas, perennials, and shrubs. Rhododendrons, hardy camellias, ferns, trees, and conifers.

Sweetbay Farm

4260 Enon Road

Coolidge, GA 31738

(912) 225-1688

Specializes in magnolias and pawpaws.

Transplant Nursery, Inc.

1586 Parkertown Road

Lavonia, GA 30553

(706) 356-8947; fax (706) 356-8842

Native deciduous azaleas, choice evergreen azaleas, rhododendrons, and other companion plants.

Woodlanders, Inc.

1128 Colleton Avenue

Aiken, SC 29801

(803) 648-7522; fax (803) 648-7522

Good selection of Southeastern native and newly introduced trees, shrubs, vines, perennials, ferns, and ground covers.

Yucca Do Nursery

Route 3, Box 104

Hempstead, TX 77445

(409) 826-4580

Unusual trees, shrubs, and perennials; native plants. Many plants adapted to the Southwest and Southeast.

HERBS

Dabney Herbs
P.O. Box 22061
Louisville, KY
40252
**(502) 893-5198;
fax (502) 893-5198**
Comprehensive catalog of herbs and herbal toiletries. Includes teas, oils, and potpourri.

'Opal' basil

The Flowery Branch Mail Order Seed Co.
P.O. Box 1330
Flowery Branch, GA 30542
(770) 536-8380; fax (770) 532-7825
Rare European herbs at home in a greenhouse or sunny window; perennials, herbs, and everlastings.

Sandy Mush Herb Nursery
316 Surrett Cove Road
Leicester, NC 28748-5517
(704) 683-2014
Wide selection of herb seeds and plants; also ornamental grasses and perennials.

Story House Herb Farm
587 Erwin Road
Murray, KY 42071
(502) 753-4158
Nearly 100 different certified organic herbs for the kitchen garden.

INDOOR PLANTS AND TROPICALS

Brudy's Exotics
P.O. Box 820874
Houston, TX 77282-0874
(800) 926-7333
Bananas, cannas, gingers, plumerias, and exotic seeds.

Glasshouse Works
Church Street, P.O. Box 97
Stewart, OH 45778-0097
(740) 662-2142; fax (740) 662-2120
http://www.rareplants.com
Large selection of exotic and tropical plants, including ferns, bromeliads, gingers, aroids, and euphorbias. Specialty is variegated plants.

Ivies of the World
P.O. Box 408
Weirsdale, FL 32195
(352) 821-2201
Oddities, unique variegation, or unusual leaf shapes. Specializing in exotic and common ivies for the enthusiast.

Logee's Greenhouses
141 North Street
Danielson, CT 06239
(860) 774-8038; fax (860) 774-9932
http://www.logees.com
Enormous collection of begonias, vines, and other rare and exotic plants.

Stokes Tropicals
P.O. Box 9868
New Iberia, LA 70562
(800) 624-9706; fax (318) 365-6991
Bananas, bromeliads, gingers, heliconias, and plumerias.

Scarlet passion vine

ORGANIC GARDENING SUPPLIES

Gardens Alive!
5100 Schenley Place
Lawrenceburg, IN 47025
(812) 537-8650
Natural pesticides, weed killers, fertilizers, animal repellents, pheromone traps, floating row covers, beneficial insects.

Natural Gardening Company
217 San Anselmo Avenue
San Anselmo, CA 94960
(707) 766-9303
Composters, tools, earthworms, beneficial insects, wildflower seeds, animal repellents, pheromone traps, drip irrigation kits, and heirloom tomatoes.

Peaceful Valley Farm Supply
P.O. Box 2209
Grass Valley, CA 95945
(916) 272-4769
Organic fertilizers, seeds, and weed- and pest-control products, including beneficial insects. Gardening tools, greenhouses, and cold frames. Catalog features over 1,300 items, tips, and features.

TOOLS AND SUPPLIES

Duncraft
Penacook, NH 03303-9020
(800) 593-5656
Outstanding source for bird supplies, including feeders, birdhouses, seed, hummingbird supplies, and squirrel baffles.

Gardener's Supply Company
128 Intervale Road
Burlington, VT 05401
(800) 863-1700
http://www.gardeners.com
Plant labels, tools, watering supplies, floating row covers, seed germination kits, plant supports, water timers, garden ornaments, composters, containers, and greenhouses.

Kinsman Company
River Road
Point Pleasant, PA 18950
(800) 733-4146
High-quality tools, planters, garden ornaments, topiary frames, watering cans, metal arches, brackets, hooks, and hangers.

Smith & Hawken
2 Arbor Lane
Florence, KY 41022-6900
(800) 766-3326
http://www.vgmarketplace.com
Upscale garden ornaments; teak, wicker, and other furniture; clothing, accessories; high-quality tools.

Solving the Mystery of
BOTANICAL
NAMES

Campsis radicans

Although Southerners feel comfortable with common names, botanical names are often intimidating. So why do we need botanical names at all? For a very good reason—common names for plants vary from region to region and even from town to town. One plant may live under several common names. Or a single common name may refer to several plants that don't look anything alike.

ARE COMMON NAMES PRECISE?

A common name may refer to several different plants. A good example of this is the plant commonly known as "dusty miller." This name actually applies to four similar plants that have silvery foliage—*Senecio vira-vira, Senecio cineraria, Centaurea cineraria,* and *Artemisia stellerana.* Only the first of these plants is frequently sold at garden centers.

Rudbeckia hirta

Thunbergia alata

And some plants that share a common name aren't the least bit similar. "Black-eyed Susan," for example, applies to a golden-flowered perennial *(Rudbeckia hirta),* as well as to a vine usually planted and grown as a summer annual *(Thunbergia alata).* "Texas sage" is a shrub with silvery leaves and purple flowers *(Leucophyllum frutescens)* and also a perennial with purple-blue flowers *(Salvia texana).*

Having multiple common names for the same plant also causes confusion. For instance, if you call a shrub with brilliant-red autumn foliage "burning bush" and someone else knows it as "winged euonymus," you may not realize that you're both talking about the same plant—in this case, *Euonymus alata.*

So there are practical reasons for using botanical names. They provide the most accurate means we have for identifying a plant. And they're still the best way to ensure that the plants you buy are ones you really want.

KEEP AN EYE OUT FOR CLUES

Botanical names, once you break them down, reveal important clues to the natures of plants. The first word of a botanical name is the genus, which tells you the group of plants to which this one belongs. The second word is the species name, which is usually descriptive and easy to decipher once you know how to look for clues.

Descriptive words used often in species names are listed at right. When you know the meanings of these words, many plant names become easy to understand and can help you identify plants. For example, the species name for twinleaf *(Jeffersonia diphylla)* combines *di* (double or two) with *phylla* (leaves) to mean "two leaves."

The easiest botanical names to remember are those directly translated into common names. For instance, bigleaf magnolia *(Magnolia macrophylla)* does have huge leaves. And *macro* means large, *phylla* means leaves.

Some botanical names are so much like English words that they offer immediate clues to that plant's appearance. We can easily gather the meaning of words like *compacta, contorta, canadensis, deliciosa, fragrans,* and *micro.*

A GUIDE TO BOTANICAL NAMES

Color of Flowers or Foliage

alba—white
argentea—silvery
aurantiaca—orange
aurea—golden
azurea—azure, sky blue
caerulea—dark blue
caesia—blue-gray
candida—pure white, shiny
cana—ashy gray, hoary
cereus—waxy
citrina—yellow
coccinea—scarlet
concolor—one color
cruenta—bloody
discolor—two colors, separate colors
glauca—blue-gray, blue-green
incana—gray, hoary
lutea—yellow
pallida—pale
purpurea—purple
ruber, rubra—red, ruddy
rufa—ruddy
viridis, virens—green

Dodonaea viscosa 'Purpur

Form of Leaf (*folia*—leaves or foliage)

acerifolia—maplelike
angustifolia—narrow
aquifolia—spiny
buxifolia—boxwoodlike
ilicifolia—hollylike
laurifolia—laurel-like
parvifolia—small
populifolia—poplarlike
salicifolia—willowlike

Lavandula angustifolia 'Hidcote'

Shape of Plant

adpressa—pressing against, hugging
alta—tall
arborea—treelike
capitata—headlike
compacta—compact, dense

conferta—crowded, pressed together

contorta—twisted

decumbens—lying down

depressa—pressed down

elegans—elegant, slender, willowy

fastigiata—branches erect and close together

humifusa—sprawling on the ground

humilis—low, small, humble

impressa—impressed upon

nana—dwarf

procumbens—trailing

prostrata—prostrate

pumila—dwarf, small

pusilla—puny, insignificant

repens—creeping

reptans—creeping

scandens—climbing

Where It Came From

A number of suffixes are added to place names to specify the habitat where the plant was discovered or the place where it is usually found.

africana—of Africa

alpina—from the mountains

australis—southern

borealis—northern

campestris—of the field or plains

canadensis—of Canada

canariensis—of the Canary Islands

capensis—of the Cape of Good Hope area

caroliniana—of the Carolinas

chinensis—of China

hispanica—of Spain

hortensis—of gardens

indica—of India

insularis—of the island

japonica—of Japan

montana—of the mountains

riparia—of riverbanks

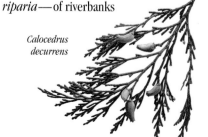
Calocedrus decurrens

saxatilis—inhabiting rocks

texana—of Texas

virginiana—of Virginia

Plant Parts

dendron—tree

flora, florum, flori, florus—flowers

phyllus, phylla—leaf or leaves

Cestrum elegans

Zephyranthes grandiflora

Elaeagnus pungens

Ligustrum japonicum

Passiflora caerulea

Brachychiton acerifolius

Plant Peculiarities

armata—armed

baccata—berried, berrylike

barbata—barbed or bearded

campanulata—bell or cup shaped

ciliaris—fringed

cordata—heart shaped

cornuta—horned

crassa—thick, fleshy

decurrens—running down the stem

densi—dense

diversi—varying

edulis—edible

florida—free flowering

Hydrangea macrophylla

fruticosa—shrubby

fulgens—shiny

gracilis—slender, thin, small

grandi—large, showy

-ifer, -ifera—bearing or having; e.g., *stoloniferus,* having stolons

imperialis—showy

laciniata—fringed or with torn edges

laevigata—smooth

lobata—lobed

longa—long

macro—large

maculata—spotted

micro—small

mollis—soft, soft-haired

mucronata—pointed

nutans—nodding, swaying

obtusa—blunt or flattened

officinalis—medicinal

-oides—like or resembling; e.g., *jasminoides,* like a jasmine

patens—open, spreading growth

pinnata—constructed like a feather

platy—broad

plena—double, full

plumosa—feathery

praecox—precocious, early

pungens—piercing

radicans—rooting, especially along the stem

reticulata—net-veined

retusa—notched at blunt apex

rugosa—wrinkled, rough

saccharata—sweet, sugary

sagittalis—arrowlike

scabra—rough feeling

scoparia—broomlike

Gardenia jasminoides

INDEX

Gardening Terms and Topics

INDEX

Scientific and Common Names

Italic page numbers refer to pages on which there are relevant photographs. The **boldface** page number after each name refers to the plant's encyclopedia entry.

Photography Credits

For pages with six or fewer photographs, each image has been identified by its position on the page: Left (L), center (C), or right (R); top (T), middle (M), or bottom (B). On other pages, such as those in "A Guide to Plant Selection" or the Dictionary Visual Guides, photographs are identified by their position in the grid (shown right).

	L	LC	RC	R
1	1	1	1	1
2				
3				
4				
5				

Acadaemy of Natural Sciences, Phildelphia/VIREO: 65 L1. **Max E. Badgley:** 420 C, L1, L2,L3, LC2, RC1, R1, R2; 450 R2; 455 MR; 456 L1, L3, RC1, RC4; 475 LC1, LC2, R2, R3. **BIOS (Klein-Hubert)/Peter Arnold, Inc.:** 50 L1. **BIOS (W. Lapinski)/Peter Arnold, Inc.:** 54 R3. **T. Boylan:** 456 LC5. **Ron Boylan:** 475 R4. **Marion Brenner:** 39 R4; 41 L4, L3, L5, R1; 45 L1, L4, L5, R1; 46 R3; 47 R3; 50 R2; 52 R2; 54 L5; 55 R2; 56 R3; 57 L1, R3; 59 L2; 63 L1, R3; 70 R3; 71 L3; 72 L1, R2; 74 L2, L5, R1, R3, R4; 76 R5; 77 L1, L2; 82 R1, R3, R4; 84 L1, R5; 87 L4, R3; 86 L3; 97 R1, R2, R4; 99 R4; 100 R4; 101 L1, L3, L4, R5; 112 L1. **Kathy Brenzel:** 54 R2. **Lisa Butler:** 66 R5; 70 R2. **Scott Camazine:** 455 ML, MT, TL. **James L. Castner:** 455 C; 475 RC2. **Peter Christiansen:** 488 B. **Jack K. Clark:** 456 R2, R5; 476 LC4. **Clovis/WVU:** 78 L3; 102 L3. **Comstock:** 456 L2. **Ed Cooper:** 100 L1. **R. Cowles:** 455 BM; 456 L4, LC3, R3; 475 R1, R5; 476 R2. **Crandall & Crandall:** 456 LC4; 476 L4. **Whitney Cranshaw:** 476 R1. **D. Cudney:** 475 L2, LC3, RC1; 476 L1, LC3. **Claire Curran:** 39 R2, 43; 40 R5; 41 L5, R2; 42 L5; 43 R2, R3, R4; 46 L4, R1, R5; 47 L3; 48 L3, L4, R1; 51 L1; 54 L3, R1; 56 L3, R1, R2; 57 L5; 59 L4, R3; 60 L2, L3, L4, R4; 61 L1, L2, L3, L4, L5, R1, R2, R4; 62 L2, L3, R4; 63 L3, L4, R1, R2, R4; 67 L4, R4; 69 R3; 70 L2, L3; 71 R2; 74 L4, R1, R2; 75 L3; 76 R3; 77 L4; 81 L4, R3; 82 L3; 83 L3, R2, R3; 86 L5; 87 L5; 96 L1, L2, R3; 98 L1, L4; 99 L1, L2, L4, L5, R3, R4, R5; 100 L2, L4; 101 L5, R1, R2, R3; 487 R; 488 T. **R. Todd Davis:** 49 L2; 58 R5; 66 R4; 69 L4; 78 L1, R2; 79 L3; 80 R4; 86 L1, R2. **Alan & Linda Detrick:** 79 R1. **William B. Dewey:** 67 R1; 68 L4, R2, R4, R5; 71 L4; 83 L2; 84 L5; 96 L1. **Wally Eberhart:** 476 RC2. **Derek Fell:** 40 R4; 42 R4; 54 L1, R5; 60 L4, L5, R2; 64 L5; 67 R5; 68 L2; 72 L2; 73 L1; 74 R4; 75 L2; 78 L2, R3; 80 L3; 81 L2; 82 L2, L4; 85 L2, R2, R4; 86 R4; 456 LC1. **E. Ferguson:** 476 L2. **FourbyFive:** 67 L1, 69 L1. **Dan Gurlach/Researchers, Inc.:** 476 RC1. **Jessie M. Harris:** 42 R5; 72 R4; 76 R4; 70 L1; 79 L1; 80 R3; 86 R3, R5. **Walter H. Hodge/Peter Arnold, Inc.:** 54 R4; 66 R3. **Saxon Holt:** 39 L1, L3, L5; 40 L2, L3, R1, R2; 44 R1, R2, R3; 49 R1, R2; 50 L2, L5, R1; 52 R3; 53 L2, L3, R2; 54 L2; 55 L1; 58 L3, R2, R4; 64 L4; 65 R3; 66 L4; 69 R4; 77 R4; 87 L2; 102 L2, R4. **Dr. Jerral Johnson:** 456 RC2. **Stephen J. Krasemann/Peter Arnold, Inc.:** 66 R1.

Ray Krine/Grant Heilman Photography: 455 TR. **Michael Landis:** 49 R5; 51 L4. **Charles Mann:** 39 L2; 43 L2; 44L2; 49 L3; 51 R4; 53 L4; 56 L2, L4; 57 L2, L3; 62 R2, R3; 64 L3; 67 R3; 71 L1, R3; 73 R2; 75 R2; 76 R2; 77 R3; 80 R2, R5; 82 R2; 83 R4, R5; 84 R3; 87 L2; 95 R1, R2, R3, R4; 97 R3; 98 L5; 100 L3, R3; 101 L2, R4; 102 R1; 489 B. **David McDonald:** 40 L1, R3; 41 R1; 46 L5; 47 L4; 48 R2, R4, R5; 55 L2, R3, R5; 62 L4; 65 L3; 66 L1, L2; 71 R1, L1, L3; 76 L4; 77 R2; 94 L2, L3, L5, R2, R3; 95 L2, L3, L4, L5, R5; 96 R2, R4; 99 L3, R2. **Shep Ogden:** 487 TL. **Jerry Pavia:** 49 R4; 51 L3, R2; 53 L1; 56 L5; 59 R4; 64 L2, R2; 65 R2; 66 R2; 68 L3; 80 L4; 94 L1; 95 L1; 100 R2; 489 T. **Norman A. Plate:** 47 L5; 48 R3; 69 R1; 486 B, T; 487 BL. **Ed Reschke/Peter Arnold, Inc.:** 53 R4. **Paul Rezendez/Positive Images:** 78 L4. **J.H Robinson:** 455 BL. **Susan Roth:** 52 R1, R4; 54 L4; 55 L4; 65 R4; 67 R2; 75 L1; 79 R2; 80 L2. **Clyde H. Smith/Peter Arnold, Inc.:** 49 L1. **Pam Spaulding/Positive Images:** 59 R2; 78 R4; 79 L4. **Albert Squillace/Positive Images:** 58 L2, R3. **David M. Stone/PhotoNats:** 475 L1. **Joseph G. Strauch, Jr.:** 43 L4; 50 L4, R4; 51 L2; 52 L2; 55 R4; 59 L1; 64 R4; 65 L2, L4, R5; 66 L3, L5; 75 R5; 76 L2, L3, R1; 77 R1, R5; 79 L2, R3, R4; 81 R1, R2; 85 R3; 86 R1; 102 R3. **Superstock:** 64 L1. **Michael S. Thompson:** 40 L4; 51 R3; 55 L5; 64 R1; 69 L3; 80 L1; 86 L2; 87 R2; 94 L4; 96 L2; 87 R2; 94 L4; 96 L4. **Tom Stack & Associates:** 476 LC2. **Darrow Watt:** 62 L1; 420 LC1; 491 T. **Doug Wilson:** 39 L4; 42 L3; 48 L1; 55 L3; 56 L1; 57 R2; 69 L2; 70 L4; 72 L5, R1; 490 T. **Tom Woodward:** 41 R4; 42 L1; 46 L3; 46 L3, R6; 47 L1; 51 R5; 53 R1; 55 R1; 59 L5, R1, R5; 60 L1, R5; 62 R1; 63 L5, R5; 65 R1; 67 L3, L5; 68 R4; 69 R4; 70 L1, R5; 71 R4; 72 L3; 73 R1; 81 L1; 82 L2; 83 L1; 84 R1, R2; 94 R1; 96 R1; 97 L2; L5, R5; 100 R1; 102 R2, R6; 112 R2; 456 RC3, R1, R4. **Cythia Woodyard:** 50 R3; 57 R4; 79 L5; 80 R1; 87 R4; 98 R3. **Josephine Zeitlin:** 83 L5.

Acknowledgments

Illustrations: Mary Davey Burkhardt, Ireta Cooper, Lois Lovejoy, Dennis Nolan, Bill Oetinger, Rik Olson

Our thanks to the following for their contributions to this book: Lisa Anderson, Charles D. Batte, Lory Day, Vasken Guiragossian, Laurie Kinary, Britta Swartz, Sandra Snow, George Taylor